Freedom in the World

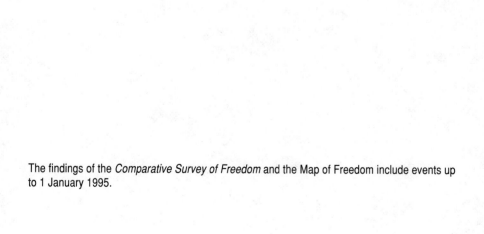

The findings of the *Comparative Survey of Freedom* and the Map of Freedom include events up to 1 January 1995.

Freedom in the World
The Annual Survey of Political Rights & Civil Liberties 1994-1995

Freedom House Survey Team

Adrian Karatnycky
Survey Coordinator

Kathleen Cavanaugh
James Finn
Charles Graybow
Douglas W. Payne
Joseph E. Ryan
Leonard R. Sussman
George Zarycky

James Finn
General Editor

Freedom House

First published in 1995

Cover design and maps by Emerson Wajdowicz Studios, N.Y.C.

The Library of Congress has catalogued this serial title as follows:

Freedom in the world / —1978-
New York : Freedom House, 1978-
v. : map; 25 cm.—(Freedom House Book)
Annual.
ISSN 0732-6610=Freedom in the World.
1. Civil rights—Periodicals. I. R. Adrian Karatnycky, et al. I. Series.
JC571.F66 323.4'05-dc 19   82-642048
AACR 2   MARC-S
Library of Congress   [84101]
ISBN   0-932088-81-3 (pbk.)
          0-932088-82-1 (cloth)

Distributed by arrangement with:

University Press of America, Inc.
4720 Boston Way
Lanham, MD 20706

3 Henrietta Street
London WC2E 8LU England

Contents

Foreword

Freedom in the World is an evaluation of political rights and civil liberties in the world's nations and related territories, now numbering 191 and 58 respectively, that Freedom House provides on an annual basis.

Freedom House is a nonprofit organization based in New York that monitors political rights and civil liberties around the world. Established in 1941, Freedom House believes the effective advocacy of human rights at home and abroad must be grounded in fundamental democratic values and principles.

Freedom House first began to evaluate political rights and civil liberties during the 50s, when racial violence broke out in the United States. The first year-end review of freedom was completed in 1955. During those early years, the project was called the Balance Sheet of Freedom, and later the Annual Survey of the Progress of Freedom. By the late 1960s, the Freedom House Board of Trustees felt there was a need to create a single standard by which to measure and record the development of freedom around the world.

When Freedom House's *Comparative Survey of Freedom* was established in the early 1970s, democracy was in a perilous condition in many states and on every continent: Spain, Portugal and Greece were under military rule; the world's largest democracy, India, was sliding toward martial law; an American president faced the possibility of impeachment; Africa was torn by both factional strife and racial conflict; and the prospects for liberalization—not to say democratization—in Eastern Europe, Latin America and Asia were dim. By the 1980s this dispiriting picture had changed and we witnessed a decade of unprecedented gains in democratization and freedom in much of the world. The years of 1993 and 1994, however, revealed the fragility of many of those gains, as they were undercut by corruption, interfactional feuding, ethnic rivalry, open conflict, economic stress and citizen dissatisfaction.

The *Survey* project has continued to develop over the years, being incorporated in the late 1970s into *Freedom in the World*, where it is now complemented by regional essays and country-by-country reports. In 1989 it became a year-long effort produced by our regional experts, consultants, and human rights specialists. As the resources listed at the back of this book attest, the *Survey* acquires its information from a wide range of diverse sources.

Freedom House has become known, over the years, as a dependable and fair advocate for those deprived of civil liberties and political rights. Because of that record, it has the privilege of being the recipient of information provided by many human rights activists, journalists, editors, and political leaders from around the world. The transmission of this information often exacts a high price from those who send it, as they frequently risk endangering their livelihoods, their health and lives, and sometimes the lives of their families. Much of the material in this book is, therefore, the contribution of heroic figures, many of whose names will go unremarked in the history of our times.

Western journalists have a long tradition of putting themselves in physical danger to obtain information, of finding ingenious ways to penetrate almost inaccessible places. They do this today in some places where there are few if any human rights advocates. We have benefited from their reports from areas such as Somalia, Bosnia, Rwanda, and Chechnya. They have brought back, or sent back, reports of horrendous human rights abuses, often humanizing gruesome reports that statistics seem to deaden by giving the names of particular families and individuals who have been subjected to the deprivation of their basic rights.

We have been pleased to note and to benefit from the increasing number of human rights organizations that are forming in the Far East, in Asia and its neighboring countries. Operating under the most trying conditions, economic and political, these nongovernmental organizations (NGOs) face the same obstacles that other human rights organizations know so well. But in addition they must make the case for the protection of individual human rights in political cultures that would often subordinate them to the demands of the state, as those demands are interpreted by autocratic or dictatorial leaders. Even as they struggle to defend their fellow citizens, they must combat charges that they are operating under the sway of foreign influences, specifically those from the West.

Throughout the year Freedom House personnel regularly conduct fact-finding missions to gain more in-depth knowledge of the vast political transformations affecting our world. During these week-to-month long investigations, we make every effort to meet a cross-section of political parties and associations, human rights monitors, religious figures, representatives of the private sector, trade union movement, academics and the appropriate security forces and insurgent movements where they exist. The *Survey* project team also consults a vast array of published source materials, ranging from the reports of other human rights organizations to newspapers and magazines, large and small, from around the world.

During 1994 Freedom House personnel traveled to Antigua and Barbuda, Austria, Canada, Dominican Republic, El Salvador, France, Haiti, Hungary, India, Japan, Kashmir, Kenya, Mexico, Nepal, Nicaragua, Poland, Russia, St. Vincent and the Grenadines, South Africa, South Korea, Sudan, Switzerland, Ukraine and the UK.

The *Survey* project team also consults a vast array of published source materials, ranging from the reports of other human rights organizations to often rare, regional newspapers and magazines.

The coordinator of this year's *Survey* team is Adrian Karatnycky, president of Freedom House. Other members include Dr. Joseph E. Ryan, *Survey* methodologist, Kathleen Cavanaugh, James Finn, Charles Graybow, Douglas W. Payne, Leonard R. Sussman and George Zarycky. The general editor of *Freedom in the World* is James Finn; the deputy editor and assistant editor are Mark Wolkenfeld and Pei C. Koay, respectively. This year's research assistants were Art Boguslaw Artman, Shahrzad Elghanayan, Sarah Gershman, and Gillian Lipton

Substantial support for *Freedom in the World, 1994-1995* has been generously provided by The Pew Charitable Trusts, the Lynde & Harry Bradley Foundation, Inc, and the Smith Richardson Foundation.

Ed.

The Comparative Survey of Freedom 1994-1995: Democracies on the Rise Democracies at Risk
Adrian Karatnycky

As the year 1994 drew to a close, the Freedom House Survey of Freedom documented a major increase in the level of freedom in 8 countries, and a major decline in freedom in 4 nations. Additionally, 14 countries experienced a less significant expansion of freedom, while 19 countries registered a more modest decline. Nearly 20 percent of the world's population now live in Free societies and enjoy a full range of political rights and civil liberties. The total represents an increase of 1 percent—some 70 million people. Forty percent of the world's population lives in Partly Free societies, in which some basic rights are abridged, while 40 percent live in countries that are Not Free—societies in which basic rights are denied.

The year saw a gain in the ranks of countries judged Free by Freedom House. Today, there are 76 Free countries—an increase of four over the figures for last year. There are six new entrants into the ranks of Free countries—Latvia, Malawi, Panama, Slovakia, South Africa and Palau (formerly a Free territory). One free society—The Gambia—registered a deep erosion in political rights and civil liberties and joined the ranks of the Not Free. Kazakhstan and Yemen saw the erosion of their political rights and civil liberties and likewise joined the ranks of the Not Free.

There are 61 countries that are Partly Free. Haiti, which saw the restoration to power of its democratically elected president, joined the ranks of Partly Free countries, along with Mali, Mozambique and Uganda.

In 1993 Freedom House reported a major trend: freedom in retreat. While that alarming trend has not been reversed in this year's *Survey*, the modest increase in the number of free societies in 1994 indicates that the dramatic erosion in political rights and civil liberties of last year has subsided.

Despite the new opportunities afforded by the more open international order since the collapse of Soviet communism and the end of the Cold War stalemate, there has been little evidence of a sustained global momentum in the direction of societies which provide strong protections for basic political rights and civil liberties. Freedom, therefore, continues to elude the vast majority of the world's people, with nearly 80 percent living in Partly Free and Not Free states.

More democracies than ever—and more at risk

Perhaps the most significant trend of 1994 has been the further enlargement of the number of countries with governments elected on the basis of relatively free and competitive elections. There is a growing acceptance in most countries of the principle of seeking the consent of the governed. Thus, 1994 saw a net increase in the number of democracies, from 108 to 114—the largest number in history and more than double the number of democracies since the early 1970s. Never before have there been as

Freedom in the World—1995

The population of the world this year is estimated at 5.607.0 billion persons, who reside in 191 sovereign states and 58 related territories—a total of 249 entities. The level of political rights and civil liberties as shown comparatively by the Freedom House *Survey* is:

Free: 1,119.7 billion (19.97 percent of the world's population) live in 76 of the states and in 44 of the related territories.

Partly Free: 2,243.4 billion (40.01 percent of the world's population) live in 61 of the states and 5 of the related territories.

Not Free: 2,243.9 billion (40.02 percent of the world's population) live in 54 of the states and 9 of the related territories.

A Record of the Survey
(population in millions)

SURVEY DATE	FREE		PARTLY FREE		NOT FREE		WORLD POPULATION
January '81	1,613.0	(35.90%)	970.9	(21.60%)	1,911.9	(42.50%)	4,495.8
January '82	1,631.9	(35.86%)	916.5	(20.14%)	2,002.7	(44.00%)	4,551.1
January '83	1,665.1	(36.32%)	918.8	(20.04%)	2,000.2	(43.64%)	4,584.1
January '84	1,670.7	(36.00%)	1,074.8	(23.00%)	1,917.5	(41.00%)	4,663.0
January '85	1,671.4	(34.85%)	1,117.4	(23.30%)	2,007.0	(41.85%)	4,795.8
January '86	1,747.2	(36.27%)	1,121.9	(23.29%)	1,947.6	(40.43%)	4,816.7
January '87	1,842.5	(37.10%)	1,171.5	(23.60%)	1,949.9	(39.30%)	4,963.9
January '88	1,924.6	(38.30%)	1,205.4	(24.00%)	1,896.0	(37.70%)	5,026.0
January '89	1,992.8	(38.86%)	1,027.9	(20.05%)	2,107.3	(41.09%)	5,128.0
January '90	2,034.4	(38.87%)	1,143.7	(21.85%)	2,055.9	(39.28%)	5,234.0
January '91	2,088.2	(39.23%)	1,485.7	(27.91%)	1,748.7	(32.86%)	5,322.6
January '92	1,359.3	(25.29%)	2,306.6	(42.92%)	1,708.2	(31.79%)	5,374.2
January '93	1,352.2	(24.83%)	2,403.3	(44.11%)	1,690.4	(31.06%)	5,446.0
January '94	1,046.2	(19.00%)	2,224.4	(40.41%)	2,234.6	(40.59%)	5,505.2
January '95	1,119.7	(19.97%)	2,243.4	(40.01%)	2,243.9	(40.02%)	5,607.0

many countries attempting to play by democratic rules. Many of these democracies, however, remain fragile and often are incapable of providing for the basic rights of their citizens. And a growing number of democracies confront serious challenges to their stability and cohesiveness.

Many of these fragile democracies are at risk because of internal division, rampant corruption, overarching influence by militaries and oligarchies, and destabilization from abroad. As a result 37 democracies are only Partly Free.

Inter-ethnic and inter-sectarian strife is a major contributing factor in the erosion of political rights and civil liberties in many formal democracies. The outstanding case is Bosnia, whose democratic government's inability to protect its citizens and to maintain civil order amid inter-ethnic strife gives it the unhappy status of the world's only Not Free democracy. Other democracies facing inter-ethnic and inter-sectarian strife and tension include India, confronting insurgencies and terrorism from Sikh, Assamese, Kashmiri, Tamil and fundamentalist Islamic movements, and Turkey, whose democracy confronts a Kurd insurgency and occasional acts of terror by fundamentalist Muslims. Both India and Turkey are ranked Partly Free. Inter-ethnic conflict has contributed to the erosion of basic rights in Mali and Niger, two Partly Free African democracies.

Albania, Romania, Russia and Ukraine are undergoing a wrenching transition from Communist rule. Though these new democracies have made significant progress toward the expansion of freedom, they still risk regressing. They still lack a full range of stable institutions of civil life, have economically vulnerable news media and do not yet have sufficiently well developed systems of rule of law based on an independent judiciary. A similar challenge confronts countries trying to build the infrastructure of civil society after prolonged periods of guerrilla insurgencies, terrorism and civil war. These countries include El Salvador, Nicaragua and Mozambique.

Another group of democracies at risk are countries where the political process and judicial system are tainted by high levels of corruption and/or the influence of drug cartels. These include Brazil (which this year saw the expansion of political rights), Colombia, the Dominican Republic (which registered declines in freedom), Guatemala, Honduras, Paraguay and Venezuela.

8 Gains in Freedom Changing Categories

Countries	1994	1995
Haiti	Not Free	Partly Free
Latvia	Partly Free	Free
Malawi	Not Free	Free
Mozambique	Not Free	Partly Free
Panama	Partly Free	Free
Slovakia	Partly Free	Free
South Africa	Partly Free	Free
Uganda	Not Free	Partly Free

4 Declines in Freedom Changing Categories

Countries	1994	1995
The Gambia	Free	Not Free
Kazakhstan	Partly Free	Not Free
Mali	Free	Partly Free
Yemen	Partly Free	Not Free

Regional trends

In 1994, the Survey registered several significant regional trends.

Africa was the most volatile part of the world, registering the largest number of advances and declines in freedom. While in 1994 the trend toward the extension of formal democracies in the region was unmistakable, the durability of these transitions was far from assured. In part, this is because of the weakness of independent organized life, of free trade unions, civic organizations, and the private sector. It is also due to the overarching influence of military elites in the political life of many African countries. Despite these impediments, significant gains in political rights and civil liberties were registered in Malawi and South Africa, and real progress toward greater freedom occurred in Mozambique and Uganda. As noted above, Mali and The Gambia fell out of the ranks of Free countries.

Five years after the collapse of communism, Eastern and Central Europe offer cause for hope. The expansion of political rights and civil liberties in the former Eastern bloc continued in 1994 with Slovakia's entry into the ranks of the Free. Today, with the exception of Albania and Romania, and the countries in conflict-ridden former Yugoslavia, all the Central and East European states are Free. But while this trend is heartening, the failure of NATO to put an end to the conflict in Bosnia holds the prospect of broadening strife that could destabilize several Balkan countries in transition to democracy.

In the former Soviet Union, the year saw a growing differentiation among the new independent states. In 1994 democratic gains and gains in freedom were registered in Ukraine, which held a series of parliamentary, presidential and local elections marked by high voter turnout. And after Latvia's implementation of a new citizenship law that offered the possibility of eventual full political participation for the majority of nonindigenous residents, the country joined its Baltic neighbors, Lithuania and Estonia, in the ranks of Free societies.

Russia, Belarus, Ukraine, Moldova, Georgia, Kyrgyz Republic and Armenia all are rated Partly Free in 1995. With the exception of the Partly Free Kyrgyz Republic, all the formerly Soviet Central Asian republics are Not Free. In Turkmenistan, the personality cult of President Saparmurat Niyazov reached new levels of absurdity. In Uzbekistan, repression of political opponents of the ruling elite was severe. And in Tajikistan, civil war and the consolidation of power by ex-Communist apparatchiks has contributed to the absence of basic rights. In Kazakhstan, the increasing unchecked domination of political life by President Nursultan Nazarbayev saw the country slip from the ranks of the Partly Free and into the ranks of the Not Free. The Caucasian state of Azerbaijan—which saw a failed coup launched by parts of the military and security apparatus who were encouraged and abetted by the Russian military—also was rated Not Free as its president, Gaidar Aliev, continued to imprison peaceful political opponents and broaden restrictions on civic and political groups.

A worrying trend in 1994 was the growing evidence of Russia's participation in efforts to topple indigenous authorities in what it terms its "near abroad," and to help install former Communist leaders believed by Russia to be sympathetic to a new unitary state. Russia's efforts to strengthen democratic governance were hampered by massive involvement of Russia's security forces in the autonomous republic of Chechnya.

The 21 Worst Rated Countries*

Afghanistan
Algeria
Angola
Bhutan
Burma (Myanmar)
China
Cuba
Equatorial Guinea
Iraq
Korea, North
Libya
Mauritania
Rwanda
Saudi Arabia
Somalia
Sudan
Syria
Tajikistan
Turkmenistan
Uzbekistan
Vietnam

The 6 Worst Rated Related Territories

East Timor (Indonesia)
Irian Jaya (Indonesia)
Kashmir (India)
Kosovo (Yugoslavia)
Nagorno-Karabakh (Armenia/Azerbaijan)
Tibet (China)

* For explanation of Survey Methodology see p. 672

The Not Free

In recent years, a clear pattern has emerged among countries that are Not Free. Of the 54 countries that are Not Free, 49—over 90 percent—share one or more of the following characteristics:

a) they have a majority Muslim population and frequently confront the pressures of fundamentalist Islam;

b) they are multi-ethnic societies in which power is not held by a dominant ethnic group, i.e. a nation that represents more than two-thirds of the population;

c) they are neo-Communist or post-Communist transitional societies.

Frequently, the Not Free countries have two or three of these characteristics. Significantly, these three indicators appear to be more accurate in determining whether a country is Not Free than such characteristics as levels of economic prosperity and growth rates.

14 Gains in Freedom Without Changing Categories	19 Declines in Freedom Without Changing Categories
Andorra	Albania
Belarus	Algeria
Brazil	Colombia
Burundi	Dominican Republic
Guinea-Bissau	Kenya
Italy	Liberia
Kyrgyzstan	Lesotho
Moldova	Macedonia
Peru	Mauritania
Romania	Niger
Taiwan	Nigeria
Togo	Paraguay
Ukraine	Rwanda
United Arab Emirates	St. Kitts-Nevis
	St. Vincent & the Grenadines
	Tanzania
	Trinidad & Tobago
	Turkey
	Vanuatu

The ranks of the Not Free include such prosperous states as Bahrain, Brunei, Oman, Qatar, Saudi Arabia and the United Arab Emirates. Among the Not Free states, there are also a number of countries that have made marked economic progress without any significant improvement in their political rights and civil liberties. These include China, which has experienced an average annual growth rate of more than 10 percent for five years, and Indonesia, whose per capita Purchasing Power Parity has doubled in the last seven years.

There also are a number of Free countries, whose citizens enjoy a broad range of political rights and civil liberties, and that are poor. These include Belize, Benin, Bolivia, Botswana, Dominica, Grenada, Jamaica, Kiribati, Malawi, Namibia, Trinidad and Tobago, and Tuvalu. The list also includes South Africa, more than two-thirds of whose population lives in acute poverty.

There are also many poor countries that are Partly Free democracies, whose citizens are able to openly express their political preferences. Among these are Congo, El Salvador, Guinea-Bissau, India, Madagascar and Pakistan.

These numerous examples show that while economic and social factors arising from poverty and underdevelopment can contribute to instability, strengthen movements that preach extremist solutions, and encourage mobilization along ethnic lines, many poor countries are able to adhere to democratic practices and protect a broad range of political rights and civil liberties.

While many democracies have achieved high levels of development and prosperity, this appears to be a consequence of the capacity of democracies to create a legal framework that safeguards prosperity, not an indication that wealthier societies inevitably become democracies as a consequence of their prosperity. This question is essential for policymakers to confront and to debate, particularly because of the emerging economic power and technological gains made by China. China's persistent record of repression of dissent, its expanding secret police system, the absence of tangible progress in political freedoms, and the failure to progress toward democratic reform all pose a significant challenge for the post-Cold War world.

China's economic and technological progress has far outstripped that country's political changes. According to a Rand Corporation study, by the year 2020 China will have a GNP 1.5 times as great as that of the United States. The accumulation of such productive capabilities raises the prospect of an undemocratic and unfree China as a regional, even a global, military power. China's economic growth will not inevitably lead to its political transformation. Such a transformation will require support for democratic forces.

This is why Freedom House strongly supports the establishment of an Asian Democracy Radio and its funding at an appropriate level, in keeping with President Clinton's 1992 election-year promise. A well funded Asian Democracy Radio, broadcasting the views of China's internal and exiled democrats, would be an effective mechanism for promoting democratic values within a population in which there is little open political debate and in which calls for democracy are rigorously suppressed.

The Global Trend			
	Free Countries	Partly Free Countries	Not Free Countries
1985	53	58	56
1992	76	65	42
1993	75	73	38
1994	72	63	55
1995	76	61	54

Opportunities for expanding freedom

Despite the difficulties facing many incipient and embattled democracies, these countries represent the best hope for the enlargement of human freedom. Fragile and emerging democracies, therefore, deserve to be the focal point of U.S. foreign assistance efforts. Such assistance ought to be more rigorously targeted at promoting nongovernmental organizations, strengthening the private sector and free trade unions, encouraging inter-ethnic dialogue and cooperation, strengthening the underpinnings of civil society, assisting the diversification of the news media, and strengthening the bases of an independent and impartial judicial system.

There are good practical reasons why U.S. and Western policy ought to be directed at strengthening the many "democracies at risk." Not the least of these is linked to our national security: Established democracies do not war with one another. Since 1819, out of 353 wars fought (defined as military actions in which more than 1,000 persons have been killed), none have been fought between two established democracies; 155 have been fought between nondemocracies and democracies; and 198 have been fought between nondemocracies.

Democracies also make for reliable allies. The treaties they sign endure because they reflect the will of their citizenry. Moreover, because democracies are responsive to the social and economic needs of citizens, they tend to develop the legal infrastructure and rule of law that respect property rights and promote a free market system and economic growth. Democratic development, therefore, is an important pillar of economic development.

In recent years, the US Agency for International Development (USAID) has made important progress in applying these principles to its work overseas. USAID is to be lauded for launching innovative programs aimed at strengthening the independent nongovernmental pillars of civil society and civic life, especially in Latin America and the former Soviet bloc. USAID also deserves credit for making democratic development an integral part of its strategy for sustainable development around the world and for cutting development aid to states that are undemocratic and violate basic human rights.

Yet the application of democratic principles in the allocation of U.S. foreign aid still falls far short of the U.S. government's declarations. With a diminishing foreign aid pie—there has been a reduction of 20 percent in foreign aid spending since the Bush years—there is simply no compelling reason for U.S. foreign development aid funds to be spent in assisting the economies of dictatorships. While programs aimed at strengthening democratic nongovernmental groups should be reinforced, the repressive governments in Chad, Kenya, Liberia, Tajikistan, Turkmenistan and Uzbekistan should not receive foreign development aid.

There is no strong argument for spending taxpayer dollars on development programs in Indonesia's one-party dictatorship, which was allocated over $44 million in U.S. assistance, or in Kenya's military dictatorship, which was slated to receive more than $40 million in 1994. Each of these single-country allocations is significantly more than the entire budget of the U.S. National Endowment for Democracy.

Is there a persuasive reason to spend tens of millions of dollars in foreign development aid money in Indonesia, whose government represses peaceful protest and dissent? Or in Mauritania, whose military-dominated government condones widespread slavery, but which received several millions in development assistance? And what sort of message is sent about respect for democratic rule when the U.S. rewards Peruvian President Alberto Fujimori's unconstitutional coup in 1992 against his democratically elected parliament with nearly half a billion dollars in foreign aid in the last two years?

At a time when the U.S. government faces increasing constraints on its foreign aid spending, including the amount of funding available to support fragile new democracies that respect human rights, it is time for the president and the Congress to ensure more effective targeting of that foreign assistance to poorer Free and Partly Free societies. The new Congress is likely to take a close look at foreign aid. The state of the world reflected in the 1995 Survey of Freedom indicates that the U.S. government and other prosperous industrial democracies have a historic opportunity to strengthen and solidify fragile democratic transitions by rigorously redirecting economic assistance to countries that are playing by the democratic rules of the game.

Money is not everything

But the growth of stable democracies will require more than U.S. financial support. It will also require U.S. global leadership. Institutions like the U.N. are not effective instruments for the launching of democracy-building initiatives. The large number of dictatorships within the ranks of the U.N. and their representatives within the U.N. bureaucracy make it very difficult for that agency to play an important transformational role. The lack of consensus in the U.N. over Bosnia is also indicative of the limited potential of this institution for resolving some of the world's most pressing and potentially destabilizing issues.

This is why the U.S. ought to look at strengthening the efficacy of structures that are made up of democratic states, such as NATO. There is a far better chance that NATO can act effectively and decisively with proper U.S. leadership than multilateral instruments, such as the U.N., that have within them governments that restrict basic freedoms or do not share democratic values.

The world remains a very dangerous place. There are currently some fifty inter-ethnic, secessionist, or inter-state conflicts. Many of these conflicts are encouraged by the failure of the international community to deal effectively with the crisis in Bosnia. Moreover, the record of U.N. peacekeeping in enlarging the scope of freedom is decidedly mixed. In addition to the recent failure of U.N. peacekeeping efforts in Somalia and Bosnia, U.N. peacekeeping efforts frequently freeze conflicts without permanently resolving them. Beyond peacekeeping, large-scale initiatives aimed at promoting democratic values are needed.

In this context, it is important for the U.S. to promote a policy of opening NATO up to the new and increasingly stable democracies in Eastern Europe. Such an expansion must be pursued in a way that doesn't destabilize other neighboring states—particularly Ukraine. However, an effort to fill the wide security vacuum that has developed in Central and Eastern Europe is essential to the stable evolution of these countries and to the irreversibility of their democratic and market reforms.

As the new Congress and the president begin a dialogue and debate over U.S. foreign policy priorities, the world that the 1995 Survey depicts suggests that they should focus their attention on the following priorities:

a) Targeting U.S. foreign aid development assistance to emerging democracies and to Partly Free societies in which further progress toward freedom is possible;

b) expanding the funds available to the National Endowment for Democracy to support efforts aimed at strengthening emerging democracies and promoting democratic transitions in nondemocratic states;

c) allocating substantial funds to promote the flow of democratic literature and ideas and to support democratic movements in Cuba and China;

c) strengthening the broadcasting of the Voice of America, Radio Marti, Radio Liberty and Radio Free Europe;

d) adequately funding Asian Democracy Radio to broadcast into China, Vietnam and Burma; and

e) moving quickly to resolve the problem of the security vacuum in Eastern and Central Europe to solidify the region's new democracies.

Adrian Karatnycky, president of Freedom House, is coordinator of the Comparative Survey of Freedom.

The United States: The Demands of Leadership

James Finn

When the political history of the twentieth century is written, among the events that will be recorded will be the great wars, the fall of empires, decolonization, the rise and fall of murderous, totalitarian systems, gulags, the Holocaust and nuclear weapons, the vast growth of international economic power, the spread of the democratic idea—and, threading its way through these matters, the gradual increase in the power of the United States until it emerged toward the end of the century as the sole, undisputed global superpower. At this point in history, no other country has the capacity that the United States has for exercising leadership in the world. That role may be exercised well or badly, but it cannot be avoided.

The U.S. radiates its influence by the traditional means of political, economic and military agencies, but also through the culture which it transmits through an ever increasing array of communications systems. It inevitably reveals the principles and values that it professes as well as, even when they diverge, those by which it acts. There is scarcely a corner of the globe that is untouched by American influence. For these reasons alone, what happens in the U.S. is of interest not only to its own people but to the governments and people of other countries.

And for these reasons the elections of 1992 and the stunning elections of 1994—it is well to consider them together—were and are being subjected to close analyses. What do they tell us about the United States? About what the electorate wants and expects? What are our present policies and goals? In what direction is the nation headed as it faces the large political and economic challenges of our time?

The Clinton campaign of 1992 was run on guidelines that were frequently reiterated. "It's the economy, stupid" was shorthand for the belief that among the matters in which the government should properly be involved, the American people were concerned first with jobs and income. "All politics are local," long regarded as a tested truism, told us that what really motivates people, what leads them to pull one lever rather than another in the polling booth, is how the outcome affects their local conditions. The interests of Podunk are more immediate and overriding than the national interests. A third guideline was that Washington should attend first to domestic issues, then to foreign policy. The Cold War had drawn heavily on U.S. resources for decades and, the theory ran, its end offered a respite, a chance to redirect vast human and material resources to domestic needs.

Bill Clinton campaigned on a platform built on these guidelines and on his self-description as a "New Democrat." He tried to assure the voters that our political system could respond to its many acknowledged problems and that he would provide the leadership that was needed. He would be an agent of change, operating from the political center. He would, for example, "end welfare as we know it." With the promise that this implied, he was elected with 43 percent of the vote to his principal opponent's 38 percent. (Nineteen percent went to the independent Ross Perot, whose resources included his novelty as political figure, his wit, self-confidence and acclaimed business acumen and his considerable personal wealth.)

President Clinton governed with a Democratic majority in both houses of Congress—

until the historic midterm elections of 8 November 1994. The long-term effects of this election became matters for prolonged intense debate, but the short-term effects were immediate and sharp. There was no anti-incumbency fever among the voters, as some had predicted. Not one single Republican incumbent in the Senate, the House or a governor's office lost, but Democrats were swept from office wholesale. The Democratic majority of 56-44 in the Senate was transformed into a Republican majority of 53-47. (This was aided by a Democratic incumbent who changed party allegiance.) In the House the Democratic majority of 256-178 was overturned to give the Republicans a majority of 231-203 (with one independent), and control of the house for the first time in forty years.

Stunning results

Grim or glorious, depending from which side they were viewed, the statistics were, from either side, stunning. Nevertheless, they told only one part of the story. For among those who lost were such long-term, nationally known stalwarts as Representative Dan Rostenkowski of Chicago; Representative Jack Brooks of Texas, who first went to Washington in 1952; Governor Mario Cuomo of New York, long the liberal's liberal; Governor Ann Richards of Texas, who was replaced by George W. Bush; and Speaker of the House Tom Foley, the first Speaker to lose since 1860.

"It's the economy, stupid." This assertion was badly damaged if not, indeed, politically invalidated. For the Clinton administration could point to a number of encouraging signs in the American economy: a reduction in the deficit, a relatively low and stable rate of inflation, a gradually expanding economy, an increase in jobs and decreasing rates of unemployment. In the logic of the slogan this should have translated into Democratic votes. Why didn't it? According to Treasury Secretary Lloyd Bentsen, who said the "economy numbers" were good, the Democratic loss was the consequence of "a great product and a lousy sales pitch." Others, however, could give other reasons. They could, for example, point to findings of The Economic Policy Institute, a Democratic think-tank: Since 1989 the median wage in the U.S., adjusted for inflation, fell from $10.21 per hour to $9.41. For males alone, the median wage fell from $11.78 to $11.23 in the same period. Workers did not feel the beneficial effects of the "good numbers." And for many workers who were "downsized," the numbers were irrelevant. This may account for Mr. Bentsen's subsequent comment that the biggest problem in this country is that "middle-income job holders have not seen their incomes expanding."

Most commentators and analysts agreed, however, that no matter how one read the economic indicators, the economy was not the determining factor in the vote. Other candidates for that honor were the failed health reform plan proposed by the administration, a race-based agenda advanced by the Democrats, and an array of social issues that include the breakdown of the traditional family structure, poor or misguided education, drugs, crime, poverty and welfare.

• *Health care*: The basis for nominating the health care plan was that only 25 percent of Americans thought Congress should enact a major reform of the present system, 41 percent opted for modest change and 25 percent said no change was needed. For those who saw the plan as a return to big government spending and centralized decision making, it stripped away Clinton's image as a "new Democrat." A recent massive poll by the Times Mirror Center for the People and the Press showed that more than two-thirds of Americans agree that "when something is run by the government, it is usually inefficient and wasteful." The reform plan ran headlong into this attitude.

• *Racialism*: Polling also revealed that an increasing majority of Americans, including blacks and whites, are critical of race-based policies, whether they are labeled affirmative action or reverse discrimination. A policy that was deemed acceptable as a temporary necessity became increasingly unpopular as it came to be seen as a policy with no end in sight, and one that some of its supporters were willing to push to extremes. In California, for example, the policy led the Democratic-controlled state assembly to legislate that by the end of the century the proportion of graduates of state universities should reflect a pre-determined set of racial guidelines. The measure was vetoed by the Republican governor. A pattern of such actions caused the Democrats to be seen as the party of racialism. Before the 1994 elections, a centrist Democrat affiliated with the Democratic Leadership Council (DLC) predicted that large numbers of Democrats would defect from their party on "the racialist issue."

• *Family*: Thirty years ago Daniel Patrick Moynihan produced a study that analyzed the black family in the United States and spoke of an impending breakdown if the nuclear family continued to give way and the rate of births out of wedlock continued to rise. The paper was buried under a relentless and general onslaught as a racist tract. Today many regard that study as prescient. It pointed to conditions in the black family that both blacks and whites now agree need national attention. At present the illegitimacy birth rate among whites is higher than it was among blacks when Moynihan's study was completed. An unavoidable conclusion is that conditions of the white family also need serious national attention. Today there is widespread agreement among those who study family structures that a number of social ills flow from the growing rate of births by poor, uneducated, teenage, single parents. These ills form a constellation that includes continued poverty, drugs, violence, inferior education and welfare dependency. Among large segments of the public this constellation is associated with a general moral decline and a lack of personal responsibility.

• *Crime*: "I remember when I chased these two juveniles up three flights of stairs, but I got them," said the officer. "You should have," said his partner. "They were only seven years old."

As the wry smile fades, the import of this true incident begins to sink in. According to F.B.I. reports, serious crimes in this country have declined steadily since 1992. During the first half of 1994, homicides, rape and burglary have all gone down. Yet the expressions of fear and feelings of insecurity among the citizenry, especially among the elderly and the disabled, have not diminished. Why not? Because these statistics must be placed against another set leading up to 1992. In late 1994 the Center for Disease Control and Prevention released a study which shows that between 1985 and 1992 the annual rate at which men fifteen to nineteen years old were being killed jumped 154 percent. Over 95 percent of these deaths involved guns. All the statistics show that younger and younger people—going down to pre-teenagers—are committing serious crimes, including murder. These troubling statistics are supported by anecdotal evidence of people, particularly the elderly, who fear to leave their apartments, especially if they live in projects where police protection is scarce or nonexistent. According to a typical observation by one inner city social worker, these are "children who don't care how they get money. Children who have a complete depletion of moral values." Others have noted that a large jump in the number of violent young people coincided with the introduction of crack, highly distilled cocaine, into their schools and playgrounds.

"All politics are local." The results of the 1994 elections belie that supposed truism. The Republican leadership made strong efforts to nationalize the issues of the pre-election debate, and they succeeded. They could not have succeeded, however, if the political ground was not already lying fallow, ready to receive such arguments. The concern about crime, the family, illegal immigrants, health care and schools may have varied in intensity from region to region, from locality to locality, but the election returns leave no doubt that the concern extended across the country. From coast to coast and skipping no large areas in between, the voters expressed the same discontents and fears, and the same kind of preferences.

An overall assessment of the U.S. during and at the end of 1994 must, it is clear, attempt to understand the midterm elections. A major difficulty is not that there are no compelling analyses, but that there are so many. In addition to those already offered, two others merit attention. Representative Dave McCurdy, chairman of the DLC and a loser in the elections, rendered a sharp judgment of his friend Bill Clinton. "While Bill Clinton has the mind of a New Democrat, he retains the heart of an old Democrat." The result is that he "has pursued elements of a moderate and liberal agenda at the same time, to the great confusion of the American people." If this reading is accurate, one could legitimately conclude that the American people have not turned from left to right, as many analysts assert, but that they wanted a centrist and failed to find him in Bill Clinton, and that they are still seeking that center. At the end of 1994 it was too early to ascertain whether they had found such leadership in the new Congress.

A more emphatic reading of the present condition of the American political process was provided by David L. Boren, who predicted the Democratic debacle and who, with two years left to serve as Democratic senator of Oklahoma, decided to retire with the end of the 103rd Congress. The latest vote is, he said, potentially the last fling with the traditional two-party system in this country. "I think there's a great likelihood that there will be a centrist independent political movement in this country" and a centrist independent president. He did not speculate about what would happen to the two-party system, but he did about the immediate future. "I think this is the beginning of a period of great turmoil in this country, not the end of it."

What unites McCurdy and Boren is their reading that American voters are weary of political extremes and are looking for a vigorous center that will attend to their real voiced concerns. The remaining years in this decade and this century will test that proposition, as they will test those who dispute it.

First domestic issues, then foreign

Bill Clinton campaigned for president with strong interest in domestic issues but with little interest or experience in foreign affairs. Even before Clinton was elected, Prime Minister Felipe Gonzalez of Spain observed: "I think the U.S. has an international dimension which appears little in the campaign. But whoever sits in the White House has no choice but to assume it." What President Clinton assumed with his office was an agenda that included policies, both domestic and foreign, advanced by his predecessor but far from concluded: the North American Free Trade Agreement (NAFTA) and the General Agreement on Tariffs and Trade (GATT), nuclear weapons and their disposal, famine and war lords in Somalia, Haiti and its refugees, Bosnia and the inept efforts to end the fighting there, China's Most Favored Nation (MFN) status and human rights, Arab-Israeli relations, Russia and its neighboring, newly independent states, NATO's changing role, the U.N. and its peacekeeping forces. Even such a truncated list indicates the heavy foreign responsibilities thrust upon the man who sits in the White House. There was never a possibility that these could be put aside while domestic issues were tended to. As always they required to be dealt with simultaneously.

As president, Clinton has experienced both successes and failures. He did, for example, with great personal effort succeed in pushing approval of NAFTA through Congress. He could not, of course, assuage many of its critics, who remain skeptical of its alleged merits. Even after the 1994 elections, he oversaw congressional approval of GATT—a most ambitious, complex trade agreement involving over 100 countries that has been many years in the making, but which has attracted critics across the political spectrum. Even critics of the bill praised Clinton's consistency and clarity of purpose as he fought for bills that, he strongly argued, would enhance international trade to the benefit of all countries.

On other issues, however, observers perceived different characteristics of the president. For example, at year's end Haiti was experiencing relative stability after a long period of turmoil and Jean-Bertrand Aristide, the duly elected but subsequently deposed president was back in the presidential office, restored there by virtue of United States armed intervention. A positive accomplishment by the administration. But even before the military intervention, observers had raised a number of unsettling questions. Are Haiti and its problems a matter of vital national interest to the United States? If so, on what grounds? If not, what justifies the use of military intervention, with the accompanying risk to American lives? Instead of answering such traditional questions, different and sometimes conflicting evaluations were issued by the policymakers. Sanctions, threats and the withdrawal of threats followed by renewed threats had come to be the expected procedures. And when the time for armed intervention actually came, the inconsistencies continued. Jimmy Carter, Sam Nunn and Colin Powell were dispatched as emissaries to Haiti, followed by the president's address that diplomacy had been exhausted and action was necessary. Aircraft were launched even as the emissaries were still negotiating. The near-impasse resolved, Jimmy Carter did come to an agreement with the generals, but not before saying that he was ashamed of his government's Haitian policy and praising the generals whom President Clinton had just called thugs and murderers. Continuing skeptics recalled that the last time the U.S. sent troops into Haiti they stayed for nineteen years.

For foreign observers, what transpired in Haiti was less important than the policymaking procedures of the U.S. As more than one foreign journal noted, the idea of applying such methods to significant policies was highly unsettling. It is not, they added, a promising perspective from which to view the efforts of the U.S. to make decisions about Bosnia or NATO. It is not, domestic observers said, a promising way to deal with Boris Yeltsin, the newly assertive Russian president who, at a fifty-two-nation summit conference early in December, pointedly asserted: "History demonstrates that it is a dangerous illusion to suppose that the destinies of continents and of the world community in general can somehow be managed from one single capital." Nor to work with allies on Bosnia when the French foreign minister is willing to criticize in the French National Assembly, just as pointedly, "governments that want to give us lessons when they have not lifted a finger to put even one man on the ground."

What both foreign and domestic political leaders expect from the United States in foreign policy, and would hope to get from other countries, is clarity of purpose and a degree of consistency. Ambiguity and abrupt shifts in policy are disconcerting and easily lead to dangerous misunderstandings. The U.S. has never been unaware of power and its uses in international affairs, but it has never fully embraced *Realpolitik*. On the basis of history—and whether they approve or not—other countries have a right to expect from the U.S. policies that are imbued with, not merely cloaked by, moral principles. It is by virtue of its present power and its historic principles that the United States has gained its preeminent role in world affairs today, and it is on those grounds that the performance of the present administration is being judged.

Canada: The gathering cloud, again

Once again, the cloud of Quebec separatism hangs over Canada, casting shadows over the political and cultural landscape. In the elections of September 1994, the Quebecers elected Jaccques Parizeau, a strong separatist, to be their next premier. Although Parti Quebecois (PQ), which he headed, won 77 of the 125 legislative seats, those numbers do not indicate the narrowness of his victory. The popular vote is a more precise indicator of separatist sentiment, and there his party's 44.7 percent barely edged the Liberal Party's 44.3 percent. Nevertheless, he has pledged to have the National Assembly pass a declaration that the people of Quebec want to separate from the rest of Canada. One of the great problems with such a declaration is that, according to polls, the majority of Quebecers want no such thing.

One of the great divides in Quebec, which derives from its history, is language. It is upon that significant cultural hook that the separatists hang their political arguments. Approximately 80 percent of Quebec is Francophone, 18 percent having English as their first language (although many of these can do quite well in French). Most of the English-speakers live and work in Montreal, Quebec's largest city, and many have said they would leave if the separatists won. This would not be the smallest disruption to Quebec or to the rest of Canada should separation take place, even though separatists argue that the severance would be cost-free to Quebec.

Could not some reasonable accommodation be made between francophones and anglophones before a divorce takes place? The theoretical answer is yes. Not only have other countries made such accommodations, but federal Canada has done so. For federal Canada, with 20 percent French speakers, gives equal status to French and English. In contrast, Quebec, with 18 percent English speakers, adamantly refuses to do so. It places high obstacles in the way of those who wish their children to be educated in English, and imposes what the English speakers regard as petty laws concerning the language on commercial signs.

But Canadian observers stress that neither economics nor common sense are reliable guides to the separatist sentiment. It is driven by nationalism, by what former prime minister Pierre Elliott Trudeau years ago termed tribalism. Anti-separatists say that a glance at world affairs today indicates what a powerful but also destructive force nationalism can be.

Although Parizeau was shaken by the slim margin of his victory in September, he continues to proclaim that he wants Quebecers to become "a normal people." He promises to call a referendum on the question before the end of 1995, and if that vote goes against the separation—as it did in the first referendum—he might call up referendum III, IV and V.

Parizeau is aided in his crusade by the ex-Conservative Lucien Bouchard, leader of Bloc Quebecois, the opposition party in the federal government. An illness and an operation he underwent at the end of the year may, however, limit his activities.

The noted Canadian writer Mordechai Richler has pointed out one possible outcome of Parizeau's strategy of calling successive referendums on the question. Even though most Quebecers to date say they do not want to separate, the rest of Canada, "weary of the endless, wasting quarrel, will boot la Belle Province out of the confederation." This would be, for the separatists, a most welcome reaction. What they could not win at the polling booth, they would have won by attrition. But Canadians, who have much at stake, and the rest of the world, which has little or none, must wait until the promised referendum measures accurately the sentiments of the Quebecers. In the meantime a sour mood prevails in large parts of Quebec.

James Finn is senior editor of Freedom Review.

Latin America: Ballots, Neo-Strongmen, Narcos and Impunity Douglas W. Payne

Democracy is in the balance in Latin America and the Caribbean, but you would hardly know that from listening to the region's political leaders. The declaration by heads of state from throughout the region at the eighth annual Rio Group summit in September 1994 devoted but a single paragraph to the issue. And then, only to express "satisfaction" with the many elections taking place and conclude, "This demonstrates the vitality of democracy in our region."

To assume that elections alone are an accurate gauge of the health of democracy is naive at best. But the Rio Group declaration came just a month after President Joaquín Balaguer had himself installed for a seventh term in the Dominican Republic following an election judged fraudulent by an array of international observers. The refusal to acknowledge this affront to the principle of free and fair elections made the 1994 declaration just another in a long line of self-congratulatory, ultimately cynical statements by the region's political leadership.

Nowhere in the Rio Group declaration was there a reference to the rule of law, the issue that remains at the heart of the question of whether democracy will succeed in Latin America. Luis Rubio, a noted Mexican political and economic analyst, and Beatriz Magaloni put it well in a recent essay: "Without a profound respect for the law in all its forms and meanings no society can advance, because none of its members can be certain about what others, including the government, will do."

The reality is that in the region today, rule is still based more on power than on law. The exceptions are Costa Rica, Chile, most of the English-speaking Caribbean and to a lesser extent, Uruguay. In a majority of countries the traditionally dominant sectors of society—political elites, the wealthy, armies, police—continue to enrich themselves at public expense, while the human rights of ordinary people are violated with impunity. Judicial systems are less about justice than providing protection for those who can pay for it and punishing those who cannot. Voters can chase presidents and legislators through the ballot box in most countries, but government remains a racket dominated by the powerful and the well-connected.

Not only will there be no advances without an established rule of law. But the formal structures of democracy will erode and become distorted, prey to the autocratic impulse deeply rooted in Latin American culture, and the international criminal syndicates spawned by the drug trade. The trend is already evident in a number of Latin American nations, and in the new lexicon that has emerged to describe the ensuing deformations—*Fujimorismo*, constitutional despotism, authoritarian democracy, narco-democracy.

Fujimorismo

Peruvian President Alberto Fujimori, backed by the military, dissolved Peru's congress and suspended the constitution in 1992. He then danced around protests by the thirty-four-member Organization of American States (OAS) by holding a state-engineered election for a new congress. The congress produced a new constitution that, in effect, ratified Fujimori's *autogolpe*, or self-coup, by codifying nearly paramount executive authority and allowing for reelection.

That was good enough for the OAS, which gave its approval to Fujimori's acrobatics and, in effect, overturned the OAS declaration of 1991 to defend representative democracy against all threats. Good enough, too, for the Rio Group, in which Fujimori continues to play a prominent role. Fujimori, having broken the law and gotten away with it, is one reason why the rule of law gets no endorsement in Rio Group statements. First, he would never countenance it. Second, a number of his peers may want to keep the *Fujimorismo* option open for themselves, given the international financial community's embrace of Fujimori because of his state-imposed market reforms.

In fact, there have been frequent rumors and allegations that "a Fujimori" was brewing in a number of Latin countries where scorn for politics-as-usual runs deep—for example, in Ecuador and Bolivia in 1994. There actually has been one attempted "Fujimori," in Guatemala in 1993. But the Guatemalan military backed out once it realized that it made little sense to risk international economic sanctions when it could dominate the country no matter who was president or what the constitution said. President Ramiro de Leon Carpio, the former human rights ombudsman who replaced Jorge Serrano when his autogolpe failed, was powerless in 1994 to do anything about the worst wave of extrajudicial executions—at least one per day—and other human rights abuses in Guatemala in five years.

Fujimori has basked in his notoriety, expressed disdain for representative democracy and gone so far as to advocate the Chinese dictatorship as a model for Latin America. After a visit with China's rulers in Beijing in mid-1994, Fujimori told Andres Oppenheimer of the *Miami Herald* that Latin America should copy much of what has been done in that country. In Latin America, he said, "We must not be dogmatic and impose the so-called democratic system." Rather, he suggested that Latin America address its problems the way he did in Peru—"fix it with a machete."

By letting Fujimori off the hook the OAS and the U.S. have given a green light to aspiring autocrats throughout the region. When the Clinton administration announced it would host a hemispheric summit in Miami in December 1994, the gathering was billed as a celebration of democracy. Fujimori received an invitation because the standard for admission was no higher than that used by the Rio Group—those invited merely had to be democratically elected, which in fact Fujimori was in 1990. In the end, the Clinton administration did not hold to that standard any better than the Rio Group. Despite the election fraud in the Dominican Republic, President Balaguer still had a reserved seat in Miami.

The only hemispheric leader not invited by Washington to the summit was Cuba's Fidel Castro. The implicit and unfortunate message was that authoritarian behavior will not incur the loss of democratic credentials as long as it falls short of the totalitarian repression and severe deprivation under which the Cuban people continued to suffer.

The green light for antidemocratic behavior appeared to become brighter still with the election in 1994 of former Colombian President Cesar Gaviria as secretary general of the OAS. Gaviria received strong backing from the Clinton administration because he is a proponent of free trade. But Colombia under Gaviria had one of the worst human rights records in the hemisphere, notwithstanding the spin by high-priced U.S. public relations firms, and his stated commitment to democracy in Latin America remained questionable.

When asked by journalists whether his support for democracy would extend to Peru, Gaviria replied, "The question of Peru is totally behind us." Fujimori, who had vocally supported Gaviria for the OAS, must have been pleased. By the time Gaviria assumed his new post, Fujimori had already deployed the Peruvian military and state intelligence, the principal pillars of his regime, with the aim of engineering his reelection in April 1995. Fujimori's principal rival looked to be former United Nations Secretary General Javier Perez de Cuellar. What will be Gaviria's response, or Washington's, if Perez de Cuellar makes a legitimate claim of fraud?

Free speech = treason

Venezuelan President Rafael Caldera, a seventy-eight-year-old populist throwback who quit the Christian Democratic party (COPEI) in 1993, has entertained the idea of making the "Fujimori" option legal. After obtaining a weak mandate in the December 1993 election, he proposed a constitutional amendment that would allow him to dissolve the legislature "when it does not carry out the will of the people." But it appeared the Venezuelan military, responsible for two coup attempts in 1992, might not go along. After taking office in 1994 Caldera settled for suspending constitutional guarantees regarding arbitrary arrest, property rights and freedoms of expression, movement and financial activity. He did this, he said, "in the name of social justice and solidarity."

When Venezuelan journalists working for international news agencies reported critically on Caldera's actions, he declared to the Venezuelan National Journalists Convention in July, "This is treason against the homeland! This is a crime against Venezuela!" Caldera's allies and apologists asserted that governing Venezuela required a strong hand, that some form of "constitutional despotism" was justified. Amid bank collapses, high inflation, and violent street protests, the question was how strong a hand Caldera, or the military, was willing to impose in what has become one of the most volatile countries in the region.

The autocratic impulse is also alive and well in Argentina and Paraguay. Argentine President Carlos Menem has effectively ruled Argentina by decree for the last five years, bypassing Congress and packing the Supreme Court. He has also been obsessed with duplicating the feat of Juan Perón, the founder of Menem's Peronist party and the only Argentine president to secure reelection. To overturn the constitutional ban against a second term, Menem cut a backroom deal with former president Raúl Alfonsín, the leader of the opposition Radical party. Alfonsín, hoping to salvage his declining career, agreed to reelection in exchange for reforms that in theory would limit executive powers.

Menem's popularity seemed to be waning by the time the constitutional reforms were finally pushed through Congress in mid-1994. Key Peronist figures were defecting, some to join a new center-left coalition, the Grand Front, that had sponsored the largest demonstration against Menem since he took office. How far was Menem willing to go to secure reelection in the vote scheduled for May 1995?

Menem's antidemocratic behavior has been especially evident in his antagonism toward the Argentine media, which have been at the forefront in exposing the rampant corruption in his government. He has initiated campaigns to entangle journalists in a web of lawsuits and done little to curb intimidation by Peronist bullies. Journalists continue to be killed in Latin America at an alarming rate, particularly in Colombia, Mexico and Guatemala. But the assault on the media in Argentina and Venezuela reflects a newer pattern of more sophisticated, selective intimidation by Latin America's new breed of strongman.

In Paraguay the man to watch is Gen. Lino Oviedo. Oviedo has consistently flouted the ban against military interference in politics. He helped engineer the primary election fraud that made businessman Juan Carlos Wasmosy the presidential candidate of the ruling Colorado party. Wasmosy won the presidency in 1993, but only after Oviedo threatened a coup if the Colorado party was voted out of power, stating that the military "would govern together with the glorious Colorado party forever and ever." Wasmosy took office beholdened to Oviedo and has since become Oviedo's stepping stone for achieving the presidency himself. Wasmosy, as nominal commander-in-chief, has allowed Oviedo to eliminate rivals from within the military by retiring them. In November 1994, when three former generals publicly criticized Wasmosy and Oviedo, they were jailed and sentenced to ten to thirty days.

"Authoritarian democracy"

For the last sixty-five years Mexico has remained apart from Latin America's cycles of upheaval and military rule. It has done so through a corporatist, state-party system maintained since 1929 by the Institutional Revolutionary Party (PRI). After the fall of the Soviet Communist Party, the PRI became the longest ruling party in the world. Many observers of Mexico, particularly those who favor the free-trade policies of former President Carlos Salinas and his successor Ernesto Zedillo, have sought a diplomatic way of describing Mexico's party-dominant state. Many eventually latched onto "authoritarian democracy," a resonant oxymoron that Fujimori apologists like to apply to Peru and that can be heard, too, when Argentina, Venezuela or the Dominican Republic are discussed.

In 1994, however, the PRI state-party system took a battering and Mexicans began to wonder what would come next if it finally came undone. In January the Chiapas Indian rebellion in Mexico's poorest state, shook the political system to its foundations. Chiapas, where conflict was beginning to simmer again in late 1994, was also a reminder that despite NAFTA and Mexico's newly achieved membership in the Organization for Economic Cooperation and Development (OECD), Mexico remains highly and increasingly unequal, its society strung out between the first world and the third. At the top, twenty-four *Forbes*-certified billionaires. At the bottom, the nearly half of ninety million Mexicans who are poor, the pool from which flows the tide of immigrants causing such a political ruckus from California to Washington.

Chiapas was followed by the assassination of PRI presidential candidate Luis Donaldo Colosio. Colosio had advocated political reform, leading to suspicions he had been murdered as part of the ongoing internecine battle between PRI reformers and hardliners. Whatever differences existed within the PRI, however, all sectors of the party got behind Zedillo, who had been anointed by Salinas to replace Colosio, to ensure the PRI retained power in the August 1994 election. Under intense international scrutiny the PRI eschewed more traditional instruments like ballot-stuffing and outright intimidation. Rather, it relied on the enormous resources available to it as the electoral arm of the state, on its control of the broadcast media and on the support of the billionaire set to defeat the conservative National Action Party (PAN) and the left-wing Party of the Democratic Revolution (PRD). The election was freer than in the past but far from fair.

After the vote the PRI went back to war. Francisco Ruiz Massieu, the PRI secretary general and a proponent of political reform, was assassinated in September, his murder evidently ordered from somewhere within the PRI. His brother, Mario Ruiz Massieu, the assistant attorney general in charge of the case, resigned from his post and from the PRI in November after accusing top PRI officials of blocking the investigation. It was during this period that Mexican analysts Rubio and Magaloni published the essay quoted earlier. The title they chose: "Without Respect for the Law, We are Just One More Banana Republic."

President Zedillo, a technocrat in the Salinas mold, campaigned as a reformer. Before taking office on 1 December he even promised to make the PRI independent of the government—in essence, to dismantle the state-party system. Rare is the leader who is willing to undo the structures upon which his power is based. But even if Zedillo is serious, would PRI hard-liners let him get away with it?

Not underdeveloped, but unjust

Fernando Henrique Cardoso of Brazil is another newly elected president who will be severely challenged. Since 1992 Brazil has seen one president fall because of corruption and a caretaker replacement who at times seemed so overwhelmed many Brazilians expected, and some called for, the military to step in. As finance minister, Cardoso authored in 1994 a new currency program that brought down the hyperinflation that has bedeviled Brazil for years. He was rewarded in October with an easy election victory over Luis Inacio "Lula" da Silva, a fiery labor leader who initially had been the front-runner.

Cardoso, a social democrat who believes in market economics, promised reform and committed himself to addressing social issues in what is the world's most unequal society. His supporters believed the mandate he won in 1994 was strong enough to enable him to channel the benefits of economic growth to the lower two-thirds of the population. But Cardoso will be up against a political culture marked by entrenched corruption, a constitution that mandates spending on behalf of a vast array of special interests and makes structural reform nearly impossible, and a country divided into a network of regional political fiefdoms that spans the impoverished north and the industrialized south.

The Rio Group declaration of 1994 specifically linked social development to economic growth. The fact is that in the 1990s, Latin America, led by Mexico and Brazil, has already achieved significant levels of growth. But the result has been a widening of what was already the biggest income gap in the world, rising unemployment in every country and an increase in social unrest. The Chiapas rebellion, the riots in Argentina's northwestern city of Santiago del Estero in late 1993, the Indian demonstrations that paralyzed Ecuador in spring 1994 are among the most recent examples of mounting discontent over a lack of promised progress from market reforms.

The lesson is that without political accountability, the rule of law and greater respect for worker rights, market-fueled economic growth will create only more billionaires and more poor people. That is a sure formula for continued unrest and enhances the likelihood that Latin America's historical pendulum will swing back toward instability and repression. Before his inauguration on 1 January President Cardoso stated, "Brazil is no longer an underdeveloped country. It is an unjust country." Such a clear admission of the problem puts Cardoso ahead of most Latin American political elites and suggests he is serious about doing something to correct it. Whether he actually can remains to be seen.

The countries of Central America, with the exception of Costa Rica, remain unjust *and* underdeveloped. There are elected governments, but they are steeped in corruption. Militaries have evolved into armed corporations feasting on national economies, and grave human rights violations continue to be committed with impunity, particularly in Guatemala and Nicaragua.

The picture may have brightened somewhat in El Salvador in 1994. The peace process overseen by the United Nations led to an election in which the former FMLN guerrillas not only participated for the first time, but emerged as the second political force in the country. New President Armando Calderon Sol seemed to be taking a more moderate approach than his roots in the conservative wing of the incumbent right-wing ARENA party might have indicated. But the U.N. monitors were scheduled to depart in early 1995, and prospects for establishing even a semblance of a rule of law appeared to be a long way off.

There was also an election in Panama, where voters returned to power the former party of ousted dictator Gen. Manuel Noriega. However, under the guidance of Ernesto Pérez Balladares, who was elected president in the most free and fair election in Panama's history, the Democratic Revolutionary Party seemed to have shed the authoritarian legacy of Noriega. What has not changed in Panama is that it remains a major hub in the hemispheric drug and money-laundering trade that no country in Latin America and the Caribbean has been able to resist.

"Narco-democracy"

Ask a drug kingpin what the optimum conditions would be for conducting his operations, and the answer would be: weak rule of law and low trade barriers. Those are the conditions that prevail in much of Latin America today. What is at risk is not just democracy but the very sovereignty of nations.

The so-called "drug war" initiated by Washington in the 1980s has been won by the traffickers. Nearly $100 billion spent on interdiction has hardly made a dent in the northward flow of drugs. But the war was really over once the traffickers realized they did not have to fight it. They learned that what alarms Latin American governments most is not drug-trafficking per se, but the violence associated with it.

Medillin cartel leader Pablo Escobar took on the Colombian state with all guns blazing. When he was killed by Colombian security forces in December 1993, it was proclaimed a great victory by then-President Gaviria. The Cali cartel, meanwhile, has become a global, multi-billion-dollar narcotics empire, the central star of a criminal constellation that spans three continents. Cali does not confront governments, it infiltrates, then emasculates them.

A few months after Escobar went down, Gilberto and Miguel Rodríguez Orejuela, the two brothers who run the Cali cartel, were on the phone agreeing to give $3.75 million to the presidential campaign of Ernesto Samper. Tape recordings of the conversations surfaced in June after Samper, a former minister in the Gaviria government, had won the election to succeed him. Samper denied receiving the money. But even if he did not, the "narco-cassettes" show that the Cali cartel at least thought it could buy the president of a country.

And why not? The Cali cartel has already purchased a sizable chunk of the Colombian state—judges, prosecutors, police and soldiers. It has bought sufficient influence in the Congress to make sure extradition to the U.S., the only thing traffickers fear, was banned in the new constitution promulgated in 1991. In 1993 cartel lawyers virtually dictated penal code reforms which allow traffickers who turn themselves in on a single drug-related charge to have their sentences reduced by two-thirds, while any pending charges to which they do not plead are forever dismissed. It is not inconceivable the cartel will be able, in effect, to have itself legalized, with minimal penalty and little disruption of its operations.

The Samper government expressed outrage when Joseph Toft, a retired chief of the U.S. Drug Enforcement Administration office in Bogotá, described Colombia as a "narco-democracy." But numerous Colombian officials, speaking to international reporters on condition of anonymity, said they agreed. One judicial official told the Reuters news agency, "It is very sad to say it, but unfortunately when he says most of Colombia's institutions are corrupted by traffickers, he is right."

The Cali cartel and its myriad subsidiaries are thriving. In Latin America there is not one country where traffickers and launderers cannot operate with relative ease. The networks of patronage, payoffs, graft and illegal transactions that define Latin American political culture from Mexico to Argentina make governments, banking systems, judiciaries and electoral campaigns highly receptive to penetration and compromise.

In 1993, for example, Venezuela witnessed the spectacle of then-President Ramon Velasquez inadvertently signing a pardon for a prominent trafficker after it somehow found its way to his desk. In Mexico, drug-related corruption has so penetrated politics, financial institutions and private business that "Colombianization" has become part of the national discourse.

Moreover, declining trade barriers and reduced border controls now make it even easier for traffickers to move drugs and to launder money through investments. If free trade promotes the growth of legitimate business, consider the advantage for a beyond-the-law corporation like the Cali cartel and its offspring, equipped with the best intelligence networks, technology, money-managers and lawyers that money can buy. Before NAFTA was implemented, Mexico's major cartels were already working with the Colombians to set up new factories, warehouses, transport companies and currency exchanges to exploit the expected flood of cross-border commerce.

Storm watch in the Caribbean

Among the twelve nations of the English-speaking Caribbean, democracy and the rule of law have proved to be more effective and durable than in any other subregion of the developing world. Today, the only exception is Antigua and Barbuda, which the Bird family has dominated for decades. In 1994 Lester Bird replaced his father as prime minister following an election that was neither free or fair.

Nonetheless, the difficulties faced by the Caribbean democracies and the potential for setbacks should not be underestimated. These nations, important voices on behalf of democracy and human rights within the OAS and the U.N., have been left out in the economic cold with the emergence of giant trading blocs in North America and Europe. Citizens in many Caribbean countries are beginning to lose confidence in the ability of politicians to adjust. But the greatest concern is that social and economic pressures have left these mostly small nations vulnerable to drug traffickers and money-launderers that have already begun to corrupt governments and law enforcement agencies in the region.

Investigations by U.S. and European drug agencies show that the Cali cartel and the Sicilian Mafia have combined forces to make the Caribbean and Venezuela (with a 750-mile Caribbean coastline) a major route for moving cocaine to the expanding European market. At the same time, they are laundering money in casino, resort and real estate operations throughout the area. Every Caribbean government is now grappling with increases in violent crime and official corruption tied to the encroachment of the drug trade.

Little noticed outside the Caribbean were the events in tiny St. Kitts and Nevis in 1994. In October the director of the police unit that provides security for top government officials was shot dead with a machine pistol in broad daylight outside his home. He had been investigating the disappearance of one of the deputy prime minister's sons, who was subsequently found murdered. Two other sons were arrested as suspects in their brother's murder and found to be in possession of a large shipment of cocaine. The deputy prime minister was forced to resign and opposition parties demanded that Prime Minister Kennedy Simmonds do the same.

As long as the global demand for drugs continues and Latin America remains such an accommodating host, the drug juggernaut will keep on rolling. How long can Caribbean nations withstand the assault?

Hope in hell

Three years after the military overthrow of President Jean-Bertrand Aristide, a reluctant U.S. finally intervened to halt that country's descent into absolute hell. A few Latin American countries applauded, while others grumbled platitudes about non-intervention. Most just seemed happy to be relieved of any further responsibility for the fate of a fellow OAS member whose democratically elected president had been overthrown.

Although Haitians have suffered greatly, they are a remarkably resilient people and deserve another chance at democracy. They now have it, but the challenges are enormous. President Aristide has only a year left in his term to somehow prepare his country for elections in December 1995. He will need to display more political acumen and common sense than he did during his first brief tenure in office. Moreover, Haiti's institutions and economic infrastructure were decimated under military rule. The U.S. and the U.N., whether they want to admit it or not, have undertaken the responsibility for rebuilding a nation. If they falter in their determination the likelihood is that Haiti will spin out of control yet again.

Douglas W. Payne is director of hemispheric studies for Freedom House.

Africa: Trade, Aid, Finance, People, Poverty

Thomas R. Lansner

Across sub-Saharan Africa, the year past has indeed seen the best of times and the worst of times. In a continent so vast and so varied, this should perhaps be little surprise. Yet even for those long accustomed to watching the high drama of societies in transformation, the polarity of 1994's most pressing events traveled an emotional roller coaster. But while the world's hope and horror focused on a few lands, Africa's progress and Africa's peril were also visible in more prosaic scenes.

An international pact, even if sadly underfunded, is finally taking aim at the galloping desertification that threatens tens of millions of Africans. Scientists announced a vaccine against malaria that could control one of the continent's worst scourges. Telecommunications links crucial to economic development are gaining ground. And in several more African countries, democratic elections brought closer the stability and accountability in governance that is a baseline requirement for long-term economic progress.

Basic fears, ardent hopes

These positive signs are amply offset by problems that provide fertile ground for the many "Afropessimists." Droughts and wars today put tens of millions Africans in danger of hunger or even famine. Ten thousand children die each day of preventable diseases. Ethnic wars are rending the national fabric of several countries and driving hundreds of thousands of people into uncertain exile. Terms of trade in the international marketplace continue to deteriorate. Unbridled population growth consumes resources far faster than economies are expanding, likely dooming some countries to a poverty trap in perpetuity.

Serious scrutiny of these seemingly intractable dilemmas lies beyond the scope of most media, where graphic images of joy and despair are the mainstay. Yet, ironically, in stark juxtaposition and thousands of miles apart, the most basic fears and most ardent hopes for the continent's future were arrayed for all the world to watch. Rwanda's ethnic holocaust provided the archetypal nightmare and raised anxieties that something similar could recur elsewhere. South Africa's triumphant, if still tenuous, transition to multicultural tolerance offered the counterpoint—politics as the art of compromise winning over the power of the gun, or the sharp edge of a machete.

Deservedly, these stories garnered vast international attention and involvement. Other contrasts were equally evident, even if eliciting little global engagement: Nigeria's descent into deeper dictatorship against Malawi's emergence to multiparty democracy; Liberia's bloody tailspin toward ethnic anarchy and Uganda's steady consolidation of a society too long ravaged by boundless brutality; Ghana's economic revival versus Zaire's continued disintegration.

The interplay of modern and traditional politics, shifting international economic realities and forces of nature plays havoc with prediction or prescription. Even the basic question of systems of government remain contentious. Acceptance of democratic systems and institutionalization of the rule of law in many countries remain weak. But we must still ask: can the gloomy prognostications of the Afropessimists be avoided? The year's perplexing panoply of pain and progress perhaps offers some guideposts and allows a few generalities. The issue of governance must be addressed first as the foundation for resolving Africa's many other problems.

Governance: Escaping the zero-sum game

Too often in Africa, politics has been played as a zero-sum game. State control over large portions of small national economies is a central cause of this conundrum. Government is where the money is, and to leave power is to forfeit access to scarce resources. The lack of a strong private sector economy and a thinly developed modern civil society reinforce state power. Exercised more benevolently as patronage or blatantly through the police, such concentrated and generally unaccountable power is a prime blockage to political and economic development in Africa.

Nelson Mandela's election as president of a nonracial—and "non-ethnic"—South Africa is widely hailed as the model for all Africa to emulate. A massive voter education campaign, independent election and media commissions, and the cooperation of the extant state power, the ruling National Party, combined to promote a free and fair election. Many other countries could draw important lessons in creating the "level playing field" needed for genuine elections, as well as the broad citizen participation by nongovernmental organizations and the voters themselves required to make the vote credible.

An equally central notion is that power-sharing, even among seemingly implacable enemies, is a realistic possibility. South Africa's electoral mechanism allowed minority parties, *de facto* representatives of the country's largest ethnic minorities, the Afrikaners and the Zulus, to take meaningful roles in the new "government of national unity." Whether South Africa's political parties will transcend their ethnic bases before the next national elections in 1999 is unclear. But the present formula of broad inclusion at least allows minority voices to be clearly heard.

The South African model is most compelling in societies sharply divided on non-ideological markers such as race, ethnicity or language. It modifies normal Western parliamentary practice, in which the victorious party typically forms the government and the losers serve as the loyal opposition while awaiting their next turn at the polls. It provides for the empowerment of participation, helping forge political consensus even where respect for the institutions of law is not deeply rooted.

Rwanda's bloody tragedy underlines this point. The genocidal assault on the Tutsi minority was no spontaneous explosion of ethnic fury. Long lists were drawn and mountains of machetes were imported in preparation for the bloodletting that began on 7 April. Among the very first targets were moderate Hutu leaders willing to share power with the minority. The "winner-keep-all-forever" mentality of Hutu extremists made compromise for them unthinkable. In neighboring Burundi, radicals in both ethnic camps threaten conflagration. The installation of a new president, Sylvestre Ntibantungarya, in October, has apparently lessened tensions, though killing goes on.

Governments of national unity help create consensus. But respect for the rule of law encourages acceptance of any elected government. An independent judiciary enforcing constitutional and legal rights reassures citizens that an elected government—

even if dominated by a different group—will not be able to trample their rights or block their opportunities. It convinces people that there is security of physical and economic life for people and groups other than those holding the reins of power. In some African countries, including Benin, Botswana, Guinea-Bissau, Madagascar, Mali, Namibia, Niger, São Tome and Zambia, multiparty politics with genuine elections seems to be taking hold. In Malawi, octogenarian and infirm President Hastings Kamuzu Banda accepted his party's sound defeat in May elections and left office after thirty years. In Mozambique, elections held at the end of October under U.N. auspices seem to have finally ended a long and devastating civil war.

A different "African solution" is being applied in Uganda, where President Yoweri Museveni is pursuing "nonparty democracy." Uganda suffered through two decades of ethnic strife that left hundreds of thousands of people dead. President Museveni, like many observers, blames political parties for stoking ethnic hatred. In March, voters turned out in large numbers to elect delegates to a constitutional convention. Candidates could not use party, ethnic or religious affiliation as the basis for their candidacy. The draft constitution that delegates are now considering provides for five more years of nonparty government, including presidential and legislative elections next year, before a referendum on returning to a multiparty system.

Whether a nonparty system offers genuine democratization is subject to debate both inside and outside Uganda. What is certain is that whatever the shape of any democratic transition, the strength of the rule of law in upholding individual rights and maintaining constitutional order is crucial to its success. And even democratized systems exclude minority voices at their peril. A case in point: both Mali and Niger conducted successful elections, yet each has faced fierce rebellion by desert-dwelling Tuareg rebels who feel marginalized by the system.

Generals and autocrats: Against the tide

If the democratic wave will eventually prove irresistible, some soldiers still seek to rule and some leaders still envision lifelong tenure. A July junior officers' coup in Gambia ended that country's long democratic tradition. Sierra Leone's twenty-something military council seems in no hurry to return to civilian rule. In southern Africa, tiny Swaziland's ruling royal clan is still evading genuine elections. Lesotho's army mutinied but returned to barracks, though it is grumbling in the wings once again. And, most important, in the continent's most populous nation, Nigeria, the generals refuse to go back to barracks, instead locking up the winner of the 1993 presidential election, Moshood Abiola. Suppression of the press and trade unions has helped keep a lid on dissent. Military repression has also struck the Ogoni people, who inhabit Nigeria's richest oil-producing region and are demanding a share of the wealth produced from their land.

Most notable among long-reigning autocrats is Zaire's Marshal Mobutu Sese Seko, who by late 1994 seemed to have escaped the Western world's recent opprobrium by cooperating with relief efforts for Rwandan refugees. Around him, his country continues to disintegrate amidst reports of government instigation of ethnic strife. But after nearly three decades of world-class kleptocracy, his political acuity has not abandoned him, and he remains a master manipulator on both the domestic and international political scene. Other autocrats cling to power elsewhere in Francophone Africa, bolstered by French guns and money and intricate webs of finance and friendship with France's political and economic elite.

Even despotic leaders now seek the mantle of legitimacy a democratic mandate provides. However, polls they organize often offer the trappings rather than the substance of genuine elections—what one electoral consultant classes as "charitably, D+ elections." In February, Gabon's President Omar Bongo unleashed his presidential guard to suppress protests against his proclaimed re-election. The victor in another such contest in 1993, Kenyan President Daniel arap Moi, has again tightened his grip on power by arresting journalists and harassing political opponents. Kenya's promise of democratization has faded, and ethnic violence—here also reportedly abetted by the regime—has wracked several areas of the country.

The wars (mostly) go on

Ethnic strife simmering in many countries has blown into full-scale conflagration in others. Liberia threatens to disappear entirely as a nation-state as various ethnic groups and subgroups revive long-dormant rivalries, now with modern weapons and far more deadly consequences. Somalia is another candidate for "failed-state" category. At the least, it faces the sort of partition that saw Eritrea win full recognition as an independent country last year. The "Republic of Somaliland" has set up a functioning *de facto* state in the northern area of Somalia that was once a British colony, though it, too, is beset by internal rivalries. Across the continent in Angola, nearing its twentieth anniversary at war, severe fighting went on for most of 1994, though at year's end government and rebels were warily testing the strength of yet another peace pact. Ethnic conflicts of greater or lesser intensity also flared during the year in Burundi, Djibouti, Ethiopia, Ghana, Kenya, Mali, Niger, Rwanda, Sierra Leone, South Africa (before April's election), Sudan and Zaire.

Sudan continues to present calamity on a huge scale. It has been embroiled in bloody civil war for twenty-eight of the thirty-eight years since independence in 1956. Its borders, like many other African countries, are mostly an expression of imperial mapmakers' convenience or conceit. The colonial mélange of an Arab north and a black, non-Muslim south, stitched together under a *pax Brittania*, has never stood on its own. The highly repressive Muslim fundamentalist regime in Khartoum that seized power in a 1989 coup is propped up by Iranian support and Chinese arms. This year, it recorded a string of costly battlefield victories over the southern rebels, whose ranks have been hit by famine and internecine strife. The civil war has driven millions of people from their homes. The exact number of people lost to battle, butchery and famine will never be known, but the dead already run into the hundreds of thousands, and millions of people remain at risk.

Sudan's war is in a land far from television cameras, front pages and any great power's national interest. There is no chance of outside intervention to halt the carnage, and little likelihood that even a serious international effort could achieve a negotiated peace.

Africa and the world: *plus ça change...*

But Sudan was not entirely forgotten. Reports in the Paris press described French intelligence cooperation with the Khartoum regime—amidst speculation that it was not merely coincidental with Sudan's decision to extradite Ilyich "Carlos the Jackal" Ramirez Sanchez to face trial for terrorist crimes in France. France's role in Africa today is arguably the most important of any outside power. Its aid budget of over $3 billion is nearly four times official U.S. assistance. French troops are garrisoned in Cameroon, Central African Republic, Djibouti, Gabon, Ivory Coast and Senegal, and have intervened many times to prop up the failing fortunes of strongmen closely linked to France. An exception was the 1979 expeditionary force that deposed self-proclaimed Emperor Jean-Bedel Bokassa, of the then-Central African Empire—his delusional megalomania became too much even for France to countenance when he began murdering schoolchildren detained for protesting his dictatorship.

Just slightly less egregious behavior is tolerated. France's relations with other autocrats across Francophone Africa remain intimate. Mobutu in Zaire, Cameroon's Paul Biya, Gabon's Omar Bongo and Gnassingbe Eyadéma of Togo all have close personal ties with France's political and business elite, as did the late leaders of Ivory Coast and Rwanda, Félix Houphouët-Boigny and Juvénal Habyarimana. These African dictators, who became among the world's richest men while leading the earth's poorest peoples, have reportedly contributed heavily to French political parties. And close family members of top French politicians have garnered extremely lucrative contracts doing business in these countries.

A brief breeze of change appeared to alter France's course in Africa in 1990, when President François Mitterrand urged Francophone African leaders to accept democratization. Policy since has clearly reverted to the belief that much of Africa is France's *chasse gardeé*, its private preserve. While visiting Togolese dictator General Eyadéma in September to announce resumption of aid—suspended in 1993 after a fraudulent presidential election and massacres of government opponents—French Cooperation Minister Michel Roussin proudly proclaimed that France "never abandons its friends in need."

France's "Operation Turquoise" in Rwanda was launched too late to save another "friend in need." French forces could not preserve even a toehold in Rwanda for the shattered government army, which had been largely armed and trained by France. Yet there are signs of change. Some of the new generation of democratic leaders in Francophone Africa are quietly seeking American and other Western investment in hopes of reducing French influence. The devaluation of the African franc, long backed by France at an unrealistic exchange rate, could also loosen traditional bonds. But among old-line politicians—in France and in Africa—the power and the money are too attractive to let even the possibility of democracy interfere. French paratroopers and legionnaires still stand ready to protect this French connection.

Today, over 250 million Africans—more than a third of the continent's population—live in absolute poverty. Thirty-four million are right now threatened by hunger, according to the U.N.'s Food and Agricultural Organization. At least 10 million people are infected with AIDS. Average life expectancy is only fifty-one years. The percentage of children attending school drops every year. Half the world's refugees are in Africa, and hundreds of millions of dollars badly needed for development projects is diverted to emergency care.

The problems are more daunting in the face of diminishing international aid levels in a post-Cold War world in which Africa is increasingly politically and economically marginalized. The Eastern bloc, once a source of finance and technical assistance to many African states, now absorbs much of Western Europe's and America's aid and investment.

Further, Africa's terms of trade—the relative value of its mainly commodity exports versus the manufactures it imports—sank by 5.5 percent in 1993. The General Agreement on Tariffs and Trade (GATT), hailed as a boon to the world economy, will at least in the short run hurt Africa as its agricultural trade preferences in Europe diminish. Structural Adjustment Plans imposed by the International Monetary Fund (IMF) have had some success in reviving several moribund economies. This stern economic medicine certainly carries a price, though, in reduced government spending that cuts sharply into health, education and social welfare programs. And the race against explosive population growth makes even catching up with world standards a long haul. In Ghana, the IMF's showcase for African economic success, it could be as long as fifty years before the average Ghanaian clears the international poverty line.

This litany of obstacles does not exclude hope. But the obstacles certainly will never be overcome so long as countries squander scarce resources on arms and repression. Political stability is a base requirement for economic progress in Africa. Elections in several countries in 1994 could be important stepping stones in this direction. Western governments should press for, and provide increased aid to help, democratic transitions; develop the rule of law; and strengthen the free media and other institutions of civil society. Absent transparency and accountability in governance, conflict and corruption will continue to be rife. Consensus on hard decisions will be unlikely. And the enormity of Africa's problems means that *harambee*—pulling together—is now more necessary than ever.

Thomas R. Lansner writes frequently on Africa.

The Middle East: A Dynamic of Peace—and Terror

David A. Korn

That famous September 1993 White House lawn handshake between Yitzhak Rabin and Yasir Arafat brought something altogether novel to the Arab-Israeli conflict in 1994: a dynamic of peace. But also something depressingly familiar: a counterdynamic of terror.

For the first time, the parties to the conflict found themselves pushed in the direction of compromise rather than confrontation. It didn't happen that way in 1979. Arab states denounced the Egyptian-Israeli peace treaty and many broke off relations with Egypt. The 13 September 1993 agreement between Israel and the Palestine Liberation Organization (PLO) had the opposite effect. It engendered a dynamic that impelled Israel and Jordan, and to a lesser extent even Syria, forward along the path of peace.

Jordan and Israel

For decades Israelis talked and dreamed of a settlement with their neighbors to the east. Israeli and Jordanian leaders had met secretly innumerable times; still, the two countries remained formally at war. King Hussein seemed destined to go down in history as the Hamlet of Middle Eastern politics, a man who would forever be unable to make up his mind to run the risk of peace with Israel. Hussein had his reasons. Over half the population of his kingdom was Palestinian. In 1970 he only barely survived a Palestinian uprising. He feared another if he should move prematurely for peace with Israel. He feared the reaction of Syria and Iraq, and of Saudi Arabia and the Persian Gulf emirates. And he remained haunted by the memory of the day in July 1951 when, as a boy, he looked on as his grandfather, King Abdullah, was slain by Palestinian gunmen who opposed Abdullah's peace talks with Israel.

One by one the grounds for Hussein's hesitations were swept away. The first to go was Hussein's own claim to sovereignty over the West Bank, which he formally renounced in 1988. Then came the fall of the Soviet empire, which deprived both Syria and the PLO of a powerful external patron; then the Gulf War that isolated and weakened Iraq; and then the September 1993 Israeli-PLO agreement. If the PLO, the universally (in the Arab world) recognized representative of the Palestinian people, could come to terms with Israel, why should Jordan be barred from doing so?

Hussein was helped to his decision to make peace with Israel by the success of the experiment in graduated democracy that he launched in Jordan in 1989. Despite an initial surge of Islamic fundamentalist voting, free elections that year and in 1993 showed a solid base of support for the king's moderate policies and gave him and his ministers confidence in the domestic strength of their government. And the cancer with which Hussein was diagnosed in 1992 put him on notice that he had finite time left in which to secure his place in history as peacemaker.

On 14 September 1993, just twenty-four hours after Yasir Arafat and Yitzak Rabin exchanged their historic handshake, Israel and Jordan signed a "Declaration of Principles" that set out guidelines for peace between the two countries. Israeli Foreign Minister Shimon Peres went to Amman at the beginning of November and in nine hours of talks with Hussein and his ministers hammered out the draft of an agreement that would commit Jordan to a formal peace and Israel to accepting Jordan's water and land rights in the Jordan and Arava valleys.

Momentum stalls

But then momentum stalled, in part owing to prematurely enthusiastic public statements by Peres; but mainly because negotiations for the implementation of the Israeli-PLO agreement had fallen behind schedule. Hussein didn't want to be left out on a limb. Before taking the next step he required assurance that Israel was actually going to give the Palestinians the self-rule it had promised them in the September 1993 document.

Then, on 25 February, a Jewish settler in Hebron slipped into a Muslim prayer service at the Cave of the Patriarchs and opened fire with an automatic weapon, killing at least twenty-nine and wounding some one hundred others. Arafat suspended all negotiations with Israel. Hussein let Rabin and Peres know he couldn't proceed until talks with the PLO got back on track and showed progress. Arafat demanded that the U.N. deploy an international security force in the West Bank and Gaza and that Israel dismantle settlements in Hebron and certain other locations and disarm all settlers. Rabin refused but offered to allow international civilian observers. Israel began releasing Palestinian prisoners—596 left Israeli jails on 1 March and another 400 on 3 March—and outlawed Kach and Kahane Chai and arrested violent right-wing extremists. The United States dangled before Arafat the incentive of Western economic aid. By the end of March, Israel and the PLO were back at the negotiating table. On 4 May 1994 they reached agreement on handing over Gaza and Jericho to Palestinian administration.

Full speed toward a peace treaty

From that point on, Israeli-Jordanian negotiations moved ahead at full speed. On 19 May, the day after Israel completed its redeployment in Gaza, Hussein met secretly with Rabin in London and let him know that he was ready to go for a peace treaty. On 25 July the king of Jordan and the prime minister of Israel, in their first public appearance together, shook hands at a ceremony on the White House lawn and announced an end to the state of belligerence between Israel and Jordan. The following day Hussein and Rabin went before a joint session of Congress; and the Clinton administration, making good on a carrot it had dangled before Hussein, forgave $220 million of Jordan's nearly one-billion-dollar debt to the U.S. Three months more and the deal was done. On 26 October the Treaty of Peace between Israel and Jordan was signed in a gala ceremony at the border just north of Elat and Aqaba with President Clinton in attendance.

A dynamic of competition and reward

A dynamic of competition and reward pushed this process at every stage. Jordanians feared that the Israeli-PLO agreement would put their economic and political interests in jeopardy. They sought and won assurance against this in their November 1993 accords with Israel. The knowledge that Jordan required progress in Israeli-Palestinian negotiations spurred Israel to the 4 May 1994 agreement under which it handed Gaza and Jericho over to Palestinian administration. That agreement, in turn, made it possible for Jordan to proceed with the steps that led to the conclusion of the peace treaty with Israel.

For Israel the 26 October treaty meant more than just wrapping up a second peace with an Arab neighbor. It meant that Israelis should not have to worry about trouble from across their eastern border as they proceeded to enter the difficult next stages of negotiations with the Palestinians, when they would have to come to grips with the gradual transfer of authority over the West Bank. For Jordanians it offered ground floor entry to the economic benefits of peace, Israel's support for Jordan's claim to administration of the Muslim holy places in Jerusalem and, most important of all, assurance against the prospect of the Hashemite Kingdom's being made over into the eastern half of a Palestinian homeland.

And as Israeli-PLO negotiations moved forward, slowly, painfully, but inexorably, Israel's ties with other Arabs multiplied. Morocco and Tunisia agreed to the opening of Israeli trade offices; Qatar and Oman received Israeli trade delegations; Israel's environment minister, Yossi Sarid, paid an official visit to Bahrein; and an Arab-Israeli economic summit convened in Casablanca. Arab-Israeli negotiations assumed the aspect of a giant chessboard with multiple contestants, each of whom had constantly to gauge the effect of his moves, or non-moves, on the positions of all the other players. And the players were not just Israel, the PLO and Jordan. There was Syria as well.

And then came Syria

The prospect that President Hafez al-Assad might be ready to move toward peace with Israel, first whispered about in the late 1980s, generated something akin to euphoria at the State Department and among America's other Middle East watchers. The vision of a settlement with Israel's fiercest and most threatening Arab enemy transfixed Israeli diplomacy, too. Getting Syria's signature on a peace treaty, after having already gotten Egypt's, would effectively mean the end of the Arab-Israeli conflict. The Bush administration launched a full court press to bring Syria into the Middle East peace negotiations. The Clinton administration picked up where its predecessor left off. President Clinton met with Assad in Geneva in January 1994 and declared himself persuaded that the Syrian was ready to normalize relations with Israel. Secretary of State Warren Christopher visited Damascus five times between May and October. Christopher's labors narrowed the gap between Israel and Syria, but at year's end, and despite a visit by President Clinton to Damascus on 27 October, the gap had not been closed.

For despite official optimism, the signals from Syria were mixed. Assad had stopped talking about war with Israel and had started talking publicly about peace. The Syrian media toned down (but did not stop) their attacks on Israel. The Syrian ministers of Foreign Affairs and Economy and Foreign Trade gave on-the-record interviews to Israeli journals, and handshakes were exchanged between Syrian and Israeli officials abroad. But while professing a wish for peace with Israel, at the 1993 United Nations General Assembly, Syria voted against a resolution expressing hope for rapid progress in Arab-Israeli peace negotiations. At his January 1994 press conference with Clinton in Geneva, Assad announced his desire for peace with Israel but wouldn't let Israeli journalists be there to hear him say it. In May 1994 Syria launched an effort to keep the economic boycott of Israel in place, just as other Arab countries were beginning to talk about lifting it; and in October Syria turned down an invitation to the Casablanca Arab-Israeli economic summit which most other Arab states attended.

More ominously, while talking about peace Syria has energetically pursued its military buildup. Assad's government is reported to have spent $1.4 billion on military modernization since the Gulf war. A new armored division has been deployed and a Scud-C missile brigade is in formation. Syrian missiles are now capable of reaching almost every city in Israel, and Damascus has thousands of chemical bombs and warheads and is said to be developing a biological weapons capability.

So does Assad want peace or is he just playing games? He insists on full Israeli withdrawal from the Golan Heights and southern Lebanon. For Israel, pulling out of Golan while still testing an agreement that commits it to give the West Bank over to Palestinian authority comes dangerously close to political and security overload. For Assad, peace has its risks as well. It could spark violent opposition within Syria. And over the longer term it means shrinking the role of the military, the mainstay of Assad's regime. So far, Assad appears to consider peace worth the risk only if he can get the full price he is demanding.

The counterdynamic of terror

In the history of the brutal rejectionist onslaught that followed the Israeli-PLO accord, two names will stand out: Baruch Goldstein and Saleh Abdul Rahman al-Souwi. Goldstein was the Jewish settler who on 25 February gunned down Muslims at prayer in the Cave of the Patriarchs. Al-Souwi was the twenty-seven-year-old Palestinian human bomb who on 19 October blew to pieces a bus in rush hour traffic in the heart of downtown Tel Aviv, killing himself and twenty-two others and maiming or wounding some fifty. They were, without knowing one another, both the bitterest of enemies and the closest of collaborators in the common enterprise of killing peace between their two peoples.

But it would be a mistake to judge them or what they stand for equally. Goldstein's was an individual act, endorsed in its aftermath by some right wing Jewish extremists but not planned or sponsored by any organized group. Al-Souwi, though no doubt a volunteer, was the instrument of a well organized and heavily funded terrorist conspiracy, recruited, trained, equipped and sent to his sacrifice by the Islamic fundamentalist group Hamas. Goldstein snuck out of his home telling no one of his plan. Al-Souwi spent his last hours before a videocamera boasting of his intention to kill, calling himself a "living martyr," proclaiming that "it is good to die...for Allah" and—anticipating the reward of his gruesome deed—that "sages end up in paradise."[1]

Today the main terror organizations operating against peace between Israel and the Arabs are Hamas, Islamic Jihad and Hizbollah. All proclaim themselves Islamic fundamentalist. Hamas, an Arabic acronym for Islamic Resistance Movement, seized center stage in 1994 with a series of spectacular actions: an Israeli bus blown up in Afula in April, killing eight and wounding some twenty; a busy street in Jerusalem sprayed with gunfire early in October; the kidnapping, attempted ransom and killing days later of an Israeli soldier, Corporal Nahshon Waxman; and then the blowing up of the Tel Aviv bus. In the thirteen months following the September 1993 ceremony on the White House lawn, ninety-five Israelis died in terror attacks and well over 300 were wounded, double the figure for the previous period.

And the onslaught continues. Can peace survive it?

The conventional wisdom among Washington's corps of Middle East experts is that, despite the Islamic terrorism offensive, full Arab-Israeli peace is now more or less a sure thing. The Middle East has entered a new era, one hears; matters have gone too far for Israel and the Arabs to pull back. Now that he has lost his Soviet patron, even Assad, according to this view, has no place else to go, no choice now but to put aside his hesitations and sign with Israel.

There is a problem with this analysis. It is that the Arab-Israeli peace that has been achieved so far is the work of the leaders. None was pushed to it by his public; all had to drag along constituencies that ranged from hesitant and fearful to outright opposed. Arabs and Israelis continue to harbor deep animosities toward one another. And the leaders who are showing the way toward peace are no longer young men. Rabin and Peres are well into their seventies, and Rabin, in particular, shows it. They have only a little more than a year in which to lay rock solid, irreversible bases for peace between Israelis and Palestinians before Israel's next elections which will very likely pit Rabin against a much younger Likud candidate. Arafat will be sixty-six this year. He is surrounded by many able younger advisors but he has no strong deputy, and time has taken its toll on him as it has on the PLO. In Gaza and on the West Bank, Hamas has made dangerous inroads into the PLO's power base. It aims first to destroy the PLO's agreement with Israel and then to destroy Arafat and the PLO, and its chances of doing so appear to be improving all the time.

Assad too is in his sixties (he looks considerably older) and not in good health— conditions not ordinarily conducive to the taking of bold new steps.

The challenge for the year ahead will be to make the 13 September 1993 Israeli-Palestinian agreement work. That agreement was the cornerstone of everything else that has been achieved, the Israeli-Jordanian peace treaty and the Arab states' opening to Israel. Unlikely as this may now seem, if it were to collapse, it could bring the rest of the edifice tumbling down with it. Making the agreement work will not be easy. Turning Gaza and Jericho over to the PLO was a relatively easy first step. All the really hard part lies ahead. Negotiations for the empowerment of a Palestinian Authority on the West Bank, for the creation of a Palestinian council (or an assembly?) and for the holding of elections and the withdrawal of Israeli forces are yet to be concluded; and the explosive issues of water rights, Jerusalem, the disposition of Israeli settlements and the boundaries of an ultimately independent Palestinian state have not yet even begun to be dealt with.

One must pray that Washington's conventional wisdom turns out to be right. Nothing, however, can be taken for granted. An extraordinary dynamic has propelled the Middle East much further down the road to peace this past year-and-a-half than anyone would have thought, but there is no inevitability that it will last.

Political Islamic fundamentalism

Political Islamic fundamentalism emerged in 1994 as the main threat to peace between Israel and the Palestinians after having positioned itself at the beginning of the decade as the main challenger to Arab governments. Just what does it portend?

The attempt to answer that question has spawned scores of symposia in the U.S. and Europe, thousands of hours of talk and hundreds of articles and books. As a general rule, the more learned the analysis the less connected it has been to reality. Scholars have concluded that "no inherent and necessary conflict exists between democracy and Islam,"[2] but if by this it is meant that political Islamic fundamentalism is compatible with democracy, the proposition has yet to be demonstrated other than in theory. In Iran fifteen years of theocratic rule have produced a sad record of oppression, gross violations of basic human rights, persecution of minorities, corruption, economic stagnation and growing public discontent. Tehran has become the world's foremost sponsor of international terrorism, linked to bombings of Jewish institutions in Argentina and Britain, and to killings of Iranian opposition figures throughout Europe. Six years of semi-Islamic rule in Sudan behind the skirts of a military regime have brought more repression, more torture and killing, more poverty and ever more ferocious civil war to that country and a reputation for sponsorship of terrorism second only to Iran's.

Few who have seriously considered the question believe that democracy and human rights, as we know them in the twentieth century, could survive in a polity ruled by the absolutist precepts of religious dogma (be it Islam, Christianity or Judaism), which in effect is what political Islam is all about. More important still, the learned apologists for political Islam have yet to explain away the most damning evidence against it: that so many of those that claim its name preach xenophobia and religious hatred and employ murder as a paramount weapon for attaining their ends.

Political Islamic fundamentalism is nonetheless a force everywhere in the Middle East today. No state escapes its impact, but Algeria and Egypt have become its major battlegrounds. In Algeria this past year, between forty and sixty persons have been killed every day in the struggle between Islamic fundamentalists and the country's secular, military-dominated government. Islamic fundamentalist groups have killed journalists, teachers, secular intellectuals, women and girls who refused to wear traditional dress, civil servants, military and police officers and senior political figures. The army and security services have tortured and killed Islamic activists, members of their families and persons suspected of association with them. The government has sent tens of thousands of suspected Islamic militants off to desert detention camps. The struggle between the two sides dates to January 1992 when, facing the prospect of a landslide electoral win by the Islamic Salvation Front (FIS in its French initials), the Algerian army seized power and arrested FIS leaders. Two even more extreme fundamentalist organizations soon arose, the Armed Islamic Group and the Armed Islamic Movement. This past year they have taken to killing FIS members they consider too moderate or ready to compromise with the government. In September 1993 these groups ordered foreigners to leave Algeria, threatened to kill any who remained and then quickly began making good on their threat. They have murdered French businessmen and diplomats, Eastern European technicians in the oil and gas industry and Italian sailors on a ship docked in port to unload a cargo of grain, to name a few. By the end of October 1994, Islamic fundamentalist killers had murdered sixty-eight foreign nationals in Algeria. The last to be added to the list at that date were two elderly Spanish nuns who had lived in the country for twenty years doing charitable work.

General Lamine Zeroual, the new president installed by the Algerian army in January 1994, has sought to negotiate with the FIS, but FIS leaders, outflanked by the two extreme terrorist groups, have been unable to stop the violence. Some confidently predict an Islamic takeover of Algeria. For the moment Algeria's military government appears to be holding on. Should it eventually reach the end of its rope, an Islamic takeover is perhaps less likely than a descent into chaos, on the model of Yugoslavia, Liberia, Somalia or Afghanistan, with warring Islamic fundamentalist and secular factions and the large Berber population (Muslim but for the most part not Islamic fundamentalist) staking out competing territorial claims.

Egypt is the other major site of confrontation between political Islamic fundamentalism and an established government. Egypt's Armed Islamic Group fundamentalists have used many of the same tactics as Algeria's. They have targeted government officials, security forces, journalists, educators, Coptic Christians, secular Muslim intellectuals and even Egypt's sole Nobel laureate, Naguib Mahfouz, who was severely wounded in a knife attack by fundamentalist terrorists in October. They have also targeted foreign nationals, with the aim of closing off one of the country's principal sources of foreign currency earnings, the tourism trade. The attacks on tourists have emptied hotels and cut tourism revenues drastically.

The fundamentalist assault, however, has been less successful in Egypt than in Algeria. Through energetic police and military action over the past year President Husni Mubarak's government has largely succeeded in suppressing the most serious manifestations of fundamentalist terrorism. Security has for the most part been restored in Cairo, albeit at substantial cost in violations of law and human rights. Nonetheless, political Islamic fundamentalism continues to draw wide support in Egypt. Several quarters of Cairo and much of what is called upper Egypt (the Nile valley south of Cairo) are fundamentalist bastions. In and around the city of Assiut the government finds itself for all practical purposes in the role of occupying power, barricaded behind sandbagged administrative buildings and police and army outposts in the midst of a hostile population. It appears incapable of undertaking political and economic reforms that would offer the Egyptian public the prospect of a better life and democratic government.

Still, it is generally thought that Islamic fundamentalism has little chance of taking over the Egyptian state. Over the short term, this view may be right; Egypt's pro-Western government, backed by a powerful military that enjoys a substantial subsidy from the U.S., should be able to hold on. But one wonders just how long the system can bear up without cracking. Over the past thirty years Egypt's population has doubled, from 30 million in 1967 to 60 million today; and in almost every one of those years population growth exceeded economic growth. The theological state that Islamic fundamentalists propose offers no solution to the country's ills, but that cannot be counted on to prevent poverty, overcrowding and despair from pushing Egyptians into their arms. The Egyptian state might be classified as accident prone. With luck, it may avoid upheaval for many more years. But a jolt—a severe natural catastrophe, a failure of food supplies or of foreign aid—could bring it crashing down at any time.

Elsewhere, a sad scorecard

Progress toward Arab-Israeli peace aside, the Middle East didn't present a pretty picture for democracy and human rights during 1994. As in the previous year, the best performances were turned in by the two liberal Arab monarchies, Jordan and Morocco, where limited parliamentary democracy offered popular representation and a degree of protection from state abuse; and in the Kurdish region of Iraq. The

Kurdish experiment in democracy, launched when elections were held in May 1992, was set back this past year by an outbreak of fighting between the two main parties, the Kurdish Democratic Party and the Patriotic Union of Kurdistan. In addition, the Kurdish region continues to suffer severe economic hardship owing to the wholly paradoxical application to it of U.N. economic sanctions against Saddam Hussein's government—as though the Kurds were the accomplices, not the victims, of the Iraqi dictator's outrages! Its citizens nonetheless enjoy far greater measures of freedom and protection from governmental abuse than do any of their neighbors.

In the field of worst abusers there are two that deserve special mention this year: Iraq and Turkey.

Iraq

Saddam Hussein's Iraq comes in for scrutiny this time not on the usual grounds of torture, extrajudicial arrest, killing, denial of all basic human freedoms and repression of its Kurdish and Shiite populations. All those things it continues to do, but now there is a new charge: the deliberate starvation and physical, moral and social degradation of the Iraqi people. Reports from Iraq tell of children suffering malnutrition and dying of the diseases it unleashes, of a population that is assured only of rations that amount to one-third of internationally recognized requirements, of the impoverishment of the professional middle class, of the breakdown of medical and social services and a plague of crime and prostitution. Of Iraq's population of 18 to 20 million, only the favored million or so who form the core of Saddam Hussein's regime escape these conditions.

Saddam Hussein's spokesmen blame the U.N. economic sanctions, which bar Iraq from selling oil on the international market, for the Iraqi public's suffering. They and others accuse the U.N., and the United States, of trying to starve the people of Iraq into revolting against their government. What they conveniently neglect to mention is that the U.N. has offered the Iraqi government the means for alleviating its citizens' suffering even while it fails to satisfy requirements for lifting of the sanctions. In 1992 the U.N. proposed to allow Iraq to sell $1.6 billion worth of oil provided that the proceeds be used exclusively for the purchase and delivery of food, medicine and other humanitarian supplies under U.N. monitoring. That proposal still stands. The Iraqi government rejected it at the time and continues to reject it, alleging infringement on its sovereignty. The truth of the matter is that Saddam Hussein callously subjects the Iraqi people to semi-starvation in the hope of getting the international community to excuse Iraq from the sanctions, which would allow him to resume unrestricted oil sales that could then be used to finance a new military buildup.

In October Saddam Hussein sent his army back to the Kuwaiti border in a move that he hoped would force removal of the sanctions. It proved a monumental miscalculation. The U.S. promptly despatched forces to Kuwait and Saudi Arabia and the Iraqi army retreated. The sanctions remain on (although Russia and to a lesser degree France are again pressing for their removal) and Saddam Hussein's regime continues to subject the Iraqi people to a slow starvation that may undermine its physical and intellectual health for generations to come.

Turkey

Turkey is struggling with a problem that it only barely admits it has: its Kurdish minority. Prime Minister Tansu Ciller has gutted the late President Turgut Ozal's policy of conciliation and gone foursquare for repression. In March of this past year, Mrs. Ciller's center right government lifted the immunity of six members of parliament from the country's only Kurdish political party, the Democracy Party, arrested them and proceeded to prosecute them on charges of undermining the unity of the Turkish Republic. In May the Turkish Constitutional Court, acting at the behest of the government, banned the Democracy Party. Earlier, right-wing death squads connected to the government's security services had murdered two Democracy Party parliamentarians.

Mrs. Ciller acted after the Turkish army's chief of staff publicly accused the Kurdish parliamentarians of complicity with Kurdish insurgents operating in Turkey's southeast under the banner of the PKK, or Kurdistan Workers Party. The PKK insurgency has been going on since 1984. Every year the army has promised to wipe it out; and every year, or almost, it has grown in scope and intensity. The chief of staff's remarks reflected his and the army's frustration over their failure. The politicians' prompt response reflected their fear that if they didn't act the army might act for them.

Martial law is in effect and legal and human rights protections are suspended in ten provinces of predominantly Kurdish southeastern Turkey. Over 13,000 people are said to have been killed in the struggle between government security forces and the PKK, more than half of them during the past year. Kurdish political activists, journalists, intellectuals and ordinary citizens suspected of sympathizing with the PKK have been arrested, tortured and murdered; and the PKK has murdered government officials and Kurds it has labelled as collaborators. The Turkish army has embraced the tactic—reminiscent of Vietnam and the French colonial war in Algeria—of forcible displacement of populations in order to deprive the PKK of its base of popular support. Altogether, some 2 million Turkish Kurds have been expelled from their homes and driven off their land, left to fend for themselves with practically no help from the Turkish government. The population of the major Turkish cities has surged as destitute displaced Kurds sought refuge there.

The Turkish state's refusal to come to terms with the reality of its Kurdish minority is costing it dearly. In 1994, Turkey spent an estimated $8.2 billion—one fifth of the entire budget of the state—on the war against the Kurdish insurgency while inflation ran at over 100 percent, banks failed and companies went bankrupt at record rates, and unemployment rose past the 20 percent mark. Repression is increasingly pushing Turkish Kurds into the ranks of the PKK and of political Islamic fundamentalism, both inimical to democracy.

How to deal with its Kurdish population is the biggest challenge facing Turkey today. So long as its leaders, and a large part of the ethnically Turkish public, persist in clinging to policies of denial and repression, Turkey will have scant prospect of achieving stability, prosperity and genuine democracy.

Notes

1 - As quoted in the *New York Times,* 21 October 1994.

2 - United States Institute of Peace, *In Search of Political Islam,* August 1994.

David A. Korn is a writer and former diplomat. He is the author of Stalemate: The War of Attrition and Great Power Diplomacy in the Middle East, 1967-1970 *(Westview Press, 1992) and, most recently,* Assassination in Khartoum *(University of Indiana Press, 1993).*

Asia: Democracy or Development...or Both? Charles Graybow

In most years the annual meeting of the Association of Southeast Asian Nations (ASEAN), a trade and regional security bloc, draws little outside interest. The July 1994 ASEAN meeting in Bangkok was different. The six-member organization invited the outlaw Burmese military junta as an observer, thereby undermining the efforts of Burmese dissidents, Western governments and human rights advocates in its own member countries to diplomatically isolate the regime. Burma is one of Southeast Asia's richest countries in terms of natural resources, and its neighbors want preferential access to a potential bonanza.

The Burmese government's transformation from pariah to player symbolized a disturbing trend. In the 1990s authoritarian governments in East Asia are increasingly using their economic leverage to override human rights concerns. South Asian governments may not be far behind: India is skillfully capitalizing on its size and economic potential to brush aside criticism of its rights record in Kashmir, Assam and other areas.

Asian governments have found a powerful ally: Western businesses eager to expand their market share in some of the fastest growing economies in the world. In June United States President Bill Clinton "de-linked" China's Most Favored Nation trade status from human rights considerations after conceding that the policy had largely failed to produce any improvements in Beijing's record. In August China delivered the goods. U.S. Commerce Secretary Ronald Brown visited Beijing and Shanghai accompanied by twenty-four American corporate leaders. The delegation signed agreements potentially worth up to $6 billion for American corporations.

Trade concerns have also sidetracked efforts at promoting labor rights. The U.S. government has reviewed labor rights violations in several Asian countries including Indonesia, Malaysia, Maldives, Pakistan and Thailand but has deferred ruling on whether to lift tariff privileges under the General System of Preferences (GSP). Many developing countries have responded by going on the offensive, accusing the U.S. of trying to protect its workers from low-wage foreign competition.

In East Asia there are now eight countries—Brunei, Burma, China, Indonesia, Laos, Malaysia, Singapore and Vietnam, with a combined population of 1.5 billion people—that have market-oriented economies but no discernible trend toward democratization. Authoritarian leaders say heavy-handed restrictions on political rights and civil liberties are necessary to promote stability and growth in developing countries. But are democracy and development really incompatible, or is this just a false trade-off cooked up by elites trying to maintain their hold on power?

The Asian way?

Pundits trying to explain the success of the East Asian "miracle" economies have coined the term "The Asian Way" to describe the supposedly consensus-oriented politics, and emphasis on society over the individual, characterizing these countries. The intellectual giant of the Asian Way is Lee Kuan Yew, the former prime minister of Singapore. When Singapore achieved independence from Britain under Lee in 1959, it was little more than a squalid backwater. By the time Lee stepped down in 1990 the city-state had become one of the four renowned "Little Dragons," along with Taiwan, South Korea and Hong Kong.

In an interview in the March-April 1994 *Foreign Affairs*, the seventy-year-old Lee noted that East Asia's Confucian-based cultural values, stressing family and society, sharply differ from the Western emphasis on individual liberties. Lee believes that these East Asian cultural norms are responsible for the region's economic success, while in the West "The expansion of the right of the individual to behave or misbehave as he pleases has come at the expense of orderly society."

But while most authoritarian leaders in Asia are committed to economic development, their use of the state's security apparatus against political dissidents and tight control over the media are geared primarily toward maintaining power. There are of course levels of repression. Hardline authoritarian regimes such as China and Vietnam ban all political opposition. In so-called "soft authoritarian" countries such as Singapore and Malaysia opposition groups are allowed to participate in the political process but face significant barriers to coming to power. Indonesia allows two parties besides the ruling Golkar party, but they are wary of even referring to themselves as the opposition. In fact, since President Suharto came to power in the late 1960s, the Indonesian parliament has never initiated or blocked a single piece of legislation.

Most Asian authoritarian governments rely on harsh, broadly drawn internal security laws (some dating from periods of colonial rule) to threaten and detain political dissidents. While China, Vietnam and Indonesia still rely on torture to silence their critics, drawing censure from the West, Singapore has found more subtle measures. The government has brought at least one opposition politician, J.B. Jeyaretnam, to near financial ruin through a series of court actions, and has harassed critics through the threat of libel suits, dismissal from public sector jobs and revocation of academic tenure.

Another commonality is the use of highly restrictive speech and press laws to limit or stifle open political debate. Citizens of China, Vietnam and Laos cannot criticize their respective communist parties' monopoly on power. But in other countries, the level of official tolerance is not much greater, as evidenced by several incidents around the region in 1994. In October and November the authorities in Singapore filed criminal and civil charges against American academic Christopher Lingle for an article in the 7 October *International Herald Tribune* in which he referred to "intolerant regimes" in the region and criticized their lack of independent judiciaries. Lingle managed to leave the country, but several staff members at the *Tribune* still face charges.

Indonesia's brief experiment with modest press liberalization came to a halt in June when the government banned three outspoken newsweeklies. One of the magazines had written an article on the government's controversial purchase, without the military's approval, of thirty-nine ships of the former East German navy, breaking a taboo on reporting on the regime's internal political schisms.

Malaysia's Prime Minister Mahathir Mohamad showed his contempt for a free press in February when he banned British companies from receiving government contracts after an article in London's *Sunday Times* suggested a British firm may have offered the premier a bribe. The ban was not lifted until September. In March the Malaysian authorities announced that foreign journalists who wrote reports critical of the government would be thrown out of the country. In April it expelled Filipina correspondent Leah Makabenta on national security grounds over an article on the treatment of migrant laborers.

Hong Kong's journalists increasingly have been practicing self-censorship as the colony's reversion to Chinese authority in June 1997 approaches. To hammer home the message, in April a Beijing court sentenced Xi Yang, a mainland-based correspondent of the Hong Kong newspaper *Ming Pao*, to twelve years in prison for leaking alleged "state secrets," in reality information on central bank monetary policy.

China further shook up the colony's media when it shut down the Beijing outlet of Hong Kong businessman Jimmy Lai's popular clothing chain, Giordano, allegedly for licensing problems. Lai had called Chinese premier Li Peng a "turtle's egg," an extremely offensive Chinese idiom, in an editorial in the magazine he publishes, *Next*. As prominent pro-democracy politician Martin Lee told the *Far Eastern Economic Review*, Beijing was "warning other publishers and businessmen that it can and will sabotage the business stability of those who are critical of Chinese leaders or policy."

In November Cambodia's freely elected government showed its authoritarian stripes in announcing it would submit a draft press law to the National Assembly that would throw journalists in jail for one to three years for articles considered defamatory against the government and monarchy. During the year, two newspaper editors died in mysterious circumstances in the capital, Phnom Penh; numerous papers received official warnings over their political coverage; and the authorities detained *Morning News* editor Nguon Nonn for suggesting certain officials were involved in a July coup attempt.

Authoritarian democrats in South Asia

At first glance, authoritarian government would not appear to be the main problem in South Asia, where five of the seven countries in the region have parliamentary democracies. When Pakistan held its freest elections ever in October 1993, it joined Bangladesh, India, Nepal and Sri Lanka as South Asian countries holding competitive elections.

Yet the rule of law is weak in all of these countries, allowing the police and security forces to violate human rights with impunity under the cover of broadly drawn internal security laws. Perhaps the most infamous is India's Terrorist and Disruptive Activities Prevention Act (TADA), which the government introduced in 1985 to combat terrorism in Punjab but subsequently applied to Kashmir, Assam and other states. TADA allows the authorities to detain suspects for speech and other nonviolent acts, permits courts to use confessions obtained through torture, and allows security forces to destroy structures allegedly used to shield terrorists, a provision the army has used to burn down entire rows of houses in Kashmir.

TADA has been widely used to detain journalists and human rights activists. According to the *Economist*, of the 65,000 arrests made under TADA from its inception through mid-1994, 19,000 occurred in the western state of Gujarat, where there are no insurgencies. The Gujarat authorities have even used TADA to throw environmental activists in jail. In March 1994 the Supreme Court upheld TADA, and in October the government concluded a review by deciding against scrapping the act.

Bangkok and beyond

The contempt that many Asian leaders have for universal human rights standards got a public airing in late March and early April 1993, when forty-nine countries met in Bangkok to draft a regional agenda for the June United Nations World Conference on

Human Rights in Vienna. The document that emerged from this meeting, the Bangkok Declaration, rejected the fundamental liberties enshrined in the 1948 Universal Declaration of Human Rights. It said that freedoms such as speech, religion and assembly are not inalienable, but instead must be considered in the context of regional, cultural and historical backgrounds, the so-called "cultural relativism" argument. The Declaration also said Western attempts to link development aid to human rights infringed on the national sovereignty of developing countries.

Although China, Indonesia and Singapore were among the strongest supporters of the Declaration, several South Asian governments also signed on. Authoritarian leaders are particularly brazen in using cultural relativism arguments to justify widespread restrictions on political rights and civil liberties. Particularly in East Asia it is not uncommon to hear officials cite traditional village consensual decision-making arrangements in the context of banning political parties or throwing dissidents in jail.

In the 5 March 1994 *Financial Times*, Bangkok bureau chief Victor Mallet noted that for many Asian leaders the Asian Way boils down to "a reaction to Western liberalism rather than a set of ideas in its own right." He feels this aversion to the West has been caused in large measure by the experience with colonialism. But by shamelessly using the notion of an Asian Way to countenance restrictions on free speech and political opposition, the ruling elites ignore the need for public debate on the challenges facing authoritarian countries, including political succession problems and income gaps between rich and poor.

Who's afraid of NGOs?

The Bangkok Declaration's message that democracy is an alien, Western concept is not borne out by the behavior of ordinary Asians. In East and South Asia there are thousands of indigenous nongovernmental organizations (NGOs) fighting to promote basic rights. Unfortunately most Asian leaders consider NGOs to be the enemy rather than partners in progress. This is disappointing but not surprising. The work of NGOs in the fields of women's rights, child welfare, minority rights and assistance to backward castes and "untouchables" involves grassroots empowerment, and this threatens to shake up entrenched political interests.

There are few countries in Asia where NGOs are allowed to work unimpeded. China, North Korea, Vietnam, Laos, Singapore, Bhutan, Brunei and the Maldives either ban NGOs outright or place such heavy restrictions on speech and association that in practice none exist. In other countries NGOs can operate but their leaders are frequently detained or otherwise harassed. NGOs are under particularly heavy pressure in Indonesia. In 1992 the Indonesian government prohibited NGOs from receiving financial assistance from their counterparts in the Netherlands, the country's former colonial ruler. In the fall of 1994 the government circulated a draft presidential decree giving the government new powers to shut down NGOs and to restrict their activities.

U.S. policy

Many business leaders in Asia hold the United States government in contempt for its advocacy of human rights. The Clinton administration, in addition to its criticism of China's human rights abuses, is also nominally committed to placing workers' rights on the trade agenda. Many developing countries are eligible for preferential tariff rates on certain exports to the U.S. under the General System of Preferences (GSP). However, GSP rights are conditional on a country adhering to International Labor Organization standards on workers' rights and working conditions.

The Clinton administration faces several test cases in Asia. The Office of the U.S. Trade Representative (USTR) is reviewing the Malaysian government's refusal to allow the 120,000 workers in the electronics industry, many of whom are employed by American companies, to form a national union. Malaysia is the biggest beneficiary of GSP privileges, with nearly $3 billion worth of goods covered.

In Indonesia, which exports $650 million in goods to the U.S. under GSP, conditions for workers are worse. At least three labor activists have died in suspicious circumstances since May 1993; the minimum wage of $1.80 per *day* is among the lowest in the region; and factory conditions are abysmal. In January 1994 the government revoked a decree allowing the military to intervene in strikes, but soldiers reportedly still get involved in labor disputes. The government uses a set of stringent restrictions to withhold recognition of the country's largest independent confederation, the Welfare Labor Union of Indonesia, which claims 250,000 members nationwide despite being outlawed.

In response to an AFL-CIO petition, the USTR gave Indonesia a February 1994 deadline to improve its labor situation or face a loss of its GSP status. In February, the USTR extended the deadline for six months. In April labor tensions came to a head in the northwestern city of Medan, where striking workers, mostly ethnic Malays, staged riots in some of the most serious unrest in the country since the 1970s. According to the respected Legal Aid Foundation in Jakarta, evidence suggests that the government covertly instigated the riots and whipped up anti-Chinese sentiment in order to discredit the independent labor movement.

The United States and several European countries have also been pressuring South Asian countries over the issue of child labor. According to a July 1994 U.S. Department of Labor report, by some estimates there are up to 100 million child laborers in India, and perhaps 37 million more in Bangladesh, Nepal and Pakistan. Many work in the carpet industry, putting in fourteen-hour days, or longer, in cramped, dangerous conditions.

South Asia

On the ground, there were important political and social developments in South Asia in 1994. In India, the ruling Congress Party suffered heavy losses in four state legislative elections in November and December, raising doubts about Prime Minister P.V. Narasimha Rao's ability to lead the party at general elections scheduled for 1996.

Another critical issue facing the country is conflict between upper- and lower-caste Hindus. Some 70 percent of Indians are backward castes, scheduled castes (ex-"untouchables"), or tribesmen, and in recent years they have used their numerical superiority to win political power. Most notably, in the November 1993 elections in Uttar Pradesh, India's most populous state, lower castes combined with Muslim voters to win control of the state legislature.

In Uttar Pradesh and elsewhere, lower castes are demanding greater reservation, or quotas, of university admissions slots and government jobs. This puts them in direct and often violent conflict with the numerically smaller upper castes. Matters came to a head in Uttar Pradesh in fall 1994 as upper-caste protestors clashed with police after the state government increased lower caste reservations to 50 percent of all university slots and civil service positions. Similar rioting four years earlier killed 2,000 people across northern India.

Elections in both Nepal and Sri Lanka swept incumbents out of office. Nepal's November elections marked the first time in Asia that a communist party came to power through a relatively free vote, albeit one marred by widespread irregularities.

The Communist Party of Nepal-United Marxist Leninist (CPN-UML) took 88 seats in the 205-seat parliament to beat out the incumbent Congress Party, which took 83 seats. The CPN-UML's Man Mohan Adhikary, a seventy-four-year-old former dissident who was at the forefront of the prodemocracy movement that toppled the absolute monarchy in 1990, subsequently formed a minority government that faces a mandatory vote of confidence in early January.

In Sri Lanka, a year after a suicide bomber killed President Ranasinghe Premadasa the conservative United National Party's (UNP) seventeen-year rule ended with losses in both parliamentary and presidential elections. In August Chandrika Bandaranaike Kumaratunga, the daughter of two former prime ministers, led the center-left People's Alliance to victory by securing a 105-seat plurality in the 225-seat parliament. The new prime minister pledged to end the eleven-year-old civil war in the north, which has pitted the country's Buddhist Sinhalese majority against Hindu Tamil separatists who claim discrimination in jobs and educational opportunities. In late October a suicide bomber killed the UNP's candidate for the upcoming presidential elections, Gamini Dissanayake. Two weeks later premier Kumaratunga routed Dissanayake's widow to win the presidential vote.

Pakistani prime minister Benazir Bhutto's woes include a severe law-and-order crisis in many parts of the country, including Karachi, the commercial capital, and the Northwest Frontier Province. In Bangladesh, parliamentary activity came to a halt in March when the opposition launched a boycott to demand fresh elections run by a neutral caretaker government. The crisis, which continued at year's end, was the latest episode in a long-running personal feud between prime minister Khaleda Zia and her chief rival, Sheik Hasina Wajed of the opposition Awami League.

Ethnic cleansing in Shangri-La

The most troubled country on the subcontinent is the tiny Himalayan kingdom of Bhutan, which has one of the worst human rights records in the world. Since 1985 King Jigme Singye Wangchuk's government, dominated by the northern-based, Tibetan-descended Ngalong Drukpas, has systematically persecuted the ethnic Nepalese population in the south. In late 1990 this escalated into an ethnic cleansing campaign of rape, torture and burning of houses that has since forced more than 100,000 southern Bhutanese into exile. Most live in cramped refugee camps in southeastern Nepal. In June 1994 a group of dissident northerners launched the Druk National Congress (DNC) in exile, indicating discontent within the King's own ethnic group. The DNC leadership pledged to bring democracy to one of the world's last absolute monarchies.

East Asian bleakness

The human rights situation got bleaker in China in 1994. Chinese authorities detained or arrested dozens of dissidents in Beijing and Shanghai, introduced new restrictions on religious freedom, and stepped up the pace of executions for drug trafficking, corruption and other noncapital offenses. Premier Li Peng signed a law in June criminalizing many of the means human rights activists use to peacefully publicize their cause, including working with foreign nongovernmental organizations.

The government's crackdown on dissident activity reflects its concern that the country's economic growth is chipping away at the Communist Party's tight control over the population. Since late 1978, when Deng introduced free market reforms, economic growth has averaged 9 percent per year, including 13 percent growth in

1992 and 1993. Although there are still 900 million peasants, most of them living in oppressive poverty, for the first time in generations millions of other Chinese are no longer struggling simply to survive. Many are now participating in the private sector and have removed themselves from dependence on the danwei (state work unit) with its stifling social controls. Shortwave radios and satellite dishes provide more and more people with the BBC and other foreign news services.

A report released in March by the London-based International Institute for Strategic Studies concluded that Beijing's authority over the provincial governments has been greatly weakened, particularly in the area of economic decision making. Local authorities frequently levy arbitrary, crushing taxes on peasants and seize land illegally. Peasants have fought back against local officials and police in hundreds of incidents of rural unrest over the past several years. There has also been a general breakdown in authority in parts of the countryside, where warlordism and banditry have returned at a level not seen since the 1920s.

China's economic growth has been highly concentrated in the cities and southern coastal areas. At the same time, the country has a "surplus" of more than 200 million agricultural workers. As a result, peasants have left their villages in search of jobs in staggering numbers, creating a "floating population" of some 105 million people. Most have taken part in a massive migration to the cities.

Vietnam has paralleled China in recent years, with the Vietnam Communist Party (VCP) maintaining tight political control but allowing citizens greater economic opportunity. In both countries, citizens are becoming increasingly less dependent on the Communist party.

Rogue regimes: Burma and North Korea

In the fall of 1994 the state-controlled Burmese media devoted considerable attention to a pair of meetings between the country's most famous dissident, Nobel Laureate Aung San Suu Kyi, who has been under house arrest since July 1989, and two of the top generals who run Burma's State Law and Order Restoration Council (SLORC). Although the SLORC has benefitted from increased foreign aid and diplomatic recognition, Suu Kyi's continued detention has been an obstacle to getting international aid sanctions lifted. In playing up its meeting with Suu Kyi, whom the SLORC has vilified for years, the junta may have been laying the groundwork for her eventual release.

The death in July of North Korea's Stalinist leader Kim Il-Sung, who ruled for forty-six years, did little to open one of the most tightly controlled countries in the world. Following the shaky accession of Kim's son, Kim Jong-il, as his successor, in October North Korea signed a pact with the U.S. agreeing to freeze its atomic weapons program and eventually allow full inspections of its facilities in exchange for modern nuclear reactors and other concessions.

Power politics

Malaysia's ruling National Front consolidated its rule at the state level. At the start of the year there were two state governments—Kelantan and Sabah—in opposition control. In February Sabah's voters went to the polls and gave the incumbent United Sabah Party (PBS) 25 seats in the 48 seat state assembly. But then PBS members began defecting to the ruling National Front Coalition, allegedly because of massive payoffs. Within days the National Front had control of the state government.

Meanwhile, in August, the government began a highly publicized crackdown on the Al-Arqam Muslim messianic sect. The government accuses the group of deviant teachings, but some observers suggest that the authorities view the wealthy group, with 100,000 members, as a political threat.

Of the sixteen countries in East Asia (a region broadly defined to include Southeast Asia), only three—Japan, Mongolia and South Korea—are free democracies. In 1994 Japan continued a sweeping reorganization of its postwar political order, a process that began in the summer of 1993 when the conservative Liberal Democratic Party (LDP) lost its lower house parliamentary majority for the first time since 1955. In April Morihiro Hosokawa, who in August 1993 became prime minister of a seven party coalition that threw the LDP into the opposition, resigned over charges of illegal financial dealings. The accusations were particularly stinging since Hosokawa had come to office promising to reform a system that for decades had been characterized by the cozy relationship between the LDP and big business.

Hosokawa's replacement, Tsutomo Hata, led a short lived minority government that fell in June when the Socialists bolted. The Socialists, who for decades had functioned as something of an institutional opposition to the LDP, now joined into an unlikely coalition with the LDP and the smaller New Harbinger party. Tomiichi Murayama became Japan's first-ever Socialist prime minister.

In November parliament approved an overhaul of the country's electoral laws designed to reduce corruption and give the cities equal representation as the rural areas. Meanwhile, the real action continued in the backrooms, where new alignments are shaping up to contest the next general election, which will probably be held in 1995. In December nine conservative parties reorganized themselves as the New Frontier Party to challenge the LDP on the right.

South Korea's parliament also passed reform legislation this year, in March, aimed at reducing corruption in election campaigns. But the luster seems to be fading around President Kim Young Sam, who took the oath of office in February 1993 as the country's first civilian leader in more than three decades and waged an intense anti-corruption campaign during his first year in office. Many feel Kim has merely shaken up a corrupt political establishment but has not yet institutionalized the reforms.

South Koreans are also concerned with the government's continued application of the harsh National Security Law (NSL) that was used by previous military governments to detain thousands of dissidents, including Kim himself. In 1994 police arrested dozens of people for allegedly pro-North Korean activities, which under the NSL can include the peaceful exercise of freedoms of speech, association and assembly.

Shaky democracy

Both Thailand and the Philippines have lively multiparty systems, but fall short of being free democracies. In the Philippines the political system is weakened by the dominant role of entrenched economic interests and by widespread bureaucratic corruption. To his credit, President Fidel Ramos, who was elected in May 1992 with just 23 percent of the vote, has managed to bring political stability within a democratic framework through skillful consensus building.

Thailand has alternated in this century between military and civilian authority, and as a result the rule of law has not been firmly established. The military still plays an influential role in business and politics, and controls the illegal cross-border trade with Burma in drugs, arms and timber. Despite Prime Minister Chuan Leekpai's stated determination to crack down on child prostitution, the practice is rampant. In July the U.S. Department of Labor reported that

Thailand uses at least four million child workers in the garment industry and other areas. Overall, working conditions are among the most dangerous in the developing world.

Chuan's five-party coalition government suffered a setback in April and May 1994 as right-wing opposition parties in the lower house combined with the military-dominated Senate to defeat seven prodemocracy amendments to the 1991 constitution, which was drafted by a military junta. The defeated amendments sought to make the Senate, which was appointed by the military junta, smaller and more accountable.

Taiwan's democratic transition continued in 1994 as the country held its first-ever elections for the island's governor, the second most important post behind President Lee Teng-hui. The ruling Kuomintang (KMT) party's James Soong, the incumbent, scored an easy victory over the opposition Democratic Progressive Party's (DPP) candidate. But the DPP won the mayoralty of the capital, Taipei, its most significant electoral victory ever over the KMT. The DPP is hoping to make big gains in the December 1995 legislative elections, but its platform of declaring formal independence from China could scare off voters at the national level, given Beijing's threat to invade if Taiwan takes that step.

Hong Kong's voters also have reason to be wary of China. Beijing has pledged to disband all of Hong Kong's elected bodies after the British colony reverts to Chinese sovereignty in June 1997, in response to governor Christopher Patten's reforms that have broadened the franchise for district board and Legislative Council elections. In September's local district board election two prodemocracy parties took nearly a third of the 346 local district board seats, with half going to independents and the remainder going to business and pro-China parties. The Democratic Party and the Association for Democracy and People's Livelihood hope to replicate their success in the September 1995 Legislative Council elections.

An Asian basket case

In spring 1994 Cambodia's King Norodom Sihanouk told a visiting Australian television crew that the United Nations' two-year, $2.2 billion effort at bringing democracy to his country was a waste of money. Sadly, even many supporters of democracy would be forced to agree. In May 1993 the U.N. staged the country's freest elections ever, which brought an 89 percent turnout and resulted in a power-sharing arrangement between the royalist United Front for an Independent, Neutral and Free Cambodia (FUNCINPEC) and the incumbent, ex-Communist Cambodian People's Party.

The government has been unable to dislodge Khmer Rouge guerrillas from the 15 percent of the country they occupy. Outside of the capital, Phnom Penh, much of the country is in a state of lawlessness. In October co-premiers Norodom Ranariddh and Hun Sen sacked Finance Minister Sam Rainsy, who had won widespread praise from the international financial community for his prudent fiscal policies but made too many enemies at home with his attacks on official corruption.

South Pacific

So where can one find the largest collection of democracies in Asia? In the South Pacific, where eleven of fourteen countries, mostly poor and isolated, are free democracies. Never heard of Nauru, Kirabati, Vanuatu and Tuvalu? Neither, apparently, have many of Asia's ruling elites–nor their Western apologists–who don't seem to believe that ordinary Asians can handle democracy.

Charles Graybow is a consultant at Freedom House.

Western Europe: The Dream of a Great Civilization

Roger Kaplan

In 1994, the European Union, the federation of western European states that Winston Churchill in 1948 prophetically had called into being, expanded northward into Scandanavia and embraced the heart of Mitteleuropa, bringing back into the heartland of Western civilization peoples who had been cut off from it for the better part of this century.

Answering the call of duty, the Union applied its powerful military arm, the West European Union, to saving the embattled Republic of Bosnia & Herzegovina. At Christmas, a joint French-German-Spanish armored division was in control of Belgrade while the Royal Air Force, renewing the finest traditions of the World War II Bomber Command, reduced Pale, site of the Bosnian Serb regime, to rubble. A company of the legendary British SAS commandos captured Bosnian Serb president Radovan Karadzic and brought him to The Hague to face charges of crimes against humanity, while a battalion of the famed French 1 ere division de chasseurs alpins (mountain troops) mopped up in the Krajina, whence Serb attacks on the Muslim enclave of Bihac in November had provoked, at last, a forceful response from the Free World.

A team of experts from the EU's nuclear agency, Euratom, made important progress in repairing faulty nuclear power installations in Russia and Ukraine, while other teams of doctors and environmental scientists proceeded in an accelerated program of cleaning up the after-effects of the disastrous Soviet energy policies. Hope was even expressed that something might be done for the devastated Aral Sea region, ruined by decades of a mad cotton monoculture and toxic fertilizers.

Aware that Europe's roots and its future are in the Mediterranean and the Middle East, the EU organized a major conference on Europe-Maghreb relations which had the double aim of calming the civil strife between Islamic fundamentalists and the military regime in Algeria while laying the basis for a long-term development plan for the entire region, founded on enhanced commerce and investment. In Jerusalem, outgoing President of the EU Commission Jacques Delors and his successor Jacques Santer met with Israel's Prime Minister Yitzhak Rabin and PLO leader Yasir Arafat to put the final touches on a settlement that includes the creation of a Middle East common market closely associated with the European community.

Thanks to an ingenious combination of tax cuts and public works financed by new Euroconsortia in transportation and energy, the EU unemployment level was reduced from some 12 percent (average) to under 7 percent. The distaste for public service brought on by corruption scandals in almost every EU country was to a significant degree replaced by a renewed confidence in democratic institutions as a young generation of politicians, prosecutors and high-ranking civil servants, often grouped in parties that had broken away from the socialist and Christian Democrat establishments that have dominated west European life, swept municipal elections in several countries and prepared to force early elections in France, Germany, Italy and Great Britain.

And the dreamers dreamed on.

A detestable year

Of course, it was not this way at all. There was nothing, really nothing, that Europe, since 1993 officially a Union of twelve members with 326 million people and covering 2,305 million sq km, with an overall GDP of $6,090 billion and over a million men and women under arms, could not do, if it set its collective mind to it. The problem was that the now fifteen-member EU did not have a mind, or if it did, it was feeble indeed.

Instead of an intervention in ex-Yugoslavia, the Europeans moaned, groaned, and turned the other way. The wonders of modern communication allowed them to see, live on television, images that immediately brought to mind the Nazi persecutions of Jews and others, as the Bosnian Serb forces invested the Bosnian pocket—a zone officially declared to be protected by the U.N.—in late November and subjected captured soldiers to racist humiliations.

Instead of a serious effort to pre-empt the spreading civil war in Algeria—declared by German Chancellor Helmut Kohl to be Europe's gravest security threat and which most experts agreed could, and sooner than later, have the consequence of sending up to 4 million desperate refugees into France (unemployment 12.5 percent), Italy (unemployment 15.4 percent), and Spain (unemployment—officially—22 percent)— the EU made twisted gestures with its collective crooked hands and hemmed and hawed as France put in place a system of military and political assistance to the regime whose only policy is to kill as many young men as necessary to squelch the revolt. The result is that the Muslim parties, or "Islamists," as they are called to underscore their insistence on Islam as a political ideology as well as a spiritual vocation and a way of life, continued their policy of terror aimed at journalists, intellectuals, businessmen, and now children: late in the year they began to try to enforce their order to shut down the "secular" public schools by entering villages and raping all the girls in sight.

Instead of figuring out how to put the best-educated populations in the world to productive jobs, the EU governments fidgeted with budget deficits and the margins of health insurance and social security accounts and watched as the jobless rolls inexorably increased, with small exceptions (notably in England), while in almost every "industry of the future" (information, robotics, medicine) the North Americans and Asians widened their leads.

Confidence in democracy faltered, as politicians were indicted for corruption, caught in sex scandals, and viewed as far more interested in electoral combinations than in the issues of the day, let alone their compatriots' problems; political parties were torn by fratricidal rivalries, such as the war on the French Right for the succession of President François Mitterrand in May 1995. Not untypical (if specifically British) was John Major's threat to resort to the "atomic bomb" of dissolving Parliament to force the traditionally well-oiled Tory machine into some semblance of discipline; or the proposed legislation of a conservative French deputy, Alain Marsaud, to ban all newspaper coverage of corruption inquiries and indictments; or the endless

problems of Italian PM Silvio Berlusconi—"Mr. Clean" only a few months earlier—
as prosecutors zeroed in on allegations of bribes to Treasury officials to lay off his
Fininvest Company's tax returns. By December, Berlusconi was facing the fall of his
government, as Umberto Bossi, leader of the Northern League, threatened to bolt from
the governing coalition. The underlying problem, as in other countries, remained how
to reform democratic institutions, strengthen a supra-national framework, maintain
expensive welfare states, and boost growth and job creation all at once. In a sense, the
rejection of membership in the EU by Norwegian voters—despite the "yes" votes weeks
earlier by their Swedish and Finnish neighbors—appeared symptomatic of a widespread mood: Europe stinks, the hell with Europe.

The shame of a civilization

To be sure, nothing could possibly be more significant in the year 1994 than the European failure in Yugoslavia. "Why is that?" a British trade union leader asked me.
Why indeed should England be concerned for what hard experience has taught it to
call the "bloody Balkans"? And were they not already giving enough in lives and trea-
sure, alongside France, Spain, and a few others, through the furnishing of some 20,000
U.N. Blue Helmets?

I have no answer, except to say that the question says it all. Any attempt to convince a west European that he shares in the responsibility for the Yugoslav tragedy
and has an interest in repairing the little that can still be fixed is bound to sound sen-
timental, puerile, ill-tempered, unrealistic. In one of the few articles worth reading
about what happened in Bosnia (*New Republic*, 1 August 1994, revised for the French
quarterly *Commentaire*, Fall 1994), Albert Wohlstetter explains that the Serb aim, in
Belgrade no less than in Pale and the Krajina, was from the start the creation of a
Greater Serbia in which at best there might be room for a few non-Serb reservations,
and that the totally absurd military "strategy" under the disjointed U.N.-NATO non-
command could have been imagined only by "leaders" in the Quai d'Orsay, Whitehall,
and Foggy Bottom, determined to resist any move that might deny the Serbs their
victory.

In this regard, the stated desire of the Bonn government, during the sixty-fourth
French-German Summit in November, to lift the arms embargo on Bosnia, sounded
as sadistic as the Clinton administration along the same lines, several months earlier,
had sounded vapid.

In point of fact, there has been a German will to break the embargo since at least
1992, when it was proposed by Christian Schwarz-Schilling, who at least had the grace
to resign his ministerial post when his policy was not followed. This time, both newly
elected (with a thin majority) Chancellor Helmut Kohl and his designated successor
as CDU leader Wolfgang Schauble supported the idea, which was passed at a CDU
congress. Kohl himself had proposed it at an EU (then EC) summit at Copenhagen in
1993.

But a will is not a deed, and Germans are notorious for wanting what they per-
ceive the rest of the world wants them to want. The CDU's approach, with its appeal
to public opinion, is, in practice, phony. The U.S. does exactly the same thing when,
in a condescending and counterproductive appeal to "Arab" opinion (which fits in
with current State Department strategy of distinguishing "moderate" Islamists from
Iranian-style "radicals"), it pretends to cry over poor little Bosnia. The fact is that the

poor little Bosnians did not want pity. If there had been any sort of military assistance worthy of the name during the battle for Bihac in November—instead of the perfectly pointless bombing run against an unused military target, by some of the best flyers, in the best machines, available to any air force—something might have been saved.

A union of fakers

Nineteen-ninety-four was, if you viewed it superficially, a year of expansion for the European Union. Referenda in Austria, Finland and Sweden turned a club of twelve into one of fifteen and the nations of central Europe were encouraged to believe their turns would come soon enough, while even Turkey, Israel and Morocco, and of course Russia and Ukraine, were assured that no good Europeans ever let them be far from their thoughts.

Of course, looking at the Bosnians, no sharp-witted Turk could help but wonder just what good it might do to be in, or even near, Europe. The original intent of the Community was to prevent a fourth French-German conflict (and hence third World War), but this acknowledged accomplishment has now become a jaded cliché. At what cost to civilized values are the West Europeans going to perennially congratulate themselves for preserving the peace in an area that can be crossed from one end to another in scarcely more than a day's travel in high speed trains?

That this is clearly understood and the cause of a profound bad conscience on both sides of the Rhine is revealed, too, in the no-longer-masked disagreements over the future of Europe that the members of the "hard core" entertain. The term "hardcore," proposed by a German parliamentary committee in September to describe what is, after all, the reality and the original *raison d'etre* of what is supposed to be a living, dynamic, vital political-economic entity, is disputed. The Germans—admittedly in a somewhat clumsy way—simply meant that as Europe grows bigger, it should be formally recognized that some of its member-states are more united, and are acting more in concert, than others. This was meant to reconcile the Germans' federal vision with the more confederal vision of most of their EU partners and, if anything, it demonstrated a respect for their opinions.

For example, there is a good deal of recalcitrance regarding monetary union, even though it represents an important part of the Maastricht Treaty which is the legal basis for the 1993 transition from Community to Union. The Germans themselves were very unhappy about monetary union, complete with a single Euro-currency, because the sound Deutschmark is the foundation of their economic health. But they went along with it and they then said that there was no need to rush things, those who wanted it would do it—the "hard core" of France, Belgium, Luxembourg, Netherlands and themselves—and the rest would not, until they were able and willing. Ditto defense; no one would force Portuguese boys or Danish boys or Irish boys to go where they did not want, but if the "hard core" or some part thereof decided it was timely and right to restore order in the Balkans or the Coasts of Barbary, then they would do so.

But even this seemed too much to ask. The French-German summit brought out differences which the unstable political situation in France was, if anything, bound to render even more problematic in the months and year ahead. The Germans want, in keeping with their federal vision of Europe, to diminish the powers of the *Bundestag, Assemblee nationale* and other parliaments (even as, rather ominously, they move their own federal capital to Berlin, presently in the midst of a major real estate boom despite crushing German taxes—but as they say, "*Wir sind wunderbar!*") in favor of what they (and the widely despised and seldom read Maastricht Treaty) view as a "democratic reinforcement" of the European Parliament in Strasbourg (currently still little more than a play assembly despite the presence of capable and committed Europeans like Otto von Habsburg and Claudia Roth, both German Eurodeputies, one from the right and one from the left), and other institutional changes.

The French are more inclined toward what in political theory would be called a "confederation," a union of completely sovereign states. They give little weight to governing structures at the Eurolevel, preferring to see the Commission (the executive) and the Council of Ministers (which the Germans view as a potential Senate) as only the administrative appendages of decisions taken government-to-government. The French always have tended to view the EC, now EU, as that "super-state" which British and Norwegian "Euroskeptics" fear: a super-state which France could control and which would be useful for carrying out policies which they desire but would prefer not to take direct responsibility for.

The discord regarding how fast Europe might become something that it is not yet cuts lines within, as well as between, nations and even governments. The German foreign minister, Klaus Kinkel, leader of the small FDP (liberals), disagrees with the CDU "hard core" ideas as well as with the lifting of the Bosnian arms embargo. France's interior minister, Charles Pasqua, though he belongs to the same RPR (neo-Gaullist) party as prime minister Edouard Balladur, is a known anti-Maastrichian and has been blocking federalist policies desired by the Germans, for example turning Interpol (presently little more than a crime data bank) into a Euro-FBI.

Europe has thus become an issue, perhaps the issue, around which to stake out political positions and fight elections. Europe periodically threatens to split the Conservative Party in Great Britain. The Labor Party wants more, not less, Europe. Although the political landscape keeps shifting, it would not be too risky to generalize by saying that there is a kind of conservative-left alliance across Europe against Europe, and a broad centrist alliance (Christian Democrat-Social Democrat) across Europe for Europe. This was very clear in the Norwegian campaign, which pitted an internationally known figure of the social democratic establishment, Prime Minister Gro Harlem Brundtland, against Anne Enger Lahnstein, leader of the conservative Center party but supported by left-social democrats (including many labor unionists). The Greens, dispersed and divided, tend to favor a utopian anti-nation-state Europe with a powerful parliament dictating pollution and health standards, disbanding armies, moving toward negative population growth, and bicycles for transportation.

European democracy under strain

Divided and temperamental, the Europeans perhaps should not be blamed for expending as much energy as they do to accomplish so little. The fact that they cannot get their EU act together is merely a reflection of the fact that they cannot get their houses in order. Throughout the year, the French, Italian and Spanish governments were beset by financial corruption scandals of appalling proportions, as if kleptocracies oppressing Third World countries were becoming the norm in the established democracies.

There is something paradoxical in the idea that liberal democracy seems to be jaded and worn down in the very years of its triumph over totalitarianism. But, very broadly, there are two explanations for the spectacle of kickbacks and sex-and-favors scandals besetting politicians across borders and ideologies, from John Major's Tories to Silvio Berlusconi's Forza Italia, passing by French conservatives (the socialists had their turn already) and Spanish socialists. The left said that the problem was that there was not enough democracy, the right that there were not strong enough moral values.

Democratic deficit

Both points were true, and false. There is, in most of Europe outside Scandanavia, a "democratic deficit" which expresses itself in different ways but which has the effect of alienating citizens from the state and nation. It is also true that there is a great deal of moral confusion. This is not to say that there are more dishonest people in Europe than elsewhere—such a generalization would be silly. However, there were several factors that contributed to making Europe vulnerable to moral rot.

First, all EU countries—and the substantial agencies of the EU as well—have state-supported sectors that have got out of control. The question is not why "Thatcherism" never took hold in continental Europe (it was well understood only in Denmark, which for historical and demographic reasons has been able to ally a "Thatcherian" conception of entrepreneurial capitalism with a highly developed welfare state, however contradictory this may sound). The point, rather, is that the Europeans in their diverse ways believe in their states' efficacy as economic and social agents, in a way the English or Americans do not. Every country in Europe has its adepts of libertarian economics. There are plenty of excellent continental authors on the political no less than the economic aspects of "liberalism." After all, Tocqueville was French, as was the late Jacques Rueff; the Germans produced Ludwig Erhardt and the famous "miracle" (which was at root the lifting of economic controls, trusting the people); the Italian foreign minister, Antonio Martino, is a member of the Mont Pelerin Society.

The issue is that the Europeans wanted to have, and do have, states which got out of control before anyone quite noticed it. Germany's finance minister, Theo Waigel (a liberal in the European sense) speaks glowingly of reducing the state share of GNP to under 50 percent. This is the statist reality of Europe. Berlusconi at year's end was engaged in titanic negotiations with the trade unions to reduce the state's budget by some billions that would still leave Italy's public deficit beyond the bounds set by the EU (in fact, only Luxembourg is within the debt-to-GNP parameters.)

A conservative French government embarked on a major ad campaign to explain to people that AIDS could be beaten with educational programs, free condoms in schools, complete taxpayer-supported medical assistance for victims of the disease, and so forth. But the French state (through the National Blood Agency) knowingly distributed HIV-contaminated blood to hemophiliacs (and others) a few years ago. A European liberal would argue that they should give cash to the victims and get out of the business altogether. But the French, and Europeans generally, simply do not conceive of public policy this way.

A real liberal (see Hayek's *Constitution of Liberty*) would argue that regardless of the honesty of the men involved—and no one has accused Laurent Fabius, prime minister at the time of the blood disaster, of moral turpitude—statism will engender corruption because of the lack of competition-induced control. But it does little good to say this. The state, the states, are everywhere in Europe. The corruption of politicians is, in an almost Marxian—or Hayekian—sense, almost preordained.

Consider France. In fifteen years, the public sector share of GNP went from an already high 40 percent to some 55 percent today. In Germany it represents 50 percent. (U.S.: 33 percent.) Among other things, of course, this means far less private investment in these countries. There may be other reasons for the rise of unemployment in the EU, but it is a fact that it is up by some 130 percent in France in the past fifteen years (close to 12 million people) and 65 percent in Germany (about 7 million.)

The fight against political corruption in France, Italy and Spain has been led for the past two years by courageous, civic-minded magistrates (investigating attorneys). The public supports them. The news media support them. Most politicians, for that matter, support them. But if the state is everywhere, no one can bypass the state. Periodic purges, as are occurring now in the Latin countries, are just that; the system's perversions will return. There is no sign that anyone in public life really grasps the implications. In Italy, Berlusconi, egged on by ministers like the libertarian Martino, makes important—even courageous—gestures to dismantle excessive statism and reduce the public debt and the government's budget, even as he puts such pressure on the judiciary that Antonio di Pietro, the crusading Milan magistrate who has been leading the fight for clean public life, feels forced to resign. The gestures will be only that, with the rest of the political class clamoring for a "clean" state. The same refrain is heard in France: there is a consensus for "restoring the state," and an accompanying cacophony on the dignity of the state's vocation, the honor of those who serve it. In a typical case, neo-Gaullist presidential candidate Jacques Chirac, who once had proclaimed himself a "Reagano-Thatcherian," has rediscovered the Gaullist virtues of service to a strong state. The Socialists proclaim the goal of a "social Republic."

There is nothing wrong with a "strong state," under democratic control, if there are well understood limits. The European states are asphyxiating their nations' economies, which one would think is outside their vocations, while they are unable to prevent mass murder, verging on genocide, in Bosnia, which, one would like to believe is one of the reasons for their being.

Roger Kaplan is editor of Freedom Review.

Russia: A Year-Long Holding Action

Pierre Lorrain

The year 1994 in Russia was characterized by a search for balance and normality: a steady economic course and a place in the concert of nations. Neither goal was fully attained on the eve of 1995. However, despite colossal adjustments in the Russian economy, which bring with them no less colossal dysfunctions, and despite what looks at times like a trial-and-error approach to foreign affairs, Russia has not slid back, as some observers feared, into a mode, despotic at home and imperial abroad, to which it is supposedly condemned by history. Nineteen-ninety-four saw the strengthening of a real, albeit still fragile, civil society, as well as a more assertive, confrontational foreign policy marked by an opposition to NATO's proposed eastward expansion and reestablishment of Russian influence in the "near abroad."

"Industrialists" in power

The elections of 12 December 1993, which brought in a State Duma with a majority of agrarians, Soviet-era throwbacks, and neo-Communists, marked the end of the period when reformers dominated Russian political life. Although former Prime Minister Yegor Gaidar's group, Russia's Choice, had been expected to win, it found itself outpolled by the Russian Liberal Democratic Party, which captured 24 percent of the vote. Its leader, Vladimir Zhirinovsky—who is neither liberal nor democratic and is suspected of having been a KGB officer with the job, during perestroika, of discrediting the young democratic parties—stepped on the political stage and, with his extremism, made the Communists and other nostalgics look moderate.

For Boris Yeltsin this was a serious blow. For two years he had fought against the old parliament led by Ruslan Khasbulatov and Alexander Rutskoi, who competed with him for power and prevented him from governing, and Yeltsin had only got the upper hand, in October 1993, by bringing in the army. A referendum ratifying the new constitution and elections for a new bicameral parliament were meant to lay down new rules for the political game, at last imposing the rule of law.

Under the new constitution, to which dubious voters accorded a slight "yes," the president can dissolve the State Duma only after a year. Short of wrecking all chances of attaining political stability, Yeltsin had no choice but to accept the new situation. To govern, he could rely on the Federation Council, the parliament's upper chamber (made up for the most part of regional officials who are less "politicized" than the deputies in the lower chamber) and, by moving to the center, seek a certain degree of consensus rather than conflict with the new Duma.

Here Yeltsin had a sizeable asset in the flexible government of Prime Minister

Viktor Chernomyrdin, in which the "industrialists" (statists) worked with the "liberals" (market reformers). The goal of the former was to maintain high employment and the productive capacities of the country (including in the defense sector) by means of state subsidies, without regard for profitability or for the risks of inflation (over 800 percent in 1993). However, the "liberals" controlled the government through the main economic ministries (economy, finance, privatization).

In January, after affirming that reforms would continue, Yeltsin nonetheless shifted Chernomyrdin's government toward the industrialists. Deputy Prime Minister Yegor Gaidar, in charge of the Economy Ministry, and Finance Minister Boris Fyodorov both resigned, citing a shift in favor of the industrialists that ended all hopes of economic stabilization. The prime minister confirmed the liberals' worst fears by announcing: "The romantic era of the market is over."

These words had a positive effect on the Duma, all the more so since the new government included men whom the deputies could trust, notably First Deputy Prime Minister Oleg Soskovets, formerly responsible for heavy industry and defense, and the agriculture minister, Aleksandr Zaveryukha, an "agrarian" who had made his name by promising the *kolkhozniks* (collective farm managers) that the state would buy their products at world prices, and who was also promoted to the rank of deputy prime minister.

Peaceful coexistence between parliament and government was underscored in the spring by the nomination (as minister without portfolio) of Nikolai Travkin, then-president of the Democratic Party and allied to the agrarians and the Communists.

This did not mean the State Duma had lost all hostility toward Yeltsin. As early as February, the deputies passed an amnesty law that quashed the indictments against the authors of the August 1991 putsch and the instigators of the insurrectionary riots of October 1993, particularly Rutskoi and Khasbulatov. For the Russian president, this amnesty was a slap in the face.

Nor has the Duma missed an opportunity to oppose the foreign policy of Yeltsin and his foreign minister, Andrei Kozyrev, particularly regarding the conflict in ex-Yugoslavia and Russo-Ukrainian relations.

However, conflicts were mitigated, thanks largely to Duma Speaker Ivan Rybkin (agrarian), a former Communist official who, unlike his predecessor Khasbulatov, behaves more as a mediator than as a faction leader and has even acquired sufficient respect to be mentioned as a possible presidential candidate in 1996. For its part, the government carefully avoided making legislative proposals that the deputies would have found too difficult to swallow.

A schizophrenic economy

Most commentators described the Russian economic situation in 1994 in catastrophic terms. During the first half of the year production fell by close to 30 percent, prices nearly doubled and the ruble lost half its value against the dollar. Cash being scarce, firm-to-firm debt grew geometrically, jeopardizing the survival of firms that would be viable if normal credit lines were available. Taking advantage of the state's disorganization and the vagueness of the laws, some 4,000 criminal gangs, generically referred to as mafia, in effect robbed the entire country, engaging in every conceivable racket and accumulating immense fortunes. An absurd and dysfunctional fiscal system placed a serious handicap on foreign investors. Capital flight reached collossal levels; for each foreign dollar invested in Russia, 365 left the country.

And yet, behind this gloomy picture there were positive signs. The liberals' fear that the economy would crash proved unfounded: from February to September, Chernomyrdin continued the same austerity policies as his predecessors and inflation fell from 22 percent in January to less than 10 percent, and finally to less than 5 percent, monthly.

Despite the slide in industrial production, one of the significant facts of 1994 is that the Russian economy is trying to respond to consumer demand.

The emancipation of civil society

Contrary to conventional wisdom, household consumption did not drop in 1994. Non-food purchases (televisions, cars, furniture, for example) even showed a marked increase. In one year, real household income increased by 20 percent. This is due to the fact that employees are switching from the industrial to the service sector. Even those who continue to be officially on the payroll of state enterprises on the brink of bankruptcy moonlight for far more than their official salaries. The service sector, which represented less than 20 percent of the economy in the Soviet era, now represents about 50 percent, and it is composed, for the most part, of private enterprises.

The market has definitely emerged in Russia. Preoccupied with internal competition for power, the government has loosened its grip on the population, allowing a real civil society to emerge and facilitating its economic emancipation. The state, which prided itself on running the economy in the Communist period, has retreated from the field, giving way to entrepreneurs. To be sure, this retreat is due mainly to the regime's incompetence. Government agencies and ministries publish regulations, but these are ignored and cannot be enforced. Moreover, the entrepreneurs have an important weapon in their fight for economic independence: the hands of public officials in their businesses. Anywhere else this would be called corruption. But one sign of the private sector's vigor is that despite the kickbacks and payments to the mafia, which amount to 10-15 percent of earnings, profits are being made.

To be sure, optimism should be tempered. Consumption is not in itself proof of a healthy economy. Entrepreneurs prefer the quick profits of commerce over long-term returns on substantial investments in production. The ruble crisis in October, a clumsy attempt by the government to let it find its real value, led to the resignation of Finance Minister Sergei Dubinin, Central Bank governor Viktor Gerashchenko, and Aleksandr Shokhin, who was replaced at the Economy Ministry by Anatoly Chubais, the last of the great liberal ministers still in the government. Russian commerce is characterized by far too many imports, compared to a limited export sector. But before they can export, Russian producers must be competitive in their home markets.

Illusions of power

While the economy remained, generally, on a reform course, political discourse hardened, as the "patriotic" camp, which ranges from Communists to all manner of nationalists, gained in popularity. For even if, objectively, household income can be shown to be on the increase, there is a widespread feeling that things are worse and poverty is spreading. There is, in fact, no doubt that a great many people are worse off.

The idea has spread that Russia's hardships are due not to economic inefficiency but to an obscure Western plot whose instruments are Russian liberals and democrats.

Accustomed to thinking of their country as a superpower, most Russians had no idea of the real state of the Soviet Union. In 1991, most Russians thought, quite seriously, that once the Communists left the scene the country would rapidly attain the West's living standards.The Soviet economy was a lie.

Until his death, Richard Nixon believed that the U.S. had to respect the only country in the world that could destroy it. However weak Russia may be, it has inherited the Soviet military might, and Yeltsin can hardly do less than the late American leader in expecting respect for his country and himself.

Yeltsin supporters and "conservatives" agree on this, but draw different conclusions. For Yeltsin, Russia must join the concert of nations as a "normal" power, no more and no less, and no longer be a destabilizing force on the world stage.

Realpolitik and national interests

This perspective was clearly noticeable in 1992 and the beginning of 1993, when the foreign policy debate was not muddied by conservative agitation. In June 1992, during the START II treaty negotiations, President Yeltsin stated: "We do not want this wretched [military] parity that condemns half the Russian population to living below the poverty line."

Unfortunately, imperial habits persist. The sacrifices for military power had to stand for something. In an unstable new world, people grasp at the idea that a country is as great as it is feared. The Russian contradiction today is that it is caught between a realistic foreign policy that will gain it access to the rest of the world, while keeping it, in the short term, in a minor international role, and a policy of power, that would inspire fear in other countries but that would again condemn Russia to isolation.

Addressing this problem, the government presented two faces. It respected international commitments, especially in matters of disarmament, to assure other countries that it is a reliable partner rather than an adversary; at the same time it tried to assert Russian power, to undercut the opposition's arguments that the government is making Russia weak.

The hardening of Russia, in foreign policy, is shown mainly in the so-called "near abroad," the former Soviet republics now independent states. There has been a noticeable change in this regard. Moscow's official position is to consider the "near abroad" as an "area of interests" which Russians must defend. The Russians would like to see their interests accepted, all the more so as the economic interdependence in the ex-USSR may lead to pressures tending toward a new de facto Russian hegemony in the territory of the former Soviet Union.

CIS: Return to reality

Thus, some republics, including Ukraine and Belarus, aimed at closer cooperation with Russia in 1994 rather than the assertion of independence, which was understandable in the years immediately following the Soviet meltdown. The elections of Leonid Kuchma to the presidency of Ukraine and Alexander Lukashenko to the presidency of Belarus should encourage a rapprochement, even if marred by occasional rifts and quarrels.

Russia's military presence in most of the republics—by way of defense pacts, peacekeeping, or border guards—is one of the major elements of Russian power in the "zone of influence." There are Russian troops in all the former Soviet republics, though only a handful of military personnel remain in the Baltics.

At the U.N., Russian diplomats argue that the troops are there for peacekeeping missions, and the U.N. should therefore pick up the tab. But such demands (in practice they concern only Moldova, Georgia, Armenia and Tajikistan) are incompatible with Yeltsin's statements regarding Russia's obligation to defend the some 25 million Russians living outside the borders of the Russian federation. Russian "blue helmets" could scarcely intervene in a neighboring independent state to defend the rights of the Russian minority.

The case of Chechnya is special in that this Caucasian republic, led by former Soviet Air Force Gen. Dzhokhar Dudaev, is the only constituent Russian republic that unilaterally proclaimed independence (in 1991). Unlike Tatarstan, for example, which rejected outright secession and successfully negotiated for greater powers within the Russian federation, the predominantly Muslim Chechens chose sovereignty. On 11 December, Russian television reported that as many as 40,000 Russian troops were sent to Chechnya to, according to a statement by Yeltsin, prevent a "threat to the integrity of Russia." By late December, the conflict escalated, as Russian forces engaged the Chechen militia, bombing the capital, Grozny. All out war followed, then unrestrained massacres.

The limitations of double talk

This contradiction in the Russian position explains its hesitations with regard to the Partnership for Peace that would associate the countries of central and eastern Europe with NATO, but without making them members. It also helps to explain the ambiguities of the Russian position on Bosnia: protesting against any moves by NATO, participating in the contact group seeking diplomatic settlement, and all but openly defending the Serbs. In a characteristic mark of double talk, in April, when the Serbs were assaulting Gorazde, a high foreign ministry official said, off the record: "The West can nuke Belgrade if it desires, so long as it asks us nicely."

Boris Yeltsin was welcomed courteously to the G-7 summit in Naples, in July, as an equal and not a petitioner, as Gorbachev had been. Though Russia was not a participant in the economic part of the meeting, the West was, by this invitation, recognizing Russia as a power, capping Yeltsin's efforts in this regard with success.

Yet, Russian indulgence toward Serb aggression in Bosnia, alongside a divided West's timorousness, did nothing to resolve the Yugoslav catastrophe, while overbearing moves in the "near abroad" were cause for worry. The year concluded with Yeltsin's angry performance at the CSCE meeting in Budapest in December, where he accused the U.S., via NATO, of seeking a "new division" of Europe.

While not reassuring, Russian foreign policy in 1994 must be viewed in perspective. Yeltsin used foreign policy, to some extent, to appease domestic critics. More importantly, it would be wrong to compare Russia's claims (on its own behalf or the Serbs') to the peculiarly aggressive Soviet foreign policy, driven by a messianic claim of leading a world revolution. Russian foreign policy in 1994 was not "easy," but it could be called "normal." This could well serve as a verdict on Russia as a whole for 1994, and in this regard, at least, it was a good year.

New nations

Notwithstanding reassertions of Russian hegemony inside the boundaries of the former Soviet Union, the most symbolic event in the Baltic states was the withdrawal of virtually all Russian troops on 31 August from Estonia and Latvia (they had quit Lithuania in 1993). This put an end to one of the most important events of the twentieth century, the alliance between Hitler and Stalin that helped start World War II and that left much of Eastern Europe, including, precisely, the Baltics, under Soviet rule for nearly half a century.

The Baltic states helped spark the dissolution of the Soviet empire by means, in particular, of Estonia's "singing revolution." In 1994, the Baltic states' vigorous economies gave credence to the thesis that the best way out of "post-Soviet" economic stagnation is the sort of shock therapy that Estonia has been willing to apply to itself, thus far with quite good results.

The Balts have a clear advantage, as they chart their post-Soviet destinies, of having a close link to Scandinavia and the commercial ports of northern Germany and Poland. They are also, of course, small, manageable countries and, despite the fifty-year Soviet occupation, less scarred than Ukraine and Belarus.

Ukraine, however, acquitted itself well, considering the pressures it was under. These included the ecological ravages that came with carrying the brunt of the Soviet nuclear energy policy for decades. Politics in both countries revolved around issues of reparation and reconstruction, and how to humor Russia while maintaining the necessary links to the West. In this regard, the most important single event was Ukraine's signing in November of the Nuclear Non-Proliferation Treaty, which brought it much praise in Washington.

Both Ukraine and Belarus struggled with the question: Just what should be the relationship to the former "center"? Free and fair elections did not completely resolve the issue, giving decisive edges neither to "pro-Russian" nor to Western-oriented parties. This may have been a blessing in disguise, as it forced governments to seek prudent policies even as they pushed for reforms.

In Ukraine, Leonid Kuchma defeated incumbent Leonid Kravchuk, a former Communist party ideologue, in the July presidential election; and in October Kuchma unveiled a program of radical economic reform, aimed first at currency stabilization and dampening inflation, as well as privatization. Under the leadership of Viktor Pynzenyk, Kuchma's choice as first deputy prime minister for economics, Ukrainian reformers pushed market-oriented reforms through a conservative parliament, with President Kuchma insisting that reform was not negotiable. Currency stabilization was on the agenda, but American generosity (Ukraine is the fourth largest U.S. aid recipient, after Israel, Egypt and Russia) was not matched by the European Union. Nevertheless, the EU package approved at the Essen meeting on 5 December was better than some had feared.

With the exception of the Kyrgyz Republic, in the lands of what used to be called Soviet Central Asia, authoritarian rulers remain in charge, sometimes with quasi-Stalinist personality cults around them. Parliamentary elections were held (or "staged") in Kazakhstan—in which the supporters of former Communist party strongman President Nursultan Nazarbayev won two-thirds of the seats.

Ethnic tensions appeared in Central Asia, particularly in Tajikistan, where talks between the government (controlled by ex-Communists) and the opposition failed to put an end to sporadic violence.

Uzbekistan remained one of the most repressive former Soviet republics, with opposition newspapers banned and opposition leaders harassed and jailed. In

Turkmenistan, President Separmurot Niyazov signed a pipeline deal with Iran which would make it possible for Iranian oil to transmit to Europe without going through Russia.

Despite Russian- and Western-led mediation efforts and several cease-fires, war continued in Nagorno-Karabakh, the Armenian enclave in Azerbaijan. In Georgia, torn by separatists in Abkhazia and South Ossetia, President Eduard Shevardnadze secured some humanitarian assistance from President Clinton, and reluctantly accepted Russian-led CIS peacekeepers.

Conflicts in the Caucasus are a test of what Russia means by its interests in the "near abroad." Georgian leaders have long contended that Moscow helped arm and encouraged Abkhazian rebels. Azerbaijani President Gaidar Aliyev has implicitly blamed Russia for orchestrating a coup attempt and political destablization, particularly after his government inked a $7 billion oil deal—vigorously opposed by Russia—with a consortium of Western companies to explore huge oil reserves in the Caspian Sea. Russia has deployed several thousand peacekeeping troops in Nagorno-Karabakh and Georgia. The question is whether Russia will play a police role, or whether there will be a sort of neo-imperialism, encouraged by the presence of ethnic Russian residents and military forces throughout the "near abroad."

Pierre Lorrain, reporter, essayist and novelist, is the editor of the monthly newsletter Bulletin de Russie, *published in Paris by the Institut d'Histoire Sociale.*

East-Central Europe: Between Berlin and Bihac

George Zarycky

The fifth anniversary of the fall of the Berlin Wall passed without fanfare. Since the dramatic collapse of the Soviet-Communist empire, the liberated nations of East-Central Europe moved toward economic reform and political democracy. Integration with the rest of Europe, eagerly sought, seemed a realistic goal, as the fifteen-member European Union (EU), at its December summit at Essen (Germany), indicated that "enlargement" eastward was on the agenda. But the carnage in Bosnia and the U.N.'s ineffectiveness in protecting the "safe haven" of Bihac provided a sobering counterpoint to this good news.

Countering pessimists' chiliastic predictions of rack and ruin, ethnic upheaval, irreversible economic collapse, intra-state border conflicts, and mass migrations westward, most East-Central Europeans in 1994 concentrated on consolidating new political, social and economic institutions. Integration with the West revolved around a constellation of institutions—EU, NATO, GATT, IMF—representing the interdependent world of liberal-democratic capitalist states. Commenting on the last five years, Czech Prime Minister Vaclav Klaus remarked, "Europe as a whole has become more free, more democratic, more open, more integrated, more united, less ideological and more pragmatic than at any time in living memory...The people of Europe's post-Communist countries are demonstrating that they are no less 'European' in their habits and aspirations than are their neighbors who were fortunate enough not to live through the Communist trauma."

Klaus's unvarnished optimism may be premature. Governments from the Czech Republic to Romania grappled with balancing the contingencies of rapid privatization, deregulation and liberalization—the imperatives for joining the global economy—with the social needs of citizens. Accustomed to paternalistic centralism, people were unnerved by IMF demands for the elimination of state subsidies to inefficient industrial and agricultural sectors and the ending of price controls. Even where impressive economic gains were made, they were accompanied by high levels of unemployment, social dislocation and poverty. A side effect of democratization and a stronger civil society compelled governments to contend with often obstreperous multiparty parliaments, weak party structures, obstructionist bureaucracies, the enormous challenges of codifying and implementing new legal codes. Organized crime and corruption were troublesome by-products of the venture into what, for many, were uncharted waters. Nevertheless, Eastern Europe as a whole continued on the path toward political pluralism and market economics, truly a remarkable development after over four decades of communism.

Politics: Neo-Communists and neo-post-Communists

The year confirmed a regional resurgence of "post-Communist" Communists, that in 1993 had seen the ascension of the Democratic Left Alliance in Poland. May elections in recession-plagued Hungary were won by the Hungarian Socialist Party (HSP), a successor to the (Communist) Hungarian Socialist Workers Party. Political inexperience and fragmentation weakened the ruling conservative Hungarian Democratic Forum (MDF), already hobbled by the December 1993 death of its moderate leader, Prime Minister Josef Antall. The HSP, which took 209 of 386 parliamentary seats, tapped into Hungarians' natural pessimism (in a pre-election poll, only 18 percent said they were better off in 1994 than under the Communists) and an economy plagued by spiraling inflation, 12 percent unemployment, and 4 million people (out of 10 million) living below the poverty line. In Bulgaria, parliamentary gridlock forced the collapse of the fifteen-month government of non-Party technocrat Lyuben Berov, leading to the election of the (ex-Communist) Bulgarian Socialist Party (BSP). In Macedonia, former Communist and moderate President Kiro Gligorov won presidential-parliamentary elections boycotted by the opposition Internal Macedonian Revolutionary Organization-Democratic Party for Macedonian National Unity (VMRO-DPMNE). In Slovakia, populist firebrand Vladimir Meciar and his Movement of Democratic Slovakia (HZDS), ousted in March, were re-elected in the fall. But the former Slovak interior minister, with reputed ties to the former Czechoslovak secret police, could not forge a governing coalition until mid-December. With Poland, Hungary, Bulgaria, Romania, Slovenia, Serbia and, arguably, Croatia, at least partly governed by former Communist functionaries, only Albania and the Czech Republic bucked the neo-Communist trend, though leftist-socialists and Communists made up the largest opposition in these countries.

The return of the Communists did not signal a reversion to Soviet-era Communist ideology. Ironically, Communists had so thoroughly discredited the concept of socialism that nascent social democratic parties could not get a foothold in the period following the crumbling of Marxist-Leninist regimes. Subsequently, the political landscape left of center was occupied by Communists who, utilizing superior organization, quietly transformed themselves into "socialists, " though their democratic credentials remain to be proven. They benefited, too, from the unraveling of the broad-based coalitions, often headed by dissident-intellectuals unsullied by communism, that toppled Soviet-era regimes, but were unprepared for the responsibilities and politics of leadership. In Poland, then-Czechoslovakia, Bulgaria and Hungary, early non-Communist governments ultimately collapsed amid infighting and economic inexperience.

But the steady consolidation since 1989-90 of democratic institutions, civil society, independent media and civic and labor associations, as well as a burgeoning legal or quasi-legal private sector and its increased share of economic activity, put institutional and structural constraints on the retooled Communists' ability to concentrate and abuse power and roll back market reforms.

Moreover, the exigencies of restructuring dysfunctional economies to reassure Western investors and international lending institutions necessitated fiscal, monetary and industrial policies that obliged neo-Communist leaders to implement measures that ran contrary to their own campaign rhetoric and past inclinations.

Another encouraging development in much of the region was the marginalization of ultra-right, nationalist parties. In Hungary, the right-wing MDF splinter group led by Istvan Csurka, who blamed the country's ills on Jews, international bankers and liberals, was shut out of parliament. Several small neo-fascist groups were organized in 1994, but their appeal was minimal. In Slovakia, Meciar's former coalition partner, the ultra-right Slovak National Party (SNS), won just nine seats, though it became part of the ruling coalition in December. In Romania the minority coalition government of Prime Minister Nicolae Vacariou and his ruling (former Communist) Party of Social Democracy of Romania (PSDR) was tethered to the nationalist Greater Romania Party (PRM). In August, the government granted two cabinet post to the Transylvania-based, ultra-nationalist and anti-Hungarian

Romanian National Unity Party (PRNU), who held a pivotal 10 percent of the seats in a deadlocked parliament. Ultra-nationalists stayed on the fringes of Bulgarian politics.

Economies: Pain and gain

Throughout the region governments faced the difficult tasks of establishing viable banking and financial services institutions, mass privatization and budget cuts to meet IMF restructuring specifications. Slovakia's short-lived government of Prime Minister Jozef Moravcik implemented stringent macro-economic measures, cutting social spending, raising taxes and slashing farm subsidies. In Hungary, Prime Minister Gyula Horn's newly elected reform-Communist government announced its most important task was reducing a $3 billion budget deficit, swollen by Communist-era social insurance programs. Bulgaria's technocrat-dominated government came under pressure after fiscally reasonable but highly unpopular increases in electricity and heating charges and the introduction of an 18 percent value-added tax. Poland's neo-Communist-dominated parliament passed a tough budget that limited social spending, as well as anti-inflationary wage-control legislation. Romania also adopted an unpopular austerity budget. Albania's government cut unemployment benefits, reduced wage subsidies, closed money-losing enterprises, and liberalized prices.

Despite bickering parliaments and underdeveloped capital markets, privatization moved forward, albeit in fits and starts in some countries. After much delay, Poland's government removed the last obstacles to a mass privatization program, establishing fifteen national investment funds (NIFs) to oversee the privatization of 460 companies, though by year's end political wrangling threatened to impede the process. In Romania, the State Ownership Fund, with a 70 percent stake in over 6,000 state-run companies, announced a sell-off of several companies through public offering. Slovakia implemented a second wave voucher privatization, though the re-election of Meciar in the fall raised doubts as to the scope and rate at which it would proceed. In Hungary, the new government promised to accelerate privatization halted under the MDF, unveiling a three-year program that envisaged the complete sale of state companies by 1998. After two years of contentious debate, Slovenia expanded privatization to include 2,500 companies over two years. In late June, the Czech government announced the last big sell-off of stakes in mostly commercial and industrial companies; a voucher privatization system, in which 8 million Czechs bought vouchers enabling them to bid for shares on two tranches of companies, resulted in partial or complete privatization of nearly 2,300 Czech companies, representing over 80 percent of the country's economic activity. Bulgaria lagged behind, as sales of state-owned companies were held up by political infighting over mass privatization legislation.

Frayed safety nets and rising joblessness at a time when revenues from taxes on state companies declined sharply did have social ramifications. In 1994, over 7.5 million people were unemployed, an average of about 14 percent of the labor force. Outside the Czech Republic, over 30 percent of the unemployed were out of work for at least a year. Housing shortages made it harder for the unemployed to move in search of work, and unemployment was markedly higher in rural than urban areas where private sector job opportunities in services and other fields were greater. The fact that regional unemployment rates were generally lower than in Spain was small consolation to workers used to guaranteed, lifelong employment, state pensions and healthcare.

Social fallout was manifest in work stoppages and demonstrations. In Poland, the Solidarity trade union staged several strikes over wage controls and social policy. Romania was hit by sporadic labor unrest, with workers protesting low wages, high unemployment and inflation. Unions in Bulgaria launched a series of warning strikes urging that incomes reflect inflation pressures and that key industrial sectors be protected. Even in the Czech Republic—with unemployment an enviable 3.8 percent, budget surpluses and successful public works programs—some 30,000 people demonstrated in Prague against proposed changes in pension and labor laws and the loss of jobs when state-run enterprises were privatized. It was the largest demonstration since the 1989 "velvet revolution." Significantly, job actions and protests failed to generate much popular support, suggesting an acceptance of the inevitability and desirability of change.

So reforms continued more-or-less apace in Poland, the Czech Republic, Hungary, Slovenia and Slovakia. The private sector of most East-Central European states constituted between 40 and 65 percent of the economy. Most had 50 percent of their trade with the EU. Millions of jobs were created in the trade and service sectors and small- and medium-sized private businesses. Successful foreign debt reduction and rescheduling agreements in 1994 helped Poland and Bulgaria. Despite recession, Hungary continued to attract foreign investment and a slight growth in GDP was predicted for 1995. Albania (struggling to overcome an autarkic past), Bulgaria (whose economy was the most closely linked to the Soviet Union and whose trade with the former Yugoslavia has been restricted by U.N. sanctions), Romania (where the Ceausescu regime eradicated economic and civil society structures) and Croatia (faced with military conflict) pressed on with market reforms.

Corruption, rule of law, media and more...

A troubling phenomenon was the persistence of lawlessness. While crime statistics actually declined in the Czech Republic, corruption continued throughout the region, particularly among political and private business elites. Weak domestic controls, a legacy of bribery as accepted business practice, vague laws and lack of experience in international markets resulted in several well-publicized scandals. In Poland, saddled with one of Eastern Europe's fastest-growing crime rates, bribery, automobile smuggling and embezzlement scandals involving high-ranking police officials led to proposals to stiffen the penal code. In Bulgaria, the proliferation of weapons and racketeering were major problems, as sanction-busting gangs smuggled arms and materials into the former Yugoslavia. Allegations persisted about official corruption in banking, privatization, agriculture, energy and the tourist sector. Hungary's incoming government launched an inquiry into corruption in the privatization of state companies under the previous administration. In Slovakia, Meciar's role as head of privatization and the Fund for National Property raised eyebrows. In the Czech Republic, a major securities fraud scheme followed a series of scandals that linked senior officials, politicians and businessmen to activities ranging from tax evasion to insider trading and extortion.

Many countries were plagued by organized extortion gangs that preyed on private businesses. In Poland, shop owners in Warsaw's Old Town shut down their stores for one day to protest a lack of police protection against gangsters. More menacing has been a rise in drug-trafficking, as heroin from Central Asia and Turkey found new channels to the West through Bulgaria, Romania and Hungary. Poland was a pipeline for homemade and smuggled amphetamines and designer drugs. Albania and the Albanian enclave of Kosovo in Serbia became new distribution zones, suggesting collusion between Kosovo Albanians and established Serb criminal gangs in the area. Drugs also took a social toll; there are an estimated 10,000 heroin addicts in the Czech Republic, and 20,000 Bulgarians reportedly had sampled the drug.

Though high-level graft and a corrupt privilegentsia were endemic during the Communist era, many in the region saw the new high-visibility crime and the accompanying social and individual pathologies as direct products of consumerist capitalism. Growing frustration at the exploitation of power and privilege by new elites as well as the growing gap between rich and poor awakened nostalgia in some for more authoritarian methods to restore order and stamp out graft. Spreading cynicism and voter apathy, reflected in declining participation figures in national and local elections, posed a threat to fragile democratic institutions not yet immune to authoritarian forces on the left and the right.

One reason for what often seemed like an absence of law and order was that modern judicial systems with truly independent judiciaries had yet to be fashioned out of the politicized institutions left by the Communists. The region remained handicapped by a dearth of qualified lawyers and jurists, sluggish reform of penal codes, and continued political interference with judges and prosecutors. However, Poland, the Czech Republic, Slovenia, Slovakia and Hungary have made significant progress in judicial reforms, Bulgaria passed a controversial law that called for all top judicial posts to be filled by those who served as judges or prosecutors for five years, suggesting the imminence of a purge of post-Communist jurists. Opponents argued that the BSP-backed law was aimed at removing Supreme Court Chairman Ivan Grigov and Prosecutor General Ivan Tatarchev, a staunch anti-Communist who actively pursued the prosecution of former Communist officials. In Croatia, the judiciary still was not wholly free from government interference, and the power of judicial appointments and dismissals remain firmly in the hands of an influential parliamentary committee dominated by the right-wing faction of the ruling HDZ.

The year also saw the ongoing struggle over media control. Opposition groups in Hungary, Croatia, Slovakia and Romania claimed government control of most television and radio denied them equal access. In Hungary, still without a press law, the second year of the so-called "media wars," included dismissals of journalists by both the conservative MDF government and later by its neo-Communist successor. In March, 30,000 demonstrated in Budapest over the MDF government's firing of 129 journalists at state-run radio and TV stations. Prior to the May elections, prominent journalists were sacked amid charges the government was trying to muzzle the airwaves. After victorious neo-Communists appointed new chiefs of radio and television, they reinstated the 129, and then proceeded to purge other journalists, including a reporter of the major TV evening news program, Hirado. In Slovakia, journalists faced intimidation and harassment, as well as limited access to government and HZDS officials. The Polish penal code retained provisions proscribing "insulting" government officials and institutions, and President Walesa was accused of removing two members of the putatively independent commission of broadcasting, leading to parliamentary censure and the conclusion by the country's ombudsman that the move was illegal. Some legal restrictions, distribution controls and economic pressures on press freedom remained in Albania, Bulgaria, Romania and Croatia.

Discrimination and ethnic tensions continued throughout the region. Gypsies were favorite targets of attack and discrimination in housing, employment and education, notably in Hungary, Romania and the Czech Republic. Crimes against Gypsies frequently were ignored by police. Serbia continued its repression of 2 million ethnic Albanians in Kosovo, and the brutalization of the beleaguered Muslim community in Sandjak along the Montenegrin-Bosnian border. While the Moravcik administration in Slovakia sought to ameliorate concerns of the 560,000-strong Hungarian minority by pushing through laws to safeguard the Hungarian language, the electoral return of Meciar, whose campaign, as well as his allies in the SNS, were marked by anti-Hungarian and anti-Semitic rhetoric, threatened to reignite tensions with Budapest. The rise of neo-fascists in Italy caused friction with Croatia and Slovenia over the territory of Istria, home to some 40,000 ethnic Italians, which Italy lost after World War II. Romanian-Hungarian relations remained strained over the substantial Hungarian minority in Transylvania, where rabid nationalist and mayor of Cluj, Gheorghe Funar, and his ultra-nationalist PRNU harassed and provoked Hungarians. Albania and Greece remained at loggerheads over the treatment of the Greek minority in Albania.

In a positive development, Macedonia's ethnic Albanians, one-third of the population, refused to take part in an opposition boycott of elections. They were encouraged to do so by Albanian President Sali Berisha. Macedonia's radical Albanian separatists apparently lost ground to elements committed to strengthening the country's democratic institutions. In Bulgaria, extreme nationalists with visions of a Greater Bulgaria, including parts of Macedonia, remained on the fringes. But given the historic volatility of ethnic relations, and the possible spread of the Bosnia war to the rest of the Balkans, minority issues continued to be a potential flashpoint.

Knocking on Europe's door

During the year, East-Central European nations stepped up efforts toward greater integration into Western economic and security bodies: the EU and NATO. Poland, the Czech Republic, Hungary, Slovakia, Bulgaria and Romania, already EU associate members, reiterated their goal of full membership. At its summit in Essen, the EU approved full membership for the six associate members by the year 2000. The EU's principal argument for forestalling eastward enlargement was the oft-repeated prerequisite that East-Central European states needed "functioning market economies" to join the club. Domestic political and economic factors also played a role, as EU quotas, duties and other barriers protected its own uncompetitive industries by restricting market access to East European products. Yet, the region's marked progress in implementing market economies made the argument for eastern expansion more compelling. Of the six associate members, all had private sectors that accounted for increased percentages of GDP; the level of subsidies in Eastern Europe was little higher than in many West European countries; budget deficits had been brought under control. To be sure impediments existed: high inflation, low incomes, underinvestment in infrastructure and restructuring of enterprises. Between 1990 and 1993, the EU associates together got less than $10 billion in direct foreign investment, compared with $15 billion to Singapore alone. As for income levels and rate of growth, Poland and Albania had the fastest growing economies in Europe, and East Europeans maintained that many of their economies compare favorably with Greece and Portugal and that rapid integration into the EU would boost investment and exports.

East European leaders continued to cite fears of Russian neo-imperialism, the war in Bosnia, the potential for ethnic wars, and Western resistance to an East-Central European collective security alliance as factors for their inclusion into NATO. However, prospects for early integration dimmed significantly in December when Russian President Boris Yeltsin bluntly told the fifty-two-nation Budapest summit meeting of the Conference on Security and Cooperation in Europe (CSCE) that NATO's eastward expansion was an attempt to split Europe.

Bosnia: Bihac and beyond

By year's end, the war against Bosnia-Herzegovina's legitimate government ground toward end-game. A desperate breakout from the Bihac pocket by government forces was thwarted by Bosnia Serbs and their Croatian Serb allies who threatened to overrun the U.N.-mandated "safe haven." Bickering between Western governments, the U.N. and NATO, which half-heartedly lobbed a few bombs at Serb targets in Croatia, resulted in the possibility of a U.N. withdrawal, sure to embolden Serb aggressors and Croat opportunists. The Bihac breakout was likely a last-ditch effort to prompt the West to intervene or lift the arms embargo, which had been tantalizingly dangled as an option by President Clinton, then dropped. Bosnia's sense of isolation increased, as several secret meetings in Austria and Knin (capital of the self-proclaimed Serb republic in Croatia's occupied Krajina section) between high-level Croat and Serb officials suggested a rapprochement between Belgrade and Croatia, notwithstanding the latter's stated commitment to an essentially unworkable U.S.-brokered "federation" between Bosnian Croats and Muslims with ties to Zagreb. Previous secret Serb-Croat meetings over Bosnia in the last two years boosted fears that Serbia and Croatia had always meant to carve up Bosnia between them. For the Bosnian government, Croatia could not be trusted, particularly after Croatian Army regulars joined the indigenous Croatian Defense Council (HVO) in Bosnia in bloody assaults on Bosnian Muslims early in the year. At year's end, diplomats went back to map-making, and the Bosnian government vowed a war of attrition. In a bitter speech to the CSCE meeting in Budapest, Bosnian President Alija Izetbegovic excoriated European and U.S. failure in Bosnia that portended "a worse world in which the relations between Europe and the U.S., the West and Russia, and the West and the Muslim world shall never again be the same."

Looking to the twenty-first century

The symbiosis between democratization and market reforms remained the principal dynamic in charting the region's course. But banks, stock markets, casinos and private kiosks are only part of the equation. With comparatively little Western aid, there has been an economic revolution in East-Central Europe. The habits of democracy are harder to instill and maintain, particularly when these traditions have been absent for generations, if not centuries. Yet steady progress has been made here too; all the countries have had several multiparty, free-and-fair elections, a range of civic, political and labor associations, an emerging free press, access to information and communication spurred by global technological revolution that has helped wed them to the rest of Europe.

To ensure the viability Vaclav Klaus's vision, enlightened Western engagement and commitment must continue. The nations of East-Central Europe need help with infrastructure. According to a December report by the U.N. Economic Commission for Europe they need a substantial increase in foreign investment, access to international capital markets, liberalization of trade with the West, and full integration in international economic structures. But Western economic planners should avoid a laissez-faire slash-and-burn strategy based on the arrogant misperception that nothing functioned in the region before IMF "shock therapy." The appeal of neo-Communists in the vast rural areas around the region has less to do with ideology and ignorance than with fears that functioning, relatively productive collective-private farm hybrids would be scrapped in the capitalist zeal to start from scratch.

East-Central Europe needs continued governmental, NGO and private assistance for ethnic mediation and conflict resolution, independent broadcast media development, judicial and legal reforms, and establishing modern police forces. And in light of Western failure in Bosnia, and the forces of deracination, revanchism and ativistic nationalism deeply-rooted in the regions' history, they must be integrated in European security structures, regardless of the concerns of Russia or others.

George Zarycky is Central European specialist for Freedom House.

The Survey of Press Freedom: "Pressticide" and Press Ethics

Leonard R. Sussman

Ironically, during the bloodiest "pressticidal" year on record—113 journalists murdered in 27 countries—governments in 1994 seemed more interested in "press ethics" than in journalists' safety.

While press ethics was debated even in the Council of Europe, 35 journalists in 16 countries were kidnapped or "disappeared." Another 265 newspersons were beaten or otherwise assaulted, and 311 arrested. Most were targeted for their reporting.

Thirty-seven were murdered in Rwanda since the massacres began 6 April. Seventeen were killed by religious extremist in Algeria. Eleven died, including 8 in Bosnia, covering wars or insurgencies. Most widespread were the 1,460 less fatal but no less censorious attacks in 108 countries—physical, psychological and economic assaults on journalists and news services. In 1993, 74 journalists were killed and 47 kidnapped.

In Russia in October, Dmitry Kholodov, a prominent investigative journalist, was blown to bits as he took a parcel supposedly containing, evidence of corruption in the military. Some 10,000 people attended his memorial service. "The journalist is everyone's enemy now," said a spokesman for the journalists' union. "Our whole society, the government, everyone is working against the press." Headlined the *Moscow News,* "We will not retreat from threats." At least 15 journalists were killed in the former Soviet Union this year, five in Russia alone.

When gunmen executed Mirwais Jalil, the British Broadcasting Corporation's best-known correspondent in Afghanistan, the BBC said plaintively, "We don't have our own guns to go out and take revenge. We only have our limited moral authority...and the weapon of publicity."

In Algeria, religious extremists murdered 25 journalists in eighteen months. Two were shot and beheaded. They were all "deliberately targeted," says the Committee to Protect Journalists. Similarly, the CPJ names 26 reporters and editors killed in Tajikistan the past 30 months. The government has total control over all Tajik media. Opposition papers have been closed.

Thousands of Nigerian newspersons were driven from their jobs in 1994 when the government banned 14 publications, including the three most influential media firms. Publicity to reveal such catastrophic attacks on the flow of in formation was hampered in at least forty countries which bar foreign news services or control the domestic news in monopoly.

The Council of Europe, a presumed bastion of Western freedoms, in December recommended that countries examine press "duties and responsibilities." That rationale for government intervention can have influence far beyond Western Europe. More than thirty governments in East/Central Europe, the former Soviet states, and some African countries are

Press Freedom Violations—1994

[ ]countries

A Journalists Killed	126 [27]
B Journalists Kidnapped; Disappeared	38 [17]
C Journalists Arrested; Detained	345+ [58]
D Journalists Expelled	43 [17]

A. Afghanistan-1; Algeria-24; Armenia-1; Belarus-2; Bosnia-8; Brazil-1; Burundi-1; Cambodia-3; Colombia-5; Egypt-2; Georgia-2; Guatemala-2; India-2; Iraq-1; Madagascar-1; Mexico-3; Nepal-1; Pakistan-2; Palestinian Territory-1; Philippines-1; Russia-11; Rwanda-37; Somalia-3; South Africa-3; Tajikistan-5; Turkey-1; Zaire-2.

B. Afghanistan-1; Algeria-7; Bosnia-1; Dominican Republic-2; Ethiopia-3; Guatemala-2; Haiti-2; India-2; Japan-1; Mexico-6; Namibia-2; Pakistan-1; Serbia-1; Sudan-1; Turkmenistan-1; Turkey-3; Yemen-1; Zaire-1.

C. Albania-36; Algeria-1; Angola-6; Austria-1; Azerbaijan-5; Bangladesh-2; Bosnia-2; Burundi-1; Cambodia-1; Cameroon-3; Cape Verde-1; Central African Rep. -1; China-13; Congo-2; Croatia-3; Dominican Republic-1; Egypt-10; Ethiopia-23; Gabon-2; Gambia-3; Georgia-1; Guatemala-1; Haiti-11; India-13; Indonesia-4; Israel-9; Ivory Coast-5; Jordan-1; Kazakhstan-1; Kenya-11; Malawi-1; Maldives-2; Mali-2; Mexico-1; Morocco-1; Myanamar-1; Nepal-4; Nigeria-9; Pakistan-6; Palestinian Terr. 11; Peru-5; Romania-1; Rwanda-1; Serbia-4; Sierra Leone-5; Slovakia-1; Sudan-5; Taiwan-1; Tajikstan-2; Tanzania-2; Togo-1; Turkey-83; United States-1; Uzbekistan-3; Yemen-1; Zaire-6; Zambia-9; Zimbabwe-1.

D. Albania-10; Azerbaijan-3; Bosnia-2; China-4; Egypt-1; Gabon-1; Gambia-1; Haiti-3; Indonesia-6; Kenya-1; S. Korea-1; Malaysia-1; Mali-1; Nigeria-3; Tunisia-1; Yugoslavia-3; Zaire-1.

OTHER STATISTICS

Journalists wounded	82+ [19]
Journalists beaten	59+ [21]
Journalists otherwise assaulted	134+ [32]
Death threats & other threats to journalists	118 [35]
Journalists' homes/offices raided; destroyed	26 [14]
Charges/sentences against journalists	83 [26]
Films, manuscripts; issues confiscated	55 [27]
Press credentials refused; expulsion threats	51+ [16]
Harassment of journalists	135+ [38]
Closed publications; radio/tv	35 [14]
Banned/suspended publications; radios/tv	152+ [28]
Bombed; burned publications; radios/tv	14 [10]
Occupied publications; radios/tv	3+ [3]

Total violations against journalists: I,499 (in 111 countries)

—Jessie Miller

—Kristen Guida

devising press laws. The flexible Western European approach, rather than America's strict First-Amendment protection of the press, is a welcome guide for new press-controllers.

In free countries, legislating, ethical performance leads to clashes of rights. Press freedom is challenged, for example, when a law guarantees the right of a citizen to reply when he disagrees with a published statement about him. Germany's Saarland passed a press law in October requiring newspapers to make equal space available to an individual seeking, to rebut a published article. France has a similar law, seldom invoked. The U.S. Supreme Court has several times declared the right of reply unconstitutional, saying only a journalist can decide what he should publish. The Council of Europe now recommends instituting the right of reply.

Journalists in free societies understand that an ethical lapse is an abuse of freedom, yet they believe statutes should not dictate what is or is not responsible journalism. Where press freedom exists, practices that raise ethical questions diminish the public's trust in the press and eventually in the society.

The Associated Press managing editors (APME) in October approved a revised code of ethics after a year-long debate. Some 27 percent of the editors, though, voted against the code. Some believed it would give lawyers a chance "to take us to court." The majority, however, wanted to display its principles for an increasingly mistrustful public. The code addresses such issues as diversity in staffing and coverage, plagiarism and electronic photo manipulation.

Intervention by government, however, threatens not only press freedom but the right of citizens to the free flow of information. Not surprisingly, then, many governments open press-ethics debates to influence the content of the news flow. A classic example of governmental enforcement of journalists' ethics is the warning issued by Slovak Prime Minister Vladimir Meciar, who told Slovak journalists:

A citizen has the right to obtain truthful information, and the state has to guarantee it....[E]ither you, the journalists, do it of your own free will, and protect citizens from lies and manipulations, or...the state has to do it....Of course...the state organs [c]ould divide the dailies and media into the "vulgar press" and the "serious press." [and] differentiate your incomes according to the tax code.

The Russian case

Throughout the year, the Russian Duma (parliament) tussled with draft press laws. The Russian Federation statute on the mass media signed into law by Boris Yeltsin in 1991 is being redrafted. As in freer countries, some journalists act irresponsibly. To bring some order to the scene, the Union of Russian Journalists this year drafted a code of ethics. The code, said the union secretary, would have journalists "voluntarily assuming serious responsibilities and a readiness to civilize the activities of the Russian press."

To be sure, the most draconian provisions in the Russian statute have gone unenforced. There is great diversity among Russian newspapers, though radio and television remain under strict central control. The lower chamber of the Duma early in 1994 approved an amendment to control the content of broadcast news, but it was not likely to go forward. Later, the Duma voted to bar the government from owning newspapers. The practice had enabled non-Communists to establish newspapers since there were still 157 pro-Communist papers. Another bill proposed financial support for newspapers, the funds to be doled out by the Duma. The Duma would thus bar control of the press by the Executive, but assume control for the Parliament. President Yeltsin publicly opposed the plan.

It will take time for the new democracies in the East to develop the ingrained standards of civil and ethical concerns reflected in traditional Western press relationships. This requires tolerance toward opposition views, airing of conflicting positions, and respect for political processes. Most of these requirements, though sometimes skirted in the West, are generally absent in states formerly in the Soviet empire. Western governments, which bridle at what they regard as press excesses in their own countries, do little to insist on greater press freedom in the newly liberated nations. While a responsible press is desirable, it is impossible to legislate "responsibility"; or, given freedom of expression, rule out errors of fact, poor judgment or insensitivity in the press.

How ethical, how free?

What, then, of the press's moral authority? This rests mainly on the degree of press freedom permitted by the respective government. (See table on page 66.) In 57 countries, 31 percent of the nations, the press is not free and has little authority, moral or otherwise. In 62 countries (33 percent), the press is partly free, and in 67 nations (36 percent) the news media are free. Even in many of these, their moral authority is repeatedly challenged, most notably by political debates over press ethics. Draft statutes assigning moral standards for journalism subtly avoid the onus of government censorship, while placing newspersons on the defensive for acts labeled licentious or subversive, unprotected by guarantees of press freedom.

Press freedom is judged by the independence from government of the news media, and the absence of political, economic, social and occupational influences on journalists and media managers by government officials.

In The Gambia, relatively free until the military coup in July, the constitutional provision protecting freedom of expression was negated. A military decree gives the government far-reaching powers of censorship, specifically banning reports deemed political. The Gambia's media are now listed as "not free."

Malawi and Guyana entered the free-press category from partly free. Antigua & Barbuda and Venezuela went from free to partly free. Cameroon, Haiti, Kuwait and Uganda rose from not free to partly free. Entering the not-free group were Indonesia, Kazakhstan, Kenya, Nigeria, Yemen and Zambia-all had been partly free.

The government of Kenya is trying to "bully us into self-censorship," said David Makali, a writer for *The People* who was beaten in prison and forced to break stones for five hours a day. Charges of sedition and contempt of court, rather than direct censorship, have served to restrict press freedom in recent years. The government promises to present a new press law in 1995 to address access and dissemination of information, as well as the latest concern for professional ethics and standards.

Elsewhere in Africa, parliaments have pondered press laws linked to ethical standards. The Botswana legislature passed an anti-corruption bill which could threaten press freedom. The bill permits the confiscation of documents and information from the media which could force them to reveal their sources. It would also empower the government to search newsrooms. Anyone who "fails to provide any information or to answer any questions ... shall be guilty of an offense." Botswana's press, long free, is under fire.

Tanzania again theoretically expanded press freedom, only to crack down when some liberty was used by journalists to criticize the government. For months, the government tried unsuccessfully to create a media council in which journalists under official guidance would regulate press ethics and responsibility. That failed, the government turned to intimidation of the press by police and the courts. Under the 1976 Newspaper Act the minister of information can ban papers said to be a "danger" to the nation. A reporter and the publisher of *Express* were arrested and charged with sedition for claiming in graphic terms that Tanzania has become a dumping ground for expired medicines, food and chemicals. Meanwhile, the government encouraged the expansion of television and radio outlets, including several privately owned. But government propaganda over Radio Tanzania makes it impossible for opposition parties to be heard. There was competition between two independent TV channels, however, for beaming World Cup soccer.

Official censorship was lifted in Cameroon because the journalists pledged to adopt a code of ethics and establish a national journalist body to implement the code "rigorously." This code of press ethics, hardly voluntary at the outset, will be watched to see whether it results in government-sponsored self-censorship or an earnest effort by journalists and the government to permit professional integrity, if not self-censorship, to develop.

In Uganda, the government's mass media bill would create a media council to license journalists and register newspapers. The journalists association said the act would "severely limit press freedom." The association acknowledged that official censorship had not been applied for some time, and that the media had, on occasion, outraged public sensibilities. The journalists submitted their own draft law to meet "the government's sworn need to have statutory control of the press, and the journalists' own need to remain independent and autonomous."

Press licensing in the Americas

The licensing of the press became a contentious issue again in South and Central America this year. The journalists association of Costa Rica, known as the Colegio de Periodistas, formally proposed that the nation's constitution be amended to make licensing of journalists obligatory. For many years, Costa Rica's licensing of journalists has prevented all but members of the Colegio from working in the news media. When this law was challenged in 1985, the Inter-American Court of Human Rights ruled that mandatory licensing denies freedom of expression, and is "incompatible" with the American Convention on Human Rights. Costa Rica and a dozen other countries in the hemisphere, however, continue to license journalists. The Costa Rica Colegio argues that licensing maintains the standard of journalism and protects the working conditions of journalists. The practice also limits competition for jobs, while giving censorious governments a tool to de-license journalist critics. At year-end, Venezuela made a Colegio certificate mandatory for work in the press.

Costa Rica's Supreme Court surprised journalists throughout the hemisphere in July by imposing restrictions on the right of the press to report an investigation in progress. To protect privacy, the court ruled the press cannot identify the subjects of a criminal investigation. The same week, a columnist became the first reporter ever convicted of *desacato*, "irreverence," or offending the honor of a public official. This offense increasingly appears in proposed codes of press ethics in many countries. Costa Rica still is in the free-press column.

Europe and Asia/Pacific

The Turkish press, particularly those reporting Kurdish demands, suffered the greatest harassment anywhere (except for the number of murders elsewhere). In addition to one killing and 3 disappearances in Turkey, there were 49 arrests, 18 physical assaults on journalists and some 30 other cases of harassment. Although the government promised to amend the Law to Fight Terrorism, often used to intimidate journalists, little progress was made. The Turkish press is partly free.

In Romania amendments were proposed to the penal code that would condemn journalists to two years longer in prison than nonjournalists for slandering or insulting a civil servant. If a journalist publishes information "proven true" he would face prison from six months to three years. The lower house of parliament was considering even harsher penalties for journalists who insult or slander the president of Romania.

The Cambodian government in November asked the National Assembly to approve a draft press laws to make defamation punishable by a prison term. Insulting the king would draw a three-year jail sentence. Newspapers have been shut down, and three journalists murdered. The press generally is under attack.

In November, China sentenced Gao Yu, a dissident journalist, to six years in prison. She had been held in detention since October 1993, just days before she was to start a one-year research fellowship at Columbia University. She was tried without counsel for "leaking state secrets." Her arrest has particular significance for press freedom in Hong Kong after China resumes control there in 1997. Ms. Gao had written for *Mirror Monthly*, a Chinese-language magazine in Hong Kong.

Singapore explained its pervasive velvet censorship in handling the case of Christopher Lingle, an American academic who criticized Singapore's "compliant judiciary" in the *International Herald-Tribune*. The country's ambassador to the U.S. repeated earlier official threats to Lingle, and said he may be charged with "contempt of court or criminal defamation." Clearly, full freedom of the press-even the right of a foreign national to write in a foreign newspaper about Singapore—does not exist in that country's tightly controlled press. Lingle left Singapore, rather than face extensive litigation—or worse.

Some brighter signs

Throughout the year, advocates gained ever-widening approval for detailed declarations of press freedom (see box, page 67).

Better rating can be given the British news media after the broadcasting ban on certain Northern Ireland activists was lifted 16 September. The ban—imposed October 1988 by the Home Secretary—applied to the British Broadcasting Corporation (BBC) and the Independent Broadcasting Association (IBA). They were forbidden to carry words spoken by, or soliciting support for, representatives of illegal Republican or Loyalist paramilitary organizations. Also banned were several legal political organizations such as the political arm of the Irish Republican Army (IRA), Sinn Fein, and the Ulster Defense Association, a Loyalist armed group from the Protestant community. The ban was repeatedly opposed by British journalists as a restriction of their freedom.

A landmark victory was won in May by UK journalists who sought to protect their sources. The European Commission of Human Rights in Strasbourg upheld the claim of William Goodwin, a reporter four years earlier for *The Engineer*. A British

High Court had ordered Goodwin to reveal a confidential source of information. He refused and was fined for contempt. The European Commission ruled that "protection of the sources from which journalists derive information is an essential means of enabling the press to perform its important function of 'public watchdog' in a democratic society." American Supreme Court decisions, however, hold that a journalist is a citizen first and must respond to a court's subpoena to supply information needed to provide a fair trial to a defendant.

Elsewhere, restrictions on news media were eased. The upper house of the Polish Parliament in October rejected a proposed law to protect state secrets. This Official Secrets Act would impose stiff prison terms for disclosing information the government considers vital to its interests. If the lower house overturns this decision, President Lech Walesa would decide whether to veto this bill.

In Malawi, following the May election which ended thirty years of dictatorial rule, there was an outpouring of private newspapers. Censorship ended. The laws permitting it must now be repealed. The interim constitution does, indeed, pledge freedom for the media.

Following the Israeli-PLO handshake and peace with Jordan, journalists in Israel have begun seeking an end to military censorship. The censor provides a daily list of topics that must be submitted for approval. The chief censor does not see an end to his job, but journalists are more restive than ever. A decision will clearly depend on how arrangements with the PLO, and eventually Syria and Lebanon, work on the ground.

Ethics in the U.S.

A Times-Mirror national poll in October found 71 percent of Americans agreeing "the news media get in the way of solutions [in solving problems], while 25 percent said they help." This malaise seems to reflect not solely the performance of the news media but the interaction between them and the political candidates taking the lowest roads during the 1994 electoral campaigns. The high percentage of negative advertising by politicians of all parties created spectacular charges, distortions of facts, and some blatant lies. The news outlets received blame for more than their own lapses of ethical performance.

Peter Kann, publisher of the *Wall Street Journal,* told the Inter-American Press Association, "Journalism that puts too high a priority on entertaining is almost destined to distort and mislead. Entertainment that masquerades as news is even more insidious because it taints and tarnishes real journalism," said Kann. He also criticized the blurring of lines between news and opinion, the pitfalls in "pack journalism" (peer pressure to convey "conventional wisdom" and "political correctness"), an exaggerated tendency toward pessimism, fascination with the bizarre, the perverse and pathological, coupled with a "strain of puritanism" that prosecutes public figures for lapses in their private lives which have little to do with their public performance.

Leonard R. Sussman is senior scholar in communications of Freedom House, and adjunct professor of journalism and mass communication at New York University.

The Map of Freedom—1995

(Numbers refer to the map, pages 77-78)

FREE STATES

6 Andorra
10 Argentina
13 Australia
14 Austria
17 Bahamas
20 Barbados
22 Belgium
23 Belize
24 Benin
27 Bolivia
30 Botswana
34 Bulgaria
40 Canada
42 Cape Verde
48 Chile
57 Costa Rica
60 Cyprus (G)
62 Czech Republic
63 Denmark
65 Dominica
68 Ecuador
73 Estonia
78 Finland
79 France
85 Germany
88 Greece
90 Grenada
96 Guyana
100 Hungary
101 Iceland
106 Ireland
109 Israel
110 Italy
112 Jamaica
113 Japan
118 Kiribati
120 Korea (S)
126 Latvia
131 Liechtenstein
132 Lithuania
133 Luxembourg
139 Malawi
143 Malta
144 Marshall Islands
147 Mauritius
150 Micronesia
152 Monaco
153 Mongolia
158 Namibia
159 Nauru
161 Netherlands
164 New Zealand
172 Norway
176 Palau
177 Panama
183 Poland
184 Portugal
193 St. Kitts-Nevis
194 St. Lucia
196 St. Vincent and the Grenadines
197 San Marino
198 Sao Tome & Principe
204 Slovakia
205 Slovenia
206 Solomon Isls.
208 South Africa
209 Spain
215 Sweden
216 Switzerland
227 Trinidad & Tobago
232 Tuvalu
236 United Kingdom
237 United States
238 Uruguay
240 Vanuatu
248 Western Samoa

FREE RELATED TERRITORIES

2 Aland Is. (Fin.)
5 Amer. Samoa (US)
8 Anguilla (UK)
12 Aruba (Ne)
16 Azores (Port)
25 Bermuda (UK)
32 Br. Vir. Is. (UK)
41 Canary Is. (Sp)
43 Cayman Is. (UK)
45 Ceuta (Sp)
47 Channel Is. (UK)
50 Christmas Is. (Austral.)
52 Cocos (Keeling Is.) (Austral.)
56 Cook Is. (NZ)
75 Faeroe Is. (Den)
76 Falkland Is. (UK)
80 French Guiana (Fr)
81 French Polynesia (Fr)
87 Gibraltar (UK)
89 Greenland (Den)
91 Guadeloupe (Fr)
92 Guam (US)
108 Isle of Man (UK)
137 Madeira (Port)
138 Mahore (Mayotte) (Fr)
145 Martinique (Fr)
148 Melilla (Sp)
154 Montserrat (UK)
162 Ne. Antilles (Ne)
163 New Caledonia (Fr)
168 Niue (NZ)
169 Norfolk Is. (Austral.)
171 No. Marianas (US)
182 Pitcairn Islands (UK)
185 Puerto Rico (US)
187 Rapanui (Easter Is.) (Chile)
188 Reunion (Fr)
192 St. Helena and Dependencies (UK)
192a Ascencion
192b Tristan da Cunha
195 St. Pierre-Mq. (Fr)
213 Svalbard (Norway)
224 Tokelau (NZ)
231 Turks & Caicos Isls. (UK)
244 Virgin Isls. (US)
246 Wallis & Futuna Isls. (Fr)

PARTLY FREE STATES

3 Albania
9 Antigua & Barbuda
11 Armenia
19 Bangladesh
21 Belarus
31 Brazil
35 Burkina Faso
38 Cambodia
44 Central African Republic
53 Colombia
54 Comoros
55 Congo
58 Croatia
66 Dominican Republic
70 El Salvador
77 Fiji
82 Gabon
84 Georgia
86 Ghana
93 Guatemala
95 Guinea-Bissau
97 Haiti
98 Honduras
102 India
114 Jordan
123 Kuwait
124 Kyrgyz Republic
127 Lebanon
128 Lesotho
135 Macedonia
136 Madagascar
140 Malaysia
142 Mali
149 Mexico
151 Moldova
155 Morocco
156 Mozambique
160 Nepal
165 Nicaragua
166 Niger
175 Pakistan
178 Papua New Guinea
179 Paraguay
180 Peru
181 Philippines
189 Romania
190 Russia
200 Senegal
201 Seychelles
203 Singapore
210 Sri Lanka
212 Suriname
218 Taiwan (China)
221 Thailand
225 Tonga
229 Turkey
233 Uganda
234 Ukraine
242 Venezuela
252 Zambia
253 Zimbabwe

PARTLY FREE RELATED TERRITORIES

61 Cyprus (T)
99 Hong Kong (UK)
122 Kurdistan (Iraq)
134 Macao (Port)
170 Northern Ireland (UK)

NOT FREE STATES

1 Afghanistan
4 Algeria
7 Angola
15 Azerbaijan
18 Bahrain
26 Bhutan
29 Bosnia-Herzegovina
33 Brunei
36 Burma (Myanmar)
37 Burundi
39 Cameroon
46 Chad
49 China (PRC)
59 Cuba
64 Djibouti
69 Egypt
71 Equatorial Guinea
72 Eritrea
74 Ethiopia
83 The Gambia
94 Guinea
103 Indonesia
104 Iran
105 Iraq
111 Ivory Coast
116 Kazakhstan
117 Kenya
119 Korea (N)
125 Laos
129 Liberia
130 Libya
141 Maldives
146 Mauritania
167 Nigeria
174 Oman
186 Qatar
191 Rwanda
199 Saudi Arabia
202 Sierra Leone
207 Somalia
211 Sudan
214 Swaziland
217 Syria
219 Tajikistan
220 Tanzania
223 Togo
228 Tunisia
230 Turkmenistan
235 United Arab Emirates
239 Uzbekistan
243 Vietnam
249 Yemen
250 Yugoslavia
251 Zaire

NOT FREE RELATED TERRITORIES

67 East Timor (Indo.)
107 Irian Jaya (Indo.)
115 Kashmir (India)
121 Kosovo (Yugo.)
157 Nagorno-Karabakh (Armenia-Azerbaijan)
173 Occupied Territories & Palestinian Autonomous Areas (Isr.)
222 Tibet (China)
245 Vojvodina (Yugo.)
247 Western Sahara (Mor.)

This Map of Freedom is based on data developed by Freedom House's Comparative Survey of Freedom. The *Survey* analyzes factors such as the degree to which fair and competitive elections occur, individual and group freedoms are guaranteed in practice, and press freedom exists. More detailed and up-to-date *Survey* information may be obtained from Freedom House.

89

101

75

PACIFIC OCEAN

40

237

ATLANTIC OCEAN

108
170
106   236

79

16

184   209

25

137   87 45
       155   14

41
247   146   142

35
200   86
83   94
95   202   111
129

192a

237

149

17
59   185 244
      231   32
97   8 193 9
           154
43   91
23   65
112   162 66   145
      227 90   194
12   196
165   20
96   242 212 80
57   53
177   68
       180   31
       27
48   179
      238
10

5
168   81
56
182   187

76

FREEDOM
HOUSE

FREE ☐   PARTLY FREE ▨   NOT FREE ■

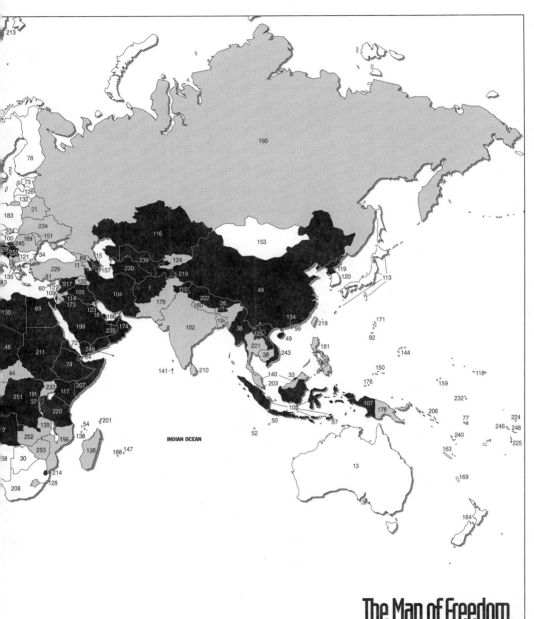

The Map of Freedom

JANUARY 1995 ©FREEDOM HOUSE

INDIAN OCEAN

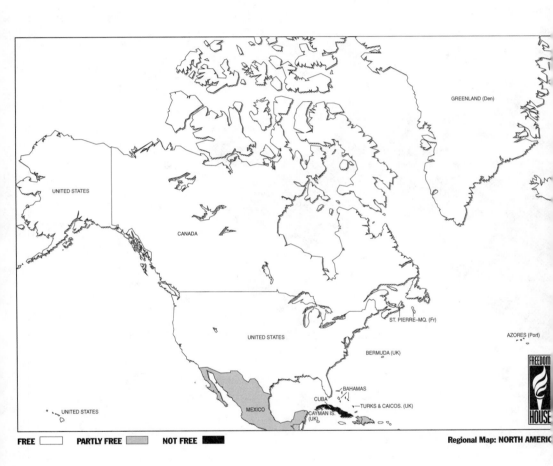

GREENLAND (Den)

UNITED STATES

CANADA

UNITED STATES

ST. PIERRE–MQ. (Fr)

AZORES (Port)

BERMUDA (UK)

BAHAMAS

CUBA

TURKS & CAICOS. (UK)

MEXICO

CAYMAN IS.
(UK)

UNITED STATES

FREEDOM HOUSE

FREE   **PARTLY FREE**   **NOT FREE**   **Regional Map: NORTH AMERIC**

MEXICO

GUATEMALA
BELIZE
HONDURAS
EL SALVADOR
NICARAGUA
COSTA RICA
PANAMA

CAYMAN IS. (UK)
JAMAICA

CUBA
HAITI
DOMINICAN REP.
NE. ANTILLES (Ne)
ARUBA (Ne)

TURKS & CAICOS. (UK)

PUERTO RICO (US)
VIRGIN IS. (US)
BR. VIRGIN IS. (UK)
ANGUILLA (UK)
ST. KITTS–NEVIS
ANTIGUA & BARBUDA
MONTSERRAT (UK)
GUADELOUPE (Fr)
DOMINICA
MARTINIQUE (Fr)
ST. LUCIA
ST. VINCENT AND THE GRENADINES
GRENADA
BARBADOS
TRINIDAD & TOBAGO

VENEZUELA
COLOMBIA
GUYANA
SURINAME
FRENCH GUIANA (Fr)

ECUADOR

PERU

BRAZIL

BOLIVIA

RAPANUI/EASTER IS. (Chile)
PITCAIRN IS. (UK)

PARAGUAY

CHILE

URUGUAY

ARGENTINA

FALKLAND IS. (UK)

FREEDOM HOUSE

FREE ☐   PARTLY FREE ▒   NOT FREE ▓   **Regional Map: SOUTH AMERICA**

FREE ☐ PARTLY FREE ▨ NOT FREE ■

Regional Map: EURO

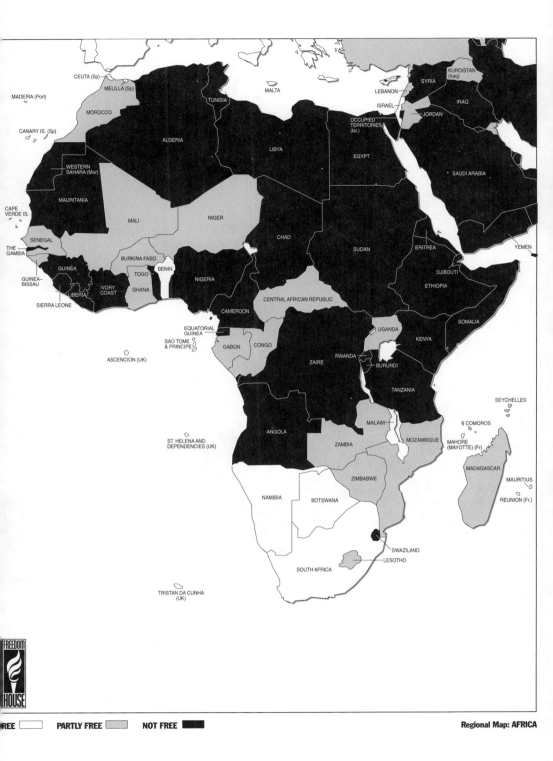

CEUTA (Sp)
MELILLA (Sp)
MADEIRA (Port)
MOROCCO
CANARY IS. (Sp)
WESTERN SAHARA (Mor)
CAPE VERDE IS.
MAURITANIA
SENEGAL
THE GAMBIA
GUINEA-BISSAU
GUINEA
SIERRA LEONE
LIBERIA
IVORY COAST
GHANA
TOGO
BENIN
BURKINA FASO
MALI
NIGER
ALGERIA
TUNISIA
MALTA
LIBYA
EGYPT
NIGERIA
CHAD
SUDAN
CENTRAL AFRICAN REPUBLIC
CAMEROON
EQUATORIAL GUINEA
SAO TOME & PRINCIPE
ASCENCION (UK)
GABON
CONGO
ZAIRE
UGANDA
RWANDA
BURUNDI
KENYA
ERITREA
DJIBOUTI
ETHIOPIA
SOMALIA
SEYCHELLES
TANZANIA
MALAWI
COMOROS
MOZAMBIQUE
MAHORE (MAYOTTE) (Fr)
ST. HELENA AND DEPENDENCIES (UK)
ANGOLA
ZAMBIA
ZIMBABWE
MADAGASCAR
MAURITIUS
REUNION (Fr.)
NAMIBIA
BOTSWANA
SWAZILAND
LESOTHO
SOUTH AFRICA
TRISTAN DA CUNHA (UK)
KURDISTAN (Iraq)
SYRIA
LEBANON
ISRAEL
OCCUPIED TERRITORIES (Isr.)
JORDAN
IRAQ
SAUDI ARABIA
YEMEN

FREEDOM HOUSE

REE ☐ PARTLY FREE ☐ NOT FREE ■ Regional Map: AFRICA

RUSSIA

KAZAKHSTAN

MONGOLIA

TURKMENISTAN

UZBEKISTAN

NAGORNO
KARABAKH
(Arm./Azer.)

GEORGIA

ARMENIA

LEBANON

SYRIA

AZERBAIJAN

KURDISTAN
(Iraq)

IRAQ

IRAN

KUWAIT

KYRGYZ
REPUBLIC

TAJIKISTAN

AFGHANISTAN

PAKISTAN

KASHMIR
(India)

NEPAL

BANGLADESH

TIBET
(China)

BHUTAN

CHINA (PRC)

KOREA (N)

KOREA (S)

JAPAN

TAIWAN
(ROC)

FREEDOM HOUSE

FREE   PARTLY FREE   NOT FREE

Regional Map: RUSSIA AND CENTRAL AND EAST AS

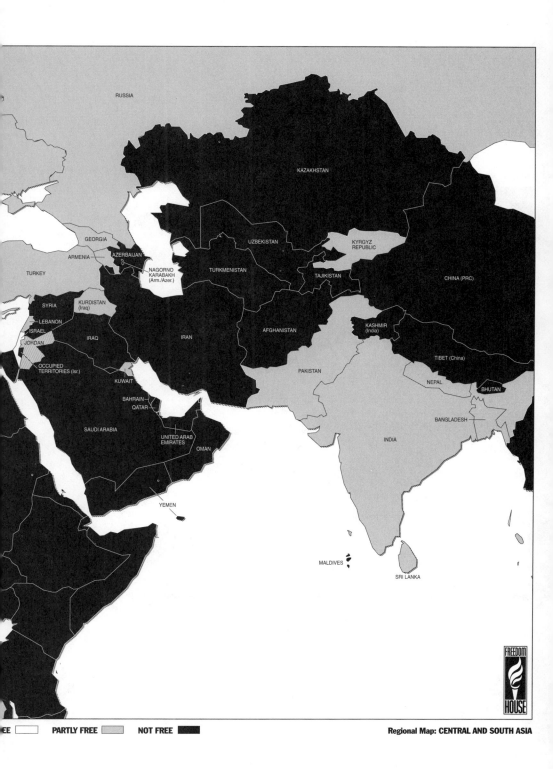

RUSSIA

KAZAKHSTAN

GEORGIA

ARMENIA   AZERBAIJAN

TURKEY

NAGORNO
KARABAKH
(Arm./Azer.)

UZBEKISTAN

KYRGYZ
REPUBLIC

TURKMENISTAN

TAJIKISTAN

CHINA (PRC)

SYRIA   KURDISTAN
(Iraq)

LEBANON

ISRAEL
JORDAN   IRAQ   IRAN   AFGHANISTAN

KASHMIR
(India)

OCCUPIED
TERRITORIES (Isr.)

TIBET (China)

KUWAIT

PAKISTAN   NEPAL   BHUTAN

BAHRAIN
QATAR

BANGLADESH

SAUDI ARABIA   UNITED ARAB
EMIRATES   OMAN

INDIA

YEMEN

MALDIVES   SRI LANKA

FREE   **PARTLY FREE**   **NOT FREE**   Regional Map: **CENTRAL AND SOUTH ASIA**

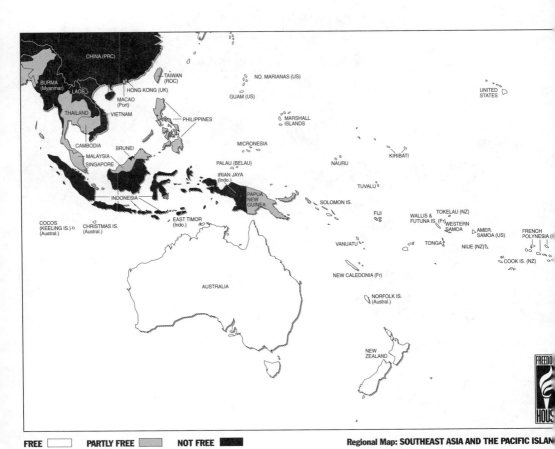

CHINA (PRC)

BURMA
(Myanmar)

LAOS

THAILAND

VIETNAM

TAIWAN
(ROC)

HONG KONG (UK)

MACAO
(Port)

CAMBODIA

BRUNEI

MALAYSIA
SINGAPORE

INDONESIA

COCOS
(KEELING IS.)
(Austral.)

CHRISTMAS IS.
(Austral.)

PHILIPPINES

PALAU (BELAU)

IRIAN JAYA
(Indo.)

EAST TIMOR
(Indo.)

PAPUA
NEW
GUINEA

NO. MARIANAS (US)

GUAM (US)

MICRONESIA

MARSHALL
ISLANDS

NAURU

SOLOMON IS.

KIRIBATI

TUVALU

FIJI

VANUATU

NEW CALEDONIA (Fr)

NORFOLK IS.
(Austral.)

WALLIS &
FUTUNA IS. (Fr)

TOKELAU (NZ)

WESTERN
SAMOA

TONGA

AMER.
SAMOA (US)

NIUE (NZ)

COOK IS. (NZ)

UNITED
STATES

FRENCH
POLYNESIA (

AUSTRALIA

NEW
ZEALAND

FREEDO
HOUS

FREE PARTLY FREE NOT FREE

Regional Map: SOUTHEAST ASIA AND THE PACIFIC ISLAN

Introduction to Country and Related Territory Reports

The *Survey* team at Freedom House wrote reports on 191 countries and 58 related territories.

Palau changes from territory to country in this edition. Four black homelands that were territories in previous *Survey*s appear no more, because they were integrated into South Africa in 1994.

Each report begins with brief political, economic, and social data. This information is arranged under the following headings: **polity, economy, political rights, civil liberties, status, population, purchasing power parities (PPP), population, life expectancy,** and **ethnic groups.** There is also a brief explanation of **ratings changes and trends** since the last yearbook. When actual events changed the rating and trends, a succinct explanation follows. Readers interested in understanding the derivation of the ratings in this *Survey* should consult the chapter on methodology.

More detailed information follows in an **overview** and in an essay on the **political rights** and **civil liberties** of each country.

Under **polity**, there is an encapsulated description of the dominant centers of freely chosen or unelected political power in each country. Most of the descriptions are self-explanatory, such as Communist one-party for China or parliamentary democracy for Ireland. Such non-parliamentary democracies as the United States of America are designated presidential-legislative democracies. European democratic countries with constitutional monarchs are designated parliamentary democracies, because the elected body is the locus of most real political power. Only countries with powerful monarchs (e.g. the Sultan of Brunei) warrant a reference to the monarchy in the brief description of the polity. Dominant party polities are systems in which the ruling party (or front) dominates government, but allows other parties to organize or compete short of taking control of government. There are other types of polities listed as well. Among them are various military and military-influenced or -dominated regimes, transitional systems, and several unique polities, such as Iran's clergy-dominated parliamentary system. Countries with genuine federalism have the word "federal" in the polity description.

The reports label the **economy** of each country. Non-industrial economies are called traditional or pre-industrial. Developed market economies and Third World economies with a modern market sector have the designation capitalist. Mixed capitalist countries combine private enterprise with substantial government involvement in the economy for social welfare purposes. Capitalist-statist economies have both large market sectors and government-owned productive enterprises, due either to elitist economic policies or state dependence on key natural resource industries. Mixed capitalist-statist economies have the characteristics of capitalist-statist economies plus major social welfare programs. Statist systems have the goal of placing the entire economy under direct or indirect government control. Mixed statist economies are primarily government-controlled, but also have significant private enterprise. Developing Third

World economies with a government-directed modern sector belong in the statist category. Economies in transition between statist and capitalist forms may have the word "transitional" in the economy description.

Each country report mentions the category of **political rights** and **civil liberties** in which Freedom House classified the country. Category 1 is the most free and category 7 is the least free in each case. **Status** refers to the designations "free," "partly free," and "not free," which Freedom House uses as an overall summary of the general state of freedom in the country.

The ratings of countries and territories that are different from those of the previous year are marked with an asterisk (*). The reasons for the change precede the "Overview" of the country or territory.

Each entry includes a **population** figure which is sometimes the best approximation that is available. For all cases in which the information is available, the *Survey* provides **life expectancy** statistics.

Freedom House obtained the **Purchasing Power Parities (PPP)** from the U.N. Development Program. These figures show per capita gross domestic product (GDP) in terms of international dollars. The PPP statistic adjusts GDP to account for real buying power. For some countries, especially for newly independent countries, tiny island states, and those with statist economies, these statistics were unavailable.

The *Survey* provides a listing of countries' **ethnic groups**, because this information may help the reader understand such questions as minority rights which the Survey takes into account.

Each country summary has an **overview** which describes such matters as the most important events of 1994 and current political issues. Finally, the country reports contain a section on **political rights** and **civil liberties**. This section summarizes each country's degree of respect for the rights and liberties that Freedom House uses to evaluate freedom in the world. These summaries include instances of human rights violations by both governmental and non-governmental entities.

Reports on related territories follow the country summaries. In most cases, these reports are comparatively brief and contain fewer categories of information than one finds in the country summaries.

Afghanistan

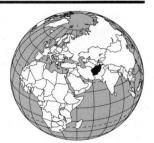

Polity: Competing war- **Political Rights:** 7
lords, traditional rulers, **Civil Liberties:** 7
and local councils **Status:** Not Free
Economy: Mixed-statist
Population: 17,846,000
PPP: $700
Life Expectancy: 42.9
Ethnic Groups: Pashtun, Tajik, Uzbek, Hazara

Overview: The near total collapse of governance and civil society in Afghanistan continued in 1994 as rival Islamic militias laid waste to the capital, Kabul, in a fierce power struggle. Nominal President Burhanuddin Rabbani and his main rival, radical fundamentalist Gulbuddin Hekmatyar, were the main protagonists in battles that had more to do with power than ideology.

Decades of Russian and British influence in Afghanistan ended in 1919 when the British relinquished control over the country's foreign affairs. A series of coups and assassinations brought instability until King Mohamed Zahir Shah came to power in 1933. King Shah ruled until 1973, when his cousin deposed him in a coup and established a republic. In April 1978 the Khalq faction of the Communist People's Democratic Party of Afghanistan (PDPA) came to power in another coup.

On 24 December 1979 the Soviet Union began airlifting tens of thousands of troops into Kabul and three days later deposed unpopular President Hafizollah Amin in favor of his rival, Babrak Karmal of the PDPA's Parcham faction. The Soviets soon had 115,000 troops in Afghanistan but were unable to overcome fierce resistance from rebel *mujahideen* fighters supported directly by Iran and Pakistan, and covertly by China, the U.S. and others. In May 1986 the Soviets replaced Karmal with secret service head Mohammad Najibullah, who proved no more effective against the mujahideen. Faced with a stalemate as well as mounting domestic problems, the Soviet Union withdrew its last troops in February 1989.

The collapse of the Soviet Union in December 1991 hastened the fall of the Afghan government. In January 1992 powerful General Abdul Rashid Dostam, an Uzbek, defected to the mujahideen and established his own militia. In April Kabul finally fell to the mujahideen, and the rebels proclaimed the Islamic Republic of Afghanistan. A Pashtun cleric, Sigbatullah Mojaddidi, took over as head of state under a two-year, three-phase, power-sharing plan designed to lead to elections.

Fighting immediately broke out among the mujahideen forces. Gulbuddin Hekmatyar, the ethnic Pashtun leader of the anti-Western, militant fundamentalist Hizb-i-Islami (Islamic Party), turned his troops on the Jamiat-i-Islami (Islamic Society) headed by Burhanuddin Rabbani, an ethnic Tajik, and military commander Ahmed Shah Masoud. The majority Pashtuns, who have ruled the country in various forms for 250 years, and the Tajiks are the two largest ethnic groups, and the Hekmatyar-Rabbani feud reflected in part long-standing power disputes between the two groups.

In June 1993 the second phase of the transitional power-sharing plan began as Rabbani took over as president of a Leadership Council for a planned four-month term. Fighting continued among the militias, particularly between the Sunni Muslim Ittehad-i-Islami group backed by Saudi Arabia, and the Iranian-backed, Shiite Hizb-i-Wahadat group, which demanded greater representation in the interim government. By late August several thousand civilians were killed and 6,000 others driven out of the capital.

On 30 December a Grand Council of tribal elders, religious leaders and militia commanders elected Rabbani to a two-year presidential term. However, five of the nine mujahideen factions boycotted the vote, including Hekmatyar's Hizb-i-Islami. By this point four major groups controlled most of the country. In the north, Dostam's Uzbek-dominated militia, the most powerful armed group, ruled six provinces from a base in Mazar-i-Sharif, 180 miles north of Kabul. The Jamiat-i-Islami controlled most of the capital and parts of other areas. The Hizb-i-Wahadat controlled six provinces in central Afghanistan. The largest area, in the south and east, was dominated by Pashtuns loyal to Hekmatyar.

As fighting continued, on 1 January 1993 the Grand Council formed a parliament from among 20 percent of its 1,355 members. A peace accord brokered by Pakistan in early March called for Rabbani to remain president until mid-1994 and for Hekmatyar to be named prime minister. The Islamabad Accord also stipulated elections would be held within eight months for a constituent assembly, which would draft a new constitution. A new Leadership Council shared power among eight mujahideen parties, but at Hekmatyar's bequest the factions excluded Dostam because he was a former Communist.

In September the government announced that rebel leaders had approved an interim constitution to carry the country through general elections in mid-1994. However, factional fighting broke out in the capital again in October, as the Shiite Wahadat militia objected to the constitutional provision calling for the country's Islamic law to be based on Sunni tradition. Some 18,000 civilians were killed or wounded during the year.

On 1 January 1994 government troops came under attack from an unlikely alliance of Hekmatyar's Hizb-i-Islami forces and Dostam's militia. Fighting also spread beyond the capital for the first time in months to Dostam's northern base at Mazar-il-Sharif. By March food had become scarce in the capital as Hekmatyar's troops blocked relief trucks.

In late June government troops launched a fierce attack in the capital which succeeded in pushing back Hekmatyar's troops and capturing several of Dostam's positions. President Rabbani, who under the Islamabad Accord was to have organized elections and ceded power at the end of June, announced he would remain in office until at least the end of the year. Rabbani said he no longer recognized the Accord since Dostam and Hekmatyar had allied against him. By September fighting during the year had killed at least 4,500 people, mainly civilians, left more than 25,000 wounded, and driven a more than a half million civilians from their homes.

Most of the refugees from Kabul fled to the Sar Shahi camp outside Jalalabad, near the Pakistani border. The 118,000 residents of the camp face brutal conditions that include outbreaks of disease and temperature extremes. Some 3.3 million refugees from earlier fighting remain in Iran and Pakistan, giving Afghanistan the highest number of refugees in the world.

Political Rights and Civil Liberties: **A**fghans cannot change their government democratically. The unelected nominal government in Kabul lacks authority over much of the countryside, which is controlled by rival militias. Tens of thousands of people, mostly civilians, have been killed in clashes between rival Islamic groups since the Communist regime fell in April 1992. While most of the civilians killed were caught in indiscriminate shelling, others were killed in attacks by militiamen.

There are credible reports of torture and extrajudicial killings carried out by the rival groups against their opponents. Members of the Sikh and Hindu minorities are often targeted for crime and random violence, and thousands have fled the country. In the absence of a rule of law, small tribal feuds and disputes over drug turf frequently turn deadly.

The new government has attempted to establish Islamic law over the parts of the country it controls. In January 1993 a newly formed Grand Council of religious and tribal leaders declared that only Muslims can work for the government. It also banned all non-Muslim organizations and ordered television programming and print media to conform with Islamic principles. Freedoms of speech, press and association are sharply restricted by these decrees. There are few independent publications in the country. The state radio and television stations are controlled by President Rabbani's Jamiat-i-Islami group and rarely if ever air views of other groups. Other large factions control their own broadcast facilities, and the content of their programs is highly regulated. On 29 July gunmen abducted and murdered BBC reporter Mirwais Jalil, who had earlier been reproached during a tense interview with Hizb-i-Islami leader Gulbuddin Hekmatyar for alleged biased reporting.

Justice is administered according to Islamic law by the government, Islamic law or tribal customs by the factions controlling the countryside—in either case without regard for due process rights. There are credible reports of summary executions following trials. Although there is no effective civil administration in most areas, in the nine provinces controlled by warlord Rashid Dostam there is a reasonably efficient system of tax collection and customs, as well as electricity and drinking water.

Women are frequently raped and abused by soldiers of the various militias. Since the fundamentalists overthrew the Communist government women have come under increasing pressure to submit to Islamic religious norms. Some women have had acid thrown in their faces for wearing makeup, and women are routinely harassed for wearing Western clothes or not wearing an Islamic veil.

Civilians have been permitted to hold peaceful demonstrations in some areas outside the capital. Freedom of movement is hampered by the continued factional fighting, banditry and the millions of uncleared landmines strewn across the country. Afghanistan had no independent labor movements during the Communist regime, and it appears doubtful that free trade unions will be permitted in the current political climate.

Albania

Polity: Presidential- parliamentary democracy
Economy: Transitional
Population: 3,403,000
PPP: $3,500
Life Expectancy: 73.0

Political Rights: 3*
Civil Liberties: 4
Status: Partly Free

Ethnic Groups: Albanians (two main ethnic/linguistic groups: Ghegs, Tosks, 96 percent), Greeks (2.5 percent)
Ratings Change: *Albania's political rights rating changed from 2 to 3 because the government placed some restrictions on the Greek minority.

Overview: In 1994, President Sali Berisha faced continued political uncertainty as Albanians overwhelmingly rejected a constitutional draft on 6 November. The document would have shifted the balance of power from Parliament to an already powerful presidency. Other issues facing this small, Balkan country included maintaining a fast-growing economy, fueled in part by remittances from Albanians abroad, and continued deterioration of Greek-Albanian relations.

Situated on the southern Adriatic coast of the Balkan peninsula, this predominantly Muslim country gained independence in 1912 after 450 years of Ottoman rule. It was annexed by Italy in 1939. A one-party Communist regime was established in 1946 under World War II partisan Enver Hoxha, who died in office in 1985. Hoxha outlawed religion, and razed mosques and churches. His autarkic economic policies left Albania the poorest country in Europe.

In 1990, following the collapse of Communist regimes throughout East-Central Europe, Ramiz Alia, who had succeeded Hoxha as first secretary of the Albanian Party of Labor (Communist), was elected president as head of the Socialist (former Communist) Party (SP) in elections marred by irregularities.

In March 1992 elections, preceded by months of intense social unrest and a mass exodus of Albanians to Greece, Italy and elsewhere, Berisha's Democratic Party (DP) won ninety-two parliamentary seats (to the SP's thirty-eight) in the 150-member People's Assembly. The rest of the seats were filled by proportional representation from national party lists. The Social Democratic Party (SDP) picked up seven seats; the Union for Human Rights of the Greek Minority, two; and the right-wing Republican Party, one. President Alia resigned. Lawmakers elected Berisha to succeed him by a margin of 96-35. Alexander Meksi was named prime minister.

A key political issue in 1994 was the constitutional referendum to replace the Law on Major Constitutional Provisions, a revised Communist-era document in force since 1991. The constitutional debate highlighted continued political polarization, as some leaders of the SDP and the Democratic Alliance, which split from the ruling DP after moderates were purged, criticized the draft for leaving too much power in presidential hands. In September, more than a third of government MPs abstained in a parliamentary vote, depriving Berisha of the majority needed to legalize a referendum by which he sought to bypass parliament.

Following its national assembly meeting in October, the Democratic Alliance called for a boycott of the referendum. The party stated that the referendum was "unlawful" because it breached the existing provisional document that reserved to Parliament, not the president, the right to draw up and approve a new constitution. It also maintained that the proposed constitution did not clearly delineate the division of legislative, judicial and executive powers. The constitution would have given the president the power to appoint and dismiss the prime minister, appoint ministers and preside over the supreme court. On 6 November, more than 60 percent of voters rejected the draft constitution.

In other issues, Albanian-Greek tensions were enflamed by the prosecution of five leaders of the Greek minority organization, Omonia (Harmony), who were charged with espionage. [The number of Greeks, mostly in southern Albania's Northern Epirus region, is put at 400,000 by Athens, 60,000 by Tirana, and 280,000 by the U.S. Central Intelligence Agency.] The five were arrested in April after a border incident in which two Albanian conscripts were killed inside Albania. Albania accused Greece of staging a cross-border raid, prompting angry denials from Athens. On 7 September, the five were sentenced to between six months and eight years for spying for Greece and illegally possessing weapons. The Greek government retaliated by expelling more than 70,000 of the estimated 250,000 Albanians working illegally in Greece. A major border crossing between the two countries was also closed. The move had substantial economic consequences because Albanians working in Greece send home more than $350 million a year, bolstering an otherwise lackluster economy.

Former president and Communist party leader Alia and nine former government officials were charged on 21 May with abusing power, misusing state funds and violating the rights of Albanians. In July, Alia was sentenced to nine years' imprisonment.

In 1994 the government continued economic reforms launched two years earlier, which included cuts in unemployment benefits, reduction of wage subsidies, price liberalization, privatization of agriculture, and gradual privatization of most state enterprises, trade, transportation and the fishing and mining industries. Privatization included closing large loss-making enterprises, vouchers for citizens, cash purchases and private foreign investment. Thanks mainly to emigrant remittances and the abolition of all restrictions on foreign exchange dealings and foreign trade, thousands have rapidly found employment in a fast-growing private trade sector. Remittances, estimated at $500 million, have allowed the government to finance large imports of consumer goods and raised disposable incomes, thereby stimulating small business, particularly in the service sector. Nevertheless, high prices, unemployment, housing shortages and a controversial land restitution law allowing former landowners dispossessed by the Communists, or their heirs, to reclaim property continue to undermine economic growth.

Political Rights and Civil Liberties: Albanians can change their government by democratic means. The 1992 election to the 150-member Assembly was generally regarded as free and fair, although there were some reports of irregularities. Voters' rejection of a new constitution on 6 November leaves in force a jerry-rigged document adopted in 1991 that still contains many Communist-era provisions.

Judicial restructuring and implementation of the rule of law are proceeding slowly. Police have wide-ranging authority with little supervision. There is a shortage of legal experts and lawyers. The executive branch has interfered with the judiciary and procuracy by dismissing judges and prosecutors on political grounds.

Political parties, civic organizations, independent trade unions and student groups may organize, but there have been restrictions of the rights of expression, assembly and association, particularly on the Greek minority. The trial and conviction of five Greek activists for espionage drew international condemnation. An unofficial report written for the International Federation of Human Rights said that "much of the evidence against the defendants (was) circumstantial and vague." In the last two years, other former senior officials have been sent to jail on overtly "political crimes," including Fatos Nano, the former prime minister and head of the opposition Socialist Party, who is serving a nine-year term for corruption. In 1993, Idajet Beqeri of the Albanian Unity Party was imprisoned for "slandering" the president.

Political parties control much of the independent press. Newspapers face a poor delivery system and shortages of newsprint and independent printing presses. In August, six newspapers accused government agencies of favoring the government press, claiming the government "exhibited the outlines of a strategy to bankrupt the independent and opposition press," a charge the government denied.

The 1993 press law is restrictive and includes provisions susceptible to abuse. On 28 February, Martin Leka, a reporter for *Koha Jona*, was sentenced to eighteen months in prison for publishing details of a defense ministry document ordering some areas of the military to be disarmed.

On 3 May President Berisha pardoned five journalists convicted under the press law on the occasion of World Press Freedom Day, including Leka. All had received sentences ranging from five months to two years for charges that included slandering Albania's secret service, publishing state secrets and insulting President Berisha. Radio and television are state monopolies, and Radiotelevisione Shqiptar is a government facility. Throughout 1994 opposition groups alleged persistently that television and radio were biased toward the regime and refused to cover opposition positions and events.

While the in-force constitution mentions "equality under the law" and "human rights" for all groups, minority rights remain a potentially incendiary issue. The trial of five Omonia members was seen as a political slap at the Greek community. Albanian authorities have shut down some Greek-language, village primary schools for allegedly having too few pupils. There are no Greek-language high schools; ethnic Greeks claim that they have been prevented from setting up their own private schools. Moreover, several hundred ethnic Greek officers have been kicked out of the Albanian army in the past two years and many ethnic Greek civil servants have lost their jobs. Ethnic Greeks have been prevented from bidding when state enterprises are privatized at southern auctions.

Restrictions on religious activity have been officially lifted in this predominantly Muslim country. There are Roman Catholic and Orthodox minorities. In 1994, there were no expulsions of Greek Orthodox clerics as happened in 1993. Fearful of pro-Greek activism and propaganda, the authorities continue scrutinizing Greek Orthodox activities. Macedonians, Vlachs, Gabels and Gypsies also have been pressing cultural demands.

Freedom of movement and foreign and domestic travel are guaranteed and generally met in practice. The Law on Major Constitutional Provisions does not specifically address women's rights. Most Albanians are nonpracticing Muslims but Islamic and cultural traditions do not accord women equal treatment with men. Women do have equal access to education and some professions.

Workers obtained the right to form independent trade unions in 1991. The Independent Confederation of Trade Unions of Albania (BSPSh) is an umbrella organization for several smaller unions. The rival Confederation of Unions cooperates closely with the Socialist Party. It is a continuation of the "official" federation of the Communist period. In 1993, municipal employees and communication and bakery workers founded their own independent associations. Some unions have organized workers in foreign-owned shoe and textile factories. According to the Law on Major Constitutional Provisions, all workers (excluding employees of military enterprises) have the right to strike.

Algeria

Polity: Civilian-military **Political Rights:** 7
Economy: Statist **Civil Liberties:** 7*
Population: 27,895,000 **Status:** Not Free
PPP: $2,870
Life Expectancy: 65.6
Ethnic Groups: Arabs (75 percent), Berbers (25 percent)
Ratings Change: *Algeria's civil liberties rating changed from 6 to 7 because violence increased in the struggle between Islamists and the government.

Overview: Throughout 1994 President Zeroual's efforts to negotiate a compromise solution to a three-year-old crisis was stifled by internal opposition within Algeria's ruling military-dominated Higher State Council, deep divisions among radical Islamic groups, and opposition from secular parties against making any concessions to the Islamists. However, on 31 October President Zeroual announced presidential elections would be held before the end of 1995, shortening the scheduled transition period to elected rule by one year. An increasing number of civilians, intellectuals, women, journalists and foreigners were killed at the hands of either the government forces or the armed Islamists. The terrorism, reminiscent of the violent struggle for independence in the 1950s, began with the cancellation of election results in January 1992.

President Chadli Benjedid's democratization process ended abruptly after the first round of parliamentary elections in December 1991 when the radical Islamic Salvation Front (FIS) captured 188 out of the 230 seats. The military cancelled the second round of elections, scheduled for January 1992, because it was clear the FIS was going to win.

The FIS had vowed to establish a theocratic state and impose *Shari'a*, the Islamic law, as the supreme law of the country. The widespread support for the fundamentalist FIS was a protest against the National Liberation Front (FLN), which had ruled Algeria since its independence in 1962 after a bloody liberation war against France. The majority of Algerians viewed the FLN as corrupt and blamed it for high unemployment, inflation and an acute housing shortage for the rapidly growing population, 70 percent of whom are under the age of thirty. With the Arabization of the education system in the 1970s, most youth are excluded from the higher-level positions more accessible to francophones.

In addition to stopping the elections, the army forced President Benjedid to resign, instituting a collective presidency, the Higher State Council (HCE), with Mohammad Boudiaf, a veteran of the war of independence, as its chairman. Shortly thereafter, amid increasing violence, the HCE imposed a year-long state of emergency, arresting the FIS leaders and activists and banning the party. Despite the ban, the violence escalated with shootouts between the militants and the security forces, and the number of assassinations grew. In June 1992 HCE President Boudiaf was killed by a person presumed to be a fundamentalist soldier.

In January 1993 HCE Chairman Ali Kafi invited political parties to initiate a dialogue on holding a referendum on a new constitution. The talks collapsed because secular parties such as the Front of Socialist Forces (FFS), the Movement for a Democratic Algeria (MDA), and the Berber-based Rally for Culture and Democracy (RCD) opposed the participation of Hammas and Ennahda, moderate Islamic parties. In June the government created a blueprint for constitutional changes that promised a modern Muslim state with a free-market economy. Meanwhile, violence between government forces and the radical Islamic opposition escalated.

The FIS is composed of three major factions: a moderate faction of intellectuals, nationalists and ex-socialists disappointed in the FLN headed by Abdelkader Hachani; a traditionalist group that follows Ali Belhajd, a preacher; and a third faction headed by university professor Abbasi Madani. FIS leaders contend that they have lost hold on other militant forces such as the Armed Islamic Group (GIA), which have an estimated 5,000 to 10,000 fighters. After the government arrested the moderate leaders of the FIS, traditionalist Belhadj supporters, who include GIA members and those who returned from the war in Afghanistan, gained the upper hand.

In January 1994 President and Defense Minister Zeroual, promising to seek dialogue with the fundamentalists while being tough on violence, headed a National Consensus Conference to choose a president and two vice-presidents to replace the HCE, scheduled to step down at the end of January 1995, and to name a 180-member body to act as parliament for a three-year transitional period leading to elections. Five of the six largest political parties, the FLN, the FFS, the RCD, the MDA, and the Movement for Islamic Renaissance, boycotted the conference. It was attended by the moderate Movement for an Islamist Society-Hamas, also called Rally for an Islamic Republic.

In April President Zeroual, who had reportedly tried to establish indirect contacts with the outlawed FIS as early as January, continued secretly to seek a political settlement with the fundamentalists. Meanwhile, as minister of defense, he bolstered the authority of the chief of staff, General Mohamad Lamari, who, with the interior minister, Selim Saadi, is pressing for a fight to the end with the fundamentalists.

In April Algeria suspended payments on its foreign debt while it negotiated with creditors demanding economic reforms. The French-supported plan to restructure its foreign debt made valuable progress. In May, however, President Zeroual replaced the hard-line prime minister and the interior minister with Moghdad Sifi and Abderrahmane Meziane Cherif.

Months later, the president encouraged opposition parties to meet with jailed FIS leaders. Ali Belhadj sent the president a letter from military prison demanding recognition for armed groups. In September, Abassi Madani suggested a truce so that FIS conditions for peace talks could be discussed. These conditions included the release of all members of its ruling council held in Algeria and permission for those in exile to return, and the guarantee that they can meet freely in Algeria with the Islamic Salvation Army.

In the fall, due to pressure by parties who refused to participate in the National Transition Council in May in the absence of the FIS, Abassi Madani and Ali Belhajd, along with three other leaders were released from prison and placed under house arrest. The FIS said it insisted that militant Islamic factions, particularly the GIA, participate in any talks. Three days before the GIA, led by a former army officer, had called for a general mobilization of its guerrillas throughout Algeria.

The FIS leaders asked for a referendum on an "Islamic state" and on holding early parliamentary elections. However, since they were prevented from holding a meeting of the party's ruling council, the *Majlis Es Shura*, and a consultation with leaders of the Islamic Liberation Army, which owes allegiance to the party, they did not attend the talks held on 20 September. Five opposition parties drew a fourteen-point list of demands that included the release of jailed Muslim leaders, the shutting of internment camps in Western Sahara and a lifting of restrictions or bans on political parties and newspapers. Secular, democratic parties that opposed a compromise with the fundamentalists were absent. The next day the GIA burned down a $10 million technical school.

The U.S. urged Algeria's rulers to start serious negotiations with the Muslim opposition to broaden the governments narrow political base. Algeria signed a contract with the U.S. oil company Arco to develop a Saharan oil field.

Both the Algerian government and the armed Islamists are responsible for the escalating violence. Muslim militants progressively widened their targets. The armed wing of the FIS, the Armed Islamic Salvation (AIS), attacked officials and clashed with security forces, while the GIA is responsible for killing scores of journalists, intellectuals, entertainers and foreigners.

The GIA led a campaign against foreigners to drive out foreign investments without which an already beleaguered economy might be ruined. More than half a dozen European, East European and Asian countries either asked their citizens to leave Algeria or closed their embassies after businessmen, missionaries and nuns, consular workers and seamen bringing food to Algeria were killed.

On 10 March, a guerrilla group freed 400-900 prisoners—estimates vary—including Islamic radicals sentenced to death, from Tazoult, Algeria's toughest prison. This attack, the first of its kind, was a blow to the government's struggle to contain the insurgency. Security forces killed sixty-four escapees and captured seventy-nine.

On 20-21 August, the FIS warned foreign governments and companies that all contracts signed since the elections could be considered illegal if FIS came to power.

Deadly clashes followed the government's promise to hold presidential elections by the end of 1995. An attempt by a Catholic religious association in Italy to mediate the conflict in mid-November collapsed after the government declined to participate.

On 24 December, the GIA ordered the hijacking of an Air France flight from Algiers to Paris. The four hijackers demanded the release of three leaders under house arrest, including Madani and Belhajd. Before the plane landed in Marseilles, where French commandos killed the gunmen and rescued the hostages, the gunmen killed three passengers and left their bodies on the tarmac. Shortly after the 171 hostages were freed on 26 December, the GIA killed four European priests in Algeria in reprisal for the killings of the hijackers.

Political Rights and Civil Liberties: Algerians lost their right to change their government democratically after the cancellation of the 1992 elections. The elected members of the local council were replaced with government appointees.

The state of emergency reinforced the power of the security forces to set up detention centers, order house searches, ban marches, dismiss local authorities and order trials by military courts. The security forces conducted a crackdown on citizens, especially suspected militants and their sympathizers. In October 1992 the HCE established special courts to issue sentences to suspected terrorists, bypassing regular judicial safeguards. A January 1994 report by Middle East Watch stated that the special courts routinely convict suspects on the basis of confessions extracted under torture. Government forces are also subject to armed attacks. The government is responsible for politically motivated extrajudicial killings.

In January 1993 the HCE introduced a tighter press law limiting journalists' access to information on political violence and requiring police permission before publication of such information. The introduction of the law followed the temporary suspension of the independent daily *El Watan* for announcing the killing of five police officers before the official news agency released the information. Terrorists have been increasingly targeting journalists. Middle East Watch has found that more journalists were assassinated in Algeria than in any other country in the first eleven months of 1993, with the exception of Russia. Some terrified journalists have asked to have their bylines omitted from columns. In December two journalists were beheaded. On 6 December independent newspapers did not publish in a gesture of mourning for a prominent editor who had been assassinated.

On 22 March, widows and women's groups unwilling to submit to a fundamentalist vision of their role in society led marches in three cities against assassinations and threats against unveiled women. Women who walk around without the Islamic head scarves have been shot in the street. Different women's associations have multiplied. The GIA has demanded that students be separated by sex and have burned down 300 schools that refuse to abide by strict Islamic rules.

Although the law prohibits discrimination against the Berbers, who comprise a quarter of the population, there have been many restrictions placed on the Berber language schools and culture during the Arabization program. On 21 September they staged a strike in Tizi Ouzou, the capital of the Kabile region, in a show of force against the government and militants. In October 10,000 Berbers staged a march to demand the release of a Berber singer.

Although Islam is the official religion, other faiths are legal but may not proselytize. Following the imposition of a state of emergency, the government replaced most of the pro-FIS clergy in mosques. Roadblocks, nightly curfews and frequent random searches of travelers limit the rights to travel freely within the country. Men may travel freely, but women must obtain travel permits from their male guardians.

In November 1992 new laws allowed the government to shut down associations, labor unions, private companies and local councils deemed to support fundamentalist organizations. The main trade union, General Union of the Algerian Workers (UGTA), has openly opposed the idea of a theocratic Algeria and has joined the HCE in organizing rallies condemning the fundamentalist violence.

Andorra

Polity: Parliamentary democracy
Economy: Capitalist
Population: 64,000
PPP: na
Life Expectancy: 81 female, 75 male
Ethnic Groups: Andorran (Catalan), Spanish, Portuguese, French, other European
Ratings Change: *Andorra's political rights rating changed from 2 to 1 because the country had its first full year under a new, democratic constitution.

Political Rights: 1*
Civil Liberties: 1
Status: Free

Overview:

In 1994 Andorra experienced its first full year as a sovereign nation with a constitution and U.N. membership. From 1278 through early 1993, Andorra had been a territory under the joint control of France and the bishop of Urgel, Spain. The country's new constitution and independence resulted from an internal power struggle and outside pressure from France and Spain.

For centuries, there was no clear power structure to rule the country. As co-princes, the French president and the Spanish bishop had representatives there, but Andorra had no locally chosen head of government until 1981. In 1991 Andorra joined the European Community customs union. Its neighbors are forcing the principality to modernize and liberalize the economy. Andorra is feeling inflationary pressure from prices in Spain and France, whose currencies circulate there.

Andorra began 1992 in political deadlock. Oscar Ribas Reig, the head of government, had been unable to pass a budget for eleven months. Although the General Council (Parliament) had decided in 1990 to draft the territory's first constitution, conservatives blocked Ribas's attempt to codify rights in a written constitution. The French and Spanish governments had pressed Andorra to legalize trade unions and to establish other rights. Ribas had only twelve supporters in the twenty-eight-member General Council. After a technically illegal demonstration, the parliament voted to dissolve itself. In a two-round election in April 1992, reformist Ribas backers won seventeen of the twenty-eight seats. On 2 February 1993, the pro-Ribas majority adopted a constitution with entrenched human rights, parliamentary democracy and a highly limited role as a combined constitutional monarch. Andorran voters approved the constitution overwhelmingly in a referendum on 14 March 1993. This vote affirmed the country's sovereign status and paved the way for its admission to the U.N. on 28 July 1993.

The number of Spanish and Portuguese immigrants is growing faster than the native population. The government has proposed easing citizenship requirements.

Political Rights and Civil Liberties:

Andorrans have the right to change their government by democratic means. Women have had the franchise since 1970. There are some limitations on voting rights for young, first-generation Andorrans. Otherwise, there is universal suffrage at age 18. Only a minority of the population is Andorran, so only about 10,000 may vote. Before the adoption of the constitution, technically, there were no political parties, but there were factions and associations which had effective party functions. Article 26 of the constitution accords Andorrans the right to create political parties, which must be democratic and conduct lawful activities. The judiciary has the responsibility to dissolve parties not meeting these standards. Andorra has democratically elected local (parish) governments.

There are two competing, private weekly newspapers. There is local public radio and television service. French and Spanish media are easily available. The constitution guarantees freedoms of expression, communication and information, but it also allows for laws regulating rights of reply, correction and professional confidentiality. There is freedom of assembly, but organizers of demonstrations must give authorities advance notice and take care not to "prevent the free movement of goods and people."

In 1990 the co-princes issued the first Andorran penal code, which eliminated the death penalty. The constitution confirms this prohibition. Convicts go to French and Spanish prisons. The country is building its own independent judicial system. By tradition, when a corpse turns up, judges ask it three times, "Who killed you?"

Economic groupings have freedom of association. However, the sovereign government was slow to recognize the Andorran Workers Union, which sought to become the country's first official trade union. The right to strike is absent from the constitution, but that document outlines social and economic rights, including employment, housing and social security. Andorrans have a largely tax-free private enterprise economy. There is religious freedom, subject to limitations "in the interests of public safety, order, health or morals, or for the protection of the fundamental rights and freedoms of others." The constitution guarantees the Roman Catholic Church "the preservation of the relations of special co-operation with the State in accordance with the Andorran tradition."

Angola

Polity: Transitional　**Political Rights:** 7
Economy: Statist　**Civil Liberties:** 7
Population: 11,206,000　**Status:** Not Free
PPP: $1,000
Life Expectancy: 45.6
Ethnic Groups: Ovimbundu (38 percent),
Kimbundu (25 percent), Bakongo (17 percent), other

Overview:　Nineteen years after gaining independence from Portugal, Angola's internecine war continued. A framework for peace, mediated by the U.N., was agreed to in November 1994 by both government and UNITA (the National Union for the Total Independence of Angola) negotiators in Lusaka, Zambia. However, repeated cease-fire violations jeopardized Angola's fragile peace process. The Lusaka Proposals call for a cease-fire, disarmament of UNITA rebels and the establishment of an inclusive National Army.

Negotiators from both parties as well as U.N. mediator Alioune Blondin Beye are hopeful that the approved framework will pave the way toward reconciliation and power-sharing. Such optimism may be premature. The transport and communications infrastructure within Angola is ravaged and will likely impede any cease-fire implementation. Increasingly, the war has assumed an ethnic, as opposed to an ideological, focus and coupled with the logistical difficulties are deep-seated ethnic divisions and distrust. Although support for UNITA leader Jonas Savimbi has reportedly ebbed in the wake of widespread disease and famine, his continued support of the peace initiative remains crucial.

Angola has four primary political movements: the Popular Movement for the Liberation of Angola-Labor Party (MPLA-PT), UNITA, and two smaller groups, the National Front for the Liberation of Angola (FNLA) and the Front for the Liberation of the Enclave of Cabinda (FLEC).

Founded in 1956, the MPLA was successful in winning the 1975-76 civil war and now forms the government led by President Jose Eduardo dos Santos. Long believed to have a Marxist ideology, and previously supported by the former USSR and Cuba, the party is based on the Kimbundu tribe of north-central Angola.

MPLA's main rival party is UNITA. Founded in 1966 by a former deputy of the FNLA, Jonas Savimbi, this party is based on the Ovimbundu tribe (the largest in Angola) of central and southern Angola. Since his defeat in the 1975-76 civil war, Savimbi continued to lead a rebellion based on his tribal homeland, with substantial support from, among others, the United States, South Africa and Zaire.

Militarily moribund since the mid-1970s, the FNLA was established in 1960 by Holden Roberto and is based on the Bakongo tribe of northern Angola and Zaire. The FLEC was founded in 1963, and is dedicated to securing independence for the oil-rich province of Cabinda in Southeast Angola.

Much like Mozambique, Angola emerged from a fifteen-year war for independence from Portugal (1961-1975), only to find itself embroiled in an internal power struggle. Angola became a bloody battleground spurred on by Cold War rivalries. UNITA, led by Jonas Savimbi, successfully campaigned for support from the West (and, in particular, from the Reagan administration), portraying himself as a "freedom fighter" leading a pro-democratic party against the then-Marxist regime of the MPLA. As the Cold War came to a close, so, too, did much of the financial and military support from the U.S. and the USSR. In a reversal of U.S. foreign policy, the Clinton administration formally recognized the Angolan government in May 1993 and recently has threatened UNITA with sponsoring U.N. sanctions if it did not agree to a cease-fire.

While the U.N. had made a number of failed attempts to negotiate an end to the conflict, a permanent cease-fire agreement between the MPLA government headed by Jose Eduardo dos Santos and the rival UNITA party led by Jonas Savimbi was successfully engineered in May 1991. The adoption of the Bicesse Peace Accord was to have marked the beginning of a democratization process. Under the provisions of the accord, multiparty national elections were held in September of 1992 under United Nations' supervision. Shortly after the elections, however, fighting resumed between the government forces of the MPLA and UNITA amid reports of gross human rights violations by both sides.

In charging the government with embezzlement and citing delay in the establishment of the National Electoral Commission (CNE; a provision of the accord) just prior to elections, the stage was set for Savimbi's eventual rejection of the results. Although elections were remarkably quiet and had a high voter turnout (with approximately 90 percent of the population casting votes), the U.N.'s decision to forge ahead with the 1992 election may have been premature. Provisions in the Bicesse Accord for a demobilization process and an establishment of an inclusive National Army were not completed before the elections took place. Despite declarations that the elections were generally free and fair, the 400 international monitors had only a limited mandate and were unable to monitor the 5,000 polling stations satisfactorily. Unsurprisingly, it was against this background that UNITA rejected its defeat at the polls, declared the elections to be fraudulent and resumed fighting. While UNITA forces commanded a majority of territory in Angola during 1994, beginning in October 1994 government forces had begun to regain control of key cities.

Should the accord hold, the U.N. appears determined to avoid past mistakes. It has pledged to send in an unspecified number of peacekeepers and to ensure that demobilization is complete before new elections are held.

Political Rights and Civil Liberties:

While there is tempered optimism over Angola's prospects for peace, Angolans remain unable to change their government by democratic means. Despite the U.N.'s continued efforts to negotiate an end to Angola's bloody civil war, the fighting continues. Since the end of colonial rule in 1975, an estimated 500,000 people have been killed and over three million people (one third of the population) have been displaced as a result of the ongoing power struggle between the MPLA and UNITA. According to U.N. representative Beye, estimates that famine and disease continue to claim 1,000 casualties daily "must be considered conservative." In July 1994, the United Nations estimated that up to 3 million Angolans faced death by starvation and disease unless emergency food and medical airlifts—which have been blocked by both sides—are resumed.

To date, human rights violations continue unabated. While both sides deny allegations, aid workers maintain that thousands of politically and ethnically motivated killings have been systematically carried out by special police loyal to the MPLA and by UNITA rebels.

The U.N. has reported that UNITA forces have laid siege to a number of cities including Kuito, Malanje, Menongue and Huambo. The siege of Kuito began in January of 1993 and within the first ten months, an estimated 18,000-35,000 (about 20 percent) of the population died. The United Nations World Food Programme (WFP) reports that UNITA forces routinely prevent emergency food and medical airlifts to UNITA-controlled areas. The result in many regions has been described by the WFP as an "apocalypse."

For its part, the government has been accused of summarily executing UNITA military and civilian sympathizers. UNITA has claimed, with some independent media corroboration, that supporters have been executed in Benguala, Lobito and Lubango. Reports also indicate that the government has illegally detained UNITA members. UNITA members charged that during their detention they were subjected to cruel and inhumane treatment by government forces. International media reports confirm UNITA contentions that South African mercenaries have been deployed to assist MPLA-PT forces—a violation of international humanitarian law.

Angolans are not free from torture or inhumane treatment. According to the International Committee of the Red Cross (ICRC), prisoners of war are routinely subjected to torture during interrogation. This is especially true in the government holding center of Laboratorio, where ICRC and international human rights monitors have been denied access. It is reported that prisoners are denied food, held incommunicado for long periods and subjected to physical torture (electric shocks).

Angolans are not free from undue government and rival party interference into personal and family life. Both the MPLA and UNITA have exchanged accusations of arbitrary search and seizure of personal and business property. The judiciary system within Angola is not free from government interference. While the 1991 Angolan Constitution provides detainees with the right to both legal counsel and habeas corpus, these provisions are reportedly ignored as a result of the ongoing tensions between the MPLA and UNITA.

Angola's press is, on the whole, not free. The government controls the only daily newspaper, television station and national radio. The sole Angolan news agency is also under government control. Following the 1991 peace accords, some degree of independence in the media began to emerge. An independent media workers union, Sindicato dos Jornalistas Angolanos (SJA), was established and a few allegedly nonaligned media appeared. As the fighting resumed, however, intimidation, arbitrary detention and execution of journalists by both UNITA and the MPLA increased dramatically. The Media Institute of Southern Africa (MISA) reported that at least ten media workers were killed and an additional seven were listed as missing.

While the Bicesse Accords provided for freedom of movement for both people and goods within Angola, the WFP reports that in UNITA-controlled areas, access is virtually impossible.

Antigua and Barbuda

Polity: Dominant party
Economy: Capitalist-statist
Population: 65,000
PPP: $4,500
Life Expectancy: 74.0
Ethnic Groups: Black (89 percent), other (11 percent)

Political Rights: 4
Civil Liberties: 3
Status: Partly Free

Overview: Following the victory of the long-ruling Antigua Labour Party (ALP) in the 8 March 1994 elections, Lester Bird replaced his aging father, Vere Cornwall Bird, as prime minister. However, because of serious deficiencies in the electoral system and a grossly uneven playing field, the elections could not be judged free and fair.

Antigua and Barbuda is a member of the British Commonwealth. The British monarchy is represented by a governor-general. The islands became self-governing in 1969 and gained independence in 1981. Based on the 1981 constitution, the political system is a parliamentary democracy with a bicameral parliament consisting of a seventeen-member House of Representatives elected for five years and an appointed Senate. In the House, there are sixteen seats for Antigua and one for Barbuda. Eleven senators are appointed by the prime minister, four by the parliamentary opposition leader, one by the Barbuda Council and one by the governor-general. Barbuda has limited self-government through the separately elected Barbuda Council.

Antigua and Barbuda has been dominated by the Birds and the ALP for over two decades. Rule has been based more on power and the abuse of authority than on law. The constitution has consistently been disregarded and the Bird tenure has been marked by a long series of corruption scandals. A commission headed by prominent British jurist Louis Blom-Cooper concluded in 1990 that the country faced "being engulfed in corruption" and had fallen victim to "persons who use political power as a passport to private profit."

In 1992, amid mounting opposition protests, Vere Bird announced he would step down after completing his term in 1994. Meanwhile, the United National Democratic Party (UNDP), the leftist Antigua Caribbean Liberation Movement (ACLM) and the Progressive Labour Party (PLM) united to form the United Progressive Party (UPP). Labor activist Baldwin Spencer of the UNDP became UPP leader and Tim Hector, ACLM head and editor of the outspoken weekly *Outlet*, deputy leader.

A bitter succession battle between Lester and his brother Vere, Jr., ended in 1993 when Lester was elected to lead the ALP. In the 1994 election campaign Lester, aware of mounting anti-ALP sentiment, tried to portray himself as an agent of reform. The UPP, in the face of great disadvantages—the ALP's domination of the broadcast media and its use of state resources and patronage—campaigned on a social democratic platform emphasizing rule of law and good governance.

In the election the ALP won eleven of seventeen parliamentary seats, down from fifteen in 1989. The UPP won five, up from one in 1989. The Barbuda People's Movement (BPM) retained the Barbuda seat, giving the opposition a total of six seats. Despite the unfair conditions, the UPP opted to accept the outcome because it believed that political momentum was now on its side. UPP leaders said the UPP wanted to prove that it presented a viable alternative to the Bird dynasty

Lester, sensing the shift in the political mood of the country, seemed to appropriate much of the UPP's platform after taking office. He moved to fill the post of government ombudsman, a constitutional requirement ignored by his father, and vowed to take measures against corruption. He also said he would make government accounts open to public review, another previously ignored constitutional requirement.

However, in the fall of 1994 Lester was implicated in a scandal involving the sale of passports to Hong Kong nationals. He denied any wrongdoing and fired a few minor officials, but some in the opposition called for him to step down pending a full inquiry. There were also fresh allegations by U.S. drug enforcement agencies that public officials were participating in, or acquiescent to, drug-related activities.

Political Rights and Civil Liberties: Constitutionally, citizens are able to change their government by democratic means. But the March 1994 election was not free or fair because 1) the balloting system did not guarantee a secret vote; 2) the ruling party dominated the broadcast media to the exclusion of the opposition; 3) the voter registration system was deficient; 4) the voter registry was inflated by possibly up to thirty percent with names of people who had died or who had left the country, and; 5) the electoral law allows the ruling party to abuse the power of incumbency with impunity and without limit.

Political parties, labor unions and civic organizations are free to organize. An Industrial Court exists to mediate labor disputes, but public sector unions are under the sway of the ruling party. The free exercise of religion is respected. Opposition demonstrations are occasionally subject to harassment by the police, who are politically tied to the rulng party, as is the ninety-member Antigua Defense Force.

The judiciary is nominally independent but weak and subject to political manipulation by the ruling party. It has been nearly powerless to address the entrenched corruption in the executive branch. There is an inter-island court of appeals for Antigua and five other former British colonies in the Lesser Antilles.

The ALP government and the Bird family control all the country's television, cable and radio outlets. Television and radio are the two most important media for reaching the public. During the 1994 election campaign, the UPP opposition was allowed to purchase time only to announce its campaign events. The government barred the UPP from the broadcast media through a strict interpretation of the country's archaic electoral law, which prohibits broadcast of any item "for the purpose of promoting or procuring the election of any candidate or of any political party." Meanwhile, the ALP rode roughshod over the law, filling the airwaves with a concerted political campaign thinly disguised as news about the government.

The government, the ALP and the Bird family also control four newspapers, including *Antigua Today*, an expensively produced weekly established in late 1993 as an election vehicle for Lester Bird. The opposition counts solely on *The Daily Observer,* a small but vocal twelve-page publication, and Tim Hector's weekly *Outlet*, which the government is continually trying to throttle, albeit unsuccessfully, through intimidation and libel suits.

Argentina

Polity: Federal presiden-
tial-legislative democracy
Economy: Capitalist
Population: 33,913,000
PPP: $5,120
Life Expectancy: 71.1
Ethnic Groups: Europeans (mostly Spanish and
Italian), mestizo, Indian, Arab

Politic Rights: 2
Civil Liberties: 3
Status: Free

Overview: **P**eronist President Carlos Menem pushed through a package of constitutional reforms that allows for presiden-tial re-election. However, mounting popular discontent over official corruption and the widening gap between rich and poor were indications that winning re-election on 14 May 1995 might not be as easy as Menem once thought.

The Argentine Republic was established after achieving independence from Spain in 1816. A federal constitution was drafted in 1853. Democratic governance has frequently been interrupted by military takeovers. The end of authoritarian rule under Juan Peron (1946-55) led to a period of instability marked by left-wing violence and repressive military regimes. After the military's defeat in the 1982 Falkland/Malvinas war, Argentina returned to elected civilian rule in 1983.

Most of the constitutional structure of 1853 was restored in 1983. As amended in 1994 the constitution provides for a president elected directly for a four-year term, with the option of running for re-election for a second consecutive term. The leading candidate must win more than 45 percent of the vote to avoid a run-off. The legislature consists of a 257-member Chamber of Deputies directly elected for six years, with half the seats renewable every three years, and a 48-member Senate nominated by provincial legislatures for nine-year terms, with one-third of the seats renewable every three years. Two senators are directly elected in the Buenos Aires federal district. Starting in the year 2001, all senators will be chosen directly, there will be three senators, at least one from the opposition, from each province and their terms will be reduced to six years. Provincial and municipal governments are elected.

Menem won a six-year presidential term in 1989, defeating Eduardo Angeloz of the incumbent, moderate-left Radical party. Confronting a severe economic crisis, Menem turned away from Peronist traditions and initiated a market-based reform program. A rapid drop in inflation and a renewed sense of economic security enhanced his popularity.

By 1992 Menem was maneuvering to overturn the constitutional ban against re-election. Unable to secure the necessary two-thirds support in the legislature, Menem resorted to a backroom deal with former President Raul Alfonsin, leader of the Radical party. At the end of 1993 Alfonsin agreed to support re-election in exchange for a modified form of parliamentary government, judicial and other reforms and a mandated spoils system that gave the Radicals control of certain federal agencies.

Implementing the agreement required a constituent assembly, which was elected in April 1994. However, in the vote the Peronists made their worst showing in an election since 1987, winning only 36 percent of the vote. The decline was attributed to anger over a long series of corruption scandals involving government officials and members of Menem's family, record levels of unemployment, Menem's propensity to implement policy by executive decree and his naked ambition to perpetuate himself in office.

The Grand Front, a newly formed, mostly left-wing movement founded by renegade Peronists, Marxists and liberals seized, on the discontent over old-school politics, corruption and increasing poverty to win a surprising 13 percent of the vote. That catapulted its leader, Carlos Alvarez, into the forefront of national politics .

The Radicals made their worst election showing in decades. They won only 19 percent of the vote, a reflection of the widespread disgust over Alfonsin's dealings with Menem. The defeat exacerbated divisions in the party and left it weakened with the approach of the 1995 election. Nonetheless, the combined Peronist-Radical majority was able to engineer passage of the Menem-Alfonsin reforms in the constituent assembly. Along with the reforms described above, the assembly established the post of cabinet chief, similar to a prime minister, who will be designated by the president but subject to removal by the legislature.

Menem launched his re-election campaign in September. However, amid continuing strikes and street protests, his opinion poll ratings had declined. The Peronists suffered a blow when a young and popular Peronist senator, Jose Octavio Bordon, defected with five other Peronist legislators, formed his own party and began negotiating with Alvaraz about running on the Grand Front ticket in 1995.

Menem took another political hit in November. Attempting to placate the military, which was angry over budget cuts and the ending of the draft, Menem thanked the armed forces for winning the "dirty war" against guerrilla groups in the 1970s, during which thousands of people were "disappeared" by security forces. Menem was widely criticized and expelled from the Argentina's Permanent Assembly on Human Rights. His response: "What do you want me to do, cry?"

Although the Radicals looked weak and the Grand Front remained a wild card, Menem became increasingly concerned about the 1995 vote. One indication was his effort at the end of 1994 to get the legislature to approve voting for foreigners living in Argentina for more than ten years, 60 percent of whom backed Menem, according to polls.

Political Rights and Civil Liberties:

Citizens are able to change their government through elections. Constitutional guarantees regarding freedom of religion and the right to organize political parties, civic organizations and labor unions are generally respected. There are more than a dozen political parties, from Communist to fascist, many of them represented in the Congress and in municipal governments.

However, the separation of powers and the rule of law have been undermined by President Menem's propensity to rule by decree and his manipulation of the judiciary. He has invoked emergency laws to issue more than 250 "decrees of necessity and urgency," more than 90 percent of all such decrees issued since 1853. Attempts by legislators to challenge Menem in court have been blocked since 1990, when Menem pushed a bill increasing the number of Supreme Court justices from five to nine through the Peronist-controlled Senate and stacked the court with politically loyal judges.

Menem also has used the Supreme Court to uphold decrees removing the comptroller general, whose main function is to investigate executive wrongdoing, and other officials mandated to probe government corruption. Some top prosecutors have been removed and replaced with officials who had been targets of their investigations. In late 1993 Menem forced a number of Supreme Court judges to resign as part of the deal with Alfonsin to secure presidential reelection. Overall, the judicial system is politicized and riddled with the corruption endemic to all branches of the government, creating what Argentines call "juridical insecurity."

Despite nearly two dozen major corruption scandals and the resignations of at least that many senior government officials since 1989, no investigation has ended in a trial. Polls show that more than 80 percent of Argentines do not trust the judicial system, and that corruption ranked second—behind low salaries—among issues that most concern them.

It remains to be seen whether the 1994 constitutional reforms will temper Menem's autocratic impulse if he is re-elected in 1995, or strengthen the rule of law. The next president will have to appoint a cabinet chief who, like a prime minister, will be subject to legislative removal. Moreover, the president's freedom to rule by decree will be legally restricted and a nominally independent council of jurists is to be formed to select judges and oversee management of the judiciary.

The vibrant human rights community condemned Menem's 1990 pardon of military officers convicted for human rights violations committed in the "dirty war," and have since been subject to anonymous threats and various forms of intimidation. In 1993 the Inter-American Commission on Human Rights of the Organization of American States determined that the 1990 pardons were incompatible with Argentina's treaty obligations under the American Convention on Human Rights.

Newspapers and magazines are privately owned, vocal and reflect a wide variety of viewpoints. Television and radio are both private and public. Menem's authoritarian style has been evident also in his antagonism toward the media, which has created a climate in which journalists have come under increasing attack. Since 1989 there have been an increasing number of incidents of media intimidation, including more than fifty cases of physical attacks by security forces and shadowy groups apparently linked to the ruling Peronist party. Journalists and publications investigating official corruption are the principal targets. They have also been subject to a libel-suit campaign and cuts in government advertising. The newspaper *Pagina 12* has endured five bomb attacks in the last seven years. In 1994 Menem said he was going to sue the newspaper to foil "a plot" to undermine his leadership, and also proposed an "ethics tribunal" to judge journalistic conduct.

Amid a sharp increase in street crime in recent years, there have been frequent reports of arbitrary arrests and ill-treatment by police during confinement. Police brutality cases rarely go anywhere in civil courts due to intimidation of witnesses and judges. Since 1993 nearly every criminal court judge in Buenos Aires has received anonymous threats.

The 18 July 1994 car-bombing of a Jewish organization in Buenos Aires provided Menem with an excuse to establish by decree a security super-secretariat encompassing the foreign, interior, intelligence and defense ministries, and answerable directly to the president. Critics charged that Menem was less concerned about terrorism than about being able to confront, especially with elections approaching, a renewed outbreak of the type of violent unrest that has occurred in a number of provinces since 1993.

The nation's Catholic majority enjoys freedom of religious expression. The Jewish community, numbering up to 250,000, is occasionally the target of anti-Semitic vandalism. In January Argentina's top rabbi was physically attacked and received anti-Semitic insults in broad daylight on a Buenos Aires street. There were allegations that local neo-Nazi organizations or other anti-Semitic groups were involved in the July bombing of the Jewish center,

Labor is well organized and dominated by Peronist unions. But union influence has diminished because of corruption scandals, internal divisions and restrictions on public sector strikes decreed by Menem to pave the way for his privatization program.

Armenia

Polity: Presidential-par-
liamentary (transitional)
Economy: Mixed-statist
(transitional)
Population: 3,676,000
PPP: $4,610
Life Expectancy: 72.0
Ethnic Groups: Armenians (93 percent), others

Political Rights: 3
Civil Liberties: 4
Status: Partly Free

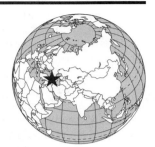

Overview:
The central issues for beleaguered President Levon Ter-
Petrossian in 1994 were political polarization over a new
constitution, war in the predominantly Armenian Nagorno-
Karabakh enclave in Azerbaijan, and economic problems exacerbated by the
continued railroad blockade by Azerbaijan and Turkey.

This landlocked, predominantly Christian Transcaucus republic was ruled at
various times by Macedonians, Romans, Persians, Mongols and others; it was
obtained by Russia from Persia in 1828. Prior to their defeat in World War I,
Ottoman Turks controlled a western region, and between 1894 and 1915, engaged
in a systematic campaign of genocide. The Russian component came under
Communist control and was designated a Soviet Socialist Republic in 1922,
western Armenia having been returned to Turkey.

Armenia officially declared independence from the Soviet Union on 23 September
1991. A unicameral, 249-member parliament had been created following multiparty
elections in May 1990. Ter-Petrossian's umbrella Armenian National Movement
(ANM) won fifty-six seats. Opposition parties included the Armenian Revolutionary
Party (ARF-Dashnak) with eleven members and the Armenian Democratic Party
(Ramgavar) with fourteen. Subsequent defections have weakened the ANM's strength in
parliament. On 16 October 1991 Ter-Petrossian was overwhelmingly elected president.
Armenia became a member of the Commonwealth of Independent States (CIS) in
December 1991, and joined the United Nations in March 1992.

Nineteen-ninety-four opened with an Azeri offensive in Nagorno-Karabakh and
renewed opposition pressure on Yerevan over the government-sponsored draft constitution. In 1993 five opposition parties—the Democratic Party, the Republicans, the
Liberal-Democratic Party, the ARF-Dashnak, and the Union of Constitutional Law—
had joined forces to create a "constitutional council" of civil consent. In January 1994
leaders of six opposition parties signed and submitted to Parliament the draft of an
alternative constitution, which stipulated a parliamentary republic whose president
was to be elected neither by universal suffrage nor by parliament; a clear delinea-
tion of powers of the legislative, the executive and the judiciary; the devolution of
power to local authorities; and the right of all ethnic Armenians, regardless of their
current citizenship, to participate in the construction of the Armenian state.

In early March 1994 several opposition parties formed a thirty-nine-member
shadow cabinet led by former Prime Minister Vasken Manukian of the National
Democratic Union (NDU). It included members of the NDU, ARF-Dashnak and

former Communist party first secretary Karen Demirchyan. Further undermining President Ter-Petrossian, the cabinet included ten members of the government.

Provisions in the government's constitution that strengthened the presidency at the expense of parliament became a focus of opposition. On 25 April Parliament opened debate on the constitution, with the president backing a national referendum to adopt the document. Controversial articles included a provision stipulating that ethnic Armenian immigrants must have been citizens of the Republic of Armenia for seven to ten years in order to be eligible to run as candidates for parliament or the presidency. This restriction would have seriously affected prominent members of diaspora-based political parties such as ARF-Dashnak and the Liberal Democrats. The government draft also called for the establishment of a unitary state, with the president as chief executive authority.

The opposition's alternative draft called for the formation of a constituent assembly, rejecting the proposal for a national referendum. A principal objection was that the ANM-drafted constitution provided no real counterweights to presidential power.

After much debate 113 deputies voted in favor of a referendum and fifty for creating a constituent assembly; neither variant received the necessary two-thirds majority. On 13 June Parliament convened an extraordinary session to discuss what were now five constitutional drafts and three drafts of a law on parliamentary elections. President Ter-Petrossian reiterated his support for a presidential system. In August Parliament revised some articles in the government's draft, but by year's end, the country still lacked a post-Communist constitution.

The constitutional crisis highlighted the increasingly bitter, fractious relationship between the government and the opposition. On 1 July some 20,000 people took part in an antigovernment demonstration in Yerevan organized by the National Democratic Union. NDU spokesmen accused the government leadership of condoning political persecution, and called for the arrest and trial of the president and top aides. Two weeks later, an NDU-sponsored rally drew an estimated 50,000 demonstrators in Yerevan to protest the grave economic conditions, corruption and political repression. NDU leader Manukian, a former close ally of the president, accused the government of instigating the assassination of several political figures, including former KGB chairman Marius Yuzbashyan. Vigen Sarkissian, a reporter for *Golos Armenii*, cited evidence that Armenian authorities had threatened, blackmailed and exerted pressure on the editorial board of the newspaper. A third massive rally was held at the end of the month. By midsummer, the government's popularity had fallen. A poll found that the most popular party in the country was the renewed Armenian Communist Party (18 percent), followed by the ARF-Dashnak (14-15 percent). Ter-Petrossian's ANM, which enjoyed over 50 percent support in 1990, had fallen to 5-6 percent support. On 12 August an NDU protest rally attracted 70,000 people. The same day Ashot Mamajanian, chairman of the regional interior ministry in the Dilijan district, was killed by a grenade. Like other killings of public officials, the case remained unsolved.

On 5 October leading opposition parties formed a political alliance calling for the government to step down and for early elections. The ARF-Dashnak and four smaller parties, the NDU, the Society for Self-Determination, the Union of Constitutional Law and the Democratic Party, released a statement calling for a fair settlement in Nagorno-Karabakh and the resignation of the president.

Despite mediation efforts by the Conference on Security and Cooperation in

Europe (CSCE) the so-called Minsk Group and Russia, the Nagorno-Karabakh conflict dragged into its sixth year, marked by Azeri incursions into Armenian territory, a string of broken cease-fires and tensions between Russia and the CSCE over the composition of peacekeeping forces. Over 25,000 have died in the conflict and more than 1.3 million have become refugees.

In early March a Russian-mediated truce collapsed before it took hold, with heavy fighting in the Fizuli-Dzehbrail regions of Armenia that lie between Nagorno-Karabakh and the Iranian border. On 27 April Russian Defense Minister Pavel Grachev asked President Ter-Petrossian to influence Karabakh's ethnic Armenians to accept another cease-fire offer; the Armenian president reiterated Yerevan's official line that Armenia is not involved in the fighting. In May, the Azeris refused to sign a cease-fire agreement in Moscow, complaining that Armenian troops would be allowed to remain on occupied Azerbaijani territory. Fierce fighting continued in early May despite a truce worked out in Bishkek, capital of the Kyrgyz Republic. On 16 May Armenia, Azerbaijan and Nagorno-Karabakh signed a cease-fire agreement in Moscow that called for peacekeepers from Russia and other ex-Soviet republics to separate the warring sides, but talks collapsed the following day. On 31 May Azerbaijan accused Armenian forces of launching a major offensive with hundreds of soldiers against Nakhichevan, a mountainous Azerbaijani region surrounded by Armenia. Fighting along the Armenian border continued in July despite a cease-fire.

On 8 August, the eve of President Ter-Petrossian's visit to the United States, a prominent U.S. human rights group cited numerous examples of Armenian volunteers and army draftees backing ethnic Armenians in Nagorno-Karabakh. While in Washington, Ter-Petrossian said he would welcome several thousand Russian peacekeepers. President Clinton said he was not opposed to the move so long as the CSCE approved and provided for proper safeguards to oversee the peacekeeping force.

After further clashes Azerbaijan's President Gaidar Aliyev and President Ter-Petrossian met in Moscow. A preliminary agreement called for an end to military hostilities, the disengagement of all armed forces in the region, the deployment of peacekeeping forces from the CIS and the eventual return of refugees to the region. Outstanding issues included the status of Azeri territory outside Karabakh in Armenian hands, and the composition of the peacekeeping contingent. A short time later, President Ter-Petrossian said that the Russia-CSCE split over who should play the main peacekeeping role was hindering attempts to solve the Karabakh conflict.

On 27 September a New York meeting between presidents Aliyev and Ter-Petrossian mediated by U.S. Ambassador to the U.N. Madeline Albright yielded no "effective results." On 30 October U.N. Secretary-General Boutros Boutros-Ghali, speaking after a meeting with President Aliyev, said the U.N. was ready to play a role in coordinating Russian and CSCE peace efforts. He also urged Armenia to withdraw its troops from Azerbaijani territory.

The war and subsequent blockade by Azerbaijan and Turkey continued to have a deleterious impact on Armenia's economy. Severe fuel shortages crippled industry, while homes, schools and hospitals went unheated in winter. In September, Yerevan reached a $120 million agreement with Turkmenistan for 5 million cubic meters of natural gas that would be paid for by "jewelry" and consumer goods. In late October the International Monetary Fund announced plans to grant Armenia a $500 million credit line contingent on liberalization of prices of bread, transportation fares, electricity rates and communal utilities, as well as on reducing the budget deficit and raising taxes. The increases were slated to be effective as of 1 November. Unemployment and inflation remained high throughout the year. In January Parliament approved a plan to privatize 4,700 state-owned enterprises. In September the minister of economics reported that by year's end, 20 percent of medium and large enterprises would be privatized as joint-stock companies with employee participation. A delay in the formation of investment funds necessary for the servicing of trade in vouchers impeded the effectiveness of the privatization program.

Political Rights and Civil Liberties: Armenians can change their government democratically despite the absence of a new constitution. There are over thirty political parties. In late August, the Conservative-Democratic Party of Women of Armenia was registered, the first women's party in the country's history.

There has been no comprehensive reform of the criminal code, which has largely been carried over from the Soviet period. The judiciary and court system are not fully independent from the other branches of government.

Freedom of expression is generally recognized, but the press faces restrictions. Over 250 news media are registered. In 1993 the government deprived three opposition newspapers and one independent news agency of accreditation for allegedly discrediting political figures. Of the four major privately held dailies, two are owned by leading opposition parties. The press practices self-censorship, avoiding controversial and sensitive subjects such as the military structure and commentary on the Karabakh war that deviates too far from the government line. Shortages of supplies, access to printing facilities and lack of advertising revenue have hurt many independent publications. State-run television and radio have limited access to certain political groups. The first independent radio station was due to begin broadcasting four hours a day in Armenian and English on 19 September.

Freedoms of movement, association and assembly are guaranteed and generally respected. There were several large, peaceful political demonstrations organized by the opposition in 1994. International travel and emigration are hampered by a Soviet-era bureaucracy. Over 400,000 Armenian refugees have fled Azerbaijan to escape ethnic persecution, and their return is doubtful in light of the ongoing conflict in Nagorno-Karabakh.

The 1991 law on religion established the separation of church and state, but recognized the Armenian Apostolic Church, to which 80 percent of the population nominally belong, as the dominant denomination.

While deeply engrained attitudes make Armenia a male-dominated society, employers are prohibited by law from discriminating against women. The law is frequently violated in practice, and women face obstacles to advancement. Unemployment among women is several times that of men.

The lack of a constitution hinders the advancement of legal guarantees for workers. Small, independent trade unions have been organized, but most labor organizations are holdovers from the Soviet era. About 80 percent of the workers are unionized, according to official sources. A 1992 law guarantees the right to strike.

Australia

Polity: Federal
parliamentary democracy
Economy: Capitalist
Population: 17,843,000
PPP: $16,680
Life Expectancy: 76.7
Ethnic Groups: European (95 percent), Asian (4 percent),
aborigines (1 percent)

Political Rights: 1
Civil Liberties: 1
Status: Free

Overview: In 1994 Prime Minister Paul Keating's government
wrestled with the issue of compensating Aboriginal groups
for native land claims. Meanwhile, nineteen months after
Keating's Australian Labor Party (ALP) won an upset election victory, a late
October poll showed a healthy 46 percent of voters supporting the party.

The British claimed Australia in 1770 and initially used the Botany Bay area as
a penal colony. In January 1901 six states formed the Commonwealth of Australia,
adding the Northern Territory and capital city of Canberra as territorial units in
1911. The queen of England is the nominal head of state in this parliamentary
democracy. The directly elected bicameral parliament consists of a seventy-six-
member Senate, drawing twelve members from each state plus two each from the
capital and the Northern Territory, and a 147-member House of Representatives.

Since World War II political power has alternated between the center-left ALP and
the conservative coalition of the Liberal party and the smaller National Party. Prime
Minister Bob Hawke led the ALP to four consecutive election victories between 1983
and March 1990 and took steps to sharpen the resource-rich country's economic
competitiveness, including floating the currency, deregulating the financial system and
reducing tariffs. In December 1991, during a deep recession, then-Treasurer Paul Keating
beat out Hawke in a vote of confidence among Labor MPs to become prime minister.

Going into the 13 March 1993 parliamentary elections unemployment still stood at
over 11 percent, making the economy the primary campaign issue. Opposition leader Dr.
John Hewson pitched his Fightback Mark II program, which called for greater
privatization and decentralization, further tariff reductions, extensive labor relations
reforms that would diminish union power, and a controversial Goods and Services Tax
(GST). The ALP offered a continuation of its more gradual liberalization program.

With the ALP taking a beating in pre-election polls over the poor state of the
economy, Keating skillfully played to voters' fears over the opposition's proposed
GST, warning of higher taxes and prices. On election day the ALP pulled off the
country's greatest electoral upset in post-War history, taking 80 seats; the Liberal
Party, 49; the National Party, 16; and independents, 2. Elections for 40 of the 76
Senate seats left the ALP with 32 seats; the Liberal Party, 29; the center-left
Democrats, 8; the National Party, 5; and the Greens, 2.

One of the most important issues facing the Keating government is the resolution of
aboriginal land claims. In June 1992 the High Court formally overturned the concept of
terra nullius (no man's land), which had considered Australia to have been vacant when

the British settlers arrived. The Mabo Decision formally recognized that native groups inhabited the land prior to British arrival, and that native titles to the land would still be valid in government-owned areas, provided the indigenous peoples had maintained a "close and continuing" connection to the land.

The ruling, based on a claim filed by Eddie Mabo in 1982, awarded actual title only to the tiny area in the Torres Straight off the northern coast that had been under review. Almost immediately, aboriginal groups around the country announced several major land claims. Farmers and mining companies feared the Mabo decision would threaten the long-term leases they held on government land.

In December 1993 Parliament passed the Native Title Act, requiring the government to compensate aboriginal groups with valid claims to land that had been put to other uses. Aborigines will also be allowed to convert their own pastoral leases into native title. The more controversial aspect of the Act involves mining leases, which upon expiration will be subject to native land claims. If these claims are upheld, the indigenous holders will have a "right to negotiate over future use."

In 1994 the parliament grappled with the implementation mechanisms for the Native Title Act, in particular the establishment of a land-procurement fund to assist those aboriginal groups not directly benefiting from the Mabo decision. Since many groups have been pushed off their traditional land, in practice only about 10 percent of their people would be able to take direct advantage of the law. During parliamentary negotiations, aboriginal groups criticized the $1.11 billion fund as too small, and called the establishment of a supervisory Indigenous Land Corporation, to be responsible to the federal finance minister, paternalistic. At year's end the implementing legislation remained stalled in the Senate.

In other events, in January the country's worst fires in at least 200 years ripped through the suburbs of Sydney, killing four people and burning more than 200 homes. On 5 September gunmen killed an MP of the New South Wales state parliament in the country's first-ever assassination of a serving politician. Police linked John Newman's death to his outspoken denunciation of organized Asian criminal gangs. On the economic front, unemployment hovered just below 10 percent during the year and the current account deficit remains uncomfortably large at 4 percent of GDP.

Political Rights and Civil Liberties: Australians have the democratic means to change their government. Although the constitution does not include a bill of rights, fundamental freedoms are respected in practice, and the judiciary is fully independent of the government.

The country's major human rights issue is the treatment of its indigenous population of 229,00 aborigines and 28,000 Torres Straights islanders. Life expectancy for aborigines is fifteen to twenty years lower than for nonaborigines, and unemployment six times higher. An April 1991 Royal Commission Report found aborigines are incarcerated at a rate twenty-nine times higher than the white population, often after having been unable to afford a fine or denied bail for minor offenses. Most arrests are alcohol related. Once in jail they are far more likely to commit suicide or be abused by guards than nonaborigines. The government now provides "bail hostels" for aborigines denied bail for lack of a fixed address. The Aboriginal and Torres Straight Islander Commission has been set up to give these groups greater control over governmental programs established for them.

Domestic violence is believed to be fairly common but has only recently been receiving public attention. In 1994 ethnic tensions between the country's Greek and Macedonian communities resulted in the firebombing of several churches and community centers in Sydney and Melbourne. The violence came after Australia recognized the former Yugoslav republic of Macedonia, angering the Greek community, and then offended Macedonians by deciding to refer to them officially as "Slav Macedonians."

Australian trade unions are independent and vigorous. As a backup to the regular collective bargaining process, the government establishes centralized minimum wage awards. However, in recent years the government has encouraged management and labor to rely less on centralized awards in order to tie wage agreements more closely to productivity.

Austria

Polity: Federal parliamentary democracy
Economy: Mixed capitalist
Population: 7,984,000
PPP: $17,690
Life Expectancy: 75.7
Ethnic Groups: Austro-German majority, Slovene minority, Eastern European immigrant and refugee groups

Political Rights: 1
Civil Liberties: 1
Status: Free

Overview: The coalition government lost ground to the right-wing populist Freedom Party in the parliamentary election on 9 October 1994. This followed the government's victory in a referendum on 12 June on Austrian membership in the European Union.

The Republic of Austria began in 1918 after the defeat of its predecessor, the Austro-Hungarian Empire, in World War I. Austrian independence ended in 1938 when Nazi Germany annexed its territory. After Germany's defeat in World War II, the Republic of Austria was reborn in 1945, but the Western Allies and the Soviet Union occupied the country until 1955, when they signed the Austrian State Treaty. This agreement guaranteed Austrian neutrality and restored its national sovereignty.

The Austrian system of government features a largely ceremonial president, chosen directly for a six-year term. Thomas Klestil, a member of the Christian Democratic Austrian People's Party (OVP), replaced Kurt Waldheim as president in 1992. After the controversies over Waldheim's activities under the Nazis, Austrians hoped Klestil would be a symbol of steadiness and reliability. However, his wife left him on New Year's Eve and the public learned in January 1994 that Klestil had an affair with one of his aides. Newspapers demanded his resignation, but Klestil held on to his job after his lover was reassigned to a new post.

The president appoints the chancellor, the government's chief executive, whose party or coalition commands majority support in the National Council, the 183-member lower house of Parliament. Its members are elected directly for four-year terms. The upper house is the sixty-three-member Federal Council, which the provincial assemblies choose by proportional representation. Federal Council members have four- to six-year terms, depending on the term of their respective provincial assemblies. The chancellor is Social Democrat Franz Vranitzky, who took office in 1986. The Social Democrats govern in coalition with the OVP.

In the federal elections held on 9 October 1994, the ruling coalition lost its commanding majority in Parliament. In the race for the 184 lower house seats, the Social Democrats remained the largest party with 35 percent of the vote and 66 seats, down from 80 seats previously. The People's Party took 28 percent and 52 seats, a loss of 8 seats. Threatening to overtake the OVP, the anti-immigrant Freedom Party snared 23 percent and 42 seats, a gain of 9. The environmentalist Greens won 13 seats, up from 10. The Liberal Forum, a comparatively moderate group that broke away from the Freedom Party, won 10 seats in its first federal election.

Led by Jörg Haider, the Freedom Party has made significant gains in local and regional elections in recent years. For example, it finished with 33 percent in the Carinthian provincial vote in 1994.

The Freedom Party and the Greens campaigned against Austrian admission to the European Union in the referendum held on 12 June. Despite this opposition, 66.4 percent of the voters approved joining the EU. The Austrian government had softened opposition to Europe by limiting Alpine truck traffic through Austria for a decade.

Since the collapse of communism in Eastern Europe in 1989, Austria has sought to redefine its international role. It used to present itself as a bridge between the two camps in Europe, but has now joined the European Union (EU). The EU is positive toward Austrian membership on political and economic grounds, but is concerned that Austrian neutrality could cause problems if the Community gets involved in defense policy. Austria is moving away from its reluctance to join a Western security structure.

In March 1993 former Chancellor Fred Sinowatz and two other ex-ministers went on trial for illegal weapons sales to Iran. The jury cleared them of charges that they had covered up the sales, but it convicted former Interior Minister Karl Blecha of falsifying documents and suppressing evidence.

Political Rights and Civil Liberties: Austrians have the right to change their government democratically. Voting is compulsory in some provinces. The country's provinces have significant local power and can check federal power by choosing the members of the upper house of Parliament.

Nazi organizations are illegal, and the 1955 State Treaty prohibits Nazis from enjoying freedoms of assembly and association. However, for many years old Nazis found a home in the Freedom Party, which still seems sympathetic to the Nazi period. In 1992 the Parliament made the following criminal offenses: belittling the Holocaust and publicly denying, approving or justifying Nazi crimes against humanity. These limits on expression apply to print, broadcast and other media. The same legislation also lightened jail sentences for Nazi activities, because juries often acquitted people in cases for which they felt the sentences were too harsh. The Austrian police enforce anti-Nazi statutes unevenly, tending to act more when extremist activities get international attention.

There is a Slovenian minority which has had some disputes with the Austro-Germans over bilingual education. This conflict became violent in August 1994 when a bomb exploded after extremists had planted it outside a bilingual school in Klagenfurt. The explosion blew the arms off a police bomb expert and injured two others.

The media are generally very free. There are a few, rarely used restrictions on press freedom which allow the removal of publications from circulation if they violate laws on public morality or security. Broadcast media belong to an autonomous public corporation. In June 1994, police banned demonstrations against Chinese Prime Minister Li Peng, who was visiting Vienna. There is freedom of religion for faiths judged consistent with public order and morality. Recognized denominations must register with the government.

The judiciary is independent. Refugees have long used Austria as the first point of asylum when leaving Eastern Europe and the former Soviet Union. Until 1990 Austria had an open-door policy for people fleeing Eastern Europe. Since 1990, Austria has required that all prospective newcomers apply for a visa first. The country had concluded that it needed to draw a distinction between economic refugees and politically persecuted arrivals. Xenophobia motivated extremists to send letter bombs in June 1994 to a monastery and several other institutions that were assisting asylum-seekers. Police defused the packages.

Business and labor groups are strong and play a major role in formulating national economic policy. Most Austrian workers must belong to Chambers of Labor, which represent workers' interests to the government. Trade unions, on the other hand, negotiate for workers with management.

Austria has generous welfare provisions and several state enterprises. However, the current government is trimming the size of the public sector.

Azerbaijan

Polity: Presidential-military
Economy: Statist transitional
Population: 7,386,000
PPP: $3,670
Life Expectancy: 71.0
Ethnic Groups: Azeris, other Turkic, Russians

Political Rights: 6
Civil Liberties: 6
Status: Not Free

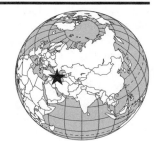

Overview: A coup attempt, assassinations of public officials, war in the predominantly Armenian enclave of Nagorno-Karabakh and surrounding Azeri territory, economic deterioration and increased repression by the regime of President Gaidar Aliyev made for a turbulent year in Azerbaijan. Events signaled the third year of political instability in this former Soviet republic bordering Russia, Georgia, Armenia and Iran.

Persia and the Ottoman Empire competed for Azeri territory in the sixteenth century, with the former gaining control in 1603. The northern sector, ceded to

Russia in the early nineteenth century, joined Armenia and Georgia in a short-lived Transcaucasian Federation after the 1917 Bolshevik Revolution. It proclaimed its independence the following year, but was subdued by Red Army forces in 1920. In 1922 it entered the Soviet Union as part of the Transcaucasian Soviet Federal Republic, becoming a separate Soviet Socialist Republic in 1936.

After the collapse of the Soviet Union in 1991, the Azeri electorate voted for independence in a referendum. In September 1991 Ayaz Mutalibov, a hard-line Communist, was elected president. The Azerbaijan Popular Front (AzPF), led by Abulfaz Elchibey, held only forty of the 360 seats in the Communist-dominated Supreme Soviet elected in a fraud-marred vote in 1990. Amid anti-government rallies in October, the Supreme Soviet created a National Council, a permanent fifty-seat legislature half of whose members would be picked by the president, half by the opposition.

On 7 June 1992, after months of instability, AzPF leader Elchibey was elected president with 59 percent of the vote. He promised to withdraw from the Commonwealth of Independent States (CIS) and keep Nagorno-Karabakh.

In 1993 Azeri battlefield setbacks in the Karabakh war and political uncertainty led to open rebellion against the Elchibey government. Forces loyal to renegade commander Col. Suret Guseinov, in control of the several-thousand-strong 709th Division, seized Gyandzha, the country's second-largest city. The fighting and instability led President Elchibey to ask former Communist Party boss Aliyev to become premier, but he refused. On 15 June, with rebel forces in control of over half the country and moving on the capital, Baku, the National Council elected Aliyev chairman of the Azerbaijani Parliament. Aliyev immediately began negotiations with Guseinov. On 18 June President Elchibey fled to his home town in Nakhichevan. Several days later, the National Council voted to transfer presidential power to Aliyev, and subsequently agreed to appoint Guseinov prime minister.

In presidential elections held on 3 October, Aliyev won an overwhelming victory, allegedly getting 98.8 percent of the vote. The election was boycotted by the AzPF and declared "undemocratic" by Western observers.

In 1994 the key political crisis was an October palace coup attempt allegedly engineered by Prime Minister Guseinov that threatened to thwart a $7 billion oil deal with Western investors. Two men close to Aliyev—Deputy Parliament Speaker Afiyaddin Jailov and security chief Shamsi Ragimov—were assassinated less than two weeks after Azerbaijani officials signed a 20 September deal worth an estimated $7 billion with a consortium of Western partners. These partners, including Amoco Corporation, Statoil and British Petroleum, were to explore three oil fields in the Caspian Sea. Despite the involvement of the Russian company, Lukoil, in the agreement, the deal enraged Moscow, which claimed that Azerbaijan did not have exclusive rights to the oilfields. Moscow's reaction raised speculation that Russia was behind the coup attempt, but Moscow vigorously denied the allegations.

On 3 October anti-Aliyev troops took Public Prosecutor Ali Umarov hostage in an apparent attempt to hinder authorities from bringing the assassins of Aliyev's two close aides to justice. Umarov was released the next day, but his kidnappers later skirmished with government troops on the outskirts of Baku.

On 4 October Aliyev declared a sixty-day state of emergency, and later deployed hundreds of government troops and fifteen tanks around the compound where Prime Minister Guseinov's troops were stationed. The next day, Aliyev told a crowd of thousands he had called to support him outside the presidential palace in Baku that the political crisis was over. Interior ministry officials later announced that government troops had reclaimed the airport and other buildings in Gyandzha, Guseinov's power base. Aliyev officially sacked the prime minister, who vigorously denied the charges against him, but the National Council voted thirty-one to one to dismiss him. Aliyev appointed Deputy Prime Minister Faud Guliyev to succeed Guseinov, who fled the country and was reportedly in Russia.

The year also saw sporadic political violence, assassination attempts and crackdowns on the opposition, particularly the AzPF. In February police in Baku sealed off AzPF headquarters after a search of the premises allegedly yielded arms and ammunition. More than 100 members of the AzPF and the Musavat Party were arrested; most were eventually fined and released. The offices of the Front's newspaper, *Azadlyq,* were also searched. In March, a remote-controlled bomb exploded in a crowded Baku subway station, killing at least twelve people. A similar explosion in July killed seven. AzPF offices were raided again on 17-18 March by policemen without warrants. In mid-May a group of 150 members of the Azerbaijani Society for the Defense of Women were forcibly prevented by police from picketing Parliament. That night some 300 armed persons attacked the Baku headquarters of the opposition National Independence Party (NIP). On 31 May at the prompting of the Parliament speaker, former foreign minister Tofik Gasymov and AzPF first deputy chairman Ibrahim Ibrahimly, both of whom had criticized the policies of the Aliyev regime, were expelled from parliament by a majority vote.

In early August Azeri militia units in Baku dispersed a demonstration of over 200 supporters of former Defense Minister Rakhim Gaziyev, on trial for military losses in Nagorno-Karabakh. Demonstrators, who demanded an open trial, were severely beaten. Tensions heightened when ten leading AzPF members were arrested. Days earlier, ousted President Elchibey released a statement from Nakhichevan charging the government with dispatching an assassination team to kill him.

In early September police prevented an opposition rally in Baku, leaving 400 people hurt. The rally had been planned to protest the Aliyev government's policies on Nagorno-Karabakh. AzPF deputy chairman, Ali Kerimov, was arrested on criminal charges, and launched a hunger strike. Minister of National Security Nariman Imranov was removed after the escape of former defense minister Gaziyev and four other senior military officers. Reports in Baku indicated that the national security minister may have been involved in the escape as part of a larger conspiracy to overthrow the Aliyev government. Following the alleged coup attempt in October, several government ministers were fired.

Growing political discord was exacerbated by military and political setbacks in the six-year Nagorno-Karabakh conflict. In January Azeri forces sought to reverse losses, and fighting continued throughout the year despite mediation efforts and cease-fires brokered by Russia and, to a lesser extent, the so-called Minsk Group of the Conference of Security and Cooperation in Europe (CSCE). Conflict also arose between Moscow and the CSCE on the composition of peacekeeping forces, with the former favoring Russian and CIS personnel and the latter calling for a multinational contingent. An escalation in fighting in May caused hundreds of casualties; 50,000 people had to flee their homes.

On 22 September President Aliyev met with Armenian President Levon Ter-Petrossian in Moscow to renew discussion of a Russian peace plan for Nagorno-Karabakh. Negotiations were slowed by major differences over the timing of a withdrawal of Armenian Karabakh forces from Azeri territory bordering the enclave, as well as the Azeri preference for Turkish troops to serve in a peacekeeping role as part of a CSCE force, rather than a predominantly Russian force within the CIS contingent. While in Baku in late October U.N. Secretary General Boutros Boutros-Ghali called for a U.N. supervisory role over CSCE and Russian mediation efforts for Karabakh.

Despite rich off-shore oil reserves and the multibillion-dollar deal with a Western energy consortium, Azerbaijan faced severe economic conditions in 1994. In October, as a result of an overall decline in energy-related revenue, the government introduced a number of sharp price increases for many goods and commodities. Oil and gas prices more than tripled, and electricity and heating costs were raised, as were bread prices and mass transit fees. Inflation hovered at over 14 percent. With the Karabakh war consuming 70 percent of the national budget, the country flirted with bankruptcy. Despite privatization legislation in 1991 and 1993 that outlined a loose framework for dismantling the command economy, the government has no coherent strategy. In July, then-Prime Minister Guseinov criticized a privatization plan submitted to the National Council, stressing that the state should maintain control over large, monopolistic enterprises. Lack of government leadership has led to a so-called "gray zone" private economy rife with corruption.

Political Rights and Civil Liberties: The current government wrested control of the country by force, ousting democratically elected President Elchibey in June 1993. Presidential elections that October were won by acting President Aliyev in a vote that was deemed "undemocratic" because it excluded most major parties and was fraught with irregularities.

The so-called National Council continues to act as an interim legislature pending parliamentary elections tentatively scheduled for June or July 1995. A new 150-member Parliament will replace the National Council.

There are some forty-three political parties registered, according to official sources. The year saw an upswing in repressive measures against opposition parties, particularly the AzPF. On 25 April the parties of the Boz Gurd, United Azerbaijan and the Azerbaijan National-Democratic Party created an alliance. There was a spate of assassinations and assassination attempts against public officials, some political, others criminal; in July the deputy procurator general escaped an assassination attempt, while in the same month the police chief of the Apsheron district was shot dead. On 30 September two close aides to President Aliyev were gunned down in Baku. Following the alleged coup attempt in October, a state of emergency was imposed for sixty days, curtailing civil liberties.

The judiciary is not independent and is structured like the old Soviet system. In July defendants in a trial of former Elchibey officials accused of the 1993 violent uprising in Gyandzha charged then-Prime Minister Guseinov of interfering with the case. Both the judge and the prosecutor were dismissed. There were several political trials, including the in-camera trial of former Defense Minister Rakhim Gaziyev and four senior military officers for losses in Nagorno-Karabakh (Gaziyev and three others escaped, allegedly with the aid of the national security minister;

one of the escapees subsequently turned himself in). There are an estimated thirty-five political prisoners in Azerbaijan, according to human rights groups.

The Aliyev regime has censored opposition newspapers and the Turan news agency. Under the Aliyev regime the press is restricted to "constructive criticism" and there are penalties for insulting public officials. There are some 525 Azeri- and Russian-language newspapers registered, and some do criticize government policies without sanction.

Freedoms of assembly and association have been periodically curtailed, as during the state of emergency, and several demonstrations were brutally dispersed by police and militia.

There is no state religion, though most Azeris are Shiite Muslims. There are significant Russian and Jewish minorities that can worship freely. Christian Armenian churches have been vandalized or closed. The Karabakh conflict has limited freedom of movement. All citizens wishing to travel abroad must first obtain exit visas; minorities wishing to emigrate face harassment from officials seeking bribes.

There have been reports of continued persecution of the small Kurdish minority, and the Lezhgin people have demanded greater autonomy. In June, violence erupted in the Lezhgin areas of the Kusarskiy region in northern Azerbaijan after police moved in to escort deserters back to the army.

Cultural norms and the Karabakh war have led to in discrimination and violence against women, who are often exchanged for hostages and forced into sexual slavery.

Unions join international organizations and form federations, and workers have the right to strike. In August, striking workers at two Baku oil facilities suspended their collective strike after successful negotiations with government officials. A strike was also held at a Baku machine-building plant, and there were sporadic work stoppages in other enterprises.

Bahamas

Polity: Parliamentary democracy
Economy: Capitalist-statist
Population: 272,000
PPP: $12,000
Life Expectancy: 71.9
Ethnic Groups: Black (85 percent), white (15 percent)

Political Rights: 1
Civil Liberties: 2
Status: Free

Overview: During his second year in office Prime Minister Hubert A. Ingraham of the ruling Free National Movement (FNM) received some credit for improvements in the economy, but was criticized for delays in implementing promised government reform.

The Commonwealth of the Bahamas, a 700-island nation in the Caribbean, is a member of the British Commonwealth. It became internally self-governing in 1967 and was granted independence in 1973. The British monarchy is represented by a governor-general.

Under the 1973 constitution, there is a bicameral parliament consisting of a forty-nine-member House of Assembly directly elected for five years, and a sixteen-member Senate with nine members appointed by the prime minister, four by the leader of the parliamentary opposition, and three by the governor-general. The prime minister is the leader of the party that commands a majority in the House. Islands other than New Providence and Grand Bahama are administered by centrally appointed commissioners.

After twenty-five years in office the Progressive Liberal Party (PLP), led by Lynden O. Pindling, was ousted by Ingraham and the FNM in the August 1992 elections. The PLP had been dogged by allegations of corruption and high official involvement in narcotics trafficking, and had lost ground to the FNM in the two previous elections. Ingraham, a lawyer and former cabinet official expelled by the PLP in 1986 for his outspoken criticism regarding drug and corruption allegations, had become the FNM leader in 1990.

Ingraham vowed to bring honesty, efficiency and accountability to government. Pindling, at the time the Western hemisphere's longest-serving, freely elected head of government, relied on his image as the father of the nation's independence. But many voters were born since independence and many workers had been left unemployed as a result of a five-year economic downturn. The PLP and the FNM are both centrist parties, but the FNM is more oriented to free enterprise and a "less government is better" philosophy.

With 90 percent of the electorate voting, the FNM won thirty-two seats in the House of Assembly to the PLP's seventeen. Pindling held his own seat and became the official opposition leader. He and other members of the former PLP government became targets of a wide-ranging corruption probe by the Ingraham government that continued through 1994.

Under Ingraham, the country's economic picture has brightened somewhat, with renewed growth and a dip in unemployment. However, a number of state enterprises remained in poor shape, the bankrupt Bahamas Broadcasting Corporation, for instance. Moreover, in 1994 Ingraham came under fire, especially from within his own party, for not attending to a politicized government bureaucracy, a legacy of the Pindling years. Ingraham renewed his vow to put an end to "obscene patronage" and "blatant victimization."

Political Rights and Civil Liberties: Citizens are able to change their government through democratic elections. Unlike previous balloting, the 1992 vote was relatively free of irregularities and allegations of fraud. In 1992 the use of indelible ink to identify people who had voted was used for the first time.

Constitutional guarantees regarding the right to organize political parties, civic organizations and labor unions are generally respected, as is the free exercise of religion. Labor, business and professional organizations are generally free, and unions have the right to strike. Nearly 30 percent of the work force is organized and collective bargaining is prevalent.

There is an independent Grand Bahama Human Rights Association, as well as at least two other independent rights groups. In recent years, there has been an increase in violent crime and continuing reports of police brutality during the course of arrests and interrogations. Human rights groups have also criticized the "subhuman conditions" and overcrowding in the nation's prisons. The Fox Hill prison, built for 500 prisoners, held more than three times that many in 1994.

A major concern is the condition of the Haitian immigrant population, estimated at between 20,000 and 50,000, with the government citing a figure of 40,000. Tight citizenship laws and a strict work permit system leave Haitians in legal limbo and with few rights. The influx has created tension because of the strain on government services. Following through on a campaign pledge, the Ingraham government began taking a tougher stand on illegal Haitian immigrants in the fall of 1992. Human rights groups have since charged that Haitians are treated inhumanely by the police and the public and that they are deported illegally.

Full freedom of expression is constrained by strict libel laws. These laws were used by the former Pindling government against independent newspapers, but the Ingraham government has refrained from the practice. Under Pindling, radio and television were controlled by the government and often failed to air pluralistic points of view. At the end of 1992 the Ingraham government amended media laws to allow for private ownership of broadcasting outlets. Since then at least two newspaper companies were awarded the first-ever licenses to operate private radio stations and dozens of applications were received from investors wanting to set up cable television stations..

The judicial system is headed by a Supreme Court and a Court of Appeal, with the right of appeal under certain circumstances to the Privy Council in London. There are local courts, and on the outer islands the local commissioners have magisterial powers. Despite antidrug legislation and a formal agreement with the United States in 1987 to suppress the drug trade, there has been evidence that drug-related corruption continues to compromise the judicial system and the Bahamian Defense Force, although to a far lesser extent than during the Pindling years.

Bahrain

Polity: Traditional monarchy
Economy: Capitalist-statist
Population: 564,000
PPP: $11,536
Life Expectancy: 71.0
Ethnic Groups: Bahraini (63 percent), other Arab (10 percent), Asian (13 percent), immigrant groups, Iranian

Political Rights: 6
Civil Liberties: 6
Status: Not Free

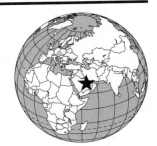

Overview:

This Persian Gulf archipelago off Saudi Arabia achieved full independence from the British on 14 August 1971. The Al Khalifa family has held the throne since 1782. The current emir, Sheik 'Isa ibn Salman Al Khalifa, assumed power in 1961, and rules with his brother, Prime Minister Khalifa ibn Salman Al Khalifa, and his son, crown prince Hamad ibn 'Isa Al Khalifa. The 1973 constitution provides for a National Assembly consisting of the cabinet and thirty popularly elected members. However, the emir dissolved the National Assembly in August 1975, ostensibly for debating "alien ideas," and has not reconvened it since then.

On 16 December 1992 the government created a thirty-member, appointed *majlis al-shura*, a consultative council consisting of business and religious leaders. This body has convened several times since January 1993, but has had little practical impact.

On 5 December 1994 police arrested Shiite cleric Sheikh 'Ali Salman, who had called for the restoration of parliament. Throughout the month Shiite protesters clashed with police, who arrested hundreds of demonstrators in some of the worst unrest in the country's history.

Political Rights and Civil Liberties: Citizens of Bahrain lack the democratic means to change their government. Political parties and opposition movements are not permitted. The emir rules by decree and appoints all government officials, including the fifteen-member cabinet, the municipal councils in urban areas and the *mukhtars* (local councils), which govern in rural areas. The only political recourse for citizens is to submit written petitions to the government, and to appeal to the emir and other officials at *majlises*, regularly scheduled audiences. The ruling family is from the Sunni Muslim minority, which dominates top government positions.

The Interior Ministry handles internal security through the police and its Security Service, and maintains informal control over most activities through pervasive informer networks. Although done infrequently, the Ministry's agents can enter homes without a warrant. The 1974 State Security Act (SSA) allows the government to detain those accused of antigovernment activity for up to three years without a trial. "Antigovernment" activity can include membership in outlawed organizations and holding peaceful demonstrations.

Ordinary civil and criminal trials feature the right to council, open proceedings and the right of appeal, but cases tried in security courts are exempted from these guarantees, and defendants do not receive fair trials. Some convictions in security courts are reportedly based on forced confessions. Nevertheless, defendants are acquitted reasonably often in security cases, indicating a fair degree of judicial independence.

Despite constitutional guarantees of free speech, citizens do not publicly criticize the regime for fear of being detained. The privately owned newspapers also refrain from criticizing the government. Public political meetings and political organizations are not permitted, and the few private associations allowed to operate are closely monitored by the government.

Women face fewer cultural and legal restrictions than in most Islamic countries, but are still discriminated against in the workplace through unequal wages and opportunities. The Islamic *Shari'a* courts rule on matters of divorce and inheritance, and occasionally reject divorce requests. Sunni women inherit only a portion of all property, even in the absence of a direct male heir. Foreign domestic workers are occasionally beaten and sexually abused.

The 1963 Bahraini Citizenship Act denies full citizenship to some 3,000-5,000 Persian-origin Shi'as, known as *bidoon* (those without). Bidoon are restricted in business activities and cannot obtain government loans. Islam is the state religion, but Christians, Hindus, Jews and others are generally permitted to worship freely. The majority Shi'a Muslims face discrimination by the ruling Sunni minority in employment and social services.

The government discourages the formation of labor unions, and none exist. Workers do not have the right to bargain collectively or strike. The government has instead encouraged the formation of closely controlled joint labor-management consultative committees (JCC), which do advocate workers' interests to the extent permitted. Thirteen JCCs have been set up, representing 70 percent of the industrial workforce.

Bangladesh

Polity: Parliamentary democracy
Economy: Capitalist-statist
Population: 116,602,000
PPP: $1,160
Life Expectancy: 52.2
Ethnic Groups: Bengali (98 percent), Bihari (1 percent), various tribal groups (1 percent)

Political Rights: 2
Civil Liberties: 4
Status: Partly Free

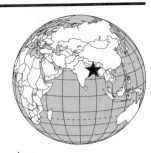

Overview:
In December 1994, following a ten month walkout by opposition lawmakers, Bangladesh Prime Minister Khaleda Zia agreed to resign one month before elections due by February 1996.

Bangladesh won independence in December 1971 after India invaded then-East Pakistan and defeated the occupying west Pakistani troops. In its short history two political leaders have been assassinated, and there have been nineteen coup attempts and two successful military takeovers. The last, in March 1982, brought army Chief-of-Staff Gen. H.M. Ershad to power. The country's democratic transition began with Ershad's resignation on 6 December 1990, following weeks of intense pro-democracy demonstrations.

Bangladesh's freest ever elections were held on 27 February 1991 for the 300 directly elected seats in the 330-member National Assembly. (Thirty seats are reserved for women.) The contest centered on two dominant personalities: the Bangladesh National Party's (BNP) Khaleda Zia, widow of assassinated president Ziaur Rahman, and the secular Awami League's Sheik Hasina, daughter of assassinated independence premier Sheik Mujibar Rahman. The BNP took 138 seats; the Awami League, 89; the jailed Ershad's Jatiya (National) Party, 35; the fundamentalist Islamic League, 19; the remainder split among smaller parties and independents. The Islamic League threw its support behind the BNP, enabling it to name twenty-eight of the thirty women's seats and secure a parliamentary majority. In March, BNP leader Zia became the country's first female prime minister.

In September 1991 a referendum on scrapping the presidential system in favor of a parliamentary democracy won 84 percent approval. Parliament subsequently reappointed Zia as head of government with executive powers, and approved the BNP-nominated Abdur Rahman Biswas for the new, largely ceremonial presidency.

Since Zia took office Bangladeshi politics has been dominated by the intense, personal rivalry between herself and Sheik Hasina. From the outset Hasina attempted to undermine the government by criticizing its tacit alliance with the fundamentalist Islamic League and its controversial leader, Golam Azam, considered by many Bangladeshis to be a traitor for having supported Pakistan during the 1971 war. Hasina has also repeatedly called for the government to resign over alleged corruption and inefficiency.

An important test of the government's support came on 30 January 1994 as the country held mayoral elections in four major cities for the first time in 129 years. In a clear blow to the government, the Awami League won the capital, Dhaka, as well as Chittagong. Many observers attributed the Awami League's success to popular discontent over the country's sluggish economic growth under an IMF-designed austerity program.

In March the BNP won a by-election in the Magura district in western Bangladesh, which had been an Awami League stronghold. The Awami League claimed fraud and began a parliamentary boycott to force Zia to appoint a neutral, caretaker government to preside over the next parliamentary elections, which must be held by February 1996. The government's main parliamentary ally, the Islamic League, defected to join the opposition in the boycott.

Adding to Zia's troubles was the mounting controversy over feminist writer Taslima Nasreen. In July 1993 the government banned Nasreen's book, *Lajja* (Shame), for fear it could provoke communal tensions. The book criticizes Muslim revenge attacks on Hindus in Bangladesh following the December 1992 destruction of a mosque in northern India. In May 1994 the Calcutta-based *Statesman* quoted Nasreen as saying that the Koran should be "thoroughly revised." Although the writer claimed she had been misquoted, fundamentalists called for her death.

On 4 June the government charged Nasreen under a statute banning speech or writings that would offend religious believers. In August Nasreen fled for Sweden, but the country was left to cope with rising fundamentalism. Islamic groups continued to urge the government to pass a blasphemy law, and called for a holy war against Western-financed nongovernmental organizations working to spread literacy and to provide health care, family planning assistance and other aid to women. Fundamentalists also vandalized some 1,400 girls' schools around the country to underscore their demands.

By September, as the parliamentary boycott dragged on, politics consisted mainly of street clashes between the opposition and the police. On 28 December, 147 of the 154 opposition lawmakers resigned from Parliament. The next day Zia agreed to resign one month before the next general election, but the impasse continued as the opposition responded by demanding that she resign immediately.

Another key issue is the low-grade insurgency waged since 1973 by the Chakmas and other Buddhist tribes in the southeastern Chittagong Hill Tracts (CHT). For years the government tacitly encouraged Muslims to settle in the CHT, and by the time it discontinued its policy in 1985 some 300,000 Bengali-speakers had settled in the area. Indigenous Buddhist tribes now make up only 60 percent of the population in the CHT, down from 90 percent four decades ago. Although three local district councils have been set up to give CHT residents greater autonomy, there is still a heavy military presence, and law and order and control over land tenure are still not under local control. In 1994 a cease-fire called one year earlier remained in effect, but several rounds of peace talks between the government and the Shanti Bahini (Peace Force) insurgents failed to make much headway in ending a conflict that has claimed 4,000 lives.

Political Rights and Civil Liberties: Citizens of Bangladesh have the democratic means to change their government. Partisan violence continues to mar political rallies and elections. During the January 1994 mayoral elections, six people were killed and 200 were wounded in Dhaka, and armed activists took control of some polling stations at gunpoint.

Key human rights problems center around the police, army and paramilitary units. Police frequently torture suspects during interrogations, leading to several deaths each year. Abuse of prisoners in the lowly Class "C" cells is rampant. In the Chitagong Hill Tracts (CHT) the indigenous Chakmas accuse the security forces of rape, torture and illegal detention of Buddhist villagers. Cycles of attacks by Shanti Bahini insurgents and reprisals by Muslims living there are common.

The 1974 Special Powers Act (SPA) allows police to detain suspects considered "a threat to the security of the country" for an interim period of thirty days before being formally charged, although suspects are frequently held longer before being charged. In the CHT the government has used the SPA against political opponents and tribal dissidents.

The judiciary is independent of the government. However, the system is weakened by a severe backlog of cases, some dating back ten years, and rampant corruption. Due process rights are occasionally ignored in rural areas, where the population is mainly illiterate and people are often ignorant of their rights.

Women face discrimination in health-care, education and employment opportunities. Domestic violence is reportedly common. In rural areas a *shalish*, an informal council of fundamentalist leaders, often levies unofficial sanctions against women for alleged moral offenses. The *Economist* reported that in punishment for allegedly having sex with a married man in a neighboring village, a fourteen-year-old girl received 74 of a mandated 101 lashes before blacking out. Many observers feel that harsh sentences such as this are a reaction to the growing economic and social power of women in the country.

Freedoms of speech and press are generally respected. Publications can freely criticize the government. However, most are heavily dependent on the government or state-owned enterprises for advertising revenues, and in practice advertising apportionment is politically slanted. The government has periodically floated the idea of formally tying advertising revenue to "objectivity" in reporting. Newspaper offices and journalists are occasionally attacked by fundamentalists and party militants. The broadcast media are state-owned and coverage favors the government.

Freedom of peaceful assembly is generally respected, but political protests frequently degenerate into violence between activists and police. In a surprising move, in September the government temporarily banned rallies in the capital after the opposition called a mass demonstration to demand early elections. More than 100 students have been killed in campus violence over the past three years.

Although Islam is the official religion, Buddhist, Christian and Hindu minorities worship freely. However, Hindus are subject to random violence, and reportedly receive less police protection in some areas than their Muslim counterparts.

Sexual exploitation of children is rampant in urban areas, and throughout the country children are occasionally kidnapped and sold into bondage. On 10-13 September police arrested 540 street children in Dhaka during a wave of political protests to prevent parties from hiring the youths as demonstrators.

Some 240,000 Bihari Muslims, who opted for Pakistani citizenship after independence, live in Bangladesh pending resettlement, mostly in sixty-six refugee camps throughout the country. In the southeast, refugee camps house Rohingya Muslims, who have been fleeing Burma since 1989. At the peak, in 1992, some 265,000 Rohingyas lived in the camps, although the U.N. is confident that a repatriation program will be completed by the end of 1995. The Rohingya refugees are frequently abused by Bangladeshi troops.

Most civil servants are forbidden from joining unions, and are limited to forming associations that cannot engage in collective bargaining. The Industrial Relations Ordinance favors employers' interests, allowing, for example, workers suspected of union activities to be transferred. Strikes are often accompanied by violence. Child labor is a serious problem and laws against it are rarely enforced.

Barbados

Polity: Parliamentary democracy
Economy: Capitalist
Population: 260,000
PPP: $9,667
Life Expectancy: 75.3
Ethnic Groups: Black (80 percent), white (4 percent), mixed (16 percent)

Political Rights: 1
Civil Liberties: 1
Status: Free

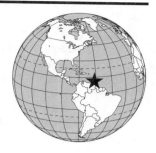

Overview:

Following a no-confidence vote against the Democratic Labour Party (DLP) government in June 1994, new elections were held in September and won by the Barbados Labour Party (BLP). BLP leader Owen Arthur replaced Erskine Sandiford as prime minister and promised economic change and job creation.

Barbados, a member of the British Commonwealth, became internally self-governing in 1961 and achieved independence in 1966. The British monarchy is represented by a governor-general.

The system of government is a parliamentary democracy. The bicameral parliament consists of a twenty-eight-member House of Assembly elected for five years by direct popular vote, and a twenty-two-member Senate, with twelve senators appointed by the prime minister, two by the leader of the parliamentary opposition and seven by various civic interests. Executive authority is invested in the prime minister, who is the leader of the political party commanding a majority in the House.

Since independence, power has alternated between the two centrist parties, the DLP under Errol Barrow, and the BLP under Tom Adams from 1976 until Adams's death in 1985. Adams was succeeded by his deputy, Bernard St. John, but the BLP was defeated in the 1986 elections and Barrow returned as prime minister. Barrow died in June 1987 and was succeeded by Sandiford, who led the DLP to victory in the 1991 elections.

Under Sandiford, Barbados suffered through a prolonged economic recession as revenues from the twin pillars of sugar and tourism declined. In 1991 Sandiford's economic austerity program sparked a two-day general labor strike, backed by the BLP, and mass demonstrations, a level of turbulence not seen in Barbados in decades.

By 1994 the economy appeared to be improving, but unemployment remained over 20 percent. Meanwhile, Sandiford's popularity continued to plunge and he was increasingly criticized for his authoritarian style of rule, from within his own party as well as by the opposition. In June Sandiford lost a no-confidence vote, fourteen to twelve, when the nine BLP legislators were joined by four DLP backbenchers and one independent legislator who had quit the DLP.

Sandiford was not forced to resign, which would have required the vote of fifteen members of Parliament. However, he called for new elections in September and gave up the leadership of the DLP. The DLP elected David Thompson, the thirty-two-year-old finance minister, to replace him.

In the election campaign Owen Arthur, the forty-four-year-old economist elected in 1993 to head the BLP, promised to build "a modern, technologically dynamic economy," create jobs and restore investor confidence. Thompson argued the economy had turned the corner and that the DLP should be able to continue its work. In the end, the widespread anti-Sandiford sentiment was overpowering as the BLP won nineteen seats, the DLP eight and the New Democratic Party (NDP), a disaffected offshoot of the DLP formed in 1989, one.

Voter participation dipped to 60.6 percent, down from 62 percent in 1991 and 76 percent in 1986. According to one noted local analyst the trend reflected "a growing disenchantment with voting, particularly among the youth where the scourge of unemployment is the greatest."

Political Rights and Civil Liberties: Citizens are able to change their government through democratic elections. Constitutional guarantees regarding freedom of religion and the right to organize political parties, labor unions and civic organization are respected.

Apart from the parties holding parliamentary seats and the NDP, there are other political organizations, including the small left-wing Workers' Party of Barbados. There are two major labor unions and various smaller ones, which are politically active and free to strike. Human rights organizations operate freely.

Freedom of expression is fully respected. Public opinion expressed through the news media, which are free of censorship and government control, has a powerful influence on policy. Newspapers are privately owned, and there are two major dailies. There are both private and government radio stations. The single television station, operated by the government-owned Caribbean Broadcasting Corporation (CBC), presents a wide range of political viewpoints. The highlight of the 1994 election campaign was a first-ever televised debate between the leaders of the three main political parties,

The judicial system is independent and includes a Supreme Court that encompasses a High Court and a Court of Appeal. Lower court officials are appointed on the advice of the Judicial and Legal Service Commission. The government provides free legal aid to the indigent.

In 1994 human rights concerns continued to center on the rising crime rate, much of it fueled by an increase in drug abuse and trafficking, occasional allegations of police brutality during detention to extract confessions, and excessive use of force during arrests. In 1992 the Court of Appeal outlawed the practice of public flogging of criminals. Also in 1992, a Domestic Violence law was passed to give police and judges greater powers to protect women against battering in the home.

Belarus (Byelorussia)

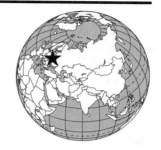

Polity: Presidential-parliamentary

Economy: Statist transitional

Population: 10,330,000

PPP: $6,850

Life Expectancy: 71.0

Political Rights: 4*

Civil Liberties: 4

Status: Partly Free

Ethnic Groups: Belarussians, Russian, Ukrainians, Poles

Ratings Change: *Belarus's political rights rating changed from 5 to 4 because the country had a competitive presidential election.

Overview:

Recent major developments in this economically troubled former Soviet republic included the ouster of reformist parliamentary chairman, Stanislaw Shushkevich, adoption of the country's first post-Communist constitution and presidential elections that saw a surprise victory by populist Alyaksandr Lukashenka. Other issues were the pace and scope of economic reforms and the degree of monetary and security integration with neighboring Russia.

The territory that is now Belarus was part of the tenth-century Kievan realm. After a lengthy period of Lithuanian rule, it merged with Poland in the sixteenth century. It came under the Russian Empire after Poland was partitioned three times in the eighteenth century. It became a constituent republic of the USSR in 1922.

In March 1990 multicandidate elections, the democratic Belarusian Popular Front (BPF) gained 37 of 360 seats in the Belarus Supreme Council (Parliament), Communists winning most of the rest. On 17 March 1991 Belarus participated in Soviet President Mikhail Gorbachev's Union-wide referendum on the preservation of the Soviet Union. Eschewing the post of president, Shushkevich, a nationalist-minded centrist, became head of state as well as Supreme Council chairman. The prime minister, Vyacheslav Kebich, was a pro-Russian conservative whose cabinet consisted largely of former Communists. Throughout 1993 Shushkevich, Kebich and Parliament were at loggerheads over economic reform, relations with Russia, the constitution and other issues, virtually paralyzing the political process.

On 26 January 1994 the political conflict came to a head when legislators voted 209 to 36 to oust Shushkevich, who had almost single-handedly battled politicians and bureaucrats opposing free-market reforms. The removal was based on dubious charges of corruption. Prime Minister Kebich survived a vote to dismiss him, 175 to 101. Shushkevich's first deputy, Vyacheslaw Kuznetsow, who served during the Soviet era, took over as acting chairman of Parliament. He was later replaced by Mechislav Grib, a former Communist Party member and Belarusian police general. BPF leader Zenon Poznyak called the move "a betrayal of Belarusian sovereignty," and "a creeping Communist coup."

On 15 February about 30,000 workers downed their tools to back opposition demands for the government's resignation and new parliamentary elections. The strike committee, backed by the BPF, the Social Democrats, Christian Democrats and independent trade unions called for Kebich's removal and multiparty elections. Several union leaders were detained, including Vyacheslav Kozel, head of the Independent Trade Union at the giant Minsk Tractor Factory.

On 1 March Parliament voted to create the post of president by a vote of 266-16. The president would be head of state, appoint the cabinet, serve as commander-in-chief of the military and have the power to introduce a state of emergency, but not to dissolve Parliament. The post was confirmed on 15 March as Parliament overwhelmingly adopted the country's first post-Communist constitution and ordered presidential elections before July. Under the charter, presidential candidates were required to gather the signatures of seventy Parliament members or 100,000 citizens within two weeks. It also reduced the number of parliamentary deputies from 360 lawmakers to 260, though no date for parliamentary elections were set. In addition to creating the presidency, the twenty-four-page document declared Belarus "a free...democratic state" and guaranteed individuals the right to own land. It also stated the goal of becoming a nonnuclear, neutral country.

By the end of May six candidates had registered for the 23 June presidential elections—Prime Minister Kebich; Shushkevich; BPF leader Poznyak; Vasily Novikov, secretary of the Central Committee of the Communist Party; Alexander Dubko, an Agrarian Party activist and chairman of the Union of Collective Farmers; and thirty-nine-year-old Alyaksandr Lukashenka, a firebrand populist and chairman of Parliament's anticorruption commission.

In an electoral surprise, Lukashenka trounced the front-runner Kebich, getting 45 percent of the vote to the prime minister's 17 percent. Over 80 percent of eligible voters turned out on 23 June, and the elections were judged free and fair. BPF chairman Poznyak got 13 percent, and Shushkevich, 10 percent. With no candidate polling the necessary 50 percent, a run-off was scheduled for 10 July. In defeating Prime Minister Kebich, Lukashenka won 4.2 million votes, or 80 percent of those cast; turnout was about 70 percent.

The new president, a poorly educated former director of a state farm with no party affiliation, had campaigned as a man outside of the state structure and promised to crush high-level corruption, halt inflation by fixing prices on goods and forge closer ties with Moscow. Kebich had the backing of Russian Prime Minister Viktor Chernomyrdin, who shortly before the vote visited Belarus and signed a tentative monetary union plan to boost the prime minister's chances.

The primary issue facing Lukashenka, who had been endorsed by Russian extremist Vladimir Zhirinovsky, was a rapidly deteriorating economy. Compared with the first six months of 1993, production had dropped by more than 50 percent and inflation had reached monthly rates of 40 to 50 percent. Some experts put unemployment at 50 percent. In the days immediately after his election, he promised to "do everything possible" to conclude an economic union, including a single currency, with Russia, and said "there is no way out of our economic crisis without Russia." He said he regretted the collapse of the Soviet Union, adding that he was "categorically against" withdrawal of the 40,000 Russian troops from Belarus. After his inauguration on 20 July President Lukashenko asked Parliament to confirm commercial banker Mikhail Chihir as prime minister, a move that surprised experts because of Chihir's reputation as a pro-market reformer.

A comprehensive economic integration with Russia was clouded on 3 August when President Lukashenka and Russian President Boris Yeltsin, meeting in Moscow, agreed to develop closer economic ties, but merging the currencies of the two countries was put off until Belarus pushed ahead with market reforms.

By September, the Belarusian president was rethinking his campaign pledges. With President Yeltsin refusing to burden Russia with the costs of an economic and currency union with Belarus, Lukashenka's election promises, including a pledge of full employment and the wholesale sacking of "corrupt" officials, were all but scrapped. That month, the president announced that the Belarusian ruble, the zaitsev (hare), would be the sole legal tender, reinforcing the position of Stanislav Bogdankevich, the pro-reform president of the central bank who was one of the officials threatened with dismissal in Lukashenka's election campaign. Instead of the promised bailout by Moscow, the "program of economic priorities" outlined by the president emphasized self-help and painful macro-economic stabilization aimed at reducing inflation.

On 11 August, which President Lukashenka told a television audience was "the hardest day of my life," the government ended price subsidies for milk and bread. Bread prices rose ten times, and the price of milk went up twentyfold. A week earlier, the government ended subsidies on beef, which tripled in price, and increased the cost of housing, heating and electricity for noncommercial users. To cushion the impact of ending subsidies, the government imposed a ceiling on producer profit margins. The president said that Belarus's crumbling economy could no longer support food subsidies, noting that the relatively cheap cost of food in Belarus encouraged the smuggling of local products to neighboring Russia, Latvia and Lithuania. On 12 October the government, which had been pressing for monetary union with the Russian ruble, banned its use, along with other foreign currency, in all cash and domestic transactions.

By year's end the Belarus economy continued to be plagued by high inflation and unemployment. Most of the big military plants, which provided over 70 percent of industrial output, were idle, while the country remained dependent on Russian oil and gas. Adding further gloom, grain harvests were estimated to be 25 percent less than in 1993. Meanwhile, there was no significant privatization in 1994.

In other issues U.S. President Bill Clinton stopped in Belarus in January and pledged at least $50 million in additional aid, including $25 million to help the government carry out its pledge to surrender all eighty-one of the old Soviet SS-25 nuclear missiles left on its soil.

Political Rights and Civil Liberties: The new constitution enshrines democratic principles, and the country's first post-Communist presidential elections were free and fair. The Communist-dominated legislature was elected in 1990, and no date has been set for new elections.

There are approximately twenty-six political parties and organizations which are allowed to exist and function openly, though membership tends to be small and concentrated in urban areas. On 5 October Parliament passed controversial legislation that may keep most political parties off the next nationwide ballot, prompting opposition criticism that the new law is antidemocratic. Most of the country's parties may find it hard to meet the new requirement that parties convene a founding meeting of at least 500 signed members in order to be registered. The opposition BPF and the Hramada parliamentary factions said the restrictions favored the Communists. But a top presidential aide praised the law, saying it would help curb the political ambitions of small parties' leaders.

The judicial system is essentially the three-tiered structure from the Soviet era, and judges continue to be influenced by the political leadership. The KGB retains broad intrusive powers, and can set up structures such as political parties, trade unions, civil movements and other organizations. On 2 February then Parliament Chairman Grib (later prime minister) announced that he had asked the KGB to investigate the national strike called for February by opposition groups and unions.

There are limitations on freedom of the press. Belarusian law bans publications of any material that "insults human dignity," giving aggrieved subjects leeway to take any journalist to court for virtually any criticism. "Technically we're under the laws of the former Soviet Union," said Roman Yakovlevsky, political editor of *Belarusian Market*, an economic weekly. The government continues to own and control nine major publications with a total press run of over 1.5 million. Government subsidies give mainstream papers a financial edge over independent publications, which are forced to match subsidized cover prices in order to sell. Shortages of printing supplies, especially paper imported from Russia, can upset printing schedules of independent newspapers, since state publications get priority. For radio and television journalists, a controversial story can have serious repercussions. The independent television station MM4 lost its broadcasting license on 31 December 1992, after only one year of operation, primarily for competing with the official news. MM4 stayed afloat in 1993 by producing programs on art and fashion for Minsk's less censored cable network, as well as a popular weekly crime-news show for state television. Independent Belarusian journalists have described their country as "an information hole in the center of Europe."

Freedom of movement and travel are respected. Adults are issued internal passports and the *propiska* (pass) system requires Belarusians to register their place of residence; they may not move without official permission.

Freedom of religion is guaranteed by law and usually respected in practice. Catholics (with strong links to Poland) and Jews have complained about government foot-dragging in returning churches and synagogues.

Women's organizations have been established to document discrimination and abuses, including domestic violence. There are no legal restrictions on the participation of women in politics and government, though social barriers to women in the public arena exist.

There are several independent unions, such as the Independent Trade Union of Belarus. Independent union leaders have faced harassment and intimidation. Several union leaders were detained after organizing a day-long national strike in February. The Federation of Trade Unions of Belarus, a direct descendent of the former Soviet trade union council, enjoys unofficial government support, and retains the administration of various social functions and pension funds.

Belgium

Polity: Federal par-liamentary democracy   **Political Rights:** 1
Economy: Capitalist   **Civil Liberties:** 1
Status: Free
Population: 10,137,000
PPP: $17,510
Life Expectancy: 75.7
Ethnic Groups: Fleming (55 percent), Walloon (33 percent), mixed and others, including Moroccan, Turkish and other immigrant groups (12 percent)

Overview:
A national bribery scandal and big gains for right-wing nationalist parties in local elections were the major developments in 1994.

Modern Belgium dates from 1830, when the territory broke away from the Nether-lands. A constitutional monarchy, Belgium has a largely ceremonial king who symbol-izes the unity of this ethnically divided state. The death of King Baudouin in 1993 shook the country emotionally, because he was a popular, stabilizing figure during thirty-two years of often bitter linguistic strife. His brother, Albert, succeeded him.

Belgium is divided into separate linguistic zones for the Flemings, Walloons, Germans and multicultural Brussels, the headquarters of the European Commission. Since summer 1993, Flanders and Wallonia, the Flemish and Walloon zones, have been operating their own powerful regional parliaments. Brussels and the German area also have elected legislatures. The disastrous ethnic conflict in Bosnia-Herzegovina has tempered somewhat the demands for Flemish separatism. However, there are frequent disputes between the two dominant language groups. For much of Belgian history, the Walloons dominated culture and the economy, while the Flemish had no legal status. To inspire Flemish enlistment in World War I, the king promised "equality in right and in fact."

Due to ethnic divisions, Belgian political parties are split along linguistic lines. Both Walloons and Flemings have parties ranging across the political spectrum. Governments come and go rapidly. There have been more than thirty cabinets since World War II. However, many of the same politicians and political parties reappear frequently in coalition governments. The bicameral parliament has a Senate, which combines directly and indirectly elected members, and a Chamber of Representatives, which the people elect directly on the basis of proportional representation. Each house has a term of up to four years. The heir to the throne has the right to a Senate seat. The current Senate has 181 members, while the Chamber of Representatives has 212.

After forming a governing coalition of four Socialist and Christian Democratic parties, Jean-Luc Dehaene became Belgium's new premier in February 1992. Dehaene, a Flemish Christian Democrat, formed the four-party coalition after two other politicians had failed to do so following the inconclusive general election of November 1991.

That election produced losses for the Christian Democrats, Socialists, Francophone Liberals and Volksunie, a moderate Flemish party. The right-wing Flemish Bloc, the Greens, Flemish right-wing Liberals, Flemish Libertarians and the Francophone National Front made gains. The small Francophone Federalists held their ground. Nationalist pressure on the government is bound to increase, because the Flemish Bloc and two right-wing Walloon parties (the National Front and Agir) made big gains in local elections in October 1994. Running with the slogan, "Our People First," the Flemish Bloc became the largest party in Antwerp. Mainstream parties scrambled to prevent local councils from naming right-wing nationalist mayors.

The Francophone Socialists suffered major losses in local elections following their implication in a bribery scandal earlier in the year. Word leaked out from an investigation that three party leaders, Deputy Prime Minister Guy Coeme, Wallonian Minister-President Guy Spitaels, and Wallonian Internal Affairs Minister Guy Mathot, known as "The Three Guys," had awarded a helicopter contract to an Italian company in 1988 in exchange for a contribution. The scandal forced all three to resign their posts. The Flemish Liberals sent a delegation to Rome to investigate the case, thereby triggering some political and communal tensions.

The Dehaene government has a deficit-reduction program aimed at meeting the standards for European currency union. Austerity measures include stricter welfare policies, higher social security taxes and the closing of tax loopholes. Communal tensions arose over austerity, because the more prosperous Flemings subsidize the Walloons heavily through taxes. In 1994, the economy recovered from recession, but employment and trade union bargaining power in traditional industries continued to decline.

In early 1994 Dehaene was a candidate to succeed Jacques Delors as president of the European Commission, but a British veto in June left him in place in the Belgian government.

Political Rights and Civil Liberties:

Belgians have the right to change their government democratically. Nonvoters are subject to fines. Political parties organize freely, usually along ethnic lines. Each language group has autonomy within its own region. However, tensions and constitutional disputes arise when members of one group get elected to office in the other's territory and refuse to take competency tests in the regionally dominant language.

In general, there is freedom of speech and of the press. However, Belgian law prohibits some forms of pornography and incitements to violence. Libel laws may have some minor restraining effects on the press, and restrictions on civil servants' criticism of the government may constitute a small reduction of freedom of speech. The four-way zoning of the country has provoked numerous disputes over the rights of outsiders and local linguistic minorities to move across internal cultural borders and to use their preferred languages. The municipalities around Brussels have the right to refuse to register new residents from countries outside the European Community.

Autonomous public boards govern the state television and radio networks, and ensure that public broadcasting is linguistically pluralistic. The state has permitted and licensed private radio stations since 1985. There is freedom of association. Most workers belong to Catholic and Social Democratic trade union federations. On 29 November public sector unions held a one-day strike against privatization.

Freedom of religion is respected. The state recognizes and subsidizes Christian, Jewish and Muslim institutions. Other faiths are unrestricted. The monarch and his consort have a religious role. According to Belgian tradition, the seventh son or seventh daughter born to any Belgian family has the king or queen as godparent.

The judiciary is independent. The government appoints judges for life tenure. Belgium has a generally good record on the rights of the accused, but there have been some problems with extended pretrial detentions. A central government commission handles political asylum cases.

Linguistic zoning and racism against immigrants limit opportunity. However, Belgium has taken important steps toward sexual equality, including prohibition of sexual harassment.

Belize

Polity: Parliamentary democracy
Economy: Capitalist
Population: 207,000
PPP: $3,000
Life Expectancy: 68.0
Ethnic Groups: Majority of mixed ancestry, including black, Carib, Creole and mestizo, with small Indian minority

Political Rights: 1
Civil Liberties: 1
Status: Free

Overview: The primary concerns for Prime Minister Manuel Esquivel, in his second year after returning to power as head of the United Democratic Party (UDP), were escalating violent crime and Guatemala's renewed territorial claim to Belize. Belize is a member of the British Commonwealth. The British monarchy is represented by a governor-general. Formerly British Honduras, the name was changed to Belize in 1973. Internal self-government was granted in 1964 and independence in 1981.

Because neighboring Guatemala refused to recognize the new state, Britain agreed to provide for Belize's defense. In 1991 Guatemala recognized Belize and diplomatic relations were established. However, Guatemala reaffirmed its territorial claim to Belize in March 1994, three months after Britain began withdrawing its 1,600 troops.

Belize is a parliamentary democracy with a bicameral National Assembly. The twenty-nine-seat House of Representatives is elected for a five-year term. Members of the Senate are appointed, five by the governor-general on the advice of the prime minister, two by the leader of the parliamentary opposition, and one by the Belize Advisory Council. In the 1984 election the center-right UDP overturned thirty years of rule by George Price and the center-left People's United Party (PUP). Businessman Manuel A. Esquivel became prime minister. Price returned to power in the 1989 elections.

Price called snap elections for June 1993, apparently feeling compelled to renew his mandate in the wake of political instability in neighboring Guatemala and the announcement that Great Britain would be withdrawing most of its troops in 1994.

In a tumultuous campaign the UDP assailed Price for being soft on the Guatemala threat. It accused the PUP government of corruption, including being involved in a $30 million passport scam in which wealthy Asians were allowed to purchase citizenship. The UDP also charged the PUP with awarding citizenship to Central American immigrants to bolster the PUP vote.

The UDP won the election, taking sixteen seats to the PUP's thirteen. Five seats were won by margins of five votes or less and the PUP actually won the popular vote with 51.2 percent. The determining factor in the election may have been the support of the National Alliance for Belizean Rights (NABR) for the UDP. The NABR, which split from the UDP in 1992, takes a hard-line position on the Guatemala issue.

In local elections held in March 1994 the UDP captured all seven of the country's local councils, or Town Boards.

In response to Guatemala's renewed claim to Belize, Esquival made a futile attempt to get London to reverse its decision to withdraw troops, but did win a commitment for joint British training with the 900-member Belizean Defense Force. Esquival also issued defense bonds to help fund an expansion of the force.

In August Said Musa, deputy leader of the PUP, was cleared by a magistrate of charges that he had attempted in 1993 to bribe a UDP parliamentarian to cross the floor of the House. Meanwhile, the PUP joined civic groups in decrying the government's apparent inability to cope with a surge in gang- and drug-related criminal violence and its toll on Belize's traditional peaceable society.

Political Rights and Civil Liberties:

Citizens are able to change their government through free and fair elections. There are no restrictions on the right to organize political parties. Civic society is well established, with a large number of nongovernmental organizations working in the social, economic and environmental areas.

Labor unions are independent and free to strike. There are about half a dozen trade unions, but the percentage of the workforce that is organized has declined in recent years to less than 20 percent. Disputes are adjudicated by official boards of inquiry, and businesses are penalized for failing to abide by the labor code. There is freedom of religion.

The judiciary is independent and nondiscriminatory and the rule of law is generally respected. The Belize Human Rights Commission is independent and effective.

In recent years, human rights concerns have focused on the plight of migrant workers and refugees from neighboring Central American countries—primarily El Salvador and Guatemala—and charges of labor abuses by Belizean employers. A majority of the estimated 40,000 Spanish-speaking immigrants since the 1980s do not have legal status. Some have registered under an amnesty program implemented in cooperation with the United Nations High Commissioner for Refugees. In 1994 there were reports of migrant workers being detained, mistreated and summarily deported.

A small community of Maya Indians in the Toledo district have few rights of ownership to their ancestral lands, which have been targeted by foreign agricultural investors.

Belizeans have been outraged and frustrated over the increase in violent crime, much of it related to drug trafficking and gang conflict. At least three police officers have been killed since the end of 1993. Because most of the 600-member police force goes unarmed, a policy of joint patrols between the police and the 900-member Belize Defense Force was instituted. There have been some allegations of unlawful use of force in making arrests.

There are five independent newspapers representing various political viewpoints. Belize has a literacy rate of over 90 percent. Radio and television have played an increasingly prominent role in recent years, especially in the last two elections when they were saturated with political ads. There are fourteen privately owned television stations including four cable systems. There is an independent board to oversee operations of government-owned outlets.

Benin

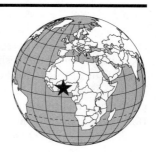

Polity: Presidential-parliamentary democracy
Economy: Statist-transitional
Population: 5,265,000
PPP: $1,500
Life Expectancy: 46.1
Ethnic Groups: Aja, Barriba, Fon, Yoruba

Political Rights: 2
Civil Liberties: 3
Status: Free

Overview:

In 1994 the government of President Nicephore Soglo faced the economic ramifications of France's decision to devalue the African franc (CFA) and a conflict with the National Assembly and Constitutional Court over a presidential decree on the budget.

The republic of Dahomey, a former center for the black African slave trade, achieved independence from France on 1 August 1960. Gen. Ahmed Kerekou seized power in a 1972 coup. He renamed the country Benin in 1975 and established a Marxist-Leninist state under the banner of the Benin People's Revolutionary Party (PRPB). By 1988 Benin was effectively bankrupt, plagued by official corruption and incompetence and besieged by widespread work stoppages and student-led strikes. In December 1989, after a series of moves to consolidate its hold on power, the regime entered into negotiations with the exiled political opposition in an effort to fend off economic and political disaster. The resulting Paris agreement laid the foundation for the country's transition to a multiparty democracy.

A national conference assumed sovereign control in early 1990, appointing an interim government. Stripping Kerekou of his effective power as president, though not his formal position as head of state, the conference selected Soglo as interim prime minister. A former World Bank official, the prime minister led a year-long transition to competitive elections. Local multiparty elections in late 1990 were followed by legislative and parliamentary elections during the first quarter of 1991. In addition, a new democratic constitution was ratified by a popular referendum. In March 1991 two rounds of balloting for president resulted in a conclusive victory for Soglo over Kerekou.

The Soglo administration set out to address the acute economic problems facing this largely agricultural society. He implemented an unpopular austerity program that included budget cuts under International Monetary Fund (IMF) restructuring guidelines. In 1993 a national conference of twenty-three opposition parties and three organizations created a platform for consultation called the National Convention of Forces of Change (CNFC).

The key issue in 1994 was France's 11 January decision to devalue by half the CFA, the currency of Francophone Africa. The move came after France bowed to Western pressure to end what amounted to a subsidy. The attendant price increases for pharmaceutical products and essential food items had political and social repercussions through much of West Africa.

On 25 January the Beninese government banned a demonstration organized by a six-union inter-union labor committee and prevented thousands of people from rallying in front of the Labor Exchange in Cotonou, the capital. Two days earlier, President Soglo reiterated that a price freeze on basic commodities and a series of fiscal relief measures had been decided, but while agreeing to the "principle" of salary adjustment, urged workers to accept a reasonable salary decrease. In a March interview the president acknowledged that the measures would be difficult "to explain to the population, even if this devaluation enables us to win back our internal markets, especially in the agricultural sphere."

On 7 March government offices and businesses were paralyzed by a renewable seventy-two-hour strike called by ten trade union federations demanding a salary increase of 30 percent to compensate for the CFA devaluation. Two weeks later, security forces and students clashed in Cotonou as 3,000 demanded an audience with the president to press for doubling of scholarships. The same day, the inter-union crisis committee called for a five-day renewable strike. The large National Federation of Workers' Union of Benin pulled out of the strike after negotiations with the government yielded some progress.

In May the constitutional court invalidated President Soglo's appointment of the former justice minister as Supreme Court president, maintaining that the term of office of the incumbent had not expired. The government accepted the decision, and a presidential spokesmen said that Benin exists as "a state of law." In July, the president became chairman of the Benin Renaissance Party.

On 1 August, following a decision by the president to resort to exceptional measures provided under Article 68 of the constitution to push through its own budget, the sixty-four-member National Assembly convened an extraordinary session on 2 August in Porto-Novo. On 28 July, the Assembly had adopted its own budget by a vote of fifty-four to six and four abstentions. On 25 August the Constitutional Court, after days of deliberation, declared the president's 1 August decrees unconstitutional for faulty procedure.

In mid-September the president decided to execute the 1994 budget, thus ignoring the opinions of Parliament and the Constitutional Court, the highest jurisdiction in Benin. The cabinet met in extraordinary session to examine the procedure to be followed to implement the budget. Meanwhile, the Constitutional Court admitted that the president's resorting to Article 68 was a discretionary act and not subject to any judiciary control. September also saw 6,000 striking students rioting at the National University over the university's policy not to let students retake exams they had failed.

Political Rights and Civil Liberties:

Benin's citizens can change their government democratically. Over twenty parties are represented in the sixty-four-member National Assembly. In January the National Convention of Forces of Change (CNFC) adopted a series of recommendations on the organization of the country's next election to ensure "openness and democratic character." It urged political parties to examine the possibility of creating a national and independent electoral commission. It also urged greater access to state media.

The judiciary is generally free of government interference. The constitution provides that judges and other appointed officials are answerable only to the law. In 1994, the Constitutional Court invalidated several presidential decrees and blocked a presidential Supreme Court appointment. The year also saw the trial of twenty-seven men (sixteen were in hiding or out of the country) accused of being in a 1992 coup plot; in September the court sentenced *in absentia* coup leader Pascal Tawes and fifteen others to life imprisonment with hard labor. Others got lighter sentences, and three were acquitted.

Parties, professional organizations and nongovernmental groups are permitted. In 1994 several new parties were registered, among them the Party of Beninese Workers Rally (PROB), the Generation Progress and the Action Front for Renewal and Development-Alafia (FARD-Alafia). The steering committee of the Pan-African Union for Democracy and Solidarity (UPDS) merged with the president's Benin Renaissance Party in October.

Although government control of radio and television has raised the issue of access to the broadcast media, there is a lively and often irreverent free press, including *Le Soleil*, *Tam Tam Express*, and *L'Observateur*.

There are no major restrictions on religion, though tensions have flared up between Muslims and animists. Of Benin's 5 million people, about one-fifth are Catholics, about one-eighth are Muslims and the rest follow vodun, the form of spiritual worship that gave voodoo its name.

Both domestic and international travel are generally unrestricted for political reasons, though roadblocks and checkpoints have been set up to exact bribes from travelers. Women continue to face discrimination and violence in rural areas. Female circumcision is common; one reliable non-Beninese source has estimated that 50 percent of the country's women have gone through the procedure.

There are at least ten independent labor unions and federations, which organized a series of strikes and work stoppages in 1994 after the devaluation of the CFA.

Bhutan

Polity: Traditional monarchy
Economy: Pre-industrial
Population: 804,000
PPP: $620
Life Expectancy: 47.8
Ethnic Groups: Ngalongs, Sarchops, Nepalese, others

Political Rights: 7
Civil Liberties: 7
Status: Not Free

Overview:　　　The Bhutanese government's ethnic cleansing campaign against Nepali-speaking southerners continued in 1994 with little sign that King Jigme Singye Wangchuk is prepared to take back some 100,000 refugees who have fled the country since 1990.

The British began guiding Bhutan's affairs in 1865; India took over this role in

1949, agreeing not to interfere in domestic matters. The Wangchuk dynasty has ruled as an absolute monarchy since being installed by the British in 1907. In 1972 nineteen-year-old Jigme Singye Wangchuk succeeded his father to the throne.

The king governs the country with the assistance of a Council of Ministers and a Royal Advisory Council. A 150-member National Assembly holds little independent power and meets only twice a year to enact laws and approve senior appointments. Although the king cannot veto legislation, in practice his influence is always enough to ensure passage of legislation he considers important. Every three years 105 National Assembly members are elected by village headmen in Buddhist areas, and by family heads in Hindu regions. Twelve Assembly seats go to religious groups and thirty-three are appointed by the king. Political parties are discouraged and none exists.

Since the mid-1980s the government has systematically persecuted ethnic-Nepalese citizens, who are also known as *Lhotshampas*, or southern Bhutanese. Many of these Hindu, Nepali-speaking southern Bhutanese trace their roots in the country to the mid-nineteenth century or earlier. The stringent 1985 Citizenship Act confirmed the primary basis for citizenship to be residence in Bhutan in 1958, the year in which a Nationality Law granted citizenship to most ethnic Nepalese. It also tightened the requirements for transmitting citizenship to persons born after 1958 by requiring that both parents be Bhutanese citizens. Previously, only the father had to be a Bhutanese citizen for citizenship to be transmitted. To prove citizenship, southern Bhutanese had to show a land tax receipt for 1958 (evidence that predates or postdates 1958 would not be acceptable), which amounted to asking a largely illiterate population to suddenly produce documentation that had been of little importance when issued three decades earlier. The 1985 Act also allowed the government to revoke citizenship from any naturalized person who "has shown by act or speech to be disloyal in any manner whatsoever to the King, country and people of Bhutan," which could include nonviolent protest.

The country's sixth five-year plan (1987-92) introduced a program of "One Nation, One People" that discriminated against southern Bhutanese through measures that included the promotion of a national dress code based on the culture of the ruling Ngalong Drukpa ethnic group. The Ngalong Drukpas, who are Buddhists of Tibetan origin, live in northern and western Bhutan and comprise only one-fifth of the population.

In 1988, after a census showed ethnic-Nepalese to be in the majority in five southern districts, the government began using the 1985 Citizenship Act to arbitrarily strip thousands of southern Bhutanese of their citizenship. People losing their citizenship could be naturalized only by meeting the nearly impossible requirements of proficiency in the Dzongkha language and proof of residency during the previous fifteen to twenty years.

A February 1989 royal decree made *Driglam Namzha* (traditional Ngalop Drukpa dress and customs) mandatory for all Bhutanese, enforceable through fines and imprisonment. The government also banned instruction in the Nepali language in schools, and required candidates for the civil service to speak Dzongkha.

In the summer of 1990 the newly formed southern-based Bhutan People's Party (BPP) organized several protests in the south against Driglam Namzha and against the imprisonment of Tek Nath Rizal, a former Royal Advisory Council member, and other dissidents. In September 1990 soldiers fired on a group of protestors, killing several civilians. The government outlawed the BPP shortly thereafter, accusing it of engaging in terrorist attacks on officials, arrested thousands of southern Bhutanese as "anti-nationals" and shut down scores of schools and hospitals in the region.

In late 1990 and early 1991 the government began expelling from the country the first of tens of thousands of southern Bhutanese. Officials forced many to sign "voluntary departure" statements that forfeited their land and property. Throughout southern Bhutan, soldiers randomly raped and beat villagers, hastening the exodus. The flow peaked in 1992, but by 1994 there were 86,000 southern Bhutanese in eight refugee camps in eastern Nepal and 15,000 others in India. Bhutan claims that most of the refugees were illegal immigrants. However, according to the Nepalese government 97 percent of the refugees possess some form of Bhutanese citizenship documentation.

In 1994 there was growing evidence that the government is encouraging northern Bhutanese to resettle in depopulated areas in the south. In another development, on 21 June a group of northern Bhutanese launched the Druk National Congress party in exile in Nepal to press for democratic reforms.

Political Rights and Civil Liberties:

Bhutanese citizens lack the democratic means to change their government. The king wields absolute power, and policymaking is centered around the king and a small number of Buddhist aristocratic elites. Ethnic Nepalese hold a disproportionately small number of seats in the National Assembly. The two major ethnic-Nepalese-based political parties, the Bhutan People's Party and the Bhutan National Democratic Party, are both outlawed and operate in exile in Nepal.

The Bhutanese army and police are responsible for grave human rights violations against ethnic-Nepalese citizens. These include arbitrary arrests, beatings, rape, destruction of homes and robbery. Security forces regularly search houses without apparent justification. There are at least 200 southern Bhutanese political detainees, and several detainees and prisoners have reportedly died in custody in recent years due to torture and poor conditions.

Southern Bhutanese are required to obtain from the government "No Objection Certificates" (NOC) to enter schools, take jobs and sell farm products. In practice NOCs are frequently denied. The 1989 Driglam Namzha decree requiring all Bhutanese to wear traditional Ngalop Drukpa clothes is enforced infrequently in the north, but fairly strongly in the south. The teaching of the Nepali language in schools remains banned, and many of the southern schools and hospitals closed by the authorities in 1990 have yet to reopen. The government charges southern Bhutanese with terrorist actions, but according to the U.S. State Department most attacks in the south appear to be the random work of armed robber gangs with no political or ideological affiliation.

The king appoints and can dismiss judges, and the judiciary is not independent of the government. Judges handle all aspects of a case, including investigation and prosecution. There are no jury trials or lawyers, although a defendant has the right to the services of a *jambi*, a person familiar with the law.

Only 12 percent of the population is literate, so the print media has little impact. The state-owned weekly *Kuensel* is the country's only regular publication and is essentially a government mouthpiece. Foreign publications are available but the authorities ban editions carrying articles critical of the king or government. The country has no television stations, and since 1989 the kingdom has banned satellite dishes to prevent people from receiving foreign broadcasts. Freedom of speech is restricted and criticism of the king is not permitted, except indirectly during National Assembly discussions. There is no freedom of association, and there are no nongovernmental organizations or other elements of civil society.

The Druk Kargue sect of Mahayana Buddhism is the official state religion. Monasteries and shrines are subsidized by the government and some 6,000 Buddhist *lamas* (priests) wield fairly strong political influence. Most southern Bhutanese are Hindus; due to persecution against them, they lack the means to worship freely. Southern Bhutanese reportedly also face difficulty in traveling freely throughout the country. Only 3,000 visitors are allowed into the kingdom each year. Trade unions and strikes are not permitted. According to UNICEF preteens are sometimes put on roadbuilding teams.

Bolivia

Polity: Presidential-legislative democracy
Economy: Capitalist
Population: 8,214,000
PPP: $2,170
Life Expectancy: 60.5
Ethnic Groups: Quechua Indian (30 percent), Aymara Indian (25 percent), other Indian (15 percent), mixed (10-15 percent), European (10-15 percent)

Political Rights: 2
Civil Liberties: 3
Status: Free

Overview: President Gonzalo Sanchez de Losada made some headway in implementing an ambitious economic reform and privatization program. However, few Bolivians expected to benefit in the short term, and because he had difficulties handling protests by coca growers, the president's popularity waned in the second half of 1994.

After achieving independence from Spain in 1825, the Republic of Bolivia endured recurrent instability and extended periods of military rule. The armed forces, responsible for over 180 coups in 157 years, returned to the barracks in 1982 and the 1967 constitution was restored. The 1985 election of President Victor Paz Estenssoro of the Nationalist Revolutionary Movement (MNR) marked the first transfer of power between two elected presidents in twenty-five years.

The constitution provides for the election every four years of a president and a Congress consisting of a 130-member House of Representatives and a 27-member Senate. Following reforms made in 1993-94, the terms will be extended to five years beginning in 1997. Currently, if no presidential candidate receives an absolute majority of votes, Congress makes the selection from among the three leading contenders. Starting in 1997, the outcome will be decided by a run-off election between the two leading candidates. Municipal elections are held every two years.

Sanchez de Losada, the former planning minister under Paz Estenssoro and architect of an austerity program that ended hyperinflation, won a plurality in the 1989 election. Retired Gen. Hugo Banzer, head of the conservative National Democratic Action (ADN) came second. Jaime Paz Zamora of the social democratic Movement of the Revolutionary Left (MIR) came third. Sanchez de Losada lost out when the ADN joined the MIR in a coalition to elect Paz Zamora president in exchange for half the cabinet positions.

Paz Zamora's term was marked by factionalism, corruption scandals, student protests and paralyzing labor strikes. Widespread discontent with traditional politics led to the emergence of populist, anti-establishment alternatives, the Civic and Solidarity Union (UCS) led by beer magnate Max Fernandez and the Conscience of the Fatherland party (CONDEPA) led by talk-show host Carlos Palenque.

The 1993 election campaign came down to a duel between Sanchez de Losada and Banzer for the incumbent ADN-MIR. Sanchez de Losada's reputation as a successful and honest entrepreneur apparently gave him the edge.

Sanchez de Losada took 33.8 percent of the vote; Banzer, 20 percent; Palenque, 13.6; Fernandez, 13.1; and Antonio Aranibar of the leftist Free Bolivia Movement (MBL), 5.1. The MNR won 69 seats in the bicameral legislature. Sanchez de Losada secured the backing of Fernandez, whose UCS took 21 seats, and Aranibar, whose MBL took 7. The three-party coalition elected Sanchez president. Running mate Hugo Cardenas, an Aymara Indian, became vice president, the first indigenous leader in Latin America to hold such a high national office. Both the UCS and the MBL were rewarded with cabinet positions.

In 1994 Sanchez de Losada managed to get Congress to agree in principle to his economic centerpiece, a privatization scheme he calls "capitalization." It would bring in foreign investors to make a strategic equity stake in six major state companies, then distribute up to 50 percent of the remaining shares to the estimated 3.8 million adult Bolivians. However, full implementation required a heavy legislative program, and Sanchez de Losada had difficulties maintaining his governing coalition. In September Fernandez defected. Only after seven UCS legislators made a separate peace with the MNR was Sanchez de Losada able to retain a slim majority in Congress.

Meanwhile, the president had raised great expectations during his campaign by promising to create thousands of jobs. However, austerity cuts in the public sector work force, followed by a series of strikes, left many Bolivians disillusioned.

Sanchez de Losada also mishandled a September march by coca growers who were protesting stepped-up measures against coca production by Bolivian drug police advised by the U.S. Drug Enforcement Agency. First, the government used force against the marchers. Then, after widespread criticism, Sanchez de Losada about-faced, inviting protesters to the presidential palace. In the end, little was settled and Sanchez de Losada had reinforced his image as an indecisive leader.

By October, Sanchez de Losada saw his rating in the opinion polls, once as high as 70 percent, drop to nearly half that. Still, he stood well above his political rivals. The ADN seemed paralyzed by an internal fight over who would succeed the aging Banzer as party chief. The MIR also was in turmoil after Paz Zamora stepped down as party leader in the face of allegations that he and other MIRistas had links with drug traffickers during his administration.

Political Rights and Civil Liberties: Citizens are able to change their government through democratic means. In 1991 a new electoral court consisting of five relatively independent magistrates was created, and a new voter registration system was implemented.

Constitutional guarantees regarding free expression, freedom of religion, and the right to organize political parties, civic groups and labor unions are generally respected. But political expression is restricted by recurring violence associated with labor strife and the billion-dollar-per-year cocaine trade. Also, the emergence of small indigenous-based guerrilla groups has caused an overreaction by security forces against legitimate government opponents. The languages of the indigenous population are officially recognized, but the 40 percent Spanish-speaking minority still dominates the political process.

The political landscape features political parties ranging from fascist to radical left. There are also a number of indigenous-based peasant movements, including the Tupac Katari Revolutionary Liberation Movement headed by Victor Hugo Cardenas, the nation's vice president.

There is strong evidence that drug money has penetrated the political process through the corruption of government officials and the military, and through electoral campaign financing. The drug trade has also spawned private security forces that operate with relative impunity in the coca-growing regions. Bolivia is the world's second largest producer of cocaine. A U.S.-sponsored eradication program has drawn political fire from peasant unions representing Bolivia's 50,000 coca farmers, the Bolivian Workers Confederation, the nation's largest labor confederation, and nationalist sectors of the military.

Unions are permitted to strike and have done so repeatedly against the economic restructuring programs of three successive governments that have left more than a quarter of the work force idle. Strikes are often broken up by government security forces.

The judiciary, headed by a Supreme Court, is the weakest branch of government. Despite recent reforms it remains riddled with corruption, over-politicized and subject to the compromising power of drug traffickers. A revamped Supreme Court won accolades in early 1993 for convicting fugitive former dictator Gen. Lucas Garcia Mesa (1980-81) and a number of his cronies on murder and corruption charges. Later, however, seven of the twelve justices faced charges in the Congress for soliciting bribes in an extradition case. In 1994 two of them, including the chief justice, were impeached by the Senate. It remained to be seen whether the creation of a Constitutional Tribunal and a "people's defender" branch would improve the judicial system.

Human rights organizations are both government-sponsored and independent. Their reports indicate an increase in police brutality, torture during confinement and harsh prison conditions since 1991. There has been occasional intimidation against independent rights activists. Prison conditions are poor and nearly three-quarters of prisoners have not been formally sentenced.

The press, radio and television are mostly privately owned and free of censorship. Journalists covering corruption stories are occasionally subject to verbal intimidation by government officials, arbitrary detention by police and violent attacks. There are a number of daily newspapers including one sponsored by the influential Catholic church. Opinion polling is a growth industry. Seven years ago there was no television, but now there are more than sixty channels. The impact has been most evident in the media-based campaigns of the prominent political parties.

⬇ Bosnia-Herzegovina

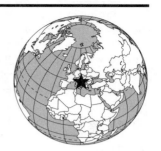

Polity: Presidential-par- **Political Rights:** 6
liamentary democracy **Civil Liberties:** 6
(mostly foreign-occupied) **Status:** Not Free
Economy: Mixed-statist
(severely war-damaged)
Population: 4,600,000
PPP: na
Life Expectancy: na
Ethnic Groups: Pre-war—Slavic Muslim (44 percent),
Serb (33 percent), Croat (17 percent)
Trend Arrow: The country suffered a downward trend as war intensified.

Overview: **A**s 1994 drew to a close, former U.S. President Jimmy
Carter helped broker a cease-fire after a counteroffensive
by Bosnian Serbs, Croat Serbs and antigovernment Muslim
renegades threatened to overrun the U.N.-designated "safe haven" of Bihac in the
northwest after a temporarily successful breakout effort by Bosnian Muslim forces.
To some, the Bihac setback spelled military defeat for the multi-ethnic Bosnian
Muslim government led by President Alija Izetbegovic.

Bosnia-Herzegovina became one of six constituent republics of Yugoslavia in
November 1945. During World War II, brutal internecine conflict left 700,000
dead, mostly Serbs. As Yugoslavia began to unravel, multiparty elections were
held in September 1990, with the three nationalist parties representing Muslim,
Serb, and Croat constituencies winning a majority in the 240-member Assembly. In
a February 1992 referendum boycotted by Serbs, 99 percent favored secession
from Yugoslavia. President Izetbegovic issued a declaration of independence 3
March. Two weeks later, Muslim, Croat and Serb leaders agreed to divide Bosnia
into three autonomous units based on the "national absolute or relative majority" in
each area. The agreement was never enforced.

The U.S. recognized Bosnia on 7 April. As fighting intensified, outgunned Muslims
and their Croat allies faced an estimated 100,000 Serbs supplied by the Serbian government of Slobodan Milosevic. By year's end, Serbs controlled over 70 percent of the
country, and a systematic policy of "ethnic cleansing" had killed or displaced hundreds
of thousands of Muslim, Croat and Serb civilians. The Vance-Owen plan—named for
former U.S. Secretary of State and U.N. mediator Cyrus Vance and European Community negotiator Lord David Owen—which called for the partition of Bosnia into ten
autonomous provinces, was widely criticized and never implemented. The presence of
over 20,000 U.N. peacekeepers did not deter Serbian aggression.

January 1994 opened with renewed Serbian shelling of Sarajevo and intense
fighting between the Bosnian Croatian Defense Council (HVO) forces and
government troops, particularly around Mostar in central Bosnia. Despite denials
from Zagreb, the Croat capital, regular Croatian army troops, including forced
conscripts, were involved in the fighting to halt Bosnian government advances. The
U.N. also confirmed that troops from Serbia were aiding Bosnian Serbs. In mid-

month, President Izetbegovic met with Croatia's President Franjo Tudjman in Bonn to end the fighting, but no agreement was reached. Meanwhile, Geneva peace talks mediated by Lord Owen and Thorvald Stoltenberg, named U.N. negotiator in 1993, went nowhere, as the Bosnian government again rejected a partition plan that consolidated Serb territorial gains.

In early February, after a Serb mortar attack that killed sixty-one and wounded 200 in Sarajevo, NATO set a ten-day deadline for Bosnian Serb forces to withdraw heavy weapons twenty kilometers from the encircled capital or risk air strikes. Russia moved to undercut the NATO deadline, calling on the U.N. Security Council to discuss demilitarization of the capital and placing it under U.N. administration. Bosnian Serbs demanded that the government pull back its infantry in exchange for a Serbian withdrawal of artillery.

Just days before the 20 February U.N. deadline and with Geneva peace talks suspended, the U.S., in another policy shift, backed the European partition plan and agreed to pressure the Bosnian government to accept the Owen-Stoltenberg plan. Concurrently, Bosnian Serb leaders began withdrawing artillery from around Sarajevo after Russia surprisingly announced that it was sending 800 troops to the capital. Vitaly Churkin, Russia's Yugoslav envoy, met publicly with Serb President Slobodan Milosevic, who thanked the Russian for helping avert NATO air raids. On 28 February, U.S. F-16 fighters shot down four Serb military aircraft for violating the year-old "no-fly zone."

On 23 February warring Muslims and Croats agreed to a cease-fire after the U.S. put pressure on the Croatian government to restrain militant Bosnian Croats. President Tudjman had earlier been behind the dismissal of Mate Boban, the hard-line president of the self-styled Croatian republic in Bosnia. In early March, Tudjman endorsed a Washington-engineered peace accord signed by Bosnian Muslims and Croats, who agreed to form a federated state in a loose union with Croatia. On 2 June the election of a president, Croat Kesimir Zubak, and vice president, Muslim Ejup Ganic, of the new Croat-Muslim federation in Bosnia signaled a renewed Croat-Muslim alliance.

On 3 March Serbian gunners violated the short-lived truce and shelled Sarajevo, using howitzers in a zone from which heavy weapons were banned under the NATO ultimatum. Serb forces also blocked seven U.N. convoys in Bosnia, including Manglaj, in direct defiance of the U.N. Security Council. Later that month, the Bosnian government and Serb leaders did agree to allow limited movement of people, food and medicine across siege lines around Sarajevo.

In April Serbs launched an assault on the U.N. "safe haven" of Goradze with a force that included members of the Yugoslav Army corps from Uzice, Serbia. Scores of civilians were killed. On 10-11 April, American fighter planes bombed Serbian targets near the besieged city. Russian Yugoslav envoy Churkin, exasperated by the duplicity of Bosnian Serb leaders, accused them of being "sick with the madness of war." Bowing to another NATO ultimatum, the Serbs withdrew some forces from Goradze, but not before intense shelling and infantry assaults. On 25 April American, French, German, British and Russian foreign ministers meeting in London agreed to form a "Contact Group" to work more closely with the U.N. for a settlement of the Bosnia war.

In May the Contact Group agreed to back a solution that would award the new Croat-Muslim federation 51 percent of Bosnia-Herzegovina, with the Serbs taking

49 percent. But on 25 May Serb and Muslim forces battled around Tesanj, sixty miles north of Sarajevo.

On 9 June in Geneva, Bosnian government officials, citing Serb withdrawal from a two-mile exclusion zone around Goradze, returned to the table and agreed to a month-long cease-fire, the thirty-fifth cease-fire in twenty-six months. But one Bosnian army official dismissed the document as "a piece of paper" that would "just give people time to get ready for the next round of war." The U.S. also moved closer to the view of France and Britain on the need to apply pressure on all sides, including the Bosnian Muslims. European officials indicated that part of the strategy would be the removal of some sanctions against Serbia if the Muslim government rejected the plan. Meanwhile, the U.S. House of Representatives, in a nonbinding resolution, called on the U.S. to lift the arms embargo and supply weapons to the Bosnian government. (The Senate later defeated a similar motion.)

In mid-June government troops stepped up efforts against Muslim troops loyal to renegade Fikret Abdic, a businessman and convicted embezzler who denounced President Izetbegovic as a destructive fundamentalist-nationalist, signed a non-aggression agreement with the Serbs and claimed control of territory around Bihac. Croatian Serbs unleashed heavy artillery fire across the Bosnian border to support Abdic's rebels, threatening an escalation in the fighting.

The Contact Group peace settlement was further jeopardized when fighting between government and Serb forces erupted around the Serb-held city of Doboj and the adjacent Mount Ozren region. At the same time, Serb leader Karadzic condemned a proposed map that would require Serbs to surrender to Muslims and Croats nearly a third of the territory under their control. His reluctance put him on a collision course with Serbian President Milosevic, who indicated he might support the plan if it meant the removal of economic sanctions against rump-Yugoslavia.

On 5 July the Contact Group unveiled a new map that put the crucial Brcko corridor into what would be Serb territory. Bosnian Prime Minister Haris Silajdzic said his government would study the plan. But by the end of the month, the Bosnian Serb parliament and leaders rejected the plan, demanding territorial concessions. President Izetbegovic then withdrew his conditional support for the plan, saying that in view of the Serb rejection, Sarajevo wanted conditions of its own.

Serb rejection divided the Contact Group; while the U.S. and Europe saw the Serbs as spurning the peace process, Russia insisted that the Serb response offered promise and that further negotiations were warranted. The Serbs reimposed the blockade of Sarajevo, lifted in March. At the end of July, the Contact Group meeting in Geneva failed to agree on a coordinated strategy to pressure the Bosnian Serbs and Serbia, Russia proving reluctant to tighten sanctions on Belgrade. On 2 August Serb President Milosevic, facing the prospect of stiffer sanctions, urged Bosnian Serbs to accept the plan, but Bosnian Serb leaders rejected the plan for the third time despite warnings from Russia. On 4 August President Milosevic announced that most political and economic links with nationalist Serb rebels in Bosnia were being severed because of their rejection of the peace initiative. A day later, NATO jets launched an attack in Bosnia after Serb forces seized heavy weapons under U.N. control near Sarajevo.

On 12 August President Bill Clinton set a deadline of 15 October for Bosnian Serbs to accept of the Contact Group plan or the U.S. would urge the U.N. Security Council to lift the arms embargo on Bosnia. The proposal won swift support from France, while

U.N. officials suggested that such a move would only fuel the war. On 28 August Bosnian Serbs overwhelmingly rejected the international proposal in a referendum.

In the first week of September, Serbs drove more than 2,500 Muslims, Gypsies, and Croats from areas around Banja Luka and Bijeljina, and forced non-Serb males into labor camps. On 9 September Serb forces from Bosnia and Croatia launched an assault near Bihac. By the end of the month the U.N. had monitored several hundred flights over northeastern Bosnia by helicopters originating in Serbia. Nevertheless, the Security Council voted on 23 September to ease sanctions on Yugoslavia for 100 days in response to President Milosevic's support of the peace plan. The Clinton administration decided not to press for a binding Security Council resolution to end the arms embargo on the Bosnian government.

In early October Serbs again blocked U.N. convoys around Sarajevo and launched a new wave of "ethnic cleansing" around the capital, expelling non-Serbs from several villages in eastern Bosnia. With Bosnian Serbs putatively abandoned by their patrons in Belgrade and facing fuel shortages, Bosnian government forces led by the Muslim V Corps and Croats launched a breakout offensive from Bihac, quickly capturing over ninety square miles of territory, forcing Bosnian Serb soldiers to retreat into Serb-controlled areas in Croatia.

By November Bosnian Serb forces renewed shelling in Sarajevo and, supported by Croatian Serbs who were getting logistical help from Serbia, recaptured territory around Bihac and bombed the city from the air. The U.S. announced it would unilaterally stop enforcing the arms embargo, but never followed through after rebukes by NATO allies. With government forces in retreat, the Serbs threatened to overrun the Bihac "safe haven." On 16 November President Izetbegovic appealed to the U.N. and NATO for immediate action to halt the Serb offensive. On 22 November NATO aircraft carried out a heavy bombing raid against missile sites in Serb-held territory in Croatia, which did little to stop the Serb drive. The U.N. and NATO bickered over how to respond to the fighting, particularly after U.N. spotters on the ground refused to guide NATO aircraft to their targets. The U.N. actions so angered the Bosnian government that Prime Minister Silajdzic expelled the U.N. commander, Lieut. Gen. Sir Michael Rose, from a meeting.

On 29 November the U.N. threatened to withdraw its 22,000 peacekeepers from Bosnia. By mid-December, 1,200 Bangladeshi U.N. troops were trapped in Bihac. Bosnian Serb leader Karadzic invited former President Jimmy Carter to mediate the war. Carter's involvement angered Bosnian government officials. But the Serbs refused to honor any of the conditions set by Carter, such as lifting the blockades of U.N. "safe havens," reopening the airport at Sarajevo and guaranteeing human rights in Serb-held territory.

On 19 December Bosnian Serbs offered a four-month cease-fire in Bosnia and agreed to open negotiations to modify the same plan they had rejected on several occasions. At year's end, Croatian Serb forces and renegade Muslims under Abdic, not included in the Carter agreement, continued attacking Bihac. The Bosnian government reiterated warnings that it would refuse to sign the four-month cease-fire if assaults on Bihac did not stop.

Political Rights and Civil Liberties:

War, *de facto* partition and "ethnic cleansing" seriously undermined the ability of the democratically elected government of Bosnia-Herzegovina to govern, notably in over 70 percent of territory in rebel Serb hands where rule of law has broken down. The country is run by a ten-member, multi-ethnic collective presidency chaired by President Alija Izetbegovic.

Human rights violations were rampant throughout 1994. Civilians faced deportation, execution, torture and unlawful imprisonment in labor camps. Thousands of non-Serbs were expelled from areas around Sarajevo, Banja Luka, Bihac and Bijeljina. In some cases, entire villages were forced to pay Serbian businessmen to arrange their escapes. Non-Serb men and women were pressed into forced labor, including trench-digging, around the country. Hundreds of men and women were confined for forced labor purposes in Siprage, a village near Banja Luka. Similar camps existed throughout Serb-held areas in Bosnia and Croatia. Croats also admitted inhumane conditions in prison camps that hold thousands of Muslims. The Muslim-Croat federation called for returning those who had fled the war, but local political resistance and lingering mistrust prevented mass returns.

Most newspapers stopped printing in 1993. The Sarajevo daily, *Oslobodjenje*, continued printing despite shortages of supplies, and an English-language edition was introduced with Western aid. The Independent Journalism Foundation expressed some concern over political influence at Bosnian Radio and Television. War made domestic travel risky and restrictive. Refugees and relief convoys were frequently stopped or attacked. Freedoms of association and assembly have been circumscribed by war. Muslims, Catholic Croats and Orthodox Serbs practiced their religion in areas they controlled. Mosques, churches and cemeteries were intentionally targeted in war zones. Trade unions exist, but their functions have been limited by economic and social dislocation.

Botswana

Polity: Parliamentary democracy and traditional chiefs
Economy: Capitalist
Population: 1,439,000
PPP: $4,690
Life Expectancy: 60.3
Ethnic Groups: Tswana, Baswara, Kalanga, Kgagaladi, European

Political Rights: 2
Civil Liberties: 3
Status: Free

Overview:

In 1994, Botswana held national parliamentary elections, in which the Botswana Democratic Party (BDP) retained its strong majority. The opposition party, the Botswana National Front (BNF), gained considerable support. Economic decline and financial scandals helped to weaken public confidence in the BDP.

Botswana, a landlocked country located in southern Africa, has one of the world's lowest population densities. Formerly a British colony, it gained independence in 1966 and became one of Africa's few working democracies. Since independence, the BDP has won all the elections and has ruled the country without interruption, withstanding charges of electoral rigging. The opposition parties include the Botswana National Front (BNF), the Botswana's People's Party (BPP), the Botswana Independence Party (BIP) and the Botswana Progressive Union (BPU). The country's president is Sir Ketumile Masire, who is also the leader of the BDP.

In the 15 October national elections, the BDP captured twenty-two of the thirty-five contested seats. The BNF won a total of thirteen—four times the amount it held before. Of the estimated 370,000 registered voters, more than 60 percent cast ballots. The increase in BNF seats showed a general voter swing to the left, as the BNF strongly promotes social welfare programs. Support for the opposition also indicated voter dissatisfaction with the declining economy.

Botswana's diamond industry suffered major setbacks in 1994. Botswana's earnings from diamond exports have been shrinking since 1992 as demand fell and Angola's rebels flooded markets with diamonds to finance their war. With the end of sanctions against South Africa, Botswana's diamond industry was further threatened by competition. Botswana's decreasing diamond revenue and an increase in urban population have caused unemployment to rise to 20 percent.

Threatened with an increasingly uncertain source of hard currency, the government made attempts throughout 1994 to try to diversify the economy by promoting eco-tourism in the Okovango Delta and the Kalahari. Other economic reforms include focusing less on minerals and more on labor-intensive industries such as meat-processing.

In May, the *Botswana Gazette,* an independent newspaper, released a report that seven cabinet members, seven members of the parliament and the president himself had all failed to honor their financial obligations to the National Development Bank, which was nearing bankruptcy. The government appointed a team of Irish consultants to investigate the matter and to determine how to revitalize the bank.

Political Rights and Civil Liberties:

Citizens of Botswana can change their government democratically. Although the BDP has governed the country since independence, the BNF's showing in the 1994 election proved the system is open to opposition.

The judiciary is independent. Citizens are protected from arbitrary arrest, and in most cases, suspects must be charged before a magistrate within forty-eight-hours. Suspects charged under the National Security Act (NSA) may be detained indefinitely. The NSA has rarely been invoked, however.

The right to assemble is usually respected, but permits for gatherings may be denied if there is a risk of violence. In February 1994 university students were denied permission to demonstrate against the retrenchment of 129 workers at the National Development Bank. Police prohibited the protest because of "lack of manpower." The students went ahead with the protest and were prevented from leaving the university.

The constitution prohibits discrimination based on ethnicity, but in 1992 the Botswana Christian Group, a religious consortium, charged that the Bushmen (*Baswara* or *San*) are subjected to pervasive discrimination, widespread torture, and forced departure from their ancestral land. The government charged that the report had been prepared by "foreign agitators" and refused to answer the charges. Of the 39,000 Bushmen, only 3,000 continue to lead a nomadic life, while the majority has been forced to settle in government approved areas and rely on public assistance.

Although the government-owned media, such as Radio Botswana, the Botswana Press Agency (BOPA) and the *Daily News* newspaper, tend to present government views, the four independent weeklies favor the opposition. The independent press has become increasingly aggressive in recent years in criticizing the opposition. Journalists can be charged with sedition if they promote discontent with the government, invite the use of violence or ridicule the government. This law against sedition is rarely enforced, however, and was carried over from the colonial period, when it was used to suppress the anti-British struggle.

Free trade unions in the private sector exist, but the right to strike is severely circumscribed. Public servants may form professional associations, but are not allowed to enter into wage bargaining.

According to a 1994 *Human Rights Watch* report, the Botswana Citizenship Act discriminates against women and their children. Under the terms of the Act, Botswana women married to foreign men may not pass citizenship on to their children unless their children obtain a special residence permit. This law does not hold for Botswana men who marry foreign women. In 1992, this law was challenged in the Supreme Court case *Dow v. State*, which ruled that the law must be rewritten. This still has not been done.

Brazil

Polity: Federal presiden-
tial-legislative democracy
Economy: Capitalist-
statist
Population: 155,254,000
PPP: $5,240
Life Expectancy: 65.8
Ethnic Groups: Caucasian (53 percent), black mixed (46 percent),
pure Indian (less than 1 percent)
Political Rights: 2*
Civil Liberties: 4
Status: Partly Free

Ratings Change: *Brazil's political rights rating rose from 3 to 2 principally as a result of the holding of relatively free and fair national elections.

Overview: Former finance minister Fernando Henrique Cardoso, whose Real Plan reduced inflation and restored a degree of national optimism, won a first-round victory in the October presidential elections. His challenge was to end the cycle of political paralysis and social decay that has seized Brazil for most of the last decade.

After gaining independence from Portugal in 1822, Brazil retained a monarchical system until a republic was established in 1889. Democratic rule has been interrupted by long periods of authoritarian rule, most recently under military governments from 1964 to 1985. The return to civilian rule in 1985, the result of a controlled transition transacted by the military with opposition political parties, led to the presidency of Jose Sarney, the first civilian leader in two decades. A bicameral Congress elected in 1986 produced a new constitution.

The 1988 constitution provides for a directly elected president and a bicameral Congress consisting of an eighty-one-member Senate elected for eight years and a 503-member Chamber of Deputies elected for four years. In 1994 the Congress reduced the presidential term from five to four years. Brazil is divided into twenty-six states and the Federal District of Brasilia. State governors and legislatures are elected, as are municipal governments.

In 1989 Fernando Collor de Mello defeated Luis Ignacio "Lula" da Silva of the leftist Workers' Party (PT) in a second round run-off presidential election. Collor vowed to end corruption and modernize the economy. But shock programs failed to control inflation and plans to overhaul the statist economy were undermined by a hostile Congress wielding the 1988 constitution, a populist document that mandates spending on behalf of a vast array of special interests and makes structural reform virtually impossible.

In 1992 Collor was tied to a $55-million graft and influence-peddling scheme. Pressured by the media and mass protests, the Congress—a diverse and generally feckless group of parties tied to labor, big business and regional interests— impeached him. Collor resigned in December 1992.

Itamar Franco, the vice president, took over. By the end of 1993, with inflation still rising and violent crime out of control, Franco's poll ratings were barely above single digits.

The constitution mandated that it be reviewed by Congress in 1993. The process was derailed by a massive corruption scandal involving dozens of legislators, cabinet ministers, state governors and assorted captains of industry. The effort finally fizzled out in mid-1994.

By that time, Lula da Silva was the clear front-runner in a field of eight presidential candidates for the October election. One of the eight was Cardoso, a market-oriented centrist and the author of the anti-inflation Real Plan that involved issuing of a new currency. Cardoso resigned as finance minister in April and cobbled together a center-right, three-party coalition centered around his own Social Democratic Party (PSDB). His plan went into effect in July. By September monthly inflation had plummeted from 50 to less than 2 percent. The whole campaign turned around as Cardoso, backed by the media and the business establishment, jumped to a twenty-point lead over da Silva in the polls.

On 3 October Cardoso won the presidency with 54 percent of the vote. Da Silva took 27 percent as other candidates trailed badly. However, the congressional balloting appeared to reinforce the amorphous and factionalized political system. The Senate was left divided among eleven parties and the Chamber of Deputies among eighteen parties. Even so, Cardoso did appear to command a majority based on his loose and unwieldy coalition, and coalition candidates fared well in key gubernatorial elections.

Nonetheless, as Cardoso approached his 1 January 1995 inauguration, he still faced the problem of how to get the legislative support necessary to carry out the program of political reform and economic liberalization he promised in his campaign. His Real Plan had lifted national morale, but keeping inflation down required further structural changes and the types of constitutional reforms Brazil's political parties had previously rejected. His showing in October gave him a strong popular mandate, but he needed quickly to find a way to overcome the tradition of corrupt, gridlocked politics before the mood turned sour again.

Cardoso also had to come to terms with the 300,000-member military. The political and economic chaos that reigned prior to the Real Plan caused former President Franco to embrace what local analysts called the "military anchor," giving the military inordinate influence in politics. Some even raised the specter of a "Fujimori" solution—the dissolution of Congress in favor of presidential-military rule as in Peru. The military did not interfere in the 1994 campaign and was pleased that Cardoso rather than da Silva won. But it remained anxious over the prospect of cuts to its budget and, like many Brazilians, uncertain whether Brazil had finally turned the corner.

Political Rights and Civil Liberties: Citizens are able to change their governments through elections at the national and local levels. Overall, the 1994 elections were relatively free and fair. However, there were not insignificant irregularities at the local level, particularly in some of the northeast states and in the state of Rio de Janeiro, as well as evidence that candidate Cardoso benefited from government support.

Constitutional guarantees regarding freedom of religion and expression and the right to organize political and civic organizations are generally respected. In the last decade civic society has grown rich and vibrant. However, escalating criminal violence, much of it fueled by the burgeoning drug trade, and a national breakdown of police discipline have created a climate of lawlessness and generalized insecurity in which human rights are violated on a massive scale with impunity. Polls show that Brazilians rank violence as their first or second concern, but it was hardly addressed in the 1994 election campaign.

Brazil's national police are among the most violent and corrupt anywhere. Going back to military rule, police in each state receive military-style training. Although nominally commanded by elected officials, military police are under the jurisdiction of military courts in which they are rarely held accountable. Below the military police are the local civil police whose inefficiency and corruption are used by the military police to justify their tactics of simply eliminating suspected criminals.

In October 1994, the federal government was forced to send the army into Rio de Janeiro's 400 slums, most of which had been taken over by drug gangs in league or in competition with corrupt police and local politicians. Brazil is now a principal bridge between cocaine-producing Andean countries and consumers in Europe and the U.S.

Brazil's numerous independent human rights organizations have documented killings by the military police and systematic abuse in police detention centers. In 1992 111 inmates were summarily executed by military police during a riot at a São Paulo prison. None of the police was jailed and ten were promoted. Conditions in Brazil's overflowing, violence-plagued penal system are wretched and the military police are responsible for quelling disorders.

Vigilante "extermination" groups linked to the police and financed by local merchants are responsible for thousands of extrajudicial killings a year. According to Amnesty International, in Rio de Janeiro alone 1,200 poor people were killed by such groups between September 1993 and June 1994.

Violence, including disappearances, against the 35 million children living in poverty, at least a fifth of them living in the streets of burgeoning urban centers, is systematic. About five "street kids" a day are murdered in Brazil, according to researchers at the University of São Paulo, yet only very rarely are their killers caught. About 80 percent of the victims are of African descent. In June 1994 two human rights workers investigating child murders were found shot to death in Rio de Janeiro.

The climate of lawlessness is reinforced by a weak judiciary. It is headed by an eleven-member Supreme Court whose members must be approved by the Senate, and is granted substantial autonomy by the constitution. However, the judicial system is overwhelmed (with only 7,000 judges for a population of more than 150 million) and vulnerable to the chronic corruption which undermines the entire political system. It has been virtually powerless in the face of organized crime, much of it drug-related.

There is little public confidence in the judicial system, and poorer citizens, beset by inflation and unemployment, have resorted to lynchings, with hundreds of mob executions reported in the last three years. The middle class, unable to afford costly private security measures, is targeted by kidnappers-for-ransom who often operate in league with police.

Violence associated with land disputes continues unabated. Brazil's landowners control nearly 60 percent of arable land, while the poorest 30 percent share less than 2 percent. The income gap between rich and poor in Brazil is wider than in any other country in the world. Every year, hundreds of activists, Catholic church workers and rural unionists are killed by paramilitary groups and hired killers in the pay of large landowners, with very few cases brought to court.

There are continued reports of forced labor of thousands of landless workers by ranchers, often with the complicity of local police, in the Amazon and other rural regions. Workers are held in virtual slavery by large landowners through debt bondage and coercion. Although forced labor is against Brazilian and international law, the judicial response to forced labor can most generously be described as indifferent and the practice continues with impunity.

Rubber tappers and Indians continue to be targets of violence, including assassination, associated with Amazon development projects initiated under military rule and the gold rush in the far north. The constitution gives Brazil's quarter million Indians legal sanction, but the government has only reluctantly tried to stop invasions by settlers and miners into Indian reserves.

Violence against women and children is endemic, much of it occurring in the home. Protective laws are rarely enforced. In 1991 the Supreme Court ruled that a man could no longer kill his wife and win acquittal on the ground of "legitimate defense of honor," but juries tend to ignore the ruling. Forced prostitution of children is widespread.

Industrial labor unions are well organized, politically connected and prone to corruption. The right to strike is recognized and there are special labor courts. The constitution makes it virtually impossible to fire public-sector workers and there have been hundreds of strikes in recent years against attempts to privatize state industries. Child labor is prevalent and laws against it are rarely enforced.

The press is privately owned, vigorous and uncensored. There are daily newspapers in most major cities and many other publications throughout the country. The print media have played a central role in exposing official corruption. Radio is mostly commercial. Television is independent, politically conservative and a powerful political instrument. Roughly two-thirds of the population is illiterate, while 85 percent of households have television sets. The huge TV Globo dominates, but there are three other networks, plus educational channels. At least one journalist was killed in 1994.

Brunei

Polity: Traditional monarchy
Economy: Capitalist-statist
Population: 285,000
PPP: $14,000
Life Expectancy: 74.0
Ethnic Groups: Malay (65 percent), Chinese (20 percent), other (15 percent)

Political Rights: 7
Civil Liberties: 6
Status: Not Free

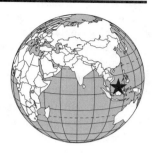

Overview:

Located on the northern coast of the Southeast Asian island of Borneo, Brunei became a British protectorate in 1888. The 1959 constitution provided for five advisory councils: the Privy Council, the Religious Council, the Council of Succession, the Council of Ministers and a Legislative Council. In 1962 the leftist Brunei People's Party (PRB) took all ten of the elected seats in the twenty-one member Legislative Council; late in the year British troops crushed a PRB-backed rebellion. The sultan then assumed constitutionally authorized emergency powers for a stipulated two-year period. These powers have been renewed every two years since then, and elections have not been held since 1965. Sultan Haji Hasanal Bolkiah Mu'izzadin Waddaulah ascended the throne in October 1967.

Following a period of gradually decreasing British participation in internal affairs, full independence came on 1 January 1984. The sultan serves as prime minister and has nearly complete authority over the country. Currently only the Council of Ministers, composed largely of the sultan's relatives, and the Legislative Council, with all members appointed by the sultan, are convened. In 1985 the government recognized the moderate Brunei National Development Party (PKDB), followed a year later by the offshoot Brunei National United Party (PPKB). However, in 1988 the government dissolved the PKDB and detained two of its leaders for two years, reportedly after the party called on the sultan to hold elections. The PPKB currently has fewer than 100 members and wields no influence.

Political Rights and Civil Liberties:

Citizens of Brunei lack the democratic means to change their government in this hereditary sultanate. Nearly all political power is wielded by the sultan and his inner circle of relatives. Since 1992 there have been local elections for village chiefs, who serve life terms. All candidates must have a knowledge of Islam (although they can be non-Muslims) and cannot have past or current links with a political party. The only other means of popular participation is through petitions to the sultan. The constitution does not protect freedoms of speech, press, assembly or association, and these rights are restricted in practice. The threat of government sanction has meant that, in practice, criticism of the government or opposition activity rarely occurs.

A 1988 law makes forty-two criminal offenses, including drug-related crimes, subject to corporal punishment although, given the low crime rate, it is rarely administered. Police have broad powers to make arrests without obtaining warrants. The Internal Security Act (ISA) allows the government to detain suspects without trial for renewable two-year periods. There have been no detentions under the ISA since the government released several dissidents in 1990.

The judiciary is independent of the government. Hong Kong provides judges for the High Court and Court of Appeals. Defendants receive reasonably adequate procedural safeguards, with the notable exception of the right to trial by jury. The country's one independent newspaper frequently practices self-censorship by avoiding discussion of religious issues and of the sultan's paramount political role. The only television station is state-owned.

Although the constitution guarantees the right of non-Muslims to practice their religion freely, since 1991 the government has been asserting the primacy of Islam through a national ideology of Malay Muslim Monarchy (MIB), which allegedly dates back more than 500 years. The government frequently refuses non-Muslims permission to build new places of worship, and has closed some existing ones. Other restrictions on non-Muslims include a ban on proselytizing and on the importation of religious books or educational materials, restrictions on religious education in non-Muslim schools and a requirement that Islamic education and MIB be taught at all schools.

Ethnic Malays enjoy advantages in university admission and employment. While the Chinese community is influential in business and commerce, most Chinese were not granted citizenship when the country became independent, and the rigorous Malay-language citizenship test makes it difficult for them to become naturalized. Women face discrimination in matters of divorce and inheritance, and in obtaining equal pay and benefits. Muslim women are strongly encouraged to wear the *tudong*, a traditional head covering, although there is no formal sanction against those who do not. Foreign domestic servants are occasionally beaten or otherwise treated poorly.

Citizens can travel freely within the country. Some expatriate workers are limited in traveling abroad during their first year under contract. The government must approve all trade unions, but does not interfere in their affairs. Four exist, covering just 5 percent of the workforce. The constitution neither recognizes nor prohibits strikes, and in practice none occurs.

Bulgaria

Polity: Parliamentary democracy
Economy: Mixed statist transitional
Population: 8,393,000
PPP: $4,813
Life Expectancy: 71.9
Ethnic Groups: Bulgarian (85 percent), Turkish (9 percent), Gypsy (3 percent), Macedonian (3 percent)

Political Rights: 2
Civil Liberties: 2
Status: Free

Overview:

In 1994 the beleaguered technocrat-led government of Prime Minister Lyuben Berov collapsed following a vote of no-confidence, leading to 18 December national elections that saw the (formerly Communist) Bulgarian Socialist Party (BSP) win 43.5 percent of the vote and 120 seats in the 240-member National Assembly (Parliament).

Berov's ouster came after the ruling coalition made up of the BSP and the Turkish-based Movement of Rights and Freedoms (MRF) withdrew their support for the government in a year that saw a political stalemate over such issues as privatization and market reforms.

Bordered by the Black Sea on the east, Bulgaria is nestled between Romania, Turkey and Greece on the north and south and the former Yugoslavia to the west. It was occupied by Ottoman Turks from 1396 to 1878, and did not achieve complete independence until 1908. It was on the losing side in both World Wars, and Communists seized power in conjunction with the "liberation" of Bulgaria by the Soviet Army in 1944. From 1954-1989, the country was in the grip of Communist Party strongman Todor Zhivkov, who was forced to resign one day after the fall of the Berlin Wall in November 1989.

The Berov government was formed in December 1992 after the collapse of the Union of Democratic Forces (UDF) government under reformist Filip Dimitrov. Berov, a nonparty technocrat and former economic adviser to President Zhelyu Zhelev, was backed by the BSP and MRF. In 1991 elections to the National Assembly (Parliament), the UDF, a coalition of some 13 opposition groups, won 111 seats, the BSP 106, and the MRF 23. In 1993 the government survived several no-confidence motions for failure to implement privatization laws passed the year before and to fulfill a budget draft which included an indirect offer for aid to a wide range of state enterprises, and the continued control of much of the economic sector by the nomenklatura, including members and former members of the BSP.

In April 1994 President Zhelev announced that he could no longer support the government, criticizing the slow pace of privatization, agricultural reform, the absence of improvements in communications infrastructure and the Cabinet's failure to deal effectively with the dramatic devaluation of the lev. The UDF under Dimitrov called for the government to step down, while the BSP and MRF said their support was conditional on major policy changes. The government also came under fierce pressure after the introduction of financially reasonable but highly unpopular increases in electricity and heating charges and the introduction of an 18 percent value-added tax on 1 April.

In April and May the Confederation of Trade Unions in Bulgaria (KNSB), which had backed the government in the past, staged several warning strikes to protest social policies, urging that incomes be protected against inflation and that key industry sectors be protected. On 8 May the prime minister proposed to reshuffle the cabinet, naming BSP member Rumen Gechev as his deputy in charge of economic reform to replace UDF Trade Minister Velentin Karabashev, who resigned in April. Finance Minister Stoyan Alexandrov threatened to resign if Parliament failed to adopt legislation on bankruptcy and substantial amendments to the privatization law. In mid-May, amid nationwide strikes of hundreds of thousands of workers in public and private sectors, the MRF and the centrist New Union for Democracy (NUD) rejected the cabinet reshuffling, saying they could not accept transforming a nonparty "government of experts" into a BSP cabinet. Polls showed that 60 percent of respondents opposed Berov's ruling until the end of his term.

Berov barely won a no-confidence motion on 27 May, leading the UDF to declare that it would not participate in the plenary sessions of Parliament. It charged that the government had systematically replaced UDF appointees in the ministry of foreign affairs, the state-run media, the judiciary and major state companies. At its sixth conference in May, the UDF adopted a rule stating that not only former leading Communists but also their children would be excluded from higher positions in the coalition. At its congress in early June, the BSP passed a resolution calling for early elections.

The besieged government won a small victory when the Assembly passed the final text of amendments to the 1992 privatization law, which paved the way for mass privatization of state enterprises under a voucher system not envisaged in the original law. The Assembly voted to establish a Center for Mass Privatization. President Zhelev signed the law on 23 June.

Throughout the summer political groups were preparing for the likelihood of early elections. In July, there were reports that three members of the UDF—the right-wing Democratic Party, the Radical Democratic Party and the centrist Bulgarian Agrarian National Union—were leaving the coalition.

In early September the government announced its intention to resign, with Berov acknowledging that Parliament was so hamstrung by contradictory opinions that new elections were the only solution to break the deadlock. President Zhelev subsequently named Renata Indzhova as caretaker prime minister and elections were set for 18 December.

After the vote the BSP held 120 seats. The UDF won only 24 percent of the vote and 69 seats. The agarian Popular Union won 6 percent; the MRF, 5 percent; and the Bulgarian Business Block, just under 5 percent. Most of the forty-seven parties that contested the election did not clear the 4 percent hurdle necessary for representation in parliament. Turnout was more than 75 percent. By 28 December President Zhelev urged the BSP to form a government.

A key issue throughout the year was the economy, particularly the scope and pace of privatization. Early in the year, it was estimated that the private sector contributed 37 percent of the national economy, lagging behind other countries in Central Europe. However, the absence of a well-functioning financial system and bureaucratic resistance held up mass sales of state-owned companies, despite the passage of mass privatization legislation. The economy, which was hard-hit by the collapse of the COMECON markets and the U.N. embargo against neighboring Serbia, did show some signs of a slow recovery. Over 46 percent of foreign trade in 1994 was with Western countries, compared to just 9 percent in 1990. Inflation, which reached 64 percent in 1993, was expected to fall to 30-35 percent. Foreign investment began to increase.

Crime and corruption were other key concerns. In August, the cabinet approved an anticrime package providing for an additional 5,000 police officers and the establishment of an intergovernmental crime prevention working group. Smuggling and racketeering were major problems; organized gangs continued to smuggle arms and materials into the former Yugoslavia, and illicit drug-trafficking remained a issue. Some 20,000 Bulgarians are believed to have experimented with heroin. There were persistent allegations of government corruption among BSP and MRF officials in banking, the privatization apparatus, agriculture, energy and the tourist trade. A business lobby group, the Group of 13, had close ties to the Communist regime or the secret police. Allegations of corruption also surfaced against the Podkrepa free trade union. Illegal currency speculation and unregulated, *de facto* privatization and corruption in state bureaucracies were endemic.

Other issues included a controversial Law on the Judiciary that said that those in top positions in the judiciary needed to have served at least five years as judges or prosecutors, raising the possibility that most jurists would be from the Communist era. Parliament overrode President Zhelev's veto of the measure. Local elections in June saw an extremely low voter turnout that nullified most results.

Political Rights and Civil Liberties: Bulgarians have the right to change their government democratically under a multiparty system enshrined in the 1991 constitution.

Under the constitution, the judiciary is guaranteed independence and equal status with the legislature and executive branch. A controversial law passed in June calls for all top judicial posts to be filled by those who served as judges or prosecutors for five years, leaving the possibility of a purge of post-Communist jurists.

Bulgarians can express themselves freely, and there is a lively independent press that has criticized the government. However, there are some restrictions. Article 187 of the Penal Code allows investigation of the press, though not of the journalist, on "alleged stated facts." However, the Bulgarian Helsinki Committee concluded that the prosecution of a television journalist for slander was based on the grounds that threatened freedom of the press. In March, Bulgaria's major newspapers ceased publications for one day, and six private radio stations stopped broadcasting to protest the 18 percent value-added tax that would adversely affect advertising revenue. In October, the Central Electoral Commission allocated air time during the campaign in a way that clearly favored the BSP and the MRF at the expense of smaller parties, drawing protests from President Zhelev.

Freedoms of association and assembly are generally respected. Political parties can organize freely although there are restrictions on parties being formed strictly along ethnic, religious or racial lines. Two new parties were formed by splinter groups from the Turkish-based MRF: the Party of Democratic Changes and the Turkish Democratic Party.

Ethnic tensions have lessened in the last few years, but there were reports of discrimination against Turks, Pomaks (ethnic Bulgarian Muslims) and especially Gypsies (Roma). In July, a MRF parliamentary leader was investigated for allegedly calling on ethnic Turks serving in the army to disobey orders if the Bulgarian language were made compulsory for soldiers carrying out their duties. Gypsies continue to be the victims of job discrimination and police brutality, and crimes against Gypsies are often not investigated by authorities.

Freedom of worship is generally respected, although the government regulates churches and religious institutions through the Directorate on Religious Beliefs. New amendments to the Law on Persons and the Family, adopted in February, however, were interpreted by some as violating the spirit of freedom of religion and separation of church and state. Article 133a said that "the non-profit juridical entities which have religious or related activities or perform religious education should be registered...after the approval of the Council of Ministers." In June, twenty-four organizations were prohibited from registering.

There are a number of women's organizations, and women have held prominent government offices, including caretaker prime minister. There is *de facto* discrimination in employment.

Bulgaria has two large labor union confederations, the Confederation of Independent Trade Unions (KNSB), a successor of the official, Communist-era union, and Podkrepa, an independent federation founded in 1989. Workers have and exercise the right to strike. In 1994, there were allegations of corruption against some Podkrepa officials related to aid from the West.

Burkina Faso

Polity: Dominant party
Economy: Mixed statist
Population: 10,069,000
PPP: $666
Life Expectancy: 47.9
Ethnic Groups: Bobo, Mossi, Samo, other

Political Rights: 5
Civil Liberties: 4
Status: Partly Free

Overview:

Under the leadership of President Blaise Compaore, a series of controlled democratic reforms and a government reconstruction were introduced in 1991. During 1994, the political landscape in Burkina Faso remained unchanged. However, the economic adjustment programme, initiated under the auspices of the World Bank and the International Monetary Fund (IMF) as part of the government reconstruction in 1991, continued. An additional $25 million was pledged by the International Monetary Fund (IMF) in 1994.

Since gaining independence from France in 1960, Burkina Faso has been governed by successive military dictatorships. Burkina Faso's current head of state, President Blaise Compaore, seized power in a military coup in 1987. Originally opposed to a multiparty system, Compaore allowed several independent political parties to join the ruling Organization for Popular Democracy/Labor Movement (ODP-MT) and its allies in 1991. As the number of opposition forces continued to grow, the Coordination of Democratic Forces (CDF) was formed. While opposition parties were able to organize, they were not able to exercise any control over the rate and substance of political change. The opposition parties called on the government to convene a sovereign national conference of all Burkinabe political forces to take interim control of state affairs pending multiparty elections. President Compaore denied this request.

Following Compaore's refusal to convene a sovereign national conference, opposition candidates refused to participate in the presidential elections. Amid violent protests, the election was held. Only 25 percent of those registered to vote took part and the low voter turnout denied Compaore the mandate he sought. The government subsequently condemned the violence and indefinitely postponed multiparty legislative elections that were to be held in January 1992. He did agree to convene a "national reconciliation forum" to begin political dialogue between the government and opposition party members. The forum was quickly suspended when the government would not comply with opposition parties' demand that the proceedings be televised.

The CDF coalition proved tenuous, however, as one key coalition member joined Compaore's administration as minister of state. Other members soon decided to contest rather than boycott the rescheduled multiparty legislative elections. In May 1992, the legislative elections were held. Voter turnout was only 35 percent, and Compaore's Organization for Popular Democracy (ODP-MT) claimed 78 out of a possible 107 seats.

In January 1994 the Convention of the Forces of Progress was formed as an umbrella organization of eleven smaller political parties. The aim of the coalition was to shape a national policy agenda and promote the democratization process.

Political Rights and Civil Liberties: Burkinabes continue to have limited ability to change their government. The first multiparty presidential elections in 1991 were plagued with accusations of irregularities and were held against a background of violence and intimidation. As Compaore's ODP-MT party continues to dominate political life in Burkina Faso, it is too early to tell whether opposition party members will have any substantive influence on government policy. However, there appears to be some independent political party movement.

Reports of human rights abuses in Burkina Faso continue. During 1993 security forces were suspected of a number of extrajudicial killings in the wake of disturbances at the University of Ouagadougou. Despite continued pressure from international human rights groups, the government has refused to investigate the 1991 assassination of Clement Ouedraogo, a prominent opposition leader, or the 1989 disappearance of Professor Guillaume Sessouma and Dabo Boukary, a medical student.

Civil and criminal court cases are adjudicated fairly by a regular court system. However allegations of mistreatment during detention continue. Detainees allege that they were subjected to beatings during interrogations.

The 1991 constitution guarantees freedom of speech and press. Burkina Faso has both independent print and broadcast media and the media do have some degree of freedom and independence from government interference. However, scattered attempts at intimidation of the press have occurred and while the government has tolerated some degree of critical reporting, all papers practice some degree of self-censorship.

The implementation of the government's rapid economic growth plan caused some labor unrest during 1994. Burkina Faso has a strong trade union movement and the General Labour Confederation of Burkina Faso (CGTB) organized a three-day strike in April 1994 to demand higher wages. No government retaliation was reported. All but essential workers can join unions and trade unions are allowed to form, strike and bargain collectively. The right to strike is provide for in the Constitution. There is limited freedom of association. Foreign travel for business and tourism appears to be unrestricted, but internal travel is subject to routine identity and customs checks.

Women do not share equal rights with men. Women continue to occupy subordinate positions in education, employment, property and family rights. There are disproportionately fewer women in schools. A high rate of domestic violence and practices of female genital mutilation continue. The government has made some attempts to educate people through the media on issues of domestic violence and genital mutilation. In a 1994 pledge to the World Bank and IMF, the government of Burkina Faso committed itself to eliminate the practice of female genital mutilation as part of a package aimed at receiving favorable economic assistance loans.

Burma (Myanmar)

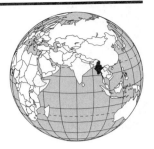

Polity: Military
Economy: Mixed statist
Population: 45,423,000
PPP: $650
Life Expectancy: 56.9
Ethnic Groups: Burman (68 percent), Karen (7 percent), Shan (6 percent), Rakhine (4 percent), Chin, Kachin, Mon and Arkanese totaling 1 million

Political Rights: 7
Civil Liberties: 7
Status: Not Free

Overview: In securing an invitation to the annual meeting of the Association of Southeast Asian Nations (ASEAN) in July 1994, Burma's military government took a major step toward easing its international isolation. Junta leaders also held a pair of talks with detained Nobel laureate Aung San Suu Kyi that appeared aimed at softening the regime's outlaw image.

Occupied by the Japanese in World War II, Burma achieved independence from the British in 1948. Prime Minister U Nu led a parliamentary democracy for a decade before resigning when his Anti-Fascist People's Freedom League splintered. A caretaker government under army commander General Ne Win organized elections in 1960, which briefly brought U Nu back to power. The army overthrew the civilian government in 1962 amidst an economic crisis, political turmoil and threats from ethnic rebel groups.

During the next twenty-six years, Ne Win's Burmese Socialist Program Party (BSPP) turned one of Southeast Asia's richest countries into an impoverished backwater. In September 1988 the army cracked down on massive, peaceful pro-democracy demonstrations, killing some 3,000 people. Army leaders General Saw Maung and Brigadier General Khin Nyunt placed the country under the military rule of the State Law and Order Restoration Council (SLORC).

The SLORC organized the country's first free elections in three decades on 27 May 1990. The National League for Democracy (NLD) attracted widespread support, mostly due to its charismatic secretary general, Aung San Suu Kyi, who remained in detention after being placed under house arrest in June 1989. The party won 392 of the 485 parliamentary seats, while the SLORC-sponsored National Unity Party, the successor to the BSPP, won just 10.

The SLORC refused to recognize the results and jailed hundreds of NLD members, including several elected MPs. In December 1990, a core of NLD MPs set up a government-in-exile in rebel-held territory at Mannerplaw near the Thai border, but no country has recognized it. In December 1991 Aung San Suu Kyi received the Nobel Peace Prize in absentia.

In 1992 the SLORC carried out a series of superficial liberalizations, no doubt intended to persuade Western governments to quit an aid embargo that has cost the country hundreds of millions of dollars. In April General Than Shwe replaced hardliner Saw Maung as prime minister and junta leader. Over the summer the regime held three rounds of meetings with twenty-eight representatives of seven parties, including the NLD, and announced it would hold a constitutional convention in early 1993. In August the SLORC re-opened universities following an eight month hiatus, and in September the junta lifted a nationwide curfew and removed two martial law decrees that had allowed military judges to try civilians in Mandalay and Rangoon.

The SLORC convened the constitutional convention in January 1993. The junta clearly expected the delegates to draft a document that would formalize the military's leading role in politics while providing a veneer of democracy for Western consumption. The 699 handpicked delegates, representing the NLD and nine other parties, as well as ethnic minorities, peasants and professional groups, were sequestered and warned against being too outspoken.

By June the SLORC had forwarded to the delegates guidelines for an Indonesian-style polity in which the military would have one-quarter of the parliamentary seats, and the president would be a military figure and hold broad executive powers. However, the delegates refused to sign off on the guidelines, forcing a frustrated SLORC to adjourn and restart the convention several times throughout the year before closing it for the year in September.

In 1994 the junta again convened the constitutional convention several times throughout the year. By year's end the delegates had still not approved the controversial proposal for a fixed number of seats in Parliament for the army.

In a surprising development, the junta also held a pair of high-level, high-profile meetings with Aung San Suu Kyi, the detained pro-democracy leader. On 20 September and again on 28 October two top military leaders, Lieut.-Gen. Khin Nyunt, the head of the Directorate of Defense Services Intelligence and reportedly the most powerful member of the SLORC, and nominal junta leader Gen. Than Shwe met with Suu Kyi in her family compound. Some observers feel the regime is laying the groundwork for some sort of negotiations between Suu Kyi and Khin Nyunt.

Although Suu Kyi's detention poses a problem for the SLORC, overall the junta is in a fairly strong position. In 1994 Burma received an invitation to attend the annual meeting of the Association of Southeast Asian Nations (ASEAN) in Bangkok in July as part of that group's policy of "constructive engagement." The regime has also benefited from the $1.23 billion that foreign corporations have invested in Burma since 1988. Overall, there has been a shift away from the isolationist policies of eighty-two-year-old ailing former strongman Ne Win, who does, however, continue to wield some influence over the junta.

The SLORC has also strengthened its position by acquiring $1 billion worth of Chinese arms in recent years, and by signing cease-fire deals with nine of the most powerful ethnic-based rebel armies active in the border areas. For decades these guerrillas having been fighting the central government, dominated by ethnic Burmans, for greater autonomy for their people. In 1989 the Communist Party of Burma's four Wa-dominated armies agreed to a cease-fire in return for being allowed to keep their weapons and maintain control over their respective areas. The junta subsequently struck similar deals with the Shan State Army, the Pa-O National Army, the Palaung State Liberation Army and others. Many of these former rebel armies are now involved in lucrative cross-border trade with China in timber, gems, jade and opium.

More recently, in October 1993 the government agreed to a cease-fire with the

6,000-strong Kachin Independence Army in the north. In 1994 it appeared that the strongest remaining guerrilla army, the 6,000-man Karen National Union, is moving toward accepting a cease-fire.

Political Rights and Civil Liberties: Burmese citizens cannot change their government democratically. The ruling military junta has all but decimated any political opposition. Several dozen political parties have been banned, and the remaining ten are closely monitored and restricted. Despite some cosmetic liberalizations in recent years, the junta still denies its citizens fundamental rights. Freedoms of speech, press and association are severely restricted. Trade unions, collective bargaining and strikes are illegal.

In the border areas sporadic fighting continues between the government and the few rebel armies that have not yet agreed to cease-fire deals, as well as between the army and druglord Khun Sa's Maung Tai militia in eastern Shan state. In February 1994 the U.N.'s Special Rapporteur for human rights in Burma, Yozo Yokota, reported that "atrocities are being committed consistently and on a wide scale by soldiers" of the government's army. Soldiers rape women, force villagers to act as human minesweepers ahead of troops and compel civilians to act as porters, often until they die of exhaustion or hunger. Young teenagers have been pressed into battle against rebel groups, often stiffened first with shots of liquor. Captured rebels have been subjected to torture and extrajudicial executions.

Diplomats and the U.S. State Department estimate there are at least 1,000 political prisoners in the country. The regime claims it has freed more than 2,000 "political prisoners" since 1992, although many appear to have been common criminals. The Law to Safeguard the State from the Dangers of Subversive Elements authorizes officials to detain dissidents for up to five years without trial. Nobel laureate Aung San Suu Kyi has been under house arrest since July 1989 under this law. In October 1994 a court sentenced five dissidents to prison terms of between seven and fifteen years, reportedly because they provided information to the U.N. special rapporteur.

The Directorate of Defense Services Intelligence maintains an elaborate network of spies and informants, and routinely searches homes, intercepts mail and monitors telephone conversations. Universities in particular are closely watched by informers. Immediately prior to the reopening of universities in August 1992, professors were forced to attend re-education camps and were told to report on student activities.

Political prisoners and common criminals are often beaten and mistreated. Prison conditions are especially harsh. The judiciary is wracked by corruption and is not independent in security cases. Nevertheless, some basic due process rights are observed in ordinary civilian trials.

Throughout the country the government uses forced labor for everything from building roads to beautification projects. In July the *Washington Times* reported that in Mandalay each family is being forced to provide labor for massive urban renewal projects. In the south the army is using 30,000 people, some of them convicts, to build an eighty-mile road-and-railway line from Ye to Tavoy in conjunction with a planned oil-and-gas pipeline. Meanwhile thousands of Burmese women and young girls have been trafficked across the Thai border by criminal gangs to work in brothels.

In eastern Kayah and Karen states, the army has in recent years forcibly relocated thousands of villagers into government-controlled towns for fear they might provide support to the rebels. The government has also forcibly relocated 500,000 residents of the capital, Rangoon, to squalid satellite "new towns."

Religious freedom is restricted. The army killed several monks and arrested hundreds in an October 1990 raid on monasteries suspected of supporting pro-democracy activities. At least 300 monks reportedly remain in detention and monasteries are closely monitored. Christians and Muslims have trouble openly practicing their religion.

In 1994 the fate of some 200,000 Rohingya Muslims from Burma's western Arakan state, now living in eighteen refugee camps in eastern Bangladesh, remained unresolved. The Rohingyas began crossing the border in late 1990 to escape rape, torture and destruction of their homes by the Burmese army; by 1992 more than 250,000 had reached Bangladesh. In November 1993 the Burmese government signed a Memorandum of Understanding with the United Nations allowing for independent monitoring of conditions in Arakan. However, only about 60,000 Rohingyas have been repatriated, with the remaining 190,000 saying they still fear persecution by the army if they return home.

Meanwhile, an additional 78,000 Burmese refugees from other ethnic minority groups live in camps straddling the Thai border. In July the army attacked two ethnic Mon refugee camps, and reportedly kidnapped several camp residents and burned houses in a nearby village.

Burundi

Polity: Civilian-military
Economy: Statist
Population: 6,039,000
PPP: $640
Life Expectancy: 48.2
Ethnic Groups: Hutu (85 percent), Tutsi (14 percent), Twa pygmy (1 percent)

Political Rights: 6*
Civil Liberties: 7
Status: Not Free

Ratings Change: *Burundi's political rights rating changed from 7 to 6 because a new civilian leadership was chosen through a somewhat representative process. Ethnic killings continued from 1993, but at a reduced level.

Overview: Political instability has beset the Republic of Burundi since 1993. Following the death of Melchior Ndadaye of the Burundi Front for Democracy (FRODEBU), FRODEBU's cofounder Cyprien Ntaryamira, a moderate Hutu, was elected head of state. In April 1994 Ntaryamira died in a suspicious plane crash along with Rwandan President Juvenal Habyarimana, also a Hutu. While the incident plunged Rwanda into an ethnic civil war between Hutus and Tutsis, Burundi remained compara-tively calm with only scattered ethnic clashes. In late September, a forum com-

prised of representatives from thirteen political parties, two bishops, a business-person and a trade unionist met to consider the qualifications of six presidential candidates. In October 1994, Sylvestre Ntibantunganya, a Hutu, was appointed as president of the Republic of Burundi.

Since independence from Belgium in 1962, Burundi has been governed primarily by leaders who came to power as a result of military coups. The country is ethnically divided between the majority Hutu tribe, which comprises about 85 percent of the Burundi population, and the minority Tutsi tribe, which makes up about 14 percent, with the remaining 1 percent comprised of the Batwa (Pygmies). Despite the clear majority, the Hutus were dominated by the ethnic Tutsi minority who commanded top military, judicial, educational and governmental posts since Burundi's independence from Belgium.

In June 1993, Burundi held its first multiparty presidential elections. Melchior Ndadaye, a Hutu and member of FRODEBU, defeated incumbent President Jean Pierre Buyoya, a Tutsi, by gaining 60 percent of the popular vote. Legislative elections followed, with FRODEBU securing 72 percent of the vote. The multiparty elections were to mark the beginning of Burundi's transition to democracy. On 21 October 1993, Ndadaye and six top aides were killed when the newly elected government was overthrown in a military coup. The coup, orchestrated by senior military officers from the minority Tutsi tribe, was an attempt to nullify the results of Burundi's first multiparty elections and abort Burundi's transition to democracy.

Burundi has four main political movements: the Party for the Liberation of the Hutu People (PALIPEHUTU), the Burundi Front for Democracy (FRODEBU), the Unity for National Progress (UPRONA), and the People's Reconciliation Party (PRP). Until April 1992, UPRONA was the country's only legal political party. Both PALIPEHUTU and FRODEBU were initially established to oppose Tutsi dominance of society and government in Burundi. While PALIPEHUTU carried out a violent campaign of resistance, FRODEBU sought to attain independence through nonviolent methods. FRODEBU condemned PALIPEHUTU's use of violence while PALIPEHUTU claimed that FRODEBU was willing to compromise on the Hutu right to rule.

In the wake of Ndadye's assassination, Amnesty International reported that between October and December 1993 up to 100,000 civilians, mostly Hutu, were killed. While most of the large-scale killings halted at the end of 1993, sporadic ethnic killings, mainly in the capital Bujumbura, continue. Most of those killed were Hutu allegedly killed by Tutsis, aided by the Tutsi-dominated security forces.

Political Rights and Civil Liberties:

As a result of political and ethnic instability in 1994, Burundi's political leaders determined that a national election was impossible and chose current President Ntibantunganya at a representative forum. It is unclear whether the appointment of Ntibantunganya will impart stability in Burundi. Opportunity exists to achieve a balance of power between the Tutsi-dominated military and the Hutu-led government. However, the situation remains tense, with sporadic ethnic violence continuing. As well, Ntibantunganya's fragile coalition government continues to unravel as UPRONA announced its intention to withdraw in late December 1994, fueling speculation that ethnic violence may ensue. Observers warn that Burundi's fragile peace could easily dissolve.

Amnesty International reports continued violations of human rights including torture and extrajudicial executions. In March 1994, Amnesty reported the execution of 500 civilians, all Hutu (including women and children), in the Kamenge district of Bujumbura. The killings were reportedly carried out by the Tutsi-dominated security forces. In May 1994, nine people, Hutus and Zairian nationals, were arrested by the security forces and have since disappeared. Also in May an additional twenty-eight residents of the Kamenge district were arrested by security forces during an operation to disarm the region. It is alleged that these detainees were subsequently subjected to torture. In June 1994, eighteen civil servants were arrested by security forces in the Karuzi and Gitega provinces of central Burundi. Reportedly, the men were subject to severe torture, and one of the detainees was close to death. In September 1994, Amnesty reported that thirteen men were executed extrajudicially by members of the security forces in Bujumbura, and an additional five men had reportedly disappeared after being arrested.

Burundi's media are not free and independent, and it remains unclear whether this will change under Ntibantunganya. Amnesty International has reported that one of those extrajudicially executed in September 1994 was a journalist. Burundians do not have access to an independent judicial system. During August 1994, Amnesty International asserted that the criminal justice system "has all but completely broken down."

In Burundi's fragile climate, it is unlikely that the new government will allow freedom of assembly or demonstration. Previously, while serving as interim leader, Ntibantunganya jailed opposition leader Mathias Hitimana, a Tutsi and leader of the PRP, after Hitimana allegedly called for a protest march through Bujumbura in March 1994. In demonstrations that followed his arrest, at least fifteen people were killed by security forces.

Cambodia

Polity: Monarchy, constituent assembly, and Khmer Rouge occupation
Economy: Statist
Population: 10,265,000
PPP: $1,250
Life Expectancy: 50.4
Political Rights: 4
Civil Liberties: 5
Status: Partly Free

Ethnic Groups: Khmer (93 percent), Vietnamese (4 percent), Chinese (3 percent)
Trend Arrow: Growing lawlessness in the countryside and the government's authoritarian tendencies indicated a downward trend.

Overview: Following a two-year, $2 billion United Nations operation that led to Cambodia's first free elections in May 1993, the country's human rights and security situation deteriorated sharply in 1994. Fighting continued between the army and Khmer Rouge guerrillas, the countryside reverted to lawlessness and the governing coalition, wracked by corruption and infighting, became increasingly authoritarian.

Cambodia achieved independence from France in 1953 under King Norodom

Sihanouk. The king abdicated in 1955, becoming Prince Sihanouk, to serve as head of government. In 1970 army general and prime minister Lon Nol ousted the prince in a bloodless coup. In April 1975 the Maoist Khmer Rouge overthrew Lon Nol's right-wing regime. Led by Pol Pot (Brother Number One), the Khmer Rouge ruthlessly emptied cities in a genocidal attempt at creating a classless agrarian society. More than one million Cambodians died through torture or starvation. Vietnam invaded in December 1978 and installed the Communist Kampuchean People's Revolutionary Party (KPRP), led largely by Khmer Rouge defectors.

In 1982 three anti-Vietnamese groups joined in an uneasy coalition to fight the government and the occupying Vietnamese. Led by Prince Sihanouk, the three groups were the Chinese-backed Khmer Rouge; the Prince's Sihanouk National Army; and the Khmer People's National Liberation Army, led by a former prime minister, Son Sann. Vietnam removed its last main contingents of troops in September 1989.

In 1991 several rounds of internationally supervised talks led to a peace accord signed in Paris on 23 October. Signatories included Prince Sihanouk, Son Sann, nominal Khmer Rouge leader Khieu Samphan, Cambodian prime minister Hun Sen, and representatives of eighteen countries. The Paris Accord called for a United Nations Transitional Authority in Cambodia (UNTAC) to run five key ministries in advance of national elections to be held in May 1993. To reduce the threat of armed conflict, UNTAC planned to place troops in temporary canton-ments and return 70 percent of each of the armies' soldiers to civilian life.

In 1992 the process threatened to unravel as the Khmer Rouge continued fighting and refused to comply with the cantonment and demobilization phase of the peace process, claiming that Vietnamese soldiers and advisers remained in the country and controlled the government. The Khmer Rouge removed itself from the political process by ignoring the January 1993 deadline for party registration.

The 23-28 May election opened with some 22,000 UNTAC troops bracing for Khmer Rouge rocket and mortar attacks on polling stations. But throughout the vote, violence was minimal and random. An astonishing 89 percent of the 4.7 million registered voters cast ballots, and twenty political parties participated. Final results for the 120-seat National Assembly gave 58 seats to the royalist opposition United Front for an Independent, Neutral and Free Cambodia (FUNCINPEC), headed by Prince Sihanouk's son, Prince Norodom Ranariddh; the government's Cambodian People's Party (CPP), 51; Son Sann's Buddhist Liberal Democratic Party, 10; and Moulinaka, a FUNCINPEC offshoot, 1.

On 12 June Prince Norodom Chakrapong, another Sihanouk son and a CPP official, unexpectedly led a secession attempt in seven eastern provinces. The movement collapsed on 15 June, but it served notice to FUNCINPEC that it would have to share power with Hun Sen's CPP, which still carried substantial clout through the loyalty of thousands of soldiers and police, and its control of the country's administrative apparatus.

A compromise announced on 17 September made Prince Ranariddh first prime minister and Hun Sen second prime minister of a new government. The National Assembly adopted a constitution on 21 September that created a constitutional monarchy in which the king "reigns but does not rule," has the power to make governmental appointments after consultation with ministers, and can declare a state of emergency if the prime minister and cabinet agree. On 24 September

Sihanouk formally returned to the throne after thirty-eight years and ratified the constitution, having gained power without standing in any election.

In early February and March 1994 the newly integrated CPP-FUNCINPEC national army suffered a pair of humiliating defeats at the hands of the Khmer Rouge, taking the strategic northwestern towns of Anlong Veng and Pailin only to lose both to guerrilla counterattacks. As the guerrilla group increased its attacks on government positions in the western provinces of Battambang and Banteay Meanchey in the spring, some 55,000 civilians temporarily fled their homes to escape the fighting.

By the summer the fragile governing coalition appeared ready to unravel in the face of its impotence in confronting the Khmer Rouge. A new crisis erupted on 3 July as the government announced that it had foiled a coup attempt by Prince Norodom Chakrapong and senior general Sin Song. The failed coup led to fresh accusations that CPP hardliners permeated the governing coalition.

On 7 July Parliament overrode King Sihanouk's advice and passed a law outlawing the Khmer Rouge. Sihanouk and others had favored bringing the rebels into a unity government. The Khmer Rouge responded by declaring a Provisional Government based in the jungle. Meanwhile, throughout the summer Hun Sen's plan to investigate the aborted coup led to a widening interparty rift between himself and two powerful CPP leaders, National Assembly President Chea Sim and Deputy Premier Sar Kheng.

On 20 October the National Assembly approved a cabinet reshuffle, sacking Finance Minister Sam Rainsy, who had won international approval for his reformist policies but had made too many enemies within the government for his attacks on official corruption. Three days later Foreign Minister Prince Norodom Sirivuddh resigned to protest Rainsey's dismissal, meaning that the government had lost its two most competent and honest officials.

Political Rights and Civil Liberties:

Cambodians elected a new government in May 1993 in what was easily the freest vote in the country's history. Prior to the election, the U.N. registered 95 percent of the eligible voters, and repatriated most of the 370,000 refugees who had fled to Thai border camps during the civil war.

The Cambodian People's Party (CPP), nominally the junior member of the coalition government, effectively runs the country due to the numerically superior position of its soldiers in the newly integrated army and through its control of the police, the bureaucracy and the provincial governorships. The Khmer Rouge controls at least 15 percent of the country's territory, and citizens living in these areas are denied most basic rights. Villagers are frequently caught up in indiscriminate shelling by the both the government and the Khmer Rouge.

Outside of the capital, Phnom Penh, a state of lawlessness exists throughout most of the country. Soldiers from both the national army and the Khmer Rouge frequently rape women and are accused of summarily executing enemy prisoners. Government soldiers, often unpaid for months at a time, roam the countryside committing acts of banditry, extortion, widespread looting, forced conscription and illicit commerce. Khmer Rouge guerrillas use civilians for portering and frequently attack trains and kidnap civilians, including at least nine foreigners in 1994. Three Westerners kidnapped by the Khmer Rouge in July were later executed; overall the Khmer Rouge reportedly killed hundreds of civilians in 1994.

In August a confidential U.N. report surfaced detailing a campaign of terror by the army's B-2 intelligence units in northwestern Cambodia beginning prior to the May 1993 elections. The report implicated soldiers in widespread arrests, torture and extrajudicial executions, often while extorting money from merchants and traders. The report also identified a secret detention center in Cheu Kmao village in Battambang Province where, between August 1993 and May 1994, military intelligence officers reportedly executed at least thirty-five civilians.

Between November 1992 and the May 1993 election, UNTAC documented political killings of seventy-four opposition party members, carried out mostly by the CPP, with 126 others injured. Other estimates suggest a much higher figure, perhaps upwards of 200 party workers, along with sixty-five U.N. personnel.

Although political violence dropped off in 1994, the government appeared unable or unwilling to safeguard the wide range of rights guaranteed in the September 1993 constitution, particularly in the area of press freedom. In May the government suspended the newspaper *Sokal* (Universe) for publishing articles and cartoons critical of King Sihanouk and arrested Noun Nonn, editor of *Dom Ning Pei Prek* (Morning News), for an article suggesting that top Interior Ministry officials may have been involved in the recent coup attempt. On 7 September gunmen killed Nuon Chan, the editor of *Sam-leng Yuachun Khmer* (The Voice of Khmer Youth) who had criticized official corruption. At least two other journalists were killed during the year.

In November the government announced plans to introduce a press law that would impose prison terms of up to one year and a fine for writing an article considered defamatory, and up to three years and a fine for insulting the king. Parliamentary approval is expected.

Prior to its departure UNTAC revamped the country's legal system, but there is a severe shortage of judges, lawyers and court administrators, and due process rights are still inadequate. Overall the judiciary is not independent of the government. Prison conditions have reverted to the abysmal state they were in prior to UNTAC's arrival. Government officials routinely search homes without proper authorization.

A key human rights issue is the treatment of the country's Vietnamese minority. Many of the estimated 200,000-500,000 Vietnamese in Cambodia have roots in the country going back several generations, although perhaps half entered following Vietnam's 1978 invasion of Cambodia. Since the 1991 Paris Accord, Khmer Rouge guerrillas, in a blatant effort to tap nationalist sentiment, have massacred scores of Vietnamese living along the Tonle Sap Lake and the Mekong River, including more than forty villagers in 1994. Some 30,000 Vietnamese have fled to Vietnam. Some 6,000 others who tried to flee remain stranded on the border after Vietnam refused to let them in, while the Cambodian authorities refuse to allow them to return to their villages.

The September 1993 constitution extends human rights guarantees only to ethnic Khmer (Cambodian) people. In addition, an immigration law signed in September 1994 allows the government to summarily expel undocumented foreigners, and in the absence of a nationality law defining citizenship observers fear the new law will be used to arbitrarily expel ethnic Vietnamese.

In recent years there has been a noticeable increase in street children and child prostitution in Phnom Penh and other cities. Travel within much of the country is restricted by land mines and banditry, and the Khmer Rouge tightly restricts travel in its areas. Trade unions and collective bargaining are guaranteed in the constitution, although in practice independent unions have not formed and collective bargaining is not practiced.

Cameroon

Polity: Dominant party (military-dominated)
Economy: Capitalist
Population: 13,132,000
PPP: $2,400
Life Expectancy: 55.3
Ethnic Groups: Adamawa, Bamiléké, Beti, Dzem, Fulani, Mandari, Shouwa, other—over 100 tribes and 24 languages

Political Rights: 6
Civil Liberties: 5
Status: Not Free

Overview:

In 1994, anglophone and other opposition parties demanded that President Paul Biya's two-year-old government advance the constitutional reform process. Previous attempts to organize national conferences to address constitutional issues in 1993 had failed.

After President Biya legalized opposition parties and adopted democratic reforms, he and his ruling Cameroon People's Movement (CPDM) and the main opposition parties agreed in 1991 to hold multiparty parliamentary elections in the fall of 1992. However, Biya scheduled the elections for March 1992, leaving the opposition little time to prepare. Half of the registered parties participated; others, including the strongest opposition group, the Social Democratic Front (SDF), boycotted the elections. The SDF, under the leadership of John Fru Ndi, has its main base in the anglophone, western part of the country. With eighty-eight of the 180 legislative seats, the CPDM formed a coalition with the six elected members of the Democratic Movement for the Defense of the Republic (MDDR). The largely northern and Muslim National Union for Democracy and Progress (UNDP) won sixty-eight seats and formed the chief opposition. Although presidential elections were scheduled for mid-1993, President Biya set the date as 11 October 1992, leaving less than thirty days for campaigning.

According to official results, Biya received almost 40 percent of the vote, while John Fru Ndi, who represented a coalition of opposition groups called the Union of Forces for Change (UFC) received 35 percent. According to the opposition, international observers and even some members of government, the elections were fraudulent. In the ensuing dispute both Biya and Fru Ndi declared themselves winners. Faced with protests denouncing electoral irregularities, Biya declared a state of emergency in the opposition stronghold of western Cameroon, and placed Fru Ndi under house arrest.

Shortly after his election, Biya nominated the first anglophone prime minister, Simon Achidi Achu, from the same constituency as Fru Ndi. Because the powers of the prime minister were circumscribed, the opposition dismissed him as window dressing. Following his release from house arrest in January 1993, Fru Ndi demanded new presidential elections. He also distanced himself from separatist organizations calling for the independence of the anglophone provinces.

At the end of 1993 the government banned a press conference organized by Fru Ndi to evaluate Biya's performance. Thirty-two opposition activists and five reporters on their way to the conference were detained for two days. The government was allegedly offering money to nearly sixty leaders to enter into alliance with the CPDM. Fru Ndi dismissed the SDF secretary general, accusing him of having tried to approach the government for SDF participation in a government of national unity. On 9 January 1994, Jean Michel Tekam, the leader of the SDF, created a new opposition front open to the SDF in preparation against the incumbents in the next municipal elections. However, in October, sixteen opposition parties formed the Allied Front for Change (FAC) bringing together members of the former coalition of the UFC, including the SDF and Jean-Jacques Ekendi's Progressive Movement. On 15 October the FAC held a ghost city operation, shutting down all business, in major English-speaking towns to coerce the government into readopting a democratic timetable and decreasing privatization plans. They held a demonstration during which the police injured several people. The new coalition subsequently held another demonstration in which six SDF members were arrested and released six days later.

The authorities also banned a conference organized by the Cameroon Anglophone Movement (CAM), later renamed the Southern Cameroon People's Conference, which advocates a two-state federation between the majority francophones and the minority anglophones. From 29 April to 2 May at the second All-Anglophone Conference, a final document called the Bamenda Proclamation called for an Anglophone federated state within a federal republic. However, not all anglophone parties advocate this solution. Union of Populations of Cameroon leader Ndeh Ntumazah advocates a decentralized form of government with an elected governor for each of the ten provinces.

In July, for the second time in two years, the government postponed municipal elections on the grounds that it needed more time to reorganize constituency boundaries and that the Nigerian occupation of the Bakassi Peninsula would prevent a complete poll from taking place.

The following month, Biya demoted Joseph Owona from secretary general of the presidency to health minister. The demotion took away Owona's responsibility for constitutional reform and delayed reform. The Consultative Constitutional Review Committee (CCRC) began deliberations on 15 December. The opposition boycotted the debate, claiming it was excluded from drawing up the agenda and some of its members were not selected to participate in the committee.

A border dispute with Nigeria over the oil-rich Bakassi Island intensified because Cameroon applied to the International Court of Justice, claiming other parts of Nigeria. On 22 March violent clashes between the Choa Arab and the Kotoko communities in the north forced over 200 people to flee to Chad. Ten Cameroonian soldiers were killed in mid-September during clashes with Nigeran soldiers.

Cameroon suffered the impact of the devaluation of the franc CFA by half in January 1994. Some 150 teachers were dismissed for demanding better salaries to make up for the consequent loss of buying power.

Political Rights and Civil Liberties:

The citizens of Cameroon have not been able to change their government democratically. Despite two elections, the country continues to be ruled by the CPDM, the former single party of Cameroon. Major opposition parties boycotted the 1992 legislative elections, citing the government's refusal to reform electoral laws and to have an independent interim government to supervise the vote. The presidential elections were fraudulent. The constitution favors the executive over the parliament without legislative or judicial oversight. The president has the right to dissolve the National Assembly for new elections within forty days and can govern by decree during the ten months a year the Assembly is not in session. Although Cameroon has over seventy parties, and opposition parties occupy half of the National Assembly, the ruling CPDM still dominates the bureaucracy. Members of the president's ethnic group, the Beti, have a disproportionate share of political power.

The judiciary is part of the executive, subordinate to the Ministry of Justice. The government usually does not interfere in civil and criminal cases. However, in political cases, courts often render decisions favorable to the government.

Following the presidential elections some 200 opposition supporters were detained and many tortured. Although the law proscribes beating suspects, torture is common. Despite constitutional promises of free assembly, the government regularly bans meetings. In 1994, the government banned several anglophone party conferences and a UNDP meeting.

The rights to free speech and freedom of the press are restricted. Some seventy private newspapers are published and criticize the government often. Censorship was officially abolished in September 1994 when journalists adopted an ethics code to replace pre-publication censorship. The 1990 press law authorizes licensing journalists, suspending publications and restricting foreign journalists. Journalists in government media are civil servants. After the presidential election, the government increasingly harassed the independent press, banning several editions of *Le Messager* and a humorous weekly called *Populi*, charging two senior journalists with libel and sentencing an editor-in-chief to six months in prison.

The law does not restrict domestic travel. Document checks to control illegal immigration and the opposition are common. Passports of government critics are often confiscated.

The law guarantees freedom of religion, but religious organizations must register. The 1992 Labor Code allowed workers to form and join independent trade unions. The only labor confederation is the Confederation of Cameroonian Trade Unions (CSTC) formerly affiliated with the ruling CPDM party under the name Organization of Cameroonian Trade Unions. The CSTC formally declared its political independence in 1992. However, no other labor organizations have been legalized. Louis Sombes, CSTC secretary general, was fired because he organized a strike over civil servants' pay. Following his reinstatement, he presided over a vote to oust the union's president accused of working too closely with the government.

Canada

Polity: Federal parliamentary democracy
Economy: Capitalist
Population: 29,112,000
PPP: $19,320
Life Expectancy: 77.2
Ethnic Groups: British, French, other European, Asian, Caribbean black, aboriginal or native (Indian and Inuit), others

Political Rights: 1
Civil Liberties: 1
Status: Free

Overview:

Canada's long-running dispute over its national identity continued in 1994 as separatists won the legislative election in the predominantly francophone province of Quebec. The *Parti Quebecois* (PQ) victory on 12 September threatened to spark a constitutional crisis, because the winners promised a referendum on Quebec's independence in 1995. Polls showed that Quebeckers voted for PQ not out of a desire for independence (which most of them opposed in 1994), but because they felt it was time for a party change after an economic recession and years of Liberal Party rule.

Political change in Quebec intensified the political upheaval that began with Canada's general election in 1993. In that contest, Canadian voters threw out Prime Minister Kim Campbell and her Progressive Conservative Party (Tories). Jean Chretien became the new prime minister as his Liberals took 177 of the 295 seats in the House of Commons. The Liberals pledged to reinvigorate the economy. Hurt by high unemployment and an angry electorate, the Conservatives lost all but two seats.

Regional parties wiped out the Tory bases in the western provinces and in Quebec. Led by ex-Conservative Lucien Bouchard, *Bloc Quebecois*, a party favoring Quebec's independence, became the leading opposition party with 54 seats. The right-wing, Western-based Reform Party captured 52 seats under leader Preston Manning. Audrey McLaughlin's socialist New Democratic Party (NDP) lost more than 30 seats, retaining only 9. An independent ex-Conservative won the remaining seat.

The regional divisions in the election stem from Canada's history. The French and British colonized different parts of Canada in the seventeenth and eighteenth centuries. Following the Treaty of Paris in 1763, Britain governed both the Francophone and Anglophone areas until it granted home rule in 1867. The British monarch remains the titular head of state, acting through the largely ceremonial Canadian governor-general. Britain retained a theoretical right to overrule the Canadian Parliament until 1982, when Canadians established complete control over their own constitution.

The Canadian Parliament is bicameral. The House of Commons has 295 members elected from single-member districts (ridings). The Senate has more than 100 members whom the government appoints to represent the country's provinces and territories. There is growing sentiment to abolish the Senate, which many Canadians view as a superfluous chamber of political patronage appointees. The provinces have some significant local powers, including interprovincial trade restrictions. However, in July 1994 Prime Minister Chretien and provincial premiers signed an agreement to lower domestic trade barriers.

At the federal and provincial levels, there is an increasingly fractious multiparty system. The governing Liberal Party is headed by Chretien, an anti-separatist Quebecker. It supports activist government economic policies, but the Liberal government's interventionism is tempered by budget cuts to reduce the deficit. The Progressive Conservatives (Tories), who support free trade and business-oriented economic policies, held power under Prime Minister Brian Mulroney from 1984 until his resignation in 1993. Hampered by dismal poll ratings, Mulroney stepped down in order to give a new leader a chance. Defense Minister Kim Campbell replaced Mulroney after she defeated Environment Minister Jean Charest for party leader at the Conservative convention.

Following defeat in 1993 Campbell resigned the Tory leadership. Charest replaced her and is struggling to revive the party. The NDP also has serious problems. It barely survived in the House of Commons. Although New Democrats control three provinces including Ontario, Canada's largest, the NDP's provincial governments have undermined its national support. Public sector austerity and other NDP provincial policies in Ontario have caused some trade unions to disaffiliate from the party. Since 1991 Bloc Quebecois has been the federal affiliate of Parti Quebecois, the provincial independence party headed by Jacques Parizeau. In the House of Commons, the BQ's Bouchard has positioned his party as a social democratic defender of labor rights and social security.

In the 1993 general election Preston Manning's fast-growing, anti-bilingual Reform Party swamped the Tories in the West. Manning emphasizes strict budget cuts and smaller government as alternatives to the federal budget deficit. In 1994, Reform activists demanded that the party establish provincial affiliates and contest provincial elections. The Confederation of the Regions Party (CoR), another anti-bilingual party, is the chief opposition in New Brunswick, the only officially bilingual province. In the west, the Social Credit Party controlled provincial governments in the past, but it is declining. Founded as a movement to control the economy through currency manipulation, the "Socreds" are a now a populist conservative party.

In 1982 Canada's constitution added a charter of rights and freedoms, which common law had covered previously. Limiting the binding nature of the rights and freedoms, one constitutional clause, known as the "notwithstanding clause," permits provincial governments to exempt themselves from applying the charter within their jurisdictions. Quebec invoked the "notwithstanding clause" to keep its provincial language law, which restricts the use of English in signs. After holding out against the new constitution, Quebec agreed to accept it in 1987 in return for a recognition by the federal government and the other provinces that Quebec constitutes a "distinct society" within Canada. This distinct status was at the heart of two federal-provincial constitutional reform pacts, the Meech Lake accord (1990) and the Charlottetown agreement (1992), named after the places where the constitutional negotiations took place. The Meech Lake deal, which required unanimous provincial approval, died because two provinces failed to ratify it.

Responding to Quebec's anger at the failure of Meech Lake, the federal and provincial governments tried again with the Charlottetown deal. Consequently, Quebec put off the sovereignty issue, and Canadians voted in a referendum on

Charlottetown in October 1992. With 56 percent of the voters disapproving, the package lost.

Following the referendum, Quebec's parties prepared for the 1994 provincial election. After Liberal Premier Robert Bourassa retired in early 1994, Quebec Liberals picked Daniel Johnson as premier. In his campaign, PQ leader Jacques Parizeau attacked Johnson on economic issues, while Johnson warned voters about the difficulties an independent Quebec would face. Parizeau promised a referendum on Quebec's independence in 1995, and hoped for a decisive mandate. In the voting on 12 September 1994, Quebeckers gave PQ 44.7 percent of the vote to 44.3 percent for the Liberals and 6.5 percent for *Action Democratique,* which favors independence, but not yet.

Although PQ won 77 of the 125 legislative seats, its popular vote was no ringing endorsement of separatism. However, the very idea of scheduling a referendum on independence has triggered sometimes bitter Canadian arguments. Western provincial politicians have been especially harsh. British Columbia's Premier Michael Harcourt said that Quebec's independence would make the two entities "the worst of enemies." Calling Parizeau and Bouchard "master illusionists," Saskatchewan's Premier Roy Romanow accused separatists of a "con job" when they suggest that independence would be painless. The possible breakup of Canada has many serious implications.

Liberals charge that an independent Quebec would lose $8 billion (Canadian) by dropping out of cost-sharing programs with Canada. On the basis of population, an independent Quebec could inherit one-fourth of Canada's national debt. Quebec would have to negotiate its economic relationship with Canada and new trading arrangements with other countries, especially with the U.S. and Mexico. Some financial institutions have predicted that even the fear of Quebec's separation could drive down the Canadian dollar, raise interest rates and eliminate jobs. Other possible costs of independence include loss of territory for Quebec, especially if Indians were to attempt secession. However, Bouchard claims that Quebec's boundaries are inviolable, but that somehow the U.S. might annex Western Canada.

Political Rights and Civil Liberties: Canadians have the right to change their government by democratic means. Due to government canvassing, Canada has nearly 100 percent effective voter registration. Prisoners have the right to vote in federal elections. In the 1993 general election, the federal government extended voting rights to Canadians living abroad for less than five years. The government also encouraged turnout with three days of advance voting for people unable to vote on election day.

Canada prohibits the broadcasting of new, scientific public opinion polls within three days of the general election. Old or unscientific polls are exempt from this regulation. In 1993 the House of Commons passed a "gag law," legislation limiting individuals and groups other than political parties to $1,000 (Canadian) spending on advocacy advertisements during election campaigns. The National Citizens Coalition, a conservative-libertarian group, filed and won a lawsuit to overturn this limit, on the grounds that the law restricted freedom of expression.

The provinces, especially Quebec, have significant powers. In recent years, Canada and the provinces have given more autonomy to the aboriginals. As power devolves to native groups, questions arise about the constitutionally guaranteed equal rights of native women under the traditionally patriarchal tribal governments. At the U.N. Human Rights Conference in Vienna in 1993, the Canadian government allegedly objected to the letter "s" in a reference to rights of "indigenous peoples." Reportedly, the government feared that putting the plural form in a declaration might imply a right of aboriginals to secede from the country. However, in 1992-93 the Canadian government negotiated with the Inuit to create Nunavut, a largely Inuit homeland, out of the Northwest Territories. Once operational in 1999, the new jurisdiction will have one-fifth of Canada's territory.

In general, civil liberties are protected by the Charter of Rights and Freedoms. However, the "notwithstanding clause" allows liberties to be curtailed. There are also several limits on freedom of expression, ranging from unevenly enforced restrictions on hate crimes and pornography to rules on reporting. Willful promotion of racial hatred is against the criminal code, but there are increasing levels of harassment and vandalism against minorities. Toronto, the world's most multicultural city with 140 ethnic groups is also the home of several hate groups. In 1994 there was controversy over attempts to ban Sikh headgear in local veterans' groups.

On 5-6 October authorities discovered that five people in Quebec and ten Quebeckers in Switzerland had been killed with dozens of other members of the Solar Temple Cult, a fringe religion. One of the victims was the mayor of Richelieu, Quebec. The cult had specialized in recruiting dozens of affluent and influential citizens in French-speaking countries, including fifteen managers with Hydro Quebec, the provincial utility.

The media are generally free, but there are some restrictions. Canadian law prohibits "split runs" for foreign-based publications, meaning, for example, that an American magazine may not duplicate its U.S. edition with a mere change of advertisements for the Canadian market. The law also prohibits tax deductions for Canadian advertisements placed in magazines printed outside the country. There is an autonomous government broadcasting system, the CBC, which has both English and French channels. There are also private broadcasters, magazines and newspapers.

Private cable and satellite television are expanding. Effective 1 January 1994, broadcasters adopted a code to limit televised violence. This amounted to self-censorship to stave off government regulation. In 1991 the Canadian Radio Television and Telecommunications Commission (CRTTC) relaxed regulations dictating the precise mixtures of music radio stations could play, but there are still rules defining and encouraging "Canadian musical content." The CRTTC is expanding the number of specialty television channels and has eased rules for religious broadcasting. The Inter-American Press Association (IAPA) attacked the Canadian judiciary in 1993 for barring the press from reporting on some court cases, including ones dealing with freedom of expression. The IAPA also reported that courts banned the reporting of such restrictions, which the group called a "striking new affront to freedom of the press."

A generous welfare system supplements a largely open, competitive economy. Property rights for current occupants are generally strong, but increasing Indian land claims have led to several rounds of litigation and negotiation. Canada has a significant and growing underground economy. Recognizing this, the federal government cut cigarette taxes in 1994 in order to discourage illegal cigarette sales.

Trade unions and business associations are free and well organized. In 1993, the Canadian Auto Workers and Chrysler negotiated an equity clause in a contract giving workers the right to strike if management cannot or will not resolve a complaint of harassment based on sex, race or religion. Ontario bans replacement workers during strikes.

Religious expression is free and diverse, but there are special rules about religious education. Since the founding of the Canadian government in 1867, in various provinces there have been state-supported religious (or "separate") school systems, but not all denominations have government-backed systems. In 1994, Newfoundland's provincial government introduced legislation to undo the church-run public school systems that have been segregated by denomination. Ontario's Education Act has a vague requirement that teachers must uphold Judeo-Christian virtues. There are growing disputes about government recognition of holy days, especially over whether to close schools and government offices for Muslim observances.

The judiciary is independent, and the courts often overturn government policy. In 1994 there were allegations that Canadian intelligence agencies spied on the CBC, the Canadian Jewish Congress, the Reform Party and France-Quebec communications.

Homosexuals won the right to serve in the armed forces in 1992 when the Supreme Court applied the equal rights provisions in the Charter to them. In 1994, the Ontario legislature rejected legislation that would have extended various economic and social benefits to homosexual couples.

Quebec's language laws limit the cultural and educational rights of non-French Canadians. Immigrants may not send their children to Anglophone schools in Quebec, although Anglo-Canadians may do so under some circumstances. Since 1993, new rules have expanded these circumstances for Anglophone children. The U.N. Human Rights Commission condemned Quebec's law banning English on outdoor commercial signs in 1993. The U.N. called the law a violation of the International Covenant on Civil and Political Rights, which guarantees freedom of expression. The provincial Liberals moved to allow English on signs as long as the French lettering predominates. The Quebec ruling party also abolished the language police, who had fined La Brecque Auto Service $7,000 (Canadian) for not having its sign say "Service Auto La Brecque." Parti Quebecois has promised to relax the language laws in an independent Quebec. However, PQ wants more French required in business.

In the 1990s Canada has expanded the opportunities for political asylum to include refuge on the grounds of spousal abuse and sexual orientation. The Canadian government announced cutbacks in immigration in 1994. Skilled and wealthy people will get precedence over other applicants who seek to enter Canada for family reunification.

Cape Verde

Polity: Presidential-par-
liamentary democracy
Economy: Mixed statist
Population: 407,000
PPP: $1,360
Life Expectancy: 67.3
Ethnic Groups: Mestico/Mulatto, black African, European

Political Rights: 1
Civil Liberties: 2
Status: Free

Overview:

A small archipelago off the coast of west-central Africa, Cape Verde began its post-colonial existence in 1975 politically linked to Guinea-Bissau, another former Portuguese dependency. The relationship was severed in 1979 after the government in Guinea-Bissau was overthrown in a coup. The 1980 constitution established a one-party state under the leftist African Party for the Independence of Cape Verde (PAICV), led by President Aristides Pereira. Legislative authority was vested in a unicameral National People's Assembly.

Cape Verde's move toward a multiparty system began officially at a PAICV party congress in February 1990. The leadership advocated constitutional amendments to pave the way for competitive elections and eliminate reference to the guiding role of the PAICV in society. The Assembly later voted to permit alternative party slates in parliamentary polling and direct elections for president.

Carlos Veiga, a former PAICV activist, led the eight-month-old opposition party, Movement for Democracy (MPD), to a convincing win in January 1991 parliamentary elections. The MPD won 56 of 79 seats, the PAICV, 22 seats. In February's presidential election, MPD-supported independent candidate and former Supreme Court justice Antonio Mascarenhas Monteiro, beat incumbent Pereira, who had ruled for fifteen years.

Divisions in the MPD appeared in late 1993 after several ministers resigned, blaming the prime minister for retaining the country's ambassador to Portugal, who was accused of using government money for personal use. In 1994, the MPD faced growing internal strife. In February, the reappointment of Prime Minister Veiga as MPD chairman led to the resignation of many party leaders, including former labor and justice minister Ernesto Monteiro, who announced that he would create a new party. The PAICV, which had ruled the country for seventeen years, called for early elections due to the crisis in the MPD, but the latter's comfortable parliamentary majority precluded approval of early elections. In April, MPD dissidents formed a new party led by Monteiro and former Foreign Minister Jorge Carlo Fonseca.

A key priority for the government was the privatization of certain industries and the reduction of the civil service. The country's per capita income is among the highest in West Africa. Many citizens survive on remittances sent by expatriates working abroad or from Social Security checks sent to retirees who spent their working lives in the United States. Agricultural opportunities are limited on the arid islands, and the fishing industry is still underdeveloped.

Political Rights and Civil Liberties: Citizens are able to change their government through free and fair elections under a multiparty system. Criminal and civil cases are generally adjudicated fairly and expeditiously; there are no known political prisoners.

Public criticism of the government is tolerated, but the regime has on occasion warned the press to avoid sensationalism. The most widely read newspaper, and radio and television are controlled by the government, but coverage is generally fair and balanced. National Assembly sessions are broadcast live in their entirety.

Freedoms of assembly, association and religion are guaranteed by law and respected in practice in this predominantly Catholic country. There are no restrictions on domestic or foreign travel.

The constitution prohibits sex discrimination and guarantees full equality of men and women; in practice, however, women are excluded from certain jobs and are often paid less then men. Domestic violence against women remains common in rural areas.

Workers are free to form and join independent unions; seven were created in 1992. The largest confederations were the Coordinated Council of Free Labor Unions (CCLS) and the National Union of Cape Verde Workers, formed and controlled by the former government.

Central African Republic

Polity: Presidential-parliamentary-democracy (military influenced)
Economy: Capitalist-statist
Population: 3,142,000
PPP: $641
Life Expectancy: 47.2
Ethnic Groups: Baya (34 percent), Banda (27 percent), Mandja (21 percent), Sara (10 percent)

Political Rights: 3
Civil Liberties: 4
Status: Partly Free

Overview: In 1994 the Central African Republic marked its first full year under the democratically elected government headed by President Andre-Felix Patasse. The government faced economic and social problems inherited from the old regime under General Andre Kolingba. The French decision to devalue the CFA franc resulted in civil strife and forced the government to begin to reform the economy.

This sparsely populated country received its independence from France in 1960 but continues to remain economically and politically dependent on its former metropolis. Following the 1979 overthrow of the self-styled Emperor Bokasssa I, who ordered massive human rights abuses and led the country toward financial disaster, the country held presidential elections in 1981, in which the CAR's first elected President David Dacko was reelected. Dacko's reign ended after only six months when a military junta formed by General Andre Kolingba ousted him.

In September 1993 CAR held its first democratic elections in more than a decade.

General Kolingba was replaced by President Patasse, the head of the Central African People's Liberation Movement (MLPC) and former health minister under the Bokassa regime.

Although the 1993 elections were considered mostly free and fair, the Supreme Court reviewed candidates' complaints in 1994 and decided that there had been irregularities in six districts where the race had been particularly close. The Court suspended the six parliamentarians and called for new elections for those six seats, five of which were held by opposition members. On 4 December elections for the six seats were held. The president's Party still did not win any of them. One of the six seats was again repealed by the Supreme Court because of alleged election irregularities. A new election date for the seat was not yet determined.

In January, the French government decided to devalue the CFA franc by 50 percent. While the devaluation is predicted to have long-term benefits, it caused short-term economic downfall. Following the devaluation, the CAR issued a price-freeze to curb inflation. This caused a wave of protest from traders who responded by taking items, including basic foodstuffs, off the supermarket shelves. The price-freeze ended a month later.

In February, Patasse attended an economic summit of Central African heads-of-state in Libreville, Gabon, to discuss long-term measures for economic recovery. These included strategies to increase domestic savings, attract foreign capital and reduce unemployment. In addition, the leaders announced the creation of the Economic and Monetary Commission of Central Africa (CEMAC) to deal with the consequences of the devaluation.

CAR's economic conditions provoked social strife and unrest throughout 1994. Students, civil servants and army troops continued to hold demonstrations protesting the miserable economic conditions and demanding the payment of scholarship money and salary arrears.

Political Rights and Civil Liberties: The people of the Central African Republic have the potential to change their government democratically. For only the third time since independence, they exercised that right in August 1993, when democratic elections ended twelve years of autocratic government by General Kolingba.

The independence of the judiciary is compromised by corruption and insufficient funding. The court system is underdeveloped and inefficient, and the executive branch can and has influenced Supreme Court decisions. Although legal counsel and public trials are prescribed for the accused, in many cases prisoners are held without a trial.

The freedom for individual citizens and groups to express their views has increased since the 1993 election. All radio and television media, however, are government controlled. Although there is freedom of the press, print media are virtually nonexistent, largely because of lack of funding.

There are twenty-two registered political parties in the CAR. Opposition groups voice their opinions openly, but the police and military have been known to arrest arbitrarily persons suspected of attempting to subvert the government.

Since 1989, when a new Labor Code went into effect, workers have been free to organize and join the trade union of their choice. However, the law requires that union officials be employed as full-time wage earners, thus restricting union activities to their spare time. There are currently five labor federations, each composed of several individual unions. The two most active federations held marches in 1994 demanding that the government pay salary arrears.

Although the constitution stipulates equality of all citizens, there is a wide gap in economic opportunities and political influence among the eighty ethnic groups. The indigenous forest dwellers, Ba'aka (pygmies), who lead traditional lifestyles based on hunting and gathering, are subject to various forms of exploitation which the government does not condone, but fails to address.

Women are under-represented in universities, the workplace, and the political arena. Polygamy is still legal, although educated women are resisting the practice more and more. Despite a 1966 law against female genital mutilation, it is still widely practiced, especially in rural areas.

Chad

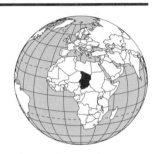

Polity: Transitional
Economy: Capitalist
Population: 6,494,000
PPP: $447
Life Expectancy: 46.9
Ethnic Groups: Arab, Bagirmi, Sara,Wadai, Zaghawa, Bideyat Gorane, other

Political Rights: 6
Civil Liberties: 5
Status: Not Free

Overview:

In August 1994 a cease-fire agreement was reached between the government of President Idriss Deby of the Patriotic Salvation Movement (MPS) and the opposition movement of the Committee of National Revival for Peace and Democracy (CSNPD), led by Moise Kette. Despite an earlier cease-fire agreed to by the government and Kette's southern rebel movement in June 1993, clashes between government forces and rebels had continued. Negotiations which began in Bangui, the capital of the Central African Republic, in February 1994 culminated in a signing of the Bangui accord on August 10, 1994. The accord calls for an immediate cease-fire, the withdrawal of the Presidential Republican Guard from the southern area of Chad, respect for the freedom of movement of peoples and formal recognition of the CSNPD. Also under the accord, a new National Army incorporating rebel forces was to be established. The Armed Forces for a Federal Republic (FARF), a CSNPD splinter group headed by Laokein Barde, did not participate in the negotiations.

Since gaining independence from France in 1960, Chad has endured an intermittent civil war spurred on by tribal and factional rivalry. Chad is divided roughly between the Saharan and Arab Muslims living in the northern, central and eastern regions, and the Sudanian zone ethnic groups (predominately Christian farmers) in the south. Despite the fact that there are over 200 ethnic groups in Chad, substantive power remains in the hands of a few minority ethnic groups from northern and eastern Chad.

Deby, a member of MPS, seized control of Chad's government from Hissein Habre in December 1990. In March, the MPS enacted a National Charter which annulled the 1989 constitution, convened a thirty-month transitional government and concentrated power in the office of the presidency. The Charter also outlined the government's commitment to protecting fundamental rights and freedoms including the freedom of speech and association, freedom of the press, freedom of movement, property rights and the rights of trade unions to organize. In 1992, the Charter was amended to designate the prime minister as chief of government and to allow twenty-six political parties to operate.

In October 1992, the government announced that it would convene a National Conference comprised of members of government as well as independent organizations and opposition groups. The purpose of the conference was to review Chad's political and social problems and to discuss ways to achieve both stability and democracy and to protect human rights. The conference took place in January-April 1993. General and presidential elections were promised for the end of the one-year period. In March 1994 ten opposition parties operating under an umbrella group, Alternative 1994, called for a twelve-month extension of the transitional democratic period in order to prepare for elections. In addition, the group called for revisions in the National Charter and a formation of a new government. In April, the Higher Transitional Council (CST) adopted a motion to extend the transition period by twelve months. Legislative elections are scheduled for January 1995, to be followed by presidential elections in March 1995.

Following a ruling by the International Court of Justice at the Hague in February 1994, in May, Libya completed its withdrawal of troops from Aouzou after twenty-one years of occupation. The territory, located along Chad's northern border with Libya, is said to be rich in minerals including uranium and has been a source of dispute between Libya and Chad for forty years.

Political Rights and Civil Liberties: Chadians do not have the right to change their government democratically. Multiparty elections originally scheduled for 1994 have been postponed until 1995. While the National Charter provides for freedom of speech and assembly, open political activity continues to be curtailed by the security forces. Restrictions have been eased on journalists since Deby came to power. While journalists who criticize the government continue to be subject to intimidation, on 9 July 1994 the CST adopted a Press Bill to implement the freedom of speech provisions adopted by the National Conference in 1993.

Despite assurances by Chadian President Idriss Deby that human rights and democratization would be the primary objective of his government, more than 800 people have been killed since he took office in 1990. According to Amnesty International, many of those killed were extrajudicially executed while in custody or were targeted by government security forces because of suspected association with opposition parties or their respective ethnic groups.

Ethnic clashes continue, and Amnesty International has reported gross human rights violations by security forces loyal to Deby. In August 1994 Amnesty International and the Chadian League of Human Rights (LTDH) reported the extrajudicial execution of more than twenty-five villagers from the Logone district of southern Chad by the Chadian army. In addition, Amnesty reports army clashes with the FARF led to additional civilian casualties in the district of Kaga. The Chadian army was also responsible for torching several villages, including Korotrois, Bemboura, Mbala, Kagain and Heuri. No attempt has been made by Deby's government to investigate allegations of human rights violations or restrict the use of lethal force by government forces against noncombatants or detainees.

Political power remains concentrated in the hands of a small number of minority groups and persecution solely on the grounds of ethnic origin continues unabated. Chadians are not protected from political terror and are subject to torture. Despite commitments to a democratization process, opposition leaders in Chad continued to be harassed during 1994. In March 1994, Yoronger Lemohiban, leader of FARF (an illegal opposition party), was arrested and detained without charge. In July 1994 elements of the Presidential Republican Guard reportedly harassed southern civilian populations, targeting supporters of the CSNPD. Chad continues to hold political prisoners.

Chadians do not have equal access to an independent, nondiscriminatory judicial system. Ordinary courts have been partially replaced by the Military Court and Special Court of Justice where defendants, who are usually held on politically motivated crimes, are often presumed guilty. Sentences are commonly subject to manipulation by the regime.

The rights of trade unions to operate are protected in the National Charter. In April 1994, a general strike was called by the Federation of Chadian Trade Unions and Chadian civil servants, in order to force the government to sign a social pact and to increase wages following the devaluation of the CFA franc. Chad, along with thirteen other African countries, found its currency devalued by France in January 1994. In July, the government and the Union of Chadian Trade Unions (UST) signed a social pact which, in part, provided a moderate wage increase.

Chad is a secular state and freedom of religion is respected. International travel is not guaranteed. While internal travel is allowed (except in military zones), the U.S. State Department continues to report that travelers are subject to roadblocks set up by security forces and criminals who demand money before allowing passage.

Women do not enjoy equal status in Chad. Women's rights are not protected by traditional law or through the Penal Code. The UNDP reports that the female literacy rate is significantly lower than that of the male and that, on average, females receive one third of the education of males. Domestic violence against women is common and victims have only limited legal recourse against the batterer. Female genital mutilation is widespread. The percentage of Chadian women who have been subject to this procedure may be as high as 60 percent. The Deby government has made no effort to stop this practice.

Chile

Polity: Presidential-legislative democracy
Economy: Capitalist
Population: 14,030,000
PPP: $7,060
Life Expectancy: 71.9
Ethnic Groups: Mestizo, Spanish, other European, Indian

Political Rights: 2
Civil Liberties: 2
Status: Free

Overview: President Eduardo Frei, son of former President Eduardo Frei (1964-70), took office on 11 March following his victory in the 11 December 1993 election as the candidate of the incumbent Concertacion for Democracy coalition. It was soon apparent that Frei, like his predecessor Patricio Aylwin, would have trouble exerting greater civilian authority over the armed forces.

The Republic of Chile was founded after independence from Spain in 1818. Democratic governance predominated in this century until the overthrow of the socialist government of Salvador Allende in 1973. Gen. Augusto Pinochet became head of state, dissolved Congress and brutally repressed dissent. The 1980 constitution installed by the military regime provided for a plebiscite in which voters could reject another presidential term for Pinochet. In 1988, 55 percent of Chilean voters said "no" to Pinochet, which meant the government had to hold competitive presidential and legislative elections in 1989.

After the plebiscite the Command and the government agreed on a number of constitutional reforms, including raising the number of elected senators in the Congress from twenty-six to thirty-eight (but with eight still appointed by the Pinochet government) and lifting the ban on Marxist parties.

The center-left Concertacion for Democracy (formerly the Command for the No) nominated for president Christian Democrat Patricio Aylwin, who vowed not to make major changes in the free-market, free-trade thrust of the economy. Civil-military relations were a major campaign issue, with Aylwin advocating reform of the constitution that now allows army commander Pinochet and other military chiefs to remain until 1997.

In December 1989 Aylwin handily defeated two right-wing candidates for the presidency. The Concertacion won a majority in the 120-member Chamber of Deputies, and twenty-two of thirty-eight elected Senate seats. But with eight additional senators appointed by the outgoing government, it fell short of a majority in the Senate.

Aylwin oversaw a broadly representative, remarkably clean government that was responsive to a wide social base. His administration successfully combined market economics with social policies that made substantial reductions in poverty. That provided a strong base for Frei, also a Christian Democrat, who was nominated in the Concertacion primary in May 1993. However, Aylwin's attempts to reform the constitution were consistently blocked by the right-wing bloc in the Senate.

Frei, a fifty-two-year-old businessman, easily won the presidency on 11 December 1993, taking 58 percent of the vote against 24 percent for right-wing candidate Arturo Alessandri. Prior to the election the Congress amended the constitution to make the presidential term six years.

During his campaign Frei vowed to maintain the fight against poverty, strengthen the educational system and continue pursuing greater civilian authority over the armed forces. However, the Concertacion lost a seat in the Senate and two seats in the Chamber of Deputies, leaving it still short of the four-sevenths majority needed to reform the constitution.

Frei's first test came in March when a judge charged Gen. Rodolfo Stange, the national police commander, with neglect of duty for failing to prevent or investigate the 1985 murders of three human rights activists. Frei made it clear that Stange should resign, although legally he could not remove him. Stange made a show of putting a subordinate in charge of day-to-day police affairs. But in June a military court, where the case had been referred, declined to pursue the charges and Stange announced he would resume his full duties.

Chastened, Frei opted for a less ambitious, more incremental approach. In October the government announced it would pursue constitutional reform in four stages, starting with the elimination of the designated senators and including direct election of mayors and presidential recourse to plebiscites to resolve intractable differences with the legislature.

Frei's reform agenda did not include restoration of the president's power to appoint and remove military commanders. A number of local analysts predicted that would not come about until 1997, when the constitution requires that Pinochet, now seventy-nine-years-old, and the other commanders step down.

Political Rights and Civil Liberties:

Citizens are able to change their government through free and fair elections at the national, regional and municipal levels. Democratic institutions are better established than in any other Latin American country outside of Costa Rica.

However, the 1980 constitution installed under military rule, while substantially reformed, still limits civilian authority over the armed forces. The president cannot change armed force commanders until 1997 or reduce the military budget. The constitution also allowed the former Pinochet regime to appoint eight senators to eight-year terms.

The Aylwin government (1990-94) was able to whittle away some of the military's autonomy. The armed forces now send top brass to the Congress to explain military expenditures and the navy and air force have invited legislators on inspections and military maneuvers.

In 1990 a Truth and Reconciliation Commission was formed to investigate human rights violations committed under military rule. The Commission's report implicated the military and the secret police at the highest levels in the death or disappearance of 2,279 people between September 1973 and March 1990. However, in 1978 the Pinochet regime had issued an amnesty for all political crimes, and the Supreme Court, packed by Pinochet before leaving office, has blocked government efforts to lift it. Chilean rights groups in 1994 formally asked the Inter-American Human Rights Commission to declare the amnesty invalid.

But the amnesty has not stopped civilian governments from investigating thousands of human rights cases brought to light by a government commission in 1991. Hundreds of cases have been brought to civilian courts. In March 1994 fifteen police officers and one civilian agent were found guilty in the 1985 murder of three rights activists and given tough penalties including three sentences of life imprisonment.

The Supreme Court, after persistent coaxing by former President Aylwin, made a dramatic turnaround in the case of the 1976 murder in Washington of former Chilean ambassador to the U.S., Orlando Letelier, and his assistant, Ronni Moffit. In 1991 the Court ruled that the alleged authors of the crime—retired Gen. Juan Manuel Contreras and Col. Pedro Espinosa—be tried in civilian courts. Under Pinochet the power of military courts was greatly expanded at the expense of the civil court system. Contreras and Espinosa were convicted in November 1993, the first time a civil court had convicted ranking officers for crimes committed during the Pinochet era. They were sentenced to seven and six years in prison, respectively, pending appeal.

In 1993 three right-wing opposition senators voted with pro-government senators to impeach a Supreme Court justice charged with dereliction of duty in handling human rights cases. The vote was an important step in strengthening congressional oversight of national institutions.

Most of the laws limiting political expression were eliminated by the 1989 constitutional reforms and the political spectrum runs from Marxist to fascist. Religious expression is unrestricted, although Mormon temples are occasionally the targets of attacks by left-wing radicals.

Nearly complete media freedom was restored after the return to civilian government There are scores of publications representing all points of view. Radio is both private and public. The national television network is owned by the state but independently operated. In 1994, however, it appeared the Frei government was trying to influence news coverage. There are three noncommercial television stations run by universities.

A licensing law for journalists remains in place, and a number of restrictive laws remain on the books, including one that grants power to military courts to convict journalists or others for sedition or libeling members of the armed forces. Human rights lawyer Hector Salazar Ardiles was charged with sedition in April 1994 for making critical comments in the media about Gen. Stange, the police commander.

There have been significant reforms of the draconian labor code inherited from the Pinochet regime. Strikes are legal, but organizational and collective bargaining provisions remain weak. Following a major labor demonstration in July 1994, the Frei administration proposed legislation to strengthen labor rights guarantees.

There were more than 350 political prisoners in 1990. By the time former President Aylwin left office in March 1994, he had made good on his promise to see that all were released. Since 1990 about 150 people have been incarcerated for violent political crimes and rights groups have expressed concern about whether they have access to adequate legal representation.

There continued to be sporadic terrorist actions by remnants of the Manuel Rodriguez Patriotic Front (FPMR), the former armed wing of the Communist Party, and the anarcho-hedonist Lautero Front. Human rights groups remain concerned about anti-terrorist legislation which broadened police powers. There are still frequent reports of police abuses, including torture, but there are also signs of greater accountability. There are continuing reports of excessive force used against political demonstrators.

An indigenous rights law was passed in 1993 but implementation has been slow because, according to the government, of a lack of resources.

In 1990 Chile ratified the Inter-American Convention on Human Rights and formally recognized the jurisdiction of the Inter-American Human Rights Court for the interpretation and enforcement of the provisions contained in the convention.

↑ China

Polity: Communist one-party
Economy: Mixed statist
Population: 1,191,976
PPP: $2,946
Life Expectancy: 70.5
Political Rights: 7
Civil Liberties: 7
Status: Not Free

Ethnic Groups: Han Chinese (93 percent), Azhuang, Hui, Uygur, Yi, Miao, Manchu, Tibetan, Mongolian, others
Trend Arrow: There is a trend towards more private enterprise.

Overview: On the forty-fifth anniversary of China's 1949 Communist revolution, the country's leadership struggled to reign in an economy that is racing out of control. In May the government secured an unconditional renewal of its Most Favored Nation (MFN) trade status with the United States despite its continued poor human rights record.

Chinese Communist Party (CCP) Chairman Mao Zedong proclaimed the People's Republic of China on 1 October 1949 following victory over the Nationalist Kuomintang. From 1958-60 Mao attempted to accelerate industrialization and agricultural collectivization through the disastrous Great Leap Forward, which created a rural famine that killed upward of 30 million peasants. In 1966 Mao began his most infamous mass movement, the Cultural Revolution, in a bid to regain control over a fractious CCP. By 1976 up to one million people had died, and millions more had been disgraced, including party secretary Deng Xiaoping. Following Mao's death in September 1976, Deng assumed several top-level posts, and in December 1978 began introducing free-market reforms.

In December 1986 students protested in several cities demanding political reforms. In January 1987 CCP hardliners sacked party secretary general Hu Yaobang for having permitted the protests and replaced him with Zhao Ziyang.

In April 1989 several thousand students gathered in Beijing's Tiananmen Square to mourn Hu's death, later boycotting classes to demand democratic reforms and to protest rising prices. By mid-May the protests had spread to other cities. The Beijing demonstrations ended with a bloody army assault on Tiananmen Square on 3-4 June, in which hundreds, perhaps thousands, were killed. Party hardliners seized the opportunity to sack liberal officials and arrest some 10,000 students and workers. Hardliner Jiang Zemin replaced the relatively moderate Zhao as party chief.

In the five years since Tiananmen the government has concentrated on raising living standards through economic reforms while continuing to crack down on political dissent. Policies are ultimately shaped by a core of six aging revolutionary veterans. Deng no longer holds any official titles but remains the country's ultimate arbiter by virtue of his leading role in the Communists' rise to power in the 1930s and 1940s.

Nineteen-ninety-two may ultimately be remembered as the year when Deng rooted the economic reforms deep enough so as to make them irreversible after his death. In January Deng made a highly symbolic visit to the booming Shenzhen and Zhuhai Special Economic Zones in southern Guangdong Province. At the CCP's 14th Party Congress in October 1992, the party formally adopted the goal of a "socialist market economy," a seemingly innocuous phrase that in fact buried the orthodox Marxist ideology of the 1949 revolution.

With Deng's health getting progressively worse, in 1993 the government focused on ensuring a smooth transition of power after his death. In March the rubber-stamp National People's Congress (NPC) elected CCP party secretary Jiang, who is Deng's hand-picked successor, to succeed Yang Shankun as president. However, Jiang, who holds a third title as Chairman of the Central Military Commission, lacks a power base; a leadership struggle after Deng's death is likely.

The NPC also re-elected premier Li Peng to a second five-year term, although 11 percent of the 2,977 delegates voted no or voided their ballots. Most Chinese abhor Li for his leading role in ordering the Tiananmen Square crackdown. In addition, the NPC named as its new chairman Qiao Shi, the CCP's former internal security chief.

In May 1993 U.S. President Bill Clinton set a June 1994 deadline for China to show improvements in its human rights record in return for extending the country's MFN trade status. Specifically, Clinton called on China to ease emigration restrictions for the families of dissidents living abroad and to move toward ending the export of goods made with prison labor, as well as to show "overall, significant progress" in areas including the release of political prisoners and the protection of Tibet's cultural heritage (a separate report on Tibet appears in the Related Territories section). In May 1994, following months of rising bilateral tensions during which China showed little if any improve-ments in the areas outlined, Clinton shifted tack and formally "de-linked" MFN from human rights considerations.

During the year, evidence continued to suggest that the economic reforms are having far-reaching political and demographic effects. A March 1994 report by London's International Institute for Strategic Studies (IISS) concluded that the increasing prosperity has greatly weakened Beijing's control over the provincial governments. Local authorities have largely ignored Beijing's call to slow infrastructure investment and to exercise fiscal restraint.

As a result, Zhu Rongji, the deputy premier overseeing the reforms, and his colleagues are finding it increasingly difficult to slow inflation, a major concern given that rising prices contributed to the student unrest in 1989. The government, meanwhile, adds to the infla-tionary pressure by subsidizing loss-making state-owned factories, fearing that an acceler-ated program of closures and privatization would cause severe unemployment and unrest. In the fall, following reports that consumer prices rose 27.4 percent in the twelve months to September 1994, the government reimposed price controls on many staple food items.

Researchers have also noted a dramatic population shift: in the 1990s more than 100 million peasants have left their rural villages in search of jobs, most of them becoming part of a massive migration to the cities. Although GDP growth has averaged 9 percent per year since 1978, including increases of more than 13 percent in 1992 and 1993, most of the gains have been in the southern coastal areas and in the cities. The new "floating popula-tion" has been attracted to the cities by wages that average 2.5 times more than those in the countryside, where there are an estimated 260 million "surplus" agricultural workers. In a related development, in recent years there have been hundreds of peasant riots to protest illegal land seizures and arbitrary taxes levied by rogue provincial authorities.

In other key issues, Deng turned ninety in August and is reportedly near death, raising new anxiety about a potential succession crisis. The country's most severe drought of the century hit several central and eastern provinces in the spring and summer. In foreign affairs, on 8 August China and Taiwan reached their first substantive bilateral agreements since 1949, involving repatriation of airline hijackers and illegal immigrants, and on ways to resolve fishing disputes.

Political Rights and Civil Liberties: Chinese citizens lack the democratic means to change their government. The Chinese Communist Party (CCP), controlled by a handful of aging revolutionaries, wields ultimate authority. Although economic reforms have given many ordinary Chinese somewhat greater freedom from government intrusion in their day-to-day lives, the regime continues to have one of the worst human rights records in the world.

Approximately 90 percent of the country's village committees are now chosen through local elections, although only CCP candidates and non-party independents can compete. According to the International Republican Institute, the fairness of these elections varies; in some elections independents have won seats, while in other villages there are marked irregularities.

It is impossible to estimate accurately how many political prisoners are held in China. The government acknowledges holding some 3,000 people convicted of "counterrevolutionary" crimes. However, in recent years the government has increasingly charged dissidents with ordinary crimes rather than with counterrevolutionary offenses in an effort to avoid international censure. Therefore, the number of political prisoners is probably considerably higher than 3,000. In June 1994 Premier Li Peng signed the "Detailed Implementation Regulations" for the 1993 State Security Law. A July report by Human Rights Watch/Asia and Human Rights in China noted that the Regulations criminalize peaceful acts of dissent that were formerly labeled counterrevolutionary, including working with foreign human rights organizations and articles or speech harmful to "state security."

In the months prior to the U.S. government's May 1994 decision on China's MFN status, (*See Overview above*), the government released several prominent dissidents, apparently as token gestures, but in February and March detained and harassed dozens of others in Beijing and Shanghai. In March the authorities re-arrested the country's most prominent dissident, Wei Jingsheng. By year's end there had been no word on his whereabouts. Following the May MFN decision, the government ceased releasing dissidents and in July began proceedings for a trial of fifteen dissidents and labor activists who had been detained for "counterrevolutionary" offenses since mid-1992. In December nine of the activists received sentences of up to twenty years.

The lack of accountability at all levels of government is most evident in the penal system and judiciary. Suspects are frequently tortured to extract confessions. Abuse of prisoners, particularly ordinary workers, is routine and widespread. In April the government broke off negotiations with the International Committee of the Red Cross on prison inspections. The judiciary is subservient to the CCP and due process rights are generally ignored. The accused are presumed guilty and over 99 percent are convicted. Defense lawyers ordinarily appeal for leniency rather than truly defend the accused.

Two special types of punishment exist: the *laojiao*, or "re-education through labor" camps, and the *laogai*, or "reform through labor" camps. The laojiao provide for administrative detention for up to four years without a hearing, bypassing the formal judicial process and trial system. At the end of 1993 Chinese authorities reported that 120,000 prisoners were undergoing "re-education through labor," although the actual number may be higher.

In recent years there has been a chilling rise in the number of people executed during mass crackdowns on corruption and drug trafficking, often after summary trials. The Associated Press reported on 27 June that in a three-day period seventy smugglers and traffickers had been executed, including a Tibetan accused of selling 2.2 pounds of narcotics.

Religious practice is tightly controlled by the state and is officially limited to government-sanctioned "Patriotic" churches. Students attending seminaries run by state-approved churches must pass exams on political as well as theological knowledge. The government regulates the publication and distribution of religious books and other materials. Small, unofficial Catholic and Protestant churches are often tolerated provided they maintain a low profile. However, scores of such churches have been closed in some provinces, and hundreds of bishops, priests and ordinary worshippers have been arrested and detained for months—in some cases, years. Muslims face restrictions in building mosques and in providing religious education to youths under eighteen. On 31 January the government codified into law long-standing bans against proselytizing by foreigners, and banned Chinese from worshiping with their foreign co-religionists. In February the authorities detained seven foreign Christians, including three Americans, in central Henan Province for four days.

China's harsh one-child planning policy is applied inconsistently from region to region. The policy is zealously enforced by some local officials through sanctions and even forced contraception and sterilization. Couples adhering to the policy receive preferential education, food and medical benefits, while those failing to comply face a loss of benefits and are fined. Failure to pay the fine often results in seizure of livestock and other goods and destruction of homes.

Expecting mothers often use ultrasound machines to determine a baby's sex. Female fetuses are frequently aborted, and infanticide is practiced in a small fraction of births. According to an official study obtained by the *New York Times* in July 1993, the ratio of male to female births in 1992 reached 118.5:100; a normal ratio is roughly 105:100. In December 1993 the government aroused international concern by proposing national legislation aimed at preventing "births of inferior quality" through sterilization of women considered likely to pass genetic diseases to their children. According to the U.S. State Department, since 1988 five provinces have already approved eugenics regulations designed to prevent severely retarded people from having children. In March the government withdrew the draft law, but then in November announced that the measures would take effect in January 1995, along with a ban on ultrasound testing.

Freedoms of press, political expression and association are nonexistent. In March a Beijing court sentenced Xi Yang, a mainland-based correspondent of the Hong Kong newspaper *Ming Pao*, to twelve years in prison for leaking alleged "state secrets"—in reality information on central bank monetary policy. In November, a court sentenced fifty-year-old journalist Gao Yu to six years in prison for leaking state secrets, apparently a reference to economic articles she wrote for the Hong Kong-based *Mirror Monthly* magazine. During the year, police detained and interrogated several Western journalists. An October 1993 regulation sharply restricts private ownership and operation of satellite dishes, although in practice they are tolerated.

Women face discrimination and sexual harassment in the workplace. In rural areas women are frequently abducted for sale as prostitutes. The government recognizes fifty-five ethnic minorities, although few people from these groups hold key positions in the CCP or government hierarchies.

Independent trade unions are illegal, and all unions must belong to the CCP-controlled All-China Federation of Trade Unions. The 1982 constitution does not recognize the right to strike. In practice strikes are permitted to protest dangerous or inadequate working conditions and low wages, and occur most often in foreign-owned factories. The 4 August *Far Eastern Economic Review* reported that at least sixteen labor activists had been arrested since March, including the leadership of the League for the Protection of Workers' Rights, a newly formed, underground organization. Almost all prisoners are required to work, receiving little if any compensation. The U.S. in particular remains concerned about the export of goods made with prison labor.

The successes of both the Special Economic Zones in the south and the small-scale township and village enterprises in the countryside have helped remove millions of Chinese from dependence on the *danwei*, or state work unit, eroding the once-pervasive influence of the CCP. However, for some 100 million others still working in state enterprises, the danwei controls everything from the right to change residence to permission to have a child.

The system of *hakou*, or residence permit, has also been loosened to give workers more flexibility in filling jobs in areas of fast economic growth. However, in September the Beijing municipal government announced that beginning 1 November a fee of $5,800 would be levied on outsiders wishing to live in the capital.

Colombia

Polity: Presidential-
legislative democracy
(insurgencies)
Economy: Capitalist-
statist
Population: 35,578,000
PPP: $5,460
Life Expectancy: 69.0

Political Rights: 3*
Civil Liberties: 4
Status: Partly Free

Ethnic Groups: Mestizo (58 percent), Caucasian (20 percent),
Mulatto (14 percent), Black, (4 percent), Indian (1 percent)
Ratings Change: *Colombia's political rights rating declined
from 2 to 3 principally as a result of advancing penetration of
the political system by drug traffickers.

Overview:

Ernesto Samper of the incumbent Liberal Party won the
presidency on 19 June 1994 in an election overshadowed
by evidence of drug money contributions to his campaign.

Colombia won independence from Spain in 1819. The Republic of Colombia
was established under the 1886 constitution. Politics has been dominated by the
Liberal and Conservative parties, which in 1957 joined forces to rule as the
National Front. After 1974 the two parties divided to compete in direct presidential
and congressional elections. Municipal governments have been elected since 1988.

President Cesar Gaviria (1990-94) initiated a process of political reform. In 1990 a
constituent assembly was elected. It produced a new constitution that provided for an
expanded bicameral Congress and the election of governors in the nation's thirty-one
departments. It limited presidents to single four-year terms and gave Congress veto powers
over the Cabinet. It abolished the system of discretionary funds that allowed members of
Congress to pay for patronage and re-election campaigns at public expense, prohibited
legislators from holding second jobs and barred relatives from running for office.

Nevertheless, the Liberal and Conservative political machines have continued to
operate in traditional ways and still dominate the political system, as was evident in
congressional and municipal elections in 1991 and 1992. In 1993 more than a hundred
current and former legislators, dozens of municipal officials, and members of the Gaviria
government, including Gaviria himself, had to answer corruption charges.

Gaviria sought to reduce drug-related violence. In December 1993 Medellin
cartel leader Pablo Escobar was killed by security forces. The cartel split into
dozens of independent operations headed by a new generation of traffickers. The
Cali cartel, in turn, having avoided a direct confrontation with the state, absorbed
many of the Medellin traffickers and cemented its status as the largest, most
efficient cocaine- and heroin-trafficking operation in the Western hemisphere.

Gaviria also tried to entice guerrilla groups to join the political system. But intermittent
talks with the Revolutionary Armed Forces of Colombia (FARC) and the National Liberation Army (ELN), the two main forces with about 9,000 members combined, went nowhere. The guerrillas have raised substantial funds through kidnapping and drug trafficking.

The ELN and the FARC unleashed a terrorist offensive in late 1993 that targeted police, government officials and the economic infrastructure, especially oil pipelines. As the 1994 election campaign got underway, they bombed the offices of a dozen congressional and presidential candidates. In the 13 March 1994 legislative elections the Liberals retained a majority in both the Senate and the Chamber of Deputies. Voter abstention was nearly 70 percent, high even by Colombian standards.

The Liberals selected Ernesto Samper, a forty-three-year-old former economic development minister, as their presidential candidate. The Conservatives backed Andres Pastrana, a thirty-nine-year-old former mayor of Bogota. Both candidates, political moderates, vowed to continue the free-market, free-trade reforms of Gaviria and increase social spending.

On 8 May Samper took 45.2 percent of the vote, Pastrana 44.9 percent, with six other candidates trailing. As no candidate garnered an absolute majority a runoff was held on 19 June. Samper won, taking 50.4 percent of the vote to 48.6 percent for Pastrana.

Drugs were hardly mentioned during the campaign, except in veiled hints by both candidates that the other was financed at least in part by drug money. However, after the vote four tape recordings surfaced in which the top Cali cartel leaders, the brothers Gilberto and Miguel Rodriguez Orejuela, discussed million-dollar contributions to Samper's campaign.

An audit of Samper's books showed no irregularities. But the scandal prompted U.S. drug enforcement agencies, as well as some Colombian analysts, to affirm that Cali narco-bosses had already purchased through bribery and threats up to a third of the government. It may never be known whether Samper solicited or received Cali money. But as Fabio Castillo, a columnist for the daily *El Espectador*, put it, "The press is bombarded daily with evidence of ties between political bosses and the Cali traffickers."

Samper took office in August promising to renew peace efforts with the FARC and the ELN and to take stronger antidrug measures. He was greeted by a nationwide guerrilla offensive that lasted through the gubernatorial and municipal elections on 30 October, dimming hopes for a cease-fire. In the elections the Liberals lost control of Colombia's four main cities, but won a majority of the other municipalities and about half the governorships.

Political Rights and Civil Liberties: Citizens are able to change their government through elections. The 1991 constitution provides for broader participation in the political system, including two reserved seats in the Congress for the country's small Indian minority and a voter system that gives all parties equal billing on the ballots. There are more than a dozen highly diverse political groups.

However, because of fear of political violence and a widespread belief that politics is too corrupt for elections to matter, voter participation rarely exceeds 40 percent of eligible voters. Political candidates campaign under heavy security and tend to limit themselves to indoor appearances. In 1994 dozens of candidates were killed, kidnapped or injured during election campaigns. There were indications that left-wing guerrillas controlled up to 15 percent of the nation's 1,000-plus municipalities.

Evidence mounted in 1994 that the Cali cartel and other traffickers have deeply penetrated the political system. The "narco-cassette" scandal (see "Overview") implicated President Samper himself and seemed to indicate the penetration had reached the highest level of government. Whether the Samper administration had come under the sway of the Cali cartel was not known, but the tapes indicate the narco-bosses believed they could bring it about.

When Joe Toft, the outgoing U.S. Drug Enforcement Agency chief in Bogota, said in September that Colombia had become a "narco-democracy," more than a few Colombian justice ministry officials were quoted anonymously in the international media saying he was correct, that most of the nation's institutions had been corrupted by traffickers. In fact, there is strong evidence the Cali cartel, through its lawyers, virtually dictated to the Congress the 1993 penal-code reform that allows traffickers who turn themselves in as much as a two-thirds sentence reduction and the dismissal of any pending charges they do not plea to. Traffickers also appeared to influence the constituent assembly in 1991 to ensure that it banned extradition in the new constitution.

Constitutional rights regarding free expression and the freedom to organize political parties, civic groups and labor unions are severely restricted by political and drug-related violence and the government's inability to guarantee the security of citizens, institutions and the media.

Political violence in Colombia continues to take more lives than in any other country in the hemisphere, with about ten killings and disappearances per day in 1994. The military and security forces are responsible for most of these, followed by right-wing paramilitary groups, left-wing guerrillas, drug-traffickers and hundreds, possibly thousands, of paid assassins. All perpetrators of political violence operate with a high degree of impunity.

Another category of killings is "social cleansing"—the elimination of drug addicts, street children and other marginal citizens by vigilante groups often linked with the police. Overall, criminal violence results in dozens of murders per day. Homicide is the number-one cause of death in Colombia. Kidnappings occurred in 1994 at a rate of more than two per day, about half by left-wing guerrillas.

There are numerous human rights organizations, but activists, as well as labor, peasant and student organizations, are consistently the targets of violence and intimidation. Dozens of trade unionists were killed in 1994 as Colombia retained its status as the most dangerous country in the world for organized labor.

Over the last decade the entire judicial system has been severely weakened by the onslaught of the drug cartels and generalized political violence. Much of the system has been compromised through corruption and extortion. In the last eight years, more than 300 judges and court personnel, as well as a justice minister, an attorney general and dozens of lawyers, have been killed.

Under the new constitution, the judiciary, headed by a Supreme Court, was revamped. A U.S.-like adversarial system was adopted and government prosecutors are able to use government security services to investigate crimes. Previously, judges investigated crimes without the help of major law enforcement agencies.

The new measures have brought some success in dealing with common crime, but the judiciary remains overloaded and ill-equipped to handle high-profile drug cases. To protect the judiciary from drug traffickers, the Gaviria government instituted a system of eighty-four "faceless judges." But traffickers are able to penetrate the veil of anonymity and judges remain under threat.

The military was untouched by constitutional reform. No demands were made on spending accountability and mandatory military service was left intact. Cases involving police and military personnel accused of human rights violations are tried in military rather than civilian courts. In effect, the military and police remain accountable only to themselves, reinforcing the atmosphere of impunity that pervades the entire country.

Radio is both public and private. Television remains mostly a government monopoly and news programs tend to be slanted. Moreover, the "right to reply" provision of the new constitution has resulted in harsh judicial tutelage over all media.

The press, including dozens of daily newspapers and weekly magazines, is privately owned. Although no sector of Colombian society has been left untouched, the press has been hit especially hard by drug-related and political violence. Dozens of journalists have been murdered in the last decade, nearly one a month in the first ten months of 1994. Numerous others have been kidnapped. A number of newspapers have been forced to close regional offices.

The new constitution expanded religious freedom by ending the privileges of the Catholic church, which long enjoyed the advantages of an official religion. In 1994 there were at least two bomb attacks against Mormon temples, apparently by left-wing radicals.

Comoros

Polity: Dominant party
Economy: Capitalist
Population: 530,000
PPP: $700
Life Expectancy: 55.4
Ethnic Groups: Majority of mixed African-Arab descent, East Indian minority

Political Rights: 4
Civil Liberties: 4
Status: Partly Free

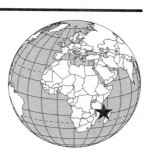

Overview:

Challenged by opposition parties demanding his resignation in 1994, President Mohamad Said Djohar was also faced with infighting within his ruling party, the Rally for Democracy and Renewal. A document published on 17 January by all Comoran opposition parties accused the president and his son-in-law, Mohamad Said M' Changama, who is Speaker of the National Assembly, of consistently violating the constitution. Exiled opposition leader Abdallah Ahmed Mohamed called for President Djohar's resignation at a 23 January rally in Paris. On 20 March 1994, the government arrested two members of the opposition for "crimes against the state." The power struggle between the executive and legislative which dominated the political scene in 1993 ended with Prime Minister Madi's dismissal in October 1994 over rows about economic reforms. Under pressure to act against Madi in a power battle with M'Changama, considered the government strongman, Djohar replaced Madi with Halifa Houmadi.

The Federal Islamic Republic of the Comoros, a tiny three-island state in the Indian Ocean off Madagascar, declared independence from France in 1975. It also claims Mayotte, still governed by France. The first president, Ahmed Abdallah Abderrahman, served briefly before being ousted in a coup. Abdallah resumed leadership in 1978 after seizing power with the assistance of Col. Bob Denard, a French mercenary. Abdallah stood for election unopposed in 1978 and 1984, consolidating the power of his one-party regime. He fought off several coup attempts, but was assassinated in 1989, allegedly on Denard's orders. Supreme Court Justice Djohar became interim president and, under French pressure, Denard's mercenaries left the country.

Djohar became president in his own right in 1990. The elections were fraudulent. First-round winner Mohamad Taki challenged the results, but the Supreme Court validated them. Subsequently, the state charged Taki with complicity in an alleged coup attempt. Under French influence, Taki formed a coalition with Djohar. A national reconciliation conference followed. In December 1991, all Comoran parties acknowledged the legitimacy of Djohar's presidency.

In 1992 Djohar sacked Taki as prime minister after the latter hired a French mercenary as an adviser. Army mutineers and two sons of former President Abdallah attempted a coup. Taki was accused of backing the coup. Those who plotted the coup were convicted by the court and sentenced to death in 1993, but their execution was suspended after Amnesty International's intervention.

Disturbances and irregularities undermined the two-round legislative election in November 1992. After rescheduling the vote several times, the regime seemed to have a majority in December elections. However, in May 1993 Said Ali Mohamed succeeded Prime Minister Halidi after Parliament voted no confidence by a margin of 23 to 2 with 16 abstentions. In June, Djohar dissolved the legislature after a majority introduced a censure motion against the government. New elections, scheduled for November, took place 12-29 December. After four rounds of voting marred by accusations of government gerrymandering and sporadic violence, the government won 21 seats to 18 for opposition parties, which pledged to boycott the legislature. Three seats remained vacant. Nine political parties finally formed an opposition despite Djohar's design to reduce the twenty-four parties to three. He set up his own party, the Movement for Democracy and Renewal to succeed the Movement for the Triumph of Democracy.

Economic life in the Comoros depends largely on international aid. In 1993, Comoros became the twenty-second member of the Arab League. Because the Central Bank enjoys relative stability, the currency was devalued by only 25 percent instead of 50 percent following France's decision to devalue the CFA franc by half in all its former colonies.

Political Rights and Civil Liberties:

Comorans have a theoretical right to change their government by democratic means, but electoral fraud and irregularities, constant coup attempts and elite intrigues are what actually changed the government. Numerous political parties exist, but President Djohar attempts to restrict them through political imprisonment and alleged gerrymandering. In 1993, he attempted to reduce the number of parties running for legislative elections from twenty-four to three.

The legal system is based on both Islamic law and remnants of the French legal code. The judiciary is largely independent. Most disputes are settled by village elders or by a civilian court of first instance.

There is generally free expression. However, security measures taken around coup attempts reduce these freedoms intermittently. The government also bans assemblies sporadically. The frequent civilian riots and army mutinies leave the country with poor civilian-military relations and only spasmodic protection from political terror. Prison conditions are grim. Women are somewhat better off in the Comoros than in other Muslim countries. They have both political and property rights. Islam is the state religion. Other faiths may function, but may not proselytize.

The population, which increases at one of the fastest rates in the world, has only limited economic opportunities. Trade unions may exist and workers may strike, but collective bargaining is weak.

Congo

Polity: Presidential-
parliamentary democracy
(military-influenced)
Economy: Mixed statist
Population: 2,447,000
PPP: $2,800
Life Expectancy: 51.7
Ethnic Groups: Kongo, Lari, Bembe, M'bochi, Vlli, pygmy, other

Political Rights: 4
Civil Liberties: 4
Status: Partly Free

Overview: In 1994 bloody, often ethnic-based clashes continued between armed supporters of the opposition and armed forces of President Pascal Lissouba of the Pan-African Union for Social Democracy (UPADS). The conflict was sparked by disputed results of the May 1993 legislative elections, although tribal and regional alliances and animosities were key factors in the violence.

Ten years after winning independence from France in 1960, the African Republic of the Congo was established as a one-party, Marxist-Leninist state ruled by the Congolese Workers Party (PCT). Gen. Denis Sassou-Nguesso seized power in a 1979 coup and ruled as both president and PCT chairman until 1991, when a national conference limited the president's functions. The PCT's rubber-stamp legislature was disbanded and a High Council of the Republic oversaw a one-year transition to multiparty democracy.

In 1992 a 125-seat National Assembly was elected. The UPADS won 39 seats; the Congolese Movement for Democracy and Integral Development (MCDDI), 29; the PCT, 19, and two smaller parties split the rest. Then-Prime Minister Andre Milango finished fourth in the first round of presidential elections behind Sassou-Nguesso, who threw his support to Lissouba, allegedly in exchange for immunity from prosecution on corruption charges. In the second-round presidential vote, Lissouba got 61 percent, with the MCDDI's Bernard Kolelas garnering 39 percent. President Lissouba aggravated ethnic tensions when he replaced Lari and Kongo officials with people from his own ethnic group, the Nibolek.

By the fall, the PCT joined with a new seven-party coalition, the Union of Democratic Renewal (UDR), to bring down the government of Prime Minister Stephane Maurice Bongho-Nouarra of the pro-Lissouba, forty-three-party National Alliance for Democracy (AND). With a parliamentary majority of 66, the PCT-UDR bloc demanded that President Lissouba choose a prime minister from its ranks; instead, he dissolved the Assembly and called for new elections in May 1993, and Claude Antoine da Costa was selected to head an interim government consisting of 60 percent PCT-UDR ministers and 40 percent from the AND.

The first round of voting for the new National Assembly began on 2 May 1993 with charges by the opposition of fraud and irregularities that included improper voter registration, incomplete voter lists and instances of persons voting more than once in Brazzaville and in many of the 2,000-plus polling stations. After the interior minister announced that pro-Lissouba parties had won 62 seats, the PCT-UDR said it would boycott the second round. Violence erupted in June, as armed opposition supporters in

Brazzaville's Bacongo, Makelekele and Talangai areas set up barricades, ostensibly to protect the homes of Kolelas and former military ruler Sassou-Nguesso. Protests were fueled by a government announcement that the second round of voting had given Lissouba's supporters an overall majority in the Assembly. Former head-of-state Gen. Yhombi-Opango, who led the country from 1977-79, was appointed prime minister by the president. The PCT-UDR formed a parallel government and legislature, and some fifty opposition members boycotted the new Assembly.

By mid-July the clashes began to take on an ethnic dimension, since the country's political parties were divided on ethnic, tribal and regional lines. The fighting pitted Bembe supporters of the president against the Lari people of opposition leader Kolelas. The fighting escalated, and included mutilations and other atrocities, prompting a state of emergency and the appointment of a special envoy by the Organization of African Unity (OAU). After negotiations in Gabon's capital, Libreville, all sides agreed to an accord that, among other provisions, confirmed the first round of elections but called for a new vote for eleven disputed seats. After an October vote, it was announced that of the eleven seats contested, the Kolelas opposition won eight and the presidential group, three.

Tensions erupted in November 1993, when government security forces moved against opposition militia in the Bacongo section of the capital. The government maintained that under conditions of the Libreville Accords, opposition militias, such as Kolelas's "Ninjas," should be disbanded. By December "ethnic cleansing" operations had begun in Brazzaville as Bembe and Lari people continued to kill each other. In Brazzaville's Mfilou suburbs journalists reported mounds of decomposing bodies with limbs hacked off.

Clashes continued in January 1994, as forces loyal to Kolelas launched attacks into Makelekele, a southern district in the capital. The government retaliated by destroying a bridge connecting Brazzaville to the neighboring Pool region, and blockaded the Bacongo district, where nearly one-third of Brazzaville's 600,000 people live. Meanwhile, an arbitration committee composed of seven international magistrates examined fifty-eight appeals for the cancellation of the first-round of the 1993 legislative elections. At the end of the month, all sides agreed to a cease-fire and an end to inter-ethnic violence, and the arbitration committee canceled on the basis of fraud the results in eight of fifty-eight constituencies.

By February, however, the cease-fire had broken down. A mediation force of 400 men was deployed to create a buffer zone between warring factions in Brazzaville. In early April, the force began collecting arms from opposition and pro-presidential groups. But on 15 April the force was withdrawn with no official explanation. In late May, a huge cache of arms was stolen from an officer's training school in Gamboma, an opposition stronghold.

In early June President Lissouba proposed a power-sharing agreement he said was based on the example of South Africa. He suggested that the opposition be awarded the post of vice president, an idea initially supported by Kolelas. Meanwhile, sporadic fighting and kidnapping continued in Brazzaville. Moreover, members of the 2,000-strong private pro-presidential militias created to fight the opposition marched in front of the presidential palace demanding to be integrated into the National Army. Over 200 pro-president militiamen were eventually enrolled in the army and police.

In July the town councillors of Brazzaville unanimously elected Kolelas as mayor of the capital. The appointment was seen as a step toward restoring peace and order in Brazzaville. The new mayor announced the creation of a new municipal force to restore order and security in the capital. In August, the interior minister, in an address to Parliament, threatened to arrest deputies who continued to support various militias. He accused the opposition of setting up a new militia, called the "Sharks," in the port city of Pointe-Noire.

Despite agreements between the government and opposition, September saw several clashes between the army or police and militias in Brazzaville, and there were numerous incidents of looting. While some of the violence was ethnically or politically motivated, much was criminal mayhem carried out by opposition militia and elements in the army. On 28 September President Lissouba ordered the deployment of troops in Brazzaville to restore order. In October, the government faced increased unrest in the northern part of the country, and an ad hoc parliamentary commission was established to meet with deputies from the northern constituencies.

On 3 November three labor union federations issued an indefinite general strike notice in the civil service and state-owned enterprises following the failure of negotiations with the government. The three federations, all close to the opposition and including the Confederation of Congolese Labor Unions (CSTC)—the biggest in the country—demanded salary increases and improved pensions. Five days later, the government and the unions signed a protocol agreement in which the government promised to pay five months' salary arrears to workers, and the unions pledged not to strike.

Political Rights and Civil Liberties:

Congolese nominally have the right to change their government democratically, but fraud-marred parliamentary elections in 1993 led to the escalation of violence and lawlessness as anti- and pro-government militias battled each other through much of the year. The ethnic, tribal and regional dimension to the violence created refugees and charges of "ethnic cleansing" by government and antigovernment forces.

The 1991 national conference that launched the democratic transition led to a constitution that called for an independent judiciary, but the judiciary is not wholly free from government interference. The violence of 1994 brought charges of brutality and extrajudicial murders by the army, police and pro-government militias. Prisons are in deplorable condition, and inmates are frequently released for hours at a time because the government does not have money to feed them. In October, thirty-one prisoners nearly died of malnutrition at Brazzaville's Central Prison.

Unrest also inhibited freedom of expression. Over sixty political parties and groupings exist, but ethnic and tribal tensions made it dangerous for some citizens to proclaim their political affiliation.

State-run radio and television were barred from airing political views. Parliamentary deputies from both the opposition and pro-government factions decided in the spring that state media would be allowed to broadcast only official news. The deputies said the measure was taken to prevent political parties issuing communiqués that might provoke violence.

Political and ethnic violence encumbered freedom of movement; tens of thousands have reportedly been displaced. Freedom of assembly has been circumscribed, as several demonstrations and protests were broken up by police. There are no serious restrictions on freedom of worship, and many denominations are represented in government and other social institutions.

Northern Pygmies face discrimination, particularly in employment, where they have been exploited and underpaid. International organizations have characterized some as living in virtual slavery. Pygmies are excluded from government posts.

While sex discrimination is officially banned, discrimination against women in terms of employment and education is widespread. Adultery is considered illegal for women, but not for men, and male polygamy is accepted. There have been positive developments, including pay equity and opportunities in the white-collar and government sectors.

The Confederation of Congolese Labor Unions (CSTC) is the largest of several trade union federations; workers enjoy and utilize the right to strike.

Costa Rica

Polity: Presidential-legislative democracy
Economy: Capitalist-statist
Population: 3,248,000
PPP: $5,100
Life Expectancy: 76.0
Ethnic Groups: Spanish with large mestizo minority

Political Rights: 1
Civil Liberties: 2
Status: Free

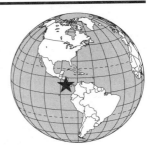

Overview:

Jose Maria Figueres of the National Liberation Party (PLN) was elected president on 6 February 1994, defeating Miguel Angel Rodriguez of the incumbent Social Christian Unity Party (PUSC) in the closest, most bitter race in the country's history.

The Republic of Costa Rica achieved independence from Spain in 1821 and became a republic in 1848. Democratic government was instituted in 1899 and briefly interrupted in 1917 and 1948. The 1949 constitution, which bans the formation of a national army, has been the framework for democratic governance ever since.

The constitution provides for three independent branches of government—executive, legislative and judicial. The president and the fifty-seven-member Legislative Assembly are elected for four years and are prohibited from succeeding themselves. The Assembly has co-equal power, including the ability to override presidential vetoes.

President Rafael A. Calderon, Jr., of the center-right PUSC defeated Carlos Manuel Castillo of the social democratic PLN in the 1990 election. The PLN had held the presidency for two straight terms, and sixteen out of the previous twenty years.

Calderon implemented a structural adjustment program to reduce a widening public-sector deficit and a mounting foreign debt. The program received high marks from international creditors, but provoked a widespread backlash, including a series of public-sector labor strikes, from a population used to the some of the best social services in Latin America.

Rodriguez, a businessman and legislator, won the PUSC primary in 1993. Figueres prevailed in a fierce six-candidate PLN primary. The forty-year-old Figueres is the son of former President Jose "Pepe" Figueres, a national hero for leading the fight to preserve democracy in the 1948 civil war.

Figueres campaigned against the PUSC's "neo-liberal" economic policies and promised "to govern for those who have the least and need the most." Rodriguez proposed to deepen structural reforms. However, the campaign was dominated by acrimonious personal attacks to such a degree that the electoral tribunal, following the electoral law, banned 161 advertisements from both parties that it deemed to be slanderous or libelous.

Figueres had to contend with unsubstantiated allegations that as a policeman in 1973 he was involved in the murder of a drug dealer, and with reports implicating him in a scandal dating back a decade in which foreign investors lost their money. Rodriguez was dogged by corruption charges—that he sold tainted meat to the U.S., illegally imported cattle and used his influence as a legislator to further the interests of his brewery. Rodriguez denied the allegations and countered that he, too, was being smeared.

On 6 February Figueres took 49.7 percent of the vote, just 2.2 points ahead of Rodriguez. He was inaugurated on 8 May. The PLN won twenty-eight seats in the Assembly, one short of a majority, and the PUSC won twenty-five. The Democratic Force, an alliance of leftists, nationalists and centrists won two seats. Two small regional parties won the remaining two.

The acrimony between the two main parties carried over into the first months of Figueres's term, as he and the PLN waged a campaign to discredit the outgoing PUSC. After a public outcry, the two parties agreed in August to open a dialogue.

In November Figueres angered many supporters when he reversed his campaign pledge by supporting passage in the Assembly of a structural adjustment package introduced by the PUSC. The package was necessary to secure loans from international lenders, which Figueres said Costa Rica had to have given its gaping budget deficit. His policy switch seemed to fit the Costa Rican pattern in which governments first fill public coffers, then empty them at the end of their terms in election-year spending.

Political Rights and Civil Liberties: Citizens are able to change their government, at both the national and local levels, through free and fair elections. In fall 1993, and for the eleventh time since 1949, the executive branch turned control of the police over to the independent electoral commission for the duration of the election period. The political landscape is dominated by the PLN and the PUSC, but more than a dozen other parties run candidates in elections.

Numerous allegations implicating both major parties in drug-tainted campaign contributions were made during the 1990 election. New campaign laws have since been instituted to make party financing more transparent. But Costa Rica, with no army, navy, or air force, remains an easy target for drug-traffickers and there is great concern about increasing drug-related corruption and money laundering.

In 1994 a multiparty electoral reform commission stepped up its work in the legislature in 1994. Proposals under consideration included presidential re-election and the election of deputies by district rather than from party lists.

Constitutional guarantees regarding freedom of religion and the right to organize political parties and civic organizations are respected. However, in recent years there has been a reluctance to address restrictions on labor rights and mounting threats to press and media freedom.

The former Calderon government supported Solidarity, an employer-employee organization that business uses as an instrument to prevent independent unions from organizing in the private sector. The government, pressured by the International Labor Organization and the International Confederation of Free Trade Unions, and threatened with the loss of U.S. trade benefits, changed tack in late 1993. It agreed to change labor laws to conform to international standards regarding the freedom to organize and bargain collectively. But in 1994, there were delays in enacting the necessary legislation.

In May the government used excessive force during a banana workers' strike.

Eighteen workers were wounded when riot police fired rifles into a demonstration. The labor ministry mediated an end to the strike, but workers complained months later that union activists were being summarily fired.

Labor abuses by multinational corporations operating in free trade zones are prevalent. Minimum wage and social security laws are often ignored and fines for noncompliance are minuscule. Women workers frequently suffer sexual harassment, are often worked overtime without pay and are fired when they become pregnant. There have also been reports of abuse of Nicaraguan workers on Costa Rican farms.

The press, radio and television are generally free. There are a number of independent dailies serving a society that is 90 percent literate. Television and radio stations are both public and commercial, with at least six private television stations providing an influential forum for public debate. But freedom of expression is marred by a twenty-three-year-old licensing requirement for journalists.

Moreover, there have been a number of alarming incidents in recent years involving censorship. Pilar Cisneros, an influential television anchor, left Channel 7 in January 1994, alleging she had been forced out under pressure from candidate Figueres's advisers. In March a commission appointed by the government-sanctioned journalist union (which all journalists are legally bound to join) sided with Channel 7 and criticized Cisneros for trying to damage Figueres's reputation.

In July award-winning journalist Bosco Velarde of the daily *La Nacion* became the first journalist in Costa Rica to be found guilty of breaking a law against offending the "honor" of a public official. Velarde had written a column critical of the Supreme Court. He was sentenced to three years' probation.

The judicial branch is independent. Its members are elected by the legislature. In 1993 the legislature passed new laws to guarantee selection of judges based on experience and ability. There is a Supreme Court with power to rule on the constitutionality of laws, as well as four courts of appeal and a network of district courts. The members of the national election commission are elected by the Supreme Court.

The judicial system has been marked by delays, creating a volatile situation in overcrowded prisons and increased inmate violence. The problem is linked to budget cuts affecting the judiciary and the nation's economic difficulties, which has led to a rise in violent crime and clashes in the countryside between squatters and landowners.

In recent years the judiciary has been called upon to address numerous charges of human rights violations made by the independent Costa Rican Human Rights Commission and other rights activists. A number of cases, including allegations of arbitrary arrests and accusations of brutality and torture in secret jails, have been made against police units.

A number of killings of suspected drug traffickers in recent years heightened the controversy over the large amounts of military training the nation's various police branches have received in the last decade. In 1994 the police were overhauled and reorganized under one statute, with new standards for hiring within a civil service structure that allows for "eminently civilian training."

In 1993 the government established an official ombudsman as a recourse for citizens or foreigners with human rights complaints. The ombudsman has the authority to issue recommendations for rectification, including sanctions against government bodies, for failure to respect rights.

Croatia

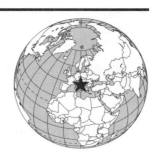

Polity: Presidential-parliamentary democracy (partly foreign-occupied) **Political Rights**: 4
Civil Liberties: 4
Status: Partly Free
Economy: Mixed-statist
Population: 4,800,000
PPP: na
Life Expectancy: na
Ethnic Groups: Croats (77 percent), Serbs (12.2 percent), Muslims (1 percent), Hungarians, Slovenes, Czechs, Albanians, Montenegrins, Ukrainians, others

Overview: The key issues facing President Franjo Tudjman in 1994 were the November NATO air strikes on the Serb-controlled Krajina region, shifting relations between Croat and Muslims in Bosnia that led to a federation agreement, negotiations with separatist Croatian Serbs and a split in the ruling Croatian Democratic Union (HSZ).

From the twelfth century until after World War I, most of what is Croatia was ruled by Hungary. In 1918, it became part of the Kingdom of Serbs, Croats and Slovenes, renamed Yugoslavia in 1929. Following the Nazi invasion in 1941, a short-lived independent state was proclaimed by the pro-fascist *Ustasa* movement that oversaw the massacre of thousands of Serbs. In 1945, Croatia became one of the republics of the federal People's Republic of Yugoslav under former Communist partisan leader Josip Broz (Tito).

On 25 June 1991 Croatia and Slovenia declared independence from an unraveling Yugoslav federation. Within a month, forces of the Serb-dominated Yugoslav People's Army (YPA) backed by armed Serb militias seized large parts of Croatia. By year's end, Serbs controlled about one-third of the country and declared an autonomous region, the Krajina Serbian Republic (RSK). The fighting killed over 10,000 and left 700,000 displaced. In December, all sides agreed to the deployment of U.N. peacekeeping troops (UNPROFOR) in three regions with predominantly Serb populations. In 1992, Croatia accused the 16,000-strong U.N. forces of maintaining the status quo of Serb dominance by failing to disarm Serb paramilitary forces, confiscate heavy weapons and repatriate refugees. Meanwhile, Serb forces continued "ethnic cleansing" in areas under their control. In 2 August presidential elections, President Tudjman (HSZ) won 56.7 percent of the vote, followed by Drazen Budisa of the Croatian Social-Liberal Party (HSLS), 21.8 percent; and Slava Dabcevic-Kucar of the Croatian People's Party (HNS), 6 percent. Finishing fourth with 5.4 percent was Dobroslav Paraga of the neo-fascist Croatian Party of Rights (HSP), named for the far-right party that produced the *Ustasa*. Nikcia Valentic was named prime minister in April 1993.

Nineteen-ninety-four opened with continued fighting between Bosnian Croats and their erstwhile Muslim allies. In early January, the Croatian government, ignoring possible international sanctions, threatened to send regular army units to bolster forces of the Croatian Defense Council (HVO) battling Muslims in Bosnia. Young Croatian men were conscripted, many of then forcibly, and sent to Bosnia to support the HVO.

Later in the month, President Tudjman was strongly criticized by the opposition for discussions with Serbian President Slobodan Milosevic on normalizing relations. The opposition charged that the government had no business talking with Belgrade unless the latter recognized Croatia within Tito-era frontiers. Tudjman's opponents also stressed the importance of rebuilding the alliance with Bosnian Muslims to fight a common enemy, Serbia. On 31 January, after a long and stormy discussion, the upper house of the Croatian parliament voted to support Serb-Croatian dialogue as "a step toward peace." Meanwhile, the Bosnian government urged the U.N. Security Council to take strong action against Croatia, accusing Zagreb of open intervention in aiding the HVO.

In early February, the European Union (EU) discussed sanctions against Croatia after U.S. intelligence reports indicated that 10,000 Croatian soldiers had moved into Bosnia. The U.N. drafted an ultimatum warning that Croatian regular forces must withdraw from Bosnia by 17 February. In the face of growing international pressure, President Tudjman was instrumental in the 10 February dismissal of Mate Boban, the hard-line president of the self-styled Croatian republic in Bosnia.

In March, breaking with hard-line nationalists, President Tudjman endorsed a Washington-engineered peace accord signed by Bosnia's Muslims and Croats. He added that in supporting the pact, under which Bosnian Croats and Muslims agreed to form a federated state in a loose union with Croatia, he had been "explicitly promised" help in regaining Croatian control over Serbian-occupied regions, as well as reconstruction aid and membership in NATO's Partnership for Peace.

March also saw the first high-level meetings, held at the Russian Embassy in Zagreb, between RSK representative and Croat officials since the start of hostilities in 1991. On 28 March, the two sides signed a cease-fire agreement. By early April, the Croatian army and rebel Serb forces began pulling back heavy weapons under U.N. supervision.

In April, President Tudjman faced a long-anticipated ideological split in the ruling HDZ. Upper house speaker Josip Manolic, who had been stripped of his top HDZ posts, and his counterpart in the lower house, Stipe Mesic, announced the formation of the moderate Croatian Independent Democrats (HND). They accused the president of increased authoritarian style and kowtowing to hard-line nationalists in spurring the war against Muslims in Bosnia. Eighteen HDZ legislators joined the HND, making it the largest opposition party. The HDZ continued to hold an overwhelming edge in public opinion polls. On 25 May, Mesic was stripped of his parliamentary speaker post and replaced by Nedjeljko Mihanovic. The same day, Croatian opposition parties launched a boycott of Parliament. Though the HDZ retained a seventy-six-seat majority in the 140-seat lower house, it had serious problems gathering the seventy-member quorum for sessions.

On 14 June President Tudjman visited the Bosnian capital of Sarajevo for the first time in the twenty-six-month war to discuss the nascent Bosnian federation of Muslims and Croats allied to Croatia that was formalized in Geneva a month before. At the same time, sporadic Croat-Muslim fighting continued around Mostar in Bosnia, and antagonism to the pact by local Muslim and Croat leaders impeded progress in organizing the federation.

On 16 June talks between Croatian and RSK representatives broke down amid speculation that the Serbs had torpedoed talks for fear that they would amount to a forum in which Krajina would be pressured into abandoning its ultimate objective of union with Serbia. To break the gridlock in Croatia, the so-called "Contact Group" of U.S., Russian, French, German and British mediators unveiled a plan in July to partition the country between the warring factions. Mediators hoped to reach agreement on local autonomy for the two Krajina municipalities that had pre-war Serbian majorities, something Croatia said it would accept.

In mid-August, hoping to get international sanctions lifted, Serbia's President Milosevic closed his country's western border, isolating rebel Serbs in Croatia with the aim of coercing RSK leaders back to the negotiating table.

On 19 September opposition parties announced they were returning to Parliament, as opinion polls released earlier in the month showed growing support for President Tudjman. A week later, Parliament voted against renewing the mandate of the U.N. peacekeepers in Croatia for more than 100 days unless the U.N. was given some muscle to return Serb-held lands to government control. Nevertheless, U.N. Resolution 947 extended the UNPROFOR mandate for another six months.

In October Croat and Serb officials held secret meetings in Graz and Knin, the RSK capital, concerning Serb-Croatian rapprochement. In early November, in the midst of a renewed Muslim offensive in Bosnia, Yugoslav Foreign Minister Vladislav Javonic and his Croatian counterpart, Mate Granic, held talks on finding a formula for the reintegration of Krajina. Meanwhile, the so-called "Z-4 group"—U.S., Russian, EU and UN representatives—continued work on an initiative granting Serbs a high degree of autonomy in two Krajina municipalities in exchange for returning most of the land under their control. Croatian Serbs, however, continued to resist surrendering territory, and Serb President Milosevic said he would not recognize Croatia until Krajina Serbs were offered a deal that "would safeguard their legitimate interests."

The situation was complicated by the Bosnian Muslim offensive, as RSK leader Milan Martic, elected earlier in the year, said Croatian Serbs would send forces to support their Bosnian brethren. Bosnian Croats joined the Muslim side. A Bosnian Serb counteroffensive in midmonth included the bombing of the Muslim-held "safe haven," Bihac, by aircraft launched from Krajina. On 21-22 November, about thirty NATO aircraft bombed Serb positions in Croatia, threatening an escalation in the conflict. U.N. officials said that Croatian Serb bombings may have been "staged" to draw Croatia and Serbia into the conflict.

In economic issues a year-old comprehensive, three-phase macro-economic stabilization program had driven down inflation. In February, as part of the second phase, the government began selling some forty of its leading companies in a debt-for-equity swap scheme enabling citizens to draw on foreign currency savings blocked since the breakup of former Yugoslavia. However, privatization efforts remained modest. On 30 May, Croatia adopted a new currency, the kuna, while doing away with the dinar. In July, U.S. advocacy won Croatia a $128 million World Bank loan and $400 million more was expected before year's end.

Political Rights and Civil Liberties: Citizens have the means to change their government democratically, but a constitutionally strong presidency has led to repressive measures by the Tudjman government. Critical decisions are made in the name of the National Security Council, a sixteen-member body packed with the president's supporters.

The fact that one-third of the country remains in control of rebel Serbs has also placed limits on free political expression, the right to vote and freedom of movement.

Opposition parties are allowed to organize; many have charged HDZ meddling in fomenting internal disputes. In 1994, three new parties were formed: the Croatian Independent Democrats (HND), which split from the HDZ; the pro-market Croatian Democratic-Peasant's Party (HDSS); and the far-right New Croatian Right (NHD), which splintered from the Croatian Party of Rights (HSP).

The judiciary is not wholly free from government interference. The power of judicial appointments and dismissals is firmly in the hands of an influential parliamentary committee dominated by the right-wing faction of the HDZ.

The government remains in strict control of radio and television, effectively denying equal access to the opposition. It continues to use its ownership interest in print media and its near monopoly of the distribution system to limit media independence. Private publications such as the daily *Novi List* and the weekly *Globus* continue to maintain an independent editorial line.

In December President Tudjman struck against *Vjesnik*, a leading Zagreb newspaper, by arranging for a friendly bank to buy it and dismiss its independent-minded editor and publisher.

The record of guaranteeing minority and civil rights has been spotty. There were several well-publicized cases of evictions from their homes of Serbs and Croats opposed to President Tudjman. In 1993, the government took over some 2,000 apartments. Some Serbs continue to be denied citizenship. Laws from Zagreb also threatened Italian schools and cultural institutions in Istria, home to 30,000 ethnic Italians. Treatment of refugees remained a troublesome issue. Early in the year, Croat-Muslim hostilities in Bosnia led to actions against the 350,000 Muslim refugees and other Muslims in Croatia. The U.N. High Commissioner on Refugees reported expulsions, forcible conscription and harassment. By May, 2,400 Muslim and Croat refugees fled Serb atrocities and "ethnic cleansing" in and around the Bosnian city of Banja Luka. There were persistent reports of Croat officials barring or expelling refugees, or demanding bribes for allowing them into Croatia. In August, Croatian authorities, already burdened with hundreds of thousands of refugees, refused to accept 14,000 Muslims fleeing fighting in northwestern Bosnia.

The realities of conflict have limited freedom of movement for Croats and Serbs within the RSK. Freedom of religion is nominally assured, but Roman Catholic Croats were persecuted or expelled from Serb-controlled areas, their churches destroyed, and Orthodox Serbs face a shortage of clergy, many of whom fled when war began in 1991. There is an active Jewish community in Croatia; in February, President Tudjman publicly apologized for earlier writings widely regarded as anti-Semitic.

There are several independent union federations, among them the Croatian Unified Trade Union (HUS), the Coordinating Committee of Croatian White-Collar Trade Unions and a coalition patched together from the Federation of the Independent Trade Unions of Croatia, the Confederation of the Independent Trade Unions of Croatia and the Union of Trade Unions of Public Employees. In September, primary- and second-grade teachers went on a strike organized by three teachers' unions demanding wage hikes.

Cuba

Polity: Communist
one-party
Economy: Statist
Population: 11,064,000
PPP: $2,000
Life Expectancy: 75.6

Political Rights: 7
Civil Liberties: 7
Status: Not Free

Ethnic Groups: Caucasian (estimated 40-45 percent), and
black and mulatto (estimated 55-60 percent)

Overview:

In August Fidel Castro unleashed a wave of raft-born
migrants, bargaining chips in a futile effort to get the U.S.
to lift its economic embargo of Cuba. The mass exodus
underscored the desperation of vast numbers of Cubans whipsawed between
deprivation and repression.

Following the Spanish-American War, the Republic of Cuba was established in
1902, but remained subject to U.S. tutelage under the Platt Amendment until 1934. In
1959 Castro's guerrillas overthrew the long-running dictatorship of Fulgencio Batista.

Since 1959 Castro has dominated the Cuban political system, transforming it
into a one-party Communist state. Communist structures were institutionalized by
the 1975 constitution installed at the first congress of the Cuban Communist Party
(PCC). The constitution provides for a National Assembly which, in theory,
designates a Council of State which, in turn, appoints a Council of Ministers in
consultation with its president, who serves as head of state and chief of government. In reality, Castro is responsible for every appointment. As president of the
Council of Ministers, chairman of the Council of State, commander-in-chief of the
Revolutionary Armed Forces (FAR) and the first secretary of the PCC, Castro controls
every lever of power in Cuba. The PCC is the only authorized political party and it
controls all governmental entities from the national to the municipal level.

Since the collapse of the Eastern bloc, Castro has consistently reaffirmed
Cuba's adherence to Marxism-Leninism. At a Latin American summit in Colombia
in July 1994 Castro seemed to endorse the Chinese model, which he interpreted as
economic reform, but not "capitalism," and the maintenance of a one-party
Communist state.

The end of the Soviet Union, and its estimated $6 billion annual subsidy, left
Cuba adrift. In deals with former Soviet republics Cuba has been able to reconsti-
tute only about one quarter of its lost trade. International credits have dried up
because Cuba cannot service its $6 billion-plus debt with Western lenders. Since
1990 Cuba has been in a "special period in peacetime," meaning a drastic austerity
program involving severe cutbacks in energy consumption and tighter rationing of
food and consumer items. At the fourth PPC congress in 1991 priority was given to
wooing foreign investment and developing tourism.

The establishment, in principle, of direct elections to the National Assembly in 1993
was designed to convince Spain and Latin America that Cuba was open to political

reform and therefore deserving of greater economic cooperation. But little aid was forthcoming. Rather, some European and Latin governments continued to press Castro to open the political system to avoid a violent breakdown of his regime, but to no avail.

Since mid-1993, with Cuba on the verge of devolving into a pre-industrial society, Castro has made a series of economic reforms—legalization of the U.S. dollar, the opening of farm and industrial and consumer goods markets, and the opening of more state-run industries to foreign investment. However, dollarization heightened social tensions as the minority with access to dollars from abroad began emerging as a new monied class, and the majority without became increasingly desperate as state-paid salaries dwindled to three dollars or less per month.

Desperation boiled over in August 1994, when thousands rioted in Havana as police tried to stop a group of Cubans from launching a raft. The following day Castro said the government would no longer stop people from leaving the island. Thus began an exodus of over 35,000 people, most of whom were picked up by the U.S. Coast Guard and sent to camps at U.S. military bases in Panama and Guantanamo. The U.S., trying to force Castro to stop the flow, banned Cuban exile remittances, which amount to an estimated $400 million annually, and cut charter flights between Miami and Cuba.

In September Washington and Havana reached an agreement: Cuba would stop the flow of rafters, and the U.S. would allow entry to at least 20,000 Cubans each year in a variety of immigration categories. The U.S. also agreed to continue talks on immigration, with Havana hoping to expand talks to include the embargo. But, in discussions in October the U.S. refused even to discuss lifting the sanctions imposed in August.

Meanwhile, the Cuban government imposed yet another crackdown by police and security forces against the August rioters and against Cuba's diverse and battered dissident movement. Since Castro began making economic reforms that threaten to unleash social forces he might not be able to control, cycles of repression have become more frequent and severe. Other measures in 1994 included the removal of all Havana high school students to rural boarding schools, an effort to control increasingly disaffected youth. Castro's greatest fear seemed to be an outbreak of disturbances so severe that the Cuban military, under his brother Raul, would be needed to quell it. There were indications that not all soldiers would follow orders to fire on fellow Cubans, raising the specter of the armed forces splintering and civil war.

Political Rights and Civil Liberties:

Cubans are unable to change their government through democratic means. All political and civic organization outside the PCC is illegal. Political dissent, spoken or written, is a punishable offense. The elections for the National Assembly held in 1993 were totally controlled by the state, with only candidates that supported the regime allowed to participate.

With the possible exception of South Africa, Indonesia and China, Cuba under Castro has had more political prisoners per capita for longer periods than any other country. In 1994 there were at least 600 political prisoners, most of them locked in with common criminals, about half convicted on vague charges of "disseminating enemy propaganda" or "dangerousness." Numbers could not be confirmed because access to Cuba by international human rights monitors remains restricted. Since 1991 the U.N. has voted annually to assign a special investigator on human rights in Cuba, but the Cuban government has refused to cooperate.

Although there has been a recent, slight thaw in cultural life, the educational system, the judicial system, labor unions, professional organizations and all media are tightly controlled by the state. Outside of the Catholic church, whose scope remains limited by the government, there is no semblance of independent civil society. Members of four small labor groups that have tried to organize independently remain subject to blacklisting and arbitrary arrest.

Since 1992 Cuba's community of human rights activists and dissidents has been subject to particularly severe crackdowns. Hundreds of human rights activists and dissidents have been jailed or placed under house arrest. In the extended crackdown that began in August 1994, over thirty dissidents were detained, some beaten while in custody. Dissidents are frequently assaulted in the streets and in their homes by plainclothes police and the "rapid action brigades," mobs organized by state security, often through the Committees for the Defense of the Revolution (CDRs). Nonetheless, rights and opposition groups continue to emerge, with possibly as many as 100 existing in 1994.

There is continued evidence of torture and killings in prisons and in psychiatric institutions, where a number of the dissidents arrested in recent years have been incarcerated. Since 1990 the International Committee of the Red Cross has been denied access to prisoners. According to Cuban rights activists, more than 100 prisons and prison camps hold between 60,000 and 100,000 prisoners of all categories. In 1993 vandalism was decreed to be a form of sabotage, punishable by eight years in prison. Men and women infected with the HIV virus are subject to compulsory medical quarantine.

Freedom of movement and freedom to choose one's residence, education or job are restricted. Attempting to leave the island without permission is a punishable offense and crackdowns have been severe since 1993, except during the month-long exodus in 1994 (see "Overview"). The punishment for illegal exit is three years, with the number incarcerated for this crime estimated at 1,000 in 1994. There are frequent incidents in which Cuban marine patrols fire on people trying to flee the island by sea.

Official discrimination against religious believers was lifted by constitutional revision in 1992. The measure was welcomed by the Catholic church, which has seen an increase in membership in recent years. However, it remained unclear whether discrimination had actually ended in practice. In September 1993 the Catholic Bishops Conferences, headed by Havana Archbishop Jaime Ortega, issued its most critical pastoral in three decades. Publicly backed by Pope John Paul II, the letter called for an end to one-party rule and the state security system, and the beginning of a national dialogue. The government responded with blistering attacks in the state-controlled media. In 1994 the Pope reinforced his support by appointing Archbishop Ortega as cardinal.

As has been evident during the trials of human rights activists and other dissidents, due process is alien to the Cuban judicial system. The job of defense attorneys registered by the courts is to guide defendants in their confessions.

The government has continued restricting the ability of foreign media to operate in Cuba. Journalist visas are required and reporters whom the government considers hostile are not allowed entry. In April 1994 plainclothes police forced a crew from the U.S.-based "MacNeil-Lehrer NewsHour," on its way to interview political dissident Elizardo Sanchez, to hand over $50,000 worth of video equipment.

Cyprus (Greek)

Polity: Presidential-legislative democracy
Economy: Capitalist
Population: Entire island: 741,000, Greeks: 579,000
PPP: $9,844 (sector not specified)
Life Expectancy: 76.7 (sector not specified)
Ethnic Groups: Greek majority, Turkish minority, and small Maronite, Armenian, and Latin communities

Political Rights: 1
Civil Liberties: 1
Status: Free

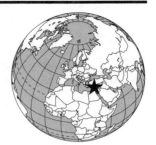

Overview:

In 1994 U.N.-sponsored talks between Greek Cypriot President Glafkos Clerides and Turkish Cypriot leader Rauf Denktash failed to break the deadlock in negotiations to reunify the two communities. The prospects for a federal solution waned after the European Union (EU) decision in June to extend membership to the Greek part of the island in the next EU enlargement.

Cyprus gained independence from British colonial rule in 1960. Since independence, the country has been plagued by tensions and sporadic violence between Greek and Turkish Cypriots. The U.N. established a 2,000-member peacekeeping force in 1964. Turkey, responding to an unsuccessful coup attempt aimed at unifying Cyprus with Greece, invaded in 1974 and occupied the northern portion of the island, installing 35,000 troops and Turkish settlers. As a consequence, approximately 200,000 Greek Cypriots were forced to flee their homes and settle in the south of the island. In 1983, the Turkish Cypriots declared independence, a move condemned by the U.N.

The Cyprus House of Representatives is a unicameral body formerly encompassing thirty-five Greek and fifteen Turkish members, although Turkish participation ceased in December 1963. In 1985 the parliament was enlarged and composed of 56 Greek members. In the last legislative elections held on 19 May 1991, the Democratic Rally garnered 20 seats; the Progressive Party of the Working People, 18; the Democratic Party 11; and the Socialist Party 7. There are also 24 seats nominally reserved for Turkish Cypriots.

On 15 February 1994, U.N. special representative Joe Clark met with both leaders to discuss confidence-building measures. The following week, Denktash met Turkish officials for discussions on breaking the deadlock in peace talks. Another round of talks on 23 March failed. Denktash refused the year-old confidence-building package which includes opening Nicosia international airport for both communities and handing over Varosha, a Greek tourist resort, to U.N. troops. Denktash said he would reject them until the Turkish Republic of Northern Cyprus (TRNC) is officially recognized. Boutros Boutros-Ghali extended a 31 March deadline for determining preliminary conditions and blamed the deadlock on both conflicting parties.

On 30 August Turkish Cypriots formally abandoned the search for a federal solution after the EU declared its readiness to embrace the Greek part of Cyprus, and the European Court of Justice banned most Turkish Cypriot goods from being sold in EU countries. In 1992 the U.N. secretary general offered a proposal to unite both communities on a federal basis, which would guarantee each of them wide-ranging autonomy in conducting their communal affairs. At the end of August 1994, the Turkish Cypriots passed a motion to coordinate foreign, defense and security police with Ankara, in effect endorsing partition and supporting formal integration with Turkey.

In 1993, Glafkos Clerides of the Democratic Rally (DISY) campaigned for peaceful reunification of the Greek and Turkish parts of the island, and defeated the incumbent George Vassiliou, an independent. The president welcomed the European invitation in 1994 and said that efforts to achieve membership would be stepped up irrespective of developments in the negotiation efforts with the Turkish Cypriots.

Political Rights and Civil Liberties: Greek Cypriots can change their government democratically. Suffrage is universal and compulsory, and elections are free and fair. The government is a multiparty political system. The president is elected for a five-year term and appoints his own cabinet.

The judiciary is independent and operates under the tradition of the British legal system, including the presumption of innocence and the right to due process. Cases are usually tried before a judge, although a request for trial by jury is usually granted. Allegations of police brutality have become more common, particularly in Limassol.

Freedom of speech and freedom of press are respected. Independent and party-affiliated newspapers and periodicals are numerous and frequently criticize authorities. Since 1990, in addition to government-owned radio stations, several independent ones have been allowed to operate. In 1992, the first independent television began to broadcast. In addition, cable services from around the world are available throughout the island.

Freedom of assembly and association is respected. Workers have the right to strike, and more than 90 percent of the labor force belongs to trade unions. Due to high economic growth rates in recent years and a labor shortage, the government relaxed the issuance of work permits to foreign workers, who often work below the level of Greek Cypriot wages.

Freedom of movement for the residents is respected, with the exception of traveling to the north, which is discouraged if it involves filling out entry cards issued with the Turkish Republic of Northern Cyprus (TRNC) inscription.

The Greek Orthodox Church has the character of a state institution; all its property and activities are exempt from taxation, and the church wields a considerable influence in the direction of public policy. However, freedom of worship is respected, and other religious groups are allowed to operate.

Women generally have the same legal status as men. Although women are legally entitled to equal pay for performing the same job as men, many women's rights advocates complain that women fill lower-paying jobs.

Czech Republic

Polity: Parliamentary
democracy
Economy: Mixed
capitalist
Population: 10,342,000
PPP: na
Life Expectancy: na
Ethnic Groups: Czechs (94 percent), Slovaks (4 percent),
Roma (2 percent)

Political Rights: 1
Civil Liberties: 2
Status: Free

Overview: The coalition government of Prime Minister Vaclav Klaus
in 1994 balanced accelerating privatization and steady
economic growth with the social needs of those not
touched by one of East-Central Europe's more prosperous and promising economies. Other issues included corruption in business and government; regional
government; and integration into European economic and military structures.

Czechoslovakia was created in 1918 with the collapse of the Austro-Hungarian
empire. Until then, Czechs and Slovaks existed separately for a millennium. The
Czechs had their own state—the Kingdom of Bohemia—which experienced
periods of independence and subjugation by Austria and Germany. The Slovaks
endured a long history of Hungarian rule. Soviet troops helped establish the
Communist People's Republic of Czechoslovakia in 1948, a one-party dictatorship
renamed the Czechoslovak Socialist Republic in 1960. In 1968, after Warsaw Pact,
Russian-led forces crushed the so-called "Prague Spring" led by Communist
reformist leader Alexander Dubcek, it became one of the East Bloc's most repressive regimes. In November 1989, however, the government was forced to negotiate
with the grass-roots oppositionist Civic Forum led by playwright and former
political prisoner Vaclav Havel. The so-called "velvet revolution" peacefully ended
forty-one years of hard-line Communist rule.

By 1992, strains between the country's two constituent republics worsened
over such issues as the pace and scope of reform, disproportionate Western
investment in the Czech Republic and increased Slovakian nationalism. On 25
November, the Federal Assembly voted to dissolve the seventy-four-year federation, and thus itself and other federal institutions, on 1 January 1993. Havel was
elected president of the new state on 26 January 1993.

Former finance minister and free-market advocate Klaus and his Civic Democratic
Party (ODS)-led, four-party coalition won the June 1992 elections in the Czech republic.
In 1993, the government moved ahead with the second phase of a privatization program
launched in 1991-92. The Klaus coalition faced little resistance in Parliament, mainly
because of a badly fragmented opposition. With 105 of 200 seats, the ruling coalition,
consisting of the ODS, the Civic Democratic Alliance, the Christian Democratic Union-
People's Party and the Christian Democratic Party, pushed through reform legislation.
Meanwhile, the Communist Party of Bohemia and Moravia, which in 1992 captured
slightly more than 14 percent of the vote and thirty-five seats, had split into rival

factions. The Social Democratic Party also fractured, while the right-wing Republican Party hovered at a popularity rate of around 6 percent.

In 1994 Prime Minister Klaus continued to campaign aggressively around the country for his economic program, spurred partly by earlier Communist electoral victories in Poland and Lithuania, and a resurgence of support for Communists in Hungary. Early in the year, unemployment stood at 3.8 percent, compared to 15 percent in Poland. Nineteen-ninety-three had ended with a budget surplus and a 16 percent growth in trade with Western Europe.

Although Czechs enjoyed one of the highest standards of living in Eastern Europe, there was social discontent spurred by corruption and the economic difficulties facing the poor. On 22 March, more than 20,000 people demonstrated in Prague against proposed changes in labor and pension laws. Protesters opposed government plans to ban trade unions in state services, allow employers to hire on short-term contracts and raise the legal retirement age. Many demonstrators feared that workers would lose their jobs when large, state-run enterprises are privatized.

In April the government was embarrassed by a scheme to raise $1.2 billion through the sale of fraudulent securities, which highlighted weak domestic controls and inexperience in the international capital markets. The U.S. Securities and Exchange Commission discovered the scheme. The fraud came on top of a series of scandals that have hit the republic since the fall of communism. Senior officials, politicians and businessmen had been linked to tax evasion, insider trading and extortion. In early November, the director of the country's coupon privatization program, Jaroslav Lizner, was arrested and charged with taking a bribe to manipulate a stock tender.

However, the government continued to enjoy the support of labor unions. Although Klaus admires former conservative British Prime Minister Margaret Thatcher, he follows a statist-corporatist approach to reform that incorporates labor unions as partners; relies heavily on social welfare measures to keep social peace; and supports an extensive social safety net to soften the effects of wrenching economic reforms. In 1994 the prime minister continued to rely on such regulations as a law barring state-owned enterprises from declaring bankruptcy while they were being privatized. Yet, 61 percent of 767 industrial enterprises were insolvent as of 31 March.

The government also had dipped heavily into the Czech National Property Fund, set up in August 1991 to handle receipts from state companies sold to foreign or local investors. By the end of 1993, it had collected $1.7 billion and used nearly half to pay off the debts of privatized state enterprises. In late May, the prime minister announced that the government would take another $230 million from the fund to cover the debts of state-owned farms.

The government also implemented make-work projects to create "publicly useful jobs" such as street sweeping to keep another 100,000 to 140,000 employed. In addition, the government paid a "living minimum" wage to 300,000 or more Czechs classified as below the poverty line.

In late June, the government began selling off big stakes in several hundred mainly commercial and industrial companies in which the National Property Fund held a majority interest. The move was seen as the last big sell-off by the government. Its voucher privatization system, in which 8 million Czechs bought vouchers enabling them to bid for shares in two tranches of companies being privatized, resulted in partial or complete privatization of nearly 2,300 Czech enterprises, representing over 80 percent of the country's economic activity. In August, the government announced it would repay its entire outstanding debt of $471 million to the International Monetary Fund (IMF).

Local government caused tensions between the ODS and its coalition partners. The key disagreement was over the size and number of administrative units. The ODS originally proposed 81; the rest of the coalition and some ODS members wanted 13 more, on the ground that larger regions would have the revenue and clout to govern effectively. Klaus denied that he favored centralization at the expense of regional democracy, stating he favored decentralization without splitting the republic "into self-governing entities" that would "cantonize the country."

Klaus favored a first-past-the-post election of senators, while the rest of the coalition supported proportional representation. Disagreement over an election law for the Senate precluded a vote for the constitutionally mandated Upper House.

In March President Havel, speaking in Strasbourg, urged the EU to welcome members from Eastern Europe or risk instability. The Czech Republic joined NATO's Partnership for Peace.

Political Rights and Civil Liberties:

Czechs can change their government democratically under a December 1992 constitution that enshrines a multiparty democratic state. Besides electing representatives, citizens are able to exercise power through referenda.

The definition of "judicial power" in the constitution corresponds to the European concept of a state based on the rule of law. The four-tiered judicial system (the Supreme Court and the chief, regional and district courts) also includes a Constitutional Court composed of fifteen members appointed by the president for terms of ten years. There is a lack of fully qualified lawyers in public administration. Prison conditions are generally poor, and there is a complete lack of post-penitentiary care. People accused of crimes sometimes have long delays before trial. So-called lustration laws, passed in 1991 to bar top-level Communists, security officials and collaborators from public life, continued to be controversial. Under the law, which is due to expire in October 1996, over 200,000 people had been vetted by the Interior Ministry; but of seventy cases appealed in 1993, the government lost sixty-five. On 9 July 1993 Parliament passed a law that lifted the statute of limitation on some crimes committed in the Communist era back to 1948.

Political parties, professional organizations, cultural groups and other nongovernmental associations can organize freely, but they must register with the government and face some limits to their activities.

Independent publications are flourishing, though they vary in quality and objectivity. In 1994 the Constitutional Court abolished a penal code provision permitting prosecutions for defaming Parliament, the government and public officials. In February, Eastern Europe's first nationwide commercial television station, NOVA TV, went on the air in Prague after a three-year struggle symbolic of broadcasting battles in former Communist states. The station, an offspring of CET 21, a private group of five owners, was the first to win the rights to a nationwide, government-held frequency. In August, Radio Free Europe/Radio Liberty got permission from the U.S. Congress to relocate from Munich to Prague.

Although ethnic and minority rights are protected under law, there have been problems, particularly for the Gypsy (Roma) population numbering anywhere from the official estimate of 150,000 to 300,000, many of them from Slovakia. Roma-nies are officially recognized as a national minority and allowed to use their language, form political parties and establish cultural organizations, but they have often been denied equal access to housing, education, employment and public services. The 1993 Czech citizenship law deprives a significant number of people, mostly those considered Slovaks under a 1969 law, of their right to citizenship in the country and town where they were legal citizens before the law was passed. They are disenfranchised and deprived of social services. In February Parliament threw out a bill that would have handed back Jewish property confiscated during the war to survivors of the Holocaust or their descendents. The government also dragged its feet over whether the small Jewish community of Bohemia and Moravia should be given back its former collective possessions, such as syna-gogues, cemeteries and community centers. Sudetan Germans, displaced from Czech lands after World War II, continued to agitate for the return of their land or compensation. The property of some 2.5 million Sudetan Germans was confiscated between 1945 and 1947, and thousands died during the forced repatriation.

Freedom of religion is guaranteed and respected, and there is no official church. Restitution of Roman Catholic Church property nationalized by the Communists in 1948 remained largely unresolved.

There are no major restrictions on domestic and foreign travel. There are several women's organizations, and there are no legal obstacles based on gender. Women have held key government and public posts.

Workers enjoy and exercise freely the right to organize and join unions, the major one being the CKOS (the Czech Confederation of Trade Unions). The government has maintained a close working relationship with unions; a Tripartite Council brings together the government, union federations and employer associations to hammer out agreements on wage, price and rent controls and other social policies. The Czech-Moravian Chamber of Trade Unions represents 3.5 million workers.

Denmark

Polity: Parliamentary democracy
Economy: Mixed capitalist
Population: 5,214,000
PPP: $17,880
Life Expectancy: 75.3
Ethnic Groups: Overwhelmingly Danish, a small German minority, various small immigrant groups

Political Rights: 1
Civil Liberties: 1
Status: Free

Overview:

On 21 September 1994 Denmark held parliamentary elections. The Liberal Party made significant gains and Prime Minister Poul Nyrup Rasmussen, head of the center-left Social Democratic Party, lost his majority coalition, winning an overall 43.8 percent of the vote. His minority coalition still gained enough support to continue heading the government.

Denmark is the oldest monarchy in Europe. Today the role of royalty in state functions is largely ceremonial. Queen Margrethe II has served as the head of state since 1972.

Real political power in Denmark rests with the parliament, the *Folketing,* a unicameral chamber consisting of 179 members, 135 of whom are elected in seventeen districts. The autonomous regions Greenland and the Faroe Islands each send two representatives to the Folketing. The remaining forty seats are allocated on a proportional basis to representatives chosen from parties that receive more than 2 percent of the popular vote. Because of the large number of parties and the low 2 percent hurdle needed to enter the Folketing, Danish parliamentary politics are marked by shifting and collapsing coalitions.

The parliamentary elections on 21 September were no different. The Social Democratic Party was forced to resign its majority coalition when it dropped from holding eighty-nine to seventy-five of the possible 179 seats. The failure of one of its four members, the Christian People's Party, to win enough votes to stay in the Parliament contributed to the drop.

The competitors of the Social Democratic Party also fared poorly. No coalition won a majority of seats. The Liberal-Conservative opposition coalition came closest, gaining ten seats to win a total of sixty-nine. Most of the gains were made by the Liberal Party, which captured forty-two of the sixty-nine seats. The Socialist People's Party, which split off from a now-defunct Communist Party, won thirteen seats. The newly formed Unity Party captured six seats.

One independent seat was won by Jacob Haugaard, a popular comedian who promised to improve the weather, put God back in the church and support the rights of impotent men.

On 27 September, in a Denmark tradition called the "Queen Rounds," Rasmussen ceremonially presented to the queen his minority government coalition, consisting of his own Social Democratic Party, the Center Democrats, and the Radical Liberals. Having shown that his coalition had the most parliamentary support, Rasmussen reestablished his position as head of government.

The welfare state, defended by Rasmussen, was a central issue in the election. The Liberal-Conservative coalition campaigned for restraints on welfare spending in an effort to lower taxes. Government spending accounts for 64 percent of the GDP, second only to Sweden among industrialized nations.

Political Rights and Civil Liberties:

Danes have the right to change their government by democratic means. There is a wide range of political parties, including various Communists, a radical right-wing party, a green party and a party advocating the philosophy of the nineteenth-century philosopher Henry George. There is freedom of assembly and association.

The Danish intelligence agency has been criticized for collecting too much information on its citizens. In April 1994 Copenhagen University investigated a twenty-year-old practice in which university directors gave the Police Intelligence Agency lists of all students containing names, the courses they were taking, social security numbers and home addresses. In their defense, the intelligence agency has argued that the files are used, like telephone directories, as means of idenfication.

Denmark has a free press. Forty-five newspapers are printed on a daily basis. The state finances radio and television broadcasting. The state-owned television companies, however, have editorial boards that operate independently of the state. The state permits independent radio stations, but regulates them tightly. The media as a whole reflect a wide variety of political opinion and are frequently critical of the government.

The Lutheran Church is the established church of Denmark, receiving its finances from the state. Over 90 percent of the Danish populace is affiliated with the state church. There is freedom of worship for all.

Discrimination against people based on race, sex, and language is illegal in Denmark, although there have been reports of attacks by civilians on recent non-Nordic immigrants and refugees, many of whom arrived from the former Yugoslavia. The state has not made any major attempts to combat the rise of racism in Denmark, but the media have made significant efforts to educate the people about the newcomers.

Denmark has pioneered equality for homosexuals. In 1989, Denmark became the first country officially to sanction marriages between people of the same gender.

Workers have the right to organize and strike. Ninety percent of the wage earners are affiliated with free trade unions. The umbrella organization in the labor movement is the Danish Federation of Trade Unions, which is linked with the Social Democratic Party. Labor organizations not affiliated with the Danish Federation of Trade Unions have organized, but not without meeting fierce resistance from the more established unions and their federation.

Djibouti

Polity: Dominant party
Economy: Capitalist
Population: 569,000
PPP: $1,000
Life Expectancy: 48.3
Ethnic Groups: Issas, Afars, Arabs

Political Rights: 6
Civil Liberties: 6
Status: Not Free

Overview: In June 1994 the government led by Hassan Gouled Aptidon, an Issa from the Popular Rally for Progress party (RPP), and the armed resistance movement of the Front for the Restoration of Unity and Democracy (FRUD) reportedly agreed to a cease-fire. However, the significance of the announcement is unclear. Negotiations for FRUD were conducted by Ougoureh Kifle, whose status as secretary general of the movement has been called into question by Ahmed Dini, the FRUD leader. FRUD infighting between Kifle and Dini was reported in March 1994, when Kifle announced the dissolution of the political bureau led by Dini and the establishment of a thirteen-member "executive council."

Since gaining independence from France in 1977, Djibouti has been governed by Aptidon. Largely as a result of the armed insurgency, Aptidon announced a series of measures intended to institute "reasonable multipartyism" and a new democratic constitution to protect a number of political and civil rights. A national referendum in September 1992 adopted the proposed constitutional changes.

In May 1993 Djibouti held its first contested presidential election. President Hassan Gouled Aptidon defeated four other candidates and gained 60 percent of the popular vote, securing his fourth term in office. International observers to the elections and the four opposition party candidates declared that the voting was plagued with irregularities. The four opposition candidates, all from the Issa ethnic group, included the Party for Democratic Renewal (PRD), the National Democratic Party (PND), United Movement for Democracy (MUD) and one independent candidate. The election was boycotted by the Revolutionary Front for Unity and Democracy (FRUD).

Djibouti is a small country covering only 9,000 square miles. Its 500,000 inhabitants are ethnically divided between the Afar ethnic group, which comprises about 35 percent of the population and occupies the northern and western regions of Djibouti, and the southern Issa ethnic group, which comprises about 50 percent of the total population. Since 1991, armed insurgents representing the Afar people (FRUD) have been waging a violent campaign to secure greater rights for the Afars, claiming that political power is concentrated in the hands of Issa people. As a result Amnesty International indicates that Djibouti's security forces have committed "gross human rights violations including rape, torture and extrajudicial executions...in reprisal for losses inflicted" by FRUD.

Political Rights and Civil Liberties:

Djiboutians are not able to change their government democratically. During the legislative elections in December 1992 and the presidential elections in May 1993, international monitors reported widespread fraud.

As a result of the FRUD guerrilla campaign, security forces have targeted those from the Afar ethnic group for reprisals. FRUD has accused the government of gross human rights violations. In March 1994, Dini accused the government of carrying out 227 extrajudicial executions. Amnesty International confirms that the Afars have been the victims of gross human rights violations. In March 1994, Amnesty reported the rapes of a dozen girls and women in the Oueima and Mabla regions by government soldiers. Earlier, Amnesty reported extrajudicial executions by government forces of thirty-six Afar civilians in the same regions.

The new constitution protects the freedom of assembly and association; however, the government has effectively banned political protest. In June 1994 in the Afar district of Arhiba, demonstrators protested the police torching of temporary shelters used by internal refugees displaced by the war. Amnesty International reported that security forces employed tear gas and rubber bullets against demonstrators, reportedly killing two and wounding at least twenty others. Approximately 600 people were arrested but subsequently released. Police and demonstrators again clashed in the Afar Ahabia District when homes in the district were bulldozed. According to the United Opposition Front of Djibouti, four people were killed and more than thirty people, including the Front's president, Muhammad Ahmad Issa, were arrested.

While the constitution also permits opposition parties to form, the ruling party determines which opposition groups can be legalized. In January 1994, four leaders of the United Front were arrested and accused of providing public support for FRUD. They were held until May 1994 and eventually sentenced to three months in jail. They were subsequently released.

Djiboutians do not have access to an independent judicial system. It is common for the government to interfere with the judicial process. The constitution states that imprisonment cannot occur unless an arrest decree is presented by a judicial magistrate. In practice, however, security forces frequently arrest demonstrators and others involved in political activity without proper authorization.

Article 15 of the new constitution does protect freedom of speech. Despite this provision, freedom of speech continues to be severely curtailed. While workers have the right to join unions and strike, the government does not allow the unions to operate freely. As a result of the civil war, internal travel between north and south is not possible. International travel is generally not restricted. Although Djibouti is predominately Sunni Muslim, there is no state religion and freedom to worship is respected.

Dominica

Polity: Parliamentary democracy
Economy: Capitalist
Population: 75,000
PPP: $3,900
Life Expectancy: 72.0
Ethnic Groups: Black and mulatto with a minority Carib enclave

Political Rights: 2
Civil Liberties: 1
Status: Free

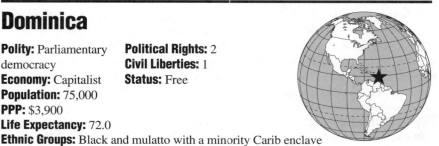

Overview: The country prepared for elections to be held before May 1995. The vote should mark the end of the Charles era, as Prime Minister Eugenia Charles, the first woman to head a government in the English-speaking Caribbean, has announced that she will retire at the end of her third term.

Dominica has been an independent republic within the British Commonwealth since 1978. Internally self-governing since 1967, Dominica is a parliamentary democracy headed by a prime minister and a House of Assembly with twenty-one members elected to five-year terms. Nine senators are appointed, five by the prime minister and four by the opposition leader. Over half the island's population depends directly or indirectly on banana production.

Charles narrowly won a third term in 1990, as the ruling Democratic Freedom Party (DFP) won only eleven of twenty-one seats. The newly formed United Workers Party (UWP) led by Eddison James, former head of the Banana Growers Association, took second with six seats and displaced the leftist Dominica Labor Party (DLP), with four seats, as the official opposition.

In August 1993, after the now-seventy-five-year-old Charles said she would relinquish the DFP leadership, External Affairs Minister Brian Alleyne defeated three other candidates in a vote of DFP delegates to become the new party leader.

In the fall of 1994 the DFP narrowly lost a by-election to the UWP, which some local observers interpreted as giving the UWP the edge in the run-up to the coming elections. In November, the campaign heated up when the UWP alleged that the DFP had plotted to spy on the opposition through a bugging operation. The DFP vehemently denied the charge.

Political Rights and Civil Liberties: Citizens have the right to change their government democratically. Mrs. Charles was criticized in some quarters for not stepping down as prime minister after relinquishing the ruling party leadership in 1993.

There are no restrictions on political or civic organizations. In 1994 a group of prominent Dominicans formed an organization for "good and accountable government" and called for the appointment of an ombudsman and an independent auditor to investigate allegations of official corruption.

Since 1990 the 3,000 indigenous Carib Indians, many of whom live on a 3,700-acre reserve on the northeast coast, have been represented in the House of Assembly by an elected Carib parliamentarian. In 1994 Hilary Frederick was elected chief of the Carib people for a five-year term, defeating Irvince Auguiste, the incumbent. A policeman was charged with the murder of a young man during the ensuing celebration.

Freedom of religion is generally recognized. However, the small Rastafarian community has charged that their religious rights are violated by a policy of cutting off the "dreadlocks" of those who are imprisoned, and that Rastafarian women are harassed by immigration officials who single them out for drug searches.

Government welfare officials have expressed concern over the growing number of cases of child abuse.

The press is generally free, varied and critical. Television and radio, both public and private, are open to pluralistic views. Opposition parties have charged that the board appointed to oversee state-run media is manipulated by the government. Nonetheless, since 1990 television has been used as an effective campaign tool by all parties.

There is an independent judiciary and the rule of law is enhanced by the court system's embrace of the inter-island Eastern Caribbean Supreme Court. A state of emergency was imposed, in accordance with the constitution, in response to clashes during a week-long bus strike in April 1994. Calm was restored after the government scaled back an increase in license fees.

The Dominica Defense Force (DDF) was disbanded in 1981 after it was implicated in attempts by supporters of former Prime Minister Patrick John to overthrow the government. John was convicted in 1986 for his involvement and given a twelve-year prison sentence. He was released by executive order in 1990 and now heads the National Workers Union.

Dominican Republic

Polity: Presidential-legislative democracy
Political Rights: 4*
Civil Liberties: 3
Economy: Capitalist-statist
Status: Partly Free
Population: 7,769,000
PPP: $3,080
Life Expectancy: 67.0
Ethnic Groups: Mestizo and mulatto (70 percent), Caucasian (15 percent), and black (15 percent)
Ratings Change: *The Dominican Republic's political rights rating changed from 3 to 4 because of substantial fraud in the 1994 election.

Overview:

Following an election steeped in fraud, eighty-eight-year-old President Joaquin Balaguer was sworn in for a seventh term in August. Under international pressure he agreed to a shortened term, with new elections expected in 1996.

Since achieving independence from Spain in 1821 and Haiti in 1844, the Dominican Republic has endured recurrent domestic conflict. The assassination of Gen. Rafael Trujillo in 1961 ended thirty years of dictatorial rule but led to renewed turmoil. The military overthrow of the elected government of leftist Juan Bosch in 1963 led to civil war and U.S. military intervention in 1965. In 1966, under a new constitution, civilian rule was restored with the election of the conservative Balaguer.

The constitution provides for a president directly elected for four years, a Congress consisting of a 120-member Chamber of Deputies and a thirty-member Senate, also elected for four years. The governors of the twenty-six provinces are appointed by the president. Municipalities are governed by elected mayors and municipal councils.

Balaguer was reelected in 1970 and 1974 but defeated in 1978 by Silvestre Antonio Guzman of the social democratic Dominican Revolutionary Party (PRD). The PRD repeated in 1982 with the election of President Salvador Jorge Blanco, but Balaguer, heading the right-wing Social Christian Reformist Party (PRSC), was elected again in 1986 and 1990 in elections marred by serious irregularities.

As in 1990, the main contenders against Balaguer in 1994 were fellow octogenarians Bosch of the leftist Dominican Liberation Party (PLD) and the PRD's Jose Francisco Pena Gomez. During most of the campaign, polls showed Pena Gomez, a fifty-eight-year-old charismatic black, with a significant lead over Balaguer. Voters seemed motivated by resentment over poverty and 25 percent unemployment in the fourth poorest country in the hemisphere. The Balaguer machine then unleashed a campaign of race-based attacks that falsely branded Pena Gomez as a Haitian who secretly planned to unite the neighboring countries. The attacks, ugly even by Dominican standards, were effective and narrowed the gap in the polls.

On election day, 16 May, substantial numbers of registered voters, principally Pena Gomez supporters, were excised from the official voter list. International observers, including the Organization of American States, concluded that between

50,000 and 100,000 voters were disenfranchised, significant numbers given that on 2 August the Balaguer-controlled electoral board declared him the winner over Pena Gomez by 22,281 votes.

Pena Gomez cried foul and threatened to call a general strike. Amid street protests and mounting international pressure, especially from the U.S., Balaguer blinked. On 10 August Balaguer and Pena Gomez reached an OAS-mediated accord: New presidential elections to be held in November 1995, a ban on presidential re-election, a new electoral board and the legislators elected on 16 May to complete their four-year terms. The PRD and its allies took 57 seats in the Chamber and 15 in the Senate. The PRSC took 50 in the Chamber and 14 in the Senate. The PLD took 13 in the Chamber and one in the Senate.

However, when the Congress convened, the PLD backed a PRSC subterfuge to lengthen Balaguer's shortened term from eighteen months to two years, with elections to be held in May 1996. The PLD was evidently exacting revenge for 1990, when Balaguer narrowly beat Bosch in a disputed vote that the PRD sanctioned. Balaguer added a sweetener by having the PRSC make a PLD legislator president of the Chamber. The PRD walked out of the congressional session and boycotted Balaguer's inauguration on 16 August.

In the fall Pena Gomez became ill and spent months abroad receiving medical attention. The PRD eventually took its seats in the Congress to press for passage of the electoral reforms agreed on in the August accord. It tacitly conceded a two-year term for Balaguer by announcing Pena Gomez would be the PRD candidate in 1996. Meanwhile, Jacinto Peynado, Balaguer's running mate, began campaigning to succeed Balaguer the moment he took office as vice president. Peynado is the head of a wealthy business family. His grandfather was, like Balaguer, one of dictator Trujillo's puppet presidents.

Political Rights and Civil Liberties:

Citizens are unable to change their government through free and fair elections. The 16 May national elections were steeped in fraud as tens, possibly hundreds, of thousands of principally opposition voters were systematically disenfranchised by manipulation of the electoral rolls. President Balaguer controls the police, the armed forces, the bureaucracy and the national electoral board, and it was clear that he used all these instruments in 1994 to keep himself in power. It remains to be seen whether he will comply with the August 1994 accord that calls for the establishment of an independent electoral board and a complete revision of the electoral rolls in time for new elections in May 1996.

Constitutional guarantees regarding free expression, freedom of religion and the right to organize political parties and civic groups are generally respected. There are over a dozen political parties from left to right that run candidates in elections. But political expression is often restricted by the climate of violence associated with political campaigns and government-labor clashes and by the repressive measures taken by police and the military. In the 1994 campaign there were reports of up to thirty deaths and hundreds of injuries during interparty clashes.

Human rights groups are independent and active. In 1994 they reported that prison conditions remained abysmal, and that nearly nine out of ten prisoners had yet to be tried. There also were continuing allegations of police brutality, including torture, and arbitrary arrests by the security forces. Criminal violence, much of it drug-related, and police corruption threaten the security of citizens. Poor women are vulnerable to criminal rings that promise jobs in Europe for a fee, then press the indebted women into prostitution in Spain and Germany.

Labor unions are well organized. Although legally permitted to strike, they are often subject to government crackdowns. Peasant unions are occasionally targeted by armed groups in the hire of large landowners. A new labor code in 1992 established standards for workplace conditions and strengthened the right to bargain collectively. But companies in the twenty-seven industrial free zones, employing almost ten percent of the nations's workforce, remain reluctant to comply. Worker conditions in the zones remain below international standards and discriminatory practices against women workers are prevalent. In July 1994 workers at one free-zone company were able to secure an unprecedented collective bargaining contract. That resulted in the U.S. lifting its threat to revoke the country's trade privileges. Soon after, however, there were renewed reports of workers at other free-zone companies being fired for union organizing.

The government continues to receive criticism for the slavelike conditions of Haitians, including children, working on state-run sugar plantations. The new labor code recognizes the right of sugar workers to organize, but reports of abuses continued in 1994 as the influx of refugees fleeing repression in Haiti heightened anti-Haitian sentiment.

The media are mostly private. Newspapers are independent and diverse but subject to government pressure through denial of advertising revenues and taxes on imported newsprint. There are dozens of radio stations and at least six commercial television stations. Journalists critical of the government are occasionally threatened. Narciso Gonzalez, a journalist and government critic, disappeared on 27 May 1994, apparently after being arrested by state security forces. The government denied knowledge of the arrest or his whereabouts.

Supreme Court judges are elected by the Senate. The Court appoints lower court judges and is also empowered to participate in the legislative process by introducing bills in the congress. But the judicial system is over-politicized and, like most other government institutions, riddled with corruption. The courts offer little recourse to those without money or influence. Again, it remained to be seen whether the government would comply with the last point of the August 1994 accord that called for the formation of a national judicial council that in theory was to make the judiciary more independent.

⬇ Ecuador

Polity: Presidential-
legislative democracy
Economy: Capitalist-
statist
Population: 10,566,000
PPP: $4,140
Life Expectancy: 66.2

Political Rights: 2
Civil Liberties: 3
Status: Free

Ethnic Groups: Complex, Indian (approximately 40 percent),
mestizo (40 percent), Caucasian (10 percent), black (10 percent)
Trend Arrow: The down trend arrow is due to increasing deterioration of
democratic institutions and corruption.

Overview:
President Sixto Duran Ballen's economic modernization plan encountered fierce resistance in a year marked by mass Indian demonstrations, labor strikes and political war between the executive and the opposition-dominated legislature.

The Republic of Ecuador was established in 1830 after achieving independence from Spain in 1822. Its history has been marked by interrupted presidencies and periods of military rule. The last military government paved the way for a return to civilian rule with a new constitution approved by referendum in 1978.

The 1978 constitution provides for a president directly elected for four years, with a second round of voting between the two front-runners if no candidate wins a majority in the first round. There is a 77-member unicameral National Chamber of Deputies with 65 members elected on a provincial basis every two years and 12 elected on a national basis every four years. Municipal governments are elected.

The presidency of Rodrigo Borja (1988-92) of the social democratic Democratic Left (ID) saw extended executive-legislature conflict as opposition parties ganged up on the government, using a legislative majority to impeach six cabinet ministers. Impeaching government officials, allowed by the constitution, has been a staple of the country's fragmented, gridlocked politics since the return to civilian rule.

The leader in the 1992 election campaign was Duran, who had split from the right-wing Social Christian Party (PSC) to form the Republican Union party (PUR). He was followed by the PSC's Jaime Nebot, Abdala Bucaram of the populist Ecuadoran Roldosist Party (PRE), and Raul Baca of the incumbent ID. On 17 May 1992 Duran took 31.9 percent of the vote. Nebot, with 25 percent, edged out Bucaram for second.

With both Duran and Nebot espousing market economics, the runoff was a clash of personalities. Duran, a seventy-two-year-old architect, offered the patrician style associated with the elite of Quito, the nation's highland capital where he was once mayor. The forty-five-year-old Nebot, a lawyer and businessman, displayed the fiery demeanor characteristic of coastal Guayaquil, the nation's largest city and business hub.

Duran won the runoff with 57 percent of the vote, but took office with a weak hand. His PUR had won only 13 of 77 legislative seats. The PSC had won 21, Bucaram's PRE 13, the remaining 26 being divided among ten other parties. Nebot opted to stake out opposition turf, underscoring the fact that personal rivalries count more than ideology in Ecuadoran politics.

After taking office Duran imposed unpopular austerity measures that led to two partially successful general strikes led by the 400,000-strong United Workers Front (FUT). A third strike, against the government's privatization scheme, was held in February 1994. Duran denied widespread rumors he was thinking of resigning or seeking military support to shut down the legislature.

In midterm legislative elections on 1 May 1994, Duran's PUR dropped to ten seats and the PSC rose to twenty-five. Notably, the radical left Popular Democratic Movement (MPD) jumped to seven seats and an independent nationalist, Frank Vargas, a former general who led a failed coup attempt in 1986, won a seat.

In June Duran resorted to emergency procedures to implement an agrarian law that threatened to end a land distribution program begun in 1964. In protest, CONAIE, one of the hemisphere's few Indian organizations with a national base, called a national strike, which was backed by the FUT. As protesters paralyzed highways and clashed with security forces, Duran imposed a state of emergency. The government blinked in July, agreeing to modifications of the land law, and the protests tailed off.

In an August referendum voters approved a proposal to begin reforming the constitution. In the fall the government offered a reform package that it said would make government more efficient by giving greater power to the executive. It was broadly opposed by left and right, all claming it was a ruse to impose market reforms. The legislature had until January 1995 to pass or reject Duran's reforms.

The legislature continued its assault on Duran's cabinet. By October, three ministers had been impeached in as many months, and others who had been targeted had resigned. The principal attackers were the PSC and the PRE, that had been bitter enemies until August. Opinion polls showed that most Ecuadorans frowned on such political fisticuffs, and that the legislature remained the least respected institution in the country.

Political Rights and Civil Liberties: Citizens are able to change their government democratically. Constitutional guarantees regarding freedom of expression, religion and the right to organize political parties, labor unions and civic organizations are generally respected. There are more than a dozen political parties ranging from right to left. Competition is fierce and election campaigns are marked by sporadic violence.

Opinion polls and rising voter abstention indicate that the credibility of political institutions is in deep decline. Local analysts note the repeated gridlock between the executive and the legislature and warn of a "crisis of governability." There is evidence that drug traffickers have penetrated the political system through campaign funding and sectors of the police and military through bribery. Ecuador is a transshipment point for cocaine passing from neighboring Colombia to the U.S. and a growing money-laundering haven.

The judiciary is headed by a Supreme Court appointed by the legislature. Reforms passed in 1992 were designed to decentralize the system and make it more efficient. The Supreme Court was also given authority to act as a court of appeals. The Court, however, is frequently caught in political tugs-of-war between the executive and the legislature and its impartiality is often in doubt. The judiciary, in general, is undermined by the corruption that afflicts the entire political system. Prisons are overcrowded and conditions poor.

There are numerous independent rights organizations, and activists are occasionally targets of intimidation. Overall, there are frequent allegations of arbitrary arrest and police brutality, including torture and rape of female detainees. The armed forces are responsible for a significant percentage of abuses, particularly when they are deployed under states of emergency during labor strikes, demonstrations and land disputes. The government has instituted a human-rights training program for police and the military. But rights groups charge that abuses are still committed with impunity because police and military personnel are tried in military rather than civil courts.

The government and the military have generally sided with landowners and multinational oil companies as they continue to infringe upon land rights granted to Indians in the eastern Amazon region by the former Borja government. Paramilitary units employed by landowners against indigenous organizations operate with a high level of impunity. Under the state of emergency imposed during the June national strike led by the CONAIE Indian confederation, at least seven Indian activists were killed and dozens of others injured.

Labor unions are well organized and permitted to strike. Hundreds of national and local work stoppages have taken place in recent years in response to government efforts to restructure the statist economy. Strikes are often marked by violent clashes with police and a number of labor activists have been killed. Unions have protested amendments to the labor code that limit public-sector strikes.

Newspapers, including at least six dailies, are privately owned or sponsored by political parties. They are free of censorship and outspoken. Radio and television stations are privately owned, although the government controls radio frequencies. Broadcast media are supervised by two independent associations. There are nearly a dozen television stations, mostly commercial, that play a major role during political campaigns.

⬇ Egypt

Polity: Dominant party (military-dominated)
Political Rights: 6
Civil Liberties: 6
Economy: Mixed statist
Status: Not Free
Population: 58,873,000
PPP: $3,600
Life Expectancy: 60.9
Ethnic Groups: Eastern Hamitic (90 percent), Greek, Syro-Lebanese
Trend Arrow: Increased Islamist violence was a negative trend in 1994.

Overview:
Pitched battles between security forces and militants trying to turn Egypt into an Islamic state continued in 1994. The consequent loss in tourism revenues continued to put more pressure on an already stagnant economy.

The British granted Egypt independence in 1922. In July 1952 military leaders overthrew the monarchy, establishing a republic one year later. Coup leader Col. Gamel Abdel Nasser took formal power as prime minister in 1954 and as president in 1956, and led the country until his death in 1970.

The 1971 constitution adopted under Nasser's successor, President Anwar al-Sadat, granted full executive power to the president, who is nominated by the

People's Assembly and elected for a six-year term in a national referendum. The president names the cabinet and appoints military leaders, provincial governors and other officials. Most policies are implemented through presidential decrees, which have the power of law. The 454-member People's Assembly primarily approves rather than initiates policy. In 1978 President Sadat organized the governing National Democratic Party (NDP), and by May 1980 a series of laws, constitutional amendments and referenda cleared the way for additional parties.

In March 1979 Sadat signed an unprecedented peace treaty with Israel, securing the return of the Sinai Peninsula which Egypt had lost in the 1967 Six Day War. However, Egypt's recognition of Israel's sovereignty enraged Islamic militants, leading to Sadat's assassination in October 1981.

Under Sadat's successor, Hosni Mubarak, the military-backed NDP continues to dominate politics. At the November 1990 parliamentary elections the NDP took 383 seats; the leftist National Progressive Unionist Party, 6; independents, 55. Ten seats were set aside for presidential appointees. Seven opposition parties boycotted to protest the government's refusal to appoint an independent committee to run the elections.

On 4 October 1993 the sixty-five-year-old Mubarak won a third presidential term by winning 96.3 percent approval as the sole candidate in a national referendum. Despite this seemingly overwhelming show of support, many Egyptians are extremely disillusioned with the country's lack of democracy, endemic bureaucratic corruption and widespread poverty and unemployment. This discontent has been tapped by Muslim fundamentalist groups, including the nonviolent Muslim Brotherhood and the militant Islamic Group, itself composed of some forty-five factions.

Mubarak has tried to counter the fundamentalists' influence by promoting the government as a staunch supporter of Islam in an effort to win support from orthodox Muslims. State media frequently offer programming on religious themes, and the government bans or censors books, films and plays considered offensive to the religion.

Despite these efforts, in spring 1992 the Islamic Group sharply stepped up its drive to topple the government and set up an Islamic state. The militants targeted not only security forces but also tourists in an effort to wreck a $2.2 billion per year industry that provides the government with its largest source of revenue. In December thousands of police raided the Cairo slum of Imbaba as well as militant strongholds in Assiyut in southern Egypt, detaining some 1,700 suspected radicals. In 1993 the militants made assassination attempts on several top officials, including Prime Minister Atef Sedki.

In spring 1994 the authorities began a crackdown on the nonviolent Muslim Brotherhood, detaining and interrogating scores of the movement's leaders. The move reflected an assessment within the government that the Brotherhood's influence in local politics and the professions, and its sponsorship of health clinics and charitable institutions, had aided the Islamic Group by contributing to an overall rise in fundamentalism. Meanwhile, in the summer and fall the major flashpoint between police and the militants shifted from Assiyut to the area around the town of Mallawi, 160 miles south of Cairo.

Political Rights and Civil Liberties: Despite the trappings of a multiparty system, the ruling National Democratic Party's (NDP) control of the media, the large public sector and labor unions, as well as official restrictions on political organizing, effectively prevent Egyptians from having the democratic means to change their government. Both the government and Islamic militants are responsible for widespread human rights violations. According to a July 1994 report by the Egyptian Organization for Human Rights (EOHR), in 1993 militants killed 137 people, including forty-five civilians and two tourists, while police killed fifty-nine militants and eleven bystanders.

Since President Anwar el-Sadat's assassination in 1981 the country has been under a state of emergency, renewed periodically by Parliament. The Emergency Law grants the police broad powers against militants and other suspects. The interior minister can authorize police to detain suspects without charge for up to ninety days, and for an additional six months with a court order. Often after a court has ordered the release of a detainee the authorities prolong the detention by issuing a new order. According to a U.S. State Department estimate, at the end of 1993, 3,000 people were being detained under the Emergency Law.

The authorities have widespread powers to place suspects under surveillance and to conduct searches without warrants. These powers are frequently used not only against militants, but also against activists, journalists and writers.

The Interior Ministry's General Directorate for State Security Investigations has been accused of repeated, systemic human rights violations, including torturing suspects to extract information and coerce confessions, and detaining women and children to persuade suspects who are relatives to turn themselves in. The EOHR claims at least fourteen people died from torture in prison in 1993. In August 1993 a civilian court aquitted twenty-four fundamentalists charged with murder due to the "hideous methods used to extract confessions." In a case that attracted widepread attention, in late April 1994 prominent fundamentalist lawyer Abdel-Harith Madani died in police custody. Medical officials and employees who saw his body at a morgue said he had been badly tortured. Local police also routinely abuse detainees held for ordinary criminal offenses.

In recent years the judiciary has shown increasing independence. However, the use of civilian and military "state security courts" to try terrorism cases has severely undermined the regular judicial system. Under the Emergency Law, there is no judicial review from state security courts and only one appeal, to the President. Defense attorneys in military state security courts generally lack adequate time to prepare for trial. Since October 1992 the government has tried civilians accused of terrorist acts in military state security courts in order to expedite trials. By July 1994 thirty-seven militants had been executed since the military courts began trying terrorism cases.

In recent years militants have attacked several anti-fundamentalist intellectuals. Most notably, in June 1992 gunmen killed professor Farag Foda, and in October 1994 an unidentified assailant stabbed and seriously wounded Nobel Prize-winning author Naguib Mahfouz.

The rise in fundamentalism has also compromised academic freedom. Notably, in December 1993 the government agreed to grant conservative Muslim scholars at Cairo's Al Azhar University the right of prior approval over books scheduled for publication by the Culture Ministry.

Egyptian citizens can freely criticize the government. The government has broad control over the media and, although private publications are outspoken, there are occasional crackdowns. A press law prevents direct criticism of the president or foreign heads of state, although journalists can generally criticize the president mildly without receiving sanction. The prosecutor general can and does ban media coverage of sensitive issues. In April 1994 a military court jailed a reporter for the opposition newspaper *Al-Shaab* for writing on U.S.-Egyptian military maneuvers. In May the Information Ministry banned distribution of the weekly *Middle East Times* twice in three weeks over articles on Muslim militants, domestic violence and other topics. All newspapers must be licensed by the government, and the government-influenced Higher Press Council must approve applications for new publications.

Most major newspapers are state-owned and uncritically endorse official policies. In the run-up to Mubarak's October 1993 re-election these newspapers functioned as campaign mouthpieces. The state-owned broadcast media heavily promote government policies, and opposition candidates and issues are generally denied coverage. This is especially significant in a population that is 70 percent illiterate and relies heavily on broadcast media for its news.

The government places significant restrictions on cultural freedom as part of its effort to promote itself as a supporter of Islam. Plays and films must be approved by the Ministry of Culture, and the Ministry of Information exercises prior censorship over television productions.

Freedoms of assembly and association are restricted. Under the Emergency Law the Interior Ministry must grant approval for public meetings and demonstrations. Permits are rarely granted for outdoor events. The NDP-influenced Parties Committee must approve all new political parties. The Private Organizations Law requires the Ministry of Social Affairs to license "private organizations" and allows it to dissolve private or nongovernmental organizations (NGO) for engaging in political or religious activities. The Ministry can also merge two or more NGOs and has used this power to shut down undesireable groups. The government refuses to license the EOHR because it allegedly engages in political activities.

Women face discrimination in many areas, including inheritance rights and employment. Female genital mutilation is practiced in rural areas.

Islam is the state religion. In an effort to curb the spread of fundamentalism, in November 1992 the government placed all mosques under the control of the Ministry of Religious Affairs. The Ministry exercises influence over the content of sermons and police have closed many unlicensed mosques. In addition the Interior Ministry frequently confiscates books, pamphlets and cassettes distributed by the fundamentalists.

The conflict between the government and the fundamentalists has spilled into the country's primary and secondary schools. In 1993 Education Minister Hussein Bahaeddine prohibited girls from wearing the *niqaab* to school, a garment covering the hair, face and neck. Many girls have continued to wear the niqaab in a show of defiance. In May 1994 Bahaeddine further ordered girls to get parental permission to wear the less restrictive *hijab*, which covers only the hair and neck, later modifying this to include only primary school students. However, in response to a lawsuit by fundamentalists, in September a court ruled the order to be an infringement of civil liberties. In 1994 the government dismissed scores of teachers for allegedly promoting fundamentalism in the classroom.

The small Jewish minority is generally not bothered, but Coptic Christians, who constitute roughly 11 percent of the population, face persecution. Fundamentalist militants have murdered dozens of Copts in recent years, and Copt houses, shops and churches have been burned and vandalized. In March 1994 gunmen killed two priests and three others in an atttack on a monastery in southern town of Qussiya. This was the bloodiest single incident since militants killed thirteen Copts near the southern town of Dairut in May 1992. Copts have only token representation in top government and political positions and face widespread discrimination in employment. Public school teachers frequently emphasize Islamic precepts and often ridicule Coptic students. An archaic, 1856 Ottoman Empire-era law requires non-Muslims to obtain a presidential decree to build or repair places of worship. Coptic groups say they frequently have trouble obtaining this.

Egyptians are free to travel internally. Unmarried women under twenty-one must obtain permission from their fathers to travel abroad, and married women must get permission from their husbands.

In February 1993 Parliament passed a law designed to prevent fundamentalists from taking advantage of low turnout to win union elections. The new law makes voting in these elections compulsory and requires 33 percent participation to validate a union election. The government-influenced Egyptian Trade Union Federation is the only legal labor union federation. The 1976 law on labor unions sets numerous regulations on the establishment and operation of unions, including the conduct of elections. The government can also revoke the charter of any union. There is no explicit right to strike, but strikes do occur. Child labor remains a serious problem.

↑ El Salvador

Polity: Presidential-legislative democracy (military-influenced)
Economy: Capitalist-statist
Population: 5,237,000
PPP: $2,110
Life Expectancy: 65.2
Ethnic Groups: Mestizo (89 percent), with small Indian and Caucasian minorities
Trend Arrow: The up trend arrow is due to the inclusion of left-wing former guerrillas in the 1994 election

Political Rights: 3
Civil Liberties: 3
Status: Partly Free

Overview: Armando Calderon Sol of the incumbent, right-wing National Republican Alliance (ARENA) won the presidency in a runoff election in April. The electoral process, despite disorganization and irregularities, was an important step toward consolidating peace, as the former guerrillas of the Farabundo Marti National Liberation Front (FMLN) emerged from the vote as the country's second political force.

El Salvador declared independence from the Captaincy General of Guatemala in 1841. The Republic of El Salvador was established in 1859. More than a century of civil strife and military rule followed.

A 1979 coup by reformist officers was the first breach in the historical alliance between the military and the landed oligarchy. Reform was undercut by civil war as the Marxist FMLN squared off against the military and right-wing forces.

A constituent assembly was elected in 1982 and a new constitution drafted in 1983. It provides for a president and vice president elected for a five-year term, and an eighty-four-member unicameral National Assembly elected for a three-year term. Municipal elections are held every three years.

In 1984 Jose Napoleon Duarte of the Christian Democratic Party (PDC) was elected president, defeating Roberto d'Aubuisson, a cashiered army officer linked to right-wing death squads who founded ARENA in 1981. In 1987 exiled political allies of the FMLN returned to form the Democratic Convergence (CD). ARENA took a moderate turn as businessman Alfredo Cristiani replaced d'Aubuisson as ARENA chief. Cristiani won the 1989 presidential election, defeating the PDC's Fidel Chavez Mena and the CD's Guillermo Ungo.

In 1990 the government and the FMLN agreed to U.N.-mediated negotiations, which led to a complicated peace accord signed in January 1992. The FMLN agreed to disarm and the government agreed to cut the 60,000-member military by half and eliminate counterinsurgency units. The U.N. agreed to monitor the process and assist in the formation of a civilian-led police force that would include former guerrillas and replace the old security forces.

The accord also called for investigations and removal of military officers responsible for rights abuses, a program to transfer land to former FMLN combatants and peasant sympathizers, reorganization of the judicial and electoral systems and FMLN participation in economic reconstruction programs.

The FMLN demobilized in December 1992 after Cristiani agreed to remove over 100 officers accused of rights violations. The military balked, but after the release in 1993 of the U.N.-sponsored Truth Commission report, which found the military to be the worst rights violator during the war, the purge of officers was carried out.

The FMLN, after gaining legal recognition, opted to back Ruben Zamora, a former ally and the CD candidate, for president in the March 1994 election. The PDC nominated Chavez Mena. ARENA nominated Armando Calderon Sol, the mayor of San Salvador with roots in the conservative wing of the party.

Tensions rose in the months before the vote as two high-level FMLN leaders were assassinated amid assaults on and killings of political activists, apparently by reactivated death squads. In the campaign, ARENA, a well-oiled political machine, sounded populist themes and attacked the FMLN as Communists and terrorists. The FMLN-CD coalition, operating at a severe financial disadvantage, was less confrontational, offering a progressive but moderate platform and calling for compliance with the peace accord.

On 20 March 1994 Calderon Sol took just under 50 percent of the vote, setting up a runoff against Zamora, who came second with 25 percent. In the legislature ARENA won 39 seats, the FMLN 21, the PDC 18, the CD one, and the Unity Movement (MU), a small evangelical party, one. The right-wing National Conciliation Party (PCN) won four seats, giving ARENA an effective right-wing majority. ARENA won about 80 percent of 262 municipal elections.

In the 24 April runoff, conducted with substantially less confusion, Calderon Sol defeated Zamora by 68 percent to 32 percent. He took office on 1 June and committed his administration to full compliance with the peace accords. But as the end of the year approached, the U.N. noted a paralysis of the land transfer program, delays in the ex-combatant reintegration program, and problems in completing the deployment of the new National Civilian Police.

Meanwhile, the three main parties suffered from internal rifts. At the ARENA congress in the fall Calderon Sol had to fight off charges of government corruption by ultra-conservatives to retain control of the party. The PDC, after its electoral drubbing, went on a finger-pointing spree. And the FMLN seemed on the verge of splitting between its three militant factions and the two factions that had adopted social democracy. The moderates had incurred the wrath of the militants by helping to vote in the ARENA president of the legislature in exchange for two seats on the legislative directorate.

Political Rights and Civil Liberties: Citizens are able to change their governments through elections. The 1994 vote was the first in which all political groups from right to left were able to participate, a significant step toward consolidating the peace process following the 1992 accords that ended the civil war.

However, the electoral process was marred by right-wing violence during the campaign, the inordinate financial advantage of the incumbent ARENA party, irregularities in voter registration that disenfranchised tens of thousands of eligible voters and a high level of disorganization, at least during the first round of voting in March. Many of the problems were rooted in a politicized national electoral commission and the reluctance of ARENA to use its position as the ruling party to ensure a more independent commission and a more level playing field.

The opposition parties accepted the outcome despite the flaws in the process. Though the Left was hurt the most by the irregularities that were duly noted by thousands of international monitors, it recognized that the results nonetheless reflected the relative electoral strength of the competing parties.

The constitution guarantees free expression, freedom of religion and the right to organize political parties, civic groups and labor unions. Although the 1992 peace accords have led to a significant reduction in human rights violations, political expression and civil liberties are still restricted to an extent by sporadic political violence, still-existing right-wing death squads that operate with impunity, and a mounting crime wave.

A U.N. observer mission has issued regular human rights reports since 1991 but was expected to depart in 1995. Under the peace accord the government established a human rights ombudsman office. There are a number of independent rights groups, including the highly professional Tutela Legal.

The assassination of former guerrilla commander David Faustino in November 1994 was the first killing of an FMLN leader since 1993. It came on the heels of a report by the Joint Group, a U.N.-government panel established in early 1994, that confirmed the continued existence of death squads with direct links to the military and people in government and the judiciary. The report stated that some of the actions of these groups were politically motivated, including the goal of destabilizing the peace process, while others were purely criminal. In fact, with the sharp increase in criminal violence in recent years, it remained difficult to discern motive in many murder, robbery and kidnapping cases.

The Joint Group report concluded that while the government appeared serious about going after the death squads, the underlying problem was the justice system that "continues to give the margins of impunity that these organizations require." An important step toward judicial reform came in mid-1994 with the naming by the new legislature of a new, more politically representative fifteen-member Supreme Court, which in El Salvador controls the entire judiciary. Still, the challenge remained of overhauling a system riddled with corruption and with a tradition of functioning as an enforcement arm of the military and the ARENA party.

Two amnesty laws have added to the sense of impunity. The FMLN and the government agreed to the first in 1992, which covered most rights violations by both sides during the war. In 1993 the Cristiani government pushed a blanket amnesty through the legislature that immunized the military from charges subsequently recommended by the U.N.-sponsored Truth Commission.

The peace accord called for a new National Civilian Police (PNC) incorporating former FMLN guerrillas. But training remained slow and underfunded, and up to 500 former members of disbanded security forces were apparently integrated into the new force. In late 1994 the U.N. pressed the government to finish dismantling the old paramilitary National Police and to complete the formation and deployment of the PNC. In November 1994 the government came under fire for calling out the military to augment the PNC during a violent transport strike. At the same time, rights groups protested a government program of establishing neighborhood security committees as a crime deterrent, noting that such groups led to rights abuses in the past.

Prisons are overcrowded, conditions are wretched, and up to three-quarters of prisoners have not been sentenced. Dozens of inmates were killed during prison riots in 1994.

Most media are privately owned. Election campaigns feature televised interviews and debates between candidates from across the political spectrum. The FMLN's formerly clandestine Radio Venceremos operates from San Salvador and competes with nearly seventy other stations. Left-wing journalists and publications are occasionally targets of intimidation.

Labor, peasant and university organizations are well organized. The archaic labor code was reformed in 1994, but the new code was enacted without the approval of most unions because it significantly limits the right to organize, including in the export processing zones. Unions that strike remain subject to intimidation and police crackdowns.

Equatorial Guinea

Polity: Dominant party (military-dominated)
Economy: Capitalist-statist
Population: 389,000
PPP: $700
Life Expectancy: 47.3
Ethnic Groups: Fang (75-80 percent), Bubi (15 percent), Puku, Seke and others (5-10 percent)

Political Rights: 7
Civil Liberties: 7
Status: Not Free

Overview:

In 1994, tension mounted in Equatorial Guinea as the government arrested and tortured scores of people suspected of opposing a population census issued in September. Opposition parties objected to the census on the grounds that it violated the terms of a June agreement they had made with the government.

Since gaining independence from Spain in 1968, Equatorial Guinea has been governed ruthlessly by its two presidents, Macie Nguema and his nephew, Teodoro Obiang Nguema Mbasogo. Obiang overthrew Macie in 1979, and had him executed for his genocidal policies against the population. Soon after gaining power, however, Obiang continued the repressive policies, albeit on a smaller scale. Pressured by donor countries to institute democratic reforms, he has presented himself since 1991 as a moderate leader willing to accept political opposition.

After Obiang's announcement of an "era of pluralism" in January 1992, the political opposition and exile groups demanded the unconditional legalization of political parties in addition to Obiang's Democratic Party of Equatorial Guinea (PDGE). The opposition also called for the release of political prisoners and abolition of torture, access to the media and financial assistance to political parties, and an electoral timetable.

President Obiang agreed to the legalization of political parties, and by late January 1993 ten opposition groups were formally registered. What followed was a government crackdown on the opposition. The opposition parties chose to boycott the November 1993 election, in which the PDGE scored a lopsided victory.

In response to the opposition parties' boycott of the 1993 elections, the government arrested eight opposition leaders in February 1994 as part of a strategy to close down the offices of opposition parties.

Faced with international pressure, Obiang again tried to present himself as ruling in a multiparty society. In June, he held negotiations with leaders of the ten opposition parties. They reached an agreement that stated that the government and opposition parties would jointly compile an electoral census that would serve as a precondition for the municipal elections scheduled to take place at the end of 1994. The government instead issued a population census that excluded the participation of the opposition. The opposition parties claimed that the government would manipulate the outcome of the census by undercounting the opposition using false signatures as a basis for the elections.

Following the opposition's call to boycott the population census, the government began a crackdown in which many political activists were arrested and tortured. In October, as a sign of government protest, the speaker and deputy speaker of the National Assembly resigned their posts. "As representatives of the suffering masses," they said on *Radio Exterior de Espana,* "we could not continue to stick to our posts." The state-controlled radio offered no explanations for the resignations.

Political Rights and Civil Liberties:

Citizens of Equatorial Guinea lack the means to change their government democratically. The single-handed rule of the self-appointed President Obiang and his party prevents most citizens from influencing public policy in any meaningful way. The opposition parties, registered by a presidential decree, face harassment, intimidation, arrest and torture, especially outside of the capital.

In a 1990 report, Amnesty International reported that a "culture of terror" had developed in the Equaguinean society. This culture remained in 1994. There were reports of police torture to extract confessions from accused criminals and political opponents, often resulting in death. Commonly used torture methods included truncheon blows over the kidneys and hanging victims from poles and wall hooks.

The judiciary cannot act independently of the executive, and many detainees are reportedly tortured without trial. Freedom of association, with the partial exception of members of legalized political parties, is illegal and repressed.

Equaguineans do not have freedom of assembly. Any gathering of ten or more people for purposes the government considers political is illegal. There is only one opposition newspaper. In April *Radio Exterior de Espana* was reportedly jammed.

The Catholic Church, representing a large majority of the population, has been persecuted in a move to rid the country of "foreign influence."

No free trade unions exist. Citizens and residents of the country must obtain permission for travels within the country and abroad. Political activists are often stopped by security guards and forced to pay bribes.

Eritrea

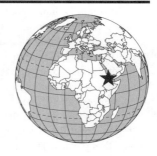

Polity: One-party
Economy: Mixed statist
Population: 3,482,000
PPP: na
Life Expectancy: na
Ethnic Groups: Afar, Arab, Beja, Bilin, Jabarti, Kunama, Saho, Tigrawi

Political Rights: 6
Civil Liberties: 5
Status: Not Free

Overview:

In 1994 the Eritrean government appointed a forty-two-member constitutional committee, responsible for producing a draft for ratification in two years. It became apparent, however, that it will be several more years before Eritrea begins to establish a multiparty system. Other main issues included Eritrea's deteriortating relations with Sudan over issues of Islamic fundamentalism and a narrowly averted famine.

After a thirty-year insurgency by the Eritrean People's Liberation Front (EPLF), Eritrea won independence from Ethiopia in 1991. The coincident overthrow of the Marxist-Leninist regime of Mengistu Haile Mariam in Ethiopia by their comrades-in-arms allowed the new Ethiopian rulers to confirm the right of Eritreans to self-determination. The EPLF leadership transformed itself into the Provisional Government of Ethiopia (PGE), headed by EPLF's secretary-general Isaias Afwerki.

In 1993 Eritrea became an internationally recognized country, following a referendum in which 99.8 percent of voters opted for independence from Ethiopia. The EPLF quickly dominated the PGE, the provincial and local councils, and the military and hence became the *de facto* new state administration.

In February 1994 the PGE held its third conference, in which the EPLF party officially changed from a military front to a national movement called the Popular Front for Peace and Justice (PFDJ). This drew a separation between the Government of Eritrea and the only political party. The following month, the fourth conference took place and a forty-two-member constitution commission was formed. The constitution is unlikely to be ratified before 1997 and elections are unlikely to take place before mid-1999. While the government promises democratic, multiparty elections, officials say that parties based on ethnicity or religion will be banned.

Relations between Eritrea and neighboring Sudan continued to deteriorate. In 1993 and 1994, the Eritrean Islamic Jihad (EIJ), the militant fundamentalist group based in Sudan, launched several guerrilla attacks into Eritrea. In April 1994 the Eritrean Government accused the Sudanese government, under the direction of the National Islamic Front (NIF), of having armed, trained and instructed the EIJ. A few days later, Eritrea signed a defense treaty with Ethiopia—a sign to Sudan and to the NIF that violence perpetrated by Sudanese-trained Islamists would not be tolerated. Despite such strong preventive action, the Eritrean Islamic fundamentalist movement seemed to grow stronger, particularly in Muslim schools. Tensions between the two countries culminated on 5 December, when Eritrea broke off all diplomatic relations with Sudan.

Due to poor rains and pestilence, Eritrea experienced a 70-80 percent crop failure in 1993. An effective early warning system, as well as prompt and efficient donor assistance managed to avert a famine. An estimated 1.5 million people, however, were still in need of food, and trade was reduced to almost nothing, as Eritrea's neighbors, Sudan and Ethiopia, also suffered greatly. In an effort to ameliorate the situation, the government introduced a campaign to promote fish-eating. Seafood, which is plentiful in the Red Sea, has traditionally been considered by Eritreans as inedible or taboo. Much of the program was aimed at introducing seafood to school children.

A new law requires all citizens over the age of eighteen to serve eighteen months of national service. The law is part of a national reconstruction plan aimed at rebuilding Eritrea's infrastructure, which was devasted in the thirty-year independence war. The national service program is also an effort to begin to wean the country away from foreign dependency and assistance.

Political Rights and Civil Liberties:

The citizens of Eritrea lack the possibility to change their government by democratic means. A constitution commission responsible for setting up a multiparty system was formed, but elections are unlikely to take place before 1999. The present government consists almost entirely of members of the PFLJ, formerly the EPLF, and came to power in May 1991 after a prolonged guerrilla war. The PFLJ, claiming to represent the interest of the entire population, has monopolized the political life of the country, from the village councils to the National Assembly, the interim legislature.

Despite Eritrea's ethnic and cultural differences, opposition to the PFLJ has been virtually nonexistent. Most of the opposition leaders remain in exile and the PFLJ refuses to allow them to take part in the government.

In 1993, the decree that established the interim government granted the judiciary formal independence from the legislature and the executive. The National Assembly has yet to adopt a new constitution and a set of civil and criminal laws.

Freedom of the press is severely limited. There is only one newspaper covering political and social issues, the government-owned *Hadas Eritra* (New Eritrea), which appears twice a week in a Tigrinya and an Arabic version. The circulation is 25,000 and 5,000 respectively. Three other newspapers are owned by the Catholic and Orthodox Churches and report mostly on church activities and religious and social issues. Most of the population relies primarily on the government-owned radio station, *Dimsti Hafash* (Voice of the Masses). The station broadcasts in the six major languages of the country. The emigre opposition groups have criticized government control over the media and have argued that as long as there is no multiparty system, there can be no independent media.

In its attempt to monopolize the political and social life of the new state, the government has discouraged the creation of independent associations. Nevertheless, nongovernmental organizations are slowly beginning to develop. In 1991 the PGE promulgated a new labor code allowing workers to form and join a trade union of their choice. The code also established the National Confederation of Eritrean Workers (NCEW), composed of five industry-based trade federations. In addition, the Labor Code legalized the right to bargain collectively and strike as a final resort. The NCEW was not officially launched until September 1994. The fledgling 20,000-member confederation began to confront the government on issues of vacation, paid maternity leave and other benefits.

Freedom of religion is generally respected and, in a society equally divided between Christians and Muslims, the government strives to maintain a balance in the appointments to public office. This effort proved particularly important in 1994, as a rise in Islamic fundamentalism had the potential to turn Muslims away from the government.

Although women comprise half of the constitution committee, they are treated as secondary citizens. During the war for independence, women fought alongside men and made up a third of the fighting force. With the end of the war, women found that they were forced back into the traditional domestic female roles. A new law, however, gives women (married or not) equal rights to use residential and agricultural land. Previously, land was held by communities and periodically rotated among male members. While the government has sought to ban child marriages, dowry payments, and female circumcision, they are still widely practiced in the region.

Estonia

Polity: Presidential-parliamentary democracy (ethnic limits)
Political Rights: 3
Civil Liberties: 2
Status: Free
Economy: Mixed Capitalist
Population: 1,542,000
PPP: $8,090
Life Expectancy: 71.2
Ethnic Groups: Estonian (61 percent), Russian, Ukrainians, Germans, others (39 percent)

Overview: In 1994 key developments in this Baltic state were the appointment of a new prime minister in October, the withdrawal of the last 2,300 Russian troops, a robust economy that was the best of all former Soviet republics and uneasy relations with Russia on border issues and the Russian minority.

Dominated by Sweden in the sixteenth and seventeenth centuries and annexed by Russia in 1704, Estonia became independent with the collapse of the Russian Empire in 1918. Two decades of independence ended when Soviet troops occupied the country during World War II as a result of the 1939 Hitler-Stalin pact, which forcibly brought Estonia, Latvia and Lithuania into the Soviet Union. Under Soviet rule, over 100,000 Estonians were deported or died in labor camps. Government-sponsored Russian immigration substantially changed the ethnic composition of Estonia's population during the Soviet occupation; ethnic Estonians constituted 88 percent of the population before Soviet rule and just over 61 percent in 1989.

Estonia took its first tentative steps toward independence in 1988-89 by declaring its laws superseded Soviet authority and making Estonian the official language. March 1990 saw the country's first free elections since 1940. A year later, voters approved a plebiscite on independence, and after the coup attempt against Soviet President Mikhail Gorbachev, the Supreme Council made it official. A new constitution was ratified in 1992. In parliamentary elections, the Pro Patria coalition of five free-market-oriented parties gained one-third of the seats. Pro Patria formed a narrow majority with the Estonian National Independence Party and the Moderates, initially a 1990 coalition of the Estonian Social Democratic Party and the Estonian Rural Center Partly. Parliament elected Lennart Meri president. Mart Laar was named prime minister. By year's end, the Supreme Council was replaced by a new 101-seat State Assembly (Riigikogu).

A controversial 1992 citizenship law was essentially a restoration of 1938 regulations, disenfranchising a large majority of the 600,000 Russians living in Estonia. Proponents of the law claimed that 50,000 were eligible for automatic citizenship but never bothered to apply for it. A 1993 Law on Aliens officially designated all noncitizens as aliens.

A key political issue in 1994 was growing dissension in the ruling Isamaa (Fatherland) coalition government. On 19 May, amid in-house bickering, mounting discontent over the government's "shock therapy" economics and rumors of corruption, two rebel ministers, Justice Minister Kaido Kama and Defense Minister Indrek Kannik, resigned. Leading members of the coalition insisted that personality clashes, not differences over policy, sparked the discord. But the government's popularity had plummeted even as it had won praise abroad for slashing virtually all state subsidies and dropping trade tariffs. Consumers, farmers and the elderly complained about world-market prices and a high monthly inflation rate of 8 percent. On 11 June Prime Minister Laar survived an attempt to oust him as leader of the Fatherland Party after he threatened to step down unless he was re-elected chairman at a special party congress. Laar received 191 votes while former justice minister Kama got 86 votes. However, against Laar's wishes, delegates also passed a resolution that the party chairmanship and premiership were not necessarily linked. Two days later, the "small coalition"—the other parties in the ruling coalition with Fatherland—announced that they would leave open the issue of whether they would propose an alternate candidate to Laar.

In September, after months of political turmoil, the government faced charges that it misappropriated $5 million when Soviet rubles were withdrawn from circulation in December 1992. Prime Minister Laar denied any wrongdoing, but said he would consider resigning after consulting with the Fatherland leadership. The opposition Coalition Party accused him of diverting state funds to private firms. Polls showed growing discontent with the government. Only 5 percent supported the Fatherland Party, the dominant party in the ruling coalition.

On 27 September deputies accused Laar of destroying public confidence by deceit, high-handedness and promoting secrecy in government, but they made clear pro-market reform polices would continue.

On 28 October Parliament backed Environment Minister Andres Tarand as prime minister, averting the prospects of early elections. Deputies voted 63 in favor, with 15 abstentions and 1 against, in support of Tarand. The new prime minister said given that elections were scheduled for March 1995, he did not intend to initiate any major changes in government policy.

A contentious and emotional issue was the withdrawal of 2,300 Russian troops, a persistent reminder of Soviet-Russian occupation. Early in the year, Russia hedged on its promise to remove the troops by 31 August, maintaining the withdrawal was conditional on Estonia's resolving the issue of citizenship for ethnic Russians and granting social guarantees to 9,000 retired Russian servicemen. On 26 July Presidents Lennart and Yeltsin, meeting in Moscow, formally agreed to the 31 August withdrawal. They compromised on the fate of the 9,000 retired Soviet officers. Russia recognized Estonia's right to establish a commission to review residency applications on a case-by-case basis, while Estonia agreed to allow all retirees to apply for residency rather than give preference according to age and date of retirement. On 31 August the last Russian troops withdrew, fifty-four years after the Soviet annexation.

The Estonian economy continued to flourish. Officially, GDP was expected to grow 6 percent, but factoring in unrecorded private activity, real growth may have exceeded 10 percent. The government's "shock therapy" included closing bankrupt industries, introducing free trade—even in farm products—liberalizing prices, abolishing nearly all subsidies, and introducing a modern tax system. In 1991 over 90 percent of the country's trade was with former Soviet republics; in 1994 over 60 percent of trade was with European Union countries. Privatization, overseen by the Privatization Agency, was 90 percent complete. In August, the government announced plans to allow individuals to purchase share vouchers in four leading companies: the Tallinn Department Store, as well as a brewery, a tobacco company and a chocolate factory. The government had budget surpluses in 1993 and 1994.

The Russian minority issue and unresolved border questions colored relations with Russia. In 1945, the Soviets incorporated the disputed territory into Russia. In 1994, Russia began marking the border with barbed wire. Estonia claimed the land under the 1920 Treaty of Tartu.

By mid-1994, only about 48,000 ethnic Russias in Estonia had opted to become Russian citizens, while some 65,000 were already entitled to Estonian citizenship even though not all had taken it. Those who are neither Russian nor Estonian were considered resident aliens under the 1993 Aliens Law.

Political Rights and Civil Liberties:

Estonians have the rights and means to change their government democratically, although restrictive citizenship and alien laws have disenfranchised some non-Estonians, particularly Russians, from the political process.

The constitution enshrines a multiparty system, and parties function freely, including several organizations representing the Russian minority.

The citizenship, alien and local election laws, even in amended form, continued to draw criticism. Under the law, an overwhelming majority of the Russian-speaking population could not participate in the constitutional referendum or parliamentary elections.

In February 1993 Parliament waived the residency and language requirements for about 40,000 persons who had registered for citizenship by 24 February, 1990, under the auspices of the Congress of Estonia. The following month, in order to bring the legislation in line with European standards, the law was amended to provide citizenship at birth through either parent who was entitled to become a citizen, a step which removed an inequity in the 1938 law.

The May 1993 Law on Local Elections widened the gap between citizens and noncitizens. It permitted noncitizens (and, with five years' residency, citizens of other countries) to vote for local office, but not to run for office. Noncitizens in heavily Russian areas charged that their local interests would not be protected.

Partly to regularize the status of noncitizens, and partly in response to international pressure to give formal status to the Russian-speaking population, Parliament on 21 June 1993 passed the Law on Aliens. It designated post-1940 arrivals and their descendants without citizenship as "aliens" and required them to apply formally for residence within one year of the law's adoption. After criticism and consultation with the CSCE and the Council of Europe, Parliament reconsidered the law on 8 July 1993. The requirement that "permanent residents" would have to repeat the registration process every five years was dropped, and conditions for denial of aliens passports were made clearer. In their defense of the Law on Aliens, many Estonian leaders referred to the law giving persons the opportunity to "choose Estonian, Russian, or other citizenship" as if the choice of permanent alien residence was not an option. According to the CSCE, limiting the pool of potential resident aliens "does not appear consistent with international law."

The judiciary is independent and free from government pressures. Estonians can freely express their views and there is a lively independent press, including English- and Russian-language publications. Estonian television and radio networks have been converted to joint-stock operations. There are commercial FM-band stations and television stations.

Freedom of religion is guaranteed by law and honored in practice. There are no significant restrictions on emigration or domestic or international travel, though Russian noncitizens must apply for a visa to re-enter and are not guaranteed that they will be able to return.

Women possess the same legal rights as men and are legally entitled to equal pay for equal work.

The Central Organization of Estonian Trade Unions (EAKL) was created in 1990 to replace the Soviet confederation. There are some thirty unions in the country and the right to strike is legal and has been used without government interference.

⬇ Ethiopia

Polity: Dominant party **Political Rights:** 6
Economy: Statist **Civil Liberties:** 5
Population: 55,228,000 **Status:** Not Free
PPP: $370
Life Expectancy: 46.4
Ethnic Groups: Afar, Amhara, Harari, Oromo, Somali, Tigrean, others
Trend Arrow: Increased ethnic tension and restrictions on expression were negative trends in 1994.

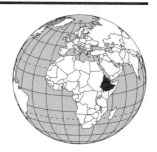

Overview:
In 1994 it became clear that the Transitional Government of Ethiopia (TGE) has little intention of giving up power. The June 1994 elections for a constitutional assembly were fraught with irregularities, including opposition boycott, which enabled the ruling party, the Ethiopian People's Revolutionary Democratic Front (EPRDF), to score a lopsided victory. Faced with increased antigovernment sentiment, the EPRDF used repressive measures throughout the year to crack down on the protesters. In December the long-awaited war trials for leaders of Col. Mengistu Haile Mariam's former regime finally began. Famine again plagued the region, although the government showed more openness in dealing with the crisis.

Colonel Mengistu was the Communist dictator of Ethiopia from 1974-1991. His regime was one of the most ruthless and deadly on the African continent. In 1975 the Tigrean People's Liberation Front (TPLF), a Marxist-Leninist student group, formed to oppose Mengistu's ruthless policies. Within the multimember EPRDF coalition, which characterized itself as "revolutionary democratic," other ethnically based movements committed to its political program were launched, including the Oromo People's Democratic Organization (OPDO) and the Amhara-based Ethiopian People's Democratic Movement (EPDM). The Tigrean ethnic minority, however, still controls most of the party.

Mengistu's regime was overthrown in 1991 and replaced by the self-proclaimed "transitional" government led by the EPRDF. Shortly thereafter, twenty-six Mengistu opposition groups assembled and agreed to set up the Transitional Government of Ethiopia (TGE), which was to serve for two years, and elected the TPLF/EPRDF leader, Meles Zenawi, as the country's interim president.

The 1992 regional elections, viewed as the "beginning of opening up the political system" by international observers, were marred by EPRDF's heavy-handedness in assuring its own and its allies' electoral victory.

In June 1994 elections were held for a national assembly responsible for drawing up the final constitution, which was begun in 1991 and is due to be completed by early 1995. Ninety percent of the 15 million registered voters turned out to elect the 502-seat constituent assembly from among 1,470 candidates. Sixty percent of the candidates were independents. The rest were affiliated with thirty-eight political parties. The EPRDF won 449 seats. Twenty-six seats went to the different political parties and twenty-eight went to independent candidates.

While no serious violence occurred, non-EPRDF candidates and voters were harassed, especially in regions dominated by the OPDO, the EPRDF-affilated group which originated from the Mengistu armed forces. In some cases, voters were "guided" by election officials to EPRDF-sponsored candidates.

The election results were distorted because the main opposition groups and their supporters boycotted the polls. Following the election, opposition parties stated their intentions to boycott the national legislative elections, which are anticipated but not officially scheduled for mid-1995. With these elections, the transitional government, including the constituent assembly, would in theory be dissolved. Some of the opposition groups apparently wished to participate in the constituent assembly elections but were unable to meet the strict registration requirements. The centrist All Amhara People's Organization (AAPO) boycotted the elections on the grounds that a clause in the draft of the constitution, which allows regional ethnic groups to secede from Ethiopia by democratic process, will lead to the fragmentation and destruction of the country. Opponents to the clause argue that by encouraging ethnic divisions, the government is essentially ensuring its own political monopoly. Indeed, small groups of enemies would be too busy fighting to form an effective, united opposition.

This fear of the AAPO that Ethiopia will become balkanized is fueled by the fact that several ethnic groups in Ethiopia have expressed discontent with the TGE and desire autonomy. While none of these groups alone holds enough military power to challenge the EPRDF, the growing number of discontented groups raises the question as to whether or not the government will be able to keep the country's forty ethnic groups together under peaceful terms. On 2 December 200,000 people demonstrated in Addis Ababa against the secession clause.

The EPRDF cracked down on antigovernment protesters throughout 1994. On 20 September the government arrested and detained hundreds of Ethiopians who were peacefully demonstrating against the arrest of Professor Asrat Woldeyes, a human rights leader charged with "inciting violence." The protesters were hurled onto trucks and taken to prisons in Sendafa. This action is representative of a general EPRDF effort to repress dissent.

After two years of relatively good weather, 1994 proved to be a year of little rain and impending famine. While the level of drought was tragically similiar to the Mengistu-era famine of 1983-84, the government's response to the crisis shows greater willingness to deal with the problem. The government welcomed foreign relief and made successful efforts to increase international awareness about the crisis. In September Ethiopia signed an $8.6 million financial and technical aid agreement with Germany. In 1994, Ethiopia was also the second largest recipient of foreign aid from the U.S. Despite this help, vast regions of the country, mainly inaccessible rural areas, still remained neglected. An estimated 60 percent of children under five-years of age living in rural areas were malnourished.

On 3 December prosecutors opened the long-awaited war crimes trials against former Mengistu officials. Forty-six of the sixty-six living defendants were brought handcuffed from prison to the courtroom, where the three-judge panel identified them and began reading 209 charges of genocide and crimes against humanity. Twenty of the defendants, including Mengistu, are in exile or hiding and are being tried in absentia. The remaining seven died in prison or elsewhere. The Mengistu regime, apparently confident that it would remain in power, carefully documented the imprisonment, torture and killing of victims. The documents remain intact and provide one of the best records of atrocities since the Nazi concentration camp reports. On 16 December, the trials were adjourned for three months to give the defense time to prepare.

Political Rights   **A**lthough the government claims to be in a transition to
and Civil Liberties: democracy, Ethiopians are not able to choose their
   government in free and fair elections. The 1994 constituent
assembly elections were marred by the boycott of the opposition, and democratic
elections in which the opposition parties are duly represented do not seem likely to
take place in the near future.

The judiciary is formally free, although most of the judicial appointees have
been EPRDF nominees. The court system is underdeveloped, poorly funded and
inefficient. Mengistu government and military officials waiting for war trials were
held in detention for over three years. Unable to meet its May 1994 deadline to
begin the trials, the trials finally began in Decmber 1994.

A 1993 press law prohibits the publication of information "leading to great
harm," such as inciting ethnic groups against each other. In 1994, the government
issued a crackdown on journalists from the independent press. Throughout the year,
at least eighteen journalists were arrested and detained. Despite the crackdown,
Ethiopia's print media remain a vibrant form of political expression. Broadcast
media are controlled by the government and devote little coverage to opposition
activists.

The stated intention of the TGE to institute a market economy has been only
partially achieved, as the question of property rights has yet to be resolved. All of
the farmland and most of the industry remain in government hands, although
farmers are free to sell their produce at market prices, and retail trading and other
services are in private hands. According to the EPRDF, the government wants to
retain the title to the farmland for the time being in order to prevent it from being
purchased by the affluent Amhara elite, from whom it had been confiscated under
the Mengistu regime. One of the tasks of the Constitution Commission is to
provide a legal solution to the question of land ownership.

Although the National Charter guarantees freedom of movement outside and
inside the country, the latter was made difficult in practice by continued armed
clashes in various parts of the country and by the policies of local and regional
governments that discouraged some people from moving out of the area of their
jurisdiction and prevented others from moving in.

The population is almost equally divided between Christians and Muslims and
freedom of religion is guaranteed. The right of workers to organize in trade unions
is guaranteed in the interim charter. Five-hundred-and-six unions, which are
grouped under nine trade federations, have so far been organized. In November
1993 the interim government established the nationwide Confederation of Ethiopian Trade Unions (CETU).

Fiji

Polity: Parliamentary democracy and native chieftains (ethnic limits)
Economy: Capitalist
Population: 764,000
PPP: $4,858
Life Expectancy: 71.1
Ethnic Groups: Indians, Fijians, other Pacific islanders, Chinese

Political Rights: 4
Civil Liberties: 3
Status: Partly Free

Overview:

Prime Minister Sitiveni Rabuka began a second term in office in February 1994 following a strong showing by his Fijian Political Party (SVT) in early elections. During the year Rabuka made little headway on his pledge to set up a commission to review the country's racially biased 1990 constitution.

Fiji's paramount chiefs ceded sovereignty over these South Pacific islands to the British in 1874 to end frequent territorial conquests among rival kingdoms. In 1879 the British began bringing Indian laborers to the islands to work on sugar cane and cotton plantations. At independence in 1970 the country's ethnic Fijian and Indian communities were roughly equal in size.

The April 1987 elections brought to power a coalition of two Indian-based parties, the National Federation Party (NFP) and the Fiji Labor Party (FLP), breaking the seventeen-year rule of the ethnic-Fijian Alliance Party. Alarmed by the emerging political influence of the Indian community, Lieutenant Colonel Sitiveni Rabuka led bloodless coups in May and September 1987 that overthrew Dr. Timoci Bavadra's government and a subsequent provisional government.

In January 1990 the country returned to full civilian rule. In July an interim government promulgated a controversial new constitution guaranteeing ethnic Fijians a perpetual majority in Parliament. The constitution reserved for ethnic Fijians thirty-seven of the seventy seats in the House of Representatives, and twenty-four of the thirty-four seats in the unelected Senate. The constitution allocated the Indian community twenty-seven of the remaining thirty-three House seats, with five reserved for "other races," mostly Chinese and Europeans, and one to the northern island dependency of Rotuma. The unelected Great Council of Chiefs, a group of traditional rulers, secured the right to select the president and appoint the ethnic Fijian Senate seats.

The May 1992 elections, though held under the racially biased constitution, restored the country to partial democracy. The SVT took thirty of the ethnic Fijian seats, while the Indian seats were split between the moderate NFP with fourteen, and the more confrontational FLP with thirteen. Rabuka formed a government with the help of the General Voters Party (GVP), which took the five seats reserved for "others," and several independents. Rabuka promised a review of the 1990 constitution and in December floated the idea of inviting the Indian parties into a national unity government.

In August 1993 the militant right-wing *Taukei* (Indigenous) Movement publicly warned of another coup if the Indian parties continued to press for changes in the constitution. On 29 November Rabuka faced a crisis after seven SVT MPs joined the opposition in rejecting the government's 1994 budget proposal. The prime minister received permission from President Ratu Sir Kamisese Mara to dissolve Parliament, and called elections for February 1994. Although the dissident SVT MPs were motivated in part by the budget's high spending plans, the move also reflected concern over official mismanagement and corruption, as well as a personal rivalry between Rabuka and former finance minister Joseveta Kamikamica.

Key issues in the campaign for the February 1994 elections were the continued controversy over the 1990 constitution and the status of the 1966 Agriculture Land and Tenant Act (ALTA). Under ALTA ethnic Fijian-owned land is leased on a long-term basis to canegrowers, who are predominantly Indian. ALTA is due to expire in 1996. While Indians favor its extension so they can maintain their businesses, many ethnic Fijians, who own 83 percent of the land, want it abolished so they can reassert control over their property. During the campaign Rabuka took a moderate line by proposing a biracial parliamentary committee to review ALTA.

In the 18-25 February vote, results of the ethnic Fijian polling gave the SVT thirty-one seats; the upstart Fijian Association Party led by Kamikamica, five; independents, one. The militant Fijian National United Front lost all five of its seats. In the Indian voting the NFP took twenty seats at the expense of the FLP, which took seven.The GVP took four of the seats reserved for other races, with the fifth going to an independent. On 28 February Rabuka began a five-year term as head of a coalition government consisting of his SVT, the GVP and the two independents.

In May the government rejected an opposition request that a foreign national head a planned eleven-member commission that will review the 1990 constitution.The commission, which is due to give a final report by the end of 1996 will, however, include representatives of all the major political parties.

Political Rights and Civil Liberties:

Fijians have voted twice under a constitution that ensures ethnic Fijians a parliamentary majority. An unelected interim government promulgated the 1990 constitution without a referendum, casting serious doubt on its legitimacy. In addition to rejecting the concept of "one-man, one-vote," it allows Parliament to suspend its civil liberties protections in emergency situations. To perpetuate politics along traditional lines, Parliament's ethnic Fijian seats are heavily weighted toward the rural areas, where voters tend to support ethnic Fijian nationalist parties and traditional leaders in greater numbers.

Occasional police abuse of detainees is a persistent problem, and police convicted of such abuse generally receive light punishments. The judiciary is modeled on the British system and is independent of the government. Defendants receive adequate due process rights.

Fijians of all races can speak freely on political issues, although the Public Order Act, which prohibits speech or actions likely to incite racial antagonism, remains on the books. Several restrictions on press freedom exist. The Press Correction Act (PCA) allows the minister of information to order a paper to print a "correcting statement" to an article. If a paper refuses and a court finds it guilty, individuals involved can face a fine and/or imprisonment for up to six months. Under the PCA the government can also arrest anyone it considers to have published "malicious" material, including false news that can cause public disorder. Although the government rarely exercises these restrictions, their existence leads newspapers and private radio stations to practice self-censorship regarding sensitive political matters. The government-produced "Nightly News Focus" does not grant equal time to opposition news and viewpoints. In July the new, permanent Fiji TV replaced the temporary service which had operated since 1991 and only served parts of the country.

Rape and domestic violence are serious problems. *Pacific Islands Monthly* (PMI) columnist Atu Emberson-Bain has noted that in some rape cases the practice of *Bulubulu* (traditional reconciliation) is applied, allowing the offender to apologize to the victim's father or family. If accepted, the felony charge is dropped. Women are generally paid less than men for equal work. Child abuse is also a growing problem. Members of the Indian community are occasionally subject to racially-motivated harassment.

Freedom of religion is respected. Freedom of movement at home and abroad is unrestricted. Workers have the right to join independent unions and strike. The government has begun repealing anti-union legislation passed in November 1991 by reinstating the automatic dues checkoff system and eliminating a prohibition on union leaders holding multiple offices. The May 1994 *PMI* exposed grim working conditions at the state-owned Pacific Fishing Company cannery in Lekuva. Women on the production line face stifling heat, dangerous conditions and low wages.

Finland

Polity: Presidential-parliamentary democracy
Economy: Mixed capitalist
Population: 5,095,000
PPP: $16,130
Life Expectancy: 75.4
Ethnic Groups: Finns, Swedes, Lapps (Saami)

Political Rights: 1
Civil Liberties: 1
Status: Free

Overview:

In 1994 Finland held its first direct presidential election. Previously, presidents were chosen through electoral colleges. Martti Ahtisaari, a Social Democrat, replaced former President Mauno Koivisto, also a Social Democrat. Voters approved a referendum to join the European Union (EU), and the ferry *Estonia* sank off the Finnish coast, killing more than 900 people.

The present constitution of Finland dates from 1919. It provides for a 200-seat Parliament elected by universal suffrage, based on proportional representation, for a four-year term. The head of state is the president, who serves a six-year term and has some significant powers. The president appoints the prime minister from the party or coalition that commands the majority of the parliament. The prime minister heads the cabinet. The president can initiate and veto legislation and is directly responsible for foreign affairs and some domestic affairs. In addition, the president may dissolve the parliament at any time and call for elections.

In 1994, in the first direct presidential election since the country gained independence from Russia in 1917, Ahtisaari, a former United Nations diplomat, defeated defense minister Elizabeth Rehn to become the new president of Finland. Ahtisaari replaced Mauno Koivisto, who retired in March after serving two six-year terms. In his campaign, Ahtisaari focused on improving Finland's sluggish economy. From 1990 to 1993, Finland's gross domestic product has dropped 15 percent. The collapse of the Soviet Union eliminated a large market for Finnish goods. Unemployment also increased from 5 percent to 20 percent.

Finland began to show signs of economic recovery in 1994, largely a result of the 8.5 percent rise in exports, which created a $3 billion trade surplus. In addition, the unemployment rate dropped from 20 percent to 17.9 percent, although it is still the worst rate in Europe after Spain.

The Finnish government hopes to reorient the country toward the West by joining the EU. In April 1994, the EU approved Finland's entry and promised Finland special aid to its farmers. On 16 October voters approved a referendum proposal to join the EU. Fifty-seven percent favored the measure, and 43 percent opposed it. Earlier in the year, a dispute over Finland's possible EU membership led to a split in Prime Minister Esko Aho's center-right coalition when the anti-EU Christian Party pulled out of the government. The remaining three parties in Aho's coalition retained an absolute majority in the Parliament.

According to a study by the Ministry of Trade and Industry, Finland's economy would be further strengthened by its membership in the EU. Membership would encourage foreign investment and decrease inflation, as Finnish exports would no longer be subject to EU customs duties. In addition to strengthening the economy, membership also signifies Finland's continued move away from Russia's shadow and towards building closer ties with Western Europe.

Finland's entry is also significant to the EU, giving the EU its first direct frontier with Russia in the form of the 1,270 km-long Finnish-Russian border. Further, Finland's membership enables EU territory to extend for the first time to the Arctic Circle, which contains expansive forestry resources.

On 28 September, the ferry *Estonia* sank off the Finnish coast. Over 900 lives were lost. A three-nation investigation commission based in Helsinki set out to determine how more people could have been rescued. Because faulty locks on the *Estonia*'s door were blamed for the disaster, Finland's National Board of Navigation ordered bow doors welded shut on all cruise ships and ferries departing from Helsinki.

Political Rights and Civil Liberties: Finns have the right to change their government by democratic means. The indigenous Swedish and Lappic (Saami) have full political and cultural rights.

There is a wide selection of publications available to the Finnish public. Newspapers are private. Traditionally, many parties have owned or controlled newspapers, but several dailies have folded in the 1990s. For years, the press restrained itself on issues sensitive to the Soviet Union, but this self-censorship died with the Soviet Union, if not before. The Finnish Broadcasting Company controls most of the radio and television programming. There are programs for both Finnish and Swedish speakers. Limited private broadcasting is also available.

There are two established churches in Finland, one Lutheran and the other

Orthodox. The state finances both of the established churches through a special tax from which citizens may exempt themselves. There is freedom of worship for other faiths. Approximately 88 percent of the population belongs to the Lutheran church.

It is illegal to discriminate on the basis of race, religion, sex, language or social status in Finland. There have been cases of civilian attacks on non-Nordic immigrants, but the government has condemned this violence and has taken action to fight racism. In addition, the Finnish state investigates cases of sex discrimination.

Workers have the right to organize, bargain and strike. An overwhelming majority of Finns belongs to free trade unions. The Central Organization of Finnish Trade Unions (SAK) dominates the labor movement in Finland.

⬇ France

Polity: Presidential-par- **Political Rights:** 1
liamentary democracy **Civil Liberties:** 2
Economy: Mixed **Status:** Free
capitalist
Population: 57,999,000
PPP: $18,430
Life Expectancy: 76.6
Ethnic Groups: French, regional minorities (Corsican, Alsatian, Basque, Breton), and various Arab and African immigrant groups
Trend Arrow: New restrictions on immigrants and on expression were negative trends in 1994.

Overview: In 1994 the center-right governing coalition was unable to consolidate the enormous gains made in 1993's legislative elections. Competition within the Rally for the Republic (RPR) between Prime Minister Edouard Balladur and Paris Mayor Jacques Chirac to succeed President François Mitterrand in 1995 tempered the influence of the neo-Gaullist RPR, the chief center-right coalition party that shares a legislative majority with the Union for French Democracy (UDF), led by Charles Million. The outcome of the 1994 European Parliamentary elections reflected voter disapproval of mainstream parties, and signaled the difficulty their presidential candidates have to secure a solid majority in 1995. The mainstream parties RPR, UDF and Socialist together garnered 40 percent of the total votes, while Bernard Tapie, a radical candidate, collected 11.8 percent, Roman Catholic traditionalist, Phillippe de Villiers, won 12 percent, and Jean-Marie Le Pen of the National Front, 10 percent. Moreover, as if to confirm voter dissatisfaction, a clampdown on corruption implicated dozens of politicians and businessmen, including two ministers charged with receiving illegal funds.

The current system of government, the Fifth Republic, dates from 1958. As designed by Charles de Gaulle, the presidency is the dominant institution in this mixed presidential-parliamentary system. The people elect the president directly through a two-round system. In the first round, candidates of all parties appear on the ballot. If no candidate wins a majority, a runoff takes place between the top contestants. Socialist François Mitterrand became president in 1981 and won reelection in 1988. The parliamentary bodies are the 577-member National Assembly, which the people elect directly in two rounds, and the 318-member Senate, which is chosen by an electoral college of local elected officials. The Assembly is elected for five years and can be dissolved by the president.

In 1993 the electorate overturned the Socialist-Communist coalition, which was replaced with a center-right coalition of the RPR and the UDF that won 80 percent of the seats. For the second time during his presidency, Mitterrand entered a period of "cohabitation" with a conservative Parliament. Throughout 1994 the government was beleaguered by social unrest. In January, teachers and students protested after the government announced a plan to increase public funding of private schools, most of which are Roman Catholic.

In March, in an effort to deal with unemployment, Balladur planned to establish entry-level wages for workers under twenty-five, allowing employers to pay less than minimum wage in return for professional training. Top officials of the Socialist and Communist parties rallied against the wage plan with students and union leaders. After proposing other plans, which were rejected, the government capitulated. It decided to subsidize companies by paying $175 a month for nine months for every young person given a first job and $350 a month for every job created before 1 October 1994. One in four people between eighteen and twenty-five is unemployed.

In a massive clampdown on corruption, dozens of corporate executives and high-level politicians were indicted on charges linked to kickbacks for illegal funding of electoral campaigns. Several ministers, including Defense Minister François Léotard, Industry Minister Gérard Longuet, Development Minister Alain Madelin and Communication Minister Alain Carignon, were charged with receiving illegal funds. Longuet and Carignon resigned. In December the National Assembly approved a bill barring businesses from financing election campaigns and political parties. It also voted to make ineligible for election for a period of five years any politician convicted of corruption. Former Socialist Premier Laurent Fabius and two former ministers were charged with complicity in poisoning hemophiliacs who died after receiving HIV-tainted blood products.

As France celebrated the fiftieth anniversary of the liberation of Paris, the trial of Paul Touvier, the first French citizen to be tried for crimes against humanity, and the disclosure of President Mitterrand's friendship with René Bousquet, a senior police official who oversaw the deportation of French Jews to concentration camps, reopened the debate about France's wartime past. *A French Youth,* written by Pierre Pean, with Mitterrand's collaboration, described Mitterrand's support of the Vichy regime before he joined the Resistance.

Paul Touvier, the intelligence chief for the Vichy regime's militia in the Lyon area, stood trial in 1994. He had managed to elude authorities, thanks to support from nearly fifty Roman Catholic institutions. Maurice Papon, also a former official in the Vichy government, and a high official in the Fourth and Fifth Republics, indicted in 1981, requested to stand trial soon or have the charges dropped.

After the assassination of five Frenchmen in Algeria on 3 August, France braced itself for possible attacks by Islamic radicals. Refusing to free seventeen detained fundamentalists, Interior Minister Charles Pasqua also banned five Islamic publications and ordered vigilance for signs of terrorism. On 31 August, the government expelled to Burkina Faso twenty of twenty-six people interned because of their suspected sympathies with Islamic extremists in Algeria. Foreign Minister Alain Juppé advocates a discussion among all parties to the Algerian conflict while Interior Minister Pasqua unequivocally supports the military-backed regime.

In November, Jean-Louis Bruguiére, France's chief anti-terrorist judge, ordered a massive crackdown on Islamic militants active within France's Muslim population. The police arrested ninety-five people believed to be linked to Algeria's Armed Islamic Group (GIA), some of whom are French citizens of Algerian descent. Fearful that Islamic fundamentalists are trying to infiltrate the country's Muslim minority, France also expelled three foreign Muslim clerics on accusations of preaching subversion. On 24 December French commandos freed hostages held in an airplane on a flight from Algiers to Paris. The commandos stormed the plane and killed four hijackers linked to the GIA.

France undertook a humanitarian mission, Operation Turquoise, in Rwanda in July. The motives remained suspect among the Tutsi-led rebels because of past French support for the deposed Hutu-led government. France is the largest contributor to a two-year U.N. peacekeeping force in the Balkans, with 6,800 troops deployed in Croatia and Bosnia. France belongs to the five-nation "contact group" that drew up peace plans for partition that were subsequently rejected.

Political Rights and Civil Liberties: The French have the right to change their government by democratic means. Under the Fifth Republic constitution, the president has significant emergency powers and the right to rule by decree under certain circumstances. These represent potential threats to democracy. France has democratically elected local governments, but there is a strong tradition of centralized government. Political parties receive public financing. Prime Minister Balladur proposed limiting campaign spending and requiring annual financial statements by politicians.

Political surveillance is common. On 19 June police were caught eavesdropping on a private Socialist meeting in which Henri Emmanuali was chosen to succeed Michel Rocard as head of the party. One month later, Interior Minister Pasqua abolished the entire section of the General Information Bureau dealing with political surveillance. After the tapping incident, the National Assembly passed a bill demanding that the presidents of both houses of Parliament be informed about plans to tap a member's telephone.

The press is largely free, but there are some restrictions on expression. The government partially subsidizes journalism and registers journalists. The broadcast media became competitive and increasingly free from the government in the 1980s. Despite the liberalization, the French government's reign on the media infuriates the EU. In 1994, the conservative government was accused of seeking control of Canal Plus, an independent TV station, after the founder and chairman resigned in protest against shareholders he believed were government cronies conspiring to exert control over the station.

In a battle against "franglais" (a mixture of French and English), Minister of Culture Jacques Toubon introduced legislation in May requiring the use of French on all products and public announcements and translations in French of all papers presented at scientific forums in France. However, the Constitutional Court voided it.

France's anti-terrorist policy includes the expulsion of suspected Basque and foreign terrorists. On 17 November police arrested several suspected leaders of the Basque

Homeland and Liberty (ETA) commando group in a crackdown campaign of cooperation with Spain to round up suspects linked to separatist movements in the Basque
region. The government can legally expel foreigners without any possibility to
appeal the decision. On 6 April two Algerian youths hastily expelled from France
for allegedly attacking police during the student riots were allowed to return,
striking a blow against Pasqua's tough restrictions on immigrants, which include
rapid expulsions for lawbreakers deemed to be a "threat to the public order."

Breaching international anti-terrorist laws, in 1994 the conservative government sent
back to Iran two men who were supposed to be extradited to Switzerland to face charges
of murdering the brother of the leader of the exiled Mojaheedeen organization.
However, Ali Vakili Rad, the man charged with the assassination in France of
former Iranian Prime Minister Shapour Bakhtiar, stood trial in November 1994.
The constitutional right to asylum was amended in 1993 to bring it into conformity
with the new rules set out under the Treaty of the European Union.

On 4 November, the National Front for the Liberation of Corsica, a nationalist
militant group fighting for Corsican independence, held a clandestine news conference in
which reporters were blindfolded in an undisclosed location. The group, which has
committed scores of bombings in recent years, announced they wanted a political
settlement rather than armed conflict.

In October 1994, Amnesty International (AI) reported continued police brutality. In
1993 and the first half of 1994, AI reported the shooting to death by police of eleven
people. One died from injuries while being interrogated at a police station.

There is freedom of religion. French law prohibits wearing religious garb and
symbols in state schools. The dispute over the Islamic scarf (*hijeb*) has been a
national controversy since three Muslim girls were expelled from a junior high
school in 1989. The emergent consensus between many immigrants and French
society is coming under increasing strain. The Grand Mosque of Lyons, which
opened on 30 September 1994, is the seventh large mosque in France.

The government may place up to five years of restrictions on the political rights of
anyone convicted of committing racist, anti-Semitic or xenophobic acts. Although
France has strict antiracist legislation, "ghettos" have developed in areas where immigrants from black Africa, the Maghreb and Asia are concentrated.

Out of a population of some 57 million, France currently has about 4 million immigrants, most of whom are from its former North African possessions. Pasqua wants France
to be a country of "zero immigration." New nationality laws went into effect 1 January
1994. Children born to foreigners in France must apply for French nationality between the
ages of sixteen and twenty-one. A new bureau was created in Pasqua's ministry to take
charge of controlling immigration and fighting employment of illegal immigrants.
Beginning in April 1995, foreigners from thirteen countries, considered as "sensitive," as
well as Palestinians, will have to obtain exit visas before leaving the country.

Under the constitution, groups have the right to demonstrate, but French authorities
sometimes prohibit demonstrations and rallies on the ground that they could disturb
public order. On 9 September, the government prohibited planned protests in Paris and
in Marseilles on the arrival of Chinese President Jiang Zemin. Rallies by Kurds and the
far-right National Front have been banned in the past. On 11 October the National
Assembly approved a law that would allow police to search vehicles near a demonstration. However, the Senate wants to amend the bill before a final version is approved.

Gabon

Polity: Dominant party   **Political Rights:** 5
Economy: Capitalist   **Civil Liberties:** 4
Population: 1,139,000   **Status:** Partly Free
PPP: $3,498
Life Expectancy: 52.9
Ethnic Groups: Duma, Fang, Mpongwe, Shogo, others

Overview: **F**ollowing the fraudulent election of President Omar Bongo in December 1993, a wave of chaos and government repression swept over Gabon in 1994. The situation stabilized in September when Bongo held negotiations with opposition leaders about reforming and democratizing the political system.

Situated on the west coast of central Africa, Gabon gained independence from France in 1960. Its first president, Leon M'ba, created a one-party state under his Gabon Democratic Bloc (BDG). M'ba died in 1967 and was succeeded by Bongo, who outlawed all opposition groups and maintained a one-party rule of the BDG, renamed the Democratic Party of Gabon (PDG). He was elected president in 1986 to a seven-year term, running as the sole PDG candidate.

The Gabonese have long enjoyed the highest standard of living in Sub-Saharan Africa. The country's economic backbone is its oil reserves, controlled mostly by the French. The Bongo regime has promoted a free-market system, but at the same time has neglected to develop an economic infrastructure necessary to attract foreign investment. Due to corruption and mismanagement—Bongo's personal wealth is estimated at several billion dollars—by the early 1990s, Gabon had the highest capital flight in the developing world, double its GDP, according to the World Bank. In August 1993, the government introduced austerity measures to control the swelling budget deficit. In January 1994, the French government devalued the CFA franc by 50 percent. Despite the IMF's promise to Gabon of $1.5-1.7 billion worth of aid, economic conditions deteriorated.

In December 1993 Bongo won a renewed term in office. In January 1994, evidence of fraud undermined the validity of the election. The ballots from three of the nine Gabonese provinces had not even been counted when Bongo declared his victory. The African American Institute (AAI) declared the election "an electoral *coup d'état*."

Violent civilian protests erupted after the election. The government responded by arresting protesters and issuing a curfew, which was lifted on 12 February.

One week later, violence broke out again. Opposition leaders and the Confederation of Free Trade Unions declared a general strike, protesting the deteriorating economic conditions. Crowds of civilians took to the streets, looting and burning over fifty vehicles and 100 stores. Nine people were killed in the strike, which lasted for four days. The government launched a crackdown on the violence; soldiers rolled through the streets in armored cars, arresting demonstrators. On 22 February, soldiers ransacked and torched *Radio Liberté*, the only functioning opposition radio station. Bongo later described the attack as "a punitive measure." The regime re-issued a curfew and announced a "State of Alert," defined by the government as "an emergency decree restricting public liberties." The curfew remained in effect until 8 April.

On 26 May students at University Omar Bongo in Libreville went on strike, demanding a 19 percent stipend increase to cushion the blow of the currency devaluation. On 16 June, the strike exploded into a violent protest; government authorities closed down the school, and various student leaders were arrested.

Increased public dissent and international pressure forced Bongo in July to agree to negotiate with the High Council for the Resistance of Democracy in Gabon (HCR), composed of representatives from the various opposition groups. On 29 July the talks had to be postponed when Bongo broke the pre-negotiation agreements by appointing himself mediator between his own regime and the opposition. Negotiations began on 7 September. A month later, an accord was signed in which Bongo agreed to work with the HCR to form a new transitional government in charge of reforming the political system in preparation for the April 1996 National Assembly elections.

On 31 October Dr. Paulin Obame Nguema, the appointed transitional prime minister, announced the transitional cabinet. The HCR objected to the fact that only six out of the twenty-seven cabinet members were opposition members. Also subject to question was the appointment of Pierre-Louis Agonjio, an opposition leader, who was made justice minister without his knowledge or consent.

Political Rights and Civil Liberties: The people of Gabon cannot choose their government democratically. By manipulating the election process, Bongo has kept himself in power for the past twenty-seven years.

Since 1992, when the legislature granted greater autonomy to the courts and improved the career paths of the judges, the judiciary has strengthened its independence from executive interference. Nevertheless, the pressure on the courts from the executive remains strong, particularly in opposition and security related cases. Bongo's wife heads the Constitutional Court.

Torture remains an accepted practice to extract confessions from suspects. Prison conditions are poor, with insufficient food, inadequate medical facilities, crumbling buildings and frequent beatings of inmates. In February 1994 sixty-four prisoners were found dead in a tiny prison cell in Libreville. They apparently died of suffocation and lack of food.

Since 1991 the state and private press have become more critical of the government. The state media, including the main daily, *L'Union*, expanded their coverage of opposition activities. In February 1994 government soldiers torched the last opposition radio station, *Radio Liberté.* The other private station, *Radio Frequence Liberté,* was destroyed by the military in December 1993.

Government authorization is required for all public meetings, although in practice protests and rallies often take place without permits. The right to protest was suspended this year when the government declared a state of alert.

Freedom to form and join political parties is generally respected, although civil servants may face harassment because of their convictions. During the military crackdown in February 1994, soldiers stormed the house of Father Paul Mba Abessole, leader of the opposition group, the National Lumberjacks. He was not at home.

Freedom of religion is generally respected, and there is no state religion. The majority of the population is Christian. President Bongo, however, is a member of the Muslim minority.

The Gabonese have the right to travel and migrate internally and externally.

This right, though, was also suspended during the 1994 state of alert. In June, soldiers used tear gas and automatic weapons to prevent a delegation of opposition leaders from leaving the country to meet with leaders in Washington, D.C., and Paris. The delegation was told that their right to travel was suspended under a 1959 French colonial statute that is still in place.

Since 1992, when the monopoly of the PDG-affiliated Gabonese Labor Confederation (COSYGA) was lifted, workers have had the right to form and join trade unions of their choice.

The Gambia

Polity: Military
Economy: Capitalist
Population: 1,061,000
PPP: $763
Life Expectancy: 44.4
Ethnic Groups: Mandingo, Fulani, Wolof, Jola, Serahuli
Ratings Change: *The Gambia's political rights rating changed from 2 to 7 and its civil liberties rating from 2 to 6 following a military coup and numerous restrictrions on freedom. As a result The Gambia's status changed from Free to Not Free.

Political Rights: 7*
Civil Liberties: 6*
Status: Not Free

Overview: **W**hen Lieut. Yahya Jammeh seized power in a bloodless coup in this tiny West African country on 22 July 1994, he broke one of the continent's longest traditions of electoral democracy. Governing by decree with four junior officers, Jammeh barred all political activity, detained many of his superiors in the 800-man armed forces, and confined government ministers to house arrest.

The republic of Gambia is a narrow country surrounded on three sides by Senegal. Under British rule since 1588, it became a separate colony in 1888, achieved internal self-government in 1963, and became fully independent in February 1965.

Until the coup, President Sir Dawda K. Jawara and his People's Progressive Party (PPP) had ruled since independence. He had been directly elected under a multiparty system since 1982, most recently in April 1992. In legislative elections the same year to the unicameral, 51-member House of Representatives, thirty-six seats were contested, of which the PPP won twenty-five. Other parties included the Gambian People's Party, the United Party, the leftist People's Democratic Organization for Independence and Socialism, and the right-of-center People's Democratic Party.

After the July coup, which began as a military protest march against unpaid wages and the presence of Nigerian military officers, President Jawara, the first of his two wives, and fourteen of his nineteen children were spirited away from Banjul aboard a U.S. warship and subsequently granted asylum by Senegal. Within a week of the coup, two of the original four coup leaders were imprisoned by the twenty-eight-year-old Jammeh. Several army officers and government ministers were arrested. Jammeh accused the old regime of "exploiting the country's riches for a privileged minority while the vast majority of Gambians lived in poverty for the last thirty years." The four-man Armed Forces Provisional Ruling Council announced an anticorruption drive and a 2 A.M.-5 A.M. curfew.

In August the Ruling Council issued two stringent decrees. Decree No. 3 State Security (Detention of Armed and Police Personnel) provided the vice-chairman of the Council, Lieut. S.B. Sabally, with the power to arrest and detain any member of the forces "in the interest of the security of the Gambia." No court would be able to hear any evidence on behalf of any armed forces members. Decree No. 4 (Political Activities Suspension) effectively disallowed political activity, including the function of political parties. It read in part: "No person shall engage in any political propaganda by means of a newspaper publication or any other media form for spreading the ideas or ideology of any political party." On 3 August the new military rulers freed all ten former government ministers detained after the coup but placed most of them under house arrest. A dozen former ministers were arrested on 13 September in Banjul; they were released three days later, but six were subsequently re-arrested.

By late September several senior police officials were sacked. The government assured the World Bank and other institutions that it would continue the "sustained development" economic policies inherited from the previous administration that had led to a relatively healthy economy. The World Bank suspended for six months the disbursement of funds for several projects while waiting to see if the junta would actually follow through on the macro-economic reforms launched under Jawara. The United States Agency for International Development (USAID) threatened to freeze further aid altogether. Aid donors demanded the restoration of democracy and the release of some thirty army officers detained since the coup.

In October Bakary Dabo, finance minister under the Jawara administration and the only one to be retained by the military government, was dismissed. On 18 October Jammeh lifted the curfew but retained the ban on political parties. He also said the junta would hand over power to a civilian regime in 1998. Nevertheless, the European Union (EU) suspended military cooperation and economic aid, stating that there should be "no obstacles to a rapid return to a constitutional regime," adding that "the repeated arrests of former ministers and the trial of journalists for their opinions" were repressive.

In early November, Vice President Sabally announced an attempted coup by several army officers against the military regime. The government said three people were killed, including Lieut. Bassiru Barrow, a battalion commander and the alleged leader of the coup attempt. Meanwhile, more former ministers were arrested, detained and released. At the end of the month, the British Foreign Office called on its tour operators to bring more than 2,000 vacationers back from Gambia because of the deteriorating political situation.

Political Rights and Civil Liberties:

Until the July 1994 coup, citizens of Gambia had the means to change their government democratically. After the takeover by the Armed Forces Provisional Council, political activity and parties were suspended, government ministers were arrested, released and re-arrested throughout the year and journalists faced detention and intimidation. The cabinet has been reshuffled several times.

Before the coup, the judiciary was independent and based on the British model, while Islamic *shari'a* law governed marriage, divorce and inheritance for Muslims and tribal customary law applied to non-Muslims. The military junta passed several decrees restricting due process and the rule of law. By year's end, some thirty military officers arrested after the coup remained in detention.

The principal newspaper and national radio station are government-owned. Several independent newspapers exist, but the military junta has muzzled the press by arresting and harassing journalists. In October, Kenneth Y. Best, managing editor of the Banjul-based *Daily Observer*, was deported. Military rule and a three-month curfew put limits on freedom of assembly and association.

Religious freedom is guaranteed and respected in practice. The U.N. has reported that Koranic schools in Gambia often enlist young boys, known as *almudos*, to beg alms in urban areas and work on the farms of their teachers in rural regions.

Women's rights are circumscribed by custom and tradition. Marriages are often "arranged," and the circumcision of women is common; some 60 percent of women have reportedly undergone the procedure. In late July two women were brought into the new government as minister of information and minister of health.

The Gambian Workers' Confederation and the Gambian Workers' Union are competing labor federations. Union functions, particularly political activity, was limited by the junta.

Georgia

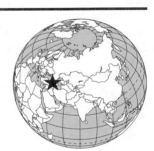

Polity: Parliamentary democracy (foreign military-influenced)
Economy: Statist transitional
Population: 5,450,000
PPP: $3,670
Life Expectancy: 73.0
Ethnic Groups: Georgians (70 percent), Russians, Abkhazians, Armenians, Azeris, Ossetians, others (30 percent)
Trend Arrow: Separatist insurgencies in South Ossetia and Abkhazia were negative trends in 1994.

Political Rights: 5
Civil Liberties: 5
Status: Partly Free

Overview: In 1994 President Eduard Shevardnadze faced growing political opposition for agreeing to accept Russian peace-keeping forces for the breakaway region of Abkhazia, for bringing the country into the Commonwealth of Independent States (CIS), a moribund economy and separatism in the province of South Ossetia.

Absorbed by Russia in the early nineteenth century, Georgia proclaimed independence in 1918, gaining Soviet recognition two years later. In 1921, it was overrun by the Red Army and became a Soviet Republic. In 1922, it entered the USSR as a component of the Transcaucasian Federated Soviet Republic, becoming a separate union republic in 1936.

Georgia declared independence from the Soviet Union after a referendum in April 1991. Nationalist leader and former dissident Zviad Gamsakhurdia was overwhelmingly elected president in May. By late 1991, his erratic, authoritarian behavior led to his violent ouster by opposition units led by former Prime Minister Tengiz Sigua and Jaba Ioseliani, head of the 2,000-man *Mkhedrioni* (Knights of Georgia) militia. After fierce battles in the capital, Tblisi, Gamsakhurdia fled in early 1992 to the Chechen region in Russia. Former Soviet Foreign Minister Shevardnadze was asked by the State Council, which had temporarily assumed legislative and executive powers, to head a new government. On 24 August, Shevardnadze announced he would run for the office of Speaker of Parliament, and he was elected in October. Sigua was named prime minister.

In 1993 Georgia experienced the violent secession of Abkhazia and an armed insurrection by supporters of Gamsakhurdia. Abkhazian insurgents drove Georgian forces from the province in September, violating a Russian-brokered peace agreement that called for the disengagement of forces. Georgia, which had abided by the pact and withdrawn its troops, accused the Russians of orchestrating the debacle. More than 3,000 people reportedly died in the conflict, and as many as 300,000, mostly ethnic Georgians, were driven from their homes. Shevardnadze blamed rogue Russian army units, some from Moldova, for supplying the mostly Muslim Abkhazians, who constituted only 18 percent of the region's 538,000 people, with troops, heavy weapons and aircraft. In exchange for legalizing the presence of some 19,000 Russian troops in five Georgian bases, Russia sent forces to help a desperate Shevardnadze quell the Gamsakhurdia rebellion, which was put down by November. The former president fled and committed suicide in December.

The key government concern in 1994 was to resolve the Abkhazia issue, specifically the role and makeup of peacekeeping forces and the repatriation of Georgian refugees. On 13 January Georgian and Abkhazian representatives meeting in Geneva agreed to ask the United Nations to send peacekeepers to potential conflict zones. There was tentative agreement on a U.N.-sponsored program for returning refugees, but only limited progress toward a political settlement on the future status of Abkhazia.

In February, on the eve of a visit to Tblisi by Russian President Boris Yeltsin, Russian Defense Minister Pavel Grachev arrived to discuss the possibility of extending Russian control of five army bases beyond the 1995 expiration date. The visit sparked anti-Russian demonstrations by Abkhazian refugees and nationalists near the parliament building. A few hours before Yeltsin arrived on 3 February, Georgia's deputy defense minister was assassinated by a bomb at his home. A second bomb later in the day injured Defense Minister Georgy Karkarashvili, who earlier had offered his resignation to protest closer ties with Russia.

Yeltsin signed a friendship treaty and about a dozen other agreements that represented a rapprochement between Tblisi and Moscow and provided for close security cooperation, including arms sales to Georgia and training Georgian troops. Grachev and the Georgian chief of staff signed a separate protocol of intentions, allowing Russia to maintain at least three military bases in Georgia.

The month also saw renewed fighting in Abkhazia by Georgian partisans and Abkhazian forces, backed by Chechens, that led to the destruction of several villages and left more than 100 civilians dead. Each side accused the other of instigating the violence. Georgia asked Russia to stop what it called further "ethnic cleansing" by the Abkhazians. On 25 February mediators in Geneva proved unable to break a deadlock between Georgia and Abkhazia over wording that stressed the territorial integrity of Georgia.

On 1 March, after a heated debate, Parliament approved Georgia's entry into the Moscow-dominated CIS. Of 193 legislators present, 125 voted in favor, 64 against and 4 abstained. Several high-ranking Shevardnadze allies, including Deputy Prime Minister Irina Sarishvili, resigned in protest, arguing that joining the CIS meant losing sovereignty.

During his trip to the United States in March, Shevardnadze asked the U.S. to contribute to a U.N. peacekeeping force, underscoring his desire to avoid the deployment of a Russia-dominated CIS contingent. President Bill Clinton said the U.S. would back a U.N. force, but that no American troops would be involved. On 26 March, Abkhazian separatists captured a village outside the province's borders.

On 14 April CIS leaders meeting in Moscow agreed to send peacekeepers to Abkhazia if the U.N. failed to provide troops. A month later, Georgians and Abkhazians signed an agreement in Moscow that called for a cease-fire and stationing CIS troops under Russian command along the Inguri River, effectively separating the rebel region from Georgian control. Despite Georgia's preference for U.N. troops, Russia asked for U.N. Security Council approval to deploy the CIS forces. On 24 May, Russia canceled an economic blockade of Abkhazia.

Under a U.N.-brokered peace plan, some 5,000 Georgian villagers returned home to Abkhazia on 1-3 July, despite sporadic fighting in the Kodori Gorge. On 9 July a political demonstration, organized by opposition parties and calling for Shevardnadze's resignation, attracted several thousand protesters in Tblisi. The protest was violently dispersed by police, sparking the All-Georgian Association for the Protection of Human Rights to criticize the government.

In August internal opposition to Shevardnadze intensified. The opposition demanded that Shevardnadze release all political prisoners, but he agreed only to review all cases of political detainees within one month. On 11 August, an emergency parliamentary session was convened, but it failed to reach the necessary quorum, only 80 of 235 deputies being present. Two weeks later, representatives of thirty-seven Georgian opposition parties met in Tblisi, denounced the government and vowed to wrest Georgian independence from Russian control.

On 31 August U.N.-sponsored talks in Geneva on a political settlement in Abkhazia foundered on the issue of Georgian refugees. On 2 September, Georgian and Abkhazian representatives reached an agreement on the refugee issue. To date, the U.N. had registered more than 20,000 ethnic Georgians who wanted to return home. Despite the agreement, repatriation was held up by flare-ups in fighting, delayed negotiations, and Abkhazia's insistence that repatriation was "practically impossible" without substantial economic aid.

The government also faced separatist pressures in South Ossetia and Ajaria, a small, pro-Moscow enclave bordering Turkey. On 23 July the government created a commission to investigate the situation in Ajaria in response to claims by Ajarian officials that terrorist groups of former Gamsakhurdia supporters had been sent to the autonomous republic to destabilize the region. The pro-Communist government of South Ossetia, which in a June 1992 war drove out all the Georgians, who had made up one-third of the population, continued to push for incorporation into the Russian Federation, thus joining the Russian autonomous republic of North Ossetia.

Civil war and violent and clannish politics inextricably mixed with criminal gangs pre-dating independence, left a once vibrant economy in tatters. In May 1994 Shevardnadze signed several decrees speeding up privatization. But parliamentary inertia, obstructionist state structures and criminal activity muddled the privatization picture. In February, Georgia announced it was rationing electricity. On the eve of his

U.S. visit, Shevardnadze said his country was on the verge of famine. In late October, an official from the U.N. World Food Program predicted that 483,000 Georgians risked starvation in the winter without massive international aid, which his agency was not in a position to provide. On 3 November International Monetary Fund (IMF) officials expressed concern that Georgia had failed to liberalize bread prices and reduce public sector jobs as required in return for $100 million. In March President Clinton announced $70 million in relief goods and services, in addition to the $233 million Washington had contributed to Georgia over the previous two years.

Political Rights and Civil Liberties: Georgians have the right to change their government democratically, but the government's *de facto* loss of control over Abkhazia, South Ossetia and, to some extent, Ajaria, has affected the scope of the government's power and representation. The country operates on a mixture of the Soviet-era constitution and the 1921 constitution dating from Georgia's brief interwar independence in 1918-21. Work by the State Constitutional Committee on a new constitution continues.

Forty-six parties and blocs participated in the October 1992 elections to the 235-member Parliament, though voting was postponed in parts of Abkhazia, South Ossetia and western Georgia. There were numerous cases of fraud and other irregularities. Organizations loyal to ex-President Gamsakhurdia face repression and harassment. Several opposition demonstrations in 1994 were dispersed by brutal force. Nongovernmental Georgian human rights groups report that scores of political prisoners are subjected to poor prison conditions, torture, beatings and other abuses, as well as to violations of due process and their legal rights.

Georgia's entire legal structure is a hybrid of laws from Georgia's brief period of pre-Soviet independence, the Gamsakhurdia presidency and the State Council period. Many "political" crimes remain on the books as a means to deter and prosecute opponents, and the system is plagued by documented instances of illegal arrests, arbitrary dismissal of defense attorneys and other related problems. Members of the judiciary have engaged in corrupt practices, including accepting bribes and bending to the influences of individuals in and out of government, including gangsters.

The political crisis has led to repression of the independent press. In addition to censoring news from Abkhazia, the government has closed independent newspapers and detained journalists. Irakli Gotsiridze of the liberal newspaper *Iberia Spektra* has been repeatedly detained and his paper illegally banned by executive order. Under a 1991 press law, journalists are obliged to "respect the dignity and honor" of Georgia's president and not impugn the honor and dignity of citizens or undermine the regime. The independent *Droni* has been prosecuted for "inciting cruelty and treason." The government controls newsprint and the distribution network, as well as radio and television, which reflect official views and deny access to the opposition. Ibervision, the putatively independent TV station, has faced government pressure.

Ethnic and minority rights are under stress. Georgians in Abkhazia and along the border have been victimized by "ethnic cleansing" carried out by Abkhazian separatists. Atrocities against Georgian civilians in these areas have included rape and mutilation of women.

Freedom of religion is generally respected in this predominantly Christian Orthodox country. There are some restrictions on domestic and foreign travel, particularly in the separatist enclaves. Government concern about the status of and discrimination against women is minimal. Access to education is unimpeded, but women are found mostly in traditional, low-paying occupations.

The Georgian Confederation of Trade Unions (GCTU), the successor to the official Communist-era structure, claims 2 million members, an unrealistic figure given the country's skyrocketing unemployment and worker apathy. There is a legal right to strike.

Germany

Polity: Federal par-
liamentary democracy
Economy: Mixed
capitalist
Population: 81,175,000
PPP: $19,770
Life Expectancy: 75.6
Ethnic Groups: German and numerous immigrant groups

Political Rights: 1
Civil Liberties: 2
Status: Free

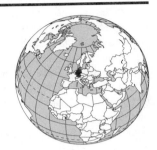

Overview:

Nineteen-ninety-four seemed like an election marathon, with nineteen assorted polls culminating on 16 October, when Chancellor Helmet Kohl's ruling conservative-liberal coalition won a ten-seat majority in the 672-member *Bundestag* (National Assembly). Social Democrat-led coalitions remained dominant in the *Bundesrat* (Federal Council). Among key issues were financing the cost of unification, social spending and a large budget deficit, tax reform, illegal immigration, right-wing violence, crime and the pace of European integration.

Following the defeat of Hitler's Third Reich by the Allies in 1945, Germany was divided into Soviet, U.S., British and French occupation zones. In 1949, the Allies helped establish the Federal Republic of Germany (FRG) under a democratic parliamentary system; the Soviets formed the German Democratic Republic (GDR), dominated by the Communist Party. Berlin remained a divided city, reinforced by the Soviet-led construction of the Berlin Wall in 1961. After the collapse of the hard-line GDR regime of Erich Honecker in 1989, symbolized by the destruction of the Wall in March 1990, citizens voted in that country's first and only free parliamentary election, backing parties that supported a speedy reunification with the FRG.

The absorption of eastern Germany was complete on 3 October 1990. The formerly centralized east was divided into five states (*Laender*), bringing the total of states in a unified Germany to sixteen. On 2 December, the first post-unification election to the 662-seat *Bundestag* was won by Chancellor Kohl's coalition: the Christian Democratic Union (CDU)/Christian Social Union (CSU, the CDU's Bavarian partner) and the liberal Free Democrats (FDP). The CDU/CSU won 319 seats and the FDP captured 79. The Social Democrats (SPD) took 239 seats, the (ex-Communist) Party of Democratic Socialism (PDS), 17; and the Greens, 8. In 1994 the Bundestag was enlarged to 672 seats through a mixed system of proportional and first-past-the-post constituency voting.

In 1993 a poor economy, Europe-wide recession, delayed prosperity for eastern

Germans and attendant anti-foreigner and anti-immigrant sentiments led to growing voter discontent, reflected in fringe rightist and left-wing parties scoring well in local and state elections.

In January 1994 the CDU nominated the country's top judge, Bavarian Roman Herzog, as its candidate to succeed Richard von Weizsäcker in the largely ceremonial post of president. His SPD-backed opponent was State Premier Johannes Rau of North Rhine-Westphalia. Even as Chancellor Kohl exhorted the CDU during February's party conference, warning that a defeat for the ruling coalition would mean the ascension of a "red-green" alliance of the SPD and the Greens, polls showed him trailing SPD leader Rudolph Scharping, minister president of Rhineland-Palatinate. On 13 March the CDU suffered a setback in Lower Saxony, gaining only 37 percent of the vote for the state legislature; this was down from 42 percent in 1990 and the party's worst showing in the largely industrial, Protestant area in thirty-five years. The SPD won 44 percent.

In late April Kohl hit another snag when some Free Democrat leaders announced that they were considering voting for Rau over Herzog, the chancellor's handpicked presidential candidate, when the special assembly met to vote in May. The FDP had a pivotal role because the 1,324 Presidential Assembly (consisting of all 662 members of Parliament and an equal number of representatives from the sixteen state governments) are chosen proportionally to reflect party strengths, and because not all CDU members of Parliament, who would be members of the assembly, were enthusiastic about Herzog. In the first two ballots, in which an absolute majority is required to win, the Free Democrats planned to support their own candidate, Hildegard Hamm-Brucher, a former government minister. The hard-fought campaign for the non-partisan presidency was seen as a prelude to the race for chancellor.

On 23 May Chancellor Kohl won an important victory when the special assembly chose Herzog to be the next German president. In the decisive third round, the Free Democrats supported Herzog.

The ex-Communist PDS (known as the Red Socks) advanced in local summer elections in eastern Germany. In the northern state of Mecklenberg-Vorpommern, where thousands of shipyard workers had lost jobs to closures and privatization, the PDS won 25 percent, 6 percentage points more than in 1990; it also gained in Saxony-Anhalt, Saxony, Brandenberg and Thuringia. Key factors in the gains were inherited local grassroots organizations, the perception that the PDS was a viable social democratic party and the notion that it was an indigenous "regional" eastern party that held the former east's interests paramount. Nevertheless, the CDU managed to maintain its hold, albeit through coalitions, in much of the region. In Saxony-Anhlat, the CDU gained 34.4 percent of the vote, the SPD, 34 percent. In a political gamble aimed at bolstering its stagnating popularity, the SPD rejected a CDU-SPD coalition, opting instead to join with the eco-leftist Alliance 90-Green Party (5.1 percent) and the PDS (20 percent). With an eye toward the national election, the CDU-CSU was quick to label the arrangement "Reds on the Rhine."

By late summer, with the economy strongly rebounding from recession, Chancellor Kohl, bolstered by improving poll numbers, stepped up his attacks, portraying the SPD as an irresponsible, tax-and-spend party that would share power with the PDS. Analysts concluded that the SPD-PDS coalition in Saxony-Anhalt was hurting SPD standard-bearer Scharping and the national campaign. In an effort to prop up his campaign, Scharping, a lackluster campaigner, brought in two former rivals, Gerhard Schroder, the high-profile state premier of Lower Saxony, and Oskar Lafontaine, the Saarland state premier, as part of what he called a new SPD leadership team.

By September, six weeks before the election, polls showed Kohl with a commanding thirteen-point lead. SPD strategists conceded that they would be able to take power only if the FDP, the weak link in the ruling coalition virtually shut out of state and local voting, failed to clear the 4 percent hurdle necessary for representation in the *Bundestag*. The FDP, led by Foreign Minister Klaus Kinkel, was shut out of the state legislatures in Brandenberg and Saxony in mid-September voting; the CDU won in Saxony and the SPD in Brandenberg. In the last state election before the national poll, the ruling CSU won an absolute majority in Bavaria. However, once again the FDP failed to gain the 5 percent threshold to gain seats.

On 16 October Chancellor Kohl's ruling coalition squeezed out a victory, seeing a 134-seat majority whittled down to ten. The narrowness of the victory raised speculation about whether the coalition could hold for a full four-year term. The CDU/CSU won 41.5 percent of the vote and 294 seats; the FDP won just 6.9 percent of the vote and 47 seats (down from 79); the SPD took 36.4 percent and 252 seats; the Greens, 7.3 percent and 49 seats; and the PDS won 4.4 percent and 30 seats. The governing coalition, which initially had its majority reduced to two, managed to increase it by eight because of the "overhang mandates," a peculiarity of the German political system. If a party gains more seats on the first vote (for the directly elected individual constituency seats) than its share based on the second vote (for the party) then the number of seats is increased by the difference. This is done on a state-to-state basis. The SPD gained four extra seats in this way.

On 15 November Chancellor Kohl was officially elected by Parliament to a fourth term by only one vote over the necessary absolute majority of 337. Even though the ruling coalition won 341 seats, the secret ballot made it possible for party renegades to vote against the chancellor. In mid-December FDP leader Kinkel faced mounting pressure from his party to resign.

The election results clearly weakened the chancellor and enfeebled the coalition. Possible political and regional polarization was suggested by the showing of PDS, which took nearly 18 percent of the vote in its home region. The chancellor also faced a hostile majority in the *Bundesrat*, the second house of Parliament representing the sixteen federal states. Although it has veto powers where specified state interests are involved, under the constitution it is limited to those policy areas that fall under joint federal-state responsibility. The *Bundesrat* represents a complex mix of state governments which range from grand coalitions between the CDU and the SPD through "rainbow coalitions of many parties—SPD, Greens, FDP—to single-party rule in a minority of states. The SPD's leading role in a majority of the state governments means that it has the capacity to block legislation, above all where finance is required. This means that the states will continue to wield considerable power in Bonn.

Kohl's prospects were somewhat bolstered by Germany's rapid economic recovery. Unemployment fell sharply in 1994, company profits boomed and the government made progress toward cutting the federal budget by 1996. Truehandanstalt, the state-owned agency charged with privatizing eastern Germany, wound up its work at the end of the year. In September, after three years of wrangling over terms and funding, the *Bundesrat* passed a law to compensate former property owners in eastern Germany.

In other issues, the last Russian troops left Germany in August, followed a week later by the withdrawal of the Western allies. On 12 July Germany ended its self-imposed ban on sending troops to fight abroad when the Constitutional Court ruled that German troops could join foreign military ventures under the aegis of the U.N. or other international groups to which the country belongs. Germany continued to be a leader in calling for the widening of the European Union (EU) and deeper economic integration.

Political Rights and Civil Liberties: Germans have the right to change their government democratically. The federal system allows for a considerable amount of self-government among the sixteen states. In July Parliament voted to amend the post-Nazi German Basic Law (constitution) to take unification into account. Deputies voted for stronger commitments to the rights of women and the handicapped and for a pledge to protect the environment for later generations. But they rejected clauses on respecting ethnic minorities and on the division of power between the federal government and the states.

The constitution requires all parties to be democratic, and several neo-Nazi organizations have been banned by the government. All parties, regardless of ideology, receive federal money; since 1990 the government has given $20 million to the radical-right Republikaners. This and other radical-right parties failed to win a seat in the 1994 parliamentary elections. Court cases upheld the right of radical parties to demand equal access to the airwaves of private networks.

The judiciary is independent and free from government or party interference. There are limits on freedom of expression. The display of Nazi paraphernalia is forbidden, though the law is only sporadically enforced. Members of extremist organizations are banned from employment in the civil service.

Right-wing, skinhead, neo-Nazi violence against immigrants, foreigners and Jewish institutions continued to be an issue, particularly in eastern Germany. In the last three years, 6,000 far-right attacks were recorded, with thirty people killed. Law enforcement officials have been accused of ignoring or mishandling right-wing violence. In June a three-judge panel in Mannheim gave a leader of the far-right National Democratic Party a suspended sentence for inciting racial hatred, calling him a "strong-charactered, responsible personality with clear convictions." After an outcry two of the judges were replaced. In July right-wing youths rampaged at the former Nazi concentration camp at Buchenwald, smashing windows; all but one were released. In May the *Bundestag* passed a wide-ranging crime bill. Under its provisions, propagating the "Auschwitz Lie"—essentially denying the existence of the Holocaust—would become a punishable criminal act. In August the government began shutting down the right-wing extremists, preventing planned neo-Nazi demonstrations to mark the anniversary of Nazi henchman Rudolph Hess's death.

A tough new immigration law has thwarted some asylum-seekers. Under its provisions, any refugee arriving overland into Germany via a "safe third country"—a democracy where human rights are observed—is ineligible for asylum. A key element involved assessing whether the home country of a refugee practices political persecution. Early in the year, Germany changed its mind about expelling 100,000 Croatian refugees.

In October, a leftist and confessed informer for the East German Stasi (secret police) resigned from Parliament after her party, the PDS, withdrew its support. On 2 November, a Cold War lawyer and spy trader went on trial for helping the Stasi blackmail former clients. A call by SPD leader Scharping for partial amnesty for those who cooperated with the Stasi led to sharp rebukes by the government.

German press and broadcast media are free and independent and offer pluralistic points of view. By law, television channels are required to provide equal opportunities for expression of opinions. But they are not required to give equal time to each party outside party political broadcasts.

Freedom of religion is respected, although members of some fringe religions and occult groups, among them Scientology, may be barred from employment in the civil service. In October, leading German politicians called on the government to ban Scientology, calling it a conspirational movement with global political aims.

There are numerous women's organizations addressing a range of issues from spousal abuse and violence to pay equity and sexual harassment. Parliament has been committed to women's rights.

Labor, business and farming groups are free, highly organized and influential. In March employers and leaders of the IG Metall union averted a potentially crippling strike in the crucial engineering industry.

Ghana

Polity: Dominant party
Economy: Capitalist-statist
Population: 16,944,000
PPP: $930
Life Expectancy: 55.4
Ethnic Groups: Some fifty in number, the majority being Akan (including the Fanti), followed by the Ashanti, Ga, Ewe, and the Mossi-Dagomba

Political Rights: 5
Civil Liberties: 4
Status: Partly Free

Overview:
In 1994 Ghana's free-market-oriented economic reforms garnered worldwide recognition and praise. Fighting between the Nunumba and Kokumba ethnic groups forced President Jerry Rawlings to declare a six-month state of emergency in the Northern region. On the political front Ghana's four main political opposition parties negotiated with the government for political reforms and took steps to unite their efforts.

Formerly known as the Gold Coast, Ghana became, in 1957, the first black African country to gain independence from Britain. Since independence, Ghana has oscillated between civilian and military rule. The last military *coup d'état* against the elected government of President Hilla Limann was led by Flight Lieutenant Jerry Rawlings in 1981. Since then, Rawlings and his National Democratic Congress (NDC) have dominated the political life of the country.

In 1991, Rawlings proposed convening a Consultative Assembly to draft a new constitution. Despite criticism for its lack of representation and circumscibed agenda, closely controlled by Rawlings and the Provisional National Defense Council (PNDC), the Assembly began its work that fall. The constitution was completed with a referendum in April 1992, in which the overwhelming majority of the voters approved the new constitution, the alternative being continued rule by the PNDC.

Following their legalization in May 1992, political parties were formed on the basis of traditional Ghanaian ideological bipolarity that stemmed from the early years of the independence struggle. The populist platform derives from the socialist ideology espoused and implemented by the country's first president, Kwame Nkrumah. The other major ideology is based on the free-market ideas of J.B. Danquah, one of the leading pre-independence activists, and former President K.A. Busia.

Due to disagreements, the populist politicians were unable to form a united party, splitting into factions that include the National Independence Party (NIP), the People's National Convention (PNC), the National Convention Party (NCP) and the People's Heritage Party (PHP). The pro-market forces were able to unite, establishing the National Patriotic Party (NPP), Ghana's largest opposition group. Rawlings established the National Democratic Congress (NDC) to act as the continuation of the PNDC.

Following the dubious November 1992 presidential elections, in which Rawlings renewed his term in office, the NPP, PNC, PHP and the NIP formed the Inter-Party Coordinating Committee (ICC) to express the common position of the opposition toward the government. In October 1994 the NPP, PCP and PNC held a unity rally, in which they agreed to put up only one candidate in order to challenge Rawlings most effectively in the 1996 presidential elections.

In preparation for the 1996 elections, negotiations had begun in November 1993 between the government and the NPP. The talks, which continued into 1994, set the terms for two major political reforms: the establishment of an independent electoral commission and amnesty for all opposition exiles. In May 1994, the NPP withdrew from the talks because they believed that no constructive dialogue was taking place.

Ghana's privatization reforms received world recognition in 1994. As Ghana began to sell off state-owned companies and open its markets to foreign investors, donor countries called the nation an "African success story." Since the mid-1980s Ghana has enjoyed an annual growth rate of 5 percent. Ghanaians, however, have been feeling the short-term costs of the transition, including a cost of living increase and plummeting currency values.

Ethnic violence erupted in February 1994 when a member of the Nanumba tribe killed a Kokumba man at a market in the northern town of Tamale. The two men had been bargaining over the price of a black guinea-fowl. Following the murder, Kokumbas rampaged through towns, torching property and killing and injuring villagers. It was not the first time that a minor dispute triggered a major clash. In 1981, a dispute between the two groups over a game of cards eventually led to 1,500 deaths.

Days after the guinea-fowl murder, seven ethnic groups began fighting across much of the north. The ongoing conflict between the seven tribes is rooted in territorial claims. The Nanumbas, Dagombas and Gonjas all have paramount chiefs and are entitled under customary law to own land. The Kokumbas, who are settlers from Togo, do not have paramountsy and thus cannot own property. The Nawuris and Nchumuris are also not indigenous to the region and cannot own land. The Kokumbas, Nawuris and Nchumuris all object to this landowning policy, claiming that they were the original inhabitants of the region before the British colonial period.

Rawlings sent army troops to the north to quell the violence. Water distribution, schools, banking and health services all became paralyzed. The government responded to the crisis by declaring a state of emergency and setting up a committee of cabinet ministers and chiefs to organize relief efforts and restore order.

In March, after a short period of calm, ethnic violence again exploded when a mob of Dagomba youths besieged the Agricultural Development Bank, threatening to lynch a Kokumba man who had entered the bank to cash a check. After unsuccessfully trying to disperse the mob with peaceful means, soldiers fired into the crowd, killing fourteen people and wounding fifteen.

In June the seven ethnic groups signed a cease-fire accord. The Ghanaian parliament continued the state of emergency, however, because of isolated clashes. The state of emergency was finally lifted in mid-August. In total, as a result of the 1994 ethnic clashes, 1,000 people were killed and 150,000 were displaced, many of whom fled to neighboring Togo.

In April the Ghanaian intelligence service exposed a coup plot that had been scheduled to take place that month. Alleged death threats on two private newspaper editors were revealed to be part of the coup plan, a ploy of diversion. While it remained uncertain who was behind the plot, intelligence officials stated that retired service personnel and exiled politicians were likely suspects.

The second highest contributor to the peace effort in war-torn neighboring Liberia, Ghana threatened in June to withdraw its troops from the region, claiming that the military involvement was draining its resources. In August, however, Ghana became even more immersed in the Liberian civil war when Rawlings became the new chairman of the Economic Community of West-African States (ECOWAS) and arranged a series of negotiations among the seven warring Liberian factions aimed at enacting the Akosombo peace accord. Despite Rawling's efforts, the negotiations proved unsuccessful.

Relations between Ghana and Togo remained tense, the Togo government accusing Rawlings of harboring Togolese opposition and aiding them militarily. In November, relations between the two nations improved with the appointment of an Ghanaian ambassador to Togo. The Ghanaian mission had previously been run by a charge d'affaires.

Political Rights and Civil Liberties:

Despite multiparty elections in 1992 and the introduction in 1993 of a constitution that guarantees the right to elect and be elected to public office, Ghanaians still lack the means to change their government democratically. Although international observers declared the November 1992 presidential elections free and fair, the opposition provided a long list of abuses before and during the election.

Two types of courts exist in Ghana: the traditional common law courts, based on the British model, and the people's tribunals set up by Rawlings in 1982. Both are subject to government control and interference. The common courts are composed of legal professionals and follow a lengthy practice of due process, but the tribunals restrict the procedural rights of defendants and are staffed with appointees with little or no experience in legal matters. There is no appeal from their verdicts, which include the death penalty. Prisons are overcrowded and, as a result, have poor security. In 1994, there was a particularly high incidence of jail breaks.

Freedoms of speech and assembly remain circumscribed. The government controls broadcast media and the major newspapers. Ghana's private press, the main voice of the opposition, faces harassment and financial difficulties. In December 1993, Isaac Frimpong, the armed forces sergeant-major, stated to a several private newspapers that since there was freedom of speech in Ghana, there should also be freedom of beatings and assassinations. After that infamous remark, various top government officials, including the first lady, also denounced the private press. Such high-level government condemnation often led to self-censorship. Nonetheless, private newspapers remained active, and stories were printed which unleashed scandals aimed at embarrassing the government. In January 1994, for example, the independent *Free Press* made allegations about the first lady's hedonistic sexual exploits.

Freedom of religion is generally respected in this predominantly Christian country, which also has a sizable Muslim minority. As one of its final acts, the PNDC abolished the Religious Bodies Registration Law, which restricted the full exercise of religious practices by the Jehova's Witnesses and the Mormons.

Trade unions are still governed by a 1965 law that grants the government broad regulatory powers over their registration and activities. In recent years, however, the once PNDC-affiliated Trade Union Congress (TUC) became more independent and active on behalf of its members. Although Ghanaians are generally free to travel within and outside the country, members of the opposition are often denied the right.

In April 1994 the government drafted a bill to outlaw female circumcision. In certain parts of the Volta region, the *trokosi* system is still in effect: Young girls are forced to almost a lifetime of servitude at fetish houses in order to atone for the misdeeds of relatives.

Greece

Polity: Parliamentary democracy
Economy: Mixed capitalist
Population: 10,380,000
PPP: $7,680
Life Expectancy: 77.3
Ethnic Groups: Overwhelmingly Greek with Macedonian and Turkish minorities

Political Rights: 1
Civil Liberties: 3
Status: Free

Overview: In 1994 Greece placed a trade embargo on neighboring Macedonia in order to pressure the former Yugoslav republic to change its name and guarantee that it will make no claims on Greek territory. The action received strong criticism from the European Union (EU), which took the case to the European Court of Justice in April. Relations with Albania also deteriorated over the issue of the treatment of the Greek minority in that country.

Located on the southern tip of the Balkan peninsula, Greece fought for independence from the Ottoman Empire in the 1820s and 1830s. After its victory, the country became a monarchy in 1835. In a series of wars in the early twentieth century, Greece increased its territory in Europe. Following the Axis occupation in World War II, civil war broke out between Communist and royalist forces. With Western aid, the constitutional monarchy prevailed. In 1967, a military junta took control and held power until 1974, when the country returned to parliamentary democracy, but without the monarchy.

The Greek parliamentarians serve a maximum term of four years. The political party or coalition that wins a majority of seats forms the government. The parliament elects the president, who is largely a ceremonial figure. In the October 1993 general election, former Prime Minister Andreas Papandreou and his Pan-Hellenic Socialist Movement (Pasok) defeated Constantine Mitsotakis's New Democracy Party and returned to power.

Upon election, Papandreou reversed many of Mitsotakis's privatization reforms. In order to make up for the revenue loss, he cracked down on tax evaders, who constitute as much as 40 percent of the population. The tax collectors, however, are often corrupt, and Athenian shopkeepers resent being major targets of the new policy. Papandreou also renationalized public transportation and ended the privatization of telecommunications.

Papandreou's efforts at reform failed to end Greece's six-year-old economic recession. In 1994, Papandreou took a turn back to privatization by re-appointing the same international investment bankers who had previously served as privatization advisers during the Mitsotakis adminstration. The government also made plans to partially reprivatize the telecommunications system. In November, however, the government decided to postpone this reprivatization until 1995.

On 16 February Greece suspended its diplomatic relations with Macedonia and cut off its main trade route, Salonica. Greece threatened to maintain the embargo until Macedonia agreed to change its name and flag. The Greek government felt that Macedonia's name choice implied a desire to control the Greek province of the same name. Furthermore, the Macedonian flag, which displayed a sun symbol associated with Alexander the Great, was also perceived by Greece as a territorial threat. The conflict over land dates back to the 1946-1949 Greek civil war. Thousands of Macedonians were driven from Greece into the Yugoslav republic when Athens confiscated land belonging to Communist fighters.

The EU criticized the trade embargo and accused Greece of violating the Treaty of Rome, which provides for the free circulation of goods inside the EU. According to EU rules, a country's border may be closed only if there is a security threat to one of the member nations and if all its members act together.

Despite pressure from the EU, Greece refused to end the blockade. In April, the EU's executive agency, the European Commission (EC), took the case to the European Court of Justice. The court, however, refused the Commission's request for an emergency interim ruling to force Greece to end the blockade.

Issues of land ownership and minority rights also fueled the conflict between Greece and neighboring Albania. The Greek minority in Albania lives in a region in a southern part of the country that Greeks call "northern Epirus." Greece and Albania cannot agree on the actual size of the Greek minority; Greece asserts that there are 300,000 of these "ethnic Greeks," while Albania claims that there are only 70,000. Greeks allege that Albania victimizes its Greek minority.

In August, Albanian police arrested five ethnic Greeks accused of working with the Greek Intelligence Service to encourage a Greek separatist movement in Albania. On 7 September, an Albanian court sentenced the five men to serve between six and eight years in jail. The trial provoked an angry response from Greece. In August and September, Greece deported 45,000 Albanians, most of whom were illegal aliens. On 9 September, Greece closed a major border-crossing with Albania.

In September, the Greek parliament indicted former Prime Minister Mitsotakis on charges of bribery and breach of trust in the 1992 sale of a cement company. Mitsotakis denied the charges, accusing the ruling Socialist party of manipulating the case for political purposes. Earlier in the year, Mitsotakis was charged with having authorized wiretaps and with having stolen archeological antiquities during his administration.

The ruling Socialist party suffered losses in the 15 October local elections. The New Democracy Party came out ahead in the major cities, but the socialists retained popularity in the rural areas.

Political Rights and Civil Liberties: The citizens of Greece have the right to change their government by democratic means. Voting is compulsory for people aged eighteen to seventy. The bureaucracy is so cumbersome that when people move, they do not transfer their voting addresses. Consequently, about 650,000 people needed holidays around the 1993 general election to go back to vote in their old home towns and villages.

The media have substantial freedom, but there are several politically related restrictions. In 1994, strict self-censorship by Greek television and newspapers suppressed information concerning Papandreous's weakening health, including the fact that the seventy-six-year-old prime minister could only work a few hours a day. The media also censored debate over whether the ailing prime minister should retire and allow a younger leader to take his place. Publications deemed offensive to the president or to religious beliefs may be seized by order of the public prosecutor. Greece also has a controversial law that bans "unwarranted" publicity for terrorists, including terrorists' proclamations after explosions.

There is freedom of association and all workers except the military and the police have the right to form and join unions. Unions are linked to political parties, but are independent of party and government control. Strikes against the government are permitted. In May 1994 culture ministry employees shut down the Acropolis, the nation's most important tourist attraction, in a strike for higher pay.

Greece refuses to acknowledge the presence of a Macedonian minority in the country, instead referring to them as "Slav speakers." The minority faces obstacles in trying to preserve its language and cultural traditions.

Greek Orthodoxy is the state religion and claims 98 percent of the population, at least nominally. The Orthodox bishops have the privilege of granting or denying permission to other faiths to build houses of worship in their jurisdictions. The constitution prohibits proselytizing by religious groups. Sometimes police arrest Jehovah's Witnesses for seeking converts. Despite objections from Catholics, Jews, Muslims and other religious minorities, national identity cards, required since 1992, list each person's religion. Greece offers non-combatant military service, but does not provide a non-military alternative to the universal conscription of men for national service. Jehovah's Witnesses and others who refuse to serve can be tried and sentenced to three-to-five-year terms in military prisons.

The Turkish Muslim minority, whose religious rights were guaranteed under the 1923 Treaty of Lausanne, objects to the Greek government's choosing the *mufti*, the leader of the Muslim community. The state prevents Muslims from controlling their own charities.

The Greek government places severe restrictions on former King Constantine. When he returned to Greece on a family vacation, all major parties denounced the trip, as Constantine is prohibited from visiting populated areas. The government had two missile boats and a plane tail him during his journey. In April 1994, Constantine declared to the government that he would use any lawful means to retain his Greek citizenship.

The Greek parliament abolished the death penalty in December 1993.

Grenada

Polity: Parliamentary democracy
Economy: Capitalist-statist
Population: 94,000
PPP: $3,374
Life Expectancy: 70.0
Ethnic Groups: Mostly black

Political Rights: 1
Civil Liberties: 2
Status: Free

Overview: **P**rime Minister Nicholas Braithwaite resigned as head of the ruling National Democratic Congress (NDC) in August 1994 and was replaced by George Brizan. With elections due by March 1995, no less than seven political parties were in the running, underscoring the fragmented nature of Grenadian politics.

Grenada, a member of the British Commonwealth, is a parliamentary democracy. The British monarchy is represented by a governor-general. The Caribbean island state became self-governing in 1958 and gained independence in 1974. The nation includes the islands of Carriacou and Petit Martinique.

Prime Minister Eric Gairy was overthrown in a 1979 coup by Maurice Bishop's Marxist New Jewel Movement. In October 1983, Prime Minister Bishop was murdered by New Jewel hardliners. Bernard Coard and General Hudson Austin took control of the country and declared martial law. Sir Paul Scoon, the governor-general and the only duly constituted executive authority in the country, formally asked for international assistance. A joint U.S.-Caribbean military intervention removed Coard and Austin, and Scoon formed an advisory council to act as an interim administration.

In the 1984 elections the New National Party (NNP) of Herbert Blaize defeated Gairy's rightist Grenada United Labour Party (GULP). The NNP, a coalition of three parties, took fourteen of fifteen seats in the House of Representatives. The bicameral parliament also consists of an appointed Senate, with ten members appointed by the prime minister and three by the leader of the parliamentary opposition.

In 1989 the NNP coalition unraveled, leaving Prime Minister Blaize with the support of only six representatives in the House. Blaize formed The National Party (TNP) from among remaining supporters. When he died in December 1989, he was replaced by his deputy, Ben Jones, and elections were called.

The five main contenders in the 1990 campaign were: the TNP, headed by Jones; the centrist National Democratic Congress (NDC), led by Nicholas Braithwaite, former head of the 1983-84 interim government; the New National Party (NNP), headed by Keith Mitchell; the leftist Maurice Bishop Patriotic Movement (MBPM) led by Terry Marryshow; and the GULP.

On 13 March 1990 the NDC won seven seats, the GULP four, and the NNP and TNP two each. After the GULP, NNP and TNP failed to form a coalition government, Braithwaite was appointed prime minister by the governor-general. One of the

GULP's winning candidates defected to the NDC, leaving the new government with a one-seat majority.

After taking office the Braithwaite government maintained a shaky parliamentary majority as it came under pressure from opposition parties and labor unions because of its structural adjustment and privatization programs. Polls in 1993 and 1994 indicated deepening popular discontent in the face of rising unemployment and general economic hardship.

In August 1994 Braithwaite announced his retirement as NDC chief, saying he had tired of political intrigues. Aides said he was also angered by corruption within the government. At the September NDC convention, agricultural minister George Brizan won the NDC leadership, narrowly defeating attorney general Francis Alexis in a hard-fought contest by a vote of 230 to 204. The question was whether Brizan could reunite the party in time for elections due by March 1995.

A poll conducted in October showed the NNP's Keith Mitchell leading with 25 percent, followed by Gairy, now in his seventies and blind, with 14 percent. Brizan came third, followed by the TNP's Ben Jones and Marryshow of the MBPM. About 40 percent remained undecided.

Political Rights and Civil Liberties:

Citizens are able to change their government through democratic elections. However, local analysts warned that many people were losing confidence in the political system because of fragmented politics and increased allegations of corruption. Constitutional guarantees regarding the right to organize political, labor or civic groups are generally respected.

There are numerous independent labor unions, but labor rights have come into question since 1993. A law passed in 1993 gives the government the right to set up a tribunal empowered to make "binding and final" rulings when a labor dispute is considered of vital interest to the state. The national trade union federation claimed the law was an infringement of the right to strike. The government countered that the law was pro-worker because it guaranteed the reinstatement of persons fired for trade union activities. In 1994 a union was formally recognized even though it did not have the necessary support of a majority of workers at the country's largest hotel.

The exercise of religion and the right of free expression are generally respected. Newspapers, including a number of weekly political party organs, are independent. Radio is operated by the government but open to independent voices. Television is independently operated.

There is an independent, nondiscriminatory judiciary whose authority is generally respected by the police. In 1991 Grenada rejoined the Organization of Eastern Caribbean States court system, with right of appeal to the Privy Council in London. The Braithwaite government set up a five-member committee, including independent public figures, to monitor worsening prison conditions. Like many Caribbean island nations, Grenada has suffered from a rise in violent drug-related crime, particularly among increasingly disaffected youth.

In 1986, after a two-year trial, thirteen men and one woman, including Bernard Coard and General Hudson Austin, were found guilty of the 1983 murder of Maurice Bishop and sentenced to death. In July 1991 the Grenada Court of Appeals turned aside the last of the defendants' appeals, and reports circulated that Coard and four others would be hanged. After a series of appeals by international human rights organizations, however, the government decided to commute the death sentences to life imprisonment for all fourteen defendants.

Guatemala

Polity: Presidential-leg- **Political Rights:** 4
islative democracy **Civil Liberties:** 5
(military-dominated) **Status:** Partly Free
(insurgencies)
Economy: Capitalist-statist
Population: 10,322,000
PPP: $3,180
Life Expectancy: 64.0
Ethnic Groups: Complex, more than 60 percent Mayan and other Indian
Trend Arrow: The down trend arrow is due to increasing political violence
and human rights abuses, and further weakening of civilian rule vis-à-vis
the military.

Overview: **A**s the military remained the final arbiter in how the nation
was run, President Ramiro de Leon Carpio seemed
powerless to respond to the worst levels of political
violence and human rights abuses in five years. Former dictator Efrain Rios Montt
(1982-83) returned to the fore as his political party made a strong showing in
congressional elections.

The Republic of Guatemala was established in 1839, eighteen years after
independence from Spain and following the breakup of the United Provinces of
Central America (1824-1838). The nation has endured a history of dictatorship,
coups d' état, and guerrilla insurgency, with only intermittent democratic government. After a thirty-year stretch of repressive military rule, Guatemala returned to
civilian government in 1985 with a new constitution and the election of President
Vinicio Cerezo of the Christian Democratic party.

Amended in 1994, the constitution provides for a four-year presidential term
and prohibits re-election. An eighty-member unicameral Congress is elected for
four years. The governors of twenty-two departments and the capital, Guatemala
City, are appointed by the president. Municipal governments are elected.

In the 1990 presidential campaign, the frontrunner was the tough-talking
retired Gen. Rios Montt, but he was ruled ineligible because the constitution bars
former dictators from returning to power.

Jorge Serrano, a right-wing businessman, inherited Rios Montt's following. In
the November 1990 election Serrano ran second to newspaper publisher Jorge
Carpio Nicolle of the National Centrist Union (UCN). In the January 1991 runoff
Serrano handily defeated Carpio.

In May 1993 Serrano, backed by the military, dissolved the congress and fired
the Supreme Court. Amid mass protests and threats of economic isolation by the
U.S. and the Organization of American States (OAS) that frightened conservative
economic elites, the military changed its position. The military sent Serrano
packing to Panama. The congress, under pressure from an alliance of unions,
business sector moderates and civic groups, chose as president de Leon Carpio, the
government human rights ombudsman.

De Leon Carpio, who took office vowing to purge the government of corruption, demanded the resignation of the congress and Supreme Court. They refused, setting off an institutional crisis. Amid rumors of a military coup, de Leon Carpio ended up cutting a deal with congress on a package of constitutional reforms that would lead to elections in mid-1994 for an interim congress which would appoint a new Supreme Court.

The reforms were passed in a national referendum in January 1994, but many in the broad alliance that helped bring de Leon to office labelled the reforms a sell-out, and only 15.85 percent of the electorate voted. The military, satisfied that its interests were not threatened, and unaccountable and immune to popular demands that its power be curbed, went about its business of hunting the left-wing guerrillas of the Guatemalan National Revolutionary Unity (URNG).

In congressional elections held on 14 August, Rios Montt's Guatemalan Republican Front (FRG) won 32 of 80 seats in the new body. The conservative National Advance Party (PAN) won 24, the Christian Democratic party 13, the UCN seven, the National Liberation Movement (MLN) 3, and the Democratic Union (UD) 1. Only one of five eligible voters turned out. The interim congress will be replaced by a congress elected for a four-year term in November 1995.

In the 1994 campaign Rios Montt's law-and-order rhetoric appeared to strike a chord amid mounting criminal violence and persistent government corruption. It was clear he planned to use the congress as a platform for a presidential run in November 1995. On 2 December 1994 Rios Montt secured the support of the Christian Democrats, his arch-enemies less than a decade ago, to win the presidency of the congress. Three days later one of Rios Montt's closest aides was assassinated. The two events underscored the opportunism and violence at the heart of Guatemalan politics.

Meanwhile, U.N.-mediated talks between the URNG and the government resulted in an accord on human rights in April. Further talks stalled as political violence and rights abuses increased sharply thereafter. The military seemed intent on derailing peace negotiations at all costs. Talks started again with the arrival of a U.N. rights-monitoring mission at the end of the year. But by then the abuses and the violence, including bombings and clashes between protesters and security forces during a nine-day transport strike, had reached levels unprecedented in the last five years, and de Leon Carpio appeared weaker than at any time since taking office.

Political Rights and Civil Liberties: Citizens are able to change their governments through elections at the national and muncipal levels, but voter participation rates of less than 20 percent reflect a profound disillusionment with electoral politics. The powers granted to civilian administrations by the constitution are greatly restricted by the armed forces, the dominant institution in the country. The rule of law is undermined further by the endemic corruption that afflicts all public institutions, particularly the legislature and the courts.

The constitution guarantees religious freedom and the right to organize political parties, civic organizations and labor unions. There are more than a dozen political parties, from social democratic to radical right, most representing small interest groups.

However, political and civic expression is severely restricted by a climate of violence, lawlessness and military repression. Since President de Leon Carpio took office in 1993 there has been a dramatic increase in political and criminal violence including murder, disappearances, bombings and death threats. Politicians, student organizations, street children, peasant groups, labor unions, Indian organizations, human rights groups, and the media have all been targeted.

The principal human rights offenders are the 40,000-member military, particularly the intelligence unit; the rural network of paramilitary Self-Defense Patrols (PACs), which are an extension of the army and have about 500,000 members; the police (under military authority); and a network of killers-for-hire linked to the armed forces and right-wing political groups. There is also evidence that the military runs a network of clandestine jails in which people suspected of ties to the URNG guerrillas are tortured during interrogation.

President de Leon Carpio announced in 1993 that the dreaded Presidential Military Staff (EMP) was being "restructured." But the indications are that the unit was actually absorbed into military intelligence. In a dramatic sign of weakness, de Leon Carpio acceded to military pressure in April 1994 and named the head of military intelligence to the number-two post in the interior ministry, overseeing the police. In the last two years there has been a steady increase in rights violations and a reversion to systematic brutality—killings, abductions, torture, bombings. The principal targets were members of rights organizations and civic groups calling for political reform and the reigning in of the army. Guatemala remains one of the most dangerous places in Latin America for human rights activists.

In 1992 de Leon Carpio, then the official human rights ombudsman, characterized the situation as "a government without the power to stop impunity." Unfortunately, there has been little improvement since then. Those few judges who have brought the first successful prosecutions against members of the security forces for rights violations—usually cases where great international pressure was applied—have been targets of death threats. The respected president of the Constitutional Court, the highest court in the land, was murdered outside his home in April 1994 in a case still unresolved by the end of the year.

One question was whether penal code reforms implemented in mid-1994 would make the judicial system something other than a virtual black hole for most legal or human rights complaints. Reforms included trying soldiers accused of common crimes in civilian rather than military courts. But most civil courts remained corrupted and politicized. In October 1994 a new Supreme Court was seated, its thirteen members chosen by the narrow majority of the anti-Rios Montt bloc in the newly elected congress.

The Runejel Junam Council of Ethnic Communities (CERJ) is an advocate for the country's Indians, a majority of the population and probably the most segregated and oppressed indigenous community in the Western hemisphere. CERJ is a principal advocate of dismantling the PACs, which are a violation of the constitutional article that states no individual can be forced to join any type of civil-defense organization.

Labor unions have the right to strike. But they are frequently denied the right to organize and subjected to mass firings and blacklisting, particularly in export-processing zones where a majority of workers are women. Unions were also targets of systematic intimidation, physical attacks and assassination, particularly in rural areas during the increasing numbers of land disputes in 1994. The International Confederation of Free Trade Unions classifies Guatemala as among the ten most dangerous countries in the world for trade unionists. Child labor is a growing problem in the agricultural industry.

The press and most of the broadcast media are privately owned. There are several independent newspapers and dozens of radio stations, most of them commercial. Five of six television stations are commercially operated. However, journalists are at great risk. In 1994 three were murdered, thirty-six more suffered physical attacks, and eight media outlets were attacked in a number of ways including bombings. Numerous others received threats. The 1993 murder of former presidential candidate and newspaper publisher Jorge Carpio Nicolle, de Leon's cousin, remained unresolved in 1994. Carpio's relatives who claimed it was a politically motivated murder received death threats, forcing some to leave the country. In recent years at least fifteen Guatemalan journalists have been forced into exile.

Guinea

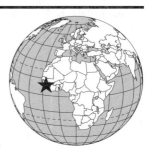

Polity: Military (transitional)
Economy: Capitalist
Population: 6,392,000
PPP: $500
Life Expectancy: 43.9
Ethnic Groups: Fulani (35 percent), Malinke (25 percent), Susu (15 percent), others

Political Rights: 6
Civil Liberties: 5
Status: Not Free

Overview: In 1994, Guinea's military ruler, Gen. Lasana Conté, excluded the opposition when, eight months after his election, he formed the new government.

Under the leadership of Ahmed Sekou Touré, Guinea declared independence from France in 1958. Touré ruled the country until his death in 1984. Three days after he died, a group of army officers under the leadership of Lasana Conté took power in a coup.

In October 1989, Conté promised to bring multiparty democracy to Guinea. In December 1990, Guineans approved a new constitution, which calls for a presidential system and a unicameral legislature to be set up within five years.

In April 1992, when the new constitution went into effect, political parties were legalized. Legislative elections were scheduled for 27 December 1992, but two weeks prior to the election date Conté bowed to the demands of the opposition for their postponement.

By the end of 1993, forty-three political parties, mostly ethnic based, were registered. Of the three largest parties, members of the pro-Conté Party of Unity and Progress (PUP) are largely Susu, those of the Union for the New Republic (UNR) are predominantly Fulani, and members of the Rally of the Guinean People (RPG), led by charismatic former exile, Alpha Condé, are almost entirely Malinke.

Guinea's first presidential elections, which took place on 19 December 1993, were preceded by mass rallies and violent demonstrations. The opposition parties protested against Conté's single-handedness in determining the electoral process. Following the vote, the Interior Ministry declared Conte the winner with 50.93 percent of the vote. Condé finished second with 20.85 percent of the vote.

On 29 January 1994, Conté was officially sworn in as president. The ceremony was boycotted by the opposition, who refused to accept the results, claiming electoral rigging.

The first eight months after the election were marked by political deadlock. Conté left the old government in place until August. During that period, the twenty-three old cabinet ministers remained inactive, as they did know when they would finally be replaced.

In May, several senior military officers were detained for allegedly plotting to overthrow the government. The officers, who denied the charges, were released on 16 June.

Protests flared in August when Conté finally announced the new cabinet, which included no members of the opposition. Although disappointing to the opposition, Conté's appointments were no great surprise, since he had stated in January that if he formed a government including people from all political trends, his administration would run the risk of being taken hostage. After the appointments were made, vigorous campaigning began for the parliamentary elections, the dates of which have yet to be scheduled.

While meeting party supporters in Upper Guinea, opposition leader Condé narrowly escaped an assassination attempt by the government. September brought further difficulties to the RPG when its deputy secretary general, Ahmed Tidiane Cisse, resigned, causing a split in the party. Cisse left the party because he objected to Condé's authoritarian leadership.

In 1994, Guinean military forces engaged in U.N. peacekeeping missions in Rwanda, Liberia, Sierra Leone and Western Sahara. Violence in Liberia spilled over into Guinea throughout the year. In June thirty Guineans were killed when Liberian fighters launched an attack on the Guinean border town of Koyama. Guinea had previously closed all borders with Liberia in 1993 following an attack in which many civilians were killed. Thousands of Liberian refugees have escaped into Guinea during the course of the civil war.

A cholera epidemic struck 3,000 Guineans in 1994. In August, the European Union (EU) donated money to build three medical centers to deal with the epidemic.

Political Rights and Civil Liberties:

Both the government's high-handedness in controlling the December 1993 elections and President Conté's refusal to include the opposition in his new cabinet impeded Guineans' right to change their government democratically.

The judiciary lacks independence from executive government interference. The judges are employed as civil servants and have no guarantee of tenure. The courts often defer to government authorities in politically sensitive cases. In addition, the lower court judges are often poorly trained, and there is a shortage of practicing attorneys. Corruption and nepotism are extensive. Minor cases are often handled by customary courts presided over by village chiefs or wisemen. Prison conditions are poor; torture and ill treatment of prisoners are prevalent.

A recent press law restricts the dissemination of information and the free flow of ideas. The law permits the arrest of journalists and editors in cases of vaguely defined defamation and slander, including anything offensive to the president, disturbance of peace and incitement to violence or racial and ethnic hatred. In 1993, the Human Rights Association expressed concern about physical threats against journalists by supporters of the ruling and opposition parties. In September 1994 Guinea radio broadcast reports that made references to clashes between soldiers and the opposition. It was the first time that the government-controlled radio admitted that these types of clashes take place.

Government authorization is required for public gatherings and, under Article 22 of the constitution, when there is a doubt about state security or when there is a threat of violence, the central government or a local authority has the right to ban demonstrations. In August 1994, the military fired shots in the air and used tear gas to break up a public demonstration organized by the RPG.

The government encourages the formation of nonpolitical and non-ethnic-based organizations. Freedom of movement is largely respected, although the government may withhold the passports of opposition activists. Women, except those who are financially independent, must obtain permission from a male family member in order to travel.

Freedom of religion is respected, and the constitution states that the country is a secular republic. Muslim and Christian holidays are observed by the state, however, and the state media provide Muslim and Christian broadcasts.

Since 1988, workers have had the right to form and join independent trade unions. The strongest trade union remains what was the only official National Confederation of Guinea (UGTG). In February 1993, thirty-three associations formed the National Federation of Guinean Unions and Associations (FNUAG). Its founders specifically rejected union involvement in politics and promised to concentrate on advocating communal welfare and economic development for its members.

Guinea-Bissau

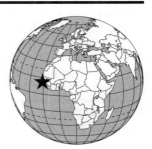

Polity: Presidential-parliamentary democracy
Economy: Mixed statist transitional
Population: 1,050,000
PPP: $747
Life Expectancy: 42.9
Ethnic Groups: Balanta, Fulani, Malinke, Mandjague, as well as mulatto, Moorish, Lebanese and Portugese minorities
Ratings Change: *Guinea-Bissau's political rights rating changed from 6 to 3 and its civil liberties rating from 5 to 4 because of a peaceful and fair election—the first in its history.

Political Rights: 3*
Civil Liberties: 4*
Status: Partly Free

Overview:

In 1994 Guinea-Bissau's fourteen-year ruler, General Joao Bernardo Vieira, was declared the winner in the country's first democratic multiparty elections. Despite several chaotic irregularities and delays in the electoral process, Guineans held an election that was generally fair and peaceful.

Guinea-Bissau won independence from Portugal in 1973. The current president, Joao Bernardo Vieira, came to power in 1980, in a coup that overthrew the country's first civilian president, Luis de Almeda Cabral. The 1984 constitution codified the supremacy of Vieira's African Party for the Independence of Guinea-Bissau and Cape Verde (PAIGC). In 1989 Vieira won another five-year term in an indirect election.

At a party congress in January 1991, the PAIGC formally ended its role as the single official party. The leadership concluded that it had to allow political pluralism in order to receive Western investments needed for its economic liberalization program. The congress voted to propose a thorough constitutional revision.

In May 1991 the National Assembly passed a law legalizing political parties. At first, the regime proposed a three-year transition to multipartyism, with elections at the end of 1993. In March 1992 the timetable was moved forward; the presidential election was slated for 15 November, and legislative elections for 13 December. Despite opposition protest, the government postponed the elections until March 1993, and again until 27 March 1994. Three weeks before the election, the opposition called for a futher postponement, as the electoral census had not even begun. This census, the first of its kind in the country's history, was completed on 23 April.

On 5 May six major opposition groups formed an alliance as a strategy to defeat Vieira. The alliance chose as their single candidate Kumba Ialla, the charismatic leader of the Party of Social Renovation (PRS). Throughout his campaign, Ialla stressed the need for change, in particular the need to revitalize the debt-ridden economy. In 1994 Guinea-Bissau's national debt was three times greater than its GDP.

National elections began on 3 July. Eight candidates ran for president, and 1,136 candidates ran for the 100-seat Parliament. Thirteen political parties had registered for the election.

In many voting locations, the National Election Commission (CNE) failed to distribute election materials, causing delayed poll openings. In an attempt to salvage the integrity of the election, the CNE mobilized civilians to distribute the materials voluntarily. Despite the civilian effort, ten voting booths opened so late that the voting had to be extended to the following day.

Torrential rains failed to dampen the determination of the 400,000 Guineans who turned out to cast their ballots. Guineans used campaign posters as raincoats, and many went all day without food or drink waiting to vote. Voters were educated on the electoral process by cartoon posters, funded, ironically, by the Chinese government.

The PAIGC won a majority in Parliament, but Vieira fell short of a majority in the presidential race, winning only 46 percent of the vote. Yalla came in second, winning 22 percent. A run-off election between the two candidates was scheduled for 7 August. The opposition, which had previously suspected electoral rigging, accepted the results as legitimate. The U.N.'s observer mission also pronounced the election free and fair.

The second round was better organized; most of the voting was completed by midday. Vieira won the election, capturing 51 percent of the vote. Ialla was elected as a member of the Parliament. Vieira received most of his support from the rural areas, while Ialla won a majority in the capital, Bissau. At first, Ialla refused to accept the results, claiming that Vieira had bought votes. He finally conceded his defeat on 20 August.

Political Rights and Civil Liberties:

As shown for the first time in 1994, citizens of Guinea Bissau are able to hold democratic elections. The long-ruling party continues to stay in power, but the opposition is gaining political strength.

The judiciary remains a part of the executive branch, and the regime retains the arbitrary power to detain individuals suspected of antigovernment activities. Political trials are held in secret by military tribunals. Arrests and the conduct of trials in civil and criminal cases are often arbitrary, due to executive interference and the lack of qualified judges. In rural areas, customary law prevails.

Freedoms of assembly and expression have recently become more open. In the 1994 election campaign, political parties were allowed to hold rallies. In one PRS-sponsored campaign rally, opposition candidate Kouamba Iala was able to publicly denounced the PAIGC without any government interference.

Despite the establishment of two independent newspapers in recent years, freedom of speech and freedom of the press remain curtailed; journalists rarely directly criticize the president or high government officials, unless the latter lose the former's favor. There is no daily newspaper. Because of the 80 percent illiteracy rate and sparse distribution of newspapers, the population relies more on radio for information. The broadcast media have become more bold in criticizing specific government policies and in giving coverage to the opposition.

Although religious groups must be registered by the government, freedom of worship is respected. Proselytizing is permitted and no religious group has been denied registration since 1982. The major religions are Christianity, Islam and Animism.

Despite the existence of informal police checkpoints on major roads to monitor the movement of people and goods, Guinea-Bissauians enjoy the right to unhindered travel within the country. Although there are no legal restrictions on foreign travel or emigration, in 1994 there were reports of political opposition leaders who were prevented from leaving the country.

Until 1992, the only labor union in existence was the National Trade Union Confederation (UNTG), which had close ties to the ruling party. Since then, several branch unions have broken away from the UNTG and pressed the government to negotiate with them directly, forcing the Confederation leadership to pursue workers' interests more closely. The government limits citizens' right to strike. In February 1994, the National Union of Teachers held a five-day strike, demanding better working conditions and salary increases. The government condemned the strike and threatened to use violence to force the teachers to go back to work. Luis Nacassa, the union leader, was arrested without legal notice for initiating what the government called the "illegal strike."

Guyana

Polity: Parliamentary democracy
Economy: Mixed statist
Population: 825,000
PPP: $1,862
Life Expectancy: 64.6
Ethnic Groups: Complex, East Indian (52 percent), black (36 percent), mixed (5 percent), Amerindian (4 percent), and the remainder European

Political Rights: 2
Civil Liberties: 2
Status: Free

Overview: The ruling People's Progressive Party/Civic alliance (PPP-Civic) fared well in the first local elections held since 1976. But Hamilton Green, a former leader of the opposition People's National Congress (PNC) now heading his own party, won the mayoralty of Georgetown, the nation's capital.

A member of the British Commonwealth, Guyana was ruled from independence in 1966 until 1992 by the black-based PNC. Under President Forbes Burnham (1964-85), Guyana was designated a socialist "cooperative republic" and the PNC retained power through fraudulent elections and repression. In 1980 Burnham installed a constitution that provides for a president with strong powers and a sixty-five-seat National Assembly elected every five years. Twelve seats are occupied by locally elected officials.

After Burnham died in 1985, the PNC's Desmond Hoyte became president and was reelected to a full term in a fraudulent election. With the statist economy in shambles, Hoyte began restructuring and seeking Western assistance.

In 1990 key U.S legislators and international human rights organizations convinced Washington to tie economic assistance to political reform. As the Guyanese opposition stepped up demands for free elections, Canada and Great Britain also applied pressure.

Cheddi Jagan's East Indian-based, Marxist PPP, the social democratic Working People's Alliance (WPA) and three smaller parties joined in the Patriotic Coalition for Democracy (PCD). A civic movement, the Guyanese Action for Reform and Democracy (GUARD), was formed, backed by the Anglican and Catholic churches, the Guyanese Human Rights Association (GHRA), independent labor unions and business and professional groups.

Hoyte gave ground in 1990 when he asked the Council of Freely Elected Heads of Government, headed by former U.S. President Jimmy Carter, to help with electoral reform. Carter brokered two major changes demanded by the opposition—a new voter registry and a revamped election commission. Hoyte agreed to election-monitoring by Carter's group and a Commonwealth team.

After two postponements, two election commissions and two efforts to create a valid voter registry, the vote was finally scheduled for 5 October 1992. In the campaign, Hoyte touted recent economic growth and promised improved living conditions. But the social costs of the PNC's austerity program in what was already one of the poorest countries in the Western hemisphere had been severe.

Jagan believed the PPP could win on its own and the PCD unraveled. Jagan, who had moderated his Marxist rhetoric since the collapse of communism, presented himself as a democrat and formed an alliance, PPP-Civic, with some noted civic figures. As always, race looked to be a key factor. Since the first elections under internal self-rule in the 1950s, the PNC and the PPP leaned on *apan jhaat*, a Hindi expression meaning "vote your race." With Indo-Guyanese outnumbering Afro-Guyanese by nearly 20 percent, the PPP won every election until 1964, when Burnham won, thanks to the covert assistance of London and Washington.

The WPA, the only mixed-race party in the country, campaigned on a platform of multiracial cooperation. It was also the only party other than the PPP and PNC to run a full slate of candidates. As expected, the Indo-Guyanese majority turned out for Jagan. The PNC orchestrated violent disturbances, apparently trying to establish a pretext for annulling the vote. But Carter and the Commonwealth observers pressed Hoyte to call off the PNC cadres and the vote count was completed.

Jagan was elected president with 52 percent of the vote, as Hoyte took 41 percent, percentages that mirror the country's racial composition. The WPA message was lost amid the racial polarization as its candidate, economist Clive Thomas, won less than 2 percent. In the legislature, the PPP won 36 of 65 seats, the PNC took 26, the WPA 2, and the centrist United Force (UF), one.

Jagan promised the PPP would not seek revenge against the former rulers. And, despite charges of discrimination by the PNC, Jagan has governed in a relatively evenhanded manner. Meanwhile, the electoral loss led to severe infighting within the PNC and the expulsion in 1993 of former prime minister Hamilton Green, who apparently had been behind the riots on election day.

Jagan oversaw new electoral reforms, supported by the main political parties, which paved the way for municipal and local elections held 8 August 1994, the first since 1976. PPP-Civic won forty-eight of sixty-five neighborhhod councils and three of six municipalities. But in the capital, the Good and Green for Georgetown (GGG) movement surprised by winning twelve of thirty city council seats. When the PNC, with ten seats, and the PPP-Civic, with eight, could not agree on a rival candidate, Hamilton Green became mayor.

Political Rights and Civil Liberties:

Citizens are able to change their government through elections. However, the 1980 constitution gives the president of the country inordinate powers. The incoming PPP-Civic promised to reform the constitution to make it more democratic. In 1993 it negotiated with opposition parties an amendment that allows for a broader and more independent electoral commission. But not until late 1994 did the government offer a draft proposal for deeper reforms.

The rights of free expression, freedom of religion and the freedom to organize political parties, civic organizations and labor unions are generally respected. However, without more explicit constitutional guarantees, political rights and civil liberties rest more on government tolerance than institutional protection.

The judicial system remains understaffed and underfunded. In 1994 the government proposed to establish courts headed by community-backed citizens to hear minor and civil claims. Prisons are overcrowded and the conditions deplorable.

The police force remains ill-trained and vulnerable to corruption, particularly given the penetration of the hemispheric drug trade into Guyana. There were continued reports of police brutality in 1994. The Guyana Human Rights Association (GHRA) is independent, effective and backed by independent civic and religious groups.

Domestic violence against women and the government's reluctance to address the issue are a cause for concern.

Although racial clashes have diminished since the 1992 election, long-standing animosity between blacks and Indo-Guyanese remains. The Jagan government took steps to form a multiparty race relations committee to promote tolerance.

Labor unions are well organized, and the right to strike is generally respected. Public sector unions, which tend to be PNC-linked, crippled state operations in May 1994 during a six-day shutdown. Agricultural unions are mostly allied with the PPP.

There are a number of independent newspapers that operate relatively freely, including the *Stabroek News* and the *Catholic Standard*, an outspoken church weekly. Television and radio are mostly controlled by the government, but allow for far more pluralism than under the former PNC regime. Aside from government-controlled television there are a number of stations that rely primarily on foreign programming via satellite.

The 40,000 Amerindians residing in the interior of the country were either shunned or repressed under the PNC. President Jagan created a cabinet ministry of indigenous affairs, and in 1994 proposed a development plan to address the social concerns of Amerindians. But the three main Amerindian organizations continued to demand more land and local control.

Haiti

Polity: Presidential-par-
liamentary democracy
Economy: Capitalist-
statist
Population: 7,035,000
PPP: $925
Life Expectancy: 56.0
Ethnic Groups: Black (majority) and mulatto
Ratings Change: *Haiti's political rights rating changed from
7 to 5 and its civil liberties rating from 7 to 5 reflecting the
improvement in conditions following the U.S. intervention and
the restoration of the elected government.

Political Rights: 5*
Civil Liberties: 5*
Status: Partly Free

Overview: **F**aced with an imminent U.S. invasion in September, the
military junta agreed to step down, paving the way for the return
of President Jean-Bertrand Aristide. Haiti's institutions and
economy were devastated under military rule, and there remained enormous challenges
and pitfalls for Aristide, the U.S. and the U.N. as they sought to rebuild the nation.

Since gaining independence following a slave revolt in 1804, the Republic of Haiti
has endured a history of poverty, violence, instability and dictatorship. A February 1986
military coup ended twenty-nine years of rule by the Duvalier family, but the army ruled
directly or indirectly for the next five years, often in collusion with remnants of the
Tontons Macoute, the sinister paramilitary organization of the Duvaliers.

Under international pressure, the military allowed for the election of a constituent
assembly that drafted a democratic constitution that was approved in a 1987 referendum.
Elections were aborted amid the mass killing of voters. In 1990 the military gave way to
a provisional government, which reinstated the constitution and called for elections.

The 1987 constitution provides for a president directly elected for five years, an
elected parliament composed of a twenty-seven-member Senate and an eighty-three-
member House of Representatives, and a prime minister appointed by the president.

In the internationally monitored December 1990 elections, Aristide, a charismatic left-wing priest, took 67 percent of the vote in a landslide over Marc Bazin, a
former World Bank official.

Aristide formed a government from among loyal but politically inexperienced
associates, and initiated a program to strengthen the judicial system, establish
civilian authority over the military and end corruption. The result was a dramatic
reduction in political violence and greater respect for political rights and civil
liberties than at any other time in the nation's history.

Haiti's mostly mulatto elites were furious over Aristide's bid to end their
control over the economy. The military, used to enriching itself through graft,
contraband and drug-trafficking, opposed Aristide's effort to create a civilian-led
police force, as required by the constitution.

Aristide on occasion overstepped his constitutional authority by calling on supporters to defend the government through violent means. When Aristide returned from a trip

abroad in September 1991 there were unmistakeable signs that the military was preparing to overthrow him. He suggested in a speech that supporters prepare to dispatch government opponents by "necklacing," burning tires around their necks.

Aristide was overthrown on 30 September 1991 and narrowly escaped from the country. Over the next three years Haitians were subjected to severe repression and the consequences of ever tighter international economic sanctions. There were two civilian puppet presidents, but the true rulers were the military triumvirate of Gen. Raoul Cedras, Gen. Philippe Biamby and Lt. Col. Michel François.

In 1993 the U.S. and the U.N. imposed a global trade and oil embargo. The military agreed to negotiate with Aristide, but reneged on an accord for his return by unleashing the *attaches*, a military-sponsored network of tens of thousands of armed civilian thugs that, for Haitians, was the second coming of the Tontons Macoute. The military then built a political base by creating an armed front group headed by avowed Duvalierists called the Front for the Advancement and Progress of Haiti (FRAPH).

In 1994 the Clinton administration, pressured by Aristide supporters in the U.S. and the tide of Haitian refugees, tried to get the junta to negotiate again by tightening economic sanctions. When the junta did not budge, the U.S. began a military buildup in the Caribbean and prepared for invasion. Soon after an ultimatim by Clinton in September an invasion was underway.

Facing imminent invasion, Cedras and Biamby came to a last-minute agreement on 18 September with a U.S. delegation headed by former U.S. President Jimmy Carter. They agreed to step down by 15 October in exchange for a vaguely described amnesty. They also agreed to a U.S. military presence during Aristide's restoration.

U.S. troops took control of the country with little resistance and within weeks violence by junta supporters had tailed off. François resigned on 4 October and left for the neighboring Dominican Republic. The parliament reconvened and approved an amnesty for political offenses, but not for crimes like murder, rape, torture and other human rights abuses. Facing potential prosecution, Cedras and Biamby resigned on 10 October and went to Panama.

Aristide returned on 15 October amid a great outpouring of joy. He underscored his call for reconciliation by naming Smarck Michel, a prominent member of the mostly hostile business community and free-market advocate, as prime minister and appointing a broad-based cabinet that included close associates, but also a number of technocrats and a conservative. He then dismantled the military command and appointed as military chief Brig. Gen. Bernardin Poisson, an officer with the least association to the former junta.

The tasks ahead for Aristide, whose term ends in February 1996, and for the U.S. and the U.N. remained enormous. The country in many respects had been pushed back to a nineteenth-century barter system, and delays were expected in a $550 million international aid package. Legislative elections had to be postponed until at least March 1995 because the electoral commission, like most of the nation's institutions, had to be rebuilt practically from scratch. Moreover, Aristide's conciliation efforts and restraint seemed to disappoint many of his mass of supporters. There were concerns about increased restlessness unless the Haitian poor, denied the satisfaction of revenge, did not soon see improvement in their daily lives.

The greatest concern was the looming security vacuum. Political violence had been minimal in the first weeks after Aristide's return but tens of thousands of armed attaches and members of FRAPH remained free and criminal gangs were beginning to emerge. There were serious doubts about the loyalty of a scaled-down military and the effectiveness of a hurriedly U.S.-trained police force. By the end of the year U.S. forces were to have been reduced by two-thirds to 6,000 soldiers. Aristide and the U.N. asked the U.S. to help disarm the society before it gave way in early 1995 to a U.N. force, but Washington appeared reluctant to do so.

Political Rights and Civil Liberties:

The restoration of the freely elected President Aristide returned the country to constitutional rule. However, a third of the senators in the reconvened parliament had been elected in a sham vote in 1993, and political parties remained weak, most of them personal vehicles with little organization. New parliamentary elections constitutionally due by the end of 1994 had to be postponed at least until March 1995 because the electoral system, like most of the nation's institutions, had been decimated. Before leaving power the military had gutted virtually all government ministries and facilities.

By December there remained a void in legal authority and enforcement. Security still depended on the presence of 6,000 U.S. troops, down from an original 20,000, and about 800 international police monitors. In November and December there were increasing reports of robberies and assaults from towns and villages across the country, and sporadic incidents of politically motivated violence.

Aristide and the U.N., concerned by the continued existence of up to tens of thousands of attaches and FRAPH members, asked the U.S. to disarm Haitian society before it handed responsibility off to a U.N. peacekeeping force in early 1995. But the U.S., afraid of a Somalia-like "mission creep," seemed reluctant to do so, and pressed ahead with a program to create a foreign-trained police force from civilian recruits and existing police, to be placed under civilian authority as per the constitution. Human rights groups expressed concern that the new force would include former police responsible for rights abuses.

By December Aristide had dismantled most of the old military command structure and promoted younger officers with reputations as technocrats to leadership posts. Eliminating the military, as demanded by many in Aristide's grassroots Lavalas movement, would require a constitutional amendment. Aristide appeared reluctant to address the issue, evidently not wanting to further alienate soldiers and officers and encourage them to plot against him. Rather, his goal was a scaled-down military of a few thousand restricted to its constitutional duties of guarding the border, assisting in development projects and providing disaster relief. How that would be accomplished remained much in question.

Aristide also ordered the dismantling of the network of 565 rural section chiefs, many of them former Tontons Macoutes, most of whom controlled their turf through extortion, repression and torture. The question was whether the military, assigned with the task, would or could carry it out. Moreover, the ensuing vacuum of authority in the countryside could not be filled until the election of a new parliament that would initiate procedures for the creation of new administrative section councils.

The judiciary, purged of Aristide appointees after the coup and totally corrupted, had functioned as a virtual arm of the military. Record-keeping was poor when records were kept at all, and prisons devolved into medieval dungeons. The entire judicial system needed to be overhauled and rebuilt. Although international assistance was available, the task of establishing even a semblance of legitimate legal authority appeared overwhelming.

There also was the question of justice for prior human rights violations. An estimated 3,000 people were killed under military rule and 300,000-500,000 out of a population of 6.5 million were driven into hiding. Tens of thousands were subjected to arbitrary arrest, torture, rape and extortion. The amnesty passed by the parliament in October 1994 applied only to political offenses, not to human rights abuses. In early December the government announced it would create, in conjunction with the Canadian government, a Truth Commission to investigate rights violations and recommend judicial action.

Under the military, the independent media were either physically destroyed, repressed or intimidated into operating under a high degree of self-censorship. After Aristide's return, the climate for free expression improved appreciably. Independent newspapers and radio stations came back to the fore, and the Aristide government reassumed the operation of state radio and television, although the facilities had been looted by military loyalists. With security still uncertain, many ordinary citizens remained reluctant to speak freely in public, particularly in rural areas.

The civil society which had been emerging under Aristide—peasant groups, cooperatives and community organizations—was severely weakened under military rule. But by the end of 1994 many had started to reorganize. Many labor unions had been able to preserve some of their organization by establishing an underground network, like Solidarity in Poland, with international assistance.

Under military rule, grassroots organizations connected to the Catholic church were subject to repression, and a number of pro-Aristide priests and nuns were threatened and forced underground. Most of the Catholic bishops, however, remained staunchly anti-Aristide and criticized U.S. intervention. After his restoration, Aristide tried to alleviate the tension with the church hierarchy by finally agreeing to leave the priesthood. But his conciliation effort did not sit well with the progressive priests and grassroots movements of the so-called "little church."

Honduras

Polity: Presidential-legislative democracy (military-influenced)
Economy: Capitalist-statist
Population: 5,315,000
PPP: $1,820
Life Expectancy: 65.2
Ethnic Groups: Relatively homogeneous mestizo, approximately 7 percent Indian

Political Rights: 3
Civil Liberties: 3
Status: Partly Free

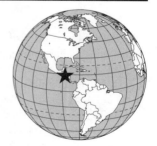

Overview: President Carlos Reina made only limited progress in attempts to curb corruption and reduce the power of the military, as his first year in office was marred by economic woes, an energy crisis, rising criminal violence, labor unrest and coup rumors.

After achieving independence from Spain in 1821, and after the breakup of the United Provinces of Central America (1824-1838), the Republic of Honduras was established in 1839. Its history has been one of military rule and intermittent elected government. A democratic trend began with the election of a constituent assembly in 1980 and the promulgation of a democratic constitution. Reina is the fourth consecutive elected civilian president since 1982.

The constitution provides for a president and a 130-member, unicameral Congress elected for four years. Muncipal governments are elected. Governors of eighteen regional departments are appointed by the president.

The administration of President Rafael Callejas (1990-94) of the conservative National Party (PN) was marked by economic restructuring, layoffs, labor unrest and gross corruption. The poverty level rose to more than 70 percent. The 24,000-member military, under Gen. Luis Alonso Discua, continued to exert inordinate political influence and used its clout to become a major economic player. The constellation of military-owned businesses has made the armed forces one of the ten largest corporations in the country.

In the 1993 primary elections, the incumbent PN nominated Oswaldo Ramos Soto, a table-pounding right-winger and former Supreme Court president. The Liberal Party (PL), which had been in power during most of the 1980s, nominated Reina, a sixty-seven-year-old progressive and former president of the Inter-American Court of Human Rights. The vulgar and often inane campaign saw vicious personal attacks by both sides, and little attention to issues of concern to the electorate—poverty, corruption and the status of the military.

On 28 November 1993 Reina won with 52 percent of the vote. Ramos Soto took 41 percent. The PL won 70 seats in the congress, the PN 56, and two small left-wing parties took the other four. The PL won a majority of the 290 municipal elections.

Reina took office on 27 January 1994, promising a "moral revolution" and limits on the military. In March a new Public Ministry was opened with a mandate to root out corruption. By the end of the year, however, little had been accomplished, in part because corruption is so entrenched and in part because the 1906 penal code is extremely weak and hardly recognizes administrative wrongdoing as a criminal offense.

Meanwhile, there was constant tension between Reina and Gen. Discua. Amid rumors of a military coup, the congress in May passed Reina's bill outlawing forced military recruitment. There was more saber rattling when congress approved bills putting the treasury and intelligence departments of the police under civilian rather than military authority starting in 1995.

However, power blackouts caused by a year long drought and energy crisis had led to a violent crime wave that overwhelmed the police, who were already occupied with labor strikes in the critical banana industry. Under pressure to respond, Reina was compelled to turn to Discua. After a tense meeting in August, Discua agreed to put troops in the streets in exchange for a decree by Reina that "temporarily" restored the military draft, and an apparent increase in the defense budget.

By the end of the year Reina's image as a reformer had been damaged and his weakened administration was widely criticized, including from within his own party. There were also rumors of unrest within the armed forces as many officers appeared unhappy with Discua's political maneuvering.

Political Rights and Civil Liberties:

Citizens are able to change their governments through elections. The 1993 vote, however, was marred by administrative errors that left up to 100,000 registered voters incorrectly listed and unable to vote.

The military exerts inordinate influence over elected governments. By law, the congress elects the armed forces commander for one three-year term from a list of nominees provided by the military. In reality, the military always gets its way. Gen. Discua, former head of military intelligence, became military chief in a barracks coup in 1990. In January 1993 he secured a second three-year term after he strong-armed his subordinates and cowed the congress by threatening to expose corrupt activities.

The military has the final say in most matters that affect it, it is the principal violator of human rights in the country and it generally operates above the law. Some significant initiatives were taken in 1994 to put the police under civilian authority, but there were delays in the process and more legislation needs to be passed in 1995. The military controls vast business and banking enterprises, as well as the country's seaports, borders, airports and customs. After President Reina overturned the new law abolishing the military draft in September 1994, the military returned to gang-pressing poor young men into uniform.

Constitutional guarantees regarding free expression, freedom of religion and the right to form political parties and civic organizations are generally respected. There are numerous parties ranging from left to right. A handful of tiny left-wing guerrilla groups remains active, but under an amnesty, a number of radical-left groups have disarmed and formed political parties.

In 1993 a government human rights office was established. As a result of pressure from the public and the U.S., a colonel was convicted in 1993 of the 1991 rape-murder of a young girl, the first time an officer had been convicted of a crime against a civilian. The sixteen-year prison sentence was upheld in 1994.

Still, the military has continued to violate rights and generally refused to cooperate with the government rights office. Independent rights monitors report that extrajudicial killings still occur, and some allege that Battalion 3-16—a virtual army death squad in the 1980s—still exists in some form despite the military's claim to have disbanded it. In December 1993 a government commission attributed 184 disappearances during the 1980s to the military. Rights groups called for the repeal of amnesties implemented in the late 1980s in order to protect the military.

Rights groups say many violent attacks now stem from greed rather than politics, as economic interests, including the military and drug traffickers, compete for profit and leverage. Targets include businessmen, trade unionists and peasant leaders, who are also subject to arbitrary detention and torture by police. Rights activists report receiving death threats.

The judicial system, headed by a Supreme Court, is weak and rife with corruption. A few judges have asserted themselves in rights violation cases, but most are political appointees with no desire to confront the military or powerful elites. It was hoped that the new Public Ministry, established in 1994 with newly trained prosecutors, would make the courts more responsive, but the traditional inertia of the system seemed to weigh against quick results. Most cases against the armed forces remain in the purview of military courts and usually result in dismissal of charges.

Labor unions are well organized and have the right to strike. However, strikes in 1994 frequently led to violent clashes with security forces. Labor leaders, religious groups and indigenous-based peasant unions pressing for land rights remain subject to repression and violent attacks. Unions have achieved collective bargaining agreements in some export-processing zones, but management abuses remained widespread, including firings for union activities. These resulted in a series of strikes in 1994 and renewed government promises to enforce labor laws. Women workers are a majority in the zones and are subject to sexual harassment, forced overtime without pay and physical abuse.

The press and broadcast media are mostly private. There are several newspapers representing various political points of view, but the practice of journalism is restricted by a licensing law. Some media have become targets of intimidation as they have become bolder in covering human rights cases and corruption.

Hungary

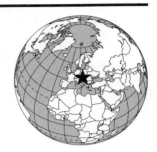

Polity: Parliamentary democracy
Economy: Mixed capitalist
Population: 10,262,000
PPP: $6,080
Life Expectancy: 70.1
Ethnic Groups: Hungarians (95 percent), Slovak, German, Romanian minorities, Croat and Bosnian Muslim refugees

Political Rights: 1
Civil Liberties: 2
Status: Free

Overview: The national election triumph of Hungarian Socialist Party (formerly, the ruling Communists) led by Foreign Minister Gyula Horn, a nagging economic slump, attempted integration with European economic and security structures, and contention over media control were key developments in Hungary in 1994.

With the collapse of the Austro-Hungarian empire after World War I, Hungary lost two-thirds of its territory under the 1920 Trianon Treaty, leaving 3.5 million Hungarians as minorities in neighboring Romania, Slovakia, Serbia and Croatia. Hopes of regaining lost territory was partly responsible for Hungary's alliance with Hitler during World War II. After the war, Soviet forces helped install and uphold a Communist regime. In 1956, an armed uprising by Hungarians was brutally quashed by the Soviets and Hungarian Stalinists. Under Janos Kadar, Hungary, while politically repressive, enjoyed comparative economic well-being under so-called "goulash communism," which had aspects of a market economy. By the late 1980s, with the economy deteriorating, the ruling Hungarian Socialist Workers Party (MSzMP) lost its sense of legitimacy. The ouster of Kadar in 1988 led the way to political reform and the eventual introduction of a multiparty system in 1989.

In May 1990 elections to the unicameral, 386-member Parliament, the conservative Hungarian Democratic Forum (MDF) won 165 seats, and formed a ruling coalition with the Smallholders and the Christian Democrats. The head of state was President Arpad Goncz of the opposition Alliance of Free Democrats (SzDSz); Jozef Antall became prime minister.

Antall's death in December 1993 further undermined an already splintered MDF. President Goncz nominated Interior Minister (and acting prime minister) Peter Boross to fill Antall's post.

Public opinion surveys at the start of 1994 indicated strong support in the May elections for the Hungarian Socialist Party (MSzDP), a successor to the MSzMP made up largely of "reform" Communists who had paved the way for the country's transition in the late 1980s. The trend had begun earlier as the Socialists won some significant by-elections. Painful economic restructuring that had led to spiraling inflation of more than 20 percent, unemployment of 12 percent, steep price rises and public spending cuts, and 4 million people living below the poverty line helped fuel social discontent. The country's foreign debt stood at $20 million, the highest per capita in Central Europe. Under Foreign Minister Gyula Horn, an admitted member of a volunteer militia that hunted insurgents after the 1956 uprising, the Socialist Party stressed its commitment to market economy, multiparty democracy and continued reform. Its probusiness agenda included lowering corporate taxes, increasing investment incentives and even speeding up privatization, which had ground to a halt under the MDF.

The Socialists' popularity came at the expense of the Young Democrats (FiDeSz), whose leads in the polls plummeted after political infighting and a controversy involving the party's ownership of a luxury car rental firm.

Trailing badly in the polls, the MDF in February named Defense Minister Lajos Feuer as chairman to succeed the late Jozef Antall. Prime Minister Boross said he did not want both a party and government post. In an effort to undermine the Socialists, Parliament on 8 March approved a law by 177-12 (with 50 abstentions) to establish a review board that would screen former members of the Communist secret police, its informers, and those who participated in the repression of the 1956 uprising. The law seemed aimed at Horn's past.

As the first round of the election neared, opinion surveys showed the Socialists with 30 percent, despite a rush of TV ads showing their complicity in the 1956 suppression. Only 18 percent of Hungarians said they were better off than under communism, fewer than in any other former East Bloc country except Russia. This was in spite of dramatic economic gains that led to 50 percent of economic output coming from private firms.

More than fifteen parties, ranging from the far-right to Marxists, fielded 1,876 candidates who competed for 8 million voters in the 8 May first round. Ballots were cast for individual candidates and party lists to fill the 386 seats. The complex system meant that most seats would be decided in the 29 May runoff. Early after the first round, the Socialists had 32.3 percent, with 80 percent of the returns in. Second was the Alliance of Free Democrats, with 19.9 percent. The MDF trailed with 11.7 percent, followed by the Smallholders with 8.8 percent and the Christian Democrats with 7.7 percent. Some 69 percent of eligible voters turned out.

After the runoff, the Socialists gained 209 seats, giving them a majority of 32. The Alliance of Free Democrats came in second with 70 seats, the MDF capturing 37. The Smallholders took 26 seats; the Christian Democrats, 22; and FiDeSz, 20.

In the immediate aftermath of the election, some businesses expressed concern about future reforms and the Socialists' close relationship with labor unions. The main challenge facing the new government was reconciling campaign promises of providing a more extensive social safety net with the austerity needed to ease the country's financial squeeze.

On 23 June the Socialists agreed to share power with the liberal, aggressively pro-market Alliance of Free Democrats. Prime Minister-designate Horn announced the concession of three of twelve ministries to the SzDSz, which also won a right to consultation which came close to that of veto power over government policies and appointments. Gabor Kuncze, a central figure in the Free Democrats' campaign, was slated to become interior minister. On 15 July Horn was sworn in as prime minister.

The new government said the most important task would be to reduce the $3 billion state budget deficit, swollen by Communist-era child support subsidies, income supplements and other spending. Spokesman said citizens could not expect immediate relief from inflation, and pledged to speed up transfer of state-owned enterprises to private business, and provide tax breaks to encourage foreign investors.

In August the forint was devalued by 8 percent. Finance Minister Laszlo Bekesi warned of impending recession in 1995, and the government embarked on negotiations with trade unions and employers on a wide-ranging program to cut back surges in wages. Budget cuts were expected to meet IMF 1995 targets. The Socialist austerity program did not sit well with voters, who thought the former Communists would ease economic hardship. In late September,the prime minister told Parliament that the World Bank and the IMF had written the new government to express concern over the country's poor financial and economic situation. He said that the slowdown in reform under the MDF had cost Hungary its advantage as a pioneer of market-led reforms in the 1980s and that the government would draw up a three-year economic program with the help of the two institutions and the European Union (EU), which would be presented to Parliament in April 1995. He promised to accelerate privatization and urged unions and employers to accept pay constraints.

In early October the government fired eight of ten board members of a state holding company and began investigating its general manager for alleged corruption as part of a wide-ranging shake-up of privatization. In early November, the government approved sweeping changes to privatization regulations, with the aim of completing the sale of most state companies by the end of its term in 1998. To make administration of privatization more efficient, the finance minister said that the state property agency (AVU) and the state holding company (AV Rt) would merge into a single company. The ruling coalition won all but one of nineteen counties as well as several large towns in nationwide local elections on 10 December.

Hungary's so-called "media war" over the control of broadcasting continued in 1994. On 15 March, 30,000 people demonstrated in Budapest over the government's dismissal of 129 journalists at its radio and television stations. On the other side of the issue, a crowd of 5,000 heard ultranationalist politician Istvan Csurka applaud the government because the news media were in the hands of "Bolsheviks." In Parliament, the MDF ruled out the possibility of Western communications companies investing in new national television or radio outlets.

On 7 July President Goncz approved the dismissal of the acting heads of state radio and TV after the Socialists beat the MDF in May elections. The Socialists and Free Democrats agreed on film director Adam Horvath to head state TV. Janos Sziranyi, a Socialist, was named chief of Hungarian Radio, a move protested by the opposition. He agreed to suspend his party membership.

Sziranyi pledged to reinstate the 129 journalists dismissed in March. Meanwhile, Horvath dismissed a TV reporter of the major evening news program, Hirado, prompting opposition charges of political purges.

On 8 February, the country joined NATO's Partnership for Peace, becoming the fifth former Warsaw Pact nation to join the group. In March, Hungary stepped up pressure to join the EU and to force the EU to open its doors to Eastern Europe by the end of the decade.

Political Rights **H**ungarians can change their government democratically.
and Civil Liberties: May parliamentary elections were free and fair. The
constitution and statutes guarantee an independent,
impartial judiciary and a Constitutional Court.

In 1993 the Constitutional Court lifted a statute of limitations on the persecution of former Communist officials who suppressed the 1956 revolution. In February 1994 five former militiamen were arrested for firing into a crowd during an antigovernment demonstrations in 1956. Since 1989, the government opened twenty-seven cases involving the uprising. In June, twelve former militiamen went on trial for "crimes against humanity" for shooting unarmed civilians. The issue continued to be debated, raising concerns about a "witch hunt."

Citizens are free to express their views, with some minor restrictions. In 1993, the president signed a law banning the public use of extremist symbols such as the swastika, the SS badge, the fascist arrow-cross, the hammer-and-sickle, and the five-pointed Red Star. On 17 March a municipal court aquitted a pizzeria owner of displaying banned Communist symbols on his menu, ruling that "the display of the Red Star cannot be deemed dangerous to society."

While Hungary has a broad range of independent newspapers and magazines, the government and opposition remain at odds over control of television and radio. Parliament argued but could not agree on a media law in 1993, and the incoming Socialist government promised to rectify the matter. In June, an international journalists' organization said the government-controlled radio and television coverage leading up to the first round of elections showed a pro-government bias. The new government's dismissals of broadcast journalists sparked charges of political interference.

Freedom of assembly and association is guaranteed and respected. There are tens of thousands of civic and nongovernmental organizations. Political parties can organize freely.

On 7 July 1993 parliament passed a Bill on National and Ethnic Minority Rights, banning discrimination against minorities and regarding their rights to national and ethnic self-identity as part of universal human rights and basic freedoms. Nevertheless, the country's estimated 500,000 Gypsies (Roma) continued to suffer *de facto* discrimination in employment and housing. A law effective October 1994 allows police to enter private homes and check up on foreigners as part of a campaign to clamp down on illegal immigrants. The law drew protests from foreign embassies and business groups.

Freedoms of conscience and religion are viewed as a fundamental liberties not granted by the state. In March, Budapest's Jewish community opened a museum as part of a series of events marking the fiftieth anniversary of the Holocaust in Hungary. While the MDF government resisted attempts by Jews to reclaim communal property such as synagogues, schools and hospitals, the Socialists set up a four-member commission to deal with the claims.

An estimated 2.5 million Hungarian workers are members of independent trade unions. The largest is the Confederation of Hungarian Trade Unions. In 1993, the former Communist trade union picked up nearly half the vote in labor elections. The Socialists have maintained a close relationship with some unions. In mid-December rail workers struck for eighteen hours over wages, effecting 750,000 passengers. The government granted demands for an extra 4 percent wage increase.

Iceland

Polity: Parliamentary democracy
Economy: Capitalist
Population: 267,000
PPP: $17,480
Life Expectancy: 78.1
Ethnic Groups: Icelander

Political Rights: 1
Civil Liberties: 1
Status: Free

Overview: In 1994, Iceland celebrated its fiftieth anniversary as an independent state. Fishing disputes with Norway and a continued economic recession were the dominating issues of the year.

After disaffected Norsemen settled the country in the tenth century, Iceland flourished as an independent republic until the thirteenth century, when it came under Norwegian rule. In the fourteenth century, Iceland came under the rigid colonial control of Denmark until 1874, when it received limited autonomy within the Kingdom of Denmark. It was not until 1944, however, when British and American forces occupied Denmark, that Iceland achieved full independence.

Iceland has a parliamentary tradition dating from the tenth century. The parliament, called the *Althing,* is a bicameral legislature subject to dissolution and composed of sixty-three members elected to four-year terms. Forty-nine Althing members are selected on the basis of proportional representation from eight districts. The remaining members are chosen on the basis of parties' percentage of national vote. The Althing splits into two houses after elections—an upper house composed of twenty-one members selected by and from the Althing's representatives, and a lower chamber.

Every four years, voters elect a president, the ceremonial head of state, who chooses the prime minister from the ruling party or coalition.

Iceland's prime ministser is David Oddsson of the conservative pro-Europe Independence Party. In the 1991 parliamentary elections, his party obtained twenty-six seats in the legislature to become the strongest caucus. It then formed a new coalition government with the Social Democrats, which held ten seats. The Progressive Party, which had been the ruling party for twenty years, went into opposition with only thirteen seats. The remaining fourteen seats were captured by the left-wing People's Alliance and the Women's List.

Disputes with Norway over fishing rights intensified in 1994. In a desperate attempt to replace its own depleting stock of fish, Iceland sent an armada of fishing boats inside a 200-mile commercial zone which Norway had previously claimed. In September, two Icelandic trawlers were boarded and their crews arrested by the Norwegian coast gaurd.

Iceland has faced a serious economic recession for three years. While declining fish prices and sluggish demand for other exports keeps the economy stagnant, inflation has been brought down from double digits to 1-2 percent.

Political Rights and Civil Liberties: Icelanders have the right to change their government by democratic means. There is freedom of association. While the people have the right to assembly, some restrictions may apply when it appears that a riot may develop.

Icelanders enjoy complete freedom of expression. The newspapers are a mixture of independent and party-affiliated publications. There is a public broadcasting service, which is run by an autonomous board of directors. The U.S. Navy also broadcasts from its NATO base in Iceland. The constitution forbids censorship.

Over 95 percent of the population belongs at least nominally to the state-supported Lutheran church. There is freedom of worship for nonestablished churches.

It is illegal to discriminate on the basis of race, language, gender and social class. The Women's List, however, alleges that there are cases where women have been deprived of equal pay. The government maintains a generous welfare system. Workers have the right to organize and to stike. Over 95 percent of all eligible workers are members of free labor unions.

India

Polity: Parliamentary democracy (insurgencies)
Economy: Capitalist-statist
Population: 911,576,000
PPP: $1,150
Life Expectancy: 59.7

Political Rights: 4
Civil Liberties: 4
Status: Partly Free

Ethnic Groups: Indo-Aryan (72 percent), Dravidian (25 percent), other

Overview: India's ruling Congress Party suffered huge losses in four state elections in November and December 1994, raising the possibility that Prime Minister P.V. Narasimha Rao's government will have to scale back its economic reform program. During the year caste-based tensions threatened to open new political fault lines.

India achieved independence from Britain in February 1947. Faced with escalating political and religious tension, in July 1947 the country was partitioned into largely Hindu India, under Prime Minister Jawaharlal Nehru of the center-left Congress Party, and Muslim Pakistan. Nehru's daughter, Indira Gandhi, led India from 1966 to 1977 and from 1980 until October 1984, when her Sikh bodyguards killed her to avenge the army's storming of a holy Sikh temple. Her son, Rajiv Gandhi, immediately took over as prime minister.

In the November 1989 elections V.P. Singh of the socialist Janata Dal Party led the centrist National Front Coalition to victory, sending the Congress Party into opposition for only the second time since independence. The Singh government's August 1990 proposal to increase the reservation (quotas) of university slots and government jobs for members of lower castes led to widespread rioting across northern India. In November the government lost a vote of confidence, and in March 1991 a subsequent minority government under Prime Minister Chandra Shekhar collapsed. On 21 May, with balloting underway for a new parliament, Tamil separatists assassinated Rajiv Gandhi as he campaigned for the Congress party in Madras, throwing the country into turmoil.

When voting concluded on 15 June, the Congress Party (226 seats) and its smaller allies took 243 out of the 511 contested seats to the National Front's 131. The right-wing Hindu fundamentalist Bharatiya Janata Party (BJP) and its allies took 123 seats. Veteran Congress politician P.V. Narasimha Rao became prime minister of what many predicted would be a short-lived minority government.

On 6 December 1992 a mob of 200,000 Hindu fundamentalists, encouraged by BJP activists, destroyed a sixteenth-century mosque allegedly sitting on a holy Hindu site in the northern town of Ayodhya. This touched off a week of violence across the country during which 1,200 people were killed and 5,000 injured. In the aftermath, Rao sacked the four BJP-controlled state governments and temporarily banned three Hindu fundamentalist groups.

In January 1993 communal violence flared in Bombay and Ahmedabad, leaving 600 dead and wounding 2,000. Most of the victims were Muslim, and thousands of Muslim businesses and homes were looted and burned. Police tapes obtained by the *New York Times* revealed that the Bombay police purposely avoided aiding Muslim victims and in some cases even participated in the violence.

In November elections in the four northern states placed under federal rule after the Ayodyha riots, the major parties suffered a setback in Uttar Pradesh, the country's most populous state. Two parties representing lower-caste Hindus and backed by poor Muslims formed a governing coalition. This marked the first time that openly caste-based parties took power at the state level. At the federal level, on 30 December ten Janata Dal MPs defected to the Congress Party, giving the Rao government its first majority.

Heading into 1994, the Uttar Pradesh election results foreshadowed growing conflict in the Hindu community along caste lines. Some 70 percent of Indians come from lower castes, and increasingly they are forcing state governments to reserve for them more university spots and government jobs. The constitution provides a 23 percent reservation of slots for scheduled castes (ex-"untouchables") and scheduled tribes, and the Supreme Court has held that an additional 27 percent of slots can be reserved for backward castes and Muslims.

Several state governments want to exceed this 50 percent reservation limit. In 1994 Parliament passed a law allowing southern Tamil Nadu state to set reservations at 69 percent, and may soon approve similar allowances for Karnataka and other states. In the fall sporadic violence rocked Uttar Pradesh after the state government increased reservations to 50 percent.

In another development, the Congress Party was routed in three state elections held in November and December, and lost its majority in a fourth. Analysts said voters were angered with widespread government corruption.

On 25 December Arjun Singh, the Human Resources minister and Rao's main rival within the Congress Party, resigned to protest the premier's handling of a $1.5 billion stock market scandal in 1992 and a sugar import scandal earlier in the year.

The Congress party's electoral debacle may force the government to scale back its economic reform program. Since 1991 the government has carried out currency, banking, tariff and regulatory reforms, although it has avoided deeper structural measures such as privatizing loss-making state-owned industries and reducing the civil service.

In another development, in September and October the world's worst outbreak of the pneumonic and bubonic plague in decades led to fifty-five deaths across the country.

Political Rights and Civil Liberties: Indian citizens can change their government democratically. However, a general lack of accountability permeates government and leads to human rights abuses by security forces and widespread corruption. During elections outright cash bribes are common in rural areas. Politics in several states, particularly Bihar, is increasingly dominated by criminal gangs.

Police, army and paramilitary forces are accused of extrajudicial executions, rape, torture, arbitrary detentions, "disappearances" and the destruction of homes, particularly in crackdowns in Kashmir, Punjab and Assam and other northeastern states. *(A separate report on Kashmir appears in the Related Territories section).*

In Punjab, a peaceful Sikh separatist movement turned violent in the early 1980s, escalating sharply in June 1984 after Indira Gandhi ordered an army assault on the sacred Sikh Golden Temple in Amritsar to flush out suspected militants. Some 18,000 police, separatists and ordinary civilians have been killed since 1982, although the death toll has fallen sharply since police began a massive crackdown in July 1992. The 1983 Armed Forces (Punjab and Chandigarh) Special Powers Act grants security forces wide latitude in using lethal force in the state. Local human rights groups charge police with staging "encounter" killings, essentially killing suspects after capture and claiming death came during the chase, and in dozens of unresolved "disappearances."

In the northeast, large numbers of Hindus from other parts of the country and Muslims from northern Bangladesh have moved into the region since independence, and indigenous tribal groups say they have lost control over their lands. According to the U.S. State Department there are eighteen tribal-based insurgent groups fighting for greater autonomy in the seven northeastern states. The 1958 Armed Forces Special Powers Act grants security forces wide latitude in using lethal force in Assam and four nearby states. During the army's September 1991-January 1992 "Operation Rhino" campaign against the United Liberation Front of Assam, soldiers raided thousands of villages, raping women and torturing and killing detainees and suspects. In 1994 human rights groups in Assam again reported rights violations by the army and police against civilians, human rights activists and suspected terrorists.

Militant groups are also accused of atrocities. In July 1994 the tribal-based Bodo Security Force (BSF) killed more than 100 villagers near the town of Barpeta in Assam. In December 1993 the federal government imposed direct rule on another northeastern state, Manipur, following terrorist attacks by the National Socialist Council of Nagaland. (The government lifted direct rule in December 1994.) In October 1994 the *Christian Science Monitor* reported that fighting between Naga and Kuki tribesmen in Manipur had killed 300 people during the past year. Elsewhere in India, in the eastern states of Bihar and Andhra Pradesh, the Maoist People's War Group and other Naxalite guerrillas frequently target politicians and wealthy landlords.

The broadly drawn 1980 National Security Act (NSA) allows police to detain security suspects for up to one year (two in Punjab) without charges or trial, subject to approval by a board of three high court judges. According to the U.S. State Department the NSA had been invoked in 16,000 detentions as of 1993. The 1985 Terrorist and Disruptive Activities Prevention Act (TADA) allows the authorities to detain individuals for up to one year for action, speech or other form of expression which "questions, disrupts or is intended to disrupt, whether directly or indirectly, the sovereignty or territorial integrity of India." Under TADA, "voluntary" confessions made to a superior officer are admissible as evidence; in practice police frequently torture detainees, particularly in Punjab and Assam, to extract confessions or as a form of extrajudicial punishment.

Evidence suggests that the authorities widely misuse TADA as a means of holding political dissidents, human rights activists and journalists without trial. Although the government initially introduced TADA as a means of fighting terrorism in Punjab, it has been invoked in almost every state, including Gujarat, Tamil Nadu and others where there is no terrorist activity. According to the *Economist*, of the 65,000 arrests made under TADA from its inception through mid-1994, 19,000 occurred in Gujarat. In March 1994 the Supreme Court upheld TADA, although it admitted that torture of TADA detainees is a serious problem.

The judiciary is considered independent of the government in ordinary cases, although the system is severely backlogged and is often inaccessible to poor people. Nonsecurity trials are generally conducted with adequate procedural safeguards, although judges are frequently bribed. In cases tried under TADA and other security acts defendants charged with certain crimes are presumed guilty and, as noted above, evidence obtained during interrogation is admissible in court. In Punjab most courts remain closed due to threats by militants against judges.

In Bihar the Naxalite Maoist Communist Center has instituted extrajudicial "people's courts" that hand down harsh punishments, including amputation of hands and facial parts. In other areas tribal customs often supersede the law and punishments occasionally defy accepted norms of decency.

Police frequently abuse ordinary prisoners, particularly those belonging to lower castes, and there are occasional deaths in police custody. Female prisoners are often raped by guards and male convicts. There are frequent reports of prison officials using inmates for domestic labor. Conditions are most brutal in the lowly Class "C" cells, reserved for prisoners who cannot prove they are either taxpayers or college graduates.

The country's vigorous press is often strongly critical of the government and of human rights abuses by police and security forces. The Official Secrets Act allows the government to ban publication of articles dealing with sensitive security issues. Journalists say that in practice this is occasionally used to limit criticism of government actions, particularly in Punjab. Journalists are frequently harassed by Sikh militants in Punjab and by right-wing Hindus in Gujarat and Maharashtra.

The state-run monopolies on radio and television are accused of biased reporting. In September the government announced it would soon reverse a 1956 prohibition and allow foreigners to own minority interests in Indian publications.

Dowry payments, under which the family of the bride gives cash and gifts to the family of the groom, have been illegal since 1961. In practice, dowries are fairly common in rural areas, and brides are frequently killed over dowry disputes. In August, the government said that 5,582 dowry deaths were reported in 1993.

Hindu women are often denied their proper inheritances, and Muslim daughters generally get one-half the inheritance of a male. Forced prostitution is widespread. More than 150,000 Nepalese women, many under sixteen, have been trafficked to brothels in large Indian cities. In Bihar women are occasionally killed as "witches."

Due to a preference for male offspring, by some estimates upward of 10,000 cases of female infanticide occur each year. Most Indian cities have large numbers of street children, and child prostitution is very common.

Although discrimination based on caste status is illegal, in practice caste frequently determines an individual's occupation and marriage options. Lower castes are often subjected to killings, beatings, rape and arson.

Freedom of association is not restricted. Numerous human rights organizations operate relatively freely, although human rights activists are frequently harassed by police and occasionally tortured or killed. The right to peaceful assembly is generally respected, although the government occasionally bans demonstrations on security grounds.

Freedom of religion is respected in this secular country, but communal violence has characterized India since independence. Citizens can travel freely within the country, except in certain border areas. The authorities occasionally use the 1967 Passports Acts to bar dissidents, generally Sikh activists, from traveling abroad.

In northeastern Arunchal Pradesh state, student groups have campaigned for the expulsion of the 70,000 Buddhist Chakmas who have entered the state since the 1950s after fleeing conflict with Muslims in neighboring Bangladesh. Some 50,000 Chakma refugees also live in six camps in Tripura state. There are 80,000 Tamil refugees from Sri Lanka living in 131 refugee camps in Tamil Nadu.

Workers can join independent unions. The central government can ban strikes in certain "essential" industries, and it occasionally uses this power. Bonded labor is illegal but exists in rural areas. The International Labor Organization estimates there are up to 44 million child laborers, many of them working in conditions of servitude.

Indonesia

Polity: Dominant party (military-dominated)
Economy: Capitalist-statist
Population: 199,717,000
PPP: $2,730
Life Expectancy: 62.0
Ethnic Groups: A multi-ethnic state—Javanese (45 percent), Sundanese (14 percent), Madurese (7.5 percent), Coastal Malays (7.5 percent), other (26 percent)
Trend Arrow: Negative trends included continuing labor rights violations and the government's shutdown of critical publications.

Political Rights: 7
Civil Liberties: 6
Status: Not Free

Overview:　The government of Indonesian President Suharto shut down three outspoken independent newspapers in June 1994, apparently marking the end of a brief period of relative *keperbukaan*, or openness. Overall, the human rights situation deteriorated as the government sought to stifle dissent in advance of the Asia Pacific Economic Cooperation Forum summit hosted by Indonesia in November.

Indonesia, the fourth most populous country in the world, consists of 13,677 islands of the Malay archipelago, containing 350 distinct ethnic groups, including the politically dominant Javanese. The Dutch began colonizing the islands in the late sixteenth century. In August 1945, following the surrender of the occupying Japanese, the fiercely nationalist President Sukarno unilaterally proclaimed independence from the Dutch. In September 1965 the Army Strategic Reserve, led by General Suharto, thwarted a coup attempt by the Indonesian Communist Party (PKI). In the ensuing turmoil, more than 300,000 leftists and suspected sympathizers were killed, many of them ethnic Chinese. In March 1966 Suharto assumed key political and military powers, and one year later became acting president. He formally became president in March 1968.

Suharto's "New Order" administration has stressed economic development and stability. The official *Pancasilla* philosophy consists of five principles–monotheism, justice for all citizens, political unity, democracy through consensus and social justice. In practice, the government cites Pancasilla to justify its tight political control and severe civil liberties restrictions. The country is 87 percent Muslim, and the government and army remain wary of fundamentalist influences. The military nominally backs Suharto but is wary that a trend toward "civilianization" of some top political posts will erode its influence. The army also wants to insure that the president's successor is chosen from within its ranks.

Suharto's political organization, Golkar, is a coalition of social and advocacy groups rather than a true party. Besides Golkar, two significant parties exist, but neither considers itself an opposition party in the traditional sense. The Indonesian Democratic Party (PDI) is a coalition of Christian and nationalist groups that appeals to urban blue-collar workers and younger voters. It favors a more open political system, a greater focus on individual rights, and a more equitable distribution of income. The United Development Party (PPP) is a coalition of Islamic groups.

The 500-member Parliament has 400 elected legislators and 100 seats set aside for the military. During Suharto's tenure the parliament has never initiated or blocked a single piece of legislation. The 1,000-member People's Consultative Assembly consists of the entire parliament, plus 500 members appointed by the president and provincial governors. The Assembly meets once every five years to elect the president and vice president. Suharto has never faced any opposition, and these "elections" simply confirm his desire to hold another term.

Golkar's share of the popular vote fell from 73 percent in 1987 to 67.5 percent in the June 1992 parliamentary elections, but the party still took a commanding 282 of the 400 contested seats. The PPP won 62 seats and the PDI, 56.

On 10 March 1993 the People's Consultative Assembly, without bothering to vote, formally gave Suharto a sixth five-year term. The next day the Assembly elected fifty-seven-year-old armed forces commander General Try Sutrisno, who also ran unopposed, as vice president. Suharto had never made it clear whom he backed for the number two post, but since the military establishment had endorsed Sutrisno since the beginning of the year, the president had to go along or risk an open rift with the armed forces.

Following the election Suharto announced a new cabinet that dropped three key Berkeley-educated "technocrats" who favor a pragmatic economic program of continued deregulation, a balanced budget, and emphasis on low-wage manufacturing exports. The new economic team consists largely of "technologists," led by influential Research and Technology Minister B.J. Habibie, who favor a substantial state role in backing expensive, high-tech industries. In October Suharto backed Information Minister Harmoko's election as Golkar's first nonmilitary chairman, continuing the cautious civilianization process.

In mid-April 1994 the northwestern city of Medan exploded in labor riots following strikes involving some 50,000 workers. The striking workers' grievances included factory owners' refusal to pay the minimum wage of $1.40 per day, the suspicious death of Rusli, a labor activist who had led a strike at a Medan rubber factory, and the government's refusal to recognize the independent Indonesian Workers' Welfare Union. The strikes degenerated into violence that took on anti-Chinese overtones, as workers clashed with riot police, looted shops and killed an ethnic-Chinese factory owner. According to the Indonesian League Aid Foundation, the government appears to have covertly instigated the violence in order to discredit the independent labor movement, which had organized the strikes.

On 21 June the Information Ministry shut down *Tempo*, the country's premier newsmagazine, along with two other weeklies, *Editor* and *DeTik*. The three had reported on issues including the government's controversial purchase of thirty-nine ships of the former East German navy, which had been opposed by the military but favored by Research and Technology Minister Habibie, and speculation on a successor to President Suharto. In October the government shut down a short-lived successor to *DeTik*. The closures appeared to be part of a concerted effort to stifle dissent in advance of the 15 November opening of the annual Asia Pacific Economic Cooperation Forum summit in Jakarta (*See Political Rights and Civil Liberties below*).

Political Rights and Civil Liberties: Indonesian citizens can not change their government democratically due to institutional barriers, the prominent role of the military in politics and President Suharto's political dominance. Members of *Abri* (the armed forces) hold 20 percent of seats in national, provincial and district legislatures, and officers hold many key administrative posts. Official corruption is rampant. The military has a constitutionally established *dwifungsi* (dual function) of external and internal security, and in practice the armed forces violate civilians' rights with impunity.

All political parties must embrace the consensus-oriented Pancasilla philosophy. This effectively limits the scope for political discussion. Prior to the June 1992 parliamentary elections, the government repeatedly restricted campaign activities of the PPP and the PDI. The government also banned seminars on politics and political debates from private television and radio stations. Candidates were allowed fifteen minutes per day on state radio and television, but speeches were reviewed in advance.

The government faces armed separatist movements in Aceh, East Timor and Irian Jaya (*Separate reports on East Timor and Irian Jaya appear in the Related Territories section*). In Aceh province, on the northern tip of Sumatra, the army has killed some 2,000 civilians and *Aceh Merdeka* (Free Aceh) guerrillas since 1989. According to the U.S. State Department, security forces in Aceh frequently detain suspects without charge or trial for lengthy periods, and torture is routine.

The judiciary is not independent. Judges are appointed by and can be dismissed by the executive branch, are frequently pressured by the government and the military, and can often be bribed. The safeguards outlined in the Indonesian Criminal Procedures Code (KUHAP) are often ignored. Torture of suspects and prisoners is common and confessions are often forced. Police frequently use excessive force in routine situations.

The broadly defined 1963 Antisubversion Law allows suspects to be detained without the regular KUHAP protections. In 1993 the U.S. State Department estimated that 300 persons were serving sentences for subversion, although scores or even hundreds of others, many of them political dissidents, are reportedly imprisoned under felony sedition or hate-sowing statutes. The Agency for Coordination of Assistance for the Consolidation of National Security (BAKORSTANAS) has wide latitude in dealing with suspected national security threats and is legally exempt from KUHAP protections. Forced entry and surveillance of citizens are common.

The largely private print media face numerous official restrictions. The state-sponsored Indonesian Journalists Association (PWI) must approve journalists before they can work for a publication, and must approve editors-in-chief before a paper can get a publishing license. The government also regulates the amount of advertising and the number of pages allowed in newspapers. Article 11 of the Press Act prohibits articles on topics considered at odds with the state's Pancasilla philosophy.

Following the closure of three leading newsweeklies, the Information Ministry warned at least five other publications about being too outspoken. Editors are often pressured by the government not to run particular stories and journalists frequently practice self-censorship.

The government operates the national television and radio networks. The private companies serving some regions are required to use government-produced news reports, although radio stations frequently supplement these.

In February the Interior Ministry announced a draft decree that gives the government wide latitude to shut down nongovernmental organizations (NGO) for threatening public security and for receiving foreign aid without official permission. Police frequently break up peaceful demonstrations and detain protesters.

In the months prior to the annual Asia Pacific Economic Cooperation Forum summit, held in Jakarta in November, the authorities took numerous measures to stifle dissent. In Jakarta police carried out "Operation Cleansing," detaining labor activists, dissidents and common criminals. Police reportedly executed some criminals without judicial proceedings. In September and October police harassed several outspoken critics of the regime, including prominent academic George Aditjondro.

Indonesia is the largest Muslim country in the world. Minority religious groups are generally allowed to regulate their affairs and worship freely. The Association of Batak Protestant Churches in Sumatra is a notable exception. In November 1992 a regional military commander installed officers in the organization's top two positions. In June 1994 the Church reported that a priest had been tortured and shot to death by the authorities, and that in recent months scores of followers had been arrested and detained. Advocating a Muslim state is illegal. Chinese citizens are forbidden to operate all-Chinese schools, cultural groups and trade associations, or publicly display Chinese characters. The vernacular papers of the majority Malay community occasionally publish racist articles about the Chinese community.

Women face discrimination in receiving equal pay for equal work, and in access to health and educational services. Domestic violence and rape are reportedly fairly widespread though underreported. Female genital mutilation is reportedly practiced in Indonesia.

Under Indonesia's controversial "transmigration" policy, approximately 2.5 million people have been voluntarily relocated since 1969 from the densely packed island of Java to Sumatra and Kalimantan. Critics say the policy, which has slowed in recent years, is environmentally destructive and disruptive to those already living in the outlying areas.

The Department of Manpower's requirements for trade union registration are stringent: offices in at least twenty of the country's twenty-seven provinces, branch offices in at least 100 districts and representation in at least 1,000 plants. Only the government-controlled All Indonesian Workers Union has managed to satisfy the conditions. On 6 August the government formally declared the independent Indonesian Welfare Labor Union (SBSI) to be illegal because it had not met the necessary requirements.

Factory owners frequently pay workers less than the minimum wage and treat them poorly. In January 1994 the government revised Manpower Decree No. 342, which had allowed the military to intervene in labor disputes, although such intervention continues. Workers have the right to strike, although organizers often lose their jobs. Since May 1993 three labor activists have died under mysterious circumstances. On 7 November a court in Medan sentenced SBSI leader Muchtar Pakpahan to three years in prison for inciting the Medan riots even though he was in Semarang, Java, at the time. Earlier, a Medan court sentenced SBSI regional director Amosi Telaumbanua to fifteen months in jail for incitement.

Iran

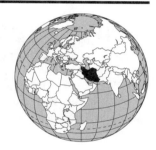

Polity: Presidential-parliamentary (clergy-dominated)
Political Rights: 6
Civil Liberties: 7
Status: Not Free
Economy: Capitalist-statist
Population: 61,168,000
PPP: $4,670
Life Expectancy: 66.6
Ethnic Groups: Persian, Turkic, Arab, other

Overview:

In 1994 radical hard-line clerics continued to gain political ascendancy in Iran, thwarting President Ali Akbar Hashemi Rafsanjani's efforts to introduce modest market reforms. As the economy continued to spiral downward, signs of unrest with the fundamentalist regime included an attempt on the president's life and a spate of bombings and riots throughout the country.

Iran (then Persia) nominally gained independence from Great Britain following World War I, although it remained heavily influenced by London. In 1921 Reza Khan established a military dictatorship, and in 1925 set himself up as the hereditary monarch Reza Shah Pahlavi. In 1941 the British accused Reza Shah of collaborating with the Axis powers and installed his son, Mohammad Reza Pahlavi, in power.

In 1951 the leftist National Front gained control of the parliament under Premier Mohammed Mossadegh. In 1953 a coup briefly ousted the Shah from the throne before a countercoup against Mossadegh restored him to power. By the late 1970s the Shah's authoritarian rule had led to widespread dissatisfaction among the poor. In January 1979, amidst mounting turmoil, the Shah went into exile and fundamentalist religious leader

Ayatollah Ruhollah Khomeini returned from exile in France. In February the secular government fell and the fundamentalists established the world's only Islamic republic.

The December 1989 constitution vests formal power in a directly elected president and a twelve-member Council of Guardians. The latter must certify that all bills passed by the directly elected 270-member *Majlis* (Parliament) are in accordance with Islamic law. The Council of Guardians also must approve all candidates for the presidency and the *Majlis*, which in practice maintains the political dominance of Shiite Muslim clerics and their supporters. The eighty-nine member Assembly of Experts, a body of Islamic scholars, decides the succession of the nation's religious leaders. Ayatollah Khomeini assumed full executive powers in January 1981 and unleashed a period of mass executions of political moderates and non-Muslim leaders.

The 1980-88 war with neighboring Iraq took a heavy toll on the economy. Following Ayatollah Khomeini's death in June 1989, Ayatollah Ali Khamenei assumed the role of supreme religious leader. In September 1989 Ali Akbar Hashemi Rafsanjani won the presidential election with 94.5 percent of the vote.

During his first term Rafsanjani introduced limited free-market reforms, gaining the support of the *Bazar*, the powerful, traditional merchant and money-lending class of which the president himself is a member. Rafsanjani managed to overcome opposition from more radical clerics who favor statist economic policies and whose power base consists of five main Islamic *bunyods* (charity foundations) that operate large industries employing hundreds of thousands of workers.

In early 1992 the Council of Guardians rejected some 1,100 extreme hard-line candidates for the Majlis elections held over two rounds in April and May. This cleared the way for pro-Rafsanjani candidates to win roughly three-quarters of the seats in the non-party vote, giving the president an apparent mandate for cautious economic reform. However, in May and June unskilled laborers in several major cities demonstrated against municipal governments that were trying to destroy their squatter settlements. Many of the president's supporters in the Majlis blamed the agitation on the economic liberalizations, and shifted their allegiance to Ayatollah Khamenei, who opposed the reforms.

On 10 June 1993 Rafsanjani easily won a second four-year term, but despite running against three weak contenders captured a relatively low 63.2 percent of the vote. In 1994 Rafsanjani's power continued to wane amidst declining economic conditions and widespread unrest. On 1 February Sunni Muslims in the southeastern city of Zahedan rioted to protest the demolition of a Sunni mosque. The same day in Teheran a gunman fired at Rafsanjani at an outdoor rally, reportedly the seventh assassination attempt since he took office. On 13 February Ayatollah Khamenei named hardliner Ali Larijani as head of the country's television and radio programming, ousting Rafsanjani's brother from the position. Nine days later Parliament approved hardliner Mostafa Mirsalim's nomination as minister of culture and Islamic Guidance.

In June Ayatollah Khamenei announced that the five-year-old *fatwah* (death edict) on the writer Salman Rushdie for blasphemy cannot be reversed, overriding Rafsanjani's past suggestions that a reversal might be possible. On 20 June a bomb exploded in a mauso-leum in the northeastern city of Mashad, killing at least twenty-six people. Coming on the anniversary of the seventh-century death of one of the holiest Shiite religious figures, some observers speculated that a disgruntled Sunni faction had planted the bomb. At least four bombs inflicting lesser damage also exploded in Teheran during the year.

In early August two days of riots rocked the northwestern city of Qazvin after the national parliament voted down the city's application to secede from Zanjan Province. The city had been hoping to increase its share of revenues from the central government. The *Economist* reported that senior officers in the armed forces, which had been sent in to quell the riots, later wrote a letter to Khamenei expressing their dissatisfaction that the military was called in to put down internal unrest. In October and November students at Teheran University held a series of antigovernment rallies, an almost unprecedented public show of discontent in such a tightly controlled country.

The outlook for the economy remains bleak. Inflation stands at 60 percent, and there are severe shortages of food, jobs and housing.

Political Rights and Civil Liberties: Iranians cannot change their government democratically. Although there are elections for the presidency, the parliament and the Assembly of Experts, all candidates must be formally approved by the Council of Guardians. The criteria, which include being "pro-revolution" and "being Iranian, with practical belief in and commitment to Islam and the Islamic Republic of Iran, and loyal to the constitution," effectively prevent opposition candidates from running. In practice, the country is run by a Shiite clergy elite. Political parties exist but do not participate in elections and have little influence.

State control is maintained through arbitrary detention, torture, and summary trials and executions, carried out by the Revolutionary Guards and other security forces. In February Reynaldo Galindo Pohl, the U.N. Special Rapporteur for human rights in Iran, released his annual assessment, which described the continuation of "persistent and widespread torture and ill treatment, chiefly to force detainees to confess, make public statements of repentance, or inform on the organizations they belong to." Pohl estimated there are 19,000 political prisoners in Iran.

The U.S. State Department estimates that several hundred people are executed each year for political reasons, often on trumped-up drug or other criminal charges. There are no legal limits on detention or avenues of appeal, so suspects can be held indefinitely. On 1 November Parliament approved a bill allowing police to shoot on demonstrators and giving them immunity if a fatality occurs.

The Intelligence and Interior Ministries operate networks of informers, and frequently tap telephones and monitor mail. In 1994, for the first time in five years, the Islamic Revolutionary Councils, which monitor government employees for appropriate religious fervor, reappeared and carried out purges of dozens of civil servants.

The government encourages fundamentalist gangs, known as the *Komiteh*, to enforce strict Islamic dress guidelines for women, regardless of their faith, through arrests and fines. During a particularly harsh three-day crackdown in June 1993, fundamentalist squads arrested some 800 women, some for wearing sunglasses. Women have also been physically attacked for wearing Western clothes or other clothes deemed immodest.

Even more radical are the *Bassij* (literally, "those who are mobilized"), a 3 million-strong group of state-supported hard-line enforcers. The Bassij frequently receive military training and carry guns. In order to boost recruitment, the government has guaranteed Bassij members 40 percent of all university slots, regardless of their grades.

The judiciary is not independent. Judges, as with any political positions, must meet strict political and religious qualifications. Bribery is common and lawyers have been punished for zealously defending clients. A two-tiered court system consists of civil courts dealing with criminal cases and Revolutionary Courts that try political or religious offenses. The civil courts are pre-1979 holdovers and feature some procedural safe-guards. In the Revolutionary Courts there are no procedural safeguards. According to the U.S. State Department defendants are often charged with vague crimes including "siding with global arrogance" (i.e., Western interests), and some cases are decided in less than five minutes. Revolutionary Courts may overturn rulings of the civil courts.

There are substantial restraints on freedoms of speech, press and assembly. In March 1993 an editorial in the fundamentalist newspaper *Salam* candidly described the extent of official censorship, noting there is a "forbidden realm of news." In April police arrested the paper's editor.

In March 1994 police arrested sixty-three-year-old author Saidi Sirjani on espionage and drug abuse charges, although diplomats said his arrest was clearly related to his criticism of the regime in numerous essays. On 27 November the authorities announced Sirjani had died of a heart attack, although his daughter told the *New York Times* that her father had no history of heart problems.

The Ministry of Islamic Culture and Guidance must approve all books prior to publication. All radio and television stations are state-owned, and broadcasts promote government views. Academic freedom is limited and university admission is often based more on political acceptability than on educational qualifications. In early November the government banned "pen-friends" clubs, which correspond with people abroad, and police arrested at least one man for running such a club. In December 1994 Parliament banned private satellite dishes.

Independent organizations that speak out against the government face severe harassment. The government banned one such group, the Freedom Movement, in 1991. Only government sponsored religious and nationalist assemblies and rallies are permitted.

In 1994 persecution of Christians increased and three Protestant leaders were murdered. Church officials told the *New York Times* in July that scores of churches had been shut down since the beginning of the year.

The government rarely grants the necessary approval for the publication of Christian texts, and church services are routinely monitored. Both Christians and Jews are subject to restrictions on operating schools, and face discrimination in education, employment, property ownership and other areas. All students, regard-less of religion, must receive education on Islam, and Islamic knowledge is a requirement for university admission and civil service jobs. In July the *Economist* reported that an elderly rabbi, Feizollah Muchubad, had been executed in February. Entire Jewish families cannot travel abroad together.

The 300,000-strong Bahai minority is not officially recognized and faces significant persecution. In March 1993 the U.N. Human Rights Commission made public a secret legal code, drafted by the government in February 1992, outlining discriminatory policies against the Bahai that included denial of employment and educational opportunities and plans to curb the growth of the religion. Bahais are denied university education, face heavy restrictions on employment, may not teach their faith and are frequently subject to arbitrary detention. The estimated 5-8 million Iranian Kurds are compelled to use the official Farsi language in education and other official and public matters.

The government-controlled Worker's House is the only authorized national labor federation, and smaller labor councils and guild unions are closely allied to the government. There are no independent labor unions. Strikes have occurred more frequently in recent years but are still relatively rare.

Iraq

Polity: One-party   **Political Rights:** 7
Economy: Statist   **Civil Liberties**: 7
Population: 15,890,000   **Status:** Not Free
PPP: $3,500
Life Expectancy: 65.7
Ethnic Groups: Arabs (75 percent), Kurds (15 percent),
Turks, others

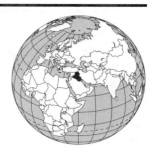

Overview: Three years after the end of the Gulf War, Iraq's economy is in a free-fall largely due to a U.N.–imposed oil embargo, but strongman Saddam Hussein remains entrenched in power.

Iraq won independence from the British in 1932. Since then Sunni Arabs, comprising no more than 15 percent of the population, have held the leadership positions in the country under successive governments. A July 1958 military coup overthrew the Hashemite King Faisal and established a left-wing republic. Another coup in 1968 brought the Arab Baath (Renaissance) Socialist Party (ABSP) to power. In 1979 Saddam Hussein, considered the strongman of the regime since 1973, formally took on the titles of president, chairman of the Revolutionary Command Council and secretary general of the Regional Command of the ABSP.

In September 1980, following months of border clashes, Iraq attacked Iran, touching off a fierce eight-year war. In August 1990, while still recovering from that conflict, Iraq invaded its tiny, oil-rich neighbor, Kuwait. The U.N. Security Council immediately imposed an embargo preventing Iraq from selling oil. A twenty-two-nation, United States-led coalition began air and missile attacks in January 1991, and liberated Kuwait in February. An estimated 100,000 Iraqi soldiers and civilians were killed or wounded.

Immediately following its defeat, the army ruthlessly crushed a nascent Shiite uprising in the south. By late March 1991 the government had also put down a Kurdish uprising in the north, causing hundreds of thousands of Kurds to flee to the mountains. To protect the Kurds, the U.S. and other allied countries set up a military task force in southern Turkey and established a no-fly zone for Iraqi warplanes north of the 36th Parallel. In April the U.N Security Council passed Resolution 687, requiring that before the embargo is lifted Iraq must destroy its chemical, biological and nuclear weapons capability and accept long-range monitoring to ensure that new programs are not initiated.

In 1992 the Iraqi army attacked both the Shiites and Kurds. In August the U.S., Britain and France established a no-fly zone south of the 32nd Parallel to protect the Shiites. In January and April 1993 the U.S. carried out air strikes against Iraqi targets in response to a series of military provocations. In June the U.S. launched a cruise missile attack against the Iraqi intelligence headquarters in Baghdad following reports that Iraq had backed a plot to assassinate former U.S. President George Bush during an April visit to Kuwait.

In 1993 and 1994 economic conditions continued to deteriorate. By January 1994 prices had risen an estimated 6,000 percent since August 1990. On 29 May the fifty-seven-year-old Hussein sacked Prime Minister Ahmed Hussein Khudayir al-Samarral and assumed the post himself after the dinar plunged to new lows against the dollar on the black market.

On 2 October Iraq began moving troops southward toward Kuwait, massing 70,000-80,000 troops on or near the border within a week. The U.S. began sending the first of an eventual force of 30,000 ground troops to the region; by 15 October the Iraqi troops had headed away from the border area. Analysts suggested that Hussein had been trying to pressure the U.N. into lifting the oil embargo through the threat of another invasion. On 17 October the U.N. Special Commission charged with installing the weapons monitoring system announced that the system was largely in place.

On 10 November Iraq formally recognized Kuwait for the first time ever, timing its announcement to coincide with a routine U.N. Security Council vote four days later on whether to continue the oil embargo. Prior to the vote Iraq claimed that with the weapons monitoring mechanisms in place it had met the conditions set out in Resolution 687 for the embargo to be lifted. Although the Security Council voted unanimously to continue the embargo, three of its five members—France, China and Russia—favored taking steps toward lifting it. The U.S. and Britain argued that the monitoring systems and Hussein's actions should be observed for a period of time before any timetable for lifting the embargo is set.

During the year new evidence emerged concerning the army's ruthless campaign against Shiite rebels and villagers in the southern marshlands. Since the end of the Gulf War the army has burned and razed Shiite villages, attacked some 10,000 die-hard insurgents in the marshlands and diverted food and medicine heading to the region. The army has accelerated the process of diverting water from the Tigris and Euphrates Rivers via canals and dikes in order to drain the southern Amara and Hammar marshes. This has facilitated moving army vehicles into Shiite areas.

On 24 April the Iraqi government announced it had completed a major sixty-five-mile irrigation canal in the south. On 5 May the London-based Assist Marsh Arabs and Refugees released a study showing that only 57 percent of the southern marshland recorded in 1985 still existed in 1992. An accompanying video, shot two months earlier by Royal Air Force fighters, showed smoke rising from several burning villages that had been attacked by army troops. In September the U.S. Central Intelligence Agency released a report documenting similar devastation. One agency official estimated that more than 100,000 of the 150,000 Shiites originally living in the wetlands had been driven out. Many have fled to Iran, while thousands of others have been killed by the Iraqi army. The draining has all but destroyed the 6,000-year-old culture of the Marsh Arabs.

Throughout the year the security situation in the country remained tense, particularly in Baghdad. In January *The European* reported that Saddam Hussein had survived an assassination attempt earlier in the month and another in December 1993. During the year there were several bombing incidents in the capital carried out by unknown groups. The 8 April *Associated Press* reported that travelers from Baghdad have described unrest among the minority Sunni Muslim population, long the core support of the regime, due to the economic difficulties and arbitrary purges of some Sunnis from the government.

Political Rights and Civil Liberties: Iraqi citizens cannot democratically change their government. Saddam Hussein holds supreme power in one of the most repressive regimes in the world, and has installed close friends and relatives from his birthplace, Tikrit, in many sensitive positions. The rubber-stamp, 250-seat National Assembly holds no independent power.

Citizens are denied all basic freedoms. All media are state-run and promote the government's views. State control is maintained through widespread arbitrary detentions, routine torture and summary executions. The U.N. has documented the disappearance of more than 16,000 Iraqi citizens in recent years, many of them in northern Kurdistan *(A separate report on Kurdistan appears in the Related Territories section)*. In February 1992 the U.N. special rapporteur investigating Iraqi abuses, Max van der Stoel, reported that "scarcely a day passes without executions or hangings."

According to the rapporteur there are more than 100 detention and interrogation sites throughout the country. Security officials are rarely required to obtain a warrant to conduct searches. The security services rely on informers to spy on the population, and frequently monitor personal communications.

Defendants in ordinary cases receive fairly adequate judicial safeguards. Although the Revolutionary Courts were abolished in 1991, in practice security or political cases are still tried in separate courts that are subject to the whim of the government. In these courts defendants are frequently held incommunicado, confessions extracted through torture are admissible as evidence and there are no procedural safeguards.

In both regular and security courts, punishments are generally out of proportion to the crime committed. The death penalty is frequently used for political offenses, which are broadly defined by a series of presidential decrees to include any speech or acts that can be construed as disloyalty to the regime. Merchants accused of violating price controls and currency speculators are sometimes executed. Local Baath Party Committees can also jail individuals suspected of these crimes without a trial.

In June 1994 the government announced that convicted thieves would have the left hand amputated and their foreheads branded with an "X"; the left foot would be amputated for a second offense; and persons committing crimes with weapons would be executed. In August the government announced that draft evasion or desertion from the army would be punished by cutting off the ear and branding the forehead. There are credible reports that these punishments have been carried out.

The Shiite Muslim majority faces particularly strong persecution. The worst abuses occur in the southern marshlands, where in addition to the ground campaign *(See Overview above)* the army has arrested hundreds if not thousands of Shiites and brought them to detention centers in and around Baghdad. Some have reportedly been executed. Throughout the country Shiite clergy have been arrested, and the government directly administers many Shiite holy sites. Bans on some Shiite public ceremonies and the publication of Shiite books remain in effect. In some predominantly Shiite cities the government has also banned the call to prayer.

Other restrictions on religion apply to both the Shiite and Sunni communities. A 1981 law gives the Ministry of Endowments and Religious Affairs control over mosques, the appointment of clergy and the publication of religious literature. The small Jewish and Christian minorities can generally practice without harassment, although Jews face restrictions in traveling abroad and in contacting Jewish groups outside the country.

In September the government halved basic rations of staple food items that even before had met only 70 percent of basic needs. Humanitarian relief is often diverted to the army and other privileged groups. As a result, food shortages have caused particular hardship for children. The U.N. has authorized Iraq to sell $1.6 billion worth of oil in order to purchase humanitarian goods, but the regime has refused.

Numerous areas are off-limits for travel inside the country. According to the *Economist*, citizens who arrived in Baghdad after the Gulf War, mostly Shi'as, are being forced out of the capital; those who cannot prove residency in the city before 1975 can no longer buy property. Citizens are limited to two foreign trips per year, and in 1994 the government imposed heavy exit taxes that make it nearly impossible for ordinary Iraqis to leave the country. There are no independent trade unions and the right to strike does not exist.

⬆ Ireland

Polity: Parliamentary democracy
Economy: Capitalist
Population: 3,604,000
PPP: $11,430
Life Expectancy: 75.0
Ethnic Groups: Irish (Celtic), English, and small immigrant communities
Trend Arrow: The peace process in Northern Ireland reduced violence and had a positive effect on civil liberties.

Political Rights: 1
Civil Liberties: 2
Status: Free

Overview:
The dramatic breakthrough in the Northern Irish peace process and the shocking resignation of *Taoiseach* (Prime Minister) Albert Reynolds were the major events in 1994. Reynolds, leader of the *Fianna Fail* (Soldiers of Destiny) party, resigned the premiership on 17 November 1994. He had precipitated his own demise by appointing Attorney General Harry Whelehan as president of the High Court over the strenuous objections of Deputy Prime Minister Dick Spring, leader of the Labour Party. Following Whelehan's appointment to the bench, Labour withdrew its support from the coalition government. Labour accused Reynolds of misleading them over Whelehan's role in delaying the extradition of a pedophile priest to Northern Ireland. Whelehan's office had sat on nine extradition warrants for the priest for seven months. The new judge followed Reynolds's resignation with his own.

Fianna Fail's parliamentary deputies selected Finance Minister Bertie Ahern to be Reynolds's successor as party leader. Ahern and Spring almost reformed the coalition government in early December. However, at the last minute, press reports suggested that several Fianna Fail ministers besides Reynolds knew that he was misleading the Dail (lower house of Parliament) about Whelehan while he was doing it. Reportedly, Reynolds was defending Whelehan publicly a day after seeking the judge's resignation privately. These stories broke the fragile trust between the two parties, leaving Spring with the alternatives of trying to form a Left-Right "Rainbow Coalition" with other parties or triggering an unpopular general election right after the holidays in January 1995. By late December, Labour had formed a coalition with the conservative *Fine Gael* and the Democratic Left. Fine Gael's John Bruton became the new prime minister.

Reynolds had received great international credit for his role in encouraging the Provisional Irish Republican Army (IRA) to announce a cease-fire, effective 1 September 1994. The cease-fire came nine months after the Downing Street Declaration, an agreement between Reynolds and British Prime Minister John Major that recognized the Irish right to self-determination and offered the IRA a role in negotiations following a cessation of violence. The Provisionals had conducted an armed struggle against British rule in Northern Ireland for a generation. (*See Northern Ireland under United Kingdom, Related Territories.*) The cease-fire allowed the IRA's political wing, *Sinn Fein*, to move closer to the Irish political mainstream. Sinn Fein's leader, Gerry Adams, met with Reynolds in Dublin on 6 September, symbolizing his newfound acceptability. Loyalist paramilitaries, groups committed to continuing British rule in Northern Ireland, announced their own cease-fire on 13 October. Ireland seemed poised for its most profound political changes since the 1920s. On 28 October the Forum for Peace and Reconciliation began in Dublin, bringing together Sinn Fein and other Northern and Southern Irish parties. Even though the British and most Northern parties boycotted the meeting, it reinforced Sinn Fein's new role.

Following centuries of British domination and occupation, twenty-six of Ireland's thirty-two counties won home rule within the British Commonwealth in 1921. The six counties of Northern Ireland have remained part of the United Kingdom. In 1948 Ireland proclaimed itself a republic outside the Commonwealth. The Irish constitution's Articles 2 and 3 claim Northern Ireland, but the Republic has only a consultative role in the North under the Anglo-Irish Accord of 1985. The Unionist parties, which represent the North's Protestant majority, oppose the Anglo-Irish Accord, because they fear that the mostly Catholic republic's involvement in the six counties could cause Irish unification. The Northern Protestants have claimed for decades that Ireland's Catholic majority could jeopardize their traditions. Throughout negotiations with the British and the Northern parties in 1994, the Irish government sought some cross-border institutions, but stressed that change could come only with Northern consent.

The Republic of Ireland has a bicameral legislature, consisting of a Senate and the Dail. The upper house of 60 members is comparatively powerless but can delay legislation. Its term lasts as long as that of the Dail, a maximum of five years. The Taoiseach (prime minister), universities, and occupational panels name or elect senators. The Dail has 166 members elected by the single transferable vote method of proportional representation. Mary Robinson, the largely ceremonial, popularly elected president of the Republic, is head of state and appoints the Taoiseach from the party of coalition able to command a majority in the Dail. Her liberal views have encouraged major politicians to advocate changes in laws on such lifestyle and morality issues as divorce, birth control, homosexuality and abortion. In February 1994 Robinson triggered a constitutional crisis. A committee on the future of the U.N. invited her to be its chairman. The government and then-Attorney General Whelehan ruled that the chairmanship of such a committee lay outside her constitutional role. Robinson hired lawyers who advised her otherwise. Ultimately, Robinson backed down, and withdrew from consideration for the U.N. position.

The Irish political party system is a mixture of parties formed early in the twentieth century around the issues of nationalism or class and more recent ones founded on other bases. The oldest major parties are Fianna Fail, Fine Gael, and Labour. Fianna Fail is a generally conservative party with roots in republican nationalism. Fine Gael (Family of the Gaels), led by John Bruton, is a decidedly more conservative party descended from the politicians who accepted Ireland's divisive treaty with Britain in the 1920s. Facing very low popularity, Bruton survived a leadership challenge in February 1994. Labour is a social democratic party with roots in the trade union movement. The significant newer parties include the Progressive Democrats (PD), Democratic Left, the Workers' Party, and the Greens. The Progressive Democrats are a socially liberal, pro-business party that split off from Fianna Fail. PD leader Mary Harney is the first woman to head a major Irish party. Democratic Left is a new, left-wing party that broke away from the Workers' Party, a formerly Soviet-backed group. The environmentalist Greens have gained ground in local, national and European elections. In the general election of November 1992, Fianna Fail had its worst showing since the 1920s, 39.1 percent of the vote and 68 seats. Fine Gael received only 24.5 percent and 45 seats, its worst result since the 1940s. Labour won 19.3 percent and 33 seats, doubling its representation from the previous Dail. The Progressive Democrats captured 4.7 percent and 10 seats. Democratic Left took 2.8 percent and 4 seats. The Greens garnered 1.4 percent and 1 seat. Independents took five seats. After the election, Fianna Fail and Labour formed their first short-lived coalition with each other.

Political Rights and Civil Liberties:

Irish voters can change their government democratically. Citizens register to vote through a government-sponsored household survey. However, only diplomatic families and security forces abroad have the right to absentee ballots overseas. There may be a referendum in 1995 on extending voting rights to ordinary Irish citizens living abroad.

The press is comparatively free, but there is censorship on moral and political grounds on issues such as sexually oriented material and interviews that might promote violence. In January 1994 the government dropped Section 31 of the Broadcast Act, a provision that had long prohibited Sinn Fein representatives and members of paramilitary and "subversive" groups from the broadcast media. However, the government could still censor on the basis of Section 18, which forbids the broadcast of anything likely to undermine state authority or promote violence. Satellite broadcasts make pornography available despite national laws. In July 1994, RTE, the public broadcasting corporation, banned a public screening of an abortion documentary, because it believed the film was too sympathetic to abortion. Despite a 1992 referendum allowing the distribution of information on abortion, there was still no follow-up legislation by late 1994.

Many homes receive British and other international broadcasts through cable television. British newspapers are gaining an increasingly large share of the Irish market, undercutting domestic publications that bear the highest value-added tax on newspapers in the European Union. Harsh libel laws provide politicians a tool for attacking critics. In September 1994 the director of Public Prosecutions ordered the arrest of Susan O'Keeffe, the journalist who uncovered a major scandal involving the government and the beef industry. She had refused to reveal her sources to the authorities. Ironically, none of the guilty parties in the scandal was arrested.

Terrorist organizations, such as the Provisional IRA, are illegal, but Sinn Fein, the IRA's political wing, is legal. The Irish government allows Sinn Fein to organize and campaign for elections and it made gains in local council elections in 1994.

Due to occasional spillovers from Northern Irish violence in the past, the police have special powers to detain and question suspected terrorists. In 1994, as a follow-up to the paramilitary cease-fire, the Irish Council for Civil Liberties (ICCL) called for the abolition of the Offenses Against the State Act and the special criminal courts that have tried alleged terrorists. Both the ICCL and Dick Spring advocated ending the country's long-standing state of emergency. Security forces estimate that the IRA has stashed away over 1,000 good-quality firearms and tons of supplies, most of it in the Irish Republic.

In August 1994, before the cease-fire, the IRA killed Martin ("The General") Cahill, the boss of Dublin's organized crime. The IRA took responsibility for the death after the Irish National Liberation Army, a more extreme republican group, had already done so. The loyalist Ulster Volunteer Force (UVF) said that it, too, wanted to kill him. The IRA apparently killed Cahill to make "an example" of him for his alleged cooperation with the UVF's June attack on a Sinn Fein fund-raiser. That attack left one man dead and another wounded. Loyalists also carried out a few letter bomb attacks in the Republic earlier in the year. A UVF bomb exploded on a Belfast-to-Dublin train in September, injuring two. On 22 October, Special Branch agents raided twenty-four homes of alleged members of Republican Sinn Fein, a republican splinter group. The raid turned up publications, videos, ammunition, one gun and a box of Twinkies. In July, the ICCL criticized the government for not living up to the promise to the U.N. Human Rights Committee to allow Irish prisoners abroad to serve their sentences in Ireland. The government had signed but not ratified the European convention on prisoner transfers.

The judiciary is independent, but many male judges appear prejudiced about crimes against women, giving light sentences or release to alleged rapists.

Ireland is a temporary haven for some refugees from Communist and formerly Communist countries. However, there is also a government policy of imprisoning some asylum-seekers. Amnesty International has called for a change of this policy.

There may be a referendum on divorce in 1995. The voters rejected divorce in a 1986 referendum. At that time, fears about loss of property influenced the negative result. Women are playing an increasingly important role in the economy; the number working outside the home has grown by over 40 percent in the last twenty years. However, only 30 percent of women work outside the home, the lowest rate in the European Union. Moved by AIDS, the government liberalized condom sales in 1993. Responding belatedly to a 1990 ruling by the European Court of Human Rights, Ireland legalized homosexual acts in 1993.

The Roman Catholic Church remains strong, but other faiths have religious freedom. There have been Protestant presidents and a Jewish mayor of Dublin. Most schools are controlled by boards dominated by the Catholic and Protestant churches. Few schools are multidenominational. The Irish-speaking minority forms the only significant, indigenous minority cultural group. Irish-speakers are concentrated in a small collection of areas called the *Gaeltacht*, located chiefly along the west coast. The government protects their linguistic tradition through various subsidies and other programs. Business is generally free, and free trade unions and farming groups are influential.

Israel

Polity: Parliamentary
democracy
Economy: Mixed
capitalist
Population: 5,432,000
PPP: $13,460
Life Expectancy: 76.2
Ethnic Groups: Jewish majority, Arab minority

Political Rights: 1
Civil Liberties: 3
Status: Free

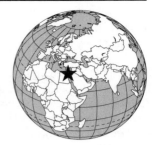

Overview:

Israeli Prime Minister Yitzhak Rabin's government enjoyed only shaky public support at midterm despite having signed peace pacts with the Palestinian Liberation Organization (PLO) in 1993 and with Jordan in October 1994. As terrorist attacks continue, Rabin has been hard-pressed to show tangible benefits from his diplomatic initiatives.

Israel was formed in May 1948 out of less than one-fifth of the original British Palestine Mandate. Its Arab neighbors, having previously rejected a United Nations partition plan that would have also created an Arab state, attacked the new country immediately following independence. Israel fought Egypt in 1956, and in the Six-Day War of June 1967 routed several Arab armies after Egypt closed the Gulf of Aqaba to its ships, capturing the Gaza Strip, the West Bank, the Golan Heights (which it annexed in 1981) and East Jerusalem. In 1979 Israel signed a peace treaty with Egypt that led to the return of the Sinai in 1982. The same year, Israel invaded southern Lebanon to neutralize PLO guerrillas operating there; currently its troops maintain a small "security zone" in southern Lebanon.

Israel has functioned as a parliamentary democracy since independence. Arabs and other minorities can and do elect representatives to the 120-seat *Knesset* (Parliament). Voters choose parties rather than individuals; a party then draws MPs from its list depending on how many seats it wins.

The conservative Likud party formed a governing coalition under Prime Minister Menachem Begin after the 1977 parliamentary elections, ending twenty-nine years of center-left rule. At the 1984 elections, Likud failed to attract enough smaller parties to form a "blocking majority" in the Knesset, and entered into an uneasy coalition with the Labor Party. After another close Likud victory in 1988, the two major parties again entered a "national unity government," but Labor withdrew in March 1990.

Under Yitzhak Shamir, the Likud government firmly ruled out any "land for peace" compromise involving territory occupied in 1967, citing national security reasons. In October 1991 Israel entered into U.S.–brokered multilateral peace talks with its Arab neighbors that made little progress.

At the 23 June 1992 elections, former prime minister Yitzhak Rabin led the Labor party to resounding victory, taking 44 seats. Having been the victorious army commander during the 1967 War, Rabin offered voters both a pragmatic approach to the peace negotiations and strong credibility in protecting Israel's security interests. Likud took 32 seats; the leftist Meretz, 12; the right-wing Tzomet, 8; the Sephardic, ultraorthodox Shas, 6; the National Religious Party, 6;

United Torah Jewry, 4; the Arab-Communist Democratic front, 3; the right-wing Moledet, 3; and the Arab Democratic Party, 2. Rabin formed a sixty-two-seat coalition including Labor, Meretz and Shas that drew the support of the two Arab parties.

Through a series of seventeen secret, unrelated negotiations, mostly in Norway, Israel and the PLO reached a breakthrough agreement on 20 August 1993 providing for gradual Palestinian self-rule in the occupied territories (*A separate report on the Occupied Territories and Palestinian Autonomous Areas appears in the Related Territories section*). In September Israel and the PLO signed mutual recognition agreements, as well as a Declaration of Principles outlining the steps toward Palestinian autonomy.

In 1994 the autonomy process with the PLO bogged down. Although the government reaffirmed its commitment to the Declaration of Principles in December, delays in the implementation included PLO Chairman Yasir Arafat's failure to revoke parts of the organization's charter calling for the destruction of Israel, and questions over the timing and extent of the withdrawal of Israeli troops from populated areas of the West Bank and the timetable and nature of Palestinian elections in the West Bank and Gaza Strip.

On another front, on 25 July Israel and Jordan formally declared an end to their forty-six-year state of war. Prime Minister Rabin also reaffirmed Jordan's King Hussein's role as the guardian of Muslim holy sites in Jerusalem in an effort to reassure the Israeli public that his government would not negotiate with the PLO over the status of East Jerusalem, which Israel annexed in 1967. On 17 October the two countries initialed a peace treaty, which was signed in a formal ceremony nine days later.

During the year there was little progress in U.S.–brokered negotiations with Syria, which demands that Israel agree to cede sovereignty over the entire Golan Heights before it discusses its terms for peace. Prior to 1967, Syria had used the plateau to shell towns in northern Israel. In September Rabin floated plans for an initial, modest pullback of Israeli troops as a good faith measure during a three-year test period, but repeated his pledge that any significant Israeli withdrawal from the Golan Heights would be put to a national referendum.

With elections due by November 1996, Rabin may not have time to demonstrate that his peace initiatives will produce tangible benefits including an improved security situation. Since the September 1993 accords, more than ninety Israelis have died in terrorist attacks.

In economic affairs, in June the government announced plans to sell 51 percent of El Al, the national airline.

Political Rights and Civil Liberties: Israeli citizens can change their government democratically. Parties representing Arabs and far-right Jewish groups hold seats in Parliament, although the extremist *Kach* party of the late Rabbi Meir Kahane, and an offshoot, the Kahane Lives party, are banned under a 1988 law outlawing racist parties. The Declaration of Independence describes Israel as a Jewish state that respects the rights of minorities.

Sporadic terrorist violence continues to plague Israeli society. A 19 October 1994 bomb blast on a Tel Aviv bus killed twenty-two people and wounded forty-eight others in one of the worst terrorist attacks in the country's history.

The *Shin Bet* (General Security Service) is responsible for internal security, and is accused of practicing psychological and physical torture against Arabs and Arab sympathizers. Internal security regulations from 1987 allow security forces to apply "moderate physical pressure" to suspects during interrogation. In November 1994, following a fresh wave of terrorist violence, the government admitted it had eased the regulations on physical force when dealing with suspects who might have knowledge of imminent terrorist attacks.

A 1979 law provides for administrative detention without charges of suspects for up to six months, subject to automatic review after three months. The order is renewable upon expiration. A detainee must be brought before a district judge within forty-eight hours of arrest; if the order is confirmed it must be renewed after three months. A detainee may appeal to the Supreme Court, but the government can withhold evidence on security grounds.

The judiciary is independent of the government, and procedural safeguards are adequate. Security cases can be closed to the public on limited grounds, and access to some sensitive evidence can be withheld from defense attorneys. However, that evidence cannot be used for a conviction. Ordinary prisons and police detention facilities are overcrowded. Detention facilities run by the Israeli Defense Forces to hold security prisoners do not meet international norms.

The government places some restrictions on press freedom. Newspaper and magazine articles dealing with security matters must be submitted to a military censor, which provides a list of topics falling under its discretion. A 1989 Supreme Court decision narrowed the grounds for censorship to information that has a "near certainty of damage to the security of the state," although in practice censorship often reflects a desire to withhold sensitive news from the general public. Editors can appeal a censorship decision to a three-man tribunal which includes two civilians, although not to the Supreme Court. Arabic-language publications are censored more frequently than are Hebrew-language ones. All newspapers are privately owned, and can and do vigorously critique government policies.

Freedoms of assembly and association are respected. In January 1993 the Knesset repealed a law banning contact with the PLO. Israeli recognition of the PLO in September 1993 led to a repeal of bans on displaying Palestinian flags and expressing open support for the organization.

Women frequently do not receive equal work for equal pay, and face discrimination in employment opportunities. All religious believers worship freely. Each community has jurisdiction over its members in questions of marriage and divorce. Orthodox Jewish authorities have jurisdiction over marriage, divorce and burial affairs for the entire Jewish community.

The 76,000 Druze citizens serve in the army, but frequently face social ostracism and discrimination in employment opportunities and government services. Arab citizens do not receive the same level of government funding for services as Jewish citizens. In 1993 the New Israel Fund reported that 60 percent of Arab children live below the poverty line, compared with 10 percent of Jewish children. It also reported that the Education Ministry spent $123 per Jewish schoolchild in 1991, compared to $67 for each Arab child. The Rabin government has pledged to close the gap in education and other areas. A policy introduced in 1993 made geography and not ethnic composition the basis for a municipality to receive priority funding. Arabs are at a disadvantage by not being subject to the draft, since army veterans receive preferential access to some economic benefits, such as housing subsidies. Arabs are barred from employment with security-related companies.

Workers can join unions of their choice and enjoy the right to strike. Three-quarters of the work force either belongs to unions affiliated with *Histadrut* (General Federation of Labor in Israel) or is covered under its social programs and collective bargaining agreements.

Italy

Polity: Parliamentary democracy
Economy: Capitalist-statist
Population: 57,150,000
PPP: $17,040
Life Expectancy: 76.9
Ethnic Groups: Italian (Latin), various immigrant groups, and small Austro-German and Gypsy minorities
Ratings Change: *Italy's civil liberties rating changed from 3 to 2 reflecting the system's ability to reform after major corruption.

Political Rights: 1
Civil Liberties: 2*
Status: Free

Overview:

In 1994 Italy elected the first right-wing government in which there was no Christian Democrat (DC) participation since World War II. Media tycoon Silvio Berlusconi entered politics and became prime minister after forming a winning rightist coalition consisting of his own *Forza Italia* party, the rightist Northern League, and the fascist-oriented MSI/National Alliance. Aided by the scandals undermining the DC and the Socialists (PSI), Berlusconi's government faced crisis after crisis in 1994, including several corruption scandals of their own. The crises peaked in December, forcing Berlusconi to resign and call for new elections. Meanwhile, the government stepped up efforts to fight corruption as new scandals continued to rock the nation, causing political upheaval and social unrest.

Modern Italian history dates from the nineteenth-century movement for national unification. Most of Italy had merged into one kingdom by 1870. Italy began World War I on the side of Germany and Austria-Hungary, but then switched to side with the Allied Powers. From 1922-1943, the country was ruled by the fascist dictator, Benito Mussolini. A 1946 referendum ended the monarchy and brought in a republican form of government.

Since the abolition of the monarchy, the president has had a largely ceremonial role. He is elected for a seven-year term by an assembly of parliamentarians and delegates from the Regional Councils. The president is responsible for choosing the prime minister, who is often, but not always, a member of the largest party in the Chamber of Deputies, the lower house of Parliament. Members of the upper house, the Senate, are elected on a regional basis. The president can appoint five senators for life and becomes one himself upon leaving office.

From the 1940s to the early 1990s, short-lived governments dominated by the Christian Democrats (DC) ruled Italy. An electoral system based on proportional representation, multimember districts and ballots with party lists created a parliamentary system with many small parties. Since 1990, frustrated voters and party dissidents fought to give the voters more leverage in choosing individual candidates for Parliament. Under proportional representation, electors voted for party lists of their choice, but party bosses determined both the candidates and their order of appearance on the ballot lists. In 1993 a series of electoral reforms was instituted in order to curb the power of the party. The reforms allowed voters to choose from a list of individual candidates rather than from a selection of party names, thereby encouraging a move away from small-party politics toward the establishment of a bipolar system. The reforms also converted 75 percent of both houses to the British-style first-past-the-post approach. The remaining 25 percent are to be elected by proportional representation.

On 16 January President Luigi Scalfaro dissolved Parliament and called for new elections on 27 March. The date was extended to 28 March in response to a Jewish protest at having to vote on Passover. On 19 January the Christian Democrats changed their name to the Italian Popular Party, hoping to regain support and salvage their corrupt reputation. A week later, Silvio Berlusconi, media tycoon and champion soccer team owner, announced his entry in politics to save the country from "men tied to political and economic failure." Berlusconi was able to unite the Italian right by forming a three-way coalition composed of his own Forza Italia movement, named after a soccer team slogan; the right-wing Northern League, led by Umberto Bossi; and the highly controversial fascist-oriented MSI/National Alliance party. Berlusconi was forced to turn to the fascists when he failed to get support from the former Christian Democrats. In the face of public criticism for his connections with the National Alliance, Berlusconi stated his belief that the alliance would weed out the extremist elements of the party and force the group into the political mainstream.

Indeed, 27 and 28 March were red-letter days for the right-wing coalition, which captured 366 of the 630 Chamber seats and 155 out of 315 seats in the Senate. The left-wing coalition won 213 in the Chamber and 122 in the Senate. The centrists came in third, winning 46 Chamber seats and 31 Senate seats. The remaining 5 Chamber seats and 7 Senate seats went to various other parties. Berlusconi's control of the media contributed to his victory. The owner of three major television stations, Berlusconi was able to broadcast his election propaganda throughout the campaign. In the face of growing suspicion concerning his media control, Berlusconi offered in July to hand over control of the three stations to special overseers.

Following his victory, Berlusconi faced the task of forming a new government. On 11 May he was sworn in as prime minister. Eight days later, his cabinet barely won a confidence vote in the Senate (159-155). Berlusconi's cabinet included five members from the neo-fascist National Alliance. The victory of the right sparked new concern that Italy could be edging in the direction of its fascist past. One legislative seat was won by the former dictator's granddaughter, Aleasandra Mussolini. However, the National Alliance is not directly connected to Mussolini's Fascist party, which was declared illegal.

Soon after Berlusconi became prime minister his government and business empire faced high-level corruption charges, including the arrest of two media executives in July. Also that month, public outrage forced the leader to withdraw a controversial detention decree that freed certain corruption suspects. During the first hundred days of the administration, the government moved from crisis to crisis and managed to maintain power largely because of the weakness of the opposition.

On 5 October an investigating magistrate accused high-level members of Berlusconi's media empire of "mafia-style" corruption. Berlusconi responded by saying that the allegations were "completely unfounded." To make matters worse, on 22 November Berlusconi himself was named in corruption charges because his media empire had allegedly bribed tax inspectors.

In October and November, unions and opposition parties organized a series of demonstrations protesting the government's efforts to slash the budget. On 12 November over one million protesters demonstrated against the austerity budget— the largest rally in Rome since World War II. In the face of these end-of-the-year crises, the Democratic Party of the Left (PDS), led by Massimo D'Alema, slowly gained ground to become the leading political party in the nation.

Berlusconi's final beating occurred on 17 December, when the Northern League withdrew its support for the rightist coalition, forcing the collapse of the government. On 22 December Berlusconi resigned and called for early elections in order to avoid defeat in the upcoming no-confidence vote in the Senate. President Scalfaro was then given the power either to form a new government or declare new elections in 1995.

For the past three years a team of magistrates has launched a massive anti-corruption campaign. The probe has unearthed the vast scale of corruption in Italy and has led to the arrests and indictments of more than 3,000 prominent political and business figures.

Political Rights and Civil Liberties: Italians have the right to change their government democratically. Elections to the national, regional and local levels are competitive and feature a plethora of political parties ranging from the far-left to the far-right. The 1993 electoral law, however, encourages fewer parties and places more emphasis both on individual candidates and on the formation of coalitions. There is freedom of political organization, but Mussolini's Fascist movement is outlawed. Some friction remains between Italians and the Austro-German minority in the northern area of Alto Adige, which was part of the Austro-Hungarian empire until World War I.

The media are generally free and competitive, but there are some minor restrictions on the press in the areas of obscenity and defamation. In 1994, Berlusconi's extensive control of the broadcast media raised questions about ownership and the relationship between politics and business. In October Bossi, the leader of the Northern League, banned all contact with eleven newspaper journalists in response to their stories concerning the League's links to Berlusconi's corruption charges.

The court system is notoriously slow. The judiciary is independent, but political pressures may affect some proceedings. Since the start of the anti-corruption probe in 1992, prosecutors and judges have shown vigor in indicting and prosecuting business and political leaders.

With the exception of overtly fascist and racist groups, Italians have freedom of association. After a skinhead rally on 14 May 1994, Italy's chief of police ordered police nationwide to ban such rallies "out of concern for public order."

Italians have religious freedom. Although the Catholic Church is still dominant, it is no longer the state church. Italians who do not evade the income tax can designate contributions to churches on their tax forms.

Since 1992, an edict has allowed authorities to expel foreigners accused of serious crimes. Human rights groups complained that the edict created a separate and summary justice for foreigners. Anti-foreigner violence exploded in December 1994 when a fifteen-year-old Italian girl was hit and killed by a Moroccan driver. African and Arab immigrants were insulted and struck by fists, at least three blacks were killed and an Indian was stabbed as he boarded a bus in the town where the girl lived.

Women face some obstacles to advancement in employment, but have had increasing legal equality since the 1960s.

Ivory Coast

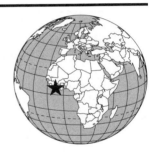

Polity: Dominant party
Economy: Capitalist
Population: 13,896,000
PPP: $1,510
Life Expectancy: 51.6
Ethnic Groups: Baule (23 percent), Bete (18 percent), Senufo (15 percent), Malinke (11 percent), other

Political Rights: 6
Civil Liberties: 5
Status: Not Free

Overview: After thirty-three years of rule, Ivory Coast President Felix Houphouet-Boigny of the Democratic Party of Cote d'Ivoire-African Democracy Rally (PDCI-RDA) died on 7 December 1993. Since gaining independence from France in 1959, Felix Houphouet-Boigny guided the Ivory Coast from colonial to independent rule. During his rule Ivory Coast's development was notable for its ability to escape internal religious and ethnic wars that have engulfed much of post-colonial Africa. Upon his death Henri Konan Bedie, former president of the National Assembly and also from the PDCI-RDA, was appointed successor.

Antigovernment demonstrations in 1990 forced Houphouet-Boigny to authorize the formation of opposition parties. To date, the Ivory Coast has forty-one recognized political parties. Among the new parties to form is the Ivorian Popular Front (FPI), led by Laurent Gbagbo, a long-time adversary and critic of Houphouet-Boigny. In October 1990, Gbagbo, along with a number of other opposition candidates challenged Houphouet-Boigny in the country's first multiparty election. Houphouet-Boigny's subsequent victory was marred by charges of rampant vote-rigging. The government subsequently conceded that the elections were "poorly organized." National Assembly elections followed in November and critics again charged that there was widespread vote-rigging. The ruling PDCI-RDA won 163 seats, the FPI nine, independent candidates' two, and the Ivorian Workers' Party only one. Gbagbo and former prime minister Alassane Dramane Ouattara (PDCI) are likely to be the main challengers in presidential elections scheduled for 1995.

Until the 1980s, the Ivory Coast was one of the wealthiest nations in Africa, a leading exporter of cocoa and the third in the world for coffee production. Its robust economic growth, aided by the World Bank, International Monetary Fund (IMF) and other Western institutions, was dubbed the "Ivorian miracle." In the early 1980s coffee and cocoa prices dropped dramatically, and in subsequent years the Ivory Coast faced a growing IMF debt and an economy close to collapse. Like a number of other African nations, the Ivory Coast agreed to an economic stabiliza-tion program to reduce the deficit, reform tax and labor codes, institute an income distribution plan and begin a program of privatization. In January 1993 Ivory Coast, along with thirteen other African countries found its currency (CFA franc) devalued. The result was immediate price increases, which led to social unrest and protest. Despite this setback, the Ivory Coast is now said to be in a period of economic recovery bolstered by a March 1994 decision by the Paris Club of official creditor nations to cut the Ivory Coast debt by $2.5 billion.

Political Rights and Civil Liberties: Ivorians cannot change their government democratically. Although multiparty elections are scheduled for 1995, earlier multiparty presidential and legislative elections in 1990 were plagued with irregularities, rendering them unfair. Opposition candi-dates have predicted similar practices for 1995 and the likelihood that elections will be accepted as free and fair, should the PDCI-RDA again emerge victorious, is slim.

While freedom of speech is provided for in the Constitution, it does not exist in practice. The radio and television stations in the Ivory Coast are state-controlled and criticism of the government is rare. Opposition newspapers are in circulation but it remains an offense, punishable by three months' to two years' imprisonment, to offend the president, prime minister or other government leaders or to defame institutions of the state. A press law enacted in 1991 created a commission to oversee the press and to enforce laws barring publication of defamatory materials or information that would "undermine the credit of the nation."

In 1992, under the Houphouet-Boigny government, five Ivorian journalists were imprisoned for violating the 1991 law and their respective newspapers' activities were suspended. Since Bedie has taken office, further press restrictions have been imposed. The Media Institute of South Africa (MISA) reports that in July 1994 two journalists from the *La Voie* were sentenced to three years in prison for "inciting violence" and "disturbing public order." Their arrest followed a published article calling for civil disobedience. Other journalists have been sentenced to jail and a fine for "insulting the head of state."

The constitution allows for freedom of assembly and association. In practice, however, these freedoms are severely restricted. The government requires that all organizations register before operating and reserves the right to deny any request. Permits are required to hold public meetings and these requests are frequently denied. In 1992, the government enacted a ban on all outdoor public meetings "until further notice" and the ban has not yet been rescinded. The ban has been selectively applied to exclude some government-organized gatherings. The government also bans organizations from forming along political or religious lines.

In July 1992 the National Assembly passed an "anti-vandal" law, which states that organizers of a meeting that becomes violent are subject to imprisonment regardless of whether they participated in or were present at the meeting. Human rights groups as well as opposition parties denounced the law as being too vague and for imposing collective punishment for the actions of a few. Since its passage, the law has been arbitrarily imposed and has allowed the government to detain non-violent political leaders and student activists.

In February 1994, student demonstrators demanding payment of their scholarship arrears were violently abused by the police. The Federation of University and High School Students of the Cote D'Ivoire (FESCI) was officially banned and a student leader alleged that he was detained and subject to torture following the demonstrations. Amnesty International reports that on 15 May, twenty-five student members of FESCI were arrested and held incommunicado for two weeks, violating the ninety-six-hour limit permitted under Ivorian law. The students were subsequently released in late May 1994. The students had been on strike protesting the imprisonment of FESCI activist Eugene Gonthy, who was sentenced to one year in prison in March 1994. In an appeal trial, Gonthy was sentenced to two years' imprisonment for involvement in violent activities. Amnesty contends that Gonthy was sentenced without corroborating evidence, and it is likely that he was prosecuted solely as a result of his FESCI activities.

The judicial system is not free from government influence. There is no clear separation between the judicial and executive branches of government. In theory, criminal cases are to be tried independent of the executive branch. In practice, verdicts and sentencing in cases that involve crimes committed during protests or marches have been influenced by political pressures. In contrast, there are reports of lenient sentences given to individuals with government contacts. While all those accused of committing capital crimes or felonies have the right to legal counsel, those who cannot afford private counsel often are not represented, since court-appointed attorneys are not readily available.

There is no state religion and freedom of worship is respected. Freedom of international travel is generally respected. While government control on internal travel is limited, the U.S. State Department has received reports of arbitrary roadblocks and harassment of travelers. It is alleged that money is sometimes extorted for passage.

Workers have the right to organize and strike under the constitution. Until 1992, most union activity took place within the government-sponsored General Union of Ivory Coast Workers (UGTCI). In 1992 eleven formally independent unions joined to form the Federation of Autonomous Trade Unions of Cote d'Ivoire (FESCACI). A third, smaller trade union known as Dignite also formed. While the UGTCI rarely approves a strike, the newly formed trade unions have exercised their right to strike. There was no reported government interference with trade unions during 1993.

Jamaica

Polity: Parliamentary democracy
Economy: Capitalist
Population: 2,452,000
PPP: $3,670
Life Expectancy: 73.3
Ethnic Groups: Black majority (about 75 percent), with mixed race, European and Asian minorities

Political Rights: 2
Civil Liberties: 3
Status: Free

Overview:

The economic restructuring effort by the government of Prime Minister P.J. Patterson received high marks from the international financial community. But that could not obscure rising levels of crime and poverty, and the increasing popular disillusionment with politics.

Jamaica, a member of the British Commonwealth, achieved independence in 1962. It is a parliamentary democracy, with the British monarchy represented by a governor-general. The bicameral parliament consists of a sixty-member House of Representatives elected for five years, and a twenty-one-member Senate, with thirteen senators appointed by the prime minister and eight by the leader of the parliamentary opposition. Executive authority is invested in the prime minister, who is the leader of the political party commanding a majority in the House.

Since independence, power has alternated between the currently ruling, social democratic People's National Party (PNP) and the conservative Jamaica Labour Party (JLP). The PNP's Michael Manley was prime minister from 1972 to 1980, and again from 1989 until his resignation for health reasons in 1992. JLP leader Edward Seaga held the post from 1980 until 1989.

In his final tenure Manley adhered to the market reform program begun by Seaga. But falling income, high inflation and unemployment caused the PNP's approval ratings to drop. After Manley resigned, PNP party delegates elected Patterson, a former deputy prime minister and party moderate, over Portia Simpson, an outspoken populist, to succeed Manley.

Patterson continued the economic restructuring program and worked to ease tensions within the PNP. When the PNP moved ahead of the JLP in the polls, Patterson called for early elections. On 30 March 1993 the PNP won in a landslide, taking fifty-two parliamentary seats against eight for the JLP.

The two parties differed little on economics. The JLP was hurt by long-standing internal rifts. Race played a role as Patterson, who is black, appealed to the black majority. Seaga is of Lebanese descent. Also, many Jamaicans saw Patterson's low-key, technocratic style as a stabilizing influence on the nation's traditionally fractious political scene.

The vote was marred by irregularities and violence. That prompted the JLP to boycott the Parliament for a number of months, the start of a prolonged fight between the PNP and the JLP over electoral reform that remained unresolved by the end of 1994.

The JLP tried to organize a "stay-at-home" protest on the one-year anniversary of the 1993 elections, but outside of some neighborhoods in Kingston, the nation's capital, few citizens participated. As the attempt at bipartisan reform dragged on, the JLP boycotted two by-elections in 1994, and local elections, which had been due in 1993, were postponed yet again.

In October the PNP was pleased when the International Monetary Fund gave Jamaica's structural reforms good grades and removed it, after nearly two decades, from its list of sick member-states. However, the news was tempered by increasing labor unrest, eroding purchasing power, high unemployment, an unrelenting crime wave that threatened tourism and a poverty level of more than 30 percent.

Political Rights and Civil Liberties:

Citizens are able to change their government through elections. However, the 1993 elections were marked by thuggery on both sides in urban areas, police intimidation, large-scale confusion, scattered fraud and voter turnout of 59 percent, the lowest since the pre-independence 1962 elections.

There was little progress toward electoral reform in 1994 and the main opposition JLP boycotted two by-elections, one of which saw numerous irregularities. Local elections were postponed for the second straight year. A poll in 1994 showed that nearly half the population preferred neither the PNP nor the JLP, which seemed to indicate a declining confidence in politics in general.

Constitutional guarantees regarding the right to free expression, freedom of religion and the right to organize political parties, civic organizations and labor unions are generally respected. While the JLP and PNP dominate, there are a number of small parties ranging from left to right. Labor unions are politically influential and have the right to strike. There were numerous public-sector strikes in 1994. The critical sugar industry was crippled by a strike in May 1994 before it was resolved by the Industrial Disputes Tribunal.

Electoral violence remains a staple of Jamaican politics. But codes of conduct endorsed by both major parties and supported by civic and religious groups have reduced violence in the last two elections. More than 750 people died in election-related violence in 1980, thirteen in 1989, and fourteen in 1993.

Criminal violence, fueled by poverty and drugs, and human rights violations by the police are of great concern. Violence is now the major cause of death in Jamaica. There were a record number of killings in 1994, 688, compared with 653 in 1993. Jamaicans were stunned by the separate murders of two priests. Much of the violence is due to warfare between drug gangs, known as posses. However, domestic violence, particularly against women, common criminal activity and vigilante actions in rural areas are major factors. The government-supported Bureau of Women's Affairs estimates that only 10 percent of abuse and rape cases are reported, primarily because of the indifferent attitude of law enforcement bodies.

The police, in turn, have been responsible for the deaths of over 2,000 people in the past eight years, as well as numerous cases of physical abuse of detainees. The work of the Jamaica Council for Human Rights has led to successful prosecution in a number of cases, with victims receiving court-ordered, monetary reparations. But officers found guilty of abuses usually go without punishment and many cases remained unresolved. The controversial twenty-year-old Suppression of Crime Act, which gave police extraordinary powers of search and detention, was finally scrapped in 1994. But police can still be granted special powers in emergencies.

In 1993 the Patterson government responded to criticism of police abuses by decentralizing the command structure and appointing a commissioner from outside the force.

The judicial system is headed by a Supreme Court and includes several magistrates' courts and a Court of Appeal, with final recourse to the Privy Council in London. The system is slow and inefficient, particularly in addressing police abuses and the deplorable, violent conditions in prisons and police lockups. There is a mounting backlog of cases due to soaring crime, a shortage of court staff at all levels and a lack of resources. In 1994 international rights groups protested the detention of children in adult police jails.

To stem the crime wave the government has taken the controversial steps of restoring capital punishment, which had been suspended in 1988, and flogging. Rights groups protested both measures. Critics charged that flogging was unconstitutional because it could be characterized as "inhuman or degrading punishment."

Newspapers are independent and free of government control. Journalists occasionally are the targets of intimidation during election campaigns. Broadcast media are largely public but open to pluralistic points of view. Public opinion polls play a key role in the political process and election campaigns feature televised debates on state-run television.

⬆Japan

Polity: Parliamentary democracy
Economy: Capitalist
Population: 125,023,000
PPP: $19,390
Life Expectancy: 78.6
Ethnic Groups: Japanese, Korean, and small immigrant groups
Trend Arrow: Electoral reform and the breakup of old party structures augur well for a more competitive political system.

Political Rights: 2
Civil Liberties: 2
Status: Free

Overview:

The restructuring of Japan's post-War political order continued in 1994 as the conservative Liberal Democratic Party (LDP) returned to power in June in an unlikely old-guard coalition with their longtime opponents, the Socialists. Tomiichi Murayama took office as Japan's first Socialist premier since 1948 and promptly repudiated his party's leftist ideology. Later in the year nine reform-oriented parties united in a single large conservative party.

Following its defeat in World War II, Japan adopted an American-drafted constitution in 1947 that invested legislative authority in the *Diet* (Parliament), renounced war and ended the emperor's divine status. The U.S. took responsibility for Japan's security, allowing the country to focus on rebuilding bombed-out cities and rejuvenating the war-ravaged economy. In October 1955 the two wings of the opposition Japan Socialist Party (JSP) merged, and in November the two main conservative parties merged to form the ruling Liberal Democratic Party (LDP). This "1955 system" remained in place throughout the Cold War as the LDP guided Japan through a spectacular industrial expansion and the Marxist JSP, failing to establish itself as a credible alternative, functioned as an institutional opposition.

The staunchly anti-Communist LDP left most policy decisions up to the powerful bureaucracy. Corporations seeking preferential treatment in landing contracts and bypassing regulations would funnel legal and illegal contributions to the LDP, which would then exert influence on the bureaucracy. The LDP itself consisted of several factions, which were driven more by influence and patronage than ideology. The presence of several LDP candidates competing against each other in the Diet's multiple-seat constituencies inevitably fostered corruption, as contests hinged on fundraising and patronage.

By the late 1980s Japanese began to question the LDP's nominally democratic but corrupt rule on several fronts. The end of the Soviet threat made a vote for the LDP on national security grounds less compelling. Many citizens favored a more open, competitive political system which would be responsive to the needs of ordinary consumers rather than big business. Moreover, a series of political scandals revealed the magnitude of the corruption to be greater than previously believed.

In August 1989, a month after losing its majority in the upper House of Councilors, the LDP named the obscure, "clean" Toshiki Kaifu as prime minister. In October 1991 party leaders replaced Kaifu with Kiichi Miyazawa after Kaifu tried to pass an electoral reform package featuring a proportional representation system that would have cost his party seats.

In August 1992 MP Shin Kanemaru, who had used his backroom influence to virtually dictate the rise and fall of the past four prime ministers, admitted he had received an illegal $4 million contribution from the Sagawa parcel delivery company in 1990. Prosecutors also revealed that in 1987 Kanemaru had used an organized crime syndicate to silence the sound trucks of a right-wing group protesting Nobura Takeshita's impending election as party president and prime minister. Public outrage forced Kanemaru to quit politics in October. In March 1993 prosecutors arrested him on unrelated charges of evading taxes on political contributions. Investigators found a $50 million horde of cash, gold and securities in his home.

In June 1993 the LDP's leadership announced that the government would shelve plans for an electoral reform package until after the 1995 upper house elections. On 18 June 39 pro-reform LDP MPs joined the opposition in a 255-220 vote of no-confidence against the Miyazawa government. With fresh elections now one month away, the LDP began to fracture, as forty-seven MPs defected to join new reform parties.

At the 18 July elections, the LDP lost its lower house majority for the first time since the party's founding, taking a 223 seat plurality. Only 67.2 percent of the voters turned out, a postwar record low for a lower house election. The JSP's share plunged from 136 seats to 70; the newly formed Japan Renewal Party (JRP) took 55; the Buddhist Komeito party, 51; Japan New Party (JNP), the original pro-reform party founded in May 1992, 35; the Democratic Socialist Party, 15; the Japan Communist Party, 15; the newly formed New Harbinger Party (NHP), 13; with 34 seats going to minor parties or independents.

On 29 July the left-wing JSP and six smaller conservative and centrist parties united in a 255-seat coalition. On 6 August the coalition elected JNP founder Morihiro Hosokawa as prime minister, breaking the LDP's streak of naming nineteen consecutive premiers and throwing the party into the opposition for the first time ever. Hosokawa pledged to make electoral reform his top priority. In November the lower house approved four bills that would scrap the multiple-seat constituency system in favor of a mixed proportional and single-seat district system, and would ban corporate donations to individual politicians. However the LDP and the JSP, both fearing a loss of seats under the new system, blocked the bills in the upper house.

On 21 January 1994 the upper house of Parliament formally voted down Hosokawa's reform package. Eight days later Hosokawa won parliamentary approval of a compromise package that dropped the proposed ban on corporate contributions to individual politicians in favor of an annual cap of $4,600 from each company per politician. The package also placed stricter limits on contributions to political parties. The next election will be for a 500-seat parliament with 300 single-seat districts and 200 seats chosen on a proportional basis, each representing one of eleven new super-districts.

In March the opposition began questioning Hosokawa about a $970,000 interest-free loan he received in 1982 from a construction company currently being investigated for corruption. On 8 April Hosokawa unexpectedly resigned over the charges. On 25 April Parliament approved Tsutomo Hata of the JRP as the new prime minister. However, early the next morning the JSP withdrew from the governing coalition after learning that its six conservative partners had joined in parliamentary bloc in an effort to marginalize the leftist party. The JSP's withdrawal forced Hata to form the country's first minority government since 1948.

On 25 June Hata resigned rather than face a vote on a no-confidence motion submitted by the LDP. Four days later the LDP returned to power in an unlikely alliance with the JSP, its longtime ideological rival, along with the smaller NHP, as Parliament voted seventy-year-old Tomiichi Murayama of the JSP as Japan's first Socialist premier since 1948. The LDP-JSP alliance represented an old-guard reaction against reformist policies championed by Ichiro Ozawa, the backroom strategist of the previous two coalition governments. Ozawa and his allies favor faster economic deregulation, a more open political system and a more assertive foreign policy. In July Murayama formally abandoned the JSP's extreme pacifist positions.

In early December nine conservative opposition parties that had formed the backbone of the two previous governments joined together as the New Frontier Party (NFP) and named former premier Kaifu as party leader. At year's end the NFP held 187 seats to the ruling coalition's 293 seats. Although the country appeared to be heading toward a two- or three-party system, many Japanese saw little distinction between the groups. A December poll showed that 44 percent of voters did not support any party.

Political Rights and Civil Liberties: Japanese citizens can change their government democratically. The current parliament was elected in 1993 under an electoral system heavily weighted in favor of the rural areas. Reform legislation passed in 1994 reduced the disparity in population between urban and rural districts, tightened campaign finance laws, and scrapped the multiple–seat constituencies that were blamed for fostering corruption. It remains to be seen whether the new measures can root out the political corruption that has characterized post–War Japanese politics.

A continuing human rights concern involves the 2 million Korean permanent residents, many of whom trace their ancestry in Japan for two or three generations. Ethnic Koreans regularly face discrimination in housing, education and employment opportunities, are not automatically Japanese citizens at birth and must submit to an official background check and adopt Japanese names to become naturalized. In 1993 the government dropped a requirement that Koreans be fingerprinted, although they and other permanent residents must still carry alien registration cards at all times. Both the *Burakumin*, who are descendants of feudal–era outcasts, and the indigenous Ainu minority face discrimination and social ostracization.

Japanese law allows police cells to be used to detain suspects because of a shortage of detention facilities. Police occasionally physically abuse suspects to extract confessions. The Criminal Procedure Code allows the authorities to restrict the right to counsel during an investigation, and in practice access to council is often limited, particularly during interrogation.

The judiciary is independent of the government. Freedoms of expression, assembly and association are guaranteed by the Constitution and respected in practice by the government. Exclusive privately run press clubs provide journalists with access to top politicians and major ministries, and in return journalists often practice self–censorship. The press clubs have only recently begun admitting foreign news organizations and smaller Japanese papers. Foreign news services must negotiate with each club directly, and entry is occasionally denied.

For decades the Education Ministry has censored passages in history textbooks that describe Japan's military aggression in the 1930s and 1940s. In March 1993 the Supreme Court ruled that the Ministry has the right to screen textbooks on "reasonable grounds." In a landmark October 1993 ruling, the Tokyo High Court ruled that the Ministry had overstepped its authority on three of the eight passages deleted in the latest version of a textbook written by historian Saburu Ienaga, and awarded the author partial compensation.

Women face discrimination in employment opportunities and are frequently tracked into clerical careers. A 1989 Labor Ministry report found that female workers receive on average less than half the wages of male workers. There is complete freedom of religion; Buddhism and Shintoism have the most adherents. Workers, with the exception of police and firefighters, are free to join unions of their choice.

Jordan

Polity: Monarchy and elected parliament
Economy: Capitalist
Population: 4,224,000
PPP: $2,895
Life Expectancy: 67.3
Ethnic Groups: Palestinian and Bedouin Arabs, small minorities of Circassians, Armenians, Kurds

Political Rights: 4
Civil Liberties: 4
Status: Partly Free

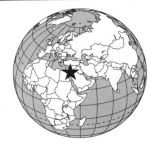

Overview: Jordan's King Hussein signed a peace treaty with Israel in October 1994, formally ending a forty-six year state of war between the two countries.

The British installed the Hashemite monarchy in 1921, and granted Jordan full independence in 1946. Palestinian refugees flooded the Kingdom following the 1948 Arab-Israeli war. King Hussein came to the throne in 1952 and formally assumed constitutional powers in May 1953. The 1952 constitution vests executive power in the king, who appoints the prime minister and Council of Ministers, and convenes, adjourns and dissolves a bicameral National Assembly. The Assembly consists of a forty-member Senate appointed by the king, and an elected eighty-member House of Representatives. The king makes most policy decisions while the prime minister and Council of Ministers run day-to-day affairs.

The country held multiparty elections in 1956, but the king banned political parties a year later following a coup attempt by leftist pan-Arab parties, one of many coup and assassination attempts Hussein has weathered. In the 1967 Six Day War with Israel, Jordan lost the West Bank of the Jordan River, which it had seized in 1948 after the British Mandate in Palestine ended. In September 1970 the king began a crackdown on Palestinian guerrillas operating in his country. The king suspended elections throughout the 1970s and much of the 1980s.

In April 1989 rioting erupted in Karak and other southern cities over price increases under an IMF-mandated austerity program. The king responded by lifting restrictions on freedom of expression and ending a ban on party activity. Hussein prohibited candidates from holding party affiliations in the first elections in twenty-two years in November 1989, but allowed the fundamentalist Muslim Brotherhood to compete under its status as a charitable organization. The Brotherhood took 22 seats, while other fundamentalist groups took 10; tribal and clan groups, 17; pan-Arab leftists, 11; with 20 others appointed by the king representing minority groups.

In October 1992 the government legalized the formation and licensing of political parties. Jordan held its first multiparty elections in thirty-seven years on 8 November 1993. The polling consisted of 534 candidates competing for the 80 seats, and drew a 68 percent turnout. The Islamic Action Front (IAF), the Muslim Brotherhood's political party, took sixteen seats, but none of the nineteen other parties had much impact. Progovernment conservative independents and Bedouin leaders fared well, taking fifty-four seats.

The country's tentative democratization process has been complicated by a complex regional demographic and political situation. Currently "East Bank" Jordanians—those of non-Palestinian descent, including the Hashemites—are a minority and dominate the army and civil service, while Palestinians, who form a 60 percent majority, control business and commerce. After losing the West Bank, Jordan had assumed that any potential Palestinian entity formed in the territory would be part of a Jordanian-dominated confederation. This view held even after the country relinquished its legal and administrative claim to the West Bank in 1988.

The sudden peace agreement announced by Israel and the Palestinian Liberation Organization in late August 1993 shattered this conventional wisdom. With the Palestinians gradually assuming autonomy over the West Bank and potentially expanding their economic influence, many Hashemites feel the very existence of their monarchy is threatened.

King Hussein had also hoped that any peace agreement with Israel would involve Syria and Lebanon as well as Jordan. However, having been taken by surprise by the PLO-Israeli accord, the king now feared being left behind if Syria and Lebanon also struck private deals, and he accelerated the Jordanian-Israeli negotiating track. In June 1994 Prime Minister Abdul Salam Majali reshuffled his cabinet to bring nearly all of the parties represented in Parliament, with the exception of the IAF, into the government. The government hoped to secure broad support in advance of a peace agreement with Israel.

On 25 July King Hussein and Israeli prime minister signed a Washington Declaration ending the forty-six-year state of war between their countries. On 17 October the two leaders initialed a draft peace treaty, and held a formal signing ceremony nine days later. The accord demarcated the two countries' borders, approved a plan for cooperation on water disputes, set security arrangements and pledged cooperation on trade and tourism. The accord also recognized Jordan's "historic role" as a guardian of Islamic holy sites in Israeli-controlled East Jerusalem, pre-empting a similar claim by Palestine Liberation Organization Chairman Yasir Arafat. Domestically, Islamic fundamentalists strongly opposed the accord, although other Jordanians appeared cautiously optimistic that their country would reap economic benefits.

Political Rights and Civil Liberties: Although the country held multiparty elections in November 1993, Jordanians cannot change their government democratically. King Hussein holds broad executive powers and must approve all laws. Any change to the constitution without the king's approval is highly unlikely, since the king appoints the entire forty-member Senate, and two-thirds of the 120-member bicameral National Assembly must approve amendments. Observers rated the elections generally free, although bribery was reported in several districts.

Police frequently abuse prisoners in detention and during interrogation, and often hold prisoners without charge for lengthy periods of time. The judiciary is generally independent of the government in civil cases, although there is some question about the impartiality of the military judges in State Security Courts. Defendants in civil court trials generally receive adequate safeguards, although bribery of judges is relatively common. Defendants in State Security Courts are denied access to lawyers during pre-trial periods and lack an adequate avenue of appeal. The High Court of Cassation automatically reviews State Security Court decisions involving a death sentence or imprisonment of more than ten years, but does not examine the facts or the decision, only whether the court properly applied the law. Separate Islamic Shari'a and Christian courts handle family and religious matters.

Jordanians freely criticize the government's policies and express diverse political viewpoints, although direct criticism of King Hussein is rare. State law prohibits political commentary in mosque sermons. After King Hussein signed an agreement with Israeli premier Yitzhak Rabin in July ending the two countries' state of war, the government took measures to limit dissent by the Muslim Brotherhood and its political wing, the Islamic Action Front (IAF). The *Christian Science Monitor* reported in early August that the Ministry of Islamic Affairs had suspended twenty-four preachers from giving sermons, and that the Ministry of

Education had begun purging pro-IAF teachers from public schools. The 8 August *Associated Press* reported that police arrested Tahir Abdul Hamid, a preacher belonging to the radical Hezb al-Tahrir party, after he delivered a sermon criticizing Jordan's peace overtures with Israel.

Journalists reportedly practice self-censorship on sensitive issues, and the government occasionally pressures editors not to run certain stories. In April 1993 King Hussein approved a relatively restrictive press law permitting only official news dispatches to be published on matters regarding the king, the royal family and the armed forces, as well as regional security issues, and banning "defamation" of the diplomatic corps and heads of state of friendly foreign countries. The law also required the licensing of journalists and editors and the licensing of publications, and required foreign news organizations to have a Jordanian national as editor. The new law repealed the government's right to penalize journalists and revoke newspapers' publishing licenses without due process rights. In September 1994 police detained Nidal Mansour, chief editor of *Al-Bilad*, an Arabic language weekly, under the press law following an August article which said that twelve members of the Jordanian contingent of the U.N. peacekeeping troops in Croatia had been infected with AIDS.

Since 1989 the government has freely granted permits for peaceful public demonstrations. Local human rights groups can operate freely but are subject to regulations concerning publication of information about the police and armed forces, thus making it nearly impossible to report on instances of torture.

Islam is the state religion and most other groups are allowed to worship freely. However, the government does not recognize the Baha'i faith. As such, Baha'i are not permitted to run schools, must register property as individuals rather than as a religious entity and their family legal matters are handled in the Islamic Shari'a courts. Citizens can travel freely within the country, although women must receive permission from a male guardian to travel abroad. Women also are legally discriminated against in inheritance and divorce matters, and frequently do not receive equal pay for equal work. In recent years there has been a growing population of street children, and the government is attempting to provide for their welfare.

The Israeli-PLO September 1993 Declaration of Principles did not address the fate of the approximately 1.5 million Palestinian refugees living in Jordan. Although Jordan has granted them full citizenship, many desire to return to Israel, the West Bank or the Gaza Strip.

All nongovernmental workers are free to unionize. The government can legally prohibit private sector strikes by referring a dispute to an arbitration committee. Some government employees can form unions, such as in the state-owned airline, but none is allowed to strike. The International Confederation of Trade Unions has criticized the government for not adequately protecting workers from anti-union discrimination by employers.

Kazakhstan

Polity: Dominant party
Economy: Statist
transitional
Population: 17,087,000
PPP: $4,490
Life Expectancy: 69.0

Political Rights: 6
Civil Liberties: 5*
Status: Not Free

Ethnic Groups: Kazakhs (43 percent), Russians (35 percent), Ukrainians (6 percent), others (16 percent)
Ratings Change: *Kazakhstan's Civil Liberties rating changed from 4 to 5 because of increasing Kazakh-Russian ethnic tensions and President Nazarbayev's increasing dominance of the country.

Overview:

Among the major issues facing President Nursultan Nazarbayev in 1994 were the country's first post-Soviet parliamentary elections, economic reforms and tensions with Moscow over Russian participation in the development of Kazakhstan's large oil and gas fields.

This sparsely populated, multi-ethnic land the size of India stretching from the Caspian Sea east to the Chinese border was controlled by Russia from 1730-1840. After a brief period of independence in 1917, it became an autonomous Soviet republic in 1929 and a union republic in 1936. Kazakhstan formally declared independence from a crumbling Soviet Union in December 1991.

President Nazarbayev, a former first secretary of the Kazakhstan Communist Party, was directly elected in 1991. In January 1993 the Soviet-era 358-member Supreme *Kenges* (Parliament), which was elected in 1990, adopted a new constitution that established a strong presidency. The president has the power to appoint the prime minister and deputy prime minister, the foreign, defense and interior ministers, the chairman of the National Security Council and all the country's ambassadors. There are no provisions for impeachment of the president. A month after the document's adoption, President Nazarbayev became chairman of the newly established, progovernment People's Unity Union (SNEK or PUUK), which adopted a program backing radical economic reform and political pluralism. Parliament dissolved itself in December 1993.

In 1994, President Nazarbayev continued to rule as a popular but authoritarian leader who put economic modernization before political reform. Ruling a country with a population that is 40 percent ethnically Russia, or Slavic, he sought to maintain political and ethnic stability while attracting aid and investment to exploit the country's tremendous mineral wealth, including large deposits of oil, natural gas, gold and uranium.

The run-up to the March 1994 parliamentary elections brought opposition charges of irregularities and intimidation by the government. More than 750 candidates competed for 177 seats, 42 of which were to be chosen from a "state list" drawn up by Nazarbayev. Socialists (former Communists), led by Nazarbayev until he formed the Unity Union, complained that the president forced the old parliament to resign because it was blocking his reforms. Several Socialist Party candidates were unfairly barred from registering for the election, even though they had garnered more than the 3,000 signatures required to run. Ethnic Russians noted that of the parliamentary candidates, only 128 were Russians, who make up 39 percent of the population, and 566 were Kazakhs, who account for just over 40 percent. Nazarbayev's control of the media also hampered opposition candidates.

Official and unofficial international observers of the 7 March vote agreed that it was not up to democratic standards, an assessment supported by Nazarbayev himself. Pro-Nazarbayev centrist parties won 60 percent of the seats. The new parliament was composed of 105 Kazakhs, 49 Russians, 10 Ukrainians, 3 Germans, 3 Jews, 1 Uzbek, 1 Tatar, 1 Korean, 1 Pole, and 1 Uighur. Turnout estimates ranged from 60 percent to 73 percent of 9.4 million registered voters at over 2,400 polling stations. Observers said that flaws included a too short campaign period, requirements that discouraged real opposition candidates, restrictions on media, and provisions that allowed individuals to vote on behalf of family members.

A key domestic issue continued to be the economy and the pace and scope of market reforms. Multinationals continued to flock to Kazakhstan, which was second only to Russia among the fifteen ex-Soviet republics in attracting foreign investment. Chevron was developing the Tengiz oil field on the Caspian's northeastern shore, said to be one of the world's ten largest fields. A consortium of Western multinationals was also exploring the Kazakh part of the Caspian Sea bed. Some sixty U.S. firms had branches in Almaty, the capital.

In April the government launched a mass privatization program, which called for selling some 3,500 medium-sized state enterprises, accounting for about 70 percent of the country's businesses and 30 percent of the entire economy, over a fifteen-month period. Citizens were handed out coupons that could only be exchanged for shares in 140 investment funds, which would use the coupons for buying up companies. The program ran into trouble in September when Parliament tried to suspend privatization of medium- and large-scale enterprises, alleging that auctions had been fixed to benefit powerful families. Privatization of small-scale enterprises, such as shops and restaurants, proceeded normally.

In June Kazakhstan accused Russia of cutting off most of the country's oil exports as part of a campaign of political and economic pressure. Russia had demanded an equity share in the giant Karachagnak gas field and a stake in the rich Tengiz oilfield. Throughout the year, Moscow had demanded veto rights over any resource development project on the Caspian Sea, claiming that without its approval any deal with Kazakhstan and Azerbaijan was illegal. The dispute was defused in November, when the Russian gas company, Gazprom, was included in a $6 billion proposal to develop the Karachagnak field. The agreement opened the way for the field's production to be shipped through Russia's pipeline system to the West.

To countervail undue Russian influence, Kazakhstan signed numerous economic, trade and friendship treaties with Britain, the United States and regional powers, including Iran and China. In April Chinese Prime Minister Li Peng visited Almaty as part of a swing through former Soviet Central Asia to "build a new Silk Road," a reference to the ancient Asian trading route. Peng was also concerned about Islamic unrest among the Uighur peoples in western China; Uighurs across the borders in Kazakhstan have called for an independent "Uighurstan." While in Washington in February, President Nazarbayev was promised a $311 million aid package for 1995, triple the $91 million appropriated for 1993-94.

In October, frustrated with the rate of reform, President Nazarbayev forced the resignation of Prime Minister Sergei Tereshchenko and his cabinet. He was succeeded by his deputy, Akhezan Kazhegeldin. One problem was inflation, which was 7 percent a month, above the 4.3 percent target promised by the government under a 1993 deal with the International Monetary Fund (IMF). Parliament had derailed portions of the so-called economic "crisis program" launched in the summer. Proposals to free bread and flour prices were rejected by Parliament fifteen times.

On 15 December Parliament refused to discuss President Nazarbayev's proposals to amend the constitution affecting private property, two official languages and reforms of the legislation process. After the voting, the president said that government and parliamentary representatives should "sit down at the negotiating table" to iron out differences.

The Clinton administration negotiated to transfer some 1,300 pounds of enriched, bomb-grade uranium to the United States. The deal was hammered out between the U.S., Kazakhstan and Russia. The material was flown to the U.S. in late November.

Political Rights and Civil Liberties: Citizens of Kazakhstan have the power to change their government democratically under a 1993 constitution that enshrines a multiparty, presidential system. Nevertheless, *de facto* power has been centered in the hands of President Nazarbayev, whose regime has cracked down on the opposition, controls the media and monitors the opposition. March parliamentary elections failed to meet Western democratic standards, according to international observers.

There are numerous opposition parties, among them the Socialists, the Azat (Freedom) Party, the nationalist Republican Party, the ethnic Russian-dominant Unity, the Public Slavonic Movement (LAD) and several smaller groups. In December, a republican Agrarian Party was launched. Articles 55 and 58 of the constitution prohibit ethnic- and religious-based public associations and parties. Opposition parties have complained of harassment, surveillance, denial of access to state-run media, and irregularities that led to several parliamentary candidates being denied the right to run despite having garnered the requisite number of signatures.

Minority and citizenship rights were an issue in light of the country's large, non-Kazakh population. Russians, Germans and others charged discrimination in favor of ethnic Kazakhs was prevalent in government, state-run businesses, housing and education. Kazakhs made up the bulk of the over 750 candidates running for Parliament. While Kazakh is the official language, Russian is enshrined as the language of "interethnic communication." President Nazarbayev extended a deadline to March 1995 to let residents decide if they want Kazakhstan citizenship. Ethnic Russian have left in droves, particularly from the northern industrial cities such as Karaganda. About half of the 140,000 ethnic Germans who originally resided in the city of 650,000 have emigrated to Germany. In December, foreign ministers of Kazakhstan and Russia initialed a treaty on the legal status of citizens of one country who live on the territory of another country, as well as an agreement simplifying the procedure of granting citizenship.

The judiciary is not wholly free from government interference. In 1993, the president and Parliament seriously weakened the power of an activist Constitutional Court which had sought criminal code reform and had rejected several presidential decrees.

Obstacles to press freedom include economic factors as well as some government interference. Although over 800 media outlets (475 newspapers) are registered, many are beset by problems such as access to state-run printing operations, paper and distribution. Supplies have been denied to *Birlesu*, a Russian-language trade union publication. With most newspapers dependent on some government subsidies, and with laws against criticizing the president and parliamentary deputies, self-censorship is a problem. There are Russian-, German- and Korean-language papers. The quasi-governmental Kazakh Radio and Television company has removed journalists for political reasons. There are several independent television stations.

The constitution guarantees freedom of religion, but religious associations may not pursue political goals. Christians, Muslims and Jews can worship freely.

Domestic and international travel, as well as emigration, is generally unencumbered. Government control of housing and requirements for residence permits are obstacles to freedom of movement. Several independent women's groups exist to address such issues as discrimination in hiring and education, and domestic violence.

There are several trade unions, including the Independent Trade Union Center (ITUC), with twelve member unions, one of which is the important coal miners' union in Karaganda.

Kenya

Polity: Dominant-party   **Political Rights:** 6*
Economy: Capitalist   **Civil Liberties:** 6
Population: 26,975,000   **Status:** Not Free
PPP: $1,350
Life Expectancy: 58.6
Ethnic Groups: Kikuyu (21 percent), Luhya (14 percent), Luo (13 percent), Kalenjin (11 percent), Somali (2 percent), other
Ratings Change: *Kenya's political rights rating changed from 5 to 6, reflecting a crackdown on opposition.

Overview: Tribal violence, the prospects of widespread drought, and persistent allegations of human rights abuses and political repression dogged the regime of President Daniel arap Moi in 1994. A key issue was economic reforms mandated by international lending institutions.

Kenya came under British control in the late nineteenth century and was organized in 1920 as a colony (inland) and protectorate (along the coast). From 1952-56, the Kikuyu, the country's largest tribe, led the Mau Mau rebellion to protest British rule. A May 1963 election established the predominant position of the Kenya African National Union (KANU) led by Mau Mau leader Jomo Kenyatta, a Kikuyu. Kenyatta's authoritarian rule led to conflicts with other tribes, particularly the Kalenjin, who lived in the fertile Rift Valley. After his death in

1978, Kenyatta was succeeded on an interim basis by Vice President Moi, a Kalenjin, who was elected to a full term in November 1979. In June 1982 he formally banned all opposition parties and in 1990 forcibly put down several pro-democracy demonstrations. After tribal clashes in the fall of 1991, Moi was pressured by international financial and lending institutions into legalizing opposition parties, and a multiparty constitution took effect in December of that year.

In December 1992, in the first multiparty presidential and parliamentary elections since 1966, Moi was elected with barely 36 percent of the vote. He defeated Kenneth Matiba, a Kikuyu of the Forum for the Restoration of Democracy (FORD)-Asili faction, who got 26 percent; former Moi ally Mwa Kibaki of the Democratic Party, who got 19.4 percent; and Oginga Odinga, an ethnic Luo and leader of FORD-Kenya faction, who got 17.4 percent. In the vote for the 188-member unicameral National Assembly (Parliament), KANU took 100 seats; FORD-Asili, 31; FORD-Kenya, 31; Democratic Party, 23; and three tiny parties took one seat apiece. The voting in both elections largely followed tribal lines. Moi used his constitutional power to appoint twelve additional MPs, all from KANU.

International observers concluded that the elections could not "be given an unqualified rating of free and fair." The team's report noted irregularities in the voter-registration process; problems with the nomination process that prevented several candidates from registering; threats and harassment of opposition party supporters; bans on opposition speakers in several areas; partisan coverage by the state-run media; and a "failure to de-link the ruling party from the government," allowing public funds to be used for political purposes.

The election results revealed what a one-party state could conceal: that President Moi headed a government of minority tribes that had deliberately marginalized the larger ethnic groups, particularly the Kikuyu tribe, which had dominated political life under Kenyatta.

In 1994 tribal violence, much of it instigated by the government, continued to wrack the country. The government blamed the conflict on the multiparty democracy introduced in 1991-92. In January 1994 approximately 4,000 Kikuyus fled their homes in the Narok province after their farms were attacked by Maasais. In February Kalenjins raided Kikuyus in the Laikipia District, resulting in one death and scores of injuries. In March, violent clashes broke out again in the Burnt Forest area in the Rift Valley, the scene of much violence in the previous two years. According to official sources, the fighting between Kikuyus and Kalenjins left eighteen people dead. As the violence continued, there were persistent charges that the government was behind much of the violence or was doing nothing to stop attacks on the Kikuyu. Church and human rights groups reported that the fighting between the tribes had caused over 1,500 deaths and displaced more than 300,000 people since 1991. Three independent reports charged the government with complicity or involvement in the violence. Government officials and close associates of President Moi were named as the principal instigators of the Rift Valley clashes.

The government denied any involvement in the conflict, which in the first half of 1994 began to take the form of "ethnic cleansing"—the removal of all ethnic groups except the Kalenjin, Maasai, Turkana and Sambura from the Rift Valley. In July attention focused on the massacre of 10,000 Turkana over a three-year period with the connivance of the Kenyan and Sudanese governments. The Turkana were besieged both by the Toposa people backed, by Sudan, and the Pokot people, backed by Nairobi, in return for their support for President Moi, a fellow member of the Kalenjin-speaking ethnic group. Throughout the year, the government also persecuted activists from the illegal Islamic Party of Kenya (IPK), arresting leaders and members.

Politics in 1994 was marked by continued acrimonious relations between the government and the opposition. In March KANU won a by-election in Lugari. In May an election court nullified the 1992 election of FORD-Asili MP Geoffrey Macharia. The following month Kenyan opposition parties formed a new alliance, the Kenya National Democratic Alliance (KENDA), at a rally attended by fifty opposition deputies. In November five people were killed and several injured when violence erupted in Nairobi after a by-election won by FORD-Kenya. There were several fistfights in Parliament; in one incident, Kenya's assistant minister for lands and settlement bit off the ear of an opponent at a public meeting, and his victim was charged with assault. After the January death of FORD-Kenya leader Odinga, President Moi announced that KANU would no longer cooperate with the political opposition. A favorite tactic used to harass and arrest opposition MPs was to detain them on the pretext that public meetings they attended were not licensed or to withhold licenses for opposition applicants.

In the economic sphere, Kenya continued the tough structural adjustment program imposed by the World Bank and the International Monetary Fund (IMF), which required that government finances be closely managed, state companies privatized, agriculture and other marketing boards abolished, the Kenyan shilling floated and the civil service was sharply cut. By year's end, only four minor companies had been privatized, but the shilling had strengthened and inflation had dropped from 100 percent annually to 13 percent. The strong shilling made it tough for manufacturers, exporters and farmers. In response, the World Bank earmarked $70 million for schools, $70 million for farmers and $100 million for small businessmen. A number of Moi's supporters were hostile to privatization, notably the so-called "Rift Valley mafia," led by former Energy Minister Nicholas Biwott, Vice President George Saitoti and the minister for local government, William Ntimama.

A major concern of the government was drought and the possibility of famine. In February President Moi established a special relief department to coordinate drought recovery programs, including the supply of seeds and fertilizers. By March the government said that one-fifth of the population was in need of emergency relief, and that crop failures and massive loss of livestock could have catastrophic results. Western donors complained of theft and corruption in government agencies.

Political Rights and Civil Liberties: Although Kenya held multiparty elections in December 1992, the right of citizens to change their government is severely restricted. The president and government officials have railed against democratization imposed, they say, by international organizations. "Multi-party elections were forced on us by the donor community," according to the KANU general secretary and education minister, John Joseph Kamotho.

In January 1993, a month after the elections, a Commonwealth observer team concluded that the elections "cannot be given an unqualified rating of free and fair," citing numerous violations.

The judiciary is not independent of the government. The president appoints the attorney general and top judges, and can remove the attorney general and all judges upon the recommendation of a presidentially appointed tribunal. Under a 1989 High Court ruling, the courts lack the power to enforce the country's Bill of Rights. There are no jury trials, and defendants do not have the right to free legal representation.

Police often violate constitutional provisions by holding criminal suspects incommunicado for two or more weeks before bringing charges. Suspects can also be detained indefinitely without charge for security reasons under the Preservation of Public Security Act. Police often abuse or torture suspects to extract confessions, and frequently use unwarranted force in dealing with civil disturbances as well as peaceful demonstrations.

Political parties are allowed to organize, and there are ten registered parties. In May, the National Development Party was registered. However, the Islamic Party of Kenya repeatedly has been denied registration. The Public Order and Police Act restricts peaceful assembly by requiring permission to hold meetings of three or more people. This law was repeatedly used in 1994 to arrest, interrogate and detain opposition MPs and to prevent political meetings by opposition parties, in violation of constitutional guarantees on freedom of association and expression. Critics have been imprisoned on trumped-up criminal charges, according to independent human rights and church groups.

Freedom of the press is restricted. In recent years, police have arrested numerous journalists and publishers on charges of "rumormongering" or sedition. In March, Bedan Mbugua, editor of *The People*, and reporter David Makali were arrested and sentenced to four months in prison for calling an Appellate Court ruling a "judicial lynching...tailored to meet the political expedience of the executive." Makali was placed in solitary confinement and badly beaten. In March and April editors and workers from *The Standard* and *The Nation* were charged with sedition for reporting on tribal violence. Between January and October eighteen Kenyan journalists were fined, arrested or jailed for contempt of court for violating libel laws. In September the Ministry of Information threatened to evict an American correspondent for the British *Daily Telegraph* "for filing inaccurate and misleading stories about Kenya," after he wrote stories on violence and crime.

Women generally occupy subservient roles in society, business and government, but there are women in Parliament and government. Although the government discourages female genital mutilation, it is practiced by some ethnic groups. There are women's organizations, but they face restrictions and harassment if their work is deemed political. In March, because the keynote speaker at a seminar was an opposition MP, anti-riot police dispersed the seminar of about 100 representatives from women's groups in the Kisimu Rural constituency who were to discuss the role of nongovernmental ogranizations in development. On 9 June, heavily armed police stopped a meeting organized by the League of Kenyan Women Voters to discuss "civic education and the legal rights of women."

Swahili Muslims charge discrimination in employment and property rights. Swahili Sheik Kalid Salim Balala, leader of the IPK, has been arrested several times for antigovernment speeches and for calling for strikes in Mombassa.

Workers, except for central government civil servants, can join independent trade unions. Most unions are affiliated with the Central Organization of Trade Unions (COTU), which is considered progovernment. Workers must give the minister of labor a three-week notice before striking. In late August the government sacked most of the 3,000 public-sector doctors on strike since June. The government also refused to register University Academic Staff Union (UASU); university lecturers have been on strike since November 1993.

Kiribati

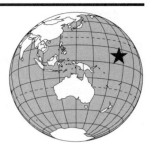

Polity: Parliamentary democracy
Economy: Capitalist-statist
Population: 78,000
PPP: na
Life Expectancy: na
Ethnic Groups: Kiribatian (Micronesian, 84 percent), Polynesian (14 percent), other (2 percent)

Political Rights: 1
Civil Liberties: 1
Status: Free

Overview: The Republic of Kiribati consists of thirty-three islands of the Gilbert, Line and Phoenix groups scattered over two-million square miles of the Pacific Ocean. It became an independent member of the British Commonwealth on 12 July 1979.

The unicameral *Maneaba ni Maungatabu* (Assembly) has thirty–nine members directly elected every four years, along with one representative from Banaba Island elected by the Banaban Rabi Council of Leaders. The president is directly elected from a list of three to four candidates nominated by the Maneaba from among its members, and is limited to three four–year terms. In July 1991 founding President Ieremia Tabai served out his third term and threw his support in the presidential election behind Teatao Teannaki, who beat out his main competitor, Roniti Teiwaki.

On 24 May 1994 Parliament voted to set up a select committee to investigate misuse of public funds by a cabinet minister for hotel, transportation and entertain-ment expenses. Reading this as a vote of no–confidence in the administration, Parliamentary Speaker Beretitara Neeti dissolved Parliament and President Teanaki resigned from office. A Council of State, consisting of the speaker, the chief justice and the chairman of the Public Service Commission (PSC), took over as a caretaker administration. On 1 June, in what acting head of state Tekire Tameura, head of the PSC, termed an "administrative coup," police forcibly removed him from his office on the grounds that his tenure at the PSC had expired three days earlier.

Tameura's ouster had little discernible effect on the political situation. On 21–22 July the country held early elections for a new parliament, with 206 candidates compet-ing. Following runoff balloting on 29–30 July, the Christian Democratic Party (CDP) took a plurality of the seats, ousting the National Progressive Party. Owing to the informal nature of the country's political parties, the exact breakdown of the seats was not available. In September voters elected the CDP's Teburoro Tito as president.

Political Rights and Civil Liberties: Citizens of Kiribati can change their government demo-cratically. Local Island Councils are established on all inhabited islands. Politics are generally conducted on a personal and issue-oriented basis rather than on a partisan level. The three existing parties—the National Progressive Party, the Christian Democratic Party, and the United Kiribati Party—lack platforms and offices.

The government respects human rights, and fundamental freedoms of speech, press, assembly, religion and association are respected in theory and practice. The independent judiciary is modeled on English common law, and provides adequate due process rights. In July 1993 the parliament voted unanimously to amend the Broadcasting Act to end the government's monopoly on radio and, although no government television currently exists, on television. The sole radio station and two government-owned newspapers offer pluralistic viewpoints, and churches publish newsletters. Women are entering the work force in increasing numbers in this male-dominated society. Citizens are free to travel internally and abroad. Workers are free to organize into unions and strike. The Kiribati Trade Union Congress includes seven trade unions with approximately 2,500 members.

Korea, North

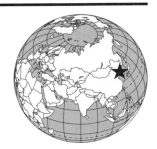

Polity: Communist one-party
Economy: Statist
Population: 23,067,000
PPP: $1,750
Life Expectancy: 70.7
Ethnic Groups: Ethnically homogeneous—Korean

Political Rights: 7
Civil Liberties: 7
Status: Not Free

The sudden death in July 1994 of North Korea's Stalinist leader Kim Il Sung, who ruled this tightly controlled police state for forty-six years, raised questions about whether his son, Kim Jong Il, could assume power as planned despite being reportedly unpopular with the military. In October North Korea signed an agreement with the United States pledging to freeze and eventually dismantle its nuclear program, which is suspected of harboring atomic weapons technology, in return for modern reactors.

The Democratic People's Republic of Korea was formally established in September 1948, three years after the partition of the Korean Peninsula. Marshall Kim Il Sung, installed as leader with Soviet backing, created a Stalinist personality cult based largely on his supposed leading role in fighting the Japanese in the 1930s. For decades Kim used an all-encompassing "ideology," *Juche* (I Myself), stressing national self-reliance and independence, to justify isolating the country from the rest of the world. Meanwhile the government nurtured a slavish devotion to the "Great Leader" Kim and his son, "Dear Leader" Kim Jong Il, by indoctrination through the media, the workplace, the military, mass spectacles, cultural events and some 35,000 Kim statues and ubiquitous portraits.

In December 1991 the younger Kim replaced his father as Supreme Commander of the 1.2-million-man armed forces (the fourth largest in the world), in what appeared to be the first stage of an anticipated transfer of power from father to son. The same month, with its Soviet patron collapsing, North Korea signed a nonaggression pact with the South. The two Koreas, which have never formally ended their 1950-53 war, also pledged to ban nuclear weapons from the peninsula and agreed to form a Joint Nuclear Control Commission to inspect potential atomic weapons facilities.

In April 1992 North Korea agreed to allow International Atomic Energy Agency (IAEA) inspectors access to its three declared nuclear facilities. This included a controversial complex of more than 100 buildings at Yongbyon, sixty miles northwest of Pyongyang, the capital, which the U.S. believes contains a reprocessing plant capable of producing weapons-grade plutonium. In January 1993 inspectors discovered that North Korea had produced more plutonium than the small amount it had previously declared. The IAEA, concerned that the "missing" plutonium may be enough to make a nuclear weapon, requested access to two suspected nuclear waste sites at Yongbyon. Pyongyang refused, and on 12 March North Korea became the first nation to pull out of the Nuclear Non-Proliferation Treaty (NPT).

Despite having no formal relations, the U.S. and North Korea began a series of urgent negotiations that led Pyongyang to agree to "suspend" its treaty withdrawal in June. However, throughout the year North Korea continued to deny inspectors access to its facilities. On 25 December the *New York Times* reported that U.S. intelligence agencies had estimated that there is a "better than even" chance that North Korea has developed one or two bombs.

On 3 June 1994 the IAEA told the U.N. Security Council that North Korea had dismantled so much of the Yongbyon reactor's core that it was not possible to determine if plutonium had been reprocessed from spent fuel rods. Tensions rose as the U.S. began seeking support on the Security Council to impose economic sanctions, a move that the North broadly hinted could lead to war. In a surprise development, former U.S. President Jimmy Carter visited Pyongyang on 15-18 June and reported that Kim Il Sung was willing to freeze his nuclear program if the U.S. would begin high-level talks focusing on a permanent shutdown of North Korea's plutonium-producing complex in exchange for advanced reactors.

Kim Il Sung' sudden death from a heart attack on 8 July at the age of eighty-two threw uncertainty into these plans. However, bilateral U.S.-North Korean negotiations resumed in August in Geneva. The breakthrough came on 21 October as the U.S. and North Korea signed a complex, three-stage agreement under which Pyongyang agreed to a ten-year timetable for dismantling its nuclear program.

In the first stage, the North agreed to freeze its nuclear program while the U.S., South Korea, Japan and other countries would provide the country with oil to alleviate widespread electricity shortages. Work would also begin on two light-water reactors, to be financed primarily by South Korea and Japan. These are less useful in producing weapons-grade plutonium than are the North's existing graphite reactors. In the second phase, North Korea would allow inspections of its two controversial waste sites and allow spent fuel rods to be sent to a third country to ensure that plutonium is not reprocessed from them. During phase two, the first light-water reactor would be completed. In the third phase, which probably would not begin until 2003, the North would dismantle its existing reactors and the second light-water reactor would be completed.

As tensions eased, in November South Korea announced it would begin lifting restrictions on business activity with North Korea. With North Korea's economy a shambles, South Korea does not favor rapid reunification, which economists estimate could cost Seoul $40 billion or more, and is focusing more on building the country's infrastructure. On 16 December North Korea shot down a U.S. military helicopter that reportedly strayed over the Demilitarized Zone separating the two Koreas. The helicopter's copilot died immediately, and the North released the captured pilot on 30 December.

Another area of concern is North Korea's leadership. By year's end the fifty-two-year-old Kim Jong Il had still not assumed the two top positions held by his father, President of the country and general secretary of the Workers' Party. Although analysts have long reported that Kim is unpopular with the military, it was unclear whether he was having difficulty assuming the top posts or simply observing the Confucian tradition of not grabbing power too quickly after a death.

Kim's long-term survival will depend on opening up an economy that reportedly contracted by an average of 5.2 percent per year between 1990-93. Defectors report severe food shortages and, in April 1994, the Supreme People's Assembly issued a statement acknowledging a "food problem," a rare admission in a country where such information is usually suppressed. In July, just after the elder Kim's death, there were unconfirmed reports that the government had begun using military rice reserves to feed hungry civilians.

Political Rights and Civil Liberties:

North Koreans live in the most tightly controlled country in the world and cannot change their government democratically. The government denies citizens all fundamental freedoms and rights. The Supreme People's Assembly holds no independent power. It consists of state-approved candidates from the government-backed Korean Workers' Party and from smaller state-run parties, and meets for only a few days each year. Opposition parties are illegal, and owing to the regime's repressive and isolationist policies and the effects of severe economic hardship, there appears to be little organized opposition. Citizens face a steady onslaught of state propaganda from loudspeakers and from radios and televisions that are built to receive only government stations.

Authorities conduct monthly checks of residences and electronic surveillance is common. Children are encouraged at school to report on their parents' activities. The government assigns a security rating to each individual that, to a somewhat lesser extent than in the past, plays a role in determining access to education, employment and health services.

Persons committing the slightest effrontery to the Kim family, criticizing the government or committing any other act deemed threatening to the regime are subject to imprisonment or summary execution. Citizens have been severely punished simply for listening to the Voice of America or the BBC World Service.

The judiciary is controlled by the government. Defense lawyers attempt to persuade defendants to plead guilty rather than advocate for them. Prison conditions are reportedly brutal. Entire families are sometimes imprisoned together. The regime operates "re-education through labor" camps where forced labor is practiced. South Korean analysts estimate up to 150,000 or more political prisoners and their families are held in remote camps. Defectors say some political prisoners are "re-educated" and released, while others languish in brutal conditions.

Religious practice is restricted to state-sponsored Buddhist and Christian services. Government escorts frequently take foreign visitors to observe these places of worship, indicating that they exist simply to burnish the regime's image. Permission to travel outside one's town is generally granted only for state business, weddings or funerals. The government reportedly forcibly resettles politically suspect citizens. Access to Pyongyang, the capital, is tightly controlled. Few citizens are permitted to travel abroad. Unions are controlled by the state, and strikes do not occur.

Korea, South

Polity: Presidential-
parliamentary democracy
Economy: Capitalist-
statist
Population: 44,454,000
PPP: $8,320
Life Expectancy: 70.4
Ethnic Groups: Ethnically homogeneous—Korean

Political Rights: 2
Civil Liberties: 2
Status: Free

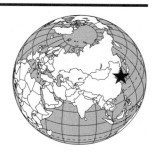

Overview:

A year after being sworn in as South Korea's first civilian president in three decades, Kim Young Sam has enacted substantial reforms aimed at weakening the security apparatus and rooting out corruption. Nevertheless, the continued application of the National Security Law remains a key human rights concern.

The Republic of Korea was established in August 1948 in the U.S.-controlled southern Korean Peninsula, three years after the occupying Japanese were defeated in World War II. General Park Chung Hee took power in a 1961 military coup, and guided the country through a period of intense industrialization and authoritarian rule. Following Park's assassination in 1979, Chun Doo Hwan took power in another military coup. In May 1980 the army crushed widespread anti-government protests in the southern city of Kwangju. In June 1987 violent student-led protests rocked the country after Chun picked another army general, Roh Tae Woo, as his successor. On 29 June Roh announced sweeping reforms including direct presidential elections and a restoration of civil liberties suspended under martial law.

The country's best-known dissidents, Kim Young Sam and Kim Dae Jung, both ran in the December 1987 presidential election, dividing the opposition and allowing Roh to win with just 35.9 percent of the vote. A revised constitution took effect in February 1988 guaranteeing basic rights, limiting the president to a single five-year term and taking away his power to dissolve Parliament. In January 1990, Kim Young Sam and another opposition leader Kim Jong Pil, startled their supporters by merging their parties with the governing Democratic Justice Party, forming the Democratic Liberal Party (DLP). In 1991 Kim Dae Jung, now the country's leading opposition figure, merged his Party for Peace and Democracy with two minor opposition parties to form the center-left opposition Democratic Party.

At the 24 March 1992 elections for the Assembly's 237 directly elected and 62 proportionately distributed seats, the DLP lost its majority, taking 149 seats. The Democratic Party won 97 seats; the upstart United National Party, headed by billionaire Hyundai founder Chung Ju Yung, 31; the tiny Party for New Political Reform, 1; along with 21 mostly progovernment independents.

The 18 December presidential vote, the cleanest in the country's history, was the first in three decades in which none of the candidates had a military background. Kim Young Sam, running for the ruling DLP, was elected with 42 percent of the vote, followed by Kim Dae Jung, 34 percent; and Chung, 15 percent.

In January 1993 Kim Dae Jung quit politics, leaving the Democratic Party without a dynamic leader. By 20 February defections had left the UNP with less than the twenty MPs required to be recognized as a parliamentary negotiating caucus, and gave the DLP a 170-seat majority.

Kim took office on 25 February 1993 as the first civilian president since 1961, and pledged to root out corruption and curb the powers of the security apparatus. In March the Agency for National Security Planning announced it would end three decades of widespread internal surveillance. In the spring Kim sacked twelve top generals. Most were close to former president Chun Doo Hwan, and were members of the *Hanahoe* (One Mind) Society, a group of some 100 top active and retired generals favoring a strong military role in society.

In June Parliament enacted the Public Officials Ethics Law, requiring the country's top 7,000 politicians and civil servants to reveal their wealth. On 12 August Kim introduced a real-name financial system, ending the practice of allowing individuals to maintain bank accounts under false names. The government said the change would make it easier to track political bribes and kickbacks. On 16 December Kim sacked Prime Minister Hwang In Sung, replacing him with Lee Hoi Chang, in response to public anger over the lifting of a long-standing ban on rice imports.

On 4 March 1994 parliament passed a political reform package aimed at reducing corruption in election campaigns. The measures placed caps on spending for presidential and parliamentary campaigns, and authorized public subsidies to candidates to reduce dependency on outside contributions. In other developments, on 22 April Kim sacked premier Lee, who had wanted to strengthen the office of the prime minister by having a greater say in policy decisions. Kim named Lee Young Duk, a former North Korean refugee, as the new premier. On 17 December Kim replaced Lee with Lee Hong-koo. On 29 October the Seoul District Prosecutor's office announced that although it had concluded that former presidents Chun and Roh had carried out a "premeditated military rebellion" in their December 1979 military coup, it would not press charges due to the contributions the two had made to the country.

The key foreign affairs issue involved continuing tensions with North Korea. The death of longtime Stalinist leader Kim Il Sung in early July shelved plans for an unprecedented summit between the presidents of the North and South, which had been slated for 25-27 July. Following a pact between the U.S. and North Korea in October, in which Pyongyang agreed to freeze its nuclear program in exchange for modern reactors and other concessions, South Korea eased restrictions on business ties with the North.

Political Rights and Civil Liberties: South Koreans can change their government democratically. The 1992 Assembly elections were marred by fraud charges, including claims that military officers rigged up to 560,000 absentee ballots. However, according to the U.S. State Department these and other alleged irregularities did not appear to influence the outcome of the vote. Mayoral and gubernatorial elections are scheduled for June 1995. The incumbents in these positions are governmental appointees.

President Kim Young Sam has taken numerous steps to ease the formerly pervasive role of the state security apparatus, including removing the National Security Planning Agency's once-widespread internal surveillance powers. In December 1993 the National Assembly passed a law formally curbing the powers of the Agency by limiting it to cases involving terrorism, espionage and international crime, and by establishing a oversight National Assembly Committee. The Assembly also passed an anti-wiretapping law establishing tighter rules for surveillance of personal communications. President Kim granted extensive amnesties in 1993. According to the U.S. State Department there are fewer than 100 political prisoners in South Korea.

The continued application of the National Security Law (NSL) remains the country's key human rights issue. The NSL broadly defines espionage to include cooperation, encouragement or praise of "anti-state," (i.e. North Korea) organizations. In practice, this can include speech or possession of literature considered supportive of North Korea. Unauthorized contact with North Korea is also banned.

Following the death in July of North Korean leader Kim Il Sung, the South Korean government took numerous measures to curb expressions of sympathy. The government sent 28,000 riot police into campuses around the country, and the authorities arrested several student leaders. Clashes between students and police in mid-August at Seoul National University caused nearly 200 injuries, and police arrested more than 1,400 students. During the year, police reportedly arrested dozens of people under the NSL.

The judiciary has become independent of the government in recent years, and due process rights are generally observed for trials. Under the NSL, a judge can allow the authorities to detain individuals suspected of "serious" violations such as spying for an additional twenty days beyond the thirty-day period allowed in non-NSL cases. Detainees, especially in NSL cases, are frequently beaten and deprived of sleep to extract confessions. Suspects are generally not allowed access to an attorney during interrogation. Conditions in prisons are generally harsh.

The Law on Assembly and Demonstrations requires that the authorities be notified of all demonstrations, and prohibits those considered a threat to public order. During the Kim administration the authorities have been more lenient in granting permits, and the police have generally shown greater tolerance toward protesters. Radical students often intimidate professors, occasionally through violence, posing a threat to academic freedom. The government reportedly posts informers at universities.

There is full religious freedom in South Korea. Korean Confucian tradition has given women a secondary social status. In the country's first successful sexual harassment suit, in April 1994 a judge ordered a professor at Seoul National University to pay damages to a female assistant he allegedly fired for resisting his advances. According to the International Labor Organization, South Korean women earn only 54 percent as much as men. Domestic violence is reportedly fairly widespread.

Citizens can move freely within the country but travel to North Korea requires government permission and is heavily restricted. Prior to 1993 the government recognized only two labor federations—the Federation of Korean Trade Unions and the independent Korean Federation of Clerical and Financial Workers. In 1993 the government recognized four independent federations. Each firm can represented only by one union. Strikes are not permitted in government agencies, state-run industries and defense industries.

Labor actions have become less militant since President Kim took office. A walkout by railway engineers and subway workers in late June lasted just seven days after failing to trigger sympathy strikes in other industries or gain public support. A sixty-three-day walkout over the summer by 20,000 workers at Hyundai Heavy Industries, known for the militancy of its workers, was the only major prolonged strike of the year and ended peacefully.

Kuwait

Polity: Traditional mon-
archy and limited
parliament
Economy: Mixed
capitalist-statist
Population: 1,272,000
PPP: $13,126
Life Expectancy: 74.6
Ethnic Groups: Kuwaitis and other Arabs, and various foreign workers

Political Rights: 5
Civil Liberties: 5
Status: Partly Free

Overview: In 1994 Kuwait's opposition-dominated National Assembly
continued to expand its supervisory powers over the government, chipping away at the power of the ruling al-Sabah family.

The al-Sabah family has ruled Kuwait since 1756. Britain handled the
emirate's foreign affairs and defense from 1899 until 1961. The 1962 constitution
vests broad executive powers in an emir from the al-Sabah family, who rules
through an appointed prime minister and a Council of Ministers.

In 1976 the emir suspended the National Assembly after MPs criticized his
selection of ministers. The current emir, Sheik Jabir al-Ahmad al-Sabah, reopened
the Assembly in 1981 but suspended it again in 1986 over calls for a public
inspection of the country's financial records. Following the August 1990 Iraqi
invasion, many citizens blamed the government for failing to recognize the Iraqi
threat and prepare for it adequately. In October, while in exile in Saudi Arabia, the
emir agreed to hold elections in 1992. In February 1991 a thirty-two-nation, U.S.-
led military coalition liberated the country from Iraq.

The government limited the suffrage in the 5 October 1992 elections to "first-
class" males, who were over twenty-one and could prove that they or their ancestors had lived in Kuwait before 1920 and had maintained a residence in the country
until at least 1959. This left just 15 percent of the population eligible. Although a
1986 ban on political parties remained in effect seven informal opposition groups
participated. Only the radical Islamic Popular Grouping openly challenged the
ruling family's constitutional status as a hereditary emirate.

On election day opposition candidates took thirty-one of the fifty seats, split
between nineteen candidates linked to Islamic groups and twelve with generally
left-wing views. The royal family named a cabinet that minimized the opposition's
gains. The emir reappointed Crown Prince Sheik Saad as prime minister, who in
turn gave the key Foreign Affairs, Defense, Interior and Information posts to
members of the al-Sabah family.

Since the election the National Assembly has steadily increased its supervisory
power over the government. In January 1993 Parliament began investigations into
huge losses in the country's once-solid financial holdings, and passed a law
requiring any company that is at least 25 percent government-owned to disclose
new investments. In January 1994 Parliament rescinded a 1990 government decree
that had allowed ministers to be tried outside the regular judicial process in special

tribunals. This cleared the way for a criminal court to begin trying Sheik Ali 'Khalifa al-Sabah, a former minister, and member of the royal family, who along with four others is accused of embezzling $100 million from the state-owned Kuwait Oil Tanker Company. The investigations and trials continued throughout the year.

Political Rights and Civil Liberties: **K**uwaiti citizens cannot change their government democratically. The hereditary, nonelected emir holds executive powers and under the constitution can suspend Parliament at any time, declare martial law, and suspend articles of the constitution. From 1976-81 and from 1986-92 the emir suspended Parliament and suspended the article in the constitution requiring him to hold new elections within two months of suspending Parliament. Through strict eligibility rules the government limited the suffrage in the October 1992 National Assembly elections to 15 percent of the population. Political parties are officially banned, although several groups function essentially as parties. National Assembly elections are due in 1996.

Following Kuwait's liberation from Iraq in February 1991 numerous extrajudicial executions were carried out against suspected Iraqi collaborators and sympathizers. Nearly all of the killings remain unresolved. According to the U.S. State Department, there are also more than 100 unresolved disappearances dating from the period after liberation.

Foreigners, particularly Jordanians, Palestinians and Iraqis, are sometimes briefly kidnapped by unidentified Kuwaitis as a form of harassment. There are reports of abuse and torture at detention facilities, often against Iraqis, Jordanians, Sudanese and Palestinians. Members of these same groups are occasionally subject to arbitrary arrest by the authorities. The Kuwait Security Service frequently detains suspects without charge beyond the legal four-day period.

The judicial system consists of regular courts, the State Security Court (SSC), the Court of Cassation, which reviews cases from the SSC, and military courts, which can try nonmilitary cases during periods of martial law. The independence of the judiciary is compromised by the fact that the executive branch controls its administration and finances. In the regular courts defendants receive reasonably fair public trials. However, in the State Security Courts and the military courts there are credible reports that cases are decided on the basis of confessions obtained through torture in trials that did not meet international standards. Many of those convicted of collaborating with Iraq during the Gulf War were tried in military courts. This includes twenty-two foreigners convicted in April 1991 of working for a pro-Iraqi newspaper, *Al-Nida*, during the Iraqi occupation. The foreigners claim the Iraqis forced them to work on the newspaper, and that Kuwaiti courts did not grant them fair trials. Several hundred Palestinians, Iraqis and *bidoon* (stateless persons of Bedouin origin) are detained under administrative deportation orders, from which there is no right of judicial review.

Some 100,000 domestic servants, mostly from the Philippines, Sri Lanka and India, are forced to work long hours, are often refused permission to leave the house, are subjected to beatings and are occasionally raped. Several domestic servants have died from physical abuse. Most employers retain the servants' passports to prevent them from leaving the country. Hundreds of domestics have sought refuge in their countries' embassies.

Kuwaiti women, in addition to being denied suffrage, face discrimination in some areas of employment and do not receive social security benefits. Under Islamic law Muslim women receive less inheritance than men. Domestic abuse reportedly occurs.

Another concern is the status of the 100,000 bidoon. While some were born in Kuwait, others apparently arrived during the 1960s and 1970s. Bidoon cannot own houses, travel abroad or work for private companies. Before the war the government dropped the bidoon from the census roles and stripped them of their identification cards, which had allowed them access to social services.

Citizens freely criticize the government's policies, but are prohibited from criticizing the al-Sabah family or Islam. The press law prevents publication of articles criticizing the royal family, as well as articles that might "create hatred, or spread dissension among the people." This broad definition leads to some self-censorship. In February 1993 the Attorney General banned publication without his permission of articles dealing with corruption at the official Kuwait Investment Office. Journalists said the ban could set a dangerous precedent and that it appeared intended to protect members of the royal family.

Public gatherings, and private meetings that result in the issuance of a statement, require prior government approval. The government occasionally denies permits for political gatherings, although during the 1992 election campaign opposition groups were generally allowed to hold large public gatherings without interference.

Freedom of association is restricted. In 1985 the government placed a moratorium on the licensing of new nongovernmental organizations (NGOs), and since then has made exceptions only for NGOs with ties to the royal family. A 1988 amendment to the 1962 Law of Public Interest Associations gave the executive branch complete authority over the licensing of associations, a process not subject to judicial review. In August 1993 the government announced a decree shutting down all unlicensed organizations on the grounds that they were operating illegally. This mainly affected six human rights groups that have been denied permits since their formation in 1991. The groups, including the country's main human rights organization, the Kuwaiti Association to Defend War Victims, had been pressing the government for an accounting of some 600 Kuwaitis believed to be held by Iraq, as well as on rights issues within the country.

Islam is the state religion. While Christians are allowed to worship freely, Hindus, Sikhs and Buddhists cannot build places of worship. Proselytizing is illegal, and non-Islamic religious education is prohibited but generally tolerated. Citizens can travel freely within the small country, but women must receive permission from husbands to travel abroad. The government is attempting to reduce the number of bidoon, Iraqis, Palestinians, Sudanese and Yemenis in the country through deportations and tacit pressure on employers not to hire them.

The government maintains significant financial control over unions through subsidies that in practice account for 90 percent of union budgets. Only one union is allowed per industry or profession, and only one labor federation, the Kuwaiti Trade Union Federation, is permitted. New unions must have at least 100 members, at least fifteen of whom must be Kuwaiti. In practice this prevents most blue-collar occupations, which have few Kuwaitis, from forming unions. Foreign workers must reside in the country five years before joining a union and cannot hold union office. Strikes are permitted, but the labor law mandates arbitration if a settlement cannot be reached. Foreign workers say they endure poor food and housing, and are not given adequate time to visit families.

Kyrgyz Republic

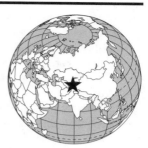

Polity: Presidential-par- **Political Rights:** 4*
liamentary (transitional) **Civil Liberties:** 3
Economy: Statist   **Status:** Partly Free
(transitional)
Population: 4,519,000
PPP: $3,280
Life Expectancy: 68.0
Ethnic Groups: Kirgiz (52.3 percent), Russian (21.5 percent),
Uzbek (12.9 percent), Germans, others
Ratings Change: *The Kyrgyz Republic's political rights rating
changed from 5 to 4, reflecting continuing democratization.

Overview: In 1994 President Askar Akayev, faced with a recalcitrant
                  Soviet-era parliament, won two key referenda in the fall
                  when voters approved changes to the constitution and the
creation of a new bicameral legislature. But the highly regarded reformer faced
charges of increased authoritarianism in issuing decrees and closing two newspapers critical of the government. Other issues included the resignation of the
government, corruption and stimulating economic growth.

In 1991 this small, impoverished Central Asian country bordering China and
Uzbekistan declared independence from the Soviet Union. In what subsequently
became known as the "Silk Revolution," President Akayev, a respected physicist,
committed the country to multiparty democracy and market reforms. The 1993
constitution enshrined the powers of the executive, legislature and judiciary.
President Akayev remained head of state, but Prime Minster Tursunbek
Chyngyshev became head of government. The main provisions ensured human
rights, equality of forms of ownership and land ownership rights. Finally, all
languages, including Russian, were guaranteed free development and use.

At the end of 1993, President Akayev fired the prime minister and cabinet after
a parliamentary no-confidence vote brought on by allegations of embezzlement
surrounding a gold-mining deal. Apas Dzhumagulov was asked to form a government.

In January, with resentment rising over declining living standards, President
Akayev called a national referendum on his leadership. On 31 January he won an
overwhelming 96 percent vote in a plebiscite participated in by 95 percent of the
people. His administration faced severe obstacles, including loss of subsidies from
Moscow, inflation, obstructionism from the old economic and political bureaucrats,
and confusion about market reforms.

These issues came to a head on 6 September when the government resigned,
apparently to strengthen the hand of President Akayev against the conservative-
dominated Parliament, a cumbersome, 350-member institution elected in 1990. The
confrontation, launched when more than half the members of Parliament declared
they would boycott the next session, pitted Communist deputies, many of them
representing the large Russian diaspora, against a minority in parliament who

supported the president's reformist strategies. Parliament had impeded privatization efforts and other free-market structural changes.

To circumvent a truculent legislature, President Akayev dissolved Parliament and decreed that a national referendum be held in October in conjunction with local elections that would seek public approval for changes in the constitution and the creation of a bicameral, 105-member Parliament. The referenda would be deemed valid if more than 50 percent of registered voters took part, and its resolution would be valid if more than 50 percent of participants approved. The president's decision angered the opposition, which was condemned in several newspapers, and caused concern among some Western analysts who feared that the country was taking an authoritarian turn.

On 22 October nearly 75 percent of voters approved the proposal that changes to the constitution and other important matters should be decided by referendum. Nearly 75 percent approved of the new parliament; turnout was reportedly 87 percent. Under the parliamentary restructuring, thirty-five deputies would be elected to a lower house, responsible for drafting new laws. The upper house of seventy members would meet twice a year to scrutinize proposed legislation.

The local elections were for local soviets (councils). Over 8,500 candidates were registered, including 3,800 from working collectives, 3,700 from residential localities, and 538 from various parties and movements. After the referenda, president Akayev set elections for Parliament and local self-government bodies for February 1995.

In December, President Akayev told the Constitutional Assembly in Bishkek that the role of the prime minister as head of government must be strengthened. He said that under the existing system, "the prime minister has practically no rights in the face of parliament."

In economic issues, in November, the World Bank scheduled a foreign investors meeting in Paris to try to get capital flowing into the Kyrgyz republic. By year's end, the national currency (the som) had stabilized, and inflation was down to 1 percent a month. The Overseas Private Investment Corporation (OPIC) had signed a deal committing more than $250 million of U.S. government support to an American-Kyrgyz joint venture to extract and process gold from the Jerooy field. Economic problems persisted. Most enterprises were working at 25 percent capacity, and Uzbekistan threatened to cut off the supply of gas in mid-December. The president acknowledged that corruption and bribe-taking continued to be an issue that hampered greater foreign investment, and said that the war on crime had become a priority.

Political Rights and Civil Liberties:

Citizens have the power to change their government democratically under a multiparty system enshrined in the 1993 constitution. President Akayev's dissolution of Parliament following a vote of no-confidence in the government angered the opposition and caused some concern that the president was exercising too much power.

There are numerous political parties representing a political spectrum. The constitution enshrined the principle of an independent judiciary, and steps have been taken to reform the judicial system and to limit interference in practice.

The press laws do place some restrictions on journalists, including the publication of state secrets, materials that advocate war, violence or intolerance of ethnic groups. In 1994 the Kyrgyz press, among the freest in Central Asia, complained of government attempts to censor them. Some outspoken newspapers were temporarily banned. The *Res Publica* newspaper, the voice of the Kyrgyz intelligentsia, was banned, but resumed publication before the October voting. It condemned the referendum and the dissolution of Parliament as undemocratic. The press also faces problems of costs, access to materials and distribution difficulties. The government owns all radio and television facilities, raising the issue of self-censorship and political interference.

There are no significant restrictions on domestic and foreign travel. Although the constitution ensures minority rights and the government has shown sensitivity to the Russian minority, 1994 saw a continued "brain drain" as educated and skilled Russians and Germans continued to leave the country, albeit at slower rates than the previous year. In December the Kyrgyz Folksrat (People's Council of Germans) and the government began implementing a program to support ethnic Germans and stem their migration. It planned to provide social and economic support to Germans, and to develop business, education and culture in cooperation with Germany.

Freedom of religion is respected in this predominantly Islamic country, where Christians and Jews can worship freely and openly. President Akayev is committed to the rights of women, and many women serve in government posts. In October, the Democratic Women's Party of Kyrgyz was registered with the justice ministry.

Workers are represented by the Federation of Independent Trade Unions of Kyrgyzstan (FITUK). Workers have the right to organize and strike.

Laos

Polity: Communist one-party
Economy: Mixed-statist
Population: 4,702,000
PPP: $1,760
Life Expectancy: 50.3
Ethnic Groups: Multi-ethnic—Lao (50 percent), Thai (20 percent), Phoutheung, Miao (Hmong), Tao and others

Political Rights: 7
Civil Liberties: 6
Status: Not Free

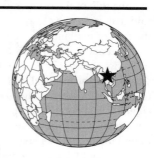

Overview:

The opening of a bridge linking Laos with Thailand in April 1994 is expected to provide an economic boost to this impoverished country at a time when the ruling Lao People's Revolutionary Party (LPRP) continues to follow the Chinese model of combining a single-party political system with free-market liberalizations.

This landlocked, mountainous Southeast Asian country became a French protectorate in 1893. Following the Japanese occupation during World War II, the Communist *Pathet Lao* (Land of Lao) fought the returning French, winning complete sovereignty on 23 October 1953. Royalist, Communist and conservative factions formed a coalition government in 1962 but began fighting each other in 1964. In the late 1960s and early 1970s the United States heavily bombed North Vietnamese and Pathet Lao forces that were fighting the royalist government of

Souvanna Phouma. In May 1975 the Pathet Lao overran the capital, Vientiane, and seven months later established the one-party Communist Lao People's Democratic Republic under Prime Minister Kaysone Phomvihane.

The LPRP introduced the New Economic Mechanism (NEM) in 1986 to revive an economy that had been decimated by a decade of central planning. Under the NEM, farms have been privatized, state-owned companies have either been privatized or granted autonomy, and price controls have been abandoned. Inflation has dropped to around 10 percent since the government tightened the money supply and offered higher interest rates to attract private savings.

In August 1991 the rubber-stamp National Assembly approved the country's first constitution, which mixes socialist rhetoric with market-based economic principles. It formally makes the LPRP the "leading organ" of the political system and places the government under the Leninist doctrine of "democratic centralism." At the same time it requires the state to protect private ownership by "domestic capitalists and foreigners who make investments" in the country. Notably, opposition parties are not expressly banned, giving the government the option of allowing rival parties in the future. The constitution established a newly enlarged presidency. The president is the head of the armed forces, can remove the prime minister, and can ratify and abolish foreign treaties. Prime Minister Kaysone moved up to the new presidency, while veteran revolutionary Khamtay Siphandone succeeded him as prime minister.

Kaysone's death on 21 November 1992 created a serious leadership gap. The president had been the undisputed head of an "Iron Troika" that had led the Laotian Communist movement since the mid-1950s. The National Assembly predictably named the remainder of the Troika—Assembly Speaker Nouhak Phoumsavan and prime minister Khamtay—to succeed Kaysone as president and LPRP chairman, respectively. At the December National Assembly elections, the government allowed non-LPRP independents to participate for the first time, although all candidates had to be pre-approved by the LPRP. Several independents are believed to have won seats in the eighty-five-member Assembly, although the government did not provide a breakdown. In February 1993 an extensive ministerial shakeup brought several younger, educated technocrats, including new foreign minister Somsavath Lengsavath, into a new sixteen-member cabinet.

Kaysone's successors are expected to continue liberalizing the economy while maintaining the LPRP's political monopoly. In April 1994 the Australian-financed Thailand-Laos Friendship Bridge over the Mekong River officially opened, linking the two countries for the first time. With 40 percent total investment, Thailand is already the biggest investor in the country and this share is expected to increase. Many Laotians fear being economically and culturally swamped by Thailand and other neighboring countries.

In related developments, in the spring of 1994 Laos required emergency foreign assistance to head off a potential famine following a rice harvest that was 17 percent below normal in 1993. In June 1994 a United Nations-organized donor roundtable pledged to support a $1.4 billion government investment program focusing on irrigation and road-building programs. Although 85 percent of the population is engaged in subsistence farming, and agriculture accounts for almost 60 percent of GDP, the country has reserves of gold and other minerals as well as substantial hydroelectric resources.

Political Rights Laotians cannot change their government democratically.
and Civil Liberties: The Lao People's Revolutionary Party (LPRP) is the only existing political party.

Some elements of state control have been relaxed in recent years, including widespread, direct police monitoring of civilians. However, the security services still search homes without warrants, monitor mail and international telephone calls and maintain networks of neighborhood and workplace informers. Workers' committees monitor Laotians who are employed by foreign governments or organizations. The Interior Ministry frequently inspects households to insure that residents are registered with the police.

The Hmong, the largest of several tribal groups that collectively comprise half the population, have conducted a small-scale insurgency since the Communist takeover. Both the Hmong guerrillas and the government are accused of human rights violations, including extrajudicial killings. The Hmong accuse the government of carrying out chemical warfare against them, but according to the U.S. State Department this cannot be confirmed.

The government is committed to promoting a rule of law in civil and commercial affairs, and is developing a legal framework to deal with these matters. However, the judiciary is subservient to the government, and trials lack adequate procedural safeguards. The government suspended the bar in late 1992 pending the introduction of a new set of rules regarding private lawyers, although private lawyers can still assist defendants. Torture and mistreatment of detainees and prisoners are apparently rare, although prison conditions are reportedly harsh. Prisoners are often forced to do manual labor, sometimes in private enterprises, without compensation.

The government has released nearly all of the tens of thousands of people who were sent to "re-education camps" following the Communist victory in 1975. However, it continues to hold at least six officials of the former government. In addition, in December 1992 the government gave fourteen-year terms to three high-level LPRP ministers who had been held since 1990 for denouncing official corruption and calling for a multiparty system.

Freedoms of speech and press are nonexistent. Newspapers and electronic media are controlled by the government and reflect its views. In Vientiane and other towns along the Mekong River, Thai broadcasts are available. All associations are controlled by the LPRP. Political assemblies, except for those organized by the government, are illegal. The government's record on religious freedom is mixed. Buddhists, Protestants and Roman Catholics can generally worship freely. However, Laotians must obtain government approval to associate with their co-religionists abroad, and foreign missionaries are generally denied approval to enter the country. Christian seminaries have been closed since the Communist takeover.

The government is dominated by ethnic Lao but is slowly trying to integrate minority groups into the political system. The government lacks sufficient resources to adequately provide for children's welfare. According to UNICEF Laos has one of the highest mortality rates for children under five years of age in Asia.

The 1990 Labor Code permits the formation of labor unions representing private-sector workers, but these unions must belong to the LPRP-affiliated Federation of Lao Trade Unions and are not permitted to organize and bargain collectively. Strikes are not permitted.

Latvia

Polity: Presidential-
parliamentary democracy
(ethnic limits)
Economy: Mixed cap-
italist transitional
Population: 2,549,000
PPP: $7,540
Life Expectancy: 71.0

Political Rights: 3
Civil Liberties: 2*
Status: Free

Ethnic Groups: Latvians (52 percent), Russians (34 percent),
Ukrainians, Poles, Byelorussians, Lithuanians, Jews
Ratings Change: *Latvia's civil liberties rating changed from 3 to 2
following the passage of a new citizenship law. As a result Latvia's status
changed from Partly Free to Free.

Overview:

Key issues for this former Soviet Baltic republic in its third
year of independence from the Soviet Union were tensions
with Russia over the withdrawal of some 16,000 Russian
troops and a controversial citizenship law that Moscow charged discriminated against
the large ethnic Russian minority. The July resignation of the government led by Prime
Minister Valdis Birkavs presented a political crisis for President Guntis Ulmanis.

Latvia was an independent republic from 1918 to 1940, when it was forcibly
annexed by the Soviet Union after the Hitler-Stalin Pact. During the more than fifty
years of Soviet occupation there was a massive influx of Russians accompanied by
the deportation of ethnic Latvians; the proportion of Latvians fell from 77 percent
in 1940 to 52 percent by 1991. Latvia declared independence from a disintegrating
Soviet Union in 1991.

In October of that year, the *Saeima* (Parliament) adopted a series of guidelines for
defining who qualified for citizenship. Only those who were citizens in 1940 and their
descendants were automatically granted citizenship. For others, certain conditions were
set, including: a conversational knowledge of Latvian; knowledge of Latvian legal
structures; sixteen years of residence; and renunciation of citizenship from another state.
The guidelines, which disenfranchised the mostly Russian non-Latvians, were criticized
by Moscow and Western human rights groups. Right-wing nationalist parties such as
Fatherland and Freedom, which supported unforced repatriation of those who had come
to Latvia since 1940, considered the guidelines not exclusionary enough.

In June 1993 Latvia held its first parliamentary elections since the fall of the
USSR. In a vote observers called free and fair, 90 percent of eligible voters chose
among twenty-three lists to elect a new Saeima. Parties needed at least 4 percent of
the total vote in a proportional electoral system. Of the eight parties clearing the
hurdle, Latvia's Way (LC), led by then-President Anatolijs Gorbunovs and
including the old elite of Latvia's Communist Party-turned nationalists, as well as
émigrés of Latvian descent, gained 36 seats. Other winners were the ultra-nationalist, anti-Russian, Latvian National Independence Movement (LNNK), 15 seats; the
centrist Harmony for Latvia-Rebirth of the Economy, 13; Farmer's Union (LZS),

12; Equal Rights, 7; Fatherland and Freedom (TUB), 6; Christian Democratic Union (LKDS), 6; and the Democratic Center Party (DCP), 5. Surprisingly, the ruling Latvian Popular Front (LTF), which had led the anti-Communist movement and engineered Latvia's independence drive, failed to gain the required 4 percent. Although about 300,000 Latvians of non-Latvian origin could vote in the election, about 700,000 people (almost one-third of the voting-age population)—largely Russians, Ukrainians and Jews—could not vote for lack of a new law on citizenship and naturalization.

One month after the election, the new *Saeima* unexpectedly chose economist Guntis Ulmanis as president. Ulmanis, the grandnephew of Karlis Ulmanis, the authoritarian leader of pre-1940 Latvia, was a virtual unknown in political circles. Former President Gorbunovs was named to the powerful post of parliamentary speaker. Ulmanis nominated Valdis Birkavs of Latvia's Way as prime minister, and he was approved by parliament.

In early 1994 Latvian-Russian tensions increased, with some senior Russian politicians declaring that the Baltics remained in the Russian sphere of influence and that Latvia had violated the human rights of ethnic Russians by restricting their ability to become citizens. During a visit to Washington in late January, Latvian Foreign Minister Georgs Andrejevs was assured by U.S. Secretary of State Warren Christopher that Russia intended to withdraw its troops from Latvia by late August in exchange for a four-year extension of Russian civilian control of the early-warning anti-ballistic missile installation near Skrundra near the Latvian coast. In a February letter to President Ulmanis, Russian President Boris Yeltsin said the rights of ethnic Russian "have become a prime concern" of his.

On 16 March, after more than two years of often bitter negotiations, Russian and Latvian diplomats agreed on a 31 August deadline for the pullout of Russian troops and an extended four-year lease on the Skrundra installation. A Latvian spokesman also said that Russian military pensioners would be allowed to stay in their old apartments. The agreement met with resistance from the opposition, particularly the LNNK and the TUB, which accused negotiators of treachery for permitting Russian personnel to remain at Skrundra. Passions were further aroused when Russian announced—then withdrew—plans for a new military base in Latvia.

In late April Latvian and Russian negotiators meeting in Jurmala agreed on the issue of payment of pensions and other benefits for the 22,300 Russian military veterans living in Latvia. The officers would be allowed to stay in Latvia, but not to obtain citizenship. On 11 July President Yeltsin said that all Russian troops would leave Latvia by 31 August, and most had withdrawn by September. The U.S. Senate had put pressure on Russia by passing an amendment to the foreign aid bill that would have cut off all American credits to Russia unless Moscow's troops were out of Estonia and Latvia by the August deadline. On 28 October the Russian State Duma approved the Latvian-Russian accords on the troop withdrawal and the status of Russian military retirees in Latvia.

The removal of Russian troops was played out in a political atmosphere charged by the issue of citizenship for the mostly Russian non-Latvians. In June the Saeima approved a controversial nationality law that set a limit of 230,000 Latvian-born non-Latvians who could become citizens by the end of the century. European officials said the law was so harsh that Latvia could not qualify to join the Council of Europe or, eventually, the European Union (EU).

On 23 July, bowing more to pressure from Europe than from Russia, the *Saeima* amended the law by eliminating the quota proviso. The new law, which was passed by a vote of 58 to 21, provided for the naturalization of most noncitizens born in Latvia by the year 2000; those residents born outside Latvia could become full citizens beginning in the year 2000. Applicants needed to speak conversational Latvian, know some history and swear an oath of loyalty. Noncitizens who worked with the Soviet secret police encouraged Moscow to keep Latvia by force, or were active Communists would not be naturalized. The law was endorsed by President Ulmanis on 11 August. President Yeltsin said the law "legalized ethnic discrimination."

Politically, the year marked a series of setbacks for the ruling LC-LZS coalition that saw the resignation of the Birkavs government in July. In 29 May local elections the government coalition partners were trounced by centrist-right and nationalist parties, suggesting a mixture of popular discontent with economic reforms and a wariness about attempts to mend relations with Russia. In early July three LZS ministers resigned. The defection was triggered by increased farmers' demands for more price supports and protection from imported food. On 13 July Prime Minister Birkavs announced his government's resignation on national television. He said the LC would be ready to form a new government with another coalition partner.

On 25 July President Ulmanis asked Andrejs Krastins and his ultra-nationalist LNNK to try and form a new governing coalition. But on 18 August, President Ulmanis's efforts to patch together a formula to end government paralysis collapsed when Parliament withheld endorsement of the LNNK-led conservative team, fearing that it might embark on nationalist policies that would jeopardize the Russian troop withdrawal and a free trade accord with the EU.

By the end of August, President Ulmanis had named LC leader and Minister of Government Reform Maris Gailis as prime minister-designate. On 10 September the LC endorsed the ministerial candidates, many of them incumbents, named by Gailis. Former-Prime Minister Birkavs was selected as foreign minister.

Latvia continued to implement market reforms, and reduce inflation. The Bank of Latvia, while allowing the lat (introduced as the national currency in 1993) to float, adopted a "strong lat" policy and maintained high interest rates to stamp out inflationary pressures. Foreign investment continued to increase, but privatization remained sluggish. Tensions between the newly established privatization agency and government ministries over responsibility for sell-offs and whether to opt for hard currency or voucher sales hindered progress. Although Latvia aimed to sell about 200 companies a year, only 85 out of a list of over 700 had actually changed hands by midyear.

On other issues, Latvia in February signed up for NATO's Partnership for Peace program. In September, the government announced plans to help form a Baltic peacekeeping battalion which would have "inter-operability with NATO."

Political Rights and Civil Liberties:

Citizens of Latvia can change their government democratically. Under provisions of a controversial citizenship and naturalization law, a substantial percentage of mainly Slavic residents is excluded from citizenship and voting rights. On 19 October, the U.N. High Commissioner on Human Rights Jose Ayala Lasso, citing U.N. and CSCE reports, said that Latvia observed human rights and welcomed the government's plans to establish an independent body for the protection of human rights.

The judiciary is generally free from government interference, and reforming the system continues. A former KGB colonel, eighty-six-year-old Alfon Noviks, went on trial for "crimes against humanity" for sending thousands of Latvians to their deportation and death more than fifty years earlier.

The rights of association and assembly are respected, and there are several well-organized political parties, including Equal Rights, mainly supported by Russians dissatisfied with Latvia's citizenship policies; it won seven seats in the 1993 parliamentary elections. Business, cultural and ethnic organizations are allowed to exist, among them the League of Non-Citizens.

There is an independent press in both Latvian and Russian, but newspapers and other publications continue to face economic difficulties in terms of distribution, commercial viability and resources. A 1992 law specified the creation of separate administrative bodies for radio and television, and guaranteed their independence from political interference.

Freedom of movement is unrestricted, and religious rights are respected in this largely Lutheran country. The church hierarchy's opposition to ordaining women caused internal rifts and alienated the church from branches in Europe and the Americas.

Women have the same legal rights as men, and are granted daycare and maternity benefits. Women face discrimination in hiring and pay.

Independent unions are allowed to organize and workers in most sectors have and exercise the right to strike. On 2 September some 47,000 teachers and school employees staged a warning strike over low salaries and unresolved problems in Latvia's educational system. Their trade union chairman said participation was about 90 percent.

Lebanon

Polity: Presidential-parliamentary (military- and foreign-influenced, partly foreign-occupied)
Economy: Mixed statist
Population: 3,620,000
PPP: $2,500
Life Expectancy: 68.1
Ethnic Groups: Eastern Hamitic (90 percent), Greek, Syro-Lebanese

Political Rights: 6
Civil Liberties: 5
Status: Partly Free

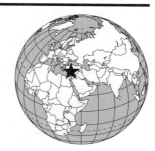

Overview:

The February 1994 bombing of a Maronite Christian church north of Beirut led to a crackdown on Lebanon's strongest Christian opposition party. Many accused Prime Minister Rafik Hariri's Syrian-backed government of using the church bombing as an excuse to weaken the Christian opposition movement. In the spring the Hariri government barred private radio and television stations from reporting news.

Lebanon declared independence from France in 1941, and full sovereignty followed the final withdrawal of French troops in 1946. The genesis of the country's 1975-90 civil war lay in the unwritten 1943 National Pact, which gave Christians political dominance over the Muslim population through a perpetual 6:5 ratio of parliamentary seats.

Following three decades in which non-Christian groups tried unsuccessfully to end this religion-based political system, civil war broke out in 1975 between Muslim, Christian and Druze militias. Syria sent troops into the country in 1976 to support the government, which ultimately collapsed. The country's reconciliation process began at Taif, Saudi Arabia, in November 1989, with an Arab League-sponsored accord that provided for a new power-sharing constitution. The accord continued the tradition of a Christian presidency, who is chosen by the Parliament for a six-year term, but transferred many of the executive powers to the cabinet, to be headed by a Sunni Muslim prime minister as before. Future parliaments were to be split evenly among Muslims and Christians. The accord also allowed Syria to maintain up to 40,000 troops in Beirut and other cities until September 1992.

In October 1990 Lebanese and Syrian troops defeated Christian troops loyal to General Michel Aoun, who had refused to relinquish power to the central government. Aoun's defeat ended a civil war that had killed more than 150,000 people. In December 1990 President Elias Hrawi named a thirty-member, half-Christian, half-Muslim cabinet that included the leaders of several warring militias. In May 1991 the government signed a treaty allowing Syria to maintain troops indefinitely in the Bekka Valley and linking the two countries' economic and security policies, a deal that effectively ceded control of the country to its more powerful neighbor.

The country held its first elections in twenty years in three stages in August and September 1992. At stake was a new parliament with 128 seats, split evenly among Muslims and Christians. However, most Christians boycotted to protest the continuing Syrian army presence in major cities. In balloting for the sixty-four Muslim seats, two hard-line fundamentalist militia groups, Amal and Hezbollah, took eighteen and twelve seats respectively, while independents linked to various political figures took thirty-four seats. Due to the boycott, the sixty-four Christian seats were won by independents or by candidates who ran on Muslim tickets. Altogether, three-fourths of the seats were won by nominally pro-Syrian candidates.

In October 1992 President Hrawi named billionaire businessman Rafik al-Hariri as prime minister. Although the major steps in the Taif Accord had been completed, in November Syria announced it would not redeploy its troops to the Bekka Valley until further political changes were carried out, including abolishing the practice of awarding junior government posts along religious lines.

Efforts to ease religious tensions in the country received a setback with the 27 February 1994 bombing of a Maronite Christian church north of Beirut that killed eleven people and wounded fifty. The government claimed that the Maronite Christian-based Lebanese Forces (LF), a former militia turned political party, carried out the bombing in order to instill a fear of Muslim domination in the Christian community. In the aftermath the army cracked down on Christian areas north of Beirut, the capital, searching houses and detaining more than 100 people. The government banned the LF in March, and in June indicted LF leader Samir Geagea and seven other LF members in the February bombing as well as in earlier crimes, including the 1990 assassination of Christian leader Dany Chamoun. Many felt the government was simply trying to emasculate the strongest Christian opposition group. In the spring the government also placed restrictions on the media linked to the church bombing (*See Political Rights and Civil Liberties below*).

In December Premier Hariri briefly threatened to resign after accusing powerful parliamentary speaker Nabih Berri of delaying the country's $11 billion reconstruction program. Many parliamentarians had accused Hariri of corruption in administering the program. During the year sporadic fighting continued in and around Israel's "security zone" in southern Lebanon. Israel originally invaded southern Lebanon in 1982 to clear out Palestinian Liberation Organization (PLO) guerrillas launching rocket attacks into northern Israel. The 440-square-mile security zone, established in 1985, is manned by Israeli soldiers and by the Israeli-backed, Christian-based South Lebanese Army.

Political Rights and Civil Liberties: Lebanese citizens changed their government in 1992 for the first time in two decades in elections that were not free or fair. Christians largely boycotted the vote to protest a Syrian army presence in major cities. There were numerous charges of irregularities in drawing up the electoral rolls, in the voting itself, and in tallying the ballots, and there were no official foreign observer teams. Independent candidates reported being harassed and intimidated by party workers. The government also redrew the six electoral districts to favor pro-Syrian candidates. The president is not directly elected but is chosen by parliament for a six-year term. Parliamentary elections are due in 1996.

The government still lacks full control of the country. Syria exercises substantial political and military leverage with 40,000 troops in Beirut, the Bekka Valley and northern Lebanon. Meanwhile, the South Lebanon Army (SLA) administers Israel's 440-square mile security zone, the Hezbollah militia is still active in many southern towns and Palestinian factions administer several refugee towns in the south. All of these extra-governmental groups detain suspects and administer justice, generally without due process, in areas under their control.

Thousands of disappearances during the 1975-90 civil war remain unresolved. Politically motivated killings still occur, but far less frequently than during the civil war. Most involve some seventeen Palestinian factions, which are also accused of torturing members of rival groups. Syrian troops and SLA troops are also accused of torture.

Security forces are accused of using excessive force against detainees, particularly against members of the former Lebanese Forces militia. Prisons are severely overcrowded. The judiciary is generally independent of the government, although influential politicians reportedly intervene in some cases to protect supporters and corruption is fairly common. The army arbitrarily arrests opponents of the government and of Syria's role in Lebanon.

The Interior Ministry must grant a permit for all demonstrations, and such permits are frequently denied to Christian groups. In September 1993 army troops killed eight Islamic fundamentalists and wounded at least forty-one others during a protest against the Israeli-PLO peace accord.

There are significant restrictions on press freedom. On 24 March 1994 the government barred the country's 200 private radio and 50 private television stations from broadcasting news and political commentary, citing an emergency stemming from the 27 February bombing of a church (*See Overview above*). In July Parliament approved a repeal of the ban, but broadly stipulated that the private stations could not air sensitive political, economic and religious news.

The government's Lebanon Television (LTV) has a legal monopoly on television until 2012. The government has refused to license private television stations, which operate illegally, and periodically threatens to shut them down. The prosecutor general can shut down newspapers for up to one week without the possibility of a judicial appeal for publishing articles deemed inimical to state security or religious and ethnic harmony. There are also legal restrictions on publishing articles considered insulting to the head of state or foreign leaders. In the spring of 1993 the government used these restrictions to temporarily shut down three newspapers and a television station. Journalists frequently practice self-censorship.

Police must approve all leaflets and other nonperiodical materials, and citizens have been imprisoned for not gaining this approval. The authorities frequently exercise prior censorship of art and other cultural works.

Women must obtain permission from their husbands before going into business. Incidents of rape reportedly occur fairly frequently. Muslim women receive less inheritance than do males. The country has a growing population of street children, and children often work in conditions of servitude. The government does not extend normal legal rights to some 180,000 stateless undocumented persons, many of whom live in disputed border areas. There are also some 350,000-500,000 Palestinian refugees in Lebanon. Most live in camps and are not allowed to conduct normal commercial affairs outside of the camps.

Freedom of religion is respected. Internal travel is generally unrestricted, except in areas of southern Lebanon under Israeli or Hezbollah control. Citizens can travel abroad freely. Government workers do not have the right to join trade unions or hold strikes, although in practice such employees do stage brief strikes to press their demands.

Lesotho

Polity: Parliamentary democracy (military- and royal-influenced
Economy: Capitalist
Population: 1,929,000
PPP: $1,500
Life Expectancy: 59.8
Ethnic Groups: Sotho (99 percent)

Political Rights: 4*
Civil Liberties: 4
Status: Partly Free

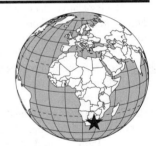

Ratings Change: *Lesotho's political rights rating changed from 3 to 4 after the temporary overthrow of the democratic government. Elected officials, the military and the royals are competing for power.

Overview: On 17 August 1994 King Letsie III orchestrated a royal coup, dissolving the year-old Basutoland Congress Party (BCP) parliament and dismissing Prime Minister Mokhehle and his government. Opposition party Basotho National Party (BNP) had petitioned the king on 14 July to dismiss the government and prepare new elections. Less than a month later, after South African military maneuvers near Lesotho's border, threats of international economic sanctions and civil unrest, negotiations with a delegation from South Africa, Namibia and Zimbabwe led King Letsie to reinstate the old ruling bodies. Since King Letsie III had never wanted the throne, a bill was passed in Parliament to reinstate former King Moshoeshoe II. A January army mutiny over pay raise, the assassination of the deputy prime minister and other civil unrest plunged Lesotho into chaos in the months preceding the coup.

Lesotho, a small mountainous kingdom completely enclosed by South Africa, with a homogenous Basotho population, gained independence from Britain in 1966, while choosing to remain a member of the British Commonwealth. The political struggle for independence began in 1952 with the formation of the BCP that opposed Lesotho's incorporation into South Africa. The party wanted democratically elected councils and a devolution of power from the influential traditional chiefs.

In 1958 the BNP was established as a counterweight to the BCP and favored a policy of retaining the traditional patterns of governance through the village headmen. The BNP was more inclined toward a market-oriented economy and did not oppose ties with South Africa. In 1957, the Marematlou Freedom Party (MFP) was established, favoring a monarchy with strong legislative and executive authority.

In 1965 the BNP won a narrow victory over the BCP in pre-independence parliamentary elections. With Chief Leabua Jonathan as prime minister, the parliament adopted a Westminster-style constitution, installing King Moshoeshoe II as the head of state. During the 1970 elections, when it appeared that the BCP had won, Jonathan declared a state of emergency, invalidated the vote, and imprisoned members of the opposition. In 1986 a group of army officers led by General Justin Lekhanya, overthrew Jonathan. In 1990 another group of army officers led by Colonel Pitsoana Ramaema overthrew Lekhanya and forced Moshoeshoe II to abdicate in favor of his son, Letsie III, over a dispute on the extent of the royal legislative and executive authority. In 1991 Ramaema appointed a Constituent Assembly to draft a new constitution, in preparation for the reintroduction of civilian rule.

The legislative election, originally scheduled for June 1992, was postponed several times and finally took place on 27 March 1993. The constituent assembly published the final draft of the constitution after weeks of public meetings throughout the country, in which voters were consulted on the text of the constitutional provisions.

Fourteen political parties participated in the 1993 election, in which the BCP won a resounding victory, taking all of the sixty-five Assembly seats. The seventy-year-old opposition veteran, Ntsu Mokhehle formed a government on 2 April, following the BNP's failed attempt to invalidate the vote on the grounds of alleged voter fraud and rumors of an army coup. The BNP rejected Mokhehle's offer to appoint two BNP members to the thirty-three-member Senate, a second parliamentary chamber consisting of representatives of village chiefs and winning party appointees.

On 18 January 1994 Makoanyane barrack soldiers, loyal to opposition parties, and government-backed Ratjomose barrack soldiers clashed in the capital city of Maseru over the former's demand for a 100 percent pay raise. The fighting claimed the lives of five soldiers, and wounded eleven civilians. Numerous explanations for the conflict were given following the mutiny.

On 11 May members of the Royal Lesotho Mounted Police, soldiers and prison officers went on strike, demanding a 60 percent pay raise. The following day, with the help of the British, the government established a Ministry of Defense to take up responsibility for all matters relating to the Lesotho defense force. During talks to address the crisis, the opposition walked out after the prime minister accused the BNP of stirring unrest. Gunfire broke out in Maseru, claiming the life of Selabalo Mathie, the BCP youth leader.

On 13 July, following several weeks of police strikes in April and the murder of Deputy Prime Minister Selometsi by dissident soldiers, who also detained four cabinet members, the government appointed an independent commission of inquiry from Botswana, South Africa and Zimbabwe to investigate why its army was in disarray.

On 14 July, the BNP presented a petition to King Letsie III asking him to step down in favor of his deposed father, former King Moshoeshoe II. The petition also called on King Letsie to dismiss Prime Minister Mokhehle's BCP government and form a government of national unity with new elections. In a public broadcast on 17 August, King Letsie III dissolved Parliament on charges of alleged corruption, dismissed the prime minister and his government and suspended certain sections of the Constitution.

Following the coup the prime minister's supporters staged anti-monarchy demonstrations. A delegation of BCP officials tried to present the king with a petition protesting the unconstitutional dissolution of the government. Security forces opened fire on progovernment demonstrators, reportedly killing four people. A dusk-to-dawn curfew was imposed. The Lesotho Order 1994, instituted by the king on 17 August, vested all legislative authority in the king. BNP members, notably party leader Evaristus Sekhonyana, formed a provisional council.

A two-day national strike, beginning 22 August, was called by nongovernmental organizations headed by Kelle Bsilo, chairman of the Lesotho Council of nongovernmental organizations, to protest the king's action. They called a stay-away during which banks and businesses stopped work. The U.S. suspended all aid to Lesotho. The presidents of Botswana, South Africa and Zimbabwe met in Pretoria during the last week of August, and sent an ultimatum for the king to retract the dissolution of the government.

After some delays in the negotiations, on 14 September the king restored the government. As early as December 1992, King Letsie had announced that the military had forcibly installed him as king, and had asked for a *pitso* (public meeting) to vote for reinstating his father as monarch. The Council banned the meeting, and Letsie canceled the pitso after a dispatch of soldiers confined him to a house arrest. After the coup's reversal, Parliament passed a bill in December 1994 to restore King Moshoeshoe II to the throne because King Letsie had never wanted to be king. However, the right to succeed his father is preserved.

Political Rights and Civil Liberties:

Despite the 1993 democratic parliamentary elections, after which the winning party was able to occupy its seats in Parliament and form a government in the first elections in twenty-three years, the events of 1994 showed that the monarchy and the deeply entrenched military are able to undermine a democratically elected parliament.

Even though the BCP holds all the parliamentary seats, political pluralism exists, with a number of small but lively political parties, often critical of the government, ranging from the monarchist MFP to the Communist Party. On the local level, the chieftaincy remains the most powerful authority. Some have suggested a new system of proportional representation for the 1998 general elections.

The judiciary consists of a modern court system based on Roman-Dutch law, and a customary system operating on the village level. The judges on the High Court are largely independent of government, but judges on the lower courts are often susceptible to central government or local chieftain pressure. In recent years, the High Court acted on several occasions to limit the authorities' infringement of the law, and to investigate cases of human rights violations. In 1988, the court annulled the state of emergency on procedural grounds and in 1991 sentenced two officers for the abduction and killing of two former ministers in 1986.

The government controls the official media, consisting of two weekly newspapers, a radio station and a one-hour newscast on the local television channel. In 1992, the military authorities assigned time slots for each of the fourteen parties contesting the election to air their views on radio and television. With the continued postponement of the electoral date, however, public exhaustion with the programs caused the Military Council to cancel them. In early 1993, the BCP and the minor parties accused the official media of being strongly biased in favor of the BNP. Following the BCP takeover of the government, the party avoided wide-scale purges of the official media. The BCP and the minor parties received more coverage in the two Lesotho-language newspapers affiliated with the Roman Catholic and Lesotho evangelical churches, and the two independent English-language newspapers. In September 1994, neither party spoke to the media as an agreement to reinstate the government was being discussed.

Freedom of religion is respected in this largely Christian country. Travel within the country and to neighboring South Africa is generally unrestricted. In September 1994 the government banned officials from foreign travel while discussions between Lesotho and the neighboring countries were taking place. The high cost of obtaining an "international" passport for travel to other countries, including the other countries in South Africa, makes foreign travel inaccessible to all but the most affluent.

Trade union activities are restricted due to the peculiar nature of employment in Lesotho. Most miners working in South Africa belong to the South African National Union of Mineworkers (NUM); since this is a foreign organization it is not allowed to operate in Lesotho. Most previous attempts by the workforce to organize have been resisted by the military authorities, who have relied on inexpensive labor costs to woo foreign investment, most notably from the Far East.

Liberia

Polity: Monrovia: interim civilian goverment (foreign military and foreign-influenced); elsewhere: rival warlords
Economy: Capitalist
Population: 2,941,000
PPP: $850
Life Expectancy: 54.7
Ethnic Groups: Sixteen major tribes, including the Krahn, Mandingo, Gio and Mano (95 percent), Americo-Liberians (5 percent)
Ratings Change: *Liberia's political rights rating changed from 6 to 7 as the war intensified and hopes for elections faded.

Political Rights: 7*
Civil Liberties: 6
Status: Not Free

Overview: In 1994 Liberia's five-year-old civil war reached new levels of devastation and mayhem. An estimated 250,000 civilians have been killed since the war began, and 95 percent of the population has been forced to flee their homes. The three warring factions splintered into seven, increasing chaos and complicating the negotiation process. The appointment of a transitional council and attempts at disarmament failed to ameliorate the situation.

Liberia was founded in 1847 by freed American slaves, known as Americo-Liberians, whose unchallenged political domination ended in 1980, when Samuel Doe, a member of the small Krahn ethnic group, became Liberia's first indigenous leader. Doe consolidated his power by brutally repressing other ethnic groups. In December 1989, the rebel National Patriotic Front of Liberia (NPFL), operating from the neighboring Ivory Coast, attacked government troops. Led by Charles Taylor, an Americo-Liberian and former Doe cabinet member, most NPFL soldiers are of the Gia and Mano ethnic groups. In July 1990, an NPFL offshoot group killed Doe while he was in custody.

By mid-1990, members of the Economic Organization of the West African States (ECOWAS) sent an armed monitoring group (ECOMOG) to defend the remnants of the government against NPFL assault. An ECOWAS-sponsored Interim Government of National Unity (IGNU), with Amos Sawyer as president, was set up later in the year. The NPFL formed an alternative government headquartered in the interior town of Gbarnga.

Following a cessation of hostilities that lasted throughout much of 1991, later ECOWAS-sponsored talks failed to resolve the country's division and provide for lasting peace. In September 1991 the armed clashes resumed, with a third faction gaining ground. The Sierra Leone-based United Liberation Movement (ULIMO), composed of armed anti-Taylor refugees, mainly Krahns and Mandingoes, was led by General Alhaji Kromah, the former officer of President Doe's Armed Forces of Liberia (AFL). The ECOMOG placed the AFL remnants under the IGNU's nominal control, although the latter was unable to exercise full control of its operations.

In July 1993 increased U.N. and ECOWAS pressure helped to bring the three enemies together in Cotonou, Benin, to work out a peace agreement. A week later the Cotonou accord was signed by all three factions. The accord called for a cease-fire starting 1 August; the formation of a unitary transitional government composed of all the factions, with legislative and presidential elections to follow by February 1994; an expansion of ECOMOG to include military units from African countries outside the region; and simultaneous disarmament of all the factions prior to the elections.

For seven months after the signing of the Cotonou accord, negotiations were held to try to set up a transitional government. The talks were overshadowed by continued guerrilla violence throughout the country. The proposed February 1994 elections were rescheduled for 7 September 1994.

On 7 March, the five-member Liberian National Transitional Government (LNTG) was formally installed. Composed of representatives from all three factions, the coalition of enemies planned to serve as an interim government until the September elections. The installation of the LNTG marked the first time since the war began that the country was united under one national government.

At the same time, ECOMOG troops began the disarmament process. The goal of the effort was to disarm 60,000 guerrillas under the supervision of over 300 U.N. observers.

The slow disarmament process became paralyzed when the Krahn and Mandingo elements of the ULIMO faction clashed over which of the two sub-divisions would represent ULIMO in the transitional government. The conflict divided ULIMO into two groups: ULIMO-K represented the Krahns; ULIMO-M, the Mandingoes. The violence intensified, and by late April the disarmament process had come to a complete halt. Only 2,500 out of the 60,000 guerrillas had relinquished their weapons.

By August the three factions had splintered into seven, and the five-year civil war had deteriorated into a state of anarchy. Each of the factions suffered from tremendous command and control problems. At the same time, every group remained determined to rule the country and saw no advantage in seeking peace and negotiating a compromise.

In August a series of violent clashes involved all seven enemies. The fighting began in Nimba county, home of the Taylor headquarters, but soon spread throughout the country. Typical of the Liberian civil war, the fighting consisted of guerrilla warfare rather than major battles. As a result, civilians, rather than combatants, suffered.

Also in August, Ghanaian president Jerry Rawlings became the new leader of ECOWAS, replacing President Nicephore Soglo of Benin. Rawlings held a series of negotiations that led to the formation of a peace accord, Akosombo I. An extension of Cotonou, the accord broadened the executive council to include representatives from all seven factions, as well as the Liberian National Conference, which includes hundreds of delegates who represent the majority of the unarmed population. The accord, signed on 12 September, never had the chance to be implemented, however, because it was immediately shot down by the original council members, who did not want to lose their positions.

Once Akosombo I was repudiated, Rawlings again began a series of negotiations. In October he secured the approval of the seven factions, the original LNTG members and civilian representatives to meet in Akkra, Ghana, on 20 November to sign Akosombo II.

Meanwhile, in September, Taylor's mansion was stormed by General Charles Julue and his Krahn-based group, "New Horizons." ECOMOG forces bombed the mansion, preventing the coup from succeeding.

Akosombo II negotiations began in Akkra in early November. By 30 November no agreement had been reached and Rawlings had the factions leaders, along with a peacekeeping delegation, flown back to Monrovia in order to continue discussions there. Elections were postponed indefinintely.

In December, guerrillas stormed into Monrovia and hacked and burned forty-eight civilians to death. Hundreds of Liberians carried bodies of victims to the city cemetary and then marched through the streets demanding an end to the fighting. The slayings marked the first such violence in the capital since 1993. On 21 December representatives of the seven factions signed yet another agreement calling for a cease-fire to begin on 28 December; disarmament of the 60,000 guerillas to start in March 1995; and national elections to be held in November 1995. Civilians remained skeptical about the agreement, which allowed the warlords to maintain control of Liberia until the elections.

Political Rights and Civil Liberties: Liberians lack the means to change their government democratically. Despite the establishment of the interim transitional government, anarchy reigns in this decimated nation. Ninety-five percent of Liberians have been forced to flee their homes. An exorbitant number of the displaced—including many women and children—suffer from malnutrition, dehydration and bullet wounds. Approximately 250,000 people have been killed since the start of the civil war.

All of the contestants, including the ECOMOG forces, have been accused of horrible human rights abuses against the civilian population. According to Human Rights Watch/ Africa, the LPC stepped up its campaign against civilians in 1994. The faction was responsible for a chain of atrocities, including widespread looting, arbitrary arrest and detention, forcible recruitment, beatings, torture, rape and extrajudicial executions. Africa Watch also reported that members of the Nigerian contingent of ECOMOG consistently aided the LPC in carrying out these abuses.

Thousands of children under the age of thirteen have been forced to serve as soldiers for the NPFL and ULIMO. Many have been killed or wounded, and many have been forced to take part in the killing, maiming and raping of civilians, reported Africa Watch. Some children had to undergo brutal initiation rites, such as commiting an atrocity against an enemy in order to prove their loyalty to a particular faction. Former child soldiers suffered from post-traumatic nightmares, flashbacks, sleep disorders, anxiety, and depression. An estimated 10 percent of the 60,000 fighters are children under fifteen.

Liberia's court system, which practically collapsed in 1990, began to be reconstituted two years later, following an agreement between IGNU and NPFL to re-establish a five-member Supreme Court. Lower courts have also been set up in the LNTG- and NPFL-controlled territories. Outside Monrovia, utter lawlessness prevails. The police and military indiscriminately and arbitrarily arrest and torture civilians. Soldiers are subject to courts-martial, often involving capital cases, without recourse to legal counsel or the right to appeal. Customary law is used extensively in rural areas. In some cases, the accused suffer "trial by ordeal" and undergo physical travails in processes intended to determine guilt or innocence.

The freedoms of speech and the press, and the rights to organize and join independent organizations are generally respected in Monrovia. Outside the capital, the media are virtually nonexistent, and information is mostly spread by word of mouth. The major newspapers in Monrovia are *The Inquirer, The Eye* and *The Daily News*. Sporadically during the course of the civil war, the IGNU engaged in censorship of war-related stories. In June 1993 the Information Ministry announced that it and the Justice Ministry had to clear any war-related news stories before their publication. The Press Union of Liberia (PUL) subsequently denounced the directive as "aiming at curtailing press freedom under the guise of security of the state." The PUL demanded that the Ministry instead publish a set of written guidelines for journalists to follow in war reporting. Shortly thereafter, the Information Minister and the PUL compromised on these guidelines.

A number of independent organizations exist in Monrovia, including human rights groups such as the Catholic Peace and Justice Commission and the Center for Law and Human Rights Education. Relief groups include the Christian Health Association of Liberia (CHAL) and various other church, student and child assistance organizations. Outside the capital, freedom of association is impeded by political repression and general chaos. Most relief organizations have ceased to exist outside Monrovia.

Freedom of worship is generally respected by all sides. Freedom of movement within the country is generally limited by checkpoints and the requirement to show travel permits when crossing borders controlled by the different factions.

Libya

Polity: Military   **Political Rights:** 7
Economy: Mixed statist   **Civil Liberties:** 7
Population: 5,057,000   **Status:** Not Free
PPP: $7,000
Life Expectancy: 62.4
Ethnic Groups: Arab, Berber, Tuareg

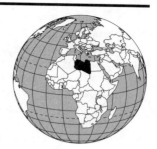

Overview:

In 1994 Colonel Mu'ammar al-Qadhafi's twenty-fifth year of rule in Libya was marked by continued economic troubles caused by U.N.-backed trade restrictions against the country. The six-year-old impasse over Qadhafi's refusal to extradite Abdel Basset Ali al-Megrahi and Lamen Khalifa Fhimah, the two suspects wanted for the bombing of Pan Am Flight 103, which blew up over Lockerbie, Scotland in December 1988, did not break. Libya retreated from the Aouzou strip, relinquishing the territory to Chad. Mansour Kikhia, a former Foreign Minister and the leading exiled opposition figure, was reported missing throughout the year.

The Libyan regime began with a bloodless coup on 1 September 1969, when twenty-seven-year-old Qadhafi and fellow army officers ousted King Idris while the monarch was out of the country.

Libya has been under U.N. economic sanctions since April 1992 because of Qadhafi's opposition to United Nations Resolution 748, which orders him to hand over the two suspects to either the U.S. or Scotland. Both countries reject a Libyan proposal to try the alleged bombers at U.N. or Arab League proceedings. On 1 December 1993 the U.N. tightened restrictions by freezing Libyan assets abroad and banned all oil technology export to Libya. The Vatican, concerned that the sanctions were increasingly provoking violence and despair, offered in March 1994 to broker a solution to the case. Pressed on by mounting domestic discontent over the country's decaying economic situation, Saad Mujber, a high ranking Libyan politician, announced the possibility in March 1994 that the suspects could be tried before Scottish judges at the International Court of Justice. In Lebanon, Youssef Shaaban, a Palestinian follower of guerrilla leader Abu Nidal, declared in June 1994 that he was responsible for the bombing. However, prosecutors denied he had made the confession, and continued to hold Libya responsible for the bombing. On 20 October Radio Monte Carlo announced that a spokesman for the British Foreign Office said that talks between Libya and Britain are set to take place in Cairo.

Qadhafi will not turn in the suspects because he fears an internal split in the country. One of the bombing suspects belongs to his tribe, the other to Major Abdel-Salaam Jalloud's tribe, the Megraha. A power struggle between Qadhafi and Jalloud, his second in command, escalated in 1993. Jalloud made only a brief appearance with Qadhafi on the twenty-fourth anniversary of his coup on 1 September 1993. Throughout 1993, the power struggle between the two men continued. Jalloud opposed the possibility of giving oil profits directly to the public as well as a government-approved surprise pilgrimage to Israel by 200 Libyans to win favor with Israel at the U.N. Palestinians and, apparently, Jalloud criticized the trip, which was aborted when the tourists denounced Israel and abruptly returned home. Unofficial reports in September 1994 announced that Jalloud was under semi-house arrest after refusing to resume his duties in protest of the visit. In a memorandum to Qadhafi, he said Qadhafi alone is the cause of the suffering in Libya.

The weight of the U.N. embargo on the economy, which derives 90 percent of its export income from oil, along with political and tribal problems have fomented opposition on several fronts. In an effort to placate the fundamentalist opposition, the regime announced in 1994 that it would extend the scope of the *Shari'a*, Islamic law, over the existing legal structure. In October 1994, praising the Shiite Muslim Hezbollah in southern Lebanon, Qadhafi urged Muslims to form a united Islamic front to safeguard Islam and the Koran.

In October 1993 Qadhafi crushed an attempted coup by the Wurfala tribe and military officers sympathetic to the exiled National Front for the Salvation of Libya. Furthermore, former Foreign Minister Mansour Kikhia, the leading opposition figure abroad, vanished while attending a human rights conference in Cairo in December 1993. In 1973, he had resigned from the government because he disapproved of Qadhafi's ties with terrorist movements. After a brief return in 1975 as Libya's representative to the United Nations, he broke definitively with the government during Qadhafi's rigorous crackdown on dissent in 1980.

In 1994 Libya abandoned its twenty-one-year-old claim on the Aouzou Strip in northern Chad. On 3 February the World Court ruled that the occupied territory belongs to Chad under a treaty Libya signed with France in 1955, when Chad was still a French colony. In May Libya withdrew from Aouzou, a potentially uranium-rich strip of land over which two wars, claiming thousands of victims, have been fought.

Political Rights and Civil Liberties:

Libyans do not have the right to change their government democratically. Qadhafi rules with the help of layers of committees around the country. There is no constitution. Governing principles come from Qadhafi's *Green Book*. Qadhafi, his aides, and committees acting in his name make major governmental decisions. He appoints officials ranging from military figures to junior-level personnel.

Qadhafi rules through a series of Revolutionary Committees and intelligence agencies under his personal control. Nominal power lies with the secretary of the General People's Congress, which is elected by municipal groups called People's Committees. The Revolutionary Committees oversee the People's Committees and screen all candidates. All committees have security functions. Qadhafi redesigned his regime in 1992, holding local elections in October. This was designed to give the appearance of popular control over thirteen ministries by creating thirteen separate 1,500-member bodies, consisting of one representative from each community. However, ultimate power and authority remain in Qadhafi's hands.

The system prohibits political parties or any other types of associations. Participation in elections is mandatory.

The human rights situation has not changed much since the end of 1993. However, in 1994 Libya passed new Islamic laws covering execution and compensation for killing, inheritance, theft, and marriage and divorce to nurture an image of Libya as an Islamic state, apparently to pre-empt the growth of fundamentalism.

Freedom of speech is severely limited. People's Committee meetings allow only some limited debate. Citizens generally refrain from criticizing the regime because they fear the extensive surveillance network inside the country. Informers monitor the population. The government does not respect the right to privacy. The state owns and controls the Libyan media and the government censors available foreign broadcasts. JANA, the official news agency, broadcasts the official news. Publishing opinions contrary to government policy is prohibited. Occasional criticism of government policy could be orchestrated. Journalists muzzle themselves through self-censorship so that very few cases of harassment exist. The only documented case by the Committee to Protect Journalists involves Abdallah Ali al-Sanussi al-Darrat, a journalist who has been in jail for twenty years. However, since the regime strictly limits access to information, it is difficult to ascertain the number of such cases.

There is no freedom of assembly or association. Only government-sponsored demonstrations are allowed, and only government affiliates have the right to organize. Any activity that opposes the basic principles of the "Revolution" may be punishable by death.

Prisoners are reportedly tortured during interrogations. The security forces hold political prisoners in secret detention centers. Libya's arbitrary judicial system does not provide fair trials. Detainees are often sentenced without trial, and death sentences are applied for many offenses.

Discrimination exists based on ethnic status, specifically against Berbers and Tuaregs in the south. In an attempt to eliminate the Berber identity, Qadhafi has tried unsuccessfully to get Berbers to marry non-Berbers. Cultural norms make women second-class citizens, but Qadhafi has tried to expand their access to higher education and employment opportunities. Women receive basic military training and are subject to the military draft. A husband's permission is required for women to travel abroad. Female circumcision is still practiced among tribal groups in the south.

Libya is predominantly Muslim. The regime has banned the Sanusiyya Muslim sect. The government allows the small Christian population to practice and conduct services; there are two churches in Libya. The regime opposes Islamist extremists inside the country but praises extremist organizations such as the Hezbollah operating outside of Libya. The mosques are monitored for political activity. Libyans are free to travel within the country, except in certain security areas. Exit permits are required for travel abroad. Libyan students studying abroad are subject to interrogation upon returning home and are usually placed under surveillance.

Trade unions are under strict government control, and Libyan workers do not have the right to join unions of their own choice. There is no collective bargaining, and no right to strike. Labor laws do not apply to foreign workers in Libya. Although Qadhafi has proclaimed a policy of privatization of major economic sectors, the economy still remains largely statist.

Liechtenstein

Polity: Prince and
parliamentary democracy
Economy: Capitalist-
statist
Population: 31,000
PPP: na
Life Expectancy: na
Ethnic Groups: Alemannic German, Italian, other European

Political Rights: 1
Civil Liberties: 1
Status: Free

Overview:

In November 1994 Liechtensteiners voted to join the European Economic Area (EEA), a free trade zone linked with the European Union. Local business interests campaigned hard for the EEA, in order to maintain high levels of European investment in their tiny country. The vote capped two years of unusual political turbulence. In the general election held in February 1993, the first of two that year, the environmentalist Free List won seats for the first time, taking two of the twenty-five seats in the *Landtag* (legislature). The Free List won seats at the expense of the moderate Patriotic Union (VU). VU leader Hans Brunhart resigned as head of government. Markus Buechel, leader of the conservative Progressive Citizens' Party (FBP), which won twelve seats, became the new head of government. He formed a short-lived coalition with the VU.

Prince Hans Adam II, the head of state, dismissed the parliament in June 1993 after it handed Buechel a no-confidence vote. Buechel had upset the political elites by hiring an outside professional, not a patronage appointee, to head the principality's personnel department. Hans Adam asked Buechel to remain in office after the dissolution of parliament. There was a new parliamentary election in October 1993. The VU won an absolute majority of seats, but formed a grand coalition with the FBP. Mario Frick of the VU is Prime Minister. The instability in 1993 followed a struggle in 1992 in which Hans Adam and the legislators fought over scheduling referendums. The government would like to clarify the division of powers between the monarch and parliament, but that issue will await a resolution of the principality's relationship with the rest of Europe.

The Principality of Liechtenstein was created in its current form in 1719. Most of Liechtenstein's native residents are descended from the Germanic Alemanni tribe. Over one-third of the population is foreign. Prince Hans Adam's Austrian ancestors purchased the country's land. The royal family lived primarily in Moravia (once part of the Austro-Hungarian Empire, now a Czech land) until 1938, when the spread of Nazism forced them to flee to Liechtenstein. Between Czecho-Slovakia's independence in 1918 and the Communist takeover in 1948, that country confiscated Liechtenstein's royal estates without compensation. Since the fall of communism in 1989, Hans Adam has attempted to reclaim the family's Czech properties, but the Prague government has refused to give him either land or compensation.

The prince appoints a head of government from the majority party or coalition in the twenty-five-member Landtag, which has a maximum term of four years.

Called "hallowed and sacrosanct" by the constitution, the monarch has the right to veto legislation. Hans Adam's father vetoed only one bill, a proposed hunting law. Parties with at least eight percent of the vote receive representation in the Landtag. Major local issues include overdevelopment and the large number of foreigners in the labor force. The Swiss handle many of Liechtenstein's defense and foreign affairs, but the principality has had its own U.N. membership since 1990.

Political Rights and Civil Liberties: Liechtensteiners can change their government democratically. Control shifts between parties. However, the monarch retains more executive powers than other constitutional monarchs in Western Europe. Hans Adam is more involved than his father was in setting the legislative agenda. Voters may decide issues directly through referendums. Woman have had voting rights nationally since 1984, and won legal equality through a constitutional amendment in 1992. Major parties publish newspapers five times each week. Residents receive radio and television freely from other countries. Liechtenstein has no broadcast media. The country is too small to have numerous organizations, but association is free. A small, free trade union exists. The prosperous economy includes private and state enterprises. The state religion is Roman Catholicism, but other faiths are free to practice.

The native population can grant citizenship to foreigners by local vote after five years of residence. There are significant numbers of second and third generation residents without citizenship. Prime Minister Frick wants to liberalize citizenship laws.

Lithuania

Polity: Presidential-parliamentary democracy
Economy: Statist transitional
Population: 3,726,000
PPP: $5,410
Life Expectancy: 72.6
Ethnic Groups: Lithuanian (80 percent), Russian, Ukrainian, Byelorussian, others

Political Rights: 1
Civil Liberties: 3
Status: Free

Overview: A controversial national referendum on corruption and economic reform, improved ties with neighboring Poland and Russia, and possible membership in the North Atlantic Treaty Organization (NATO) were among the key issues President Algirdas Brazauskas faced in 1994.

Lithuania was an independent state from 1918 to 1940, when it was forcibly annexed by the Soviet Union under provisions of the Hitler-Stalin Pact. It regained independence from a disintegrating Soviet Union on 1991 after the failed hard-line coup attempt against Soviet President Mikhail Gorbachev. In the parliamentary elections of 1992 the ex-Communist Lithuanian Democratic Labor Party (LDLP) won 44.9 percent of the vote and 79 of 141 seats in the *Seimas* (parliament). Sajudis, the independent coalition formed in 1988 and which spearheaded independence, won 19.9 percent. Sajudis chairman and President Vytautus Landsbergis was replaced as head of state by LDLP Chairman Brazauskas, who was elected chairman of parliament, a post that made him acting president of Lithuania. In February 1993, he became the country's first directly elected president, easily defeating the ambassador to Washington, Stasys Lozoraitas. The bulk of Soviet troops withdrew from Lithuania on 31 August 1993.

On 27 August a referendum that would have obliged the government to compensate Lithuanians for savings lost to inflation was defeated when only 35 percent of eligible voters cast ballots (50 percent turnout was need to validate the vote). Other provisions of the eight-question referendum, which was backed by the opposition led by Landsbergis, dealt with high-level corruption and law enforcement. The opposition maintained that the plan would have benefited Lithuanians suffering in the market economy, arguing that funding for the measure would come from privatizing state industries. The government, as well as the International Monetary Fund (IMF) and the World Bank, said the plan would bankrupt the treasury. The government of Prime Minister Adolfas Slezevicius accused the opposition of blatant populism.

The economy was a key issue throughout the year. In February, farmers went on strike to demand higher prices for their goods and more stable subsidies. Strike organizers also condemned the system of state-owned processing plants. While over 90 percent of farmland has been privatized, most farmers still had to sell their produce to refineries that are inefficient state monopolies. And while inflation dropped sharply during the year to 36 percent by June, Lithuania suffered annual price rises of over 1,000 percent as the Soviet Union collapsed and the republic struggled to introduce its own currency, the lita. The country is also totally dependent on Russia for oil. In April, after furious debate, the government pegged the lita to the U.S. dollar.

The country has made bigger strides toward privatization than the other Baltic states, and more than two-thirds of companies slated for sale have been privatized. Over 50 percent of the workforce is employed in the private sector economy, and trade with the West increased to 45 percent. GDP rose nearly 2 percent and was expected to go up to 6 percent in 1995. Western investment, however, has been slow, though in October the IMF approved a $201 million standby agreement loan to continue economic reforms.

There was great concern about Russian military transit through Lithuania to Kaliningrad (formerly the German port of Konigsburg), the Russian Baltic enclave where some 150,000-250,000 troops are stationed and where Moscow planned to build a new naval base. Russia had hinted that it would double customs duties on Lithuanian goods until the Kaliningrad issue was resolved, leading the government to accuse Russia of using military and economic pressure to intimidate the Baltics. In January, Russia reacted harshly to Lithuania's decision to apply for NATO membership and a subsequent decision to join NATO's "Partnership for Peace." In September, the Russians objected to the troop transit rules being incorporated into a general law that also regulated the transport of hazardous waste through Lithuania. The issue was unresolved by year's end.

Poland's President Lech Walesa made steps toward Lithuanian-Polish reconciliation when he paid a late April visit to Vilnius, the capital. Presidents Brazauskas and Walesa signed a friendship treaty that had taken two years to complete. The main obstacle had been Lithuania's demand that it include a condemnation of Poland's occupation of Vilnius from 1921 to 1939. There had also been discord over Lithuania's 200,000-strong Polish community, which had pressed for greater autonomy and cultural rights.

Political Rights and Civil Liberties:

Citizens have the means to change their government democratically. There are numerous political parties covering the range of the political spectrum. The 1992 parliamentary elections were free and fair. In 1993 the country held its first direct election for president.

In February 1993, the *Seimas* passed a law on the nine-member Constitutional Court, providing that it would rule whether any laws or government decrees conflict with the constitution or other legislation. The judiciary is independent and free from government interference. In late November *Seimas* Deputy Chairman Juozas Bernatonis said that as of the beginning of 1995 a new system of courts would begin functioning: a Supreme Court, a Court of Appeals and regional courts. Parliament had appointed thirteen out of twenty-three judges to the Supreme Court and eleven to the Court of Appeals. In 1993, several tough laws were passed to combat rapidly spreading, often violent organized crime activities.

The press is generally free. There are private radio and television stations, and a variety of independent newspapers, periodicals and journals. Journalists have been victimized by organized crime gangs.

Freedom of religion is guaranteed and respected in this largely Roman Catholic country. Ethnic minority rights are generally respected, though Polish and Russian communities have complained of discrimination. In late November, the Russian Community of Lithuania (RCL) released a communiqué charging that the government does not support the development of Russian culture and seeks to create an "information and cultural vacuum." The RCL said that the cultural needs of Russians are disregarded, that the number of radio and television programs in Russian has been reduced, and that Russian schools face critical shortages of funds.

Freedom of domestic and international travel is guaranteed. Women are underrepresented in certain professions and in managerial sectors, but are entitled to day-care and maternity benefits. There are several women's organizations that are working to increase government and public awareness of spousal abuse.

Various independent trade unions established the Lithuanian Trade Union Association in 1992, and workers in most sectors have the right to strike.

Luxembourg

Polity: Parliamentary democracy
Economy: Capitalist
Population: 402,000
PPP: $20,800
Life Expectancy: 75.2
Ethnic Groups: Luxembourgers (70 percent) and other Europeans (30 percent)

Political Rights: 1
Civil Liberties: 1
Status: Free

Overview:
National elections on 12 June 1994 returned the Christian Social Party-Socialist Workers' Party coalition to power. The coalition has been in office since 1984. After the election, Christian Social Prime Minister Jacques Santer prepared to leave office in January 1995 to assume the presidency of the commission of the European Union (EU). Luxembourg is pro-European unity, but has some anxiety about being overwhelmed by bigger countries.

The Grand Duchy of Luxembourg received international recognition as an independent neutral country in 1867. However, Germany occupied the country during both world wars. Since World War II, Luxembourg has advocated a united Europe, and belongs to both the EU and NATO.

Grand Duke Jean is head of state. He appoints the prime minister from the party or coalition able to command a majority in the sixty-member Chamber of Deputies. Voters elect deputies by proportional representation for a maximum term of five years. There is also an appointive Council of State, a twenty-one-member body with life terms. The Chamber can overturn the Council's decisions. In addition to the dominant Christian Social and Socialist Workers' Parties, the country has smaller groups: the liberal Democratic Party, the Green Alternative, the Communist Party, and the Five-Sixths Party, which favors pensions worth five-sixths of all workers' final salaries.

As European institutions expand, Luxembourgers fear that Germany, France and other larger countries will exclude the duchy and other small countries from automatic membership in the European Commission and other European bodies. Many Luxembourgers are suspicious of the EU's constitutional review, set for 1996, because it could downgrade their European role. Fernand Rau, the Five-Sixths leader, opposes a common European citizenship. Small business people hope that the single European market will not overwhelm home-grown enterprises.

Luxembourg has based its prosperity on a strong industrial base. However, the long-term decline in the steel industry worldwide has taken its toll. In April 1993 the government announced that Arbed, the money-losing, semi-state steel company, would have to borrow heavily and restructure in order to stay alive through the year 2000. The company is cutting personnel and reinvesting borrowed capital.

Political Rights and Civil Liberties:
Luxembourgers have the right to change their government by democratic means. Voting is compulsory. Since foreigners constitute about one-third of the residents and

half the work force, Luxembourg's politicians worked out a deal with the EU to exempt the country from the voting rights provision of the Maastricht treaty on European union. This provision would have granted generous local voting rights to other EU nationals resident in Luxembourg. However, Luxembourg negotiated successfully to prevent resident citizens of other EU countries from voting until after five years' residence. Such residents would have to wait another five years before becoming candidates for local office. As of 1994, only 6,000 foreigners had registered to vote.

There is freedom of speech and of the press. Print journalism is private and uncensored, except for restrictions on pornography. Broadcast media are state-chartered and free. Publications appear in various languages. The schools use both French and standard German, but the courts use French. In ordinary conversations and in some of the media, most Luxembourgers prefer Letzebuergesch, their own Germanic language. There is a movement to have the tongue made an officially recognized European language, in order to protect the small country's distinct identity.

The judiciary is independent and fair. The country has freedom of association. The steel industry, agricultural interests and small businesses all have lobbying groups. Affiliated with the Socialist and Christian social parties, two competing labor federations organize workers. The population is mostly Catholic. There is religious freedom and no state church. The productive economy is largely private.

Macedonia

Polity: Presidential-parliamentary democracy
Political Rights: 4*
Civil Liberties: 3
Economy: Mixed statist
Status: Partly Free
Population: 2,090,000
PPP: na
Life Expectancy: na
Ethnic Groups: Macedonians (64.6 percent), Albanians (21 percent), Turks (5 percent), Macedonian Muslims (2.5 percent), Romanies (2 percent), Serbs (2 percent),
Ratings Change: *Macedonia's political rights rating changed from 3 to 4 because there were electoral irregularities.

Overview:　　　In 1994, seventy-seven-year-old President Kiro Gligorov was re-elected and Macedonian nationalist parties lost ground in the country's fraud-marred first parliamentary elections since achieving independence from a disintegrating Yugoslav federation in 1991. Long-standing tensions with neighboring Greece about the republic's name were exacerbated by a trade blockade by Athens, which put a further stranglehold on an already impoverished economy suffering from the United Nations embargo on trade with rump-Yugoslavia. Other sensitive issues concerned a national census and restiveness among the large Albanian minority.

Macedonia is a multi-ethnic Balkan state bordering Serbia, Bulgaria, Greece and

Albania. It was ruled by the Ottoman Turks for 500 years prior to the Balkan Wars in 1912-1913, after which its territory was divided among Greece, Serbia and Bulgaria. In 1941, Macedonians rose up against Nazi and Bulgarian occupiers. After World War II, Communist partisan and subsequent Yugoslav leader Josip Broz (Tito) launched military campaigns to unite Macedonian territories in Greece with Yugoslavia during the Greek civil war in 1946, further fueling Greek distrust of Macedonian motives. Several of Macedonia's neighbors have contended that there is no distinct ethnic Macedonian identity.

In the 1990 elections to the unicameral 120-seat Macedonian Assembly (parliament), the nationalist Internal Macedonian Revolutionary Organization-Democratic Party of Macedonia (VMRO-DPMNE) won thirty-seven seats; the Social-Democratic Alliance for Macedonia (SDLM)—formerly the Alliance of Communists of Macedonia—gained 31; and the predominantly Albanian Party for Democratic Prosperity (PDP) carried 26 seats. SDLM leader Gligorov was named president. In September 1992, three months after the collapse of the technocrat-dominated government of Nikola Kljusev, a new three-party coalition government was formed consisting of the SDLM, the centrist Reform Forces-Liberal Party (RF-LP), and the Albanian-dominant Party for Democratic Prosperity-National Democratic Party (PDP-NDP). It was headed by Prime Minister Branko Crvenkovski of the SDLM.

At the end of 1993, the government announced it had uncovered a wide-scale operation to smuggle weapons into the country to arm a 20,000-man army to establish an autonomous Albanian region that would ultimately unite with Albania. Several prominent ethnic Albanian political figures, including Assistant Defense Minister Hisen Haskaj, were arrested. In 1992, Albanians in Sturga had briefly proclaimed a so-called Republic of Albanians in Yugoslavia, known as Ilirid. The PDP and NDP and the Albanian government denied involvement in the plot.

On 9 February 1994 the United States finally recognized the independence of Macedonia. Angered by Western recognition, in mid-February Greece cut off diplomatic relations with the government in Skopje, the Macedonian capital, and imposed a trade embargo, declaring the northern port of Salonica off limits to Macedonian ships until Macedonia stopped using its name. The port was the chief route for importing fuel and other goods to landlocked Macedonia. The move by Greece, which held the European Union's six-month rotating presidency, set off friction with its partners in the twelve-nation trade bloc, six of whom had already extended diplomatic relations to what was temporarily referred to as the Former Yugoslav Republic of Macedonia (FYROM) when it was admitted to the U.N. in April 1993. On 17 February Greek border guards closed the frontier with Macedonia to most goods, and continued to argue that Macedonia had designs on Greece's eponymous northern province.

In April the EU announced it would take legal action against Greece for refusing to lift the trade embargo by bringing Greece before the European Court of Justice. In June the Court rejected a bid by the EU's executive agency for a temporary restraining order against the Athens government.

In June 1994 the government of Macedonia launched a controversial census designed to answer the delicate issue of who Macedonians are. A 1991 census had been boycotted by ethnic Albanians. It estimated that 65 percent of the country's

2.2 million people were Macedonians and 21.7 Albanians. Albanian leaders claimed that they comprised 30-40 percent. Fearing that the 1994 census would enable authorities to claim that many Albanians were not Macedonian citizens because they came from the Albanian enclave of Kosovo in Serbia, Albanian leaders started to raise "technical problems" in Albanian areas. Albanian census-takers in three Albanian-dominated regions of western Macedonia did not show up for work. Problems also arose in Serb areas. Final results are not expected until sometime in 1995.

The issue of the Albanian minority was a major concern of the government. In February, a radical Albanian group with links to Albania split from the moderate PDP, accusing the party leadership of servility to the government. An Albanian diplomat admitted ties between the radicals and the government in Tirana, the Albanian capital. Arben Xhaferi, a leader of the radicals, based in Tetovo, the main city in the western region bordering Albania, said in May that his group was concerned with human rights, asserting that the government denied Albanians equal rights. In June two prominent ethnic Albanian leaders and eight others were convicted of masterminding the 1993 mutiny plot and sentenced to prison terms of up to eight years.

The Greek embargo, a stagnating economy and ethnic relations had political ramifications in an election year. On 15 July, the embattled government of Prime Minister Crvenkovski survived the third no-confidence motion of its twenty-two-month tenure, rustling up last-minute support from ethnic Albanian parties. The nationalist opposition led the vote against the government. PDP and NDP deputies, who had boycotted parliament to protest the jail sentences against the ten Albanians convicted in the mutiny plot, returned to the assembly at the last minute for the vote.

The economy was the key issue in the presidential and parliamentary campaigns. While President Gligorov faced weak opposition from nationalist Ljubisha Georgeievski, a theater director with little political experience, the ruling coalition faced a challenge from the free-market nationalist Democratic Party of Petar Goshev, founded in 1993. Goshev's call for "clean" government underlined the resentment felt at the way those close to the governing coalition appeared to be prospering, and his plan for an easing of taxes and accelerated privatization through a voucher system strongly appealed to voters. More than 40 percent of Macedonia's work force was unemployed or on forced leave from factories that had been shut down. Welfare benefits and pensions were months in arrears, and many families survived on remittances from Macedonians working abroad. U.N. sanctions on the rump-Yugoslavia cost the economy some $2.5 billion, while the Greek embargo cost another $60 million monthly in lost exports and higher transport costs. Nevertheless, the governing coalition pressed on with a stabilization plan agreed to with the International Monetary Fund (IMF) in late 1993, although payment of a $35 million standby loan was frozen when Macedonia, in June, missed repaying $100 million to creditors abroad.

The first round of the vote was held on 16 October and President Gligorov was easily re-elected by direct vote, capturing 52 percent to Georgeievski's 14 percent. But parliamentary results were held up as international observers and opposition forces charged serious flaws in the balloting, with a "high number" of voters—as many as 10 percent of 1.3 million voters—left off eligibility lists at polling stations. Opposition parties threatened to boycott the 30 October second round. According to the government election commission, ten parliamentary candidates—eight from Gligorov's Alliance—earned seats in the first round, and some 389 of 1,765 candidates had advanced to the second round. "Democracy lost in these elections, but subconsciously I'm relieved that extremists on all sides lost as well," said Miftar Zyberi, an ethnic Albanian candidate from Tetovo.

On the day before the runoff, both the VMRO and the Democratic Party called for a boycott. After the second round, President Gligorov announced that his alliance had won 88 of 120 parliamentary seats. The president pledged to press for reforms and privatization.

In other issues, Macedonia in late June protested to rump-Yugoslavia about several incursions into Macedonian territory. At the same time, an estimated 3,000 trucks a week crossed the border, violating U.N. sanctions. In May, the U.S. Army added thirty-seven soldiers and three helicopters to its observer force in Macedonia, joining the nearly 500 Army personnel already deployed as patrols near the Serb border along with nearly 1,000 U.N. peacekeepers.

Political Rights and Civil Liberties: Macedonians can change their government democratically, although the October parliamentary elections were marred by vote-rigging and fraud according to international and Macedonian observers. The opposition boycotted the second round to protest the irregularities.

An independent judiciary has yet to be established, though President Gligorov, in a post-election address, promised reforms would continue in this area.

Political parties are free to organize and function, and there are several ethnic parties representing the interests of Albanians, Serbs and others. In the area of minority rights, the constitution refers specifically to Macedonians, Albanians, Turks, Roma (Gypsies), and Vlachs, but makes no mention of Serbs. Albanians have consistently criticized discrimination in employment and limitations on Albanian television and radio broadcasts, Albanian-language schools, and underrepresentation in the military and police forces.

The independent press faces economic constraints, and government-owned printing presses limit competition. There are four daily newspapers in Skopje and numerous other publications. There is an Albanian newspaper (*Flaka*), which comes out only sporadically. Editors have accused the government of restricting access and withholding information. The state-owned Macedonian Radio-Television has 2,300 salaried employees working for three television stations, only fifteen with Albanian backgrounds. There are an estimated 200 private small radio and TV stations, most run on shoestring budgets. Serbs, Albanians and the VMRO claim they are denied fair access to the government-run broadcast media.

Freedom of religion is respected, and the dominant faiths are Macedonian Orthodox and Muslim. There are some restrictions on domestic and foreign travel. There are an estimated 35,000 refugees from Bosnia in the country.

The constitution and laws guarantee men and women equal rights, but women face discrimination in employment and education, particularly in rural areas.

The Union of Independent and Autonomous Trade Unions (UNNIA) confederation was formed in 1992, with six member unions. The Council of Trade Unions of Macedonia (SSSM) is the successor to the old Communist labor federation. Strikes are permitted in most industries and sectors.

Madagascar

Polity: Presidential-parliamentary democracy
Economy: Mixed statist
Population: 13,702,000
PPP: $710
Life Expectancy: 54.9
Ethnic Groups: Malayan-Indonesian highlanders; coastal peoples of Black African and racially mixed origins; small groups of Europeans, Asians and Creoles

Political Rights: 2
Civil Liberties: 4
Status: Partly Free

Overview:

A horrible cyclone and economic restructuring were the major new stories in 1994 as Madagascar experienced its second year of democratic rule. In February, Geralda, the worst cyclone to hit Madagascar since 1927, killed more than seventy people, rendered 150,000 homeless, wrecked 80 percent of the homes in Taomasina, the main port, and did severe damage to the island's already rickety infrastructure. This disaster intensified Madagascar's grinding poverty and uneven development. In October the government announced that it would emphasize help from the World Bank and the International Monetary Fund, rather than other channels, in its plans to restructure the economy.

Madagascar, a large island and five small isles off the southeastern coast of Africa, won independence from France in 1960. Admiral Didier Ratsiraka headed a leftist authoritarian regime from 1974 to 1993, when Professor Albert Zafy defeated him in a democratic presidential runoff in 1993.

In 1990, a High Constitutional Court decree permitted independent political parties. Thereafter, several ideologically diverse parties gained legal status.

In June 1991, partisans of the Active Forces coalition that opposed Ratsiraka launched a series of major protests in the capital and other major cities. The opposition demanded a new constitution, a sovereign national conference, and Ratsiraka's resignation. Hundreds of thousands of people rallied for several weeks of nonviolent demonstrations. Following continued unrest, in October 1991 Ratsiraka and Prime Minister Guy Razanamasay formed a new unity government that included the opposition. They also dissolved the National Assembly and the Supreme Revolutionary Council, and established a transitional High State Authority. The transition also included promises of a new constitution and a constitutional referendum. In November 1991, Zafy became president of the High State Authority.

As the opposition had sought, a national conference took place in 1992. Several violent incidents disrupted its proceedings, but the conference did produce a new constitution. The proposed document provided for a unitary state and a strong presidency in order to reduce the power of pro-Ratsiraka regionalists (called "federalists") after a national opposition victory. Voters approved the constitution in August 1992.

According to his own original timetable, Ratsiraka did not have to face the voters until 1996, but he joined seven other candidates for the first round of presidential elections in November 1992. Zafy and Ratsiraka led the field, but no candidate received more than 50 percent of the vote, forcing a run-off. In February 1993 Zafy, leader of the Active Forces opposition coalition, carried five of the six provinces with nearly 67 percent of the vote, and swept Antananarivo, the capital, with 77 percent. The opposition parties consolidated their victory by winning a majority in the parliamentary elections in June 1993.

The country's poor economy is the most urgent problem facing Zafy's regime. Serious environmental problems are also mounting. For example, only 20 percent of the country's forest cover remains. Continued use of slash-and-burn agricultural methods could wipe out the forest by some point in the next century. Soil is eroding rapidly, endangering the farmers' ability to grow crops. Zafy is leaving most details of these and other domestic issues to his prime minister and cabinet. The government must also deal with tensions between the coastal provincials and the more elite population of the central plateau. Ratsiraka recognized the potential for a social explosion, and predicted that after his departure the presidential palace would be "an abbatoir."

Zafy faced a major crisis in April 1993 when government commandos clashed with armed, pro-Ratsiraka rebels. A radio station owned by the ex-president charged that the fighting killed four people and that pillaging followed in the northern town of Antsiranana. Authorities placed three captains involved under house arrest. In April 1994 Zafy charged an unnamed ambassador stationed in Madagascar with destabilizing his government. Zafy claimed that the diplomat was someone who had backed Ratsiraka in the 1993 election.

In parliamentary elections in June 1993, Active Forces and other anti-Ratsiraka elements won a commanding majority of seats. As a result of electoral irregularities, there had to be repeat elections in a few districts. In August 1993 Francisque Ravony, Deputy Prime Minister in the transitional government, became Prime Minister after defeating Roger Ralison in a parliamentary vote. Ralison was the candidate of the Active Forces political department. Ravony belongs to the pro-presidential majority, but was not a top anti-Ratsiraka leader. In response to an unsuccessful no-confidence vote in parliament, Zafy reshuffled the cabinet in August 1994. Ravony remains in office, but the membership of the cabinet reflects the factions that rejected the no-confidence resolution.

Political Rights and Civil Liberties:

Malagasy voters can change their government by democratic means. There were a few irregularities in parliamentary voting in 1993, but the anti-Ratsiraka opposition won in generally free and fair elections. Pro-Ratsiraka elements in the provinces may threaten the newly democratic system.

There is a vibrant private press. The government abolished censorship officially in 1990. When Ratsiraka attempted to reimpose censorship under the 1991 state of emergency, the private press refused to cooperate. However, some self-censorship remains. Television is government controlled and under some pressure to slant news coverage, but there are now private radio stations.

An independent judiciary functions without government interference. Upon his inauguration, Zafy granted a general amnesty to political prisoners and reduced sentences for certain crimes. Thereby, the new president undid several abuses of the old regime. However, prison conditions remain horrible for the remaining inmates. Several free labor organizations exist, many with political affiliations. Workers have the right to join unions and to strike. Widespread poverty and significant regional differences limit equality of opportunity. The traditional elite is of Malayan-Indonesian descent, but most of the population is of African origin. A South Asian minority forms a significant part of the commercial class.

There is religious freedom. Clergymen played a major role in the anti-Ratsiraka opposition. Christianity, Islam, traditional Malagasy religions and other faiths coexist.

In the context of a generally poor economy, women have significant economic and social rights. Citizenship passes to children matrilineally.

Malawi

Polity: Presidential-parliamentary democracy
Economy: Capitalist
Population: 9,532,000
PPP: $800
Life Expectancy: 44.6
Ethnic Groups: Chewa, Nyanja, Tumbuku, other

Political Rights: 2*
Civil Liberties: 3*
Status: Free

Ratings Change: *Malawi's political rights rating changed from 6 to 2 and it civil liberties rating from 5 to 3 following successful democratic elections. As a result Malawi's status changed from Not Free to Free.

Overview: After the National Consultative Council drafted a new constitution for Malawi in 1994, the country held its first multiparty presidential and legislative elections on 17 May, ending Dr Hasting Kamuza Banda's thirty years of despotic rule. The second president of Malawi, Bakili Muluzi, whose United Democratic Front (UDF) party failed to garner a majority of parliamentary seats, formed a minority government after a lengthy impasse on negotiating a coalition government with the Alliance for Democracy (AFORD). The new government inherited major economic problems whose prospects for improvement were grim given the crop failure caused by a drought.

Banda, who had ruled Malawi with an iron fist since independence from Britain in 1964, slowly relinquished power in 1993, twenty-one years after making himself President-for-Life. During his reign, he stifled dissent with the help of his Malawi Congress Party (MCP) and paramilitary thugs known as the Young Pioneers, instituting one of the most repressive regimes in Africa.

After a Catholic bishops' pastoral letter in March 1992 criticized human rights abuses, Banda faced increasing domestic and international pressure to legalize multipartyism. His rejection of reforms and his crackdown on churches and opposition groups misfired after Western donor countries suspended aid in May 1992, pending reforms. On 18 October Banda announced an unexpected referendum on multipartyism.

The referendum, scheduled for 15 March 1993, was postponed until 14 June after the opposition and U.N. Secretary General Boutros Boutros-Ghali rejected the date because it left too little time to campaign. In the referendum, 63 percent of the electorate chose multipartyism.

Following the crushing blow to Banda and the MCP, the president initially refused to step down and order new elections. However, on 23 June 1993 Banda and the opposition agreed to advisory councils to oversee pre-election preparations. Two councils, the National Consultative Council (NCC) and the National Executive Council (NEC), were formed and respectively worked parallel to the National Assembly and the cabinet. In November 1993, parliament made constitutional amendments including a bill of rights, the repeal of life presidency and of the presidential right to nominate MPs exclusively from the MCP.

In the run-up to the 17 May 1994 elections, as early as February 1994, there were allegations of widespread voter intimidation at the hands of the MCP. The Malawi Young Pioneers (MYP), paramilitary Banda thugs who have not been entirely disbanded and 2,000 of whom continue to operate from Mozambique, attacked several schools in the capital Ligongwe, beating teachers for their role in the registration of voters. After the ruling party decided to retain the aging and critically ill Banda as its presidential candidate, relations between the government and the opposition deteriorated further.

UDF candidate Bakili Muluzi, AFORD candidate Chakufwa Chihana, Kamlepo Kalua of the Malawi Democratic Party and Tim Mangwazu of the Malawi National Democratic Party (MNDP) ran against Banda and his running mate, home affairs minister Gwanda Chakuamba. The UDF and AFORD were the two largest internal opposition movements to emerge in the early 1990s. In 1993 UDF chairman Muluzi was arrested and charged with misappropriating MCP funds in the 1970s when he was its secretary general. Prior to that, in April 1992, the regime had arrested Chihana, the secretary general of the Southern Africa Trade Union Coordination Council and later AFORD founding member, for meeting with the opposition in exile in Zambia.

Muluzi, a southern Muslim businessman, and former member of the MCP and the MYP, won with 42 percent of the presidential votes, followed by Banda who took 33 percent and Chihana with 23 percent. Muluzi's party formed a common electoral group with the Congress for the Second Republic party and the United Front for a Multi-Party Democracy.

In separate elections for the 177-seat parliament contested by eight political parties, UDF won eighty-five seats, MCP garnered fifty-five seats, AFORD thirty-six and John Tembo, the *eminence grise* Banda depended on to run the government when his health broke down, took one seat. John Tembo was a member of the triumvirate that ruled Malawi when Banda underwent brain surgery in South Africa in October 1993.

The voting followed geographical lines, setting the scene for possible regional division. Muluzi carried the populous Yao-speaking south and fifteen or so seats from the central region, Banda retained the MCP's leadership, doing well in the Chewa-speaking central region, and Chihana virtually swept the less populous Tumbuka-speaking north.

President Muluzi's priorities are the alleviation of poverty and food supplies. Malawi is one of the world's poorest countries and has an illiteracy rate of 60 percent. The new government inherited a national budget dependent on foreign aid. Food production is far from meeting the country's needs and hardship was extended in 1994 as the already drought-stricken country did not receive its normal seasonal rains. On 30 September, Malawi and the United States signed three grant agreements totaling about $120 million to support development programs in agriculture, education and transport. On 11 November, the World Bank granted $40 million in aid to import maize and support economic reforms.

Coalition talks between UDF and AFORD stalled because the UDF failed to meet AFORD's demands for several key ministerial posts and the post of vice president for Chihana. Instead the UDF was offered the ministries of forestry and physical planning. UDF ruled out any coalition with the MCP, and formed a minority government that faced strong opposition in parliament where AFORD and MCP held ninety-one seats. The impasse over the formation of government and parliamentary coalitions also sparked a short-lived demand from some Malawians in the north to break away from the country.

Shortly after AFORD abandoned talks with the UDF, the MCP approached the latter in formulating an alliance. Chihana, who had called the MCP the party of death and darkness, said that it was better to convert the devil to work with them. The two parties signed a "memorandum of understanding," under which the two parties would work more closely to preserve the unity and security of the country.

In October, however, Muluzi teamed up with AFORD, making Chihana second vice-president despite criticism that the post is unconstitutional.

On 24 August, Malawi and the United Nations signed a joint declaration on human rights. President Muzuli announced upon his return from Botswana on 30 August that the southern African states had agreed not to condone nondemocratic actions in Malawi in its process of democratization.

On 10 November MCP and AFORD legislators voted themselves a 50 percent pay increase and free health care.

Political Rights and Civil Liberties: The people of Malawi exercised the right to change their government democratically on 17 May 1994 when they held their first multiparty elections, electing a new president for a five-year term, and members of a 177-seat parliament. The voting age was lowered from twenty-one to eighteen. The army was prohibited from voting to prevent it from being divided into factions.

Although the international election monitors considered the elections free and fair, in the months preceding the elections several incidents of elections-related violence claimed several civilian lives. Malawi's independent electoral commission named the MCP as the main violator of electoral law in April. The commission charged that MCP officials had been seizing or buying voter registration certificates to be used in the elections in nine of the country's twenty-four districts. It said chiefs, who play an influential role in rural politics, and MCP officials were the main culprits in snatching voter certificates. The commission also reported apprehending AFORD members who attempted to seize registration certificates. In March, opposition parties uncovered a plot in which the MCP allegedly hired Kenya African National Union (KANU) strategists to help manipulate the elections in its favor. The Malawi Broadcasting Corporation reported that six poll manipulators had been posing as international election monitors. During the election, the commission was forced to nullify the results of two constituencies following complaints of irregularities.

The new constitution, which includes twenty-seven individual rights, is under a twelve-month review scheduled to end in May 1995. Under this period of transition, the constitution can be subject to amendment. One of the major amendments is the creation of a second vice-president, a post which satisfied one of Chihana's conditions for participating in a government of national unity. The National Assembly legalized opposition parties on 23 June 1993.

The constitution provides for a Senate composed of indirectly elected members and traditional village chiefs.

The judiciary, long a tool of Banda, has become increasingly independent. In March 1993 Minister of Justice and Prosecutor General Friday Makuta resigned, accusing the government of interference with trials. In 1994 the courts challegenged the constitutionality of the post of a second vice-president.

The new constitution guarantees freedoms of speech and press. Under Banda, the authorities restricted these freedoms in the run-up to the elections. The electoral commission accused the MCP of trying to intimidate the media. Article 19, a censorship watchdog group in London, reported that Banda's government restricted its rivals by retaining control of the only national radio station. In response the MCP accused journalists of the Malawi Broadcasting Corporation (MBC), former MCP mouthpiece, of bias towards the UDF because they "point their microphones in UDF direction." Newspapers also faced intimidation at the hands of groups outside the government. In February 1994 the *Malawi Democratic*, an opposition weekly newspaper, said its editors received several death threats for alleging Muluzi was jailed for six months for stealing government funds twenty-five years ago while working as a civil servant.

In June President Muluzi announced plans to reintroduce the Tumbuka language on national radio, MBC. Television was also aired for the first time.

Muluzi ordered the closure of prisons that had been used to abuse human rights. He also ordered the release of all political prisoners and commuted death sentences to life imprisonment and invited international observers to visit the prisons. The new constitution abolished detention without charge or trial.

The public is reportedly taking justice into its own hands. Eleven suspected thieves were "necklaced," burned alive. The police had not arrested those who committed the necklacing.

Freedom of assembly is permitted. In October 1994 striking government workers demanded a 100 percent pay raise. The police did not take any action against those boycotting work and blocking streets. The civil servants accepted a 25 percent raise.

Malaysia

Polity: Dominant party   **Political Rights:** 4
Economy: Capitalist   **Civil Liberties:** 5
Population: 19,486,000   **Status:** Partly Free
PPP: $7,400
Life Expectancy: 70.4
Ethnic Groups: Malays (50 percent), Chinese (35 percent),
Indians (15 percent)

Overview: After winning control in March 1994 of one of two state governments that had been in opposition hands, Malaysian Prime Minister Mahathir Mohamad's ruling National Front coalition focused on national elections due in 1995.

Malaysia was established in September 1963 through a merger of the formerly British, independent Federation of Malaya with the British colonies of Sarawak, Sabah and Singapore. (Singapore withdrew two years later). The ceremonial head of state is a King chosen for a five-year term by and from among the hereditary sultans of the nine Malay states. The King, currently the Sultan of Perak, can delay federal legislation for thirty days. Executive power is vested in the prime minister and a cabinet. The parliament consists of a Senate, with thirty-two members appointed by the king and twenty-six elected by the thirteen state legislatures, and a 180-member, popularly elected House of Representatives. Each of Malaysia's thirteen states has its own parliament and constitution and shares legislative powers with the federal government.

Reaction to the economic success of the ethnic Chinese minority triggered race riots in 1969. At the time the Malays made up half the population but owned only 2 percent of the wealth. In 1971 the government responded with the New Economic Policy (NEP), which discriminated in favor of Malays through racial quotas in education, civil service opportunities and business affairs. Malays now hold a 20 percent economic share, although the urban elite has prospered much more than the rural *Bumiputras* (sons of the soil). A new National Development Policy adopted in 1991 has the same basic goals as the NEP.

The ruling National Front coalition has captured at least a two-thirds majority in the lower house in all eight general elections since 1957. The coalition's dominant party is the United Malays National Organization (UMNO), a secular, conservative party representing ethnic Malay interests. The coalition's nine other parties are also ethnic-based. By tradition, the top two UMNO leaders serve as the country's prime minister and deputy prime minister. In July 1981 Dr. Mahathir Mohamad won the UMNO presidency and became prime minister. The party's claim to represent all Malays through consensual decision-making was shattered in April 1987, when top UMNO figures tried to oust Mahathir for alleged mismanagement and corruption. The party split on factional lines, and a court deregistered it in February 1988. The pro-Mahathir faction subsequently formed the present UMNO-Baru (New).

In late 1988 former Trade Minister Razaleigh Hamzah led disgruntled UMNO members in forming Semangat '46 (Spirit of '46, the year UMNO was founded in Malaya). In May 1989 this new party joined with the Muslim fundamentalist Pan-Malaysian Islamic Party (Pas) and two smaller parties in a Malay-based opposition called the Muslim Unity Movement (APU). At the October 1990 national elections, the ruling National Front won 127 seats (UMNO, 71; the Malaysian Chinese Association, 18; the Malaysian Indian Congress, 6; the social democratic Malaysian People's Movement, 5; the United Sabah National Organization, 6; affiliated independents, 21). The opposition won 53 seats, a gain of 25 from 1986, led by the center-left, Chinese-based Democratic Action Party (DAP) with 20; the multiracial United Sabah Party (PBS), 14; Semangat '46, 8; Pas, 7; independents, 4.

In 1993 UMNO faced a potentially divisive split over Mahathir's eventual successor. Heading into the November party elections the vote for the deputy president post pitted the incumbent, Deputy Prime Minister Ghafar Baba, against Finance Minister and UMNO Vice President Anwar Ibrahim. Ghafar, who appeared to be nominally in line to succeed Mahathir, represented UMNO's conservative, rural rank-and-file voters who still adhere to the party's traditional Malay-nationalist roots. By contrast Anwar epitomized a younger generation of urbanized, business-oriented Malaysians. Many UMNO supporters doubted Ghafar's ability to carry out Mahathir's ambitious program of making Malaysia a fully industrialized country by 2020, and threw their support behind Anwar. Anwar romped to victory and subsequently assumed the deputy prime minister post.

At the beginning of 1994 the National Front controlled eleven of the thirteen state governments, while opposition groups held Sabah and Kelantan. Days before the 1990 national election, then-Chief Minister Joseph Kitingan of Sabah pulled the PBS, the state's ruling party, out of the National Front coalition. In response Prime Minister Mahathir sharply cut development funds to the state, and in January 1992 the federal government placed Kitingan on trial on corruption charges. At the 18 February 1994 Sabah state elections, the PBS took twenty-five seats in the forty-eight seat legislature against twenty-three seats for National Front parties. However the Sabah state governor inexplicably refused to swear in Kitingan for another five-year term. In March the National Front gained control of the state legislature after three PBS deputies defected, allegedly after being paid off.

Political Rights and Civil Liberties:

Malaysians have a limited ability to change their government democratically due to the dominant political role of the United Malays National Organization as well as numerous institutional barriers. A Commonwealth team rated the 1990 parliamentary elections free but not entirely fair, largely due to the government's control of the media, irregularities in voting roles, and a ban on political rallies. In addition, the government uses numerous security laws against dissidents, causing a chilling effect on political activity. In the 1994 Sabah state elections, the ousted party accused the ruling National Front coalition of allowing illegal immigrants to vote in return for receiving Malaysian identity cards, and of widespread bribery. Parliamentary elections are due by December 1995 but will likely be held earlier in the year. Official policy favors ethnic Malays in education, the civil service, and business licenses and ownership.

The government continues to detain former Communists, religious extremists, and others under the broadly drawn 1960 Internal Security Act (ISA) and the 1969 Emergency (Public Order and Prevention of Crime) Ordinance (EO). Under the ISA police can detain suspects for up to sixty days without filing formal charges; the Ministry of Home Affairs (a portfolio currently held by Premier Mahathir) can authorize a further detention of up to two years. The government frequently places speech and association restrictions on former ISA detainees. Under the EO the country is still under the state of emergency declared in the wake of the 1969 communal riots. The Home Affairs Minister can use the EO to detain persons for up to two years.

Police are accused of abusing suspects to extract confessions. The judiciary is independent in civil and criminal cases, but less independent in political cases. The 1994 Constitution (Amendment) Act authorizes the government to draw up a code of ethics for judges, and this is under consideration. Defendants generally receive fair trials. Caning is applied for criminal offenses including drug possession and rape, and in December the government authorized mandatory caning for white collar crimes.

Freedom of speech is restricted by the 1970 Sedition Act Amendments, which prohibit discussion of issues considered sensitive, including the privileges granted to ethnic Malays. The 1984 Printing Presses and Publications Act requires domestic and foreign publications to renew their permits annually. A 1987 amendment to this Act bars the publication of "malicious" news, expands the government's power to ban or restrict publications and prohibits publications from mounting legal challenges to bans or restrictions. The government occasionally uses these powers to shut down newspapers. Journalists practice self-censorship, although newspapers published by the Chinese community are fairly outspoken. All major newspapers and all radio and television stations are owned by the government or by companies owned by parties in the ruling National Front coalition, and their coverage of opposition views is limited. The Mahathir government has ignored a September request by the Election Commission for the authority to order remedies for politically biased coverage in state-run media. On 1 April the government expelled Leah Makabenta, a Filipina journalist, over an article on the treatment of migrant laborers, and another comparing Malaysia's 1969 race riots to the current situation in Bosnia.

The 1967 Police Act requires permits for all public assemblies. Political rallies have been banned since the 1969 riots; currently only indoor "discussion sessions" are permitted. Under the 1966 Societies Act any association (including political parties) of more than six members must register with the government. The government can refuse permits or revoke existing permits. A similar law applies to student groups, which are barred from political activity. The independent National Human Rights Association functions without harassment.

Female genital mutilation is practiced in some Malay communities. In an effort to crack down on illegal immigrants, the government has arbitrarily detained thousands of foreign workers. On 27 March 1994—Palm Sunday—the authorities detained some 1,200 Philippine women gathered outside a Kuala Lumpur church, later releasing all but twenty-one of them.

Islam is the official religion in this secular country, but non-Muslim minority groups worship freely. In July 1994 the government began a crackdown on the Al-Arqam messianic Islamic sect, which it accuses of deviant teachings. Some observers feel that Prime Minister Mahathir viewed the wealthy group as a political threat. In July and August police arrested scores of Al-Arqam followers and banned the movement under the Societies Act. In early September police detained al-Arqam leader Ashaari Muhammad under the ISA. In October Ashaari appeared on national television and "confessed" he had "deviated" from Islamic principles, and subsequently disbanded the sect.

The government must approve of and can dissolve all unions. Each union and each labor federation can cover only one particular trade or occupation. In the 120,000-worker electronics industry the government permits only "in-house" unions rather than a nationwide union.

Strikes are legal but restricted. Under the 1967 Industrial Relations Act unions must provide advance notice in several "essential services," some of which are not considered essential by the International Labor Organization.

Maldives

Polity: Nonparty, presi-
dential-legislative (elite-
clan dominated)
Economy: Capitalist
Population: 244,000
PPP: $1,200
Life Expectancy: 62.6
Ethnic Groups: Mixed Sinhalese, Dravidian, Arab, and black

Political Rights: 6
Civil Liberties: 6
Status: Not Free

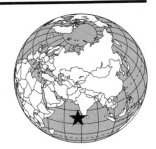

Overview: The poor, Islamic, Republic of Maldives is a 500-mile-long string of twenty-six mostly uninhabited atolls in the Indian Ocean. The British granted independence to Maldives in July 1965. In 1968 a referendum ended the ad-Din sultanate's 815-year rule, and a new constitution gave the president extensive powers, including the right to dismiss the prime minister and appoint top officials. The *Majlis* (parliament) has forty directly elected seats and eight appointed by the president. Every five years the Majlis elects a single presidential candidate, and forwards this choice to the electorate for a yes-or-no referendum. Political parties are not banned but are strongly discouraged, and none exists.

Successive governments have faced several coup attempts. Most recently, in 1988 President Maumoon Abdul Gayoom called in Indian troops to crush a coup attempt by Sri Lankan mercenaries allegedly hired by a disgruntled Maldivian businessman. In the aftermath, the president increased the National Security Service (NSS) to 2,000 troops and named several relatives to top posts. The February 1990 Majlis elections brought in a crop of activists who sought to enact democratic reforms. This encouraged journalists to report on official corruption and nepotism. By June the government banned all independent media, and late in the year it arrested several journalists.

In June 1993 the president sacked his brother-in-law, Minister of Atolls Administration Ilyas Ibrahim, allegedly for using witchcraft to influence lawmakers in order to win the August parliamentary nominations for the October presidential referendum. On 23 August the president won the parliamentary nomination with twenty-eight votes, but Ibrahim, who had fled to Singapore, won a surprising eighteen votes and his brother, Fisheries Minister Allyas Ibrahim, took one. On 5 October President Gayoom, South Asia's longest serving head of state, won a fifth term with a 92 percent approval in the yes-or-no referendum. The president pledged to change the constitution to allow more than one candidate in the next referendum, scheduled for 1998.

Following the election a court tried Ibrahim in absentia and found him guilty of treason for attempting to usurp the parliamentary nomination process by actively campaigning for the nomination, and for allegedly trying to bribe MPs. According to the U.S. State Department, the government also detained at least twenty of Ibrahim's supporters on charges of assisting his presidential campaign, and sentenced at least four to lengthy prison terms.

In October 1994 the Indian government accused two Maldivian women of using sex and money to gain secret information from officials of the Indian Space Research Organization. The space secrets affair threatened to upset bilateral relations.

Political Rights and Civil Liberties: Maldivians cannot change their government democratically. The president, who under the constitution must be a male and a Sunni Muslim, holds broad executive powers and is nominated by the parliament to be the sole candidate in a national referendum. The government has successfully discouraged organized political opposition, and although political parties are not expressly banned, none exists. The 2 December 1994 Majlis elections were held on a nonparty basis, but following the vote President Gayoom claimed the government was considering a multiparty system.

Citizens can lodge complaints through certain channels, such as petitioning members of the Majlis, but the Penal Code prohibits actions that could "arouse people against the government" and this is broadly interpreted as a ban against political dissent. A 1968 law prohibits speech or writing considered inimical to Islam or threatening to national security.

In December 1990 the Majlis passed a strict Prevention of Terrorism Act that could be applied retroactively. In November and December 1990 police arrested and charged several journalists under the Act. In December 1991 a court sentenced Mohammed "Saape" Shafeeq, former editor of the magazine *Sangu*, to eleven years in prison for planning to blow up a conference center, although there appears to be scant evidence to support the charge. No lawyers were willing to defend Shafeeq, whom the government released in May 1993. *Sangu* had published articles on government corruption and other sensitive issues. Several other journalists were also convicted, but most appear to have been released.

The government can shut down newspapers for publishing allegedly unfounded criticism, and a similar broadly drawn provision allows the government to take action against journalists. In 1990 the government revoked the licenses of *Sangu* and *Hukuru*, and they remain closed. Journalists practice significant self-censorship. The state-run media carry only official views.

The constitution guarantees freedom of assembly, but citizens rarely gather for political purposes. The president exercises partisan control over the judiciary through his power to appoint and remove judges. The legal system is based on both Islamic law and civil law, and does not afford adequate procedural protection to the accused. Persons suspected of terrorism, conspiring to overthrow the government or drug offenses can be detained without trial indefinitely. Criminals can be flogged and banished to remote islands, and prison conditions are harsh. The NSS occasionally monitors personal communications and searches homes without a warrant.

Clubs and civic associations are permitted only for nonpolitical purposes. Under Islamic inheritance laws, a woman receives half the amount of an inheritance accorded to a man. The constitution defines all citizens as Muslims, and conversion to other religions can lead to a loss of citizenship. It is illegal to practice any religion except Islam, although in practice private worship by non-Muslims is tolerated. The authorities discourage migration to the overcrowded capital island of Male. The government denies workers the right to form unions, stage strikes or bargain collectively.

Mali

Polity: Presidential-par-
liamentary democracy
Economy: Mixed statist
Population: 9,113,000
PPP: $480
Life Expectancy: 45.4

Political Rights: 2
Civil Liberties: 4*
Status: Partly Free

Ethnic Groups: Arab Bedouin, Bambara, Berabish Berber,
Dogon, Fulani, Malinke (50 percent), Songhai, Tuareg, other
Ratings Change: *Mali's civil liberties rating changed from 3 to 4 because the
Tuareg insurgency flared up again. As a result Mali's status changed from
Free to Partly Free.

Overview: In 1994 President Alpha Oumar Konaré's administration faced a
continuing student crisis and a crippled economy. These led to
the resignation of the ten-month-old government of Prime Min-
ister Abdoulaye Sekou Sow over policy disagreements with the radical wing of his party,
Alliance for Democracy in Mali (ADEMA). The armed Tuareg rebellion in the north
resumed between Tuaregs opposed to the 1992 peace treaty and Malian armed forces.

Mali, known as Soudan at the time of its rule by France, declared its independence in
1960. Under the leadership of its first president, Modibo Keita, the country became a
Marxist, single-party state with close Soviet and Communist Chinese ties. In 1968 a group
of army officers under the leadership of Moussa Traoré ousted Keita, reversing his collect-
ivist policies. In 1979 the military formally relinquished power, Traoré became a civilian
president, and his Mali People's Democratic Union (UDPM) the sole new political party.

Military officers deposed Traoré in March 1991. Following the coup, the military
shared the government with civilians in the Transitional Committee for National
Salvation (CTSP). A national conference of all newly constituted political parties drew
up a new electoral code and a new constitution. ADEMA garnered most of the local
council and national legislature seats in elections held throughout the spring of 1992. In
the April presidential runoff Alpha Konaré won 69 percent of the vote and susequently
appointed Younoussi Touré as prime minister. Despite claims of abuse from some of the
smaller parties, international observers generally considered the elections to be free and
fair. In February 1993 Traoré and three other high-ranking military officers were
sentenced to death over the 1990 killings of protesters who supported a multiparty
system. Up to 125 demonstrators died at the hands of security forces who sprayed the
protesters with machine-gun fire.

One of the first student demands spearheading the 1990 pro-democracy protests was
for a 200 percent grant increase. Following the formation of the interim government, the
Association of Malian Students and Pupils (AEEM) joined in the ruling coalition and
toned down their demands. With ADEMA's electoral victory, AEEM was politically
sidelined. It split into a radical faction with close ties to the opposition National Congress
for the Democratic Initiative (CNID), led by Yehia Ould Zarawana, and a pro-ADEMA
faction. The replacement of the radical faction's leader with pro-ADEMA Amadoun
Bah in February 1993 ignited a series of protests for grant increases by the radical

faction, warning of a "new one-party state." The protests escalated on 5 April 1993 as students destroyed public property. On 9 April, Younnoussi Touré resigned days after the escalation of a student protest demanding the government's dissolution for failure to meet their demands for grant increases. Following the resignation the coalition cabinet of the newly appointed Prime Minister Abdoulaye Sekou Sow, which included CNID and Rally for Democracy and Progress (RDP)`ministers, reduced the expenditures of ministers and central government agencies.

Unable to garner the support of his own party and threatened by another student strike, Sekou Sow resigned during the first few days of February 1994. CNID and RDP ministers withdrew from Ibrahim Boubacar Keita's new government and the cabinet was reshuffled into an ADEMA majority.

Shortly after the announcement of the allocation of new grants on the basis of examination results, on 15 February 1994 students protested, responding to the rise in the cost of living. The new government closed all the schools and universities after attacks on the education minister's home. Approximately twenty students were imprisoned. On 2 March the authorities arrested Yehia Oud Zarawana, AEEM's general secretary. The detention initiated another round of violence that night. In October, the government announced the conditional release of the students because they had begun a hunger strike. President Konaré made it clear, however, that the country could not afford an across-the-board bursary.

Mali has had massive economic problems for years, stemming from long-term mismanagement and corruption and from the regional drought affecting the Sahel zone. Prior to the 1992 elections, the interim government reached an agreement with the IMF providing for increased financial support for structural adjustments in the economy in exchange for reduction in spending on student grants and the civil service. Despite President Touré's criticism of the interim government's economic policy, he continued most of the austerity measures when he took office in 1992. In January 1994, following the 50 percent devaluation of the African Financial Community franc (CFA franc), prices increased sharply. On 31 January Prime Minister Sow announced fixed prices for essential daily products and a 10 percent increase of wages beginning in April. Mali managed the effects of the devaluation successfully in so far as inflation was kept within acceptable limits.

The Tuareg and Arab minorities rebellion erupted again in 1994, despite a peace treaty signed on 11 April 1992 with Algeria as mediator. More than 300 people have died since January 1994. Nearly 185,000 Tuaregs have fled to neighboring Burkina Faso, Algeria and Mauritania since 1990 when they escaped from Traoré's army, which wanted to exterminate them. On 25 February 1994 Colonel Saloum Bihal, a military leader of the Popular Movement of the Azaouad and an architect of the peace process, was killed during an attack by Tuaregs opposed to the peace treaty. The 16 April meeting to advance the implementation of the peace treaty measures failed because of demands from the Unified Movements and Fronts of the Aouazad (MFUA), the largest faction, to further integrate 2,360 MFUA soldiers into the national army, an issue which has been the main point of contention between the two sides. So far, 640 fighters have been integrated into the army. In May, the two sides signed a draft agreement whereby all the Azaouad fighters would be integrated in the Malian army, police, customs and administration and the Tuareg bases in the north would be dismantled. In June, following increased infighting among MFUA members, three groups demanded that fighters integrated into the army return to their bases. An agreement between Mali, Algeria, the

U.N. High Commission for Refugees and the International Fund for Agricultural Development was reached in August for the repatriation of Malian Tuareg refugees based in Algeria. In September the European Union called for an independent inquiry into the massacring of civilians and the wiping out of a whole village in the north by government soldiers and rebels alike.

Political Rights and Civil Liberties: In January 1992 Malians changed their government democratically for the first time. The voters overwhelmingly approved a new constitution guaranteeing political pluralism and civil liberties. ADEMA now controls 76 out of 116 National Assembly seats.

The executive branch has considerable influence on the judicial system. The Ministry of Justice appoints judges and supervises both law enforcement and judicial functions, and the Superior Judicial Council, which supervises judicial activity, is headed by the President. The Supreme Court has both judicial and administrative powers, while the newly established Constitutional Court strictly interprets the constitution. Trials are public and defendents have the right to choose their own attorney. Defendants are presumed innocent until proven guilty.

The new constitution expanded the rights of arrested persons. They must be charged or released within forty-eight hours. However, in practice, backlogs and insufficient numbers of lawyers, courts and judges often cause lengthy delays in bringing people to trial. Amnesty International reported two cases in July of women held incommunicado without charge from 12 May until 29 May 1994. They were released without charge and Amnesty believed they were prisoners of conscience detained for campaigning peacefully for the release of student prisoners.

Amnesty International also reported seventeen cases of extrajudicial executions of civilian Tuaregs by the Malian army in April and May 1994.

The constitution guarantees freedoms of speech and press with certain restrictions. The government controls the only television station and the only daily newspaper. Despite a 23 percent literacy rate, there are some thirty to fifty independent newspapers and periodicals. The media are open to a wide range of views including those critical of the president and the government. However, substantial penalties, including imprisonment for slander and for public injury to the Head of State and other officials, such as foreign diplomats, do exist. Specific injuries are not defined in the law. Since 1992, independent broadcasters have been able to operate private radio and television stations, but independent radio stations do not have statutory protection. On 17 February 1994, under "conservation measures" aimed at preserving public order, the government shut down *Radio Kaira,* which has close ties with opposition groups, for a week.

The law guarantees freedom of association and the right to peaceful protest. Permits must be obtained for mass demonstrations. Some forty-six political parties and hundreds of professional and special interest organizations are registered. Despite violent demonstrations by students, security forces respond cautiously in order to avoid a repetition of the events in 1990.

Malians no longer have to apply for an exit visa in order to travel abroad. Occasional road checkpoints are used, ostensibly to restrict the movement of contraband goods and check vehicle registrations.

An overwhelming majority of Malians in this secular republic are Muslim. Members of other religions are allowed to practice their faiths freely and establish houses of worship. The rights of ethnic minorities are generally respected. A new movement, Ganda Koi, was formed to protect members of the black African community, in response to acts of violence perpetrated against them by Tuareg rebels in the north.

The major trade union confederation still remains the National Union of Malian Workers (UNTM), the only union permitted to operate under the Traoré regime. The UNTM, however, was a major force instrumental in bringing down his regime and is an independent force. In May 1994, the UNTM threatened to strike over the government accord with the Tuaregs if ethnicity rather than qualification were the basis for civil service employment.

A new law gives women equal rights regarding property, but traditional practice and ignorance of the law prevent them from taking advantage of the law. Some active women's groups promote the rights of women. No laws exist against female genital mutilation, but the government provides media access to support educational efforts to eliminate the practice now undergone by 75 percent of women.

Malta

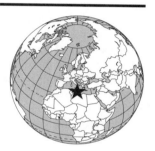

Polity: Parliamentary democracy
Economy: Mixed capitalist-statist
Population: 365,000
PPP: $7,575
Life Expectancy: 75.7
Ethnic Groups: Maltese (mixed Arab, Sicilian, Norman, Spanish, Italian, and English)

Political Rights: 1
Civil Liberties: 1
Status: Free

Overview:

In 1994 the conservative Nationalist Party government continued to lobby for membership in the European Union.

The Nationalists won office in 1987, and secured re-election in 1992 with 51.8 percent to 46.5 percent for Labor and 1.7 percent for the environmentalist Democratic Alternative. The Nationalists hold 34 seats to Labor's 31. Prime Minister Edward Fenech Adami supports full European integration and economic liberalization.

Located in the central Mediterranean, Malta was under foreign rule for most of its history. The British occupied the island in 1800. Later, it became a British colony. Malta gained independence from Britain in 1964. The Labor Party won power in 1971 and held office until 1987. In government, Labor followed a left-of-center economic policy and a neutral foreign policy. It also ordered some confiscation of church property and restricted private financing for Catholic schools. Labor turned to Libya for aid and support in the early 1980s. Even under the Nationalists in the early 1990s, Malta remained a transit point for companies doing business with Libya. Since the Nationalist victory in 1987, the conservatives have reversed Labor's economic and religious policies. The government is carrying out privatization of the state sector and deregulation of the Church.

The parliament, called the House of Representatives, has sixty-five seats, with a maximum term of five years. Voters choose representatives by proportional representation. Elected by parliament, the largely ceremonial president serves for five years, and appoints the prime minister from the parliamentary majority. Under a constitutional amendment adopted in 1987, a party getting a majority of the popular vote wins a majority of the parliamentary seats. In previous elections, it was possible for a party to receive a majority of the vote and a minority of seats.

Reacting to its recent electoral defeats, Labor has moderated its program. The party has dropped its opposition to private hospitals and free trade, and has improved its relations with the Catholic clergy.

Political Rights and Civil Liberties: The Maltese have the right to change their government democratically, and power alternates between the two major parties.

The Nationalist government has sponsored a pluralization of the broadcast media since 1991. Several private broadcast outlets now exist alongside the older public ones. Malta's constitution guarantees freedoms of speech and press. The only exception is a law passed in 1987 which forbids foreign involvement in Maltese election campaigns. The free press includes many politically oriented newspapers.

Religion is free for both the Catholic majority and religious minorities. There are tiny Protestant and Muslim communities. All groups have freedom of association. Many trade unions belong to the General Union of Workers (GWU), but others are independent. The Labor Party and the GWU severed their links to each other in 1992, in order to pursue more independent policies. A constitutional amendment banning sex discrimination took effect in July 1993, but divorce is still not legal. In 1994 Democratic Alternative demanded the dismissal of Assistant Police Commissioner Joseph Psaila, who allegedly participated in beating up prisoners and framing innocent people in the 1980's under Labor governments. However, under the Nationalists he has risen from inspector to assistant commissioner.

Marshall Islands

Polity: Parliamentary democracy
Economy: Capitalist-statist
Population: 54,000
PPP: na
Life Expectancy: na
Ethnic Groups: Marshallese (Micronesian)

Political Rights: 1
Civil Liberties: 1
Status: Free

Overview: In 1994 President Amata Kabua issued a controversial proposal offering to rent one or more of the Marshall Islands' nuclear-damaged islands as a site for atomic waste. The Marshalls received an increase in United States compensation for islanders exposed to radioactive fallout from the U.S. nuclear tests that took place from 1948-1956.

Located in the Pacific Ocean, the Marshall Islands were independent until the late 1800s, when the Germans established a protectorate. After World War I, Japan governed them under a League of Nations mandate until the U.S. Navy occupied the region in 1945. The U.S. administered the islands under a United Nations trusteeship after 1947. In 1979, the Americans recognized a distinct Marshallese constitution, causing a *de facto* change in the Marshall legal status. However, the Soviets and others waged an international legal dispute for several years over the islands' trusteeship. In 1986, the U.S. formally notified the U.N. that the trusteeship was over, and that the Marshalls had implemented a Compact of Free Association with the U.S. Under the compact, the Marshalls have self-government but still depend on American defense. Following changes in the international climate, the U.N. recognized the dissolution of the trusteeship in December 1990. In 1991, the Marshall Islands sought and received diplomatic recognition as an independent country, and full U.N.membership.

The Marshalls have a parliamentary system. Voters choose the thirty-three member parliament, *Nitijela*, from twenty-four election districts. The legislators elect a president and cabinet that are responsible to them. Members serve four-year terms. There is also an advisory body of Micronesian chiefs. The most recent legislative election took place in November 1991. In March 1994, Kabua was legally given, in addition to his title of president, the customary title of paramount chief.

The economy depends heavily on U.S. and other foreign assistance. An American base on the uninhabited Kwajalein Atoll is responsible for injecting more than 25 million dollars into the economy—over one-third of the country's annual budget. The Marshalls have a joint venture with China for additional vessels. There was concern in 1994 that the Chinese fishermen were damaging fishing stocks and crowding local boats out of the Marshall Islands' fledgling tuna industry.

In June a U.S. House of Representatives subcommittee approved a $7 million clean-up and rehabilitation fund for Rongelap, one of the islands that suffered from radioactive fallout from an American hydrogen bomb test in 1954. The decision followed the release of a document that revealed that the U.S. government knew hours in advance that the bomb explosion would contaminate the island, but proceeded with the test anyway.

High seas and huge waves destroyed or damaged 100 homes in June. The disaster served as a warning on the dangers of a rise in sea level. Indeed, a 50-centimeter (19.5 inches) rise would make the Marshalls uninhabitable.

In August, Katumba presented a proposal to rent one or more of the contaminated islands as a nuclear waste dump. The president argued that revenue from the lease would help pay for the rehabilitation of other contaminated islands. Such revenue would also be welcomed, as guaranteed U.S. aid runs out by 1992. The proposal was put on hold in order to complete a study on the feasibility of the project, which has been criticized strongly by environmentalists. The study is expected to take eight years.

Political Rights and Civil Liberties:

The Marshallese have the right to change their government by democratic means. Elections are competitive, but involve individuals, tendencies, and factions, rather than formal parties.

There is a bill of rights, which protects most civil liberties. Although there is freedom of the press, the government canceled its printing contract with a critical newspaper company in 1991. Ultimately, the government reversed the cancellation. The islands have private and public broadcast media and a private newspaper. In general, there is freedom of speech, but in 1992 the Nitijela held one of its members in contempt for having suggested the possibility of U.S. commonwealth status for the islands.

There are some minor restrictions on freedom of movement, due to defense installations and nuclear contamination. The cabinet can deport aliens who take part in Marshallese politics, but it has never done so. The government respects freedom of association, but there are no trade unions. Marshallese women have formed several associations and an umbrella organization, Women United Together for the Marshall Islands. In the traditional family structure, inheritance passes through the mother. There is religious freedom in this predominantly Christian country.

In June, President Kabua decreed that any man who enters the capital building must wear a tie. Workers protested the formality of the new dress code by wearing ties with T-shirts. The last time such a dress code was installed was three-hundred years ago, when European explorers were greeted by nude women swimming out to their ships. Missionaries soon enforced the practice of wearing clothing.

Mauritania

Polity: Dominant party (military-dominated)
Economy: Capitalist-statist
Population: 2,270,000
PPP: $962
Life Expectancy: 47.4
Ethnic Groups: White and Black Moors, Tuculor, Hal-Pulaar, Soninke, Wolof, others
Ratings Change: *Mauritania's civil liberties rating changed from 6 to 7 after human rights monitors confirmed continuing slavery and abuses. There was also a crackdown on opposition figures.

Political Rights: 7
Civil Liberties: 7*
Status: Not Free

Overview: Various oppressive practices remained an integral part of the political and social fabric in Mauritania in 1994. These include the systematic application of ethnic cleansing, slavery, repression and detention of opposition leaders, and continued human rights and civil liberties violations such as extrajudicial executions; arbitrary arrest and detention; torture; subjugation; and widespread discrimination against black Moors and blacks.

The population is divided into three main groups: white Moors, black Moors, and blacks. White Moors are culturally related to other North African Arabs. Black Moors are racially black, but culturally Moorish. The white Moors dominate the country politically and economically, but they are a minority. The non-Moorish black ethnic groups constitute about 40 percent of the population. Non-Moorish blacks and black Moors together would make a majority. However, white Moors have bolstered their domination of society by counting the black Moors as Moors, not as blacks.

Mauritania achieved independence from France in 1960. It has been under military rule since 1978, when military officers ousted President Ould Daddah and established the Committee for National Recovery, later renamed the Military Committee for National Salvation (CMSN). In 1984, Colonel Maaouya Ould Sid'Ahmed Taya of the

Social and Democratic Republican Party (PRDS) seized power in a bloodless coup. Taya became chairman of a military junta, which, until 1992, functioned as the country's legislative body. Taya was returned to power in 1992 in the country's first multi-party elections held since independence. However, both the presidential and subsequent legislative elections were marred by massive fraud and vote rigging.

Taya's primary challenger in the 1992 election was Ahmed Ould Daddah from the main opposition party, the Union of Democratic Forces (UFD), a brother of ex-president Moktar Ould Daddah. Despite an array of political support, Daddah secured only 33 percent of the vote. Although international observers reported that both the government and opposition parties participated in voting fraud, they noted that the government's efforts were more extensive and effective. Despite evidence of fraud and strong opposition party protest, the Supreme Court upheld the election results. Opposition parties boycotted the legislative elections that followed in March and April 1992, and aside from a few independent candidates, the ruling PRDS went unchallenged. Not surprisingly, all of the newly elected candidates were from the PRDS. Shortly after the election, Taya dissolved the CMSN and replaced it with the newly elected civilian Parliament.

Political Rights and Civil Liberties: Mauritanians cannot change their government democratically. The 1992 presidential and subsequent legislative elections were neither free nor fair. The executive and legislative levels of government are controlled by the PRDS. Although the CMSN was technically dissolved in 1992 and replaced by a civilian Parliament, the change was cosmetic only. Many of the military personalities from the former CMSN retained high positions in Taya's government.

Upon assuming power in 1984, Taya initially pledged that under his regime human rights would be respected. Although a limited number of concessions were made—political prisoners were freed, the use of cruel and unusual punishment (such as amputation of hands) was ended and the Mauritanian League of Human Rights was established—the progress was shortlived. Human rights violations by security forces continued unabated and in a scathing Human Rights Watch/Africa report, Taya's government is accused of implementing a systematic ethnic cleansing program against Mauritania's black population.

According to Human Rights Watch/Africa, blacks were forcibly expelled from Mauritania between 1989-1990, and the U.N. estimates that by late 1993 over 52,000 had fled to Senegal and an additional 13,000 to Mali. From November 1990-February 1991, approximately 2,500 blacks were arrested and held incommunicado without charge and subject to torture. Of these, Human Rights Watch/Africa reports "500-600 black political prisoners were executed or tortured to death by government forces." These charges have been echoed by other international human rights organizations including Amnesty International and the France-based *Agir Ensemble Pour les Droits de l'Homme*.

Government officials have repeatedly denied requests to investigate or prosecute those responsible for human rights and civil liberties violations. Although the government has denied the accusations, since 1989 requests to conduct investigations have been denied. In January 1994, delegations from Agir Ensemble and the International Federation for Human Rights (FIDH) were permitted entry to Mauritania. Following their departure, the vice president of the Mauritanian Human Rights Association (AMDH), Professor Cheikh Saad Bouh Kamara, was detained for four days without charge.

Despite repeated denials by Mauritanian officials, human rights groups, including the London-based Anti-Slavery International, maintain that slavery is still commonly practiced in Mauritania, and estimate that thousands of black Mauritanians are enslaved. Although slavery has been formally abolished in Mauritania on three occasions, the government has not attempted to provide education to black slaves on their rights or to prosecute those who continue to own slaves.

Government-sanctioned discrimination against black Moors and black Africans continues in Mauritania. Human Rights Watch/Africa states that "Black Africans in Mauritania are subjected to *de facto* discriminatory government policies, such as forced Arabization, with serious consequences for their civil and political rights. The discriminatory effects of Arabization are apparent in the suppression of the black communities' freedom of expression and association." The group also asserts that black Mauritanians in the Senegal River Valley "face great difficulties obtaining official identity documents, employment, bank loans, and land."

Mauritania's judicial system is not free from government interference. In cases which involve national security issues or political dissidents, government interference is routine. The court system is separated into different tiers and, depending on the nature of the crime, cases are tried by different courts. Islamic courts apply *shari'a*, Muslim law, and while the use of extreme physical punishment, such as amputations, no longer exists, tribal and familial relations continue to play an important role in the judiciary process. Under Mauritanian law, the accused has the right to a speedy arraignment (within seventy-two hours of arrest) and trial, access to legal counsel, and the right of appeal. However, in many cases, especially those involving political dissidents, many of these rights are not observed.

The 1991 constitution provides Mauritanians with the right to peaceful assembly and association, but these freedoms are severely curtailed. The law mandates that political parties must register and obtain permission to conduct large meetings or assemblies. The government has reserved the right to permit or deny political assembly. In practice, however, only blacks need permission to assemble and the government has been accused of continually interfering with both public and private black gatherings. Although few arrests of political opponents have been reported since the elections of 1992, Amnesty International reports that in September 1994 thirty-four Islamist activists, including the former religious affairs minister, were arrested. Unofficial estimates put the figure much higher.

The 1991 constitution protects freedom of speech and press. Beginning in 1992, press restrictions were eased. Owing to a freedom of press law adopted in mid-1991, several new independent newspapers were launched. Many of these papers criticized the government, particularly about its human rights practices. Despite these advances, numerous press restrictions are still evident. While the 1991 law helped to liberalize some aspects of the press, it remains a crime to promote "national disharmony" or to publish materials deemed to be "insulting to the president." Violators are subject to heavy fines and imprisonment. In May 1994 the bi-weekly newspaper *Le Calame* was seized following its publication of a report by FIDH. In censoring the paper, the interior minister said that he regarded the publication of the report a "threat to the security of the state." While there is some independence in the written press, the government controls both radio and television. Given the high rate of illiteracy in Mauritania, this amounts to a *de facto* control of information.

Freedom of religion is not respected. Islam is the official religion of Mauritania and, by law, all Mauritanians are Sunni Muslim and renunciation of Islam is a crime. Mauritanians are prohibited to enter the house of non-Muslims or to possess sacred texts of other religions.

With the exception of members of the military and police, workers are free to join trade unions. All unions are required to join the Union of Mauritanian Workers (UTM), a government-controlled labor federation. As a result of continual government interference, UTM's effectiveness in protecting worker's rights has been severely curtailed. The government restricts the right to strike and discourages labor participation in politics.

Mauritius

Polity: Parliamentary democracy
Economy: Capitalist
Population: 1,100,000
PPP: $7,178
Life Expectancy: 69.6
Ethnic Groups: Indo-Mauritian, Creole, Sino-Mauritian, and Franco-Mauritian

Political Rights: 1
Civil Liberties: 2
Status: Free

Overview: With a flourishing economy and political stability, Mauritius is one of the few political and economic success stories in post colonial Africa. Unemployment is estimated at just 3 percent and economic growth at 6 percent per year. While it possesses a booming textiles and tourism industry along with a well integrated multinational population, paradise has not been achieved without cost. As the result of rapid tourist growth and poor urban planning, less than one percent of the native forest remains and some of the islands' rare wildlife is in danger. In the rush toward modernization, much of the island's traditional Creole culture has also been lost.

Like the Seychelles, Mauritius does not have an indigenous people. The island's population of 1.1 million, comprised of approximately 750,000 Indians, 300,000 Creoles, 30,000 Chinese and 20,000 whites are all descendants of immigrants. Mauritius gained independence from Britain in 1968 and has maintained one of the most successful and functioning democracies in Africa. In March 1993, Mauritius became a republic within the British Commonwealth. The governor general was replaced by the president as Head of State with powers that are primarily ceremonial. Sir Veerasamy Ringadoo became the island's first president and within a few months, he was succeeded by Cassam Uteem. The government's current coalition elected in September 1991 is headed by Prime Minister Anerood Jugnauth. Mauritius has four major political parties and several smaller parties that encompass a wide array of ideological convictions.

The Mauritian Socialist Movement (MSM) was founded in 1983 by Prime Minister Jugnauth after he was expelled from the Mauritanian Militant Movement (MMM). The MSM is part of the current government's four-party coalition. The MMM enjoys substantial trade union support and is a second member of the current coalition. The Mauritian Labour Rally (RTM)and Rodriguan People's Organization (OPR) are the remaining coalition members.

Political Rights and Civil Liberties: Mauritius has an enduring colonial legacy of parliamentary democracy and holds free, fair and competitive elections on regular intervals. Ethnic and religious minorities within Mauritius are assured of legislative representation through a complicated "best loser" system in the National Assembly. Under this system, eight of the seventy parliament seats are allocated to both government and opposition parties which in turn distribute the seats to eight losing candidates who secured the most votes. Mauritius has an independent judicial system. Freedom of religion is respected and both internal and international travel are unrestricted.

While freedom of press is generally respected, journalists are subject to censorship under a 1984 act which prohibits the press from criticizing the government. There are several privately owned news publications. Both the television and radio stations are government owned, but they have increasingly developed independent news reporting. Freedoms of both assembly and association are respected. Workers have the right to organize and strike. There are nine labor federations which comprise 300 unions.

There are no known political prisoners in Mauritius and no reports of political or extrajudicial killings. While civil rights are generally respected, criminal suspects held in custody continue to report the use of excessive force by police.

Women still occupy a subordinate role in society, but the government has attempted to improve women's status by removing legal barriers to advancement. However there is no law which mandates equal pay for equal work or which protects women against sexual harassment in the workplace. Women comprise only about one-third of the student population at the University of Mauritius. Domestic violence against women is prevalent and there are no laws to address family violence crimes. Both governmental and non-governmental institutions have begun programs to educate the public on issues of domestic violence and to provide counseling to victims of abuse.

↑ Mexico

Polity: Dominant party (insurgency)   **Political Rights:** 4
Economy: Capitalist-statist   **Civil Liberties:** 4
Status: Partly Free
Population: 91,840,000
PPP: $7,170
Life Expectancy: 69.9
Ethnic Groups: Mestizo (70 percent), Indian (20 percent), Caucasian (9 percent), other (1 percent)
Trend Arrow: The up trend arow is due to an election that was freer than in the past, although not fair, and the new president's vow to make democratic reforms.

Overview: President Ernesto Zedillo took office on 1 December 1994 after an election in August that was freer than in the past, but decidedly unfair. His victory, in a year of crisis and tumult, ensured that the Institutional Revolutionary Party (PRI) would remain the longest-ruling party in the world. Zedillo promised to overhaul the state-party system and the judiciary but PRI hardliners looked to block democratic reforms. Zedillo's problems were compounded when the meltdown of the Mexican peso in December set off a severe economic crisis.

Mexico achieved independence from Spain in 1810 and established a republic in

1822. Seven years after the Revolution of 1910 a new constitution was promulgated, under which the United Mexican States is a federal republic consisting of thirty-one states and a Federal District (Mexico City). Each state has elected governors and legislatures. The president is elected for a six-year term. A bicameral Congress consists of a 128-member Senate elected for six years with at least one minority senator from each state, and a 500-member Chamber of Deputies elected for three years—300 by direct vote and 200 through proportional representation. Municipal governments are elected, except for the mayor of Mexico City, who is appointed by the president.

The nature of power in Mexico and how it functions do not correspond to the constitution. Since its founding in 1929, the PRI has dominated the state through a top-down, corporatist structure that is authoritarian in nature and held together through co-optation, patronage, corruption and, when all else fails, repression. The formal business of government takes place secretly and with little legal foundation.

Most Mexicans believe Carlos Salinas actually lost the 1988 presidential election, which was marked by massive and systematic fraud. Officially, Salinas won 50.36 percent to defeat challengers Cuauhtemoc Cardenas, who headed a coalition of leftist parties, and Manuel Clouthier of the conservative National Action Party (PAN).

Salinas, wielding the enormous power of the presidency, overhauled the economy and pursued a free trade agreement, NAFTA, with the U.S. and Canada. Political reforms were minimal and the basic structures of the sixty-five-year-old state-party system were not altered.

Under Salinas, congressional, state and local elections were marked by fraud and repression, particularly against the Party of the Democratic Revolution (PRD) formed by Cardenas after the 1988 election. Salinas conceded a number of governorships to the PAN after disputed votes in order to temper PAN demands for reform and prevent the PAN and the PRD from uniting in a pro-democracy coalition.

By late 1993 NAFTA was secured and Salinas seemed confident of being able to engineer the election of his personally chosen successor, social development minister Luis Donaldo Colosio, against challenges by the PRD's Cardenas and PAN congressman Diego Fernandez de Cevallos. But the New Year's Indian rebellion led by the Zapatista Army of Liberation in Chiapas, Mexico's poorest, southernmost state, shook the entire political system. The Zapatistas, by demanding democracy and clean elections, reset the national agenda. Under mounting international and domestic pressure, Salinas conceded to some electoral reforms and Colosio infuriated PRI hard-liners by campaigning for greater democratization.

Colosio was assassinated on 23 March. As theories abounded about whether PRI hard-liners or drug traffickers were behind Colosio's young killer, Mexicans wondered whether the political system would unravel. Salinas replaced Colosio with another close associate, Ernesto Zedillo, a forty-two-year-old U.S.-trained economist with little political experience. Zedillo promised democratic reform, too, and agreed to an unprecedented televised presidential debate in May. With Fenandez de Cevallos surging in the polls and Salinas agreeing to allow international election observers, it appeared Zedillo could actually lose.

With PRI rule on the line, hard-liners put aside their animosity for PRI moderates and put the state-party machinery firmly behind Zedillo. Under international scrutiny the PRI cut back on traditional forms of fraud like ballot-stuffing. Rather it relied on the enormous resources of the state, its control of the broadcast media and the support of wealthy business people to defeat Fernandez de Cevallo, who inexplicably seemed to lose enthusiasm in the last months of the campaign.

On 21 August Zedillo won with nearly 50 percent of the valid vote, against 27 percent for Fernandez de Cevallos and 17 percent for Cardenas. The PRI won 95 Senate seats, the PAN 25 and the PRD 8. In the Chamber of Deputies the PRI won 300 seats, the PAN 118 and the PRD 70. Both opposition parties disputed the legitimacy of the elections. In November only PRI congressmen in the Chamber voted to sanction the vote. The PRD voted against and the PAN abstained.

After the election the PRI went back to war. Francisco Ruiz Massieu, the PRI secretary general and a reform proponent, was assassinated on 28 September, his murder evidently ordered from somewhere within the PRI. His brother Mario, the assistant attorney general in charge of the case, resigned his post in November after accusing top PRI officials and hard-liners of blocking the investigation.

Zedillo took office on 1 December promising serious democratic reforms, including the separation of the PRI from the state and an overhaul of the judiciary and the police. In an unprecedented move he appointed the PAN's Antonio Lozano as attorney general, whose mandate included clearing up the Colosio and Ruiz Massieu murders. But Zedillo also appointed Ignacio Pichardo, formerly president of the PRI, to his cabinet. Pichardo, part of the hard-line group that revolves around PRI heavyweight Carlos Hank Gonzalez, was accused by Mario Ruiz Massieu of leading a cover-up of his brother's murder.

The questions therefore were how committed Zedillo was to democratic reform and how far PRI hard-liners were willing to go to stop him. There also remained the unresolved issue of Chiapas, where the Zapatistas and the PRD claimed the PRI had defeated the PRD in the governor's race in August through fraud. Finally, Zedillo's economic expertise, supposedly his forte, was severely questioned when at the end of the year the Mexican peso plummeted, setting off the worst economic crisis since Mexico's debt default in 1982.

Political Rights and Civil Liberties:

The 1994 national elections were freer than in the past, but decidedly unfair because of the ruling party's domination of the state and the broadcast media, and its still substantial control over the electoral system despite some reforms in 1994. The PRI, because of the presence of international observers and the determination of Mexican civic observer groups, had to rely less on traditional fraud like ballot-stuffing and more on the enormous power and resources at its disposal as the state party. The grossly unlevel playing field gave the PRI a decisive advantage and left the legitimacy of the electoral process in question.

Although the vote was cleaner than past elections, Mexican observer groups, particularly the National Civic Alliance, exposed a number of irregularities—for example, voter intimidation, lack of secrecy, and the "shaving" of credentialed voters from registration lists. Although such irregularities did not affect the outcome of the presidential race, they were prevalent in poor southern states where the left-wing opposition was strongest. That, coupled with the PRI's already inordinate advantages, may have affected the outcome of some local elections, and fit the pattern of recent years in which the PRI has been willing to cede more political space to the right-wing opposition than to the left.

Constitutional guarantees regarding political and civic organization are generally respected in the northern and central parts of the country. However, during the 1994 election campaign, there were reports of surveillance and harassment of left-wing opposition groups. Moreover, political expression is often restricted during rural land disputes and in poor southern states where repressive measures are frequently taken by the government against the left-wing PRD, and peasant and indigenous groups. The nearly feudal conditions in some southern states were at the root of the New Year's Indian rebellion in Chiapas.

Civil society has grown in recent years, including human rights, pro-democracy, women's and environmental groups. However, groups critical of the government remain subject to numerous forms of sophisticated intimidation that rights activists refer to as "cloaked repression"—from gentle warnings by government officials and anonymous death threats to unwarranted detention and jailings on dubious charges.

An official human rights commission was created in 1990. But only minimal progress has been made in curtailing the widespread violation of human rights—including false arrest, torture, disappearances, murder and extortion—by the Federal Judicial Police under the attorney general, and by the national and state police forces. The rights commission is barred from examining political and labor rights violations, and is unable to enforce its recommendations. Eight states do not even have laws prohibiting torture.

Targets of rights violations include political and labor figures, journalists, human rights activists, criminal detainees and, with regard to extortion, the general public. Corruption and rights violations remain institutionalized within the Federal Judicial Police, which often makes political arrests under the pretext of drug enforcement, and Mexico's other law enforcement agencies. Many police who have been dismissed for poor conduct have subsequently been implicated in kidnappings for ransom, which rose to a rate of about one per week in 1993-94.

During the Chiapas rebellion, the army was responsible for widespread human rights violations, including sweeps of towns and villages that led to the deaths of dozens of civilians, mass arbitrary arrests, torture of detainees and summary executions of at least five Zapatista fighters. The government, with the complicity of the official human rights commission, engaged in cover-ups of many of these violations. The Zapatistas also committed violations but to a far lesser extent than the army. Following the January ceasefire, peasant land seizures and landowners retaking property led to increasing violence across the state.

The judiciary is subordinate to the president, underscoring the lack of a rule of law. Supreme Court judges are appointed by the executive and rubber-stamped by the Senate. The court is prohibited from enforcing political and labor rights, and from reviewing the constitutionality of laws. Overall, the judicial system is weak, politicized and riddled with corruption. In most rural areas, respect for laws by official agencies is nearly nonexistent. Lower courts and law enforcement in general are undermined by widespread bribery. The exposure of government corruption, which is endemic, rarely results in legal proceedings. Drug-related corruption is evident in the military, police, security forces, and increasingly in government at both the local and national levels to the point where "Colombianization" is now part of the national discourse.

President Zedillo acknowledged the need for establishing a rule of law and proposed an overhaul of the judiciary and the police after taking office in December 1994. That offered the hope of ending the impunity that exists for nearly every class of crime, from high profile political assassination and corruption to drug-trafficking and kidnapping. But it remained to be seen whether and how effectively judicial reform would be carried out.

Labor is closely controlled by the government. Officially recognized unions operate as political instruments of the ruling party. The government does not recognize independent unions, denying them collective-bargaining rights and the right to strike. Independent unions and peasant organizations are subject to intimidation, blacklisting and violent crackdowns, and dozens of labor and peasant leaders have been killed in recent years in ongoing land disputes, particularly in southern states where Indians comprise close to half the population. There is also increasing exploitation of teenage women in the manufacturing-for-export sector, as the government consistently fails to enforce child labor laws.

The media, while mostly private and nominally independent, are largely controlled or influenced by the government through regulatory bodies, dependence on the government for advertising revenue and operating costs, cronyism and outright intimidation. A handful of daily newspapers and weeklies are the exceptions. A system of direct payments to journalists was ostensibly ended by the government in 1993, but there was evidence that the practice continued in 1994. Most newspapers and magazines derive over half of all advertising revenues from official sources. Although the print media showed more independence in 1994, instances abounded of self-censorship, regulatory pressures and intimidaton.

More than twenty-five journalists have been killed or disappeared in the last five years, with most cases still unresolved. At least three were killed in 1994 according to the Inter-American Press Association, the most in Latin America outside of Colombia. Dozens of others were threatened, many of whom were investigating drug-related corruption in the government.

The ruling party's domination of television, by far the country's most influential medium, is evident in the blanket, uncritical coverage of the ruling party. In the 1994 election campaign, opposition parties were given limited time on Televisa, the dominant PRI-allied network. But Televisa systematically supported PRI candidates and Jacobo Zabludovsky, the country's leading television news anchor, remained a virtual mouthpiece of the government. Two newly privatized stations have shown little inclination to buck the government line.

The government controls all radio frequencies. In 1994 it used this leverage to pressure a number of radio stations to remove commentators or program hosts the government deemed too critical. For example, Enrique Quintana, the host of the "Enfoque" news program, was forced to resign in August.

In 1992 the constitution was amended to restore the legal status of the Catholic church and other religious institutions. The right to own property and conduct religious education, which had long been accorded in practice, were given legal definition for the first time in over a century. Priests and nuns were given the right to vote for the first time in nearly eighty years. Nonetheless, activist priests promoting the rights of Indians and the poor, particularly in Chiapas, Guerrero and other southern states, remained subject to threats and intimidation by conservative landowners and local PRI bosses.

Micronesia

Polity: Federal par-
liamentary democracy
Economy: Capitalist
Population: 120,000
PPP: na
Life Expectancy: na
Ethnic Groups: Micronesian majority, Polynesian minority

Political Rights: 1
Civil Liberties: 1
Status: Free

Overview: Located in the Pacific Ocean, the Federated States of
Micronesia was a United Nations trust territory under
American administration from 1947 until 1979, when the
United States recognized the Micronesian constitution. Previously, the islands had
been successively under a German protectorate and a Japanese League of Nations
mandate. In 1982, the U.S. and Micronesia signed the Compact of Free Association, under which the U.S. retains responsibility for defense. In 1990 the U.N.
security council voted to recognize the end of the trusteeship. In 1991 Micronesia
sought and won international diplomatic recognition and full U.N. membership.

Bailey Olter is president of the four island states, Kosrae, Pohnpei, Chuuk, and
Yap. The unicameral legislature consists of one senator-at-large from each island
state elected for a four-year term, and ten senators elected for two-year terms on the
basis of island populations. The senators elect the country's president for a four-
year term from among the four at-large senators.

Pohnpei is the most modern of the four islands. The other three still have
traditional leaders and customs. In Yap, huge stone disks once used as money were
still accepted by banks as collateral in 1994.

Agriculture, tourism, forestry, and fishing are major industries, and public
sector employment is substantial. The federal and state governments play a major
role in the tuna industry. In January 1994 the government announced a plan to
develop the fishing industry. The Micronesian economy depends heavily on
American assistance, which will continue until 2001.

Political Rights   Micronesians have the right to change their government
and Civil Liberties: democratically. The people have the freedom to form
political parties, but family parties, tendencies and factions,
not Western-style parties, are the vehicles for political activity on the islands. The
states and localities have popularly elected governments.

Micronesia has a bill of rights and provisions for respecting traditional rights. Land
is not sold or transferred to non-Micronesians. Otherwise, the country respects cultural
diversity. Eight native languages are spoken. There is freedom of the press. Governmental authorities operate some media, while private enterprise and religious groups operate
others. Micronesians have religious freedom. The Congregational Church predominates
in Kosrae. Although there is freedom of association, only a few groups exist. Trade
unions are legal, but there is none. While legally, there is equality of opportunity,
traditional family status can determine one's chances for advancement. Women play

mostly traditional family roles and face the problem of traditionally tolerated domestic violence. Modernization has brought some women into paying jobs.

Moldova (Moldavia)

Polity: Presidential-parliamentary
Economy: Statist (transitional)
Population: 4,352,000
PPP: $3,500
Life Expectancy: 69.0
Ethnic Groups: Romanian (64 percent), Russian, Ukrainians
Ratings Change: *Moldova's political rights rating changed from 5 to 4 and its civil liberties from 5 to 4 following signs of more political competition.

Political Rights: 4*
Civil Liberties: 4*
Status: Partly Free

Overview:

Key events in 1994 were parliamentary elections won by parties favoring closer ties with Moscow and opposing reunification with Romania, a national referendum that underscored the country's independence, adoption of a new constitution that reduced presidential powers, and a deal for the withdrawal of Russian troops from the breakaway Transdniester region. While dealing with these issues President Mercia Snegur strove to build national consensus on the country's future course.

Moldova is a predominantly Romanian-speaking former Soviet Republic bordering Ukraine and Romania. In 1991 it officially declared independence from a fragmenting Soviet Union. Snegur, running unopposed and with the backing of the nationalist Moldovan Popular Front (MPF), was elected president by an overwhelming margin.

The conflict in the Transdniester region, the eastern sliver of territory on the left bank of the Dniester River inhabited primarily by Russians and Ukrainians, began in 1990 in response to increased demands for independence by the country's Romanian-speaking majority. In 1940 Soviet Russia had occupied the previously Romanian province of Bessarabia, establishing the Moldovian Soviet Socialist Republic. The Transdniester region was part of the Ukrainian republic until 1940, but after the Soviet annexation the region was joined to Moldova. In 1990, the Slavic minorities and the Gagauz, a Turkic people, proclaimed their own republics, the Gagauz SSR on 19 August, and the Dniester Moldovan Republic (DMR) on 2 September. Fighting broke out, lasting until mid-1992 when a cease-fire agreement was reached following negotiations between President Snegur and Russian President Boris Yeltsin. The Russian 14th Army under Lt. Gen. Aleksandr I. Lebed, which openly aided the Slavic insurgents and seized Moldovan land on the right bank of the Dniester, remained in control of the region.

The government's majority in the Soviet-era parliament, elected in 1990, consisted of 180-190 of the approximately 240 deputies who regularly attended sessions. (About eighty others, mostly left-bank Russians and several Gagauz, consistently boycotted sessions.) Deputies of the majority belonged to the Agrarian Club; the centrist Democratic and Independent Club; the majority of the Accord Club of ex-Communist Russian, Ukrainian, and other non-Moldovan deputies from the right bank, and about half of the Southern Steppe faction of Gagauz and Slavic deputies from southern Moldova. The only parliamentary groups not supporting the government were the rump-MPF and the few unreconstructed Russian and Communist deputies from the right bank. Increased polarization in parliament between Communists and nationalists over ratification of a 1991 agreement to join the Russia-dominant Commonwealth of Independent States (CIS) led to an October 1993 decision to hold early elections on 27 February 1994, a year before parliament's five-year term was due to expire.

February's first post-Soviet vote for a new 104-seat unicameral parliament marked a resounding defeat for nationalist parties that wanted the country to unite with Romania. Thirteen parties and electoral blocs were on the ballot. The Agrarian-Democratic Party, a coalition of former Communists and moderate to status-quo supporters of Moldovan statehood and closer economic ties with Russia, was the de facto ruling party in the old parliament following the demise of the MPF coalition. It took 43 percent of the vote, winning 56 seats. The fervently pro-Russian Unity/Socialist Bloc, an alliance of the former Gorbachev-era Interfront and pro-Soviet "consensus" Russian parliamentarians, came in second with 22 percent, and 28 seats. The Congress of Peasants and Intellectuals, which called for gradual reunification with Romania, won 11 seats, while the pro-Romanian Christian Democratic Popular Front (CDPF), a descendent of the original MPF, took 9 seats. No other parties broke the 4 percent parliamentary-entry barrier.

Most Moldovan citizens in the DMR boycotted the vote. The election commission reported that only 7,000 of the region's 500,000 eligible voters cast ballots. Total turnout was 79 percent, and despite a two-week delay in announcing the results, international observers deemed the election "free and fair." In Romania, the Senate reacted to the defeat of pro-unification parties with numerous speeches denouncing Moldova's leaders as "undemocratic, uneducated, anti-Romanian and pro-Russian." In Moldova, the Reform Party, an unapologetically pro-capitalist group, saw the results as evidence that "the Communist ideology is deeply infiltrated in our mentality," and CDPF leader Seregiu Mocanu asserted that "Communists have come back to power."

Less than three weeks before the election, President Snegur ordered that a national referendum be held on 6 March that asked citizens a single question— whether they supported an independent, unified and neutral Moldova "within the borders recognized by the U.N." The referendum also spoke of Moldova as a country that would maintain beneficial economic relations with any other state, without discrimination, and guarantee its citizens equal rights. Following the pattern exhibited in the parliamentary elections, 90 percent of Moldovans voted "yes" to the referendum, dealing a further setback to pro-Romania nationalists.

The outcome meant that the country would proceed on its course of moderate economic reforms, though the strong showing by the Unity/Socialists raised questions about the pace and scope of economic restructuring. In addition, the votes signaled closer economic ties with Russia and the CIS, which Moldova joined in April, and raised prospects for a resolution of the Transdniester crisis.

In July, parliament, by a vote of 81-18, approved a new constitution guaranteeing pluralism, reducing the president's power and allowing private property. The president's term was reduced from five to four years, and his powers clipped to ceremonial duties such as promoting and awarding medals to the military and receiving ambassadors.

Opposition leaders immediately criticized the document, which replaced the 1978 constitution and took effect in August, as not going far enough to ensure reforms. Valeriu Matei, leader of the Congress of Peasants and Intellectuals, said the constitution gave prosecutors a "Soviet-style role...as persecutors." The constitution upheld parliament's June decision to scrap a national anthem that was the same as Romania's, and change the state language from Romanian to Moldovan.

A paramount concern during the year was settlement of the Transdniester crisis and the removal of Russia's 2,000-man-strong 14th Army. In April, Russian and Moldovan negotiators failed to agree on a troop pullout. Lt. Gen. Lebed, a controversial figure with widespread popularity among hardliners in Russia, said his troops would not withdraw until a political settlement was reached. On 10 August, after a tense tenth negotiating round in two years, marred by the walkout of DMR observers, Russia and Moldova agreed on a Russian military withdrawal in three years, not in the eighteen months initially demanded by Moldova. Russian defense officials, in a move to undermine Gen. Lebed, said the 14th Army would be reorganized and the general reassigned. The agreement also promised a political settlement and special status for the Transdniester region.

On 2 September Grigore Maracuta, head of the DMR's parliament, said the 14th Army would stay until the Transdniester's status "as a country" was clarified. His comments came two days after the United States U.N. Ambassador Madeline Albright said Russia would proceed with the pullout.

In October, Moldovan Prime Minister Andrei Sangheli and his Russian counterpart, Viktor Chernomyrdin signed the withdrawal agreement in Chisinau (formerly Kishniev), the Moldovan capital. Meanwhile, the government tried to persuade the people of the DMR that their linguistic and ethnic rights would be secure if they joined Moldova.

The government also took steps to address the Gagauz dispute. On 23 December parliament voted to give limited autonomy to the Gagauz. The law would allow the Christian-Turkish minority of 150,000 people to have its own parliament, own government and limited rights to make its own laws as long as they did not contravene Moldovan law.

In economic issues, the country broadened privatization plans in April. Bonds were issued at workplaces, with the value of the certificates tied to the length holders had worked. The feature won over older people who generally opposed privatization. Initial plans were to sell off one-third of state-owned enterprises, or 1,530 companies. The government allowed workers to buy up to 20 percent of the nominal value of their companies before the businesses were put up for bid.

Political Rights and Civil Liberties:

Citizens of Moldova can change their government democratically. The constitution passed in 1994 enshrines a pluralistic, multiparty parliamentary system. The country's first post-Soviet parliamentary elections on 27 February were deemed "free and fair" by international observers, though there were reports of irregularities during the pre-election campaign. There are several independent political parties and blocs. The unresolved political situation in the Transdniester and the presence of Russian troops, due to withdraw in three years, undermined Moldovan sovereignty and full, participatory democracy.

Judicial reform has yet to lead to a fully independent judiciary. The new constitution, according to critics, leaves too much power in the hands of prosecutors. Western institutions, including the Center for the Independence of Judges and Lawyers, have worked with authorities to help design judicial and legal institutions and strengthen the rule-of-law.

Human rights violations and sporadic violence were reported throughout the year in and around the DMR, where six Moldovans (the Tiraspol Six) were convicted in 1993 of treason for alleged terrorism; one, Ilie Ilascu, was sentenced to death, and remains in prison.

Political parties and independent groups publish newspapers, which often take views critical of the government. The reliance of most newspapers on some type of government subsidy raises the issue of self-censorship. Government-controlled radio and television offer varied broadcasts. In June Moldova was preparing to ban Romanian financing of newspapers that opposed Moldovan statehood. Bucharest officials acknowledged subsidizing several Moldovan political weeklies and cultural periodicals and Moldovan officials believe Romania also underwrites the weeklies of Moldova's two main opposition parties which advocate a merger with Romania.

There are few restrictions on freedom of association and assembly. Freedom of worship is accepted, though the Orthodox Church has used it influence to discourage proselytizing.

The constitution guarantees the rights of minorities, but DMR leaders insist that, despite government assurances of linguistic and cultural rights, their Slavic heritage would be subsumed by the Romanian majority. Several Ukrainian villages in the DMR held referendums that supported joining Moldova. Late in the year, parliament passed a bill offering the Gagauz minority a range of autonomy. The official language was changed from Romanian to Moldovan, which is nearly identical. Chisinau, once a hub of Jewish life, has a Jewish public school and a privately owned yeshiva.

The situation in Transdniester and the presence of Russian troops mean some de facto constraints on freedom of movement. Otherwise, most domestic travel is unrestricted, as is international travel and the right to emigrate.

While women enjoy equal rights under law, they are underrepresented in government and leadership positions, and face job discrimination and/or layoffs.

The Federation of Independent Trade Unions of Moldova (FITU) has replaced the old Communist union federation. Government workers do not have the right to strike, nor do those in essential services such as health care.

Monaco

Polity: Prince and legislative democracy
Economy: Capitalist-statist
Population: 30,000
PPP: na
Life Expectancy: na
Ethnic Groups: Monegasque, French, Italian, others

Political Rights: 2
Civil Liberties: 1
Status: Free

Overview: Following an audit of the Monte Carlo Casino finances in 1994, Monaco signed an agreement with France to co-ordinate efforts against money laundering. New laws in effect since July 1993 make it a crime to launder money of "illicit origin"—including extortion, kidnapping, prostitution, drugs and arms smuggling. Banks, insurance companies, and currency exchange agencies in the principality will have to hand over details of bank accounts and transactions whenever Siccfin, the Monegasque agency responsible for tracking laundered money, suspects such illegalities.

In 1993 Monaco became a full member of the U.N., previously having held observer status. Located on the French Mediterranean coast, the Principality of Monaco has been ruled by the Grimaldi family for nearly seven centuries during which Monaco has been intermittently under the control of France, Italy or Spain. Prince Rainier, the head of state, is a member of the Grimaldi family. A 1918 treaty with France, ratified by the signatories of the Treaty of Versailles, stipulates that France must defend the independence, sovereignty and territorial integrity of the principality in exchange for the exercise of Monaco's sovereign rights in conformity with French political, military, naval and economic interests. The present constitution, replacing the one of 1911, was enacted on 17 December 1962 and is the basis of the organization of the State whose independence and sovereignty are internationally recognized. The government is a hereditary constitutional monarchy. Under arrangements with France, if the monarch dies without a male heir, France may incorporate the principality into its territory.

The Prince is the head of state. In certain matters, he is assisted by purely consultative bodies, a seven-member Crown Council and a twelve-member Council of State. The executive power is exercised, under the authority of the prince, by a minister of state, assisted by a Council of Government whose three members are appointed by the prince. The Prince selects the minister from a list of three French civil servants submitted by the French government. The three councilors are the Councilor for the Interior, the Councilor for the Finance and the Economy and the Councilor for Public Works and Social Affairs.

The Prince and an eighteen-member National Council elected by direct universal suffrage for five-year terms exercise legislative power. The prince initiates the laws which are then drafted by the Government Council in his name. The National Council, a unicameral body, passes laws, but the prince alone promulgates them. In the elections of 24 January 1988, the National and Democratic Union (UND) won all eighteen seats. The 1993 legislative elections brought a second political party into the Council for the first time. The four major parties are the ruling UND, the Communal Evolution (EC), the Communal Action (AC), and the Movement of Democratic Union (MUD).

Most of Monaco's revenue is derived from light industrial, commercial and tertiary activities. Turnover taxes on commercial transactions accounted for 46 percent of revenues in 1992. Gambling accounts for less than five percent of the total income of Monaco. Tourism is central to the economic life of the principality.

Political Rights and Civil Liberties:

The people of Monaco have the right to change their national legislature, the National Council, and the municipal government by democratic means. The powers of the Sovereign and his government must be exercised in the framework of the Constitution, the provisions of which take precedence over all institutions with the exception of international treaties.

Though judicial authority is vested in the prince, he delegates it to the Courts and Tribunals, which dispense justice in his name but independently. There is no minister of justice. A Supreme Court exists for constitutional claims and conflicts of jurisdictional powers.

Freedom of expression is guaranteed. However, the Monegasque Penal Code prohibits public denunciations of the Grimaldis. Newspapers in nearby Nice, France print Monaco editions, which they distribute freely in the principality. Radio and television are government-operated and all broadcasts from France are freely transmitted to Monaco. France has a controlling interest in Radio Monte Carlo.

There are some limits to freedom of expression and assembly. In September 1993 the police interfered with pro-Tibet demonstrators. The activists were attempting to influence the International Olympic Community (IOC) meeting in Monaco. The police arrested four Tibetan women for wearing T-shirts that read "Olympics 2000—Not in China." Riot police stopped demonstrators from approaching the IOC meeting. The police also confiscated various pro-Tibet banners, stating that Monaco bans the Tibetan flag.

In January 1992 the National Council approved legislation tightening the principality's citizenship law. Foreign women, but not foreign men, marrying Monegasque citizens would be required to stay with their spouses for at least five years to qualify as citizens. In December 1992, the Council ruled that female citizens can also pass on their nationality to their children. Women are becoming increasingly active in public life. The mayor and one member of the National Council are women.

The constitution differentiates between the rights of its nationals and the rights of residents. Whereas freedom of religion is guaranteed for both groups, nationals are given preference in employment.

Roman Catholicism is the state religion, but the constitution guarantees freedom of religion. There is freedom of association, including trade unionism. One-third of the Economic Council is composed of nominations made by the trade union movement. Unions are independent of both the government and the political parties.

Mongolia

Polity: Presidential-parliamentary democracy
Economy: Statist transitional
Population: 2,369,000
PPP: $2,250
Life Expectancy: 63.0
Ethnic Groups: Khalkha Mongols (75 percent), other Mongols (8 percent), Kazakhs (5 percent)

Political Rights: 2
Civil Liberties: 3
Status: Free

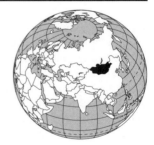

Overview: After four years of contraction, Mongolia's economy appeared to have turned the corner in 1994 by registering positive growth for the first time since the late 1980s. President Punsalmaagiyn Orchirbat continued to voice support for a free-market economy.

China controlled this vast Central Asian steppe and mountain region for two centuries until the overthrow of the Qing dynasty in 1911, and again in 1919 until Soviet-backed Marxists revolted in 1921. The Mongolian People's Revolutionary Party (MPRP) formed a Communist state in 1924 following three years of nominal rule by aging Buddhist lamas. For the next sixty-five years the country existed as a virtual republic of the Soviet Union.

The country's one-party system began to crack in December 1989 with the formation of the Mongolian Democratic Union (MDU), an opposition group under dynamic university lecturer Sanjaasurenjiyn Zorig. MDU-organized street protests and hunger strikes forced the resignation of much of the MPRP leadership in March 1990, and in May the government scrapped the party's legal monopoly. In July 1990 the country held its first multiparty elections. The MPRP took 357 of 430 seats in the Great Hural (parliament) against an unprepared opposition. In September the Hural named the MPRP's Punsalmaagiyn Orchirbat as president and the opposition Social Democratic Party's (SDP) Radnaasurenjiyn Gonchigdorj as vice president.

In February 1991 the MPRP formally abandoned Marxism-Leninism in favor of "scientific socialism." However, citizens continued to be wary of a core of hardliners within the party. In response, in August the government banned top officials, as well as police, diplomats and journalists, from belonging to any political party. Thousands of people affected, from President Orchirbat on down, left their parties to comply with the law.

Parliament passed a new constitution in January 1992 that provided the legal basis for Mongolia's transformation into a multiparty system. It provided for private land ownership, renounced socialism, and abolished the two-year-old Little Hural, transforming the Great Hural into a seventy-six seat unicameral parliament. The president is directly elected for a four-year term. The constitution granted the president the power to name the prime minister and a cabinet, subject to parliamentary approval, and to veto all legislation, subject to a two-thirds override.

On 28 June 1992 Mongolians voted for a new, smaller Great Hural. More than 91 percent of the electorate participated, many traveling for miles to reach a polling station. The MPRP, split into several factions ranging from orthodox Communist to free-market reformers, took a commanding seventy seats. The twelve opposition parties lacked clear ideological distinctions and the means to campaign effectively. The reform-oriented Democratic Coalition, headed by 1990 revolution catalyst Zorig, took four seats; the SDP one. An MPRP-affiliated independent took one seat. The MPRP formed a new government under Prime Minister Jasrai. The MPRP's victory indicated that voters blamed the country's severe economic hardship on free-market reforms instituted since 1990, and feared the opposition would extend the reforms further.

At a party congress in April 1993 hardliners in the ruling party combined forces to dump Orchirbat as the party's candidate for the June presidential election, choosing instead Lodongiyn Tudev, the hardline Communist editor of the party paper *Unen* (Truth). Two days later a coalition composed of the opposition Mongolian National Democratic Party (MNDP) and the SDP named Orchirbat as their candidate. At the 7 June election 92.7 percent of the electorate participated, and Orchirbat won with 57.8 percent of the vote to 38.7 percent for Tudev.

The main political issue in 1994 involved a thirteen-day hunger strike in April organized by younger members of the MNDP, the SDP and the MDU. The strikers initially demanded that Prime Minister Jasrai resign over alleged official corruption, later calling on the government to privatize the media and draft a new election law replacing the first-past-the post system with a proportional representation system. The strike ended with a government promise to review the media and electoral situations.

Orchirbat has pledged to continue the country's transition to a free-market economy, although privatization appeared to have slowed in 1994. The country is slowly rebounding from the loss of Soviet trade and aid. According to the *Economist*, GDP declined by a cumulative 20 percent between 1989-93, although preliminary estimates show a 2.5 percent increase in 1994.

Political Rights and Civil Liberties: Mongolians changed their government in June 1992 through free although not entirely fair elections. The electoral districts favored the rural areas, where the ruling Mongolian People's Revolutionary Party (MPRP) draws its bedrock support. Other factors in the MPRP's favor included ample funding compared to the opposition parties; control over the state–run media, printing equipment and paper; and sufficient stocks of gasoline to campaign in the countryside. In addition, the political campaign period is only twenty days, which makes it difficult for opposition candidates to build a support base. The June 1993 presidential elections appeared free and fair and resulted in victory for the incumbent, Punsalmaagiyn Orchirbat, who ran for an opposition coalition. Elections for the Great Hural are due in 1996.

Nearly all of the more than 200 newspapers are in the hands of political parties or the government and generally reflect their biases, although some state–owned newspapers do criticize the government. In 1993 the country's first truly independent newspaper, *Today*, began publishing. The government controls the allocation of newsprint imports, and opposition–linked papers say they cannot publish as regularly as the MPRP paper, *Unen*. The only full–time national radio and television stations are run by the government and generally offer pluralistic views. Freedoms of assembly and association are respected in practice.

The government admits that in recent years several prisoners have starved to death during the winter months due to acute food shortages. Police are also accused of using excessive force against criminal suspects. The once tightly controlled judiciary is being restructured and will include a new General Council of Courts to select judges and protect their independence. The Legal Code is also being revised. Currently it does not provide the accused the right to see an attorney and in practice defense attorneys are frequently denied access to their clients.

The government has established several shelters to assist a growing population of street children. The 1992 constitution provides for a complete separation of church and state, and this is respected in practice. Since the 1990 revolution Buddhist activity has blossomed throughout the country. Citizens can travel freely within the country. Some citizens are apparently arbitrarily required to surrender their passports upon returning from abroad, and must request their passports for further travel abroad. Civil servants and "essential workers" cannot strike. Collective bargaining is legal but does not appear to be practiced. As part of the country's democratic transformation unions are no longer required to be affiliated with the Mongolian Trade Unions Confederation, which in any case has separated itself from government control.

Morocco

Polity: Monarchy and limited parliament
Economy: Capitalist-statist
Population: 28,559,000
PPP: $3,340
Life Expectancy: 62.5
Ethnic Groups: Arab, Berber, Black African

Political Rights: 5
Civil Liberties: 5
Status: Partly Free

Overview: Host to the April signing of the General Agreement on Tariffs and Trade and the first Middle East-North Africa Economic Summit in November, Morocco used the forums to strengthen and forge new economic and political alliances for advancing its own policies of liberalization. In general, economic reforms have progressed at a faster pace than political liberalization.

King Hassan II has ruled Morocco since 1961, weathering two attempted military revolts in the 1970s and civil disorders in 1981 and 1990 stemming from economic problems. In 1994, King Hassan II gained recognition as an international arbitrator for Morocco's role over the past twenty years as behind the scene conciliator between Israel and its Arab neighbors.

Morocco has averaged 4 percent annual growth over the past decade, with inflation holding at 5 percent, and beginning in 1993 privatization programs were instituted to distribute state companies to Moroccans and foreign companies. Morocco has tried to diversify its relations abroad, by encouraging new business connections with Spain, Portugal, Poland and Sudan, extending trading relations with the European Union and creating a stronger strategic partnership with the U.S. The Casablanca stock market, the second biggest on the continent, is growing with the arrival of new shares from a new, extended list of privatizations.

In spite of the progress, the biggest challenge still facing the country is the creation of jobs for the expected quarter of a million new arrivals on the job market each year. More than 50 percent of the Moroccan population live in urban areas; the rate of unemployment is 20 percent countrywide, with the urban rate around 16 percent.

Meeting this challenge is a key issue for the future of Morocco, where the interior ministry keeps a tight rein on fundamentalist groups to pre-empt young and jobless Moroccans from joining their ranks and steering the country towards the anarchical situation in neighboring Algeria. As Commander of the Faithful and a direct descendant of the Prophet, King Hassan holds an unchallenged religious authority against Islamist fundamentalists who would like to see Morocco ruled by an Islamic regime. The trend in Morocco has been towards a more representative form of government in which the prime minister theoretically enjoys greater freedom of action.

In 1992, King Hassan organized a constitutional referendum after demands by the opposition Democratic Bloc, comprising the nationalist Istiqlal (Independence) Party, the Socialist Union of Popular Forces (USFP), and two smaller parties. Moroccans and Western Saharans voted overwhelmingly in favor of a new constitution, under which the King delegates some of his powers to the government and parliament.

Under the new constitution, King Hassan remains the ultimate authority, and retains the right to declare an emergency. However, the government is at present more accountable to parliament, the Chamber of Representatives. The Chamber has the power to approve ministers, the cabinet's policy, set up commissions of inquiry, and challenge the government with votes of confidence.

The 1993 parliamentary elections were the first since 1984. The Democratic Bloc withdrew from the electoral commission in February, alleging its inability to ensure a fair voting process. It rejoined the commission and withdrew its threat of boycotting the elections after a government decision to postpone the elections from 30 April to 25 June in order to finalize voter lists and print new ballots.

During two rounds of elections, a direct popular vote elects two-thirds of the parliamentarians and an electoral college drawn from trade unions, professional organizations, and communal councils elects the remaining members. According to the final official results, the conservative National Entente Coalition garnered 154 seats, the Democratic Bloc 115 seats, and the centrist National Rally of Independents 41 seats. The four Democratic Bloc parties rejected the King's invitation to join the new cabinet, urging him instead to grant his cabinet more leeway in executing policies. Following the Bloc's formal rejection of cabinet seats on 4 November, the King nominated Mohamad Karim Lamrani, a businessman and acting prime minister since August 1992, to head the conservative/centrist coalition government.

In July 1994, King Hassan asked that "the opposition come together in a coalition with whomever they wanted from the parliament and to form a majority government which would enable it to assume its role in the change of political power." In October, he announced his decision to choose a new prime minister from the opposition, replacing Abdellatif Filali, who is also minister of Foreign Affairs and Cooperation. In December talks with Istiqlal and the Socialist Union of People's Forces collapsed due to the opposition's insistence on replacing the powerful interior minister, Driss Basri, who also holds the information portfolio. King Hassan, who refused to yield, abandoned plans for a new government led by the opposition.

King Hassan told the French newspaper *Liberation* in November 1994 that Morocco would withdraw from Western Sahara, occupied by Morocco since 1975, if the Polisario Liberation Movement wins the referendum on self-determination.

Morocco established official ties with Israel in September 1994, with the two countries opening liaison offices in Rabat and Tel Aviv to deal openly with business and cultural exchange, a first step toward diplomatic relations. At King Hassan's request, a November conference that was to have been limited to the Middle East was extended to cover North Africa as well. Casablanca hosted the economic conference, and brought specific proposals including possible involvement by Moroccan companies in building a Tel Aviv-Amman motorway, hotels in Jericho and assistance for infrastructure plans of its own.

Political Rights and Civil Liberties: Moroccans have limited means to change their government democratically. Although the constitution provides for a pluralistic political system and a parliamentary form of government, ultimate power rests with the monarch. He has the power to appoint and dismiss ministers, declare states of emergency, dissolve parliament and rule by decree.

Elected opposition members may attack the government's economic record but not foreign policy, which is the King's preserve. The parliament can send back budgets, question ministers and bring up issues such as human rights. The state suppresses unauthorized groups by political imprisonment, disapppearances and torture. No party is allowed to contest elections under an Islamic banner in order to keep fundamentalist groups under control. Religious causes are mostly represented on the political scene by Istiqlal, the old national independence party.

The government limits freedom of speech and the press. Citizens face reprisals if they discuss any of the three forbidden topics: the monarchy, Morocco's claim to Western Sahara, and the sanctity of Islam. On 28 January, 1993, an appellate court upheld a two-year prison sentence against the secretary general of the Democratic Confederation of Labor, Noubir Amoui, convicted in April 1992 for criticizing the government's lack of commitment to democracy and human rights in an interview with a Spanish newspaper.

The government subsidizes and controls the news media. The weekly, *L'Economiste*, was cited by the *Financial Times* as an example of a new era in the press in which newspapers show surprising freedom. The three Berber languages can now be taught in state schools alongside Arabic. In February 1994, Islamic fundamentalist students attacked an exposition by left-wing students of Salman Rushdie's *Satanic Verses*, killing one student and injuring others. A court sentenced twenty-six fundamentalist and left-wing students at the University of Fez to prison. King Hassan opened Ifrane University, inspired by the Anglo-Saxon (as opposed to French) education system, to encourage debate on Islamic values and how they relate to the modern world. The university is built around a mosque, but it also has a synagogue and a church.

Islam is the official religion. Approximately 99 percent are Sunni Muslim. The government permits the small Jewish and Christian minorities to practice their faith, but considers other religions to be heresies and prohibits their exercise. Proselytizing by non-Muslims and conversions of Muslims to other religions is prohibited. In November 1993 a court sentenced Zmamda Mustapha, a convert to Christianity, to a three-year jail term for distribution of Christian literature. Jews, of whom there are 6,000 to 8,000, are *dhimmi*, protected persons, but first and foremost tax-payers. There are Jews in the cabinet. Since 1991 Mr. Andre Azoulay, the founder of a group of intellectuals in the 1970s that initiated the understanding of the 2,000-year history of the Moroccan Jewish community, has been King Hassan's advisor for economic and financial affairs. Mr. Serge Berdujo, who heads the Jewish community in Morocco, is minister of tourism.

Freedom of association and assembly are restricted. The government may suppress peaceful demonstrations and mass gatherings. In 1993 the government banned an attempted protest march by women's groups against sexual abuse by high public officials.

More than 400 political prisoners were amnestied in July 1994. Foreign experts say there remain about fifty political detainees, mostly fundamentalists. In 1994 there were no reported cases of opponents of the King vanishing. However, an estimated 300 to 700 political opponents have vanished in the past. The Taznamat prison in the Atlas mountains, long known as a center for torture, was reportedly razed in 1993. However, a State Department human rights report said that the interior ministry still turns to both torture and illegal detention to contain Islamist and far-left movements.

The court system is subject to occasional political intervention. The government often ignores guarantees of procedural due process. In August 1993 the authorities carried out the first death sentence since 1982, executing the former Casablanca police commissioner, Mohammed Mustafa Tabet. A court convicted Tabet of assaults and rapes of hundreds of women, which were captured on videotape.

Moroccans are free to travel within Morocco proper, but not in Western Sahara, where movement is limited in militarily restricted areas. Members of the opposition have been denied passports. Women must have permission from their fathers or husbands to obtain a passport. King Hassan has refused to give Maria-Inan Oufkir a passport to leave the country. She was released from a secret prison in which she and her familly lived for the past two decades. King Hassan imprisoned the family because General Oufkir, a former defense minister, ordered the strafing of the royal plane by air force jets in 1972.

Although there is no systematic racial discrimination, Moroccan blacks generally occupy the lowest social strata. Women have legal equality with men, except in areas of marriage and family. Moroccan women have opportunities for higher education and some have succeeded in professions and business.

The government permits independent trade unions to exist, but selection of union officials is subject to government pressure. There are sixteen trade union federations. Workers have the right to bargain collectively and these laws are usually respected in larger enterprises, while ignored in smaller ones. In February 1994 Prime Minister Lamrani banned a strike organized by the Democratic Labor Confederation, closely linked to the Popular Union for Socialist Forces. The union had called the demonstration because of an alleged absence of serious dialogue with the government and the degradation of workers' living conditions. The Association for the Defense of Human Rights in Morocco appealed for the government to release twenty-seven jailed union rights activists.

Mozambique

Polity: Presidential-leg- **Political Rights:** 3*
islative democracy   **Civil Liberties:** 5
Economy: Mixed statist   **Status:** Partly Free
Population: 15,823,000
PPP: $921
Life Expectancy: 46.5
Ethnic Groups: Lomwe, Makonde, Makua, Ndau,
Shangaan, Thonga, Yao, other
Ratings Change: *Mozambique's political rights rating changed from 6 to 3 because of a successful multiparty election in October 1994 and initial RENAMO-FRELIMO cooperation following the election. As a result Mozambique's status changed from Not Free to Partly Free.

Overview: Joaquim Chissano was re-elected president in 1994. Following intense international pressure, Afonso Dhlakama, leader of the Mozambican Resistance Movement (RENAMO) withdrew a boycott called just hours before Mozambique's first multiparty elections were held in late October 1994. With few incidents reported, elections proceeded with 90 percent of the country's 6.4 million electorate casting ballots . International observers indicated that the elections were generally free and fair.

The National Elections Commission reported that ruling President Joaquim Chissano of the Front for the Liberation of Mozambique (FRELIMO) won with 54 percent of the vote. FRELIMO won 129 of 250 seats in the national assembly, securing 45 percent of the vote compared to 38 percent and 112 seats for RENAMO. The two main parties competed with twelve smaller parties for national assembly seats. One of them, Democratic Union, won the remaining nine seats. Despite expectations that Dhlakama would contest election results, alleging pre-election fraud and vote rigging, RENAMO accepted the results.

Since Mozambique gained independence from Portugal in 1975, the former Marxist-Leninist FRELIMO regime and the 30,000-member rebel RENAMO movement waged a violent campaign for power until 1992. The civil war devastated the country. One million people died as a result of the power struggle and an estimated 3.5 million Mozambicans were internally displaced and an additional 1.7 million became refugees.

President Samora Machel led a one-party state in Mozambique until his death in 1986. Chissano succeeded him and served as both president and FRELIMO party leader. All political activity was banned in Mozambique until a new constitution drafted in 1990 legalized nonviolent political opposition. While negotiations between the government and RENAMO have been underway since 1990, the October 1992 Rome peace accord marked a breakthrough in negotiations to end the seventeen-year-old civil war.

The Rome accord between Dhlakama's RENAMO movement and President Chissano paved the way for multiparty elections. Under the October peace plan, government soldiers and rebel fighters were to report to designated U.N. assembly points to turn in their weapons and return home. RENAMO agreed to turn over territory to the state and, for its part, the government agreed to appoint three RENAMO officials from each of the country's eleven provinces to counsel provincial governors. To avoid the kind of mistakes that plagued its Angola operation, the U.N. worked to demobilize troops prior to elections and was partially successful. In addition, the U.N. posted 7,000 peacekeepers and 2,400 election observers.

Political Rights and Civil Liberties: While post-election relations between the governing FRELIMO and RENAMO remain strained, in the 1994 multiparty election, Mozambicans had, for the first time, a voice in determining political representation. The partial demobilization of troops together with a solid U.N. effort to keep peace on track helped give a promising start to Mozambique's transition to democracy. However, the tasks ahead remain daunting. After two decades of fighting, the newly formed government must work to repair the country's ravaged infrastructure, demobilize and integrate RENAMO and government troops, and repatriate both the internally displaced and those who fled to neighboring states.

Although there was a marked decrease in reported rights violations during 1994, human rights groups report that allegations of mistreatment of prisoners by soldiers, police and prison staff continued. International humanitarian relief efforts were hampered by both FRELIMO and RENAMO interference in 1994. Despite provisions under the Rome accord, RENAMO used humanitarian aid as a means of political control, while government corruption plagued relief efforts.

The judicial system in Mozambique is divided into two systems—the civil/criminal (which includes the customary courts) and the military. A 1994 report by the Law Group identified a number of inadequacies in Mozambique's judicial system. The report found that there were "...dramatic shortages of trained legal personnel in all areas..." and "...judges have little if any legal education, and legal defenders are essentially non-existent." Other shortcomings identified include placing the burden of proof on the accused and confessions.

There were continued improvements in freedom of the press, provided for in both the constitution and the new press laws (in connection with the peace accord). While broadcast media are primarily under state control, in 1993 Mozambique's first independent television station, Radio Televisao Klint (RTK), began broadcasting. There are various independent print media and, prior to the elections, opposition parties published and circulated newsletters. While some liberalization in the press is apparent, criticism of the president or investigations into high-level corruption are rare and it appears that the press is exercising self-censorship in these areas.

Freedom of religion is respected and separation of church and state is mandated in the Constitution. Workers have the right to join unions. Most trade unions belong to the Organization of Mozambican Workers (OTM) but in 1993 three unions broke away from the OTM. With the exception of government employees, police, military and other essential employees, workers have the right to strike. There were no reported government or employer reprisals against strikers during 1994.

Namibia

Polity: Presidential-legislative democracy
Economy: Capitalist-statist
Population: 1,635,000
PPP: $2,381
Life Expectancy: 58.0
Political Rights: 2
Civil Liberties: 3
Status: Free

Ethnic Groups: Ovambo (50 percent), Kavango (9 percent), Herero (7.5 percent), Damara (7.5 percent), Baster and Colored (6.5 percent), White (6 percent), Nama/Hottentot (5 percent), Bushman (3 percent)

Overview:

In 1994 Namibia held its first post-independence presidential and legislative elections. The ruling South West Africa People's Organization (SWAPO) won a resounding victory. On 7 and 8 December Namibians elected SWAPO leader Sam Nujoma, the country's four-year ruler, as president and gave his party a two-thirds majority of legislative seats. Walvis Bay citizens also participated in the elections following South Africa's formal handover of the strategic port to Namibia in February.

A former German protectorate, Namibia (formerly South West Africa) was invaded by South Africa during World War I, after which South Africa administered Namibia under a system of apartheid. In 1966 SWAPO launched an armed struggle for independence. In 1978 the U.N. adopted resolution 435 calling for Namibia's independence, which South Africa accepted only in 1988.

In November 1989 the U.N. supervised pre-independence elections, in which ten political groups vied for the seventy-two-seat National Assembly. SWAPO won forty-one seats, and the center-right Democratic Turnhalle Alliance (DTA) won twenty-one. On 21 March 1990 Namibia became formally independent, Sam Nujoma becoming its first president.

In the August runup to the December 1994 elections, the Democratic Coalition of Namibia (DCN), a new coalition party that included the United Democratic Front (UDF), the National Patriotic Front (NPF), the German Union and the South-West Africa National Union (SWANU) was launched to run against SWAPO and DTA. The DCN's effort to oust the DTA as the second biggest party was nullified when the UDF leader, Justus Garoeb, withdrew from the coalition. The DTA itself was unable to exploit the weaknesses of the Nujoma government because it was itself disabled by internal strife and tainted by its former links with South Africa's National Party. The DTA—formed in 1977 to protest the insistence of South Africa's National Party in maintaining apartheid—is criticized for holding out its hands for covert funds from the National Party in 1989.

During the 1994 elections campaign, opposition parties complained about a lack of resources needed to mount effective campaigns, alleging this favored SWAPO, which used state funds and vehicles to lobby for support. The DTA called for an inquiry by the ombudsman into a government "slush fund" made of taxpayers' money to pay the salaries of SWAPO supporters in the private sector. The ministry said the scheme was part of a job creation plan. The secretary general of SWAPO remained confident that his party would win the two-thirds majority of parliamentary seats needed to change the constitution, while acknowledging that it would be bad for democracy. He said, "Perhaps, we will have to create our own opposition."

Political enthusiasm among the voters had waned since they last went to the polls before independence. The major problem facing the government was a 40 percent unemployment rate among those who fought for independence. A Namibia-based study showed a huge disparity in the distribution of wealth and consumption patterns in Namibian society.

In 1994, the government decided to award farms to former PLAN (People's Liberation Army of Namibia) fighters as a means of compensating them for their "services during the freedom struggle." In September a long awaited Agricultural Land Reform Bill addressed the needs of black citizens who constitute the landless majority. It allowed the government to force farmers who do not fully use or have extensive farms to give up their land if they fail to negotiate a selling price with the government. About 76 percent of the arable land remains under the control of white farmers.

The SWAPO victory, which could open the field for effective one- party dominance, was won in free and fair elections with a 65 percent voter turnout. Nujoma won with 76.3 percent, his opponent, Mishake Muyongo, former SWAPO vice-president who resigned in 1984, getting 23.6 percent of the votes. SWAPO won 53 of 72 legislative seats, the DTA, 15 seats, 6 less than before, the Monitor Action Group, 1 and the UDF, 2. SWAPO's standing with the public was not hurt by revelations that the administration splurged on the purchase of an executive jet or by other corruption charges. SWAPO won votes from the north, an area populated by the Ovambo, the country's largest ethnic group. With a two-thirds parliamentary majority, SWAPO can change the constitution without consulting the opposition. The party plans to extend the presidential term limit from two to three, and get rid of several clauses which favor opposition parties. The announcement of election results was delayed because the DTA wanted an investigation into why the number of ballots cast in four constituencies exceeded the number of registered voters.

Walvis Bay's citizens, South Africans who became Namibians after the handover of the port to Namibia by its former colonial ruler, participated in the vote as well. Walvis Bay, the only deep-water port off the Atlantic Ocean coast south of Angola, was returned to Namibia on 28 February. A center for fishing and the export of copper and uranium, and linked to Kenya by a railway, Walvis Bay provides access to the ocean for landlocked countries such as Zambia, Zimbabwe, and Botswana. By creating more transport routes, Namibia plans to develop trade and business inside the continent. South Africa also transferred the presidential palace and other properties to its former colony and said it would scrap the $200 million debt Namibia acquired as a colony.

In other developments, Angola's troubles spilled over into northern Namibia when a businessman and a student were shot. The Angolan army reportedly abducted twenty Namibians near the Namibian border to be trained and deployed to fight on the side of the MPLA (Popular Movement for the Liberation of Angola). In October, Nujoma invited Jonas Savimbi, leader of UNITA in Angola, to Namibia to spur peace talks. Sam Nujoma said in December that his country would provide troops to help United Nations peacekeeping operations in Angola. On 4 December Angolans attempting to cross the closed Namibian border were shot and killed. A thousand Angolans are allegedly threatened with starvation since their main source of food from Namibia was shut off. Since late 1992, with the renewal of the Angolan civil war, approximately 100,000 Angolan refugees have crossed the Namibian border. UNITA has accused the Namibian government of providing military support to the Angolan army; the government, however, denies this.

Political Rights and Civil Liberties: Namibians can change their government democratically. The executive president elected by the National Assembly in 1989 was elected president of Namibia in elections held in December 1994. Constitutional provisions establish regular elections for a bicameral parliament. Members of the upper house, the National Council, were chosen through equal regional representation in 1992, and members of the lower Assembly, the National Assembly, were elected in December 1994.

The judiciary is independent, consisting of a three-tiered court system, with the Supreme Court being the highest appellate and constitutional review court. Trials are usually open to the public, and the accused have a right to legal counsel. However, a lack of qualified judges and attorneys has led to a backlog of cases awaiting trial. The majority of licensed attorneys are white.

Despite the constitutional prohibition against torture, over twenty allegations of abusive treatment by police and security forces were reported in 1993. These included the case of Jorge Valentim, a UNITA brigadier in detention.

The constitution prohibits discrimination based on race and specifically prohibits "the practice and ideology of apartheid." The government continued to promote the civil, economic and political rights of the indigenous majority of Namibians by implementing affirmative action and other programs to promote equal access to education. In 1993, the government also endorsed the San's rights to land. The San people have traditionally been exploited by other indigenous ethnic groups. In 1994 reports of a rift in the ranks of the police showed that the divisions between blacks and whites are still alive.

In 1994, after much criticism from South Africa, the government allowed former members of the Koevoet security forces (the former police counterinsurgency unit) who left Namibia in 1991 because of an intimidation campaign against them to return to Namibia. The constitution stipulates that no citizen through birth or of Namibian descent may be denied citizenship. The Cabinet decision could open the door to some 5,000 former San Bushmen soldiers who were taken by the South African Defense Force during the war of independence. The government also announced in 1994 that anyone with a million dollars to invest in Namibia would be eligible for a passport.

Freedoms of speech and the press have been respected since independence. The newspapers are free and vigorous. Besides one government-owned weekly, most newspapers are affiliated with political parties and are heavily partisan in their reporting. The Namibian Broadcasting Corporation airs radio and television programs in several local languages.

Freedoms of religion and movement are respected. The largest trade union organization is the National Union of Namibian workers (NUNW), a SWAPO affiliate.

Nauru

Polity: Parliamentary democracy
Economy: Mixed capitalist-statist
Population: 10,000
PPP: na
Life Expectancy: na

Political Rights: 1
Civil Liberties: 3
Status: Free

Ethnic Groups: Indigenous Nauruans (mixture of Polynesian, Melanesian, Micronesian, (58 percent), other Pacific islanders (26 percent), Chinese (8 percent), European (8 percent)

Overview: Nauru, a tiny island located 1,600 miles northeast of New Zealand, became a German protectorate in 1888. Following World War I Australia administered the island under a mandate from the League of Nations and later from the United Nations, granting independence on 31 January 1968. The 1968 constitution provides for an eighteen-member parliament that is popularly elected for a three-year term. The most recent elections were held in November 1992. Political parties are legal but none has formed; however, candidates representing a wide variety of viewpoints contest the parliamentary seats. Parliament elects the president, who serves as head of state and head of government, from among its members. In November 1992 parliament re-elected President Bernard Dowiyogo over former cabinet minister Buraro Detudamo. The Nauru Local Government Council is directly elected from fourteen districts and provides local services.

In 1993 Nauru resolved a long-standing dispute with Australia regarding compensation for phosphate mining during the trusteeship period. For years Australia denied any liability on the grounds that it had paid Nauru royalties during the trusteeship period, and in 1967 had sold the mining operation to the islanders at what it considered a generous price. However, Nauru said the royalties had been inadequate, since Australia had sold the phosphates to its domestic markets at below world-market prices. In May 1989 Nauru sued Australia in the International Court of Justice at the Hague, seeking additional royalties as well as compensation for damages done by the mining to the eight-square-mile island, 80 percent of which is now uninhabitable. In July 1993 the two sides reached an out-of-court settlement under which Australia agreed to pay $72 million in damages over twenty years.

The government's $700 million Nauru Phosphate Royalties Trust (NPRT) will provide income for future generations after the phosphates run out in about ten years. However in May 1993 the NPRT's Australian manager, Geoffrey Chatfield, quit his job after two months, claiming that several government agencies had borrowed from the fund and left it dangerously overloaded with high-risk property investments. Moreover, many of the NPRT's recent investments have been either questionable, such as providing financing in 1993 for a disastrous London musical, *Leonardo*, or careless, including being duped in 1991 into buying fraudulent "prime bank notes" in London.

In January 1994 Pacnews reported that $8.5 million is still missing from the NPRT as a result of questionable investment schemes in 1992, although in October an accountant agreed to repay the $800,000 she embezzled, plus interest. In June former presidential candidate Detudamo, the *de facto* opposition leader, died while on a plane trip to Melbourne.

Political Rights and Civil Liberties: Citizens of Nauru can change their government democratically. Political parties are legal although none has formed. Instead, parliamentary blocs coalesce according to specific ideas or issues. The judiciary is independent of the government, and the accused enjoy full procedural safeguards. Physical abuse of women occurs relatively frequently, and is generally alcohol related.

Freedoms of speech and association are generally respected. An exception occurred in July 1993 involving the People's Movement, a women's group set up to protest the NPRT's mismanagement (*See Overview above*). The government reportedly threatened to dismiss Movement members employed in the public sector if the group demonstrated during a South Pacific Forum meeting. The group staged protests with banners and placards, and no dismissals were reported.

The government-owned radio station broadcasts Radio Australia and the BBC but not local news. There is a private fortnightly newspaper and a government weekly, and news and ideas are generally transmitted via word of mouth on the tiny island. Several foreign publications are available, although the government banned the July 1993 *Pacific Islands Monthly*, which carried a cover article on the NPRT situation. The issue reportedly remained on sale despite the ban.

Freedom of religion is respected in practice. There are no restrictions on foreign travel, and all inhabited areas on the island can be reached by foot. The 3,000 foreign workers are generally housed in inadequate facilities. The constitution allows workers to bargain collectively, but the government discourages trade unions and none exists. Any foreign worker who is fired must leave the country within sixty days.

Nepal

Polity: Parliamentary democracy
Economy: Capitalist
Population: 22,050,000
PPP: $1,130
Life Expectancy: 52.7
Ethnic Groups: Newar, Indian, Tibetan, Gurung, Magar, Tamang, Bhotia, others

Political Rights: 3
Civil Liberties: 4
Status: Partly Free

Overview: Early elections in November 1994 brought the Communist Party of Nepal (United Marxist-Leninist) (CPN-UML) to power under Man Mohan Adhikary, a former dissident who helped topple the absolute monarchy in 1990. The vote reflected disillusionment with the incumbent Congress Party's factionalism and corruption.

Prithvi Narayan Shah unified this Hindu Himalayan kingdom, located between China and India, in 1769. Britain handled Nepal's foreign affairs between 1860-1923. The country's first elections in 1959 brought the leftist Congress Party to power. The next year the king accused the government of abuse of power, dissolved the Parliament, banned political parties and began ruling by decree. In 1962 the king introduced the partyless, three-tiered *panchayat* (council) system in place of the Parliament. The current monarch, King Birendra, came to power in 1972 at age twenty-six.

The country's democratic transition began in early 1990 as a coalition consisting of the Congress Party and several Communist parties organized mass prodemocracy demonstrations. As the *Jana Andolan* (People's Movement) gained strength, the situation climaxed violently on 6 April when police fired on demonstrators in Kathmandu, the capital, killing more than fifty people. The King legalized political parties three days later, and in November approved a new constitution granting most executive powers to a government headed by a prime minister. The constitution established a bicameral parliament consisting of a 205-member elected House of Representatives, and an appointed sixty-member National Council (a third of whose members must be rotated every two years), where seats are distributed in proportion to the party representation in the House. The king nominates 10 percent of the members of the upper house on the advice of the prime minister, and can assume emergency powers in national security crises, including war, insurrection, or severe economic conditions.

Nepal's first multiparty elections in thirty-two years in May 1991 gave the Congress Party 110 seats and the CPN-UML 69, the remaining 26 seats being shared by smaller parties and independents. The Congress Party's Girija Prasid Koirala, a leader of the 1990 democracy movement, subsequently formed a government.

In December 1991 Prime Minister Koirala signed a controversial agreement allowing India to build a 120-megawatt power station at Tanakpur in southwestern Nepal in return for providing the kingdom with 1 percent of the electricity. The Communist opposition claimed the prime minister had sold out the country's interests. In December 1992 the Supreme Court ruled that the Tanakpur agreement had to be ratified by parliament, but did not say whether it needed a two-thirds or simple majority.

In 1993 the CPN-UML and its six Communist allies organized a series of anti-government general strikes protesting both the Tanakpur agreement and a 92 percent price hike for electricity. On 16 May the political tensions rose after a suspicious road accident 115 miles west of Kathmandu killed CPN-UML general secretary Madan Bhandari and central committee member Jeev Raj Ashrit. Both were strong opponents of the Tanakpur agreement.

By early 1994 Koirala was coming under attack from the Communist opposition and from within his own party. The Congress Party's defeat in a 7 February 1994 by-election for the seat vacated by Bhandari's death widened an internal party rift between Prime Minister Koirala and his rival, party president K.P. Bhattarai, who had contested the seat. Bhattarai's supporters blamed the defeat on Koirala for refusing to support Bhattarai in the race.

In June Ganesh Man Singh, considered the Congress Party's de facto supreme leader, canvassed the country in a "Remove Koirala" campaign, accusing the premier of tacitly contributing to Bhattarai's defeat in order to stave off a leadership challenge. On 10 July thirty-six Congress Party MPs abstained from a parliamentary vote on the government's social and economic program, allowing the opposition to defeat the measure. Koirala immediately resigned. The following day King Birendra dissolved parliament on Koirala's advice and asked Koirala to head a caretaker government until early elections could be held in November, eighteen months ahead of schedule.

The key issues in the campaign for the 15 November elections were rising prices, criticism of the Congress Party's factionalism and corruption, frustration that three years of democracy had not produced greater social and economic change, and promises by the CPN-UML to carry out a land reform program in a country where nearly half of the productive land is held by 15 percent of the farmers. On election day 58 percent of the electorate turned out, and 1,057 candidates representing twenty-four parties as well as 385 independents competed. Final results gave the CPN-UML eighty-eight seats; the Congress Party eighty-three; the right-wing, pro-monarchist New Democratic Party, twenty; minor parties and independents, fourteen. Notably, the Congress Party topped the CPN-UML in the popular vote, 33 percent to 30 percent.

On 30 November King Birendra swore in Man Mohan Adhikary, a seventy-four-year-old former dissident who helped topple the absolute monarchy in 1990, as the head of Asia's first freely elected Communist government. The new premier gave three key cabinet posts to Madhav Kumar Nepal, a hardliner considered by some to be the party's behind-the-scenes strongman.

Political Rights and Civil Liberties: Nepalese changed their government democratically in November 1994 in elections marred by irregularities. At least five people died in political-related violence during the election campaign. On election day a shootout between rival activists in Rauthat, fifty miles south of Kathmandu, killed a party activist. Police made fifty-seven arrests nationwide. Two days after the vote the National Elections Observer Committee reported that, "Most cases of irregularities seemed to have been committed by the present ruling party (Congress Party), although other major parties were also reported." Irregularities included proxy voting, selling of votes, tampering with ballot boxes and intimidation of voters. The authorities ordered repolling in forty-two constituencies due to irregularities.

The country's primary human rights issue involves the poorly trained National Police Force. In 1992 and 1993 police fired indiscriminately into crowds of demonstrators on several occasions, killing at least twenty-five people. In January 1994 police killed up to three people in Damak, 185 miles southeast of the capital, during a clash that began after police allegedly mistreated an elderly woman. Police commonly beat suspects to extract confessions and routinely abuse prisoners. Several people have died in custody in recent years. Police are accused of using excessive force against Tibetans intercepted at the border. In June 1993 police shot and killed a monk and wounded several other Tibetans.

Legally, police must bring a detainee before a court within twenty-four hours of arrest, but in practice this is frequently ignored. The broadly defined Public Security Act (PSA) allows the Home Ministry to detain suspects for six months after first notifying a district court within twenty-four hours after arrest; this can be extended for another six months before charges must be filed. In 1993 and 1994 the Koirala government detained hundreds of antigovernment demonstrators under the PSA, generally for less than two days. The similarly constructed 1970 Public Offenses Act grants Chief District Officers broad powers to detain suspects.

The Supreme Court is considered independent, although lower courts can be influenced by the government. Defendants are not automatically assumed innocent, although other procedural safeguards exist. Indian authorities occasionally operate on Nepalese soil. In March 1994 Indian police raided several Kathmandu homes in search of a suspect.

The Constitution broadly prohibits speech and press that could threaten public order and national security, promote antagonism among different religions or castes, or violate public morals. The Press and Publications Act prevents publication of articles that would contravene these boundaries or be disrespectful of the monarchy. The Act also requires journalists to be licensed. Supplementary legislation passed in 1992 established education and experience requirements for various journalism jobs. Despite these restrictions, newspapers and magazines vigorously criticize government policies.

Under the Koirala government thugs assaulted several journalists who wrote articles critical of the government. In January 1994 Lokendra Kumar Burathoki, a journalist for a local CPN-UML newspaper, died in mysterious circumstances in his home in Rajbiraj, south of Kathmandu. In July police detained four journalists belonging to a left-wing group, *Mashal*. The television and radio stations, which are state-owned, do not cover opposition viewpoints adequately.

The constitution allows the authorities to restrict assembly on public security grounds. On several occasions in 1993 the government detained Communist leaders prior to scheduled demonstrations. Religious freedom is practiced and non-Hindus may worship freely.

Caste discrimination is prevalent in rural areas. According to the U.S. State Department, more than 100,000 ethnic Thaurus, a lower-caste group, are bonded laborers in southern Nepal. Women face legal discrimination in property rights and divorce matters, and rarely receive the same educational opportunities as men. According to Women Acting Together for Change up to 200,000 Nepalese women have been trafficked to Indian brothels. An increasing number of these women return to Nepal with AIDS and are shunned by their families. In 1992 Child Workers in Nepal estimated that there are 150,000 children working in carpet factories. There are several hundred street children in Kathmandu and other cities. Some 86,000 Bhutanese refugees live in eight camps in southeastern Nepal.

Workers are free to join unions. Strikes are prohibited in "essential services" including utilities and telecommunications, and the government can suspend a strike or the operation of a trade union if it considers this to be in the national economic interest.

Netherlands

Polity: Parliamentary
democracy
Economy: Mixed capitalist
Population: 15,378,000
PPP: $16,820
Life Expectancy: 77.2
Ethnic Groups: Dutch (97 percent), Indonesian and others (3 percent)

Political Rights: 1
Civil Liberties: 1
Status: Free

Overview:
The general election and controversies over euthanasia and other social issues were major developments in 1994.

Held on 7 May, the general election ended the coalition government of the Christian Democratic Appeal (CDA) and the Labor Party. Having lost seats, the CDA had to give up the place held in every government by major confessional parties since 1918. CDA leader Elco Brinkman upset older voters by calling for a spending freeze on old-age pensions. He resigned after the election. Two pensioners' parties took advantage of the controversy, and won a combined seven parliamentary seats. In August, after months of negotiations, Labor Party leader Wim Kok formed the first Left-Right or "purple" coalition in Dutch history with the right-wing Liberals, headed by Frits Bolkestein, and the center-left Democrats '66, led by Hans Van Mierlo. The three parties agreed to cut public spending over four years while maintaining unemployment and disability benefits. The parties also decided to reduce health costs by imposing a system of co-payments for national health patients. The coalition hopes to revive the sluggish economy by cutting taxes and insurance premiums.

Local elections in March 1994 presaged the parliamentary results. In local races, CDA and Labor lost ground, as the Liberals and Democrats '66 gained seats. The anti-immigrant Democrats Center won a few council seats, but its gain was limited by a television program that presented its leader as an arsonist who had torched blacks' homes.

The independence of the Netherlands dates from the late sixteenth century, when the Dutch provinces rebelled against Spanish rule. Located in Western Europe, the country has long-established traditions of representative government and constitutional monarchy. Queen Beatrix is the largely ceremonial head of state.

There is a bicameral parliament called the States General. Voters elect the 150-seat lower house by proportional representation. The upper house is an indirectly elected, seventy-five-member body chosen by eleven provincial councils.

In 1993-94 the Netherlands had major debates about euthanasia. In November 1993 the parliament completed passage of legislation for voluntary euthanasia. According to the law, patients must suffer irremediable pain and ask clearly and repeatedly for death before doctors may end their lives. Non-requested cases of euthanasia remain subject to prosecution. The number of reported cases of euthanasia grew from 590 in 1991 to 1,318 in 1993.

The government issued guidelines in December 1993 that left doctors confused about the circumstances that would permit legal mercy-killing versus those that would send physicians to prison. The state requires doctors to report acts of euthanasia to the authorities. Some observers believe the reporting requirement will discourage involuntary euthanasia, while others hold that reports will provide a cover for involuntary acts. The Vatican and pro-life groups condemned the legislation. Senior citizen lobbies expressed concern that the new law would allow involuntary deaths. Consequently, the Dutch government mounted an international campaign to explain the policy and soften its image. In 1994, revised guidelines allowed euthanasia of the emotionally ill. Critics feared that this policy would lead to the unwarranted deaths of psychiatric patients. One doctor admitted to killing a severely deformed infant by using a drug overdose. This became a test case of the euthanasia guidelines.

Political Rights and Civil Liberties:

The Dutch have the right to change their government democratically. Foreigners resident for five years have voting rights in local elections. Women are increasingly influential in party politics, and there is a women's party. Feminists were outraged in October 1993 when the Reformed Political Party (SGP), a Christian fundamentalist group with three parliamentary seats, voted to prohibit more women from joining its ranks. At the time, only twenty women held SGP membership. The SGP believes that God ordained males alone to exercise political authority, while the feminists and other parties believe the SGP decision contradicts legally guaranteed sexual equality.

The press is free, but it generally observes unofficial limits in writing about the royal family. Broadcasting is state-owned but autonomously operated, and offers pluralistic points of view on social and political issues. Traditionally, commercials have been restricted, and banned on Sundays for religious reasons. In general, there is free speech, but laws prohibit inciting racism and expressing racist ideas. There have been court cases against Hans Janmaat and other members of Democrats Center for making racist remarks. The Justice Ministry and the Public Prosecution Office probed that ultra-right party, and considered moving to ban it. Ultimately, the government decided that Janmaat's group did not pose a threat sufficient to justify banning it.

The judiciary is independent. In 1993, the Police Complaints Commission charged security forces with using excessive force to quell disturbances. The body recommended requiring riot police to wear identifying numbers as members of sports teams do. Local authorities have a generally tolerant attitude towards certain recreational drugs, but there is no consistent policy. For example, in 1994, Rotterdam adopted the policy of offering heroin to addicts to stop drug-related crime, and in Tilburg, marijunana cafes received immunity from prosecution. However, in July, Maastricht shut down its drug-infested "needle park," and ran the drug tourists out of town.

Immigrants from developing countries have experienced some discrimination in housing and employment. In order to prevent further discrimination, the Council of State, a constitutional body, overruled a proposed, compulsory national identity card in 1992. However, in 1993, parliament passed a law requiring identification under many (but not all) circumstances, effective in 1994. The intent of the legislation was to combat juvenile crime, illegal immigration and welfare fraud. Police may detain people who have no identifying documents for twelve hours. Human rights groups oppose the ID legislation, because they believe that police will target minorities and demand their papers. Public opinion turned against refugees in 1993. The country received about 40,000 applications for political asylum and set up tent cities to house applicants. Former Prime Minister Ruud Lubbers was ridiculed for suggesting that refugees should be cared for in the homes of Dutch families.The growing number of arrivals has tested the Dutch inclination to pay for their upkeep. At a time of austerity for themselves, the Dutch find it increasingly difficult to extend economic benefits to foreigners. Most rejected asylum-seekers assimilate successfully into Dutch life.

Religious freedom is respected. The state subsidizes church-affiliated schools based on the number of registered students. The extensive public sector regulates the private economy, and provides generous social welfare benefits. Labor is free to organize. Only civil servants lack the right to strike, but they strike anyway.

The Dutch army admits homosexuals without discrimination. Male hetero-sexual troops receive free copies of *Playboy*, and homosexual troops get compli-mentary issues of *MaGAYzine*. Brothels became legally regulated businesses as of January 1994. Other forms of prostitution were already legal or tolerated. There is a prostitutes' bill of rights that includes the right to refuse customers.

New Zealand

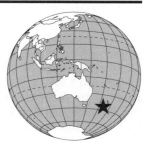

Polity: Parliamentary democracy
Economy: Capitalist
Population: 3,498,000
PPP: $13,970
Life Expectancy: 75.3
Ethnic Groups: White (79 percent), Maori (12 percent), Pacific Islander (3 percent), Other (6 percent)

Political Rights: 1
Civil Liberties: 1
Status: Free

Overview: Although Prime Minister Jim Bolger's National Party topped a November 1994 opinion poll with a 42 percent backing, his government braced for expected parliamentary defections under a new electoral system that is likely to weaken support for New Zealand's two major parties.

New Zealand achieved full self-government prior to World War II, and gained formal independence from Great Britain in 1947. Since 1935, political power in this parliamentary democracy has alternated between the mildly conservative National Party and the center-left Labor Party, both of which helped develop one of the world's most progressive welfare states. By the early 1980s these policies placed New Zealand at a disadvantage in responding to low agricultural export prices and an increasingly competitive world trading regime. In 1984 the incoming Labor government began deregulating the financial system, removing farm and industrial subsidies, reform-ing the tax code, slashing import tariffs and privatizing many industries.

The harsh effects of the economic reforms, coupled with a severe recession, led to a National Party landslide at the October 1990 parliamentary elections. The National Party took a record 68 seats; Labor, 28; the New Labor Party, a spinoff of the Labor Party, 1.

Rather than slow the reforms, as many voters had expected, Prime Minister Jim Bolger's National government extended them into two areas previously considered untouchable-welfare and labor relations. In December 1990 the government slashed welfare payments 10 percent and targeted them to a more limited group, and later raised a tax surcharge on state pensioners' supplementary earnings. The May 1991 Employment Contracts Act ended the unions' privilege to negotiate national, occupation-based awards, bringing many contracts to the factory or even the individual level. In late 1991 the New Labor Party, which favored reversing the deregulatory measures, formed a five-party, center-left coalition called the Alliance that included the Green Party, the Democratic Party, the Liberal Party and the Maori nationalist *Mana Motuhake* Party. Despite growing discontent, in February 1992 the government ended universal free hospital care, which had been a pillar of the welfare state, as part of a larger effort to create competition among health care suppliers.

Heading into the 6 November 1993 national elections the economy appeared to be turning the corner after nine years of harsh restructuring, with GDP growth forecast at 2.9 percent through 1996 and inflation within the central bank's strict target of 2 percent or lower. However, unemployment held at 10 percent, and pensioners and others hit hard by government spending cuts continued to face difficulties.

Initial election results gave the National Party 49 seats, one short of a majority; Labor, 46; the Alliance, headed by Jim Anderton, 2; New Zealand First, 2. The latter is a new populist party headed by Winston Peters, a Maori who had been thrown out of the cabinet in October 1991 for his criticism of the government's social and economic policies. On 17 November subsequent tallying of 300,000 absentee ballots gave the Labor seat in the Waitaki district to the National Party, ensuring a one-seat majority.

In a concurrent referendum, voters chose a mixed member proportional system (MMP) over the current first-past-the-post system by 54-46 percent. At an earlier two-part referendum in September 1992 held to gauge voter preferences, 85 percent of the voters had rejected the first-past-the-post-system, mainly on the grounds that it placed small parties at a disadvantage, and 70 percent chose the MMP in a choice of four alternatives. The MMP will give each citizen two votes. The first will be for one of sixty-five geographical constituency seats, and the second will go toward filling fifty-five seats through proportional representation. Small parties can win seats if they pass a 5 percent threshold.

Following the election Prime Minister Bolger dumped Ruth Richardson, the architect and staunchest proponent of the government's economic restructuring program, from the Finance portfolio as part of an effort to adopt a more consensus-oriented cabinet. In June 1994 Richardson quit politics, leaving the government short of a majority. The by-election campaign for Richardson's seat centered on the threatened closure of local hospitals under the government's health service reform program, and on cutbacks in welfare payments. On 13 August the National Party narrowly held on to the seat and regained its parliamentary majority, while the Alliance took second place and Labor came in a distant third.

The Bolger government does not have to face a general election until 1996. However the drawing of new electoral boundaries under the MMP system, expected to be completed by May 1995, will force many MPs to give up seats at the next election. Some will likely join smaller parties, and this process could force the government to call an early vote.

In September a former parliamentary undersecretary quit the National Party to form the Right-of-Centre Party, but pledged to support the government. A late November poll showed that 42 percent of the electorate supported the National Party against 25 percent for Labor, although with a razor-thin parliamentary majority and talk of more defections, Bolger's government remained on edge.

Political Rights and Civil Liberties: New Zealand's citizens can democratically change their government. Members of the indigenous Maori population can choose to be listed on a separate electoral roll and elect MPs to four specially reserved seats. The country has no written constitution, but all fundamental freedoms are respected in practice. An independent judiciary provides full due process rights for the accused. The country has a vigorous and unfettered press. All religious faiths are allowed to practice freely.

Workers can freely join independent trade unions. The 1991 Employment Contracts Act (ECA) has weakened the power of unions by banning compulsory union membership and ending the previous "national awards" system under which wage agreements were applied across the board to all employees in an industry. Wages have fallen since the introduction of the ECA. The International Labor Organization is reviewing a complaint that the ECA infringes upon freedom of association.

The indigenous Maori minority and the tiny Pacific Islander population claim discrimination in employment and education opportunities. The 1983 Equal Employment Opportunities Policy, designed to bring more minorities into the public sector, has been only marginally successful; Maori make up only 6.3 percent of the civil service, and hold only 0.7 percent of the senior management positions. Meanwhile, Maori account for half the prison population and have a 25 percent unemployment rate. According to the Social Welfare Department, in 1992 40 percent of Pacific Islander households and 43 percent of Maori households were in the bottom 20 percent of income earners.

In December 1994 the Bolger government reached a historic settlement with the Tainui, one of the three largest Maori tribes, over compensation for being displaced in 1863 by British colonists. The deal includes a $41.6 million monetary grant and the return of public land valued at $66.5 million. The government has set aside $633 million to settle all outstanding Maori land claims within ten years.

A similarly contentious issue involves the so-called Maori reserved land. Soon after the British began colonizing New Zealand, the Crown declared large tracts of land to be held in trust for the Maori, which would be leased in perpetuity to the settlers subject to twenty-one-year rent reviews. The 1955 Maori Reserved Land Act codified this arrangement. Today, the rents received by the Maori on some 2,500 leases average 1.6 percent of market valuation, against 10 percent or more for other commercial landowners. The government is examining several long term plans for raising rents to market levels and ultimately making lease arrangements subject to negotiation. The Maori base their land claims on the disputed 1840 Treaty of Waitangi, which they say grants them sovereignty over the land.

Nicaragua

Polity: Presidential-leg-
islative democracy
(military-influenced)
Economy: Capitalist-statist
Population: 4,275,000
PPP: $2,550
Life Expectancy: 65.4

Political Rights: 4
Civil Liberties: 5
Status: Partly Free

Ethnic Groups: Mestizo (approximately 70 percent),
Caucasian (16 percent), black (9 percent), and indigenous (5 percent)

Overview: With elections due in 1996, the political landscape fractured into jousting between Sandinista factions and among other foes and allies of the Chamorro government. A new law virtually legalized the separation of the Sandinista-controlled military from civil authority, ensuring its status as the country's most powerful institution amid continuing political violence, corruption and impunity.

The Republic of Nicaragua was established in 1838, seventeen years after independence from Spain. Struggles between the Liberal and Conservative parties dominated politics until Gen. Anastasio Somoza Garcia took over in 1937. The Somoza dynasty lasted until the 1979 revolution that brought the Marxist Sandinista National Liberation Front to power.

The Sandinistas suspended the 1972 constitution and ruled by decree. Daniel Ortega became president in a state-controlled election in 1984 and in 1987 the Sandinistas installed a new constitution providing for the election every six years of a president, vice president, and a ninety-six-member National Assembly.

The Sandinistas, pressured by the Contra insurgency, signed the 1987 Arias peace accord that called for democratization in Central America. In 1989 the National Opposition Union (UNO), a diverse coalition of fourteen political parties, nominated Violeta Chamorro, the publisher of opposition newspaper *La Prensa*, for president. Chamorro won the February 1990 election with 55 percent of the vote, against 40 percent for Ortega. UNO won fifty-one assembly seats, the Sandinistas thirty-nine, and two smaller parties one each.

President Chamorro has been mostly a bit player, as Antonio Lacayo, her son-in-law and presidency minister, has run her administration. After the election Lacayo secretly negotiated an agreement with Gen. Humberto Ortega, Daniel's brother and Sandinista military commander. Humberto remained as military chief after agreeing that the defense and interior ministries would be headed by civilians and state security dismantled.

But under the Sandinista military law, the defense minister, Chamorro herself, was left with practically no authority. Gen. Ortega retained complete control of the military's internal and external affairs, and simply transferred the state security apparatus from the interior ministry to the army. The Sandinistas, relying on street violence, strikes and control of the military, then leveraged Lacayo into an informal power-sharing arrangement. Left on the sidelines were UNO, private business and independent labor—the three pillars of the coalition that had supported Chamorro for president.

UNO tried to curb the Sandinistas' continued domination of the country, but it was thwarted by the defection of eight UNO legislators to Lacayo, allegedly after he bribed them. This so-called Center Group joined the Sandinistas to take control of the legislature.

The U.S. pressured the Chamorro government to exert greater authority over the military. Nicaragua, now the poorest nation in the hemisphere after Haiti, is completely dependent on foreign aid, much of it from the U.S. In early 1994 it was announced that Humberto Ortega would resign as military chief on 21 February 1995. However, the Sandinista-Center Group majority later passed a new military law that institutionalized the military's autonomy.

Meanwhile, the Sandinista party fell into factional fighting between hard-liners led by Daniel Ortega and moderates led by former vice-president Sergio Ramirez. Ortega controlled the party machine and Ramirez a majority of Sandinista legislators. The party looked to split as both fought for the party's presidential nomination in 1996. UNO, in turn, split into a number of factions—the Center Group, assorted moderates, and right-wing parties that revolved around Arnoldo Aleman, the feisty mayor of Managua who looked to be a strong presidential contender.

In late 1994 Sandinista and UNO moderates united around a proposal for constitutional reform that would limit presidential powers and ban close relatives of a sitting president from runnning for the office. Lacayo, his own presidential aspirations threatened, looked to stop the reforms, which required a second legislative ratification in 1995, in the notoriously corrupt judicial system. Daniel Ortega said he would block the reforms "in the streets."

Looming in the background was Humberto Ortega, still the most skilled political operator in the country. He had designated Joaquin Cuadra, his long-time second-in-command, to formally take over as military chief in February 1995. That meant Ortega could retain significant and possibly decisive influence over the institution he personally had constructed. Moreover, Ortega appeared to have presidential aspirations himself and some local analysts believed he might try to manipulate the division within the Sandinistas and emerge as the compromise candidate.

Political Rights and Civil Liberties: Nicaraguans have the right to change their governments through elections at the national and local levels. However, the Chamorro government's authority is severely undermined by the Sandinistas who retain control of the military and the police. The new military law passed in 1994 legalized the separation of the armed forces from civilian authority. It allows the military to act as a tax-free enterprise with substantial holdings and with full control of the national customs system. As an armed corporation accountable mostly to itself, the military is practically a state within a state.

In February 1994 regional council elections were held in the Atlantic Coast region, home to most of Nicaragua's nearly quarter-million indigenous people. However, under the 1988 autonomy law regional representatives have little power vis-a-vis the central government in Managua.

The 1987 constitution permits the organization of political parties, civic groups and labor unions. But political and civic activity are severely restricted by continuing political violence, official corruption and a mounting crime wave, much of it drug-related, all in a climate of general impunity. Because the Sandinistas control the army, the police and most of the judiciary, there is no authority citizens or non-Sandinista groups can turn to for security.

Numerous bands of former Contras continued to operate in the north, competing in their criminal activities with groups of former Sandinista soldiers in an atmosphere of lawlessness. Because there are still no effective property laws, the government has been unable to guarantee land grants or credits to former Contras, the core of the 1990 Contra demobilization agreement. Moreover, there remained about 5,000 claims involving property confiscated by the Sandinstas when they were formally in power.

In late 1993 a Tripartite Commission made up of representatives of the government, the Organization of American States, and the Catholic church concluded that political killings of both Contras and Sandinistas occurred with impunity. However, the government acted on few of the commission's recommendations in 1994 and the commission's survival appeared to be in jeopardy. There have been at least 1,000 political killings since 1990, a majority since 1992 and more than 300 in 1994. More than half the victims were demobilized Contras, UNO supporters or unaffiliated peasants. Less than 5 percent of the killings have been resolved.

In 1994 Nicaragua's independent human rights groups reported continuing intimidation, extrajudicial killings, kidnappings, false arrest, and torture during interrogation. Abuses by the military and the police are directed mostly against demobilized Contras and UNO supporters, particularly in rural areas. In November 1994 twenty Miskito indians were killed in the north but the indentity of the attackers remained unclear.

A number of high-profile murder cases remained unresolved. The military has stonewalled the investigation of the October 1990 murder of Jean Paul Genie who, according to a group of Venezuelan jurists working at the request of UNO, was killed by members of Gen. Humberto Ortega's armed escort. Frustrated by the evident impunity enjoyed by the military, the Genie family took the case to the Inter-American Human Rights Court in 1994.

The cases of at least nine former Contra leaders murdered since 1990, including former Contra commander Enrique Bermudez, remained unresolved, as did the 1992 killings of two government auditors investigating charges of government corruption. Also unresolved were the murders of Arges Sequira, a leader of a group demanding the return of property confiscated by the Sandinistas, and Leopoldo Serrano, son of a prominent anti-Sandinista business figure.

The police rarely protect people and property from the armed actions of Sandinista labor unions or rural paramilitary units. Since 1990, there have been virtually no arrests in response to the bombings, takeovers of government buildings and private property, and other incidents of Sandinista violence. At the same time the police and civil courts are overwhelmed by a surging crime wave. Prisons are overcrowded and conditions deplorable, with hundreds of detainees held for months and in some cases years before being brought to court.

The issue of labor rights is complicated by the fact that the Sandinistas wield their public unions as violent instruments to influence government economic policy. Through the public sector unions they control, the Sandinistas have managed to gain ownership of more than three dozen state enterprises privatized by the government. The legal rights of non-Sandinista unions are not fully guaranteed because they have no effective recourse when labor laws are violated by either the government or violent actions of the Sandinistas.

The print media are partisan, representing hard-line and moderate Sandinista, and pro- and anti-governmnent positions. Before leaving office the Sandinistas dismantled the seventeen-station state radio network and "privatized" it to mostly Sandinista loyalists, part of the massive, illegal transfer of state resources to the Sandinista party. They also retained possession of one of the three television stations. In 1994 hard-line Sandinistas took over *Barricada*, the party newspaper, and other Sandinista media outlets and purged them of moderate editors and journalists. The conservative daily *La Tribuna* has been pressured by the government through denial of government advertising and the placing of obstacles against importing machinery. In 1994 at least two dozen journalists were attacked, mainly by police.

The Catholic church has been outspoken in its criticism of the inordinate influence exerted by the Sandinistas and the military. In 1994 there were a number of attacks against churches, evidently by Sandinista militants, and a physical attack against the bishop of the city of Leon.

Niger

Polity: Presidential par-
liamentary democracy
Economy: Capitalist
Population: 8,813,000
PPP: $542
Life Expectancy: 45.9
Ethnic Groups: Hausa and Zherma (80 percent), Tuareg, Arabs, Daza, Fulani, others
Ratings Change: *Niger's civil liberties rating changed from 4 to 5 because of political instability and increased Tuareg rebel violence.

Political Rights: 3
Civil Liberties: 5*
Status: Partly Free

Overview:

In 1994, President Ousmane Mahamane's ruling coalition, the Alliance of the Forces for Change (AFC), lost its majority when one of its leaders resigned and switched to the opposition. Ousmane was forced to dissolve the parliament and call for new legislative elections in January 1995. The long-lasting Tuareg rebellion in the North increased in intensity following the failure of the rebels to renew a peace treaty at the end of 1993. The violence subsided in October with the signing of a peace treaty.

Niger, a landlocked West African country, gained independence from France in 1960. The military overthrew a one-party government in 1974. In 1987, the supreme military council chose General Ali Seibou as the head of state. In a move to re-establish civilian rule, the military council disbanded, naming Seibou as president. The military-backed National Movement for a Development Society (MNSD) became the sole legal party.

Faced with mass protests demanding the introduction of democracy in 1990, Seibou acceded to demands to hold a national conference to discuss political reforms. The 1991 conference stripped Seibou of all but ceremonial powers and barred him from running in the planned presidential election. The conference also appointed Amadou Cheiffou interim prime minister and André Salifou the chairman of the interim legislature, the High Council of State (HCR). In 1992, the HCR prepared a new constitution, approved on 28 December by an 89 percent majority.

In the February 1993 legislative elections, which international observers judged to be free and fair, eight opposition parties formed the AFC coalition in order to block the MNSD' return to power and obtain a majority in partliament. The following month, Ousmane, backed by the AFC, won 54 percent of the votes to become the country's first democratically elected president. In April, Ousmane nominated Mahamadou Issofou to the post of prime minister.

In September 1994, Issofou resigned his post only hours after his Niger Party for Democracy and Socialism (PNDS) announced it was leaving the AFC. The PNDS accused the AFC of "betrayal," but did not elaborate further. Without the support of the PNDS, the AFC lost its parliamentary majority. A minority government was subsequently formed, which then lost a vote of no confidence. Ousmane was forced to dissolve the National Assembly and call for new elections. The interior ministry appointed an electoral commission to organize the new round of parliamentary elections scheduled to take place in early January 1995. Opposition leaders accused the commission of being an illegal body, as the unrevised electoral code did not allow for its formation.

Violence in the North increased in early 1994 following the December 1993 lapse of a truce between government armed forces and one of the three Tuareg rebel organizations, the Liberation Front of Tamoust (FLT). French observers, who were sent to monitor the truce, left Niger on 27 November 1993 because of disputes with Nigerien authorities, which contributed to the failure of the truce renewal.

The Tuareg rebellion is based on historical conflicts and political claims. The Tuaregs, most of whom lead nomadic lives, protest the fact that the more populous Hausa and Djerma ethnic groups dominate the political system and prevent them from having access to government services.

On 19 January a Tuareg attack in the North left ten dead. The following month a fourth Tuareg movement formed, the Popular Front for the Liberation of the Sahara (FPLS). Talks opened in February between the Nigerien government and the four rebel groups. Both the president and the National Assembly rejected the rebels' demands for partition, saying that such action would lead to the fragmentation of the country.

On 16 May forty people were killed in the most violent rebel clash of 1994. Peace talks began again in August. Both sides agreed on the principles of territorial reorganization and setting up territorial administrations based more on population. Violent clashes continued that month, and negotiations resumed on 25 September. On 11 October a cease-fire was signed by the government and the four rebel groups.

In April violence erupted in the town of Kalouka when animist villagers claimed that members of the Islamic sect *Izala* were harassing them in order to make them convert. On 25 April, police tried to arrest those Islamists who were believed to be dangerous. The Islamists resisted, and ten people were killed. Months later, on 19 November, 5,000 Muslims gathered at Niamey to denounce condoms and protest the government's anti-AIDS and birth control campaigns.

Political Rights **S**ince the first parliamentary and presidential elections in
and Civil Liberties: February and March 1993, Nigeriens have had the right to
change their government democratically. Local and
regional elections, however, have been postponed several times since their original
1991 schedule. The traditional village chiefs retain their dominant power in the
countryside, where a majority of the population lives.

The judicial system is an amalgam of traditional African, Islamic, and European legal codes. The new constitution affirms the judicial principle of presumption of innocence and other safeguards, such as limits on detention without warrant
and public proceedings during trials. Even after the adoption of the constitution,
however, the army continued to detain without formal charges dozens of Tuaregs
suspected of being rebel sympathizers. In their efforts to suppress the Tuareg
rebellion, the army was responsible for a number of human rights abuses which
caused civilian deaths and property destruction.

The Superior Council of Communication (CSC), established in 1991 to protect and
regulate the media, became a permanent institution under the new constitution. Freedom
of the press has generally been respected since the country's transition to democracy.
Five French language newspapers and one in the Hausa language are published
regularly. Most of the population receives information from the government-controlled
national radio service, which airs opposition as well as government activities and views.

Freedom of association is guaranteed, with the exception of groups based on
ethnicity, regionalism, or religion. Workers have the right to join and form unions,
as stated in the 1992 constitution. Ninety-five percent of the population, however,
work in the agricultural sector, which is not unionized.

Freedom of assembly is generally unrestricted, although the government retains
the authority to deny permission for demonstrations during "tense" social conditions. When elections were announced on 15 October 1994, the government banned
all demonstrations until thirty days before the election. Campaigning was also
forbidden during that period.

Freedom of religion is respected in Niger, which is over 90 percent Muslim.
Article four of the 1992 constitution provides for the separation of mosque and
state. A growing number of Muslims actively oppose the secularization of the state.

Freedom of movement within the country is hindered by security checkpoints,
particularly in and around major cities and the northern part of the country. Travel
and emigration to and repatriation from foreign countries are unrestricted. Among
the Hausa and Fulani people in eastern Niger, many women are forbidden to leave
their homes unless accompanied by a male and generally only after dark. Women
have inferior status in most areas of society, including education, employment, and
the political procss. Domestic violence against women is widespread, even among
the upper class.

Nigeria

Polity: Military
Economy: Capitalist-statist
Population: 98,091,000
PPP: $1,360
Life Expectancy: 51.9
Ethnic Groups: Hausa, Fulani, Ibo, Yoruba, Kanuri, other
Ratings Change: *Nigeria's civil liberties rating changed from 5 to 6 because of the current government's declaration of commanding "absolute power" and its disregard for basic human rights and civil liberties.

Political Rights: 7
Civil Liberties: 6*
Status: Not Free

Overview: In presidential elections held on 12 June 1993, Chief Moshood K.O. Abiola of the Social Democratic Party (SDP), a wealthy industrialist and member of the southern Yoruba tribe, won a mandate across ethnic, geographical and religious lines. Despite his election victory, Abiola was barred from assuming political office and has been detained since June 1994, charged with attempting to "overthrow the government." Despite his ailing health and reported mistreatment during detention, human rights groups report that Abiola has been denied medical treatment.

As the military government led by General Sani Abacha tightens its control, newspapers have been closed and opposition leaders have been jailed and their passports seized. Following an oil workers' strike in July and August 1994, Abacha instituted even greater repressive legislation and declared his regime to command "absolute power." International human rights observers indicate that widespread human rights violations by government security forces, including extrajudicial executions, rape and torture, have escalated.

Since gaining independence from Britain in 1960, Nigeria has been governed by military rule for twenty-four years. Ethnic and tribal violence has played a major role in Nigeria's post-colonial period, with tensions especially high between the Muslim-dominated north and the mostly Christian south, as well as among the country's 250 tribal groups. Tribal animosity led to the 1967-1970 civil war in which an estimated 2 million people died from both fighting and starvation when the Ibos of eastern Nigeria tried to establish their own state of Biafra.

In August 1989 General Ibrahim Babangida seized power in a coup. He established the Armed Forces Ruling Council (AFRC) and assumed control as both head of state and chief executive of AFRC. Babangida pledged to clean up government corruption and to return the country to civilian rule by 1990. In May 1989, the government lifted the ban on political parties but all subsequent applications were annulled. Instead the authorities created two government-sanctioned parties—the SDP and the National Republican Convention (NRC). While the government maintained that the two differed in that "one [is] a little to the left, and the other a little to the right," in fact the parties' manifestos diverged only marginally.

The return to civilian rule was repeatedly delayed as religious, economic and ethnic violence plagued the Babangida government from the summer of 1991 through the following summer of 1992. Despite the unrest, on 4 July 1992 the country held its first parliamentary election in twelve years. The SDP emerged with forty-seven of the ninety-one seats in the Senate and 310 of the 598 seats in the House. With Presidential elections set for December 1992, primary elections scheduled in five out of thirty states were to mark the final phase of the transition. Primaries were held in August and September 1992 but in each case the elections were marred by massive fraud and vote-rigging. The government voided the primary election results, and replaced the national and local leadership of the parties with appointed caretaker committees.

On 17 November 1992 Babangida announced that presidential elections were to be postponed until 12 June 1993. Under a new plan, Babangida declared that both parties would nominate a presidential candidate through congresses in each of the thirty states plus the capital district, for a total of sixty-two. One candidate from each party would then be elected at national party conventions. Babangida dissolved the AFRC and the Council of Ministers and created a National Defense and Security Council (NDSC). He also disqualified all twenty-three candidates who took part in the earlier primaries and directed that all cabinet ministers be fired on 2 January 1993, to be replaced by a civilian-led NDSC.

Claiming that the June 1993 presidential elections were plagued with widespread irregularities, Babangida annulled Abiola's electoral victory. In an attempt to calm the widespread protest that ensued, Babangida created an interim "civilian" government led by Ernest Shonekan in August 1993. Babangida was forced from office in August 1993 by his defense minister, Abacha, and the military assumed direct control of the Government. In November 1993, Shonekan was forced to resign and Abacha became head of state. During his brief tenure in office, Shonekan attempted to win public support by freeing political prisoners, lifting press restrictions, instituting reforms in the oil industry bureaucracy and promising to hold new presidential elections. Claiming that it was in the interest of national unity, Abacha subsequently banned all existing political parties, any political assembly, the National Electoral Commission and all state, local and federal governments. He further directed that all civilian officials be replaced by military commanders.

In January 1994, Abacha announced that a constitutional conference would convene to determine the constitution of Nigeria's government. Elections for 273 of the 369 conference delegates were held in May 1994. The remaining ninety-six representatives were government-appointed. The election was boycotted in the southwest, an Abiola stronghold. Just prior to the elections, Abacha condemned opposition leaders, accusing them of driving Nigeria into chaos and anarchy. Opposition demonstrations condemning the elections were violently dispersed and Human Rights Watch reports that on election day approximately fifteen human rights and opposition party activists were detained and charged with disrupting the elections. They were subsequently released.

Political Rights and Civil Liberties: Nigerians cannot change their government democratically. Prior to the 1993 elections, opposition party and media activities were tightly controlled. Newspapers critical of the government were censored and the courts were barred from querying military decrees. Despite these constraints, opposition leader Abiola won the 1993 presidential elections but was barred from office and subsequently jailed. Provisions guaranteed under Nigeria's new constitution that were to take effect following the 1993 election have not been implemented.

Under the 1989 constitution citizens have the right to freedom of assembly and association. Shortly after assuming power, however, Abacha banned all existing political parties, and prohibited all political associations and public demonstrations or activities deemed to be political in nature. In late 1994 Abacha alleged that the ban on political parties would be lifted in January 1995. Under Abacha's regime, opposition leaders have been arrested and their passports confiscated. In an October 1994 report, Human Rights Watch/Africa alleged that government force was invovled in extrajudicial executions, shootings, bombings and harassment of prodemocracy activists. The report further states that government forces have employed violent measures, including killing, to counter university demonstrations. Students and teachers have been beaten and thirty female medical students at the University of Benin were reportedly raped.

While Nigerian law prohibits torture and mistreatment of prisoners, detainees frequently die while in police custody and there are numerous reports that police routinely use torture and beatings to extract confessions and information. Conditions in Nigerian prisons remain deplorable. Prisons are without adequate water and sewage systems. Medical supplies are in short supply and disease is prevalent in the poorly ventilated and overcrowded prison systems.

Despite some independence exercised by the judicial system in the wake of the oil strike, the criminal justice system remains under government influence and control. A federal high court judge temporarily reinstated ousted union officials in August 1994, and in November 1994 a court ruled that jailed opposition leader Abiola should be released. In an attempt to thwart judicial intervention, however, Abacha's government enacted the Military Government Supremacy and Enforcement Powers Decree which gave the military government absolute power.

Although the criminal justice procedures in Nigeria call for a trial within three months of arraignment for most prisoners, as a result of poor administrative procedures coupled with corruption there are often considerable delays. Police are empowered to make an arrest without warrant if there is reasonable suspicion that a crime has taken place or if the police witness an offense. However, this provision gives the police broad powers of arrest that are often abused.

Under the most recent constitution, the judicial branch has been separated into two divisions. Those committing common criminal offenses are tried by the regular court system. Those who are accused of certain offenses such as coup plotting, corruption, armed robbery, illegal sale of petroleum or drug trafficking are tried by military tribunals. For most cases tried before a tribunal, the accused has a right to counsel, bail and appeal. In practice, however, a presumption of guilt is often substituted for the presumption of innocence and sentences for those convicted of a crime by the tribunals reportedly exceed conviction rates of the regular courts. In cases where defendants cannot afford counsel, they can request assistance from the free Legal Aid Council. However, the Council is not adequately funded to provide counsel for all persons charged with lesser offenses.

Freedom of press is not respected in Nigeria. In the wake of the 1993 elections, newspapers were closed, and both international and national reporters have been intimidated, harassed and imprisoned. Vendors who carry critical press have also reported government intimidation. All Concord group publications (owned by Abiola), including *The Concord*, *The African Concord* and *The Punch*, were shut down by the police in June 1994. In August 1994 *The Guardian* was also closed down. Despite court rulings in favor of the publications, no damages awarded were paid, and the publications remain closed. The government has published fake editions of opposition newspapers which included anti-Abiola propaganda.

The Nigerian Labour Congress (NLC) is Nigeria's umbrella labor federation and claims to have 3 million members from a work force of 30 million. Workers, except for essential government employees and members of the armed forces, are free to join trade unions. However, the government has maintained the right to supervise union accounts and merge unions. Workers do have the right to strike although the government mandates compulsory arbitration prior to strikes. From July to early September 1994, a strike by oil workers to protest military government rule was organized by the National Union of Petroleum and Gas Workers (NUPENG) and the Petroleum and Natural Gas Senior Staff Association of Nigeria (PENGASSAN). The strike succeeded in paralyzing business and causing massive fuel shortages. Other unions, including the NLC, joined the strike. By instituting draconian measures and dissolving the leadership of the organizing unions, Abacha succeeded in ending the strike. Union leaders, including the general secretary and president of NUPENG, were arrested by the State Security Service (SSS). Senior officials of PENGASSAN were also arrested. Some of the detained union members alleged that they were beaten while in custody. Human Rights Watch reports that members of the NLC continue to be harassed and that state has ordered the arrest of the NLC chair.

In most cases, citizens are free to travel within Nigeria, but under Abacha international travel has been prevented for political reasons. In November 1994 Nobel laureate and chair of the African Democratic League, Wole Soyinka, had his United Nations' issued passport seized and was denied passage to leave Nigeria to attend a writer's conference in France. Soyinka is a fierce critic of the military government and has previously challenged the legitimacy of the regime's rule in a court case that was subsequently rejected. There is no state religion and the 1989 Constitution provides for freedom of worship.

Norway

Polity: Parliamentary democracy
Economy: Mixed capitalist
Population: 4,336,000
PPP: $17,170
Life Expectancy: 76.9
Ethnic Groups: Norwegian majority; indigenous Finnish and Lappic (Saami) minorities; and small immigrant groups

Political Rights: 1
Civil Liberties: 1
Status: Free

Overview: In a referendum on 28 November 1994 Norwegians defeated membership in the European Union (EU) by 52.2 percent to 47.8 percent. The loss was a blow to Prime

Minister Gro Harlem Brundtland, whose Labor Party split over the issue. A coalition of agricultural, fishing, environmentalist and other interests defeated the move to join Europe. The LO, the trade union federation, a traditional Labor ally, also opposed Brundtland over Europe. The result of the referendum threatened Norway with economic and political difficulties with its neighbors, because Sweden and Finland joined Denmark, the other continental Nordic state, in the EU, effective January 1995. Norway will continue to receive some trading benefits from the EU through its membership in the European Economic Area (EEA), a free-trade zone that also includes Liechtenstein and Iceland.

Opposition to European economic union has cultural and economic roots. Although most Norwegians live in towns and cities, they remain emotionally attached to their self-image as a rural nation of farming and fishing, two sectors that fear European competition. In addition, Norwegians want protection for the offshore oil that provides a substantial portion of national income.

Labor has been in power since 1990 following the collapse of a Conservative-led cabinet. The present Norwegian constitution, known as the Eisvold Convention, dates from 1814 and is one of the oldest written constitutions in the world. The largely ceremonial head of state is King Harald V. Generally, the royal family is low-key and avoids the scandals associated with other royals. However, in 1994 Princess Martha Louise was named as a co-respondent in a divorce suit in England. The *Storting* (parliament) consists of 165 members elected every four years by proportional representation from multi-member districts. After parliamentary elections, the Storting elects one-fourth of its members to serve as the upper house (*Lagting*). The remaining parliamentarians constitute the lower house (*Odelsting*). The two chambers consider some matters separately and others jointly.

In the 1993 general election, Labor captured only 37 percent of the vote, but it remained the largest party. The pro-European Conservatives lost ground to the anti-EU Center Party, whose 18 percent nearly tripled its 1989 showing. Labor formed a minority government that stays in office with the support of other parties, depending on the issue. The government introduced an anti-recession program in 1993. It aims to create jobs, improve competitiveness, and reduce taxes and tariffs. One government reform, transforming the state telephone service into a government corporation, triggered a public sector union strike in May 1994. The civil servants feared that corporate status for the telephone system would lead to privatization.

Environmentalists and several Western governments criticized Norway for its whaling in 1994. The country had resumed the practice in 1993. In July 1994 the cabinet voted to give the police and coast guard more power to detain anti-whaling activists. This decision was a reaction to the release of Greenpeace activists after the authorities were unable to make criminal damage charges stick. In another maritime clash, the Norwegian coast guard arrested Icelandic fishermen in September for fishing in Norwegian-claimed waters. The two countries tried to ease this round of the age-old "cod war" with bilateral talks in October.

Norway received great international publicity for hosting the 1994 Winter Olympics in Lillehammer. In February, at an exhibit coinciding with the winter games, anti-abortion activists stole the most famous Norwegian painting, Edvard Munch's "The Scream."

Political Rights and Civil Liberties: Norwegians can change their government democratically through free and fair elections every four years. Norwegians abroad have the right to absentee ballots. The Lappic (Saami) minority has political autonomy and its own assembly. There are few restrictions on speech, press, assembly or association. In addition to laws against slander and libel, restrictions include the prohibition of racist and sexist comments either printed or spoken in public. In September 1994, a motorist in western Norway was fined for calling a policeman an "onion." A court ruled that the word was an illegal affront. The police routinely grant permission for public demonstrations.

The state finances the established Lutheran Church, in which about 93 percent of the population holds at least nominal membership. However, there are alternative churches available to Norwegians. They receive public financing if they register with the government. Although there is significant freedom of worship, there are some minor restrictions on religion. For example, by law the King and half of the cabinet must be Lutherans. In some circumstances, employers have the right to ask job applicants whether they respect Christian beliefs.

Racial, sexual, linguistic and class discrimination are illegal. Women play a major role in politics. Three lead major political parties. There are instances of racially motivated violence committed by civilians against recent non-Nordic immigrants. However, the police and other authorities have dealt firmly with such cases.

The press is free and vibrant. The state subsidizes many newspapers, in order to support political pluralism. The state funds broadcasting, but does not interfere with editorial content on radio and television. Commercial cable television and small private radio stations operate. Censorship is minimal, but the Film Control Board has the right to prevent the public from viewing films that it deems blasphemous, overly violent or pornographic. However, the board has not censored alleged blasphemy in over twenty years. Workers have the right to organize and strike. A majority of employees belongs to unions.

Oman

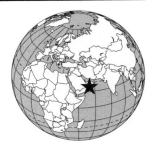

Polity: Traditional monarchy
Economy: Capitalist-statist
Population: 1,922,000
PPP: $9,320
Life Expectancy: 69.1
Ethnic Groups: Arab, Baluchi, Zanzibari, Indian

Political Rights: 6
Civil Liberties: 6
Status: Not Free

Overview: The Sultanate of Oman, an absolute monarchy located on the southeastern Arabian peninsula and several offshore islands, received independence from the British in 1951. In a July 1970 palace coup, Sultan Sa'id bin Taimur was overthrown by his son, Qabus ibn Sa'id al Sa'id, who set out to modernize what had been a severely underdeveloped country. In 1971 the left-wing Popular Front for the Liberation of Oman began an insurrection in the southern Dhofar Province, which the government finally suppressed in 1975. Since then the sultan, who rules by decree with the assistance of a Council of Ministers, has faced little opposition of any sort.

In 1981 the sultan appointed an advisory Consultative Assembly. In the spring of 1991 caucuses of prominent citizens in each of the country's fifty-nine provinces nominated three citizens per province for a new *Majlis al-Shura* (Consultative Council) to replace the Assembly. The sultan selected one nominee per province to sit in this Majlis, purposely excluding government officials in order to make the body something of a citizen's forum. The Majlis first convened in December 1991 and has met several times since then to comment on legislation, prepare development plans, and voice citizens' concerns. In 1994 the sultan named an expanded, eighty-seat Majlis that will sit through 1997.

In early 1994 diplomats and visitors to Oman reported a rise in Islamic activism, possibly related to the rising unemployment rate among youths. On 27 August 1994 *Agence France-Presse* reported that police had rounded up more than 200 Islamic activists, including politicians, soldiers, academics and students, on sedition charges in a series of raids beginning in May. The authorities released many of the detainees shortly after arrest. However, on 25 October the Cairo-based *al-Sha'b* reported that 105 activists had been sentenced to between ten and fifteen years in jail. The sentences had been handed down by a non-judicial governmental committee consisting mainly of politicians, and the defendants did not have access to lawyers. By year's end the government had not publicized the specific nature of the activists' offenses.

Political Rights and Civil Liberties: Citizens of Oman lack the democratic means to change their government. The sultan rules by decree, and although many policy decisions are made on a consensus basis there are no real checks on the sultan's power. There is no constitution or other safeguard of rights. Political parties are strongly discouraged and none exists. Participation in the nominating process to the unelected *Majlis al-Shura* (Consultative Council) is limited to prominent individuals. The only redress for citizens is through petitions to local leaders, although the effectiveness of this largely depends upon personal influence or contacts, and through direct appeals to the sultan during his annual three-week tour of the country. The sultan appoints the provincial governors, and tribal leaders wield significant authority over local matters in rural areas.

The sultan faces little organized opposition to his rule, but there are sporadic calls for independence from some Shihayeen tribesmen living in Rous al-Jibal Province on the Musandam Peninsula. The Province is geographically separate from the rest of Oman, fronting the Straight of Hormuz and bordering the United Arab Emirates on three sides, and has been administered by Oman since December 1970. In October 1993 Shihayeen representatives reported the detention of Sheikh Jumaa Hamdan Hassan al Malik, allegedly because of his links to pro-independence sympathizers. Police reportedly detained several other Shihayeen after releasing the Sheikh.

Prior to 1994 the government did not appear to be holding political prisoners. However, the reported conviction of 105 Islamic activists (*See Overview above*) on sedition charges made it likely that at least some are imprisoned for nonviolent offenses. Moreover, the trials were conducted outside of the judicial system without any safeguards. The Sultan has control over the rudimentary judicial system, which in practice operates mostly according to tradition. There is no legal provision for counsel and no jury trials, although trials are generally open to the public. The court system includes civilian courts for criminal cases and Islamic Shari'a courts to decide family matters.

All criticism of the sultan is prohibited. The 1984 Press and Publication Law gives the government control over all publications through prior censorship of domestic and imported materials. In practice Omani journalists exercise significant self-censorship, and most publications are reviewed after they are released. Two of the four daily papers are owned by the government, and the other two papers rely heavily on government subsidies. Coverage in all four dailies, and in other sundry publications, generally supports government policies. The state-controlled television and radio broadcasts carry only government views, although there are no restrictions on receiving foreign news services via satellite dish.

By law all public gatherings are government-sponsored, although this is not always enforced. All associations must be registered with the government and essentially must be nonpolitical. Islam is the official religion, and the majority of the population are Sunni Muslims. Christians and Hindus can worship freely, but non-Muslims may not proselytize. Citizens may travel freely within the country, although women must receive permission from their husbands or fathers to travel abroad. In June 1994 the government announced that women from the capital district of Muscat would be eligible to become members of the Majlis. Although most women still do not work outside the home and many are illiterate, in recent years women have gradually entered fields such as medicine and management that were once off-limits. The government enforces a law requiring women to receive equal pay for equal work. Under Islamic law women receive a lesser share of an inheritance than men. Female genital mutilation is practiced in some rural areas.

The Labor law makes no provision for trade unions, and none exists. However, employers of more than fifty workers must form a body of labor and management representatives to discuss working conditions. Wages are negotiated only through individual contracts with employees. Strikes are illegal, although brief strikes occasionally occur. Employers occasionally withhold from foreign workers the letters of release that such workers require to change jobs, essentially forcing them to remain at the job for weeks or months longer, sometimes without pay.

Pakistan

Polity: Presidential par-
liamentary democracy
(military-influenced)
Economy: Capitalist-
statist
Population: 126,415,000
PPP: $1,970
Life Expectancy: 58.3
Ethnic Groups: Punjab, Baluchi, Sindhi, Pathan, Afghan

Political Rights: 3
Civil Liberties: 5
Status: Partly Free

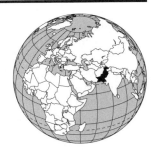

Overview:

In 1994 Prime Minister Benazir Bhutto's government faced a concerted effort by her chief political rival, Nawaz Sharif, to make Pakistan ungovernable through mass strikes, an armed uprising by tribesmen demanding the imposition of martial law, and lawlessness in the southern city of Karachi.

Formed in 1947 through the partition of India, the country originally consisted of the geographically separate regions of East Pakistan and West Pakistan. Pakistan fought India over the disputed Kashmir province in 1947-48 and in 1965. *(A separate report on Kashmir appears in the Related Territories Section.)* In 1971 East Pakistan separated to form Bangladesh; India supported the new nation by defeating the occupying West Pakistani troops. The 1973 Pakistani constitution, the third since independence, provides fc a National Assembly, which currently has 207 directly elected seats, 10 reserved for non-Muslims, and a primarily advisory 87-seat Senate chosen by the four provincial assemblies. The president is chosen every five years by an electoral college consisting of the national and provincial assemblies and the Senate.

In 1977 General Zia ul-Haq overthrew populist Prime Minister Ali Bhutto, imposed martial law and outlawed political parties. In 1985 Zia allowed political parties to function again and repealed martial law. However, he forced the Eighth Amendment through parliament giving the president broad powers including the right to nominate and dismiss the prime minister, the armed forces chief, top judges and provincial officials, and to dissolve the National Assembly and Senate. In May 1988 Zia used the amendment to dismiss the government of Prime Minister Mohammad Khan Junejo on charges of corruption and nepotism. In August, during preparations for fresh elections, Zia died in a mysterious airplane crash. Voting in November brought Bhutto's daughter, Benazir Bhutto, to power as prime minister.

In August 1990 President Ghulam Ishaq Khan dismissed Bhutto for alleged corruption, nepotism and abuse of authority, and dissolved the National Assembly. Elections in October brought the nine-party conservative Islamic Democratic

Alliance (IDA) to power under Nawaz Sharif, a businessman and the chief minister of Punjab province.

In 1992 Sharif's IDA coalition was weakened by the defection of several religion-based parties after the prime minister backed off on promises to Islamicize the legal system. In the spring of 1993 Sharif openly challenged President Khan by courting opposition support to repeal the Eighth Amendment. In April Khan dismissed the government, dissolved parliament, named a caretaker prime minister and called fresh elections.

In an unheralded decision, on 26 May the Supreme Court ruled 10-1 to restore Sharif to power, calling the dismissal unconstitutional since Khan had made no effort at mediation. In July army chief Abdul Waheed Kakar brokered a deal under which both Khan and Sharif resigned and fresh elections were called for October. Moeen Qureshi, a former World Bank official, took over as interim prime minister and quickly introduced several pragmatic financial and political reforms in order to secure emergency World Bank loans.

Some 150,000 army soldiers supervised the 6 October vote, which observers rated the country's cleanest ever. Bhutto's Pakistan People's Party (PPP) took 86 seats; Sharif's Pakistan Muslim League (PML) 72; 12 minor parties and fifteen independents took 43 seats, while legal disputes caused polling to be suspended in 6 districts. Bhutto secured the support of independents to be named prime minister, and on 13 November the parliament elected foreign minister Farooq Leghari, a Bhutto ally, as president.

Bhutto consolidated her party's strength at the 2 March 1994 indirect Senate elections. The PPP took 19 of the 37 contested seats, while no other party took more than 5, giving it 22 seats overall, the largest bloc in the 87-seat Senate.

By the fall Sharif had resorted to a strategy of making Pakistan ungovernable in order to force early elections or provoke the army into dismissing Bhutto. Sharif's PML organized a series of strikes that paralyzed parts of the country. In November the Bhutto government capped a year of official investigations into Sharif's business empire by arresting Mohammed Sharif, the former premier's seventy-five-year-old father, on charges of tax evasion. Although police released the elder Sharif after three days, the incident drew widespread condemnation from across the political spectrum.

During the year the government seemed impotent in dealing with severe law and order crises in the North West Frontier Province (NWFP) and in Karachi. In the spring fundamentalists in the NWFP began an uprising to demand the imposition of Islamic law. In early November 2,500 armed tribesmen took hundreds of people hostage and captured the airport in Swat district, while in neighboring areas some 10,000 tribesmen took hundreds of government officials hostage.

On 4 November, with a full-blown insurrection underway, the chief minister capitulated and imposed Islamic law even though the constitution granted him no authority to do so. The government sent in 10,000 paramilitary troops and quelled the uprising after two weeks of heavy fighting.

In Karachi, Pakistan's commercial capital, escalating factional, ethnic and sectarian violence killed more than 600 people during the year, nearly one-third of them in December alone. Much of the fighting occurred between rival wings of the Mohajir Qaumi Movement (MQM), which represents Muslims who migrated from India after 1947, although clashes also occurred between the MQM and ethnic Sindhis and between Sunni Muslims and the Shiite Muslim minority.

Political Rights and Civil Liberties:

In October 1993 Pakistanis changed their government in generally free and fair elections. The army supervised polling areas to prevent the widespread irregularities that had marred past votes. However, democracy is severely undermined by the concentration of political power in the hands of a tiny land-owning elite which dominates the government, army and bureaucracy. More than half of the parliamentarians come from the land-owning class, which constitutes less than five percent of the population and is responsible for widespread political corruption and nepotism. Social critic Altaf Gauhar estimates that 500 powerful families effectively rule the country. There are several million bonded laborers and nomads in the country who do not meet the eligibility criteria to vote. In the Federally Administered Tribal Areas (FATA) of the NWFP, the National Assembly representatives are elected by tribal leaders, which disenfranchises most of the two million Pashtun tribesmen living in the region.

In February 1994 President Leghari suspended the opposition-controlled, elected provincial assembly of the NWFP and sacked the chief minister. This came days after two PML members defected to the PPP, and the assembly speaker refused to hold a scheduled vote of no-confidence. The province is now run by a governor accountable only to the president.

The security forces are responsible for widespread human rights violations. Police and army soldiers reportedly kill scores of suspects each year in extrajudicial, staged "encounters." Police routinely torture detainees to extract confessions and other information. Prison conditions are brutal and, according to the independent Human Rights Commission of Pakistan, in 1993 fifty-two people died in prison due to mistreatment. Police frequently rape female detainees and prisoners, and rarely fully investigate charges of rape brought by women. In Sindh province local officials have arbitrarily detained hundreds of MQM activists for varying lengths of time.

The 1979 Hadood Ordinances authorize imprisonment, floggings and other punishment for violating Islamic behavioral codes, including a ban on extramarital sex. These punishments have never been carried out. In 1986 a military government introduced a blasphemy law, and in 1992 the government made the death penalty mandatory for blasphemy convictions. Muslims have been formally charged with blasphemy for accidentally dropping or damaging a copy of the Koran. More than 100 Ahmadis (a sect the government considers non-Muslim because its followers do not accept Muhammad as the last prophet) have been charged with blasphemy since the law was introduced, and in many cases Muslims appear to be using the blasphemy laws simply to settle scores with Ahmadis and Christians. In recent years Islamicists have killed several Christians accused of blasphemy.

Hindus claim discrimination in education and social services and are occasionally attacked by Muslims, and their places of worship are sometimes ransacked. In addition to the blasphemy laws, Ahmadis face armed attacks, harassment and other forms of discrimination.

Women face social discrimination and are frequently subject to domestic violence. Under the Hadood Ordinances a woman requires four male witnesses to prove she was raped, otherwise it is simply her word against that of the accused. The accused often files a counter charge of adultery, which carries the death penalty and likely deters many women from reporting rape. In 1994 Prime Minister Bhutto opened several all-female police stations and promised to eventually open one in each district. Bhutto has also pledged to allocate 10 percent of all senior police jobs to women and to set up special tribunals in each province to hear cases of crimes against women. Several women are killed each year in "dowry deaths" by husbands unhappy with the dowry they receive.

Random, sporadic clashes occur between Shiites and Sunni Muslims, between tribes in remote areas of Baluchistan province and the NWFP, and between rival student wings of political parties at universities. Several political parties, most notably the MQM, are accused of using "torture cells" against opponents and to enforce party discipline.

In February 1994 the Supreme Court struck down the special laws that have prevailed in the FATA since colonial days, and demanded that these areas be placed under the same laws as the rest of Pakistan. The court system is severely backlogged and some suspects remain in jail for more than a decade without going to trial. The government sometimes influences lower courts in political cases, and the president has the power to transfer judges and block tenure. The Supreme Court's May 1993 decision restoring then Prime Minister Sharif to office *(See Overview above)* set an important precedent for judicial independence at the higher levels. Suspects charged with blasphemy face difficulty in getting a fair trial due to pressure on the judicial system from fundamentalists. Local leaders in the FATA administer justice according to tribal customs, and often mete out punishment far out of proportion to the crime.

The 1975 Suppression of Terrorist Activities Act established special courts for "terrorist acts" including murder and sabotage. A 1987 law also established "speedy trial" courts for certain notorious cases. These courts generally respect procedural rights, but by their nature effectively place the burden of proving innocence on the accused. In addition, the speedy courts sometimes do not allow defense lawyers adequate time to represent clients during trials.

Both the Bhutto and Sharif governments have resorted to widespread detentions of opposition activists before and during planned demonstrations or strikes. Freedom of expression is constrained by laws against discrediting the army or Islam, by the constitutional provision mandating the death sentence for bringing the constitution into disrepute or otherwise subverting it, and by the blasphemy law. Although private newspapers criticize the government, self-censorship is practiced. Editors claimed the Sharif government discriminated against newspapers that were critical of its policies by placing fewer advertisements and allocating less duty-free newsprint. The government controls nearly all electronic media and regulates their content.

Workers in agriculture, hospitals, radio and television and export-processing zones cannot form unions. The 1952 Essential Services Maintenance Act restricts union activity in numerous sectors including education and transportation, and in some fields prevents workers from quitting jobs. Because of legally mandated cooling off periods, and the government's right to ban strikes not considered in the public interest and to call off a strike that has lasted more than thirty days, strikes rarely occur. The use of child labor, particularly in the carpet industry, is widespread. At least one landlord has been caught operating a private jail and forcing detainees to do agricultural work, and other private jails are believed to exist.

Palau

Polity: Presidential-legis-
lative democracy
Economy: Capitalist
Population: 17,000
PPP: na
Life Expectancy: na

Political Rights: 1
Civil Liberties: 2
Status: Free

Ethnic Groups: Palauan (a mixture of Micronesian, Malayan and
Melanesian) mixed Palauan-European-Asian, Filipino

Overview: Palau became the world's newest independent nation in
October 1994. After forty-nine years as a U.N. trust territory
administered by the United States, Palau became the 185th
U.N. member in December 1994. Independence came a year after Palauans approved a
Compact of Free Association with the United States with 68 percent of the vote.

Palau became part of the U.N. supervised Trust Territory of the Pacific after
World War II. In 1980, Palau adopted its constitution and changed its name to
Republic of Palau. Under the constitution, executive power is vested in a president
who is elected in a nationwide election for a period of four years. Legislative power
is vested in the *Olbiil Era Kelulau* (National Congress of Palau) consisting of a
House of Delegates and a Senate. Judicial power is vested in a Supreme Court, a
National Court and other inferior courts.

In November 1993 former Vice President Kuriwo Nakamura became president,
defeating Johnson Toribiong by a small margin. At the same time, voters approved,
by a simple majority, a constitutional amendment allowing for the approval of a
Compact of Free Association with the U.S. Palauans had previously voted seven
times on this issue since 1983, each time failing to approve the Compact due to less
than 75 percent support. The Compact adopted in 1993 provides $450 million in
U.S. aid over fifteen years in exchange for military facilities. The Americans will
build up to fifty-three miles of roads. Opponents of the Compact feared a militari-
zation of the territory and the possibility of the U.S. storing nuclear weapons or
waste. The Compact prohibits storing nonconventional weapons on the islands and
makes provisions for a U.S. cleanup of former nuclear sites.

Palau is planning significant infrastructural development, including an enhanced electric grid and bigger airport facilities for the tourist trade. About half the
40,000 yearly tourists come from Japan.

**Political Rights
and Civil Liberties:** Palauans have the right to change their government by
democratic means. Presidential and legislative elections are
competitive.

Palau is very clannish and traditional. Historically, the main chief was selected by
the highest ranking woman, the *Bilung*, and behind the scenes women held real power
on the islands, although their influence has changed since the adoption of a modern
constitution. There are tensions between the traditional leaders and the elected officials.
Traditional social rank depends on the family's standing in the home village.

The sixteen Palauan clans control land and sea rights, placing some property restrictions on foreigners. Non-Palauan citizens may not own land, but leases are available. About 5,000 foreigners, mostly Filipinos, work on the islands.

During the unsuccessful attempts to settle constitutional arrangements in the 1980s, there was some political violence. President Remeli was assassinated in 1985, and President Salii killed himself in 1988, apparently over a bribery scandal involving a power company. Palauans hope such violence is a thing of the past now that constitutional structures and independence have been settled,

There are freedoms of association and expression, but nongovernmental organizations are weak.

Panama

Polity: Presidential-legislative democracy
Economy: Capitalist-statist
Population: 2,531,000
PPP: $4,910
Life Expectancy: 72.5
Ethnic Groups: Mestizo (70 percent), West Indian (14 percent), white (10 percent), Indian (6 percent)

Political Rights: 2*
Civil Liberties: 3
Status: Free

Ratings Change: *Panama's political rights rating changed from 3 to 2 principally as a result of the holding of free and fair national elections. The ratings change altered Panama's overall status from Partly Free to Free.

Overview:

Ernesto Perez Balladares of the Democratic Revolutionary Party (PRD) was elected president in 1994 in the freest, cleanest election in Panama's history. There were concerns that followers of former dictator Gen. Manuel Noriega remained in the PRD, but Perez Balladares seemed in command as he adopted a pro-U.S., anti-corruption stance after taking office.

Panama was part of Colombia until 1903, when a U.S.-supported revolt resulted in the proclamation of an independent Republic of Panama. Until World War II the government was dominated by small groups of family-based, political elites. The next two decades saw mounting discontent over U.S. control of the Panama Canal. A 1968 military coup brought Gen. Omar Torrijos to power, followed by a renegotiation of the treaty that had granted the U.S. control of the Canal Zone in perpetuity.

After the 1977 canal treaties were signed, Torrijos promised democratization. The 1972 constitution was revised, providing for the direct election of a president and a legislative assembly for five years. After Torrijos's death in 1981, Noriega emerged as Panamanian Defense Force (PDF) chief and rigged the 1984 election that brought to power the Democratic Revolutionary Party (PRD), then the political arm of the PDF.

The 1989 elections were unfair in every aspect. Even so, Guillermo Endara, the presidential candidate of the Democratic Alliance of Civic Opposition (ADOC), defeated the PRD's Carlos Duque by nearly 3-to-1. Noriega annulled the vote, abolished the legislature and declared himself head of state.

On 20 December 1989, following Noriega's removal during a U.S. military invasion, Endara was sworn in as president. His running mates, Christian Democrat Ricardo Arias Calderon and Guillermo "Billy" Ford of the Molirena party, were sworn in as vice-presidents. ADOC occupied a majority of legislative seats, while seven went to the PRD. Overseen by the U.S., the PDF was tranformed into a civilian-led police and renamed the Public Force (PF).

Under Endara the economy grew significantly, although some analysts say it was due to the country's reemergence as a drug-trafficking and money-laundering center. But unemployment remained at 20-25 percent and poverty increased, fueling social unrest and violent crime. Polls showed that because of insecurity and economic fears up to 70 percent of Panamanians wanted U.S. troops and their economic contribution to remain after 1999, the year the U.S. bases are to be dismantled under the 1977 treaties. Meanwhile, with charges of corruption swirling around his government, Endara became increasingly unpopular and ADOC unraveled when the Christian Democrats split off in 1992.

By the end of 1993 the three main presidential candidates were Perez Balladares, singer-actor Ruben Blades, who had founded Papa Egoro, a political party whose name means "Mother Earth" in one of Panama's indigenous languages, and Ruben Carles, a former official in the Endara government. Perez Balladares, a forty-seven-year-old millionaire and former banker, removed some of the Noriega taint by re-identifying the PRD with its late founder, Torrijos. As Perez Balladares moved into the lead, former ADOC parties tried and failed to unite against him, then attempted to tar him with the Noriega legacy.

On 8 May 1994 Perez Balladares won with 33.3 percent of the vote. The surprise was the close second-place finish by Mireya Moscoso de Gruber of Endara's Arnulfista party. De Gruber had distanced herself from Endara and run under the mantle of her late husband, Arnulfo Arias, the anti-military founder of the party. Blades and Carles came in third and fourth, respectively, while the Christian Democrat candidate trailed badly. Blades resigned as Papa Egoro leader after the vote. The PRD won thirty-two of seventy-one seats in the Legislative Assembly and, with the support of allied parties that won six seats, achieved an effective majority.

Perez Balladares kept a campaign promise by choosing for his cabinet technocrats and politicians from across the ideological spectrum. His conciliatory efforts did not sit well among Noriega cronies within the PRD. Nonetheless, backed by moderates and businessmen within the party, he introduced a plan to attract foreign investment through privatization and reduced tariffs, and sought friendly relations with the U.S. Despite his pragmatic approach, opposition parties remained hostile and suspicious. He also faced a legacy of deep-seated official corruption and the transition of the control of the canal.

Political Rights and Civil Liberties:

The 1994 national and local elections were free and fair. Under the 1993 electoral code there is an independent electoral commission, direct election of municipal officials and a provision that places the police under the authority of the electoral commission during elections.

Freedom of organization, assembly and religion are generally respected. More than a dozen political parties from across the political spectrum participated in the 1994 elections.

The media are a raucous assortment of radio and television broadcasts, daily newspapers and weekly publications. There are six television stations and dozens of radio stations. The 1994 election featured a televised presidential debate. President Perez Balladares promised to eliminate restrictive media laws dating back to the Noriega regime, laws the Endara government (1990-94) used to harass journalists, but he had not done so by December 1994.

There are a number of independent human rights organizations. The Endara government was open to investigations by international human rights organizations, and accepted the jurisdiction of the Inter-American Human Rights Court. There were no indications the new Perez Balladares government would alter the policy.

The former Panamanian Defense Forces (PDF), dismantled after the 1989 U.S. invasion, constitutionally ceased to exist after the legislature formally abolished the military in October 1994. The civilian-run Public Force (national police) that replaced the PDF is poorly disciplined and prone to corruption and physical abuse. It includes former lower-ranking military officers whose loyalty to democracy remains in question. It has been ineffectual against the drug trade as Panama remains a money-laundering hub and a major transshipment point for both cocaine and illicit arms.

The judiciary, cowed into submission under Noriega through bribery and intimidation, was revamped in 1990. Then-president Endara replaced all nine Supreme Court judges. The new Court in turn appointed thirteen new members to the nineteen-seat Superior Court and replaced two-thirds of the forty-eight lower court justices.

The judicial system remains overwhelmed and its administration is inefficient, politicized, and undermined by the corruption endemic to all public and governmental bodies. During the U.S. invasion, the Supreme Court building was sacked by looters and hundreds of thousands of court records were destroyed. The disarray is compounded by an unwieldy criminal code and a surge in cases, many involving grievances against former soldiers and officials accumulated over two decades of military rule. In September 1994 Perez Balladares caused controversy by granting pardons to 217 members of the former Noriega regime who had been jailed since 1989, many without being formerly charged. The pardon did not cover a handful of ex-officials charged with serious human rights violations.

In 1994 there were nearly 18,000 court cases pending, with the numbers climbing due to a drug-fueled crime wave. Less than 15 percent of the nation's prison inmates had been tried and convicted. The penal system is marked by violent disturbances in decrepit facilities packed with up to eight times their intended capacity. The country has barely more than twenty public defenders.

Labor unions are well organized and public sector workers have generous benefits and job security. However, the Endara government was hostile to labor and did not comply with an International Labor Organization recommendation that public workers fired in a mass dismissal in 1991 be reinstated. In 1994 unions were concerned that Perez Balladares's call for a public debate on the labor code was a prelude to curtailing labor rights. According to UNICEF the workforce includes more than 60,000 children making less than the monthly minimum wage of $150.

Since 1993 indigenous groups have protested the encroachment of illegal settlers on Indian lands and delays by the government in formally demarcating the boundaries of those lands.

Papua New Guinea

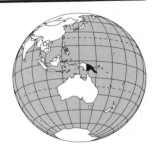

Polity: Parliamentary democracy (insurgency)
Economy: Capitalist
Population: 4,041,000
PPP: $1,550
Life Expectancy: 55.3
Ethnic Groups: A multi-ethnic, multi-tribal state—some 1,000 indigenous tribes

Political Rights: 2
Civil Liberties: 4
Status: Partly Free

Overview:
In August 1994 parliament elected Sir Julius Chan as Papua New Guinea's prime minister. This followed the Supreme Court's invalidation of his predecessor's efforts a year earlier to secure immunity from no-confidence motions. Chan's attempts at promoting a peace settlement to end a six-year-old armed secessionist conflict on Bougainville Island collapsed after rebel leaders broke off negotiations.

This South Pacific country, consisting of the eastern part of New Guinea and some 600 smaller islands, won independence from Australia on 16 September 1975. The country's parliamentary democracy has been undermined by rampant political corruption and weak party structures that cause MPs to switch parties frequently. Other obstacles arise from the extreme cultural differences between the cities and the remote highlands, and the presence of some 1,000 tribes speaking 700 languages.

The country's fifth post-independence elections in June 1992 involved some 1,650 candidates running for the 89 nationally elected and 20 provincial-based seats in the unicameral *Bese Taubadadia Hegogo* (House of Assembly). Few of the sixteen competing parties had any real platforms or ideologies. At least 89 of the 109 MPs in the outgoing parliament faced investigation on corruption charges.

Final results gave the ruling, urban-based Papua New Guinea United Party (Pangu Pati), which had held 30 seats, only 19; People's Democratic Movement (PDM) 15; People's Action Party, (PAP), 13; People's Progressive Party (PPP), 10; Melanesian Alliance, 9; League of National Advancement, 5; National Party, 2; Melanesian United Front, 1; independents, 34; vacant, 1. On 17 July the new parliament narrowly elected a former prime minister, PDM leader Paias Wingti, to the top spot again over the incumbent, the Pangu Pati's Rabbie Namaliu.

The leading political issue in 1993 involved Wingti's so-called "political coup," under which the prime minister quietly resigned on the night of 23 September and got himself re-elected with fifty-nine votes the next day. This allowed Wingti to take advantage of a 1991 constitutional amendment granting a new prime minister eighteen months of immunity from no-confidence motions.

In August 1994 the Supreme Court invalidated Wingti's election and ordered a new leadership poll. Wingti decided not to run, and on 30 August parliament elected fifty-five-year-old Sir Julius Chan, the deputy premier and leader of the PPP who had held the top job in 1980-82, in a sixty-nine to thirty-two vote over former speaker Bill Skate.

Chan took immediate steps toward ending the conflict on the island of Bougainville, 560 miles northeast of the capital, where a low-grade but deadly insurgency entered its sixth year. In December 1988 miners, landowners and their supporters began staging guerrilla attacks on the massive Australian-owned copper and gold mine at Panguna to demand compensation and a 50 percent share of the profits. The mine closed in May 1989, but the newly styled Bougainville Revolutionary Army (BRA) then declared an independent Republic of Bougainville. In May 1990 government troops began blockading Bougainville, leaving some 150,000 people without adequate supplies.

In late August 1994 the army closed in on the Panguna mine, which had been a rebel stronghold. In early September Chan signed a preliminary peace pact with BRA leaders, and a cease-fire went into effect on 9 September. However, the agreement all but collapsed after BRA leaders Francis Ona and Sam Kauona boycotted a one-week peace conference held in mid-October in Arawa, the provincial capital of Bougainville, claiming that government soldiers planned to kidnap them. By year's end the BRA had committed at least two major breaches of the cease-fire. More than 300 government soldiers and BRA guerrillas have been killed in direct fighting, and several hundred islanders have died from lack of food and medical supplies.

In a related development, in December 1994 the Chan government announced it would take legal action against the premiers of the country's four other island-based provinces to prevent them from taking steps toward independence. Former prime minister Wingti had proposed eliminating all nineteen mainland and island-based provincial governments on the grounds that they had done little to promote rural development and are riddled with corruption. This provoked the island-based provinces to consider an independent Federated Melanesian Republic.

In another issue, the 5 June 1994 *New York Times* reported that foreign logging companies continue to take advantage of mostly illiterate villagers by offering an average of $24 for trees that have market rates of $600. The companies have also largely reneged on promises to improve areas by building schools and hospitals. Government forestry officials and a judge who headed a 1989 government inquiry on logging practices have been attacked and subjected to death threats, allegedly by logging interests.

Political Rights and Civil Liberties: Citizens of Papua New Guinean can change their government democratically. The June 1992 elections were generally free and fair, but irregularities occurred in the rural highlands regions and at least thirty ballot boxes were destroyed. According to the U.S. State Department, in post-election violence following provincial elections in Simbu Province in July 1993 at least nineteen people were reportedly killed. Official corruption is rampant and politicians often resort to patronage or bribing tribal leaders to win elections.

Bands of criminals known as "rascals" have created a severe urban law and order crisis. In response, in May 1993 parliament approved changes to several laws and passed two new laws, the Internal Security Act (ISA) and the Repatriation Act. Local courts are now prohibited from granting bail for serious crimes, and national courts can refuse bail. The ISA also allows the government to restrict the movement of anyone convicted under the Act or considered likely to commit an offense covered under the Act. Stiffer penalties are provided for carrying and using firearms and illicit drugs. Parliament is considering legislation that would place the burden of proof on the defendant in trials involving rapes, armed robbery and other violent crimes. In October 1994 the assistant police commissioner of Port Moresby ordered police to shoot to kill anyone who provokes an armed confrontation with them.

The judiciary is independent of the government and the accused have due process rights. The undisciplined police force continues to commit rights abuses. Detainees and prisoners are frequently abused, often by intoxicated officers. In recent years police have reportedly burnt homes to punish highlands communities suspected of harboring criminals or of participating in tribal warfare, or to punish crimes committed by individuals.

Both the Defense Forces and the Bougainville Revolutionary Army are accused of torture, disappearances and extrajudicial executions against combatants and civilians. In April 1994 the Catholic Bishops Conference of Papua New Guinea reported that rebel soldiers are being "killed like pigs and buried like dogs" by untrained militias backed by the army that carry out "payback" murders. Civilian administration has broken down on Bougainville, and there are acute shortages of food and medicine in government and rebel-held areas. Some 45,000 Bougainvillians live in army-run "care centers" on the island, and are subject to rape and restrictions on movement.

Women face significant social discrimination according to traditional practices. Domestic violence and rape are serious problems throughout the country. Independent media have contributed to the country's democratic system, although journalists are not allowed full access to Bougainville. The state-run National Broadcasting Commission (NBC) generally exercises full independence in its news coverage. In April 1994 the Wingti government drew criticism after it banned NBC from reporting on a conference of premiers of five secessionist-minded island provinces.

Police approval for public demonstrations is occasionally refused on public safety grounds. There is full freedom of religion. Freedom of movement is unrestricted, except on Bougainville. Workers are free to join independent unions and to strike. The International Labor Organization has criticized a law allowing the government to invalidate arbitration agreements or wage awards not considered in the national interest.

Paraguay

Polity: Presidential-legislative democracy (military influenced)
Economy: Capitalist-statist
Population: 4,771,000
PPP: $3,420
Life Expectancy: 67.2

Political Rights: 4*
Civil Liberties: 3
Status: Partly Free

Ethnic Groups: Mostly mestizo; small Indian, white, black minorities
Ratings Change: *Paraguay's political rights rating declined from 3 to 4 as a result of increased influence of the military over the civilian government.

Overview:

During a year marked by peasant protests and labor strikes, the armed forces, especially army commander Gen. Lino Oviedo, asserted increased control over the government of President Juan Carlos Wasmosy, which further undermined the integrity of already weak civilian rule.

After the 1989 coup led by Gen. Andres Rodriguez, which ended the thirty-five-year dictatorship of Gen. Alfredo Stroessner, the new government initiated a period of liberalization. Rodriguez, who took over Stroessner's Colorado Party, promised full democracy by 1993 and was easily elected in May 1989 to finish Stroessner's last presidential term. Opposition parties led by the Authentic Radical Liberal Party (PLRA) had threatened to boycott the vote unless Stroessner's constitution and electoral laws were reformed. In the end they did participate and won a number of seats in the legislature.

Electoral laws were later reformed and the voting list was revised. A system of multi-party ballots and the practice of inking voters' fingers to prevent repeat voting were introduced. In 1991 Carlos Filizzola, a political independent, was elected mayor of Asuncion, the first time the Colorado Party had lost a major election since 1947.

The Colorados won a majority in the 1991 vote for a constituent assembly, which produced a constitution that went into effect in June 1992. It provides for a president, vice president and a bicameral Congress consisting of a forty-five-member Senate and an eighty-member Chamber of Deputies elected for five-year terms. The president is elected by a simple majority and reelection is prohibited. The constitution bars the military from engaging in politics. But the tradition of military interference has remained strong. In the 1992 Colorado primary election Luis Maria Argana, an old-style machine politician, defeated construction tycoon Wasmosy. Rodriguez and Oviedo helped engineer a highly dubious re-count that made Wasmosy the winner. Rodriguez backed Wasmosy because of Argana's ties to Stroessner, in exile across the border in Brazil.

Opposition parties, fearing further military interference, threatened to boycott the national election. But they went ahead after the Organization of American States (OAS), Jimmy Carter and other observers announced they would monitor the process.

The campaign became a three-man race between Wasmosy, longtime PLRA leader Domingo Laino, and Guillermo Caballero Vargas, a wealthy businessman and leader of the newly formed National Unity coalition. Wasmosy promised to modernize the economy. Laino played on his decades of resistance against Stroessner. Caballero

Vargas, a centrist, campaigned as someone free of the politics of the past. Every poll showed Wasmosy trailing until three weeks before the election. Then, Gen. Oviedo threatened a coup if the Colorado Party lost and stated the military "would govern together with the glorious Colorado Party forever and ever."

The 9 May 1993 election was marked by numerous irregularities, including vote buying, manipulation of registration lists, and military intimidation of voters. Officially, Wasmosy won with 40.3 percent of the vote, with Laino taking 32 percent and Caballero Vargas 23.5 percent. Carter and the OAS conveniently concluded the irregularities did not affect the outcome. But it was evident that fear played a key role in how people voted.

In the congress the Colorados won 20 of 45 Senate seats—ten pro-Argana and 10 pro-Wasmosy. The PLRA won 17 and National Unity 8. In the Chamber of Deputies the Colorados won 38 of 80 seats—22 pro-Argana and 16 pro-Wasnmosy. The PLRA won 33 and National Unity 9.

After the election Oviedo was promoted to army commander and has since become the most powerful officer in the armed forces. Wasmosy, constitutionally commander-in-chief but beholden to Oviedo, has allowed Oviedo to eliminate rivals from within the military by retiring them. Oviedo, backed by a hard-line Colorado faction that included a number of Stroessnerists, appeared to be using Wasmosy as a stepping stone for achieving the presidency himself.

In November 1994 three generals ordered into retirement publicly criticized Wasmosy and Oviedo. Wasmosy ordered them jailed for ten to thirty days. In December there were indications that other disenchanted officers might be moving against Oviedo, raising the specter of Paraguay returning to its coup-ridden past. Wasmosy denied there were problems within the military.

The threat of a breakdown of formal democracy came in the wake of widespread peasant and labor protests. In the spring peasant movements protesting low cotton prices and demanding land had blocked highways and demonstrated in Asuncion. Urban labor unions, protesting Wasmosy's privatization program, backed the peasants and on 2 May unions and peasant groups carried out the first general strike since 1958. The government responded with repressive tactics that led to at least one death and dozens of injuries, then offered to negotiate. Talks brought an end to the clashes but did not resolve the issues.

In October strong undercurrents of drug corruption and violence burst into the open when Gen. Ramon Rosa Rodriguez, the country's anti-drug chief, was murdered by one of his own men. Colombia's Cali cartel has expanded operations in Paraguay and accusations of high official involvement in drugs date back to the 1980s. By the end of 1994 the murder had not been resolved amid rumors that Cali had Rosa Rodriguez killed because he was involved in a U.S. Drug Enforcement Administration sting operation.

Political Rights and Civil Liberties: The 1992 constitution provides for regular elections at the national and municipal levels. However, there were serious irregularities in the 1993 national elections, including incidents of fraud and military interference. Overall, the inordinate and illegal influence of the military greatly undermines the authority of the civilian government.

Constitutional guarantees regarding political and civic organization and religious expression are generally respected. However, political and civic expression are at times restricted by the government's resort to repressive tactics during demonstrations and protests and the weak rule of law.

Peasant and Indian organizations demanding land often meet with police crackdowns, detentions, and forced evictions by vigilante groups in the employ of large landowners. More than a dozen peasants have been killed in the ongoing disputes. Activist priests who support land reform are frequently targets of intimidation. The government's promise of land reform has been largely unfulfilled, as nearly 80 percent of agricultural land remains in the hands of foreign companies and a few hundred Paraguayan families.

There are numerous trade unions and two major union federations. Labor actions are often broken up violently by the police and military and labor activists detained, as was the case during the May 1994 general strike. The 1992 constitution gives public sector workers the right to organize, bargain collectively and to strike, but these rights are often not respected in practice. A new labor code designed to protect worker rights was passed in October 1993 but enforcement has been weak.

The constitution establishes the separation of powers between the three branches of government. But the judiciary remains under the influence of the ruling party and the military, susceptible to the corruption that pervades all public and governmental institutions, and mostly unresponsive to human rights groups presenting cases of rights violations. Allegations in 1994 included illegal detention by police and torture during incarceration, particularly in rural areas. Rights groups are able to present cases to the Inter-American Human Rights Court, whose jurisdiction Paraguay recognized in 1993.

Under the 1992 constitution Supreme Court judges are to be nominated by a pluralistic magistrate council. The formation of the council was delayed by the executive as it sought to retain control of the judiciary. The council was finally formed in October 1994, but the old Supreme Court remained in place at the end of the year. Earlier, pressured by the military, the Court had declared unconstitutional a law passed by the congress that would have stripped police and soldiers of their traditional membership in the ruling Colorado party.

There are both publicly and privately owned media. State-run broadcast media present pluralistic points of view and there are a number of independent newspapers. However, journalists investigating corruption remain subject to intimidation and violent attacks, and the case of Santiago Leguizamon, a reporter murdered in 1991, remains unresolved. During the 1994 general strike, with the government sounding increasingly antagonistic toward the media, there were numerous unprovoked attacks against journalists by police and security forces. Also, while the constitution establishes safeguards for free expression, there are vague, potentially restrictive clauses regarding "responsible" behavior of journalists and media owners.

Peru

Polity: Presidential-mil-
itary (insurgencies)
Economy: Capitalist-
statist
Population: 22,914,000
PPP: $3,110
Life Expectancy: 63.6

Political Rights: 5
Civil Liberties: 4*
Status: Partly Free

Ethnic Groups: Complex, Indian of Inca descent (45 percent),
Caucasian (10 percent), and mixed (45 percent)
Ratings Change: *Peru's civil liberties rating changed from 5 to 4 as a
result of the weakening of guerrilla groups and fewer terrorist attacks.

Overview:
President Alberto Fujimori deployed the military and state
intelligence, the principal pillars of his regime, in an effort
to steamroll opposition candidates, including former
United Nations secretary general Javier Perez de Cuellar, in the presidential
elections scheduled for 9 April 1995.

Since gaining independence in 1821 Peru has been marked by periods of civilian
and military rule. After twelve years of military dictatorship (1968-80) civilian rule was
restored with the enactment of a democratic constitution and the election of conservative
President Fernando Belaunde in 1980. Alan Garcia of the center-left American Popular
Revolutionary Alliance (APRA) was the elected president in 1985-90.

In the 1990 election Fujimori, an obscure agricultural engineer and son of Japanese
immigrants, defeated novelist Mario Vargas Llosa by projecting himself as a political
outsider. Lacking an organized political party, Fujimori turned to the military to shore up
his government. By early 1992 the normally feckless Congress was uniting against his
authoritarian style, the Maoist Shining Path guerrillas were mounting a concerted attack
on urban centers and the 120,000-man army seemed overmatched.

On 5 April 1992 Fujimori, backed by the military, suspended the constitution,
dissolved the Congress and took control of the judiciary. The self-coup was popular
because of people's disdain for Peru's corrupt, elitist political establishment, their
fear of the Shining Path, and because Fujimori had ended hyper-inflation.

Fujimori's self-coup was orchestrated by Vladimiro Montesinos, the *de facto*
head of the National Intelligence Service (SIN), who engineered the support of the
military. Montesinos, a cashiered army officer and lawyer, specialized in defending
drug traffickers prior to becoming Fujimori's chief advisor in 1989. The U.S. and
other industrialized democracies suspended aid and the Organization of America
States (OAS) demanded the restoration of democratic rule.

In November 1992 Fujimori held a state-controlled election for an eighty-
member constituent assembly to replace the Congress. His patchwork New
Majority-Change 90 coalition won forty-four seats and Fujimori stated that the
exercise was "the formalization of the 5th of April."

In 1993 the assembly drafted a constitution that, in effect, ratified Fujimori's
authoritarian rule. It was narrowly approved in a state-controlled referendum and

enacted at the end of 1993. The process was inherently unfair as Fujimori drew heavily on state resources and the military for a massive "yes" campaign. He made great propaganda use of the 1992 capture of Shining Path leader Abimael Guzman.

Fujimori's political acrobatics assuaged the U.S. and the OAS and Peru was reinserted into the international financial community, which was enamored of Fujimori's economic liberalization.

By mid-1994 polls showed Perez de Cuellar, who vowed to end the Fujimori "dictatorship," running close behind Fujimori. Fujimori responded with a massive nationwide public-spending campaign that utilized all the resources of the state and was supported by the military. The SIN was employed to spy on and discredit the campaigns of Perez de Cuellar and another promising candidate, Alejandro Toledo, a mestizo and internationally trained economist.

By the end of 1994 Fujimori's poll ratings remained at around 45 percent, but Perez de Cuellar had dropped to 20 percent or less. Fujimori also seemed to benefit from the steady decline of the Shining Path since the capture of Guzman. Nonetheless, polls showed an increase in undecideds and local analysts recalled that Peru's notoriously volatile electorate had suddenly turned against Vargas Llosa, who in 1990 had been the clear front-runner only months before the vote.

Fujimori also clashed with his wife, Susana Higuchi. After she criticized his government for alleged corruption, he "fired" her as First Lady. She moved out of the presidential palace and announced she would run against him. When the electoral commission disqualified her for lacking the required number of valid signatures, she charged that the computer list of her newly formed Harmony 21st Century party had been tampered with by the SIN. In December she announced her candidacy for congress and said that she would seek to divorce Fujimori. Her political impact, however, seemed to hinge on whether she could offer proof of alleged official corruption.

Political Rights and Civil Liberties:

The Fujimori government is a presidential-military regime dressed in the trappings of formal democracy. The military functions virtually as the president's political party. Military commander Gen. Nicolas Hermoza has remained in his post for over three years even though he has surpassed the age for active duty. Management of the congress and the political landscape is conducted through the National Intelligence Service (SIN), unofficially headed by Fujimori's top aide, Vladimiro Montesinos.

Under the constitution installed in December 1993 the president can rule virtually by decree. In the event of a "grave conflict" between the executive and the legislature, the president can dissolve the congress, as Fujimori did in 1992. The constitution overturned Peru's tradition of no reelection and Fujimori's legal aides say he can stay in power until 2005, because his election in 1995 would mark his first term under the new constitution.

The old bicameral legislature was replaced by an elected unicameral Congress. Municipal governments are still elected, but the former system of semi-autonomous regions governed by elected bodies was abolished in favor of virtual military administration in the nation's twelve administrative areas.

The national election commission was purged in 1992 and brought under the control of the executive. The coalition of political parties and civic groups that campaigned against the constitution in 1993 were subject to threats and physical intimidation by the military and the SIN.

In 1994 a new, nominally independent election commission was named and it agreed to cooperate with international observers. But the commission's attempts to limit the overwhelming advantages of the presidential-military regime in the 1994-95 campaign were mostly blocked by the regime-controlled Congress. Also, the government limited the commission's budget. That meant the electoral authorities would continue to depend on the military, which traditionally has carried out the electoral legwork—including the distribution and retrieval of ballots—and conducted oversight of polling stations. There was also evidence that the military, which is barred from voting, had come into possession of an undetermined number of voter registration cards, and that the SIN was being used to spy on and sabotage opposition party campaigns.

Fujimori shut down the judicial system in 1992, overhauled it and in effect made it an arm of the executive. Files on military corruption and its involvement in drug-trafficking were removed from the courts.

Under international pressure the government implemented judicial reforms in 1994 and a new Supreme Court was named. But the independence of the judiciary remained suspect, and events earlier in the year involving the "La Cantuta" case indicated the regime remained ready to override any legal or constitutional norms when its interests were at stake.

In 1993 the government systematically tried to cover up the murders of nine students and a professor abducted from La Cantuta University in 1992. Documents leaked to opposition legislators from within the military indicated they were killed by a military death squad with the knowledge and approval of the military high command and the SIN. Under international pressure, a handful of mid-ranking officers and soldiers were arrested and charged in a civilian court. Previously, all rights abuses involving the military were handled by military courts which generally exonerated officers and soldiers.

In February 1994 the government overrode the constitution when Fujimori and the Congress pressured the Supreme Court to divert the Cantuta case to a closed military tribunal. The result was a rapid, scapegoat sentencing of the accused and impunity for Gen. Hermoza and Montesinos and their respective institutions.

Moreover, a draconian anti-terrorist law decreed in 1992 remained in effect in 1994. It practically eliminated judicial guarantees, substituting a system of military tribunals with anonymous judges installed to try alleged guerrillas. Defense lawyers are not allowed to call witnesses, government witnesses are unidentified, and sentences are handed down within hours. In 1994 there were continued reports of torture by police and prison guards. Amnesty International said there were at least two hundred prisoners of conscience in 1994, in addition to nearly 4,000 prisoners jailed under the anti-terrorism law.

The summary-trial system is probably a factor in the reduced number of disappearances (from nearly 200 in 1992 to a dozen or so in 1994) because it performs virtually the same function as physical elimination.

Peru's human rights groups calculate that since 1993 more than 15,000 people have been arrested, with hundreds receiving life sentences for alleged terrorist activities. The office of Public Defender called for by the constitution to protect constitutional rights had yet to be established by the Congress at the end of 1994.

While the government and the military respond to international criticism with commitments to improving respect for human rights, they assail Peru's human rights groups as apologists for the Shining Path, even though rights groups duly report guerrilla violations. Rights activists in 1994 continued to be subject to anonymous threats and violent intimidation by security forces.

The weakening of the Shining Path since the capture of its leader in 1992 has led to a sharp reduction in political violence. Local analysts gauged that guerrilla actions decreased in 1994 by at least 70 percent. The climate of terror that reigned throughout the country for years diminished significantly, particularly in the cities. Nonetheless, a state of emergency remained in place for over half the population.

A new labor code restricts collective bargaining rights and authorizes the government to break up any strike it deems to be endangering a company, an industry, or the public sector. Labor leaders who oppose privatizing state industries are subject to jail sentences of up to six years. In 1994 labor leaders who went to the United States to criticize the government's failure to comply with international labor standards were called "traitors to the state" by government officials and threatened with imprisonment. Labor activists remain targets of the Shining Path but to a lesser degree than in recent years. Forced labor, including that of children, is prevalent in the gold-mining regions of the Amazon.

The press is largely private. Radio and television are both private and public. State-owned media are blatantly progovernment. Since 1992 many media and journalists have been pressured into self-censorship or exile by a broad government campaign of intimidation—death threats, libel suits, withholding of advertising, police harassment, arbitrary detentions and physical mistreatment. Since 1993, between fifteen and thirty journalists have been in jail at any one time, many of them in the provinces, most of them charged with "apology for terrorism."

Philippines

Polity: Presidential-legislative democracy (insurgencies)
Economy: Capitalist-statist
Population: 68,726,000
PPP: $2,440
Life Expectancy: 64.6
Ethnic Groups: Christian Malay (92 percent), Muslim Malay (4 percent), Chinese (2 percent)

Political Rights: 3
Civil Liberties: 4
Status: Partly Free

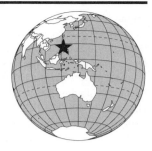

Overview:

Philippines President Fidel Ramos continued to bring political stability and respect for human rights to a country struggling to catch up economically to its generally authoritarian neighbors. The president is looking to boost his Lakas-National Union of Christian Democrats' (Lakas-NUCD) standing in House and Senate elections scheduled for 1995.

The Philippines, an archipelago of 7,100 islands in Southeast Asia, achieved independence in 1946 after forty-three years of U.S. colonial rule and subsequent occupation by the Japanese during World War II. Strongman Ferdinand Marcos ruled for twenty-one years until he was deposed in the February 1986 "people power" revolution, when thousands protested his "victory" over Corazon Aquino in massively rigged elections.

After several top military officials declared their support for Aquino, including acting army chief of staff Fidel Ramos, Marcos fled the country and Aquino took office. A new "U.S.-style" constitution approved in February 1987 provides for a directly elected president (the vice-president is elected separately) who is limited to a single six-year term and a bicameral Congress consisting of a twenty-four-member Senate and a House of Representatives with 201 directly elected members and up to fifty more appointed by the president. The president cannot impose martial law for more than sixty days without congressional approval.

In August 1987 Aquino survived the first of seven coup attempts, mostly by right wing elements of the military. During her term Aquino initiated needed macroeconomic reforms and set the groundwork for a peaceful democratic transfer of power. However, deeper reforms were impossible due to the fragile support she received from the military.

Constitutionally prevented from running again, Aquino supported Ramos in the May 1992 presidential election, which turned into a wide open, seven-candidate race. Ramos won the 11 May balloting with just 23.5 percent of the vote, beating former immigration commissioner Miriam Defensor Santiago by only 800,000 out of 23 million votes cast. Onetime actor Jaime Estrada won the vice-presidential race. In concurrent lower House balloting, the centrist Democratic Filipino Struggle (LDP) coalition won 87 seats; Ramos' Lakas-NUCD; 51; the conservative National People's Coalition, 48; and the centrist Liberal Party, 15. On 30 June Ramos took office in the first peaceful transition of power since Marcos' election in 1965.

Ramos inherited a country that had gone from being the richest in Southeast Asia in the 1950s to one in which official corruption and patronage and business oligarchies have impoverished up to 70 percent of the citizens. By 1993 Ramos had established a degree of political stability by increasing his Lakas-NUCD's representation to at least 112 seats through defections, with some 159 Representatives overall belonging to the pro-government Rainbow Coalition Alliance.

In August 1994 the Lakas-NUCD, now swelled to 130 House members, formed a coalition with the LDP to field a common slate for the twelve Senate seats up for election in 1995. The LDP had used its control of seventeen of the twenty-three Senate seats to block legislation and Ramos anticipated that the new coalition would help him get bills passed. However, by October the coalition appeared to be fraying over the choice of candidates for House of Representatives and gubernatorial elections also scheduled for 1995. The coalition had initially agreed upon an "equity of the incumbent" formula under which its support would go to incumbents who desired to run for re-election. However, Ramos later backtracked, saying that performance would also be a criterion and that five LDP-controlled provinces would not be covered under the incumbent formula. By year's end the coalition had all but collapsed.

The right-wing Reform the Armed Forces Movement, which launched the coup attempts against Aquino, has split into four groups and has not posed a threat to Ramos. However, the central government continues to face armed threats from a twenty-five-year-old Communist insurgency waged by the New People's Army (NPA) of the Communist Party of the Philippines (CPP) and a twenty-two-year-old Muslim separatist movement headed by the Moro National Liberation Front (MNLF) on southern Mindanao island that has killed some 50,000 people.

In September 1992 Ramos persuaded Congress to scrap the 1957 Anti-Subversion Act that had outlawed the CPP, and released two top Communist prisoners, Satur Ocampo and Romulo Kintanar, former head of the NPA. Ramos reasoned that bringing the movement above ground would weaken its support and make negotiations easier. The NPA is down from a peak of 25,000 guerrillas in the late 1980s to fewer than 10,000 today.

By March 1993 police had smashed the NPA's Red Scorpion Group that had been responsible for a wave of kidnappings that struck Manila in 1992, mostly against ethnic Chinese. Meanwhile, the CPP faced an internal crisis due to ideological rifts that pitted Netherlands-based leader Jose Maria Sison against a Manila-based faction headed by Filemon Lagman. In May 1994 the authorities captured Lagman, who had also controlled the CPP's Alex Boncayo Brigade, an urban terrorism outfit. Negotiations with Sison's faction bogged down in October over the group's insistence on safety and immunity guarantees that the government claimed would be tantamount to recognizing it as a sovereign body.

In January 1994 the government signed a cease-fire deal with the MNLF covering thirteen provinces on Mindanao and nearby Palawan Island. During the year the government continued peace talks with the rebels, who are calling for the government to fully implement a 1976 agreement giving autonomy to the thirteen provinces in question. The government has largely rejected this demand, citing a 1989 referendum in which only four non-contiguous provinces in Mindanao agreed to join what is now called the Muslim Autonomous Region.

The Ramos administration's economic liberalizations have resulted in lower interest rates and single-digit inflation. The Administration has also restored a normal electricity supply to the main island of Luzon, where industry had been plagued by widespread power shortages.

Political Rights and Civil Liberties: Filipinos can change their government democratically. Despite some charges of irregularities, the May 1992 elections were the freest since 1965, and altogether free of the wholesale fraud of the Marcos era. In the three months prior to the vote, pre-election violence claimed "only" seventy-one lives, less than half the total prior to the 1988 local elections. Power is disproportionately held by economic oligarchies, wealthy landowners and political elites. Official corruption reportedly costs the Philippines $3.6 billion annually.

The army and the 65,000-strong Citizens Armed Forces Geographical Units (CAFGU), a poorly trained paramilitary force used to maintain security in former Communist-controlled areas, are responsible for abuses including arbitrary arrests, disappearances and extrajudicial killings. Most of these violations occur during counterinsurgency operations, although reports of such abuses have declined in recent years. The security forces frequently link human rights activists to the Communist insurgency movement, and activists are occasionally subject to arbitrary arrest and in some cases torture and extrajudicial killings. Police and soldiers are also linked to protection rackets, illegal logging operations and other illicit activities.

The Communist insurgents are accused of extrajudicial executions, torture and kidnappings, as well as bombing attacks, assassinations and other forms of urban terrorism. Clashes between the army and Communist insurgents continue to occur. Muslim insurgents are also accused of kidnappings, extrajudicial executions and other rights violations. In June members of the Abu Sayyaf extremist group massacred fifteen Christian hostages on southern Basilan Island.

In April 1993 the Ramos administration began the largest police shakeup in the nation's history. The government ordered sixty-two top officers of the Philippine National Police Force into retirement on corruption charges, and officials said this weeding-out process may ultimately extend to 5,000 junior officers and thousands of patrolmen in the 98,000 strong force.

The government has pledged to dismantle the more than 500 private armies kept by politicians and wealthy landowners, many of which draw members from the police and the army and are responsible for extrajudicial killings. Critics say that confiscation of weapons has thus far made little practical headway, and that the strongest armies remain untouched.

The judiciary is independent of the government. The accused enjoy adequate due-process rights, but the system is backlogged and poorly administered, and judges are subject to bribery. Police are accused of torturing suspects, particularly during the interrogation phase.

Freedoms of speech and press are respected in practice, although journalists face intimidation outside Manila from illegal logging outfits, drug smugglers and others. In 1994 the Indonesian government put heavy pressure on the Philippine government to ban the private Asia Pacific Conference on East Timor scheduled for Manila in May. In a notable exception to its respect for freedom of expression and assembly, the Ramos Administration tried to ban the meeting on national security grounds. The Supreme Court overruled the government, but the authorities barred foreign participants from attending and turned away at least ten invitees at the airport including Mairead Maguire of Ireland, a 1976 Nobel Peace Laureate. During political demonstrations, police generally follow a policy of "maximum tolerance," giving nonviolent protesters substantial leeway.

Freedom of religion is respected. Trafficking of Filipino women abroad is a serious problem, and domestic prostitution is rampant. Rape and domestic violence are reportedly widespread. Child prostitution is also rampant, and cities have large numbers of street children. Citizens are free to travel internally and abroad, although military action by the army and Communist insurgents occasionally causes areas to be cordoned off.

Workers are free to join independent unions. The International Labor Organization has criticized provisions of the 1989 Labor Code that allow the government to order compulsory arbitration of disputes in industries deemed essential to the national interest. Other restrictions on the right to strike include a requirement for majority approval for a strike, and government-ordered mandatory cooling-off periods. Labor rights activists continue to be targeted for extrajudicial executions, although far less than in the past.

Poland

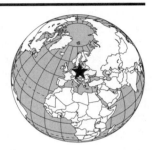

Polity: Presidential-parliamentary democracy
Economy: Mixed capitalist
Population: 38,564,000
PPP: $4,500
Life Expectancy: 71.5
Ethnic Groups: Polish, Ukrainian, Byelorussian, German, others

Political Rights: 2
Civil Liberties: 2
Status: Free

Overview:
In 1994 Poland's government of ex-Communists and their allies led by Prime Minister Waldemar Pawlak, faced political battles over the budget and the pace and scope of privatization. Other developments included worsening labor relations, local elections and growing controversy about President Lech Walesa's use of executive power in attempts to strengthen his grip on the military and media a year before presidential elections. Integration into European economic and security organizations remained a key issue.

In 1993, four years after round-table negotiations between the opposition and the ruling Communists ended decades of post-war Communist dominance, Poles swept former Communists back into power in September national elections. The Democratic Left Alliance (SLD) won 171 seats in the 460-seat Sejm (lower house), followed by the Peasant Party (PSL), a descendent of the Communist-era party, with 131 seats. The Democratic Union (UD), the mainstream Solidarity party, captured 74 seats. The year-old leftist Union of Labor (UP) won 41 seats. President Walesa's Non-Party Bloc to Support Reform (BBWR) gained 20 seats, while the nationalist Confederation for an Independent Poland (KPN) took 24. Waldemar Pawlak of the PSL was named prime minister.

In early February 1994 the first crisis of the four-month-old government was set off by the resignation of the finance minister, who authored an austerity budget favored by international financial institutions, and increased labor unrest that included a one-day strike in the arms industry and a Solidarity-led march of 30,000 urging the government to increase wages and spend more on welfare.

The fragile governing SLD-PSL coalition was divided over a program that would maintain tight monetary policy and continue market reforms. On 5 March parliament passed a $31.6 million budget draft that limited social spending and kept Poland on the road to free-market reforms. The budget, which was criticized by those who expected the new government to expand a social safety net in light of high unemployment and deteriorating living standards for many Poles, met International Monetary Fund (IMF) standards, allowing Poland to secure new loans. The passage of the budget draft led to a series of Solidarity warning strikes. On 18 March parliament approved anti-inflationary legislation aimed at curbing wage increases in state-owned enterprises. The legislation provided wage-control mechanisms that replaced a so-called excessive wage tax opposed by the trade unions.

On 7 April the ruling coalition suffered a setback in a political tug-of-war with President Walesa when it failed to muster the two-thirds majority needed to overrule his veto of the wage-control bill. The coalition's sixty-one trade union deputies voted with the opposition against the government. President Walesa had argued that the law would enable the government to extend controls to the private sector. Meanwhile, the popularity of Walesa, the former leader of the Solidarity union, continued to plummet, with one poll showing that he was less popular than Gen. Wojciech Jaruzelski, the Communist strongman who imposed martial law in 1981.

In late April, amid spreading strikes in the coal industry, Walesa approved the nomination of Grzegorcz Kolodko, an economist, as finance minister. To placate labor unrest, Kolodko said wage controls in state-run enterprises were not essential. The nationwide strike petered out following government concessions to brown coal miners and a decision by hard coal miners to suspend their protest.

On 11 May the government unveiled its economic plan, aimed at increasing the country's gross national product by 22 percent over four years. At the end of the month, tens of thousands of Solidarity supporters marched through Warsaw to demand the end of state-sector wage controls and the introduction of collective wage bargaining procedures throughout the economy. Throughout the summer there were strikes at the Fiat plant, and a seven-week sit-in strike at an Italian-owned steelworks.

In June the finance minister outlined a medium-term economic plan during IMF meetings that included reforms of the welfare system aimed at cutting budget spending, as well as consolidation and privatization of the banking system. In September, Poland signed agreements that cut nearly in half the country's $14 billion debt to foreign commercial banks. About 500 creditor banks, members of the so-called London Club, agreed to cut the debt by $6.6 billion. On 20 October Prime Minister Pawlak removed one of the last obstacles to the long delayed mass privatization program by approving over 100 companies for inclusion. The decision, which brought the number of companies to be transferred to the private sector up to 460, had been awaited by the privatization ministry since July. In signing the list, he removed sixteen entities, including meat, aluminum, grain, metal, and others he wanted to protect. The government planned to establish some fifteen national investment funds (NIFs), run jointly by foreign and local managers, which were to be handed equity in the 460 companies. At the time of the legislation, some 60 percent of Polish industry was in state hands.

In early November differences over privatization policies threatened to undermine the governing coalition. Wieslaw Kaczmarek, the SLD privatization minister, warned that delays in implementing mass privatization would jeopardize revenues from sales written into the 1995 budget.

In late November Walesa vetoed proposals to maintain income tax rates at 21, 33 and 45 percent in 1995. He said that the rates were raised from 20, 30 and 40 percent as a temporary measure in 1994 and should return to those levels in 1995. Parliament overruled his veto in early December.

By year's end Poland continued to have one of the fastest-growing economies outside southeast Asia. Industrial output rose by an extraordinary 13 percent over the first nine months of 1994. Exports in the same period increased by 23 percent, while imports were down. However, inflation jumped in the third quarter, and unemployment still stood at over 15 percent.

In the fall a new conflict between the government and President Walesa, who in June announced he would seek another term in 1995, broke out over control of the armed forces when Walesa asked Defense Minister Piotr Kolodziejczyk to resign. The move came after the defense minister opposed new draft laws that would bring the military under control of the general staff, answering directly to the president and sidelining the defense minister. Walesa faced stinging criticism from former allies, including Bronislaw Geremek, a Solidarity veteran and chairman of the UW parliamentary group, who told the president to his face: "You pose a threat to constitutional order and democracy in Poland." Parliament, in a nonbinding resolution, censured the president by a vote of 305 to 18 as a violator of the constitution and a danger to the state. Walesa was also accused of interfering in the allocation of television broadcasting licenses by the Radio and TV Council, an independent regulatory body. Licenses allegedly went to groups likely to support Walesa's political aims.

On 10 November Walesa dismissed Kolodziejczyk, one day after U.S. officials in Warsaw for talks on NATO expressed support for the defense minister by describing him as a "dedicated public servant." By late November, a permanent replacement had not been named.

In other issues, local elections on 19 June saw the SLD top other parties in votes for local councils in thirty of the forty-nine provincial capitals, but they failed to win outright majorities. Local governments were expected to be dominated by a coalition of the UW and rightist parties. At stake were over 52,100 seats in 2,383 local councils; turnout was between 25 and 30 percent, the lowest level since the fall of communism. The UW campaigned for more powers for local communities and accused the government of centralist tendencies.

In March the government announced that it would officially apply for full membership in the European Union (EU), and hoped that Poland, currently an associate member, could achieve the goal by the year 2000. In January, NATO announced that it was willing to hold joint military exercises with Polish forces in Poland. During a July visit to Warsaw, U.S. President Bill Clinton could not give Poland an official date for NATO membership, but he offered money to help the Polish armed forces convert their equipment and communications so they could work with NATO forces. In November, the last-minute postponement of a long delayed visit to Warsaw by Russian Prime Minister Victor Chernomyrdin was interpreted as confirmation that Russian efforts were under way to block new initiatives on NATO membership for Poland.

Political Rights and Civil Liberties: Poles have the means to change their government democratically under a multiparty system. In 1992 President Lech Walesa signed into law the so-called "Little Constitution," which gave considerable powers to the president and was vague on the specific division of powers between the executive, legislative and judicial branches.

The judiciary is not wholly free of interference from government, and financial and personnel woes continue to plague the justice ministry, the prosecutor's office and the courts. Most judges are holdovers from the Communist era. Political parties, parliamentary commissions, the State Security Office (under the jurisdiction of the minister of internal affairs), the government and the president's office continue to exert political pressure on the justice minister and prosecutors. In 1993 appellate courts were introduced into the judicial system. Penal and Penal Procedure Codes were reformed in 1989-90 with the removal of political provisions, and there have been far-reaching reforms in the prison system. In July the Sejm voted to reject four legislative drafts designed to screen high-ranking officials for past collaboration with the secret police. In August, two generals of the former Communist secret police were acquitted after a two-year trial in connection with the 1984 murder of Solidarity supporter Fr. Jerzy Popieluszko. Judge Jaroslaw Goral, speaking for the five-judge panel, ruled that "although the generals were probably responsible for the murder," there was no hard evidence to corroborate the accusation.

There is a bustling free and independent press, and 85 percent of the media is privatized. But significant restrictions remain on freedom of expression. Article 270 of the Penal Code states that anyone "who publicly insults, ridicules and derides the Polish nation, Polish People's Republic, its political system, or its principal organs" faces between six to eight months imprisonment. Article 273 imposes a term of up to ten years for anyone who violates Article 270 in print or through the mass media. In September, the Sejm approved the Official State Secrets Act, a measure calling for prison terms of up to ten years for anyone disclosing information interpreted as vital to Poland's interests.

The regulatory TV and Radio Council, set up in 1993 to oversee allocation of licenses for national and local radio and television, has been accused of bowing to the wishes of President Walesa, who appointed Janusz Zaorski as director of the licensing body. In August, police burst in on six local TV stations controlled by an Italian media owner, charging that his bid for a license had failed because more than 33 percent of the equity in the Polonia network was in foreign hands. In June the Constitutional Tribunal upheld a clause in the public broadcasting law requiring radio and TV programming to "respect Christian values."

Religious freedom is respected though there are charges that the Roman Catholic Church exercises too much influence on public life. The first Jewish school in Poland in twenty-five years opened in August. In 1994 both houses of parliament passed measures to ease the country's strict abortion law. President Walesa threatened to resign if he was forced to accept the law.

There is freedom of domestic and foreign travel, and no significant impediments to emigration. Freedoms of association and assembly are respected.

While the extant constitution guarantees equality of the sexes, women face discrimination in the job market. Anecdotal evidence suggests that there is a high level of domestic violence against women, particularly in rural areas and often involving alcoholism and spousal abuse.

As of January 1994 four national interbranch industrial unions were registered, along with seventeen other major independent industrial branch unions and three agricultural unions. The Independent Self-Governing Trade Union (NSZZ) Solidarity claims a membership of 2 million. Spin-offs from mainstream Solidarity include the Christian

Trade Union Solidarity (16,200 members) and Solidarity '80 (156,000 members). The National Alliance of Trade Unions (OPZZ), the successor of its Communist-era namesake, has about 3 million members and 61 parliamentary deputies. Other unions include the Free Miners' Union, which claims more than 300,000 members, and the National Teachers' Union. There were several major industrial and miners' strikes in 1994.

Portugal

Polity: Presidential-parliamentary democracy
Economy: Mixed capitalist
Population: 9,860,000
PPP: $9,450
Life Expectancy: 74.4
Ethnic Groups: Portuguese and Africans from former Portuguese colonies

Political Rights: 1
Civil Liberties: 1
Status: Free

Overview: **A**s Portugal celebrated the twentieth anniversary of the "Carnation Revolution" that ended forty-eight years of dictatorship, the country reassessed the mixed results of eleven years of Socialist leadership followed by nine years of governance by Social Democrats. In 1994 concerns about jobs and living standards were the underlying cause of public sector protests.

Located on the Atlantic coast of the Iberian peninsula, Portugal was a monarchy until a republic was declared in 1910. Antonio Salazar headed a fascist dictatorship from 1932 to 1968. His successor, Marcello Caetano, held power until 1974, when the leftist Armed Forces Movement overthrew the regime in a nonviolent half military putsch, half popular rebellion and festival. The military had become disenchanted and exhausted from fighting to retain Portuguese colonies in Africa. The transition to democracy began in 1975 with the election of a constituent assembly, which adopted a democratic socialist constitution.

The president is elected directly for a five-year term. The incumbent is the Socialist ex-Prime Minister, Mario Soares, who won election in 1986 and 1991. The president has a limited role as political arbiter and constitutional guardian. He serves as military chief of staff, and chairs the sixteen-member Council of State, a consultative body with powers of absolute veto in regard to defense and military policy. The next presidential election is scheduled for 1996. The president appoints a prime minister from the largest party or coalition in the 230-member Assembly of the Republic, the unicameral parliament.

Cavaco Silva, the current prime minister, heads the Social Democrats, the largest parliamentary party. Voters elect the parliamentarians by proportional representation for a maximum term of four years. The next general election will take place in October 1995. Cavaco Silva will either stand again as prime minister in the 1995 elections or run for the presidency in 1996.

After eight years of economic expansion, spearheaded by Silva, a technocrat who has consistently pursued a market-oriented course, Portugal plunged in 1993 into a recession that has exposed a society of stark contrasts. The benefits of the boom have been concentrated largely in the coastal region, and above all Lisbon, whereas the agrarian south known as the *Alentenjo,* is faced with an economic crisis. The flagging economy drew attention to issues less closely examined during the boom years. Lisbon, the largest beneficiary of modernization, is itself fringed with shantytowns (*bairros de lata*) that house destitute farm workers who have moved to the cities in search of work.

Other issues that have gained attention during the recession are illiteracy, child labor, and deficient education and health services. With the reversal of the post-revolutionary nationalization process, the re-privatization of banks and insurance companies has been nearly completed. Several of the seven family groups that accounted for almost three-quarters of the country's domestic product under the dictatorship of Salazar and later Caetano, have returned to Portugal to repurchase and reinvest assets confiscated after the revolution. Business confidence is weak but recovering. The recession, relatively mild by international standards, has made a strong impact in Portugal where unemployment has risen, but at 6.8 percent it is well under the 10.7 percent average EU rate.

As a result of economic stress highlighted by labor strife, the Socialists (PS) made gains at the Social Democrats' (PDS) expense in the local elections held in December 1993. Attacks on trucks of imported Spanish fish, public sector strikes in February 1994 to demand pay increases, and motorists' protests in June against toll increases were a sign of the government's waning popularity. The PDS and the PS, headed by António Guterres, who says his party represents a synthesis of traditional European social democracy and a left-wing liberalism originating in the U.S., will be the major contenders among the dozen political parties running in Portugal's elections during the next parliamentary and presidential elections.

The economic relationship between Portugal and Spain is growing through cross-border trade and investment, after decades of limited access to each other's markets. Portugal has been catching up with the rest of Europe with 0.88 percent annual growth, above the average European growth rate since Portugal joined the EU.

Political Rights and Civil Liberties: The Portuguese have the right to change their government democratically. Voters choose both the president and the parliament through direct, competitive elections. Portuguese living abroad have absentee voting rights and constitute a major portion of the electorate. Political association is unrestricted except for fascist organizations. However, members of some small extreme-right wing groups run candidates for public office without interference.

The print media are owned by political parties and private publishers. They are generally free and competitive. With the exception of *Radio Renascença,* a Catholic radio station, television and radio were state-owned until 1990. The government has introduced legislation to re-privatize state-run radio stations controlled by *Radiodifusao Portuguesa* (RDP). Television broadcasting is dominated by a state-owned station. Two independent stations, one owned by the Catholic Church, began operating in 1993. Portuguese have freedom of speech, but insulting the government or the armed forces is illegal if it is intended to undermine the rule of law. However, the state has not prosecuted anyone under this provision.

Catholicism is the religion of the majority, and there is religious freedom.

There are competing Communist and non-Communist labor organizations. Workers have the right to strike. Since 1992 the minimum employment age has been fifteen. It is to be raised to sixteen when the period of compulsory schooling is extended in January 1997. The two principal labor federations, the General Union of Workers (UGT) and the General Confederation of Portuguese Workers Intersindical (CGTP-IN), have charged that "clandestine" companies in the poor northern part of Portugal exploit child labor. There is freedom of assembly.

The status of women is improving with economic modernization. African immigrants face some discrimination. In 1993, President Soares and the parliament disputed restrictive legislation that would have ended asylum for humanitarian reasons and denied state subsidies to applicants awaiting asylum decisions. The legislators passed it twice over his objections.

Qatar

Polity: Traditional monarchy
Economy: Capitalist-statist
Population: 513,000
PPP: $14,000
Life Expectancy: 69.6
Ethnic Groups: Arab, Pakistani, Indian, Iranian

Political Rights: 7
Civil Liberties: 6
Status: Not Free

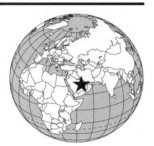

Overview: Located on the northern coast of the Arabian Peninsula, Qatar entered into a defense agreement with the British in 1916 and declared full independence in 1971. In 1972 Sheik Khalifa ibn Hamad Al Thani came to power by deposing his cousin, Emir Ahmad ibn 'Ali ibn 'Abdallah Al Thani, in a palace coup. Under the 1970 Basic Law, the Emir is chosen by and from adult males of the Al Thani family. The Basic Law also provides for a Council of Ministers and a largely elected *Majlis al-Shura* (Advisory Council). However, no elections have ever been held. Sheik Al Thani appoints the entire forty-member Majlis. In a rare public expression of political dissent, in December 1991 fifty prominent citizens signed a petition calling for democratic reforms. The government interrogated several signers and prevented three from leaving the country to attend a pro-democracy conference in Kuwait.

Key issues facing the country include security along the largely undefined border with Saudi Arabia, and economic development. In September 1992 Saudi troops attacked a Qatari border post and killed two guards. In December the countries established a committee to delineate the border by 1994, although formal boundaries have yet to be agreed upon. The country earns more than $2.5 billion a year from oil exports, and controls what is believed to be the world's largest natural gas field. A Japanese-financed project will build facilities to process and transport the gas to Far Eastern markets beginning in 1997.

Political Rights and Civil Liberties: Citizens of Qatar lack the democratic means to change their government. Political parties and political demonstrations are illegal, and there are no elections. The Emir holds absolute power, serves as prime minister and appoints the cabinet. In practice the Emir frequently consults with leading members of society on policy issues and works to reach a consensus with the appointed Majlis. The only recourse for individual citizens is to submit appeals or petitions to the Emir.

The security apparatus includes the Interior Ministry's *Mubahathat* (Investigatory Police), which handles sedition and espionage cases, and the military's *Mukhabarat* (Intelligence Service), which monitors political dissidents. Both services can detain suspects indefinitely without charge while conducting an investigation, although in practice long-term detention occurs infrequently. These two units and the Interior Ministry's regular police and General Administration of Public Security unit particularly monitor foreigners, who collectively outnumber Qataris four-to-one. Personal communications of some foreigners and dissidents are monitored.

Physical and sexual abuse of foreign nationals employed as domestic workers is a national problem. Although the authorities have investigated and punished several employers, most women apparently do not report abuse for fear of losing their residence permits.

The judiciary is not independent. Most judges are foreign nationals and the government can revoke their residence permits at any time. Civil courts have jurisdiction in civil and commercial disputes, while *Shari'a* courts handle family and criminal cases according to the country's Wahhabi Islamic tradition. In the Shari'a courts lawyers only help the participants prepare cases and are not permitted in the courtroom. Non-Muslims cannot bring suits as plaintiffs in the Shari'a courts. Caning is used as a punishment in accordance with Islamic law.

Freedoms of speech, expression and press are severely restricted. Public criticism of the ruling family or of Islam is not permitted. The privately owned press exercises significant self-censorship. The electronic media is state-owned and promotes the government's views. A government censorship board screens all locally published books as well as cultural items and performances. Academic freedom is not protected and professors reportedly practice self-censorship. Private associations are permitted but they must be nonpolitical in nature. Islam is the state religion, and followers of other faiths must worship privately and may not proselytize. Non-Muslims face discrimination in employment opportunities. Men may prevent wives and other female relatives from traveling abroad, and women must get permission from a male relative to apply for a driver's license. Children from South Asia and Africa are occasionally used as jockeys in camel races and face the threat of serious injury or death.

Workers cannot form labor unions or bargain collectively. Workers can belong to "joint consultative committees" composed of worker and management representatives that discuss issues including working conditions and work schedules. If a dispute arises, the government's Labor Conciliation Board attempts to mediate. If this fails, most workers, with the exception of government employees and domestic workers, can hold strikes. In practice, strikes rarely occur.

Romania

Polity: Presidential-parliamentary democracy
Economy: Mixed statist transitional
Population: 22,728,000
PPP: $3,500
Life Expectancy: 70.0
Ethnic Groups: Romanians (88 percent), Hungarians, Germans, Roma (Gypsies)
Political Rights: 4
Civil Liberties: 3*
Status: Partly Free
Ratings Change: *Romania's civil liberties rating changed from 4 to 3 because of the passing of a new law reforming the police.

Overview:

In 1994 the minority coalition government of Prime Minister Nicolae Vacaroiu and the ruling Party of Social Democracy of Romania (PSDR), essentially a descendant of the former Communist party, coped with the fifth no-confidence vote since 1992, a hung parliament, widespread labor unrest and sluggish economic reform.

Shaped by the geographic influence of the Carpathian Mountains and the Danube River, Romania originally consisted of the twin principalities of Walachia and Moldavia. It was overrun by the Ottoman Turks in the fifteenth century. The 1878 Berlin Congress recognized the country's independence. Romania made territorial gains as one of the victorious powers in World War I, but lost substantial areas to the Soviet Union and to Bulgaria in 1940 under threats from its neighbors and Nazi Germany. King Michael, who took advantage of the entry of Soviet troops in 1944 to dismiss the pro-German regime and switch to the allied side, was forced in 1945 to accept a Communist-led coalition government.

From 1965 to 1989 Romania was ruled by Nicolae Ceausescu, whose bizarre policies of forced urbanization, autarkic economics and cult of personality brought the country to the verge of economic ruin. A popular uprising in conjunction with a palace coup led by disgruntled Communist Party members forced him and his wife, Elena, to flee Bucharest. They were subsequently captured, tried and executed on Christmas 1989. The party's anti-Ceausescu clique had secretly established the National Salvation Front (NSF) and announced they had formed a provisional government under President Ion Iliescu, a hard-liner who oversaw extensive purges in Romania's universities in the 1950s.

The 1992 local and national elections saw growing factionalism in the NSF between the ruling neo-Communists and a more reformist opposition. President Iliescu and his newly formed Democratic National Salvation Front (DNSF) won, and were backed by the nationalist Greater Romania Party (PRM) and the pro-Communist Socialist Labor Party (SLP). Together the DNSF and the opposition coalition, the Democratic Convention (DC), won 166 of the 484 seats contested. The rump-NSF under former Prime Minister Petre Roman finished third with 61 seats. Four other parties won less than 50 seats: the ultranationalist Romanian National Unity Party (PRNU), the GRP, the SLP and the Agrarian Party. Vacaroiu, a financial expert with no party affiliation, was approved as prime minister by parliament in November.

In 1993 the DNSF merged with several smaller, extra-parliamentary parties and changed its name to the Party of Social Democracy of Romania (PSDR); in late May, the NSF merged with the Democratic Party and changed its name to the Democratic Party-NSF (DP-NSF).

Nineteen-ninety-four opened with a series of strikes and work stoppages. In January, the government asked the Supreme Court to halt a nationwide strike by 65,000 coal miners. The strike was suspended when the court ordered a thirty-day back-to-work order. In early February, about 800,000 workers joined a one-day warning strike to protest low wages in the face of 300 percent inflation and 10 percent unemployment. On 14 February, 15,000 coal miners went on strike in western Romania. At the end of the month, a nationwide one-day strike called by the Alfa Cartel and CNSLR-Fratia, the two main union blocs, brought industry to a halt. Among union demands were radical privatization and restructuring of the economy.

Labor tensions eased by June, but parliament remained gridlocked on key economic reform legislation. On 22 June the Democratic Agrarian Party, which had a pivotal position in the hung parliament, said it was withdrawing its support for the PSDR and that it intended to lodge a no-confidence motion. The Agrarians, a center-left party supported by farmers, said they were bringing the motion on the grounds that the government's economic and social policies had failed. Romania's center-right opposition parties, with control of 47 percent of parliament, said they would join the no-confidence move.

In early July the government survived its fifth no-confidence vote since the 1992 elections. Opinion polls showed that 74 percent of the public did not think the government was doing a good job.

Through the early summer, the government did manage to push through parliament a tough budget, a much-delayed securities law that would allow the establishment of the country's first stock market, and amendments to the foreign investment law giving incentives to big investors in industry. The economy showed some signs of growth for the first time since the PSDR took power, with inflation falling to 6 percent a month, rising exports, and a shrinking current-account deficit. The private sector accounted for 30 percent of official GDP. In May the International Monetary Fund (IMF) agreed on its first new loans to the country in nearly two years. In June, the Senate passed a controversial property law, granting limited restitution rights to former owners of around 250,000 residential properties confiscated after 1945 by the former Communist regime. The bill faced a possible constitutional challenge.

PSDR reactionaries remained in charge of several influential institutions, such as the privatization agencies and the foreign investment agency. Moreover, in August the government gave cabinet posts to two members of the Transylvania-based ultranationalist, anti-Hungarian PRNU. The PRNU held a pivotal 10 percent of seats in parliament. The democratic opposition charged that the appointments were unconstitutional without the approval of parliament, marked a setback for democracy and threatened to inflame ethnic tensions.

In August the main privatization body, the State Ownership Fund (SOF) said it was ready to sell controlling stakes in five state companies through a public offering. The SOF held a 70 percent stake in over 6,000 state-run companies slated for privatization over the next seven to fifteen years.

On 14 September President Iliescu, in a state-of-the-nation speech to parliament, urged the government and opposition to cooperate more closely and form a consensus on economic reform and privatization. But by year's end, critical economic measures continued to be held up in a backlog of legislation.

In September President Iliescu thanked President Clinton for helping Romania's 1993 return to Most Favored Nation (MFN) trading status after a five-year hiatus. The U.S. topped the list of overseas investors with $107 million in direct investment and 1,800 U.S.-Romanian joint-ventures.

In January Romania became the first former Warsaw Pact nation to join NATO's Partnership for Peace.

Political Rights and Civil Liberties:

Citizens of Romania have the right to change their government democratically. After the 1992 elections, the opposition claimed irregularities, particularly in light of a high number of invalid votes.

A 1992 law on reorganizing the judiciary established a four-tiered system, including the reintroduction of appellate courts. Administrative hierarchy of the magistrature permits superiors to exert pressure on junior judges. Establishing a fully staffed and qualified judicial corps has proved difficult, many professionals being attracted to more lucrative private practice.

A new law on police adopted in April 1994 represents a first step in demilitarizing the Romanian police. The nongovernmental Romanian Independent Society of Human Rights (SIRDO) has developed a program aimed at enforcing international standards in the penal system. Nevertheless, prison conditions are generally poor and inmates face abuses.

The Law on Broadcasting Media stipulates that freedom of the press is guaranteed; at the same time it forbids the defamation of country, dissemination of classified information, and production of materials offending public morals. In 1994 President Iliescu blocked legislation that journalists said would insure independence of the broadcast system. Romanian State Television remains the only broadcaster with nationwide facilities. Independent newspapers offer a wide range of views and commentaries, though government control of most newsprint and printing facilities has created problems for some. In February police freed on bail a reporter arrested for writing an article that likened President Iliescu to a fairy-tale pig; he was accused of "offending state authority." In April, the U.S.-based Christian Broadcasting Network protested state television's decision not to broadcast Easter programs the government judged to be Protestant fundamentalist proselytizing.

Free expression has also been undermined by amendments to the penal code. One amendment provides for one to five year's imprisonment for "spreading false information that undermines state security and foreign relations." A proposed new law on slandering the nation would make raising the Hungarian flag or singing the Hungarian national anthem punishable by prison terms ranging from six months to three years.

Ethnic minority rights continue to be an issue. Anti-Hungarian sentiments are rooted in the ideologies of several political parties. In November Lajos Monus, a leader of the Hungarian Democratic Union, was illegally sentenced in the Transylvanian city of Cluj to one month's imprisonment for trying to help stop Romanian authorities from an action that would have removed a statue of King Mathias, a fifteenth-century Hungarian monarch. Hungarians have been denied permission to march in Cluj. Hungarian-language education remains a contentious issue.

Gypsies (Roma) continue to be victims of racist violence and discrimination. In May villagers in northwestern Romania torched Roma houses after two Roma youths were charged with killing a shepherd. Authorities frequently fail to investigate and prosecute violence against the Roma. Roma interests are represented by the nongovernmental Romani International Union and other NGOs. A National Minorities' Council was established in 1993, but its duties and powers remain vague.

Few official restrictions are placed on travel, either domestic or foreign, and citizens have the right to emigrate. In October, President Iliescu refused entry to deposed King Michael after he landed at Bucharest airport, declaring that the king posed a threat to the country's political system.

The constitution provides for freedom of religion; there are some fifteen officially recognized religions whose clergy may receive state financial support, and another 120 denominations and faiths have received licenses entitling them to juridical status as well as certain tax exemptions. Tensions remain between the Orthodox Church (nominally, some 86 percent of Romanians are Orthodox) and Uniate Catholics over church property confiscated by the state. Jews face a barrage of anti-Semitism from the extremist press. Easter programs by a U.S.-based religious broadcaster were banned for allegedly fundamentalist Protestant proselytizing.

A labor superstructure, NCRFTU-Fratia National Trade Union Confederation was created in 1993. Workers have, and frequently exercise, the right to strike, as evinced by the numerous massive work stoppages in the country since 1989.

Russia

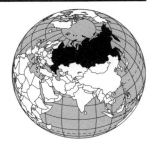

Polity: Presidential-parliamentary democracy
Economy: Mixed statist transitional
Population: 147,820,000
PPP: $6,930
Life Expectancy: 70.0
Ethnic Groups: Russian, over 100 ethnic groups

Political Rights: 3
Civil Liberties: 4
Status: Partly Free

Overview:
President Boris Yeltsin's decision to send troops to the separatist autonomous republic of Chechnya in late 1994 drew sharp criticism from the public as well as moderate and democratic forces, capping a year in which the embattled president alienated key reformers over economic policies. The election of extreme nationalists and Communists to the State Duma (parliament) in December 1993 led to the resignations of several well-known reformers.

Key domestic issues included demands for greater autonomy by several regions, crime and corruption, and the economy. In foreign policy, Russia became more assertive, deploying troops to former Soviet republics—the "near abroad"—opposing NATO's eastward expansion, and sparring with the West over Bosnia.

With the USSR's collapse in December 1991, Russia—the only constituent republic not to declare sovereignty—gained *de facto* independence under President

Yeltsin, directly elected in June 1991. In 1992, Yeltsin was repeatedly challenged by a hostile anti-reform legislature. Parliament replaced acting-Prime Minister Yegor Gaidar, a principal architect of reforms, with Viktor Chernomyrdin, a Soviet-era manager.

In 1993 the Yeltsin-parliament struggle intensified over presidential powers and a new constitution. In an April referendum, voters supported the president and his policies, but questions on new presidential and parliamentary elections did not get the necessary 50 percent of eligible voters. On 12 August parliament, chaired by hardliner Ruslan Khasbulatov, moved to amend the Soviet-era constitution and strip Yeltsin of most of his powers. The next day, Yeltsin opened a summit with leaders of the country's eighty-nine republics and regions, which established a 178-member Federation Council. Yeltsin was accused of trying to bypass parliament. In September, Yeltsin suspended hard-line Vice President Rutskoi, dissolved parliament and set parliamentary elections for December. Opposition deputies barricaded themselves in the parliamentary complex. In early October, after riots by extremists supporting the parliamentary protesters, troops crushed the uprising, arresting Khasbulatov and Rutskoi.

In November Yeltsin approved a new draft constitution giving the president considerable power to appoint senior members of the executive and judicial branches and dissolve the lower house of parliament if it repeatedly declined his choice of prime minister or repeatedly voted a lack of confidence in the president. The draft proclaimed Russia "a democratic, federative, law-governed state," and guaranteed the full spectrum of human rights, including the right to private property. It established a bicameral Federal Assembly: a Federation Council (Upper House) consisting of two representatives from the country's eighty-nine regions and territories, and a 450-member State Duma.

Before the election the Russia's Choice bloc, an umbrella group of radical economic reformers headed by Deputy Prime Minister Gaidar and backed by Yeltsin, split with the more moderate Russian Unity and Accord movement under Deputy Prime Minister Sergei Shakhrai and supported by Prime Minister Chernomyrdin.

In December voters approved the constitution but elected extreme nationalists, including Vladimir Zhirinovsky and the Liberal-Democratic Party, and Communists. The Liberal-Democrats got 22.79 percent of the vote and the most seats, 59; Russia's Choice, 15.38 percent and 40 seats; the Communist Party, 12.35 percent and 32 seats. The centrist Women of Russia won 21 seats; the Agrarian Party, 21; the Yavlinsky-Boldarev-Lukin Bloc, 20 seats; the Russian Party of Unity and Accord, 18; and the Democratic Party, 14.

In January 1994 the rift between radical reformers and the Communists/ultra-nationalists widened, illustrated by the election of Ivan Rybkin (Agrarian) as parliamentary speaker with support from Communists and far-right nationalists. The Federation Council barely elected First Deputy Prime Minister Vladimir Shumeiko, a Yeltsin supporter, as chairman. Deputy Prime Minister Gaidar, in charge of the economy, and Finance Minister Boris Fyodorov resigned, charging a lack of responsible economic policy. Prime Minister Chernomyrdin, who had sparred with Gaidar over anti-inflationary measures and with Privatization Minister Anatoly Chubais, declared the era of "shock reforms" over.

The new government consisted mainly of industrialists and farm lobbyists, including First Deputy Prime Minister Oleg Soskovets, formerly responsible for heavy industry, and Minister of Agriculture Aleksandr Zaveryukha, a former collective farm boss known by Western bankers as the "king of state credits." In a move that negated previous deficit targets, the prime minister announced additional spending in the form of writing off debts to enterprises, mostly in the defense and agro-industry sectors.

Even as parliament amnestied 1993 coup plotters, including Rutskoi and Khasbulatov, in late February, there were indications of improved relations between Yeltsin's government and the Duma, partly due to the mediating efforts of Speaker Rybkin. Opposed to radical reforms, Rybkin insisted parliament would not fuel inflation through state subsidies, and indicated he supported limited privatization.

In March, Chernomyrdin's insistence on tight credit policy, commitment to land privatization, and his statement that inefficient industries must be allowed to go bankrupt, heartened Western and Russian reformers. So did the appointment of free-marketeer Alexander Livshits to Yeltsin's team of hand-picked economic advisers. The prime minister persuaded the IMF to unlock a new $1.5 billion loan to help support new budget expenditure.

In June, re-asserting his role in economic policymaking, President Yeltsin announced a series of decrees, including measures to introduce home mortgages to Russia and to regulate the wild and fraud-ridden securities markets. Earlier decrees promised a loosening of government export controls, tax reduction, and procedures for liquidating bankrupt state-owned firms. Yeltsin also resisted attempts to expand the military budget, and chastised the government for its "bias" in favor of bloated and failing state enterprises.

The Duma failed to pass the 1994 Rbs 183,000 billion budget at a third reading and came out strongly against a Yeltsin anti-crime decree that impinged on civil liberties. The budget was rejected earlier by the Federation Council, which demanded increased military spending. A majority of deputies voted for the budget, but it failed to secure the required 226 votes.

In June Privatization Minister Chubais announced the second wave of mass privatization. In the first phase, some 14,000 medium- and large-scale enterprises had been privatized by Russian and foreign investors under a voucher program in which all citizens received investment coupons which they could exchange for shares in more than 100,000 formerly state-run companies. In the second stage, the state would offer shares for cash to the highest bidder, including 51 percent to individual investors. The plan would have led to extensive privatization, but it ran into immediate political difficulties in the Duma. In July, after G-7 countries embraced Russia as an equal partner, President Yeltsin decreed the continuation of the privatization program but made concessions to deputies who had blocked the plan in parliament. In late September Chubais announced foreign investment of $1 billion a month in Russian companies.

The government's gradualist approach failed to fully address key structural problems such as inter-enterprise debt, where companies churned out goods they were unable to sell and took delivery on goods they could not pay for. Relaxed monetary controls and renewed flows of credits to state enterprises weakened the ruble, which had dropped by 20 percent in September. On 10 October the ruble suffered its steepest one-day plunge, losing 25 percent of its value against the dollar, forcing the government to step in to stabilize its value. The crisis led to the resignation of the conservative central bank chairman, Viktor Gerashchenko, and the sacking of acting Finance Minister Sergei Dubinin.

After the ruble rebounded, the finance and economy ministries urged the cabinet to adopt a "big bang" approach to fiscal reform. They proposed a draft budget aimed at bringing inflation down to 1 percent a month in the second half of 1995. Alexander Shokhin, deputy prime minister for the economy, said the continuation of gradualism would "mean periodic crises like...the one when the ruble fell." The cabinet approved the austere budget amid criticism from the IMF that the government had failed to control spending and the macro-economic fundamentals behind the ruble's crash.

On 27 October, after a strong speech to parliament by the prime minister defending the 1995 budget draft, the government survived a no-confidence vote even though 194 deputies voted against the government, thirty-two short of the required majority of 226. To placate conservatives, Yeltsin named Alexander Nazarchuk, a leading member of the Agrarian faction, as the agriculture minister.

In early November, President Yeltsin unnerved Western creditors and reformers with a rush of new appointments that promoted both conservatives and reformers in roughly equal measure. Yevgeny Yasin, a market reformer, became economics minister. The new finance minister was Vladimir Panskov, a deputy minister in the former Soviet government and senior presidential economic adviser jailed in 1993 before bribery charges were dropped. Panskov's appointment led to the resignation of Economic Minister Shokhin. Privatization Minister Chubais was made first deputy prime minister, putting him in overall charge of economic policy.

In late December, after thirteen votes over three days, the budget was approved. However, the Chechnya intervention threatened to bust the budget. The government jeapordized Western aid by reneging on promises to remove controls on domestic energy prices. And on 30 December the new head of the main privatization agency said he was preparing a law to renationalize key enterprises such as oil and gas, aluminum and the military-industrial complex.

In politics, there was a measure of stability, due partly to the constitution, which gave the president the power to dissolve the Duma and call for new elections, and the Duma the power to bring down the government through a no-confidence motion. Neither members of the Duma nor President Yeltsin were keen on new elections. The Duma was essentially hung: conservatives could rarely muster more than 200 votes, the reformers about 170. The balance of power rested with about 100 centrist deputies. In 1994 the working relationship between the president and prime minister and the speakers of the two houses, although often testy, precluded the type of upheaval that spurred the October 1993 crisis. Throughout the year, after a series of long public absences and embarrassing incidents attributed to alcohol, concerns were raised publicly about the president's health and his drinking habits.

The escalating war in Chechnya, a Muslim-dominant Caucasus republic that declared independence in 1991, had political as well as economic consequences. In August Chechen President Dzokhar Dudayev, a former Air Force officer, declared a state of emergency, accusing Moscow of backing forces seeking to overthrow him. On 29 November President Yeltsin threatened military action because

Moscow's "vital interests and national security" were in peril. Amid public opposition, as well as criticism from the media and all political groups save for the ultra-nationalists, by mid-December 40,000 troops invaded Chechnya. At year's end, bombers and artillery pounded the capital city, Grozny, and Russian troops fought pitched battles with Chechen militias.

President Yeltsin confronted calls for greater autonomy from several other regions. In February, Russia signed a treaty with oil-rich Tatarstan, which retained its own constitution, but said it was "united" with Russia. A similar treaty was signed "defining the areas of competence" between Moscow and the Bashkortostan autonomous republic. Several of Russia's sixty-eight regions also sought status as ethno-territorial republics.

In foreign affairs, Russia grew more assertive about the "near abroad." While troops left Latvia and Estonia in August, and negotiations continued with Ukraine over the Black Sea Fleet, Russian forces were active in Georgia and Tajikistan. In Georgia, which had accused Russia of fomenting the violent Abkhazian secession, Moscow got approval for five military bases in exchange for aiding the government in defeating armed supporters of former President Zviad Gamsakhurdia. In Tajikistan, Russia got control of several key industries as payment for stationing troops along the Afghanistan border to prevent incursions by Tajik refugee militias. Kazakhstan and Uzbekistan were pressured to deal with Moscow in the energy sector.

Though Russia agreed to closer military cooperation with NATO, President Yeltsin told the Budapest summit of the Conference on Security and Cooperation in Europe (CSCE) that NATO's eastward expansion would divide Europe. A member of the five-nation "Contact Group" on Bosnia, Moscow frequently supported the Serbs and dissented over NATO air strikes and related issues.

Political Rights and Civil Liberties: Russians have the means to change their government democratically. The 1993 constitution established a strong presidency, but decentralization and institutional checks put limits on executive authority.

All but one of nineteen judges for the Constitutional Court have been chosen. Legal reforms, however, are incomplete. A July 1993 law allows for the choice of a trial by jury for crimes such as treason, rape and murder in five oblasts. A controversial presidential anti-crime decree allowed detention of suspects for thirty days without charge, the search of premises and company books and accounts without a warrant, and the use of evidence obtained by phone-tapping and infiltration of criminal gangs.

In early 1994 an independent commission report claimed serious, widespread human rights violations, citing ethnic and religious discrimination (particularly against Caucasians and central Asians), labor exploitation, attacks on the media and on prisoners' rights. The Tel Aviv-based Women's Organization for Political Prisoners documented abuses, lack of medical care and torture at the Moscobiyeh Detention Center. There are labor camps run by North Korea in Siberia, where 15,000 Korean prisoners are routinely tortured and forced to work at logging.

A multitude of political parties and groupings, as well as nonpolitical civic, human rights, social, youth, cultural, and women's organizations, operate freely. Certain extremist groups were banned after the October 1993 crisis.

Although press freedom is guaranteed by law, in 1994 the media came under increased pressure from the government, particularly after the Chechnya crisis, and from organized crime. In Chechnya, Moscow's tactics ranged from warning journalists to leave Grozny to seizing of war footage. Troops fired on Western journalists and several were detained. Misinformation was disseminated by state-run media and progovernment newspapers, and President Yeltsin publicly claimed some parts of the mass media were supported by Chechen money. Nevertheless, even though many are state-funded, dailies as well as the weeklies reported candidly on events. In October, a journalist from *Moskovsky Komsomolets* was killed by a bomb before he was to testify to parliament about Russian troops illegally selling weapons while withdrawing from Germany. Journalists faced threats, beatings and shootings to discourage reporting on criminal activity.

In December President Yeltsin ordered the government to sell shares of Russia's largest state television and radio company, Ostankino, with 51 percent of the stock to remain in state hands. There are several independent TV and radio stations, as well as foreign cable broadcasts and satellite dishes in large cities.

Freedom of religion is generally respected in this primarily Russian Orthodox country. There were reports of violence and intimidation directed at Evangelical Christians, especially in Muslim regions and southern Russia. Incidents of anti-Semitism were also reported, including a bombing attempt at Moscow's Chorale Synagogue.

While most restrictions on foreign and domestic travel have disappeared, freedom of movement is often circumscribed by "residency permits" and bureaucratic impediments. In September the Clinton administration announced Russia was in full compliance with emigration requirements to enable it to receive Most Favored Nation (MFN) trading status without seeking annual waivers.

Women are entitled to the same legal rights as men, and are well represented at many levels of the general economy. However, women face discrimination in such areas as equal pay and promotions. Women's groups have raised such issues as domestic violence and women's role in society.

The Federation of Independent Unions of Russia, a successor to the Soviet-era federation, claims 60 million members (estimates put the figure at 39 million). Newer, independent unions represent between 500,000 and 1 million workers, including seafarers, dockworkers, air traffic controllers, pilots and some coal miners. There were several strikes, including a walkout by coal miners in March.

Rwanda

Polity: Dominant party
(military dominated)
Economy: Mixed statist
Population: 7,664,000
PPP: $680
Life Expectancy: 46.5

Political Rights: 7*
Civil Liberties: 7*
Status: Not Free

Ethnic Groups: Hutu (85 percent), Tutsi (14 percent), Twa (1 percent)
Ratings Change: *Rwanda's political rights rating changed from 6 to 7 and
its civil liberties rating from 5 to 7 because of widespread genocide in 1994.

Overview:

With the murder of President Juvenal Habyarimana of the National Republican Movement for Democracy and Development (MRND) in April 1994, Rwanda plunged into a bitter and bloody ethnic war that has left an estimated 500,000 to one million dead. Up to 300,000 Rwandese fled for neighboring countries, with an estimated 2.5 million displaced within the country. Habyarimana, a Hutu, died in a suspicious plane crash along with Burundian President Melchior Ndadaye of the Burundi Front for Democracy (or FRODEBU), also a Hutu. As the world watched, ethnic cleansing and mass slaughter occurred on a massive scale. With no civil authority and with the country's infrastructure in ruins, the Rwandan civilian population continues to face death, starvation and displacement. Despite the enormity of need, the international community has remained complacent. Reluctant to call the mass killings that have taken place since April genocide (as to do so would compel the signatories to the Convention for the Prevention of Genocide to act), the international community has quietly witnessed the slaughter of over 500,000 men, women and children.

Against a background of ethnic division and tension between the majority Hutu population and the minority Tutsi population, Rwanda gained independence from Belgium in 1962. During the colonial period, the Tutsi were selected by the colonizers to administer the country. In exchange, the Tutsi elite were given educational and political opportunities denied to the Hutu. By the end of colonial rule, however, the tides had changed. Shortly before Rwanda gained independence, the Hutu seized government control. Fearing reprisals, a number of prominent Tutsi fled the country. Throughout the postcolonial period, ethnic division and violence continued to plague Rwanda. Beginning in 1962 until the late 1980s, continued ethnic violence caused thousands to flee Rwanda for neighboring countries. Most of the refugees were Tutsi fleeing ethnic violence and reprisals from the Hutu population.

Upon seizing control in a bloodless coup in 1973, Habyarimana promised to restore national unity. In the years that followed, however, Habyarimana's policies increasingly benefited the Hutu of his own region in northwest Rwanda. It was not until the late 1980s that the Rwandan government began the process of democratic reform. A poor economy coupled with internal dissent and pressure from foreign donors forced the Habyarimana regime to agree to political reforms that included the creation of a multiparty system.

The reforms coincided with an invasion by the Rwandan Patriotic Front (RPF) in October 1990. The RPF, comprised mostly of Tutsi with several Hutu leaders, claimed that their objective was to force the Rwandan government to allow thousands of refugees (most of them Tutsi) to return home. After making some initial inroads, the RPF was turned back and increasingly resorted to guerrilla tactics. As the number of RPF assaults increased, so too did the number of human rights abuses committed by government forces, particularly against those Tutsi suspected of being RPF supporters or sympathizers.

In November 1990 the government promised to hold the country's first multiparty elections in 1991. The elections never took place. The government claimed that although the elections were not held, the process of democratization had begun and that it had taken steps to allow for the return of refugees.

In August 1993 Habyarimana along with leaders of the Tutsi-led rebel RPF signed a peace pact in Arusha, Tanzania. The signing followed several unsuccessful mediation efforts by the Organization of African Unity (OAU). Under the accord, the government and the RPF were to create an interim coalition government and begin a difficult merger of their armed forces.

Habyarimana's death, allegedly at the hands of Hutu extremists, appears to have stemmed from a 1992 decision to share power with Hutu leaders outside his party. Previously, the country had been governed only by an elite comprised of family members in a circle known as the Akazu or "Little House." The Akazu controlled both the elite Presidential Guard and *Radio des Milles Collines*. When opposition members were allowed into Habyarimana's cabinet in 1992, the Akazu rebelled by forming militia known as Interahamwe (Those Who Attack Together) and Impuzamugambi (Those Who Have the Same Goal). Following the creation of these militia, Hutu opposition leaders were killed and the use of political violence became common.

Despite the OAU-backed accords, fighting continued. The RPF captured Kigali, the capital, on 4 July 1994. On 18 July the RPF proclaimed victory, declared a cease-fire and announced a new government.

Political Rights and Civil Liberties:

Rwanda is without a stable central government or any form of civilian authority. The new Rwandan "government," backed by the Tutsi-dominated RPF, contains a broad-based coalition of Hutu and Tutsi. However, the alliance is fragile at best. Rwandese have neither political nor civil rights. Human rights are routinely violated. Ethnic violence is endemic as fighting persists between the ruling RPF and Hutu opposition.

A 1994 investigation by the Arms Control Project of Human Rights Watch indicates that members of the international community have continued to contribute weaponry to Rwanda. The report alleges that France has engaged in bipartisan, linguistic politics by supporting the French-speaking Hutus and supplying arms and heavy weaponry.

Human rights violations have been committed by both government forces and members of the rebel RPF. A May 1994 Human Rights Watch Africa report charges that "At least 200,000 and perhaps as many as 500,000 unarmed and unresisting civilians have been slain" and asserts that these massacres "were planned [by the Presidential Guard and elements of the Rwandan army] months in advance." The report asserts that Habyarimana's death "was the pretext for Hutu extremists from the late president's entourage to launch a campaign of genocide against the Tutsi..."

Among the most grievous incidents reported was the slaughter of nearly 6,000

Tutsi who had taken refuge in a church in Cyahinda. A total of 6,500 people were killed in the Mibirizi, Shangi and Rukara parishes. In Kibungo, about 2,800 people who were gathered in a church were killed by the Interahamwe using weaponry and machetes; only forty survivors were reported. Children have also fallen victim to the indiscriminate violence. Human Rights Watch reports that in the Butare orphanage, "twenty one children, selected solely because they were Tutsi, were slain as well as thirteen Rwandan Red Cross volunteers who tried to protect them." In the town of Gikongoro, eighty-eight pupils were killed at their school.

For those who escaped the slaughter in Rwanda, a different kind of horror was found in refugee camps both within Rwanda and in neighboring Tanzania and Zaire. Refugees and relief agencies report intimidation and ethnic clashes. While the United Nations High Commission on Refugees (UNHCR) has attempted to provide the necessary food and medical care, the numbers have overwhelmed the operation and often refugees go for days without food or water. Human Rights Watch/Africa reports that in Kigali, RPF and army clashes have made relief attempts difficult and, at times, impossible. In other areas, its report states, "militia and authorities of the self proclaimed government have hindered or prevented assistance to the displaced." International relief organizations such as Doctors Without Borders and the International Committee of the Red Cross have reported the loss of large numbers of local staff. Attempts at encouraging refugees to return to Rwanda have found little success as many refugees are fearful of retribution if they return.

Rwandese do not have a judicial system and extrajudicial executions by both sides are commonplace. Internal travel is restricted. The role of the press since April 1994 has been reduced to inciting ethnic hostilities. The *Radio Television Libre des Milles Collines*, a privately held radio station owned by close associates of Habyarimana, has been used to deliver hate- filled propaganda against both Tutsi and opposition Hutus. As late as May 1994, the state-owned Radio Rwanda called on listeners to fight and eliminate those opposing the regime.

St. Kitts-Nevis

Polity: Parliamentary democracy
Economy: Capitalist
Population: 41,000
PPP: $3,550
Life Expectancy: 70.0
Ethnic Groups: Black, mulatto, other

Political Rights: 2*
Civil Liberties: 2*
Status: Free

Ratings Change: *St. Kitts-Nevis's political rights rating changed from 1 to 2 as a result of the weakened ability to govern of a scandal-ridden minority government. Its civil liberties rating changed from 1 to 2 as a result of increased drug-related crime and corruption.

Overview: After the already weakened government of Prime Minister Kennedy Simmonds was rocked by a drug scandal in the fall, it was agreed at a "forum for national unity" that new elections should be held no later than 15 November 1995, three years ahead of the required time.

The nation consists of the islands of St. Kitts (St. Christopher) and Nevis. The British monarchy is represented by a governor general who appoints as prime minister the leader of the party or coalition with at least a plurality of seats in the legislature. The governor general also appoints a deputy governor general for Nevis.

A federal constitution provides for a unicameral National Assembly, with members elected for five years from single-member constituencies, eight on St. Kitts and three on Nevis. Senators, not to exceed two-thirds of the elected members, are appointed, one by the leader of the parliamentary opposition for every two by the governor general.

Simmonds and the People's Action Movement (PAM) came to power in the 1980 elections with the support of the Nevis Reformation Party (NRP) and led the country to independence in 1983. The center-right PAM-NRP coalition won majorities in the 1984 and 1989 elections.

Nevis has its own Assembly consisting of five elected and three appointed members. The deputy governor general appoints a premier and two other members of the Nevis Assembly to serve as a Nevis Island Administration. Nevis is accorded the right to secession if approved by two-thirds of the elected legislators and endorsed by two-thirds of voters in an island referendum. In the 1992 Nevis Assembly elections the newly founded Concerned Citizens Movement (CCM) won three of five seats, ousting the NRP. CCM leader and businessman Vance Amory became premier.

The 1993 electoral campaign heated up when former deputy prime minister Michael Powell, ousted by Simmonds from the PAM, formed a new opposition party, the United People's Party (UPP). But the main challenger was forty-year-old SKLP leader, Denzil Douglas, like Simmonds a physician. The campaign centered on the economy, dependent on sugar and tourism, and mutual accusations of influence by drug traffickers.

On 29 November 1994 the SKLP won the popular vote on St. Kitts by more than ten percentage points over the PAM, with the UPP a distant third. But in the first-past-the-post system, the PAM and the SKLP evenly divided eight seats. On Nevis the CCM took two seats and the NRP one. The CCM said it would not join a coalition with either the PAM or the SKLP, leaving the PAM-NRP coalition with a plurality of five seats. In accord with the constitution Governor General Clement Arindell asked Simmonds to form a new government.

The SKLP called for a shutdown of the country to protest the new government, leading to violent disturbances and attacks by SKLP members on government headquarters in the capital of Basseterre on 2 December. Arindell called a state of emergency. Two church organizations sponsored a meeting between the PAM and the SKLP. Douglas demanded new elections immediately, but Simmonds said that new balloting would require a no-confidence vote when the new parliament was seated in early 1994. The state of emergency was lifted on 14 December.

In 1994 the SKLP boycotted parliament and continued to demand new elections. It also initiated a series of protests that turned violent in the early part of the year.

The Simmonds government was shaken to its foundations by a drugs-and-murder scandal in the fall. The deputy prime minister, Sydney Morris, was forced to resign on 15 November after two of his sons were arrested on drugs and firearms charges. They were also implicated in the murder of a third brother. The events followed the October killing of the police official who had been investigating the third son's murder.

When the first two sons were freed on bail, it set off a riot in the country's overcrowded prison. More than one hundred prisoners escaped after setting fire to the prison and, as during the riots in December 1993, the government was forced to call in troops from neighboring Caribbean islands to help restore order.

On 22 November a "forum for national unity" was held, chaired by the Chamber of Commerce and attended by the main political parties, church organizations and the bar association. All agreed to a political "cooling-off" period at least through the end of 1994, and the Simmonds government agreed that new elections would be held by 15 November 1995.

Political Rights and Civil Liberties:

Citizens are able to change their government through elections. The opposition SKLP argued that because it won the popular vote on 29 November 1993, the governor general should have installed a caretaker government to rule until new elections were held. But that would have abrogated the constitution which allows for a minority government in the event that opposition parties are unable to form a majority coalition.

However, the ability of the minority government to conduct the affairs of the nation proved to be weak in 1994, severely so after the drugs-and-murder scandal described above that led to an agreement for new elections in 1995.

Constitutional guarantees regarding free expression, the free exercise of religion and the right to organize political parties, labor unions and civic organizations are generally respected.

However, civil liberties were undermined in 1994 by provocative opposition demonstrations that resulted in violent clashes with police and by an upsurge in violent drug-related crime. Twice since December 1993 the government has had to call upon troops from neighboring nations to help restore order.

Moreover, the hemispheric drug and money-laundering trades have penetrated to a significant degree political parties, the government and the economy, as evidenced by the 1994 scandal involving the ruling PAM and by the business relations between SKLP leaders and Noel "Zambo" Heath, a known drug trafficker.

The judiciary is independent and the highest court is the West Indies Supreme Court (based in St. Lucia) which includes a Court of Appeal and a High Court. In certain circumstances, there is right of appeal to the Privy Council in London.

The rule of law, traditionally strong, recently has been severely tested by increasing drug-related crime and corruption. In 1994 it appeared that the police had become divided along political lines between the two main political parties. The poor, overcrowded conditions of the national prison were underscored during the riot in November 1994. There is some evidence that the ruling party has benefited illegally by catering to wealthy foreign investors.

The main labor union, the St. Kitts Trades and Labour Union, is associated with the opposition SKLP. The right to strike, while not specified by law, is recognized and generally respected in practice.

Television and radio on St. Kitts are owned by the government and the ruling party tends to restrict access to opposition parties and civic groups. There is no daily newspaper but each of the major political parties publishes a weekly or fortnightly newspaper. Opposition publications are free to criticize the government and do so vigorously. There is a religious television station and a privately owned radio station on Nevis.

St. Lucia

Polity: Parliamentary democracy
Economy: Capitalist
Population: 139,000
PPP: $3,500
Life Expectancy: 72.0
Ethnic Groups: Black, mulatto, other

Political Rights: 1
Civil Liberties: 2
Status: Free

Overview:

The government of longtime Prime Minister John Compton contended with corruption allegations, a mounting crime wave and severe damage inflicted on the crucial banana industry by Tropical Storm Debbie.

St. Lucia, a member of the British Commonwealth, became internally self-governing in 1967 and achieved independence in 1979. The British monarchy is represented by a governor-general whose emergency powers are subject to legislative review.

Under the 1979 constitution, there is a bicameral parliament consisting of a seventeen-member House of Assembly elected for five years, and an eleven-member Senate, with six senators appointed by the prime minister, three by the leader of the parliamentary opposition, and two by consultation with civic and religious organizations. The prime minister is the leader of the majority party in the House. The island is divided into eight regions, each with its own elected council and administrative services.

The leftist St. Lucia Labour Party (SLP) won the 1979 elections, but factional disputes within the SLP led to new elections in 1982. The radical faction led by George Odlum broke off to form the Progressive Labour Party (PLP). The 1982 elections saw the return to power of Compton and the United Workers Party (UWP).

In the 1987 elections the UWP won a 9-8 victory over the SLP, which had declared a social democratic orientation under the leadership of Julian Hunte. The PLP won no seats. Compton called new elections a few weeks later, but the outcome was the same. Neville Cenac of the SLP crossed the aisle later in the year, giving the UWP a 10-7 majority.

The 1992 election campaign was bitter, marked by a few violent incidents, a dispute over boundaries between electoral districts, and an exchange of personal accusations, including one by *The Star*, an anti-Compton weekly, that alleged the sixty-five-year-old prime minister had had an affair with a teenaged student. But the electorate evidently was not distracted from the core issue, the economy. In recent years, when many of its Caribbean neighbors have been struggling, St. Lucia has experienced economic growth. Despite the need for improved social services, one of the SLP's main campaign planks, voters in April 1992 returned the UWP to power, increasing its parliamentary majority to 11-6 over the SLP.

In 1993 SLP deputy leader Peter Josie, who had unsuccessfully challenged Hunte for the party leadership, was expelled from the SLP after blaming the 1992 electoral loss on Hunte.

In 1994 the Compton government continued to grapple with disruptions in the banana industry, which employs about 30 percent of the work force. Many farmers, disgruntled over low prices set by the government because of increased competition from Latin America, conducted a number of occasionally violent strikes from late 1993 until the end of 1994. A further blow came in September 1994 when Tropical Storm Debbie washed away an estimated 60 percent of the banana harvest. With unemployment at twenty percent the government looked to boost tourism.

Meanwhile, reports in the media of corruption in the civil service led to widespread demands for an investigation. Compton countered that the allegations were vague. In September Compton stunned many by appointing his old nemesis George Odlum to be St. Lucia's ambassador to the United Nations.

Political Rights and Civil Liberties:

Citizens are able to change their government through democratic elections. Constitutional guarantees regarding the right to organize political parties, labor unions and civic groups are generally respected as is the free exercise of religion.

The competition among political parties and allied civic organizations is heated, particularly during election campaigns when there is occasional violence and mutual charges of harassment. Opposition parties have complained intermittently of difficulties in getting police permission for demonstrations and have charged the government with interference.

Newspapers are mostly private or sponsored by political parties. The government has been charged with trying to influence the press by withholding government advertising. Television is privately owned; radio is both public and private. In 1994 the Compton government stepped up verbal attacks against the media and canceled "On-Line," a public affairs discussion program on state-owned radio.

Civic groups are well organized and politically active. Labor unions, which represent a majority of wage earners, have the right to strike. In September 1994, however, forty state radio workers who went on strike because of longstanding pay grievances were dismissed and the station shut down for "restructuring." Two months later the station reopened but only ten of the forty were rehired.

The judicial system is independent and includes a High Court under the West Indies Supreme Court (based in St. Lucia), with ultimate appeal under certain circumstances to the Privy Council in London. Traditionally, citizens have enjoyed a high degree of personal security. However, an escalating crime wave, much of it drug-related, and the violent clashes during banana farmer strikes have produced great concern among citizens. Prisons are greatly overcrowded.

St. Vincent and the Grenadines

Polity: Parliamentary democracy
Economy: Capitalist
Population: 110,000
PPP: $3,700
Life Expectancy: 71.0
Ethnic Groups: Black, mulatto, other
Ratings Change: *St. Vincent and the Grenadines's political rights rating changed from 1 to 2 principally as a result of irregularities in the 1994 elections.

Political Rights: 2*
Civil Liberties: 1
Status: Free

Overview:

Prime Minister James Mitchell handily won a third term in 1994 but the elections were marked by irregularities that may or may not have affected the legitimacy of the vote, a question that was still pending in the courts at the end of 1994.

St. Vincent and the Grenadines is a member of the British Commonwealth, with the British monarchy represented by a governor-general. St. Vincent became internally self-governing in 1967 and achieved independence in 1979, with jurisdiction over the northern Grenadine islets of Beguia, Canouan, Mayreau, Mustique, Prune Island, Petit St. Vincent, and Union Island.

The constitution provides for a fifteen-member unicameral House of Assembly elected for five years. Six senators are appointed, four by the government and two by the opposition. The prime minister is the leader of the party or coalition commanding a majority in the House.

On 21 February Prime Minister James Mitchell won a third term when his center-right New Democratic Party (NDP) won thirteen seats. The remaining three were won by the SVLP-MNU, an electoral alliance between two center-left parties—the St. Vincent Labour Party, which had held power from 1979-84, and the Movement for National Unity.

During the campaign the SVLP-MNU charged Mitchell with abuse of power during his previous term when the NDP had held all fifteen seats. The NDP denied the allegations and emphasized its record on economic growth. The campaign was marred by a violent clash between SVLP-MNU and NDP supporters.

In the aftermath, the SVLP-MNU disputed the validity of the elections in court. It charged that there were irregularities in voter registration and that the NDP government had failed to comply with a constitutional provision that calls for an electoral boundaries commission to review constituency lines prior to elections after a national census.

The first SVLP-MNU motion to invalidate the elections was thrown out by a High Court judge. While the SVLP-MNU initiated an appeal, another motion to invalidate the elections was made by two private citizens apparently supported by the opposition. In October another High Court judge ruled that the applicants of the second motion had a *prima facie* case as it pertained to the government's failure to undertake a boundaries review before the election. That motion was scheduled to be heard in January 1995.

Meanwhile, the SVLP-MNU formally united in October to form the Unity Labour

Party (ULP). Vincent Beache, former SVLP leader, was elected ULP leader. MNU leader Ralph Gonsalves was elected ULP deputy leader. Following the High Court decision of October the ULP demanded that Mitchell hold new elections. But Mitchell appeared determined to continue the battle in court in a case that was expected to eventually reach the Privy Council in London under right of final appeal.

Political Rights and Civil Liberties:

Citizens can change their government through elections. However, as described above, the legitimacy of the 1994 elections remained in question because of apparent registration irregularities and the government's failure to comply with a constitutional provision requiring an electoral boundaries review after a national census.

The extent of irregularities that caused some eligible voters to be disenfranchised remained unclear, but were almost certainly not so extensive as to alter the overall outcome of the vote. However, the lack of a boundaries review meant that voters may have been disproportionately distributed in some existing constituencies, which could have affected the results in those constituencies.

Constitutional guarantees regarding the right to free expression, freedom of religion and the right to organize political parties, labor unions and civic organizations are generally respected.

Political campaigns are hotly contested, with occasional charges from all quarters of harassment and violence, including police brutality. The 1994 campaign saw a particularly ugly rock-throwing clash between supporters of the main parties that left one NDP supporter dead and dozens injured on both sides.

Labor unions are active and permitted to strike. Nearly 40 percent of all households are headed by women, but the trend has yet to have an impact in the political or civic arenas.

The press is independent, with two privately owned independent weeklies, the *Vincentian* and the *News,* and a few fortnightlies run by political parties. The *Vincentian* has been charged with government favoritism by the opposition. Radio and television are government owned. Television offers differing points of view. Although equal access to radio, the medium that reaches the most people, is mandated during electoral campaigns, the ruling party abuses the state's control of programming, to the detriment of the opposition.

The judicial system is independent. The highest court is the West Indies Supreme Court (based in neighboring St. Lucia), which includes a Court of Appeal and a High Court, one of whose judges is resident on St. Vincent. There is a right of ultimate appeal in certain circumstances to the Privy Council in London.

The independent St. Vincent Human Rights Association has criticized judicial delays and the large backlog of cases caused by a shortage of personnel in the local judiciary, and has charged that the executive at times exerts inordinate influence over the courts. Prison conditions remain poor, and there are allegations of mistreatment.

Penetration by the hemispheric drug trade is increasingly a cause for concern and has led to opposition charges of drug-related corruption within the government and the police force and money-laundering in St. Vincent banks. The drug trade has also caused an increase in street crime.

San Marino

Polity: Parliamentary democracy
Economy: Capitalist
Population: 24,000
PPP: na
Life Expectancy: na
Ethnic Groups: Sammarinese (80 percent), Italian (18 percent)

Political Rights: 1
Civil Liberties: 1
Status: Free

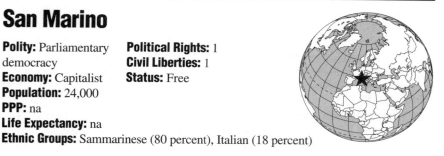

Overview:

In 1994 a coalition of Christian Democrats and Socialists continued to hold power following their combined majority in the 1993 general election.

According to tradition, a Christian stonecutter named Marinus founded San Marino in 301 A.D. Surrounded entirely by Italy, San Marino is the world's oldest republic. The country signed the first of several friendship treaties with Italy in 1862. Italy handles many of San Marino's foreign and security affairs and utilities, but otherwise San Marino has its own political institutions. The small republic became a full member of the U.N. in 1992.

The Grand and General Council has been the legislature since 1600. Its sixty members serve for a maximum term of five years. The council chooses the State Congress, which functions as a cabinet. It is chosen by the Council for six-month terms

San Marino has a lively multiparty system. In recent years, Socialists, Communists, Christian Democrats and Social Democrats have participated in coalition governments. After the collapse of communism in Eastern Europe, the Communists renamed themselves the Progressive Democratic Popular Party. Communist hardliners formed a rump Refounded Communist Party. In February 1992, the Christian Democrats broke up their coalition with the ex-Communists and formed a new one with the Socialists. In the 1993 general election, the Christian Democrats won 41.37 percent of the vote and 26 seats; the Socialists, 23.72 percent and 14 seats; the Progressive Democrats (ex-Communists), 18.58 percent and 11 seats; the Popular Democratic Alliance (ex-Christian Democrats), 7.7 percent and 4 seats; the Democratic Movement (Social Democrats), 5.27 percent and 3 seats; and the Refounded Communists, 3.36 percent and 2 seats. The Christian Democrats and Socialists formed a new ruling coalition.

The government extends official recognition to seventeen groups of Sammarinese living elsewhere. Over 10,000 Sammarinese live abroad, many of them in Italy. Recognized communities receive government subsidies for office space and communications, including fax machines. The state also subsidizes summer programs that bring young Sammarinese from abroad home for a month of education and travel.

Political Rights and Civil Liberties:

Sammarinese living at home and abroad have the right to change their government democratically. The foreign ministry covered three-fourths of the travel costs for emigrants who returned to San Marino to vote in 1993.

The media are free, and Italian newspapers and broadcasts are freely available.

Political parties, trade unions, and the government publish newspapers, periodicals and bulletins. The country has a vibrant, largely private enterprise economy that depends heavily on tourism. San Marino claims never to have refused asylum to people in need. However, refugees and other immigrants may apply for citizenship only after thirty years' residence. Women have made economic and political gains in recent decades, but, unlike men, women who marry foreigners may not pass citizenship to their spouses and children. There is freedom of religion and association. Both competing trade union movements are free.

Sao Tome and Príncipe

Polity: Presidential-par-**Political Rights:** 1
liamentary democracy   **Civil Liberties:** 2
Economy: Mixed statist   **Status:** Free
(transitional)
Population: 137,000
PPP: $600
Life Expectancy: 67.0
Ethnic Groups: Mixed race (Portuguese-Black African) majority;
small Portuguese minority

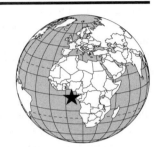

Overview: After three years in opposition, the former ruling party, the Movement for the Liberation of Sao Tome and Principe (MLSTP), is back in business. In the October 1994 legislative elections the MLSTP regained its parliamentary majority, marking the first time in the history of modern Africa that a ruling party lost its majority and then recaptured it through peaceful, democratic elections.

Located in the Gulf of Guinea 130 miles off the coast of Gabon, the Republic of Sao Tome and Principe consists of two main islands and several smaller islets. There are two provinces, twelve counties and fifty-nine localities. The country gained independence from Portugal in 1975. From that time until 1991, Manuel Pinto da Costa served as president and leader of the country's sole legal party, the MLSTP. At the end of 1989, the state embarked on a transformation from a leftist, single-party political structure into a multiparty democracy. A national MLSTP conference recommended constitutional amendments to allow for multiparty elections and term limitations for the office of the presidency. Opposition figures were granted amnesty and opposition movements were legalized.

In Sao Tome's first multiparty elections in January 1991, the MLSTP was defeated by the opposition Democratic Convergence Party (PCD). The PCD captured thirty-one seats in the fifty-five-member National Assembly, while the MLSTP won only twenty-one. In March 1991 the voters elected PCD-backed independent candidate Miguel dos Anjos Trovoada as president.

In 1994, relations between the National Assembly and the executive branch weakened to the point of crisis. The situation climaxed in June, when President Trovoada dismissed Prime Minister Norberto Costa Allegre on the grounds that the

PCD-approved leader had mismanaged funds. Soon after announcing the prime minister's removal, the president appointed a new temporary government and called for legislative elections to take place in October. The event was somewhat reminiscent of the last time that President Trovoadoa dismissed the prime minster; in 1990, Trovoada sacked Prime Minister Daniel Daio on charges of institutional disloyalty.

Six parties competed in the October election, although the only three with enough money and organization to launch workable campaigns were the MLSTP, the PCD, and the Independent Democratic Action Party (ADI). The MLSTP received most of its support from Angola, which sent Sao Tome a five-member public relations team.

Voter turnout was low. Of the 54,000 registered voters, only 40 percent actually voted, compared to the 77 percent turnout in the country's first election in 1977. The MLSTP regained its lost majority, capturing twenty-seven seats. The ADI and the PCD each won fourteen. Trovoada appointed Dr. Carlos Graca, the secretary-general of the MLSTP alliance, as the new prime minister.

In April, the National Assembly began reviewing a draft bill that calls for the Principe island to become an automonous state. The people of Principe claim that they are neglected by the Sao Tome government, 150 kilometers away.

Political Rights and Civil Liberties: Citizens of Sao Tome and Principe can change their government democratically. The October 1994 legislative elections showed that the people not only can hold fair elections, but that they are also able to peacefully re-elect a former ruling party.

The 1990 constitution provides for an independent judiciary. The judicial system, however, remains understaffed and underfunded.

The government controls most print and broadcast media, including a newspaper and a radio and television station. In May 1994 the national assembly passed a law which allows the opposition to take part in controlling the state-owned media. In addition, the new law forces the ruling party to consult with the opposition on "major issues of political interest." Also in May, two journalists were given six-month suspended sentences on charges of "abuse of press freedom." The journalists had reported that the president had withheld his signature from sixty decrees handed to him by the government in 1994.

Citizens can travel freely within the country; exit permits, however, are still required for foreign travel. Freedom of religion is respected. In 1992 labor organizers formed an Independent Union Federation (IUF), the nation's first legitimate labor confederation. The IUF seeks to represent workers in all sectors of the economy, but focuses on organizing plantation workers, the main source of employment. The underdeveloped economy limits economic opportunity. While a few women hold prominent political positions, most women still have traditional domestic roles.

Saudi Arabia

Polity: Traditional monarchy
Economy: Capitalist-statist
Population: 17,999,000
PPP: $10,850
Life Expectancy: 68.7

Political Rights: 7
Civil Liberties: 7
Status: Not Free

Ethnic Groups: Arab tribes, other Arab and Muslim immigrants

Overview:

In 1994 King Fahd's Saudi Arabian government continued to crack down on Islamic fundamentalists emboldened by the aggressiveness of their counterparts in Algeria, Egypt and Tunisia.

King Ibn Saud consolidated the Nejd and Hejaz regions of the Arabian Peninsula into the Kingdom of Saudi Arabia in 1932 and incorporated Asir a year later. Since his death in 1953, successive members of the Saud family have ruled this absolute monarchy. The king rules by decree and serves as prime minister, appoints all other ministers, and is the country's paramount religious leader. The current ruler, King Fahd ibn 'Abd al-'Aziz Al Sa'ud, assumed the throne in 1982. Crown Prince 'Abdallah ibn 'Abd al-'Aziz Al Sa'ud serves as deputy prime minister.

During the 1990-91 Gulf crisis the Kingdom allowed some 500,000 American and other Western soldiers to be stationed on its soil, widening a rift between pro-Western conservatives, including the ruling family, business interests and the middle class, and Islamic fundamentalists who feel the king is not fully implementing Islamic law and is too dependent on the West. Seeking to counteract the hardliners' influence, in March 1992 King Fahd introduced a modest liberalization program, including the eventual creation of an appointed *Majlis al-Shura* (Consultative Council) to debate policy decisions, review budgetary proposals and offer advice on domestic and foreign issues.

In November 1992, in a rare show of dissent in this tightly controlled country, 107 religious figures petitioned the king to demand a further Islamicization of society and a reduction of Western influences. In early May 1993 six fundamentalists announced the creation of the Committee for the Defense of Legitimate Rights (CDLR), headed by Muhammad al-Masaari, to press for a more rigorous application of Islamic laws in the country and to publicize alleged detentions by security forces of hardline preachers. The highest government-appointed religious body, the twenty-member *Ulemas* (Muslim Scholars) Council, ruled that groups such as the CDLR were unnecessary in a country already following Islamic law. The government stripped the six founding members of their government jobs, briefly detained several CDLR members, and held al-Masaari's son for six months.

In August 1993 the king formally named sixty pro-regime religious and tribal leaders, government officials, businessmen and retired military figures to sit in the inaugural Majlis for a four-year term. Two-thirds of the members have advanced degrees from Western universities. On 29 December King Fahd formally inaugurated the Majlis, although given the body's purely advisory role it is not expected to have much of a practical political impact.

Islamic activists in Saudi Arabia have been emboldened by the aggressiveness of their counterparts in Algeria, Egypt and Tunisia. On 26 September 1994 the government acknowledged that during the past three weeks it had arrested 110 Muslim militants, mostly in the northwest province of al-Qassim, including well-known radical scholars Salman al-Audah and Safar al-Hawali. In early October King Fahd set up a Supreme Council of Islamic Affairs, stacked with family members and technocrats and headed by a brother, Defense Minister Prince Sultan. Observers viewed the new body as an attempt to dilute the authority of the Ulemas Council, which has adopted a radical agenda.

In another issue, in June a Saudi diplomat in New York, Mohammed al-Khilewi, sought to defect on the grounds that he had knowledge of the Saudi government's human rights abuses and had been threatened by security agents. Also in June, Houston-based diplomat Ahmed Zahrani sought to defect to Britain after claiming the Saudi government had threatened him over a book on politics he had written.

In economic affairs, the government's profligate social and military spending in the past decade, combined with the collapse in oil prices since the mid-1980s, has left the country with a $12 billion budget deficit in 1993, 10 percent of GDP.

Political Rights and Civil Liberties: Saudi citizens cannot democratically change their government. Political parties are banned, the king rules by decree, and there are no elections at any level. The legal system is based on a strict interpretation of *Shari'a* (Islamic law). Beheadings are carried out for rape, murder, armed robbery, adultery, apostasy and drug trafficking. A conviction in capital-offense cases requires either two witnesses (four for adultery) or a confession. Police frequently torture detainees, particularly non-Western foreigners, to obtain confessions. Repeated thievery is punished by amputation of the right hand, while less serious crimes can be punished by flogging.

Although most suspects are charged within three days, those arrested by the Interior Ministry's General Directorate of Intelligence, also known as the *Mubahith*, are often held for weeks or months without being charged. Hundreds of Shiites and Christians have been detained simply for their religious beliefs. The number of religious detainees and political prisoners is unknown, since most persons in long-term detention are held incommunicado and have never been brought to trial. The Interior Ministry reportedly relies on a network of informants.

Western publications and alcohol are banned; women and men are segregated in workplaces, schools and restaurants; businesses must close during prayer times; and women must wear the *abaya* and other black garments covering the entire head, body and face. The official Committee for the Promotion of Virtue and the Prevention of Vice includes the *Mutawwa'in*, essentially religious police, who harass Saudi and foreign women for violating conservative dress codes or appearing in public with an unrelated male. Men are often harassed for patronizing videocassette rental shops. The Mutawwa'in occasionally enter homes to search for evidence. In May 1994 the Mutawwa'in harassed, physically assaulted and arrested a group of foreigners, including five Americans and six Canadians, leaving a party in Riyadh, the capital. Informal Islamic vigilante groups also patrol neighborhoods. Customs officials routinely open mail coming into the country.

The judiciary is not independent of the government. Judges are influenced by members of the royal family or by local officials. Defense lawyers can only assist clients during pre-trial investigations and are not permitted into the courtroom. Trials are generally closed, are conducted without procedural safeguards, are often brief and sometimes take place in the middle of the night. In some cases non-Arabic foreigners are not provided with a translator. The king must approve all capital punishment sentences.

Freedoms of speech and press are sharply restricted. Criticism of the royal family, the government or Islam is not permitted. A 1965 national security law prohibits newspapers from reporting on any public criticism of the government. The government frequently provides newspapers with official views on sensitive issues. The interior minister must approve and can remove all editors-in-chief, and the government has exercised this power on numerous occasions. The government owns all radio and television stations and news coverage reflects its views. In mid-1992 the government banned the importation and sale of satellite dishes, and on 10 March 1994 the government banned Saudis from owning and operating dishes. Political demonstrations or gatherings of any sort are prohibited, and permission must be obtained to form professional groups and other associations, which must be nonpolitical. Sheik Salman al-Audeh, whom the government arrested in September (*See Overview above*), had been banned from speaking at any pulpit because of his anti-government views,

Islam is the official religion and all citizens must be Muslims. The Shiite minority, which is concentrated in the Eastern Province, faces significant discrimination. Shiite public ceremonies are restricted to specific areas in major Shiite cities and are prohibited during the holy month of Muharram. The government generally prohibits private construction of Shiite mosques, offering instead to build the mosques but without certain Shiite symbols. Shiites are also barred from some government jobs. In October 1993 the government reached an agreement with an exile Shiite dissident group, the so-called Reform Movement, under which exiles will be allowed to return safely and an undetermined number of other Shiite dissidents freed from Saudi prisons. In return, the exiles agreed to stop publishing newsletters in Washington, D.C. and London criticizing the Saudi government. All public and private non-Muslim worship is prohibited, forcing non-Muslim foreign nationals to worship secretly. In 1993 the government banned independent charities run by fundamentalists that reportedly financed anti-government militants operating in Algeria, Egypt, Tunisia and Jordan.

Women must obtain permission from their husbands or fathers to travel to another part of the country or abroad, cannot drive cars or trucks or ride bicycles, must ride in the rear of buses, and face limited employment opportunities. Women must obtain governmental permission to marry foreigners, and in practice this is rarely granted. By law women receive only half as much of an inheritance as men and must prove specific grounds for a divorce. (Men can file for a divorce without providing cause). Domestic violence against women is reportedly relatively common. According to the U.S. State Department African nationals reportedly practice female genital mutilation.

Domestic laborers are subject to physical and sexual abuse, are forced to work long hours and are sometimes denied their wages. In 1994 two domestic workers filed a civil lawsuit in Houston claiming that Saudi agents kept them in a condition of servitude in the Ritz Carlton Hotel during a stay by a brother of King Fahd in 1991. African and Asian workers face informal discrimination in the courts and other areas. Employers generally hold the passports of foreign employees and must obtain exit visas for them, and in practice use this as leverage in resolving business disputes, or as a means of forcing employees to do extra work. The government prohibits trade unions, and collective bargaining and strikes are illegal.

Senegal

Polity: Dominant party
Economy: Mixed
capitalist
Population: 8,165,000
PPP: $1,680
Life Expectancy: 48.7
Ethnic Groups: Wolof (36 percent), Mende (30 percent),
Fulanai (17 percent), Serer (16 percent), other

Political Rights: 4
Civil Liberties: 5
Status: Partly Free

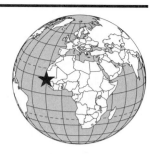

Overview:
In 1994 Senegal witnessed the aftershocks of France's decision to devalue by half the African Financial Community franc (CFA franc), the currency currently used by all its former colonies. Violent riots, allegedly fomented by President Abdou Diouf's opponents, including an Islamic movement, shook Dakar on 16 February, known henceforth as "Black Wednesday." The opposition force, adept at mustering massive support, presented a great challenge to President Diouf, struggling to consolidate his newly won victory in the wake of rising economic troubles. The two main opposition leaders, Abdoulaye Wade of the Senegalese Democratic Party (PDS) and Landing Savané of the African Party for Democracy and Socialism (PADS), were imprisoned for six months. Cuts in university subsidies continued to undermine the Socialist Party (PS) government's popularity.

After a decade of de facto one-party-rule by the PS, post colonial Senegal moved toward greater pluralism in the early 1970s under the presidency of Léopold Sédar Senghor, the poet-scholar who ruled during the twenty years following independence from France in 1960. Between 1974 and 1978, three additional parties gained recognition. In 1981, President Abdou Diouf, who replaced President Senghor, lifted the restrictions on the registration of political parties and a number of new parties emerged to challenge the ruling PS. The presidential election of 1988, in which Diouf received 72 percent of the vote, was followed by opposition party charges of fraud and periods of civil strife. In the wake of the unrest, Diouf orchestrated a rocky alliance with two opposition parties—the PDS and the Independence and Labor Party (PIT). In April 1991 the office of prime minister was reestablished and Habib Thiam was appointed to head a coalition government in which the PDS and the PIT joined the PS. The alliance held until October 1992 when Wade and three other members of the PDS left the coalition.

In the 1993 elections, President Diouf retained his post for an additional seven years, securing 58 percent of the popular vote. International observers cited minor irregularities. Despite the adoption of the 1992 electoral code, the elections were clouded by opposition party allegations of vote-rigging and election fraud. Confusion dominated the vote-certification process in the weeks following the presidential election. Madame Andresia Vaz, the head of the National Commission for Counting Votes (CNRV)—the body charged with processing and verifying election results before ratification by the Senegalese Constitutional Council—resigned, passing on the responsibility to the Constitutional Council. In March 1993 the head of Senegal's Constitutional Council, Keba Mbaye, also resigned. When the council finally disclosed the election results after weeks of delay, many opposition candidates declared the elections fraudulent.

Legislative elections followed on 9 May 1993. The ruling PS secured eighty-four seats, while the PDS secured twenty-seven seats with the remaining nine seats divided among other opposition parties. Again, a low voter turnout and allegations of election fraud marred the credibility of election results. Only six days after the election, the vice president of Constitutional Council, Babacar Sèye, was assassinated while the council was still deliberating on the formal certification of the election. In the wake of the assassination, the government arrested Wade and three top PDS associates. Earlier, Wade had criticized Seye and the Constitutional Council for promulgating flawed presidential and legislative election results. Wade and his wife were acquitted on 26 May 1994 because the court lacked evidence of complicity in the murder. In October 1994 Ibrahim Diakhate and Assane Diop were sentenced to eighteen years hard labor on charges of complicity and Mamdou Cledor Sene, considered the mastermind, to twenty years.

During the 1980s, Diouf began a program of economic reform to address Senegal's growing economic crisis. The reform program was met with much internal dissent as critics charged that it resulted in greater unemployment, a decrease in social services and a diminished purchasing power. Despite financial support from the World Bank and the International Monetary Fund and sporadic periods of progress, the economy stays fragile and the government is pressured to reverse economic policies to retain power in the face of competing parties that mobilize populist resentments against the painful side effects of reforms.

In 1994 the "Black Wednesday" riots broke out in Dakar and its suburbs to denounce the high cost of living following the devaluation of the CFA franc by 50 percent. Six policemen and two civilians died. The following day, the government banned the *Mushahidin wa al-Mashashidadi* movement, "men and women of true faith," accusing the Islamic group, and other opposition parties, of fomenting trouble.

Following reports of alleged Iranian government involvement in the financing of Islamic movements in Dakar, the authorities requested the withdrawal of the Iranian ambassador in May. The opposition umbrella group, the Coordination of Democratic Forces (CFD), which includes the PDS and the PADS, accused the government of provoking activists by barricading access routes to a public meeting scheduled for that day and authorizing the security forces to stop those who were going to the meeting. Wade and Savané were arrested for involvement in the demonstrations and convicted on 24 February along with seventy or so others including opposition politicians charged with "breach against state security." At the end of August the Criminal Court acquitted Wade and Savané, released after staging a hunger strike, along with four other politicians accused of complicity in the riots. PDS, PADS and MSU formed a new opposition coalition, *Bokk Sopi Senegal*, Wolof for Uniting to Change Senegal "to contribute to the strengthening of the law-based state." Previously, President Diouf announced in July intentions to reform the PS in the name of efficiency. Throughout the year, there was a heavy military presence in the streets of Dakar to prevent further explosion of social tensions due to economic hardship. In April the prices of imported goods soared despite government attempts to keep them down by decree.

In other social unrest, students at the University of Dakar staged a two-week long protest in June against new selection criteria and ransacked university buildings. The government is cutting expenditures by curbing its policy of universal access to free education and cutting some benefits.

On 27 February a thousand or so people were arrested for questioning during a major raid involving identity checks, drug related offenses and prostitution. Two days later, a second raid was carried out in the caves of the capital's seafront where police arrested more than 150 people, including bandits from Guinea, the Gambia and Liberia. A clash along the common border of Mali and Senegal turned deadly with incidents of vandalism.

Senegal was the only African country that put its forces on the ground in Rwanda alongside French troops, contributing 240 men.

Political Rights and Civil Liberties: Theoretically, Senegalese have the right to change their government democratically through periodic multiparty elections.

However, since independence, the ruling Socialist Party has dominated the political scene. The PS continues to benefit from the support of the religious hierarchy and low voter registration. The gain of parliamentary seats in the unicameral legislature by the opposition parties in the 1993 election may signal some limited political progress.

The judiciary is constitutionally independent of the executive and the legislative. However, the role of the Constitutional Court role became political in certifying the 1993 national elections.

Freedoms of assembly and association are protected under the constitution. Public demonstrations must receive prior government approval. An African Party for Democracy march slated for 18 February 1994 was banned on grounds of disturbing and threatening public order. The authorities also banned a rally in late June by opposition supporters of Wade.

Workers have the right to join trade unions and although union membership is confined to a small percentage of the overall population, unions are politically powerful. Workers also have the right to strike, which they exercise freely.

Freedom of the press is generally respected in Senegal. Magazines and weekly newspapers provide a spectrum of views and government criticism is frequently expressed. However, radio and television are government controlled. There are some legal restrictions on journalists that prohibit them from expressing views that discredit the State, incite the population to disorder or propagate "false news." In 1994, the director of the weekly, *Jeune Afrique* was sentenced on 2 June to a six-month suspended term *in absentia*. A magistrate sued him for libel because of an article on the murder of Babakar Seye. The distribution of the weekly was suspended in Senegal for one year.

Although Islam is the religion of 94 percent of all Senegalese, freedom of worship for all religions is respected. Senegal is a secular state, but Muslim leaders, called marabouts, play an important role in the political process. They are the link between the rural and largely illiterate masses and the elite.

As a result of a counterinsurgency operation by the government against the northern separatists, the Movement of Democratic Forces of Casamance (MFDC), the government indiscriminately shelled and burned villages suspected of harboring MFDC rebels. Extrajudicial executions, beatings, torture, and indefinite detention against suspected MFDC sympathizers have been reported. The MFDC has also been charged with similar human rights violations. The secessionist movement is composed mainly of members of the Diola ethnic group of the southern Casamance province. Many Diolas resent the national political dominance of the northern Wolof elite, mostly Muslim, as well as the presence of northern settlers in the Casamance. Thousands of citizens caught between the two forces have fled to neighboring Guinea-Bissau and Gambia. On 8 July 1993 the government signed a cease-fire agreement with the MFDC and refugees began returning to their villages.

Seychelles

Polity: Presidential-leg-
islative democracy
Economy: Mixed-statist
Population: 72,000
PPP: $3,683
Life Expectancy: 71.0
Ethnic Groups: Mixed African, South Asian, European

Political Rights: 3
Civil Liberties: 4
Status: Partly Free

Overview: **S**eychelles is an archipelago of 115 islands situated in the
Indian Ocean east of Tanzania. A geological oddity,
Seychelles are the only high-maritime granite islands. Both
Britain and France colonized the islands. French, Creole, and English are the local
languages. The country gained independence from the British in 1976. Prime
Minister France Albert Rene installed himself as head of state after overthrowing
elected President James Mancham in 1977. A year later Rene declared his
Seychelles People's Progressive Front (SPPF) to be the only legal party. Mancham
and other opposition figures operated parties and human rights groups in exile.

Rene combined authoritarian politics and substantial government ownership
with social welfare programs and environmental protection. He sought to preserve
the islands' natural beauty by prohibiting large numbers of tourists and limiting
commercial development.

In December 1991 Rene promised to legalize opposition parties and invited
political exiles to return to Seychelles to participate in a transition to multiparty
democracy. The SPPF passed a constitutional amendment that permitted new
parties. Seven opposition parties and the SPPF registered by April 1992.

Rene announced a three-stage democratic transition: an election for a constitutional commission, a constitutional referendum, and general elections. In July
1992, Seychellois voters selected a twenty-two-member commission to draw up a
new constitution. The vote gave the SPPF a 58.4 percent majority on the commission. Although Commonwealth election observers judged the voting free and fair,
the DP accused the SPPF of widespread intimidation and vote-buying.

The commission completed a draft constitution and presented it for a referendum in
November 1992. The law required the document to receive at least 60 percent approval.
Only 53.7 percent approved, however, and Rene had to reconvene the commission to
draft to amend the constitution. In June 1993, 73.9 percent of the electorate voted "Yes."

In the general election of 1993, President Rene received 59.5 percent of the vote and
James Mancham's Democratic Party, the main opposition group, received 36.72 percent.
In the race for the national assembly, the SPPF also won an overwhelming victory,
capturing 21 of the 22 directly elected seats and 6 of the 11 seats filled by proportional
representation. In 1994, Seychelles' transition to democracy continued without bloodshed.

Seaside vacationers provide approximately one-third of the island's income.
The Seychelles have the most successful tuna fishing industry in the Indian Ocean.
In 1994, plans were made to expand the fishing industry by increasing investments
in shrimp farming.

Political Rights and Civil Liberties: Seychellois can change their government democratically, but the long Rene dictatorship has left some residual authoritarian elements.

The media are partly free. During the general election campaign, the government-controlled Seychelles Broadcasting Corporation (SBC) provided substantial coverage to both government and opposition candidates. The government-owned newspaper, *The Nation,* was biased in favor of Rene and the SPPF. The opposition parties set up several weekly newspapers to rectify the imbalance in the print media. Some self-censorship remains as a result of the long dictatorship. Freedom of speech has improved since 1993.

Judges generally decide cases fairly, but they face some government pressure. There is religious freedom. The Catholic church issues a fortnightly newspaper that reports on national issues. There are no restrictions on internal travel, but the government may deny passports for reasons of "national interest." The National Workers Union is associated with the SPPF. The law permits strikes, but regulations inhibit workers from exercising this right.

⬇ Sierra Leone

Polity: Military (insurgency)   **Political Rights:** 7
Economy: Capitalist   **Civil Liberties:** 6
Population: 4,616,000   **Status:** Not Free
PPP: $1,020
Life Expectancy: 42.4
Ethnic Groups: Temme (30 percent), Mende (30 percent), Krio (2 percent), other
Trend Arrow: A growing insurgency and increasing violence were negative trends in 1994.

Overview: As the Revolutionary United Front's (RUF) insurgency in the eastern and southern regions of Sierra Leone spread to the north for the first time in the spring of 1994, the three-year-old rebellion in predominantly diamond mining and agricultural districts continued to severely drain the economy. In January the National Provisional Ruling Council (NPRC) led by Captain Valentine Strasser cancelled its unilateral cease-fire and declared "total war" on the rebels. While Strasser announced that a time limit for the return to civilian rule was not feasible while the fighting went on, government critics accused him of continuing the war to prolong his term beyond 1996, the scheduled date for presidential and legislative elections. Four Britons of Vietnamese origin, allegedly linked to former deputy head of state Solomon Musa, were charged with plotting to overthrow the government on 16 October 1993.

Sierra Leone had been on the path toward multiparty politics when unpaid troops returning from the fight against the RUF rebels protested against the civilian government of President Joseph Momoh. On 29 April 1992 a group of officers led by the twenty-seven-year-old Strasser ousted Momoh. The putschists replaced the civilian authorities with the military council, and banned all political activity. Strasser accused the regime of being corrupt and responsible for the economy's deterioration, and of being insincere in pursuing the democratic reforms forced on Momoh by student protests in 1990. Strasser pledged to prepare for a multiparty system, and end the rebellion. The NPRC established a nineteen-member Consultative Council in November 1993 to serve as an advisory body.

On 28 December 1992 the NPRC announced that the army thwarted an attempt to overthrow the Strasser-led junta by a group called the Anti-Corruption Revolutionary Movement. One of the leaders of the alleged plot was the popular Lieutenant Colonel James Yaya Kanu, a possible presidential successor to Momoh. On 29 and 30 December 1992 a special military court found twenty-six persons, including Kanu, guilty and ordered their summary execution.

Throughout 1994 Sierra Leonians were disappointed that the "kids running the country," *Nar Pikin Rule Party,* Captain Strasser's advisers, had not delivered on any of their promises. Strasser was plagued with allegations of nepotism and tribal bias in his appointments. His opponents charged him with having a Creole grand plan to take over the government.

By January 1994 the rebel war, which was initiated in March 1991 by Foday Sankoh's RUF, had claimed 20,000 lives. The military council blamed Charles Taylor's National Patriotic Front of Liberia (NPFL) of arming RUF rebels and of creating an enclave within Sierra Leone for harboring NPFL arms and men. According to Strasser, peace depends on the resolution of the Liberian war because the rebels and the NPFL share the same supply line. The RUF insurgency was born in 1991 out of the civil war in neighboring Liberia, where the NPFL gave its support to a group of Momoh opponents in retaliation for Sierra Leone's contribution to anti-Taylor West African intervention forces. The armed group dismissed Momoh's reforms as mere show, vowing to fight for "true pluralism."

Following Strasser's takeover, the fighting intensified, as the government was unwilling to enter into negotiations with the RUF. On 1 March 1993, the United Liberation Movement (ULIMO), an anti-Taylor Liberian faction, joined the Sierra Leone Army to recover a sizable territory from the RUF. Following months of a seesaw campaign in which territory changed hands several times between the government and the rebels, the government forces claimed to have pushed the rebels back to the Liberian border.

With the government's suspension of the unilateral cease-fire and the regime's declaration of "total war," in 1994 Sierra Leone witnessed offensive after counter-offensive even as the regime offered amnesty to all rebels prepared to lay down their arms. By March, the rebels had advanced their offensive to the north where they attacked a mining town near the Guinea border. In April, the government sacked several senior officers and the army chief. Fighting resumed in the eastern part of the country. Renegade army units defected to the ranks of the rebels, and rumors that the army looted and burned houses and then laid the blame on the rebels hampered efforts to end the war.

In a campaign to rehabilitate the army, two officers were arrested in connection with the murder of a Dutch family and an Irish priest. Following the disappearance of the head of a counterinsurgency unit, an investigation revealed evidence of corruption and malpractice. In July, after brutal rebel attacks on civilians crossing the ambushed Bo-Kamena road, Strasser set up a National War Council in which paramount chiefs demanded that the army begin disarming members of Liberia's ULIMO faction because they feared ethnic feuds within the ULIMO would spill over the border from Liberia.

The government proposed conditions for recognition of the RUF as a political force and for its eventual participation in the democratic process. The conditions—an immediate cease-fire, the release of all hostages, including two British aid workers, and the transformation of the RUF into a political movement—were turned down. The RUF only wants recognition from the British, whom they claim supply the government with arms. Government offensives intensified at the end of the year.

Political Rights and Civil Liberties: The citizens of Sierra Leone cannot change their government democratically. The military regime dissolved the parliament, banned independent political activity, and suspended all provisions of the 1991 democratic constitution inconsistent with its decrees. The NPRC has no set timetable to restore civilian rule because of the ongoing rebel war. A new draft constitution intended to go into effect with the return of civilian rule proscribes one-party systems, but does not ban military coups.

In late 1992 the NPRC created special military tribunals to punish treason and other capital crimes. The tribunals consist of five judges who are military officers, and who frequently lack judicial training. Both civilians and soldiers may be tried, verdicts cannot be appealed, and those convicted can be executed. The execution of the twenty-six alleged coup plotters in December 1993 came within hours of the verdict. Most of the accused lacked legal representation. In 1994, five soldiers were court-martialled for collaboration with the rebels. Their trial was the first trial conducted by the military that did not lead to the execution of soldiers suspected of collaboration.

Following the government takeover by the NPRC, the junta declared emergency legislation that gave the security forces unlimited powers of detention without charge and prevented such detention from being challenged. On 7 May 1994 the authorities arrested nineteen former ministers and deputy ministers who served under Momoh for failing to reimburse money acquired illegally during their service. The detainees were denied family visits, access to legal representation and recourse to the courts.

Both parties in the rebellion are guilty of human right violations, including looting, torture and extrajudicial execution. Rebels who surrendered to government troops to take advantage of the NPRC-announced amnesty were said to have been executed. Military officers drafted children into the army to fight the rebels. Subsequently, the NPRC decreed the immediate discharge of all soldiers under the age of fifteen. In a crackdown against a lack of discipline, on 12 November, the government executed twelve soldiers sentenced in 1992 for murder and armed robbery.

Freedom of expression, respected in the final months of the Momoh regime, has been severely curtailed. On 13 January 1993 the regime announced new guidelines for the press, requiring the newspapers to fulfill stringent administrative requirements to continue operating. The requirements call for newspapers to provide collateral equivalent to several thousand dollars, to employ at least one editor with a university degree and at least four years of experience, and the office to have a telephone. Following the decree, only fourteen newspapers continued to publish, as opposed to thirty at the time of the decree's publication. Journalists continued to be harassed and physically attacked for their criticism of the NPRC's human rights abuses and corruption. The Sierra Leone News Agency (SLENA), a government-run radio, misinforms listeners about the state of affairs in the country.

Freedom of religion is respected in this predominantly Muslim country. Other religious groups such as Christians and animists practice their beliefs freely.

All workers have the right to join trade unions of their choice. Unions are independent of government. They have the right to strike, but the government may require twenty-one days' notice. Individual labor unions customarily join the Sierra Leone Labor Congress (SLLC).

Singapore

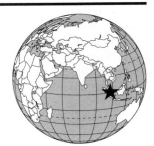

Polity: Dominant party
Economy: Mixed capitalist
Population: 2,930,000
PPP: $14,734
Life Expectancy: 74.2
Ethnic Groups: Ethnic Chinese (76 percent), Malay (15 percent), Pakistani and Indian (7 percent)

Political Rights: 5
Civil Liberties: 5
Status: Partly Free

Overview:

Midway through a five-year term Prime Minister Goh Tok Chong of Singapore continues to wield the government apparatus against dissidents and other critics. This is contrary to promises preceding the 1991 election that he would offer a more open, consultative leadership style than his predecessor, Lee Kuan Yew.

Originally established as a trading station in 1819, Singapore became a British colony in 1867. The colony became self-governing in 1959, entered the Malaysian Federation 1963 and in 1965 became fully independent under Prime Minister Lee Kuan Yew. Since then the conservative People's Action Party (PAP) has dominated politics and has spread its Confucian-based social values of savings, hard work and discipline through the media, public advertising campaigns, labor associations and the military. In the process, the country has been transformed from a squalid island into a miniature economic power. The PAP completely swept elections from 1968 to 1980 before losing a by-election in 1981.

In October 1990 Lee stepped down in favor of his handpicked successor, Goh Tok Chong, although the seventy-one-year-old former premier still exerts considerable political influence as senior minister in the government. Goh called a snap election in August 1991 to get a mandate for his leadership. Although the opposition contested only forty of the eighty-one seats, the PAP had its worse showing ever, winning seventy-seven seats with 61 percent of the overall vote. The Singapore Democratic Party (SDP) took three seats, and the center-left Worker's Party one. After the election Goh candidly admitted the PAP had become too elitist, neglecting the needs of the working-class Chinese voters who form its traditional base.

The opposition might have won more seats if not for changes in the electoral law prior to the vote. The government increased the number of Group Representation Constituencies (GRC) from thirteen to fifteen, and increased the number of seats in each from three to four. Opposition groups have trouble contesting GRCs because they must come up with four credible candidates, one of whom must be non-Chinese, in a society in which few are willing to openly challenge the government.

In August 1993 Singapore held elections for an expanded presidency. The government claimed that Singapore needed a stronger presidency, with the power to approve budgets, oversee the country's assets and approve political appointments, to protect the country's considerable foreign reserves against the possibility of a free-spending government coming to power in the future. Prime Minister Goh admitted that the strict requirements for holding office—candidates must have held one of several senior public offices, including cabinet minister, speaker of parliament and attorney general, or have run a company with paid-up capital of more than $62.5 million— left only about 400 citizens eligible to run.

Prior to the vote the government established a three-member screening committee, two of whom are government appointees, with broad powers to veto candidates. In August the committee rejected J.B. Jeyaretnam and Tan Soo Phan, both of the opposition Worker's Party, for lack of "integrity, good character and reputation."

The government ran deputy prime minister Ong Teng Cheong for the office, and persuaded Chua Kim Yeow, a retired, nonpartisan, former accountant-general, to run as a token opposition. Although Chua barely campaigned, Ong won with only 58.7 percent of the vote, a clear rebuff to the PAP, which had hoped for a minimum 65 percent tally. Many voters seem tired of the PAP's political dominance and social paternalism, which extends to a ban on chewing gum.

The main opposition SDP has been unable to take advantage of the PAP's vulnerability due to its own internal rift. In August 1993, after the party expelled secretary general Chiam See Tong for alleged breach of discipline, a breakaway faction formed a new SDP central committee. In December 1993 a court ordered Chiam reinstated in the SDP, and in January 1994 the High Court declared the new central committee to be illegal. It is unclear whether the SDP will be able to unify in time for the next elections, due by 1996.

Political Rights and Civil Liberties: Citizens of Singapore nominally have the right to change their government through free elections, although the ruling PAP maintains its political monopoly through various institutional advantages and by intimidating opposition politicians.

Under the Internal Security Act (ISA) the president can authorize detention of suspects without trial for an unlimited number of two-year periods. Currently there are no ISA detainees, although the government is using the ISA to restrict the travel, residence, speech and publishing rights of two former detainees, both political dissidents. Under the Criminal Law (Temporary Provisions) Act, which also authorizes detention without trial, the government is holding more than 300 people for being involved with secret societies, and more than 400 people for drug trafficking. In 1989 the government amended the constitution to limit judicial review of detentions under the ISA and the Criminal Law (Temporary Provisions) Act to procedural grounds, and to prevent the judiciary from reviewing the constitutionality of any anti-subversion law.

The death penalty is mandatory for certain drug offenses. In September 1994 Dutch engineer Johannes Van Damme became the first Westerner to be hanged for drug trafficking, despite evidence that suggested he had been set up by a Nigerian cartel.

The caning in May 1994 of an American teenager accused of vandalism brought publicity to a form of punishment that is carried out an average of 1,000 times a year in Singapore, and to the authorities' methods of interrogation. Caning was introduced by the 1966 Vandalism Act and is now applied for other offenses including rape, robbery and overstaying a visa. Each year scores of workers from developing countries are flogged for visa violations. The teenager, Michael Fay, insisted that he was physically coerced into making a confession and that a fifteen-year-old Malaysian youth arrested in the case was beaten so badly that an eardrum was punctured. Police reportedly regularly abuse detainees to extract confessions.

The government continues to harass opposition figures through dismissal from public sector jobs, libel suits and the threat of such suits. The government has brought Worker's Party leader J.B. Jeyaretnam to near-financial ruin through a series of controversial court cases, including a 1986 fraud conviction that was criticized by the Privy Council in London. In May 1993 the National University dismissed Dr. Chee Soon Juan for "dishonest conduct" merely for using $138 out of his research grant to courier his wife's doctoral thesis to a United States university. Chee, an SDP assistant secretary-general, ran against Goh in a December 1992 by-election and had written a series of letters to local newspapers criticizing the government's social welfare policies. Chee was subsequently sued for defamation by his department head, and in February 1994 abandoned his legal defense of the charges.

There are no jury trials although some other safeguards exist. However, persons detained under the ISA and the Criminal Law (Temporary Provisions) Act are not entitled to a public trial. The independence of the judiciary is questionable. Lower court judges are appointed by and serve at the discretion of the president; higher court judges are considered to be closely aligned with the government.

The Societies Act requires organizations of more than ten people to register with the government, and restricts political activity to political parties. However, the PAP wields strong influence over ostensibly nonpolitical associations such as neighborhood groups and trade unions while the opposition is not permitted to form neighborhood or other similar support groups. Freedom of expression is restricted. Under the ISA, public statements that could even indirectly incite ethnic or religious antagonism, or disrupt public order or security, are illegal. In December 1994 Prime Minister Goh personally warned author Catherine Lim after she had written a newspaper article comparing the leadership styles of Goh and Lee Kuan Yew.

Police approval is required for individual speakers at public functions. The government occasionally denies such permits to opposition party members seeking to address dinners and banquets. Approval is also required for any public assembly of more than five people.

The government tightly controls the media, and editorials and domestic news coverage strongly favor the ruling party. Key "management shares" in the Singapore Press Holdings, which publishes all major newspapers, must be held by government-approved individuals. The Newspaper and Printing Presses Act (NPPA) prohibits any person or group from holding more than 3 percent of a newspaper company unless exempted. The government also owns all six television channels and nine of twelve radio stations. Individual citizens are banned from owning satellite dishes.

In November the government filed contempt of court charges against American academic Christopher Lingle for a 7 October article in the *International Herald Tribune* that criticized unnamed "intolerant regimes" in Asia that rely on subtle measures including a "compliant judiciary." On 17 October police interrogated Lingle, who had been a visiting fellow at the National University, for ninety minutes and he left the country several days later. The suit also named the *International Herald Tribune*, its publisher, its Singapore corespondent, and the Singapore Press Holdings, the company that prints the local edition of the *Tribune*. On 10

December the *Herald Tribune* published a formal apology, but two days later former premier Lee filed a separate libel suit.

The broadly drawn Official Secrets Act bars the unauthorized release of government data to the media. In June 1992 the *Business Times* published "flash" GDP estimates several days before the latest figures were officially announced. In March 1994 a court found the editor of the *Business Times*, a journalist and three economists guilty of "endangering state security" and issued fines.

An amendment to the NPPA allows the government to "gazette," or restrict circulation of, any foreign publication it feels has interfered with domestic politics. In August 1993 the government capped the circulation of the London *Economist* at its current level of 7,500 after it had deleted a sentence from a government response to a June article on the *Business Times* case. Limits remain on the *Far Eastern Economic Review*, *Asiaweek* and *The Asian Wall Street Journal*, although the latter two are now allowed to distribute at their original level before they were gazetted.

Freedom of religion is generally respected in practice, although the Jehovah's Witnesses and the Unification Church are banned under the Societies Act. Citizens must carry identification cards at all times. Workers, other than those in essential industries, have the right to strike but rarely do so, in part because a labor shortage gives them bargaining leverage.

Slovakia

Polity: Parliamentary democracy
Economy: Mixed-capitalist transitional
Population: 5,342,000
PPP: na
Life Expectancy: na
Ethnic Groups: Slovak (82 percent), Hungarians (11 percent), Roma (4.8 percent), Czechs (1.2 percent)

Political Rights: 2
Civil Liberties: 3
Status: Free

Ratings Change: Slovakia's political rights rating changed from 3 to 2 and its civil liberties rating from 4 to 3 because the Moravcik government allowed freer expression and improved the sit¡utation of ethnic minorities. As a result Slovakia's status changed from Parlty Free to Free.

Overview:

The resignation of the coalition government of populist Prime Minister Vladimir Meciar and the Movement for a Democratic Slovakia (HZDS) and its subsequent return to power after October national elections marked the key political development in 1994. Other issues included conflicts over privatization and corruption, a national referendum on the purchase of state property, and increased demands for self-government by the substantial Hungarian minority.

This small central European nation was established on 1 January 1993 following the formal dissolution of Czechoslovakia that ended a seventy-four-year-old federation created after World War I. Slovakians trace their ancestry to the short-lived Great

Moravian Empire of the ninth century, during which Slovaks and Czechs united briefly. As early as the tenth century, Hungarians seized control of the region and for the next 1,000 years ruled with a system of serfdom and repression. Czech-Slovak unity after World War I was relatively brief, as Nazi Germany's dismemberment of Czechoslovakia provided an opportunity for militant Slovak nationalists to seize power and establish a nominally independent state under Josef Tiso, tainted by its allegiance to the Third Reich and its role in the deportation of Jews and Roma (Gypsies).

The "velvet revolution" of 1989 brought down the hard-line Communist system in place since Soviet tanks crushed the pro-reform Dubcek regime in 1968 but also sowed the seeds for Czech-Slovak tensions, partly because much outmoded Soviet-era industry was located in Slovakia, making economic reform and Western investment difficult. Results of the June 1992 federal and regional elections made the split inevitable; Vaclav Klaus, an uncompromising pro-market reformer was elected to head the Czech republic. Meciar, who ran on a nationalist platform, won in Slovakia. Within six months, the decision to separate was made.

In the 1992 elections Meciar's HZDS had won 74 of 150 seats in the republican parliament. The Party of the Democratic Left (SDL), made up of former Communists, emerged as the second-largest bloc with 28 seats. The Slovak National Party (SNS), the only party to stand unambiguously for Slovak independence, won 15 seats and agreed to be a junior partner in the post-election HZDS-SNS government. However, strains over policy and personalities plagued the coalition through much of 1993.

By early 1994 political bickering within the coalition and HZDS virtually paralyzed parliament. In early February, Meciar sought a nationwide referendum to end the stalemate after his deputies walked out of parliament having failed to push through a privatization law. Eight of seventy-four HZDS deputies had defected in 1993, charging the prime minister with authoritarian methods. Six of the SNS's deputies, including party leader Ludovit Cernak, broke with Meciar and sided with the opposition. Meciar said he would begin collecting signatures for a referendum on whether deputies who had left party ranks could keep their parliamentary seats. Under Slovak law, 350,000 signatures were needed to call a referendum. But under the constitution, only the president, Milan Kovac, could dissolve parliament and call general elections if citizens demanded new elections in a referendum.

A key issue in the conflict was Meciar's effort to control the country's privatization by refusing to relinquish power over the ownership of the largest state-owned industries. Meciar's role as acting minister of privatization and head of the Fund for National Property, which administered companies awaiting privatization, galvanized the opposition. The crisis deepened with the 9 February defections of ten HZDS deputies who announced the establishment of an opposition faction called the Alternative of Political Realism (APR), which called for the formation of a nonpartisan transitional government to replace Meciar's coalition until early elections.

On 11 March, after months of political gridlock, parliament toppled the government in a no-confidence motion, seventy-eight to two, with seventy abstentions, in a secret ballot. The vote followed an address by Meciar, who urged the president—who had earlier accused the prime minister of corruption— to resign and reiterated his call for June elections. He was officially dismissed on 14 March, and two days later former Slovak foreign minister Jozef Moravcik was chosen to head the government as caretaker and approved by the president. Elections were slated for 30 September and 1 October, nearly two years ahead of schedule. The new government included ministers from the Christian Democratic Party, led by former prime minister Jan Carnogursky; the SDL, led by Peter Weiss; the rebel APR; and several minor parties. Moravcik pledged to step up economic reform and privatization.

The new government moved on several important issues. It sought to ameliorate concerns of the 560,000-strong Hungarian minority by pushing through laws to safeguard Hungarian language rights. In return, the country's fourteen Hungarian parliamentary deputies joined Moravcik's four-party coalition. In economic policy, the government implemented tough macro-economic measures by cutting social spending, raising taxes and planned to cut farm subsidies. As a result, the International Monetary Fund (IMF) extended $263 million in credits. The government also moved to implement a second wave of voucher privatization involving as many as 500 companies. It also sought to strengthen anticorruption and money-laundering laws alleged to have been ignored or abused during the last days of the Meciar regime. By late summer, inflation was falling, unemployment had stabilized, and GDP had increased by 5.3 percent in the second quarter.

Nevertheless, opinion surveys showed Meciar's HZDS as the most popular party, with around 30 percent in the polls. Meciar's populist, anti-reform and anti-Hungarian rhetoric resounded among the country's 15 percent unemployed, peasants and pensioners. He promised to increase pensions and social security handouts and lambasted the government's privatization plans as "robbery of the Slovak people." Meciar relied on the HZDS's wealth and organization, including a full-time staff of 190, a fleet of vehicles and security guards. HZDS Vice President Augustin Huska promised that the HZDS would "correct" privatization, adding that the party was "for a market economy but against the accumulation of capital." Prime Minister Moravcik's Democratic Union of Slovakia got 10 percent support in the polls.

On 12 August President Kovac called for a 22 October referendum to decide whether to require all Slovak citizens buying state property in the country's privatization program to state the source of their funds. The move was forced on the government by the opposition, which claimed that a similar law passed by the government did not go far enough. Analysts saw the referendum as a ploy by Meciar and leftist forces to undermine the government's reform efforts. On 19 August the HZDS, the Slovak Green Alternative and the Farmers' Party signed a coalition, maintaining that their individual programs would by better served after the elections by a joint effort.

In September the government postponed final decisions on the range of privatization proposals until after the elections. The move was made to remove political uncertainty from the process and in response to a pledge made by the Christian Democrat members of the ruling coalition that no privatization decisions be made during the campaign. The National Property Fund did open from 1 August to 30 August for bids for stakes in state companies not included in the voucher privatization program. More than half a million people had registered to buy shares through the voucher scheme.

As the election approached, it became apparent that although Meciar was the most popular candidate, he would find it difficult to assemble a governing coalition. His former coalition, partner, the SNS, which campaigned on unbridled nationalism (it had to apologize for the publication of anti-Semitic material) and a return to Communist-era state control over the economy, was doing poorly in the polls.

The elections, which saw 18 parties compete for the 150 seats, presaged further political disarray, with Meciar's HZDS polling 35 percent of the vote, not enough to rule without coalition partners. The HZDS won control of 61 seats; the leftist Common Cause Coalition led by the SDL got 18 seats; a coalition of Hungarian parties won 17 seats; the Christian Democrats got 17; the Democratic Union, 15; the left-wing Workers Association (ZRS), 13; and the SNS, 9. Turnout was put at 75 percent.

Negotiations to assemble a governing coalition were difficult. On 31 October, a full month after the election, Meciar—in a letter to the president—formally agreed to try to form a coalition government. On 2 November a political agreement was reportedly reached between the HZDS, the SNS and the ZRS. On 11 December Meciar announced a coalition government with the SNS and ZRS. HZDS would contribute ten ministers, the ZPS three, and the SNS, two. Earlier, Meciar pushed through a series of controversial laws, effectively giving his coalition parties control of the state broadcast media and state intelligence service.

Meciar's appointment as privatization minister of Peter Bisak, a virtually unknown nominee and a fierce component opponent of selling off state companies, signalled a serious downgrading of the ministry. It left policy in this crucial area in the hands of Meciar and Sergej Kozlik, his new finance minister and chief economic adviser.

During September's election campaign the prime minister said he would introduce wholesale changes in the way state assets are sold, and to whom. Meciar was expected to push for sales to existing company management, many of whom are HZDS supporters.

Political Rights and Civil Liberties:

Citizens of Slovakia have the means under the 1992 constitution to change their government democratically; the 1994 elections were deemed free and fair. The constitution has come under fire from the 560,000-strong Hungarian minority, which has objected to the preamble which begins "We, the Slovak nation..." and not "We, the *citizens* of Slovakia." The document, which calls for a strong executive, has been criticized for leaving the door open for one-party domination, and contains ambiguous language that could be interpreted to restrict freedom of speech and expression, limit the inviolability of the home, as well as the rights to assembly and privacy of the mail.

The constitution calls for an independent judiciary, though the system is backlogged and two-thirds of current judges remain from the pre-1989 Communist period. The ten-member Constitutional Court is appointed by the president.

There are restrictions on freedom of the press. Under Meciar, the government and HZDS restricted access to government and party officials, favoring pro-government newspapers and barring independent, opposition publications. Statutory limits on criticizing the government were used in January 1994 by a city prosecutor against a newspaper editor. In February the cabinet proposed eliminating provisions that make defamation of the state and government illegal; legislation was pending. Journalists faced intimidation and harassment, and government control of the distribution system (PNS) has led to frequent complaints about the PNS refusing to carry papers out of favor with the government. State-run television and radio, overseen by the politically influenced Board for Radio and Television Broadcasting, has too often served as a noncritical, pro-government organ, particularly under the Meciar regime.

Minority rights remain a contentious issue. While the Moravcik government made some cultural concessions to the Hungarian minority and sought rapprochement with Hungary, the re-election of Meciar and the HZDS, which used anti-Hungarian rhetoric in the campaign and was anti-Hungarian while in power, raised the specter of exacerbated tensions. Early in the year, an assembly of Hungarians demanded more self-government and special status for the southern border regions where Hungarians constitute a majority. Gypsies have been vulnerable to acts of social prejudice and violence, often ignored by government authorities.

Freedom of religion in this overwhelmingly Catholic country is respected. A 1993 law dealt with the restitution of church property confiscated after 1945, and Jewish community property seized after 1938. Nationalist organizations such as the SNS continue to espouse anti-Semitism.

There are few significant restrictions on domestic and foreign travel. Restrictive refugee laws and Supreme Court decisions have drawn concern from the U.N. High Commissioner for Refugees.

Women nominally have the same rights as men, but are underrepresented in managerial posts. Workers have the right to organize and belong to trade unions, and generally have the right to strike. The Slovak Confederation of Trade Unions is the main union confederation.

Slovenia

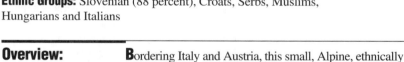

Polity: Presidential-parliamentary democracy
Economy: Mixed-statist (transitional)
Population: 1,992,000
PPP: na
Life Expectancy: 71.0
Ethnic Groups: Slovenian (88 percent), Croats, Serbs, Muslims, Hungarians and Italians

Political Rights: 1
Civil Liberties: 2
Status: Free

Overview: Bordering Italy and Austria, this small, Alpine, ethnically homogenous former Yugoslav republic entered its fourth year of independence with the most prosperous economy of the former East Bloc. Under the coalition government of Prime Minister Janez Drnovsek, leader of the Liberal Democratic Party (LDS), it also achieved relative political stability.

Slovenia, which for centuries was part of the Hapsburg Empire before being incorporated into the newly created Yugoslavia after World War I, declared independence in June 1991. Its well-armed territorial defense forces secured the nation's borders by staving off intervention by the Yugoslav People's Army. In presidential and parliamentary elections in December 1992, popular incumbent Milan Kucan, leader of the (former Communist) Party of Democratic Renewal (LCS-PDR, later changed to the Liberal Democrats) was re-elected. The LDS led the vote for a new 130-seat bicameral parliament with 23 percent of the vote. The new body replaced a cumbersome, 240-member tricameral assembly. The Christian Democrats (SKD) got 14.9 percent.

In January 1993 Drnovsek, a former president of the Yugoslav federal republic, was re-elected prime minister. The cabinet consisted of members from the Liberal Democrats, the Christian Democrats and, in the person of Defense Minister Janez Jansa, the Social Democrats.

Key issues in 1994 were the dismissal of the defense minister after allegations that he wire-tapped reporters' phones, continued economic restructuring, the arms embargo of former Yugoslavia and worsening relations with Italy over the Istrian peninsula.

Early in the year, domestic political infighting focused on President Kucan and Defense Minister Jansa. A major topic had been the 1993 Maribor arms affair brought on after a container allegedly containing humanitarian aid turned out to conceal 120 tons of weapons destined for Bosnia. The defense minister blamed the president for the affair, while the state prosecutor claimed to have documentary evidence implicating Jansa for violating the arms embargo on ex-Yugoslav republics. A final report has yet to be drafted.

Jansa, leader of a center-right coalition, also maintained that the president exercised authority not outlined in the constitution, and that members of the old political elite continued to hold key positions in government and business. President Kucan's supporters pointed out that Jansa, a former Communist Youth League functionary, was himself "part of the old structure."

On 24 March, the prime minister asked parliament to dismiss Jansa after Milan Smolniker, a former security agent, supplied copies of documents supporting bugging charges against the defense minister to the opposition weekly *Mladina*. Smolniker was detained by military security officers, badly beaten and hospitalized under police protection. Jansa stepped down.

In April, Prime Minister Drnovsek merged his Liberal Democrats with three smaller left-of-center parties to take control of one-third of the ninety-seat National Assembly.

With a per capita GDP of $6,100, almost double that of neighboring Hungary or the Czech republic, Slovenes continued to enjoy the highest standard of living of all the former Communist countries. Key issues in 1994 were measures to attract foreign investment and to expand privatization. After two years of prolonged and confusing debate, privatization expanded to include 2,500 companies over the next two years. A new law allowed for 100 percent foreign ownership of Slovene companies, although there were still restrictions limiting investment in sensitive areas such as defense, aviation, telecommunications and media.

The 1991 U.N. arms embargo on ex-Yugoslavia applied to Slovenia, and limited Slovenia's efforts to build its own army, air defense and reconnaissance. In March, Slovenia joined NATO's Partnership for Peace, which eased some security concerns. A contentious foreign policy issue developed after neo-fascist electoral gains in Italy raised fears about revanchist designs on Istria, a peninsula divided between Slovenia and Croatia. After Italy's defeat in World War II, Tito's Communist partisans incorporated the area, except for the city of Trieste, into Yugoslavia. The Slovenes saw recent disputes over compensation as an attempt by Italy, prompted by fascists, to redraw postwar borders.

Political Rights and Civil Liberties:

Slovenes have the means to change their government democratically. The 1992 elections were openly contested by many parties and candidates. Under the multiparty system, career military and police personnel may not be members of political parties.

The judiciary is independent. Judges are elected by the state Assembly on the recommendation of the eleven-member Judicial Council, five of whose members are selected by parliament on the nomination of the president, and six of whom are sitting judges selected by their peers. Nominees for the nine-member Constitutional Court are made by the president and approved by parliament.

Slovenia has lively broadcast and print media. Newspapers, many affiliated with political parties, print diverse views often critical of the government. Though the state controls most radio and television, there are private stations, among them Kanal A TV in Ljubljana, the capital. Journalists have faced limited suspension for commentary on statements by government officials, and self-censorship remains an issue.

Freedom of assembly is guaranteed and respected, though there are restrictions dealing with public safety, national security and health. There are no restrictions on freedom of religion. There are no practical restrictions on domestic and foreign travel or on emigration. In March, Slovenia refused admittance to Russian extremist Vladimir Zhirinovsky, citing an earlier visit in which he disturbed public order after a bout of drinking.

Minority rights are guaranteed by law; Hungarians and Italians are constitutionally guaranteed one seat each in parliament. The presence of 100,000 refugees from Bosnia has led to some problems of accommodation and discrimination. Women are guaranteed equality under the law.

There are three main labor federations and most workers are free to join unions that are formally independent from government and political parties, though members may and do hold positions in the legislature.

Solomon Islands

Polity: Parliamentary democracy
Economy: Capitalist
Population: 361,000
PPP: $2,113
Life Expectancy: 70.0
Ethnic Groups: Melanesian (93 percent), small Polynesian, Micronesian and European minorities

Political Rights: 1
Civil Liberties: 2
Status: Free

Overview: Solomon Mamaloni, who served as the Solomon Islands' prime minister in 1982-84 and in 1989-93, took office again in November 1994 after Francis Billy Hilly lost his parliamentary majority and resigned.

A collection of ten large islands and four groups of smaller islands in the Western Pacific Ocean, the Solomon Islands has been an independent member of the British Commonwealth since July 1978. The forty-seven-seat unicameral parliament is elected by universal suffrage for a four-year term. Executive power is held by the prime minister, who is elected by the party or coalition holding the most seats in parliament. The governor general serves as head of state.

In February 1989 the People's Alliance Party (PAP) won an eleven-seat plurality in a then-thirty-eight-seat parliament. In March the PAP's Solomon Mamaloni took office as prime minister and formed the country's first single party government. In October 1990

Mamaloni resigned from the PAP after opposition leader Andrew Nori, along with several PAP members, accused him of ruling in a non-consultative fashion. However, Mamaloni remained prime minister of a "national unity" government, dropping several PAP ministers from the cabinet and adding four opposition MPs and a PAP backbencher.

In May 1993 the country held its fourth post-independence elections. The key issues were the poor state of the economy, corruption and the lack of adequate secondary schools. Mamaloni's new "National Unity Group" took 21 seats; PAP, 7; National Action Party, 4; Labor Party, 4; Christian Fellowship Group, 3; United Party, 2; Nationalist Front for Progress, 1; independents, 5. On 18 June a coalition of five parties and several independents secured twenty-four votes to elect Francis Billy Hilly, a businessman who ran as an independent, as prime minister over Mamaloni.

In its first months in office, Hilly's National Coalition Partnership government made diplomatic overtures to neighboring Papua New Guinea, which accuses Solomon Islands residents of assisting the secessionist insurgency on nearby Bougainville Island. Papua New Guinea soldiers have launched several cross-border raids into the Solomon Islands, allegedly while in "hot pursuit" of rebel soldiers. The Hilly government also placed a moratorium on logging by foreign companies, which engage in rampant corruption and have harvested logs at up to twice the environmentally sustainable rate.

In November Hilly sacked three ministers who had allegedly expressed interest in helping the opposition to form a government. The ministers then defected to the opposition, leaving Hilly's government with only twenty-one seats. In late November one of the ministers rejoined the government and the High Court vacated one opposition-held seat for election irregularities, giving Hilly's government a one-seat parliamentary majority.

The resignations of five cabinet members plus a government backbencher in September and early October 1994 convinced Governor General Moses Pitakaka that the Hilly government lacked a parliamentary majority. On 13 October Pitakaka sacked Hilly, who claimed that the governor general lacked the authority to dismiss a prime minister and provoked a constitutional crisis by refusing to stand down. On 25 October Pitakaka swore in Mamaloni as a caretaker prime minister, giving the country two premiers. The next day the High Court sided with Hilly, ruling that only parliament can dismiss a prime minister through a vote of no confidence.

When parliament met on 31 October there were twenty-nine MPs sitting with the opposition and just fifteen with Hilly, who subsequently resigned. On 7 November parliament elected Mamaloni as prime minister over Sir Baddeley Devesi, a former governor general. Mamaloni promised to review the moratorium on logging, citing the country's bleak economic situation and the need to raise tax and foreign exchange revenues.

Political Rights and Civil Liberties: Citizens of the Solomon Islands can change their government democratically. Party affiliations are weak and tend to be based on personal loyalties rather than ideology or policy goals. Power is decentralized through freely elected provincial and local councils.

Women hold a subservient role in this traditionally male-dominated society. Domestic violence reportedly occurs relatively frequently. The independent judiciary provides adequate procedural safeguards for the accused. Freedoms of speech and press are generally respected in practice. However in May 1993 the Mamaloni government banned media coverage of border tensions with Papua New Guinea. The incoming Hilly government lifted the restriction in June. The country has two private weekly newspapers and several government publications. State radio provides diverse viewpoints. The country does not have television programming, and the government controls the use of satellite dishes because it feels that outside programs containing sex and violence could negatively affect the population. Permits are required for demonstrations but have never been denied on political grounds. The majority of citizens are Christians, but there are no restrictions on other groups. Citizens may travel freely inside the country and abroad. Workers are free to join independent unions and bargain collectively. Legally, only private-sector workers can strike. However in 1989 public school teachers staged a strike and were not sanctioned.

Somalia

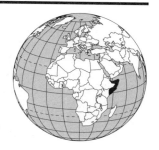

Polity: Rival warlords **Political Rights:** 7
Economy: Mixed-statist **Civil Liberties:** 7
Population: 9,845,000 **Status:** Not Free
PPP: $759
Life Expectancy: 46.4
Ethnic Groups: Somali (Hawiye, Darod, Isaq, Isa, other), Gosha, Bajun

Overview: As expected, the United States withdrew its troops from Somalia in March 1994, leaving behind a country plagued by an ongoing internecine war and food shortages. The remaining 18,000 United Nations peacekeeping troops are comprised mostly of troops from underdeveloped member-states. The U.N. has indicated its intention to end the United Nations Operation in Somalia (UNISOM) in March 1995. Despite its initial success in providing much needed food relief to combat widespread famine, the joint U.S./U.N. humanitarian relief effort was a largely a failure. While initially a humanitarian relief operation, the U.S. mission attempted to demobilize warring factions and promote nation-building. Both U.S. troops and U.N. peacekeepers soon became embroiled in the civil war and were accused by Somali factions of violating the U.N. mandate and fostering violence and instability.

Civil war, banditry and famine have dominated life in Somalia since the January 1991 coup that deposed Major Mohamed Siad Barre. Barre had seized power in a 1969 coup. At the beginning of his term, Barre was committed to ending the "clanism" that created consistent political instability within Somalia. He attempted to forge a national identity by outlawing clan names and abolishing clan-based political parties. Barre established a one-party system and tried to instill Somali nationalism with unifying ideas and symbols. In part, he succeeded. For the first five years of his term, Barre's plan met with some success. But by the late 1970s, following a military defeat in Ethiopia, Barre's hold on power began wavering.

In order to maintain power, Barre adopted a strategy which opted to exploit, rather than eliminate clan rivalries. Barre grew to rely on a small number of clans known as the MOD (Marehan-Ogaden-Dolbahante) and appointed family members to a number of key political positions. Despite the repressive nature of Barre's regime, the U.S. and Italy continued to provide support to Somalia. From 1979 to 1988, the U.S. provided $840 million dollars in aid. The aid was used to secure U.S. rights to use an airfield in Somalia deemed as "essential" for protecting U.S. interests in the Gulf. Despite the repression and corruption of the Barre regime, it was not until mid-1988 that Congress voted to freeze U.S. aid to Somalia.

By the late 1980s, internal discontent with Barre grew. The Somali National Movement (SNM), an Isaq movement created in 1981, fought the Barre regime for control of territory in northwestern Somalia. Until 1988, the SNM operated from bases within Ethiopia. Hoping to crush the movement, Barre negotiated an agreement with Ethiopia to close SNM camps within its borders. In response, the SNM moved its operations to Somalia. During May and June 1988, the SNM secured a large part of territory in northern Somalia. The Barre regime countered with a military campaign aimed against the Isaqs. Africa Watch reports that "...the government unleashed a reign of terror against Isaq civilians, killing 50,000 to 60,000 between May 1988 and January 1990."

By the time Barre's regime was toppled in January 1991, Somalia was deeply divided by clan rivalries, distrust and a legacy of brutality. Barre was ousted by members of the United Somali Congress (USC), a rebel group which draws it support mainly from the Hawiye clan. Over the objection of its military leader, Mohamed Farah Aidid, the USC appointed Ali Mahdi, of the Abgal subclan, as interim president of Somalia. In late 1991, the USC split into two rival factions—one led by Aidid and the other led by Mahdi. Shortly after the coup, the USC, led by Aidid, took control of the capital of Mogadishu and regions north. In the months that followed, factional fighting ensued. A number of rival, clan-based groups formed: The Somali Salvation Democratic Front (SSDF), the Somali National Front (SNF), and the Somali Patriotic Movement (SPM). In May 1991, the SNM established the Republic of Somaliland in the north of Somalia. However, while the SNM represent the Isaq of the region, a number of other non-Isaq minorities found themselves within the newly seceded territory. These groups opposed the secession and do not accept SNM authority. The international community has not officially recognized Somaliland and this has left the territory isolated and generally without emergency relief assistance.

Caught in the middle of the warring factions were a large number of Somalis from agricultural communities who were poorly armed, politically weak and, as a result, subject to repeated raids, looting, and rape. Africa Watch reports that the fighting "...took a heavy toll on civilians as the warring factions looted food stored in underground silos, stole or killed livestock, ruined wells, raped women of various clans and killed men of opposing clans to prevent them from taking up arms. These attacks on civilians so thoroughly disrupted production and distribution of food that, far more than the drought, they are responsible for the famine in Somalia." An estimated 700,000 Somalis sought refuge in neighboring Kenya and Ethiopia and several hundred thousand more emigrated to Gulf States, Europe and North America.

Fighting among members of clan alliances intensified during 1992 as factions attempted to profit from international food aid. Groups fought to gain control of aid distribution points—airports, ports, roads, relief centers—and relief supplies were frequently looted. The number of Somalis on the brink of starvation between 1991 and 1992 was reported to be as high as 2 million. The initial U.N. response was muted. In October 1992 the U.N. special representative to Somalia, Ambassador Mohamed Sahnoun, strongly criticized the U.N.'s inaction. After receiving a strong rebuke from the U.N. Secretary General, he resigned. Pre-occupation with the Gulf War and domestic concerns delayed international interest in Somalia. It was not until the summer of 1992, when Western news agencies began to cover the famine in Somalia, that international attention focused on the crisis and public pressure to act intensified.

In August 1992, then President George Bush assigned U.S. military aircraft to transport food aid. While this helped speed the delivery of food to some areas, it did not prevent looting. A series of diplomatic efforts to mediate the conflict in late 1992 failed. In November 1992, Bush authorized the use of U.S. troops to lead a U.N. mission in Somalia. The U.N. Security Council subsequently passed resolution 794 on December 3rd which sanctioned the use of "all necessary means..." to provide humanitarian relief in Somalia. During December 1992, over 22,000 American troops and 7,000 troops from other countries were sent to Somalia. Initially welcomed by the Somalis and accepted by the warlords, the troops were successful in securing safe routes to the feeding centers in the areas most devastated by the famine. Within just a few weeks, however, the situation had dramatically changed. The number of armed Somalis on the streets increased and U.N. troops found themselves targets of sniper fire.

By the end of December, the U.S. instituted a policy of "stabilization" which called for tighter street patrols and gave the troops authorization to disarm Somalis. Tensions between Somalis and U.N. forces grew. Attacks against U.N. forces by supporters of warlord Aidid increased. Aidid charged that the U.N. forces were favoring rival warlord Ali Mahdi. By January the U.N. mission was on the offensive. A number of encampments belonging to General Aidid were destroyed by U.S. troops and in Mogadishu a local market was raided and weapons confiscated. Fighting between Somalis and U.N. forces increased as casualties on both sides continued to grow. The mission in Somalia changed from a popular humanitarian effort to a disdained and deadly military action.

The decision by President Clinton to withdraw U.S. troops from Somalia in March 1994 was prompted by increased domestic opposition to the operation as well as a weighty domestic agenda. Following both the U.S. and U.N. troop withdrawals, attempts at negotiating a cease-fire in Somalia have met with continued failure. A cease-fire reached by Gen. Aidid and Ali Mahdi in March 1994 gave way to renewed fighting as rival clans sought to gain control of fertile farmland areas in the wake of the final U.N. troop withdrawal. In November 1994 additional fighting was reported in the breakaway Republic of Somaliland. Approximately 20,000 Somali refugees fled clashes between the "president" of Somaliland Mohammed Ibrahim Egal and troops loyal to his predecessor Abdirahman Ahmed Ali "Tur," who founded the Republic but was subsequently ousted from power in 1993.

Political Rights and Civil Liberties: The U.S./U.N. mission failed to create an interim civilian government and, since 1991, there has been a vacuum of central government authority and an abrogation of both civil liberties and political rights. Only northern "Somaliland" has some degree of local and regional authority in the wake of SNM's self proclaimed secession in 1991. Most of Somalia continues to endure factional fighting and thievery, creating a general sense of lawlessness.

As Somali factions continue to clash, unarmed civilians, relief workers and rival group members continue to be killed. The Center for Concern reports that among those most affected by the U.S./U.N. departure have been minority tribes living in the fertile farming regions between the Shabelle and Juba rivers. Rival clans seeking to take control of these lands have moved into these areas, dispossessing farmers of their land. Often farmers are forced to work on their own land as sharecroppers or be forced to pay protection money to local militia. The Center reports that many farmers have been subject to abuse and female family members have been raped.

Somalia does not have a functioning judicial system. The SNM is reported to have adopted Shari'a, Muslim law, in the northwest territory of "Somaliland," but it is not known how this has been applied. The system of "justice" administered by clans was reported to be arbitrary and unfair. Somalis are subject to arbitrary arrest and detention by rival clans and human rights groups report that detainees are subject to extrajudicial executions, beatings and torture solely as a result of their clan membership.

Freedom of speech is not permitted. While some newspapers were available in Mogadishu, publication was sporadic and distribution limited. The BBC's Somali-language services and Moscow Radio's Somali service provided Somalis with information about developments within the country. Against a background of violence, fear and intimidations, Somalis do not have freedom of assembly and association. Apart from the warring factions, no political organizations exist.

South Africa

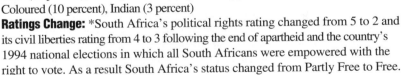

Polity: Presidential-legis- **Political Rights:** 2*
lative democracy (interim) **Civil Liberties:** 3*
Economy: Capitalist-statist **Status:** Free
Population: 41,155,000
PPP: $3,885
Life Expectancy: 62.2
Ethnic Groups: Black (Zulu, Xhosa, Swazi, Sotho,
other (69 percent), white (Afrikaner, English, 18 percent),
Coloured (10 percent), Indian (3 percent)
Ratings Change: *South Africa's political rights rating changed from 5 to 2 and
its civil liberties rating from 4 to 3 following the end of apartheid and the country's
1994 national elections in which all South Africans were empowered with the
right to vote. As a result South Africa's status changed from Partly Free to Free.

Overview: On 9 May 1994 Nelson Mandela was proclaimed South
Africa's president, ending minority rule in place since the
Union of South Africa was formed in 1910. In national
elections held in April 1994, Mandela's African National Congress (ANC) gained
62.5 percent of the vote, securing 252 of the 400-seat parliament and eighteen posts
in a twenty-seven-member cabinet. The ANC shares executive power with former
President F.W. de Klerk's National Party (NP), which has six ministers and three
deputy ministers, and the Inkatha Freedom Party (IFP), which has five ministers

and one deputy minister. De Klerk is co-deputy president with the ANC's Thabo Mbeki. Despite the ANC's landslide victory, triumphalism has given way to a spirit of conciliation and consensus-building.

Beginning in 1948 the NP ruled South Africa and developed the system of white domination and racial segregation known as apartheid. One third of the black majority and most mixed-race Coloreds and Indians live in racially segregated areas in and near large cities. An additional ten million blacks live in ten tribal homelands. The system of apartheid that was dominant for forty-six years isolated South Africa from the international community and created a cycle of political violence that, since the mid-1980s, has been responsible for approximately 16,000 deaths.

Beginning in 1990, the ANC, the then-ruling NP and seventeen opposition parties entered intensive multilateral negotiations for an end to apartheid. After losing a parliamentary seat to the Conservative Party in February 1992, De Klerk announced an extraordinary referendum for whites only, to establish whether he had a mandate to negotiate further reforms. Eighty five percent of eligible voters turned out for the March 1992 referendum and 69 percent endorsed further negotiations. Following a series of setbacks between May and September of 1992, bilateral negotiations between the government and the ANC began. On 26 September De Klerk and Mandela signed a Record of Understanding (ROU) which stated that an elected constituent assembly (CA) would draft and adopt a new constitution; a transitional executive council would be appointed alongside the CA; the existing tricameral Parliament would be dissolved; and a government of national unity would be elected following the adoption of a new constitution. Despite right-wing protest and escalating political violence, negotiations continued throughout 1992-1993.

The landmark elections of April 1994 were made possible by an accord reached by leaders of twenty-one South African parties in November 1993. Under the accord, the right to vote was extended to the country's black majority for the first time in South Africa's history. As part of the accord, a new interim Constitution was drafted which provided for a five-year Transitional Government of National Unity. A 400 member National Assembly was established to serve as a constitutional assembly and will be responsible for drafting a final constitution by April 1999. Under the accord, the country was divided into nine semi-autonomous provinces. Each province has its own legislature, premier and constitution but provincial powers will be concurrent, not exclusive, and will be deferred to the central government in matters deemed to be of "national security." The president is selected by the majority party. His cabinet must proportionally represent all parties who attain more than 5 percent of the total vote. In a break from South Africa's British style parliamentary system, sovereignty is vested in the new constitution. After three years of painstaking and precarious negotiations between the government and opposition leaders, the agreement formally ended apartheid and paved the way for majority rule in South Africa.

While 1994 ushered in a new democratic era, the task of improving South Africa's social and economic fabric remains daunting. Escalating crime, labor unrest, ongoing allegations of police brutality, internal rivalries in South Africa's Natal region and pressures by the majority population for a speedy redress of economic and social woes confront Mandela's fragile political alliance.

Political Rights and Civil Liberties:

For the first time in the country's history, all South Africans are empowered with political rights. The election of Nelson Mandela, and the pragmatic path he has taken in his first months of office, offer significant hope that democratic rule in South Africa will endure. In appointing key opposition party members, Mandela has attempted to create a "national unity" Cabinet. While the historic ANC-Inkatha rivalry continues to cause some concern, Inkatha's victory in KwaZulu-Natal may actually prove fortuitous. Despite post-election allegations by the ANC that the Inkatha election victory was the result of fraud, Mandela's decision to withdraw ANC opposition and allow the Inkatha victory to stand may signal a truce in ANC-Inkatha hostilities. Facing some opposition, Mandela appointed Inkatha leader Chief Mangosuthu Buthelezi to the senior post of Home Affairs. The inclusion of opposition party members may serve to defuse historic ethnic and political rivalries.

Despite political advancement (with concurrent social implications), South Africans are not free from human rights violations. During the first four months of 1994, the Human Rights Committee of South Africa reported that politically motivated killings occurred at a rate of nearly fourteen deaths per day. The Committee also reports that during 1994 widespread torture of prisoners by the South African Police Force continued. In a March 1994 report on KwaZulu and Bophuthatswana, Human Rights Watch Africa detailed the excess use of force by local police and called on the new South African government to employ measures that would "control the escalating political violence..." Just prior to the April elections, Amnesty International reported widespread unrest, attempted extrajudicial executions and the arrest and torture of university students in South Africa's Bophuthatswana. The unrest was the result of the pre-election activities of members of the Freedom Alliance coalition, comprising members of white right-wing extremist parties. The coalition was firmly opposed to the national elections.

During the first one hundred days following Mandela's inauguration, 457 people died and 592 were injured in politically related violence. Violence in the KwaZulu-Natal region remains endemic. Political violence resulting from ANC and Inkatha rivalries has been re-established in criminal and gang-related activities, edging the region precariously close to a return to political violence. In October 1994 Amnesty International reported that in the KwaZulu province the still-to-be disbanded KwaZulu police (KZP) had attempted to execute Prince Sifiso Zulu, a member of the Zulu Royal House, as a result of a rift between Buthelezi and King Goodwill Zwelithini. The attempts on Prince Sifiso's life underscore the tension and unrest in the province and there is concern that divisions between Buthelezi and King Goodwill will lead to internal strife. Independent reports indicate that ANC-Inkatha hostilities in the region continue. The KZP continues to harass ANC members and ANC members are accused of killing two Inkatha families in the township of Ndwedwe.

Following the April 1994 elections, members of South Africa's judiciary called for an inquiry into previous human rights abuses by State security forces as well as opposition groups (including the ANC). The call to expose apartheid crimes drew a mixed response. However, in June 1994 the government agreed to set up a Commission of Truth and Reconciliation that would address allegations of human rights violations committed under apartheid. The Commission will allow offenders to make an application for amnesty. Those applicants who can prove that their acts were politically motivated will, in most cases, be absolved of their crimes.

The judiciary is independent of the executive. Both common criminal and security-related cases are tried in criminal courts presided over by a judge or magistrate; trial by jury was abolished in 1969. Under the new system of government, sovereignty was transferred from the parliament to the constitution. During 1994, complaints alleging police complicity in violence and harassment of ANC supporters as well as excess use of force during detention continued. The Human Rights Watch Prison Project reports that, despite some improvements in 1994, prison conditions remain deplorable. A February 1994 reports states that prisoners continue to report beatings by prison guards and that these allegations are not properly investigated. The report further states that gang violence in prison is prevalent and that there are inadequate safeguards to protect prisoners from gang-related as well as other prison violence.

There remains a limited freedom of the press in South Africa. Opposition parties as well as some media groups have voiced concern over increasing press restrictions employed by the new government. Although less restrictively applied, strict censorship laws have yet to be lifted or amended in the post-apartheid government. Facing increased political pressure and scrutiny, in August 1994 the Joint Rules Committee proposed that the press be barred from reporting on the parliamentary subcommittees. In April and again in August, the Court ordered two right-wing radio stations to stop broadcasting. MISA reports that during 1994 two journalists were killed in politically motivated violence.

Workers have the right to organize and strike. Trade union membership in South Africa, estimated at just over 37 percent of the work force, is the highest in the developing world. Long at the forefront of the anti-apartheid movement, the 1.3-million-member Congress of South African Trade Unions has endeavored to redefine its role. Tensions between the new government and the trade union movement increased during the fall of 1994 as expectations that a wage increase would be part of the post-apartheid dividend had not been met. As the government sought to restructure some industries, clashes developed between trade members and the government. In September labor unrest in both the forestry and mining industries led to clashes between strikers and security forces in which the use of force led to injuries.

Spain

Polity: Parliamentary democracy
Economy: Capitalist
Population: 39,193,000
PPP: $12,670
Life Expectancy: 77.4

Political Rights: 1
Civil Liberties: 2
Status: Free

Ethnic Groups: Castilians, Basques, Catalans, Galicians, Valencians, Andalusians, Gypsies, and an immigrant population largely composed of North Africans and Latin Americans

Overview:

The ruling Socialist Workers Party led by Prime Minister Felipe Gonzalez continued to lose its political strength in 1994. In the June 1994 European Union Parliamentary elections, the center-right Popular Party (PP) soundly defeated the Socialists. And in an August 1994 parliamentary vote on regional finances held in the southern region of Andalucia, the government suffered yet another setback when the Socialist package was defeated by a consortium of opposition parties. The financial package was part of a pact between Gonzalez's Socialist Party and the Catalan nationalists and the defeat may jeopardize critical Catalan support on which Gonzalez's fragile ruling coalition relies to maintain parliamentary control.

The electoral defeats follow a series of scandals that have plagued the Socialist Party since 1993, including allegations that the Socialist Party illegally raised funds. Corruption in both the cabinet and civil service has also threatened to jeopardize Gonzalez's strained hold on power. It was revealed in the press that Luis Roldan, previously the head of the national police force (civil guard), had accumulated several million dollars on what was suppose to be a civil service salary. Also in 1994 , the former governor of the Bank of Spain, Mariano Rubio, who from 1984-1992 presided over a period of rapid economic growth in Spain, was accused of embezzlement. The press uncovered secret bank accounts and questionable financial dealings by Rubio that led to lucrative personal profit.

Despite both electoral setbacks and corruption scandals involving prominent Socialist Party members, Gonzalez has been able to retain the necessary support of the Catalan nationalists. The head of Catalonia's autonomous government and leader of Convergencia i Unio (CiU), Mr Jordi Pujol, maintained his support for the government during 1994. The support of the seventeen CiU MP's allows Gonzalez to maintain a tenuous 141-seat hold in the 350-member parliament.

Political Rights and Civil Liberties:

Political rights are respected in Spain and the Spanish have the right to change their government democratically. In a rather complex system of decentralization, Spain is divided into seventeen autonomous communities possessing varying amounts of power. Beginning in September 1994, a committee composed of senators and judicial experts met to discuss a constitutional reform package aimed at revising the country's legislative process. With a multilingual, multicultural and, for some, multinational population, Spain faces large obstacles in creating a workable, but inclusive, system of governance.

Although the government can claim significant military victories, ETA separatists remain a formidable force in the Basque region of Spain. The ETA (an acronym that stands for Basque Homeland and Freedom in the regional language) has been waging a twenty-five-year war for separation that has claimed 800 lives. In recent years, a number of ETA leaders have been arrested and the group has seen a significant decline in popular support. In the October 1994 regional elections, the group's political wing, Herri Batasuna, lost two of its thirteen seats in the Basque Parliament. In June, the party lost its sole seat in the European Parliament. Still, negotiating a permanent cease-fire has been elusive and government intelligence reports that there are currently four active ETA units capable of carrying out acts of political violence.

Approximately 500 ETA activists are jailed and reports that Basque prisoners are mistreated while in detention continue. Additionally, accusations that a government-sanctioned "death squad" has targeted Basque separatists have resurfaced. The goverment denies any complicity. Spain lacks anti-discrimination laws and ethnic minorities, especially members of immigrant populations, have reported bias and ill-treatment.

Spain has a free and vibrant press. There is one state-controlled and three independently owned and operated commercial broadcasting television stations. The state-controlled television has been accused of a progovernment bias.

Trade unions are allowed to organize and the right to strike is observed and exercised freely. Although Roman Catholicism is the dominant religion in Spain, the freedom to worship is respected and there is separation of church and state.

Sri Lanka

Polity: Presidential-parliamentary democracy (insurgencies)
Economy: Mixed capitalist-statist
Population: 17,899,000
PPP: $2,650
Life Expectancy: 71.2
Ethnic Groups: Sinhalese, (74 percent), Tamil (18 percent), Moor (7 percent), others

Political Rights: 4
Civil Liberties: 5
Status: Partly Free

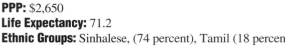

Overview:
In the August 1994 parliamentary elections Chandrika Kumaratunga led the People's Alliance, a leftist coalition dominated by the Sri Lanka Freedom Party (SLFP), to victory, ending the conservative United National Party's (UNP) seventeen-year rule. In November Kumaratunga routed the widow of an assassinated UNP candidate to win the presidential vote, and pledged to negotiate a settlement to the eleven-year-old civil war in the north that has claimed more than 34,000 lives.

Located off southeastern India, Sri Lanka (known until 1972 as Ceylon) achieved independence from the British in 1947. Since then political power has alternated between the centrist UNP and the nationalist, leftist SLFP. In 1956 Prime Minister Solomon Bandaranaike's SLFP government made Buddhism the official religion and Sinhalese the official language, and introduced laws that discriminated against Tamils in educational opportunities. Although future governments gradually repealed these measures, their initial implementation led to small-scale violence and created lasting rifts between Sinhalese and the Tamils.

Elections in 1977 brought the UNP to power. The 1978 constitution established a powerful presidency and a 225-member parliament. The directly elected president can serve two six-year terms, appoints ministers, can hold portfolios himself, presides over the cabinet, and can dissolve parliament. The parliament serves up to six years, with 196 seats elected through proportional representation from twenty-two electoral districts, and the remainder distributed according to national proportional representation.

In July 1983 Tamil separatist guerrillas in the north and east began attacks on government troops, claiming official discrimination against Tamils in housing, jobs and education. By 1985 the Liberation Tigers of Tamil Eelam (LTTE), which called for an independent homeland in north and eastern Sri Lanka, had emerged as the dominant guerrilla group. In 1987 the government agreed to allow an Indian peacekeeping force (IPKF) to disarm the rebels and maintain a cease-fire. The LTTE refused to disarm and fought the numerically superior IPKF to a standstill. The presence of the Indian troops sparked a bloody antigovernment insurgency in the south by the nationalist, Marxist People's Liberation Front (JVP).

In the 1988 presidential elections the UNP's Ranasinghe Premadasa narrowly defeated former prime minister and SLFP leader Sirima Bandaranaike. By 1990 the government had brutally crushed the JVP with the help of military-backed death squads. In May the IPKF completed a withdrawal, and fighting resumed between the government and the LTTE.

In the summer and fall of 1991 Premadasa survived an impeachment motion, supported by several UNP dissidents, accusing him of ruling in an authoritarian manner. The president dismissed eight UNP MPs from the party, who subsequently formed the Democratic United National Front (DUNF) party.

In April 1993 a gunman assassinated DUNF leader Lalaith Athulathmudali at a provincial election campaign rally in Colombo. On 1 May the country's cycle of violence claimed its most prominent victim as a suicide bomber assassinated President Premadasa and killed twenty-three others at a May Day rally. Parliament elected Prime Minister D. B. Wijetunge to serve out Premadasa's term. In November some of the civil war's heaviest battles occurred on the northern Jaffna Peninsula, the LTTE's last stronghold.

In March 1994 the People's Alliance, in a campaign led by Chandrika Kumaratunga, the daughter of Sirima and the late Solomon Bandaranaike, convincingly defeated the UNP in local elections in the Southern Province. With Kumaratunga's appeal rising, in late June President Wijetunge dissolved parliament and called for national elections in August, six months ahead of schedule. Wijetunge hoped that a UNP parliamentary victory would increase his chances of defeating the charismatic Kumaratunga in the November presidential elections.

The economy and the continuing civil war in the north were the key issues in the parliamentary campaign. While the UNP focused on its economic liberalization program that has produced steady GDP growth averaging around 6 percent in recent years, the People's Alliance pointed to a 12.6 percent unemployment rate and an 11.4 percent inflation rate, as well as to the UNP's corruption and nepotism.

Thirteen parties and 1,440 candidates contested the 16 August vote. With turnout at 76 percent the People's Alliance won 105 seats; the UNP, 94; the pro-UNP Eelam People's Democratic Party, 9; the Sri Lanka Muslim Congress, 7; minor parties, 9; independents; 1. The People's Alliance won the support of the Muslim Congress plus an independent to name Kumaratunga as prime minister.

In October the Kumaratunga government held preliminary talks with LTTE representatives. On 25 October, with the presidential campaign underway, a suicide bomber killed UNP candidate Gamini Dissanayake, who stood in after Wijetunge decided not to run, and more than fifty other people at a Colombo rally. The government immediately suspended the peace talks.

In the 9 November presidential elections, held with a 71 percent turnout, Kumaratunga took 62 percent of the vote to rout Dissanayake's widow, Srima Dissanayake, who took 35 percent. The new president appointed her mother, Sirima Bandaranaike, as prime minister, a post she had held during parts of the 1960s and 1970s. Kumaratunga promised to amend the constitution by July 1995 to transfer much of the president's executive power to the prime minister and parliament, and will undoubtedly reassume the post from her mother. The new president also pledged to resume peace talks with the LTTE.

Political Rights and Civil Liberties: Sri Lankans can change their government democratically. According to the NGO Election Observer Mission, the electoral process for the August 1994 parliamentary vote favored the incumbent UNP due to the government's biased use of state-owned media, bans on campaign posters and literature in public places and on door-to-door canvassing, and misuse of vehicles and other state resources. The UNP appeared responsible for the majority of the more than 3,000 incidents of election-related violence that included at least twenty deaths. The 600,000-800,000 persons displaced by the civil war faced difficulties in registering to vote, and only 19,000 were declared eligible.

Because 80 percent of the Jaffna Peninsula and half of the eastern Vanni district are held by the LTTE, voting was limited in these areas. (In March 1994 the government held village and town council elections in eastern Sri Lanka, the first voting of any kind in the region since 1983. However, the government has been unable to hold elections for a planned North-East provincial council.) According to Inform, the Colombo-based human rights group, during the campaign for the November 1994 presidential election there was relatively less political violence and the state-run media's political coverage was somewhat more balanced.

Upwards of 60,000 people, many of them civilians, died during the government's suppression of the JVP uprising in the late 1980s and early 1990s. In 1994 the authorities exhumed several mass graves believed to contain the victims of government-backed death squads.

Government security forces are responsible for disappearances and for extrajudicial killings of captured LTTE guerrillas and suspected civilian sympathizers. In September 1994 the Kumaratunga government lifted the state of emergency that had been in effect since 1983 from most of the country except the north and east. UNP governments detained thousands of persons under the 1979 Prevention of Terrorism Act (PTA) and the Emergency Regulations (ER), some of them in secret detention centers. Suspects may be detained for up to eighteen months under the PTA and indefinitely under the ER. Police frequently beat detainees, and under the ER confessions to police officers are admissible in court. Defendants who repudiate a confession must prove it was made under duress.

On the LTTE-held Jaffna Peninsula, 700,000 civilians are largely without running water or electricity. The LTTE rules its territory in an authoritarian manner and is responsible for arbitrary arrests, torture and disappearances. The rebels recruit child soldiers, some as young as eleven. Since 1983 the LTTE has carried out scores of politically motivated assassinations.

In recent years anti-LTTE Tamil groups have killed scores of suspected LTTE supporters. In the fall of 1993 Tamil militias allegedly helped government security agents round up LTTE supporters in Colombo. In the latter half of 1993 security forces also briefly detained tens of thousands of Tamils for security checks.

The judiciary is considered independent, and in nonsecurity cases defendants receive adequate due-process rights. Freedom of speech and press can be constitutionally restricted in the interest of national security through the PTA and ER, although this is done infrequently. The ER authorizes sentences of up to twenty years for speech that could be broadly construed to incite antagonism toward the president or government, or to create unrest among the population. The Parliamentary Powers and Privileges Act allows parliament to fine and imprison individuals for up to two years for criticizing an MP; this act was used in 1992 to call a newspaper editor before parliament for questioning.

The government controls the Lake House group, the largest media chain. Independent newspapers publish diverse opinions but small papers face intimidation by various groups, particularly by the LTTE in the north. Since the May 1993 assassination of President Premadasa, official harassment of journalists largely appears to have ended. The government owns the radio station and two of three television networks, and must approve all domestic news broadcasts. Freedom of peaceful assembly is generally respected.

Rape and domestic violence reportedly occur frequently in Sri Lanka. Domestic servants, many of them children, are routinely subjected to physical abuse. Several thousand children are trafficked in prostitution schemes catering mainly to foreign tourists. Although Buddhism is the official religion, other groups can practice without restrictions. Citizens are free to travel internally, except in areas restricted due to fighting, and can freely travel abroad. Workers may join independent trade unions. State workers are prohibited from striking, and labor activists say the Public Service Commission, with which such employees can file grievances, is biased towards the government. The 1989 Essential Services Act allows the president to declare a strike in any industry illegal, although in 1993 the government reduced the number of industries considered "essential" under the act. Child labor remains a problem.

Sudan

Polity: Military
Economy: Mixed
capitalist
Population: 28,175,000
PPP: $1,162
Life Expectancy: 51.2
Ethnic Groups: Some 600 groups—Sudanese Arabs (40 percent);
African: Dinka (11 percent), Nuba (8 percent), Neur, Shilluk, Fur, others

Political Rights: 7
Civil Liberties: 7
Status: Not Free

Overview:
In 1994 the military dictatorship of Gen. Omar Hassan Ahmad al-Bashir continued its brutal war against the factionalized Sudan People's Liberation Army (SPLA), a Christian and animist group seeking greater autonomy for the south and protection from Islamic law. Ethnically based insurgencies within the SPLA, which had split into tribal- based groups, led to violence that left thousands dead or displaced, and millions of civilians facing starvation.

Sudan, geographically Africa's largest country, won independence from Britain and Egypt in 1956, and functioned as a parliamentary democracy for thirteen years. Violence between the Arab-Muslim north and the Christian, black-African south plagued the country for decades. Following the 1969-1972 Anya Nya separatist war, the southern third of the country achieved a high level of autonomy. In 1983, however, Jafar Numeiri, who took power in a 1969 coup, partitioned the southern region into three smaller regions and introduced *Shari'a* (Islamic law). Southern Christians and animists, led by Dr. John Garang, a U.S.-educated renegade colonel, formed the SPLA and began a struggle for greater autonomy for the south. The insurgency continued even after the military toppled Numeiri in a 1985 coup and returned the country to civilian rule in 1986.

In June 1989 Gen. Bashir led a military coup that overthrew the pro-Western, elected government, suspended the constitution, dissolved the elected constituent Assembly, banned all political parties and established the National Salvation Revolutionary Command Council (RCC), which he chaired. Although Bashir became prime minister, the power behind the scene was the National Islamic Front (NIF), led by fundamentalist Hassan al-Turabi, whose supporters took control of the security apparatus, judiciary and universities, and declared Sudan to be an Islamic state. In March 1991 the government approved Shari'a for the entire country.

In August 1991 the 40,000-strong SPLA split largely along ethnic-tribal lines, when a faction headed by Reik Machar, a Neur, challenged Garang and his Dinka-dominant Torit faction. Machar's so-called Nasir faction, made up largely of Neur, called for complete independence from the north, and accused Garang of dictatorial practices and human rights abuses. Garang continued to advocate rapprochement with Khartoum and a unified secular state.

With its military supported by China and Iran, the government formed an 85,000-

man Popular Defense Force of highly motivated young Islamic militants modeled on Iran's Revolutionary Guards. In February 1992 Prime Minister Bashir announced the appointment of a 300-member Transitional National Assembly, which included all members of the RCC, a number of RCC advisors, all cabinet ministers and state governors, and representatives from the army, trade unions, and former political parties.

The end of 1992 saw a renewed government offensive against the SPLA. Some 300,000 people continued to face starvation in Juba, a government-held garrison in the south besieged by the SPLA. Seven-hundred-and-fifty-thousand refugees— most of them black African—were forced out of Khartoum into squalid refugee camps in what international diplomats and aid workers called an "ethnic cleansing" operation. Tens of thousands of non-Arab black Nuba tribesmen were relocated from their central region to camps on the pretense of giving them shelter from the civil war. The U.S. Committee of Refugees estimates that the ten-year civil war, and its attendant pestilence, starvation and disease, has killed 1.3 million southern Sudanese and involved egregious human rights abuses by all sides, including murder, rape, kidnapping, summary executions, enslavement and destruction of whole villages, livestock and crops. Over 4 million people have been internally displaced and 1 million have become refugees in neighboring states.

In 1993 fighting continued. A third SPLA faction, SPLA-Unity, led by William Nyuon, clashed with Garang's troops. Nyuon had both Dinka and Neur lineage, and had won the support of the Latukas. He ultimately merged his forces with Machar's, forming SPLA-United. The government launched a new offensive near the Ugandan border in the summer. In October Gen. Bashir announced that a new civilian government would lift a curfew imposed when he seized power. The announcement came after Bashir had been named president by the ruling junta, which then disbanded. The move was seen as an attempt by the government to give parliament more power, but it was undercut by the fact that only members of Bashir's military regime were in the new administration.

In early February 1994 the government opened a big ground and air offensive against rebels in the south. Attacks on ten relief stations forced relief organizations to halt food deliveries affecting an estimated 2 million people at a time when severe drought and crop failures threatened the worst famine since 1988. Some 100,000 people in refugee camps at Ame, Aswa and Atepi began fleeing to Uganda, amid reports that the SPLA-Torit were blocking their escape. Government forces were joined by the anti-SPLA tribal militias in trying to break out of Juba.

The government condemned a report by U.N. special rapporteur, Gaspar Biro, who chided the Sudanese not only for specific abuses, but for basing part of their penal law on principles that contravene international legal instruments that Sudan had signed. Khartoum accused Biro of blasphemy, denouncing him as "worse than Rushdie," and threatened his safety.

On 8 March the European Union approved a ban on arms shipments to Sudan. On 17 March Gen. Bashir and SPLA rivals Garang and Machar opened peace talks in separate meetings in Nairobi with a mediating committee of African presidents. Before the talks, Machar announced a unilateral ceasefire in the fighting with SPLA-Torit. The government and rebel guerrillas subsequently agreed to let aid reach famine and disease victims in the south, but little progress was made on a cease-fire or political solution to the conflict. The government rejected self-rule for the south.

In May and June continued fighting led several private aid organizations and the U.N.

to pull out of sections of southern Sudan, leaving tens of thousands facing serious shortages of food and medical supplies. The Belgian aid group, Doctors Without Borders, said children in the south suffered from "catastrophic malnutrition." The third session of the Nairobi negotiations in July produced little. The government and the SPLA said they would welcome U.S. and European assistance in drafting detailed proposals regarding distribution of power between the central government and the regions.

In mid-September efforts to revive the Nairobi peace process failed, and Gen. Bashir hinted that full-scale fighting would resume and rejected rebel demands for a referendum on self-determination in the south. Rival SPLA factions called for arms and economic sanctions against Sudan. Meanwhile new rifts developed in the rebel movement in October when the SPLA-United leader Machar, facing a challenge from a cofounder of the group, held a congress to announce a new splinter organization, the SPLA-Southern Sudan Independence Movement.

In early November Gen. Bashir announced he would not seek the presidency when national elections were held in two years time. Emulating Libya, the government called for series of elections for "popular" councils at village and district levels. Popular assemblies for the country's twenty-six states are to be elected by March 1995, and a National Assembly by late 1995 or early 1996. After that, there is to be an election for a president and his deputy.

The government intensified its offensives near Aswa and Nimule in mid-November. The government's attempts to broaden the conflict across borders included skirmishes in Chad and Eritrea amid charges that Khartoum was infiltrating returning Eritrean refugees with Islamic zealots. Eritrea broke off diplomatic relations with Sudan on 5 December. Uganda charged repeatedly that Sudan was supplying arms to rebels there. In late December, Western intelligence sources linked Sudan to Islamic extremists trying to topple the Algerian government.

Political Rights and Civil Liberties: Sudanese live under a repressive military government that has curtailed virtually all meaningful political rights and civil liberties while implementing Islamic law. The ongoing war with the SPLA, as well as internecine, often tribal-based fighting between rebel factions, have left over 1.3 million dead in over a decade. Hundreds of thousands are internally displaced or are refugees outside the country.

Illegal detentions, torture, kidnapping, rape and executions are rampant, both by government forces and rebel groups. Children as young as ten have been conscripted into government militias. All sides have used food and access to aid as a weapon against civilians. Tribal violence has included the systematic massacre and displacement of the Nuba people from 1991-94.

The judiciary is subservient to the junta. All judges are linked to the National Islamic Front and favor application of Shari'a, which includes such punishments as stoning and amputation. After the 1989 coup, the government banned all political parties, opposition newspapers and independent trade unions. Several political groups, such as al-Umma, function in exile. Those suspected of opposing theocratic rule often disappear into a clandestine prison system where torture is routine. On 5 April Sudanese authorities arrested former Prime Minister Sadek el-Mahdi, an al-Umman leader. Other activists were also arrested, including Sarra Nuqd Allah, daughter of a former interior minister.

Freedom of the press is curtailed, and journalists are often targeted for arrest, detention, or harassment. In April the government closed the Khartoum-based *al-Sudani* after two months of publishing, arresting the paper's owner and journalists. The paper had attacked the judiciary for bestowing legitimacy "on violations of basic human rights."

Penal codes have institutionalized Islamic law. Since most Christians and animists are black African, widespread "Arabization" is blatantly racist. Under Shari'a, apostasy is punishable by death. Non-Muslims are theoretically excluded from high-level government and military posts or any position in which a non-Muslim could exercise authority over a Muslim. Christians have been refused permits to build churches, and their leaders have been harassed or detained for questioning.

The imposition of Shari'a has led to systematic legal discrimination against women. Several decrees ban women from certain employment, women must sit in the back seats in transport, and certain attire is strictly forbidden. In war zones, women are forcibly kidnapped and made to serve as sex slaves. Rape is widespread.

Internal travel is limited by civil war, and security suspects have been prevented from leaving the country. Workers cannot unionize, and a violation of the ban on strikes may be punishable by death.

Suriname

Polity: Presidential-par-   **Political Rights:** 3
liamentary democracy   **Civil Liberties:** 3
Economy: Capitalist-   **Status:** Partly Free
statist
Population: 423,000
PPP: $3,072
Life Expectancy: 69.9
Ethnic Groups: *East Indian (approximately 40 percent), Creole
Amerindians (approximately 30 percent), followed by Javanese, Bush
Negroes, Amerindians, Chinese and various European minorities

Overview:
After three years in office President Ronald Venetiaan was caught amid a severe economic recession, opposition demands that he step down and hold new elections, mounting social unrest, unease within the military and the continued machinations of former dictator Desi Bouterse.

The Republic of Suriname achieved independence from the Netherlands in 1975 and functioned as a parliamentary democracy until a military coup in 1980. Col. Desi Bouterse emerged as the strongman of a regime that brutally suppressed civic and political opposition. In 1985 Bouterse announced a "return to democracy" and appointed an assembly to draft a new constitution. The 1987 constitution provided for a system of parliamentary democracy, with a fifty-one-member National Assembly elected for a five-year term and empowered to select the nation's president. But it gave the military the right to intercede in political affairs.

The Front for Democracy and Development, a three-party coalition, won the 1987 elections, taking forty of fifty-one seats in the Assembly. The National Democratic Party (NDP), the army's political front, won three seats. The Assembly elected Ramsewak Shankar president.

The Shankar government was hamstrung by the military on most policy issues, including efforts to negotiate peace with the Bush Negro-based Jungle Commando insurgency. The military deepened its involvement in cocaine trafficking and remained unaccountable for human rights violations. In December 1990 Shankar was ousted by the military in a bloodless coup and replaced by a government controlled by Bouterse.

Under international pressure, the puppet government held elections in May 1991 observed by the Organization of American States (OAS). The front-runner was the New Front (NF), essentially the same coalition of Hindustani, Creole and Javanese parties that had been ousted in 1990. Also contending were the NDP, and the newly formed Democratic Alternative 91 (DA 91), an ethnically mixed coalition led by young professionals who campaigned against corruption and for limiting the power of the military.

The NF won thirty seats in the Assembly, the NDP twelve, and DA 91 nine. The NF lacked the two-thirds majority to elect its presidential candidate, educator Ronald Venetiaan. An electoral college was convened, formed by members of the Assembly and representatives of district and municipal councils. Venetiaan won 80 percent of the 817 electoral college votes.

President Venetiaan began a process of constitutional reform to bolster civilian rule. In 1992 the Assembly approved amendments restricting the role of the military to national defense and combating "organized subversion." The changes required a two-thirds majority vote. The amendments also barred soldiers from holding representative public office and abolished conscription and the People's Militia.

After the Dutch media reported in 1992 that Bouterse had amassed great wealth at the expense of the state over the previous decade, he suddenly resigned from the military to formally head the NDP.

Venetiaan named Arthy Gorre, who had left the army in 1987 after a dispute with Bouterse, as new military chief. When ranking officers loyal to Bouterse rejected Gorre's appointment, there was fear of another coup. But the army grudgingly accepted Gorre after statements of support for Venetiaan by the Netherlands, Brazil, Venezuela, the U.S. and the OAS.

In 1993 the Dutch stopped balance-of-payment subsidies to the debt-strapped government pending the start of an IMF restructuring program. Not until fall 1994 was Venitiaan able to bring the fractious ruling coalition around to trimming the budget and floating the currency. But the measures, coupled with 120 percent inflation and nearly 75 percent unemployment for people under thirty, set off labor strikes, rioting and looting in mid-November that paralyzed the capital of Paramaribo and left dozens injured. Opposition parties demanded that Venitiaan step down and hold new elections. Bouterse, who in September had stated that Suriname must be "militarized" in order to save the country, said the NDP was ready to assume the leadership of the country.

Meanwhile, military officers and enlisted men loyal to Bouterse appeared to be conspiring to undermine Commander Gorre's authority. Amid renewed coup rumors Venetiaan and Gorre publicly exchanged barbs and there were hints Gorre might resign. Anxiety heightened in late November when a new round of protests led to the arrests of forty people.

Political Rights and Civil Liberties:

Citizens are able to choose their government in relatively free elections. The constitution guarantees the right to organize political parties, civic organizations and labor unions. Political parties are organized mostly along ethnic lines, which promotes governmental gridlock in Suriname's ethnically complex society. In 1994 the homes of the president of the parliament and a businessman were the targets of a grenade attack by unidentified people during a heated budget debate.

Labor unions are well organized and legally permitted to strike, but other civic institutions remain weak. There were numerous public sector strikes in 1994.

The constitution guarantees the right of free expression. Radio is both public and private, with a number of small commercial radio stations competing with the government-owned radio and television broadcasting system. All broadcast in the various local languages and usually offer different points of view. There are a number of independent newspapers. Although intimidation by the military has lessened, anonymous threats continue and a number of outlets practice self-censorship.

A peace accord was signed in August 1992 between the government and the two main rebel groups, the Jungle Commando and the indigenous-based, military-linked Tucuyana Amazonas. The guerrillas agreed to disarm under the supervision of the OAS but the government has been unable to comply with its commitment to new economic and social programs in the country's interior. The accord paved the way for 10,000 refugees who fled to neighboring French Guiana during the 1980s to start returning to Suriname.

In 1994 remnants of the armed insurgencies roamed the interior practicing free-lance banditry and issuing anti-government statements. One group seized a hydroelectric dam in March and demanded that the government resign. The group was routed by the army, which mysteriously let all the guerrillas flee.

The constitution provides for an independent judiciary but the judicial system is weak and ineffective, particularly against corruption in the government and the military and in addressing human rights cases. The rule of law is especially weak in the thinly populated interior.

There are a number of respected human rights groups. With the return to civilian rule in 1991 and the lessening of rights violations, they have been seeking justice for violations committed under military rule. A primary obstacle is the terms of the 1992 accord granting amnesty to former rebels and the military for rights violations committed during the conflict.

Some rights cases have been brought before the Inter-American Court of Human Rights, whose authority has been recognized by the Venetiaan government. In 1991 the government accepted responsibility for the murder of seven Bush Negroes by the military in 1987 and agreed to pay damages to the families of the victims.

Swaziland

Polity: Traditional monarchy
Economy: Capitalist
Population: 836,000
PPP: $2,506
Life Expectancy: 57.3
Ethnic Groups: Swazi, European, Zulu

Political Rights: 6
Civil Liberties: 5
Status: Not Free

Overview: Throughout 1994 Swazi workers took their grievances to the streets of Mbabane to strike against their companies' refusal to increase wages. As the government recruited journalists to join the cabinet's various ministries, the Confederation for Full Democracy in Swaziland, an umbrella group of banned political parties and human rights organizations that contested last year's elections, raised calls for a genuine multiparty system and free elections. Government critics denounced the process of appointing rather than electing ministers who cannot be accountable to voters. They also continued to describe as cosmetic changes King Mswati III's decision to allow voters to elect in 1993 a legislature which enjoys limited authority.

Swaziland is a small, land-locked monarchy tucked into an eastern corner of South Africa. In 1968 it became an independent state with a Westminster-style parliament. The first King during the postcolonial period, Sobhuza II, abolished the multiparty system in 1973, claiming that it was incompatible with Swazi traditions.

In 1991 King Mswati III appointed a *Vusela* (greeting committee) to solicit the public's view of the electoral system and propose solutions for the viability of its reform. In October 1992, the Vusela II presented its report proposing a multi-candidate election system, but stopping short of recommending multipartyism. In April 1993, following another Vusela III report, the King appointed a Delimitation Commission to study the feasibility of establishing additional *tinkhundla* (tribal councils), in addition to the forty already operating. At the same time the king stated that Swaziland was not yet ready to institute a multiparty system.

Just prior to the 11 October 1992 election, Mswati scrapped the detention law in effect since 1973, which allowed the government to detain suspects, frequently government critics, for up to sixty days without trial. However, the king replaced the 1973 act with another law that provided for suspects in nonbailable offenses, such as murder, rape and sedition, to be detained indefinitely.

During the nominating process in September, the local chiefs chose 200 from among some 2,500 candidates to compete for the fifty-five House of Assembly seats. The opposition People's United Democratic Movement (Pudemo) called for a boycott of the vote, protesting against the arbitrary selection of candidates and the unspecified powers of the future parliament. According to the Human Rights Association of Swaziland (Humeras), only 15 percent of eligible voters participated in the election.

In 1994 Prime Minister Mbilini offered the secretary of the Swazi National Association of Journalists a cabinet position in his government. Another minister recruited a political writer from the privately owned *Times of Swaziland*. Both reportedly accepted the appointments because they believe media bosses and editors give Swazi journalists second class treatment. Other journalists, however, refused the offers because they said ministers were trying to destabilize the media.

On 21 and 22 February Swazi workers held a nationwide strike for pay raises. In July, the Swaziland Manufacturing and Allied Workers' Union (SMAWA) called for thousands of private sector workers from more than five companies to strike for salary increases. Swaziland witnessed close to ten such solidarity strikes in one month by other unions. The police detained a union chief for several hours following the shooting of a sugar company employee participating in the strike on 22 July. A nationwide strike by several agricultural companies was called off on 24 July because negotiations between the union and the sugar company were advancing.

In September Sabelo Dlamini, representative of the Confederation for Full Democracy in Swaziland, visited South Africa to solicit support for a campaign to force change in Swaziland. The Confederation includes the People's United Democratic Movement, which is the most active of Swaziland's banned parties, and the Swaziland Youth Congress.

Political Rights and Civil Liberties:

The Swazis do not have the right to change their government democratically. The ultimate power to run the country's affairs is vested in the king. The parliament's role remains largely ceremonial, subject to pressures from the royalty and aristocracy. Political parties are still prohibited by law, although in recent years the democratic opposition has become much more vocal in calling for the abolition of the Tinkhundla system in favor of direct elections to parliament. In 1993, Pudemo continued its struggle for existence within the Nkhaba district, ruled by the former prime minister, Prince Bhekimpi. Security forces prevented Pudemo members from marching from the capital to the Nkhaba district to protest Bhekimpi's orders for all Pudemo members to cease their activities and leave the district. Bhekimpi vowed to attack the march with a regiment of traditional warriors. Subsequently, Bhekimpi announced the establishment of an "espionage" squad to help evict his opponents from the district.

The judiciary, whose members are appointed by the king, encompasses a High Court, a Court of Appeal, and district courts. Nonetheless, the judiciary remains largely independent of executive interference, particularly in criminal and civil cases. Judges and magistrates are frequently foreign nationals who have been "seconded" to Swazi courts based on intergovernmental agreements. In addition to the three-tiered court system based on Western law, there are also seventeen courts based on customary law, which deal primarily with minor disputes.

Public criticism of the immediate royal family and of national security policy is generally forbidden. Starting in 1990, however, the opposition began to criticize government policies more openly, including issues related to constitutional arrangements. The media, including the state-owned press and television, have expanded their coverage of opposition activities. Only the state-owned radio remains staunchly pro-government. In July 1994 the government initially refused to renew the work permit for Douglas Loffler, British owner of *The Times of Swaziland*, a paper that has been criticizing the government for nearly twenty years. Loffler filed an appeal to the government, which reviewed the matter, and the newspaper continues to operate.

Women are accorded a lower status than men both juridically and socially. In marriages conducted under traditional rules, polygamy is tolerated. Wives are treated as minors and require the husband's permission to enter into legally valid contracts. In June 1993, a tribal chief issued a ban on women wearing trousers, stating that it was "shameful" and disrespectful to tradition and the monarch.

Freedom of religion is respected. The right to travel freely within the country and abroad is limited for political opponents, women and non-ethnic Swazis. Workers have the right to freely organize. The long dominant Swaziland Federation of Trade Unions (SFTU) has faced a rival since the establishment in March 1993 of the Swaziland Federation of Labor (SFL).

Sweden

Polity: Parliamentary democracy
Economy: Mixed capitalist
Population: 8,821,000
PPP: $17,490
Life Expectancy: 77.7
Ethnic Groups: Native (Swedish, Finnish, Lappic or Saami, 88 percent), immigrant groups (12 percent)

Political Rights: 1
Civil Liberties: 1
Status: Free

Overview: The Social Democrats' victory in the general election on 18 September and the Swedish vote to join the European Union (EU) on 13 November were the major developments in 1994. A major ferry accident drew international attention.

Sweden is a constitutional monarchy governed by a parliamentary democracy. The head of state is King Carl Gustaf XVI. The head of government is Prime Minister Ingvar Carlsson, the Social Democrats' leader, who heads the largest party in the unicameral, 349-member parliament (*Riksdag*). Voters elect 310 parliamentarians directly, and the parties receiving at least 4 percent of the nationwide vote divide 39 seats. There is a three-year term.

In the 1994 general election, the Social Democrats ousted Prime Minister Carl Bildt's four-party, center-right government. On 18 September the Social Democrats captured 45.6 percent of the vote and 162 seats. They viewed the size of their vote as a rejection of Bildt's conservative economic policies. Elsewhere on the left, the former Communists, the Left Party, received 6.2 percent and 22 seats; the Environment Party garnered 5 percent and 18 seats. The left won a combined 202 seats, up from 153 in 1991. The center-right coalition parties, the Moderates, the Liberals, the Center and the Christian Democrats, won a combined 147 seats, down from 196 in 1991. The right-wing populist New Democracy Party, which had captured 25 seats in 1991 after less than a year's existence, received less than 4 percent in 1994, and lost all its seats. Women made major electoral gains, winning 41 percent of the parliamentary seats and half the portfolios in Carlsson's cabinet. The Social Democrats are governing without any coalition partners, passing legislation with the support of other parties on an *ad hoc* basis.

The most important event after the election was the passage of the referendum on EU membership, favored by most of the political establishment. The Social Democrats were split over the issue, and the Environment and Left Parties backed a No vote. In general, rural areas opposed the EU, while urban areas backed it. On 13 November Swedes voted 52.2 percent Yes and 46.9 No. There were some blank ballots. EU membership became effective as of January 1995. During the Cold War, Sweden had refrained from European and NATO memberships in order to maintain its neutrality. Since the collapse of communism in Eastern Europe, Sweden has joined NATO's Partnership for Peace program, and now has observer status with the West European Union, the defense group associated with the EU.

The biggest problem facing the Social Democratic government is the economy. Although the economy was out of recession by 1994, the large government deficit and growing national debt present threats to economic growth. Carlsson acknowledges that spending restraint is necessary, but also wants to preserve the welfare state. Shortly before the 1994 election, executives of four of the largest corporations said they would halt all new investment in Sweden unless the new government dealt with the deficit. The Social Democrats have promised a combination of spending cuts and tax increases to reduce the deficit.

Sweden will likely have a physical link to the rest of Europe during this decade. In June 1994, over the objections of the rural-based Center Party, the center-right government approved the construction of a bridge connecting Sweden and Denmark. However, environmentalists and anti-EU interests are trying to halt the project.

A major catastrophe took place on 28 September. The *Estonia*, a Baltic ferry, sank, killing more than 900 people. About half the passengers were Swedish. The size of the disaster had a devastating emotional impact on Sweden. Grief turned to anger in December 1994 when the government decided not to retrieve the vessel and the 818 bodies it contains.

Political Rights and Civil Liberties:

Swedes have the right to change their government democratically. Parliamentary elections take place at least once every three years. Aliens resident for three years have the right to participate in local elections. Swedes living abroad have the right to vote in national elections at Swedish diplomatic posts. The Lappic (Saami) ethnic minority has the right to its own parliament and significant powers over education and culture. However, in August 1994 several Saami organized roadblocks to protest a government decision to open central Sweden to small-game hunters. The protesters believed that the hunting policy was a threat to the collective hunting rights of the Saami who depend on reindeer and the land for their livelihood.

The judiciary is independent. The rights of the accused are generally respected. Sweden increased the rights of foreign suspects in 1991 by reforming the Terrorism Act. That law had allowed the state to confine alleged terrorists to their communities of residence. The government may still require that such suspects report periodically to the police. Swedes fear Russians will carry out cross-border crimes. An underground racist group, the Aryan Resistance Front, has carried out sporadic terrorist attacks in recent years.

With a few minor exceptions, freedom of expression is guaranteed, and the press is unrestricted. The government subsidizes daily newspapers regardless of their politics. Publications or videotapes that contain excessive violence or national security information are subject to censorship. Following the success of private satellite television channels, a land-based commercial television station won a license in 1991. Freedoms of assembly and association are guaranteed and almost always respected in practice. Lutheranism is the state religion, and the church gets public funding. However, other religions are free to practice.

Increasing economic problems have led to hostility between Swedes and the immigrant population. Large smuggling operations transport illegal arrivals to Sweden. In 1994, the government tightened restrictions on political asylum. However, the country gave haven to Taslima Nasrin, the Bangladeshi feminist author. Since 1991, there have been several episodes of Swedes shooting immigrants. The king has denounced the attacks as "frightening and unworthy of a democracy."

Emigration and domestic and foreign travel are unrestricted. Workers have the right to form and join trade unions and to strike. The trade union federations are strong and well-organized. The separate blue- and white-collar federations represent over 80 percent of workers. Both federations had leadership changes resulting from scandals within months of each other. In December 1993 the blue-collar federation leader quit in a dispute over payouts to former members. The white-collar federation leader resigned in July 1994 after a newspaper revealed that he and some American guests had run up a huge bill at a topless bar. Despite its historical links with the Social Democrats, the labor movement has become more independent of the party. In the 1990s, the once dominant joint labor-management guidelines for negotiations have broken down.

The social welfare system attempts to provide economic security for the population. It also attempts to enforce a degree of sexual equality. In 1994, parliament passed a law requiring fathers to take at least one of the twelve months of state-paid childcare leave given to both parents. If the father does not take that month, the parents lose a month of paid benefits.

Switzerland

Polity: Federal par-
liamentary democracy
Economy: Capitalist
Population: 7,012,000
PPP: $21,780
Life Expectancy: 77.8
Ethnic Groups: German, French, Italian, Romansch

Political Rights: 1
Civil Liberties: 1
Status: Free

Overview:

In 1994 newspaper printers held the country's first national strike since 1980 and voters continued to refrain from foreign involvement by rejecting a referendum proposal to dispatch 600 troops for United Nations peacekeeping missions. Also, forty-eight members of a religious sect called the Cross and the Rose were found dead in two Swiss villages, the first cult-related mass suicide in modern European history.

The origins of the Swiss Confederation, a landlocked, mountainous country, can be traced to 1291. Internationally recognized as a neutral country since 1815,

Switzerland is made up of twenty-three territories called cantons. There are twenty full cantons and six half-cantons. Each canton has its own political system, customs, and dominant ethnic group. While Swiss Germans predominate, French, Romansch, and Italian groups are concentrated in some areas. Switzerland is the home base of numerous institutions that have drawn people from all over the world.

The parliament, or Federal Assembly, is bicameral and sits for only three four-week sessions each year. Voters elect the 200-member lower house, the National Council, to four-year terms by proportional representation. The various parties have the following number of seats: Christian Democrats: 37; Conservative Radicals, 44; Social Democrats, 41; conservative People's Party, 25; Greens, 14; the conservative Liberals, 10; the anti-immigrant Auto Party, 8; the liberal Independent's Alliance, 6; the anti-immigrant Swiss Democrats; the Evangelical People's Party, 3; the Communist Swiss Party of Labor, 3; the Swiss-Italian Ticino League, 2; and independents, 2.

Using various local methods, the cantons elect two members each to the forty-six-member Council of States, the upper house. The executive branch is called the Federal Council, whose members function as a cabinet.

Since 1959 the governing coalition has consisted of the Social Democrats, Christian Democrats, Radicals, and the People's Party. Drawn from the Federal Assembly, one of the seven cabinet executives serves as president each year. According to a "magic formula," the small cabinet's composition must reflect the country's parties, regions, and language groups, leaving little room for any sector to dominate. In 1994, the president was Otto Stich from the Socialist Party. The cabinet's ministers carry out many trivial legislative and regulatory tasks.

Swiss voters go to the polls an average of four times a years. In one of this year's plebiscites, 57.3 percent of voters rejected a government proposal to provide 600 blue helmet soldiers for U.N. peacekeeping missions. The vote was in line with previous Swiss decisions to stay out of world affairs. In 1986, voters elected not to become a member of the U.N. and in 1992, to stay out of the European Economic Area.

Other 1994 referenda included votes to ban foreign trucks from traveling through the Alps and to give police new powers of search and detention when dealing with illegal immigrants. The former decision came under tough attack from European Union (EU) members. Italy and Germany rely on the Gothard Pass through the Alps to transport goods. The latter referendum was part of an effort to fight drug dealing. Switzerland has a high rate of addiction; with a population of 7 million, an estimated 33,000 are addicts.

In October a mass suicide sent a shock through this normally calm nation. Forty-eight members of the bizarre religious sect, Solar Temple Cult, were found dead in three fire-destroyed chalets located in two Swiss villages forty-six miles apart. The mystery deepened when five dead cult members were also found across the ocean in Quebec, where the group's leader, Belgian-born physician Luc Jouret, re-located in 1986.

Switzerland has many religious sects, but this was the first cult-related mass suicide in modern Europe's history. One week after the fires Jouret's body was identified among the suicide victims.

In November newspaper printers held a twenty-four-hour strike, protesting a new pay contract. It was the first nationwide strike in fourteen years, as such conflicts in Switzerland are generally resolved by negotiation and compromise.

Political Rights The Swiss can change their government democratically.
and Civil Liberties: The Swiss system produces coalition governments, which mitigate the chances for radical changes in policy. Voters have substantial powers of initiative and referendum, which allows them to change policies directly. Voters can trigger a plebiscite with 100,000 signatures.

Political parties have the right to organize freely, and cover the entire political spectrum. The canton system allows considerable local autonomy, which helps to preserve the linguistic and cultural heritage of the localities. The Italian and Romansch communities, however, believe that their linguistic and cultural resources are underfunded.

The government's postal ministry operates radio and television, which are political and linguistically pluralistic. Switzerland has freedoms of discussion, assembly, demonstration, and religion. The country, however, has a history of prosecuting conscientious objectors who refuse military service. Every able-bodied male must serve for three weeks in the military every two years until the age of fifty.

Feminists complain that the exclusion of women from the army and even the existence of the army itself create opportunities for male networking that put women at an economic disadvantage. Women's rights improved gradually in the 1980s. In 1993, the community of Waedenswil in the Zurich canton decided that official documents should only use the feminine form of German nouns. Swiss women may not work night shifts in factories.

Syria

Polity: Dominant party **Political Rights:** 7
(military-dominated) **Civil Liberties:** 7
Economy: Mixed statist **Status:** Not Free
Population: 13,966,000
PPP: $5,220
Life Expectancy: 66.4
Ethnic Groups: Arab (90 percent), Kurdish, Armenian and others (10 percent)

Overview: Syria's August 1994 parliamentary elections, involving only the military-backed Baath Party, its smaller allies, and state-approved independents, confirmed President Hafez al-Assad's dominant role in the country. The death of Assad's son earlier in the year in an auto accident led to speculation on the president's successor.

The French declared Syria a republic in September 1941, and granted full independence in January 1944. The country merged with Egypt to form the United Arab Republic in February 1958 but withdrew in September 1961. A March 1963 military coup brought the pan-Arab, socialist Baath party to power. Leadership struggles within the Baath party continued until November 1970 when the military wing, led by then-Lieut.-Gen. Hafez al-Assad, took power in a bloodless coup. Assad, from the minority Alawite Islamic sect, formally became president of this authoritarian, secular regime in February 1971. The 1973 constitution vests strong executive power in the president, who must be a Muslim and must be nominated by the Baath party and elected through a popular referendum. A directly elected People's Assembly, presently consisting of 250 members, serves a four-year term and nominally approves legislation and the budget, but holds little real power. There are no opposition political parties and in practice more than half of the seats are reserved for the military-backed Baath party or its allies in the National Progressive Front, with the rest going to state-approved independents.

In the late 1970s the fundamentalist Muslim Brotherhood group, drawn from the Sunni Muslim majority, began a series of anti-government attacks in Homs, Aleppo, Hama and other northern and central towns. In February 1982 soldiers crushed an armed fundamentalist rebellion in Hama, killing approximately 15,000-20,000 militants and civilians. Since then, the government has faced few overt threats from the fundamentalists.

Assad serves as head of government, commander-in-chief of the armed forces and secretary general of the Baath Party. The former fighter pilot has shrewdly given some key government positions to members of the Sunni majority and played up his devotion to Islam. Meanwhile, members of his Alawite minority hold most key military and intelligence positions, and the army and up to a dozen intelligence units keep a close watch on the population. In December 1991 Assad, running unopposed after being nominated by the Assembly, won a fourth seven-year term with a reported 99.982 percent of the popular vote. Government officials closely watched the voters, who had a "yes" or "no" choice.

The death of Major Basil al-Assad, the son of the president, in a January 1994 auto accident raised questions about who will succeed the sixty-five-year-old Assad, who is known to be suffering from heart problems. The Major had been seen as the likely candidate, and speculation is now focusing on Vice President Abdel Halim Khaddam. However Khaddam is a Sunni Muslim and may be unacceptable to the Alawite military and intelligence elite.

On 24-25 August voters elected a new parliament for a four-year term, choosing among 7,100 candidates. As expected the Baath Party and its National Progressive Front allies (consisting of five state-approved parties) took the 167 seats they contested. The remaining eighty-three seats went to independents, mainly businessmen keen on seeing the government continue economic liberalizations.

Another key issue in 1994 was the peace process with Israel. Syria has fought Israel three times since 1948, losing the strategic 483-square-mile Golan Heights in the 1967 Six Day War. Prior to 1967, Syria had shelled northern Israeli towns from the Golan. Assad refuses to discuss terms for peace until Israel recognizes Syrian sovereignty over the Golan Heights, even though Syria is motivated to negotiate with Israel by the prospect of improved relations with the U.S.

In September 1994 an Israeli cabinet minister confirmed that the two countries were holding secret negotiations, although little else is known about this process. Earlier in the month Israeli Prime Minister Yitzhak Rabin floated an offer of a limited military pullback from the Golan Heights for a three-year period, during which the two countries would normalize relations. If all went well the two sides would negotiate further withdrawals. By year's end Assad had neither embraced Rabin's plan nor offered fresh initiatives.

Investment Law Number Ten, introduced in May 1991, grants multiyear tax waivers for approved projects, removes some regulatory hurdles and allows entrepreneurs to import certain equipment duty free.

Political Rights and Civil Liberties:

Syrians cannot change their government democratically. President Hafez al-Assad maintains absolute authority in this military-backed regime. There is no outright ban on opposition groups, but in practice none is permitted and political opposition is forcibly suppressed. The parliament is elected every four years, but all candidates must be state-approved and the body has no independent authority.

Emergency laws in effect since 1963 (except during 1973-74) allow the government to suspend due process safeguards during searches, arrests, detentions, interrogations and trials in security cases. There are several internal security services and all operate independently of each other without any judicial oversight. Security forces and police engage in arbitrary arrests and disappearances, as well as torture of political and criminal detainees. The authorities monitor personal communications and conduct surveillance on persons considered to be security threats.

The government freed 2,864 political prisoners in late 1991, and 1,154 more in 1992. In 1993 the government freed at least nine political prisoners who had been imprisoned since the 1970 coup. Another, Salah Jadid, Syria's *de facto* ruler at the time of the 1970 coup, died of a heart attack in prison in August 1993. The Paris-based Committee for Defense of Democratic Freedoms and Human Rights in Syria (CDF) estimates that eleven others jailed since 1970 are still held at the Al-Mezze prison in Damascus. At least fifteen Syrian-based CDF activists arrested in February and March 1992 are either imprisoned or detained without trial. In February 1993 the U.S. National Academy of Sciences reported that in the past decade some 287 scientists, engineers and health professionals have been imprisoned, most without charge, for criticizing the government and calling for political liberalization. According to the U.S. State Department, credible estimates of the total number of political prisoners and detainees, including those held in Syrian detention facilities in Lebanon, run from 3,800 to 9,000 persons. Many are members of the Muslim Brotherhood.

The judiciary is subservient to the government. Defendants in civil and criminal cases receive some due process rights, although there is no trial by jury. Security and political offenses are handled in military-controlled State Security Courts where there are no due process safeguards.

Freedoms of speech and expression are sharply restricted. Citizens may not criticize the president or call for a change in regime, although some minor criticism of government performance is tolerated. The government and Baath party own and operate all media, and news coverage reflects state views. The government must grant permission for all assemblies, and in practice most demonstrations or other outdoor gatherings are state-sponsored. The government must also grant permission for private associations to form, and all such associations must be strictly nonpolitical.

Although there is no officially preferred religion, members of Assad's Alawite minority sect, which is considered heretical by most Sunni Muslims, hold many key security and government positions. The state forbids both Jehovah's Witnesses and

Seventh-Day Adventists from practicing together or owning church property, and some members have been arrested. The security apparatus closely monitors the Jewish community, and Jews are barred from most government jobs. In April 1992 Syria lifted restrictions on Jewish emigration abroad, and since then three-quarters of the then-4,000-strong community have left the country. Traditional conservative practices place Syrian women in a subservient position in matters including marriage, divorce and inheritance.

The government restricts travel near the borders with Israel, Lebanon, Jordan and Iraq. Individuals who have not completed required military service have difficulty in leaving the country. The government prohibits travel to Israel, and does not permit Syrian Druze to enter the Israeli-controlled Golan Heights to visit their counterparts. The government uses the umbrella General Federation of Trade Unions to dominate nearly all aspects of union activity. There is no outright ban on independent labor unions, but they are strongly discouraged and none exists. Strikes are also strongly discouraged and rarely occur.

Taiwan (Rep. of China)

Polity: Presidential-legislative (transitional)
Economy: Capitalist-statist
Population: 21,050,000
PPP: na
Life Expectancy: 74.5
Ethnic Groups: Chinese (native majority, mainland minority, 98 percent), Aboriginal (2 percent)
Ratings Change: *Taiwan's political rights rating changed from 4 to 3 and its civil liberties rating from 4 to 3 because democratization and liberalization continued in 1994.

Political Rights: 3*
Civil Liberties: 3*
Status: Partly Free

Overview: Taiwan's democratic transition continued in July 1994 as the National Assembly amended the constitution to provide for direct presidential elections in 1996. In December the ruling Kuomintang (KMT) Party won the first elections for the island's provincial governor post, as the opposition Democratic Progressive Party (DPP) took two concurrent mayoral races.

The island, located 100 miles off the Chinese coast, came under control of China's Nationalist government after World War II. Following the Communist victory on the mainland in 1949, the Nationalist leadership established a government-in-exile on Taiwan under Chiang Kai-shek. For most of the next four decades, the KMT ruled in an authoritarian manner while providing one of the highest standards of living in the region. The governments of both Taiwan and China officially consider Taiwan to be a province of China, and until recently the KMT claimed to be the legitimate government of all of China. The KMT remains pro-unification but, bowing to reality, now views Taiwan as a separate political entity of a divided nation. The government refers to Taiwan as "The Republic of China." Today native Taiwanese make up 85 percent of the population, and mainlanders or their descendants comprise the minority.

The 1947 constitution is a holdover from the KMT's rule on the mainland. It provides for a National Assembly, which can amend the constitution and until 1994 had the power to elect the president and vice president. The president serves a six-year term (to be four years after 1996) and appoints the prime minister and other top officials. The government has five specialized *yuan* (branches), each with its own head. The Executive Yuan runs most of the ministries; the Legislative Yuan enacts laws; the Judicial Yuan, consisting of fifteen grand justices appointed by the president, interprets the constitution; the Examination Yuan holds civil service tests; and the Control Yuan serves as an administrative and fiscal check on the other branches.

The country's democratic transition began with the lifting of martial law in 1987. In January 1988 Lee Teng-hui became the first native-born Taiwanese president following the death of Chiang Ching-kuo, the son of Chiang Kai-shek. In January 1989 the government formally legalized opposition parties. Lee was elected for a full term in March 1990.

In December 1991 the Taiwanese elected a new National Assembly. At the time the Assembly consisted mostly of aging mainlanders elected in 1947 or 1969 whose terms had been frozen to maintain the KMT's political monopoly and legitimize the country's claim to the mainland. Direct elections were held for 325 of its 403 seats (the remainder were held over from the limited elections in 1986), with 225 seats representing constituencies and the other 100 allotted through proportional representation. The KMT, running on a theme of stability and prosperity, won 254 seats. The DPP, which openly violated the Sedition Law by calling for the country to declare independence from the mainland, took sixty-six seats; independent candidates took five seats.

In December 1992 the country held its first full Legislative Yuan elections since the Nationalists fled to the mainland. The KMT received just 53 percent of the vote and took 96 of the 161 seats; the DPP took 50 seats; the tiny Chinese Social Democratic Party, 1; independents, 14.

Immediately following the election the KMT's native Taiwanese faction blamed the party's relatively poor showing on mainland-born premier Hau Pei-Tsun. Hau resigned in late January 1993, and on 23 February parliament swore in Lien Chan as the first native Taiwanese prime minister, continuing Lee's drive to rout aging mainlanders from top posts.

In early August the KMT formally split for the first time as six second-generation mainlander MPs led by Jaw Shau-kong defected to form the New Party, accusing Lee and the KMT's native Taiwanese faction of not being fully committed to unification with China. At the KMT's fourteenth National Party Congress in mid-August, native Taiwanese strengthened their control over the party. Lee's nominees won 151 of the 210 Central Committee seats and eighteen of thirty-one Central Standing Committee seats. At the 27 November 1993 local elections the KMT took fifteen mayoral or magistrate posts to only six for the DPP, with two going to independents. However, the KMT won only 47.5 percent of the popular vote, the first time it had received less than 50 percent in any election, while the DPP increased its share from 38 percent to 41.2 percent.

In July 1994 the National Assembly amended the constitution to provide for direct presidential elections in 1996. On 3 December Taiwan held its first elections for provincial governor, a highly symbolic but largely redundant post that maintains the KMT's claim that Taiwan is simply another province of China. The same day polls were held for the mayoralties of Tapei and Kaohsiung for the first time since 1967 and 1979, respectively.

The DPP made the KMT's corruption a leading campaign theme. In the provincial race James Soong, the KMT incumbent, won 56 percent of the vote to easily defeat the

DPP's candidate. However, DPP candidates took the two mayoral posts. Voters appear to trust the DPP's ability to govern, but are wary of its calls for independence and thus gave what is currently the island's highest elected post to the KMT. China insists it will invade if Taiwan declares independence, and this threat may limit the DPP's share of the vote at Legislative Yuan elections scheduled for December 1995.

Political Rights and Civil Liberties: Taiwanese have been gaining increasing power to change their government, with direct presidential elections due in 1996. The ruling KMT maintains significant advantages over the opposition through its control of the media and the government apparatus. The KMT listed its total business assets at $36 billion in 1992, and according to the *Financial Times* the party spends $200 million annually compared with $2 million for the DPP. Elections at all levels are marred by credible accusations of vote buying, and several elected officials have been convicted and sentenced to prison terms.

In 1992 the government eliminated several civil liberties restrictions. In April the Assembly amended the Sedition Law to cover only direct advocacy of violence, making it legal to advocate formal independence from China. In June the government abolished the "second personnel departments," commonly referred to as "thought police," that had been stationed in government offices to monitor civil servants. However, the National Security Law and the Parade and Assembly Law prohibit demonstrations advocating communism or independence, while the Civic Organization Law prohibits associations (with the exception of political parties) from advocating independence.

Police abuse of suspects in custody is a continuing problem, particularly in small, local police stations. Civil libertarians have criticized the Criminal Procedure Code's provision allowing the authorities to detain a suspect for up to four months during an investigation before formal charges are brought. Also criticized is the "Anti-Hoodlum Law," which permits police to arrest and detain alleged hoodlums on the basis of testimony by secret informers. The judiciary is not considered fully independent in sensitive cases. Trials are open but there are no jury trials.

The Publications Law allows police to censor or ban publications considered seditious or treasonous. Although censorship on political grounds no longer occurs, journalists reportedly still practice self-censorship on sensitive issues. The KMT, the Taiwan provincial government and the military maintain controlling shares in the country's three main television stations. Most radio stations are owned by the government or by the KMT-controlled Broadcasting Corporation of China. Political coverage on broadcast media is frequently biased against the opposition. In March 1993 popular television anchor Lee Yen-chiu confessed that, due to the government's influence over content, she felt like a "puppet" reading the news. During his successful campaign in 1994 for provincial governor, incumbent James Soong of the KMT had far greater television exposure than his opponents. In concurrent mayoral races television stations barely covered non-KMT rallies, leading one news anchor to quit in disgust. During the 1992 legislative election campaign the authorities apportioned advertising time on the basis of the number of candidates nominated by each party, giving the KMT a large advantage.

In 1993 the government approved applications for new radio stations for the first time since 1969, although they will be limited to local rather than island-wide broadcasting. No television stations have been approved since 1969 although the government expects to have a private station licensed and operational by 1996. In August 1994 the government was criticized for closing down fourteen popular illegal radio stations.

The Parade and Assembly Law makes the organizers of mass events responsible for the conduct of the participants. Opposition leaders have been charged with harming public order because of misconduct at demonstrations they organized. Under the Civic Organizations Law all organizations must register with the government. The authorities have refused to register some groups that have "Taiwan" in their names because this suggests a pro-independence platform. However, unregistered groups, such as the Taiwan Association for Human Rights, continue to operate openly.

Women reportedly face discrimination in salary and promotion opportunities. Enforcement of maternity leave laws is generally weak. Incidents of rape and domestic violence are widespread. Child prostitution is also a serious problem, and upwards of one-fifth of child prostitutes are from Taiwan's tiny aboriginal minority. The aboriginal population also suffers from social and economic alienation and have limited say in policy decisions regarding their land and natural resources. Citizens can travel freely within the country and abroad. The list of dissidents excluded from re-entering the country has been sharply reduced to cover only those strongly suspected of engaging in terrorism or violence. Government-run detention camps hold some 2,000 mainland Chinese illegal immigrants, as well as Vietnamese boat people and illegal foreign workers. Conditions in these camps are reportedly harsh.

There are significant restrictions on workers' rights of association. The government must approve the rules and constitutions of labor unions, and can dissolve a union for disturbing the public order. None has been dissolved, although authorities have refused to certify competing unions, asking them to file as a single union. Civil servants, defense industry workers and teachers cannot unionize. Only one labor federation is permitted, the pro-KMT Chinese Federation of Labor. Strikes must be approved by a majority of the full membership of a union, and the government must approve these vote meetings. In practice this latter power has been used to prevent strikes.

Tajikistan

Polity: Communist-dominated
Political Rights: 7
Civil Liberties: 7
Economy: Statist
Status: Not Free
Population: 5,882,000
PPP: $2,180
Life Expectancy: 70.0
Ethnic Groups: Tajiks (62 percent), Uzbeks (24 percent), Russians and Ukrainians (10 percent), Armenians, Gypsies, others

Overview:
After a year marked by violence between Russia-backed government forces and a political opposition based largely in neighboring Afghanistan, acting head of state and Parliamentary Speaker Emomali Rakhmonov was elected president of this war-torn Central Asian country in November 1994. Tajikistan's repressive regime flouted political and human rights.

Tajikistan, one of the poorest of the former Soviet republics, was carved out of the Uzbek Soviet Republic on Stalin's orders in 1929. By leaving Samarkand and Bukhara, the two main centers of Tajik culture, inside Uzbekistan, the boundaries of the republic angered Tajiks, who trace their origin to Persia. The four leading regionally based tribes are the Leninabad and Kulyab (the current ruling alliance), the Garm and the Badakhshan.

In 1990 the fledgling national movement, Rastokhez (Rebirth), sparked protests over long-neglected economic and social problems. But only Communist Party candidates were allowed to run in elections to the unicameral Supreme Soviet (parliament). In 1991 the Democratic Party and the moderate Islamic Renaissance Party (IRP) were registered. In fraud-marred elections that November, old-line Communist Rakhman Nabiyev was elected president. The opposition formed an umbrella Movement for Democratic Reforms.

In May 1992, amid political machinations and violence, the Communists and opposition reached an agreement specifying the formation of a coalition government. Nabiyev was to remain president until December presidential elections. An eighty-member Assembly (*Majlis*) was established to serve until elections for a multiparty People's Assembly. In August parliament stripped Nabiyev of the power of direct presidential rule. As fighting and instability increased, parliamentary chairman Akbarsho Iskandarov was named acting president.

In September with Russian troops in Dushanbe, the government was in the hands of secular democrats and the IRP. Forces loyal to Nabiyev staged an unsuccessful coup in October. Iskandarov urgently asked Russian troops to intervene in the conflict by imposing curfews and disarming local militias. On 10 December 1992, following months of conflict that left some 20,000 dead, the loose coalition of Islamic activists, secular democrats and nationalists was overthrown by former Communist hardliners backed by the Russians. The post of president was scrapped and Supreme Soviet Chairman Rakhmonov was named head of state.

In 1993 Rakhmonov launched a campaign of terror that drove some 60,000 people across the Armu Darya river into Afghanistan. Those targeted included not only political activists, but also people from regions, such as Garm and autonomous region of Gorno-Badakhshan in the Pamir mountains at the foot of the Hindu Kush, and clans that supported the ousted Islamic-democratic coalition. The campaign brought charges of "ethnic cleansing" against the Garm and Pamiri peoples and atrocities throughout the country. Also marked for persecution and murder were democratically oriented journalists and free-market businessmen. By year's end there were about 24,000 Russian and Uzbek soldiers along the Afghan frontier.

During a March 1994 trip to Washington to meet with World Bank and IMF officials, new Prime Minister Abdujalil Samadov told U.S. congressmen that his government planned to meet with democratic and Islamic opposition leaders and work out repatriation of 30,000 refugees then in three camps in Afghanistan (about 30,000 had returned home). Rep. Robert Andrews (D-NJ), who earlier had introduced a non-binding resolution calling on President Bill Clinton to promote political stability in Tajikistan, said there would be more support for U.S. assistance if the country showed progress in human rights and democratization.

In April talks in Moscow between representatives of the IRP-democratic coalition and the government, the IRP, countering government allegations of "Islamic fundamentalism," reiterated its commitment to a secular state. The talks made little progress save for agreement to meet again in June. Meanwhile, the

Dushanbe regime was badly fractured. The Kulyabis, represented by Rakhmonov, were openly at odds with the Uzbek-backed Leninabadis (led by Prime Minister Samadov) who ran the republic during the Soviet era.

In June, amid rising tensions, ten Russian soldiers were killed in separate incidents in Dushanbe and along the Afghan border. On 15 June gunmen killed Deputy Defense Minister Ramazan Radjabov and several soldiers with him. At night, armed gangs roamed the streets of Dushanbe. It was unclear who was responsible for the violence, with possibilities ranging from the coalition of Islamic and tribal opponents, to progovernment groups wanting to show the Russians the futility of trying to negotiate with the opposition. There were also clashes in Garm and in Gorno-Badakhshan. The increased violence came just before the opening of a second round of U.N.-sponsored peace talks in Teheran. The negotiations ended with the two sides agreeing only that it would be beneficial to have a cease-fire and national reconciliation. They agreed to continue talks in Islamabad, the Pakistani capital.

On 19 August seven Russian border guards were killed and 10 wounded in a massive attack by several hundred opposition forces along the Afghan-Tajik border. In a separate attack, fourteen Tajik interior ministry troops were killed and twenty-four wounded in a rebel ambush. It was believed the attacks were carried out by rival clans from the Garm and Pamir areas.

On 7 September Tajik lawmakers voted 153-3 to postpone that month's presidential elections and a referendum on a new constitution until November, bowing to Russian demands to open the field to opposition forces. The presidential vote had been set for 25 September, and pitted Parliament Chairman Rakhmonov against Abdumalik Abdulladzhanov, the former Tajik premier and current ambassador to Moscow. Both candidates were from the Communist ruling elite. After the postponement, Rakhmonov did not lift the ban on the IRP and the Democratic Party, the two leading opposition groups. On 9 September Akbar Turajonzoda, deputy head of the IRP living in Iran, rejected the government's offer to take part in the presidential election. He said the opposition was ready to sign a cease-fire agreement and begin peace talks on the condition that government forces be disarmed first. Rakhmonov offered to pardon rebels who laid down their arms by 20 September.

On 17 September, as government forces clashed with opposition rebels around Dushanbe, their leaders signed a Moscow-brokered temporary cease-fire to stop all fighting by 5 November, a day before the presidential vote, after U.N. observers arrived on the Tajik-Afghan border. On 19 October a team of seventeen U.N. observers was in place.

The election campaign between Rakhmonov, a Kulyabi, and Abdulladznanov, a Leninabadi, had more to do with regional and clan differences than ideology. "I have neither thugs nor armed groups at my disposal," said Abdulladznanov, alluding to well-armed government forces. Several bombs went off in Dushanbe on the eve of the vote.

The results of the 6 November election gave Rakhmonov 60 percent of the vote, and the challenger, 35 percent. Officially, turnout was 90 percent of the 2.6-million electorate. Voters also backed a new constitution that, among other things, enshrined a presidential system. Under the constitution, the president is empowered to appoint and dismiss the entire government, administration officials and judges. The president is also the head of parliament, which can dismiss him and force him to approve legislation. Serious questions about fairness surrounded the hastily called election from the outset. There were widespread charges of fraud and voter intimidation. Only one small group of international observers—sixteen people from Russia, Belarus, Georgia, Iran and Turkey—monitored the vote, and were able to visit only a handful of the 2,469 polling stations.

On 16 November the new president promised to crush the armed opposition to his authority and to improve living conditions. Despite the ceasefire, fighting continued to flare up along the Afghan-Tajik border. An influential IRP field commander was killed in early December.

On 2 December Dzhamashed Karimov, a fifty-four-year-old economist, was appointed prime minister. Parliament began deliberations on local government reforms, laws on religious rights and pensions. Parliamentary elections were set for February 1995.

Meanwhile, the Dushanbe government paid a stiff price for Russian military support. Part of the ruble zone, the impoverished country was allocated $91 million in loans since February. As collateral, it was forced to give a 50 percent share in the massive Nurek hydroelectric plant and major allotments in industrial units to Russia. Moscow owns most of Tajikistan now, so it calls the shots," said a Tajik commentator.

Political Rights and Civil Liberties:

War, government repression, and the return of a one-party Communist system have robbed citizens of the means to change their government democratically. November presidential elections were boycotted by the opposition, most of whom are abroad.

All opposition political parties, such as the IRP, the Democratic Party and the Lali Badakhshan, are banned, and most of their leaders are outside the country. An electoral law includes restrictive nomination proceedings and excludes refugees from the process. Pervasive security forces and a Soviet-era judiciary subservient to the regime effectively curtail freedom of expression, association and assembly.

Independent human rights groups have documented severe abuses, including extrajudicial killings, torture, kidnapping, and "ethnic cleansing," particularly of the Garm and Pamiri peoples. Killings and assassinations were common in 1994. There were an estimated sixty political prisoners as of October 1994, according to one human rights organization. At least two political prisoners were executed during the year. Under Tajik law, a person may be detained for up to eighteen months without trial.

The independent newspapers that flourished immediately after independence are gone, their editors and reporters now dead, jailed or exiled. Four television journalists, including the former head of the Tajikistan State Committee on Radio and Television, have been imprisoned since 1993. On 8 August 1994 state security officers entered and searched without warrants the homes of Makhsoud Husseinov of the Supreme Soviet's newspaper *Sadayi Mardom* (Voice of the People) and Muhammad Rahim Saidar, a writer and journalist. Copies of *Charoghi Ruz*, an independent newspaper published in Moscow, were found in their homes. They were detained without formal charge for several days. A February 1994 decree suspended the activities of all independent electronic media.

Islam was revived after many decades, though the regime has intruded into religious life to preclude fundamentalism and anti-government activity. On 30 December 1993 a popular Russian Orthodox priest, Father Sergy, was brutally murdered a day after sanctifying the 201st Russian Motorized Rifle Regiment. Islamic and anti-Russian sentiments caused ethnic Russians to leave Tajikistan in droves.

The war and presence of 24,000 foreign troops have severely curtailed freedom of movement. The rights of women are circumscribed in practice. There are no independent trade unions.

Tanzania

Polity: Dominant party   **Political Rights:** 6
Economy: Statist   **Civil Liberties**: 6*
Population: 29,755,000   **Status:** Not Free
PPP: $570
Life Expectancy: 51.2
Ethnic Groups: African, Asian and Arab minorities
Ratings Change: *Tanzania's civil liberties rating changed
from 5 to 6 because of continued and intensified governmental
repression against opposition and human rights leaders.

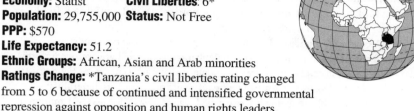

Overview: In local elections held in October 1994, the ruling Revolutionary Party of Tanzania, Chama Cha Mapinduzi (CCM), won a
landslide victory. By-elections held in the spring of 1994 also
secured power for the ruling CCM. Opposition parties were allowed to contest elections,
but limited access to media coupled with infighting among opposition parties may
have contributed to the CCM success. Although the government declared both
elections to be free and fair, there was no independent confirmation of election results.

Since gaining independence from Britain in 1961, the CCM has dominated
political power. A 1992 amendment to Tanzania's constitution legalized independent political parties. However, despite government overtures and subsequent
elections, the United Republic of Tanzania remains dominated by one party. As
national elections scheduled for October 1995 draw near, the ruling party's
commitment to a multiparty democratic system will be tested.

The East African Republic of Tanzania was formed in 1964 by the merger of
mainland Tanganyika with the islands of Zanzibar and Pemba. The politically influential
Julius Nyerere served as Tanzania's president and CCM party chairperson from post
independence until his retirement in 1985. President Ali Hassan Mwinyi succeeded
Nyerere as both president and party chairperson. In the October 1990 presidential
elections, Mwinyi ran uncontested and was returned to office for a second five-year term.

In March 1991, after much national and intra-party discussion, Mwinyi commis-
sioned a study to examine public opinion on political pluralism. At the end of the year-
long study, the commission recommended that opposition parties be allowed to register.
On 20 January 1992, the CCM executive committee officially endorsed the
commission's recommendations, but rejected the proposal for a switch to federalism to
allow greater autonomy to Tanganyika and the islands. Former President Nyerere, with
other committee members, successfully campaigned for the one-party system to continue
until Parliament's term ends in 1995. Although a number of opposition groups had
already formed by the end of 1991, the government did not allow opposition parties to
petition for legal status until 17 June 1992.

Despite its merger with Tanzania in 1964, the Island of Zanzibar exercises a
considerable degree of autonomy and has maintained a strong separate identity.
Many of the twenty-five million mainland Tanzanians are Christian; Zanzibar's
population of 750,000 is 90 percent Muslim. Within Zanzibar there is a drive for
increasing autonomy and a move towards possible secession. In August the

Tanzanian parliament accepted a proposal to create a federal system of two parallel governments—one for Tanganyika and the other for Zanzibar. Both governments would remain under the umbrella of the Tanzanian regime, but many see this move as the precursor to a breakup of the union.

With Zanzibar's economy in decay, the national government has looked increasingly to the Arab world for financial assistance and investment, a move that has disturbed many in mainland Tanzania. Adding to their concerns, in early 1993 Zanzibar became the fiftieth member of the Islamic Organization Conference (IOC), a move specifically prohibited by Tanzania's constitution. It was further revealed that the application to the IOC was made with the knowledge and approval of President Mwinyi (who is Muslim). The application was later withdrawn but the move, along with subsequent revelations of government foreknowledge, led some in the press to speculate not only on the future of the union, but also to raise concerns regarding possible conflict between Tanzania's Christians and Muslims.

Political Rights and Civil Liberties:

Despite some lessening of restrictions on opposition party organization, Tanzanians cannot change their government democratically. Opposition party organization remains restricted. Opposition parties have been denied permission to register and gain access to the press; opposition leaders have been arrested and detained.

In March 1994 Christopher Mtikila, leader of the unregistered Democratic Party and human rights activist, was arrested. Beginning in 1992 the government carried on a campaign of harassment and intimidation against members of the Democratic Party. Mtikila was arrested in February 1992 for allegedly distributing a false statement, and again in August 1992 when he was charged with various offenses including "sedition" and "intimidation." He was subsequently found guilty of illegally conducting a meeting, disobeying a police order and using abusive language. Mtikila, along with three other members who were also charged, was sentenced to nine months. A subsequent High Court ruling overturned the verdict, finding that the charges were unfounded. Mtikila was again arrested in September 1993 on sedition charges.

In nonpolitical cases, the judicial system is free from governmental interference. Arrest and harassment of political opponents, however, is routine. Under the Preventive Detention Act of 1962 (amended in 1985) the president may order the arrest and indefinite detention without bail of persons considered a threat to national security or public order. Political offenders may also be internally exiled under the Deportation Ordinance, which allows the government to restrict a person's movements or internally deport a person from one sector of the country to another. This measure has been effectively used against opposition party leaders. Abuses by local authorities in nonpolitical cases, including the unlawful detention of relatives of those wanted in connection with common crimes, has been reported. Among other repressive legislation are the Regions and Regional Commissioners Act 1962 and the Area Commissioners Act 1962 which grant Commissioners (who are usually members of the CCM party) the power to employ preventive detention without trial and the ability to restrict or deny public meetings. The Refugees Control Act 1966 provides authorities with the right to arrest, detain without trial and deport refugees.

The constitution protects freedom of speech and the press, but these rights remain restricted in Tanzania. The 1976 Newspapers Act allows the Minister of Information to ban newspapers if they are deemed a national security threat. The Act also allows the government to prosecute the owners and editors of newspapers found guilty of publishing seditious material. Opposition parties and those organizations critical of the ruling party are denied free access to broadcast media. Some autonomy in the print media has emerged but independent, nongovernmental newspapers such as *The Express* and *The Family Mirror* have limited circulation, confined mostly to the capital region. The press remains subject to government interference and the Media Institute of Southern Africa (MISA) reports that in January 1994 the weekly *Baraza* was closed "temporarily" by the government in response to an article in which the paper implicated the government in the death of a prominent religious leader. This was just the first step in what MISA alleges is a "declared war on the media, particularly the private press…" In March 1994 both the editor and publisher of the *Express* were arrested and subsequently charged with sedition for publishing an editorial that criticized the government.

Internal travel is restricted in order to control mass migration to the urban areas and to limit the mobility of opposition party members. Obtaining a passport can be difficult and, as a result, travel abroad is restricted. Mainland Tanzanians wishing to travel to Zanzibar must have a passport, although residents of Zanzibar can travel to the mainland without documentation. Freedom of religion is provided for in the Constitution and is respected in practice. In mid-1992 the government banned open air religious services and all religious demonstrations. The ban was lifted in June 1992 but was reinstated in December 1992 by the Zanzibar government because it feared that religious meetings were being used for political purposes.

Thailand

Polity: Parliamentary democracy (military-influenced)
Economy: Capitalist-statist
Population: 59,396,000
PPP: $5,270
Life Expectancy: 68.7
Ethnic Groups: Thai (84 percent), Chinese (12 percent), Malaysian, Indian, Khmer, Vietnamese minorities

Political Rights: 3
Civil Liberties: 5
Status: Partly Free

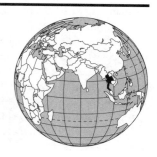

Overview: Thai Prime Minister Chuan Leekpai's governing coalition suffered a setback in the spring of 1994 as parliament defeated proposed constitutional amendments aimed at democratizing the political process, including measures to make the military-appointed Senate smaller and more accountable.

The Kingdom of Thailand is the only Southeast Asian nation never colonized by a European country. In 1932 a bloodless military coup, the first of seventeen attempted military coups in this century, introduced a constitution and limited the power of the monarchy. Since World War II a succession of pro-Western military and civilian governments has ruled. Today King Bhumibol Alduyadej's only political duty is to approve the prime minister, but he is widely revered and exerts informal political and social influence.

In 1988, following a period of military rule, Major General Chatichai Choonhaven took office as the first directly elected prime minister since 1976. In February 1991 the army deposed Chatichai in a bloodless coup, ostensibly due to high levels of corruption. But what really irked the generals was that Chatichai had tried to limit the military's influence in politics, in particular the influence of graduates of Chulachomklao Royal Military Academy's Class Five, from which the coup plotters and most of the military elite hail.

In March 1991 the army named Anand Panyarach, a widely respected former businessman, as interim prime minister. In December 1991 a pro-military, interim National Assembly approved a controversial new constitution. It allows the military to appoint the entire 270-seat Senate, meaning that in a no-confidence motion a unified Senate could bring down a government if joined by only forty-six members of the directly-elected, 360-seat House of Representatives. In addition, it permitted the prime minister to come from outside the ranks of elected MPs.

At the March 1992 lower House elections three pro-military parties won a slim 190-seat majority, and joined with two centrist parties in recommending Narong Wongwan as prime minister. After learning that Narong had been denied an entry visa to the United States in July 1991 because of involvement in drug trafficking, the coalition switched its support to coup leader Suchinda Kraprayoon, who had not stood in the parliamentary elections. Thousands of angry civilians, led by Chamlong Srimuang, the Palang Dharma (Moral Force) party leader, began weeks of protests in Bangkok, the capital. Many protesters were members of Bangkok's increasingly prosperous middle class.

On 18 May soldiers opened fire randomly into the crowd, beginning three days of confrontations. Officially, fifty-two people died, although at least forty-eight people remain unaccounted for. King Bhumibol ended the bloodshed by personally ordering Suchinda and Chamlong to broker a compromise. In June Anand began a second stint as interim prime minister and transferred authority for crowd control from the military to the police. Parliament amended the constitution to require that future premiers come from among elected MPs.

New elections were held on 13 September 1992. The Democratic Party took 79 seats; Chart Thai, 77; Chart Pattana, 60; New Aspiration (NAP), 51; Palang Dharma, 47; Social Action party (SAP), 22; minor parties, 24. On 23 September the Democrats, NAP, Palang Dharma, SAP and the tiny Solidarity party formed a 207-seat prodemocracy coalition, and elected the Democrat's Chuan Leekpai as Prime Minister. In a controversial decision, in November a special tribunal upheld an amnesty granted by the military government to generals involved in the May killings.

In 1993 Chuan had to fend off charges of being weak and indecisive on economic matters. The government survived a no-confidence motion in June. On 15 September Chuan dropped the SAP from the coalition after it hinted it might join forces with the opposition, and added the eight-seat Seritham (Liberal Democrat) Party.

In April and May 1994 Chuan's coalition suffered a string of setbacks as right-wing opposition parties in the House combined with the military-appointed Senate to defeat seven constitutional amendments providing for democratic reforms. The most controversial measure would have reduced the Senate to 120 members and made it more accountable.

In December the coalition government faced a brief crisis after the NAP helped the opposition defeat a government bill proposing elections for the thousands of village headman posts. The NAP then quit the coalition in an apparent effort to gain favor with the headmen, who use their influence to deliver votes at parliamentary elections. The Chart Pattana party joined the coalition and re-established its majority with 201 seats. However, pressure from the Palang Dharma party, the coalition's third-largest member, for faster progress on constitutional reform may force Chuan to call early elections before 1996 in order to build a stronger majority.

In another development, in May police arrested four Muslim preachers in the southern town of Songkhla on charges of planting bombs that had earlier derailed two passenger trains in March, and of involvement in other terrorist attacks dating back to 1992. The government has placed overall responsibility for the attacks on the Muslim separatist Pattani United Liberation Organization, which has campaigned sporadically for the secession of four southern provinces since the early 1960s but has been largely dormant in recent years due to a security crackdown and the positive effects of a rural development program. Some observers suggested the attacks were the work of disgruntled army officers.

Political Rights and Civil Liberties: Thais changed their government democratically in September 1992 in elections rated the cleanest in the country's history. Although army chief of staff Wimol Wongwanich has worked to professionalize the army through promotions based primarily on merit, the possibility of a future military coup cannot be discounted. Corruption is widespread, and the police and armed forces routinely engage in illicit activities. In 1994 the U.S. government refused visas to at least two opposition MPs for alleged involvement in drug trafficking, andCalifornia authorities unsealed an indictment on trafficking charges against a third MP.

Freedoms of speech and press are generally respected, but legal restrictions exist on defaming the monarchy, advocating a Communist government, inciting disturbances and insulting religion. The press is generally outspoken in its criticism of the government but exercises self-censorship in these proscribed areas and in comments on the military. The government or military controls each of the five national television networks, and news coverage is sometimes biased. In September 1992 the government authorized the establishment of two new private television channels, both of which could be operational by 1995. Radio stations are required to broadcast government-produced newscasts four times daily and a military produced commentary once, but can supplement these with their own news. A government committee reviews radio programming and occasionally censors politically sensitive material on private stations.

The judiciary is considered independent of the government. Detainees lack the right to an attorney during an investigation, although defendants receive adequate due process safeguards. The court can order a closed trial for cases involving the royal family or defamation of religion. There are credible reports of summary executions carried out by police, and police frequently abuse prisoners and torture detainees to extract confessions. In July 1994 a group of police officers murdered at least nine Asian tourists during a robbery spree. Conditions at the Suan Phlu immigration detention center are particularly harsh, and some detainees have reportedly been held for longer than a year.

In July 1994 the government withdrew visas of eleven people planning to attend a conference on East Timor in Bangkok, deported three others, and prevented several hotels from hosting the conference, which did take place. Freedom of assembly is occasionally abridged by local officials in rural areas who charge peaceful demonstrators with inciting unrest and intent to commit violence. In 1993, after farmers in the town of Kamphaeng Phet protesting falling rice prices allegedly injured several policemen, police beat one demonstrator to death and injured more than twenty others.

NGOs estimate that 300,000-800,000 prostitutes work in cities around the country. Many are from poor rural villages and turn to prostitution to raise money for their families. Others are trafficked from hill tribes and from neighboring Burma. One-fifth of all prostitutes are believed to be under eighteen years old, including boys working in brothels that cater to foreign tourists. Efforts to crack down on prostitution are undermined by the complicity of police and local officials in prostitution schemes. In 1994 the Chuan government introduced legislation, still pending by year's end, that would penalize brothel owners, pimps, traffickers and men patronizing prostitutes who are under eighteen, while reducing the penalties on prostitutes.

Freedom of religion is respected in practice. Muslims face discrimination in employment opportunities and some say the school curriculum is biased towards the Buddhist majority. Only half of some 500,000-700,000 members of hill tribes are believed to be registered as citizens, and those not registered cannot vote and have difficulty obtaining jobs and social services. Freedom of internal travel and residence is restricted for some Chinese and Vietnamese aliens. Some 76,000 Burmese living in camps in Thailand are considered illegal immigrants, and the Thai army regularly refuses entry to Burmese and Cambodians fleeing fighting in their countries, as well as to Laotians seeking asylum.

The 1975 Labor Relations Act allows private sector workers to join independent unions, but civil servants may only join "employee associations" that negotiate salaries and benefits. In April 1991 the military-appointed parliament amended the 1975 Act to exclude state enterprise workers, and passed the State Enterprise Labor Relations Act (SELRA), which dissolved unions in this sector and denied state enterprise workers the right to strike. The Chuan government pledged to amend the SELRA but has not yet done so. Trade union activists face occasional harassment, and the 1991 disappearance of activist Thanong Podhiarn remains unsolved. A July 1994 report by the U.S. Department of Labor on child labor worldwide noted that at least four million Thai children work in the garment industry and other sectors. The May 1993 fire at the Kader Industrial Company's doll factory in Nakhon Pathom east of Bangkok killed 188 mostly female workers and injured 469 others, and highlighted the lax enforcement of safety procedures at many factories.

Togo

Polity: Military dominated
Economy: Mixed statist
Population: 4,255,000
PPP: $738
Life Expectancy: 54.4
Ethnic Groups: Aja, Ewe, Gurensi, Kabyé, Krachi, Mina, Tem
Ratings Change: *Togo's political rights rating changed from 7 to 6 because of generally competitive legislative elections

Political Rights: 6*
Civil Liberties: 5
Status: Not Free

Overview:

Six months after President Gnassingbe Eyadema's undemocratic re-election, the Togolese elected a multiparty parliament in February 1994. The opposition coalition, the Togolese Union for Democracy (UTD) and the Action Committee for Renewal (CAR), split over the nomination of Prime Minister Kodjo, the UTD leader whose party won seven of the forty-three majority coalition seats. This led the CAR to boycott the parliament and the government. Prime Minister Kodjo's government, composed of UTD, independents and ministers from the former ruling party Rally of the Togolese People (RPT), pledged to work towards national reconciliation and economic recovery, and a solution of Togo's refugee problem.

In 1914 Britain occupied the western portion of then-German Togoland and France occupied the east. In 1957 the British portion became the independent state of Ghana. Western Togoland achieved independence as the Republic of Togo in April 1960. Togo's first president, Sylvanus Olympio, was assassinated in 1963 and was succeeded by his rival, Nicholas Grunitzky. In January 1967 then-Maj. Gnassingbe Eyadema deposed Grunitzky. Eyadema, a northerner and a member of the minority Kabye tribe, subsequently suspended the constitution, banned political parties, and declared himself president. In 1969, the government formed a puppet party, the Rally of the Togolese People. However, Eyadema kept the country under military rule, and in 1979 and again in 1986 won elections running unopposed.

In October 1990 the government imprisoned two opposition figures, sparking a series of demonstrations and strikes. In April 1991 the president legalized opposition parties and promised to hold multiparty elections within a year. In July a national conference convened to choose an interim prime minister. The conference was dominated by the Front of Associations for Renewal composed of ten opposition groups later called the Democratic Opposition Collective (COD). The conference declared its sovereignty from the government, stripped Eyadema of most of his powers, and elected Joseph Koffigoh as prime minister. It also formed an interim seventy-nine-member High Council of the Republic (HCR) to run the country until legislative and presidential elections, scheduled for August 1992.

In the fall soldiers continued to clash with prodemocracy protestors. On 26 November the HCR banned the RPT, accusing it of provoking the army. The next day troops loyal to the president surrounded Koffigoh's residence, and on 3 December seized the prime minister and brought him to the president who pressured him to form a "national unity government."

In January 1993 Eyadema unilaterally ended the transitional government but Koffigoh established his authority over the HCR in nominating the prime minister. In the ensuing days, protestors increasingly criticized Koffigoh for not speaking out against Eyadema. On 30 January security forces roamed in the capital of Lome, killing several people indiscriminately.

By early February some 250,000 people had fled to Ghana and Benin. In February, following failed HCR and government talks, Eyadema and Koffigoh agreed to form a new national unity government that included only three opposition figures, none of whom were from COD-2 (the successor to COD). In March dissidents attacked Lome's main military camp. The military retaliated by killing soldiers suspected of dissident sympathies.

By mid-July six opposition candidates including Gilchrest Olympio, the son of the former president, had declared they would challenge Eyadema. The main opposition candidates withdrew in protest over election conditions and of the Supreme Court's refusal to allow Olympio to run. Eyadema faced only two weak challengers.

On 23-24 August German election observers and former U.S. President Jimmy Carter pulled out of the country, claiming the credibility of the balloting had been eroded. The following day, Eyadema won the oft-postponed election with 96.49 percent of the vote and a 39 percent turnout.

As a gesture of reassurance to international observers unsatisfied with the conditions of the electoral process, Eyadema posponed the two-round legislative elections slated for 19 December 1993 and 2 January 1994 to 6 February and 20 February 1994. Several opposition groups called for a boycott of the elections on the grounds that the postpone-ment would not improve the lack of the rule of law or bring about conditions for free and fair elections and criticized the UTD and the CAR, which they consider too moderate, of legitimizing the government by running in the elections.

In the runup to the elections, on 5 January 1994 Ghana-based dissidents attacked several sites in Lome. The fight killed hundreds of civilians. The govern-ment accused Ghana of backing a coup against Eyadema to prevent elections from taking place. Ghana denied the accusation and linked the upheaval to the Togo government's refusal to create peaceful conditions for the transition towards democracy.

In the first round of voting, the ruling RPT won thirty-five of the eighty-one contested seats. On 15 February, the CAR leader, Yaovi Agboyibor, temporarily suspended his party's participation in the elections to obtain security guarantees for CAR candidates. Eyadema agreed to end army interference in the campaign to ensure its neutrality. Nonethless, the second round was marred with violence in three of the eleven constituencies. Youths wearing opposition party T-shirts alledgedly tore up ballot papers. Six polling stations were ransacked, others closed prematurely. A CAR member elected to a seat was found dead. The RPT claimed victory and blamed the unrest on the opposition, which also announced it had won an absolute majority of the seats. The National Electoral Commission did not confirm the results for several weeks after the RPT demanded that the results in five former RPT constituencies it lost be annulled. When the courts certified the results on 14 March, the opposition coalition had captured forty-three seats, with the CAR receiving thirty-six and the UTD seven, the RPT and an allied party winning thirty-eight seats.

On 21 March Prime Minister Koffigoh of the "crisis government" resigned, but controversy between the CAR and UTD over the arrangements for a new prime minister prevented the formation of a new government until May. Under the constitution, the president appoints the minister from the parliamentary majority. According to the CAR, in an agreement whose existence the UTD denies, the prime ministership would belong to the party with the most seats. On 22 April, after continued impasse over finding a list of nominees from which the president was to pick the prime minister, the president appointed Kodjo over Agboyivor, who subsequently decided the CAR would not participate in Kojdo's cabinet. Finally, on 25 May, Prime Minister Kodjo formed a new nineteen-member cabinet composed of eight ministers close to the president, eight independents and three UTD ministers. The CAR joined the National Assembly after the authorities decided to cancel the 15 May by-elections for the five disputed constituencies. However, the CAR rejected the UTD's nomination of Agboyibor as Speaker of the House.

On 20 October, in a spate of attacks by armed gangs on civilians and government officials, a presidential aide was gunned down. In November, security forces caught five heavily armed dissident commandos who said they were recruited for a sabotage mission by a group of political exiles living in Ghana.

Togo's economic crisis was aggravated by France's decision to devalue the African Financial Community's currency, the CFA franc, by half. The country received some financial support from the International Monetary Fund.

Political Rights and Civil Liberties: Togolese have limited political rights. The 1993 presidential election was marred by irregularities and the opposition's boycott. Despite some fraud and violence, the 1994 legislative election was generally free. Since the initial prodemocracy protests in 1990, several hundred people are believed to have been killed in politically related violence.

In 1994, federal troops arbitrarily executed several people suspected of having taken part in attacks on army bases.

The judicial system is nominally independent of the government, but can be influenced in sensitive cases. Defendents in ordinary cases generally receive adequate procedural safeguards, although a shortage of judges and insufficient administrative procedures cause serious backlogs. In the runup to the legislative elections, UTD insisted that the entire branch of the Supreme Court be involved in the elections petitions rather than the constitutional branch alone, which is pro-Eyadema.

The press continues to operate under restrictions. In 1994 the managing editor of the pro-opposition weekly *Tribune des démocrates* was sentenced to five years imprisonment for "insulting the head of state." Also in 1994 the editors of an independent weekly *Sentinelle* were sentenced *in absentia* to five years imprisonment and fined for defamation against the person of the president. The national assembly voted to amnesty political prisoners in December 1994. Numerous cases of police arbitrarily detaining and in some cases beating journalists were reported in 1993. In northern areas, supporters of Eyadema sometimes physically prevented opposition newspapers from being freely distributed in 1993. State-run radio and television occasionally offer opposition viewpoints, but in the main are pro-government.

Women face discrimination in education, and in inheritance and divorce matters. Religious freedom is respected. Workers can join independent unions and hold strikes. On 16 November 1993 workers conducted a general strike to demand that the military stop interfering with the transition towards democracy.

Tonga

Polity: Monarchy and partly elected legislature
Economy: Capitalist
Population: 105,000
PPP: na
Life Expectancy: na
Ethnic Groups: Tongan (98 percent), other Pacific Islanders and Europeans (2 percent)

Political Rights: 5
Civil Liberties: 3
Status: Partly Free

Overview:

This Polynesian South Pacific Kingdom of 169 islands became an independent member of the British Commonwealth in June 1970. Seventy-six-year-old King Taufa' Ahau Tupou IV has reigned since 1965. The 1875 constitution is the product of an era in which the chiefs had unlimited powers over the commoners, who were referred to as "eaters of the soil." Under the constitution the king holds broad executive powers, appoints the prime minister, and appoints and heads the Privy Council, which makes the major policy decisions. The thirty-seat unicameral Legislative Assembly consists of nine nobles selected by and from among the country's thirty-three noble families, twelve ministers from the Privy Council, and only nine "People's Representatives" elected by universal suffrage. This arrangement grants the king and the nobility a perpetual super majority.

In recent years there have been growing calls for a more broadly representative government within the framework of the existing monarchy. The campaign for a more inclusive government accelerated in August 1992 as a group of reform-oriented People's Representatives, led by Akilisi Pohiva, formed the Pro-Democracy Movement (PDM), which they stopped short of calling a political party. In November 1992 the PDM organized a seminal four-day conference on amending the constitution. Pohiva called for universal elections for the entire Legislative Assembly, and for MPs rather than the king to select the cabinet. The influential Roman Catholic and Free Wesleyan churches supported the conference, and many of the nearly 1,000 people who attended were members of the country's growing middle class. Pastor Siupeli Taliai noted that the political system is "designed to preserve old Tongan inequality, entrenched power and position." Many participants agreed on the need for change, but also concluded that the monarchy is important for preserving stability.

At the 4 February 1993 People's Representatives elections prodemocracy candidates, including Pohiva, won six seats, an increase of one over the outgoing Assembly. In September Prime Minister Baron Vaea told the Assembly that the government was considering storing 35,000 barrels of toxic waste per year from California on the northern volcanic island of Niuafo'ou. Pohiva immediately opposed the plan, and promised to make it a prominent issue in the campaign for commoners' rights.

In the fall of 1994 the PDM announced plans for the kingdom's first political party, the Tonga Democratic Party (TDP). Although Pohiva had wanted to secure constitutional reforms before forming a political party, he agreed to be part of the TDP.

Political Rights Tongans cannot change their government democratically.
and Civil Liberties: The constitution grants the King and the hereditary nobles
a perpetual super majority in the Legislative Assembly,
with twenty-four of the thirty-three seats, allowing major policy decisions to be
made without the assent of the popularly elected representatives. Roughly 95
percent of the population is represented by just nine of the thirty seats. The king
and the nobility also hold a pre-eminent position in society through substantial land
holdings. Political parties are not banned but are strongly discouraged.

Heading into the February 1993 People's Representative elections, the
government-owned Radio Tonga increasingly aired speakers opposed to the PDM.
The Minister of Police broadcast a warning that the penalty for treason is death or
life imprisonment. The electoral law prohibits the news media from publishing or
broadcasting election material on the evening before a vote, but Radio Tonga
violated the ban by broadcasting antidemocracy statements from MP Laki Niu.

The government interfered with the right of assembly prior to and during the
November 1992 conference on constitutional reform by refusing to grant visas to
foreign invitees and by intimidating participants. The government also refused to
allow Radio Tonga to air paid messages advertising the event or to broadcast live
coverage.

The judiciary can be influenced by the government in sensitive cases. Com-
moner leader and MP Akilisi Pohiva has faced three libel suits over articles in his
magazine, *Kele'a* (Conch Shell), brought by the speaker of parliament, a business
group and the crown prince. According to *Pacific Islands Monthly*, Pohiva claims
that in two of the cases the Supreme Court failed to consider information that may
have substantiated his published facts. Pohiva lost all three cases and received total
fines of nearly $80,000. Citizens generally receive adequate due process safeguards
in ordinary cases.

The country's four private newspapers freely criticize the government. A series
of libel suits brought by prominent Tongans against Akilisi Pohiva for articles in
Kele'a (*see above*) suggest a concerted effort to weaken this leading prodemocracy
activist. There is no television station and the state-owned Radio Tonga is frequently biased towards the government.

Traditional practices relegate women to a subordinate role in society. There are
no restrictions on domestic or international travel. All religious believers can
worship freely. Workers have the right to form unions, but none exists due to the
small size of the wage economy.

Trinidad and Tobago

Polity: Parliamentary
democracy
Economy: Capitalist-statist
Population: 1,287,000
PPP: $8,380
Life Expectancy: 70.9

Political Rights: 1
Civil Liberties: 2*
Status: Free

Ethnic Groups: Complex, black (41 percent), East Indian
descent (41 percent), mixed (16 percent), white (1 percent)
Ratings Change: *Trinidad and Tobago's civil liberties
rating changed from 1 to 2 principally due to sharp increases
in criminal violence and corruption.

Overview: **A**mid a prolonged economic slump and a sharp increase in
drug-related criminal violence, there were hints that the
beleaguered government of Prime Minister Patrick
Manning might hold early elections in 1995.

Trinidad and Tobago, a member of the British Commonwealth, achieved
independence in 1962. It is composed of two islands, with Trinidad accounting for
nearly 95 percent of the country's area and population. Under the 1976 constitution, the nation became a republic with a president, elected by a majority of both
houses in parliament, replacing the former governor-general. Executive authority in
the parliamentary system remains invested in the prime minister.

The bicameral parliament consists of a thirty-six-member House of Representatives elected for five years, and a thirty-one-member Senate, twenty-five appointed by the prime minister and six by the opposition. The prime minister is the
leader of the party or coalition commanding a majority in the House. Local
government (counties and major municipalities) is elected.

In 1980 the parliament established a fifteen-member House of Assembly for
Tobago, with twelve members directly elected for four years and three named by
the majority party. In 1987 Tobago was granted internal self-government.

In the 1986 elections the National Alliance for Reconstruction (NAR), an
unprecedented coalition of black and East Indian elements led by A.N.R. Robinson,
soundly defeated the black-based People's National Movement (PNM), which had
ruled for thirty years. The coalition soon unraveled when Basdeo Panday, the
country's most prominent East Indian politician, was expelled. Panday then formed
the East Indian-based United National Congress (UNC).

In July 1991 the radical Muslim group Jamaat-al-Muslimeen, led by Yasin Abu
Bakr and numbering about 300 members, seized the nation's parliament. A five-
day standoff marked by rampant looting in the capital city of Port of Spain left two
dozen dead according to official sources. The siege ended when the government
convinced Bakr the insurgents would receive amnesty if they surrendered. The
NAR never recovered from the incident, which heightened tension between the
roughly equal black and East Indian populations.

In December 1991 the PNM, under the new leadership of Patrick Manning and with a slate featuring many younger candidates, won 21 of 36 parliamentary seats. Panday's UNC won 13 seats to become the official opposition. The NAR won 2 seats and Robinson resigned as party leader. In 1992 the PNM won 10 of 14 municipal and regional council elections, with the UNC winning the other four.

Since 1993, however, the Manning government has struggled with a prolonged economic slump rooted in declining oil prices and a $2.2 billion foreign debt. In early 1994, amid public employee protests and popular outrage at rising crime and continued allegations of official and police corruption, the UNC surpassed the PNM in the opinion polls. The PNM also lost two of three by-elections to the UNC, which lowered the PNM's majority to 20 seats.

The UNC then encountered problems of its own. Hulsie Bhaggan, a young, outspoken UNC member of parliament was expelled by Panday for insubordination. She then launched her own party, the Movement for Unity and Progress (MUP), while a number of her followers sued Panday on sexual harassment charges. The sixty-one-year-old Panday claimed the charges were politically motivated and sued the attorney general for conspiracy to defame. The cases appeared likely to carry into the next election campaign. Elections were not due until 1996 but the PNM appeared ready to call an early vote in 1995.

Political Rights and Civil Liberties: Citizens are able to change their government through democratic elections, but voter apathy has been evident in low turnouts in recent by-elections. Constitutional guarantees regarding the right to free expression and the right to organize political parties, civic organizations and labor unions are generally respected.

However, civil liberties are increasingly threatened by a mounting wave of drug-related violence and corruption. The murder rate in 1994 looked to be nearly double the rate of 1993 when 108 people were killed, and the rate of other serious crimes was escalating as well. Many of the murders were carried out by contract killers in the employ of drug gangs.

In late 1993 Scotland Yard investigators concluded that drug-related and other types of corruption were endemic in the 5,000-member police force. The report noted that the police had been obstructive during the investigation and named 100 police officers that it said should be dismissed. However, the government made only a few administrative changes. Meanwhile, there were new though unconfirmed allegations of drug-related corruption in the government itself. Trinidad and Tobago is vulnerable to traffickers and money-launderers as it sits off Venezuela's coast along a prime drug-transshipment route.

An independent judicial system is headed by a Supreme Court, which consists of a High Court and a Court of Appeal, with district courts operating on the local level. There is a right of ultimate appeal to the Privy Council of the United Kingdom. The judiciary has been taxed by the mounting crime wave and the prisons are seriously overcrowded. Court cases are backlogged up to five years.

There are a number of human rights organizations. They report increasing allegations of police brutality, including a few extrajudicial killings. They have also criticized government anti-narcotics initiatives as threatening to civil rights and condemned laws that allow judges to order floggings for youthful criminal offenders. A new law passed in 1994 deprived certain repeat criminal offenders of release on bail. Rights groups challenged the law as unconstitutional. There were also scattered reports of harassment by police against the Muslim community, which comprises 6 percent of the population. Freedom of religion, however, is generally respected.

In 1994 the government resumed capital punishment, a move condemned by rights groups. In July a convicted murderer was hung, the first hanging in fifteen years, while his lawyers argued in the Appeals Court and after the Privy Council in London had said it would stay the execution. The president of the bar association called the hanging "the most serious breach of the due process of law in this country."

Domestic violence continues to be a concern. However, a 1990 law allows both men and women to obtain restraining orders against abusive spouses. The law also allows for children to be taken away from abusive parents. The recent wave of violent crime and sexual attacks against women in a predominantly East Indian region of central Trinidad has heightened ethnic tensions, as Indo-Trinidadians charged that most of the offenders were black.

In the aftermath of the 1991 coup attempt, Jamaat al Muslimeen leader Bakr and 113 others were charged with treason, murder and kidnapping. Defense lawyers claimed the charges were invalid because Bakr had given up in exchange for amnesty. A High Court agreed and all were released from jail. But in October 1994 the Privy Council decided the amnesty was not valid, but also ruled that it would be an abuse of process to have them rearrested and tried for offenses committed during the insurrection.

Labor unions are well organized, powerful and politically active. They have the right to strike and have done so frequently in recent years. An independent industrial court plays a central role in arbitrating labor disputes.

Newspapers are privately owned, uncensored and influential. There are a number of independent dailies as well as party papers. Radio and television are both public and private. Trinidad and Tobago's new media giant, Caribbean Communications Network (CCN), launched the country's second television station in 1991. The other station is state-operated.

Tunisia

Polity: Dominant party
Economy: Mixed capitalist
Population: 8,696,000
PPP: $4,690
Life Expectancy: 67.1
Ethnic Groups: Arab

Political Rights: 6
Civil Liberties: 5
Status: Not Free

Overview: On 21 March 1994 Tunisia held multiparty legislative and presidential elections that renewed President Zine el-Abidine Ben Ali's five-year mandate. They also put in place a parliament in which the opposition received the guaranteed nineteen new seats allocated in proportion to the total votes won by slates that did not win the majority in each district. Despite the new 1993 electoral law instituting these token nineteen seats, which are widely regarded as cosmetic democratic changes, the President's Democratic Constitutional Assembly (RCD) won the original 144 seats in a "winner-take-all" majority process. Throughout the year, Tunisia was criticized for the gap between its rhetoric and the reality behind its human rights record. The Tunisian government fears a fundamentalist spillover from neighboring Algeria and has banned the domestic radical Islamic *Al Nahda* party, which mainly operated in regions where the general economic growth has not alleviated poverty. As a result, Tunisia continued to liberalize its economy slowly, but several reforms to open the political scene were dismissed as tokenism by government critics barred from a deeply entrenched one-party-dominated state.

Sandwiched between war-torn Algeria and Libya, Tunisia gained independence from France in 1956. General Ben Ali succeeded the country's first longtime president, Habib Bourguiba, forcing him to retire in November 1987 on grounds of senility. The takeover was welcomed by the majority of Tunisians increasingly unhappy with government repression of the press, legal opposition parties, and other sources of dissent including the growing Islamic fundamentalist movement. Ben Ali promised to pave the way to domestic pluralism. His government initially received support as it legalized the structure of the ruling party, earlier known as the *Neo Destour* Party (Constitution Party), loosened media strictures, and amnestied more than 8,000 people.

The Islamic Tendency Movement (MTI), the radical Islamic party, refused to be signatory to the "national pact" between the regime and other political and labor groups. President Ben Ali instituted an austerity program which led to disagreements within government circles over the social repercussions of the economic policies. Sporadic unrest broke out in 1990, with critics charging that the regime's enthusiasm for democratization had waned. The opposition, including the militant Al Nahda (Renaissance) party (successor to MTI) boycotted 1990 and 1991 elections. By late 1992, most of Al Nahda's active members were either in jail or in exile. Their leader, Rachid Ghannouchi, received political asylum in Great Britain in 1993. Tunisia spent 10 percent of its 1993 budget on security services in its campaign to eliminate all Islamic militancy and establish a number of local community centers for disaffected youth.

A new challenge is to reduce the unemployment level of at least 15 percent of the workforce. Tunisia is looking to privatization policies to obtain the long term prosperity that will increase standards of living, but state-run companies are privatized very slowly in part to minimize the number of unemployed which could be potential supporters of Islamic extremism. A quiet revolution to avoid a greater drift of the rural population to the cities, to modernize agriculture and produce high quality export goods for the European Union is underway.

Running unopposed in his second presidential race, Ben Ali won the 21 March 1994 election with 99.9 percent of the votes. Moncef Marzouki, a doctor and former president of the Tunisian Human Rights League (once an independent organization currently taken over by the president's supporters) tried to run against Ben Ali, but was unable to get the required thirty endorsements from legislators or mayors, virtually all members of the ruling RCD. Abd al-Rahman al-Hani, a leader of a small nationalist party, faced the same obstacle. A group of 100 intellectuals urged the government to amend the law. In the runup to the elections, Hamma Hammami, the leader of the banned Tunisian Communist Workers' Party (PCOT) was arrested on 14 February. Following the elections, Marzouki was arrested, charged with "spreading false information to disturb public order" during an interview with a leading Spanish newspaper.

Tunisians also cast their ballots for the 163 legislative seats in the unicameral Chamber of Deputies. The ruling party took the expected 144 seats won by majority system. The Socialist Democrats won 10 of the 19 remaining seats allocated on a proportional basis. *Attajdid*, the former Communist party, won 4 seats, the Democratic Union, an Arab nationalist party, 3 and the Popular Unity Party, 2.

Political Rights and Civil Liberties:

Although Tunisia is constitutionally a parliamentary democracy, in practice the right of citizens to change their government democratically is limited. The ruling RCD holds a monopoly on power on the national and local levels. The Chamber of Deputies essentially reaffirms policy made by President Ben Ali.

All political parties require government authorization, and six opposition parties are allowed to operate. Parties based on religion, race and ethnicity are illegal. Non-governmental associations are allowed to operate, with the exception of organizations aiming to "disturb public order." According to a law adopted in March 1992, simultaneous membership in political parties and certain associations is illegal. A chapter of Amnesty International, the only one in the Arab world, is allowed to operate. Although freedoms of peaceful assembly and protest are formally enshrined in the constitution, all protests must be approved by the government three days in advance.

The authorities frequently use illegal detention and torture against suspected members of the radical opposition. During the 1992 trial of 265 suspected Al Nahda members, a number of the accused showed signs of physical abuse while testifying in court. Amnesty International accuses the government of harassing female relatives of suspected leftist and Islamic radicals, many of whom were beaten, tortured and sexually abused. The preventive detention law limits arrests without a warrant to no more than ten days, but in practice the law is often ignored.

The judicial system, which works under the authority of the Ministries of the Interior and of Justice, does not follow legal procedures in investigating disappearances or bring to justice those who commit abuses and are responsible for deaths in custody, according to a January 1994 report by Amnesty International.

Freedom of speech and press is severely curtailed. The official Press Code outlaws the dissemination of "false" information and requires editors of newspapers and book publishers to submit all publications to the Justice and Interior Ministries prior to their public release. Although in 1991 the government announced it would not enforce the prepublication censorship part of the Press Code, it continues to threaten editors and journalists with imprisonment or fines for publications critical of the government. The government severely clamped down against criticism of the regime, especially by foreign papers, around the elections period. The authorities banned the sale of the French newspaper, *Libération*, because of an opinion piece critical of the president. They expelled a foreign correspondent from the British Broadcasting Corporation and barred other writers from entering the country to cover the elections. Tunisian journalists working for international news agencies were warned against covering of the opposition.

Islam is the state religion, but the government allows relatively free practice for most other faiths, including Christianity and Judaism. The exception includes the Baha'i, considered an Islamic heresy. The government appoints and pays the salaries of Islamic clergy. Proselytizing for religions other than Islam is prohibited.

General Union of Tunisian Workers (UGTT) remains the major labor confederation. The government enacted a series of legal reforms to improve the rights of women and advance their social and professional opportunities. Many Tunisian women dislike radical Islam because they fear the movement is not sympathetic to the idea of equality between the sexes or their presence in public places.

Turkey

Polity: Presidential-parliamentary democracy (military-influenced) (insurgency)
Political Rights: 5*
Civil Liberties: 5*
Status: Partly Free
Economy: Capitalist-statist
Population: 61,799,000
PPP: $4,840
Life Expectancy: 66.7
Ethnic Groups: Turks, Kurds (12 million), Armenians, Jews
Ratings Change: *Turkey's political rights rating changed from 4 to 5 and its civil liberties rating from 4 to 5 because of government crackdown on Kurdish democrats and intensification of a campaign against the Kurdish insurgency.

Overview: In 1994 Prime Minister Tansu Ciller's government faced a severe economic crisis, surprising gains by an Islamic party in the March local elections, and continuing Kurdish insurgency that has taken more than 13,000 lives since 1984.

Mustafa Kemal Ataturk proclaimed Turkey a republic in October 1923 in territory carved out of the former Ottoman Empire. Ataturk's pro-Western, secular legacy still exerts a powerful influence over the country. Turkey joined NATO in 1952. The military used the doctrine of "Kemalism" to justify three coups between 1960 and 1980 during periods of social and political unrest. The 1982 constitution provides for a 400-seat unicameral Grand National Assembly (increased to 450 seats in 1987) elected for a five-year term. The Assembly elects the president for a seven-year term. The president appoints and can dismiss the prime minister, can dissolve the Assembly with the concurrence of two-thirds of the deputies, and appoints several top officials. Despite these powers, the office is considered largely ceremonial and the president is expected to remain above politics.

Turkey's returned to civilian rule in 1983. Elections in November gave the conservative Motherland Party (Anap) a majority, and one month later Turgut Ozal, a deputy premier during the most recent military rule, formed a government. In 1984 the Marxist Kurdistan Worker's Party (PKK) began an insurgency in southeastern Turkey to demand an independent Kurdish state. Ozal committed the army to fighting the insurgency, while his government embarked on a far-reaching economic liberalization program. In 1989 Anap used its parliamentary majority to elect Ozal to the presidency, where he focused on promoting his visionary foreign policy of making Turkey a regional power.

Heading into the October 1991 parliamentary elections Ozal's government was dogged by charges of corruption and nepotism and blamed for the country's 66 percent inflation rate. The conservative True Path Party (DYP) took a plurality of 178 seats; Anap, 115; the Social Democratic Populist Party (SHP), 66; the anti-Western, fundamentalist Welfare Party (RP), 62; the Kurdish-based People's Labor Party (HEP), 22; the Democratic Left Party (DSP), 7. DYP leader Suleyman Demirel subsequently formed a coalition with the SHP and began his seventh stint as prime minister.

The sixty-six-year-old Ozal died of heart failure in April 1993, and in May parliament elected Demirel as the country's ninth president. In June Tansu Ciller, the minister for the economy, drew strong support from the DYP's rank-and-file to win the election for the party chairman post vacated by Demirel. Ciller subsequently became Turkey's first female prime minister.

Meanwhile, clashes in May between the army and the PKK broke a fragile two-month-old cease-fire unilaterally called by the guerrilla group. Ciller appeared to give the army a free reign in dealing with the insurgency, and by year's end nearly 2,000 rebels, civilians and soldiers had died since the breakdown of the cease-fire. In July the government banned the HEP for alleged links to the PKK.

In early March 1994 parliament lifted the legal immunity of the thirteen MPs of the Kurdish Democratic Party (DEP), a successor to the banned HEP, enabling prosecutors to bring charges of separatism against them. The 27 March local elections shaped up as a test of support for the Ciller government's handling of both the Kurdish issue and of an economic crisis that included a recent 70 percent devaluation of the *lira* and an inflation rate heading toward triple digits. Ciller's DYP led the field in provincial assembly balloting with 22 percent of the total vote, while Anap took 21 percent. But the strong third place showing by the fundamentalist RP with 19 percent shook the secular establishment. The RP also took the mayoral races in Ankara, the capital, and Istanbul, Turkey's largest city, highlighting the mainstream parties' failure to alleviate conditions of the slum dwellers in major cities.

In the fall the government launched one of its largest offensives ever against the PKK in an effort to destroy vital supply routes. On 8 December a court sentenced eight Kurdish MPs to jail terms of up to fifteen years on charges of supporting the PKK and rebel leader Abdullah Ocalan. None of the alleged offenses amounted to more than vocal support for Kurdish causes.

In the economic realm, in April Ciller began an austerity program of tax increases and spending cuts that made prudent economic sense but further alienated hard-hit groups. In November parliament approved a privatization law clearing the way for the sale of more than 100 companies.

Political Rights and Civil Liberties:

Turks can change their government democratically, but the country is beset by widespread human rights abuses.

Security forces are accused of extrajudicial killings of suspected PKK terrorists, of firing randomly into crowds of demonstrators, of attacking residential areas in "retaliation" for PKK attacks, and of torturing guerrillas and dissidents. Security forces are suspected in dozens of unsolved "mystery killings" of journalists, local politicians and other alleged PKK sympathizers. Some seventy members of the DEP and its predecessor, the HEP, have been killed since 1991. According to Human Rights Watch/Helsinki the army has depopulated upwards of 1,400 villages and hamlets in southeastern Turkey to prevent their use as bases for the PKK, and frequently razes homes.

The PKK and other smaller Kurdish groups such as Dev Sol (Revolutionary Left) target government officials and buildings, schools, paramilitary "village guards," civilians suspected of cooperating with the government, and businesses. The PKK has murdered dozens of teachers for teaching in Turkish rather than Kurdish. Prior to the March 1994 local elections PKK intimidation forced at least fifteen candidates to drop out of races and dozens of villages in the southeast to boycott the vote.

A state of emergency declared in 1987 continues in ten southeastern provinces, allowing civilian governors to detain suspects for up to thirty days and to authorize media censorship. Authorities in these areas can also search residences or offices without warrants and seize materials.

The 1991 Anti-Terror Law broadly defines terrorism to include nonviolent acts by ordinary citizens. The law authorizes detentions without charge of up to fifteen days (thirty days in the areas under the state of emergency) before a person must be brought before a judge. Judges have ordered indefinite detentions that in practice have lasted several years. Parliament is considering easing the law to make it more difficult to arrest a person solely for political views.

Security forces are also accused of torturing nonpolitical detainees. Prison conditions are harsh, although incidents of torture in prisons have decreased in recent years. The constitution provides for the security of judges' tenure, and because of this the judiciary is considered independent of the government. The right of access to a lawyer during all phases of investigation and detention is sometimes denied. Defendants in ordinary cases generally receive adequate due process safeguards, although there are no jury trials. State security courts, composed of two civilian judges, two prosecutors and a military judge, try cases under the Anti-Terror Law and other terrorism cases, as well as cases involving drug smuggling and promoting seditious ideas. Trials in these courts are often closed and confessions obtained through torture are admissible as evidence.

There are numerous speech and press restrictions. The Anti-Terror Law broadly prohibits speech or writings advocating or supporting separatism. Numerous leftist and pro-Kurdish publications have had issues confiscated or have been shut down. In April 1994 the Supreme Court banned publication of the pro-Kurdish daily *Ozgur Gundem* for fifteen days for allegedly advocating separatism. The paper subsequently shut down permanently. Publications must designate an editor who is legally responsible for its contents, and several editors have faced criminal proceedings based on published articles. The national Criminal Code provides three-to-six year penalties for those who "insult" the president or other branches of government. Police occasionally detain journalists on these charges, although most such cases are eventually dismissed. In September 1994 three broadcasters went on trial on charges of violating military rules by interviewing soldiers about the country's compulsory military service.

Police often harass and occasionally torture journalists, particularly those suspected of Kurdish sympathies. Since May 1992 at least eighteen employees of the now-defunct *Ozgur Gundem* were killed. On 3 December 1994 explosions at the Istanbul and Ankara offices of *Ozger Ulke*, a leading pro-Kurdish daily newspaper, killed at least one person and wounded nearly twenty others. Due to legal restrictions and harassment, journalists practice considerable self-censorship.

In July 1993 parliament repealed the government's legal monopoly on radio and television broadcasting. State-run broadcast media air opposition views, although some groups say coverage is still biased towards the government. In April

1994 parliament approved a law allowing the government to censor any radio or television broadcast in the interest of national security.

Professors have been sentenced under the Anti-Terror Law for books they authored. In 1991 the government lifted some restrictions on the public use of the Kurdish language, although Kurdish may not be spoken at political gatherings, and publications on Kurdish culture and history are banned under the Anti-Terror Law. Kurdish-language broadcasts are still illegal.

The government must grant approval for all assemblies and demonstrations, and permission is occasionally denied on security grounds. Police often harass nongovernmental organizations, including the independent Human Rights Association. Human rights activists are frequently harassed and several have been killed.

Domestic violence is reportedly fairly common. There are some restrictions on religious freedom. Religious services can only be held in approved venues, and some minority groups cannot acquire property for churches. Evangelical Christian and Armenian and Greek churches are monitored by security forces. In July 1993 Muslim extremists in the central city of Sivas torched a hotel hosting a conference featuring Aziz Nesin, a newspaper editor who had published portions of Salman Rushdie's novel, *The Satanic Verses*. Nesin survived, but thirty-six people were killed.

Citizens can generally travel freely internally, except in the southeast where both security forces and the PKK frequently set up roadblocks, and can travel abroad without restriction. Workers, except for teachers, civil servants and security personnel, can join independent unions. The government must approve of union meetings, and can send police to monitor and record the proceedings. Workers must engage in collective bargaining and nonbinding mediation prior to striking, and security and armed forces personnel, petroleum and sanitation workers and teachers are prohibited from striking. The government can suspend strikes after sixty days on national security or public safety grounds. Collective bargaining is restricted by a law that requires a union to represent 10 percent of all workers in a particular industry in order to become a negotiating agent, which favors established unions.

Turkmenistan (Turkmenia)

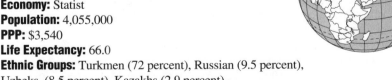

Polity: Presidential-par-
liamentary (presidential-
dominated)
Economy: Statist
Population: 4,055,000
PPP: $3,540
Life Expectancy: 66.0
Ethnic Groups: Turkmen (72 percent), Russian (9.5 percent), Uzbeks, (8.5 percent), Kazakhs (2.9 percent)

Political Rights: 7
Civil Liberties: 7
Status: Not Free

Overview: The former Soviet Central Asian republic of Turkmenistan, bordering Iran and Afghanistan, remained in the totalitarian grip of President Saparmurad Niyazov, a former first secretary of the Communist Party who renamed himself Turkmenbashi, or Head of the Turkmen, while building a cult of personality. The one-party regime continued to curtail political and human rights, while seeking foreign investment to exploit the country's vast natural gas, mineral and oil reserves and cotton-producing capacities. In December parliamentary elections, only Niyazov's Democratic Party of Turkmenistan (DPT) was permitted to field candidates.

Turkmenistan was ruled by various local leaders until the thirteenth century, when the Mongols conquered it. In the late nineteenth century, Tsarist Russia seized the country. In 1924, after the Bolsheviks ousted the Khan of Merv, the Turkmen Soviet Socialist Republic was declared.

Turkmenistan declared independence after a national referendum in October 1991; Niyazov won a one-man presidential election in December 1991. The following year, after the adoption of a new constitution, Niyazov was re-elected, claiming 99.5 percent of the vote. The main opposition group, known as Agzybirlik, formed in 1989 by leading intellectuals, was banned and its leaders harassed. Under the 1992 constitution, the country has two parliamentary bodies, the fifty-member *Majlis* (Assembly), elected in 1990, and the *Khalk Maslakhaty* (People's Council), which includes the members of the Assembly, fifty directly elected members (elected in November 1992), and leading executive and judicial officials. Niyazov is president of the People's Council.

In addition to being head of the DPT—the renamed Communist Party and the only legal party—the president has the following powers: he heads the People's Council, many of whose members he appoints with the consent of the *Majlis*, and he can prorogue the parliament if it has passed two no-confidence motions within an eighteen-month period. In addition, the president issues edicts that have the force of law, appoints and removes judges of all jurisdictions, and names the state prosecutor. He is also prime minister and commander-in-chief of the armed forces. Essentially, parliament is a rubber-stamp; during several sessions, deputies have started crying and chanting while asking Niyazov to remain president for life. "Don't elect me president for life," Niyazov told parliament. "Elect me until the year 2002." The deputies agreed.

In January 1994 Niyazov insisted that the will of the people be measured in a referendum on his presidency, even though he had no challengers to the post. The expected results of the 15 January poll showed that 98 percent of voters backed the president. Much of his popularity rides on his promise to fulfill the country's immense economic potential, using the estimated 700 million tons of oil reserves and 8,000 billion cubic meters of natural gas to turn the country into the Kuwait of Central Asia. Contracts on exploration and production have been signed with companies from Argentina, the Netherlands, the United Arab Emirates, Turkey and the U.S. Negotiations with Turkey focused on the construction of a pipeline through Iran and Turkey to provide a new outlet to Europe for the country's gas production after disputes with Russia and Ukraine over pipeline fees and the periodic blocking of transit through existing pipelines.

But serious economic problems persist. After the national currency, the manat, was introduced in November 1993, prices rose by 600 percent. Most shops are empty of anything worth buying. Some 60 percent of the country's food is still imported, as two-thirds of the country is desert and only 2.5 percent of the land is arable. Turkmenistan lacks infrastructure and the legislation needed to smooth privatization and set up a market economy. With power centralized in the president, his office does the paperwork for every foreign investment deal, leading to charges of mismanagement and corruption. In December Turkmenistan cut the value of the manat, already one of the weakest currencies in the former Soviet Union despite the country's mineral wealth. Since its introduction, the manat had been devalued by over 90 percent in stages.

Other problems of modernization are rooted in the country's tribal history. In addition to the largest tribes—the traditionally dominant Tekke in Central Turkmenistan (Niyazov's tribe), the Erasi in the southwest and the Jomudi in the west—there are nearly thirty additional tribes, each subdivided into clans. Tribal structures have not been eliminated, merely overarched by the apparatus of national government and the ruling DPT. Tribal loyalties still play a part in the political arena, so the notion of Turkmenbashi, or Head of the Turkmen, is intended to serve as an integrating force. In his years as leader of the Communist Party, Niyazov maintained that tribal and clan rivalries were an obstacle to law and order, a view he holds today.

Parliamentary elections were held on 11 December 1994. All the candidates ran unopposed and nearly all were members of the DPT. All won. Voters were given a ballot paper with a single name. Officials put turnout at 99.8 percent.

Under the foreign policy slogan "positive neutrality," Niyazov has balanced relations with Iran and Russia, and cultivated friendships and trade with Turkey and Pakistan. Under terms of a defense pact with Moscow, Russian troops patrol the Iran-Turkmenistan border. To stave off the exodus of skilled Russians, who make up about 10 percent of the population and hold key positions, Niyazov granted them dual nationality.

Political Rights and Civil Liberties:

Citizens of Turkmenistan do not have the means to change their government democratically. Power is concentrated in the hands of the president. The one-party, single-candidate elections to a rubber-stamp parliament in December 1994 were undemocratic. Candidates proposed as alternatives in some constituencies were all disqualified or withdrew on one pretext or another.

The constitution gives short shrift to individual rights and liberties, the pretext of this being the need to maintain order and stability. On the eve of passing the new constitution in 1992, the Turkmenistan Constitutional Committee removed about thirty articles and statutes, including those on freedom of the press and the creation of a constitutional court.

The judiciary is subservient to the regime; the president appoints all judges for a term of five years without legislative review.

The DPT is the only legal party. Opposition parties have been banned, and most leaders of Agzybirlik, the opposition party formed in 1989, have fled the country, many to Moscow. Those still in the country face harassment, detention and repression by the Committee on National Security (KNB), the successor to the Soviet-era KGB. Even leaving the country does not guarantee safety. In 1994 four Turkmen dissidents were arrested, two in Moscow by the Russians, and two more in the Uzbek capital, Tashkent.

Restrictions on a free press include some censorship and the denial of registration to some newspapers and journals. According to a prominent staff member of the state-owned newspaper *Turkmenskaya Iskra*, the paper exercises self-censorship. Newspapers, all state owned, mostly adhere to the old Communist style of publishing verbatim legislative texts, congratulatory speeches, letters flattering the president, and reports of successful harvests.

Local ordinances effectively ban freedom of assembly and public demonstrations. Freedom of movement and travel is circumscribed; in the past, citizens have been denied permission to travel within the country or put under house arrest to prevent them from attending meetings abroad.

Although the population is overwhelmingly Sunni Muslim, the government has kept a rein on religion to avert the rise of Islamic fundamentalism. Religious congregations are required to register with the government. Muslims have a free hand if they do not interfere in politics, and the government has built several mosques.

Although women's rights are mentioned in the constitution, discrimination in education and other social-religious limitations restrict women's freedom. Married women are not allowed to be students. There are no independent trade unions, and Turkmen law does not provide for the right to collective bargaining.

Tuvalu

Polity: Parliamentary democracy
Economy: Capitalist
Population: 10,000
PPP: na
Life Expectancy: na
Ethnic Groups: Polynesian

Political Rights: 1
Civil Liberties: 1
Status: Free

Overview:

This tiny Polynesian country, formerly the Ellice Islands, achieved independence in October 1978 as a "special member" of the British Commonwealth, participating in all Commonwealth affairs except for heads-of-government meetings. Under the 1978 constitution, executive power is vested in a prime minister, who heads a five member cabinet and is elected by and from among the twelve-member *Fale I Fono* (parliament). The fono is directly elected for a four-year term. The governor general, a Tuvalu citizen appointed by the British monarch, can delay legislation for seven days, and with the prime minister's advice appoints the other four members of the cabinet.

The country's fourth post-independence elections on 2 September 1993 saw nine of the twelve sitting MPs returned to the fono. Two of the three defeated MPs were from the informal opposition. The new fono twice failed to elect a prime minister, with both the incumbent, Bikenibeu Paeniu, and the challenger Dr. Tomasi Puapua, the opposition leader and a former premier, receiving six votes. Governor General Sir Toalipi Lauti used his constitutional powers to dissolve this new fono, and the country held fresh elections on 25 November, with a runoff in one district held five days later. On 10 December parliament elected Kamuta Laatasi, a former general manager of BP Oil in Tuvalu, as prime minister. Laatasi had been a backbencher in the Paeniu government but, supported by his wife, also an MP, crossed over and received the support of five former opposition MPs.

The tiny country has a poor resource base and is dependent on food imports. Agricultural output consists mainly of cocoa palm and its derivatives. Much of

Tuvalu's revenue comes from remittances by some 1,500 countrymen living abroad, as well as from the sale of stamps and coins. Interest from the Tuvalu Trust Fund, established in 1987 by major aid donors, covers a fourth of the annual budget. Scientists say the low-lying country is slowly sinking into the Pacific Ocean, as most of the islands are being eroded by storms.

Political Rights and Civil Liberties: Citizens of Tuvalu can change their government democratically. Political parties are legal but only one loosely organized group has formed, former Prime Minister Bikenibeu Paeniu's Tuvalu United Party. Most elections hinge on village-based allegiances rather than issues. Power is decentralized on the eight permanently inhabited islands through six-person island councils, which are elected by universal suffrage every four years. These councils are generally influenced by hereditary elders wielding traditional authority.

The judiciary is independent of the government, and citizens receive fair public trials. Freedoms of speech and press are respected. State-run Radio Tuvalu offers pluralistic viewpoints. There are no restrictions on the right to form associations or hold public assemblies or meetings. Religious freedom is fully respected, and 70 percent of the population belongs to the Protestant Church of Tuvalu. The government promotes a voluntary family planning program out of concern that a rapidly growing population will overwhelm the densely packed country's limited resources. Because of traditional norms, women face some discrimination in employment opportunities. The former Paeniu government brought women into the cabinet and other senior positions, and in 1994 the International Center for Entrepreneurship and Career Development in Ahmedabad, India opened slots in training programs for women from Tuvalu. Citizens can travel freely internally and abroad. Workers are free to join independent unions, although only the Tuvalu Seamen's Union has been organized and registered. Strikes are legal but none has occurred, largely because much of the population is engaged outside the wage economy in subsistence agriculture.

Uganda

Polity: Military
Economy: Capitalist-statist
Population: 19,823,000
PPP: $1,036
Life Expectancy: 42.6
Ethnic Groups: Acholi, Baganda, Kakwa, Lango, Nkole, Soga, Teso, other

Political Rights: 5*
Civil Liberties: 5
Status: Partly Free

Ratings Change: *Uganda's political rights rating changed from 6 to 5 following partly free elections for constituent assembly. As a result Uganda's status changed from Not Free to Partly Free.

Overview: In March 1994 Ugandans voted for a 214-member constituent assembly. While both the campaign process and the election itself showed greater political openness, unelected

President Yoweri Museveni and his National Resistance Movement (NRM) continued to control the scope and pace of Uganda's transition to multiparty politics.

Since its independence in 1962, Uganda has been afflicted with civil wars, intermittent coups and repressive dictatorships. An estimated 800,000 people died under the brutal regimes of Idi Amin and Milton Obote during the 1970s and early 1980s. Their rules were marked by economic and social disintegration of the country once known as the "pearl of Africa."

In January 1986 the Museveni-led National Resistance Army (NRA), which had been fighting against the Obote regime since 1980, overthrew Obote's successor, Lieutenant General Tito Okello, who had risen to power in a military coup. Following the takeover, Museveni set up the National Resistance Council (NRC) to act as an interim legislature. Three years later, he expanded the council with nominees from the NRM and members of social movements. At the same time, he extended the interim period until 1995.

The NRM has worked to undermine Uganda's traditional political parties, the Uganda People's Congress (UPC) and the Democratic Party (DP). The UPC, led by the exiled Obote, has a largely Protestant following and orientation, and the DP a Catholic following. Museveni has consistently opposed multipartyism, stating that it leads to religious, ethnic, and regional divisions responsible for the continuing post-independence unrest.

As an alternative to multiparty politics, Museveni offered his version of "movement democracy" based on individual candidates for elected posts running without party labels. The system enables him to permit opposition candidates to voice their opinions, while preventing them from organizing into parties and threatening his power. In recent years, the NRM has increasingly become an umbrella organization, welcoming opposition groups under its jurisdiction. This effort, along with the fact that the DP and UPC rarely agree, helps to solidify NRM political control.

On 28 March voters chose from over 1,000 candidates to elect a constituent assembly. Seventy to 80 percent of those eligible registered to vote. In keeping with his "nonparty" political agenda, Museveni barred candidates from revealing their political allegiances or holding campaign demonstrations. Nevertheless, international observers pronounced the election to be mostly "free and fair." In July election results in the eastern Mbale district were nullified because of alleged irregularities.

The National Organization for Civic and Election Monitoring (NOCEM), formed in August 1993, ran programs to educate voters, especially in rural Uganda. The NRM swept up 120 of the possible 214 elected seats. Another sixty-four were appointed by the NRM from such sectors as the military and women's groups. Seventy-five elected candidates represented the opposition. In addition, certain high-ranking NRM officials were defeated. The assembly is responsible for approving the draft of the new constitution, which took four years to write. On 15 December the government approved proposals to hold general elections in December 1995.

Prior to the election, Museveni agreed to restore on a purely cultural basis the traditional monarchies of Uganda's several ethnic groups, which had been abolished by Obote in the 1960s. Before he abolished them, the tribal kingdoms formed the regional structures of Uganda's federal systems. The *Kabaka* (king) of Uganda's largest ethnic group, the *Baganda*, was recrowned in an elaborate ceremony in July 1993. By August 1994 the *Tora* and *Bunyoro* monarchies were also reestablished.

Rebel clashes continued to rock the North. The different rebel groups represent several factions, which range from religious sects to supporters of past regimes. Particularly active is a group called the Lord's Resistance Army (LRA). Led by Roman Catholic Joseph Kony, the LRA wants to overthrow Museveni's adminstration and replace it with one that governs according to Kony's version of the ten commandments, one of which forbids people from travelling in automobiles or by road. The LRA's insurgency intensified in September, when the rebels laid landmines on roads, in keeping with the commandment. Army soldiers intervened, killing ninety-six rebels.

Conflicts in neighboring countries spilled over Uganda's borders in 1994. In June 2,000 Sudanese refugees camped in northern Uganda after fleeing intensive fighting. There are an estimated 350,000 Sudanese refugees in Uganda, some of whom have been there for twenty years.

Since Rwanda's independence in 1962, tens of thousands of Rwandan Tutsis have fled into southern Uganda. When the Rwandan government collapsed in July 1994, the majority of these refugees returned home. Militant Hutus and others accuse Museveni of supporting the Rwanda Patriotic Front (RPF) and using the refugee crisis to achieve his own regional political ambitions. Museveni denied these charges, claiming that he gave the Tutsis the same refugee status as the Sudanese.

Since 1987, when Uganda implemented an IMF-suggested economic reform program, the country's GDP growth rate has increased an average of 6 percent per year, one of the highest growth rates in Africa. In addition, Uganda has the most liberal currency exchange rate in all of Sub-Saharan Africa. Nevertheless, the country remains one of the poorest in the world. To reduce spending, the government began a disarmament process in 1992 which continued into 1994. The demobilization of troops could increase Uganda's already rapid spread of AIDS, as the rate of infection in the army is estimated at more than 50 percent. Affecting the most productive part of the population, AIDS has caused the number of orphans to reach over one million.

Political Rights and Civil Liberties:

Ugandans cannot change their government democratically, as President Museveni continues to forbid political parties from forming and allows opposition only if it does not pose a threat to his power. The 1994 constituent assembly elections, however, indicated potential for political diversification. Museveni will most likely win the presidential elections scheduled for December 1995, since the draft constitution provides five more years of nonparty government. Since the new constitution also allows the president to serve two consecutive five-year terms, Museveni could remain in power until 2006.

The LRA rebel group was responsible in 1994 for a number of human rights violations including rape, the killing of civilians, and genital and lip removal. Prison conditions for inmates remain harsh, with overcrowding, malnutrition, and the spread of AIDS causing the highest prisoner mortality rates in the world.

Independence of the judiciary is circumscribed by direct executive interference in cases involving opponents of the regime. The judiciary remains understaffed and underfunded in rural areas, especially in those with a recurrence of rebel activities. Legal representation for the accused is often unavailable; in political cases, the security forces often attempt to cajole lawyers to withdraw from representing their clients. The new constitution proposes the creation of a National Council of State to replace the checking power of the parliament. If formed, the council could jeopardize the independence of the judiciary, as it would be chaired by the president and would include parliament members.

The press covers a wide range of topics, including allegations of human rights abuses by the government and statements by members of the opposition critical of the government. Approximately twenty newspapers and newsletters are being published throughout the country, the government-owned *New Vision* having the widest circulation. Nevertheless, the government attempts to muzzle the press through the use of sedition charges against journalists, forcing many to practice self-censorship.

Political parties are prohibited from actively engaging in the political process, and political rallies are not allowed. Nonpolitical associations and human rights groups are active in society, but are often subject to unofficial harassment. Freedom of religion is respected. Rebel activities have put certain restrictions on domestic travel, but foreign travel is generally unrestricted. Workers are organized under the National Organization of Trade Unions (NOTU).

Women have inferior social, political, and family status; in some areas, women still have to kneel to men when they meet. The widespread practice of polygamy is an obstacle in the fight against the spread of AIDS, as men tend to have many sex partners, and women have little control over their sexual health. Girls aged fifteen to nineteen are six times as likely to be infected as are boys the same age, since the men tend to prefer younger women, because they believe them to be less likely to have the virus.

Ukraine

Polity: Presidential-parliamentary democracy
Economy: Statist-transitional
Population: 51,482,000
PPP: $5,180
Life Expectancy: 70.0

Political Rights: 3*
Civil Liberties: 4
Status: Partly Free

Ethnic Groups: Ukrainian (72.7 percent); Russian (22.1 percent); others
Ratings Change: *Ukraine's political rights rating changed from 4 to 3 following presidential and parliamentary elections.

Overview:

In July 1994 Leonid Kuchma, the former industrialist who was forced to resign as prime minister just nine months earlier, was elected president of the former Soviet Union's second-largest republic. In a runoff, he defeated incumbent Leonid Kravchuk, the former Communist Party ideologue who led the country in its first two-and-a-half years of independence. Kuchma was elected three months after the opening round of the country's first post-Soviet elections for the 450-member parliament. The new president's priorities included initiating a program of market reforms to rectify a sputtering economy, securing Western financial assistance, normalizing relations with Russia, facilitating parliamentary passage of the Nuclear Non-Proliferation Treaty (NPT) and addressing secessionist pressures in Crimea.

Ukraine, a major agricultural-industrial center, was the site of the medieval Kievan Rus' realm that reached its height in the tenth and eleventh centuries. The large eastern part of the country was dominated by Russia for over 300 years, while the west was ruled by Poland and Austria-Hungary. Ukraine enjoyed a brief period of independent statehood between 1917 and 1920, after which Soviet rule was extended over most Ukrainian lands with the creation of the Ukrainian Soviet Socialist Republic. Western Ukraine was forcibly annexed from Poland in 1940 under the Hitler-Stalin Pact. Ukraine declared independence from a crumbling Soviet Union in 1991, and Leonid Kravchuk was elected president by direct vote. Parliament was elected in 1990 and, although dominated by former Communists, the Democratic Bloc of over 100 deputies proved a formidable parliamentary faction that pressured hard-liners to adopt sovereignty.

In 1993, President Kravchuk, Prime Minister Kuchma and parliament, which had rejected seven successive economic reform packages since 1991, remained at loggerheads over the character and pace of economic restructuring. Kuchma, who had replaced unpopular hard-liner Vitold Fokin in October 1992, resigned in September amid labor unrest by coal miners and was replaced by Yukhym Zviahilsky, a former mine director. Zviahilsky, who was replaced in June 1994, subsequently fled to Israel amid allegations that he had embezzled $25 million in state funds.

Political gridlock over the economy and presidential powers led to early 1994 elections for parliament (27 March) and president (26 June). The legislative elections were held under a flawed and complex electoral law passed in November 1993. The law was entirely majoritarian and clearly biased against political parties (only 11 percent of candidates had party affiliations), making it difficult for them to register candidates while any "group of electors" (minimum membership of ten) or "worker collectives" (no minimum membership) could easily nominate whomever they wanted. The law set a minimum 50 percent participation rate per district for the election to be considered valid. Only 300 signatures were needed for a candidate's name to appear on the ballot, leading to 5,802 candidates, as many as twenty-seven in one Kiev district.

The election law led to a series of run-offs (in some Kiev electoral districts, voters went to the polls eight times), but by year's end some 10 percent of seats had not been filled and parliament suspended further balloting. In the first round on 27 March, 75 percent of voters turned out, but only 49 seats were decided. After the second round, 338 deputies had been elected, 38 more than the necessary quorum for parliament to meet. Subsequent rounds produced 67 deputies before elections were suspended.

While eighteen parties were represented in the new parliament, the deputies coalesced around nine major blocs, whose membership shifted during the year. After 7 August, the leftist Communist, Socialist, and Agrarian blocs accounted for 150 seats; the Inter-Regional Bloc, 53; the Centrists (many closely affiliated with Kravchuk), 38; the Reform Bloc, 27; the democratic National Rukh bloc, 29; the Statehood bloc, 27; and Independents, 49. Those who did not join any faction or were members of smaller parties made up the rest.

More than 500 international observers from fifty-three countries monitored the first-round vote. Though the elections were generally deemed "free and fair," there were major problems. The pre-election period saw a wave of beatings, break-ins, vandalism and kidnappings aimed at intimidating democratic activists. On 15 January Mykhailo Boichyshyn, head of the secretariat of Rukh—Ukraine's largest democratic party—was abducted and presumed dead. Rukh headquarters in Kiev were guarded by ex-soldiers in camouflaged army fatigues. Activists and offices were attacked in several cities.

The election results augured legislative deadlock on economic reforms and failure to reach a national consensus on regional and ideological issues. The country seemed polarized over the means to alleviate the economic morass. The eastern, industrialized part of the country, home to many of the country's 11 million Russians, voted mainly Socialist, Communist and Agrarian, suggesting a desire for closer ties with Moscow and a return to the security of a command economy. Central and nationalist western Ukraine tended to vote for moderates or business-oriented reformers. Among those elected were reform economists Viktor Pynzenyk and Wolodymyr Lanoviy, both of whom had been dismissed from government posts by President Kravchuk in 1993.

With leftists and former Communists dominating parliament, Socialist Party leader Oleksandr Moroz was elected parliamentary chairman in May. On 16 June, just ten days before the presidential vote, parliament approved President Kravchuk's nominee for prime minister, Vitaliy Masol, a former Communist who had held the post prior to Ukraine's independence but who had been ousted in October 1990. A freeze on privatization was not lifted until December, after it became clear that Western assistance and agreements with the IMF and other international institutions depended on moving ahead with market reforms.

In the presidential race campaigning focused on the shape of the new constitution, the status of the Russian language, and the extent of cooperation with Moscow. President Kravchuk, who initially announced he would not run, offered a vague platform of simply "developing Ukraine's socially oriented economy," and stressed his experienced helmsmanship in steering Ukraine toward independence. Former Prime Minister Kuchma, his main rival, sprinkled promises of market reform with pledges of close economic ties with Russia, appealing to the largely Russian-speaking eastern Ukrainians, particularly Communists and factory bosses. Lanoviy, the only candidate running on an unabashedly pro-reform platform, trailed in the polls as western Ukrainians, a natural anti-Communist constituency, backed Kravchuk to derail the putatively pro-Russian Kuchma.

In the first round, Kravchuk scored a narrow victory over Kuchma, 37.72 percent to 31.27 percent, but since neither polled over 50 percent, a runoff was needed. Turnout was 68 percent. In the 10 July runoff, Kuchma won, 52 percent to 45 percent, with over 71 percent of eligible voters taking part.

To the surprise of many, Kuchma moved quickly to assuage fears that he would strengthen ties with Russia at the expense of Ukrainian sovereignty, and he soon made it clear that he meant to pursue close economic, security and political relations with the U.S. and the West. Economic reformer Pynzenyk was made a first deputy prime minister in charge of economic reform and Lanoviy was brought in as economic adviser. Days after assuming the presidency, Kuchma met with IMF managing director Michael Camdessus, who pledged to work with the new president on such problems as inflation, macro-economic stabilization and liberalization of prices. In return for unifying the exchange rate, lifting export restrictions and raising energy prices, the IMF gave Ukraine a $365 million portion of a promised $730 million "systematic transformation facility" loan. In July, the G-7 nations, meeting in Naples, offered Ukraine $4.2 billion, including funds to shut down Chernobyl and provide Ukraine with the opportunity to qualify for large IMF and Word Bank loans. Promoted by President Clinton, the package was conditioned on the implementation of comprehensive market reforms. On 5 December the European Union (EU) lent Ukraine $108 million to help with its balance of payments.

A major step toward economic reform came on 19 October, when parliament voted 231-54 for free-market reforms by allowing Kiev to free prices, reduce state subsidies, overhaul the tax system and push ahead with privatization, including private land ownership. Privatization vouchers were delivered to Ukraine on 2 December, and citizens allowed to invest certificates in state enterprises in early 1995.

At year's end the economy remained anemic. Inflation was 70 percent in November, unemployment and prices were up and industrial production had declined. The average monthly wage stood at between (U.S.) $10 and $15. The unofficial "private economy" accounted for some 40 percent of GDP.

To move forward with economic reform, President Kuchma drafted a law that would strengthen executive powers and delineate the responsibilities of all branches of the national and local governments. Passage of the draft by parliament will be a key issue in 1995. In August, Kuchma issued several decrees to take effective control of the government and independently elected regional heads.

A key issue throughout the year was the long-simmering conflict in the Crimea, the Black Sea peninsula with a substantial non-Ukrainian, pro-Russian population. In January, pro-Russian Yuri Meshkov was elected president of Crimea and called for a referendum on the peninsula's independence to coincide with national parliamentary elections on 27 March. Then-President Kravchuk decreed the referendum unconstitutional. Even though Meshkov was snubbed by high-level Russian officials in February, in May he and the Crimean parliament moved to approve a constitution that would allow Crimea to form its own military, deal with Ukraine on a treaty basis and introduce Russian as the state language. The following month, Crimean lawmakers resolved to nullify laws and resolutions passed in Kiev. Meshkov ran afoul of his own parliament, however, when a newspaper revealed he planned to suspend parliament and assume all legislative and executive power. The government was reorganized, and Meshkov was removed as head of state by the Crimean parliament. The crisis eased somewhat in October when the father-in-law of President Kuchma's daughter was appointed prime minister of Crimea.

On the nuclear weapons issue, parliament, prodded by President Kuchma, ratified the Nuclear Non-Proliferation Treaty (NPT) in November on the eve of the president's U.S. visit. At the Conference on Security and Cooperation in Europe (CSCE) summit in Brussels in early December, President Kuchma signed the NPT, receiving security assurances from the U.S., Russia, Great Britain, and France. Ukraine joined NATO's Partnership for Peace in February, the first member of the Commonwealth of Independent States (CIS) to do so.

Ukraine maintained cautious relations with Moscow, resisting initiatives to formalize bilateral economic union. A member of the CIS Economic Union, Ukraine limited its role to specific agreements. Tensions remained over the Black Sea Fleet after negotiations stalled, and a Sevastopol City Council decision to give the city "Russian status."

Political Rights and Civil Liberties: Ukrainians can change their government democratically. Presidential and parliamentary elections in 1994 were deemed generally "free and fair" by international observers, though there were reports of irregularities and pre-election intimidation and violence directed at democratic organizations and activists. Democrats claimed the November 1993 electoral law was designed to hinder a multiparty system by weakening the role of political parties in the electoral process.

Ukraine is governed by what is essentially the 1978 constitution of the Ukrainian SSR, modified since independence by the introduction of a presidency and a multiparty system. A new constitution is likely to be drafted and debated in 1995.

An independent judiciary and rule of law remain in formative stages. Modifications of Soviet-era laws have enhanced defendant's rights in such areas as pretrial detention and appealing arrests. President Kuchma's tough anti-crime bill, signed in July, permits police to hold suspected criminals for up to thirty days; suspected criminal locations may be raided without search warrants. There are about 50,000 legal professionals in Ukraine, but most judges, especially on the regional level, were appointed during the Soviet era.

Citizens are free to organize in political groupings and associations and there are scores of political parties representing the political spectrum from far-left to far-right. Nongovernmental cultural, business, religious, women's, human rights and other groups are free to organize and operate, although some have reported administrative interference.

A 1991 press law purports to protect freedom of speech and press, but it covers only print media. There are hundreds of independent Ukrainian- and Russian-language newspapers, periodicals and journals. Many receive state subsidies, a form of indirect control. The price and availability of newsprint and print facilities, as well as an inadequate state-owned distribution system, have hampered publications. The Ukrainian State Committee for Television and Radio broadcasts in Ukrainian and Russian, and Russian TV is readily available. There are several private local TV and radio stations throughout the country, which broadcast views and stories critical of the government. Satellite dishes are available. The state grants air time to commercial channels and access to the state cable system, thereby creating the possibility of arbitrary restrictions on certain types of programs. Independent news agencies include the Ukrainian Press Agency, UNIAR and UNIAN, Vybir and Rukh Inform.

Freedom of assembly is recognized and generally respected. Although the previously outlawed Ukrainian (Uniate) Catholic and Ukrainian Autocephalous Orthodox churches are legal, conflicts between the two churches and the old Russian Orthodox Church continue over property and churches. There are three Ukrainian Orthodox churches, two with allegiances to patriarchs in Kiev and one with allegiance to Moscow. Ukraine's estimated 500,000 Jews are organized and maintain schools and synagogues.

Freedoms of domestic and international travel and emigration are generally respected, although bureaucratic restrictions exist. Ukraine has maintained relative ethnic tranquillity, but in Russian-dominant areas demands for unification with Russia persist.

Women have educational opportunities, and are represented among the professional classes. Independent women's organizations exist and have raised such issues as spousal abuse and alcoholism.

Ukrainian workers are organized in several trade unions. The Federation of Trade Unions, a successor to the former official Soviet body, claims 21 million workers. In 1992, five independent unions united under the umbrella of the

Consultative (Advisory) Council of Free Trade Unions, which interacts freely with international labor groups. Estimates of membership in independent unions range from 100,000 to 200,000; over 80 percent of the workforce is unionized.

United Arab Emirates

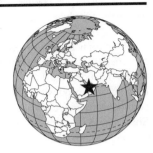

Polity: Federation of traditional monarchies
Economy: Capitalist-statist
Population: 1,686,000
PPP: $17,000
Life Expectancy: 70.8

Political Rights: 6*
Civil Liberties: 5
Status: Not Free

Ethnic Groups: Native Arabs, Arab and other immigrant groups
Ratings Change: *United Arab Emirates's political rights rating changed from 7 to 6 because the *Survey* credits the functioning of a new consultative council.

Overview: Located on the Arabian Peninsula along the Persian Gulf, the emirates were originally known as the Trucial States because of defense agreements signed with Britain in the nineteenth century and lasting until 1968. Following several attempts at unification, the United Arab Emirates formally became a state on 2 December 1971.

The seven emirates are governed internally as traditional monarchies. Under the 1971 constitution, the monarchs collectively form a Supreme Council, which elects a president and vice president from among its members for five-year terms. The President appoints a prime minister and a cabinet. A forty-member consultative Federal National Council is composed of delegates appointed by the seven rulers but holds no legislative powers. Separate consultative councils exist within several emirates. There are no political parties and no popular elections. Sheikh Zayed ibn Sultan al Nuhayyan of Abu Dhabi, the largest emirate, has been president since 1971.

The economy is based on oil and gas production and has given the emirates' citizens one of the highest per-capita incomes in the world. In June 1994 a court sentenced twelve former top executives of the collapsed Bank of Credit and Commerce International, two of them *in absentia*, to jail terms of up to fourteen years on charges of widespread fraud. The ruling family and government of Abu Dhabi had controlled 77 percent of BCCI. In another development, in September the government announced it would tighten spending to offset low oil prices.

The government maintains a pro-Western foreign policy and was a staunch supporter of the U.S.-led coalition that ousted Iraq from Kuwait in 1991. The key foreign policy issue is an Iranian claim to three islands near the Straight of Hormuz. The islands had been jointly ruled for two decades by Iran and the emirate of Sharjah until March 1992, when Iran inexplicably expelled the emirate's citizens from them. In December 1994 the United Arab Emirates announced it would refer the case to the International Court of Justice.

Political Rights and Civil Liberties: Citizens of the United Arab Emirates cannot change their government democratically. Political parties and political demonstrations are illegal. There are no popular elections, and all power is held by the seven emirates and their families. The only recourse for male citizens is to express opinions and grievances at *majlises* (gatherings) held by the rulers of each emirate, while women can attend majlises presided over by the wives of the seven rulers.

Foreign nationals are occasionally randomly detained for up to two months. Detainees can be held incommunicado until either charged or released. The dual court system includes *Shari'a* (Islamic) courts, located in each emirate, and civil courts, most of which are responsible to the Federal Supreme Court in Abu Dhabi. However, the civil court systems in Dubai and Ras al-Khaimah are separate from the federal system. Both Shari'a courts and civil courts handle criminal and civil cases, and the nature of each case determines where it is heard. The judiciary is generally independent of the government, and defendants receive adequate due process rights in both civil and Shari'a courts.

Citizens and the press exercise significant self-censorship regarding the ruling families, government policies and other sensitive issues. Television and radio stations are state owned and offer only government views. However, television stations in Abu Dhabi and Dubai broadcast the Cable News Network. All imported publications are reviewed by the Ministry of Information, which bans or censors materials considered pornographic or otherwise offensive to Islam, or critical of the ruling family.

Permits are required for organized gatherings. While some emirates permit conferences where government policies are discussed, others are more restrictive. Islam is the official religion, and most citizens are Sunni Muslims. Shiite mosques are not permitted in Ras al-Khaimah. Non-Muslims can generally practice their religion but may not proselytize or distribute literature. There are Christian, Sikh and Hindu temples, and Christian teaching is allowed for Christian children. There are no restrictions on internal travel, except near defense and oil facilities. A woman must get her husband's permission to travel abroad with her children.

Women can hold government positions and make up 70 percent of the enrollment at United Arab Emirates University, but in general they face strong traditional pressure against entering the workforce. Married women must receive written permission from their husbands to take jobs. Foreign nationals employed as domestic help are occasionally abused by their employers, although the authorities have been responsive to this problem. Strikes by public sector workers are illegal and are considered a criminal offense. There is no law either for or against the right of private workers to unionize or strike, although in practice informal government pressure prevents such activity. Similarly, collective bargaining is not expressly prohibited but is not practiced. Children, often from South Asian countries, continue to be used as jockeys in the dangerous sport of camel racing, although the government has imposed and enforces minimum weight restrictions.

United Kingdom

Polity: Parliamentary democracy
Economy: Mixed capitalist
Population: 58,370,000
PPP: $16,340
Life Expectancy: 75.8
Ethnic Groups: English, Scottish, Welsh, Irish, and various Asian, African, and Caribbean immigrant groups

Political Rights: 1
Civil Liberties: 2
Status: Free

Overview:

Prime Minister John Major's Conservative (Tory) government survived with difficulty in 1994. Intraparty disputes over Britain's role in the European Union (EU) and higher sales taxes on fuel nearly brought the government down. A series of sexual and financial scandals forced several Tories to resign their government posts. As the Conservatives plummeted in public opinion, the opposition Labour Party seemed poised to regain power. Labour's leader, John Smith, died of a sudden heart attack in May, but his party continued to top the polls throughout 1994 under the new leader, Tony Blair.

The United Kingdom of Great Britain and Northern Ireland combines two formerly separate kingdoms (England and Scotland), an ancient principality (Wales), and six counties of the Irish province of Ulster. *(See Northern Ireland section under Related Territories.)* Parliament has an elected House of Commons with 651 members chosen by plurality vote from single-member districts, and a House of Lords with over 1,000 hereditary and appointed members. The Lords have a suspensive veto, under which they can delay legislation on a bill for six months. If the House of Commons backs the bill again, it becomes law. A section of Lords serves as a supreme court. Parliament has a maximum term of five years.

Queen Elizabeth II is the largely ceremonial head of state who nominates for prime minister the party leader who has the highest support in the House of Commons. The breakup of several royal marriages in recent years has diminished public respect for the monarchy. Jack Straw, Labour's Shadow Home Secretary, suggested cutting down the officially recognized size of the royal family and its public funding.

The Conservative Party has been in power since 1979. In 1990, the Conservative parliamentary caucus unseated Prime Minister Margaret Thatcher and replaced her with the more moderate John Major. Despite a recession, Major won his own mandate with the 1992 election. The Conservatives won 41.9 percent of the vote and 336 seats. Led by Neil Kinnock, Labour improved its showing from 1987, but received only 34.4 percent and 271 seats. Paddy Ashdown's Liberal Democrats finished third with 18 percent and 20 seats. The remaining 24 seats went to regionalist and nationalist parties. Due to Labour's loss, Kinnock resigned the party leadership. John Smith, a moderate, replaced him. Under Smith, Labour democratized its internal structure and moved toward the political center. Blair has continued moderating Labour's policies, but narrowly lost a vote at the 1994 party conference to drop "common ownership" from the party constitution.

Labour crushed the Tories in local and European parliamentary elections in 1994. In the local vote in May, the Conservatives finished third with 27 percent. Labour came in first with 41 percent, followed by the Liberal Democrats. The Conservatives won control of only fifteen out of 198 local councils. In the European election in June, Labour placed first with 44 percent. The Liberal Democrats complained that they lost a Euro-seat illegitimately, because election officials had allowed a "Literal Democrat" on the ballot. The candidate siphoned off 10,000 votes from the Liberal Democrat, allowing a Conservative to win by 700 votes. A new "Conversative Party" threatens the Tories in the same way at the next general election. The Tories had their worst showing ever, winning only eighteen of Britain's eighty-seven Euro-seats.

Defeats in by-elections have thinned Conservative parliamentary ranks. In June 1994 the Conservatives lost five out of five by-elections in one day. The smaller margin of power emboldened Tory right-wing MP's to oppose Major over Europe and taxes during 1994. The Conservative right argued for British sovereignty and against a single European currency. On 24 November Major brought some party dissidents into line by threatening to call a general election that the Conservatives would lose. (Labour was running as much as thirty points ahead of the Tories in polls in 1994.) However, eight anti-EU Conservative MP's abstained from voting for Britain's contribution to the EU. Since Major had declared this matter a confidence vote in his government, he suspended the eight abstainers from the Conservative caucus. This action took away the party's official majority, but Major could count on nine votes from Ulster Unionists, Northern Irish Protestant MP's, to keep him in office. Nonetheless, on 6 December Tory defections and abstentions made the government lose a vote on raising fuel taxes. If Major had made the tax vote a matter of confidence, he might have forced a general election.

As the Conservatives lost ground in 1994, they dropped plans to privatize the postal system and moved away from proposals to eliminate county government. Major fell back on defending the British status quo, especially the continuing union of Scotland and Wales with England. At the same time, Major's government conceded that Northern Ireland had a "democracy deficit," and began face-to-face negotiations with Sinn Fein, the Irish republican party, in late 1994.

Several Tories resigned their government positions following alleged financial improprieties and sex scandals in 1994. For example, Tim Smith, MP, accepted questionable gifts from a businessman in return for raising issues at parliamentary question time. After journalists posing as businessmen got two MP's to accept checks for submitting questions, Major called for an investigation of conflicts of interest. It is legal for MP's to be paid corporate parliamentary agents. The most bizarre episode of the year was the death of Stephen Milligan, MP, who was found hanged, wearing a plastic bag over his head and women's stockings.

During a special inquiry, Major endured months of embarrassing testimony about the Conservatives' willingness to sell arms to Iraq up to the time of the Persian Gulf War, and about the government's willingness to cover it up. As a consequence of the scandals, one opinion poll showed that 61 percent of the public believed that the Conservatives gave "the impression of being very sleazy and disreputable."

Political Rights and Civil Liberties: Citizens can change their government democratically. A government survey handles voter registration. Irish and Commonwealth (former British Empire) citizens resident in Britain have the right to vote. British subjects abroad have voting rights for twenty years after their emigration. Wales, Scotland, and Northern Ireland have no regional legislatures, but they elect members to the House of Commons. Some ancient customs produce unusual effects on local government. For example, to vote in the City of London, the financial heart of the capital, a nonresident can qualify by renting property with at least ten pounds of taxable value. Corporate interests can add their employees to the voting roles by declaring their parking spaces and offices residences as rented property.

Many rights and liberties are well established by custom and precedent in Britain's largely unwritten constitution. However, Britain's contact with Europeans who have codified freedoms has influenced a growing movement for a written constitution with a bill of rights.

The lack of a written constitutional right to press freedom is raising increasing concerns about government interference. Tough libel laws may have a chilling effect on some kinds of publishing and entertainment. A strict interpretation of the right to a fair trial led a court to halt a musical about the late publisher, Robert Maxwell, on the grounds that it might prejudice a case against his sons. The Official Secrets Act provides the government with a tool to attempt halting publication of intelligence activities and other official matters. The media can deal with this restraint through appeals in the courts and publication overseas. Many opposition MP's support right-to- know legislation to replace the Official Secrets Act.

The British Broadcasting Corporation (BBC) is an autonomous public body. It responds to government pressure to censor controversial items. However, the BBC offers pluralistic points of view, and airs political broadcasts of both government and opposition parties. There are also private electronic media. They are subject to government interference on stories dealing with terrorism. From 1988 until September 1994, Britain banned alleged terrorists' voices from broadcasts. Actors did voice-overs for Sinn Fein leaders in news stories.

Since 1989, the courts have had to overturn several convictions in cases of alleged terrorism because appeals courts have discovered doctored or inadequate evidence that led to miscarriages of justice.

The Provisional Irish Republican Army (IRA) continued its violent campaign in England in early 1994. For example, it launched three mortar attacks on London's Heathrow Airport in March. IRA violence in England tapered off with the approach of the paramilitary ceasefire announced on 31 August. However, five IRA men and another prisoner attempted to break out of an English jail on 9 September. Investigations after the prisoners were recaptured revealed that the inmates had lived in luxury. Guards had bought the prisoners expensive goods, and had allowed them to make long-distance telephone calls. Middle Eastern terrorists exploded two car bombs in London on 27 July. They injured nineteen people near the Israeli Embassy and a Jewish fundraising organization.

In 1994 parliament passed the Criminal Justice Act. This legislation gutted the accused's right to silence. The government published a new warning for police to give to suspects. Among other things, the warning says, "But if you do not mention now something which you later use in your defense, the court may decide that your failure to mention it strengthens the case against you." The government intends to use this provision against suspected terrorists. The Criminal Justice Act also removed the right of Gypsies (Rom) to stop their caravans at campsites, and restricted broadcasting "rave" music. In 1994, the home secretary promised to introduce a proposal for a national identity card, in order to fight crime. The notion threatened to split libertarian and traditionalist Tories. Ethnic minorities comprise 5.9 percent of the population, and face bigotry and violence from native whites. According to a poll sponsored by the American Jewish Committee, Britons have the strongest bias against Gypsies (Rom).

There is generally freedom of movement, but the government has barred more than 100 people from traveling between Britain and Northern Ireland. However, in October 1994 the state lifted the travel bans on Sinn Fein leaders Gerry Adams and Martin McGuinness, so that they could visit London for meetings and negotiations.

Britain has free religious expression, and the Church of England and the Church of Scotland are established. The Queen is head of the Church of England. There is some possibility for political interference in religion, because the Queen appoints Anglican bishops on the advice of the prime minister. The government finances some Christian denominational schools, but denies subsidies to Muslim academies because Islamic educators reject state curriculum guidelines that include sex education.

Business and labor groups are powerful and active, but trade union membership has fallen since 1979. Under Conservative employment legislation, individual workers decide whether or not to have dues deducted automatically from their pay. The Conservatives passed this in order to weaken the unions' financial base. Both public and private sector employers have undercut collective bargaining with individual contracts. There have been some abuses of the labor law. In June the European Court of Justice ruled that Britain was in violation of EU laws protecting workers' rights during the privatization of public services. The ruling required employers to begin consulting their workers when planning layoffs and transfers.

United States of America

Polity: Federal presi-
dential-legislative
democracy
Economy: Capitalist
Population: 260,750,000
PPP: $22,130
Life Expectancy: 75.6
Ethnic Groups: Various white, black, Hispanic, Asian, Pacific,
native American (Indians, Eskimos/Inuit, Aleuts), and others

Political Rights: 1
Civil Liberties: 1
Status: Free

Overview:

In the midterm elections held on 8 November 1994, the Republicans captured control of the 435-seat House of Representatives for the first time in forty years. The Republicans also regained a majority in the Senate for the first time since 1986, and won a majority of governorships. The election results reflected dissatisfaction with Democratic President Bill Clinton, Congressional Democrats and governors. The election gave the Republicans 230 House seats and the Democrats 204. An independent socialist won the remaining seat. Thomas Foley, the Democratic Speaker of the House, became the first Speaker to lose re-election since 1860. Republican Newt Gingrich replaced him. With a combination of Republican victories and a Democratic defection, Republicans gained a 53-47 edge in the Senate.

In the 1992 presidential election, Clinton defeated Republican President George Bush with 43 percent to Bush's 38 percent of the popular vote. Independent candidate H. Ross Perot, a billionaire businessman, captured 19 percent, the best third-party performance since 1912. Clinton's running mate, Senator Albert Gore, Jr., became vice president.

In their 1994 campaign manifesto, "The Contract With America," House Republicans promised sweeping reforms to improve the efficiency and structure of Congress; lower taxes; more defense spending; less regulation; and constitutional amendments mandating Congressional term limits and balanced federal budgets.

The electoral college is the technical device for electing the president and vice president for four-year terms. The voters in each state and Washington, D.C., vote for slates of electors who usually cast their votes in the electoral college for the candidates with the most support in their jurisdiction. Occasionally, individual electors have voted for someone other than the candidates to whom they were pledged. In 1992, the Clinton-Gore team won 370 electoral votes to 168 for Bush and Vice President Dan Quayle. Perot and his running mate, James Stockdale, won no electoral votes.

Each state is guaranteed at least one representative. The rest are apportioned on the basis of population. Representatives have two-year terms. The 100-seat Senate has two members from each state regardless of population. Senators have six-year terms.

A radical overhaul of the nation's health care system topped Clinton's domestic agenda in 1994. The proposal would have guaranteed health benefits to all Americans and have required employers to provide their employees with health insurance. A complex mixture of government boards and private insurance combines would have run the system. Congressional committees debated and amended various competing health bills until September 1994. By then, it was clear that no health legislation could pass.

The failure of health legislation made Clinton look incapable of passing important legislation even with a Democratic Congressional majority. This failure may have removed an incentive for many Democratic-identifiers to vote. At the same time, right-wing religious groups were increasingly politically active in 1994, and encouraged conservative voter turnout on the basis of social issues. Voter turnout was 39 percent, a gain over other recent midterm figures.

According to election-day polls, a majority of the one-fifth of voters who claimed to have declining economic circumstances voted Republican, as did two-thirds of white males. Following the election, Clinton and the House Democrats tried to win back such voters with pledges of middle-class tax cuts.

A variety of scandals dogged the Clinton administration in 1994. An independent prosecutor continued to investigate Whitewater, a failed real estate deal in which President and Mrs. Clinton had invested. In December, former Justice Department official Webster Hubbell, one of the Clintons' closest friends, pleaded guilty to stealing from his law partners and clients. Throughout the year, Paula Jones, a former Arkansas state employee, pursued a sexual harassment case against President Clinton dating from his tenure as Arkansas Governor. A court ruling allowed Clinton to avoid the suit until after his presidency. In October, Agriculture Secretary Mike Espy resigned after he and his girlfriend allegedly accepted improper gifts from poultry companies.

The presidential residence, the White House, came under attack several times in 1994. In September a man crashed a plane below the Clintons' bedroom. On 29 October a man shot at the White House from a sidewalk, and in December an unknown assailant's bullet hit the mansion.

Political Rights and Civil Liberties: Americans can change their government democratically. Voter turnout is comparatively low. In most recent presidential elections, scarcely 50 percent of the voting age population has turned out. The 1992 contest brought out approximately 55 percent, a gain over recent contests. A few localities grant resident aliens the right to vote. U.S. citizens abroad have voting rights; about 31 percent of them voted in the 1992 presidential election. The party system is competitive. In recent years, until the Republican sweep of 1994, members of Congress seeking re-election won in overwhelming numbers . Members spend an increasing amount of their time raising campaign funds from wealthy individuals and special interest groups. Numerous states and localities have passed measures that limit terms for local, state and federal officials. Former Speaker Foley backed a lawsuit that questioned the constitutionality of states limiting terms of federal officials. In 1995 the U.S. Supreme Court will rule on this issue.

Racial minorities have gained increasing political representation since the 1960s. However, there are significant controversies over the sometimes strangely shaped legislative districts designed to guarantee the election of racial minorities. Federal district courts and the Supreme Court have issued inconsistent rulings about the requirements of redistricting under the Voting Rights Act. After the Democrats lost a majority of Congressional districts in the South in 1994, controversy raged about what role, if any, racially based redistricting had played in their loss.

In presidential election years, an ideologically unrepresentative minority chooses Democratic and Republican presidential nominees through a chaotic, complicated, and debilitating series of primary elections and local party meetings called caucuses. The early caucus and primary states play a disproportionately powerful role in reducing the field of presidential contenders. Voters in states holding later contests often have little influence in deciding the nominations, even if their populations are larger or more representative of the nation as a whole. The news media and political advertising consultants have taken over most of the traditional informational and organizational functions of parties.

Several states, such as New York, have daunting petitioning hurdles that make it difficult for small parties or major party insurgents to receive a place on the ballot. In many states, the rights of initiative and referendum allow citizens to place issues on the ballot, and to decide questions directly, sometimes overturning the decisions of their elected representatives. California is especially noted for a high number of referenda.

The American media are generally free and competitive. However, there are some worrisome trends towards monopolization. Most Americans get their news from television. Broadcast news is highly superficial, and is becoming increasingly difficult to distinguish from entertainment.

Public and private discussions are very open in America. However, a trend in universities and the media to ban allegedly racist and sexist language is subject to broad interpretation, and may have a chilling effect on academic and press freedom. The nationally publicized case of Professor Leonard Jeffries of New York's City College continued its third year in the courts. In 1992, City College refused to reappoint Jeffries as chairman of its black studies department after he had made a series of anti-Jewish speeches. A federal appeals court ruled in April 1994 that the college had violated Jeffries' free speech rights. However, the Supreme Court decided in November that the lower court had to reconsider the case, because the former tribunal had ruled in May that public employers may have some latitude to dismiss employees whose speech is likely to disrupt the workplace. There has been a growing recognition that a tendency towards left-wing conformism among university faculties results in pressure on independent thinkers to mouth "politically correct" views. Large corporations may have a chilling effect on free speech when they hit their activist opponents with lawsuits, which are known as SLAPP suits (special litigation against public participation). Several states and localities have passed legislation outlawing hateful expression.

Since the early 1980s, the Supreme Court has made increasingly conservative rulings, generally reversing the pattern of more liberal decisions in the 1960s and 1970s. Court systems at all levels of government suffer from a severe backlog of cases, delaying the course of justice in countless criminal and civil cases. In 1994, Congress passed a major crime bill that promised to add 100,000 police officers around the country, extended the death penalty for more than fifty federal crimes, and banned the possession and sale of nineteen assault weapons. The legislation also provided funds for various social programs that the Republicans pledged to abolish in 1995. Some gun owners have reacted to the crime bill and other recent gun-control legislation by forming "militias" to oppose the federal government, especially in the West. The high crime rate and growing public demand to punish criminals have led to severe overcrowding in American prisons. Federal and state prisons and local jails hold well over one million people. The rate of prisoners per 100,000 residents grew from 139 in 1980 to 373 in 1994. Police brutality against minorities and unequal sentencing based on race and class undermine the foundations of the criminal justice system. Black convicts receive the death penalty more frequently than whites who have committed similar crimes. The 1994 federal crime bill excluded a provision backed by the Congressional Black Caucus that would have allowed death row inmates to challenge their sentences as motivated by racial bias.

In 1993 and 1994 armed anti-abortion extremists killed or wounded several abortion doctors and abortion clinic employees around the country. Most notably, in December 1994 one gunman allegedly killed and wounded people at three clinics in two days in Massachusetts and Virginia. President Clinton and other political and religious leaders denounced the incidents as "terrorism."

The U.S. has freedom of association. Trade unions are free, but the labor movement is declining as its traditionally strong manufacturing base shrinks. The weak National Labor Relations Board and unenforced labor laws have made it increasingly difficult for workers to organize for better wages and working conditions. Due to management's increasing use of replacement workers during strikes, the strike has become a less effective weapon. In 1994, a bill to ban the use of replacement workers during strikes died in the Senate after a Republican filibuster. In recent years, the federal government has used anti-racketeering laws to place some local and national unions under federal trusteeship in order to remove corrupt officers and end patterns of criminal activity. The country has a regulated, largely free-market economy, with a growing number of service jobs and declining manufacturing employment. The entrepreneurial spirit remains strong. Most job growth takes place in small enterprises in the private sector.

There is religious freedom and a constitutional separation of church and state. In November 1993 President Clinton signed the Religious Freedom Restoration Act (RFRA) which overturned a 1990 Supreme Court ruling that had set a loose standard for laws that restrict religious practices. The new law requires the use of whatever standards would be least restrictive to religion.

In recent decades, the Supreme Court has issued rulings limiting religious displays on public property and prohibiting organized prayer in the public schools. After the 1994 election, Clinton sent mixed signals on the issue of a constitutional amendment to allow organized prayer in public schools. After contradictory statements from the White House, it seemed that the administration might support an officially approved moment of silence in the schools, as Clinton had done as Arkansas governor.

Most poor people in the U.S. are white, but there is a large, disproportionately black underclass that exists outside the economic mainstream. Characterized by seemingly permanent unemployment, the underclass lives to a great extent on welfare payments. Heavy drug use, high crime rates, female-headed households, and large numbers of poorly fed, badly educated, illegitimate children characterize underclass neighborhoods. The quality of life in America's older cities is in decline. In Washington, D.C., over 40 percent of young black males are in the court system as defendants, prisoners, or parolees; half of nonwhite children in the capital are on welfare.

Despite Supreme Court rulings against school segregation, some American school districts are experimenting with deliberately all-black or all-black-male schools with special black curricular emphases. These are desperate attempts to motivate black youngsters who have poor skills and low self-esteem. There is also a growing black middle class, which has made significant gains in housing, education, and employment since the civil rights legislation of the 1960s.

American women have made significant gains in social and economic opportunities in recent decades, but still lag behind men in income. Affirmative action programs have increased the number of women in business and the professions, but they remain concentrated in low-paying occupations. Even rather successful women and minorities often find "glass ceilings" limit their advancement in corporations that assign them to job slots reserved for affirmative action.

Women have had more opportunities in the military in recent years, but in 1994 senior Army generals forced the secretary of the Army to cancel plans to open thousands of combat positions to women. Military women complain that their complaints about sexual harassment go unheeded. During the 1992 presidential campaign, Clinton promised to lift the military's ban on homosexuals. In office, Clinton faced strong opposition to this promise from Congress and the military. After months of debate in 1993, the administration settled for a policy of "Don't ask, don't tell." This means that the military would no longer ask recruits about their sexual orientation, and that the services expected homosexuals in the ranks to keep their sexual activities as discreet as possible.

Immigration is a major political issue, especially in coastal and border states that have the largest amounts of both legal and illegal immigration. In 1994 the Clinton administration sent thousands of Haitian refugees to the U.S. base at Guantanamo, Cuba, and to other countries. Critics charged that the policy was racially motivated. Following the American restoration of Haitian President Aristide in September, the U.S. sent the refugees home. As unrest mounted in Cuba in the summer of 1994, thousands of Cubans fled to the U.S. After allowing the initial arrivals ashore in Florida, the American government routed Cuban refugees to Guantanamo. Ultimately, the Cuban and U.S. governments arranged for a visa lottery and an annual quota of Cuban immigrants. In November, California voters adopted Proposition 187, a referendum that mandated excluding illegal aliens from all but emergency public services. The passage of Proposition 187 sparked interest in other states. However, legal challenges to Proposition 187 delayed its effects.

The U.S. government restricts Americans' freedom of movement to a few countries, notably to Cuba. With certain exceptions, most Americans wishing to visit Cuba must apply for a U.S. government license to spend money there. Failure to obtain the license can result in five years in prison and a $100,000 fine. In 1994, the government enforced the law by blocking funds of would-be travelers and charging returning visitors with violations.

Environmentally, many parts of the U.S. have serious problems. Unacceptably high levels of air, water, and ground pollution threaten inhabitants with higher disease rates, and may lead to personal restrictions, including limits on business activity and the use of automobiles and water supplies. In the November 1994 election, Arizona voters defeated Proposition 300, a referendum that would have required state agencies to assess the effect of any regulation or action on the value of private property before the rule took effect. Environmentalists argued that the proposition would have been too cumbersome and costly. Eleven other states have passed measures similar to Proposition 300 since 1992. In June 1994 the Supreme Court decided to limit government's power to require property owners to set aside part of their land for public environmental purposes.

The U.S. seems largely indifferent to the plight of the American Indians. However, President Clinton pledged in April 1994 to "honor and respect tribal sovereignty." One-third of Indians live below the poverty line and unemployment on reservations exceeds 50 percent. The tribes argue that they need to use their sovereignty to reduce Indian dependence on the federal government. Some tribes are thriving on untaxed tobacco sales and casino gambling. Many Indian groups have cases in court against the federal government, charging violation of treaty provisions relating to control over land and resources.

In 1993 Congress passed a resolution apologizing for the U.S. overthrow of the Kingdom of Hawaii in 1893. Hawaiian natives have a growing sovereignty movement. Some seek legal status similar to that held by tribal Indians; some want national independence; others seek reparations and autonomy. In 1995 Hawaiian natives will vote in a referendum on calling a constitutional convention to discuss options for sovereignty.

Uruguay

Polity: Presidential-legislative democracy
Economy: Capitalist-statist
Population: 3,174,000
PPP: $6,670
Life Expectancy: 72.4
Ethnic Groups: White, mostly Spanish and Italian, (87 percent), Meztizo (7 percent), Black and Mulatto (6 percent)

Political Rights: 2
Civil Liberties: 2
Status: Free

Overview: Julio Sanguinetti, a center-left candidate of the Colorado Party and a former president (1985-90), won a tight three-way presidential race in November that underscored the breakdown of the traditional two-party system and presaged a continuation of the gridlock that has afflicted Uruguayan politics in recent years.

The Republic of Uruguay was established in 1830, five years after gaining independence from Spain. The Colorado Party dominated a relatively democratic political system until it lost the 1958 election. It returned to power in 1966, the year voters approved a constitutional amendment restoring a presidential system. An economic crisis, student and worker unrest, and the activities of the Tupamaro urban guerrilla movement led to a military takeover of the government in 1973.

The nation returned to civilian rule in 1985 following negotiations between the right-wing military regime and civilian politicians. Sanguinetti won the presidential election in 1984 and took office with a newly elected Congress in March 1985.

The political system is based on the 1967 constitution. The president and a bicameral Congress consisting of a ninety-nine-member Chamber of Deputies and a thirty-one-member Senate are elected for five years through a system of electoral lists that allows parties to run multiple candidates. The leading presidential candidate of the party receiving the most votes overall is the winner. In essence, party primaries are conducted simultaneously with the general election. Congressional seats are allocated on the basis of each party's share of the total vote. Municipal and regional governments are elected.

During the return to democratic rule the military backed down from demands for a permanent say in national security matters. Its defense actions and the declaration of a state of siege are now subject to congressional approval. In turn, the Sanguinetti government in 1986 pushed through Congress an amnesty for officers accused of human rights violations.

The constitution permits a referendum on laws passed by the legislature, provided that 25 percent of the electorate sign a petition requesting it. In a plebiscite held in 1989 Uruguayans voted 57-43 percent to confirm the amnesty law.

Luis Alberto Lacalle of the National Party emerged as the winner of the 1989 presidential elections with 37.4 percent of the vote. The Broad Front captured the mayoralty in Montevideo, the capital and home to nearly half the population. Lacalle vowed to liberalize what remains one of Latin America's most statist economies. But he was hamstrung by broad opposition from labor unions, the legislature and factions within his own party. In 1992 voters rejected a referendum to sell off state industries.

As Lacalle's popularity plummeted, the Colorados surged ahead in the polls and by mid-1994 the fifty-eight-year-old Sanguinetti, running on a moderately social democratic platform, was leading Tabare Vasquez by fifteen points. Sanguinetti had also gained the support of the small social democratic Party for the Government by the People (PGP). Vasquez, the popular mayor of Montevideo, had expanded the Broad Front to form the Progressive Encounter (EP), a broad leftist coalition that advocated an uncertain mix of redistributive and market-oriented policies.

In the fall the race evened as Sanguinetti's opponents hammered him on the economic downturn and unemployment that marked his first term. The National Party made up ground as its leading candidate, Alberto Volante, distanced himself from Lacalle.

The 27 November election was Uruguay's closest ever. The Colorados won 31.41 percent of the vote, the Nationals 30.23 percent and the EP 30.02 percent. Sanguinetti, as the leading Colorado vote-getter, was declared the winner. In the Chamber of Deputies the Colorados won thirty-two seats, the Nationals thirty-one and the EP twenty-eight. In the Senate the Colorados won eleven seats, the Nationals ten and the EP nine. The EP held on to the mayoralty of Montevideo.

Local analysts interpreted the outcome as evidence that a majority put Uruguay's generous social welfare provisions ahead of any desire to adopt neo-liberal economic policies. How to continue to pay for such programs remained the question. Sanguinetti appeared to see a need for liberalization, but at a slower pace than Lacalle had advocated.

But whatever Sanguinetti planned to do after taking office in March 1995, it was clear that because of the trifurcation of the political system, he would have to win significant support from among the opposition. Volante, the leading vote-getter among the National candidates, appeared to be angling for a deal. But the prospects for renewed gridlock remained likely.

Political Rights and Civil Liberties:

Citizens are able to change their government through democratic elections. Elections and referendums are overseen by an independent electoral commission. But the increasingly factionalized, gridlocked politics of recent years has led to increasing apathy and disgust among citizens.

Constitutional guarantees regarding free expression, freedom of religion and the right to organize political parties, labor unions and civic organizations are generally respected. The former Tupamaro guerrillas now participate in the system as part of the Broad Front and had one of their members elected to congress in 1994.

Political expression is occasionally restricted by violence associated with hotly contested political campaigns and labor disputes. In the 1994 electoral campaign there were a number of clashes between party supporters, a few legislative candidates were attacked and two Colorado Party offices were ransacked.

In August the government's decision to extradite to Spain three alleged members of the Basque terrorist organization ETA sparked the most violent political incident in many years. Left-wing demonstrators protesting the decision clashed with police, leaving two dead, and thirty-four civilians and forty-four police injured.

The *Guardia de Artigas* (named after a hero of Uruguayan independence), a shadowy nationalist group with links to junior and retired military officers, reemerged in early 1994 by claiming responsibility for the bombing of the home of a prosecutor who had successfully pressed a government suit against a retired general for defaming President Lacalle.

The judiciary is relatively independent, but it has proven increasingly inefficient in the face of escalating crime. It is headed by a Supreme Court appointed by the Congress. The system includes courts of appeal, regional courts and justices of the peace.

Allegations of mistreatment in the penal system, particularly of youthful offenders, have increased. In recent years several police detainees alleged they had been tortured, and a number of police personnel have been prosecuted for ill-treatment or unlawful killings. New measures to prevent such practices, which did not appear to be widespread, were implemented by the Lacalle government, but there was a lack of effective investigation in some cases.

Human and legal rights organizations played a key role in the 1991 decision by the Inter-American Commission on Human Rights of the Organization of American States that the 1986 Amnesty Law violated key provisions of the American Convention on Human Rights.

Labor is well organized, politically powerful, and frequently uses its right to strike. The leading labor confederation is the left-wing PIT-CNT, which initiated the August demonstration that turned violent. Strikes are often marked by violent clashes and sabotage.

Civic organizations have proliferated since the return to civilian rule, particularly women's rights groups and groups representing the small black minority.

The press is privately owned, and broadcasting is both commercial and public. There are numerous daily newspapers, many associated with political parties, and a number of weeklies, including the influential *Busqueda*. However, because of the government's suspension of tax exemptions for the import of newsprint, a number of publications have ceased publication. Television is an important part of the political landscape as campaigns feature debates and extensive coverage on the four channels that service the capital. In August 1994 the government suspended two Tupamaro-linked radio stations for allegedly inciting violence during the demonstration against the extradition of the reputed ETA members.

Uzbekistan

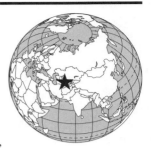

Polity: Dominant party
Economy: Statist-
transitional
Population: 22,118,000
PPP: $2,790
Life Expectancy: 69.0
Ethnic Groups: Uzbeks (70 percent), Russians (8 percent),
Tajiks, Ukrainians, Meshketian Turks, others

Political Rights: 7
Civil Liberties: 7
Status: Not Free

Overview:
In 1994 the authoritarian regime of President Islam Karimov continued to crack down on the opposition and consolidate its repressive hold on the country. December parliamentary elections were won overwhelmingly by the (former Communist) People's Democratic Party.

Located along the historic Silk Road trade route, Uzbekistan is one of the world's oldest civilized regions. In the fourteenth century, what is now its second city, Samarkand, served as a hub for Tamerlane's vast empire. It became part of the Czarist Russian empire in the nineteenth century. In 1920, it became part of the Turkistan Soviet Socialist Republic within the RSFSR. Separated from Turkmenia in 1924, it entered the USSR as a constituent republic in 1925. In 1929 its eastern Tajik region was detached and also accorded the status of a constituent Soviet republic.

President Karimov, a former first secretary of the Communist Party, was elected president on 29 December 1991 as head of the People's Democratic Party, the former Communist Party that had changed its name after the aborted coup attempt against Soviet President Mikhail Gorbachev in August 1991. He received 86 percent of the vote, defeating well known poet Mohammed Salih of the Erk (Freedom) Democratic Party, with 12 percent. The largest opposition group, the nationalist Birlik (Unity), was barred from registering as a party, and the Islamic Renaissance Party (IRP) was banned entirely, as was the Islamic Adolat group.

In December 1992 a new constitution was adopted that called for 1994 elections for a new, 250-member legislature, the *Ulu Majlis*. Though nominally enshrining a multiparty system, the document contains several undemocratic provisions that curtail political rights and civil liberties.

Through much of 1993 it appeared that the regime was obsessed with curtailing all opposition and dissent. Abdumannob Pulatov, a founder of Birlik, went on trial for "insulting the honor and dignity of Uzbekistan's president." He had been abducted a month earlier while attending a conference on human rights in neighboring Kyrgyzstan. Seven other Birlik members were already in custody and awaiting trial on trumped-up criminal charges. Pulatov was ultimately sentenced to three years' imprisonment, but the sentence was automatically commuted under a September 1992 amnesty still in force and he emigrated to the United States. The Erk Party was evicted from its Tashkent headquarters. Six members of the *Melli Majlis* (alternative parliament) were tried and convicted, though all were subsequently amnestied.

Repression continued in 1994. In May, in a case reminiscent of the Pulatov incident in 1993, Uzbek security forces crossed the border into Kazakhstan in an attempt to detain activists attending a conference sponsored by the Union of Councils for Soviet Jews. Four Uzbek security officers were ultimately deported. In June, authorities arrested two opposition activists—Vasilya Inoyatova, leader of Birlik, and Diloram Iskhakova of Erk—before they were to meet with Sen. Arlen Specter (R-PA) in Tashkent. President Karimov later told the senator during a seventy-five-minute meeting: "These two women are not so important to take up our time." Similar detentions occurred in 1993 during visits by former national security advisor Zbigniew Brzezinski and Deputy Secretary of State Strobe Talbott.

In September, Inoyatova was arrested and charged under Article 60 of the Uzbek criminal code, "anti-state activities," after police allegedly found two sacks of the newspaper *Erk*, also banned, in her apartment.

On 25 December voters went to the polls to elect a new 250-seat national legislature in the first post-Soviet parliamentary elections. The Democratic Party won 179 seats. Of these, 55 were directly elected and 124 were Democratic Party members elected on regional tickets. Nominally nonparty, progovernment legislators gained 20 seats and the pro-business, government-sanctioned Fatherland Progress Party gained 6. The remaining seats will be decided in 1995 elections.

In economic issues, the government introduced a new national currency, the som, in July, though it had no support from the International Monetary Fund (IMF) or other international backing. Despite a 1993 commitment to economic liberalization, a command system was still in place in 1994, with state enterprises still borrowing money from the government at significant negative interest rates. There has been only little foreign investment and few joint ventures, despite the country's potential agricultural and mineral wealth. Inflation in 1994 was 270 percent, down from 1,100 percent the year before. Average Uzbeks, beset by high prices, had to struggle, while old-style bureaucracy and widespread corruption stifled even small-scale private enterprise.

A key environmental issue continued to be the shrinking Aral Sea, depleted by Soviet-era irrigation schemes. As a result, drinking water in the so-called Oxus delta is a brew of pesticides, defoliants, fertilizer and raw sewage that has caused major health problems.

Political Rights and Civil Liberties: Uzbekistan is a *de facto* one-party state dominated by the former Communists, who have put severe restrictions on political opposition.

The 1992 constitution, while enshrining pluralism and a multiparty system, contains articles that undermine democratic rights. Article 62 forbids "organized activities leading to the perpetration of particularly serious state crimes and participation in anti-government organization." The judiciary is subservient to the regime, the president appointing all judges with no mechanisms to ensure their independence. The penal code contains many statutes intended to limit free expression and association. Article 60 bans "anti-state activities," Article 191 makes it a crime to defame the president, and Article 204, aimed at "malicious delinquency," has been used to stifle opposition activity.

The government continued to crack down on the opposition through a series of arrests, trials and detentions, most notably the September indictment of Birlik leader Inoyatova under Article 60.

The press faces government censorship. All nongovernment newspapers are banned.

Government-owned television and radio offer little information; the only television is in Russian, and the government has restricted broadcasts to the evenings. The Moscow newspaper *Izvestia*, which used to sell 160,000 copies in Uzbekistan, has been banned. Foreign journalists have been harassed. A local employee of the BBC was threatened by the KGB's successor organization after investigating the Uzbek government's role in the current conflict in Afghanistan. In July, a local employee for Reuters was beaten by two unidentified thugs after meeting with an opposition leader.

Freedom of religion is nominally respected in this largely Sunni Muslim nation, but the government controls the Muslim Religious Board. Because President Karimov fears Islamic fundamentalism, he has made concessions to Muslims. Although Samarkand's 20,000 Jews faced little overt persecution, many have left for Israel. German Lutherans, concentrated in Tashkent, have complained about the failure of the government to return properties confiscated under Stalin.

Freedom of movement is also curtailed. Political activists have had their exist visas or passports withheld arbitrarily. Uzbek security officers allegedly tried to kidnap Uzbek opposition figures attending a human rights conference in Kazakhstan in May.

Women are underrepresented in high-level positions throughout society. Islamic traditions also undermine the rights of women. Trade unions are legal, but their overall structure has been retained from the Soviet era and there are no independent unions.

Vanuatu

Polity: Parliamentary democracy
Economy: Capitalist-statist
Population: 170,000
PPP: $1,679
Life Expectancy: 65.0
Ethnic Groups: Indigenous Melanesian (90 percent), French, English, Vietnamese, Chinese, and other Pacific Islanders
Ratings Change: *Vanuatu's civil liberties rating changed from 2 to 3 because of some government interference with expression and labor association.

Political Rights: 1
Civil Liberties: 3*
Status: Free

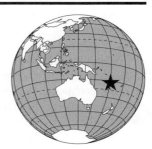

Overview:　　Located in the Western Pacific Ocean, this 800-mile-long archipelago of some eighty islands, formerly called the New Hebrides, was an Anglo-French condominium until receiving independence in July 1980. The condominium arrangement divided the islands into English and French speaking communities, creating rifts that continue today. The francophones were largely excluded from key posts in the first post-independence government, led by Prime Minister Father Walter Lini's anglophone, center-left Party of Our Land (VP). A number of islands initially faced brief secessionist movements. The independence constitution vests executive power in a prime minister chosen by and from a unicameral parliament. The forty-six member parliament is directly elected for a four-year term. A largely ceremonial president is elected for a five-year term by an electoral college consisting of the parliament and the presidents of the ten island-based Regional Councils.

Lini's VP won subsequent elections in 1983 and 1987. In May 1988 an antigovernment demonstration called by Cabinet Minister Barak Sope turned into a riot. Lini responded by throwing Sope out of the party and parliament. In December President Ati George Sokomanu, Sope's uncle, called for the support of the armed forces in order to dissolve parliament and replace it with an interim administration headed by Sope and opposition leader Maxime Carlot. All three were arrested and convicted on sedition charges. In April 1989 an appeals tribunal dismissed their sentences.

In August 1991 the VP dumped Lini as its leader for allegedly running the party in an autocratic manner, and in September parliament replaced him as premier with Donald Kalpokas. At the December 1991 elections Carlot's francophone Union of Moderate Parties (UMP) won 19 seats; the VP, 12; Lini's new National United Party (NUP), 10; Sope's new Melanesian Progressive Party, 4; the tiny Fren Melanesian Party, 1. Lini and Carlot shunted aside traditional Anglo-French animosities and joined their parties in a governing alliance. Carlot beat out Kalpokas in a parliamentary vote to become the country's first francophone prime minister.

The coalition began unraveling in August 1993 when Carlot reshuffled the cabinet and refused to give Lini a post. Lini announced that the NUP would no longer support Carlot, but four MPs broke ranks and in October formed a new coalition with the UMP. In May 1994 the four dissident members of the NUP formed the People's Democratic Party (PDP), led by deputy prime minister Sethy Regenvanu. The PDP formally entered Carlot's government, giving it a three-seat majority.

In June the government placed restrictions on log exports in response to concerns that foreign logging companies were felling trees at an unsustainable rate, and canceled the licenses of four companies. Landowners on the timber rich island of Erromango denounced the ban, which figured to be a prominent issue in the parliamentary elections due by December 1995.

On 2 March the opposition VP voted with the government to elect Jean-Marie Leye, former vice president of the UMP, as Vanuatu's third president.

Political Rights and Civil Liberties:

Citizens of Vanuatu can change their government democratically at the national and local levels.

A key problem in recent years has been government influence over the media. Critics charge that Carlot's government instructs the state-run Radio Vanuatu to limit or delay coverage of opposition events and statements. The country's only independent private newspaper, *Vanuascope*, a bilingual weekly, closed in late January 1994 for financial reasons after eleven months. It had suffered from a government ban of August 1993. The government-owned *Vanuatu Weekly* reportedly must submit its articles to the prime minister's office for approval before publication.

The judiciary is independent, and citizens receive fair trials. Freedom of religion is respected in practice. Citizens have full freedom of movement internally and are free to travel abroad. By tradition women generally occupy a subservient position in society. Domestic violence is reportedly common, although women generally refrain from bringing such cases to court.

In June 1993 the government notified six middle-level civil servants in the Finance

Ministry that they were being dismissed "on political grounds," according to a copy of the dismissal letter obtained by *Pacific Islands Monthly*. The Carlot government has set a precedent by politicizing the civil service at the middle level. The country's five unions are all independent and belong to the Vanuatu Trade Union Congress. Unions must obtain governmental permission to affiliate with international labor federations. Strikes are legal, but the Carlot government has a record of interfering with labor actions. Police briefly arrested twenty striking members of the Public Service Association (PSA) in December 1993 during a protest outside parliament. In February 1994 the government suspended 179 teachers for striking in support of the PSA.

⬇Venezuela

Polity: Presidential-legislative democracy
Economy: Capitalist-statist
Population: 21,328,000
PPP: $8,120
Life Expectancy: 70.1
Ethnic Groups: Mestizo (69 percent), White (Spanish, Portuguese, Italian, 20 percent), Black (9 percent), Indian (2 percent)
Trend Arrow: The down trend arrow is a result of the government's authoritarian tendencies manifest in the suspension of certain fundamental civil liberties.

Political Rights: 3
Civil Liberties: 3
Status: Partly Free

Overview: In 1994 President Rafael Caldera, an aging populist, responded to economic crisis with statist measures and the suspension of certain fundamental civil liberties. Amid an escalating crime wave, social unrest, and saber-rattling within the military, Venezuela remained one of the most volatile countries in Latin America.

The Republic of Venezuela was established in 1830, nine years after gaining independence from Spain. Long periods of political instability and military rule culminated with the overthrow of the Gen. Marcos Perez Jimenez regime in 1958. The election of President Romulo Betancourt and the promulgation of a new constitution in 1961 established a formal democracy.

The 1961 constitution created a federal system now consisting of twenty-one states and the federal district of Caracas. The president and a bicameral Congress are elected for five years. The Senate has at least two members from each of the states and from the federal district. All former presidents are senators-for-life. There are currently 189 seats in the Chamber of Deputies. State governments and municipal councils are elected.

Until 1993 politics was dominated by the social democratic Democratic Action (AD) party and the Christian Social Party (COPEI). Former president Carlos Andres Perez (1989-93) of the AD enacted an economic austerity program that led to violent street protests in 1989, remembered as the *caracazo*, that left hundreds dead.

By 1991 Perez's government was plagued by drug and corruption scandals, labor strikes and violent student demonstrations. In February 1992 Perez was nearly overthrown by nationalist military officers. Support for the rebels and their anti-corruption rhetoric was evident in mass demonstrations and labor and student strikes. In November 1992 air force and navy units made a second attempt to oust the government but were put down by the army. This time most Venezuelans ignored the rebel calls for a popular insurrection and looked to the elections in 1993.

In 1993 Perez was charged with corruption and suspended from office by the Congress, which then chose Senator Ramon J. Velasquez as interim president. Months later, Congress voted to remove Perez permanently.

The seventy-eight-year-old Caldera was the front-runner from the outset of the 1993 campaign. A COPEI founder and former president (1969-74), Caldera had led the calls for Perez's removal and had a reputation for honesty amid Venezuela's corruption-ridden political system. He broke from COPEI and sounded populist themes, blaming Perez's market reforms for declining wages and increasing poverty.

Caldera's main rival in a field of seventeen appeared to be Andres Velasquez, a labor leader and state governor from the leftist Radical Cause party. The AD nominated former Caracas mayor Claudio Fermin and COPEI nominated Oswaldo Alvarez Paz. With Caldera and Velasquez leading in the polls, rumors of a coup were rife. It was feared the 80,000-member armed forces would not accept a victory by Velasquez, a leftist, or by Caldera, whose sixteen-party National Convergence included Communists and other leftists, as well as right-wing groups.

Caldera was first past the post on 5 December 1993 with a mere 31 percent of the vote. Initial returns showed Velasquez second, but after more counting Velasquez tumbled to fourth, behind Fermin and Alvarez Paz. Caldera and Velasquez charged the electoral commission, still dominated by AD and COPEI, with fraud. The allegation was that numbers were changed to alter the outcome of the congressional balloting at the expense of Radical Cause and the National Convergence.

Caldera took office on 2 February 1994 amid a corruption-rooted banking collapse that precipitated a multibillion-dollar government bailout. That, coupled with high inflation and a gaping budget deficit, led to a recession. Caldera imposed statist controls to stabilize the economy but succeeded mostly in cutting the flow of foreign investment.

Caldera, faced with a Congress fragmented among AD, COPEI and a crowd of leftist, populist and independent newcomers, had proposed a constitutional amendment that would allow him to dissolve Congress "when it does not carry out the will of the people." In mid-1994, with mounting social unrest and criticism by the media, Caldera settled for suspending certain constitutional guarantees regarding arbitrary arrest, property rights and freedom of expression, movement and financial activity. The government hinted that the ensuing wave of arrests had been necessary to foil a "subversive plot."

However, the measures failed to quell escalating violent crime and social unrest and did not dampen media warnings of a "social explosion." In November, troops were deployed in urban areas in an attempt to restore public security.

Meanwhile, Hugo Chavez, an ardent Rambo-style nationalist and former colonel who led the first 1992 coup attempt, continued touring the country to preach social revolution to receptive audiences and warn of a "right-wing conspiracy." The government was clearly rattled when Chavez was embraced by Fidel Castro in Havana in December. With renewed saber-rattling in the middle echlelons of the military, possibly by Chavez sympathizers,

Caldera felt compelled to publicly warn against the politicization of the armed forces. As the end of the year approached Venezuelans braced for further tumult in 1995.

Political Rights and Civil Liberties:

Citizens are able to change their government through elections at the national, state, and local level. However, Venezuela's institutions have been severely eroded by decades of corruption and drug-trade penetration and badly damaged by the two coup attempts in 1992. Trust in the political system has been in steep decline since the 1980s. Voter abstention reached 40 percent in 1993, the highest since the establishment of elected government, and there was evidence of electoral tampering at the congressional level by the country's two traditional parties that still dominated the electoral commission.

One small step in 1993 toward greater accountability in Congress: voters directly elected half the members of the Chamber of Deputies. The other half were still chosen by proportional voting, with party leaders selecting who would fill the seats.

Constitutional guarantees regarding freedom of religion and the right to organize political parties, civic organizations and labor unions are generally respected. However, political expression and civil liberties are threatened by official antagonism toward the media and were undermined in 1994 by the suspension of constitutional guarantees regarding arbitrary arrest, property rights and freedom of expression, movement and financial activity. Moreover, 1994 saw stepped-up repressive measures taken by security forces against popular protests and labor strikes. Citizen security in general was threatened by a drug-fueled crime wave that resulted in an average of two hundred killings per month in the capital of Caracas alone.

In 1994 Venezuelan human rights organizations reported an increase in arbitrary detention and torture of suspects, as well as dozens of extra-judicial killings by military security forces and the notoriously corrupt police. Criminal suspects, particularly in poor areas, are subject to torture. Indigeneous communities trying to defend their legal land rights are subject to abuses, including killings, by goldminers and corrupt rural police. Since the 1992 coup attempts, weakened civilian governments have had less authority over the military and the police, and rights abuses overall are committed with impunity. In 1994 there was in increase in harassment of rights activists.

The judicial system is headed by a Supreme Court and is nominally independent. However, it is highly politicized and undermined by the chronic corruption that permeates the entire political system. It is slow, ineffective and generally unresponsive to charges of rights abuses by police and security forces. The judiciary is further undermined by drug-related corruption, with growing evidence of bribery and intimidation of judges.

Only about a third of the prison population totaling more than 25,000 has been convicted of a crime. The prisons are severely overcrowded and rife with drugs, while violence, which led to more than 500 prisoner deaths in 1994, is nearly out of control.

A separate system of military courts has jurisdiction over members of the military accused of human rights violations and common criminal acts. Military court decisions cannot be appealed in civilian courts. The result is that the military is rarely held accountable and most citizens view it as above the law.

The press is privately owned. There are nearly a dozen daily newspapers. Radio and television are mostly private, supervised by an association of broadcasters under the government communications ministry. Censorship of the press and broadcasting media occurs during states of emergency. The practice of journalism is also restricted by a licensing law and threatened by government control of foreign exchange required to purchase newsprint and other supplies.

In 1994 the media in general faced a pattern of intimidation. Government officials, including the president, and the military frequently leveled verbal attacks at the media, and the Congress passed a series of restrictive laws involving the right of reply and journalistic conduct. A number of journalists were subject to arbitrary arrest and interrogation.

Labor unions are well organized but highly politicized and prone to corruption. A new labor law in 1991 reduced the work week from 48 to 44 hours and made it illegal for employers to dismiss workers without compensation. However, the law is often disregarded. Numerous trade unionists were detained during strikes broken up by security forces in 1994.

↑ Vietnam

Polity: Communist one-party
Economy: Statist
Population: 73,104,000
PPP: $1,250
Life Expectancy: 63.4
Ethnic Groups: Predominantly Vietnamese, with Chinese, Khmer, and other minorities
Trend Arrow: The up trend arrow is due to a trend towards more private enterprise.

Political Rights: 7
Civil Liberties: 7
Status: Not Free

Overview: In 1994 the Vietnam Communist Party (VCP) continued to follow the Chinese model of hardline authoritarianism and free market reforms. However, in January the party promoted several old-guard Marxists to the Politburo, indicating that like their Chinese counterparts many Vietnamese leaders fear that opening the economy too fast will erode the VCP's power.

The French colonized Vietnam's three historic regions of Tonkin, Annam and Cochin-China between 1862 and 1884. During World War II a resistance movement led by Ho Chi Minh fought the occupying Japanese and later battled the returning French. The country won independence in 1954, and was divided between a Communist government in the north and a French-installed one in the south. Planned free elections to reunify the country were never held. Military forces and insurgent groups from the North defeated the French and then the United States, eventually overtook the South and reunited the country in 1976 as the Socialist Republic of Vietnam.

As the nation struggled with mounting poverty, the Sixth VCP Party Congress in 1986 began a program of *doi moi* (renovation), which has decentralized economic decision-making, encouraged small-scale private enterprises and largely dismantled agricultural collectivization. At its Seventh Party Congress in June 1991 the VCP named Do Moi as new party chairman, and in August the rubber-stamp National Assembly named veteran revolutionary fighter turned economic reformer Vo Van Kiet as Prime Minister.

In April 1992 the National Assembly approved a new constitution that codified many of the economic reforms. However, it maintained the VCP as the sole legal political party and the "leading force of the state and society," and kept the party-controlled "People's Committees" which supervise daily life at the village level. It also scrapped the collective Council of State in favor of a president, to be elected by and from within the National Assembly.

In July 1992 the country held elections for the 395-seat National Assembly. Although the new constitution allowed anyone over twenty-one to run as an independent, only two candidates out of some forty hopefuls managed to be accepted, both of whom lost their races. The government disqualified many other independents for late or incorrect forms, and neighborhood and workplace units rejected the rest. Numerous deputies of the older generation of revolutionary leaders were defeated by relatively young technocrats with university degrees. In late September the Assembly elected General Le Duc Anh as president, and re-elected Vo Van Kiet as prime minister.

In 1993 the government continued to face significant grassroots opposition from supporters of the independent Unified Buddhist Church (UBC), which the authorities banned in 1981 in favor of the official Vietnam Buddhist Church. On 24 May six monks in the central city of Hue staged a peaceful demonstration in support of Thich Tri Tuu, Superior Monk at the Linh Mu Pagoda, whom police were interrogating concerning a Buddhist layman's self-immolation three days earlier. Crowds supporting the monks blocked traffic for hours and overturned and burned an official vehicle in one of the largest anti-government disturbances in Vietnam since 1975. On 16 November a Hue court sentenced Thich Tri Tuu and three other monks to prison terms of three and four years at the end of a closed, one-day trial on charges of inciting disturbances.

The government's crackdown on the UBC continued in November 1994 as security police in Ho Chi Minh City blocked a church-sponsored humanitarian mission to the Mekong Delta, where flooding had killed 300 people and left 500,000 homeless. The authorities arrested at least five of the convoy's organizers. On 29 December police arrested Thich Huyen Quang, the Patriarch of the UBC, who had been under house arrest since February 1982, and took over his Hoi Phuoc Pagoda in Hue. On 31 December police raided the Ho Chi Minh City pagoda of Thich Quang Do, the UBC's Secretary General.

The year's key political event occurred in late January 1994 at the VCP's mid-term party conference, where the central committee drafted four new members into an expanded seventeen-member Politburo. Three of the new members, including Nguyen Ha Phan, director of the party's economic commission, reportedly are hardliners opposed to accelerating the economic reforms. Many VCP members fear that the market reforms will erode the party's power, and the changes will likely weaken the influence of Politburo members seeking faster reforms. In another development, on 3 February 1994 the United States lifted its nineteen-year-old economic embargo on Vietnam. Officials in Hanoi downplayed the announcement, saying full diplomatic ties and Most Favored Nation trade status are needed before the country can reap the full benefits of trade with the U.S.

As a result of economic reforms, the country is now the world's third-largest rice exporter. However, rural areas remain desperately poor and once-eradicated diseases are returning. Vietnam's economic development has been highly uneven. In Ho Chi Minh City and Hanoi, the two largest cities, per capita income is estimated at $500 or greater, while in the rural areas the figure is estimated at $200 or less.

Political Rights and Civil Liberties: Vietnamese citizens lack the democratic means to change their government. The ruling VCP is the only legal party. All policy decisions are ultimately made by the VCP's newly expanded seventeen–member Politburo. The VCP is the dominant member of the Fatherland Front, an umbrella organization of state–sponsored groups including peasant associations and official religious bodies.

In recent years the government has relaxed its monitoring of the population carried out through mass organizations attached to villages, city districts, schools and work units. The government still conducts surveillance through mandatory household registration, VCP–appointed block wardens, and a network of informants. Ordinary citizens have greater latitude in criticizing government corruption and inefficiency. However, questioning the one–party system or the government's commitment to socialism is illegal. Party Directive 135 criminalizes inciting opposition to the government or advocating multipartyism.

Estimates of the number of political detainees and prisoners, including many who are sent to "re–education" camps, run into the thousands. Persons released from re–education camps generally wait at least a year to regain citizenship rights and they and members of their families are barred from government employment, placing them at a disadvantage in gaining housing and other benefits provided to state workers.

In November 1990 police detained academic Doan Viet Hoat and other intellectuals for circulating a newsletter, *Freedom Forum,* that advocated peaceful political change. In March 1993 a court sentenced Dr. Hoat to twenty years imprisonment, subsequently reduced to fifteen years. In November 1993 foreign diplomats reported that the government had subjected the country's most famous political prisoner, Nguyen Dan Que, an endocrinologist, to hard labor. Dr. Nguyen has spent most of the past fifteen years in jail for criticizing the government and attempting to form a democracy movement. The government released several other political prisoners in 1994.

Police and security forces are responsible for arbitrary arrests and detentions. The authorities routinely ignore legal safeguards regarding detention, including the right to have a lawyer present during interrogation and limits on how long a suspect may be held without charge. Detainees are frequently held incommunicado.

Trials are conducted without procedural safeguards, and the judiciary is subservient to the government. The legal system is rudimentary. Some 30–40 percent of judges and lawyers lack a law degree or any professional training, and commercial and civil law codes are still being drafted. The criminal code authorizes the death penalty for fraud and bribery. Prison sentences are often handed down administratively without a trial. Prisoners face brutal conditions, and food and health-care are often denied as a punishment.

The government controls all domestic media, which reflect state views. However, many Western publications are freely available. The government permits NGOs to form but they must serve strictly nonpolitical purposes. Freedom of assembly is heavily restricted.

The government sharply restricts religious freedom. Ordinary worshippers are generally not harassed, but leading figures of all faiths have been detained and arrested on political grounds. According to the Washington–based Puebla Institute, since May 1992 police have arrested more than 300 Buddhist monks and lay persons. Major Buddhist temples are under surveillance. On 28 May 1994 Thich Hue Thau, a monk in the Mekong River Delta village of Ba Cang, committed self–immolation after authorities ordered him to demolish his temple. Since 1981 the independent Unified Buddhist Church has been driven underground, and in December 1994 police arrested its leader, Thich Huyen Quang (*See Overview above*).

The government has attempted to place Catholic religious affairs under the control of the official Catholic Patriotic Association. The government must approve all seminary students and occasionally prevents Catholic clergy from being ordained after they finish training, causing a shortage of priests. In 1994 the government announced it would exercise veto power over Vatican appointments of bishops. The southern–based Cao Dai religious movement, with 2.5 million followers, has not yet been allowed to open a seminary. In the central highlands, dozens of Protestant clergy of the Montagnard minority group have been detained for performing unauthorized religious services. Foreign clergy are not permitted to take up long term residence. Officially, VCP members may not adhere to a religion.

More than 60,000 former refugees have been repatriated since March 1989. The government is allowing the United Nations High Commissioner for Refugees to conduct long–term monitoring of the repatriation process to ensure that the authorities do not pursue legal action or otherwise discriminate against returnees. Of the 58,000 Vietnamese refugees remaining in camps in Hong Kong, Thailand and elsewhere, at least 50,000 are expected to be repatriated, the remainder to receive formal refugee status and be resettled abroad. Citizens generally need permission to relocate internally, and travel abroad is restricted.

In July an Australian parliamentary delegation canceled a trip to Vietnam after the government denied a visa to a member who told the BBC the group would be investigating human rights. In October the government permitted a visit by the U.N. Human Rights Commission's Working Group on Torture.

In June the National Assembly drafted a Labor Code providing some workers with the right to strike, but prohibiting strikes at state enterprises and in private industries considered essential to national security or economic welfare. Foreign managers frequently pay employees less than the minimum wage, provide poor working conditions and occasionally physically abuse workers.

Western Samoa

Polity: Parliamentary democ-
racy and family heads
Economy: Capitalist
Population: 212,000
PPP: $1,869
Life Expectancy: 66.0
Ethnic Groups: Samoan (88 percent), mixed race (10
percent), Europeans, other Pacific Islanders

Political Rights: 2
Civil Liberties: 2
Status: Free

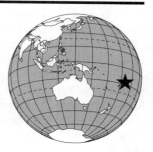

Overview:
Located 1,600 miles northeast of New Zealand, the western
Samoan islands became a German protectorate in 1899.
New Zealand claimed the islands during World War I and
administered them until granting independence in 1962. The 1960 constitution
provides for a head of state who must approve all bills passed by the *Fono Aoao
Faitulafono* (parliament). Malietoa Tanumafali, one of several paramount island
chiefs, is head of state for life, although his successors will be elected by the Fono
for five-year terms.

In an October 1990 referendum, 53 percent approved universal suffrage in
future Fono elections for all citizens over twenty-one. The Washington-based
Pacific Report newsletter noted that, due to low participation rates, only 22.9
percent of eligible voters actually approved the measure. Previously only the
25,000 *matai*, essentially family heads, could vote. However, forty-five of the
forty-seven seats in the Fono can be held only by the matai, the remaining two
seats being set aside for citizens of non-Samoan descent. In the same referendum
voters rejected the creation of an upper house both restricted to and selected by the
matai. The Fono sits for a five-year term.

Roughly 90 percent of the electorate turned out for the country's first direct
elections on 5 April 1991, held several weeks later than planned because of
difficulties in registering approximately 80,000 newly franchised voters. Several
elected MPs switched party affiliations following the vote, and when the new
parliament convened in May the ruling Human Rights Protection Party (HRPP) had
30 seats; the opposition Samoan National Development Party, 14; independents, 3.
The parliament re-elected Tofilau Eti Alesana as prime minister.

Hurricanes in 1991 and 1992 wiped out the country's copra and coconut oil
exports, sending foreign exchange reserves plummeting. In 1993 the HRPP faced
criticism that it was not extending piped water, electricity and other services
throughout the country fast enough, and over a 10 percent Goods and Services Tax
(GST) that was passed in March. The HRPP suffered a split in its ranks after three
MPs on the Public Accounts Commission recommended budget cuts with which
the prime minister disagreed. In June Tofilau expelled the three from the party,
leaving the HRPP with a three-seat majority.

Economic matters dominated politics in 1994. In March protesters in Apia, the
capital, held three weeks of demonstrations against the GST. In July Chief Auditor
Su'a Rimoni Ah Chong declared the state-owned Polynesian Airlines to be

insolvent, and criticized the government for having provided public funds to bail out the debt-ridden company. Ah Chong also accused several cabinet members of financial irregularities and corruption. Prime Minister Tofilau ordered an independent inquiry into Ah Chong's findings, and promised to resign if the findings of the inquiry went against him.

Political Rights and Civil Liberties:

Western Samoans can change their government democratically. Although two competing parties exist, political affiliations are generally formed through individual loyalties rather than ideology.

The independent judiciary is modeled on the British system and affords defendants fair trials. However, many disputes are simply handled at the local level by the 362 village *fonos* (councils of tribal chieftains) through traditional law. The 1990 Village Fono Law affirmed this authority but gave parties in certain cases recourse to the Lands and Titles Courts, and the right of direct appeal to the Supreme Court. Fonos occasionally order harsh punishments, including the burning of houses and expuslion of people from villages.

The government passed two laws in February 1993 that journalists said restrict press freedom. The Newspapers and Printers Act requires journalists to reveal their sources in libel cases or face a $2,000 fine and three-month prison sentence. The Defamation Act forbids journalists from publishing defamatory statements made in court that refer to a person not involved in the proceedings. It also requires editors to publish an apology when a member of a group that has been criticized in print requests it. There are several private newspapers and a private radio station.

There are no restrictions on freedoms of assembly and association. Although the government grants full religious freedom in this predominantly Christian country, village leaders often choose the religion of their followers. There is generally full freedom of movement internally, except for those banished from a village, and the right to travel abroad is guaranteed in practice. Wife-beating occurs fairly frequently.

Workers can join independent unions, engage in collective bargaining, and hold strikes. The only private sector union formed so far, the 800-strong Yakazi Employees Association, has yet to be recognized by management, the Japanese-owned Yakazi Samoa company. In January 1993 the Association held a brief strike to demand recognition and higher pay. Prime Minister Tofilau urged the employees to end the strike, since Yakazi, the country's biggest employer, accounts for 80 percent of export income.

Yemen

Polity: Dominant coalition (military-influenced)
Economy: Capitalist-statist
Population: 12,920,000
PPP: $1,374
Life Expectancy: 51.9
Ethnic Groups: Arab majority, African and Asian minorities
Ratings Change: *Yemen's political rights rating changed from 4 to 5 and its civil liberties rating from 5 to 6 because of civil war. As a result Yemen's status changed from Parlty Free to Not Free.

Political Rights: 5*
Civil Liberties: 6*
Status: Not Free

Overview:

The power struggle between Yemeni President Ali Abdallah Salih and Vice President Ali Salim al-Biedh, which had been festering since the May 1990 unification of North Yemen and South Yemen, erupted in April 1994 into a seventy-day civil war that ended with northern troops crushing the southern separatist movement.

Located at the southern end of the Arabian Peninsula, Yemen was formed on 22 May 1990 through the merger of the conservative, northern Yemen Arab Republic (YAR) and the Marxist, southern People's Democratic Republic of Yemen (PDRY). The two countries had never been an independent, unified entity and had fought short wars in 1972, 1979 and 1988.

In a May 1991 referendum, voters approved a new constitution that provided for a Presidential Council, composed of a president, vice president and three other officials, with broad executive powers. Under arrangements made prior to unification, the YAR's Ali Abdallah Salih became president and the DPRY's Ali Salim al-Biedh vice president pending elections scheduled for November 1992. The constitution also established a 301-seat House of Representatives, which elects the Presidential Council.

Tensions immediately emerged between the coalition partners, owing to prior political differences as well as centuries-old tribal and regional animosities. In 1992 assassination attempts were made on the prime minister, the justice minister and the speaker of parliament, and by year's end at least 120 members of the DPRY's former ruling party, the Yemeni Socialist Party (YSP), had been killed since unification. Meanwhile Sheik Abdallah Hussein al-Ahmar, the head of the powerful Hasheed tribal confederation in the north, demanded that the country be placed under Islamic law. In November the joint leadership postponed parliamentary elections until 27 April 1993. Anti-government riots in several cities in December 1992 left more than 100 people dead.

The election campaign centered on the economy. During the Gulf War Yemen had refused to join the U.S.-led coalition that drove Iraq out of Kuwait, and in retaliation Saudi Arabia expelled some 850,000 Yemeni workers and, along with several other countries, cut off aid. Overall, the country lost more than $2 billion per year, inflation soared to more than 100 percent and unemployment rose to 36 percent.

On election day some 3,700 candidates and forty parties contested the 301 parliamentary seats. Although nearly three-quarters of these candidates professed to be independent, many were quietly backed by the two ruling parties. Some 80 percent of the electorate participated, and results gave the General People's Congress (GPC) of the former YAR 121 seats; al-Ahmar's fundamentalist, Hasheed-based *Islah* (Reform), 62; the YSP, 56; minor parties, 12; independents, 47; with three seats vacant. The GPC entered into a tripartite coalition with its ally Islah and the YSP. Parliament elected Salih and al-Biedh as president and vice president, respectively, and named al-Ahmar as speaker of the assembly.

In the summer al-Biedh, frustrated by the YSP's relatively poor showing, proposed a "federal system" that would grant the south autonomy. With the centralization of power in the northern leadership, al-Biedh feared a loss of control over oil revenue from southern Hadramaut Province, and remained wary of Islah's fundamentalist agenda. On 19 August al-Biedh announced he would remain in Aden, the southern capital, rather than travel to Sana'a, the national capital, until his demands were met.

On 20 February 1994 Salih, al-Biedh, and parliamentary speaker al-Ahmar signed a Document of Accord and Agreement pledging to define executive power, fully merge the armed forces of the two former countries, and decentralize administration. However the accord would have reduced the two leaders' military and administrative authority, and implementation remained doubtful.

As tensions rose, in late February the two armies began several weeks of skirmishes. On 27 April a major tank battle in the northern city of Amran marked the beginning of full-scale conflict. On 4 May another fierce battle took place near the northern city of Dhamar, and a day later Salih declared a state of emergency and dismissed al-Biedh and other southerners from the Presidential Council and cabinet.

On 21 May a group of former DPRY officials declared the Democratic Republic of Yemen in the south, and the next day elected al-Biedh to head a five-man presidential council. By 1 June northern troops had advanced to within ten miles of Aden. On 4 July northern troops captured the southeastern city of Mukallah, the capital of Hadramaut Province, and on 7 July ended the war by capturing Aden. By then al-Biedh and much of the separatist leadership had fled to Oman and Djibouti.

In early October Salih named Abdul Aziz Abdul Ghani as prime minister and asked him to form a new government. In early December Salih appealed to southerners who had fled abroad to return. However by year's end the southern leadership remained in exile.

Political Rights and Civil Liberties: Citizens of Yemen changed their government in April 1993 in elections in which the ruling parties had significant advantages. An International Republican Institute monitoring team called the vote generally free but noted several factors compromising its fairness, including: media coverage favoring the ruling parties; irregularities in the voter registration process; the government's requirement that, in a population 80 percent illiterate voters write their choice on the ballot; and a law prohibiting the 23,000 election commission workers and some 50,000 military and security personnel from voting. The central government lacks full authority over some northern and eastern areas, where tribal leaders wield considerable influence.

The 1994 civil war and its aftermath caused a deterioration in the country's human rights situation. During the war the government indiscriminately shelled Aden, the southern capital, and both sides attacked villages. Separatist forces launched Scud missile attacks on northern cities, and attacked government troops close to a camp housing Somali refugees, near the southern town of al-Kawd, killing more than twenty refugees. According to Human Rights Watch/Middle East, fighting during the seventy-day war killed roughly 1,500 soldiers and civilians and wounded 6,000 others.

During the civil war the security forces of both sides arbitrarily detained hundreds of civilians without regard to due process rights. Following the war, militants from the Islah party took over numerous police stations in Aden and other southern cities, and joined with security officials in randomly searching homes in Aden. Islah supporters also flogged citizens in Aden for drinking alcohol. In July fundamentalists ransacked a Catholic church in Aden used by expatriates.

Prior to the war the security agencies of the two former countries had been merged into the new Political Security Organization, which continues to carry out arbitrary arrests and detentions, search homes and offices without warrants, and monitor personal communications. Some 200-300 persons who disappeared in the former DPRY remain unaccounted for.

Security forces torture detainees to extract confessions and information. Prison conditions are generally abysmal. According to the U.S. State Department, there are upwards of 4,000 persons held in prison without any documentation as to the reason for their incarceration. The Islah party, elements of the two former security services, and several government ministries reportedly run private prisons outside of the judicial system. Since early 1992 more than 200 foreigners have been briefly kidnapped in the north by tribal groups seeking government concessions or compensatory payments by foreign oil companies.

The judiciary is subject to interference by the government and well-connected interests, and procedural safeguards are inadequate. The Supreme Court, formed through a merger of the high courts of the two former countries, is reasonably independent but subject to corruption. The lower courts have not been merged. In the former YAR there are Islamic courts and commercial courts, and in the former DPRY there are magistrate courts for most criminal cases and minor civil cases, provincial courts for serious criminal cases and major civil actions, and military courts.

Prior to the war the country had more than 100 newspapers, many of them independent or linked to political groups. The media freely criticized the government on most issues, although it practiced self-censorship on certain sensitive topics. Press freedom declined sharply during and after the war. Many newspapers closed down during the war. After the war the government allowed some independent papers to re-open but appointed editors with ties to the GPC or Islah. In early October the editor of the *Yemen Times* told AFP that the government had ordered independent newspapers to obtain prior authorization to publish or "risk ceasing to appear." Many independent newspapers subsequently shut down. Radio and television stations are state-owned and rarely offer pluralistic views.

The Ministry of Social Security and Social Affairs must register associations, but this power is generally exercised fairly. Police and soldiers have violently dispersed protesters on several occasions. On 23 July northern troops fired on anti-government demonstrators in the southeastern city of Mukallah, reportedly killing several people.

Islam is the state religion. The tiny Jewish population is concentrated in two northern areas, and until 1993 Jews faced some difficulty in emigrating. The government had also occasionally denied foreign Jewish groups access to these communities, although such access now appears to be less restricted. Foreign Christian clergy may not proselytize. Citizens generally travel freely internally and most citizens can travel abroad at will. However, women are occasionally asked to prove that male relatives do not object to their departure.

Citizens with a non-Yemeni parent (known as *muwalladin*), as well as the tiny Akhdam minority, face discrimination in employment opportunities. By tradition women hold a subservient role in society. The family law allows for polygamy, and for a husband to divorce his wife without providing cause, and grants the house and children to the husband in divorce cases. Female genital mutilation is practiced in some areas, and domestic violence is reportedly common.

The labor codes of the two former countries remain in effect pending a new code. Unions are heavily influenced by the government, although strikes do occur. Child labor is prevalent. Yemeni employers sometimes have foreign employees imprisoned for theft at the end of their term of service to avoid paying their salaries and transportation back home.

Yugoslavia (Serbia and Montenegro)

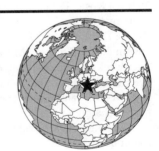

Polity: Dominant party **Political Rights:** 6
Economy: Mixed statist **Civil Liberties:** 6
Population: 6,817,000 **Status:** Not Free
PPP: na
Life Expectancy: na
Ethnic Groups: Serbs (80 percent), Montenegrin (7 percent), Muslim Slavs (Sanjak, 4 percent) Gypsies, Albanians, others

Overview: In 1994, Serbian strongman Slobodan Milosevic remained the dominant political force in rump-Yugoslavia, keeping a tight rein on the opposition, trammeling the independent media, and pressuring militant Bosnian Serbs to accept an international peace plan in an effort to ease two-year-old Western sanctions that hurt the country's economy. Nevertheless, by year's end, four months after Milosevic had closed the border between Bosnia and Serbia, fuel, troops and anti-aircraft systems were crossing the frontier to support a Bosnian Serb offensive.

The reconstituted Federal Republic of Yugoslavia (FRY), formed in 1992, was a Serb-prompted creation to maintain the illusion of a federated state after the secession of

Slovenia, Croatia, Macedonia and Bosnia-Herzegovina left Serbia—with its putatively autonomous provinces of Kosovo and Vojvodina (*see reports in Related Territories section*)—and tiny, impoverished Montenegro as the only republics that had not split from Yugoslavia in 1991-92. Under a constitution accepted by the Serbian and Montenegrin republican assemblies, the FRY was declared a "sovereign federal state based on the principles of equality of its citizens and member republics." The United States, U.N. and most of the international community do not recognize the self-styled state. The new entity faced diplomatic isolation and international economic sanctions because of Serbian aggression in Croatia and Bosnia-Herzegovina, where indigenous nationalist militias, backed by Serb-dominated remnants of the Yugoslav People's Army, launched wars against legitimately elected governments.

FRY's bicameral Federal Assembly (parliament) consists of the 42-member Chamber of Republics (divided evenly between Serbia and Montenegro) and the 138-seat Chamber of Citizens. In the December 1992 elections for the Chamber of Republics, Milosevic's Socialist Party of Serbia (SPS) won 47 seats; the ultra-nationalist Serbian Radical Party (SRS), led by suspected war criminal and paramilitary commander Vojislav Seselj, got 34; and the DEPOS opposition coalition, 20. Milosevic retained the Serbian presidency by defeating U.S. businessman Milan Panic in a fraud-marred vote. In Montenegro, President Momir Bulatovic, first elected in 1990, defeated Branko Kostic, a Milosevic ally, in a January 1993 runoff.

In 1993 Milosevic consolidated his hold on power, purging several leading intellectuals in Belgrade from government institutions, cracking down on the opposition, and moving against Seselj after the SRS-led ouster of FRY President Dobrica Kosic. Police cracked down on antigovernment demonstrations led by the charismatic Vuk Draskovic, head of the opposition Serbian Renewal Movement (SPO); Draskovic was badly beaten, arrested, then released. Zorin Lilac, a former Communist official and Milosevic ally, was elected FRY president. In October, after weeks of an anti-Seselj campaign on state-run television condemning him as a fascist and war criminal, Milosevic dissolved the 250-member Serbian parliament. In November, authorities arrested eighteen leaders of Seselj's Chetnik paramilitary forces, charging them with rape, kidnapping and illegal arms possession.

Although the SPS did not win a parliamentary majority, in 19 December elections Milosevic's position was strengthened. The SPS won 123 seats, 21 more than it had, but three short of a majority. Seselj and the SRS were the big losers, with the party's strength dropping from 73 to 39 seats. Another loser was Zeljko Raznatovic, an accused bank robber and militia leader from Kosovo, known by the *nom de guerre* Arkan. Draskovic's SPO held 46 seats, down from 50.

Nineteen-ninety-four opened with fresh allegations by Bosnian and U.N. officials that Belgrade was employing Yugoslav army forces, including paratroopers, frogmen, and elite airborne brigades, in support of Serb insurgents in Bosnia. Belgrade was also forcing Serb refugees from Bosnia and Croatia to return to their Serb-controlled regions for military service or face prosecution. The effort violated FRY laws, which forbid the mobilization of refugees unless the country is under direct military threat.

In domestic politics, the fragmented and weakened opposition parties declared a parliamentary war in May against Milosevic and the SPS. The alliance included Draskovic's SPO and Seselj's SRS. They were joined by the smaller Democratic Party and the Democratic Party of Serbia. Meanwhile, authorities brought charges against Seselj for provoking a brawl in the federal parliament. In September, he received an eight-month suspended sentence for the incident. Violence in the Serbian parliament was also an issue. In July, plainclothes police fought with opposition deputies after Tomislav Nikolic, a SRS vice president, sharply criticized Milosevic and his wife, Mirjana, a Communist Party leader, ridiculing them for monopolizing state-run television and Serbia's political scene. Opposition deputies announced a boycott to protest the presence of police in parliament, with Draskovic describing the lawmaking body as "a police academy or a torture chamber."

In August, Milosevic abandoned support for his Bosnian Serb proteges, announcing he was cutting off all political and economic ties due to their refusal to accept an international peace plan devised by the so-called "Contact Group"—the U.S., Russia, France, Britain and Germany. The plan would allot 51 percent of Bosnian territory to Bosnian Muslims and Croats, with Bosnian Serbs getting 49 percent though they controlled more than 70 percent. The state-run media changed course as well, labelling their erstwhile allies as criminals and war profiteers. *Politika*, a progovernment daily, compared Bosnian Serb leader Radovan Karadzic, who had published several volumes of poetry, to tyrants like Nero, Goebbels and Mao who "also sought refuge in the arts."

Firmly in control of the government, military, police and media, Milosevic, prompted by his Russian allies anxious to resume what once was a lucrative trade, closed the border with Bosnia to all but food and medical supplies in an effort to prod the U.N. to lift sanctions. Many questioned his sincerity, however, noting that in 1993, when Bosnian Serbs rejected the now defunct Vance-Owen proposal, Milosevic replied by closing bridges over the Drina River dividing Serbia from Bosnia. The closures, however, lasted two weeks. To avoid a repeat, the U.N. insisted that monitors be stationed along the border to verify the embargo. Milosevic countered by insisting on having the final say on the monitors' nationality and mode of deployment. The Russians criticized fellow Contact Group members for "limited flexibility" in their insistence on the deployment of observers before sanctions would be eased.

Bosnian Serbs reacted to the cut-off by proposing a parliamentary unification of all Serbian land. The notion was rejected by most political parties, even those opposed to Milosevic's gambit.

In September, U.N. diplomats announced that Milosevic had accepted a compromise plan for monitoring the trade embargo on Bosnian Serbs, agreeing to a deployment of civilian customs inspectors and similar officials rather than U.N. military personnel. The announcement came as Serbs from Croatia and Bosnia opened a major counteroffensive against the Muslim-held U.N. "safe haven" of Bihac. On 23 September the U.N. Security Council voted 11-2 to wave sanctions on the FRY for 100 days in response to Milosevic's pledge to support the peace plan, halt shipment of war supplies and accept the civilian monitors. The resolution was passed despite reports of war material being ferried into Bosnian Serb territory from Serbia. FRY's representative, Dragomir Djokic, described the easing of sanctions as inadequate and merely a political maneuver. He called for full and permanent lifting of sanctions as the best way to speed the peace process. The SRS called Milosevic's actions a "betrayal" of Bosnian Serbs.

The immediate effect of the U.N. action was t o suspend the ban on direct flights and sporting and cultural exchanges with the FRY. The most draconian sanctions—including the freezing of foreign bank accounts—remained in force and the U.N. maintained the right to reimpose punitive measures if the FRY openly resumed supplying Bosnian Serbs.

In early October, U.N. monitors reported that Belgrade was "meeting its commitment to close the border between the FYR and the areas of Bosnia under the control of Bosnian Serbs." To underscore its policy shift and silence critics in the military, the government dismissed three senior officers in the Serb-controlled Yugoslav armed forces and coverage of the war in Bosnia disappeared from the government-controlled media. There were also indications of a possible rapprochement between Serbia and Croatia, with persistent reports of secret high-level Serb-Croat meetings in Graz, Austria, encouraged by Western mediators. In November, even as the FRY foreign ministry rejected recognition of Croatia, Milosevic put pressure on Serb leaders from Croatia to halt their offensive against Bihac.

Hopes for a peace breakthrough and reconciliation dimmed substantially, however, as Bosnian and Croat Serbs pressed their attacks on Bihac and other Bosnian government strongholds, leading the U.N. to threaten to pull out besieged UNPROFOR peacekeepers. Moreover, there was mounting evidence by December that Milosevic was still aiding Bosnian Serbs, whose counteroffensive included the use of sophisticated air defense and wire-guided anti-tank missiles delivered from the FRY. Western sources also reported that troops and fuel from Serbia were being smuggled through Montenegro, where there were no U.N. monitors.

A key reason for Milosevic's initiative to lift sanctions was the economy. An austerity program and a new currency introduced in late January by little-known economist Dragolsav Avramovic, a former employee of the World Bank and the IMF, had reduced inflation from 1 million percent to 0.2 percent in September by pegging the super-dinar to the D-Mark. Industrial production rose, wages were up and shops were full despite the embargo. However, by October the super-dinar had weakened, partly because sanction-busting operations put a greater demand for hard currency. Inflationary pressure was up, and there were shortages of milk, meat and cooking oil, raising the prospect that the dramatic economic upturn was temporary.

Political Rights and Civil Liberties: Citizens of the rump-Yugoslavia can elect representatives to the federal and regional parliaments; both the president and prime minister are appointed by a parliament dominated by former Communists loyal to Serbian President Slobodan Milosevic.

December 1993 elections to the Serbian republican parliament were marred by irregularities. Milosevic's control of the media, particularly state-run television, effectively shuts out opposition views and access. The federal judiciary, headed by a Con-stitutional and a Federal Court, are subordinate to Serbia and not free from political interference.. Parliament violated the constitution and did not even bother to consult the Constitutional Court in ousting President Cosic in 1993. The government has openly flouted the rule of law, ignoring statutes that barred the forced mobilization of refugees into military units.

Freedom of assembly and expression are curtailed. Demonstrations are routinely broken up violently by police. Milosevic has strengthened the Serbian police by 20,000 men in 1993, equipping special units with armored vehicles, helicopters, and rocket launchers. The police are better equipped, trained and paid than the Yugoslav military, leading to tensions and dismissals in 1994.

The government-controlled radio and television are subservient to Milosevic and the SPS, and are staffed by Milosevic loyalists. With independent newspapers expensive or unavailable outside Belgrade, television is the main source of news and commentary. In 1994, the government launched an insidious campaign to silence the independent press by moving to gain controlling interests in leading publications. On 19 December a judge ruled that there were irregularities in the organization of the three-year private ownership consortium o f the independent paper, *Borba*. The decision placed the paper in government hands. Independent TV station Studio B and the radio station B-92 have faced similar pressure. In April, the government took away the press credentials of 13 local and foreign correspondents, including those working for CNN, Agence France-Presse, the *Christian Science Monitor*, *Le Monde*, and several others. The government also launched a campaign against the Soros Yugoslav Foundation which, in addition to providing clinics and hospitals with 140 tons of medical supplies, had helped to support 50 independent media projects. The anti-media campaign was being carried out by Milorad Vucelic, general director of the state-run radio and television and a leading SPS figure.

International sanctions limited foreign travel throughout most of the year. Ethnic Muslims in the Sandzak region between Serbia and Montenegro have faced repression and persecution. In May, 25 Sandzak Muslims charged with planning armed rebellion against Serbia went on trial in Novi Pazar. Contrary to the law, which formally allows a three-month pretrial detention, members of the group spent more than a year in Serbia's most notorious jails. Kosovo's Albanian majority faces severe persecution and oppression.

Serbs and Montenegrins are overwhelmingly Eastern Orthodox and free to practice their religion. Muslims in Sandzak and Kosovo face restrictions on freely and openly practicing their faith.

Federal and republican laws prohibit discrimination against women, but women remain underrepresented in high-level government and business sectors.

The independent Nezavisimost trade union has faced harassment and persecution, and most trade unions are directly or indirectly controlled by the government or the SPS. Despite restrictions and intimidation, workers have gone out on strike in several sectors over the last two years.

Zaire

Polity: Presidential-military and interim legislative
Economy: Capitalist-statist
Population: 42,476,000
PPP: $469
Life Expectancy: 51.6
Ethnic Groups: Some 200, including Azande, Bemba, Kasai, Kongo, Luba, Lunda, and Pygmy

Political Rights: 7
Civil Liberties: 6
Status: Not Free

Overview:

In 1994 President Mobutu Sese Seko entered his third decade in power, and Zaire continued its descent into mayhem. In June, the new Prime Minister, Leon Kengo wa

Dondo, began to pull Zaire out of the mire of political and economic disintegration. His reform efforts, however, were minute in comparison to the country's problems, which include a worthless currency, pervasive corruption, lawless militias, starvation, a dilapidated infrastructure and Mobutu's determination to block any changes that might threaten his power. Nevertheless, Kengo's reform policies, along with the country's calculated participation in dealing with the Rwanda refugee crisis, helped to earn Zaire some recognition from the West and end the country's four-year period of international isolation.

Zaire, known as the Congo until 1972, gained independence from Belgium in 1960. Since 1965, Mobutu has ruled the country through his Popular Movement of the Revolution (MPR). His regime, characterized as a kleptocracy, or rule by theft, caused this potentially rich country to become one of the poorest in the world. In 1990, facing popular pressures for reform, Mobutu legalized political parties with the ostensible aim of eventually introducing a pluralist democratic system. He refused, however, to cede any significant power and continuously sabotaged the opposition.

In July 1991 approximately 200 opposition groups formed the Sacred Union of Forces for Change. The backbone of the Sacred Union was the Union for Democracy and Social Progress (UDPS), headed by Etienne Tshisedeki, a radical opposition leader.

Beginning in 1991, the MPR and opposition forces participated in a National Conference to work out a new constitutional order. Following Mobutu's attempts to suspend the Conference and prevent it from reaching any decisions, the Conference declared its actions to be "sovereign," with the aim of passing constitutionally binding measures. It nominated Tshisekedi as prime minister.

In December 1992 the National Conference concluded its work and set up a constitution to be confirmed in a referendum scheduled for April 1993. The constitution restricted the powers of the president, removing his control over the army and police, and called for the appointment of the prime minister and individual cabinet members. The Conference established the High Council of the Republic (HCR) to act as an interim legislature, electing Catholic Archbishop Laurent Monsengo as its speaker and confirming Tshisedeki as the prime minister. Mobutu refused to recognize the Tshisedeki cabinet.

In 1993, the rift between Mobutu and the HCR increased to the point of political deadlock. In January 1993 the HCR accused Mobutu of high treason by "having blocked the functioning of the country at every level." The following month, Mobutu dismissed the Tshisekedi cabinet, a decision which was rejected by the HCR four days later.

After months of impasse, the two rival governments began negotiations in September 1993. Although some compromise was reached, the issue of the prime ministership remained unresolved, as both the radical opposition and Mobutu's National Assembly refused to compromise.

On 11 January 1994 the Mobutuist coalition and members of several opposition parties signed the *Protocol d'Accord*, a pact which called for the integration of the HCR with the National Assembly, minimizing the radical opposition's parliamentary influence. Tshisedeki denounced the accord and called for a nationwide strike. Although the strike received a large following, it did not alter the HCR's decision to approve the pact.

For the next few months, the HCR tried to find a prime minister who would be able to mediate between the opposition and the government. Tshesedeki was ruled out because he insisted on being confirmed as prime minister without a vote in parliament. Moreover, he was judged too radical and unable to talk to the government to end the political deadlock.

The transitional constitution that took effect on 9 April called for national and presidential elections, the first in Zaire's history, to take place by mid-1995. On 14 June the transitional parliament held a vote for prime minister. Leon Kengo wa Dondo captured 332 out of 421 votes. Many radical opposition members boycotted the vote. Since Kengo's appointment, Tshesedeki has lost much of his support. When Mobutuist soldiers attacked his home in July, for example, there was little popular protest. His role as the chief opposition leader seemed to have ended.

Kengo began to implement reforms almost immediately after his appointment. On 9 July, during a legislative session, Kengo discussed with candor unusual for a Zairian leader the depth and severity of Zaire's many problems and emphasized the need for change. On 22 July he ordered an audit of the records of the Bank of Zaire. Kengo also suspended the bank's governor, Ndiang Kaboul. Mobutu, who had appointed the governor and continues to control the bank, blocked this action by disregarding the dismissal and allowing Kaboul to continue to show up for work. Mobutu's virtually unlimited access to the bank's funds has allowed him to accumulate enormous wealth and buy his ministers' loyalty. Such corruption is one reason for Zaire's paralyzed economy and 12,500 percent annual inflation rate which, according to the Guinness Book of World Records, is the highest in the world. Exchange rates in Zaire change many times a day, and the government simply prints more money whenever it is needed.

Kengo also initiated reforms aimed at controlling the lawless army. Immediately after his appointment, he ruled that soldiers would no longer be permitted to roam the streets carrying arms while not on duty.

While Mobutu tried to block Kengo's reforms, his image as a strongman has been overshadowed by anarchy and deadlock. Once nicknamed "The Guide" and "The Messiah," Mobutu has lost much of his power over the people. As evidence of this change in image, the president's face no longer appears on television before broadcasts.

France, Belgium, and the United States have, for the most part, expressed support for Kengo's policies. The "troika" nations, as they are called, had united to isolate Zaire since 1990. During the Cold War, the West maintained relations with Zaire, which served as a weapons conduit for rebel forces fighting Communism in Africa. With the collapse of Communism, the "troika" nations no longer had reason to support the destructive regime. Of the three countries, France has been the most eager to re-establish relations. In August 1994 France promised Zaire 10 million dollars of humanitarian aid in 1995—a 600 percent increase over 1994. For all three nations, future aid is conditional upon continued political and economic reform.

Mobutu also earned international recognition for cooperating with relief efforts for Rwandan refugees. In July, scores of Rwandan Hutu refugees fled into the northern Zairian town of Goma, escaping an approaching Tutsi attack. The refugees flooded in at a rate of 10,000 an hour, totaling 1,200,000, creating the world's largest refugee camp. Mobutu, who was away on holiday during the crisis, was conveniently able to take credit for the Zairian effort without involving himself in its ramifications. Cholera spread rapidly through the camp, and people went for days without food, bringing the death toll to 1,800 a day. Ten days later, Zaire reopened its borders, and refugees began to trickle back into Rwanda. Many refused to leave, choosing to face disease and starvation over the possibility of being killed in Rwanda. Hutu leaders used threat and force to prevent refugees from returning to Rwanda. By then exaggerating the number of refugees, Hutu leaders attempted to show that the Rwandan government could not possibly be legitimate if so many of its citizens were forced to flee the country. By the end of 1994, an estimated 900,000 refugees still remained in Zaire.

The Zairian relief community severely lacked resources and became over-whelmed by the floods of refugees. Soldiers sent to deal with the crisis reportedly stole relief goods and extorted money from relief organizations, townspeople, and refugees. Throughout the crisis, soldiers beat, harassed, and executed refugees. On 11 August 5,000 townspeople protested the soldiers' actions. The militia responded by firing into the air, sending the protesters scattering.

The Rwandan refugee crisis caused further tensions between the Banyarwanda and the Bahunde, the two largest ethnic groups in the northern Kivu province, increasing the potential for future ethnic clashes. The Bahunde are citizens of Zaire, while the Banyarwanda (Hutu and Tutsi) became stateless following Mobutu's 1981 decision to grant citizenship only to those with pre-colonial ancestral links to Zaire. In March 1993 armed Bahunde attacked Banyarwanda-frequented markets and churches, killing thousands within a few days.

Interethnic violence in the Shaba (Katanga) province somewhat subsided in 1994, as most of the Kasaians had already been either killed or forced out of the province into internal displacement camps. Kasaians were brought to the province to work in mines, as part of Belgian colonial policy. Since independence, Kasaians have expressed a desire to secede from Shaba. Ethnic tension exploded into violence in 1992, when Tshisedeki, a Bal Oba from Kasai, became prime minister. Mobs of Shabans and paramilitary troops attacked Kasaian businesses and homes. In 1993, the continuation of violence forced several hundred thousand Kasaians to flee the province.

Political and economic chaos has led to a startling increase in the number of AIDS victims. Zaire's Project SIDA, once the largest AIDS prevention program in Africa, has crumbled because of lack of funding. In some hospitals, 80 percent of patients have been diagnosed with the virus.

Political Rights and Civil Liberties: Citizens of Zaire cannot change their government demo-cratically. Although Mobutu's image as a strongman has weakened, and Prime Minister Kengo has instituted some political and economic reforms, President Mobutu still wields absolute power. Ultimately Kengo cannot threaten Mobutu's rule, since he is half Polish and half Rwandan, and under Zairian law not able to run for president in the scheduled 1995 elections. Mobutu will likely win these elections—the first in Zaire's history—as the radical opposition has threatened to boycott them, and Mobutu is able to manipulate opposition fragmentation in order to maintain his power.

Mobutu firmly controls the judiciary. Arbitrary arrest and detention are commonplace, and security forces regularly beat, mistreat and torture detainees. The judiciary repeatedly refuses to investigate claims of torture and mistreatment.

Since 1990, dozens of independent newspapers and periodicals have been published. Following an initial period of relative liberalization, the Mobutu regime returned to its repressive measures in 1992. In November of that year, armed arsonists believed to be members of the security forces set on fire the *Terra Nova* printing press, which was used mainly to print opposition publications. In 1994, opposition newspapers often had so little funding that they were not able to be distributed, but were instead draped on strings along the roadside for passersby to read. In March 1994 Zairian journalist Kalala-Mnenga Kalao was awarded the International Freedom of the Press Award by the U.S. National Press Club. Kalao, an editor of the *Tempete des Tropiques* newspaper, was arrested in August 1993 after he published a series of articles showing how a disproportionate number of army officers belong to Mobutu's Ngbandi ethnic group. Kalao was released twenty-seven days later. Prime Minister Kengo has made some attempts at opening the media. On 15 July he formally opened the state-controlled broadcast media to opposition views.

The regime does not recognize the right to assembly and peaceful protest. Demonstrators risk being arrested, beaten, and even killed by security or armed forces. Nonpolitical associations, including religious organizations, need permission to operate, and their activities are closely monitored by government officials. The major trade union confederation remains the National Union of Zairian Workers (UNTZA), formerly the only legal labor organization, affiliated with the MPR. Since 1990, however, UNTZA has disaffiliated itself from the MPR, conducting elections for union leadership posts deemed fair by outside observers. Other nascent unions consolidate their membership along occupational lines.

All citizens, refugees and permanent residents must carry identity cards in order to travel within and leave Zaire. Corrupt officials often charge exorbitant prices for such cards. Journalists, human rights activists, and opposition leaders are often forbidden to leave the country. The constitution limits religious freedom in this primarily Christian country by granting civil servants the power to establish or dissolve religious groups.

Zambia

Polity: Presidential-par-liamentary democracy
Political Rights: 3
Civil Liberties: 4
Economy: Mixed statist
Status: Partly Free
Population: 9,132,000
PPP: $1,010
Life Expectancy: 45.5
Ethnic Groups: Bemba, Lozi, Lunda, Ngoni, other

Overview: In December 1994 the World Bank held a Consultative Group Meeting in Paris, in which Zambia reaffirmed its commitment to privatization—a commitment which it has made since President Frederik Chiluba was elected in 1991. The slow speed of this privatization process, however, as well as increased corruption and drug trafficking scandals, have dissatisfied donor countries and fueled citizens' discontent.

Zambia achieved independence from Britain in 1964. President Kenneth Kaunda and his socialist United National Independence Party (UNIP) ruled Zambia from independence until 1991. His rule, though characterized by repression, can be credited with one major accomplishment: Kaunda was able to unite Zambia's seventy-three different ethnic groups. In 1991, Zambia held its first multiparty democratic election. Kaunda lost overwhelmingly to Chiluba, a former trade union leader. In the parallel parliamentary elections, Chiluba's party, Movement for Multiparty Democracy (MMD) captured 125 of 150 seats.

Kaunda's crushing defeat showed citizens' dissatisfaction with Zambia's economic deterioration and Kaunda's authoritarian style of government. Indeed, Zambia, once one of Africa's most prosperous territories, had degenerated by the 1990s into one of the continent's poorest nations. Administrative and economic centralization, socialist experimentation, widespread corruption, and the fall of copper prices in the 1970s led to a declining standard of living, high inflation, and declining currency value.

Following Chiluba's victory, the MMD implemented an IMF-recommended Structural Adjustment Program (SAP), which enabled the government to receive additional loans and raised the possibility of rescheduling or forgiving Zambia's $7 billion debt. The program consisted of slashing public expenditures, eliminating subsidies, and ultimately privatizing most state-owned enterprises. Though some moves have been made towards privatization, Zambia Consolidated Copper Mines (ZCCM), which accounts for over 90 percent of export earnings, has barely been touched. Copper output has fallen from 700,000 to 400,000 tons per year since ZCCM was first nationalized in the mid-1970s; foreign investment is desperately needed. While debate progressed in 1994 from whether privatization should take place to how, so far little action has been taken.

Some privatization progress was made in December 1994 when the government closed down Zambia airways to replace it with a private carrier, a decision that took a year to act upon. The airways had consumed massive government subsidies: 3 to 4 percent of the GDP.

In restructuring the economy, the government is forced to mediate between the competing interests of the donor nations and the local workers. Donor nations have expressed dissatisfaction with the rate of Zambia's progress and are seriously considering slowing down disbursements in 1995. In January, finance minister Ronald Penza cut defense spending nearly in half. Then, in February, the government placed a 40 percent import tax on foreign goods in order to protect local producers—a move that donors viewed as a step backwards.

Also fueling both donor and citizen discontent are continuing governance problems. Since Chiluba was elected, over a dozen cabinet ministers have resigned. In January 1994, a corruption and drug trafficking scandal forced the resignation of Foreign Minister Vernon Johnston Mwaanga. The independent media implicated other cabinet members in the scandal and argued that the president was too weak to fire everyone involved. On 3 July Vice President Lavy Mwanawasa and Legal Affairs Minister Ludwig Sondashi also resigned, this time over differences with Chiluba.

Zambians are losing confidence in their president's ability to keep his promises and implement real change. When Zambia's renowned soccer team was killed in a plane crash in April 1993, the government collected $500,000 in donations and set up two trust funds, one for the widows and one for the upkeep of the graves. The government failed to keep its promise; the widows received but a token of the money, and the gravesites have gone untended.

In July, amidst a rising tide of public discontent, former dictator Kenneth Kaunda publicly announced his willingness to return to politics. Holding rallies throughout the country, Kaunda called for elections "now and not tomorrow." Although Kaunda's return did not pose a major threat to Chiluba, he warned the ex-dictator that he could only return to politics within the realms of democracy and placed Kaunda under surveillance in order to "preserve the peace and security of the nation." Kaunda had been receiving certain benefits from the government on the condition that he stay out of politics.

Political Rights and Civil Liberties:

Zambians have the right to change their government democratically, although critics allege that the constitution gives the executive disproportionate power over the legislature. The rise of government corruption and drug trafficking scandals threatens Zambia's transition to democracy, and decreases citizens' confidence in the government's ability to enact meaningful change.

The court system acts independently. Fair trials are often obstructed, however, by understaffing and underrepresentation for poor defendants. The police often use excessive force in apprehending suspects, and convicts face miserable prison conditions.

Freedoms of speech and press are generally respected, although the government still uses legislation inherited from the Kaunda period to stifle criticism. The president, for example, retains the right to ban any publication and requires all journalists to register through the government information department. On 29 January 1994 a photographer was temporarily detained after he shot pictures of police beating up a suspect. That week, two more journalists were arrested, one for "loitering" and one for attempting to investigate the shooting of a criminal suspect in police custody. In May 1994 Chiluba ordered police to detain two journalists who had referred to the president as a "twit," violating a Kaunda law which made it illegal to insult the president in the media. Also in May, the government approved a project to set up Zambia's first independent pay-television channel.

Independent cultural, professional and civic associations operate freely and widely. Freedom of religion is respected, although members of the MMD emphasize that Zambia is a "Christian" nation. Zambia has a strong trade union tradition. Approximately 60 percent of former workers are unionized. The country's nineteen national unions are all affiliated with the Zambian Congress of Trade Unions (ZCTU), the only legal confederation. The ZCTU, a member of the International Confederation of Free Trade Unions (ICFTU), is mostly independent from government influence.

Zimbabwe

Polity: Dominant party   **Political Rights:** 5
Economy: Capitalist-   **Civil Liberties:** 5
statist   **Status:** Partly Free
Population: 11,215,000
PPP: $2,160
Life Expectancy: 56.1
Ethnic Groups: Shona, Ndebele, white, and others

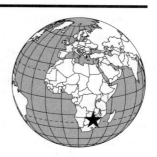

Overview:

In 1994 a corruption scandal plagued Zimbabwe President Robert Mugabe's land redistribution program, a scheme to bolster the popularity of his ruling Zimbabwe African National Union (Patriotic Front) ZANU-PF party. Deteriorating race relations, violence and poor economic performance afflicted the country.

Zimbabwe, formally called Rhodesia, achieved independence from Britain in 1980 after two decades of guerrilla warfare between the white minority government and black liberation movements. The British-mediated settlement provided a constitution equipped with a Declaration of Rights. Among other things, it prohibited the government from seizing private property without due compensation and the consent of the owners. In 1990 ZANU removed the inviolability-of-property clause and instituted the Land Acquisition Act, allowing the government to compel the 4,300 mostly white commercial farmers to sell their land to black, landless peasants.

In 1993, the government announced the forced purchase of seventy highly productive farms. In response, the Commercial Farmers' Union accused the government of breaking its pledge to acquire only underutilized land. Following the Farmers' Union decision to hire British lawyers to contest the farms' acquisitions, Mugabe lashed out at the commercial farmers and the white minority, calling them "a greedy bunch of racist usurpers" and threatening deportation. As of March 1994, close to a hundred farms were confiscated. After a regional governor denounced the allocation of farms to prominent politicians Mugabe, claiming complete ignorance of the "minister scandal," ordered an investigation into the program. On 17 April, Mugabe canceled all state land leases to individuals, while promising to resettle landless peasants. In June the government confiscated seventeen additional commercial white-owned farms. In November, the farmers lost their first legal battle against the government. Some blacks believe their lack of expertise, capital and transportation remain huge barriers to other possible solutions to redressing the country's inequities.

In 1993 Mugabe, in order to bolster his popularity, addressed the issue of the majority black landless peasants with his land reform law. At the same time, however, Mugabe seized land Ndabaningi Sithole, his opponent, had sold to 4,000 landless families in Churu. The families were thrown off the farms on grounds they were living in ramshackle homes. Sithole, the leader of the Zimbabwe African National Union (Ndonga), was not formally served with a confiscation notice. In November 1993, the farmers were allowed to return to their land. In 1994, they were ordered once again to vacate. At the close of the year, Sithole sought legal action to recover the property.

Stripped of aid and development due to long-standing enmities with the dominant Shona tribe, minority Ndebele in Matalabele formed rebel groups in January and attacked local Shonas. The trouble strained the six-year political alliance between the president and the Ndebele Vice President Joshua Nkomo. Local politicians called for demonstrations against the government policy of replacing Ndebele with Shona in top posts.

Following the incorporation of the Zimbabwe African People's Union (ZAPU) into the ruling ZANU(PF) party in 1987, Zimbabwe has effectively become a single-party state. ZAPU derived its support mostly from Ndebele in Matabeleland, the southwestern Zimbabwe, while ZANU was dominated by northern Shona.

Since 1990 several Ndebele opposition leaders have died in mysterious circumstances suggesting government involvement. In 1993 several opposition activists claimed they uncovered a government-prepared hit list which ordered their assassinations. In August 1994 Sydney Malunga, the popular Ndebele leader, died in a mysterious car accident shortly after he addressed a political meeting called by ZANU-PF in Bulawayo.

Race relations between the black and white populations further deteriorated in 1994 following reports that whites in Bulawayo were planning a march into Harare to mark the centennial of the Ndebele kingdom's defeat by colonial settlers. Nkomo warned them to leave Zimbabwe "now before it's too late." In early October about 200 black students stormed an allegedly racist club in Harare. A letter threatened that students would perform amputations on whites in public if a white doctor on trial was not given an adequately tough sentence. The issue of race divided students, and the government denied involvement in any campaign against the white population. The current round of racial tension began with a critical attack on whites in the *Sunday Mail* newspaper.

Other incidents of violence in 1994 were related to the 1995 elections. On 15 May ZANU held a warmup campaign rally at which speakers unleashed vitriolic attacks on minority parties. In June clashes between ZANU and the opposition left at least twenty-six people injured. A dozen people, many of them Ngonda members, were reportedly taken away by the police. The violence came a day after Sithole warned his supporters about violent confrontation with opponents. Enoch Dumbutshena, leader of the opposition Forum Party, called on supporters to arm themselves with axes and spears before national elections to defend themselves against ZANU youth wing members. Mugabe said he could not guarantee violence-free elections. An independent electoral commission predicted a surge in political violence before the elections.

Two opposition parties, Bishop Abel Muzorewa's United Party and the Forum Party for Democracy, announced their merger in December 1994 in a bid to unseat ZANU. The new United Parties proposed to set up a constitutional commission if elected, to examine the possible devolution of power to the provinces.

The opposition lashed out at ZANU for economic mismanagement and its socialist tendencies. In 1994 Mugabe toured the world on an investment campaign to boost an economy burdened by rising unemployment and an increased cost of living caused in part by austerity measures in place since 1990. In drought-ridden rural districts a quarter of Zimbabwe's population faced food shortages and appealed for government aid. In November, Mugabe announced that his government might consider privatizing the economy.

Political Rights and Civil Liberties:

Due to the ZANU party's monopoly on power, the citizens of Zimbabwe cannot change their government democratically. The 1990 legislative elections were marred by voter intimidation, inaccuracies and irregularities in voting registers and vote counting, and a heavily progovernment bias media coverage. Of the 150 legislative seats, ZANU won 117, with 3 seats going to two opposition groups. Thirty seats remain for tribal chiefs and the president's nominees. Zimbabwe Rights Association (Zimrights) charged that the electoral laws for 1995 are heavily biased in favor of the ruling party. In June 1994, during a Zimrights-organized conference on electoral laws in which all major parties except ZANU participated, a series of resolutions was passed to ensure free and fair elections, including the establishment of an Independent Electoral Supervisory Commission and suspension of the president's excessive powers in the Electoral Act. The opposition Democratic Party accused ZANU of planning to rig the election.

The judiciary is mostly independent. Several human rights organizations have accused the government and the police of obstructing judicial inquiry in cases related to the political opposition or high government officials.

In 1994, Mugabe, using his discretionary powers, commuted the death sentences of eighteen condemned prisoners to life imprisonment and reduced another death sentence to a five-year prison term.

Zimbabwe's constitution mentions freedom of expression but not press freedom, which is severely curtailed by a number of laws. The government labels all private media, "opposition media." It controls the bulk of mass media through its shares in the Zimbabwe Newspapers conglomerate, which controls the seven major English dailies. Journalists sometimes complain that it is difficult to bring issues to editors, whom they believe are "shadow editors." The only independent daily newspaper is *The Financial Gazette,* published in Bulawayo, in Matabeleland. Both state-owned and independent papers are increasingly outspoken in criticizing the government. In 1994 the police detained and interrogated a reporter and his editor to discover the source of a story revealing tax evasion in ZANU-owned companies. Although they were accused of breaching the Secrets Act, they were not prosecuted. A radio/television station in Matalabele was closed down on grounds that it was tribal. It was then reopened under Shona management.

In February 1993, following a Supreme Court decision denying the automatic right to residence of persons born in Zimbabwe (or Rhodesia) who retained or acquired foreign citizenship and were no longer domiciled in the country, the government clamped down on legal and illegal immigrants. In July 1994, 40,000 whites who fled Zimbabwe in 1980 made inquiries about returning home.

The Zimbabwe Congress of Trade Unions has become increasingly independent from ZANU influence and has stepped up its campaigns to defend the rights of workers in the face of mounting economic difficulties. In 1994 union leaders urged workers at the Posts and Telecommunications Corporation to protest a pay award. The government arrested a number of union leaders for breaching the Law and Order Act, which stipulates that inciting a strike in an essential service is forbidden. However, the workers were awarded their pay increase after a week-long strike. They were followed by doctors and other professionals.

In March 1994 the Supreme Court repealed a thirty-four-year-old law used by the Rhodesian and postcolonial governments to stop political opponents from holding public demonstrations. Zimbabwe Congress of Trade Unions members who were arrested in 1992 for staging a procession without police approval, challenged the law. On 11 April 1994 four people were injured by 400 ZANU members who invaded an opposition rally.

Armenia/Azerbaijan
Nagorno-Karabakh

Polity: Armenian-occupied **Political Rights:** 7
Economy: Mixed statist **Civil Liberties:** 7
Population: 150,000 **Status:** Not Free
Ethnic Groups: Armenian (95 percent),
Assyrian, Greek, Kurdish, others (5 percent.)

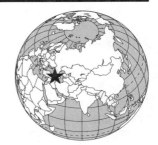

Overview: **S**everal international attempts to mediate the crisis in this predominantly Armenian enclave within Azerbaijan failed to find a permanent solution, and sporadic fighting continued even after an April cease-fire.

In 1921 Nagorno-Karabakh was transferred from Armenia and placed under Soviet Azerbaijani jurisdiction by Joseph Stalin, then the commissar of nationalities. Subsequently, the Nagorno-Karabakh Autonomous Oblast (region) was created, with a narrow strip of land bordering Armenia proper. In 1930, Moscow permitted Azerbaijan to establish and resettle the border areas between Nagorno-Karabakh and Armenia.

In 1988 Azeri militia and special forces launched violent repression in response to Karabakh Armenians' demands for greater autonomy. Since then, the region has been characterized by stop-and-start fighting in which the Armenians have gained territory at the Azeri's expense. The former now control all of Nagorno-Karabakh and have also taken swatches of bordering Azeri territory.

Attempts by the Conference on Security and Cooperation in Europe (CSCE) and Russia to broker a cease-fire have failed repeatedly, as both sides have hoped to gain advantages militarily. Thus far, 20,000 have been killed in the fighting, including civilians, and the property damage is estimated at $90 million.

During a Washington visit in August, President Ter-Petrossian of Armenia, whose official line is that his country is not involved in the fighting, despite the presence of thousands of "volunteers," said he would welcome several thousand Russian peacekeepers. President Bill Clinton said he was not opposed to the move so long as the CSCE approved. On 9 September Azerbaijan's President Gaidar Aliyev and President Ter-Petrossian, meeting in Moscow, approved a preliminary agreement calling for an end to military hostilities, the disengagement of all armed forces in the region, the deployment of CIS peacekeepers, and the eventual return of refugees to the region. A followup meeting at the end of the month foundered on differences over the timing of the withdrawal of Armenian Karabakh forces from Azeri territory, as well as the Azeri preference for Turkish troops to serve in a peacekeeping role as part of a CSCE force, rather than a predominantly Russian force within the CIS contingent.

At a meeting of the CSCE in Vienna on 24 October to discuss the war, Russian delegate Vladimir Shustov demanded that the CSCE abdicate to Russia responsibility for settling the conflict, with the CSCE playing only a supporting role. U.N. Secretary General Boutros Boutros-Ghali, after a meeting with President Aliyev, said the U.N. was ready to play a role in coordinating Russian and CSCE peace efforts. He also said the war should be resolved through the framework of U.N. Security Council resolutions 822, 853, 874 and 884, and criticized Armenian forces for balking at withdrawing forces from Azeri territory.

Another round of Russian-brokered talks between Azeri, Armenian and Karabakh representatives ended in mid-November without tangible results. On 2 December, Azeri and Karabakh representatives did agree to the release of 1,000 prisoners of war and several hundred detained citizens. The CSCE, during its summit in Budapest on 5 December, discussed a possible international peace-keeping contingent of 3,000 soldiers, but the plan was strongly opposed by Russia. While no formal resolution was reached, the CSCE approved a document granting a greater role for the Russian mediation effort. Meanwhile, with the July cease-fire holding, some 17,000 refugees returned to Karabakh, though many homes had been looted or destroyed.

Political Rights and Civil Liberties: Residents of Nagorno-Karabakh technically have the means to change their government democratically. A majority voted for secession and self-rule in a December 1991 referendum, and elections were held for an eighty-two-seat parliament. Official independence was declared on 6 January 1992, though its has not been recognized by the international community. Because of the seven-year war, *de facto* power rests in the hands of parliament's Supreme Council (equivalent to the Soviet-era Council of Ministers), partly because many parliamentarians are at the front.

On 10 November 1994 the Supreme Council convened an executive session in response to an appeal by 21 parliamentarians calling for a reconvening of the full legislature which had been informally suspended during the fighting of 1993-94. The session considered extending martial law. The following month, the Council elected a new president empowered to name a prime minister and cabinet.

The undeclared state of war has impinged on rights and civil liberties. A *de facto* state of martial law exists, and border regions have been subjected to attacks that make governing difficult. The ethnic nature of the conflict has led to charges of "ethnic cleansing" and atrocities by both sides. Freedom of movement has been curtailed by war, and martial law has led to restrictions on assembly and association. Martial law has led to self-censorship in the press. With Armenians making up 95 percent of the country, the Armenian Apostolic Church is the main religion, and the ethnic aspect of the war has constrained the religious rights of Muslims still left in the region.

Australia
Christmas Island (Kiritimati)

Polity: Appointed administrator
Economy: Capitalist-statist
Population: 78,000
Ethnic Groups: Chinese and Malay

Political Rights: 3
Civil Liberties: 2
Status: Free

Overview: Located in the Indian Ocean, Christmas Island has been under Australian administration since 1958. It is run by an administrator appointed by the governor general, Queen Elizabeth's representative in Australia. Australia dismissed Christmas island's nine-member assembly in 1982, citing fiscal mismanagement. Since then, Christmas politics have been expressed through participation in those of Australia's Northern Territory, of which the Islanders are citizens. They also vote in the Australian national elections and may opt for Australian citizenship. With the disappearance of the island's phosphate industry, plans are under review to orient the economy toward tourism.

Cocos (Keeling) Islands

Polity: Appointed administrator and elected council
Economy: Capitalist-statist
Population: 1,000
Ethnic Groups: Malay

Political Rights: 1
Civil Liberties: 1
Status: Free

Overview: An elected local council began functioning in 1978 with an Australian-appointed administrator as chief executive. A 1984 referendum made the Cocos an integral part of Australia. It is part of Australia's Northern Territory, which elects members of the Australian Parliament. The territory was a personal fiefdom of the Clunies-Ross family until 1978.

Norfolk Island

Polity: Appointed administrator and elected assembly
Economy: Capitalist
Population: 2,000
Ethnic Groups: *Bounty* families, Australians, New Zealanders

Political Rights: 2
Civil Liberties: 1
Status: Free

Overview: An Australian-appointed administrator is the chief executive and since 1979 there has been a freely elected assembly, whose executive committee acts like a cabinet. In April 1994 Norfolk Island held elections in which a record three women won seats in the nine-member legislative assembly.

Chile
Rapanui (Easter Island)

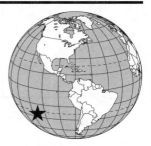

Polity: Appointed governor and elected local government
Economy: Capitalist-statist
Population: 2,000
Ethnic Groups: Spanish-speaking Polynesian natives (70 percent), and Chilean settlers (30 percent)

Political Rights: 2
Civil Liberties: 2
Status: Free

Overview: Under Chilean domain since 1888, Easter Island, 2,360 miles from Chile, subsists mainly on tourism and government subsidies. The territory has its own local government.

On 20 June 1994 the inhabitants of Easter Island went on strike, demanding the recovery of their land from the Chilean government, as well as a senator and deputy to represent them in Congress. The next day the Chilean government reaffirmed its control of the island.

Formerly run by the Chilean navy, the island became a Chilean municipality in 1966. Currently, only 20 percent of the land is owned by the original inhabitants, the Rapa Nui. The remainder, owned by Chilean authorities, serves as a national park and an agricultural testing station.

China
Tibet

Polity: Communist one-party
Economy: Statist
Population: 4,590,000*
Ethnic Groups: Tibetans, Han Chinese

Political Rights: 7
Civil Liberties: 7
Status: Not Free

* This figure from China's 1990 census indicates Tibetans under Chinese control. It includes 2.096 million Tibetans living in the Tibet Autonomous Region (TAR), and 2.494 million Tibetans living in areas of eastern Tibet that from 1950 on were incorporated into China's Qinghai, Gansu, Sichuan and Yunnan Provinces. By some estimates, the Chinese government has transferred up to 7 million ethnic Chinese into the former eastern Tibet, and to a lesser extent the TAR itself.

Overview:

In late 1949 China invaded Tibet, a fully independent state, with 100,000 troops, quickly defeated the small Tibetan army, occupied half the country, and established military and political control. In May 1951 China formally annexed the country by forcing a Tibetan delegation to sign a "Seventeen-Point Agreement for the Peaceful Liberation of Tibet." The document purported to guarantee Tibetans religious freedom and exempt the country from Communist "reforms." At the time there were 40,000 Chinese troops in Tibet. Because the agreement was signed under duress, it lacks validity under international law.

Throughout the 1950s the Chinese intensified their repression of Tibet and violated the May 1951 agreement on virtually every count. Popular pro-independence demonstrations in Lhasa, the capital, in March 1959 were followed by months of repression in which the Chinese killed an estimated 87,000 Tibetans in the Lhasa region alone. The Tibetan spiritual and temporal leader, the fourteenth Dalai Lama, Tenzin Gyatso, fled to Dharamsala, India with 80,000 supporters and established a government-in-exile.

In 1960 the International Commission of Jurists called the Chinese occupation genocidal, and ruled that prior to the 1949 invasion Tibet had possessed all the attributes of statehood as defined under international law, including a defined territory, an independent government and an ability to conduct foreign relations. In 1965 China created the Tibet Autonomous Region, including Lhasa, an entity which in reality contained only half the territory of pre-invasion Tibet. The rest of Tibet had, since 1950, been incorporated into four southwestern Chinese provinces. During the 1966-76 Chinese Cultural Revolution the authorities banned Tibetans from wearing traditional clothes and enjoying other basic cultural rights. By the late 1970s more than one million Tibetans had died as a result of the occupation, and all but eleven of 6,200 monasteries had been destroyed.

Between 1987 and 1990 Chinese soldiers broke up peaceful demonstrations throughout Tibet, killing hundreds and arresting thousands more. The authorities placed Lhasa under martial law from March 1989 to May 1990. In May 1992

China announced plans to modernize the Tibetan economy, improving transportation, but exiled Tibetans say this is meant to facilitate the mass settlement of ethnic Chinese into Tibet while accelerating environmental damage.

On 24 May 1993 some 500 demonstrators in Lhasa called for an end to the Chinese occupation and denounced the presence of prostitutes, bars and illicit drugs in the capital. Police dispersed the crowd by firing tear gas for two hours; smaller demonstrations continued for three days.

In a 10 March 1994 statement marking the thirty-fifth anniversary of the 1959 uprising, the Dalai Lama said he is reassessing his longstanding policy of calling for Tibetan autonomy within China, and may seek international support for an independent Tibet.

Political Rights and Civil Liberties:

Tibetans cannot change their government democratically. China appoints all top officials, including the governor, and continues to suppress the Tibetans' cultural identity and forcibly stifle calls for independence.

By most estimates there are between 300-400 Tibetan political prisoners in Lhasa. Political prisoners are routinely tortured, and nuns are reportedly raped. According to Human Rights Watch/Asia, Phuntsog Yangki, a twenty-year-old nun, died in a police hospital in June 1994, reportedly from lack of treatment after suffering beatings for singing independence songs.

The Chinese government has pursued a Sinification policy that includes sending 300 top Tibetan students to study in China each year, and granting economic incentives to lure ethnic Chinese into voluntarily relocating to Tibet. By some estimates in Lhasa alone there are already 120,000 Chinese and only 40,000 Tibetans, and Tibetans may already be a minority in Tibet as a whole.

Because monasteries have historically been the centers of education, authority and national identity in Tibet, the Chinese government sharply curtails religious freedom. The government limits the number of new monks and China says it will have the final say in the ongoing search for the boy who will be declared the eleventh Panchen Lama, who ranks second in the religious hierarchy to the Dalai Lama. In 1994 the government banned party members and government workers from displaying photographs of the Dalai Lama.

According to official Chinese figures Tibetans have a 25 percent literacy rate compared to 77 percent in China, reflecting the policy of educational discrimination in Tibet.

Tibetans who live outside Lhasa cannot visit the capital without going through an arduous task of obtaining permits. Although China's draconian family planning policy ostensibly does not extend to Tibetans and other minorities, sources say the one-child rule is enforced in Tibet.

Denmark
Faeroe Islands

Polity: Parliamentary democracy
Economy: Mixed capitalist
Population: 49,000
Ethnic Groups: Faeroese

Political Rights: 1
Civil Liberties: 1
Status: Free

Overview: Largely autonomous, the Faeroe Islands, which in 1994 elections saw the Sambandsflokkurim (liberal) party come to power, cedes authority over foreign affairs, defense, finance and justice to Denmark. Other government functions are run by local authorities, and the Faeroe Islanders pay no Danish taxes, while benefiting from substantial Danish subsidies.

The Faeroese have a full range of political rights and civil liberties. Eight newspapers publish freely. There are public radio and television stations. Although the established Lutheran Church represents almost 90 percent of the population, religious freedom is respected, and there are several independent churches.

Greenland

Polity: Parliamentary democracy
Economy: Mixed-capitalist
Population: 57,000
Ethnic Groups: Inuit (Eskimo), native whites, Danish

Political Rights: 1
Civil Liberties: 1
Status: Free

Overview: Greenland has had substantial autonomy since 1979. Denmark still controls Greenland's foreign and defense policies, but the local authorities handle most other matters. Greenland sends two representatives to the Danish parliament in Copenhagen.

Political rights and civil liberties are generally respected. The legislature includes parties ranging from left to right.

Finland
Aland Islands

Polity: Parliamentary
democracy
Economy: Mixed
capitalist
Population: 25,300
Ethnic Groups: Aland Islanders (Swedish)

Political Rights: 1
Civil Liberties: 1
Status: Free

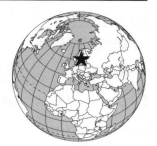

Overview:
The major political debate in the Aland Islands in 1994 concerned membership in the European Union (EU). On 16 October Alanders voted to remain outside the EU, even though Finland voted to join. The Alanders' autonomous status within Finland gave them the right to do so. A month later, however, the Alanders changed their mind and voted "Yes" along with their compatriots.

The Alands are an archipelago located between Sweden and Finland. Sweden lost the territory to Russia in the 1808-1809 war. The Alands became part of the Grand Duchy of Finland within the Russian Empire. Russia, France, and the United Kingdom recognized the Alands as a demilitarized zone in 1856. When Finland proclaimed its independence from Russia in 1917, it rejected a petition from Alanders requesting reunion with Sweden. In 1921, the League of Nations recognized the islands as an autonomous Swedish-speaking province within Finland.

The Alanders elect a thirty-member, multiparty parliament for a four-year term. The parliament can pass laws on internal affairs such as health and medical services, education, and culture. Finnish laws apply in areas where the Alanders have no legislative power. The Finnish president has veto power over local legislation only if the bill exceeds the parliament's authority or when there is a threat to national security. Alanders also elect a member of the Finnish parliament. A county governor represents Finland.

The Swedish language and local land ownership have special legal protection. There are competing newspapers and a public radio station.

France
French Guiana

Polity: Appointed com- **Political Rights:** 1
missioner and elected **Civil Liberties:** 2
assembly and council **Status:** Free
Economy: Capitalist-statist
Population: 115,000
Ethnic Groups: Complex, black (66 percent), Caucasian
(French) (12 percent), East Indian, Chinese, Vietnamese and
Amerindian (12 percent), and other (10 percent)

Overview: **A**s one of four French Overseas Departments, French
Guiana is ruled according to French law, and the administrative establishment is headed by a commissioner of the
Republic who is appointed by the French Ministry of the Interior. Representatives
to the French parliament are elected. A nineteen-member departmental council is
elected for six years, the councilors representing individual districts. Since 1982 the
Council has been given increased powers, particularly in financial matters.

When French Guiana was given regional status in 1974, a Regional Assembly was
set up, distinct from the departmental council, with limited control over the economy.
This control was expanded under the Mitterrand reforms of 1982-83. The first direct
elections to the Regional Assembly, on the basis of proportional representation, were
held in February 1983. Mayors and municipal councils are also directly elected.

In 1994 the presidents of the departmental and regional councils of French
Guiana, Guadeloupe and Martinique established a permanent conference for further
cooperation between the three departments.

There is still concern about the condition of the remaining Bush Negro and
Amerindian refugees who fled into western French Guiana during the guerrilla
conflict in neighboring Suriname.

Pluralistic points of view are presented in the media, which include two
newspapers and several radio and television stations. The United Trade Union
Movement (MSU) continued to express concerns over increased unemployment,
low European investment and the drain on the economy by a growing influx of
immigrants from Haiti and neighboring Brazil.

French Polynesia

Polity: Elected Assembly
Economy: Capitalist-statist
Population: 215,000
Ethnic Groups: Polynesian (83 percent), French and other European (11 percent), and Chinese and other Asian (6 percent)

Political Rights: 1
Civil Liberties: 2
Status: Free

Overview:
French Polynesia consists of 120 South Pacific Islands, the most populous of which is Tahiti. A High Commissioner represents the French government, but the territory has internal autonomy. Polynesians elect a member of the French Senate and two National Assembly deputies.

As a result of economic constraints following the 1992 suspension of French nuclear tests in the Mururoa atoll—which generated important income and employment—the islanders' territorial assembly and the French government agreed to a ten-year development plan to be financed in part by the islands' first income tax.

Peaceful advocates of independence have freedom of expression and association. The islanders are largely Christian. There are three daily newspapers and a public broadcasting service. The Chinese minority prospers in business, and enjoys much greater acceptance than Chinese communities on other Pacific islands.

Guadeloupe

Polity: Appointed commissioner and elected assembly and council
Economy: Capitalist-statist
Population: 423,000
Ethnic Groups: Predominantly black with white French minority

Political Rights: 1
Civil Liberties: 2
Status: Free

Overview:
As one of four French Overseas Departments, Guadeloupe is ruled according to French law and the administrative establishment is headed by a commissioner appointed by the French Ministry of the Interior. Representatives to the French parliament are elected.

A departmental council is directly elected to a five-year term, each member representing an individual district. Since 1982 the council has been given increased powers, particularly in financial matters.

When Guadeloupe was given regional status in 1974 a Regional Assembly was set up, parallel to the departmental council, with limited control over the economy. This control was expanded under the Mitterand reforms of 1983-83. The first elections to the Regional Assembly, on the basis of proportional representation, were held in February 1983. Mayors and municipal councils are directly elected.

In the Regional Assembly elections held in January 1993, the right-wing Guadeloupe Objective won 22 of 41 seats, compared with 15 in 1992. The Socialist Party (PS) dropped from 9 to 7 seats, the dissident socialist FRUI-G from 7 to 3 and the PCG from 3 to 2. The pro-independence Popular Union for the Liberation of Guadeloupe moved up from 2 to 3 seats.

In the French legislative elections held in March 1993, the right, under the banner of the Gaullist Rally for the Republic (RPR), won two of Guadeloupe's four seats, the PS and an independent leftist taking the other two.

In 1994 the presidents of the departmental and regional councils of Guadeloupe, French Guiana and Martinique established a permanent conference to further cooperation between the three departments.

There is one daily newspaper and a handful of radio and television transmitters. International news agencies maintain local offices. In recent years there has been labor unrest in the banana industry. Banana exports were severely damaged in 1994 by drought and by Tropical Storm Debbie. There is also evidence of increasing encroachment by the hemispheric drug trade.

Martinique

Polity: Appointed com-
missioner and elected
assembly and council
Economy: Capitalist-statist
Population: 374,000
Ethnic Groups: Predominantly black with French minority

Political Rights: 1
Civil Liberties: 2
Status: Free

Overview:
As one of four French Overseas Departments, the department of Martinique is ruled according to French law, and the administrative establishment is headed by a commissioner appointed by the French Ministry of the Interior. Representatives to the French parliament are elected.

A forty-five-member departmental council is elected to a six-year term, each member representing an individual district. Since 1982, the Council has been given increased powers, particularly in financial matters.

Martinique was given regional status in 1974 and a Regional Assembly was set up, parallel to the departmental council, with limited control over the economy. This authority was expanded under the 1982-83 Mitterrand reforms. Mayors and municipal councils are directly elected.

In April 1994 the PPM and the Socialist Federation of Martinique (FSM) retained the left-wing majority in elections for half the departmental council seats.

In September the presidents of the departmental and regional councils of Martinique, Guadeloupe and French Guiana established a permanent conference to further cooperation between the three departments.

The media are varied and reflect pluralistic points of view. There are several radio and television stations, one daily and several weekly newspapers. Separatist violence has nearly disappeared in recent years. Labor unions are legal and permitted to strike. There are two main labor federations, both of which were involved in strikes in 1993 to protest French government budget cuts. In recent years Martinique has become a major drug transshipment point.

Mayotte (Mahore)

Polity: Appointed com-missioner and elected council
Economy: Capitalist
Population: 93,000
Ethnic Groups: A mixture of Mahorais, French, Comoran, and Malagasy speakers of African and European descent

Political Rights: 1
Civil Liberties: 2
Status: Free

Overview:

Part of the Comoran archipelago, Mayotte is an overseas French territory, located in the Indian Ocean east of Mozambique and northwest of Madagascar. The island's ruling party is the Mahorais Popular Movement (MPM), which is opposed to the Comoran attempts to reunify Mayotte with Comoros. The Comoros, once united with Mayotte as a French colony, is now an independent republic of three islands immediately to the north of Mayotte.

The French government appoints a commissioner as chief executive, and the residents elect a seventeen-member general council, presently under the MPM control. Mayotte sends one member to the French Senate and elects one deputy to the National Assembly. Residents enjoy the same rights as French citizens. The government-owned radio station broadcasts in French and Mahorais. The economy is based largely on tourism and primary products such as ylang-ylang, vanilla, copra and coffee.

In 1993 a strike by Mahorais workers in support of wage increases degenerated into violence when demonstrators set fire to government buildings and erected street barricades. On 19 February, the French government dispatched 100 paramili-tary police to quell the riots.

New Caledonia

Polity: Appointed commissioner and elected congress and assemblies
Economy: Capitalist-statist
Population: 181,000
Ethnic Groups: Kanaky, Wallisian-Futunians, Javanese, French, Tahitians, Vietnamese, other Asian/Pacific groups

Political Rights: 2
Civil Liberties: 2
Status: Free

Overview:

New Caledonia, a group of South Pacific Islands 1,000 miles east of Australia, became a French territory in 1853 and gained internal autonomy in 1976.

Following a period of violence, in 1988 the indigenous, and largely pro-independence, Kanaks (a Melanesian people who make up 45 percent of the population) and the European and Asian settlers agreed to a French plan calling for a Territorial Assembly to govern New Caledonia until 1998, when a referendum on independence will be held.

Reunion

Polity: Appointed commissioner and elected assembly and council
Economy: Capitalist-statist
Population: 644,000
Ethnic Groups: Creole (Afro-European), French, Malagache, Malay, South Asian, and Vietnamese

Political Rights: 2
Civil Liberties: 2
Status: Free

Overview:

In March 1994, Eric Boyer, Reunion's senator in the French Parliament, was convicted of corruption and sentenced to two years in prison. He is the first French senator ever sentenced to serve time in jail. Boyer was accused of interfering in awarding contracts for school bus service and the provision of mass transit tickets in 1991 and 1992.

Located in the Indian Ocean east of Madagascar, Reunion has been in French hands since the seventeenth century. The population is multiracial and largely Catholic. A French commissioner carries out executive functions. There is a competitive multiparty system which ranges from pro-French conservatives to pro-independence Communists. Reunion has a bicameral legislature, consisting of an elected thirty-six member General Council and an elected forty-five member Regional Assembly. The territory elects three National Assembly deputies and one Senator to the French Parliament. There are three daily newspapers and a government-owned broadcasting system. High unemployment, insufficient economic opportunities, and a lack of diversions are abiding problems on the island, leading to idleness and frustration.

St. Pierre and Miquelon

Polity: Appointed commissioner and elected council
Economy: Capitalist
Population: 7,000
Ethnic Groups: French

Political Rights:
Civil Liberties: 1
Status: Free

Overview:

In June 1994 France cut off unemployment aid for St. Pierre and Miquelon, the only French possessions in North America, raising fears that all French assistance would end. One fifth of the work force lost their jobs as a result of an international moritorium on endangered stocks of cod and flounder.

The French government appoints a commissioner, and local residents, who have representatives in the French Parliament, elect a fourteen-member general council and municipal councils.

Wallis and Futuna Islands

Polity: Appointed administrator and elected council
Economy: Capitalist-statist
Population: 14,000
Ethnic Groups: Polynesian

Political Rights: 2
Civil Liberties: 2
Status: Free

Overview:

Wallis and Futuna Islands, with overwhelmingly, Polynesian populations, voted to become a French territory in 1959. The parties include local affiliates of the French center-right, but the current Assembly deputy is a leftist. In 1992, islanders voted for the Maastricht Treaty on European integration despite the Gaullist senator's plea for a "No" vote. The only radio station broadcasts in both French and Wallisian.

India
Kashmir

Polity: Indian-administered
Economy: Capitalist-statist
Population: 7,719,000
Ethnic Groups: Kashmiris (Muslim majority, Hindu minority)

Political Rights: 7
Civil Liberties: 7
Status: Not Free

Overview: In 1994 bilateral talks between India and Pakistan to resolve the future of Kashmir ended in deadlock. Pakistan's attempts at internationalizing the dispute at a U.N. human rights conference also failed. Several Kashmiri politicians were released from prison. The Indian government extended its state of emergency over Kashmir, and promised to hold local elections that the main opposition group, the All Party Freedom Party, vowed to boycott on grounds that the elections would be rigged.

In 1846 the British gained control of predominantly Hindu Jammu and Muslim Kashmir and installed a Hindu *maharajah* as leader. At the partition of India in 1947 into Muslim Pakistan and predominantly Hindu India, Muslims backed a revolt in Kashmir. Maharajah Hari Singh signed an agreement ceding control of the territories to India in exchange for protection by Indian troops.

A 1949 U.N.-brokered agreement gave a portion of Kashmir to Pakistan, while India maintained Jammu and most of Kashmir. In 1957 India formally annexed the territories as its state of Jammu and Kashmir.

Since 1959 China has occupied a section of Kashmir. In August-September 1965 and again in 1971-72, India and Pakistan clashed in the territory. During the latter conflict, India seized and subsequently annexed portions of Pakistani Kashmir.

In 1989 the Jammu and Kashmir Liberation Front (JKLF) began an insurgency seeking independence. Meanwhile, fundamentalist Kashmiris, who has fought with the mujahideen in Afghanistan, began forming several militant groups, including the Hizbul Mujahideen, seeking to incorporate Kashmir into Pakistan. In December 1989, the Indian government sent paramilitary troops into the state. In January 1990 Farooq Abdullah, who took power in 1982 after the death of his father, Shiekh Abdullah, resigned, and in July the state went under federal rule. In 1993, after years of escalating violence, India replaced hardliners with moderates to establish dialogue with pro-independence militants.

In October 1993 Indian troops began a siege outside of Kashmir's holiest shrine, the Hazrat Bal mosque in Srinagar, where some sixty-five armed rebels had encamped. As a standoff continued, in October the All Party Freedom Conference, a coalition of thirty-two anti-Indian groups uniting leaders of differing ideologies to a common platform, called on people to demonstrate against the siege.

In 1994 the All Party Freedom Conference was not invited to the negotiating table in Islamabad where India and Pakistan met to discuss Kashmir's future. Pakistan, dissatisfied with the progress, withdrew from the discussions. During the course of 1994 there were repeated acts of violence—military clashes, kidnapping, ambushes, assassinations, firebombings and riots.

At the end of the year Prime Minister Rao created a new Department of Jammu and Kashmir Affairs, which he will head because of squabbles between Home Affairs Minister S.B. Chaban and Minister for Internal Security Rajesh Pilot.

Political Rights and Civil Liberties: Kashmiris cannot change their government democratically. Since 1990, Jammu and Kashmir has been under President's Rule (direct federal rule), and citizens were not allowed to vote in the May 1991 Indian elections. The Kashmiris will accept only a plebiscite to decide their future, and opposition parties have vowed to boycott any local election they believe will serve to legitimize Indian rule. In February, New Dehli extended its ban on the JKLF until February 1996, and the All Party Freedom Conference remains unrecognized.

Since December 1989, 15,000-30,000 civilians, Kashmiri separatists and Indian soldiers have been killed in politically motivated violence. According to a 1994 Amnesty International report , there are fifty interrogation centers where detainees are kept in unacknowledged detention. Amnesty reports the Indian government stepped up its catch-and-kill campaign against the insurgents. Deaths in custody also escalated in 1994.

India maintains more than 250,000 soldiers and paramilitary troops in the state; these forces are responsible for torture and extrajudicial executions of civilians and suspected guerrillas, raping civilians, and arson attacks on shops and homes. The July 1990 Jammu and Kashmir Disturbed Areas Act and the Armed Forces (Jammu and Kashmir) Special Powers Act allow authorities to search homes and arrest suspects without a warrant.

Kashmiri militants are frequently responsible for the deaths of Indian security forces, public employees, suspected informers and members of rival factions.

The government prevents international human rights groups from conducting on site investigations in Kashmir. Local human rights groups operate under governmental pressure, and several activists have been killed.

The legal system is a shambles. Separatists routinely threaten judges, witnesses and the families of defendants, and as a result courts do not try cases involving militants or those with political overtones. In Jammu and Kashmir a district magistrate is allowed to restrict newspapers and magazines from publishing articles that allegedly provoke criminal acts or other disturbances. Both the government and the militants harass journalists, who exercise considerable self-censorship.

Indonesia
East Timor

Polity: Dominant party (military-dominated)
Economy: Capitalist-statist
Population: 778,000
Ethnic Groups: Timorese, Javanese, others

Political Rights: 7
Civil Liberties: 7
Status: Not Free

Overview: Tensions in East Timor rose in late June 1994 after two Indonesian soldiers trampled on a sacred wafer being used in a church service in the village of Remeksio, near Dili, the capital.

This, and continued clashes between the 5,000 Indonesian troops and the remnants of the FRETELIN (Revolutionary Front for an Independent East Timor) guerrillas, who are estimated to number less than 200, underscored the persistent resistance to Indonesia's annexation of this former Portuguese colony in 1976.

During the Asia-Pacific Economic Cooperation (APEC) summit held in Bogor, Indonesia in November 1994, a week of anti-Indonesian demonstrations rocked Dili. Bishop Carlos Felipe Ximenes Belo, the territory's religious leader, said police detained and beat some 135 demonstrators. Police conducted house-to-house searches to find anyone suspected of involvement. Meanwhile, a group of twenty-nine Timorese held a twelve day sit in at the American embassy in Jakarta, Indonesia, to raise international awareness of the territory's plight.

Political Rights and Civil Liberties: Since the 1976 Indonesian annexation of East Timor, the government and military have committed widespread rights abuses against dissidents and ordinary citizens. Up to 200,000 Timorese died from 1975-1979, when FRETELIN fought for independence. Freedoms of speech, press, assembly and association are nonexistent. Police continue to carry out arbitrary detentions and arrests. In May 1994 police arrested two East Timorese for staging protests in front of a hotel housing twenty-eight foreign journalists. On 23 June a court sentenced three activists to twenty months each for staging a demonstration coinciding with a conference on East Timor being held in Manila. On 27 June a court jailed two East Timorese for three years each for raising the Fretelin flag the previous July.

There are credible reports that dissidents are tortured and held incommunicado. In February 1994 the government denied imprisoned Fretelin leader Jose Gusmao permission to meet with the independent Legal Aid Foundation. The authorities occasionally detain people without charge and then require them to report to police on a regular basis. Foreign journalists must obtain special passes to enter East Timor, which are granted infrequently, and are kept under constant surveillance. The government allowed foreign journalists greater access during the November APEC summit, although police briefly detained two American reporters.

The government has closed schools that refuse to use the national Bahasa Indonesia as their primary language. According to Jose Ramos-Horta, an exile-based Timorese leader, the Indonesian government is moving as many as 1,000 Indonesians from other parts of the archipelago into East Timor each week. A New Zealand parliamentary delegation that visited the territory in November reported that over the past five years upwards of 100,000 Indonesians had been encouraged by financial inducements to move to East Timor. The majority Roman Catholic population faces frequent harassment on religious grounds. In July 1994 Bishop Belo told Reuters that "Christians are constantly being arrested, beaten and intimidated by police."

Irian Jaya

Polity: Dominant party (military dominated)
Economy: Capitalist-statist
Population: 1,700,000
Ethnic Groups: Mainly Papuan

Political Rights: 7
Civil Liberties: 7
Status: Not Free

Overview:

In November 1969 the U.N. accepted a sham referendum formalizing Indonesia's annexation of the former Dutch colony of West Papua. In 1973 it was named Irian Jaya, and in February 1984 an Indonesian army offensive against the guerrilla Free Papua Movement (OPM) sent hundreds of villagers fleeing into neighboring Papua New Guinea. In 1988 the army launched cross-border raids into Papua New Guinea against OPM rebels, and in 1989 conducted another series of anti-OPM offensives. Since then the OPM has been largely ineffective, with only about 200 poorly equipped members still hiding in jungles near the border.

The territory's rich natural resources have been exploited by foreign logging and mining companies that pay little if any compensation to the indigenous population. The April 1992 *Pacific Islands Monthly* reported that since 1989 government teams in the Kurima district in the Central Highlands area have offered villagers material incentives to relocate outside the district, and have even withdrawn services in some villages. The villages lie in the mineral exploration zone of Freeport Indonesia, the local subsidiary of the Louisiana-based multinational Freeport-McMoRan.

Political Rights and Civil Liberties:

Residents of Irian Jaya cannot change their government democratically. The Indonesian army maintains a large presence in the territory and is responsible for widespread rights abuses, including extrajudicial executions. In January 1992 the U.N. Special Rapporteur for Torture concluded that in Irian Jaya and other parts of Indonesia facing rebel movements, "torture is said to be practiced rather routinely." Several OPM guerrillas and suspected supporters remain incarcerated under Indonesia's antisubversion laws. Freedoms of speech, press, assembly and association are severely restricted. At least 3,000 Irianese refugees remain in neighboring Papua New Guinea's East Awin camp.

Since the 1970s more than 170,000 residents of Java and other overcrowded parts of the archipelago have been resettled in Irian Jaya under Indonesia's transmigration program. The local population says the settlers have taken away jobs and dominate the urban economies. According to Human Rights Watch/Asia, when foreign companies do employ Irianese the local workers often become bonded through debts allegedly run up at company stores. The government continues to restrict foreigners' access to the territory, and once in the territory foreigners need permits to go from one village to the next. Immigration officials have reduced the number of visas available to missionary workers, who provide vital social services in remote areas. In addition, since 1993 missionaries and other foreign social workers have only been able to receive two-year visas, extendible for only one year.

Iraq
Kurdistan

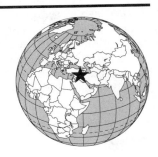

Polity: Dual leadership-elected parliament
Economy: Capitalist-statist
Population: 4,000,000
Ethnic Groups: Kurdish majority

Political Rights: 4
Civil Liberties: 4
Status: Partly Free

Overview: **B**y early 1994 the frayed Kurdistan Democratic Party (KDP)-Patriotic Union of Kurdistan (PUK) coalition led to fighting in which 600 people were killed and 25,000 displaced. By late August most of the fighting had ended, and on 24 November the KDP and PUK signed a fourteen-point peace agreement reaffirming the power sharing process. Elections are due following the completion of a census by May 1995.

In 1988 the Iraqi government, backing off from promises of limited political and cultural freedoms, engaged in a campaign against the Kurds, killing tens of thousands. Iraqi Kurdistan did not gain international attention until, in the wake of the 1991 Gulf War, Iraq suppressed an uprising and sent more than 1.5 million refugees into the mountains and neighboring Turkey and Iran. In April 1991 the U.S., Great Britain, France and the Netherlands established, and continue to maintain, a secure region for the Kurds above the 36th parallel by barring flights of Iraqi fighter aircraft over the zone. Kurdish leaders say they do not seek independence from Iraq, favoring instead autonomy in a federal system.

Presidential and legislative elections in 1992, based on universal suffrage, produced a coalition government for the secure zone, in which the KDP of Massoud Barzani and the PUK of Jalal Talabani shared power. In October of that year the Turkish army launched a massive attack on Turkish Kurdish Worker's Party (PKK) guerrillas operating out of bases in Kurdistan, killing some 1,800 rebels. The Iraqi Kurds have refused to support the PKK for fear of offending Turkey, which provides transit points for U.N. relief convoys entering Kurdistan.

In other developments, in late August Turkish warplanes launched heavy attacks against PKK targets in Kurdistan, and in November Iranian fighters bombed an Iranian Kurdish base inside the territory. The U.N. embargo on Iraq has caused food and fuel shortages and has led to widespread unemployment. An Iraqi government trade embargo against the territory is not rigorously enforced because the desperate economic situation in Iraq makes trade with Kurdistan a necessity.

Political Rights and Civil Liberties: **O**bservers report a generally open climate for dialogue on political issues. Numerous newspapers are available, including the pro-Iraq *Al-Iraq Al-Thaura*. The two major parties run four television stations, with news coverage biased towards their interests. The other parties own newspapers and radio stations. Traditional practices curtail the role of women in politics, education and the private sector. Religious groups practice relatively freely.

Iraqi laws passed prior to November 1991 remain in effect in Kurdistan, except for those judged by the Assembly to be "against Kurdish interests." In a June 1994 statement Amnesty International accused Kurdish political parties of "deliberately killing and mutilating prisoners in custody and abducting and torturing civilians based on their political ties." Iraqi agents frequently attack U.N. aid convoys. In April 1994 unknown gunmen killed Lissy Schmidt, a German journalist.

Israel
Occupied Territories
& Palestinian Autonomous Areas

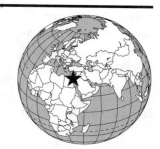

Polity: Military and PLO administered
Economy: Capitalist
Population: 2,184,000
Ethnic Groups: Palestinian Arab, Jewish

Political Rights: 6
Civil Liberties: 5
Status: Not Free

Overview:

In 1994 Israel began transferring administrative authority in the West Bank and Gaza Strip to the Palestinians. Elections for a new Palestinian Council, initially scheduled for July, have been postponed indefinitely pending Israeli-Palestinian agreement on the scope and powers of the Council.

A series of secret negotiations between Israel and the Palestine Liberation Organization (PLO) yielded an agreement in August 1993 for a five-year interim period of Palestinian autonomy in the territories, beginning with the Gaza Strip and the West Bank town of Jericho. Israeli and PLO negotiators missed the target date of 13 December 1993 for the beginning of Israeli troop withdrawal due to disputes. Intermittent Arab-Israeli violence continued to plague the territories and Israel itself. Many of the attacks against Israelis were carried out by Hamas, the militant fundamentalist movement that opposes the accord. The peace process threatened to unravel on 25 February 1994 after a Jewish settler killed at least twenty-nine Arab worshippers in a mosque in the West Bank town of Hebron. The Israeli government ordered the army to detain, disarm and place travel restrictions on settlers considered dangerous, although in practice this affected a relatively small number of settlers.

On 4 May Israel and the PLO finalized the details of the September 1993 accord, clearing the way for the Israeli troop withdrawal from the Gaza Strip and Jericho to begin. In early July PLO Chairman Yasir Arafat returned to the territories for the first time in twenty-seven years as the head of the Palestinian Authority. In August Israel transferred authority over education in the West Bank to the

Palestinians, the first step toward extending Palestinian autonomy beyond Gaza and Jericho. In the fall negotiations on holding elections bogged down over the nature of the planned Palestinian Council. By 1 December Israel had transferred responsibility for tourism, health, social services and taxation in the West Bank to the Palestinian Authority, but by year's end no date had been set for the Council elections.

Political Rights and Civil Liberties:

Palestinians living in the West Bank and Gaza cannot change their government democratically. The September 1993 Israeli–PLO "Gaza-Jericho First Accord" called for elections for a Palestinian Council for the West Bank and Gaza to be held by July 1994, although these elections have been postponed indefinitely. A twenty–four member interim Palestinian Authority headed by PLO Chairman Yasir Arafat holds legislative powers pending the election of the Council. The Palestinian Authority has appointed local councils in Jericho, Nablus and Gaza City. Municipal elections have not been held in the West Bank since 1976, and there have been no elections in Gaza since 1946, dating back to the British Mandate. Palestinians in East Jerusalem, which is not covered under the September 1993 accord, can vote in Israeli municipal elections but generally boycott.

In May 1994 the Israeli Civil Administration transferred authority over education, health, social welfare, taxation, tourism and internal security to Palestinians in Jericho and Gaza. Israel is in the process of extending Palestinian authority in these fields over the entire West Bank.

The press in Gaza and Jericho is subject to government pressure.

The judicial system in Gaza and the West Bank is in flux. In the West Bank outside of Jericho Palestinians accused of ordinary crimes are tried in local courts by Israeli–appointed Palestinian judges. In Gaza and Jericho Palestinians administer the courts themselves, and new laws are being drafted. Jewish settlers in the territories are still subject to Israeli law and are tried in Israeli–administered courts. Settlers generally receive lighter sentences for similar crimes than do Palestinians, particularly when convicted of violent acts against Palestinians.

In January 1994 the Israeli human rights group *B'Tselem* estimated that 750 to 950 Palestinians had been killed in 1993 by other Arabs. B'Tselem also accused Israeli soldiers of killing 1,067 Palestinians since the beginning of the uprising in December 1987.

Palestinian police are not yet responsible for internal security over the entire West Bank. There are credible, persistent reports of physical and psychological abuse by Israeli security forces against Palestinian detainees. Palestinians are frequently subject to administrative detention on security grounds without formal charge. In Gaza the Fatah Hawks, gangs of armed youths allied with PLO Chairman Yasir Arafat's Fatah movement, have been dispensing street justice without any regard for due process rights.

Morocco
Western Sahara

Polity: Appointed governors
Economy: Capitalist
Population: 212,000
Ethnic Groups: Arab, Sahrawi

Political Rights: 7
Civil Liberties: 6
Status: Not Free

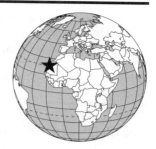

Overview:

Spain annexed the coastal areas of this northwest African region in 1884 and the interior in 1934. In 1957 Morocco renewed its claim to the territory based on informal ties with tribal leaders prior to the Spanish occupation, and in 1960 newly independent Mauritania also staked a claim.

After the last Spanish troops withdrew in February 1976, Polisario, a Marxist, Algerian-backed guerrilla group, announced the establishment of the Saharan Democratic Arab Republic, which has been recognized by more than seventy countries and by the Organization of African Unity. However in April Morocco annexed the northern two-thirds of the territory and Mauritania the southern third. In August 1979 Mauritania withdrew, and Morocco soon annexed the remainder.

In August 1988 Morocco and Polisario approved a U.N. plan calling for a referendum on self-determination. A cease-fire took effect in September 1991, and shortly afterward a 375-member U.N. Monitoring Force (Minurso) took up positions in advance of a referendum.

In late August 1994 Minurso finally began identifying eligible voters for the referendum. In mid-November the U.N., which had earlier announced plans to hold the referendum in February 1995, postponed it indefinitely due to delays in identifying voters. At the time only 4,000 people had been screened, in part because most voters have to identified by tribal elders who are scattered across the desert.

Polisario controls about 15 percent of Western Sahara, but in recent years has received declining support from Algeria, which favors a rapprochement with Morocco.

Political Rights and Civil Liberties:

Moroccan King Hassan appoints governors to the four provinces, and residents in Moroccan-controlled territory can participate in elections for ten seats in the Moroccan parliament. The population in Moroccan-controlled territory is subject to Moroccan law, and the government restricts the exercise of many basic civil liberties. Due to problems of access little is known about the exercise of civil liberties in Polisario-controlled territory, but human rights groups have accused the organization of torturing Sahrawis living in four refugee camps near Tindouf, Algeria. In Moroccan-held areas trade unions are in theory legal but none has formed. In its territory, Polisario has organized the Sario Federation of Labor, which is politically oriented rather than being an advocate of worker rights.

Netherlands
Aruba

Polity: Appointed governor and parliamentary democracy
Economy: Mixed capitalist
Population: 66,000

Political Rights: 2*
Civil Liberties: 1
Status: Free

Ethnic Groups: Black majority with Carib Indian and European minorities
Ratings Change: *Aruba's political rights rating changed from 1 to 2 because of weakened government authority caused by deepening penetration in the economy of the hemispheric drug and money-laundering trades.

Overview:

Aruba was part of the Netherlands Antilles from 1954 until 1986 when it achieved formal parity with the Netherlands and Netherlands Antilles under the Dutch crown. Under the assumption of domestic autonomy, Aruba agreed to retain economic and political links to the Netherlands Antilles until 1996.

The Netherlands is represented in Aruba by an appointed governor, but the island is largely self-governing. Domestic affairs are the responsibility of the prime minister appointed by the freely elected unicameral Staten (legislature). Full freedom of party organization and expression is respected. The Council of Ministers at the Hague remains responsible for foreign affairs and defense.

The twenty-one-member Staten is directly elected for a four-year term. The social democratic People's Electoral Movement (MEP) won the 1989 election, taking ten seats against the incumbent, center-right Aruba People's Party (AVP), which won eight seats. Three smaller parties obtained one seat each. Following the election, a three-party government was formed, headed by the MEP's Nelson Oduber.

The MEP-led coalition narrowly won again in 1993, but in April 1994 the ruling coalition unraveled. In new elections held on 29 July the AVP won ten seats against nine for the MEP. The AVP formed a coalition with the Organization for the Liberation of Aruba (OLA), a splinter of the MEP that won the other two seats, and the AVP's Heny Eman became the prime minister. As in 1993 the campaign was marked by mudslinging as the MEP and the AVP charged each other with ties to drug traffickers.

In 1990 the former MEP government and the Dutch governments agreed that any future changes in the constitutional relationship would not involve transition to full independence in 1996 as had been originally accorded. Neither the Aruban nor the Dutch government has been able to slow the steady penetration into the island's economy by South American and Sicilian drug traffickers and money launderers.

The press, radio and television are private, free and varied. Three daily newspapers are published, one in Dutch, one in English, and one in the local Papiamento. There are five privately run radio stations and one commercial television station.

Netherlands Antilles

Polity: Appointed governor **Political Rights:** 1
and parliamentary democracy **Civil Liberties:** 2*
Economy: Mixed capitalist **Status:** Free
Population: 194,000
Ethnic Groups: Black majority with Carib Indian
and European minorities
Ratings Change: *Netherlands Antilles's civil liberties rating
changed from 1 to 2, principally a result of increasing crime
and corruption, much of it drug-related.

Overview:

In 1954 the Netherlands Antilles was granted constitutional equality with the Netherlands and Suriname (which became independent in 1975). In 1986, Aruba split off and was given formal parity with the Netherlands and the Netherlands Antilles. The Netherlands Antilles currently consists of one group of two and another of three islands, the southern (Leeward) islands of Curacao and Bonaire and the northern (Windward) islands of St. Maarten, St. Eustatius, and Saba.

Although the Netherlands is represented by an appointed governor, the Netherlands Antilles is largely self-governing. Domestic affairs are the responsibility of the prime minister appointed by the unicameral Staten (legislature) of twenty-two deputies (fourteen from Curacao, three each from Bonaire and St. Maarten, and one each from St. Eustatius and Saba) elected for four years. Full freedom of party organization and expression is respected. Foreign affairs and defense remain the responsibility of the Council of Ministers at the Hague. Local government on each of the islands is constituted by elected Island Councils.

Traditionally the two main parties have been the center-right National People's Party (NPP) and the social democratic New Antilles Movement (MAN).

The NPP-led coalition government elected in 1990 unraveled in late 1993 over the issue of separate status for Curacao. In the 25 February 1994 elections a new party emerged victorious, the Antillian Reconstruction Party (PAR) led by Miguel Pourier. The PAR, formed in fall 1993 in support of maintaining the Antillian federation, won eight seats to the NPP's three. The NNP had backed separate status for Curacao.

Between late 1993 and late 1994 citizens on all five islands voted in referendums to keep the Netherlands Antilles intact, but indicated a desire for a new, more stable political structure. That was the promise of new prime minister Pourier and a proposal by his government was expected by the beginning of 1995.

The press, radio and television are private, free and varied. The islands are serviced by six daily newspapers, two in Dutch and four in the local Papiamento. Privately owned radio stations operate on all islands except St. Eustatius. There is a television station on Curacao. There have been reports in recent years of police brutality on all the islands except Saba. There has also been mounting evidence that increasing violent crime and corruption are a result of penetration by the hemispheric drug trade which neither the Dutch nor the Antillian government has been able to slow.

New Zealand
Cook Islands

Polity: Parliamentary democracy
Economy: Capitalist-statist
Population: 19,000
Ethnic Groups: Polynesian majority, European and mixed race minorities

Political Rights: 1
Civil Liberties: 2
Status: Free

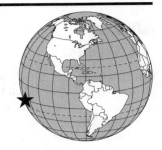

Overview: The Cook Islands are in free association with New Zealand and Cook Islanders are citizens of that country. Aside from defense and foreign affairs, they are largely self-governing. On 24 March 1994 the Cook Islands Prime Minister Sir Geoffrey Henry of the ruling Cook Islands Party (CIP) was re-elected.

Niue

Polity: Parliamentary democracy
Economy: Capitalist-statist
Population: 3,000
Ethnic Groups: Polynesian, other Pacific Islanders, Europeans

Political Rights: 1
Civil Liberties: 2
Status: Free

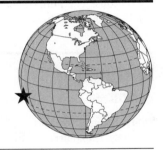

Overview: With dim economic prospects and high unemployment rates among Niue's 2,300 population, the government of Frank Lui ruled out salary and pension increases for civil servants and embarked on a program to increase the population and to expand tourism.

Tokelau

Polity: Administrator, elected leaders and elders
Economy: Capitalist-statist
Population: 2,000
Ethnic Groups: Polynesian

Political Rights: 2
Civil Liberties: 2
Status: Free

Overview: Tokelau, a group of Polynesian islands economically subsidized by New Zealand, is governed by an elected Council of Faipule (representatives) and a Fono, organized parliament. New Zealand appoints the territorial administrator. Most Tokelauers are Christian. There are no newspapers or broadcast media.

Norway
Svalbard

Polity: Appointed governor and advisory council
Economy: Capitalist statist
Population: 3,942
Ethnic Groups: Russian majority, Norwegian minority

Political Rights: 3
Civil Liberties: 1
Status: Free

Overview: The glacier-covered 24,000 square miles of the Svalbard archipelago, integrally Norwegian since 1925, are characterized by coal-mining and fishing, the latter a source of disputes with Iceland, whose trawlers are accused of violating regulations. The king of Norway appoints a governor who serves as the local head of administration and chief of police.

Portugal
Azores

Polity: Elected assembly
Economy: Capitalist-statist
Population: 269,000
Ethnic Groups: Portuguese

Political Rights: 1
Civil Liberties: 1
Status: Free

Overview: Eight hundred miles west of Portugal and internally self-governing, the Azores send representatives to the parliament in Lisbon. Statutes passed by they Azorean regional assembly remain subject to the approval of the Portugese parliament. Islanders have the same civil liberties as Portuguese mainlanders.

Macao

Polity: Appointed
governor and partially
elected legislature
Economy: Capitalist-statist
Population: 447,000
Ethnic Groups: Chinese, Mecanese, Portuguese
Ratings Change: *Macao's political rights rating changed
from 5 to 6 and its civil liberties rating from 3 to 4 because
freedom is declining as Chinese influence increases.

Political Rights: 6*
Civil Liberties: 4*
Status: Partly Free

Overview: The Portuguese established Macao in 1557 as the first
European trading station on the Chinese coast. Consisting
of a peninsula and two islands at the mouth of the Canton
River, it is an entrepot for trade with China and a gambling mecca. The 1976
Organic Statute serves as the territory's constitution. It vests executive powers in a
governor appointed by the Portuguese president, and grants legislative powers to
both the Portuguese government and Macao's Legislative Assembly.

In February 1979 Portugal and China established diplomatic relations, and
subsequently agreed that Macao was "a Chinese territory under Portuguese
administration." The May 1987 Sino-Portuguese Joint Declaration calls for China
to assume sovereignty over Macao on 20 December 1999, with the enclave
functioning as a Special Autonomous Region and maintaining its legal system and
capitalist economy for fifty years.

In the 1992 legislative elections, pro-China candidates swept all eight of the
directly elected seats. The results underscored China's dominant influence in the
colony.

On 31 March 1993 China's National People's Congress approved the Basic
Law, Macao's post-1999 constitution. The document affirmed the territory's
autonomous status after the transfer. Portuguese expatriates account for the
majority of government undersecretaries and department chiefs, and hold all
thirteen judicial seats.

Political Rights   **C**itizens of Macao lack the democratic means to change
and Civil Liberties: their government. The governor is appointed by Lisbon,
and only eight out of twenty-three legislative seats are
directly elected. In addition, citizens had no voice in the 1987 Joint Declaration
ceding control of the territory to China in 1999.

The legal system is based on Portuguese Metropolitan Law, and citizens are
extended the rights granted by the Portuguese constitution. The judiciary is
independent, and defendants receive fair trials. The government owns a controlling
interest in the television and radio stations, although opposition viewpoints are
aired. Newspapers are privately held and most are blatantly pro-China in their news
coverage and editorials. Journalists reportedly practice self-censorship in criticizing
China or government policies for fear of losing their jobs. A ban on holding

demonstrations within fifty yards of government buildings effectively bars protests from the peninsula, restricting them to the two islands. Workers can join independent unions and hold strikes. In reality, nearly all 7,000 private-sector union members belong to the pro-Beijing General Association of Workers, which is generally more involved in social and political affairs than labor issues.

Madeira

Polity: Elected assembly
Economy: Capitalist-statist
Population: 290,000
Ethnic Groups: Portuguese

Political Rights: 1
Civil Liberties: 1
Status: Free

Overview: The Madeira Islands are self-governing, with representatives in the Portuguese parliament in Lisbon. Civil liberties are the same as those on the mainland.

Spain
Canary Islands

Polity: Regional legislature
Economy: Capitalist
Population: 1,578,000
Ethnic Groups: Racially mixed, mostly Hispanic

Political Rights: 1
Civil Liberties: 1
Status: Free

Overview: With representatives in the Spanish Cortes and the status of an autonomous region, the Canary Islands, located off the northwest coast of Africa, are guaranteed Spanish rights and are self-governing. There have been periodic separatist movements, but the development of regional autonomy has reduced such sentiments.

Ceuta (Places of sovereignty in North Africa)

Polity: Municipal administration
Economy: Capitalist-statist
Population: 80,000
Ethnic Groups: Moroccan, Spanish

Political Rights: 1
Civil Liberties: 2
Status: Free

Melilla

Polity: Municipal administration
Economy: Capitalist-statist
Population: 65,000
Ethnic Groups: Moroccan, Spanish

Political Rights: 1
Civil Liberties: 2
Status: Free

Overview: Muslim city-islands off the Moroccan coast, Ceuta and Melilla are integral parts of Spain. Both cities have Muslim populations, and in 1992 Spain placed Islam on a par with other major religions.

Turkey
Cyprus (T)

Polity: Presidential parliamentary democracy (Turkish-occupied)
Economy: Mixed capitalist
Population: 178,000
Ethnic Groups: Turkish Cypriot, Turkish, Greek Cypriot, Maronite

Political Rights: 4
Civil Liberties: 2
Status: Partly Free

Note: See Cyprus (Greek) under country reports

Overview: In 1994, U.N.-sponsored talks to reunify Greek and Turkish Cyprus ended in deadlock. Following the European Union decision to extend membership to Greek Cyprus in the next EU enlargement, the new parliament formally backed the island's partition and integration with Turkey.

Divided in 1974 following an unsuccessful coup by Cyprus army officers aiming for union with Greece, Cyprus was effectively partitioned along ethnic lines. In 1992, leaders of the Turkish Republic of Northern Cyprus and the Cypriot Republic, Rauf Denktash and George Vassiliou respectively, commenced reunification talks under U.N. auspices. Despite early optimism on both sides, these collapsed in 1994.

Political Rights and Civil Liberties: The citizens of the Turkish Republic of Northern Cyprus (TRNC) can change their government democratically. The Turkish immigrants who settled in the wake of the 1974 Turkish invasion have the right to vote in TRNC elections. The 1,000-member Greek and Maronite communities do not vote in TRNC national elections but vote in Cypriot Republic elections.

The judiciary is independent and trials are fair. Civilians deemed to have violated military zones are subject to trial in military courts, which maintain all due process laws. The TRNC authorities, however, still refuse to allow for an investigation into the fate of the 1,619 Greek Cypriots who "disappeared" during the 1974 invasion.

Freedom of speech and press is generally respected, a variety of newspapers and periodicals being printed. Broadcast media are government-owned. However, the Greek press is unavailable to the remaining Greek Cypriots. The authorities control the contents of Greek-Cypriot school textbooks, and many titles are rejected on the grounds that they "violate the feelings" of Turkish Cypriots.

Freedom of religion is respected. The majority Sunni Moslems and the minority Greek and Maronite Orthodox Christians, as well as foreign residents, practice their religions freely. Freedom of movement is generally respected, although travel to and from the Cypriot Republic is strictly regulated. Workers are free to organize and join independent trade unions.

United Kingdom
Anguilla

Polity: Appointed governor and elected assembly
Economy: Mixed capitalist
Population: 7,000
Ethnic Groups: Relatively homogeneous, black minority

Political Rights: 2
Civil Liberties: 1
Status: Free

Overview: Following the establishment of the Associated State of St. Kitts-Nevis-Anguilla, Anguillans rejected governmental authority from St. Kitts and in 1969 a British commissioner was appointed. A separate constitution was provided in 1976 giving the commissioner (now governor) authority over foreign affairs, defense, civil service and internal security. In 1990 the governor assumed responsibility for international financial affairs. All other governmental responsibilities are carried out by an elected seven-member House of Assembly headed by a chief minister who commands a majority in the body.

In elections held on 16 March 1994 the incumbent Anguilla National Alliance (ANA) won only two seats. The Anguilla United Party (AUP), led by economist

Hubert Hughes, won two, as did the Anguilla Democratic Party (ADP). The seventh seat was won by an independent. The AUP and the ADP formed a coalition and former opposition leader Hughes became chief minister, replacing Emile Gumbs, who retired from politics after leading two consecutive ANA governments.

Hughes quickly clashed with Governor Allan Shave, whom Hughes accused of being partial to the outgoing ANA. In May, Hughes threatened to demand independence and charged also that Britain had ended development projects.

Anguillans enjoy all civil rights common to the homeland. The press is government owned and operated. Radio is both government owned and private.

Bermuda

Polity: Appointed governor and parliamentary democracy
Political Rights: 1
Civil Liberties: 1
Status: Free
Economy: Mixed capitalist
Population: 61,000
Ethnic Groups: Black (approximately 60 percent), large British minority

Overview: Under a constitution approved in 1967, Bermuda was granted the right of internal self-government in 1968. A British-appointed governor exercises responsibility for external affairs, defense, internal security and police. A premier is appointed by the governor but is responsible to a freely elected forty-member House of Assembly for all internal matters.

In the 1993 elections the incumbent center-right, multiracial United Bermuda Party (UBP) of Premier John Swan retained control of the House over the left-wing, predominantly black Progressive Labour Party (PLP).

Swan surprised many by re-raising the question of independence, as polls have consistently shown a majority supporting the status quo. The UBP divided over the issue and in mid-1994 backbenchers failed in an attempt to oust Swan. The PLP, traditionally more supportive of independence, tried to seize control of the issue from Swan in the House. Swan ordered the preparation of a paper on the issue that was due to be finished at the end of 1994 and proposed a referendum for 1995.

Bermudans enjoy all civil rights common to the homeland. There are several newspapers, all privately owned. There are numerous radio stations and two television stations. Labor unions, the largest being the 6,000-member Bermuda Industrial Union, are well organized. The right to strike is recognized by law and in practice. Rising drug-related crime and racial tensions have begun to taint Bermuda's image as safe tourist resort.

British Virgin Islands

Polity: Appointed governor and elected council
Economy: Mixed capitalist
Population: 13,000
Ethnic Groups: Relatively homogeneous with black majority

Political Rights: 1
Civil Liberties: 1
Status: Free

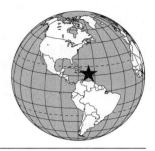

Overview:

The 1977 constitution granted the government of the British Virgin Islands greater responsibility over internal affairs. A British-appointed governor retains responsibility for external affairs, civil service, defense and internal security. On other matters the governor acts on the advice of the Executive Council whose members are the governor, the chief minister, four members of the legislature and the attorney general. The chief minister represents the majority party in the elected nine-member Legislative Council.

Residents enjoy all civil liberties common to the homeland. There is one weekly newspaper, one radio station and one television station. Since 1992 an increase in drug-related crime has raised concerns about whether the police force should remain unarmed. In late 1993 a new firearms law was implemented, providing for up to twenty years in prison for an unlicensed weapon.

Cayman Islands

Polity: Appointed governor and elected council
Economy: Capitalist
Population: 32,000
Ethnic Groups: Mixed (40 percent), Caucasian (20 percent), black (20 percent), various ethnic groups (20 percent)

Political Rights: 1
Civil Liberties: 1
Status: Free

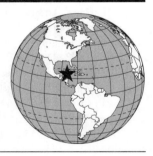

Overview:

Previously governed from Jamaica, the Cayman Islands were placed under British administration in 1962. A British-appointed governor chairs an Executive Council composed of four elected members plus an appointed chief secretary, financial secretary and attorney general. The Executive Council is drawn from the Legislative Assembly that consists of fifteen elected members, with a new Assembly elected every four years.

In 1993 the Assembly unanimously rejected a proposal by the British Foreign and Commonwealth Office to adopt a chief minister form of government. The Assembly did agree to adopt the title of "minister" for Executive Council members, to create a fifth elected ministerial post, to adopt a bill of rights and to establish a procedure for holding referenda on matters of importance.

Residents enjoy all civil liberties common to the homeland. There is a daily newspaper and a weekly publication. There is at least one radio and one television station. In 1994 the government ordered that journalists could not visit the refugee camp, housing 1,180 Cubans, unaccompanied. A government worker was fired in December after he had a letter calling for greater free speech for civil service employees published in the daily *Caymanian Compass*.

Channel Islands

Polity: Appointed executives and legislatures (varies by island)
Economy: Capitalist
Population: 147,000
Ethnic Groups: British, Norman French

Political Rights: 2
Civil Liberties: 1
Status: Free

Overview: The Channel Islands, Jersey and Guernsey and their dependencies, are Crown fiefdoms, connected to Britain through the monarch. The queen appoints her representatives, who are called lieutenant governors and commanders-in-chief. British laws do not apply unless the parliamentary legislation specifies that they do or unless the British Privy Council extends coverage of the laws to the islands.

Falkland Islands

Polity: Appointed governor and partly-elected legislative council
Economy: Capitalist-statist
Population: 2,000
Ethnic Groups: British

Political Rights: 2
Civil Liberties: 1
Status: Free

Overview: In April 1994 Guido di Tella, Argentina's foreign minister, announced that the Falkland Islands government accepted his proposals to clear 30,000 mines laid by Argentine troops during the 1982 conflict with Britain. In July, the British government chose not to prosecute any of its soldiers for alleged war crimes during the conflict.

Following the 1982 war, the Falklands experienced rapid economic growth largely due to the granting of fishing licences to foreign fishing fleets. Despite lingering tensions, Britain and Argentina are working toward a permanent fisheries conservation agreement and cooperate in oil exploration efforts.

The Islands have a mixture of appointed and elected officials, with local legislative functions vested in a six-member council. There are two newspapers, one of them government published. The public Falkland Islands Broadcasting Service operates two radio stations.

Gibraltar

Polity: Appointed governor and mostly elected assembly
Political Rights: 1
Civil Liberties: 1
Status: Free
Economy: Capitalist-statist
Population: 32,000
Ethnic Groups: Italian, English, Maltese, Portuguese, and Spanish

Overview: In December 1994, the British government protested the "intrusive" nature of car and body searches by Spanish border police, which reportedly can cause delays of several hours. Spain defended the search policy by claiming that Gibraltar had become a center of drug smuggling and money laundering. Spain still claims sovereignty over the territory, which came under British control in 1704 after the War of the Spanish Succession.

Britain appoints a territorial governor, who is advised by a Council of Ministers. Chosen through competitive, multiparty elections, the House of Assembly handles domestic affairs. Britain determines defense and foreign affairs. There are seven newspapers and a public broadcasting corporation. The Socialist government promotes a free market economy and encourages Gibraltar's use as a tax haven.

Hong Kong

Polity: Appointed governor and partly elected legislature
Political Rights: 5
Civil Liberties: 2
Status: Partly Free
Economy: Capitalist
Population: 5,847,000
Ethnic Groups: Chinese (98 percent)

Overview: Hong Kong public affairs in 1994 were characterized by China's threat to abolish the democratic institutions that have been put in place in recent years. Under the terms of the Joint Declaration of 26 September 1984, China is to obtain sovereignty over the Crown Colony (Hong Kong Island, Kowloon Peninsula, and the mainland New Territories) on 1 July 1997.

The principal political issue facing Hong Kong is whether China will permit any democracy when it takes control in 1997. The twenty-eighth colonial governor,

Christopher Patten, appointed in 1992 by British Prime Minister John Major, has encouraged a spirit of democratic resistance among Hong Kong's people. Without subverting the Basic Law which China and the UK agreed should serve as Hong Kong's constitution, Patten proposed in 1992 to broaden the franchise for the sixty-seat Legislative Council (Legco), winning legislative approval in 1994. Under the Basic Law, only twenty members are directly elected, but Patten proposed restructuring the system of occupation-based functional constituencies so that nearly all of the working population will be able to vote for one of the thirty functional constituency seats.

Claiming that Patten's reforms violated the Basic Law, China's National People's Congress announced in August that all of Hong Kong's popularly elected bodies will be dismantled in 1997. Within weeks, democratic parties swept the elections for the 346 seats to the District Board which oversees municipal affairs and, crucially, is to elect ten nondirectly elected seats at the September 1995 Legco elections.

Political Rights and Civil Liberties:

Hong Kong citizens cannot change their government democratically. The British premier appoints the governor, and a majority of the Legislative Council seats are appointed or indirectly elected. Residents had no voice in the 1984 Declaration transferring sovereignty to China in July 1997. An April 1992 report by the International Commission of Jurists condemned Britain for denying Hong Kong the right to self-determination, and recommended that it expand democracy before 1997 and extend the right of abode to the 3.4 million residents who only have British Dependent Territory Citizen (BDTC) Status and not British citizenship.

The colony has an independent judiciary, and defendants receive fair trials. In 1994 Britain and China failed to reach an agreement on the composition of the colony's post-1997 Court of Final Appeal. The Basic Law allows foreign judges to sit on the planned five-man court. Britain wants a firm agreement that at least one foreign judge will sit on the court, while China refuses to agree to a specific number. In June 1991 Legco passed a Bill of Human Rights patterned after the International Covenant on Civil and Political Rights. However, repressive laws giving the governor and police wide latitude in restricting civil liberties remain on the books, and if not removed could be arbitrarily applied by China after 1997.

As 1997 approaches, there has been a chilling effect on the media and other institutions. During the summer of 1993 eighteen leading law firms refused to represent liberal politician Martin Lee in a libel suit he brought against a pro-Beijing judge. The colony has a vigorous press, although some journalists practice self-censorship to avoid antagonizing China. In a ruling clearly intended as a message to Hong Kong's journalists, in March 1994 a Beijing court sentenced Xi Yang, the mainland-based correspondent for the Hong Kong newspaper *Ming Pao*, to twelve years in prison for leaking "state secrets," in reality innocuous data about monetary policy. In February 1994 TVB, Hong Kong's leading television station, chose not to screen a controversial BBC documentary on the life of the late Chairman Mao Zedong.

Some 24,000 Vietnamese refugees live in squalid conditions in three camps. Nearly 30,000 other refugees have voluntarily returned to Vietnam, although several hundred others have been forcibly repatriated. In April and September 1994 police used excessive force, including tear gas, against refugees, the first time while relocating refugees to another detention center, and the second time to break up a nonviolent demonstration.

Isle of Man

Polity: Appointed executive and elected legislature
Economy: Capitalist
Population: 70,000
Ethnic Groups: Mostly Manx (of mixed Celtic and Scandinavian descent)

Political Rights: 1
Civil Liberties: 1
Status: Free

Overview:

The Isle of Man is a crown fiefdom tied to Britain through the monarch, who appoints an executive, the lieutenant governor. The Court of Tynwald is the bicameral legislature. There is a twelve-member Legislative Council, of which the lieutenant governor is a member, and an elected twenty-four-member House of Keys. The Isle has its own laws. Acts of the British Parliament apply only if they state so specifically. The Isle of Man owes its success as a tax haven to its freedom from British tax laws.

Montserrat

Polity: Appointed governor and partly elected council
Economy: Capitalist
Population: 13,000
Ethnic Groups: Mostly black with European minority

Political Rights: 1
Civil Liberties: 1
Status: Free

Overview:

A British-appointed governor presides over an appointed Executive Council. Local legislative matters are the responsibility of an eleven-member Legislative Council. Of the eleven members, who serve five-year terms, seven are directly elected, two are official members, and two are nominated. The chief minister is the leader of the majority party in the Council.

In the 1991 elections, John Osborne's People's Liberation Movement (PLM) was swept from office after thirteen years by the newly formed National Progressive Party (NPP), which won four of seven legislative seats. NPP leader Reuben Meade, a thirty-seven-year-old former civil servant, was named chief minister.

Residents enjoy all civil liberties common to the homeland. There are at least two newspapers, including the opposition *Montserrat Reporter*, several radio stations and one television station. Labor unions are well organized and the right to strike is recognized by law and in practice.

Northern Ireland

Polity: British administration and elected local
councils
(military-occupied)
Economy: Mixed capitalist
Population: 1,630,000

Political Rights: 4*
Civil Liberties: 3*
Status: Partly Free

Ethnic Groups: Protestants (mostly of Scottish and English descent),
57percent; Irish Catholics, 43 percent
Ratings Change: *Northern Ireland's political rights rating
changed from 5 to 4 and its civil liberties rating from 4 to 3
following paramilitary cease-fires and the lifting of some restrictions on movement and expression.

Overview: In 1994, after twenty-five years of sectarian violence,
Northern Ireland had its best chance for peace. Following
months of internal debate, on 31 August the Provisional
Irish Republican Army (IRA) announced a cease-fire in its violent campaign
against British rule. On 13 October Loyalist paramilitaries, groups committed to a
violent defense of British rule, declared their own cease-fire.

Northern Ireland consists of six of the nine counties of the Irish province of Ulster.
At the insistence of the locally dominant Protestants, these counties remained within the
United Kingdom after the other twenty-six counties, which are largely Catholic, gained
home rule in 1921. Protestants comprise over half of the general population, but a
majority of children are Catholic. The Catholics now constitute a majority in four of the
six counties of the North and in thirteen of the twenty-six local government bodies. The
demographic trends have aroused deep anxieties among the Protestant population, which
is largely descended from Scottish and English settlers of the seventeenth century.

Generally, Protestants favor continued political union with Britain and thus have the
political labels "Loyalist" and "Unionist," while the "Nationalist" or "Republican"
Catholic population favors unification with the Republic of Ireland. Britain's Government of Ireland Act (1920), which partitioned Ireland, set up the Northern Irish parliament which functioned until the British imposed direct rule from London in 1972.
Several subsequent attempts at Catholic-Protestant power-sharing have failed.

Until the late 1960s, electoral regulations favored the economically dominant
Protestants by according property owners voting rights for both their residential and
commercial addresses. A nonviolent Catholic civil rights movement in the 1960s met
with limited success and a violent response from the Protestants. Attempting to impose
order in 1969, the British government sent in the army, which originally appealed to
some Catholics as a security force preferable to the Protestant-controlled local police.
However, Catholics soon viewed the troops as an army of occupation.

The violently confrontational situation of the late 1960s and 1970s led to
divisions in both the Unionist and Nationalist communities. There are now several
Unionist and Nationalist parties. The most important of these are: the conservative

Official or Ulster Unionist Party, led by James Molyneaux; the hard-line Democratic Unionist Party, led by Rev. Ian Paisley; the Alliance Party, a liberal, interdenominational, unionist group led by John Alderdice; the moderate, pro-Nationalist Social Democratic and Labour Party (SDLP), led by John Hume; and the militant, pro-Nationalist Sinn Fein, led by Gerry Adams. Sinn Fein is the political wing of the Irish Republican movement, whose military wing is the Provisional IRA.

In the British general election of 1992, Unionists won thirteen House of Commons seats and the SDLP took four, its highest ever. Adams lost his Commons seat, because some Protestants cast tactical votes for the successful SDLP candidate.

During 1993 Hume and Adams conducted discussions that produced the outline of an interim political settlement. Although the exact wording of their agreement was private, Hume and Adams made clear they advocated British recognition of the Irish right to self-determination and British renunciation of long-term interests in the North. In exchange, the Republican side would offer an IRA cease-fire, participate in negotiations and put off for now the question of Irish unification. The Hume-Adams proposals included implicit calls for joint Irish-British sovereignty over the North, at least for an interim period before the withdrawal of British troops and a final political settlement. Secretly, the British government held discussions with the IRA in early 1993, but denied that this was happening until late in the year. The Irish government worked on its own response to Hume-Adams, and negotiated with the British about producing a joint statement.

On 15 December 1993 Irish *Taoiseach* (Prime Minister) Albert Reynolds and British Prime Minister John Major issued a statement on Northern Ireland known as the Downing Street Declaration. The British leader acknowledged the Irish right to self-determination, North and South. However, both prime ministers agreed that there could be no coercion of the North into a united Ireland without the consent of a majority of its population. The British stated that they have no "selfish, strategic or economic interest" in Northern Ireland, and that they would encourage agreement among the Irish people even if that means Irish unification. For its part, the Irish government agreed to referenda on removing the claim to the North from its constitution, in order to provide political incentive to the Unionists. The joint document agreed in principle that there could be all-Ireland institutions. Finally, the two sides promised that after a cessation of violence, all parties, including Sinn Fein, could participate in negotiations.

Following the release of the Downing Street Declaration, the IRA took several months to debate its meaning and ask for clarifications of its terms from the British. In the meantime Republican and Loyalist terror continued. The British had no interest in letting Sinn Fein and the IRA join the peace process as long as paramilitary operations still functioned in Northern Ireland. Sinn Fein received a major boost in February 1994 when the Clinton administration allowed Gerry Adams to visit the U.S. The trip was a political and public relations breakthrough for Adams. The British government was upset that Clinton allowed Adams to generate goodwill before the IRA had agreed to a cease-fire.

By August the IRA concluded that it would try a cease-fire, in order to enable Sinn Fein to enter negotiations. The Irish government welcomed the cease-fire, and invited Sinn Fein to join the Forum for Reconciliation and Peace that began in Dublin on 28 October. Sinn Fein and the Alliance Party attended the meeting, but the main Unionist parties declined to participate. Initially, the British government hesitated to accept the cease-fire as "permanent," because that word was not in the cease-fire declaration. However, after the Loyalist paramilitaries (the Ulster Defense Association, the Ulster Volunteer Force and the Red Hand Commandos) announced their own cease-fire on 13 October, Prime Minister Major accepted the IRA truce on 21 October. Major responded with a confidence-building measure, opening eighty-eight blocked border crossings between the North and the Irish Republic. The British began separate talks with Sinn Fein and Loyalist groups (the Ulster Democratic Party and the Progressive Unionist Party) in December, but London wanted paramilitary disarmament before all-party negotiations could begin.

Albert Reynolds' resignation as Irish Prime Minister on 17 November threw the Northern peace process into confusion. However, Reynolds' successor, John Bruton, pledged in December to continue negotiations. After leaving office, Reynolds claimed in an interview with the BBC that the Irish and British governments had already agreed to an elected all-Ireland body and cross-border executive committees. Other parties to the talks variously denounced Reynolds for betraying confidences or stated flatly that there were no such agreements.

Political Rights and Civil Liberties:

The people of Northern Ireland have the right to elect members of the British House of Commons and local government bodies. However, the regional parliament remains suspended. Nationalists argue that they lack the right of self-determination, because Britain has effectively granted the Unionists a veto over the six counties' entrance into a united Ireland. Unionists, on the other hand, insist that the Irish Republic should have no role in governing them, and they resent Dublin's consultative rights in the North under the 1985 Anglo-Irish Accord. Elections appear to be conducted fairly, and have allowed Sinn Fein to win both parliamentary and local council seats. Before the cease-fires, paramilitaries limited political rights by killing and wounding elected officials and political activists.

Until September 1994 Britain had banned broadcast appearances by Sinn Fein members, except during election campaigns. However, broadcasters had used actors to dub Gerry Adams' voice on news programs. The government has banned several violent Republican and Loyalist organizations, but has included their political wings in negotiations following their cease-fires. Trial by jury does not exist for suspected terrorists. A judge tries such cases, and there is an extremely high conviction rate. Under the Prevention of Terrorism Act, the security forces may arrest suspects without warrants. The authorities may prevent suspected terrorists from entering Britain and Northern Ireland and may keep non-natives out of Northern Ireland. In 1994 Britain lifted orders that had excluded Sinn Fein leaders Gerry Adams and Martin McGuinness from England.

In 1994 sixty-five people, down from eighty-seven in 1993, died as a result of Northern violence. The death toll since the start of "the troubles" in 1969 exceeds 3,100. Following the IRA cease-fire proclamation, suspected IRA members killed a postal worker, but it was not clear on whose orders they acted. Despite the ceasefires, paramilitaries continued nonlethal violence such as beatings and kneecappings. British and Irish authorities feared that Republican splinter groups, such as Republican Sinn Fein or the Irish National Liberation Army, would replace the IRA as significant killers after the cease-fire.

All paramilitaries are potent economic forces. The Provisional IRA reaps profits through protection rackets, drug-dealing and other enterprises. Other terrorist groups (including the older Official IRA) have degenerated into pure rackets, almost totally devoid of their original political purposes.

Loyalist and Republican paramilitaries have agreed on zomes of control in Belfast. They have divided taxi services, construction projects and other legitimate business fronts among themselves.

Traditionally, Protestants have discriminated against Catholics. The British Parliament passed the Fair Employment Act of 1989, which set up a commission to monitor discrimination. Numerous organizations around the world have campaigned for the MacBride Principles, a set of standards designed to direct investment only to those Northern Irish firms that adopt affirmative action hiring practices. Catholics are two and a half times as likely as Protestants to be unemployed. According to a British government report this situation will take more than a decade to improve.

Pitcairn Islands

Polity: Appointed governor and partly elected council
Economy: Capitalist-statist
Population: 59
Ethnic Groups: *Bounty* families (Mixed Anglo-Tahitian)

Political Rights: 2
Civil Liberties: 1
Status: Free

Overview: **O**nly a few descendants of the famous *Bounty* mutineers live here, and they engage in needed public service in lieu of paying taxes.

St. Helena and Dependencies

Polity: Appointed governor and elected council
Economy: Capitalist-statist
Population: 8,000
Ethnic Groups: British, Asian, African

Political Rights: 2
Civil Liberties: 1
Status: Free

Overview: **A** British governor administers St. Helena, Ascension Island, and the Tristan da Cunha island group with an executive council of two *ex officio* members and the chairmen of the council committees. Since 1967, residents elect a twelve-member Legislative Council for a four-year term. The Ascension advisory council includes representatives of the BBC, South Atlantic Cable Company, Cable Wireless Ltd., the U.S. National Aeronautics and Space Administration, and the U.S. Air Force, all of which have facilities there. (Ascension has no native population.)

Turks and Caicos

Polity: Appointed governor and elected council
Economy: Capitalist
Population: 14,000
Ethnic Groups: Relatively homogeneous with black majority

Political Rights: 1
Civil Liberties: 1
Status: Free

Overview: **P**reviously governed from Jamaica, the islands were placed under a British administration in 1962. A constitution adopted in 1976 provides for a governor, an eight-member Executive Council, and a Legislative Council of thirteen elected, four ex-officio, and three nominated members. The chief minister is the leader of the majority party in the Legislative Council.

In the 1988 elections the People's Democratic Movement (PDM), formerly in opposition, took nine of eleven seats and Oswald Skippings became chief minister. In the 1991 elections the PNP returned to power by winning eight legislative seats to the PDM's five and PNP leader Washington Missick became chief minister.

Residents enjoy all the civil liberties common to the homeland. There are at least one weekly newspaper and several radio stations.

United States of America
American Samoa

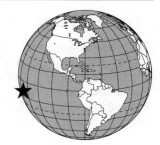

Polity: Elected governor and legislature
Economy: Capitalist
Population: 55,000
Ethnic Groups: Samoan (Polynesian)

Political Rights: 1
Civil Liberties: 1
Status: Free

Overview: **S**amoans have elected their governor directly since 1977. The *Fono,* a bicameral legislature, consists of a twenty-member House of Representatives and an eighteen-member Senate. The House is elected by popular vote for a two-year term. The *matai,* the chiefs of extended families, elect senators from among themselves for four-year terms. The territory sends a delegate to the U.S. House of Representatives. There are free and competing newspapers, a private radio station, and a government-owned television station. The American Samoan Government (ASG) is the largest employer with 40 percent of the workforce on its payroll. Labor expenses swallow 84 percent of its budget expenditures.

Guam

Polity: Elected governor and legislature
Economy: Capitalist-statist
Population: 150,000
Ethnic Groups: Guamanian or Chamorro (Micronesian) majority, U.S. mainlanders, Filipinos

Political Rights: 1
Civil Liberties: 1
Status: Free

Overview: In 1994, Guam continued its shift from a military to a civilian focus, when the United States Navy agreed to close down its Naval Air Station in the territory.

An unincorporated territory of the U.S., Guam has lobbied Washington in recent years for commonwealth status. In 1982 Guam's voters chose commonwealth, but the U.S. has not passed the required enabling legislation. Guam's leaders accuse the U.S. of perpetuating colonial rule. The U.S. Interior Department has authority to screen and approve the Guam government's disposition of land relinquished by the U.S. military.

In 1992, a federal appeals court judge declared Guam's very prohibitive abortion law unconstitutional.

Northern Marianas

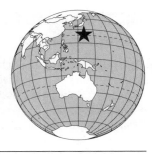

Polity: Elected governor and legislature
Economy: Capitalist
Population: 50,000
Ethnic Groups: Highly diversified populations of Pacific Islanders, Asians, Europeans, and Americans

Political Rights: 1
Civil Liberties: 2
Status: Free

Overview: The directly elected governor appoints a representative to Congress in Washington, D.C. The territorial legislature oversees island affairs, with oversight from the U.S. Congress. In recent years poor wages and working conditions for immigrants have caused friction with the U.S.

Puerto Rico

Polity: Elected governor and legislature
Economy: Capitalist
Population: 3,613,000
Ethnic Groups: Relatively homogeneous, Hispanic
Ratings Change: *Puerto Rico's civil liberties changed from 1 to 2 because of greater citizen insecurity due to mounting drug-related crime and the impingement on civil rights by the National Guard placed in public housing projects.

Political Rights: 1
Civil Liberties: 2*
Status: Free

Overview: Following approval by plebiscite, Puerto Rico acquired the status of a commonwealth in free association with the U.S. in 1952. Under its terms, Puerto Rico exercises approximately the same control over its internal affairs as do the fifty U.S. states. Residents, though U.S. citizens, do not vote in presidential elections and are represented in the U.S. Congress by a delegate to the House of Representatives who can vote in committee but not on the floor.

The Commonwealth constitution, modeled on that of the U.S., provides for a governor and a bicameral Legislature, consisting of a twenty-seven-member Senate and a fifty-one-member House of Representatives, directly elected for four-year terms. An appointed Supreme Court heads an independent judiciary and the legal system is based on U.S. law.

On 3 November 1992 Pedro Rossello of the pro-statehood New Progressive Party (PNP) was elected governor, defeating Victoria Munoz Mendoza, the candidate of the incumbent pro-Commonwealth Popular Democratic Party (PPD). After serving two terms, outgoing Gov. Rafael Hernandez Colon decided not to seek re-election.

With 83 percent of registered voters participating, Rossello took 49.9 percent of the vote against 45.8 percent for Munoz, 3.8 percent for environmentalist Neftali Garcia and 3.3 percent for Fernando Martin of the Puerto Rican Independence Party (PIP). The PNP won 36 of 51 seats in the House and 20 of 27 Senate seats, and was victorious in 54 of the island's 72 municipalities. The PNP's Carlos Romero Barcelo, a former governor, won in the race for the nonvoting delegate to the U.S. Congress.

The election reflected an anti-incumbency fever and immediate concerns over rising crime, high unemployment, government corruption and education. Nonetheless, the island's relationship with the U.S. remains a fundamental political issue. In a nonbinding referendum held in November 1993, commonwealth status received 48.4 percent of the vote, statehood 46.2 percent, and independence 4.4 percent. The vote indicated significant gains for statehood, which in the last referendum, in 1967, received only 39 percent of the vote to 60 percent for commonwealth. Any vote to change the island's status would have had to be approved by the U.S. Congress.

In November 1994 voters forcefully rejected two constitutional amendments that would have limited the right to bail and expanded the island's Supreme Court from seven to nine members. The vote, which ran contrary to most opinion polls, was a major defeat for Rosello.

As U.S. citizens, Puerto Ricans are guaranteed all civil liberties granted in the U.S. The press and broadcast media are well developed, highly varied and critical. In recent years the Puerto Rican journalists association (ASPRO) has charged successive governments with denying complete access to official information. In 1994 ASPRO charged that its president was fired as editor of *VEA* magazine because of his ASPRO activities. Labor unions are well organized and have the right to strike.

The greatest causes for concern are the steep rise in criminal violence in recent years, much of it drug-related, and the Rosello government's response to it. Since mid-1993, forty-eight public housing projects have been placed under the control of the National Guard, the first time that U.S. military units have been routinely deployed to fight crime.

The Rosello government claims the projects have been "liberated" from drug traffickers. (In 1994 the U.S. declared Puerto Rico a high-intensity drug-trafficking zone.) Critics say the projects have been unconstitutionally "militarized" through "de facto martial law" and point to civil rights abuses like unlawful search and seizure and other transgressions. After a year and a half the policy seemed to have reduced crime in some categories. However, the harrowing homicide rate reached an unprecedented level in 1994 with 950 murders (29 more than in 1993). There were also indications of increasing corruption and criminal activity within the police force.

United States Virgin Islands

Polity: Elected governor and senate
Economy: Capitalist
Population: 98,000
Ethnic Groups: Relatively homogeneous with black majority

Political Rights: 1
Civil Liberties: 1
Status: Free

Overview:

The U.S. Virgin Islands, consisting of St. Croix, St. Thomas, St. John and four dozen smaller islands, are governed as an unincorporated territory of the U.S. The inhabitants were made U.S. citizens in 1927 and granted a considerable measure of self-government in 1954. Since 1970, executive authority has resided in a governor and lieutenant governor elected for a four-year term. There is a unicameral fifteen-member Senate elected for two years, with each of the three main islands proportionately represented. Since 1973 the territory has sent one nonvoting delegate to the U.S. House of Representatives.

In a 1993 referendum 80 percent of voters opted to remain an unincorporated territory of the U.S., while 14 percent backed full integration with the U.S. and 5 percent voted for independence. Only 27 percent of registered voters turned out, less than the 50 percent required for the referendum to be valid.

Dr. Roy Schneider emerged victorious in the 1994 gubernatorial election. Outgoing two-term Governor Alexander Farrelly caused a major scandal when in December, just days before stepping down, he commuted the sentences of five convicted murderers. The most prominent was Rafael Joseph, one of five persons linked to a black power group convicted of the racially motivated machine-gunning of eight people on a St. Croix golf course in 1972. The pardons sparked angry protest marches on all three islands and were condemned by most politicians and the media.

Also in 1994 citizens gave 58 percent approval to casino gambling in a referendum. However, the outgoing legislature adjourned at the end of the year without taking action.

As U.S. citizens, island residents enjoy all civil liberties granted in the U.S. There are at least two newspapers and several radio stations. Both television stations were knocked out by Hurricane Hugo in 1989 and only one has come back. Citizen security is threatened by increasing drug-related criminal violence. In November the U.S. government designated the islands as a high-intensity drug trafficking zone.

Yugoslavia
Kosovo

Polity: Serbian administration
Economy: Mixed-statist
Population: 2,018,000
Ethnic Groups: Albanians (90 percent), Serbs and Montenegrins (10 percent)

Political Rights: 7
Civil Liberties: 7
Status: Not Free

Overview: In 1994 Kosovo, an Albanian enclave within Serbia that used to be an autonomous region in Yugoslavia, remained a tinderbox under Serbian repression. Despite pressure from Serbia, which took over administration of the region in 1989-90, Albanians elected a shadow president and parliament in 1992 to underscore the illegitimacy of the Serb-imposed administration.

Kosovo, with neither strategic nor economic importance, is the historic cradle of Serbia. Serbian President Slobodan Milosevic rose to power in 1987 over the issue of Kosovo's status. In 1989-1990, Milosevic moved to abolish the provincial government and legislature and introduced a series of amendments to the Serbian constitution that effectively removed the legal basis for Kosovo's autonomy.

In May 1992 Albanians held elections (branded illegal by Belgrade) for new members of a clandestine government. Ibrahim Rugova, leader of the Democratic League of Kosovo (LDK), was elected president of an "independent" Republic of Kosovo. Delegates to the 130-member legislature were also elected.

Serbian repression of Albanians is maintained by a 40,000-man army and militia force. Harassment, detention, intimidation and murder of Albanians is endemic. Since the Serb takeover, Rugova's government has claimed that over 120,000 Albanians out of a total work force of 250,000 have been fired, and over 200,000 left for other parts of Europe and the United States.

During a visit to Washington in February 1994, President Rugova called on the Clinton Administration to reiterate former President George Bush's threat to take military action if Serbs move to force Muslims out of Kosovo. He called for the deployment of international observers and the demilitarization of Kosovo.

By fall there were signs that militant Albanian nationalists were unhappy with the failure of the LDK's passive resistance strategy to get results.

In November tensions were exacerbated when Serb authorities announced plans to build houses for about 100,000 Serb refugees from Croatia and Bosnia. But Vojislav Zivkovic, leader in Kosovo of Serbia's ruling Socialist Party, said that "the real reason (for the resettlement) is to make the ethnic breakdown in Kosovo more favorable to the Serbs and to set up a firm obstacle to an ethnic Albanian separatist movement."

November-December saw a spate of arrests and trials. In a letter to the Conference on Security and Cooperation in Europe (CSCE), Adem Demaci, chairman of the Kosovo Committee for the Protection of Human Rights and Liberties, charged that as of December over 200 Albanians had been charged for their political views, and some 2,400 summoned and interrogated by police. In 1994, international law enforcement organizations reported that Kosovo had become a major drug-smuggling center.

Political Rights and Civil Liberties: Kosovars cannot change democratically the *de jure* government imposed by Serbia. The Parliamentary Party and the Social Democrats are technically outlawed, and the LDK may also be banned outright. Kosovo's democratically elected legislature and government were forced underground after the 1992 elections, which were not recognized by Serbia. Ultimate judicial authority lies with Belgrade.

Albanian cultural identity has been suppressed. Serbian has supplanted Albanian as the official language.

Serbian persecution has included forced displacement of Albanians, harassment by army and militia forces, arrest and detention, and murder. A Kosovo human rights group reported that as of late December, seventeen Albanians had been killed, including an eighty-year-old man tortured to death.

Albanian TV and radio have been abolished. Albanian judges, policemen and government officials have all been replaced over the last four years. Freedom of movement and other fundamental rights have been circumscribed by the Serbs.

The Independent Trade Unions of Kosovo (BSPK), an outlawed Albanian-language confederation, has been subject to repression for refusing to affiliate with the official Serbian unions or sign collective agreements approved by these unions. In 1994, scores of union leaders were arrested. There was also a rift between the union and the LDK over alleged mishandling of union funds.

Vojvodina

Polity: Serbian administration and provincial assembly
Economy: Mixed-statist
Population: 2,207,000
Ethnic Groups: Serbians (58 percent), Hungarians (14 percent), Slovaks, Bulgarians, Romanians, others

Political Rights: 6
Civil Liberties: 6
Status: Not Free

Overview: In 1993 Vojvodina, northern Serbia's agriculturally rich and most ethnically diverse province that was once an autonomous region in Yugoslavia, managed to avoid the type of violent ethnic strife that gripped most of former Yugoslavia. But political pressure and intimidation by Serb officials and paramilitary groups like the White Falcons raised tensions among the 345,000-strong Hungarian minority and the estimated 70,000 Croats.

Vojvodina enjoyed political autonomy within Yugoslavia until 1990, when the nationalist Serbian government under Slobodan Milosevic abolished most of its constitutional privileges.

In 1994, Vojvodina's Hungarians continued to work for greater autonomy. Efforts were spearheaded by the Democratic Community of Vojvodina (VMDK), led by Andras Agoston, who accused Serbs of quiet "ethnic cleansing." Janos Vekas, vice chairman of the VMDK, said that with Serbia internationally isolated for its role in Yugoslavia's civil war, Hungarians felt it especially important to make Vojvodina a separate entity.

In January VMDK leader Agoston attended a meeting with the Hungarian Foreign Minister and Serbian President Slobodan Milosevic. Agoston insisted that only dialogue could guarantee a legal framework for Hungarian demands and that open confrontation could spark an armed response that the Serbs could easily win.

The Serb campaign of quiet "ethnic cleansing" continued in 1994, and included harassment, intimidation and visits by popular Serbian ultra-nationalists.

Croats were targets of "ethnic cleansing" and intimidation but they strove to maintain Croat survival in areas where Croats had lived for centuries. Margit Savovic, Yugoslavia's human and minority rights minister, said that Croats cannot be recognized as a minority in rump-Yugoslavia because it did not recognize an independent Croatia and, hence, under international law, Yugoslavia's Croats have no parent country.

Political Rights and Civil Liberties:

In 1990, Vojvodina lost its status as an autonomous region within Yugoslavia when it was taken over by Serbia, whose territory it abuts. Citizens can elect a provincial government and take part in Serbian elections, as well as those for rump-Yugoslavia, but non-Serbs have reported harassment and intimidation. There is no truly independent judiciary.

Political parties and groupings representing Hungarian and Croat interests have been allowed to exist. In September, several Hungarian organizations reportedly formed an alliance to present a united front in future elections.

Since 1992 the parliament in Belgrade has enacted seventeen laws restricting or abolishing important minority rights. Minorities are no longer able to use their own languages before the law. Purges of non-Serbs occurred in the police, customs, and, allegedly, the judiciary.

All institutions operating in Vojvodina are essentially under the control of the government in Belgrade. Freedoms of expression and speech are curtailed, and while there are a few small independent publications in Vojvodina, the media are dominated by Serbian-government-controlled television and radio. Freedom of domestic movement and international travel are generally unrestricted. Although freedom of religion is nominally accepted, Catholics, especially Croats, face intimidation and harassment by Orthodox Serbs. In 1994, several churches were bombed, including a Franciscan church in Subotica. Trade unions are not truly independent.

The Comparative Survey of Freedom—1994-1995 Survey Methodology

Joseph E. Ryan

The purpose of the *Survey* remains what it has been since its inception in the 1970s: to provide an annual evaluation of political rights and civil liberties everywhere in the world.

The *Survey* attempts to judge all places by a single standard and to point out the importance of democracy and freedom. At a minimum, a democracy is a political system in which the people choose their authoritative leaders freely from among competing groups and individuals who were not chosen by the government. Putting it broadly, freedom is the chance to act spontaneously in a variety of fields outside the control of government and other centers of potential domination.

For a long time, Westerners have associated the adherence to political rights and civil liberties with the liberal democracies, such as those in North America and the European Union. However, there has been a proliferation of democracies in developing countries in recent years, and the *Survey* reflects their growing numbers.

Freedom House does not view democracy as a static concept, and the *Survey* recognizes that a democratic country does not necessarily belong in our category of "free" states. A democracy can lose freedom and become merely "partly free." Sri Lanka and Colombia are examples of such "partly free" democracies. In other cases, countries that replaced military regimes with elected governments can have less than complete transitions to liberal democracy. El Salvador and Guatemala fit the description of this kind of "partly free" democracy. (See the section below on the designations "free," "partly free," and "not free" for an explanation of those terms.) Readers should note that some scholars would use the term "semi-democracy" or "formal democracy," instead of "partly free" democracy, to refer to countries that are democratic in form but less than free in substance.

What the *Survey* is not

The *Survey* does *not* rate governments *per se* but rather the rights and freedoms individuals have in each country and territory. Freedom House does *not* score countries and territories based on governmental intentions or constitutions but on the real world situations caused by governmental and non-governmental factors. The *Survey* does *not* quantify our sympathy for the situation a government finds itself in (e.g., war, terrorism, etc.) but rather what effect the situation itself has on freedom.

Definitions and categories of the *Survey*

The *Survey*'s understanding of freedom is broad and encompasses two sets of characteristics grouped under political rights and civil liberties. Political rights enable people to participate freely in the political process. By the political process, we mean the system by which the polity chooses the authoritative policy makers and attempts to make binding decisions affecting the national, regional or local community. In a free society this means the right of all adults to vote and compete for public office, and for elected representatives to have a decisive vote on public policies. A system is genuinely free or democratic to the extent that the people have a choice in determining the nature of the system and its leaders.

Civil liberties are the freedoms to develop views, institutions and personal autonomy apart from the state.

The *Survey* employs checklists for these rights and liberties to help determine the degree of freedom present in each country and related territory, and to help assign each entity to a comparative category.

Political Rights checklist

1. Is the head of state and/or head of government or other chief authority elected through free and fair elections?
2. Are the legislative representatives elected through free and fair elections?
3. Are there fair electoral laws, equal campaigning opportunities, fair polling and honest tabulation of ballots?

4. Are the voters able to endow their freely elected representatives with real power?

5. Do the people have the right to organize in different political parties or other competitive political groupings of their choice, and is the system open to the rise and fall of these competing parties or groupings?

6. Is there a significant opposition vote, *de facto* opposition power, and a realistic possibility for the opposition to increase its support or gain power through elections?

7. Does the country have the right of self-determination, and are its citizens free from domination by the military, foreign powers, totalitarian parties, religious hierarchies, economic oligarchies or any other powerful group?

8. Do cultural, ethnic, religious and other minority groups have reasonable self-determination, self-government, autonomy or participation through informal consensus in the decision-making process?

9. Is political power decentralized, allowing for local, regional and/or provincial or state administrations led by their freely elected officials? (For entities such as tiny island nations, the absence of a decentralized system does not necessarily count as a negative in the *Survey.*)

Additional discretionary Political Rights questions

A. For traditional monarchies that have no parties or electoral process, does the system provide for consultation with the people, encourage discussion of policy, and allow the right to petition the ruler?

B. Is the government or occupying power deliberately changing the ethnic composition of a country or territory so as to destroy a culture or tip the political balance in favor of another group?

When answering the political rights questions, Freedom House considers the extent to which the system offers the voter the chance to make a free choice among competing candidates, and to what extent the candidates are chosen independently of the state. We recognize that formal electoral procedures are not the only factors that determine the real distribution of power. In many Latin American countries, for example, the military retains a significant political role, and in Morocco the king maintains significant power over the elected politicians. The more people suffer under such domination by unelected forces, the less chance the country has of getting credit for self-determination in our *Survey.*

Freedom House does not have a culture-bound view of democracy. The *Survey* team rejects the notion that only Europeans and those of European descent qualify as democratic. The *Survey* demonstrates that, in addition to those in Europe and the Americas, there are free countries with varying kinds of democracy functioning among people of all races and religions in Africa, the Pacific and Asia. In some Pacific islands, free countries can have competitive political systems based on competing family groups and personalities rather than on European or American-style parties.

The checklist for Civil Liberties

1. Are there free and independent media, literature and other cultural expressions? (Note: In cases where the media are state-controlled but offer pluralistic points of view, the *Survey* gives the system credit.)

2. Is there open public discussion and free private discussion?

3. Is there freedom of assembly and demonstration?

4. Is there freedom of political or quasi-political organization? (Note: This includes political parties, civic associations, ad hoc issue groups and so forth.)

5. Are citizens equal under the law, with access to an independent, nondiscriminatory judiciary, and are they respected by the security forces?

6. Is there protection from political terror, and from unjustified imprisonment, exile or torture, whether by groups that support or oppose the system, and freedom from war or insurgency situations? (Note: Freedom from war and insurgency situations enhances the liberties in a free society, but the absence of wars and insurgencies does not in itself make an unfree society free.)

7. Are there free trade unions and peasant organizations or equivalents, and is there effective collective bargaining?

8. Are there free professional and other private organizations?

9. Are there free businesses or cooperatives?

10. Are there free religious institutions and free private and public religious expressions?

11. Are there personal social freedoms, which include such aspects as gender equality, property rights, freedom of movement, choice of residence, and choice of marriage and size of family?

12. Is there equality of opportunity, which includes freedom from exploitation by or dependency on landlords, employers, union leaders, bureaucrats or any other type of denigrating obstacle to a share of legitimate economic gains?

13. Is there freedom from extreme government indifference and corruption?

When analyzing the civil liberties checklist, Freedom House does not mistake constitutional guarantees of human rights for those rights in practice. For tiny island countries and territories and other small entities with low populations, the absence of unions and other types of association does not necessarily count as a negative unless the government or other centers of domination are deliberately blocking association. The question of equality of opportunity also implies a free choice of employment and education. Extreme inequality of opportunity prevents disadvantaged individuals from enjoying a full exercise of civil liberties. Typically, desperately poor countries and territories lack both opportunities for economic advancement and the other liberties on this checklist. We have a question on gross indifference and corruption, because when governments do not care about the social and economic welfare of large sectors of the population, the human rights of those people suffer. Government corruption can pervert the political process and hamper the development of a free economy.

How do we grade? Ratings, categories, and raw points

The *Survey* rates political rights and civil liberties separately on a seven-category scale, 1 representing the most free and 7 the least free. A country is assigned to a particular category based on responses to the checklist and the judgments of the *Survey* team at Freedom House. The numbers are not purely mechanical; they also reflect judgment. Under the methodology, the team

The Tabulated Ratings

The accompanying Table of Independent Countries (pages 678-679) and Table of Related Territories (page 680) rate each country or territory on seven-category scales for political rights and civil liberties, and then place each entity into a broad category of "free," "partly free" or "not free." On each scale, 1 represents the most free and 7 the least free.

Political rights

In political rights, generally speaking, places rated 1 come closest to the ideals suggested by the checklist questions, beginning with free and fair elections. Those elected rule. There are competitive parties or other competitive political groupings, and the opposition has an important role and power. These entities have self-determination or an extremely high degree of autonomy (in the case of related territories). Usually, those rated 1 have self-determination for minority groups or their participation in government through informal consensus. With the exception of such entities as tiny island countries, these countries and territories have decentralized political power and free sub-national elections. Entities in Category 1 are not perfect. They can and do lose credit for their deficiencies.

Countries and territories rated 2 in political rights are less free than those rated 1. Such factors as gross political corruption, violence, political discrimination against minorities, and foreign or military influence on politics may be present, and weaken the quality of democracy.

The same factors that weaken freedom in category 2 may also undermine political rights in categories 3, 4, and 5. Other damaging conditions may be at work as well, including civil war, very strong military involvement in politics, lingering royal power, unfair elections and one-party dominance. However, states and territories in these categories may still have some elements of political rights such as the freedom to organize nongovernmental parties and quasi-political groups, reasonably free referenda, or other significant means of popular influence on government.

Typically, states and territories with political rights rated 6 have systems ruled by military juntas, one-party dictatorships, religious hierarchies and autocrats. These regimes may allow only some minimal manifestation of political rights such as competitive local elections or some degree of representation or autonomy for minorities. Category 6 also contains some countries in the early or aborted stages of democratic transition. A few states in Category 6 are traditional monarchies that mitigate their relative lack of political rights through the use of consultation with their subjects, toleration of political discussion, and acceptance of petitions from the ruled.

assigns initial ratings to countries by awarding from 0 to 4 raw points per checklist item, depending on the comparative rights or liberties present. (In the *Surveys* completed from 1989-90 through 1992-93, the methodology allowed for a less nuanced range of 0 to 2 raw points per question. Taking note of this modification, scholars should consider the 1993-94 scores the statistical benchmark.) The only exception to the addition of 0 to 4 raw points per checklist item is the discretionary question on cultural destruction and deliberate demographic change to tip the political balance. In that case, we subtract 1 to 4 raw points depending on the situation's severity. The highest possible score for political rights is 36 points, based on up to 4 points for each of nine questions. The highest possible score for civil liberties is 52 points, based on up to 4 points for each of thirteen questions. Under the methodology, raw points correspond to category numbers as follows:

Political Rights

Category Number	Raw points
1	31-36
2	26-30
3	21-25
4	16-20
5	11-15
6	6-10
7	0-5

The Tabulated Ratings

Category 7 includes places where political rights are absent or virtually nonexistent due to the extremely oppressive nature of the regime or extreme oppression in combination with civil war. A country or territory may also join this category when extreme violence and warlordism dominate the people in the absence of an authoritative, functioning central government. Places in Category 7 may get some minimal points for the checklist questions, but only a tiny fragment of available credit.

Civil liberties

Category 1 in civil liberties includes countries and territories that generally have the highest levels of freedoms and opportunities for the individual. Places in this category may still have problems in civil liberties, but they lose partial credit in only a limited number of areas.

The places in category 2 in civil liberties are not as free as those rated 1, but they are still relatively high on the scale. These countries and territories have deficiencies in several aspects of civil liberties, but still receive most available credit.

Independent countries and related territories with ratings of 3, 4 or 5 have progressively fewer civil liberties than those in category 2. Places in these categories range from ones that receive at least partial credit on virtually all checklist questions to those that have a mixture of good civil liberties scores in some areas and zero or partial credit in others. As one moves down the scale below category 2, the level of oppression increases, especially in the areas of censorship, political terror and the prevention of free association. There are also many cases in which groups opposed to the state carry out political terror that undermines other freedoms. That means that a poor rating for a country is not necessarily a comment on the intentions of the government. The rating may simply reflect the real restrictions on liberty which can be caused by non-governmental terror.

Typically, at category 6 in civil liberties, countries and territories have a few partial rights. For example, a country might have some religious freedom, some personal social freedoms, some highly restricted private business activity, and relatively free private discussion. In general, people in these states and territories experience severely restricted expression and association. There are almost always political prisoners and other manifestations of political terror.

At category 7, countries and territories have virtually no freedom. An overwhelming and justified fear of repression characterizes the society.

The accompanying Tables of Combined Average Ratings average the two seven-category scales of political rights and civil liberties into an overall freedom rating for each country and territory.

Civil Liberties
Category Number Raw points

Category Number	Raw points
1	45-52
2	38-44
3	30-37
4	23-29
5	15-22
6	8-14
7	0-7

After placing countries in initial categories based on checklist points, the *Survey* team makes minor adjustments to account for factors such as extreme violence, whose intensity may not be reflected in answering the checklist questions. These exceptions aside, in the overwhelming number of cases, the checklist system reflects the real world situation and is adequate for placing countries and territories into the proper comparative categories. The Survey team determines ratings for countries and territories in consultation with outside experts and the Freedom House Board of Trustees. Particular scores do not necessarily reflect the views of members of Freedom House's Board of Trustees.

At its discretion, Freedom House assigns up or down arrows to countries and territories to indicate positive or negative trends, whether qualitative or quantitative, that may not be apparent from the ratings. Such trends may or may not be reflected in raw points, depending on the circumstances of each country or territory. Only places without ratings changes since last year warrant trend arrows. The charts on pp. 678-679 also show up and down triangles. Distinct from the trend arrows, the triangles indicate changes in political rights and civil liberties caused by real world events since the last *Survey*.

Free, Partly Free, Not Free

The map on pages 78-79 divides the world into three large categories: "free," "partly free," and "not free." The *Survey* places countries and territories into this tripartite division by averaging the category numbers they received for political rights and civil liberties. Those whose category numbers average 1-2.5 are considered "free," 3-5.5 "partly free," and 5.5-7 "not free." The dividing line between "partly free" and "not free" falls within the group whose category numbers average 5.5. For example, countries that receive a rating of 6 for political rights and 5 for civil liberties, or a 5 for political rights and a 6 for civil liberties, could be either "partly free" or "not free." The total number of raw points is the factor which makes the difference between the two. Countries and territories with combined raw scores of 0-29 points are "not free," and those with combined raw scores of 30-59 points are "partly free." "Free" countries and territories have combined raw scores of 60-88 points.

The differences in raw points between countries in the three broad categories represent distinctions in the real world. There are obstacles which "partly free" countries must overcome before they can be called "free," just as there are impediments which prevent "not free" countries from being called "partly free." Countries at the lowest rung of the "free" category (category 2 in political rights with category 3 in civil liberties or category 3 in political rights with category 2 in civil liberties) differ from those at the upper end of the "partly free" group (e.g., category 3 in both). Typically, there is more violence and/or military influence on politics at 3,3 than at 2,3 and the differences become more striking as one compares 2,3 with worse categories of the "partly free" countries.

The distinction between the least bad "not free" countries and the least free "partly free" may be less obvious than the gap between "partly free" and "free," but at "partly free," there is at least one extra factor that keeps a country from being assigned to the "not free" category. For example, Lebanon (6,5) has at least some rudiments of pluralism (however perverted or fragmented) that separate this country from its "not free" neighbor, Iraq (7,7).

Freedom House wishes to point out that the designation "free" does not mean that a country has perfect freedom or lacks serious problems. As an institution which advocates human rights, Freedom House remains concerned about a variety of social problems and civil liberties questions in the U.S. and other countries that the *Survey* places in the "free" category. Similarly, in no way does an improvement in a country's rating mean that human rights campaigns should cease. On the contrary, we wish to use the *Survey* as a prod to improve the condition of all countries.

Readers should understand that the "free," "partly free," and "not free" labels are highly simplified terms that each cover a broad third of the available raw points. The labels do *not* imply that all countries in a category are the same any more than a bestseller list implies that all titles on it have sold the same number of books. Countries and territories can reach the same categories or even raw points by differing routes. We use the tripartite labels and tricolor maps to illustrate some broad comparisons. In theory, we could have eighty-eight categories and colors to match the range of raw points, but this would be highly impractical. Anyone wishing to see the distinctions within each category should look at the category numbers and combined average ratings on pages 683-684.

The approach of the *Survey*

The *Survey* attempts to measure conditions as they really are around the world. This approach is distinct from relying on intense coverage by the American media as a guide to which countries are the least free. The publicity given problems in some countries does not necessarily mean that unpublicized problems of other countries are not more severe. For example, while U.S. television networks are allowed into Israel and El Salvador to cover abuses of human rights, they are not allowed to report freely in North Korea, which has far less freedom than the other two countries. To reach such comparative conclusions, Freedom House evaluates the development of democratic governmental institutions, or lack thereof, and also examines the quality of civil society, life outside the state structure.

Without a well-developed civil society, it is difficult, if not impossible, to have an atmosphere supportive of democracy. A society that does not have free individual and group expressions in nonpolitical matters is not likely to make an exception for political ones. As though to prove this, there is no country in the *Survey* that places in category 6 or 7 for civil liberties and, at the same time, in category 1 or 2 for political rights. In the overwhelming majority of cases in the *Survey*, countries and territories have ratings in political rights and civil liberties that are within two categories of each other.

The *Survey* rates both countries and related territories. For our purposes, countries are internationally recognized independent states whose governments are resident within their officially claimed territories. In the unusual case of Cyprus, we give two ratings, since there are two governments on that divided island. In no way does this imply that Freedom House endorses Cypriot division. We note only that neither the predominantly Greek Republic of Cyprus nor the Turkish-occupied, predominantly Turkish territory of the Republic of Northern Cyprus is the *de facto* government for the entire island. Related territories consist mostly of colonies, protectorates, occupied territories and island dependencies. However, the *Survey* also reserves the right to designate as related territories places within internationally recognized states that are disputed areas or that have a human rights problem or issue of self-determination deserving special attention. Northern Ireland, Tibet, and Kashmir are examples falling within this category. The *Survey* excludes uninhabited related territories and such entities as the U.S.-owned Johnston Atoll, which has only a transient military population and no native inhabitants. Since most related territories have a broad range of civil liberties and some form of self-government, a higher proportion of them have the "free" designation than do independent countries.

The 1994-95 *Survey* has reduced the number of related territories. The territories of Bophutatswana, Ciskei, Transkei, and Venda have dissolved into post-apartheid South Africa. Palau, the last remaining fragment of the Trust Territory of the Pacific, changed status from related territory to independent country.

When analyzing the civil liberties checklist, Freedom House does not mistake constitutional guarantees of human rights for those rights in practice. For tiny island countries and territories and other small entities with low populations, the absence of unions and other types of association does not necessarily count as a negative unless the government or other centers of domination are deliberately blocking association. The question of equality of opportunity also implies a free choice of employment and education. Extreme inequality of opportunity prevents disadvantaged individuals from enjoying a full exercise of civil liberties. Typically, desperately poor countries and territories lack both opportunities for economic advancement and the other liberties on this checklist. We have a question on gross indifference and corruption, because when governments do not care about the social and economic welfare of large sectors of the population, the human rights of those people suffer. Government corruption can pervert the political process and hamper the development of a free economy.

Joseph E. Ryan is resident scholar at Freedom House.

Tables and Ratings

Table of Independent Countries
Comparative Measures of Freedom

Country	PR	CL	Freedom Rating
Afghanistan	7	7	Not Free
Albania	3▼	4	Partly Free
Algeria	7	7▼	Not Free
Andorra	1▲	1	Free
Angola	7	7	Not Free
Antigua and Barbuda	4	3	Partly Free
Argentina	2	3	Free
Armenia	3	4	Partly Free
Australia	1	1	Free
Austria	1	1	Free
Azerbaijan	6	6	Not Free
Bahamas	1	2	Free
Bahrain	6	6	Not Free
Bangladesh	2	4	Partly Free
Barbados	1	1	Free
Belarus	4▲	4	Partly Free
Belgium	1	1	Free
Belize	1	1	Free
Benin	2	3	Free
Bhutan	7	7	Not Free
Bolivia	2	3	Free
Bosnia-Herzegovina	6	6	Not Free
Botswana	2	3	Free
Brazil	2▲	4	Partly Free
Brunei	7	6	Not Free
Bulgaria	2	2	Free
Burkina Faso	5	4	Partly Free
Burma (Myanmar)	7	7	Not Free
Burundi	6▲	7	Not Free
Cambodia	4	5	Partly Free
Cameroon	6	5	Not Free
Canada	1	1	Free
Cape Verde	1	2	Free
Central African Republic	3	4	Partly Free
Chad	6	5	Not Free
Chile	2	2	Free
China (PRC)	7	7	Not Free
Colombia	3▼	4	Partly Free
Comoros	4	4	Partly Free
Congo	4	4	Partly Free
Costa Rica	1	2	Free
Croatia	4	4	Partly Free
Cuba	7	7	Not Free
Cyprus (G)	1	1	Free
Czech Republic	1	2	Free
Denmark	1	1	Free
Djibouti	6	6	Not Free
Dominica	2	1	Free
Dominican Republic	4▼	3	Partly Free
Ecuador	2	3	Free
Egypt	6	6	Not Free
El Salvador	3	3	Partly Free
Equatorial Guinea	7	7	Not Free
Eritrea	6	5	Not Free
Estonia	3	2	Free
Ethiopia	6	5	Not Free
Fiji	4	3	Partly Free
Finland	1	1	Free
France	1	2	Free
Gabon	5	4	Partly Free
The Gambia	7▼	6▼	Not Free
Georgia	5	5	Partly Free
Germany	1	2	Free
Ghana	5	4	Partly Free
Greece	1	3	Free
Grenada	1	2	Free
Guatemala	4	5	Partly Free
Guinea	6	5	Not Free
Guinea-Bissau	3▲	4▲	Partly Free
Guyana	2	2	Free
Haiti	5▲	5▲	Partly Free
Honduras	3	3	Partly Free
Hungary	1	2	Free
Iceland	1	1	Free
India	4	4	Partly Free
Indonesia	7	6	Not Free
Iran	6	7	Not Free
Iraq	7	7	Not Free
Ireland	1	2	Free
Israel**	1	3	Free
Italy	1	2▲	Free
Ivory Coast	6	5	Not Free
Jamaica	2	3	Free
Japan	2	2	Free
Jordan	4	4	Partly Free
Kazakhstan	6	5▼	Not Free
Kenya	6▼	6	Not Free
Kiribati	1	1	Free
Korea, North	7	7	Not Free
Korea, South	2	2	Free
Kuwait	5	5	Partly Free
Kyrgyz Republic	4▲	3	Partly Free
Laos	7	6	Not Free
Latvia	3	2▲	Free
Lebanon	6	5	Partly Free
Lesotho	4▼	4	Partly Free
Liberia	7▼	6	Not Free
Libya	7	7	Not Free
Liechtenstein	1	1	Free
Lithuania	1	3	Free
Luxembourg	1	1	Free
Macedonia	4▼	3	Partly Free
Madagascar	2	4	Partly Free
Malawi	2▲	3▲	Free
Malaysia	4	5	Partly Free
Maldives	6	6	Not Free
Mali	2	4▼	Partly Free
Malta	1	1	Free
Marshall Islands	1	1	Free
Mauritania	7	7▼	Not Free
Mauritius	1	2	Free
Mexico	4	4	Partly Free
Micronesia	1	1	Free
Moldova	4▲	4▲	Partly Free
Monaco	2	1	Free
Mongolia	2	3	Free
Morocco	5	5	Partly Free
Mozambique	3▲	5	Partly Free
Namibia	2	3	Free

Table of Independent Countries Comparative Measures of Freedom

Country	PR	CL	Freedom Rating	Country	PR	CL	Freedom Rating
Nauru	1	3	Free	Sri Lanka	4	5	Partly Free
Nepal	3	4	Partly Free	Sudan	7	7	Not Free
Netherlands	1	1	Free	Suriname	3	3	Partly Free
New Zealand	1	1	Free	Swaziland	6	5	Not Free
Nicaragua	4	5	Partly Free	Sweden	1	1	Free
Niger	3	5▼	Partly Free	Switzerland	1	1	Free
Nigeria	7	6▼	Not Free	Syria	7	7	Not Free
Norway	1	1	Free	Taiwan (Rep. of China)	3▲	3▲	Partly Free
Oman	6	6	Not Free	Tajikistan	7	7	Not Free
Pakistan	3	5	Partly Free	Tanzania	6	6▼	Not Free
Palau°	1	2	Free	Thailand	3	5	Partly Free
Panama	2▲	3	Free	Togo	6▲	5	Not Free
Papua New Guinea	2	4	Partly Free	Tonga	5	3	Partly Free
Paraguay	4▼	3	Partly Free	Trinidad and Tobago	1	2▼	Free
Peru	5	4▲	Partly Free	Tunisia	6	5	Not Free
Philippines	3	4	Partly Free	Turkey	5▼	5▼	Partly Free
Poland	2	2	Free	Turkmenistan	7	7	Not Free
Portugal	1	1	Free	Tuvalu	1	1	Free
Qatar	7	6	Not Free	Uganda	5▲	5	Partly Free
Romania	4	3▲	Partly Free	Ukraine	3▲	4	Partly Free
Russia	3	4	Partly Free	United Arab Emirates	6▲	5	Not Free
Rwanda	7▼	7▼	Not Free				
St. Kitts and Nevis	2▼	2▼	Free	United Kingdom*	1	2	Free
St. Lucia	1	2	Free	United States	1	1	Free
St. Vincent and the Grenadines	2▼	1	Free	Uruguay	2	2	Free
				Uzbekistan	7	7	Not Free
San Marino	1	1	Free	Vanuatu	1	3▼	Free
Sao Tome and Principe	1	2	Free	⬇ Venezuela	3	3	Partly Free
Saudi Arabia	7	7	Not Free	⬆ Vietnam	7	7	Not Free
Senegal	4	5	Partly Free	Western Samoa	2	2	Free
Seychelles	3	4	Partly Free	Yemen	5▼	6▼	Not Free
⬇ Sierra Leone	7	6	Not Free	Yugoslavia (Serbia and Montenegro)	6	6	Not Free
Singapore	5	5	Partly Free				
Slovakia	2▲	3▲	Free	Zaire	7	6	Not Free
Slovenia	1	2	Free	Zambia	3	4	Partly Free
Solomon Islands	1	2	Free	Zimbabwe	5	5	Partly Free
Somalia	7	7	Not Free				
South Africa	2▲	3▲	Free				
Spain	1	2	Free				

PR and CL stand for Political Rights and Civil Liberties. 1 represents the most free and 7 the least free category.

⬆⬇ up or down indicates a general trend in freedom.

▲▼ up or down indicates a significant change in Political Rights or Civil Liberties since the last survey.

The Freedom Rating is an overall judgment based on *Survey* results. See the "Methodological Essay" for more details.

o New country in this *Survey*.

* Excluding Northern Ireland.

** Excluding the Occupied Territories & Palestinian Autonomous Areas.

Table of Related Territories
Comparative Measures of Freedom

Country & Territory	PR	CL	Freedom Rating
Armenia/Azerbaijan			
Nagorno-Karabakh*	7	7	Not Free
Australia			
Christmas Island	3	2	Free
Cocos (Keeling) Islands	1	1	Free
Norfolk Island	2	1	Free
Chile			
Rapanui (Easter Island)	2	2	Free
China			
Tibet	7	7	Not Free
Denmark			
Faeroe Islands	1	1	Free
Greenland	1	1	Free
Finland			
Aland Islands	1	1	Free
France			
French Guiana	1	2	Free
French Polynesia	1	2	Free
Guadeloupe	1	2	Free
Martinique	1	2	Free
Mayotte (Mahore)	1	2	Free
New Caledonia	2	2	Free
Reunion	2	2	Free
St. Pierre and Miquelon	1	1	Free
Wallis and Futuna Islands	2	2	Free
India			
Kashmir	7	7	Not Free
Indonesia			
East Timor	7	7	Not Free
Irian Jaya (West Papua)	7	7	Not Free
Iraq			
Kurdistan	4	4	Partly Free
Israel			
Occupied Territories & Palestinian Autonomous Areas	6	5	Not Free
Morocco			
Western Sahara	7	6	Not Free
Netherlands			
Aruba	2▼	1	Free

Country & Territory	PR	CL	Freedom Rating
Netherlands Antilles	1	2▼	Free
New Zealand			
Cook Islands	1	2	Free
Niue	1	2	Free
Tokelau	2	2	Free
Norway			
Svalbard	3	1	Free
Portugal			
Azores	1	1	Free
Macao	6▼	4▼	Partly Free
Madeira	1	1	Free
Spain			
Canary Islands	1	1	Free
Ceuta	1	2	Free
Melilla	1	2	Free
Turkey			
Cyprus (T)	4	2	Partly Free
United Kingdom			
Anguilla	2	1	Free
Bermuda	1	1	Free
British Virgin Islands	1	1	Free
Cayman Islands	1	1	Free
Channel Islands	2	1	Free
Falkland Islands	2	1	Free
Gibraltar	1	1	Free
Hong Kong	5	2	Partly Free
Isle of Man	1	1	Free
Montserrat	1	1	Free
Northern Ireland	4▲	3▲	Partly Free
Pitcairn Island	1	1	Free
St. Helena and Dependencies	2	1	Free
Turks and Caicos	1	1	Free
United States of America			
American Samoa	1	1	Free
Guam	1	1	Free
Northern Marianas	1	2	Free
Puerto Rico	1	2▼	Free
U.S. Virgin Islands	1	1	Free
Yugoslavia			
Kosovo	7	7	Not Free
Vojvodina	6	6	Not Free

* Nagorno-Karabakh is disputed territory, contested by Armenia and Azerbaijan.

Table of Social and Economic Comparisons

Country	Real GDP per capita (PPP$)	Life expectancy	Country	Real GDP per capita (PPP$)	Life expectancy
Afghanistan	700	42.9	Denmark	17,880	75.3
Albania	3,500	73.0	Djibouti	1,000	48.3
Algeria	2,870	65.6	Dominica	3,900	72.0
Angola	1,000	45.6	Dominican	3,080	67.0
Antigua and	4,500	74.0	Republic		
Barbuda			Ecuador	4,140	66.2
Argentina	5,120	71.1	Egypt	3,600	60.9
Armenia	4,610	72.0	El Salvador	2,110	65.2
Australia	16,680	76.7	Equatorial	700	47.3
Austria	17,690	75.7	Guinea		
Azerbaijan	3,670	71.0	Estonia	8,090	71.2
Bahamas	12,000	71.9	Ethiopia	370	46.4
Bahrain	11,536	71.0	Fiji	4,858	71.1
Bangladesh	1,160	52.2	Finland	16,130	75.4
Barbados	8,667	75.3	France	18,430	76.6
Belarus	6,850	71.0	Gabon	3,498	52.9
Belgium	17,510	75.7	The Gambia	763	44.4
Belize	3,000	68.0	Georgia	3,670	73.0
Benin	1,500	46.1	Germany	19,770	75.6
Bhutan	620	47.8	Ghana	930	55.4
Bolivia	2,170	60.5	Greece	7,680	76.3
Bosnia-	na	70.0	Grenada	3,374	70.0
Herzegovina			Guatemala	3,180	64.0
Botswana	4,690	60.3	Guinea	500	43.9
Brazil	5,240	65.8	Guinea-Bissau	747	42.9
Brunei	14,000	74.0	Guyana	1,862	64.6
Bulgaria	4,813	71.9	Haiti	925	56.0
Burkina Faso	666	47.9	Honduras	1,820	65.2
Burma	650	56.9	Hungary	6,080	70.1
(Myanmar)			Iceland	17,480	78.1
Burundi	640	48.2	India	1,150	59.7
Cambodia	1,250	50.4	Indonesia	2,730	62.0
Cameroon	2,400	55.3	Iran	4,670	66.6
Canada	19,320	77.2	Iraq	3,500	65.7
Cape Verde	1,360	67.3	Ireland	11,430	75.0
Central African	641	47.2	Israel	13,460	76.2
Republic			Italy	17,040	76.9
Chad	447	46.9	Ivory Coast	1,510	51.6
Chile	7,060	71.9	(Cote D'Ivoire)		
China (PRC)	2,946	70.5	Jamaica	3,670	73.3
Colombia	5,460	69.0	Japan	19,390	78.6
Comoros	700	55.4	Jordan	2,895	67.3
Congo	2,800	51.7	Kazakhstan	4,490	69.0
Costa Rica	5,100	76.0	Kenya	1,350	58.6
Croatia	na	70.0	Kiribati	na	54.0
Cuba	2,000	75.6	Korea		
Cyprus	9,844	76.7	North	1,750	70.7
Czech Republic	na	72.1	South	8,320	70.4

Note: Freedom House obtained the figures for purchasing power parities (PPP) and life expectancy from the U.N.'s *Human Development Report 1994* (UNDP/Oxford University Press, 1994). PPPs are real GDP per capita figures which economists have adjusted to account for detailed price comparisons of individual items covering over 150 categories of expenditure. The U.N. life expectancy figures represent overall expectancy, not differentiated by sex. In some cases not covered by the U.N., the chart lists a combined average of male and female life expectancy obtained from Rand McNally. For several countries the chart lists these combined averages.

Table of Social and Economic Comparisons

Country	Real GDP per capita (PPP$)	Life expectancy	Country	Real GDP per capita (PPP$)	Life expectancy
Kuwait	13,126	74.6	San Marino	na	76.0
Kyrgyzstan	3,280	68.0	Sao Tome and	600	67.0
Laos	1,760	50.3	Principe		
Latvia	7,540	71.0	Saudi Arabia	10,850	68.7
Lebanon	2,500	68.1	Senegal	1,680	48.7
Lesotho	1,500	59.8	Seychelles	3,683	71.0
Liberia	850	54.7	Sierra Leone	1,020	42.4
Libya	7,000	62.4	Singapore	14,734	74.2
Liechtenstein	na	69.5	Slovakia	na	na
Lithuania	5,410	72.6	Slovenia	na	71.0
Luxembourg	20,800	75.2	Solomon Islands	2,113	70.0
Macedonia	na	70.0	Somalia	759	46.4
Madagascar	710	54.9	South Africa	3,885	61.2
Malawi	800	44.6	Spain	12,670	77.4
Malaysia	7,400	70.4	Sri Lanka	2,650	71.2
Maldives	1,200	62.6	Sudan	1,162	51.2
Mali	480	45.4	Suriname	3,072	69.9
Malta	7,575	75.7	Swaziland	2,506	57.3
Marshall Islands	na	72.5	Sweden	17,490	77.7
Mauritania	962	47.4	Switzerland	21,780	77.8
Mauritius	7,178	69.6	Syria	5,220	66.4
Mexico	7,170	69.9	Taiwan (China)	na	74.5
Micronesia	na	70.5	Tajikistan	2,180	70.0
Moldova	3,500	69.0	Tanzania	570	51.2
Mongolia	2,250	63.0	Thailand	5,270	68.7
Morocco	3,340	62.5	Togo	738	54.4
Mozambique	921	46.5	Tonga	na	67.5
Namibia	2,381	58.0	Trinidad and	8,380	70.9
Nauru	na	66.0	Tobago		
Nepal	1,130	52.7	Tunisia	4,690	67.1
Netherlands	16,820	77.2	Turkey	4,840	66.7
New Zealand	13,970	75.3	Turkmenistan	3,540	66.0
Nicaragua	2,550	65.4	Tuvalu	na	61.0
Niger	542	45.9	Uganda	1,036	42.6
Nigeria	1,360	51.9	Ukraine	5,810	70.0
Norway	17,170	76.9	United Arab	17,000	70.8
Oman	9,230	69.1	Emirates		
Pakistan	1,970	58.3	United	16,340	75.8
Palau	na	na	Kingdom		
Panama	4,910	72.5	United States	22,130	75.6
Papua New Guinea	1,550	55.3	Uruguay	6,670	72.4
Paraguay	3,420	67.2	Uzbekistan	2,790	69.0
Peru	3,110	63.6	Vanuatu	1,679	65.0
Philippines	2,440	64.6	Venezuela	8,120	70.1
Poland	4,500	71.5	Vietnam	1,250	63.4
Portugal	9,450	74.4	Western Samoa	na	66.5
Qatar	14,000	69.6	Yemen	1,374	51.9
Romania	3,500	69.9	Yugoslavia (Serbia	na	72.6
Russia	6,930	70.0	and Montenegro)		
Rwanda	680	46.5	Zaire	469	51.6
St. Kitts-Nevis	3,550	70.0	Zambia	1,010	45.5
St. Lucia	3,500	72.0	Zimbabwe	2,160	56.1
St. Vincent and the Grenadines	3,700	71.0			

Combined Average Ratings— Independent Countries

FREE

1.0
Andorra
Australia
Austria
Barbados
Belgium
Belize
Canada
Cyprus (G)
Denmark
Finland
Iceland
Kiribati
Liechtenstein
Luxembourg
Malta
Marshall Islands
Micronesia
Netherlands
New Zealand
Norway
Portugal
San Marino
Sweden
Switzerland
Tuvalu
United States of America

1.5
Bahamas
Cape Verde
Costa Rica
Czech Republic
Dominica
France
Germany
Grenada
Hungary
Ireland
Italy
Mauritius
Monaco
Palau
St. Lucia
St. Vincent & the
    Grenadines
Sao Tome & Principe
Slovenia
Solomon Islands
Spain
Trinidad & Tobago
United Kingdom

2.0
Bulgaria
Chile

Greece
Guyana
Israel
Japan
Korea, South
Lithuania
Nauru
Poland
St. Kitts-Nevis
Uruguay
Vanuatu
Western Samoa

2.5
Argentina
Benin
Bolivia
Botswana
Ecuador
Estonia
Jamaica
Latvia
Malawi
Mongolia
Namibia
Panama
Slovakia
South Africa

PARTLY FREE

3.0
Bangladesh
Brazil
El Salvador
Honduras
Madagascar
Mali
Papua New Guinea
Suriname
Taiwan
Venezuela

3.5
Albania
Antigua & Barbuda
Armenia
Central African Republic
Colombia
Dominican Republic
Fiji
Guinea-Bissau
Kyrgyz Republic
Macedonia
Nepal
Paraguay
Philippines

Romania
Russia
Seychelles
Ukraine
Zambia

4.0
Belarus
Comoros
Congo
Croatia
India
Jordan
Lesotho
Mexico
Moldova
Mozambique
Niger
Pakistan
Thailand
Tonga

4.5
Burkina Faso
Cambodia
Gabon
Ghana
Guatemala
Malaysia
Nicaragua
Peru
Senegal
Sri Lanka

5.0
Georgia
Haiti
Kuwait
Morocco
Singapore
Turkey
Uganda
Zimbabwe

5.5
Lebanon

NOT FREE

5.5
Cameroon
Chad
Eritrea
Ethiopia
Guinea
Ivory Coast (Cote
    D'Ivoire)

Kazakhstan
Swaziland
Togo
Tunisia
United Arab Emirates
Yemen

6.0
Azerbaijan
Bahrain
Bosnia-Herzegovina
Djibouti
Egypt
Kenya
Maldives
Oman
Tanzania
Yugoslavia (Serbia &
    Montenegro)

6.5
Brunei
Burundi
The Gambia
Indonesia
Iran
Laos
Liberia
Nigeria
Qatar
Sierra Leone
Zaire

7.0
Afghanistan
Algeria
Angola
Bhutan
Burma
China
Cuba
Equatorial Guinea
Iraq
Korea, North
Libya
Mauritania
Rwanda
Saudi Arabia
Somalia
Sudan
Syria
Tajikistan
Turkmenistan
Uzbekistan
Vietnam

Combined Average Ratings— Related Territories

FREE

1.0
Aland Islands (Finland)
American Samoa (U.S.)
Azores (Portugal)
Bermuda (U.K.)
British Virgin Islands (U.K.)
Canary Islands (Spain)
Cayman Islands (U.K.)
Cocos (Keeling) Islands (Australia)
Faeroe Islands (Denmark)
Gibraltar (U.K.)
Greenland (Denmark)
Guam (U.S.)
Isle of Man (U.K.)
Madeira (Portugal)
Montserrat (U.K.)
Pitcairn Islands (U.K.)
St. Pierre and Miquelon (France)
Turks and Caicos (U.K.)
United States Virgin Islands (U.S.)

1.5
Anguilla (U.K.)
Aruba (Netherlands)
Ceuta (Spain)
Channel Islands (U.K.)
Cook Islands (New Zealand)

Falkland Islands (U.K.)
French Guiana (France)
French Polynesia (France)
Guadeloupe (France)
Martinique (France)
Mayotte (Mahore) (France)
Melilla (Spain)
Netherlands Antilles (Netherlands)
Niue (New Zealand)
Norfolk Island (Australia)
Northern Marianas (U.S.)
Puerto Rico (U.S.)
St. Helena and Dependencies (U.K.)

2.0
New Caledonia (France)
Rapanui (Easter Island) (Chile)
Reunion (France)
Svalbard (Norway)
Tokelau (New Zealand)
Wallis and Futuna Islands (France)

2.5
Christmas Island (Australia)

PARTLY FREE

3.0
Cyprus (Turkey)

3.5
Hong Kong (U.K.)
Northern Ireland (U.K.)
4.0
Kurdistan (Iraq)

5.0
Macao (Portugal)

NOT FREE

5.5
Occupied Territories & Palestinian
    Autonomous Areas (Israel)

6.0
Vojvodina (Yugoslavia)

6.5
Western Sahara (Morocco)

7.0
East Timor (Indonesia)
Irian Jaya (West Papua) (Indonesia)
Kashmir (India)
Kosovo (Yugoslavia)
Nagorno-Karabakh (Armenia/
    Azerbaijan)*
Tibet (China)

* Nagorno-Karabakh is disputed territory, contested by Armenia and
Azerbaijan.

National Elections and Referenda

Country	Date/Type	Results and Comments
Albania 6 November 1994	referendum	Albanians voted to reject a post-Communist constitution by a margin of about 60 percent to 40 percent.
Antigua and Barbuda 8 March 1994	general	The ruling Bird family's Labour Party won 11 of the 17 parliamentary seats. The united opposition coalition increased its seats from 1 in 1989 to 6 (United Progressive Party, 5 and Barbuda People's Movement, 1). There was an apparently padded, five-year-old voters' list that included the names of ineligible emigrants and the dead. The government numbered ballots in such a way as to destroy their secrecy. The government also denied the opposition access to both public and private broadcasting outlets. Freedom House termed the election neither free nor fair.
Argentina April 1994	constituent assembly	The Peronists made their worst showing since 1987, winning only 36 percent of the vote. The Radicals had their worst result in decades, 19 percent of the vote. The Grand Front, a new, mostly left-wing coalition won 13 percent. Other parties took the remainder.
Austria 12 June 1994	referendum	With an 80 percent turnout, Austrians voted by 66.4 percent to 33.6 percent to join the European Union, effective January 1995.
9 October 1994	general	In the lower house of Parliament, the Social Democratic-People's Party Coalition government lost ground to the right-wing Freedom Party, the environmentalist Greens, and the Liberal Forum. The parties received the following: Social Demcorats, 34.92 percent of the vote and 65 seats; People's Party, 26.76 percent and 52 seats; Freedom Party, 22.5 percent and 42 seats; Greens, 7.31 percent and 13 seats; and the Liberal Forum, 5.97 percent and 11 seats. Social Democrat Franz Vranitzky remained chancellor.
Barbados 6 September 1994	general	Owen Arthur's opposition Barbados Labour Party won 19 of the 28 parliamentary seats. The governing Democratic Labour Party took only 8 seats; the National Democratic Party, 1 seat. Arthur became Prime Minister.
Belarus 23 June 1994	presidential	No candidate received the required 50 percent to win outright. Radical populist Alyaksandr Lukashekna Lukashenko finished first with 45 percent of the vote. Prime Minister Vyacheslav Kebich placed second with 17 percent. Other candidates split the rest. A run-off was scheduled Lukashenka and Kebich.
10 July 1994	presidential run-off	Lukashenko won with 80 percent to 14 percent for Kebich and 6 percent for spoiled ballots.
Botswana 16 October 1994	general	The long-ruling Botswana Democratic Party (BDP) won a majority of seats, but lost the overwhelming margin that it had in previous elections. The BDP fell from 33 of 36 elected seats to 26. The opposition Botswana National Front will have 13 seats. President Ketumile Masire has the right to name four additional legislators. Parliament reelected him to the presidency
Brazil 3 October 1994	general	With 54.3 percent of the vote, Fernando Henrique Cardoso, (center-right coalition) won the presidency. Luis Ignacio Lula da Silva (Workers Party) placed second with 27 percent. Right-wing candidate Eneas Carneiro came in third with 7.4 percent. Orestes Quercia and Leonel Brizola garnered 4.4 percent and 3.2 percent, respectively. Cardoso's majority avoided a run-off election. Pro-Cardoso forces emerged as the largest bloc in both the House of Deputies and the Senate.
Bulgaria 18 December 1994	general	The Socialists (ex-Communists) won 125 seats out of 240 in parliament. The Union of Democratic Forces won 69 seats. The other 46 seats went to other parties.
Central African Republic 3 December 1994	legislative (repeat elections)	Opposition parties won 5 out of 6 seats whose original results had been disputed since the 1993 general election. The sixth seat remains unfilled, because irregularities marred voting.
28 December 1994	referendum	By a vote of 82 percent to 18 percent, voters adopted a new constitution. Turnout was very low.
Chad 1994	general	Elections were postponed until 1995.
Colombia 13 March 1993	legislative	The Liberals retained a majority in both the Senate and Chamber of Deputies. Turnout was only about 30 percent.
29 May 1994	presidential	Ernesto Samper (Liberal) received 45.2 percent to 44.9 percent for Andres Pastrana (Conservative). Six other candidates split the rest.
19 June 1994	presidential run-off	Samper (Liberal) won with 50.3 percent of the vote, defeating Pastrana (Conservative) who had 48.6 percent. Only 7.5 million of 17 million eligible voters participated.
Costa Rica 6 February 1994	general	Jose Maria Figueres (National Liberation Party) defeated Miguel Angel Rodriguez (Social Christian Unity Party) by 49.7 percent to 47.5 percent. Six other candidates captured the rest of the vote. Thirteen parties contested the 57 legislative seats. The National Liberation Party captured 28 seats; Social Christian Unity,

National Elections and Referenda

Country	Date/Type	Results and Comments
		25 seats; Democratic Force, 2 seats; and two agrarian parties, 1 seat each.

Denmark
22 September 1994 — general

Social Democratic Prime Minister Poul Nyrup Rasmussen's coalition lost its majority in the 179-seat parliament. Rasmussen pledged to form a center-left coalition with informal support from other parties. The Social Democrats won 62 seats. Their partners, the Radical Liberals and the Center Democrats took 8 and 5 seats, respectively. The Christian People's Party, a former governing coalition partner, lost all 4 of its seats. The center-right opposition parties, the Liberals, Conservatives, and the Progress Party, won 42, 27, and 11 seats, respectively. The Socialist People's Party, an ex-Communist splinter group, took 13 seats. The left-wing Unity List captured 6 seats. Parties from the related territories of Greenland and the Faroe Islands, elected 2 seats each. Comedian Jacob Hougaard was the only independent elected.

Dominican Republic
16 May 1994 — general

President Joaquin Balaguer (Revolutionary Social Christian Party-PRSC) won re-election, using apparent vote fraud to defeat Jose Francisco Pena Gomez (Democratic Revolutionary Party-PRD). Former President Juan Bosch placed third. Opposition parties and international observers complained that the electoral system disenfranchised opposition voters in at least five cities. The complaints led to additional voting hours, during which some of the disenfranchised were allowed to vote. During the campaign, 17 people died in political violence. The government muzzled private radio and television the day of the election. It shut off CNN and other cable networks and interrupted a broadcast of "NBC Nightly News" from the United States on 16 May. The PRD won about half of the contested legislative seats in the Senate and Chamber of Deputies, finishing ahead of the PRSC. In the summer of 1994, the government certified Balaguer as the winner. However, he agreed to schedule a new election for 1996, cutting his term by two years.

Ecuador
1 May 1994 — legislative

Voters filled 65 of the 77 Congressional seats, President Duran's Republican Unity Party won only 10. The Social Christian Party won 25. The leftist Popular Democratic Movement captured 7 seats. Frank Vargas, leader of a former coup attempt, won a seat as a nationalist independent. Other parties took a combined 22 seats.

August1994 — referendum

Voters approved a proposal to begin reforming the constitution.

El Salvador
20 March 1994 — general

In the first general election since the end of the civil war, Salvadorans voted for president, vice president, and the 84-member National Assembly. Voting was generally orderly, but there were some apparent irregularities and mismanagement in the distribution of voter credentials and registration lists. The Farabundo Marti National Liberation Front (FMLN), the former guerrilla group, complained that some people waiting to vote at the time of poll-closing were turned away. In the presidential contest, Armando Calderon Sol of the National Republican Alliance (ARENA) received 49.03 percent, not enough to avoid a run-off. Ruben Zamora of the leftist Democratic Convergence and backed by the FMLN finished second with 24.9 percent. Fidel Chavez Mena (Christian Democrat) placed third with 16.36 percent. Four other candidates received a combined total of 9.71 percent. In the 84-seat legislative contest, ARENA captured 39 of the seats. The FMLN finished second with 21 seats, and the Christian Democrats third with 18. The pro-military National Conciliation Party captured 4 seats. The evangelical Unity Movement and Democratic Convergence won 1 seat each.

24 April 1994 — presidential runoff

By 66 percent to 34 percent, Calderon Sol defeated Zamora. Zamora supporters alleged that there had been irregularities, but conceded that they were not enough to alter the outcome. There were fewer logistical problems than in round one.

Ethiopia
5 June 1994 — constituent assembly

According to the government, over 90 percent of the 15 million registered voters turned out to elect constituent assembly members. About 800 of the 1,476 candidates were independents. The rest represented 39 political parties, but several major opposition groups boycotted the election. The ruling Ethiopian People's Revolutionary Democratic Front won 449 out of 502 constituencies. Other political groups won a combined 28 seats, while independents took 28. The assembly may amend the draft constitution or write a new one.

European Union
9 and 12 June 1994 — legislative

In the race for the 567-seat European Parliament, voters in most countries gave the edge to the local opposition parties. Overall, the Socialist Group, consisting of socialist, social democratic and labor parties, won 200 seats. The center-right European People's Party won 148 seats. Others won 220 seats, including 96 non-affiliated and independent deputies. The British Conservatives and Spanish Socialists suffered dramatic defeats. The French Socialists lost ground, as did major governing parties or their coalition partners in Belgium, Denmark, Greece, Ireland and Portugal. The German Christian Democrats and their Bavarian partners, the Christian Social Union, won most of their country's seats. The German Social Democrats had their worst showing in a European election since 1979. In Italy, Prime Minister Berlusconi's Let's Go, Italy! party topped the poll, improving on its showing in the 1994 Italian parliamentary election.

Fiji
18-25 February 1994 — general

Prime Minister Sitiveni Rabuka's SVT won 31 of the 70 seats. The Fijian Association (ex-SVT members) took 5 seats. The General Voters List captured 4 seats. The National Federation Party (ethnic Indian) won 20

National Elections and Referenda

Country	Date/Type	Results and Comments

seats. The Fiji Labour Party garnered 7 seats. Independents received the remaining 3 seats. The constitution reserves 37 seats for the ethnic Fijians. Rabuka expected to form a coalition government with the support of independents and small parties.

Finland
16 January 1994 — presidential

In round one of the first direct presidential election, diplomat Martti Ahtisaari (Social Democrat) led with 25.9 percent. Defense Minister Elisabeth Rehn (Swedish People's Party) finished second with 22 percent. Former Foreign Minister Paavo Vayrynen (Center Party) placed third with 19.5 percent. Former Helsinki Mayor Raimo Ilaskivi (Conservative/National Coalition) came in fourth with 15.2 percent. Seven other candidates were far behind with less than 6 percent each. About one-quarter of the electorate cast ballots during pre-election day voting at home and at embassies abroad.

6 February 1994 — presidential run-off

Ahtisaari (Social Democrat) defeated Rehn (Swedish People's Party), 53.9 percent to 46.1 percent.

16 October 1994 — referendum

Finns voted by 57 percent to 43 percent to join the European Union.

Germany
16 October 1994 — general

Electing the second all-German Bundestag, voters confirmed Christian Democratic Chancellor Helmut Kohl's center-right coalition by a narrow margin. Electors cast ballots for representatives from single-member districts and from party lists. Parties winning at least three single-member districts or at least 5 percent of the list vote were entitled to seats from their lists. The Christian Democratic Union/Christian Social Union won a combined 41.5 percent of the vote and 294 seats. Their centrist allies, the Free Democrats, took only 6.9 percent and 47 seats. The Social Democrats received 36.4 percent and 252 seats. The leftist/environmentalist Greens took 7.3 percent and 49 seats. With 4.4 percent, the ex-Communists, the Party of Democratic Socialism, just missed the 5 percent hurdle, but won in four single-member districts, entitling it to another 26 seats from its list. The new Bundestag will have 672 seats.

Guatemala
30 January 1994 — referendum

Voters approved 37 constitutional amendments including dissolving Congress and the Supreme Court, reducing the number of parliamentarians and shortening their terms. Voter turnout was under 20 percent.

15 August 1994 — legislative

Elections took place for the new 80-seat Congress. Right-wing parties led the vote. The Republican Front of former strongman, General Efrain Rios Montt, won 32 seats. The pro-business National Advancement Party, took 24 seats. The Christian Democrats won 13 seats. The National Center Union, the National Liberation Movement and the Democratic Union split the remaining 11 seats. Only about 30 percent of voters participated.

Guinea-Bissau
27 March 1994 — general

The government postponed the elections for the third time. Delayed voter registration and allegedly inadequate electoral machinery were the reasons cited.

3-5 July 1994 — general (first round)

The country's first multiparty election finally took place. Heavy rain and logistical problems caused delays in starting the vote in many areas, so polling was extended. Voters chose a president from among eight candidates and a 100-seat parliament from more than 1,136 candidates. President Nino Vieira (African Party for the Independence of Guinea-Bissau and Cape Verde-PAIGC) finished first with 46 percent of the vote. His nearest rival, Kumba Iala (Party for Social Renovation and five other parties), finished second with 22 percent. Other candidates included Domingos Fernandes Gomes (Bafata Resistance Movement) and Bubacar Djalo (Green Party). A run-off between Vieira and Iala was scheduled for 7 August. The PAIGC won 64 parliamentary seats to 36 for the Bafata Movement and three other opposition parties. Turnout was over 80 percent. The election law required presidential candidates to prove their Bissau roots through their grandparents. This discriminated against residents of Cape Verdean backgrounds. There were some allegations that Vieira used fraud.

7 August 1994 — presidential run-off

President Vieira defeated Iala 52 percent to 48 percent. However, Iala carried Bissau, the capital. Turnout was 79.8 percent.

Hungary
8 May 1994 — general - first round

The Socialists (former Communists) led with 33 percent and 53 seats. The liberal Alliance of Free Democrats was second with 19.5 percent and 28 seats. The conservative Hungarian Democratic Forum, the dominant party in the outgoing government, placed third with 11.7 percent, followed by the agrarian Independent Smallholders with 8.8 percent and the Christian Democrats with 7.7 percent. The far-right received 1.3 percent. Voters cast ballots for candidates on party lists for 210 seats and for 176 individual candidates in districts. The Socialists led in most districts. When no individual candidate receives more than 50 percent, the law requires run-offs. There were 1,876 candidates in round one.

30 May 1994 — run-offs

Candidates from round one with at least 15 percent of the vote were eligible for the run-off, but the liberal Free Democrats, Young Democrats, Agrarian Alliance and the Entrepreneurs Party united behind a single candidate in most districts. The Socialists (former Communists) won a combined 209 of 386 seats, more than enough to form a single-party government with Gyula Horn as prime minister. However, they formed a coalition with the Free Democrats, who finished with 70 seats from the two rounds. The Hungarian

National Elections and Referenda

Country	Date/Type	Results and Comments
		Democratic Forum fell to third position, winning only 37 seats. Others won a combined 70 seats.
Italy 27 March 1994	general	This was Italy's first general election under a new electoral system. Voters filled three-quarters of the Chamber of Deputies and Senate seats by first-past-the-post and one-quarter by proportional representation for parties that received at least 4 percent of the vote. A three-party, right-wing coalition of Let's Go, Italy!, the Northern League and the neo-fascist National Alliance won 366 seats in the 630-seat Chamber of Deputies and 155 seats in the 315-seat Senate. A seven-party, left-wing coalition of the Democratic Party of the'Left (ex-Communists), the hardline Communist Refoundation, the anti-Mafia Network and other groups placed second with 213 Deputies and 122 Senators. A centrist coalition of the reformist Pact for Italy and the Popular Party (the former Christian Democrats) placed third with 46 Deputies and 31 Senators. Smaller parties took the remaining seats in both houses. The Socialist Party, previously a major party, received no seats. Let's Go Italy's leader, Silvio Berlusconi, became prime minister, heading a coalition government with the Northern League and the National Alliance.
Kazakhstan 7 March 1994	legislative	In the country's first post-Soviet election, voting was partly free. Supporters of President Nazarbayev won the majority of 177 seats. The pro-Nazarbayev Union of People's Unity of Kazakhstan won 30 seats. Independents (mostly pro-government) won 60 seats. Nazarbayev appointed 42 legislators. His opponents won about 23 seats. The official trade union received 11 seats. The other 11 winners were of an unspecified loyalty. Nazarbayev issued a list of government-approved candidates before the election, thereby violating CSCE agreements. Procedures allowed family heads to cast several votes on behalf of other family members. The CSCE estimated that up to 50 percent of voters had cast ballots for electors other than themselves. Several opposition candidates were unfairly denied registration of candidacy. Three protested with hunger strikes. There were restrictions on the media's coverage of the campaign. Foreign observers were not allowed at all polling stations. The government needed a voter turnout of over 50 percent, in order to validate the results. It succeeded with apparently massaged statistics and the help of shops at the polls that sold scarce items. However, the U.S. Helsinki Commission observers stated that the government's turnout estimate, 73 percent, was a great exaggeration. An opposition leader claimed that turnout was below 50 percent.
Kiribati 21-22 July 1994 29-30 July 1994	general legislative-run-offs	There were 260 candidates for 39 seats. The Christian Democrats won a plurality of seats, ousting the National Progressives. However, the informal nature of the political system means an exact breakdown of the seats is unavailable.
September 1994	presidential	Voters elected Christian Democrat Teburoro Tito. He defeated other candidates who were also nominated by the legislature.
Kyrgyzstan 30 January 1994	presidential referendum	Voters approved President Askar Akayev 96.36 percent to 2.95 percent. Turnout was 95.9 percent.
22 October 1994	referenda	Voters decided two referenda. In the first one, with 75 percent approving, they confirmed allowing constitutional changes by referenda. In the second, 73 percent voted to restructure the unicameral parliament into a smaller, bicameral legislature. The official turnout was 87 percent.
Liberia 7 September 1994	general (canceled)	The renewed civil war prevented the vote from taking place.
Liechtenstein November 1994	referendum	Voters approved membership in the European Economic Area (EEA).
Lithuania 27 August 1994	referendum	Insufficient voter turnout invalidated an opposition-sponsored package on the economy. The opposition measures would have cost about $2 billion, and would have forced the government to compensate Lithuanians for savings depreciated by inflation. Rules required a majority turnout for a valid referendum, but only 35 percent cast ballots.
Luxembourg 12 June 1994	general	Voters returned the governing Christian Social Party-Socialist Workers' Party coalition to power. The liberal Democrats, the Greens, the Communists and the pro-pension Five-Sixths Party won the remaining seats.
Macedonia 16 October 1994	general	President Kiro Gligorov (Alliance for Macedonia) won with 53 percent of the vote. His leading opponent, Ljubisa Georgievski (Democratic Party for Macedonian National Unity), finished second with 14.5 percent. Georgievski alleged that Gligorov actually received less than half the vote. In the contest for 120 parliamentary seats, 1,700 candidates from 36 parties participated. The three-party Alliance for Macedonia led with 32.1 percent, followed by the Internal Macedonian Revolutionary Movement with 14.4 percent, and the Democratic Party for Macedonian National Unity with 11.2 percent. Voters gave only 10 candidates outright majorities, necessitating run-offs for 110 seats. Observers from the CSCE criticized the organization of the election, citing the "high number" of voters left off registration lists at polling stations. CSCE monitors also

National Elections and Referenda

Country	Date/Type	Results and Comments

attributed other irregularities to confusion and a lack of familiarity with the electoral process. Opposition leaders charged Gligorov with rigging voter lists and planning fake ballots. The electoral commission admitted that it had excluded 10 percent of eligible voters from the registration lists. What the commission called "technical difficulties" delayed the release of official returns and caused several contradictory results to appear before the above-listed results came out.

30 October and 13 November 1994 — parliamentary run-offs

Citing vote-rigging in round one, opposition parties boycotted the legislative run-offs for 110 of the 120 parliamentary seats. The opposition's poor showing in round one may also have influenced their decision to boycott. President Gligorov's Alliance for Macedonia won 95 seats; the mostly Albanian Party for Democratic Prosperity, 10 seats; People's Democratic Party, 4 seats; minor parties and independents, 11 total.

Malawi
17 May 1994 — general

In the first multiparty election since independence, former cabinet member Bakili Muluzi (United Democratic Front and other opposition parties) took 47 percent of the vote, defeating the long-ruling dictator, Hastings Kamuzu Banda (Malawi Congress Party), who had 33 percent. Chakufwa Chihana, a former political prisoner, placed third with 19 percent. Voters also chose a 177-seat parliament. The United Democratic Front won 85 seats. The Malawi Congress Party placed second with 55 seats. The Alliance for Democracy took 36 seats. John Tembo, a member of the triumvirate that administered Malawi during Banda's illness, won a seat. There were some irregularities, but the vote was generally free and fair.

Mexico
21 August 1994 — general

Getting apparently the lowest winning percentage in modern Mexican history, Ernesto Zedillo (Institutional Revolutionary Party-PRI) won the presidency with about 50 percent of the vote. Using the PRI's enormous social and political control over Mexican society and its control of the state and broadcast media, he defeated Diego Fernandez (National Action Party-PAN) and Cuauhtemoc Cardenas (Democratic Revolution Party-PRD), who garnered 28 percent and 17 percent, respectively. Minor candidates won the rest. Turnout was about 70 percent. Irregularities, especially in the southern part of the country, added to Zedillo's margin of victory. Many polling stations ran out of ballot paper. Observers reported some instances of multiple voting. Opposition party poll watchers covered the country unevenly, especially in rural areas. The PRI won control of both houses of Congress.

Moldova
27 February 1994 — legislative

Candidates contested 104 seats for a four-year term for the unicameral parliament. Parties favorable to the Commonwealth of Independent States won a combined majority. The Agrarian Democrats won 43 percent of the vote and 56 seats. The pro-Russian Socialist-Unity Bloc captured 22 percent and 28 seats. Two parties favoring unification with Romania won a combined 20 seats - the pro-Romanian Congress of Peasants and Intellectuals, 11, and the pro-Romanian Christian Democratic Popular Front, 9. There were some irregularities in the voting. Parts of the country have been in secessionist crises.

6 March 1994 — referendum

With a 90 percent Yes vote, Moldovans reaffirmed their country's independence, dealing a blow to those favoring merger with Romania.

Mozambique
27-28 October 1994 — general

The incumbent President Chissano (FRELIMO) defeated Dhlaklama (RENAMO) by 54 percent-34 percent. FRELIMO won 45 percent of the vote and 129 of the 250 seats in the legislative election, compared to 38 percent and 112 seats for RENAMO. The conservative opposition party, Democratic Union, captured 9 seats. On the first day of polling, RENAMO announced an electoral boycott, claiming fraud, but then agreed to continue participating. There were some irregularities around the country, but international observers pronounced the vote generally free and fair. Polling officials declared 500,000 ballots spoiled, necessitating a subsequent review by the elections commission. Many voters, unaccustomed to political choice, cast such ballots, because they did not know what to do.

Namibia
7-8 December 1994 — general

President Sam Nujoma (South West Africa People's Organization-SWAPO) was reelected with 76 percent of the vote to 24 percent for Mishake Muyongo (Democratic Turnhalle Alliance-DTA). In the 72-seat parliament, SWAPO took 53 seats; DTA, 15; United Democratic Front, 2; Democratic Coalition of Namibia, 1; Monitor Action Group, 1.

Nepal
15 November 1994 — general

The Communist Party of Nepal (United Marxist-Leninist) won 88 of the 205 parliamentary seats, defeating the incumbent Nepali Congress Party of Prime Minister G.P. Koirala. Congress captured 83 seats. In the popular vote, Congress took 33 percent to 30 percent for the Communists. The pro-monarchist National Democrats took 20 seats. Small parties and independents snared a combined 14 seats. There were at least six campaign-related deaths. At least eleven people were injured in bombings, riots and other election-day mayhem. A pattern of violence and irregularities caused repeat polling at sixty-four locations. The elections were re-scheduled from 13 November, a Hindu holy day.

Netherlands
3 May 1994 — general

Winning 37 of the 150 lower house seats, Wim Kok's Labor Party replaced the Christian Democratic Appeal (CDA) as the leading party. The CDA captured 22.2 percent of the vote and 34 seats; the right-wing Liberals(VVD), 19.9 percent and 31 seats; and the center-left Democrats '66, 15.5 percent and 24 seats. Smaller parties, including the Greens, the extreme right, and two senior citizen groups, captured the remaining 24 seats. Kok became prime minister in August, heading a coalition of Labor, the right-wing Liberals, and Democrats '66.

National Elections and Referenda

Country	Date/Type	Results and Comments
Nigeria 23 May 1994	constitutional conference	The military government sponsored an election for 270 delegates to a constitutional conference. The state had banned all parties and prohibited campaigning. Several groups organized boycotts. Turnout was extremely low. Most voters did not see the point of voting in a military-dominated process.
Norway 28 November 1994	referendum	Norwegians voted against joining the European Union by 52.2 percent to 47.8 percent.
Panama 8 May 1994	general	Ernesto Perez Balladares (Democratic Revolutionary Party-PRD) won with 33 percent. Mireya Moscoso (Arnulfista Party-PA) came in second with 29 percent. Ruben Blades (Mother Earth Party) placed third with 17 percent. Ruben Dario Carles received 16 percent. Three other candidates, Eduardo Vallarino (Christian Democrat), Jose Salvador Munoz (Panamanian Doctrine Party), and Samuel Lewis Galindo (Solidarity Alliance), garnered less than 2 percent each. Voters also chose two vice presidents and 71 representatives. In the legislature, the PRD won 31 of the 72 seats; the PA, 14; Mother Earth, 6; Molirena, 5; others, 16. International observers declared the results to be free and fair.
St. Kitts-Nevis 29 November 1994	general	The St. Kitts Labour Party SKLP) and the People's Action Movement (PAM) of Prime Minister Kennedy Simmonds won 4 seats each. The United People's Party (UPP) came in third on St. Kitts. On the island of Nevis, the Concerned Citizens Movement (CCM) took 2 seats and the Nevis Reformation Party (NRP), 1. The PAM-NRP coalition had a plurality of 5 seats. The CCM refused to join a coalition with either the PAM or the SKLP. Simmonds formed a new government. There were violent disturbances. The SKLP boycotted parliament and demanded new elections in 1995. After a "forum for national unity," the government agreed to hold a new election by November 1995.
St. Vincent and the Grenadines 21 February 1994	general	Prime Minister James Mitchell's New Democratic Party won 12 out of 15 seats on 54 percent of the vote. A combined opposition (Labour Party and Movement for National Unity) captured 46 percent and 3 seats.
Sao Tome and Principe 5 October 1994	legislative	The former ruling party, the Movement for the Liberation of Sao Tome and Principe, won 27 of the 55 seats. The Party for Democratic Convergence took 14 seats, down sharply from the 31 it had secured in 1991. President Miguel Trovoada's Independent Democratic Action also captured 14 seats.
Slovakia 30 September- 1 October 1994	general	Former Prime Minister Meciar's Movement for a Democratic Slovakia finished first with 35 percent and 61 of the 150 parliamentary seats. The ex-Communists of the Common Choice bloc finished with 10 percent and 18 seats; the Christian Democrats, 10 percent and 17 seats; a Hungarian ethnic parties' coalition, 10 percent and 17 seats. Outgoing Prime Minister Jozef Moravcik's Democratic Union took 15 seats; the Union of Slovak Workers, 13 seats; and the Slovak National Party, 9 seats. In December Meciar announced a coalition with the Union of Slovak Workers and the Slovak National Party.
	29 October 1994 referendum	Only 20 percent of the voters turned out for a referendum on reforming privatization. The low participation invalidated the vote.
South Africa 26, 27, 28 and 29 April 1994	constituent assembly	Following a campaign marred by bombings and numerous other acts of violence, South Africans voted in the country's first all-race election. They chose members of a 400-seat lower house on a proportional basis from 19 party lists. Each party received a seat for each .25 percent of the vote. Parties received a cabinet seat for each 5 percent of the vote. The elderly, disabled and imprisoned voters could cast ballots in 500 locations on 26 April. Current and former South African citizens abroad could vote at overseas locations beginning on 26 April. Authorities arrested white extremists on 27 April for allegedly setting off a series of bombs that they intended to disrupt voting. Due to the last-minute entry of the Inkatha Freedom Party, there were some snags in adding the party to the ballot and distributing updated voting papers. The crowds of voters were so large that many polling stations ran out of ballot papers and of the invisible ink appied to voters' hands to prevent repeat voting. In some areas, ballot-hijackings and power outages prevented voting, at least temporarily. Several parties called for extending the voting, and some areas voted on 29 April. There is also an indirectly elected upper house with 90 seats (10 members per province). Numerous irregularities took place in the voting and counting, including computer sabotage. However, the irregularities did not change the basic outcome: victory for Nelson Mandela's African National Congress (ANC) and a second place finish for F.W. DeKlerk's National Party. The Independent Electoral Commission decided not to press for precise final vote totals, because the major parties made deals to resolve their differences over the outcome. The commission made some adjustments in vote totals to take account of irregularities. Otherwise, the commission pronounced the vote "substantially free and fair." The adjusted results were: ANC, 62.65 percent and 252 seats; National Party, 20.39 percent and 82 seats; Inkatha, 10.54 percent and 43 seats; the pro-apartheid Freedom Front, 2.17 percent and 9 seats; the liberal Democratic Party, 1.7 percent and 7 seats; the militant Pan-Africanist Congress, 1.25 percent and 5 seats; the African Christian Democratic Party, 0.4 percent and 2 seats. The parliament elected Mandela president.
Sri Lanka 16 August 1994	legislative	Thirteen parties and 26 groups, 1,440 candidates in all, took part. A left-wing opposition coalition led by the Sri Lanka Freedom Party (SLFP) won 105 of the 225 seats. The incumbent United National Party won 94 seats. Other groups, including Tamil parties, won a combined 26 seats. At least 24 people died in campaign-

National Elections and Referenda

Country	Date/Type	Results and Comments

related violence. SLFP leader Chandrika Bandaranaike Kumaratunga became prime minister, heading a multiparty coalition government.

9 November 1994 — presidential

Gamini Dissanayake (United National Party) was to have faced Prime Minister Kumaratunga (Sri Lanka Freedom Party). However, on 23 October, a bomb killed Dissanayake and 51 others. Police suspected a Tamil suicide bomber. The election took place as scheduled with a new candidate, Srima Dissanayake, the late candidate's widow. Kumaratunga won with 62.3 percent to 35.9 percent for Dissananyake. Four other candidates took the rest.

Sweden
18 September 1994 — general

With 162 seats, the Social Democrats emerged as the largest party in the 349-seat parliament. Their leader, Ingvar Carlsson, pledged to lead a minority government with the support of other parties. The ex-Communist Left Party took 22 seats. The Environment Party won 18 seats. The center-right parties won a combined 147 seats, down from 196 in the previous election. The Moderates held onto their 80 seats. The right-wing Liberals, the Center Party, and the Christian Democrats all lost ground, capturing 26, 27, and 14 seats, respectively. The anti-state New Democracy Party, which had won 25 seats in 1991, disappeared from parliament.

13 November 1994 — referendum

Swedes voted to join the European Union by 52.2 percent to 46.9 percent. The rest cast blank ballots. Turnout was 82 percent, the highest in the country's history.

Switzerland
20 February 1994 — referenda

By 52-48 percent, voters approved an initiative requiring all freight to be carried by rail within ten years. This result could snarl truck traffic from European Union countries. The referendum also halts some public works projects. Voters also approved new police powers of search and detention when dealing with illegal immigrants. By 57.3 percent voters rejected providing soldiers for U.N. peace-keeping operations.

Syria
August 1994 — legislative

The National Progressive Front, dominated by the Baath Party, won the overwhelming majority of 250 seats in an election that allowed little genuine competition. State-approved independents won a few seats.

Tajikistan
6 November 1994 — presidential and referendum

Using fraud and intimidation, President Emomali Rakhmonov won with 60 percent of the vote to 35 percent for Abdulmalik Abdulladjanov, the Tajik Ambassador to Russia. Abdulladjanov charged that at least one-third of Rakhmonov's vote was fraudulent. Most opposition leaders are dead, in exile or under bans. The government controls the media strictly. According to the official count, 90 percent of voters approved a new constitution. The Conference on Security and Cooperation in Europe and the UN refused to send observers, because the election laws are seriously flawed.

Togo
6 and 20 February 1994 — legislative (two rounds)

The opposition parties, the Action Committee for Renewal and the Togolese Union for Democracy, won 36 and 7 seats, respectively, out of 81. President General Gnassingbe Eyadema's supporters, the Togolese People's Assembly, and their allies won a combined 37 seats. Transitional Prime Minister Joseph Koffigoh also won a seat. The People's Assembly contested the results, and charged the opposition with fraud and violence on 20 February. Some ballot boxes were allegedly smashed or removed from polling stations. The state media charged that an opposition party that boycotted the election ransacked six voting booths and forced sixteen others to close. The opposition charged the government with repeated harassment and threats during the campaign. An opposition leader and two supporters were assassinated between the two rounds. Opposition leader Gilchrist Olympio's party boycotted the election, because the government had barred him from the 1993 presidential election. Olympio attacked the electoral system for faulty voter registration and other irregularities that weighted the vote in Eyadema's favor. The pro-Eyadema National Electoral Commission contested the results, but the Supreme Court upheld them.

Tunisia
20 March 1994 — general

President Zine Abidine Ben Ali ran unopposed. Two opposition candidates had sought to run against him, but could not get on the ballot. Election regulations required that they receive the endorsements of 30 parliamentarians and city council members, virtually all of whom were members of the ruling party. Ben Ali won with 99.9 percent of the vote. For the unicameral 163-member Chamber of Deputies, voters chose 144 deputies from districts on a winner-take-all basis. Ben Ali's Democratic Constitutional Assembly won over 95 percent of the vote and all of the directly elected seats. New electoral laws guaranteed 19 seats to the losing parties on a proportional basis. The Movement of Socialist Democrats took 10 seats; the Renewal Movement (former Communists), 4; the Democratic Union, 3; and Popular Unity, 2. In the run-up to the election, the government expelled some foreign journalists and removed a French newspaper from circulation, in order to limit campaign coverage. The Muslim fundamentalist party, Renaissance, the chief opposition, was banned.

Uganda
28 March 1994 — constituent assembly

Ugandans voted for a 214-seat constituent assembly. Over 1,000 candidates ran as individuals without party labels, but their affiliations were generally clear: the government's National Resistance Movement or various older parties. The multiparty opposition won seats in the northern and northeastern sections of the country. The government-backed candidates generally won elsewhere. Five senior government ministers lost their races. President Museveni, the National Resistance Army and various parties and interest groups will name other constituent assembly delegates. Turnout exceeded 70 percent.

National Elections and Referenda

Country	Date/Type	Results and Comments
Ukraine 27 March 1994	legislative	Electoral laws discouraged the role of parties. Only 11 percent of the candidates had party affiliations. This hurt the opposition even before the campaign. Security forces harassed and oppositionists and detained and threatened pre-election observers. The head of the Rukh party secretariat was abducted and presumed dead. Communists and other leftists led in round one. There were some irregularities, such as voters casting ballots for several family members. Turnout was 75 percent nationwide, more than enough to validate an election that required a 50 percent turnout. Voters filled only 49 of the 450 seats in the first round. Of the 49, the Communists won 12; the moderate nationalist Rukh, 4; other parties, 9; and independents, 24. A majority of voters in Crimea and two eastern Ukrainian regions voted for closer ties with Russia. In a government-banned referendum, Crimeans approved greater Crimean autonomy and dual Russian-Ukrainian citizenship. Voters in Donetsk and Luhansk approved dual citizenship, more ties with the Russian-dominated Commonwealth of Independent States, and Russian-Ukrainian bilingualism.
3 April 1994	legislative run-off	Voters filled 24 more seats: independents, 16; Communists, 7; and Socialists, 1. Turnout averaged over 70 percent.
10 April 1994	legislative run-off	Voters filled more seats, raising the completed total to 338 out of 450. For a variety of reasons, such as restrictive rules governing parties and the large number of nominally independent candidates, it was difficult to give precise figures on parties and seats. Communists and their allies won at least one-fourth of the seats. About one-third of the seats went to various independents. Smaller numbers of seats went to Rukh and other democratic and nationalist groups.
26 June 1994	presidential first round	President Leonid Kravchuk finished first in round one with 37.7 percent. Former Prime Minister Leonid Kuchma finished second with 31.3 percent. Other candidates split the remainder.
10 July 1994	presidential run-off	With over 52 percent of the vote, Kuchma won, carrying the eastern regions of the country. Kravchuk swept the more nationalistic western areas.
24 July 1994 legislative run-offs		The government scheduled yet another round of run-offs for the remaining 112 seats, but low turnouts invalidated results in 55 districts.
7 August 1994	legislative run-offs	After still another round of run-offs, 58 seats remained unfilled due to low turnouts. Of the 392 seats filled so far, the Communists and their allies held more than 145 seats; pro-Kuchma reformers, about 75 seats; various nationalists and democrats, about 90 seats; various independents and others, about 80 seats. Officially, there were 213 independents, but most of them were close to various groups.
November 1994	legislative run-offs	Voters filled 13 more seats, leaving 45 unfilled. Additional run-offs were suspended.
United States of America 8 November 1994	legislative	The Republicans captured control of the House of Representatives for the first time in 40 years, winning 230 of the 435 seats. The Democrats took 204 seats. An independent socialist holds the remaining seat. The Republicans regained control of the Senate for the first time since 1986. With the help of a defecting Democrat, the Republicans gained a 53-47 margin over the Democrats. No incumbent Republicans lost. Many prominent Democrats lost their seats, including Tom Foley, the first Speaker of the House to lose his election since 1860. Turnout was about 39 percent.
Uruguay 27 November 1994	general	Julio Maria Sanguinetti (Colorado Party-PC) won the presidency with 31.2 percent of the vote. His nearest competitors, Alberto Volonte (National Party-PN), and Tabare Vazquez (Broad Front-FA), took 30 percent and 29.9 percent respectively. Minor candidates captured the remaining 8.9 percent. In the Senate races, the parties won as follows: PC, 11; PN, 10; FA, 9; and the New Space Party, 1. In the Chamber of Deputies, the results were: PC, 32; PN, 32; FA, 30; and New Space, 5.
Uzbekistan 25 December 1994	legislative	The former Communists, now calling themselves the Democratic Party, won 179 seats in the parliament. Independents captured 20 seats. The pro-business Fatherland Progress Party took 6 seats. The former Communists dominate the political system, taking a hardline position against dissent.

Sources: Associated Press, Caribbean News Agency, *The Christian Science Monitor, The Economist, The Financial Times, Journal of Democracy,* Liberal International, *The Miami Herald, New African, The New York Times, West Africa.*

Sources

Publications, organizations

AFL-CIO
Agence France Presse
American Institute for Free Labor Development
American Irish Education Foundation-Political Action Committee
Amnesty International *Urgent Action Bulletins*
Amnesty International: *Report 1994*
Armenian Information Service
Asian Bulletin
Asian Survey
Associated Press
The *Atlantic Monthly*
Austrian Information
Azerbaijan International (U.S.)
Balkan Medja (Bulgaria)
Caretas (Lima)
Carib News
Caribbean Insight
Caribbean Review
The *Carter Center News*
Catholic Standard (Guyana)
Center for Strategic and International Studies
Centers for Pluralism: Newsletters (Poland)
Central America Report
Central Statistical Office, Warsaw (Poland)
The *Chinese Free Journal*
Christian Science Monitor
Columbia Journalism Review
Commission on Security and Cooperation in Europe (CSCE):
    Implementation of the Helsinki Accords (Reports)
Committee to Protect Journalists *Update*
Dawn News Bulletin (All Burma Students Democratic Front)
Democratic Initiatives (Ukraine)
Eastern European Constitutional Review
The *Economist*
EFE Spanish news agency
El Financiero (Mexico City)
El Nuevo Herald (Miami)
Elections Canada
EPOCA (Mexico)
Equal Access Committee (Ukraine)
Ethiopian Review
Ethnic Federation of Romani (Romania)
Far Eastern Economic Review
Foreign Broadcast Information Service (FBIS):
    FBIS Africa
    FBIS China
    FBIS East Europe
    FBIS Latin America
    FBIS Near East & South Asia
    FBIS East Asia
    FBIS Soviet Union/Central Eurasia
    FBIS Sub-Saharan Africa
The *Financial Times*
Finnish Helsinki Commission (Reports)
Free China Review
Free Labour World
Free Trade Union Institute
Freedom Forum
Fund for Peace
The *Globe & Mail* (Toronto)
The *Guardian*
Hemisfile
Hemisphere
Himal

Hong Kong Digest
Immigration and Refugee Board of Canada
The *Independent*
Index on Censorship
Indian Law Resource Center
Inside China Mainland
Institute for European Defence and Strategic Studies (U.K.)
Inter-American Dialogue
Inter-American Press Association
International Commission of Jurists
International Committee for the Red Cross (ICRC)
International Foundation for Electoral Systems (IFES)
International Organization of Journalists
International Republican Institute
The *Irish Echo*
The *Irish Voice*
Jeune Afrique
Journal of Commerce
Journal of Democracy
La Jornada (Mexico)
Latin American Regional Reports
Latin American Weekly Report
Lawyer to Lawyer Network (Lawyers Committee for Human Rights)
London Aerogramme
Los Angeles *Times*
Miami *Herald*
Middle East International
Milan Simaka Foundation (Slovakia)
Miist (Ukraine)
Monthly Digest of News from Armenia (Armenian Assembly of America)
The *Nation*
National Bank of Hungary (Monthly Reports)
National Democratic Institute for International Affairs
National Endowment for Democracy (U.S.)
New African
The *New Republic*
New York *Newsday*
New York *Times*
New Yorker
Newsweek
North-South Magazine
North-South Center (Miami)
Organization of American States
The *Other Side of Mexico*
Pacific Islands Monthly
Political Handbook of the World: 1993
Proceso (Mexico City)
Radio Free Europe/Radio Liberty: RFE/RL *Research Bulletin*
Reforma (Mexico)
South East Asia Monitor
Sposterihach (Ukraine)
State Department *Country Reports on Human Rights Practices for 1993*
The *Statesman*
Statistical Handbook 1994: States of the Former Soviet Union (World Bank)
Swiss Press Review
The *Tico Times* (Costa Rica)
Time
The *Times Atlas of the World*
The *Week in Germany*
U.S. News and World Report
Ukrainian Center for Independent Political Research
Ukrainian Press Agency
Ukrainian Weekly
Uncaptive Minds (Institute for Democracy in Eastern Europe)
UNDP *Human Development Report*
UNICEF

Publications, organizations (*continued*)

U.S. Committee for Refugees (Special Reports)
Vueta (Mexico)
Vybir Information Service (Ukraine)
Wall Street Journal
Washington *Post*
Washington *Times*
West Africa
World Economy Research Institute (Poland)
World Population Data Sheet 1994 (Population Reference Bureau)
World Press Review
ZimRights News (Zimbabwe)

Human Rights Organizations

Amnesty International
Andean Commission of Jurists
Association for the Defense of Human Rights (Romania)
Badlisy Center
Budapest City Council Committee on Human Rights and
    Minorities (Hungary)
Caribbean Institute for the Promotion of Human Rights
Caribbean Rights
Child Workers in Nepal
Chilean Human Rights Commission
Civic Alliance (Mexico)
Committee of Churches for Emergency Help (Paraguay)
Council for Democracy (Mexico)
Croatian Democracy Project (Croatia)
Cuban Commission for Human Rights and National
    Reconciliation
Cuban Committee for Human Rights
Ethnic Federation of Romanies [Gypsies] (Romania)
Fray Bartocomé de Las Casas Center for Human Rights
    (Mexico)
Free Iraq Foundation
Group for Mutual Support (Guatemala)
Guyana Human Rights Association
Haitian Center for Human Rights
Helsinki Foundation for Human Rights (Poland)
Human Rights Centre, University of Essex (U.K.)
Honduran Committee for the Defense of Human Rights
Human Rights Commission (El Salvador)
Human Rights Organization of Bhutan
Human Rights Organization of Nepal
Human Rights Watch:
    Africa Watch
    Americas Watch
    Asia Watch
    Helsinki Watch

Middle East Watch
Independent Committee for Human Rights Protection (Bulgaria)
Inform (Sri Lanka)
Inter-American Commission on Human Rights
Inter-Hemispheric Resource Center
International Human Rights Law Group
International Human Rights Law Group (Romania)
Jamaica Council for Human Rights
Latin American Association for Human Rights
Latin American Commission for Human Rights and Freedoms of
    the Workers
Latin American Ombudsmen Institute
Lawyers Committee for Human Rights
Liberal International
Mexican Human Rights Academy
National Coalition for Haitian Refugees
National Coordinating Office for Human Rights (Peru)
Panamanian Committee for Human Rights
Parliamentary Human Rights Foundation (U.S.)
Parliamentary Human Rights Group (U.K.)
Permanent Commission on Human Rights (Nicaragua)
Permanent Committee for the Defense of Human Rights
    (Colombia)
Physicians for Human Rights
Redress Trust
Runejel Junam Council of Ethnic Communities (Guatemala)
Tutela Legal (El Salvador)
Ukrainian Center for Independent Research
Venezuelan Human Rights Education Action Program
Vicaria de la Solidaridad (Chile)
Vietnam Committee on Human Rights
Washington Office on Latin America
Women Acting Together for Change (Nepal)
Young Generation Society of Romani [Gypsies] (Romania)

Delegations/visitors to Freedom House

Africa/Middle East
Algeria
Burkina Faso
Burundi
Cameroon
Ethiopia
Ghana
Iraq (Kurds)
Israel
Ivory Coast
Kenya
Lebanon
Liberia
Mauritania
Nigeria
Rwanda
Senegal
South Africa
Tanzania
Uganda
Zaire
Zimbabwe

Asia/Pacific
Australia
Bangladesh
Bhutan
Cambodia
East Timor
Hong Kong
India
Indonesia
Korea (South)
Macao
Malaysia

Nepal
Pakistan
Papua New Guinea
Philippines
Sri Lanka
Taiwan (ROC)
Thailand

Central Europe
Albania
Bulgaria
Croatia
Czech Republic
Estonia
Hungary
Romania
Yugoslavia (Montenegro, Serbia)

former USSR
Belarus (Byelorussia)
Russia
Ukraine

Western Europe
Belgium
United Kingdom

Western Hemisphere
Canada
Columbia
Cuba
Guatemala
Peru

Delegations from Freedom House to:

Antigua and Barbuda
Austria
Canada
Dominican Republic
El Salvador
France
Haiti
Hungary
India
Japan
Kashmir
Kenya

Korea (South)
Mexico
Nepal
Nicaragua
Poland
Russia
St. Vincent and the Grenadines
South Africa
Sudan
Switzerland
Ukraine
United Kingdom